UNIVERSITY OF WINCHESTER
KT-387-437
LIBRARY

# AMERICAN FOREIGN POLICY

FOURTH EDITION

KA 0377976 9

UNIVERSITY OF WINCHESTER

# AMERICAN FOREIGN POLICY

*The Dynamics of Choice in the 21st Century*

FOURTH EDITION

BRUCE W. JENTLESON

Duke University

W • W • NORTON & COMPANY
NEW YORK • LONDON

To my students, and those of my colleagues,
with whom the choices have begun to lie

W. W. Norton & Company has been independent since its founding in 1923, when William Warder Norton and Mary D. Herter Norton first published lectures delivered at the People's Institute, the adult education division of New York City's Cooper Union. The Nortons soon expanded their program beyond the Institute, publishing books by celebrated academics from America and abroad. By mid-century, the two major pillars of Norton's publishing program—trade books and college texts—were firmly established. In the 1950s, the Norton family transferred control of the company to its employees, and today—with a staff of four hundred and a comparable number of trade, college, and professional titles published each year—W. W. Norton & Company stands as the largest and oldest publishing house owned wholly by its employees.

Copyright © 2010, 2007, 2004, 2000 by W. W. Norton & Company, Inc.
All rights reserved.
Printed in the United States of America.

The text of this book is composed in Minion with the display set in Bauer Bodoni.
Composition by Matrix Publishing Services.
Manufacturing by Worldcolor—Taunton, MA.
*Interior Book Designer:* Jo Anne Metsch
*Project editor:* Kathleen Feighery
*Production Manager:* Benjamin Reynolds

UNIVERSITY OF WINCHESTER
327.73 JEN
03779769

Library of Congress Cataloging-in-Publication Data

Jentleson, Bruce W., 1951–
American foreign policy : the dynamics of choice in the 21st century / Bruce W. Jentleson. — 4th ed.
p. cm.
Includes bibliographical references and index.

**ISBN 978-0-393-93357-4 (pbk.)**

1. United States—Foreign relations—1989– 2. United States—Foreign relations—1989—Forecasting.
3. United States—Foreign relations—21st century. I. Title.
E840.J46 2010
327.73009'05—dc22
2009054284

W. W. Norton & Company, Inc., 500 Fifth Avenue, New York, N.Y. 10110-0017
www.wwnorton.com
W. W. Norton & Company Ltd., Castle House, 75/76 Wells Street, London W1T 3QT

1 2 3 4 5 6 7 8 9 0

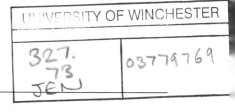

UNIVERSITY OF WINCHESTER
LIBRARY

# Contents

Lists of Maps, Boxes, Figures, and Tables xv
Preface to the Fourth Edition xix

PART I *The Context of U.S. Foreign Policy: Theory and History* 1

1 *The Strategic Context: Foreign Policy Strategy and the Essence of Choice* 2

Introduction: Foreign Policy in a Time of Transition 2

The Context of the International System 6

*Quasi-anarchy* 6

*System Structure* 7

*State Structural Position* 8

The National Interest: The "4 Ps" Framework 9

*Power* 10

*Peace* 12

*Prosperity* 15

*Principles* 16

Dilemmas of Foreign Policy Choice: "4 Ps" Complementarity, Trade-offs, and Dissensus 19

*"4 Ps" Complementarity: Optimal, but Infrequent* 19

*"4 Ps" Trade-offs: More Frequent, More Problematic* 20

*"4 Ps" Dissensus: Bitter Conflicts* 23

Summary 24

2 *The Domestic Context: Foreign Policy Politics and the Process of Choice* 27

Introduction: Dispelling the "Water's Edge" Myth 27

The President, Congress, and "Pennsylvania Avenue Diplomacy" 29

*War Powers* 31

*Treaties and Other International Commitments* 32

*Appointments of Foreign Policy Officials* 34

*"Commerce with Foreign Nations"* 36

*General Powers* 37

*The Supreme Court as Referee?* 39

Executive-Branch Politics 41

*Presidents as Foreign Policy Leaders* 41

*Senior Foreign Policy Advisers and Bureaucratic Politics* 44

Interest Groups and Their Influence 49

*A Typology of Foreign Policy Interest Groups* 50

*Strategies and Techniques of Influence* 53

*The Extent of Interest-Group Influence: Analytic and Normative Considerations* 55

The Impact of the News Media 58

*Role of the Media: Cheerleader or Critic?* 58

*Modes of Influence* 59

*Freedom of the Press vs. National Security* 61

The Nature and Influence of Public Opinion 62

*Ignorant or Sensible? The Nature of Public Opinion about Foreign Policy* 63

*The Influence of Public Opinion on Foreign Policy* 65

Summary 67

3 *The Historical Context: Great Debates in American Foreign Policy, 1789–1945* 72

Introduction: "The Past Is Prologue" 72

Brief Historical Chronology 73

*The Revolutionary War and the Consolidation of Independence, 1776–1800* 73

*Expansion and Preservation, 1801–65* 74

*Global Emergence, 1865–1919* 76

*Isolationist Retreat, 1919–41* 78

*World War II, 1941–45* 81

Great Debates over Foreign Policy Strategy 83

*Isolationism vs. Internationalism* 83

*Power, Peace: How Big a Military, How Much for Defense?* 87
*Principles: True to American Democratic Ideals?* 90
*Prosperity: U.S. Imperialism?* 95
*Key Case: U.S. Relations with Latin America—Good Neighbor or Regional Hegemon?* 98
*Key Case: The United States as a Pacific Power* 101
Great Debates in Foreign Policy Politics 103
*Going to War* 103
*National Security vs. the Bill of Rights* 106
*Free Trade vs. Protectionism* 109
Summary 110

4 *The Cold War Context: Origins and First Stages* 114
Introduction: "Present at the Creation" 114
Peace: International Institutionalism and the United Nations 116
*The Original Vision of the United Nations* 116
*The Scaled-Back Reality* 117
Power: Nuclear Deterrence and Containment 119
*The Formative Period, 1947–50* 122
*Intensification, 1950s to the Early 1960s* 127
Principles: Ideological Bipolarity and the Third World "ABC" Approach 130
*Support for "ABC Democrats"* 130
*CIA Covert Action* 132
Prosperity: Creation of the Liberal International Economic Order 133
*The Major International Economic Institutions* 133
*Critiques: Economic Hegemony? Neo-Imperialism?* 134
Foreign Policy Politics and the Cold War Consensus 135
*Pennsylvania Avenue Diplomacy: A One-Way Street* 135
*Executive-Branch Politics and the Creation of the "National Security State"* 138
*Interest Groups, the Media, and Public Opinion: Benefits and Dangers of Consensus* 141
Summary 146

5 *The Cold War Context: Lessons and Legacies* 150
Introduction: Turbulent Decades 150
The Vietnam War: A Profound Foreign Policy Setback 151
*Foreign Policy Strategy: Failure on All Counts* 152
*Foreign Policy Politics: Shattering the Cold War Consensus* 156

The Rise and Fall of Détente: Major Foreign Policy Shifts 160

*Nixon, Kissinger, and the Rise of Détente 160*

*Reasons for the Fall of Détente 167*

1970s Economic Shocks 170

*The Nixon Shock, 1971 171*

*The OPEC Shocks, 1973 and 1979 171*

*The North-South Conflict and Demands for an "NIEO" 172*

*Trade with Japan and the Rest of the World 173*

Reagan, Gorbachev, and the End of the Cold War 177

*The "4 Ps" under Reagan 177*

*Confrontational Foreign Policy Politics 183*

*The End of the Cold War: Why Did the Cold War End, and End Peacefully? 186*

Summary 192

***Readings for Part I: The Context of U.S. Foreign Policy: Theory and History*** **197**

1.1 Hans J. Morgenthau, Power: *The Mainsprings of American Foreign Policy 198*

1.2 Robert O. Keohane, Peace: *Governance in a Partially Globalized World 202*

1.3 Gabriel Kolko, Prosperity: *The United States and World Economic Power 207*

1.4 Tony Smith, Principles: *The United States and the Global Struggle for Democracy: Early 1990s Perspective 211*

2.1 Arthur M. Schlesinger, Jr., The President and Congress: *What the Founding Fathers Intended 216*

2.2 Graham T. Allison, Bureaucratic Politics: *Conceptual Models and the Cuban Missile Crisis 221*

2.3 Ole R. Holsti, Public Opinion: *Public Opinion and Foreign Policy: Challenges to the Almond-Lippmann Consensus 223*

3.1 Henry Kissinger, Isolationism vs. Internationalism: *Franklin D. Roosevelt and the Coming of World War II 231*

3.2 Walter LaFeber, Imperialism: *The American "New Empire" 239*

4.1 Melvyn P. Leffler, Cold War Revisionist Critique: *The American Conception of National Security and the Beginnings of the Cold War, 1945–48 246*

4.2 Bernard Brodie, Nuclear Deterrence Doctrine: *Strategy in the Missile Age 253*

4.3 Mr. X [George Kennan], The Sources of Containment: *The Sources of Soviet Conduct 259*

5.1 Leslie H. Gelb, Vietnam: *Vietnam: The System Worked 263*

5.2 Alexander L. George, Détente: *Détente: The Search for a "Constructive" Relationship 267*

5.3 John Lewis Gaddis, The End of the Cold War: *The Unexpected Ronald Reagan 273*

5.4 Mikhail Gorbachev, The End of the Cold War: *The Soviet Union's Crucial Role 276*

PART II *American Foreign Policy in the Twenty-First Century: Choices and Challenges* 279

6 *Foreign Policy Strategy and Foreign Policy Politics in a New Era* 280

Introduction: 11/9 and 9/11—Crumbling Wall and Crashing Towers 280
Foreign Policy Strategy for a New Era 281
*The Unilateralism versus Multilateralism Debate in the Clinton and Bush Years* 281
*The Emergence of a Global Era* 290
*Force and Diplomacy: Striking a Balance* 294
*The United Nations* 302
*WMD Proliferation* 306
*Security Threats from Nonstate Actors* 316
*The International Economy, Energy Security, and the Global Environment* 320
Foreign Policy Politics: Diplomacy Begins at Home 322
*President Barack Obama and the Obama Administration* 324
*The Internet, Blogs, and the Changing Media* 327
*Public Opinion: Continuity, Change, and Uncertainty* 329
Summary 334

7 *Post–Cold War Geopolitics: Major Powers and Regions* 342

Major Powers Geopolitics 343
Europe 346
*Western Europe, the European Union (EU), and NATO* 346
*The Future of NATO* 348
*Russia* 354
*Organization for Security and Cooperation in Europe (OSCE)* 367
Asia 368
*China* 368
*Japan* 376
*The Korean Peninsula* 379
*India* 380
*Asian Regional Organizations* 383

Latin America 383
*Cuba 384*
*Mexico 384*
*Brazil 386*
*Venezuela 387*
*Organization of American States (OAS) 387*
*Honduras 388*
Africa 391
*Somalia 392*
*Darfur 392*
*South Africa 393*
*Good Governance, Economic Development, AIDS 393*
*African Union (AU) 394*
Foreign Policy Politics: A Case Study 394
*The China Lobbies 394*
Summary 399

8 *The Middle East: A Special Focus* 405
Introduction: September 13, 1993, to September 11, 2001: From Hope to Tragedy 405
Operations Desert Shield and Desert Storm: The 1990–91 Persian Gulf War 407
9/11 and the Bush War on Terrorism 409
*The Afghanistan War under Bush 411*
*Overall Bush War on Terrorism Strategy 413*
The Iraq War 419
*Rationale for Going to War: Validity? Honesty? 423*
*Results: Winning the Peace? 425*
*Ramifications: Iraq and the "4 Ps" 430*
Key Issues and Initial Obama Strategies 435
*"Af-Pak" 436*
*Terrorism 442*
*Iran 445*
The Arab-Israeli Conflict 448
Foreign Policy Politics: Terrorism and the Iraq War 456
*National Security, the Bill of Rights, and the War on Terrorism 457*
*Domestic Politics of the Iraq War 463*
Summary 472

9 *Never Again or Yet Again? Genocide and Other Mass Atrocities* 480

Introduction: Success and Failure, Hope and Despair 480

Is the U.S. National Interest at Stake? 483

What Are the Driving Forces of Wars of Identity? 487

What about National Sovereignty? 489

Which Types of Preventive Diplomacy Strategies Can Be Most Effective? 493

When Should Military Force Be Used? 496

Who Decides on Military Intervention? 502

How to End Conflicts and Build Peace? 503

*Bosnia 503*

*Kosovo 505*

*UN Peace Operations 506*

Darfur: "Yet Again" 510

Foreign Policy Politics Case Study: War Powers, Public Opinion, and Humanitarian Intervention 515

*The Media and the "CNN Curve" 518*

*Public Opinion and Humanitarian Intervention 519*

Summary 520

10 *The Globalization Agenda* 528

Introduction: American Foreign Policy in an Era of Globalization 528

The Globalization Debate 529

*Defining Globalization: Dynamics, Dimensions, Dilemmas 529*

*The 2008 Global Economic Crisis 537*

International Trade 540

*The World Trade Organization (WTO) 542*

*Western Hemisphere Free Trade Agreements 545*

International Finance 546

*1990s Financial Crises 546*

*Policy Debates over the IMF 548*

*Shifts in International Financial Power? 550*

Global Poverty and Sustainable Development 551

*Poverty and the Human Condition 552*

*U.S Foreign Aid Policy 554*

*The World Bank 558*

*Overpopulation and World Hunger 559*

Global Public Health 563
*Global AIDS 564*
*Role of the Gates Foundation 566*
*Global Pandemics and the "DMD" Threat 567*
Global Environmental Issues 568
*Analytic Framework 569*
*Global Climate Change 571*
*Other Key Issues 575*
Foreign Policy Politics: The New Politics of Globalization and the Old Politics of Trade 577
*NGOs and the Politics of Globalization 577*
*Making U.S. Trade Policy: Process and Politics 579*
Summary 584

**11 *The Coming of a Democratic Century?* 590**
Introduction: Democracy and the U.S. National Interest 590
Global Democracy and Human Rights: Status and Prospects 593
*Post–Cold War Democratic Success Stories 593*
*Limits and Uncertainties 595*
Principles and Peace: The Democratic Peace Debate 604
*Democratic Peace Theory 604*
*Critiques and Caveats 607*
Principles and Power: Tensions and Trade-Offs 609
*From ABC to ABT? 609*
*Principles as Power: Soft Power's Significance 611*
Principles and Prosperity: The Economic Sanctions Debate 617
*Key Cases 617*
Policy Strategies for Promoting Democracy and Protecting Human Rights 620
*Who: Key International Actors 620*
*How: Key Strategies 622*
*What: Assessing Effectiveness 630*
Foreign Policy Politics: Economic Sanctions and the South Africa Case 633
Summary 636

## *Readings for Part II: American Foreign Policy in the Twenty-First Century: Choices and Challenges* *643*


6.1 Charles Krauthammer, Unilateralism: *The Unipolar Moment Revisited* 644

6.2 Kofi A. Annan, The United Nations: *"We the Peoples"* 649

7.1 Michael Mandelbaum, America as the World's Government: *The Case for Goliath* 656

7.2 Joseph S. Nye, Jr., Superpower—But Can't Go it Alone: *The Paradox of American Power* 659

8.1 George W. Bush, Bush Doctrine on Pre-Emption: *Pre-Emption and National Security Strategy* 663

8.2 G. John Ikenberry, Bush Doctrine Critique: *America's Imperial Ambition* 665

8.3 9/11 Commission, A Global Strategy against Terrorism: *Final Report of the National Commission on Terrorist Attacks upon the United States* 669

9.1 International Commission on Intervention and State Sovereignty, The Responsibility to Protect: *The Case for Humanitarian Intervention* 672

9.2 Genocide Prevention Task Force, From "Yet Again" to "Never Again: " *Preventing Genocide: A Blueprint for U.S. Policymakers* 675

9.3 Warren P. Strobel, The Media and Foreign Policy: *The Media and U.S. Policies Toward Intervention: A Closer Look at the "CNN Effect"* 677

10.1 UNAIDS, The Global AIDS Crisis: *Report on the Global AIDS Epidemic* 685

10.2 Al Gore, The Planetary Emergency of Global Warming: *An Inconvenient Truth* 690

10.3 Margaret E. Keck and Kathryn Sikkink, NGOs: *Transnational Networks in International Politics: An Introduction* 693

11.1 Francis Fukuyama, The Triumph of Democracy: *The End of History?* 702

11.2 Samuel P. Huntington, Ongoing Threats to Democracy: *The Clash of Civilizations?* 706

11.3 Edward D. Mansfield and Jack Snyder, Democratic Peace?: *Democratization and the Danger of War* 713

Credits A-1

Glossary A-5

Index A-23

# Maps, Boxes, Figures, and Tables

## Maps

The World xxiii
Africa xxiv
Asia xxv
Europe xxvi
The Western Hemisphere xxvii
The Middle East xxviii
U.S. Military Interventions in Latin America, Early Twentieth Century 98
Global Population Patterns 560
Global Income Distribution 561

## At the Source

George Washington's Farewell Address 85
Making the World Safe for Democracy 94
The Monroe Doctrine (1823) and the Roosevelt Corollary (1904) 100
The Truman Doctrine and the Marshall Plan 123
The North Atlantic Treaty 125
NSC-68 126
"Is It News?" or "Is It in the Interest of National Security?" 142
McCarthyism 145
U.S.-Soviet Détente 163
The Opening of Relations with China 169
The "Weinberger Criteria" for the Use of Military Force (1984) 179
Freedom vs. "Totalitarian Evil" 182
Enhancing Diplomacy and Building Civilian Capacity 298
Threats from WMD Proliferation 308
Obama's Speech to the Arab and Muslim Worlds 437
"Save Us From Catastrophe" 498
Millennium Development Goals 555

## *Historical Perspectives*

The Munich Analogy and Vietnam 155
Power and Peace over the Centuries 345
Arab-Israeli Conflict: Summary Timeline, 1947–2008 449
"Genocide in the Twentieth Century" 484
How "New" Is Globalization? 530
"Waves" of Democratization 594

## *International Perspectives*

Nineteenth-Century Critics 96
Support for the United States in the UN General Assembly, 1946–60 119
The Declaration of a New International Economic Order (NIEO) 174
Global Public Opinion on the United States, 1999–2008 300
African Leaders' Views 389
Support for and Opposition to the Iraq War 420
Who Provides Troops for UN Peace Operations? 507
Views on the 2008–2009 Global Economic Crisis 538
The United States and Democracy Promotion 613

## *Theory in the World*

Theories of American Exceptionalism 92
The "Wizards of Armageddon" and Cold War Nuclear Deterrence 121
Kissinger's Détente and Balance-of-Power Theory 161
Conceptualizing the Twenty-First Century 291
The Russia-Ukraine Nuclear Arms Deal and American Peace Brokering 358
International Relations Theory and the Iraq War 431
Sovereignty as Rights vs. Sovereignty as Responsibility 490
Debates about Free Trade 580
Democratic Peace Theory and the Clinton and Bush Foreign Policies 605

## *Additional Figures, Tables, and Boxes*

A Foreign Policy Strategy Typology 18
Principal Foreign Policy Provisions of the Constitution 30
Cabinet and Key Foreign Policy Officials in the Bush, Clinton, and Bush Administrations 46
A Typology of Foreign Policy Interest Groups 50
Public Support for Internationalism vs. Isolationism, 1945–2008 64
Foreign Policy Politics and the Process of Choice 67
Wartime Mobilization, Peacetime Demobilization 88
Public Opinion from Cold War Consensus to Vietnam Trauma 159
1989: Eastern Europe's Year of Revolution 187
U.S. Cold War Foreign Policy Strategy 193
U.S. Cold War Foreign Policy Politics 194
The Obama Foreign Policy Team (Initial) 326
Foreign Policy Goals 330
American Public Opinion on the United Nations, 1953–2007 332
NATO: Its Evolution, Cold War to Post–Cold War 350
The U.S. Trade Balance, 1960–2008 541
The Status of Global Democracy 596

# *Preface to the Fourth Edition*

When we went to bed on the night of September 10, 2001, the world was already going through a historic transition. The Cold War had ended, raising hopes for the future. War, though, had not ended, as the 1990s bore tragic witness in Bosnia, Rwanda, and all too many other places. New forces of globalization were sweeping the world, bringing their own combination of progress and problems. Democracy had spread but was facing the challenges of consolidation and institutionalization. All this, and more, made for quite a full foreign policy agenda for the United States.

And then came September 11. Most of us will always remember where we were when we first heard about the terrorist attacks on the World Trade Center and the Pentagon. The images were piercing. The American psyche was shaken. And the foreign policy agenda was further transformed as the war on terrorism was launched. Less than two years later, claiming that it was a crucial front in the war on terrorism, the Bush administration took the United States to war in Iraq.

We now have had to deal with both the September 10 agenda and the September 11 one. Such are the challenges and opportunities confronting American foreign policy as we move deeper into this new era and new century, for those who make that policy—and for those who teach and study it.

*American Foreign Policy: The Dynamics of Choice in the 21st Century,* Fourth Edition, is intended to help those of us who are professors and students take advantage of those opportunities and meet those challenges. This book is designed as a primary text for courses on American foreign policy. Its scope encompasses both key issues of *foreign policy strategy*—of what the U.S. national interest is and which policies serve it best—and key questions of *foreign policy politics*—of which institutions and actors within the American political system play what roles and have how much influence. Formulating foreign policy strategy is the "essence of choice," the means by which goals are established and the policies to achieve them are forged. Foreign policy politics is the "process of choice," the making of foreign policy through the institutions and amid the societal influences of the American political system.

Part I of this book provides the theory (Chapters 1 and 2) and history (Chapter 3 for 1789–1945, Chapters 4 and 5 on the Cold War) for establishing the framework of the dynamics of choice. The theory chapters draw on the international relations and American foreign policy literatures to introduce core concepts, pose debates over alternative explanations, and frame the "4 Ps" (Power, Peace, Prosperity, Principles) analytic approach to foreign policy strategy and the multiple-actors approach to foreign policy politics. The history chapters help ensure that expressions such as "break with the past" are not taken too literally. Not only must we still cope with the legacies of the Cold War, but many current issues are contemporary versions of long-standing "great debates" with lengthy histories in U.S. foreign policy. These chapters follow closely those in the First, Second, and Third Editions, with revisions and elaborations drawing on helpful feedback from reviewers, instructors, and students.

Part II (Chapters 6–11) applies the framework to the post–Cold War foreign policy agenda and the major choices the United States faces today. This part is substantially updated and expanded to cover major dynamics and developments of the past four years. Each chapter focuses on a particular issue area and applies the "4 Ps" framework to that area in a dynamic way. Chapter 6 sets this approach up, laying out overarching debates over foreign policy strategy spanning the Bush, Clinton, Bush and Obama administrations, and examining foreign policy politics and how diplomacy still begins at home. Chapter 7 focuses on the post–Cold War geopolitics of U.S. relations with other major powers and in world regions. Chapter 8 provides a special focus on the Middle East and such key issues as Iraq, terrorism, Afghanistan, Iran, and the Arab-Israeli conflict. Chapter 9 takes a hard look at ethnic conflict, humanitarian intervention, and genocide and other mass atrocities, including such cases as Rwanda and Darfur. Chapter 10 addresses the globalization agenda, its broad debates, and such key issues as international trade, international finance, global poverty and sustainable development, global public health, and the global environment. Chapter 11 examines the challenges of promoting democracy and protecting human rights, focusing on both key cases and broader debates such as that over the democratic peace, the utility of economic sanctions, and ways to asssess effectiveness. The chapters are highly comprehensive, providing students with a broad survey of the twenty-first-century foreign policy agenda. A wide range of issues is covered in a manner that both provides an initial understanding and lays the foundation for further reading and research.

This book also includes maps, boxes, and four main types of feature boxes: *Historical Perspectives*, drawing on history to provide additional insights into current issues; *International Perspectives*, giving a greater sense of how other countries view American foreign policy; *Theory in the World*, bringing out ways in which theory and policy connect; and *At the Source*, highlighting excerpts from major speeches and other primary source materials.

This fourth edition also keeps the text and the reader in a single volume. Supplemental readings are keyed to each chapter. These readings develop theories and concepts introduced in the text and delve more deeply into major policy debates. They include works both by major policy figures such as Henry Kissinger, Mikhail Gorbachev, and Kofi Annan and by scholars such as Hans Morgenthau, Robert Keohane, Walter LaFeber, Alexander George, Samuel Huntington, and John Ikenberry.

With this edition, we are offering a much-expanded and highly innovative Web site, American Foreign Policy *Student StudySpace*. You and your students will find study questions to help reinforce chapter content and concepts; Internet exercises for further research and analysis; videos that add dynamism to historical events, contemporary issues and major figures; and other engaging learning features. Periodically we will update the site with links to events, recent articles, and other current information on important foreign policy issues. Go to wwnorton.com/studyspace.

This book reflects my own belief in a "multi-integrative" approach to teaching about American foreign policy. By that I mean three things: an approach that breaks through the levels-of-analysis barriers and integrates international policy and domestic process, encompasses the full range of post–Cold War foreign policy issue areas, and "bridges the gap" between theory and practice by drawing on both perspectives. With regard to this last point, I have incorporated the perspectives and experiences gained through my own work in the policy world (at the State Department on the Policy Planning Staff, in Congress as a Senate foreign policy aide, and in other capacities) as well as from more than twenty-five years as a professor.

My interest in continuing to write this book is part of my commitment to teaching. Throughout my university education, I was fortunate to have some exceptional teachers. I was among the thousands of undergraduates at Cornell University who were first captivated by the study of foreign policy through Walter LaFeber's courses on diplomatic history. The late Bud Kenworthy, a superb and caring teacher in his own right, was instrumental in my realization as a senior that I wanted to pursue an academic career. When I went back to Cornell for my Ph.D., I was just as fortunate as a graduate student. Anyone who knows Theodore Lowi knows his intensity and passion for his work; these are especially evident in his teaching. Peter Katzenstein was my dissertation chair and has been a mentor in many ways, including in showing me how commitments to superior scholarship and excellent teaching can be combined.

In my years as a professor my good fortune has continued. In both his approach and his persona, the late Alexander George was a much-valued mentor and colleague. Thanks also to Larry Berman, Ed Costantini, Emily Goldman, Alex Groth, Miko Nincic, the late Don Rothchild, and other colleagues at the University of California, Davis, who were partners of many years in trying to make our political science and international relations majors as rich and rewarding for our students as possible. And to Alma Blount, Peter Feaver, Jay Hamilton, Ole Holsti, Judith Kelley, Anirudh Krishna, Bruce Kuniholm, Fritz Mayer, Tom Taylor, and many other valued colleagues here at Duke with whom I have been sharing similar pursuits over the past ten-plus years.

Rebecca Britton, Alexandra Pass, Kim Cole, and Sara Johnson were able research assistants on the First Edition; Seth Weinberger on the Second; Christopher Whytock, Kathryn McNabb Cochran, Christine Leach, Rachel Wald, and Tugba Gurcanlar on the Third; Marie Aberger, Sara Huff, Eric Lorber, Danielle Lupton, and Jessica Wirth on the Fourth. The librarians Jean Stratford at UC Davis, Jim Cornelius at the U.S. Institute of Peace, and

Catherine Shreve at Duke helped greatly in accessing sources and checking citations. Melody Johnson, Lori Renard, Fatima Mohamud, and especially Barbara Taylor-Keil provided tremendous support on the First Edition; Susanne Borchardt was of enormous help on the Second Edition; and Susan Alexander on the Third and Fourth. I owe many thanks to them all. Thanks also to UC Davis, Duke University, Oxford University, and the U.S. Institute of Peace for research support.

Special thanks to colleagues whose feedback as reviewers has been so helpful: Loch Johnson, Jim Lindsay, Dan Caldwell and his students, and others for the First Edition; John Barkdull, Colin Dueck, Todd Eisenstadt, Margaret Karns, Roy Licklider, Peter Loedel, F. Ugboaja Ohaegbulam, and Jon Western for the Second Edition; for the Third Edition, Charles Krupnick, Brian Lai, Alynna Lyon, Miko Nincic, Tony Payan, Rodger Payne, and Dan Caldwell and another of his classes; and for the fourth edition Susan Allen, Mark Cicnock, Shaheen Mozaffar, George Quester, and Reneé Scherlen. I also want to thank those colleagues who on a less formal basis have let me know how valuable they and their students find the book; unsolicited comments such as "my students really get a lot out of your book" mean so much.

At W. W. Norton, Roby Harrington has been there from the inception of the project and has provided the steady hand to see it through to initial completion and successive editions. Authors know that we can count on Roby to be supportive and enthusiastic yet also committed to quality and focused on getting the book done. Thanks are due also to Sarah Caldwell and Rob Whiteside on the First Edition; Avery Johnson, Andrea Haver, and especially Aaron Javsicas on the Second; Matt Arnold, Mik Awake, Pete Lesser, and Ken Barton on the Third. On this Fourth Edition it's been great to work again with Aaron Javsicas as editor as well as the Norton team of Rachel Comerford, Kate Feighery, Carly Fraser, and Dan Jost. Traci Nagle, Patterson Lamb, and especially Barbara Curialle were extremely helpful and provided the enhancements that come with skilled copyediting.

Special thanks to my family: Adam and Katie, then children and now young adults who continue to bring so much to my life and who are making their own marks on the world through their own work, and now also Britt, so exceptional in her own right; Barbara, who has been so supportive and encouraging while accomplishing so much to the benefit of so many students and community members in her own work; and the memory of my mother, Elaine, and my father, Ted, for their love, support, and understanding.

B.W.J.
November 2009
Durham, North Carolina

# The World

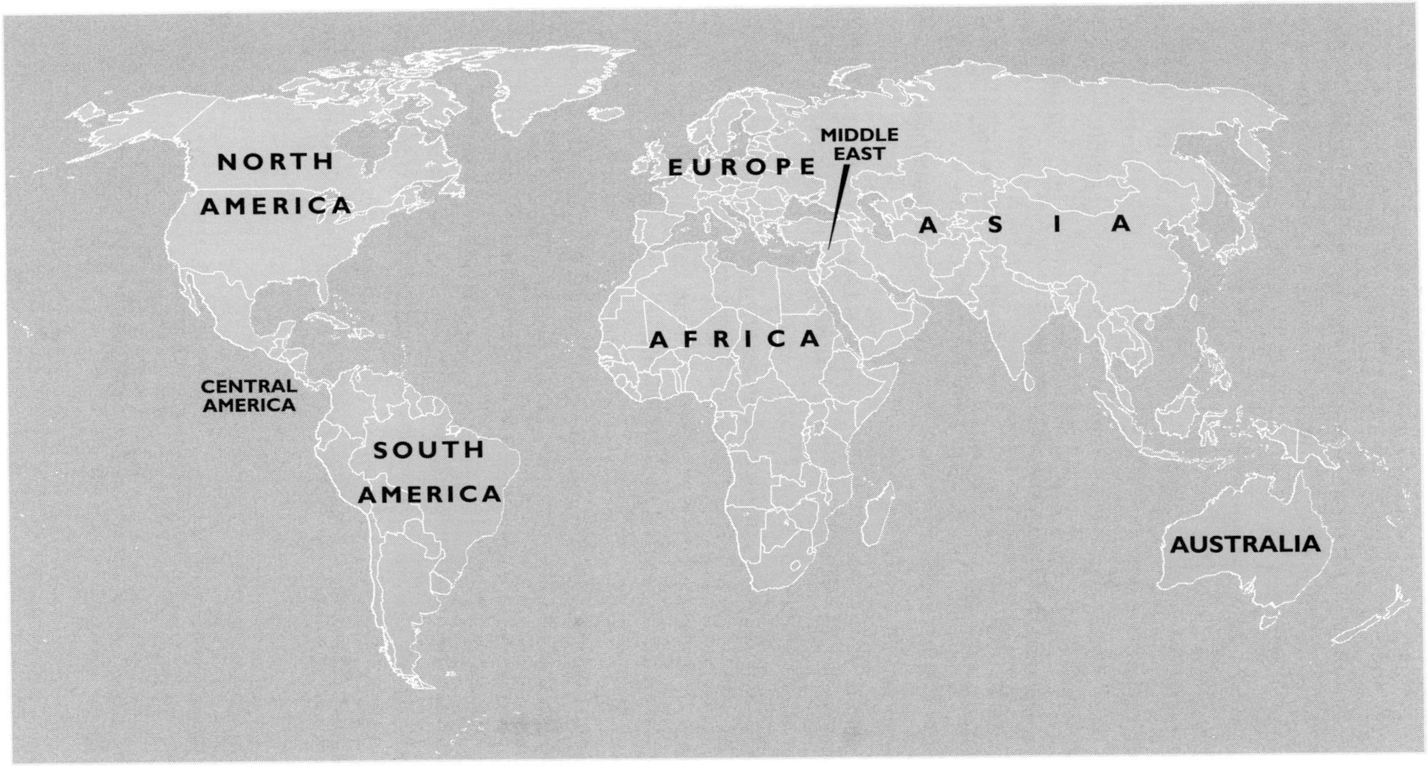
NORTH
AMERICA
CENTRAL
AMERICA
SOUTH
AMERICA
EUROPE
MIDDLE
EAST
AFRICA
ASIA
AUSTRALIA

# Africa

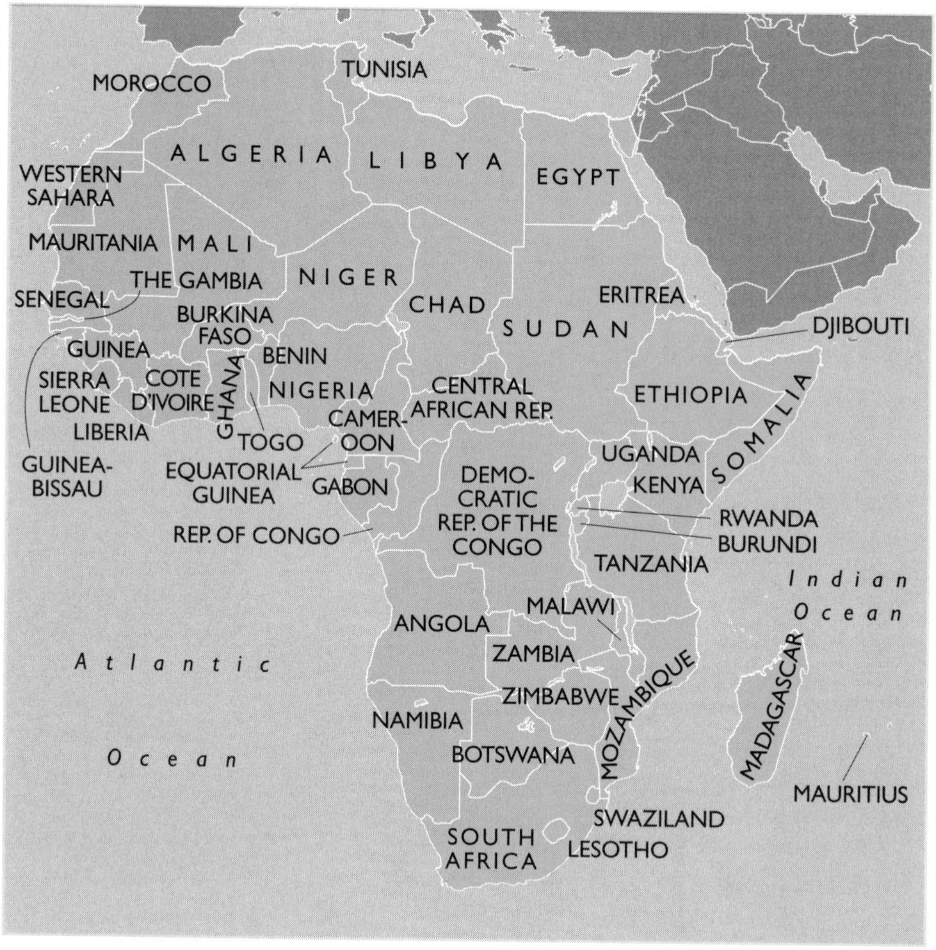
MOROCCO
TUNISIA
ALGERIA
LIBYA
EGYPT
WESTERN SAHARA
MAURITANIA
MALI
NIGER
THE GAMBIA
SENEGAL
CHAD
ERITREA
BURKINA FASO
SUDAN
DJIBOUTI
GUINEA
BENIN
SIERRA LEONE
COTE D'IVOIRE
GHANA
NIGERIA
CENTRAL AFRICAN REP.
ETHIOPIA
LIBERIA
CAMER-OON
TOGO
SOMALIA
UGANDA
GUINEA-BISSAU
EQUATORIAL GUINEA
GABON
DEMO-CRATIC REP. OF THE CONGO
KENYA
RWANDA
BURUNDI
REP. OF CONGO
TANZANIA
Indian Ocean
MALAWI
ANGOLA
ZAMBIA
Atlantic Ocean
MOZAMBIQUE
MADAGASCAR
ZIMBABWE
NAMIBIA
BOTSWANA
MAURITIUS
SWAZILAND
SOUTH AFRICA
LESOTHO

# Asia

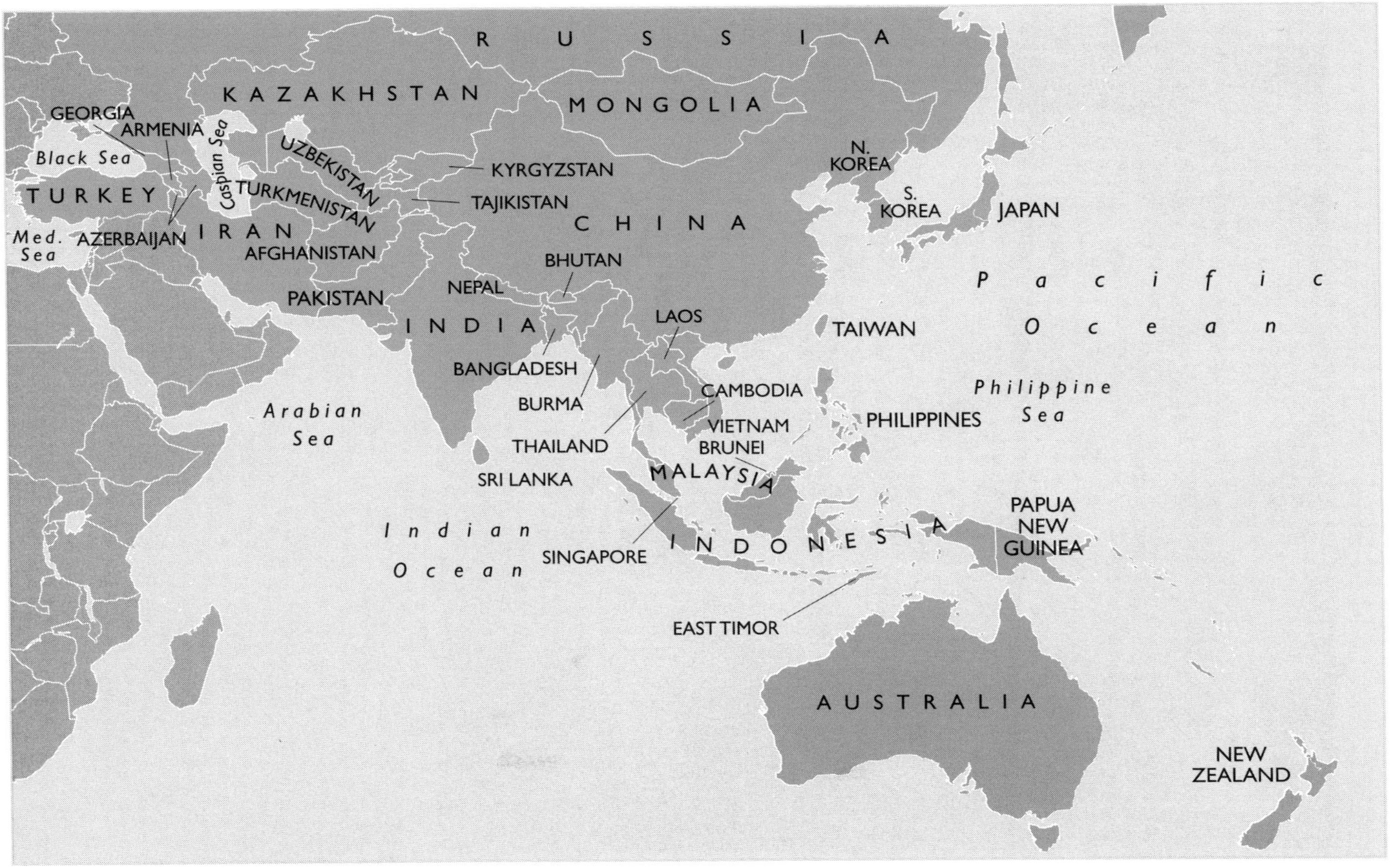
R U S S I A
KAZAKHSTAN
MONGOLIA
GEORGIA
ARMENIA
Black Sea
Caspian Sea
UZBEKISTAN
KYRGYZSTAN
TURKEY
TURKMENISTAN
TAJIKISTAN
CHINA
N. KOREA
S. KOREA
JAPAN
Med. Sea
AZERBAIJAN
IRAN
AFGHANISTAN
BHUTAN
NEPAL
PAKISTAN
INDIA
LAOS
TAIWAN
Pacific Ocean
BANGLADESH
BURMA
CAMBODIA
Philippine Sea
Arabian Sea
VIETNAM
PHILIPPINES
THAILAND
BRUNEI
SRI LANKA
MALAYSIA
PAPUA NEW GUINEA
Indian Ocean
SINGAPORE
INDONESIA
EAST TIMOR
AUSTRALIA
NEW ZEALAND

# Europe

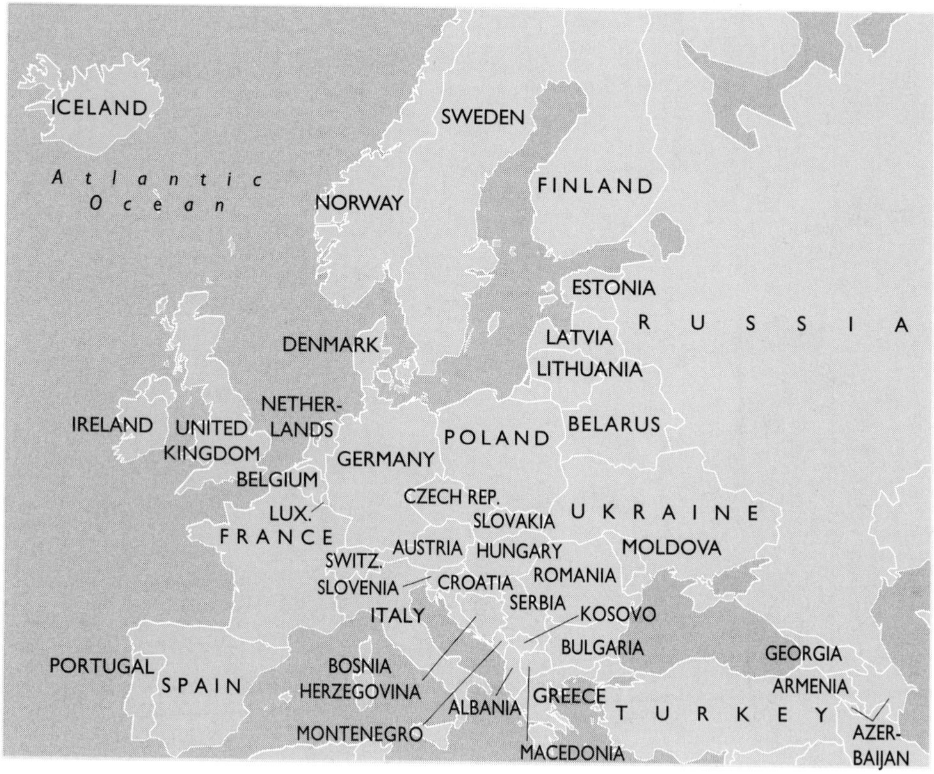
ICELAND
Atlantic
Ocean
SWEDEN
NORWAY
FINLAND
ESTONIA
RUSSIA
LATVIA
DENMARK
LITHUANIA
NETHER-
LANDS
IRELAND
UNITED
KINGDOM
BELARUS
POLAND
GERMANY
BELGIUM
CZECH REP.
LUX.
SLOVAKIA
UKRAINE
FRANCE
AUSTRIA
HUNGARY
MOLDOVA
SWITZ.
SLOVENIA
CROATIA
ROMANIA
SERBIA
ITALY
KOSOVO
BULGARIA
GEORGIA
PORTUGAL
SPAIN
BOSNIA
HERZEGOVINA
ALBANIA
GREECE
ARMENIA
TURKEY
MONTENEGRO
MACEDONIA
AZER-
BAIJAN

# The Western Hemisphere

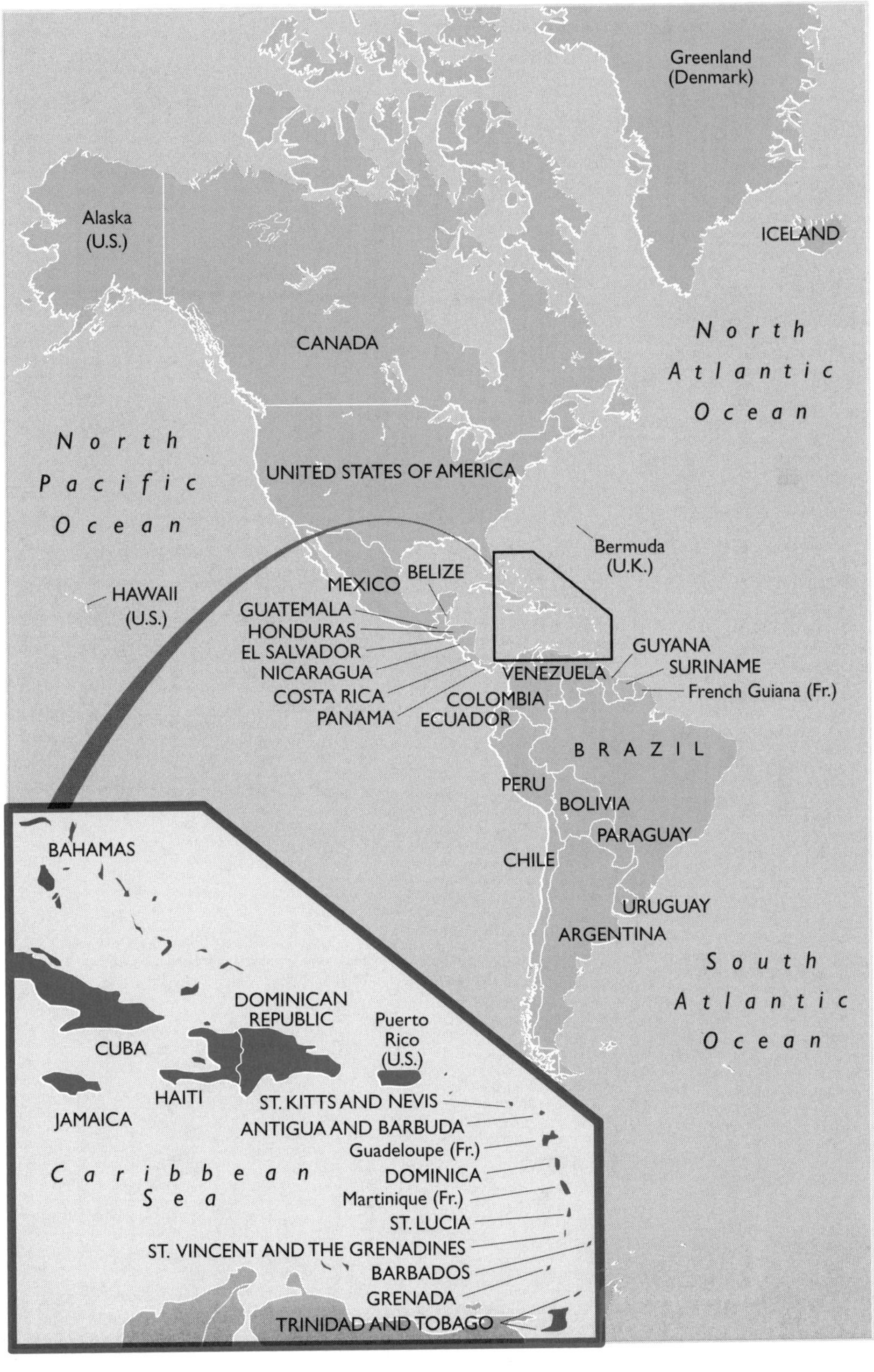

# The Middle East

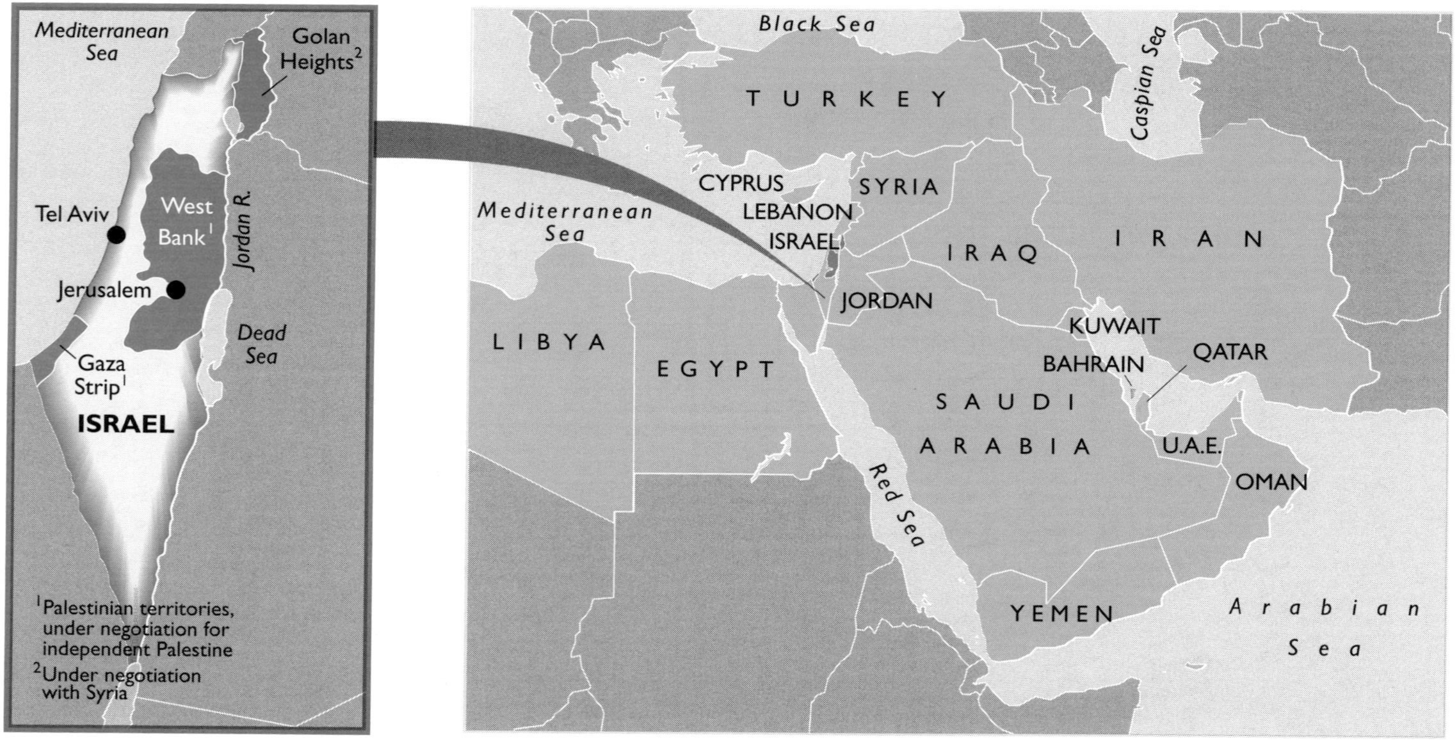

# PART I

# *The Context of U.S. Foreign Policy: Theory and History*

CHAPTER

# 1 *The Strategic Context: Foreign Policy Strategy and the Essence of Choice*

## Introduction: Foreign Policy in a Time of Transition

It was October 22, 1962, 7:00 P.M. A young boy sat on his living room floor watching television. President John F. Kennedy came on to warn the American public of an ominous crisis with the Soviet Union over nuclear missiles in Cuba. The boy's parents tried to look calm, but the fear in their eyes could not be masked. It seemed that the United States was on the brink of nuclear war.

The Cuban missile crisis ended up being settled peacefully, and the Cold War ultimately ended without nuclear war. For a while it seemed that the post–Cold War era was going to be a peaceful one. Indeed, when the Berlin Wall came down in 1989, and then the Soviet Union fell apart in 1991, a sense of near euphoria enveloped the West. President George H. W. Bush (1989–93) spoke of the end of the Cold War as "a time of great promise," an "unparalleled opportunity . . . to work toward transforming this new world into a new world order, one of governments that are democratic, tolerant and economically free at home and committed abroad to settling differences peacefully, without the threat or use of force."[1]

To be sure, the significance of families' being freed from the worry of an all-out nuclear war is not to be underestimated. In that sense the end of the Cold War left the world more secure. All too soon, however, we saw that the end of the Cold War did not mean the end of war. The 1990s will be remembered for peace agreements and the advance of democracy—but also for ethnic "cleansings," civil wars, genocide, and new setbacks for democracy and human rights. It was a decade of strides toward peace and order, but also stumbles toward anarchy and chaos. For American foreign policy, it was a decade of great successes, but also dismal failures.

The 1990s also saw the emergence of the "globalization" agenda. Globalization has been hailed by many for bringing such benefits as the spread of capitalism and economic freedom to the former communist bloc and the Third World and the closer linking through technology and markets of all corners of the globe, and for building the basis for global prosperity. President Bill Clinton spoke of "the train of globalization" that "cannot be reversed" and of how global trade could "lift hundreds of millions of people out of poverty." But he also warned that globalization needed "a more human face," that it needed to address issues such as the global environment, the global AIDS crisis, and the widening gap between rich and poor nations.[2] Indeed, a powerful antiglobalization movement emerged in the 1990s. First in Seattle at the 1999 summit of the World Trade Organization and then at international economic meetings in ensuing years in various cities around the world, this movement mounted the most extensive and violent foreign policy protests since those of the anti–Vietnam War movement in the 1960s and 1970s. On this globalization agenda as well, the 1990s ended with a mixed sense of progress and problems.

Then came the tragic and shocking terrorist assault of September 11, 2001. "U.S. ATTACKED," the *New York Times* headline blared the next day in the large print used for only the most momentous events, and the newspaper went on to describe "a hellish storm of ash, glass, smoke and leaping victims" as the World Trade Center towers crashed down.[3] In Washington, D.C., the Pentagon, the fortress of American defense, was literally ripped open by the impact of another hijacked jetliner. The death tolls were staggering. The shock ran deep. A new sense of insecurity set in, for it soon became clear that this was not an isolated incident. President George W. Bush declared a "war on terrorism," which started in October 2001 in Afghanistan against Osama bin Laden, his Al Qaeda terrorist network, and the Taliban regime. But it did not end there. "It will not end," President Bush declared, "until every terrorist group of global reach has been found, stopped and defeated."[4] Less than two years later, claiming it to be a crucial front in the war on terrorism, the Bush administration took the United States to war in Iraq.

The Iraq war proved to be the most controversial foreign policy issue since the Vietnam war of the 1960s–70s. It was one of the key issues, along with the worst national and international economic crisis since the Great Depression, that helped Barack Obama win the presidency in 2008. During the presidential campaign he acknowledged both the threats American foreign policy needed to meet and the opportunities for progress. "This century's threats are at least as dangerous as and in some ways more complex than those we have confronted in the past," he declared. Terrorism, weapons of mass destruction, more wars in the Middle East, more genocide and other deadly conflicts, global warming, global pandemics, global recession, rising powers such as China, recovering ones such as Russia—a full and complex agenda. Thinking of all this, though, was "not to give way to pessimism. Rather it is a call to action . . . [to] a new vision of leadership in the twenty-first century" geared towards a "common security for our common humanity."[5]

Any one of these sets of changes would be profound by itself. Dealing with the combined effects of all of them truly makes these times of historic transition. One era and one century ended; a new era and a new century have begun.

Just as each of the four most recent presidents has given different emphases to the U.S. role in this new era, so too have prominent scholars and analysts offered a range of views on its nature. Back in 1989, amid the sense of political and ideological triumph over communism, the neoconservative intellectual Francis Fukuyama envisioned "the end of history . . . and the universalization of Western liberal democracy as the final form of human government."[6] A few years later the Harvard University professor Samuel Huntington offered a much less optimistic view of a "clash of civilizations," particularly between the West and Islam, with prospects for political and military conflicts.[7] The *New York Times* columnist Thomas Friedman pointed rather to economics as the driving dynamic; to liberalism, clashing civilizations, and power politics as "the old system" and to globalization as "the new system."[8] The Rockefeller Brothers Fund, a prominent philanthropy, stressed the importance of "nonmilitary threats to peace and security," especially global poverty and environmental degradation, and advocated a conception of "social stewardship" for addressing these issues "before they metastasize into larger threats."[9] Even before the events of September 11, 2001, Columbia University professor Richard Betts stressed the threat of nuclear, chemical, and biological weapons of mass destruction (WMD), including those in the hands of terrorists who might "decide they want to stun American policy makers by inflicting enormous damage."[10] More recently, the scholar-journalist Fareed Zakaria wrote of a "post-American world, a great transformation taking place around the world . . . creating an international system in which countries in all parts of the world are no longer objects or observers but players in their own right. It is the birth of a truly global order."[11]

Whatever the differences among these perspectives, they share a common view of the importance of foreign policy. Time and again we hear voices claiming that the United States can and should turn inward and can afford to care less about and do less with the rest of the world. But for five fundamental reasons, the importance of foreign policy must not be underestimated.

*First are security threats. September 11 drove these home all too dramatically.* No longer was the threat "over there" in some distant corner of the globe; it had arrived right here at home. But it is not "just" terrorism. Although relations among the major powers are vastly improved from the Cold War, cooperation cannot be taken for granted, given both the policy differences that still exist and the internal political uncertainties Russia and China face. Wars continue to be fought in the Middle East, and stability remains fragile in regions such as South Asia (India, Pakistan) and East Asia (the Koreas, China, and Taiwan). Weapons of mass destruction proliferate in these and other regions, and possibly have fallen into the hands of terrorists. The United States is also at risk from newer security threats, such as diseases of mass destruction (DMD). For example, avian flu, with its potential for millions of fatalities, poses its own major security threats.

*Second, the American economy is more internationalized than ever before.* Whereas in 1960 foreign trade accounted for less than 10 percent of the U.S. gross domestic product (GDP), it now amounts to over 30 percent. Job opportunities for American workers are increasingly affected by both the competition from imports and the opportunities for exports. When the Federal Reserve Board sets interest rates, in addition to domestic factors such as inflation, it increasingly also has to consider international ones, such as foreign-currency exchange rates and the likely reactions of foreign investors. Private financial markets also have become increasingly globalized. So when Asian stock markets plunged in late 1997, and when Russia's economy collapsed in mid-1998, middle-class America felt the effects, with mutual funds, college savings, and retirement nest eggs plummeting in value. And when U.S. financial markets had their meltdown in late 2008, the negative results were transmitted around the world.

*Third, many other areas of policy that used to be considered "domestic" also have been internationalized.* The environmental policy agenda has extended from the largely domestic issues of the 1960s and 1970s to international issues such as global warming and biodiversity. The "just say no" drug policy of the 1980s was clearly not working when thousands of tons of drugs came into the United States every day from Latin America, Asia, and elsewhere. Whereas the Federal Bureau of Investigation's "Ten Most Wanted" list included mostly members of U.S.-based crime syndicates when it was first issued in 1950, by 1997 eight of the ten fugitives on the list were international criminals (and that was even before 9/11 put Osama bin Laden and other terrorists at the top of the list). Public-health problems such as the spread of AIDS have to be combated globally. The rash of consumer product-safety problems in 2007–2008 with children's toys, pet foods, and prescription drugs produced largely in China showed that product safety could no longer be just, or even mostly, a domestic regulatory issue. In these and other areas the distinctions between foreign and domestic policy have become increasingly blurred, as international forces affect in more and more ways spheres of American life that used to be considered domestic.

*Fourth, the increasing racial and ethnic diversity of the American people has produced a larger number and wider range of groups with personal bases for interest in foreign affairs.* Some forms of "identity politics" can be traced all the way back to the nineteenth century, and some were quite common during the Cold War. But more and more Americans trace their ancestry and heritage to different countries and regions and are asserting their interests and seeking influence over foreign policy toward those countries and regions.

*Fifth, it is hard for the United States to uphold its most basic values if it ignores grievous violations of those values that take place outside its national borders.* It is not necessary to go so far as to take on the role of global missionary or world police. But it also is not possible to claim to stand for democracy, freedom, and justice, yet say "not my problem" to genocide, repression, torture, and other horrors.

Foreign policy thus continues to press on Americans, as individuals and as a nation.

The choices it poses are at least as crucial for the twenty-first century as the Cold War and nuclear-age choices were for the second half of the twentieth century.

This book has two principal purposes: (1) to provide a framework, grounded in international relations theory and U.S. diplomatic history, for foreign policy analysis; and (2) to apply that framework to the agenda for U.S. foreign policy in the post–Cold War world.

The analytic framework, as reflected in the book's subtitle, is *the dynamics of choice*. It is structured by two fundamental sets of questions that, whatever the specific foreign policy issues involved and whatever the time period being discussed, have been at the center of debate:

- questions of *foreign policy strategy*—of what the national interest is and how best to achieve it
- questions of *foreign policy politics*—of which institutions and actors within the American political system play what roles and have how much influence

Setting foreign policy strategy is the *essence of choice*, establishing the goals to be achieved and forging the policies that are the optimal means for achieving them. Foreign policy politics is the *process of choice*, the making of foreign policy through the political institutions and amid the societal influences of the American political system.

Part I of this book provides the theory (in this chapter and Chapter 2) and history (Chapters 3, 4, and 5) for establishing the framework of the dynamics of choice in U.S. foreign policy. Part II then applies the framework to the major foreign policy choices the United States faces in this new era and new century.

## The Context of the International System

The United States, like all states, makes its choices of foreign policy strategy within the context of the international system. Although extensive study of international systems is more the province of international relations textbooks, three points are important to our focus on American foreign policy.

### *Quasi anarchy*

One of the fundamental differences between the international system and domestic political systems is the absence of a recognized central governing authority in the international system. This often is referred to as the *anarchic* view of international relations. Its roots go back to the seventeenth-century English political philosopher Thomas Hobbes and his classic treatise *Leviathan.* Hobbes saw international affairs as a "war of all against all." Unlike in domestic affairs, where order was maintained by a king or other recognized authority figure, no such recognized authority existed in the international sphere, according to Hobbes. Others since have taken a more tempered view, pointing to ways in which international norms, laws, and institutions have provided some order and authority and stressing the potential for even greater progress in this regard. Yet even in our contemporary era, although we have progressed beyond the "nasty, brutish," unadulterated Hobbesian world by developing international institutions like the United Nations and the International Monetary Fund, as well as a growing body of international law, the world still has nothing at the international level as weighty and authoritative as a constitution, a legislature, a president, or a supreme court. Thus, the prevailing sense is that what makes international relations "unique and inherently different from relations within states" is that "no ultimate authority exists to govern the international system. . . . As a result the existence of a 'quasi-anarchy' [sic] at the international level conditions state-to-state relations."[12]

## *System Structure*

System structure is based on the distribution of power among the major states in the international system. "Poles" refer to how many major powers there are—one in a ***unipolar*** system, two in a ***bipolar*** system, three or more in a ***multipolar*** system. In multipolar systems the key is a ***balance of power*** among the three or more states that are the major powers in the system, such that none of them can safely calculate that it can achieve dominance. The international system of the nineteenth century, when the United States was not yet a global power and the old European powers still dominated, is a frequent example of a balance-of-power system. In bipolar systems, such as the one that existed during the Cold War, peace and stability rest heavily on ***deterrence***. The general definition of deterrence is the prevention of war by fear of retaliation. In the Cold War the United States and the Soviet Union were particularly concerned with nuclear deterrence and the avoidance of nuclear war because of fear on both sides that even if one launched a first strike, the other would still have enough nuclear weaponry to strike back. In a unipolar system peace and stability depend on the ***primacy*** of a major power, and whether that major power uses its dominant position for the common international good or exploits it for its own benefit. This was one of the main debates during the George W. Bush administration, particularly over the Iraq war and more broadly over *unilateralism* versus *multilateralism.* The debate has become even more complex with questions about exactly how best to characterize the structure of an international system. Is the United States still the dominant power? Is China going to be the new dominant power? Is the system becoming a twenty-first-century version of multipolarity, with rising powers such as India and Brazil, not just China? Will the world become more regional, with stronger regional institutions? What about the increasing roles of nonstate actors, whether global terrorist groups such as Al Qaeda posing major security threats, transnational corporations and financial institutions affecting the international economy, or megaphilanthropies such as the Gates Foundation and its leading work on global public health?*

## State Structural Position

Whatever the structure, where a state ranks in it affects what it can do in foreign policy terms. Theorists such as Kenneth Waltz see system structure as very deterministic, making "[states'] behavior and the outcomes of their behavior predictable."[13] To know a state's structural position is thus to know its foreign policy strategy. Yet such claims can go too far, taking too rigid a view of how much is fixed and determined at the system level. For example, we know the Cold War went on for almost fifty years and that it ended peacefully. Waltz argues that this proves the stability of bipolarity and the success of deterrence policies. Yet it is worth asking whether the Cold War had to go on for fifty years: could it have been ended sooner had leaders on one or both sides pursued different policies? Or consider the Cuban missile crisis of 1962 (discussed in more detail in Chapter 4): the bipolar system structure raised the possibility of such a crisis but did not make either its occurrence or its successful resolution inevitable. The same logic applies to the end of the Cold War (Chapter 5) and leads us to ask whether the Cold War might have gone on longer had there been different leaders and policies on one or both sides in the 1980s and 1990s. Although it is important to take system structure into account, it should be as a context for, not a determinant of, choices of foreign policy strategy. This is especially true in the current era, when, as noted above, system structure is less clear than during the Cold War and earlier.

Another limitation of state structural explanations is conveyed through the metaphor of a game of billiards. The essence of billiards is the predictability of how a ball will move once it has been struck; hit the cue ball at a certain angle from a certain distance with a certain force, and you can predict exactly where on the table the target ball will go, regardless of whether it is solid or striped. In international systems theory, the "hitting" is done by external threats and the "angles set" by the state's position in the structure of the international system, and the "path" the state's foreign policy takes is predictable, regardless of the "stripes or solids" of its foreign policy priorities, domestic politics, or other characteristics. In reality, states are not like "crazy balls," bouncing wherever their domestic whims might take them, although they are not strictly reactive, either. Their foreign policy choices are constrained by the structure of the international system but are not determined by it. Domestic politics and institutions matter a great deal, as we discuss in Chapter 2.

---

*We take these questions up in Part II, particularly Chapters 6, 7, and 10.

## The National Interest: The "4 Ps" Framework

The national interest: all of us have heard it preached. Many of us may have done some of the preaching ourselves—that U.S. foreign policy must be made in the name of the national interest. No one would argue with the proposition that following the national interest is the essence of the choices to be made in a nation's foreign policy. But defining what the national interest is and then developing policies for achieving it have rarely been as easy or self-evident as such invocations would imply. The political scientists Alexander George and Robert Keohane capture this dilemma in a jointly authored article. They note the problems that have been encountered because the concept of the national interest has "become so elastic and ambiguous . . . that its role as a guide to foreign policy is problematical and controversial." Yet they also stress the importance that the national interest can have, and needs to have, to help "improve judgments regarding the proper ends and goals of foreign policy."[14]

Our approach in this book is to establish in general analytic terms the four core goals that go into defining the U.S. national interest: Power, Peace, Prosperity, and Principles. These "4 Ps" are not strict categories in which this policy goes in one box and that one in another. Reality is never that neat. The national interest almost always combines one or more of the "4 Ps." Indeed, although sometimes all four core goals are complementary and can be satisfied through the same policy, more often they pose trade-offs and tensions, and sometimes major dissensus. The "4 Ps" framework helps us see this complexity and especially to analyze how priorities get set and to locate the corresponding debates over what American foreign policy *is* and what it *should be*—what we earlier called "the essence of choice" in foreign policy strategy.

In setting up this analytic framework, we are not pitting the U.S. national interest against the interests of the international community. Indeed, the U.S. national interest has become increasingly interrelated with the interests of the international community. This is not and likely never will be a pure one-to-one relationship in which the U.S. national interest and other international interests are fully in sync. There is much debate about just how interrelated they are. For example, the (George W.) Bush administration criticized the Clinton administration for allegedly pursuing a foreign policy in which "the 'national interest' is replaced with 'humanitarian interests' or the interests of 'the international community.' "[15] On the other hand, among the main criticisms of the Bush administration's own policies was that they often put the American national interest at loggerheads with the interests of others in the international community, and that this proved not to be in anyone's interest. The Obama conception of "common security for our common humanity" is presenting another approach posing its own debates.

For each of the "4 Ps" we lay out three main elements:

- basic conceptualization and working definition
- the most closely associated broader theory of international relations (the IR "-isms")
- representative policy strategies and illustrative examples

## *Power*

*Power* is the key requirement for the most basic goal of foreign policy, self-defense and the preservation of national independence and territory. It is also essential for deterring aggression and influencing other states on a range of issues. "Power enables an actor to shape his environment so as to reflect his interests," Samuel Huntington stated. "In particular it enables a state to protect its security and prevent, deflect or defeat threats to that security."[16] To the extent that a state is interested in asserting itself, advancing its own interests and itself being aggressive, it needs power. "The strong do what they have the power to do," the ancient Greek historian Thucydides wrote, "and the weak accept what they have to accept."[17]

***Realism*** is the school of international relations theory that most emphasizes the objective of power. "International relations is a struggle for power," the noted Realist scholar Hans Morgenthau wrote; "statesmen think and act in terms of interest defined as power."[18] As Reading 1.1, from one of Morgenthau's classic books, *In Defense of the National Interest,* shows, he and other Realists view the international system in terms of a competition for power.* They take a very Hobbesian view, seeing conflict and competition as the basic reality of international politics. The "grim picture" is painted by the University of Chicago professor John Mearsheimer: "International relations is not a constant state of war, but it is a state of relentless security competition, with the possibility of war always in the background. . . . Cooperation among states has its limits, mainly because it is constrained by the dominating logic of security competition, which no amount of cooperation can eliminate. Genuine peace, or a world where states do not compete for power, is not likely."[19] States thus ultimately can rely only on themselves for security. It is a "self-help" system—and power is critical to the self-help states need to be secure.

1.1

For Realists, consequently, four points are central. First, states pursue interests, not peace per se. If their interests are better served by war, aggression, and other such coercive means, appeals to peace as an objective won't work very well. Peace is best served by using power to affect the calculations states make. Second, political and military power remain the major currencies of power. They are crucial to a strong national defense, to credible deterrence, and to other effective means of statecraft. The particular requirements have varied

*Marginal icons indicate a related reading; readings follow each part of the book.

dramatically over time with changes in the identity of the potential aggressor—Great Britain in early U.S. history, Germany in the two world wars, the Soviet Union during the Cold War, terrorism today—and the nature of weaponry—from muskets and a few warships to nuclear weapons, submarines, and supersonic bombers to suicide bombers and anthrax letter "bombs." But the basic strategy always has been essentially the same: to have sufficient military power to deter aggression and, if deterrence fails, to ensure the defense of the nation.

Third, economic power and other aspects of prosperity are valued by Realists less as their own international currency than as the "bullion" on which military power ultimately rests. The American economy has to be kept strong and competitive primarily so that the advanced technologies needed for next-generation weapons can be provided, and so that the political support for a large defense budget and other global commitments can be maintained. Fourth, although principles such as democracy and human rights are important, they rarely should be given priority over considerations of power. This last point emerged in the George W. Bush administration as a major difference between "neoconservatives," who stressed principles as well as power, and more traditional Realists.

The principal foreign policy strategies that follow from this line of reasoning are largely *coercive* ones. "Covenants without the sword," to go back to Hobbes, "are but words, and of no strength to secure a man at all. The bonds of words are too weak to bridle men's ambitions, avarice, anger and other passions, without the fear of some coercive power."[20] The ultimate coercive strategy of course, is *war*—"the continuation of policy by other means," in the words of the great nineteenth-century Prussian strategist Karl von Clausewitz, "an act of violence intended to compel our opponent to fulfill our will." Starting with its own Revolutionary War and then through the nineteenth century (e.g., the Mexican-American War, the Spanish-American War) and the twentieth century (e.g., World Wars I and II, the Vietnam War, the Persian Gulf War) and into the twenty-first century with the war on terrorism and the Iraq war, the wars fought by the United States have had varying success in achieving the Clausewitzian objective of "compel[ling one's] opponent to fulfill [one's] will."

***Military interventions*** are the "small wars," the uses of military force in a more limited fashion, as in the overthrow of governments considered hostile to U.S. interests and the protection or bringing to power of pro-U.S. leaders through military actions of limited scope and duration. We will see numerous historical examples (Chapter 3) as well as others during the Cold War (Chapters 4 and 5) and in the post–Cold War era (Chapters 6 and 8).

Another distinction in uses of military force concerns timing. ***Self-defense*** is military action taken in response to already having been attacked. ***Preemption*** is military action taken against an imminent threat—that is, you have strong basis for assessing that the target of the attack is about to attack you. ***Prevention*** is military action taken when the threat is less than imminent but you have strong basis for assessing that if you wait the threat will become much greater. These aspects of the use of force also have been long-standing and especially intense debates in recent years, for example, as over Iraq (Chapter 8) and humanitarian intervention (Chapter 9).

***Alliances*** against a mutual enemy are a key component of both defense and deterrence strategies. For most of American history, alliances were formed principally in wartime: for example, with France in 1778, when twelve thousand French troops came over to help the Americans fight for independence against the shared enemy, Britain; with Britain and France in World War I; with Britain and the Soviet Union in World War II; with twenty-six other nations in the 1990–91 Persian Gulf War; with an even wider coalition in the 2001 Afghanistan war; but with a much less broadly based coalition in the 2003 Iraq war. During the Cold War (officially, peacetime), the United States set up a global network of alliances, including multilateral ones such as the North Atlantic Treaty Organization (NATO), the Southeast Asia Treaty Organization (SEATO), and the Rio Treaty (with Latin American countries), as well as bilateral agreements with Japan, South Korea, Taiwan, Israel, Iran, and others. Some of these alliances and bilateral pacts have continued into the post–Cold War era; new ones also have been struck.

A related strategy is the provision of ***military assistance***, such as weapons, advisers, financing, and other forms of aid, to a pro-American government or rebel group. Here too are numerous historical examples: Lend-Lease to Great Britain in 1940–41, before the United States entered World War II; military aid to anticommunist governments during the Cold War, including major violators of democracy and human rights; current military aid to antiterrorist governments, including many with poor records on democracy and human rights.

Power can be exerted through more than just military force. Diplomacy also can be used coercively. ***Coercive statecraft*** takes a number of forms, from such low-level actions as the filing of an official protest or issuing a public condemnation, to withdrawing an ambassador and suspending diplomatic relations, to imposing ***economic sanctions*** and other, tougher measures. Then there is ***covert action***, the secret operations of intelligence agencies conducted, as former secretary of state Henry Kissinger put it, to "defend the American national interest in the gray areas where military operations are not suitable and diplomacy cannot operate."[21] Although they have been especially associated with the Cold War and now with the war on terrorism, covert actions go back to early U.S. history, as when President Thomas Jefferson secretly arranged the overthrow of the pasha of Tripoli (in today's Libya) and when President James Madison authorized a secret attack into Florida, which then was still controlled by Spain.

## *Peace*

In a certain sense, all four of the national interest objectives ultimately are about *Peace*—for that is what power is supposed to safeguard, what prosperity is supposed to contribute to, what principles are supposed to undergird. We use it to stress ***diplomacy*** in its classic sense of "the formalized system, of procedures and process by which sovereign states . . . conduct their official relations."[22] From the very beginning, when the State Department was created as one of the original Cabinet departments and Benjamin Franklin was dispatched to France seeking support for the young nation, diplomacy has been a crucial element in U.S. foreign policy strategy. Diplomacy continues on a daily basis, with U.S. ambassadors stationed in capitals around the world and foreign ambassadors in Washington, D.C. It becomes especially important in crises, wars, and other such urgent times. Although it can also take coercive forms through economic sanctions and other measures as noted above, its methods stress negotiation.

***International Institutionalism*** is diplomacy's most closely associated IR "-ism". International Institutionalism views world politics as "a cultivable 'garden,'" in contrast to the Realist view of a global "'jungle.'"[23] Although they stop well short of world government, these theories emphasize both the possibility and the value of reducing the chances of war and of achieving common interests sufficiently for the international system to be one of *world order.* International Institutionalists recognize that tensions and conflicts among nations do exist, but they see cooperation among nations as more possible and more beneficial than Realists do. Pursuing cooperation thus is neither naïve nor dangerous, but rather a rational way to reduce risks and make gains that even the most powerful state could not achieve solely on its own. To be sure, as Professor Inis Claude has written, "the problem of power is here to stay; it is, realistically, not a problem to be eliminated, but"—the key point for International Institutionalists—"a problem to be managed."[24] International Institutionalists have their own conception of power, which in contrast to that of Realists stresses diplomatic over military and other coercive means. To the extent that treaties and international institutions constrain potential aggressors, they contribute to the "general capacity of a state to control the behavior of others," which is how one international relations textbook defines power. When peace brokering is effective, it adds to the ability of the United States "to overcome obstacles and prevail in conflicts," which is another text's definition of power.[25]

Consistent with this sense that peace is achievable but not automatic, scholars such as Robert O. Keohane stress the importance of creating international institutions as the basis for "governance in a partially globalized world" (Reading 1.2). Anarchy cannot be eliminated totally, but it can be tempered or partially regulated. Indeed, it is precisely because the power and interests that Realists stress do generate conflicts that "international institutions . . . will be components of any lasting peace."[26] This also is true with regard to relations among allies. States may have friendly relations and share common interests but still have problems of collective action or even just coordination. International institutions provide the structure and the commitments to facilitate, and in some instances require, the fulfillment of commitments to collective action and coordination. "Institutions can provide information, reduce transaction costs, make commitments more credible, establish focal points for coordination

1.2

and, in general, facilitate the operation of reciprocity."[27] In doing so international institutions help states overcome the difficulties of collective action, which can persist even when states have common interests. This is a very rational argument, not just idealism. The world envisioned is not one free of tensions and conflicts. But it is one in which the prospects for achieving cooperation are greater than Realism and other power-based theories foresee. International Institutionalists also see the constraints on a state's own freedom of action that come with multilateralism as less consequential than the capacity gained to achieve shared objectives and serve national interests in ways that would be less possible unilaterally. In Part II, we explore the unilateralism-multilateralism debate and the sharp controversies it has sparked in recent years.

International institutions may be formal bodies such as the United Nations, but they also can be more informal, in what are often called "international regimes." Keohane defines international institutions both functionally and structurally, as "the rules that govern elements of world politics and the organizations that help implement those rules."[28] This definition encompasses norms and rules of behavior, procedures for managing and resolving conflicts, and the organizational bases for at least some degree of global governance, albeit well short of full global government.

We can identify five principal types of international institutions:

1. *Global,* such as the League of Nations (unsuccessful) and the United Nations (more successful)
2. *Economic,* particularly global institutions, such as the International Monetary Fund, the World Bank, and the World Trade Organization
3. *International legal,* such as the long-standing World Court and the newly created International Criminal Court
4. *Policy area,* such as the International Atomic Energy Agency (IAEA) for nuclear nonproliferation, the World Health Organization (WHO) for global public health, and the United Nations Environmental Program for the global environment
5. *Regional,* such as the Organization on Security and Cooperation in Europe (OSCE) or the Pan American Conference of the late nineteenth century.

In none of these cases has the United States been the only state involved in establishing the institutions and organizations. But in most, if not all, the United States has played a key role.

Another type of foreign policy strategy that fits here is the *"peace broker"* role the United States has played in wars and conflicts to which it has not been a direct party. Familiar contemporary examples include the 1973–75 "shuttle diplomacy" in the Middle East by Henry Kissinger, the 1978 Camp David accord between Egypt and Israel brokered by President Jimmy Carter, and the Clinton administration's role in the 1995 Dayton accord ending the war in Bosnia. But this role, too, traces back historically, as with the peace treaty brokered by President Theodore Roosevelt ending the Russo-Japanese War, for which "TR" was awarded the 1906 Nobel Peace Prize.

## *Prosperity*

Foreign policies motivated by the pursuit of *Prosperity* are those that give high priority to the national interest defined principally in economic terms. They seek gains for the American economy from policies that help provide reliable and low-cost imports, growing markets for American exports, profitable foreign investments, and other international economic opportunities. Some of these involve policies that are specifically *foreign economic* ones, such as trade policy. Others involve general relations with countries whose significance to U.S. foreign policy is largely economic, as with an oil-rich country like Saudi Arabia. Most generally they have involved efforts to strengthen global capitalism as the structure of the international economy.

Among theories that stress the economic factor in American foreign policy are two principal schools of thought. These schools share the emphasis on economics but differ on whether the prime motivator of policy is to serve the general public interest or the more particular interests of the economic elite. The first school of thought, which we dub "Economism," emphasizes the pursuit through foreign policy of general economic benefits to the nation: a favorable balance of trade, strong economic growth, a healthy macroeconomy.[29] The ultimate goal is collective prosperity, in which the interests served are those of the American people in general. This was said to have been a major part of U.S. foreign policy in the nineteenth century, when about 70 percent of the treaties and other international agreements the United States signed were on matters related to trade and international commerce.[30] It was the basis for the creation after World War II of the General Agreement on Tariffs and Trade (GATT), the International Monetary Fund (IMF), and the World Bank as the key international economic institutions of an open, market-based free trade system. It also has been evident in recent years, as in the 1995 statement by then secretary of state Warren Christopher that whereas other secretaries of state put their main emphasis on arms control, "I make no apologies for putting economics at the top of [the U.S.] foreign policy agenda."[31]

The second school includes a number of theories, most notably theories of ***imperialism*** and ***neocolonialism***, that see American foreign policy as dominated by and serving the interests of the capitalist class and other elites, such as multinational corporations and major banks.[32] The prosperity that is sought is more for the private benefit of special interests, and the ways in which it is sought are highly exploitative of other countries. The basics of this theory go back to the British economist John Hobson and his 1902 book *Imperialism*. Because the unequal distribution of wealth leaves the lower classes with limited purchasing power, capitalism creates for itself the twin problems of underconsumption and overproduction. It thus needs to find new markets for its products if it is to avoid recession and depression. Although Britain and its colonialism were Hobson's primary focus, his arguments also were applicable to the United States and its more indirect neocolonialism in Latin America and parts of Asia (see Chapter 3).

Vladimir Ilyich Lenin, while still in exile in Switzerland in 1916, the year before he would return to Russia to lead the communist revolution, wrote his most famous book, *Imperialism: The Highest Stage of Capitalism.* Lenin's version of imperialist theory differed from Hobson's in rejecting the possibility that capitalism could reform itself.* One reason was that, in addition to the underconsumption-overproduction problem, Lenin emphasized the pursuit of inexpensive and abundant supplies of raw materials as another key motive for capitalist expansionism. Giving the working class more purchasing power would not do anything about the lust for the iron ore, foodstuffs, and, later, oil that were so much more plentiful and so much cheaper in the colonial world (later called the Third World). Moreover, the essence of Lenin's theory was the belief that the capitalist class so dominated the political process and defined the limits of democracy that it never would allow the kinds of reforms Hobson advocated. Lenin's theories and their spin-offs became the basis for many highly critical views of U.S. foreign policy during the Cold War, particularly in the Third World, such as that of Gabriel Kolko excerpted in the Readings. Another version of this debate has been developing within the context of globalization (Chapter 10).

1.3

In sum, their differences notwithstanding, these two schools share an emphasis on economic goals as driving forces behind U.S. foreign policy. They differ over whose prosperity is being served, but they agree on the centrality of prosperity among the "4 Ps".

## *Principles*

1.4

The fourth core goal, *Principles,* involves the values, ideals, and beliefs that the United States has claimed to stand for in the world. As a more general theory, this emphasis on principles is rooted in ***Democratic Idealism*** (Reading 1.4).

Democratic Idealists hold to two central tenets about foreign policy. One is that when trade-offs have to be made, "right" is to be chosen over "might." This is said to be particularly true for the United States because of the ostensibly special role bestowed on it—to stand up for the principles on which it was founded and not be just another player in global power politics. We find assertions of this notion of "American

*Hobson believed that liberal domestic reforms were possible and would help capitalism break out of the underconsumption and overproduction cycle. Such reforms would create a more equitable distribution of wealth, bringing an increase in consumption, in the process both making the home society more equitable and alleviating the need for colonies, thus making foreign policy less imperialistic.

exceptionalism" throughout U.S. history. Thomas Jefferson, the country's first secretary of state and its third president, characterized the new United States of America as such: "the solitary republic of the world, the only monument of human rights . . . the sole depository of the sacred fire of freedom and self-government, from hence it is to be lighted up in other regions of the earth, if other regions shall ever become susceptible to its benign influence."[33] And then there was President Woodrow Wilson's famous declaration that U.S. entry into World War I was intended "to make the world safe for democracy": "We shall fight for the things which we have always carried nearest our hearts—for democracy, for the right of those who submit to authority to have a voice in their own government, for the rights and liberties of small nations, for a universal dominion of right by such a concert of free peoples as shall bring peace and safety to all nations and make the world in itself at last free." Democratic idealism was also claimed by many a Cold War president, from Democrats such as John Kennedy with his call in his inaugural address to "bear any burden, pay any price" to defend democracy and fight communism, to Republicans such as Ronald Reagan and his crusade against the "evil empire." It also was part of President George W. Bush's launching of the war on terrorism as not only a matter of security but also a war against "evil . . . the fight of all who believe in progress and pluralism, tolerance and freedom." So too did President Obama declare in his inaugural address that "America is a friend of each nation and every man, woman, and child who seeks a future of peace and dignity."

The other key tenet of Democratic Idealism is that in the long run "right" makes for "might," and that in the end interests such as peace and power are well served by principles. One of the strongest statements of this view is the ***democratic peace*** theory, which asserts that by promoting democracy we promote peace because democracies do not go to war against each other. To put it another way, the world could be made safe *by* democracy. For all the attention the democratic peace theory has gotten in the post–Cold War era, its central argument and philosophical basis trace back to the eighteenth-century political philosopher Immanuel Kant and his book *Perpetual Peace*. "If . . . the consent of the citizenry is required in order to decide that war should be declared," Kant wrote, "nothing is more natural than that they would be very cautious in commencing such a poor game. . . . But, on the other hand, in a constitution which is not republican, and under which the subjects are not citizens, a declaration of war is the easiest thing to decide upon, because war does not require of the ruler . . . the least sacrifice of the pleasure of his table, the chase, his country houses, his court functions and the like."[34] In Chapter 11, we take a closer look at democratic peace theory as well as at major critiques of it.

As for serving the goal of power, Professor Joseph Nye of Harvard University coined the term ***soft power*** to refer to the ways in which the values for which a nation stands, its cultural attractiveness, and other aspects of its reputation can have quite practical value as sources of influence.[35] This is not just a matter of what American leaders claim in their rhetoric, but of whether other governments and peoples perceive for themselves a consistency between the principles espoused and the actual policies pursued by the United States. It also depends on how well America is deemed to be living up to its ideals within its own society on issues such as race relations, protection of the environment, and crime and violence.

Given its strong and exceptionalist claims to principles, American foreign policy often has been severely criticized at home and abroad for not living up to its espoused ideals. Such critiques have been raised at various times throughout American history (Chapter 3); during the Cold War, especially about U.S. policy in the Third World (Chapters 4 and 5); and more recently about the war on terrorism, U.S. policy in the Middle East, and neoconservatism as an overarching foreign policy ideology-strategy (Chapters 6 and 8). Precisely because of the arguments that right should be chosen over might and that in the long run right makes for might, debates over how true American foreign policy is to its principles matter as more than just idealistic questions.

Table 1.1 summarizes the "4 Ps" of foreign policy strategy, highlighting differences among core national-interest goals, schools of international relations theory, principal conceptions of the international system, and principal types of policies pursued. It is important to emphasize again that these are distinctions of degree and not inflexible one-or-the-other categorizations. They provide a framework for analyzing foreign policy strategy in ways that push deeper into general conceptions of the national interest and get at the "essence of choice" over what American foreign policy is and should be.

**TABLE 1.1 A Foreign Policy Strategy Typology**

| Core national interest goal | International relations theory | Conception of the international system | Main types of policies |
|---|---|---|---|
| Power | Realism | Competition for power | Coercive |
| Peace | International Institutionalism | World order | Diplomatic |
| Prosperity | Economism Imperialism | Global capitalism | Economic |
| Principles | Democratic Idealism, Neoconservatism | Global spread of democracy | Political, coercive |

## Dilemmas of Foreign Policy Choice: "4 Ps" Complementarity, Trade-offs, and Dissensus

### *"4 Ps" Complementarity: Optimal, but Infrequent*

To the extent that all "4 Ps" can be satisfied through the same strategy—that is, they are complementary—the dilemmas of foreign policy choice are relatively easy. No major trade-offs have to be made, no strict priorities set. This does happen sometimes, as the following two cases illustrate.

THE 1990–91 PERSIAN GULF WAR The Persian Gulf War was a great victory for American foreign policy in many respects. The invasion of Kuwait by Iraq, led by Saddam Hussein, was a blatant act of aggression—one of the most naked acts of aggression since World War II. Furthermore, the Iraqis were poised to keep going, straight into Saudi Arabia, an even more strategic country and a close U.S. ally.

But through U.S. leadership, the *peace* was restored. "This will not stand," President George H. W. Bush declared. Resolutions were sponsored in the United Nations (UN) Security Council, demanding an Iraqi withdrawal and then authorizing the use of military force to liberate Kuwait. A twenty-seven-nation diplomatic coalition was built, including most of Western Europe, Japan, and much of the Arab world. A multinational military force went to war under the command of General Norman Schwarzkopf of the U.S. Army.

Operation Desert Storm, as it was named, was also a formidable demonstration of American *power*. It is important to recall how worried many military analysts were at the outset of Desert Storm about incurring high casualties, and even about the possibility that Saddam would resort to chemical or biological weapons. That the military victory came so quickly and with so few U.S. and allied casualties was testimony to the military superiority the United States had achieved. Striding tall from its Gulf War victory, American power was shown to be second to none.

Of course, this was not just about helping Kuwait. *Prosperity* also was at risk, in the form of oil. Twice before in recent decades, war and instability in the Middle East had disrupted oil supplies and sent oil prices skyrocketing. The parents of today's college students still have memories of waiting in gasoline lines and watching prices escalate on a daily basis during the 1973 Arab-Israeli War and the 1979 Iranian Revolution. This time, though, because the Gulf War victory came so swiftly, disruptions to the American and global economies were minimized.

Although Kuwait couldn't claim to be a democracy, other important *principles* were at issue. One was the right of all states to be free from aggression. Another was the moral value of standing up to a dictator as brutal as Saddam Hussein. Comparisons to Adolf Hitler went too far, but Saddam was a leader who left a trail of torture, repression, and mass killings.

THE MARSHALL PLAN, 1947 The Marshall Plan was the first major U.S. foreign aid program; it provided about $17 billion to Western Europe for economic reconstruction following World War II.* This was an enormous amount of money, equivalent in today's dollars to over $160 billion, which would be *over ten times greater* than the entire U.S. foreign aid budget. Yet the Marshall Plan passed Congress by overwhelming majorities, 69–17 in the Senate and 329–74 in the House. Compare these votes with today's politics, when much lower levels of foreign aid barely get a congressional majority.

The key reason for such strong support was that the Marshall Plan was seen as serving the full range of U.S. foreign policy goals. The communist parties in France, Italy, and elsewhere in Western Europe were feeding off the continuing economic suffering and dislocation, making worrisome political gains. The Marshall Plan thus was a component of the broader strategy of containment of communism to keep the *peace* in Western Europe. It also asserted American *power*, for with the foreign aid came certain conditions, some explicit and some implicit. And in a more general sense, the United States was establishing its global predominance and leadership. The glorious nations of the Old World were now dependent on the New World former colony.

American *prosperity* was also well served. The rebuilding of European markets generated demand for American exports and created opportunities for American investments. Thus, although its motives were not strictly altruistic, the Marshall Plan was quite consistent with American *principles:* the stability of fellow Western democracies was at stake.

## *"4 Ps" Trade-offs: More Frequent, More Problematic*

Not only are cases with "4 Ps" tensions more common, but they require much tougher choices. Trade-offs have to be made; priorities have to be set. The following two examples illustrate such choices.

CHINA, 1989: POWER AND PROSPERITY VS. PRINCIPLES In 1989, hundreds of Chinese students staged a massive pro-democracy sit-in in Tiananmen Square in Beijing, China's capital city. As one expression of their protest, they constructed a statue resembling the American Statue of Liberty. The Communist government ordered the students to leave. They refused. The Chinese army then moved in with tanks and troops. An esti-

*The Marshall Plan is named for Secretary of State George Marshall, who made the initial public proposal in a commencement speech at Harvard University.

mated one thousand students were killed, and tens of thousands of students and other dissidents were arrested that night and in the ensuing months.

In reaction to the Chinese crackdown, many in the United States called for the imposition of economic sanctions. The focus of these efforts was on revoking China's most-favored-nation (MFN) status. Essentially MFN status limits tariffs on a country's exports to the United States to a standard, low level; without MFN status, a country's exports to the United States are much less competitive, and that country's international trade will be adversely affected.* The pro-sanctions argument, which came from a bipartisan coalition in Congress and from human-rights groups, was based on *principles:* How could the United States conduct business as usual with a government that massacred its own people? These pro-democracy Chinese protesters had turned to America for inspiration. How could the United States not stand up for what it says are values and beliefs it holds dear?

The George H. W. Bush administration, which was in office at the time, was willing to impose only limited economic sanctions; it would not revoke China's MFN status. Its main argument was based on *power.* The administration still considered the U.S.-Soviet rivalry to be the central issue in its foreign relations and thus gave priority to its geopolitical interests—namely, continued good relations with China. Among President Bush's critics was the Democratic presidential candidate, Bill Clinton, who castigated his opponent for coddling "the butchers of Beijing." Yet as president, Clinton also refused to revoke China's MFN status. His reasons were based more on economic considerations—*prosperity*—and the calculation of billions of dollars in potential trade and investment losses for the American economy.

Both Bush and Clinton claimed that they were not abandoning principles, that other steps were being taken to try to protect human rights and promote democracy in China. But although this justification was partly true, debate still raged over what trade-offs to make in the name of the national interest. The requisites of Power and Prosperity pointed to one set of policies, Principles to another. Trade-offs were inevitable; choices had to be made.

GUATEMALA, 1954: PROSPERITY AND POWER VS. PRINCIPLES In 1945, Guatemala, the Central American country just south of Mexico, ended a long string of military dictatorships by holding free elections. A progressive new constitution was written, freedoms of the press and of speech were guaranteed, and workers and peasants were encouraged to organize. A number of military coups were attempted, but they were put

*It is not that the country receiving MFN is favored over others, but rather that all countries receiving MFN get the same "most favored" tariff treatment. In 2000 this terminology was changed from MFN to PNTR, or permanent normal trade relations.

down. In 1951, Colonel Jacobo Arbenz Guzman, a pro-reform military officer, was elected president.

One of Arbenz's highest priorities was land reform. Two percent of the population owned 70 percent of the land in Guatemala. The largest of all landholders was the United Fruit Company (UFCO), a U.S.-owned banana exporter. In March 1953, Arbenz's government included about 230,000 acres of UFCO holdings in the land being expropriated for redistribution to the peasantry. Most of this land was uncultivated, but that didn't matter to the UFCO. The compensation offered to the company by the Guatemalan government was deemed inadequate, even though it was the same valuation rate (a low one) that the UFCO had been using to limit the taxes it paid.

This wasn't just a UFCO problem, its corporate president declared: "From here on out it's not a matter of the people of Guatemala against the United Fruit Company. The question is going to be communism against the right of property, the life and security of the Western Hemisphere."[36] It was true that Arbenz had members of the Guatemalan Communist Party in his government. He also was buying weapons from Czechoslovakia, which was a Soviet satellite. Might this be the beginning of the feared Soviet "beachhead" in the Western Hemisphere?* In defending the anti-Arbenz coup d'état that it engineered in 1954 through covert CIA action, the Eisenhower administration stressed the *power* concerns raised by this perceived threat to containment. The evidence of links to Soviet communism was not that strong, but the standard that needed to be met was only what an earlier U.S. ambassador to Guatemala had called the "duck test": "Many times it is impossible to prove legally that a certain individual is a communist; but for cases of this sort I recommend a practical method of detection—the 'duck test.' The duck test works this way: suppose you see a bird walking around in a farmyard. The bird wears no label that says 'duck.' But the bird certainly looks like a duck. Also, he goes to the pond and you notice that he swims like a duck. Well, by this time you have probably reached the conclusion that the bird is a duck, whether he's wearing a label or not."[37]

An argument can be made that, given the Cold War, the duck test was sufficient from a power perspective. Even so, the anti-Arbenz coup was something of a "joint venture," strikingly consistent with Imperialist critiques of U.S. foreign policy (*prosperity*). The UFCO had close ties to the Eisenhower administration; the historical record shows evidence of collaboration between the company and the government; and one of the first acts of the new regime of General Carlos Castillo Armas, who was a graduate of the military-intelligence training school at Fort Leavenworth, Kansas, and whom the CIA installed in power after the coup, was to give land back to the UFCO.

---

*Fidel Castro had not yet come to power in Cuba. That would happen in 1959.

The critical tension here was with *principles.* The Arbenz government had come to power through elections that, though not perfectly free and fair, were much fairer than those in most of Latin America. And the military governments that ruled Guatemala for the thirty-five years following the U.S.-engineered coup were extremely brutal and showed wanton disregard for human rights, killing and persecuting tens of thousands of their own people. The U.S. role was hidden for decades but was pointedly revealed in 1999 in a shocking report by a Guatemalan historical commission, which estimated that two hundred thousand people had been killed by the U.S.-supported military regimes and provided strong evidence of U.S. complicity.[38]

## *"4 Ps" Dissensus: Bitter Conflicts*

In other situations, the debates are less about this P having priority over that one than about deep dissensus over the nature of the national interest. The Iraq war that began in 2003 exemplifies this type of situation.[39]

IRAQ WAR, 2003 Going to war in Iraq, the Bush administration contended, was very much in the American national interest. American *power* was more than sufficient to win the war and to eliminate the threat posed by Saddam Hussein and his regional aggression, alleged WMD arsenal, and links to Al Qaeda and global terrorism. Moreover, the "shock and awe" that the U.S. military would bring to bear would enhance the credibility of American power within the Middle East as well as globally. *Peace* would be strengthened in a region that had known too little of it. Saddam, who had started wars against his own neighbors as well as threatening Israel, would be gone. The Arab-Israeli peace process could be gotten back on track. Despite the immediate conflict with the United Nations, the U.S. willingness to do what needed to be done would be good for the world body in the long run.

*Prosperity* would not be hurt: budgetary estimates for the war purportedly showed that the United States would have to bear minimal costs. Indeed, U.S. and global prosperity would be helped by a post-Saddam regime's stabilizing effect on OPEC and global oil markets. Consistency with *principles* was claimed in that the war would dispense with a dictator who had used chemical weapons against his own people, tortured and murdered thousands of political prisoners, and committed countless other atrocities. The democracy that was to be created in Iraq would set a shining example for the rest of the Arab world.

Opponents asserted an equal claim to the U.S. national interest, as well as to the international interests at stake. The Bush administration, they said, was overestimating American *power.* American military superiority was a given, but converting this possession of power into actual influence over other countries was much more difficult than assumed.

Within Iraq, winning the war would be one thing, but winning the peace quite another. The line between being a liberating force and an occupying one was going to be a lot harder to walk than the Bush administration was claiming. Terrorism would be strengthened, not weakened, both within Iraq and globally. The fallout would exacerbate, not ameliorate, the Israeli-Palestinian conflict. U.S. defiance of the UN undermined rather than buttressed the UN. *Peace* was being hurt not helped.

In addition, the opponents maintained, the budget numbers were being manipulated; the White House's leading economic advisor was fired for saying so. American *prosperity* would be damaged by the hundreds of billions that would inevitably be added to the federal budget deficit. The further instability in Iraq would strengthen the forces pushing global oil prices, and the price at the pump for the average American, higher and higher. And one didn't have to defend Saddam to see how an extended military occupation could lead to the kinds of atrocities that were committed by American forces at Abu Ghraib. The Iraqi people's thirst for democracy, as shown in their first free elections, deserved praise and admiration. But all in all American *principles* were being more undermined than reinforced by the occupation.

We take these issues and debates up in more detail in Chapter 8.

## Summary

Whatever the issue at hand, and whether past, present, or future, American foreign policy has been, is, and will continue to be about the *dynamics of choice.*

One set of these choices is about *foreign policy strategy.* It is easy to preach about the national interest, but much harder to assess what that interest is in a particular situation. One or more of the four core goals—*power, peace, prosperity,* and *principles*—may be involved. Not only may basic analyses differ, but more often than not trade-offs have to be made and priorities set among these four Ps. In some cases the debates are over fundamentally conflicting positions. Views reflect different schools of international relations theory, carry with them alternative policy approaches, and can result in fundamentally different foreign policy strategies. This is the *essence of choice* that is inherent to every major foreign policy issue.

We will use this framework for analyzing U.S. foreign policy strategy historically (Chapter 3), during the Cold War (Chapters 4 and 5), and in our current post–Cold War era (Part II, Chapters 6–11). First, though, we turn in Chapter 2 to foreign policy politics and lay out an analytic framework for this other key dimension of American foreign policy, the *process of choice.*

## *American Foreign Policy* Online Student StudySpace

- For which policies has America been criticized for not living up to its exceptionalist claims to principles?
- Which are the key differences among the different schools of international relations?

For these and other study questions, as well as other features, check out Chapter 1 on the *American Foreign Policy* Online Student StudySpace at wwnorton.com/studyspace.

## Notes

[1]George H. W. Bush, "Remarks at the United States Military Academy in West Point, New York," January 5, 1993, *Public Papers of the Presidents: George Bush* (Washington, D.C.: Office of the Federal Register, National Archives and Records Administration, 1993), 2:2228–32.

[2]Bill Clinton, "Speech at the University of Nebraska," December 8, 2000, *Public Papers of the Presidents: William J. Clinton 2000–2001* (Washington, D.C.: U.S. Government Printing Office, 2002), 3:2653–61.

[3]Serge Schmemann, "U.S. Attacked: President Vows to Exact Punishment for 'Evil'," *New York Times*, September 12, 2001, A1.

[4]George W. Bush, Address to a Joint Session of Congress and the American People, September 20, 2001, www.americanrhetoric.com/speeches/gwbush911jointsessionspeech.htm; and Bush, 2002 State of the Union Address, www.c-span.org/executive/transcript.asp?cat=current_event&code=bush_admin&year=2002 (accessed 5/8/09).

[5]Barack Obama, "Renewing American Leadership," *Foreign Affairs* 86 (July/August 2007): 2–4.

[6]Francis Fukuyama, "The End of History?" *National Interest* 16 (Summer 1989): 4.

[7]Samuel P. Huntington, "The Clash of Civilizations?" *Foreign Affairs* 72.3 (Summer 1993): 22, 28.

[8]Thomas L. Friedman, *The Lexus and the Olive Tree: Understanding Globalization* (New York: Farrar, Straus and Giroux, 1999), xviii.

[9]Laurie Ann Mazur and Susan E. Sechler, *Global Interdependence and the Need for Social Stewardship* (New York: Rockefeller Brothers Fund, 1997), 9–10.

[10]Richard K. Betts, "The New Threat of Mass Destruction," *Foreign Affairs* 77.1 (January/February 1998): 26, 29.

[11]Fareed Zakaria, *The Post-American World* (New York: Norton, 2008), pp. 1, 3.

[12]Robert J. Lieber, *No Common Power: Understanding International Relations* (Boston: Scott, Foresman, 1988), 5.

[13]Kenneth N. Waltz, *Theory of International Politics* (Reading, Mass.: Addison-Wesley, 1979), 72.

[14]Alexander L. George and Robert O. Keohane, "The Concepts of National Interests: Uses and Limitations," in *Presidential Decisionmaking in Foreign Policy: The Effective Use of Information and Advice*, Alexander L. George, ed. (Boulder, Colo.: Westview, 1980), 217–18.

[15]Condoleezza Rice, "Promoting the National Interest," *Foreign Affairs* 79.1 (January/February 2000): 47.

[16]Samuel Huntington, "Why International Primacy Matters," *International Security* 17.4 (Spring 1993): 69–70.

[17]Thucydides, *History of the Peloponnesian War*, R. Warner, trans. (New York: Penguin, 1972), 402.

[18]Hans J. Morgenthau, *Politics among Nations: The Struggle for Power and Peace* (New York: Knopf, 1948), 5.

[19]John J. Mearsheimer, "The False Promise of International Institutions," *International Security* 19.3 (Winter 1994/95): 9.

[20]Cited in Caleb Carr, *The Lessons of Terror* (New York: Random House, 2002), 81.

[21]Cited in Loch K. Johnson, *America as a World Power: Foreign Policy in a Constitutional Framework* (New York: McGraw-Hill, 1991), 239.

[22]Alan K. Henrikson, "Diplomatic Method," in *Encyclopedia of U.S. Foreign Relations,* Bruce W. Jentleson and Thomas G. Paterson, eds. (New York: Oxford University Press, 1997), Volume II, 23.

[23]Michael W. Doyle, *Ways of War and Peace* (New York: Norton, 1997), 19.

[24]Claude, cited in Mearsheimer, "False Promise of International Institutions," 26–27.

[25]Bruce Russett and Harvey Starr, *World Politics: The Menu for Choice* (New York: Freeman, 1996), 117; K. J. Holsti, *International Politics: A Framework for Analysis* (Englewood Cliffs, N.J.: Prentice-Hall, 1988), 141.

[26]Robert O. Keohane and Lisa L. Martin, "The Promise of Institutionalist Theory," *International Security* 20.1 (Summer 1995): 50.

[27]Keohane and Martin, "The Promise of Institutionalist Theory," 42.

[28]Robert O. Keohane, "International Institutions: Can Interdependence Work?" *Foreign Policy* 110 (Spring 1998): 82.

[29]See, for example, Joan E. Spero and Jeffrey A. Hart, *The Politics of International Economic Relations* (New York: St. Martin's, 1997); and Richard N. Gardner, *Sterling-Dollar Diplomacy: The Origins and Prospects of Our International Economic Order* (New York: Columbia University Press, 1980).

[30]James M. McCormick, *American Foreign Policy and Process* (Itasca, Ill.: Peacock, 1992), 15–16.

[31]Michael Hirsh and Karen Breslau, "Closing the Deal Diplomacy: In Clinton's Foreign Policy, the Business of America Is Business," *Newsweek,* March 6, 1995, 34.

[32]See, for example, V. I. Lenin, *Imperialism: The Highest Form of Capitalism* (New York: International Publishers, 1939); John A. Hobson, *Imperialism* (London: George Allen and Unwin, 1954); and Richard J. Barnet and Ronald E. Muller, *Global Reach: The Power of the Multinational Corporations* (New York: Simon and Schuster, 1974).

[33]Cited in Robert W. Tucker and David C. Hendrickson, "Thomas Jefferson and Foreign Policy," *Foreign Affairs* 69.2 (Spring 1990): 136.

[34]Immanuel Kant, *Perpetual Peace,* cited in Michael W. Doyle, "Kant, Liberal Legacies and Foreign Affairs," in *Debating the Democratic Peace,* Michael E. Brown et al., eds. (Cambridge, Mass.: MIT Press, 1997), 24–25.

[35]Joseph S. Nye, Jr., *Bound to Lead: The Changing Nature of American Power* (New York: Basic Books, 1990).

[36]Cited in James A. Nathan and James K. Oliver, *United States Foreign Policy and World Order* (Boston: Little, Brown, 1985), 176. See also Stephen Schlesinger and Stephen Kinzer, *Bitter Fruit: The Untold Story of the American Coup in Guatemala* (Garden City, N.Y.: Doubleday, 1982), and Stephen Kinzer, *Overthrow: America's Century of Regime Change, from Hawaii to Iraq* (New York: Times Books, 2006).

[37]Cited in Walter LaFeber, *Inevitable Revolutions: The United States in Central America,* 2d ed. (New York: Norton, 1993), 115–16.

[38]Mireya Navarro, "Guatemalan Army Waged 'Genocide', New Report Finds," *New York Times,* February 26, 1999, A1, A8. See also Documents on U.S. Policy in Guatemala, 1966–1996, National Security Archive Electronic Briefing Book No. 11, www.gwu.edu/~nsarchiv/NSAEBB/NSAEBB11/docs/ (accessed 5/18/09).

[39]On earlier U.S. policy toward Iraq and Saddam Hussein, including inaction when he waged chemical warfare against Iraqi Kurds in 1988, see Bruce W. Jentleson, *With Friends Like These: Reagan, Bush and Saddam, 1982–1990* (New York: Norton, 1994).

CHAPTER

# 2 The Domestic Context: Foreign Policy Politics and the Process of Choice

## Introduction: Dispelling the "Water's Edge" Myth

When it comes to foreign policy, according to an old saying, "politics stops at the water's edge." In other words, partisan and other political differences that characterize domestic policy are to be left behind—"at the water's edge"—when entering the realm of foreign policy, so that the country can be united in confronting foreign threats.

The example most often cited by proponents of this ideal is the consensus of the early Cold War era, that "golden age of bipartisanship." Here is "a story of democracy at its finest," as one famous book portrayed it, "with the executive branch of the government operating far beyond the normal boundaries of timidity and politics, the Congress beyond usual partisanship, and the American people as a whole beyond selfishness and complacency. All three . . . worked together to accomplish a national acceptance of world responsibility."[1] That's how foreign policy politics is supposed to be, the "water's edge" thinking goes.

In three key respects, though, this notion of politics' stopping at the water's edge is a myth that needs to be dispelled. First, *historically, the domestic consensus that characterized the Cold War era was more the exception than the rule.* The common view is that divisive foreign policy politics started with the Vietnam War. But although Vietnam did shatter the Cold War consensus, it was hardly the first time that foreign policy politics hadn't stopped at the water's edge. In the years leading up to World War II, President Franklin Roosevelt had his own intense political battles with an isolationist Congress. In the years following World War I, President Woodrow Wilson suffered one of the worst foreign policy politics defeats ever when the Senate refused to ratify the Treaty of Versailles. We can even go back to 1794 and President George Washington, the revered "father" of the country, and his battles with Congress over a treaty with Great Britain called the Jay Treaty.

The bitter and vociferous attacks on the Jay Treaty for "tilting" toward Britain in its war with France were a rhetorical match for any of today's political battles. "Ruinous . . . detestable . . . contemptible," editorialized one major newspaper of the day, excoriating a treaty "signed with our inveterate enemy and the foe of human happiness." The Senate did ratify the treaty, but by a margin of only one vote. Indeed the whole Jay Treaty controversy was a key factor in President Washington's decision to retire to Mount Vernon instead of seeking a third term as president.

Second, *consensus has not always been a good thing.* It surely can be, in manifesting national solidarity behind the nation's foreign policy. But national solidarity is one thing, the delegitimization of dissent quite another. The most virulent example was the anticommunist witch hunt spurred by the McCarthyism of the 1950s, during which accusations of disloyalty were hurled at government officials, playwrights, professors, scientists, and average citizens, often on the flimsiest of evidence. Dissent was also criminalized during both world wars, when domestic consensus was often crucial to meeting wartime challenges; nevertheless, many Americans paid a severe price in civil liberties and individual rights during these wars. The Espionage and Sedition Acts passed during World War I permitted such repressive measures as banning postal delivery of any magazine that included views critical of the war effort—restrictions "as extreme as any legislation of the kind anywhere in the world."[2] During World War II the national security rationale was invoked to uproot 120,000 Japanese Americans and put them in internment camps, on the basis only of their ethnicity. During Vietnam, shouts of "America, love it or leave it" were aimed at antiwar critics and protesters. Consensus is not a particularly good thing when it equates dissent with disloyalty. These issues have arisen again in the context of the war on terrorism.

Third, *domestic political conflict is not necessarily always bad for foreign policy.* Debate and disagreement can facilitate a more thorough consideration of the issues. They can subject questionable assumptions to serious scrutiny. They can bring about constructive compromises around a policy that serves the national interest better than anything either side originally proposed. As the former House Foreign Affairs Committee chair Lee Hamilton wrote, "Debate, creative tension and review of policy can bring about decisions and actions that stand a better chance of serving the interests and values of the American people."[3] A good example of this was the outcome of the debate about the U.S. role in helping restore democracy in the Philippines in the mid-1980s. The policy preferred by President Ronald Reagan was to continue supporting the dictator Ferdinand Marcos, even after his forces had assassinated the democratic opposition leader, Benigno Aquino, and even amid mounting evidence of rampant corruption in the Marcos regime. But the U.S. Congress, led by a bipartisan coalition of Democrats and Republicans, refused to go along with a continued unconditional embrace of Marcos. It pushed for support for the pro-democracy forces led by Corazon Aquino, widow of the slain opposition leader. Democracy was restored, and an important U.S. ally was made more stable. This result might not have been achieved, however, had it not been for the good that can sometimes come out of conflictual foreign policy politics.

Thus, the realities of *foreign policy politics,* the process by which foreign policy choices are made, are more complex than conventional wisdom holds. Our purpose in this chapter is to provide a framework for understanding the dynamics of foreign policy politics. We do so by focusing on five sets of domestic actors: *the president and Congress,* and the "Pennsylvania Avenue diplomacy" that marks (and often mars) their interbranch relationship; the policy- and decision-making processes within *the executive branch*; the pressures brought to bear by major *interest groups*; the impact of *the news media*; and the nature and influence of *public opinion.* We provide examples to illustrate and flesh out the framework, with case studies to follow in various chapters throughout this book, including a focus on foreign policy politics in the Obama administration in Chapter 6.

## The President, Congress, and "Pennsylvania Avenue Diplomacy"

They stare at each other down the length of Pennsylvania Avenue—the White House and the Capitol: connected by the avenue, but also divided by it. The avenue: a path for cooperation, but also a line of conflict. The president and Congress: a relationship very much in need of its own "diplomacy."

Historically, and across various issue areas, presidential-congressional relations in the making of foreign policy have been characterized by four patterns: *cooperation,* when Congress has either concurred with or deferred to the president and a largely common, coordinated policy has been pursued; *constructive compromise,* when the two branches have bridged conflicts and come to a policy that proved better than either's original position (as in the 1980s Philippines case cited above); *institutional competition,* in which the conflicts have been less over the substance of policy than over institutional prerogatives and the balance between the need for executive accountability and congressional oversight; and *confrontation,* in which the policy positions have been in substantial conflict and Pennsylvania Avenue diplomacy has shown its greatest tensions.

Which pattern prevails on what issues and, more broadly, during any particular presidential administration depends in part on politics. To some extent the tensions in Pennsylvania Avenue diplomacy have been extensions of broader partisan politics. This has been especially true in cases of ***divided government,*** wherein one political party controls the White House and the other party holds the majority in one or both houses of Congress. But ***interbranch politics*** on foreign policy is not merely about partsianship. The isolationist Congress that FDR faced in the 1930s was a Democratic one. So too were the anti–Vietnam War leaders who took on the Democratic president Lyndon B. Johnson in 1966-68. In the early 1970s, conservative Republican senators opposed President Richard M. Nixon over détente with the Soviet Union. The first two years of Bill Clinton's presidency (1993–94), when Democrats controlled Congress, still were marked by extensive criticism of his policies in Somalia, Bosnia, and Haiti. As the Iraq war dragged on, some Republicans in Congress came to oppose President George W. Bush's policies.

Fundamentally, the dynamic is a structural one. Despite all the theories expounded, political positions taken, and legal briefs filed, no one has come up with a definitive answer to the question of constitutional intent and design for presidential-congressional relations in the making of foreign policy. The Constitution left it, in one classic statement, as "an invitation to struggle for the privilege of directing American foreign policy."[4] Indeed, although we usually are taught to think of the relationship between the president and Congress as a "separation of powers," it really is much more "separate institutions sharing powers."[5] A separation of powers would mean that the president has power *a*, Congress power *b*, the president power *c*, Congress power *d*, and so on. But the actual relationship is more one in which both the president and Congress have a share of power *a*, a share of power *b*, a share of power *c*, and so on—that is, the separate institutions *share powers*. This basic structural relationship is evident in five key areas of foreign policy politics (see Table 2.1).

**TABLE 2.1 Principal Foreign Policy Provisions of the Constitution**

| | Power granted to | |
|---|---|---|
| | **President** | **Congress** |
| War power | Commander in chief of armed forces | Provide for the common defense; declare war |
| Treaties | Negotiate treaties | Ratification of treaties, by two-thirds majority (Senate) |
| Appointments | Nominate high-level government officials | Confirm president's appointments (Senate) |
| Foreign commerce | No explicit powers, but treaty negotiation and appointment powers pertain | Explicit power "to regulate foreign commerce" |
| General powers | Executive power; veto | Legislative power; power of the purse; oversight and investigation |

## War Powers

No domain of foreign policy politics has been debated more hotly or more recurringly than ***war powers***. The distinguished historian Arthur M. Schlesinger, Jr., provides his view of what the founders intended in Reading 2.1. The Constitution designates the president as "commander in chief" but gives Congress the power to "declare war" and "provide for the common defense"—not separate powers, but each a share of the same power. 2.1

Both sides support their claims for the precedence of their share of the war power with citations from the country's founders. Presidentialists invoke the logic, developed by Alexander Hamilton in the *Federalist Papers,* that the need for an effective foreign policy was one of the main reasons the young nation needed an "energetic government" (*Federalist 23*); that "energy in the executive" was "a leading character in the definition of good government" (no. 70); and that "in the conduct of war . . . the energy of the executive is the bulwark of national security" (no. 75). Congressionalists, on the other hand, cite the proceedings of the Constitutional Convention. At James Madison's initiative, the original wording of the proposed constitution, which would have given Congress the power to "make war," was changed to "declare war." This is explained by congressionalists as intended to recognize that *how* to use military force ("make war") was appropriately a power for the commander in chief, whereas *whether* to use military force ("declare war") was for Congress to decide. Furthermore, as Madison stated in a letter to Thomas Jefferson, "the Constitution supposes what the history of all governments demonstrates, that the executive is the branch of power most interested in war, and most prone to it. It has accordingly with studied care vested the question of war in the legislature."[6]

Nor is the weight of historical precedent strictly on one side or the other. One of the favorite statistics of proponents of the presidency's war powers is that of the more than two hundred times that the United States has used military force, only five—the War of 1812, the Mexican War (1846–48), the Spanish-American War (1898), World War I (1917–19), and World War II (1941–45)—have been through congressional declarations of war. Perhaps another eighty-five or ninety (e.g., the 1991 Persian Gulf War, the 2001 Afghanistan war, and the 2003 Iraq war) have been through some other legislative authority. All the others have been by presidents acting on their own, which is taken as evidence of both the need for and the legitimacy of presidents' having such freedom of action.

This statistic, though, is somewhat deceptive. Many of the cases of presidents acting on their own involved minor military incidents generally regarded as the business of a commander in chief. Besides that, defenders of Congress's share of the war powers interpret this-gross disproportion—many uses of military force yet few declarations of war—not as legitimizing the arrangement, but as emphasizing the problem. They put less emphasis on the overall numbers than on key cases like Vietnam and Iraq, in which undeclared war had major consequences.

We will take war powers up again as a historical issue in Chapter 3, as an early Cold

War–era issue in Chapter 4, as a Vietnam-era controversy over the 1973 War Powers Resolution in Chapter 5, over the 2003 Iraq war in Chapter 8, and in cases of humanitarian intervention in Chapter 9. In Chapter 8 we also look at current proposals for war powers reform.

## *Treaties and Other International Commitments*

The basic power-sharing arrangement for ***treaties*** vests negotiating power in the president but requires that treaties be ratified by a two-thirds majority of the Senate. On the surface this appears to have worked pretty well: of the close to 2,000 treaties signed by presidents in U.S. history, only about twenty have been voted down by the Senate. But here, too, simple statistics can be misleading.

One reason is that although it may not happen often, Senate defeat of a treaty can have a huge impact—as with the 1919–20 defeat of the Treaty of Versailles, on which the post–World War I peace was to be based. Although European leaders also had a hand in the Versailles Treaty, it largely was the work of President Woodrow Wilson. Through the breakup of the Austro-Hungarian empire and the creation of such new independent states as Yugoslavia, as well as the founding of the League of Nations, Wilson sought to establish a new structure of peace more infused with American principles and with the Untied States playing a more central global role. But he faced opposition in the U.S. Senate. The opposition was partly political, including rivalry between Wilson and the Republican senator Henry Cabot Lodge, chairman of the Senate Foreign Relations Committee. It also was substantive, particularly over retreating into isolationism rather than joining the League of Nations. Wilson went on a cross-country speaking tour to drum up support, but to no avail (and at great personal cost as he suffered an incapacitating stroke). The Senate refused to ratify the treaty.

A more recent example was the 1998 defeat of the ***Comprehensive Test Ban Treaty (CTBT)***. The CTBT sought a total ban on the testing of nuclear weapons. Earlier treaties such as the 1963 Limited Test Ban Treaty had prohibited nuclear weapons testing in the atmosphere, under water, and in outer space, The CTBT extended this to underground testing and all other nuclear weapons testing other than as simulated in computer models and other technological mechanisms.

The CTBT debate also was partly policy substantive and partly political. In signing the CTBT in 1996, President Clinton called it "the longest-sought, hardest-fought prize in arms control history."[7] Clinton sent the CTBT to the Senate for ratification in September 1997. But it stayed bottled up in the Senate Foreign Relations Committee for almost two years. Republicans had the majority in the Senate and controlled the key committees. Senator Jesse Helms (R–North Carolina), a strong CTBT opponent, used his powers as chair of the Foreign Relations Committee to block the scheduling of committee hearings on the treaty. In July 1999, all forty-five Senate Democrats issued a joint statement calling on Helms to hold hearings and allow the treaty to go to the floor for a full Senate vote. Helms still refused. Senator Byron Dorgan (D–North Dakota) turned to another Senate procedural tactic, threatening to filibuster on the Senate floor and block votes from being taken on issues. He would put himself on the Senate floor "like a potted plant," Dorgan said. "I am sorry if I am going to cause some problems around here with the schedule. But frankly, as I said, there are big issues and there are small issues. This is a big issue. And I am flat tired of seeing small issues around this chamber every day in every way, when the big issues are bottled up in some committee and the key is held by one or two people."[8]

When hearings were finally held, they included experts on both sides of the issue. Among the most influential testimony was that from the directors of the Sandia and Lawrence Livermore National Laboratories, where much of the nuclear weapons testing was conducted. The weapons-lab directors had issued a pro-CTBT statement the previous year, expressing their view that computerized testing and other aspects of the "stockpile stewardship program" still permitted by the CTBT would suffice. But during the congressional hearings their testimony conveyed greater doubt and uncertainty. "Had the directors learned something," one scholar queried in his case study, "that made them more nervous about the adequacy of the stockpile program? Maybe they were just being typical scientists, unwilling to say that anything is 100 percent certain. . . . It is also possible that, on the contrary, they were shrewd politicians, men who understood that the treaty was going down, that the majority party on Capitol Hill was against it, and that they needed to be on the right side of the issue."[9]

All along public opinion was largely pro-CTBT, as much as 70 to 80 percent supportive. But the general public was less influential on this issue than issue activists. General public pressures brought no senator over to the pro-treaty side from a position of being opposed or undecided. The final vote was 48 in favor, 51 opposed; ratification would have required 67 votes in favor. Clinton blamed the defeat on "politics, pure and simple." He also had in mind the fallout from the congressional efforts to impeach him over the Monica Lewinsky scandal. Senate Majority Leader Trent Lott (R–Mississippi) maintained that "it was not about politics; it was about the substance of the treaty, and that's all it was."[10] Undoubtedly both foreign policy strategy and foreign policy politics came into play.

Congress also has alternative ways to influence treaties other than by defeating them. For example, it can offer advice during negotiations through the official "observer groups" that often accompany State Department negotiators. It also can try to amend or attach a "reservation" to alter the terms of a treaty, an action that can be quite controversial, since it may require the reopening of negotiations with the other country or countries.

On the other hand, presidents also have an array of strategies at their disposal to circumvent Senate objections. In particular, they can resort to mechanisms other than treaties, such as ***executive agreements***, for making international commitments. Executive agreements usually do not require congressional approval, let alone the two-thirds Senate majority that treaties do. Although in theory executive agreements are supposed to be used for minor government-to-government matters, leaving major aspects of relations to treaties, the line between the two has never been particularly clear. In addition, sometimes the most important foreign policy commitments do not come from treaties or executive agreements or any other written or legal form. Such ***declaratory commitments*** come from speeches and statements by presidents. This was the case, for example, with the Monroe Doctrine, which sprang from a speech by President James Monroe in 1823 to become the bedrock of U.S. foreign policy in the Western Hemisphere. So, too, with the Truman Doctrine (1947): its clarion call "to support free peoples who are resisting attempted subjugation by armed minorities or by outside pressures" became a basis for the containment strategy pursued in U.S. policy for the next forty to fifty years.

Some presidents also have claimed authority to withdraw from existing treaties without going to the Senate for approval, as President George W. Bush did in 2001 in withdrawing from the 1972 Anti-Ballistic Missile (ABM) Treaty. His action was different from that of President John Adams, who in 1798 terminated treaties with France but did so through an act of Congress, or that of President James Polk, who in 1846 sought congressional approval for withdrawing from the Oregon Territory Treaty with Great Britain. At least a partial precedent came from President Jimmy Carter, who did not go to Congress for approval when in 1978 he ended the U.S. mutual defense treaty with Taiwan as part of the normalization of diplomatic relations with the People's Republic of China. Still, the Bush withdrawal from the ABM treaty was hotly disputed on both policy and procedural grounds.

### *Appointments of Foreign Policy Officials*

The standard process as reflected in Table 2.1 (p. 30) is that the president nominates and the Senate confirms (by a simple majority) the appointments of Cabinet members, ambassadors, and other high-level foreign policy officials. In pure statistical terms the confirmation rate for presidential foreign policy nominees is higher than 90 percent. Yet here, too, we need to look past the numbers.

First of all, these numbers don't include nominations withdrawn before a formal Senate vote. When White House congressional-liaison aides come back from Capitol Hill reporting that "the vote count doesn't look good," a president often decides to avoid the embarrassment of a vote and instead withdraw the nomination.

Precisely because it is often assumed that nominees will be confirmed, when they are not the political impact can be substantial. Thus, for example, in 1989 far less attention was given to all of the first Bush administration's other foreign policy nominations combined than to the one case of former senator John Tower, Bush's nominee for secretary of defense, who ended up being voted down. The Senate also has left its mark on some nominees even in the process of confirming them. This was the fate of William Colby, confirmed as President Nixon's CIA director in 1973 amid controversies over Vietnam and covert action by the CIA, and of Paul Warnke, Carter's choice to head the Arms Control and Disarmament Agency, who was excoriated by conservatives as too "dovish": neither of these officials ever fully recovered from the wounds of their confirmation battles.

There also have been cases in which opposition was so strong that nominations were withdrawn before a formal Senate vote. The Clinton example is the nomination in 1997 of Anthony Lake as CIA director. Lake had been national security adviser in Clinton's first term. Although it is fair to say that there were some substantive bases for questioning Lake's CIA nomination, most observers felt these issues were not sufficient to disqualify him. Some leading Republican senators announced their support for Lake, and the votes to confirm him seemed to be there. But the Republican senator Richard Shelby of Alabama, chair of the Senate Intelligence Committee, carried on what seemed to many to be a vendetta, repeatedly delaying Lake's confirmation hearings, then dragging them out and bombarding the nominee with questions, demands for documents, and other obstructionist tactics. Ultimately Lake asked Clinton to withdraw his nomination. His letter to Clinton went beyond his own case to raise the broader concern that "Washington has gone haywire":

> I hope that sooner rather than later, people of all political views beyond our city limits will demand that Washington give priority to policy over partisanship, to governing over "gotcha." It is time that senior officials have more time to concentrate on dealing with very real foreign policy challenges rather than the domestic wounds Washington is inflicting on itself.[11]

The nomination of John Bolton as ambassador to the United Nations in 2005 is the George W. Bush administration example. The issue was not prior experience. Bolton had been undersecretary of state for arms control and international security in the first Bush term and assistant secretary of state for international organizations under the first president Bush. But even among other neoconservatives, Bolton was especially known for his sharp and derisive criticisms of multilateralism in general and of the United Nations in particular. "There's no such thing as the United Nations," he had contended in 1994 when opposing Clinton administration pro-UN policies. If the UN building in New York "lost ten stories, it wouldn't make a bit of difference." The Bush administration's argument was that a tough critic such as Bolton was the right person to represent

American interests and to push the UN for reform. Toughness and reform were one thing, opponents contended, but Bolton's in-your-face style and real questions about whether he wanted a better UN or just a less important one were quite another. As one former Clinton UN official pointed out, "neither of President Bush's first two appointees to the UN post—former Ambassador and later Intelligence Chief John Negroponte and former [Republican] Senator John Danforth—were pushovers by any stretch of the imagination. They both pressed hard on the administration's agenda, yet neither was perceived to have an axe to grind."[12] Opposition in the Senate was sufficient to block Bolton's confirmation. But Bush resorted to a "recess appointment," a technicality that allowed him to appoint Bolton while the Senate was on its Summer 2005 recess and have the appointment last "temporarily" without Senate confirmation. Bolton resigned following the Democratic victory in the 2006 elections, knowing he would not be confirmed.

None of these legislative tactics, however, applies to foreign policy officials who do not require Senate confirmation. This in particular includes the assistant to the president for national security affairs (called the national security adviser, for short) and the staff of the National Security Council (NSC). Thus such major figures as Henry Kissinger, Zbigniew Brzezinski, and Condoleezza Rice, who served as national security advisers to Presidents Nixon, Carter, and George W. Bush, respectively, did not need Senate confirmation for that position. (When Kissinger was nominated by Nixon to also be secretary of state, and when Rice switched to this position, however, Senate confirmation was required.)

## *"Commerce with Foreign Nations"*

In the area of foreign commerce the Constitution is more explicit than in others. Congress is very clearly granted the power "to regulate commerce with foreign nations" and "to lay and collect . . . duties." Presidential authority over trade policy thus has been more dependent than in other areas on what and how much authority Congress chooses to delegate.[13] For about 150 years, Congress actually decided each tariff, item by item; one result of this was the infamous Smoot-Hawley Tariff Act of 1930, which set tariffs for more than twenty thousand items—and increased almost all of them, the classic example of protectionism. The Reciprocal Trade Agreements Act of 1934, which arose from the Smoot-Hawley disaster, delegated to the president extensive authority to cut tariffs on his own by as much as 50 percent if he could negotiate reciprocal cuts with other countries. Although we often assume that the natural inclination in politics is for any institution or actor to try to maximize its own power and authority, in this instance Congress saw its own interests better served by delegating greater authority to the president. As Professor I. M. Destler astutely observes, Congress's strategy was to protect itself from going protectionist through a "pressure-diverting policy management system."[14] Congress knew it couldn't consistently resist the temptations to grant interest groups the trade protection they ask for, so by delegating authority to the executive it could say, "I can't do it" rather than "I won't do it."

Presidents and Congresses alike were generally happy with this arrangement, especially under the international free trade system set up after World War II by the General Agreement on Tariffs and Trade (GATT). But beginning again in the mid-1970s, as trade became more politically controversial, the power-sharing pulls and tugs along Pennsylvania Avenue on international trade issues grew more frequent and more wrenching. Congress began to take back some of the trade policy authority it had delegated. Although policy stayed more pro–free trade than protectionist, the politics became much more contentious (Chapters 5, 10).

Chapter 10 also goes into the process by which trade policy is made. In an initial quick summary, we can identify five key executive players:

- ***U.S. trade representative (USTR):*** a Cabinet-rank position; the principal negotiator of trade treaties and other agreements
- ***secretary of the treasury:*** one of the very first Cabinet positions created in 1789 (Alexander Hamilton was the first to serve in this position); over time has taken on an increasingly important role in international economic policy, especially amid the current international financial crisis
- ***secretary of commerce:*** trade promotion is one of the responsibilities of this position
- ***State Department:*** also plays an important role in international trade and other economic relations
- ***International Trade Commission (ITC):*** independent regulatory agency within the executive branch with responsibilities including fair trade issues of import competition

In Congress, although a number of committees are involved in trade policy, the key ones are the House Ways and Means Committee and the Senate Finance Committee.

## *General Powers*

The president and Congress both also bring to the foreign policy struggle their general constitutional powers.

EXECUTIVE POWER The Constitution states that "the executive power shall be vested in the President" and roughly defines this power as to ensure "that the laws be faithfully executed." In itself this is a broad and vague mandate, which presidents have invoked as the basis for a wide range of actions taken in order to "execute" foreign policy, such as executive agreements, as already discussed, and executive orders, which are directives issued by the president for executive-branch actions not requiring legislative approval. Sometimes executive orders are issued just to fill in the blanks of legislation passed by Congress. But they also can be used by presidents as a way of getting around Congress. Thus, for example, President Truman racially integrated the armed forces by issuing Executive Order No. 9981 on July 26, 1948, because he knew the segregationists in Congress would block any integration legislation.

Then there is the ***veto***, the most potent executive power the Constitution gives the president. The authority to block legislation unless Congress can pass it a second time, by a two-thirds majority in both chambers, is a formidable power. It is especially so in foreign policy, where the president can tap both patriotism and fear to intimidate potential veto overrides. Thus even amid the congressional activism and partisan battles of the 1970s and 1980s, presidential vetoes on foreign policy legislation were overridden only twice: President Nixon's veto of the 1973 War Powers Resolution and President Reagan's veto of the 1986 Anti-Apartheid Act against South Africa.

In many respects even more important than a president's formal executive powers are the informal political powers of the office and the skills of being a practiced politician. Stories are legion of deal making with members of Congress to get that one last vote to ratify a treaty or pass an important bill. President Lyndon Johnson was especially well known for this. So was President Reagan, who to get Senate approval of a major 1981 arms sale to Saudi Arabia doled out funds for a new hospital in the state of one senator, a coal-fired power plant for another, and a U.S. attorney appointment for a friend of another.[15]

The most significant political power a president has may well be what Teddy Roosevelt called the "bully pulpit." As Roosevelt once put it, "People used to say to me that I was an astonishingly good politician and divined what the people are going to think. . . . I did not 'divine' how the people were going to think, I simply made up my mind what they ought to think, and then did my best to get them to think it." And that was before television!

LEGISLATIVE POWER Professor Louis Henkin of Columbia University goes so far as to claim that there is no part of foreign policy "that is not subject to legislation by Congress."[16] That may be an overstatement, as demonstrated by some of the examples of executive power just cited. But it is true that the legislative power gives Congress a great deal of influence over foreign policy.

The distinction made by James Lindsay between *substantive* and *procedural* legislation is a useful one for understanding that Congress has a number of ways of exerting its foreign policy influence.[17] ***Substantive legislation*** is policy specific, spelling out what the details of foreign policy should or should not be. Disapproval of the 1919 Treaty of Versailles, approval of the 1947 Marshall Plan, ratification of the 1972 SALT arms-control treaty with the Soviet Union, approval of the 1993 North American Free Trade Agreement (NAFTA), approval of annual defense budgets—all are examples of substantive legislation.

***Procedural legislation*** is a bit subtler and requires more elaboration. It deals more with "the structures and procedures by which foreign policy is made. The underlying premise is that if Congress changes the decision-making process it will change the policy."[18] The 1973 War Powers Resolution is one example; it was an effort to restructure how decisions on the use of military force are made. The creation of new agencies and positions within the executive branch so that particular policies or perspectives will have "champions" is another form of the procedural legislation strategy.[19] Examples include the creation of the Arms Control and Disarmament Agency (ACDA) in 1961, the Office of the U.S. Trade Representative in 1974, and the Department of Homeland Security in 2001–2002. A third example is the use of the *legislative veto,* a procedure by which certain actions taken and policies set by the president can be overridden by Congress through a resolution rather than through a bill. The key difference is that whereas bills generally must be signed by the president to become law and thus give the president the opportunity to exercise a veto, congressional resolutions do not. For this very reason, the Supreme Court severely limited the use of the legislative veto in its 1983 decision in the case *INS v. Chadha,* to be discussed in the next section.

Among Congress's other powers are its oversight and investigative powers and, most important, its *power of the purse:* "no money shall be drawn from the Treasury but in Consequence of Appropriation made by Law." This power gives Congress direct influence over decisions on how much to spend and what to spend it on. In addition to stipulating the total budget of, for example, the Defense Department, Congress can use its appropriations power directly to influence more basic policy decisions, such as by setting "conditionalities" as to how the money can or cannot be spent or by "earmarking" it for specific programs or countries.

## *The Supreme Court as Referee?*

It is not that often that the Supreme Court gets involved in foreign policy politics. When the Court does become involved, it is usually because it has been turned to as a "referee" to resolve presidential-congressional conflicts over foreign policy power sharing. But the Court generally has been unable and unwilling to take on this role.

The Court has been unable to do so in the sense that different rulings seem to lend support to each side. For example, a very strong statement of presidential prerogatives in foreign policy was made in the 1936 case *United States v. Curtiss-Wright Export Corp.* Although the specific case was over whether an embargo could be imposed against an American company's arms sales, the significance of the Court's ruling was in the general principle that the president could claim greater powers in foreign than in domestic policy because of "the law of nations" and not just the Constitution: "In this vast external realm, with its important, complicated, delicate and manifold problems, the President alone has the power to speak or listen as a representative of the nation. . . . The President is the sole organ of the nation in its external relations, and its sole representative with foreign nations. . . . It is quite apparent that . . . in the maintenance of our international relations . . . [Congress] must often accord to the President a degree of discretion and freedom from statutory restriction which would not be admissible were domestic affairs alone involved."[20]

Yet the 1952 case *Youngstown Sheet and Tube Co. v. Sawyer* in many respects became the counterpart to *Curtiss-Wright,* establishing some limits on executive power. In this case, involving a labor-union strike in the steel industry during the Korean War, the Court ruled against President Truman's claim that he could break the strike in the name of national security. Going beyond the specifics of the case, the Court focused on the problems of "zones of twilight," situations for which Congress had neither explicitly authorized the president to take a certain action nor explicitly prohibited the president from doing so. In these situations the president "and Congress may have concurrent authority, or . . . its distribution is uncertain," and thus "any actual test of power is likely to depend on the imperatives of events and contemporary imponderables rather than on abstract theories of law." On these types of issues, while stopping well short of asserting congressional preeminence, the Court did not accept nearly as much presidential preeminence as it had in 1936 in its *Curtiss-Wright* decision.[21]

In other instances the Supreme Court and other federal courts have been unwilling even to attempt to adjudicate presidential-congressional foreign policy disputes. In the 1970s and 1980s members of Congress took the president to court a number of times over issues of war and treaty powers.[22] In most of these cases the courts refused to rule definitively one way or the other. Although there were differences in the specifics of the rulings, the cases generally were deemed to fall under the "political question" doctrine, meaning that they involved political differences between the executive and legislative branches more than constitutional issues, and thus required a political resolution between the branches, rather than a judicial remedy. In other words, the Supreme Court essentially told the president and Congress to work the issues out themselves.

Another key case was the 1983 case *INS v. Chadha,* mentioned earlier. In striking down the legislative veto as unconstitutional, the Court stripped Congress of one of its levers of power. Even so, within a year and a half of the *Chadha* decision, Congress had passed more than fifty new laws that sought to accomplish the same goals as the legislative veto while avoiding the objections raised by the Court. The constitutionality of some of these laws remains untested, but they still cast a sufficient shadow for the president not to be able to assume too much freedom of action.

Since September 11, 2001, the Court has heard a new wave of cases concerning presidential powers, civil liberties, and related issues. We discuss some of these in Chapter 8.

## Executive-Branch Politics

There was a time when books on foreign policy didn't include sections on executive-branch politics. Foreign policy politics was largely seen as an *inter*branch phenomenon, not an *intra*branch one. The executive branch, after all, was the president's own branch. Its usual organizational diagram was a pyramid: the president sat atop it, the various executive-branch departments and agencies fell below. Major foreign policy decisions were made in a hierarchical, structured, and orderly manner. It was believed to be a highly *rational* process, often called a "rational actor" model.

Analytically speaking, five principal criteria need to be met for an executive-branch policy process to be considered rational: (1) adequate and timely *information* must be provided through intelligence and other channels, so that policy makers are well informed of the nature of the issues on which they need to make decisions; (2) thorough and incisive *analysis* must be made of the nature of the threats posed, the interests at stake, and other key aspects of the issues; (3) the *range of policy options* must be identified, with an analysis of the relative pros and cons of each; (4) *implementation* strategies must be spelled out on how to proceed once the policy choice is made; and (5) a *feedback "loop"* must be established to evaluate how the policies are working in practice and to make adjustments over time.[23]

Yet as we will see throughout this book, the executive branch's foreign policy process often has not met these criteria. The dynamics of decision-making and policy implementation have tended to be less strictly hierarchical, less neatly structured, and much more disorderly than as portrayed in the rational-actor model. To put it more directly, the executive branch also has its own politics.

### *Presidents as Foreign Policy Leaders*

For all the other executive-branch actors that play major foreign policy roles, the president remains the key decision maker. How well the president fulfills that role depends on a number of factors.

One factor is the extent of foreign policy experience and expertise that a president brings to the office. Yet, surprisingly, it was much more common in the eighteenth and nineteenth centuries than in the twentieth for presidents to have had substantial prior foreign policy experience. Four of the first six presidents had served previously as secretary of state (Thomas Jefferson, James Madison, James Monroe, and John Quincy Adams). So had two other presidents in the nineteenth century (Martin Van Buren and James Buchanan). But no president since has had that experience. And of the seven war heroes who became president, only one (Dwight Eisenhower) did so in the twentieth century; the others were in the eighteenth (George Washington) and nineteenth (Andrew Jackson, William Henry Harrison, Zachary Taylor, Ulysses Grant, and Benjamin Harrison). As to recent presidents, George H. W. Bush ranks among those with the most prior foreign policy experience, and Bill Clinton, George W. Bush, and Barack Obama among those with the least.

The first President Bush had served in the military in World War II, the navy's youngest pilot at the time and the recipient of a medal for heroism. He had been a member of the House of Representatives (1966–70), ambassador to the UN in the Nixon administration (1971–73), head of the first U.S. liaison office in the People's Republic of China when diplomatic relations were first established (1974–75), and director of the CIA in the Ford administration (1976–77). He also served for eight years as Ronald Reagan's vice president. As president he made foreign policy a higher overall priority than any president since Nixon. He was known much more as a "foreign policy president" than as a domestic policy one. This reputation hurt him politically in the 1992 election, because the public perceived him as not paying enough attention to domestic policy, whereas Bill Clinton ran on the campaign slogan "It's the economy, stupid."

Clinton, trained as a lawyer, had spent his political career as governor of Arkansas (1978–80, 1982–92), the foreign policy component of which amounted to an overseas trade mission or two. Many attributed the foreign policy failures of his first year as president to his inexperience: "passive and changeable . . . like a cork bobbing on the waves," was one leading journalist's characterization.[24] In addition, the controversies over whether he had dodged the draft during the Vietnam War gave Clinton personal credibility problems as commander in chief. Over the course of his administration Clinton did gain experience and demonstrated greater foreign policy skills and savvy. In the first eighteen months of his second term, he made more foreign trips than in his entire first term. By 1998, the percentage of people rating his foreign policy performance as excellent or good had increased from 31 percent (1994) to 55 percent.[25] Overall he would be better known for his domestic policy, but he also did have his foreign policy successes.

The second President Bush also had been only a governor (of Texas) with the limited international agenda inherent in that office. At times during the 2000 presidential campaign, this hurt Bush's candidacy. So too in his first months in office, doubts arose about his foreign policy competence. The strength of his foreign policy team, seasoned hands who had served in his father's administration, partially compensated. Then the events of September 11, 2001 cast Bush in a new light. He was widely praised for helping rally the nation at a time of crisis. In some respects his limited prior experience was seen as a positive, in that he wasn't bogged down in details and nuances and got right to what many Americans saw as the fundamentals. The initial military victory in the Iraq war reinforced this sense of Bush as a strong foreign policy leader. But as the war dragged on, and more questions arose over the decision process for going to war as well as the strategies for seeking to "win the peace," criticisms mounted and doubts reemerged about Bush's leadership. His foreign policy approval rating, which had been over 80 percent in the wake of 9/11, was around 30 percent for most of his last year and a half in office. (We discuss President Obama in Chapter 6.)

A second set of factors influencing foreign policy decision making are characteristics of the president as an individual. As with any individual in any walk of life, the president's personality affects how and how well the job gets done. Although personality is rarely the sole determinant of behavior, in some cases it does have a very strong bearing. Woodrow Wilson's unwillingness to compromise with Senate opponents on the Treaty of Versailles has been traced in part to his self-righteousness and other deep-seated personality traits. Richard Nixon's personality significantly affected his policy making, particularly with regard to Vietnam. The consistent image of Nixon that comes through both in his own writing and in that of biographers is of a pervasive suspiciousness: Nixon viewed opponents as enemies and political setbacks as personal humiliations, had an extreme penchant for secrecy, and seemed obsessed with concentrating and guarding power. These personality characteristics help explain the rigidity with which Nixon kept the Vietnam War effort going despite the evidence that it was failing, and the virtual paranoia he exhibited by putting antiwar figures on an "enemies list" and recruiting former CIA operatives to work in secret as "plumbers" to "plug" supposed leaks—actions that, like those of the self-destructive figures of ancient Greek tragedies, led to Nixon's own downfall through the Watergate scandal.

A more cognitive approach focuses on the president's worldview, or what a number of authors have called a ***belief system***. No president comes to the job "tabula rasa," with a cognitive clean slate; quite to the contrary, as Robert Jervis states, "it is often impossible to explain crucial decisions and policies without reference to the decision-makers' beliefs about the world and their images of others."[26] Belief systems can be construed in terms of three core components:

- the analytic component of the *conception of the international system:* What is the president's view of the basic structure of the international system? Who and what are seen as the principal threats to the United States?
- the normative component of the *national interest hierarchy:* How does the president rank the core objectives of Power, Peace, Prosperity, and Principles?
- the instrumental component of a basic *strategy:* Given both the conception of the international system and the national interest hierarchy, what is the optimal strategy to be pursued?

We illustrate the importance of belief systems by contrasting those of Jimmy Carter and Ronald Reagan. The differences in their worldviews are quite pronounced, and the connections to their respective foreign policies are clear. In 1977 when he took office, Carter was convinced that the Cold War was virtually over and that the rigid structures of bipolarity had given way to a "post-polar" world. His "4 Ps" hierarchy of the national interest put Principles and Peace at the top. His basic foreign policy strategy was noninterventionist. All these characteristics were evident in many if not most of his foreign policies. In contrast, Reagan saw the world in bipolar terms and focused much of his 1980 presidential campaign against Carter on Cold War themes. He put Power rather than Peace at the top of his national-interest hierarchy, and although he too stressed Principles his conception was defined largely by anticommunism, in contrast to Carter's emphasis on human rights. In addition, Reagan's strategy was decidedly interventionist, in military as well as in other respects.

Presidents of course are also politicians, so another important factor affecting presidential foreign policy leadership is one of *political calculation*. This can work in different ways. Presidents in trouble at home may turn more to foreign policy, hoping to draw on the prestige of international leadership to bolster their domestic standing. At other times presidents feel pressured to give less emphasis to foreign policy to respond to criticisms about not paying enough attention to the domestic front. The election cycle also enters in, with foreign policy tending to get more politicized during election years. And outside the election cycle is the steady flow of public-opinion polls, which get factored in along with the intelligence analyses and other parts of the decision-making process.

## Senior Foreign Policy Advisers and Bureaucratic Politics

All presidents rely heavily on their senior foreign policy advisers.[27] In looking at presidential advisers, we need to ask two sets of questions. The first concerns who among the "big three"—the national security adviser, the secretary of state, and the secretary of defense—has the most influential role? The answer depends on a number of factors, including the respective relationships of these advisers with the president and their own prominence and bureaucratic skills. Henry Kissinger, who became so well known as to take on celebrity status, is the major example. A Harvard professor, Kissinger served as national security adviser in President Nixon's first term. When Nixon appointed him secretary of state in 1973, Kissinger also kept the national security adviser position, a highly unusual step that accorded him unprecedented influence. He continued to hold both positions under President Gerald Ford, until pressured in 1975 to give one up (national security adviser). All told, we find far more references in books on the foreign policy of that period to "Kissingerian" doctrines than to "Nixonian" or, especially, "Fordian" ones.

The other analytic question is whether *consensus or conflict* prevails among the senior advisers. Consensus does not necessarily mean perfect harmony, but it does mean a prevailing sense of teamwork and collegiality. A possible negative aspect of consensus, though, is that too much consensus among senior advisers can lead to ***groupthink,*** a social-psychology concept that refers to the pressures within small groups for unanimity that work against individual critical thinking.[28] Group cohesion is a good thing, but too much of it can be stifling. The result can be the kinds of decisions about which in retrospect the question gets asked, How did so many smart people make such a dumb decision? The Kennedy administration's decision making on the disastrous 1961 Bay of Pigs invasion of Cuba is an oft-cited example, one we will discuss in Chapter 4.

As for conflict among senior advisers, we come back to Kissinger as a classic example. While he was President Nixon's national security adviser, Kissinger clashed repeatedly with Secretary of State William Rogers, and while he was President Ford's secretary of state, with Defense Secretary James Schlesinger. Kissinger won many of these battles, adding to his prominence. But the impact of these disagreements on foreign policy often was quite negative. Such high-level divisiveness made broader domestic consensus building much more difficult. Moreover, with so much emphasis on winning the bureaucratic war, some ideas that were good on their merits, but that happened to be someone else's, were dismissed, buried, or otherwise condemned to bureaucratic purgatory.

Table 2.2 lists the key foreign policy officials of the Bush, Clinton, and Bush administrations. We take a closer look at their advisory processes and bureaucratic politics.

THE FIRST BUSH TEAM The first President Bush's principal foreign policy appointees had two characteristics in common.[29] They all had prior foreign policy and other relevant government experience, and all were longtime friends or associates of George H. W. Bush. Secretary of State James Baker had served as White House chief of staff and secretary of the treasury in the Reagan administration, and had been friends with Bush since their early days together in Texas politics. National Security Adviser Brent Scowcroft had held the same position in the Ford administration, when his friendship with Bush began, and was a retired air force lieutenant colonel with a Ph.D. from Columbia University. Secretary of Defense Dick Cheney had been White House chief of staff for Gerald R. Ford, had represented Wyoming in Congress for ten years, and had served as a member of the House Intelligence Committee. General Colin Powell, chair of the Joint Chiefs of Staff, emerged during the Reagan years first as a top Pentagon official and then as the national security adviser appointed in the wake of the Iran-Contra scandal, a man in uniform who stood for everything that Colonel Oliver North did not.

As a team, Bush and his top appointees generally were regarded as highly competent and quite cohesive. Even those who disagreed with their policies did not question their capabilities. After all the messy internal fights of prior administrations, the solidarity of the Bush team was a welcome relief. There was much less of the endruns, get-the-other-guy leaks to the press, and other bureaucratic infighting. Some critics voiced concerns that the Bush team was too tightly drawn and too homogeneous. The conservative columnist

**TABLE 2.2 Cabinet and Key Foreign Policy Officials in the Bush, Clinton, and Bush Administrations**

| | Bush (41) | Clinton | Bush (43) |
|---|---|---|---|
| Vice President | Dan Quayle | Al Gore | Dick Cheney |
| National Security Adviser | Brent Scowcroft | Anthony Lake<br>Samuel Berger | Condoleezza Rice<br>Stephen Hadley |
| Secretary of State | James A. Baker III<br>Lawrence Eagleburger | Warren Christopher<br>Madeleine Albright | Colin Powell<br>Condoleezza Rice |
| Secretary of Defense | Dick Cheney<br>William Perry | Les Aspin<br>Robert Gates<br>William Cohen | Donald Rumsfeld |
| Chair, Joint Chiefs of Staff | William J. Crowe<br>Colin Powell | Colin Powell<br>John Shalikashvili<br>Hugh Shelton | Hugh Shelton<br>Richard B. Myers<br>Peter Pace<br>Michael Mullen |
| UN Ambassador | Thomas Pickering<br>Edward Perkins | Madeleine Albright<br>Richard Holbrooke | John Negroponte<br>John Danforth<br>John Bolton<br>Zalmay Khalilzad |
| CIA Director/ Director of National Intelligence (DNI) | William Webster<br>Robert Gates | James Woolsey<br>John Deutch<br>George Tenet | George Tenet<br>Porter Goss<br>Michael V. Hayden<br>John Negroponte (DNI)<br>Mike McConnell (DNI) |
| Secretary of the Treasury | Nicholas Brady<br>Robert Rubin | Lloyd Bentsen<br>John Snow<br>Lawrence Summers | Paul O'Neill<br><br>Henry Paulson |
| U.S. Trade Representative | Carla Hills | Mickey Kantor<br>Charlene Barshevsky | Robert Zoellick<br>Rob Portman<br>Susan Schwab |

William Safire remarked on the "absence of creative tension [which] has generated little excitement or innovation. . . . As a result of the Bush emphasis on the appearance of unanimity, we miss the [Franklin] Rooseveltian turbulence that often leads to original thinking."[30] Overall, though, historians regard the Bush senior advisory process as much more positive than negative.

**The Clinton Team** The Clinton team also was marked more by consensus than by conflict. Illustrative of this was a *New York Times* profile of the National Security Adviser Samuel ("Sandy") Berger, full of complimentary quotes from his colleagues. Secretary of Defense William Cohen lauded Berger as an "honest broker." Secretary of State Madeleine Albright dubbed him "the glue for the system." Joint Chiefs of Staff Chair General Hugh Shelton praised his ability to "run a great meeting." These are hardly the comments one would have heard about Henry Kissinger in his day! Kissinger, though, did have his own assessment of Berger, portraying him as more of a "trade lawyer" than a "global strategist."[31]

The Clinton team did have its rivalries, however. Les Aspin, Clinton's first secretary of defense, did not last even a year, in part because he ended up with much of the blame for the military failure in Somalia. Warren Christopher will be remembered as a hard-working and gracious secretary of state but not the right man for the nature of the times. Earlier in his career Anthony Lake, Clinton's first national security adviser, had worked for both Henry Kissinger and Cyrus Vance. He thus was especially conscious of the damage bureaucratic warfare could cause. Some critics, though, felt he had learned these lessons too well, and played too low-key a role himself, especially given his own experience and expertise.

Two historic developments during the Clinton administration need to be noted. One was the appointment of Madeleine Albright, the first woman to serve as secretary of state. Albright's appointment was made at the beginning of Clinton's second term, and it brought a sense of historic importance and celebrity-style excitement. The other was the enhanced foreign policy role played by the vice president, Al Gore. Previous occupants of this office, dubbed by its first holder, John Adams, as "the most insignificant office that ever the invention of man contrived," typically had not had much of a substantive foreign policy role. Trips to attend funerals of foreign dignitaries were pretty much the portfolio. Gore, who had earned a reputation for foreign policy expertise in his sixteen years in Congress, took on much greater and more substantive foreign policy responsibilities. The even greater role played by Vice President Dick Cheney in the second Bush administration, whatever other issues it raised, indicates that the role of the vice presidency as an institution has been transformed.

**The Second Bush Team** As noted, the effort during the 2000 campaign to provide Governor George W. Bush with credit by association with a strong and experienced foreign policy team was a quite conscious one. Dick Cheney and Colin Powell had served in the first Bush administration, as had Condoleezza Rice, who had been a National Security Council staff specialist on the Soviet Union. So had U.S. Trade Representative Robert Zoellick, who had been a top aide to Secretary of State James Baker. Donald Rumsfeld was ambassador to NATO in the Nixon administration and secretary of defense in the Ford administration. This, then, was a new administration but with many familiar faces.

A team that began with established credentials and existing working relationships had definite advantages. They were known to the foreign policy community and the diplomatic community, and were expected to be less likely to make the mistakes of learning on the job. They appeared to start with a strong degree of intra-administration consensus.

It wasn't long, though, before questions arose as to whether there was as much consensus within the Bush team as there originally seemed to be. Within the first few months the Bush team already was showing "two faces," according to a front-page story in the *New York Times,* "an ideologically conservative Pentagon and a more moderate State Department." Although policy debates within an administration can be healthy, observers wondered whether these were becoming "ideological cleavages"—and becoming so quite publicly despite the Bush administration's claims of internal discipline.[32]

One of the earliest intra-administration splits was over North Korea and whether to continue the negotiations over its nuclear weapons program, which were initiated by the Clinton administration and the South Korean president Kim Dae Jung. On the eve of President Kim's March 2001 visit to Washington, Secretary of State Powell came out largely in support of this strategy. Stories immediately broke in the press about Powell's being out of step with others in the administration, notably Vice President Cheney and Defense Secretary Rumsfeld. Then at a joint press conference with President Kim after their White House meeting, President Bush quite candidly conveyed his own skepticism about negotiations and cooperation with North Korea. Secretary Powell was forced to backtrack and take a tougher line. And Kim, who had won the Nobel Peace Prize the previous year for his peace efforts, went home rebuffed by his country's major ally and protector.

Signs of intra-administration splits were especially evident over the war in Iraq. Vice President Cheney and Defense Secretary Rumsfeld were widely viewed as the most hawkish, and Secretary of State Powell was more moderate. "Bureaucratic tribalism exists in all administrations," Francis Fukuyama observed, "but it rose to poisonous levels in Bush's first term." Cheney and Rumsfeld and their aides were "excessively distrustful of anyone who did not share their views, a distrust that extended to Secretary of State Colin Powell and much of the intelligence community."[33] We delve more into these bureaucratic politics in Chapter 8, and the Obama team in Chapter 6.

Politics in the executive branch does not occur only at the senior advisory level. Political battles go on daily at every level of the bureaucracy. "Where you stand depends on where you sit" is the basic dynamic of ***bureaucratic politics***—i.e., the positions taken on an issue by different executive-branch departments and agencies depend on the interests of that particular department or agency. Graham Allison, among the first to develop bureaucratic politics as a model for analyzing U.S. foreign policy, defined its core dynamic as "players who focus not on a single strategic issue but on many diverse intranational problems as well; players who act in terms of no consistent set of strategic objectives but rather according to varying conceptions of national, organizational and personal goals; players who make government decisions not by a single, rational choice but by the pulling and hauling that is politics" (see Reading 2.2).[34]

Take economic sanctions as an example. The Commerce and Agriculture Departments, with their trade-promotion missions, often have opposed the Departments of State and Defense. This position can be disaggregated even further to bureaus within the same department or agency, which may also "stand" differently depending on where they "sit." Within the State Department, the Bureau of Human Rights and the East Asia–Pacific Bureau disagreed over the linkage of MFN renewal with human rights progress in China in the early 1990s. And within the military, interservice rivalry often breaks out as the army, navy, and air force compete for shares of the defense budget, higher profiles in military actions, and other perceived advantages.

On top of these interest-based dynamics are the problems inherent in any large, complex bureaucracy: simply getting things done. The nineteenth-century German political philosopher Max Weber first focused on the problems inherent in large bureaucracies in government as well as other complex organizations. Often, instead of using rational processes consistent with the criteria noted earlier, bureaucracies proceed according to their own standard operating procedures and in other cumbersome ways that remind us why the term "bureaucracy" has the negative connotations that it does.

Most of this discussion has concerned normal foreign policy decision making. When the situations faced are international crises, the challenges for meeting the criteria for a rational executive-branch decision-making process are even greater. The key characteristics of crises are a high level of threat against vital interests, a short time frame for decision making, and usually a significant element of surprise that the situation arose. Such situations tend to give presidents more power, because they require fast, decisive action. Often they also lead presidents to set up special decision-making teams, drawing most heavily on the most trusted advisers. The crisis most often cited as a model of effective decision making is the Cuban missile crisis, which we will discuss further in Chapter 4.

In sum, a rational executive-branch policy-making process is desirable but difficult to achieve. The sources of executive-branch politics are many, and the dynamics can get quite intricate. We will see these played out in ways that show both striking similarities and sharp differences over time.

## Interest Groups and Their Influence

***Interest groups*** are "formal organizations of people who share a common outlook or social circumstance and who band together in the hope of influencing government policy."[35] Three questions are central to understanding the foreign policy role of interest groups: (1) What are the principal types of foreign policy interest groups? (2) What are the main strategies and techniques of influence used by interest groups? (3) How much influence do interest groups have, and how much should they have?

## *A Typology of Foreign Policy Interest Groups*

Distinctions can be made among five main types of foreign policy interest groups on the basis of differences in the nature of the interests that motivate their activity and in their forms of organization. Table 2.3 presents the typology, with some general examples.

ECONOMIC INTEREST GROUPS This category includes multinational corporations (MNCs) and other businesses, labor unions, consumers, and other groups whose lobbying is motivated principally by how foreign policy affects the economic interests of their members. These groups are especially active on trade and other international economic policy issues. Take the infamous 1930 Smoot-Hawley Act, which raised so many tariffs so high that it helped deepen and globalize the Great Depression. Some wondered how such

**TABLE 2.3 A Typology of Foreign Policy Interest Groups**

| Type | General examples |
|---|---|
| Economic groups | AFL-CIO (organization of trade unions)<br>National Association of Manufacturers<br>Consumer Federation of America<br>Major multinational corporations (MNCs) |
| Identity groups | Jewish Americans<br>Cuban Americans<br>Greek Americans<br>African Americans |
| Political issue groups | Anti–Vietnam War movement<br>Committee on the Present Danger<br>Amnesty International<br>World Wildlife Fund<br>Refugees International |
| State and local governments | Local Elected Officials for Social Responsibility<br>California World Trade Commission |
| Foreign governments | Washington law firms, lobbyists, public-relations companies (hired to promote interests of foreign governments in Washington) |

a bill ever could have passed. Very easily, according to one senator who "brazenly admitted that the people who gave money to congressional campaigns had a right to expect it back in tariffs."[36] In the South Africa case of the 1980s, a case study in Chapter 11, many American businesses actively opposed the anti-apartheid sanctions as threatening their economic interests by damaging trade, endangering investments, and hurting profits.

With the spread of globalization, in recent years there have been even more groups whose interests have been affected, one way or the other, by trade and other international economic issues. As recently as 1970, trade accounted for only 13 percent of the U.S. GDP. Today it amounts to more than 30 percent. And trade now comprises much more than goods and services. Companies scour the world, not just their home countries, in deciding where to build factories and make other foreign investments. Millions of dollars in stock investments and other financial transactions flow between New York and Frankfurt, Chicago and London, San Francisco and Tokyo every day. Overall more foreign economic issues are now on the agenda, and those issues are much more politically salient than they used to be. Whereas during the Cold War most foreign economic policy issues were relegated to "low politics" status in contrast to political and security "high politics" issues, in recent years the North American Free Trade Agreement (NAFTA), the WTO, and other international economic issues have been as hotly contested and as prominent as any other foreign policy issues (see Chapter 10).

IDENTITY GROUPS These groups are motivated less by economic interests than by ethnic or religious identity. Irish Americans, Polish Americans, African Americans, Greek Americans, Cuban Americans, Vietnamese Americans—these and other ethnic identity groups have sought to influence U.S. relations with the country or region to which they trace their ancestry or heritage. The increasing racial and ethnic diversity of the American populace, resulting both from new trends in immigration and increasing empowerment of long-present minorities, is making for a larger number and wider range of groups with personal bases for seeking to influence foreign policy. The ethnic and national origins of American immigrants in the early twenty-first century are very different from those of the early twentieth century. Whereas 87 percent of immigrants then came from Europe, now it is only 16 percent. Immigration from Latin America has grown from 4 percent to 38 percent, from Asia from 1 percent to 36 percent, and from Africa from less than 1 percent to 8 percent.[37]

The group most often pointed to as the most powerful ethnic lobby is Jewish Americans and their principal organization, the American-Israel Public Affairs Committee (AIPAC); indeed, one book on AIPAC was titled *The Lobby.* But while the Jewish lobby unquestionably has been quite influential, it is not nearly as all-powerful or always-winning as it is often portrayed. It has lost, for example, on some Arab-Israeli issues in part because major oil companies and arms exporters with key interests in the Arab world (i.e., economic interest groups) have pressured more strongly for the opposite policy. The Jewish American community itself at times has been split, reflecting Israel's own deep political splits on issues like the Arab-Israeli peace process. Moreover, the politics of the Jewish American lobby are not solely responsible for pro-Israel U.S. policy; both Power (the geostrategic benefits of a reliable ally in a region known for its anti-Americanism) and Principles (Israel is the only democracy in the entire Middle East region) have also been served.[38]

POLITICAL ISSUE GROUPS This third category includes groups that are organized around support or opposition to a political issue that is not principally a matter of their economic interests or group identity. Among these are antiwar groups and movements, such as the anti–Vietnam War movement; the America First Committee, which tried to keep the United States out of World War II; and the Anti-Imperialist League, which opposed the Spanish-American War of 1898. During the Cold War, groups such as the Council for a Livable World and the nuclear freeze movement pushed for ratcheting down the levels of armaments and greater efforts at U.S.-Soviet accommodation. On the other hand, quite a few groups were strong advocates of more assertive foreign policies, such as the American Legion, the Veterans of Foreign Wars, and the tellingly named Committee on the Present Danger.

Other subareas of foreign policy also have their sets of political issue groups. They include environmental groups (the World Wildlife Federation, the Sierra Club), human rights groups (Amnesty International, Human Rights Watch), women's rights groups (Women's Action for New Directions), advocates of the rights of refugees (InterAction, Refugees International), and many others. Groups such as these are most commonly called *nongovernmental organizations* (NGOs) and have been playing increasingly important roles in influencing American foreign policy, as we will see in Chapter 10.

STATE AND LOCAL GOVERNMENTS Although they do not fit the term "interest groups" in the same way, state and local governments increasingly seek to influence foreign policy as it affects their interests.[39] In the early 1980s, for example, they pressured the federal government to end the arms race through groups such as the Local Elected Officials for Social Responsibility and by proclamations and referenda by more than 150 cities and counties declaring themselves "nuclear-free zones" or otherwise opposing the nuclear arms race. Conversely, states and cities with large defense industries have pressured the federal government not to cut defense spending. Local activism has been even greater on trade issues. The California World Trade Commission, part of the state government, sent its own representative to the GATT trade talks in Geneva, Switzerland. Many state and local governments actually led the effort to combat apartheid in South Africa. In fact the pressure on Congress to pass economic sanctions legislation was strengthened because so many state and local governments, including those of California and New York City, already had imposed their own sanctions by prohibiting purchases and divesting pension-fund holdings from companies still doing business with South Africa.

Foreign Governments It is of course normal diplomacy for governments to have embassies in each others' capitals. The reference here is to the American law firms, lobbyists, and public-relations companies hired by foreign governments to lobby for them. These foreign lobbyists often are former members of Congress (both Republican and Democratic), former Cabinet members, other former top executive-branch officials, and other "big guns." Indeed, by the early 1990s there were well over one thousand lobbyists in Washington who were representing foreign countries. Major controversies have arisen over foreign lobbying; one high-profile case involved Japan and, as claimed in a 1990 book provocatively titled *Agents of Influence*, its "manipulation" of U.S. policy through lobbyists to the point where "it threatens our national sovereignty."[40] Another striking case was that of Angola in the mid-1980s. American lobbyists were hired both by the Angolan guerrillas, to try to improve their image and otherwise win support for military aid, and by the Angolan government, to try to block the aid to the guerrillas. More than $2 million was paid out by the rebels and almost $1 million by the government in just one year—a hefty sum for a country so poor.

Not all issues involve all five types of interest groups. But all have at least some of these groups seeking to exert their influence.

## *Strategies and Techniques of Influence*

Interest groups seek to influence foreign policy according to many different strategies aimed at the various foreign policy actors.

Influencing Congress Foreign policy legislation generally needs to pass through five principal stages within Congress: the writing of a bill, hearings and mark-up by the relevant committees, votes on the floors of the House of Representatives and the Senate, reconciliation of any differences between the House and Senate bills in a conference committee, and the appropriations process, in which the actual amounts of money are set for defense spending, foreign aid, and other items. Lobbyists will seek to influence legislation at each of these stages. Much, of course, also goes on behind the scenes. Lobbyists regularly meet privately with senators and representatives who are allies to set strategy, count votes, and in some cases even to help write the legislation.

Interest groups also try to go even more to the source by influencing the outcomes of elections. Defense industry political action committees (PACs), for example, are major campaign contributors, especially for members of Congress who serve on defense-related committees. A 1982 study showed that almost half of the PAC contributions made by the nation's twelve largest defense contractors went to members of Congress's armed services committees and defense and military-construction subcommittees.

**Influencing the Executive Branch** Interest groups also try to directly influence executive-branch departments and agencies as they formulate and implement foreign policy on a day-to-day basis. In the 1980s, AIPAC broadened its efforts from being heavily focused on Capitol Hill to work also with mid-level officials in the State and Defense Departments who were involved in U.S.-Israeli relations. In trade policy there is a whole system of advisory committees through which the private sector can channel its influence to executive-branch officials who negotiate trade treaties.

Another strategy is to try to influence who gets appointed to important foreign policy positions. One case in which interest groups were able to have significant influence over an executive appointment involved the ability of the conservative Cuban-American National Foundation (CANF) in 1992–93 to block the nomination of Mario Baeza, a Cuban American whose views on how to deal with Fidel Castro were seen as too moderate, as assistant secretary of state for inter-American affairs. In another case Ernest LeFever, President Reagan's nominee for assistant secretary of state for human rights, was not confirmed because of opposition by pro–human rights groups who viewed him as more of a critic than an advocate of their cause.

**Influencing Public Opinion** Groups also take their efforts to influence foreign policy outside the halls of Congress and the executive branch, mobilizing protests and demonstrations to show "shoulder-to-shoulder" support for their causes. This is an old tradition, going back to peace movements in the early twentieth century, as well as to such nineteenth-century events as the Civil War veterans' march on Washington to demand payment of their pensions. The anti–Vietnam War movement was particularly known for its demonstrations on college campuses as well as in Washington. In the spring of 1970, for example, college campuses around the country were shut down (and final exams were even canceled on many campuses) and almost half a million protesters descended on Washington. An even larger demonstration was staged in 1990 on the twentieth anniversary of "Earth Day" to pressure the government for stronger and more forward-looking policies on global environmental issues.

Especially in recent years, foreign policy interest groups have become quite astute at using the media as a magnifying glass to enlarge their exposure and as a megaphone to amplify their voice. For all the econometric models that were run and other studies that were conducted to show the damage done to the American auto industry by Japanese auto imports in the 1970s and 1980s, for example, none had nearly the impact of the televised image of two members of Congress smashing a Toyota with a sledgehammer in front of the Capitol. Members of the anti-apartheid movement dramatized their cause by handcuffing themselves to the fence around the South African embassy in Washington, D.C., and staging other civil disobedience protests, a major objective of which was to get on the nightly television news. The anti-globalization movement of recent years has tried to use similar tactics, but the violence in the streets of many of these protests at times has backfired by alienating the support of broad swaths of the public.

DIRECT ACTION NGOs often work not just to influence policy in Washington but to play direct roles themselves out on the front lines by providing humanitarian assistance, monitoring human rights, supervising elections, helping with economic development, and taking on countless other global responsibilities. Proponents such as Jessica Mathews, president of the Carnegie Endowment for International Peace, argue that NGOs "can outperform government in the delivery of many public services" and "are better than governments at dealing with problems that grow slowly and affect society through their cumulative effect on individuals."[41] Others see NGOs as having problems, inefficiencies, and interests that complicate and sometimes conflict with their humanitarian and other missions (Chapter 10).[42]

CORRUPTION Popular images of suitcases stuffed with $100 bills, exorbitant junkets, and other corrupt practices at times are grossly exaggerated. Nevertheless, there have been sufficient instances of corrupt efforts to influence foreign policy that to not include it as a technique of influence would be a glaring omission. For example, Koreagate was a 1976 scandal over alleged South Korean influence peddling in Congress. Another example was the 1980s Pentagon defense-contract scandals involving bribes, cover-ups, and cost overruns that led to the purchase of "specially designed" $600 toilet seats and $1,000 coffee machines.

## *The Extent of Interest-Group Influence: Analytic and Normative Considerations*

"The friend of popular governments never finds himself so much alarmed for their character and fate," James Madison warned back in *Federalist 10*, "as when he contemplates their propensity to . . . the violence of faction." Madison defined a "faction" not just as a group with a particular set of interests but as one whose interests, or "common impulse of passion," were "adverse to the rights of other citizens, or to the permanent and aggregate interests of the community."

Madison's general political concern with what we now call the extent of interest-group influence bears particularly on foreign policy, for three principal reasons. First, if Americans have even the slightest sense that the nation is asking them to make the ultimate sacrifice of war for interests that are more group-specific than collectively national, the consequences for national morale and purpose can be devastating. Even in more ongoing, less dramatic areas of policy, the effects of such an impression on the overall state of democracy and conceptions of public authority can be deeply corrosive.

Second, this "capturing" by interest groups of areas of policy makes change much more difficult because of the many vested interests that get ensconced.[43] This is especially a problem in foreign policy, given the many threats and challenges to which the United

States must respond, including the rigors of staying competitive in the international economy. The work of the political scientist Mancur Olson asserts that throughout history it has been the sapping of the capacity for change and adaptation brought on by too many vested interests that has brought down one empire and major power after another—and into which, he warned in 1982, the United States was sinking.[44]

Third is the highly emotionally charged nature of so many foreign policy issues. The "impulses of passion" Madison warned about can be quite intense. The stakes tend to be seen not as just winning or losing, but as tests of morality and even of patriotism.

One oft-cited example of excessive interest-group influence is the ***military-industrial complex***.* Consider the warning sounded in a famous speech in 1961:

> The conjunction of an immense military establishment and a large arms industry is new in the American experience. The total influence—economic, political, even spiritual—is felt in every city, every statehouse, every office of the federal government. . . . We must not fail to comprehend its grave implications. Our toil, our resources and livelihood all are involved; so is the very structure of our society.
>
> In the councils of government, we must guard against the acquisition of unwarranted influence, whether sought or unsought, by the *military-industrial complex* [emphasis added]. The potential for the disastrous rise of misplaced power exists and will persist.
>
> We must never let the weight of this combination endanger our liberties or democratic processes.[45]

Sound like something that might have come from Nikita Khrushchev? Fidel Castro? Or maybe Abbie Hoffman or some other 1960s radical? None of the above. It is from the farewell address of President (and former general) Dwight D. Eisenhower.

Some of the statistics on the Cold War military-industrial complex really are staggering. By 1970 the Pentagon owned 29 million acres of land (almost the size of New York State) valued at $47.7 billion, and had "true wealth" of $300 to $400 billion, or about six to eight times greater than the annual after-tax profits of all U.S. corporations.[46] During the Reagan defense buildup in the mid-1980s, "the Pentagon was spending an average of $28 million *an hour*." One out of every sixteen American workers as well as 47 percent of all aeronautical engineers, more than 30 percent of mathematicians, and 25 percent of physicists either worked directly for or drew grants from the defense sector.[47]

One of the best examples of how the military-industrial complex was set up involved the B-1 bomber, a highly capable but expensive new strategic bomber whose production

---

*The formal political science definition of the military-industrial complex is a social and political subsystem that integrates the armament industry, the military-oriented science community, the defense-related parts of the political system, and the military bureaucracies. David Skidmore and Valerie M. Hudson, eds., *The Limits of State Autonomy: Societal Groups and Foreign Policy Formation* (Boulder, Colo.: Westview, 1992), 36.

President Carter sought to cancel but could not, largely because of "gerrymandered subcontracting." The main contractor for the B-1 was Rockwell International, based in California. In subcontracting out the various parts of the plane, Rockwell astutely ensured that contracts would go to companies in forty-eight states: the defensive avionics to a firm in New York, the offensive avionics to one in Nebraska, the tires and wheels to Ohio, the tail to Maryland, the wings to Tennessee, and so on. To make sure they knew the score, Rockwell spent $110,000 on a study delineating the B-1's economic benefits on a state-by-state, district-by-district basis. Thus, when Carter did not include funding for the B-1 in his version of the annual defense budget, he was threatening jobs in the states and districts of a majority of the members of both the House and the Senate. Voting records show that even many liberal Democrats who otherwise were opposed to high levels of defense spending and in favor of arms control voted against Carter and added enough funding to keep the B-1 alive.[48] When Ronald Reagan became president in 1981, the B-1 production spigot was turned on full force.

Yet there is significant debate over how extensive interest-group influence is. In their review of the literature on the military-industrial complex, professors David Skidmore and Valerie Hudson conclude that the record is mixed, that although there are numerous cases of significant influence, especially in weapons development and procurement, the more sweeping claims of dominance are not borne out by the empirical research.[49] Moreover, and more generally, we also have to go back to Madison for a note of caution about efforts somehow to ban or otherwise "remove the causes" of interest groups: "It could never be more truly said than of [this] remedy that it was worse than the disease. Liberty is to faction what air is to fire, an aliment without which it instantly expires. But it could not be a less folly to abolish liberty, which is essential to political life, because it nourishes faction than it would be to wish the annihilation of air, which is essential to animal life, because it imparts to fire its destructive agency."[50]

Others argue along similar lines that with the exception of issues of the utmost national security, foreign policy should be looked at the same way as domestic policy, with a much broader sense of the legitimacy of group interests. Many of the issues pushed by groups actually are in the broad national interest as well, such as human rights and protecting the global environment, but are not given appropriate priority within the government and thus need outside pressure to bring them to the fore.

In the work quoted above, Madison is more positively inclined toward efforts "to control the effects" of factions than toward those that would "remove their causes." Effects-controlling measures today would include such initiatives as campaign-finance reform, reforms of the defense-procurement process, tighter oversight of covert action, and broad general efforts to educate and engage the public. Experience, though, teaches that this is a problem for which there is no full or enduring solution. Reform measures such as those noted above can help correct some of the worst excesses of interest-group influence. But this is one of those dilemmas for which, as the American government scholars Theodore Lowi and Benjamin Ginsberg write, "there is no ideal answer. . . . Those who believe that there are simple solutions to the issues of political life would do well to ponder this problem."[51]

## The Impact of the News Media

It was just a few hours short of prime time, on the evening of January 16, 1991, when American bombers started attacking Iraq, live on CNN. A war was starting, and Americans and much of the world could see it (at least some of it) right there on their living-room TVs. The Persian Gulf War made the foreign policy role of the news media more graphic and more evident than ever before. So, more recently, did the war in Afghanistan and then the war in Iraq with its "embedded" journalists. Here, too, though, as with much of what we have discussed in this chapter, the key questions debated were not totally new: (1) What role should the news media play? (2) How much influence do they actually have? (3) How is the balance to be struck between freedom of the press and national security?

### *Role of the Media: Cheerleader or Critic?*

In 1916, in an effort to ensure support for a just-launched military intervention into Mexico, President Woodrow Wilson stated, "I have asked the several news services to be good enough to assist the Administration in keeping this view of the expedition constantly before both the people of this country and the distressed and sensitive people of Mexico."[52] The president was asking newspapers to be his cheerleaders. The matter-of-fact tone of his statement, made in a public speech, not just leaked from some secret memo, conveys the expectation that although the press could muckrake all it wanted in domestic policy, in foreign policy, especially during wars or other crises, it was to be less free and more friendly.

Grandparents can tell you about World War II and how strongly the media supported the war effort. Foreign correspondents filled the newspapers, and newsreels played in the movie theaters, with stories and pictures of American and allied heroism, and Nazi and Japanese evil and atrocities. This was "the good war," and there generally was a basis for positive reporting. It did get intentionally manipulative, however. A book called *Hollywood Goes to War* tells the story of how "officials of the Office of War Information, the government's propaganda agency, issued a constantly updated manual instructing the studios in how to assist the war effort, sat in on story conferences with Hollywood's top brass, . . . pressured the movie makers to change scripts and even scrap pictures when they found objectionable material, and sometimes wrote dialogue for key speeches."[53]

Even in the early days of U.S. involvement in Vietnam, the media were largely supportive. But as the war went on, and went bad, the media sent back reports that were

manipulation of
media to
gen support.

much more critical of the conduct of the war and that contradicted the official versions being put out by the Johnson and Nixon administrations. In one telling incident, a reporter who had written critical stories was dressed down by a military commander for "not getting on the team."

Cheerleader or critic? Which role have the media played? And which role should they play? These long have been and continue to be crucial questions. We return to them in Chapter 8 with reference to the 1990–91 Persian Gulf and 2003 Iraq wars.

## Modes of Influence

Three main distinctions are made as to the modes of influence the media have on foreign policy politics. First is *agenda setting*. "The mass media may not be successful in telling people what to think," one classic study put it, "but the media are stunningly successful in telling their audience what to think about."[54] Television in particular has a major agenda-setting impact. Studies by the media scholar Shanto Iyengar and others show that when people are asked to identify the most significant problem facing the nation, they name something that has been on television news recently. Mass starvation was plaguing many parts of Africa in the mid-1980s, but the outside world, the United States included, was paying little attention. Yet once NBC News went to Ethiopia and broadcast footage of ravaged children and emaciated adults to millions of television viewers back in the United States, suddenly the Ethiopian famine was on the foreign policy agenda.

Of course, the equally tragic famines elsewhere in Africa, where the TV cameras did not go, did not make it onto the U.S. national agenda. Such discrepancies raise a troubling question for policy makers: If a tree falls in the woods and television doesn't cover it, did it really fall? The media play a crucial role in determining which issues get focused on and which do not. Some issues do force their way onto the agenda, and the media are largely reactive and mirroring. But many other issues would get much less policy attention if it were not for major media coverage. Conversely, there are foreign policy issues that despite their importance don't get media coverage and thus don't get on the agenda—whole "forests" may fall down with no television cameras in sight.

As to *shaping public opinion,* in terms of its substantive content, the main impact of the media is in what researchers call "framing" and "priming" effects.[55] The stakes involved in a particular foreign policy issue are not necessarily self-evident or part of a strictly objective reality. How an issue is cast ("framed") affects the substantive judgments people make—and the media play a key role in this framing.[56] The media also influence ("prime") the relative priority the public gives to one issue over another, as well as the criteria by which the public makes its judgments about success and failure. These framing and priming effects occur both directly through the general public's own exposure to the media and indirectly through "opinion leaders"—i.e., political, business, community, educational, celebrity, and other leaders to whom the public often looks for cues.

To the extent that the media's substantive impact goes beyond these framing and priming effects, it tends to be on two kinds of foreign policy issues. One set comprises those for which the public has little prior information and few sources other than the media. The other set includes those issues that have strong symbolic significance and are heavily emotionally charged, such as the 1979–81 Iranian hostage crisis and the 2001 terrorist attacks. The intense media coverage of the Iranian hostage crisis made sure this issue stayed front-and-center on the agenda, which, given the nature of the issue, also influenced the substance of public opinion.* Even this didn't compare to the saturation coverage of the September 11, 2001, terrorist attacks. Virtually all Americans were glued to their television sets for days, arguably as much for the sense of community as for information.

Debate also continues over media bias. One aspect is over media objectivity. The Pew Research Center reports that the number of Americans who believe that news organizations are "politically biased in their reporting" increased to 60 percent in 2005 from 45 percent in 1985.[57] The usual argument has been that this is a liberal bias. Although many still hold to this view, citing the *New York Times* and the major networks among other media, many also see a conservative bias in Fox News and newspapers owned by Rupert Murdoch, and other media.[58] The debate goes further: how much does this really matter? A poll by the Annenberg Public Policy Center showed 43 percent thinking it "a good thing if some news organizations have a decidedly political point of view in their coverage of the news."[59]And one study found the effects of Fox News on voting patterns to be statistically insignificant. The public knows bias for what it is, the argument was made, and filters it out more than being shaped by it.[60]

A third type of influence is directly on *policy makers.* Although close and constant news coverage has many benefits, it does bring intense "real-time" pressure on policy makers. An American soldier gets taken prisoner, and his face flashes on the television screen time and again, all day, all night. A terrorist incident occurs, and the video plays over and over. Often policy makers must respond with little prior notice, in some cases actually first hearing about a major event on CNN rather than through official government sources. They also must respond within the immediacy of the twenty-four-hour news cycle. That makes for a very different and more difficult dynamic in key foreign policy choices.

Even in noncrisis situations, "What will the press think?" is regularly asked in executive-branch foreign policy meetings. Editorials and op-ed articles have a remarkable

*Ted Koppel's *Nightline,* which went on to be one of the top-rated news shows for the next twenty-five years, started out as nightly coverage of just the hostage crisis. Every show would be introduced as "Day 1 of the Hostage Crisis," "Day 2 . . . ," "Day 50 . . . ," "Day 100 . . . ," all the way through "Day 444," when on January 20, 1981, the last hostages were released.

influence. Highly critical opinion pieces in major papers such as the *New York Times* and the *Washington Post* have been known to prompt hastily called State Department meetings or to make officials forget about whatever else was on their schedule in order to draft a response. Read the minutes of major foreign policy meetings, and you'll see significant attention paid to media-related issues. Check out staff rosters in the State and Defense Departments, and you'll see numerous media advisers. Look at the curricula taught at the Foreign Service Institute and the National Defense University, and you'll see courses on the role of the media. Given constantly advancing technology, these emphases will only grow with time.

## *Freedom of the Press vs. National Security*

How to strike a balance between freedom of the press and national security has been a recurring issue in American politics. The First Amendment guarantees freedom of the press. Yet situations can arise when the nation's security would be endangered if certain information became public. This national-security rationale can be, and has been, very real; it also can be, and has been, abused.

Historical precedents cut both ways. For example, in 1961 the *New York Times* had uncovered information on the secret Bay of Pigs invasion of Cuba being planned by the Kennedy administration. Under some pressure from the White House, but primarily as their own self-censorship based on the national-security rationale, the *Times*'s publisher and editors decided not to print the information. The Bay of Pigs invasion went ahead, and it failed disastrously—leaving many to question whether national security would have been better served had the story been run and the plan unmasked.[61] On the other hand, in 1962, during the Cuban missile crisis, the press again restrained some of its reporting. An ABC correspondent even served as a secret intermediary for some tense negotiations between President Kennedy and the Soviet leader, Nikita Khrushchev. This time the outcome was more positive: the crisis was resolved, and many concluded that the restraint on full freedom of the press was justified.

With the Cuban missile crisis especially in mind, the historian Michael Beschloss stresses the value in times of crisis of "a cocoon of time and privacy."[62] He speculates about how differently the crisis might have turned out if the media coverage had been as intrusive and intense as it is today. What if TV network satellites had discovered the Soviet missiles on their own and broke the story on the evening news, sparking congressional and public outcry and increasing pressure on President Kennedy to take immediate but precipitous and potentially escalating action, such as an air strike? Could ExCom (JFK's decision-making group) have deliberated over so many days without leaks? Kennedy was able to shape his own story rather than being caught on the defensive; today his position would be much tougher to sell, and he probably could not get away with a number of gambits that balanced toughness with understanding of Khrushchev's situation if every move had been independently and immediately reported and discussed on radio and television talk shows.

In other instances, though, the restrictions imposed on the freedom of the press in the name of national security have been questioned for their impact both on foreign policy and on civil liberties. The Vietnam War "get on the team" view came to a head as a freedom of the press issue in the "Pentagon Papers" case. In mid-1967, at a point when the war was going very badly, Defense Secretary Robert McNamara set up a comprehensive internal review of U.S. policy. By the end of the Johnson administration, the forty-seven-volume *History of the United States Decision-Making Process on Vietnam Policy,* which came to be called the "Pentagon Papers," had been completed. It was given highly classified status, to be kept secret and for high-level government use only. But in March 1971, Daniel Ellsberg, who had been one of the researchers and authors of the Pentagon Papers but now was a critic and opponent of the war, leaked a copy to a *New York Times* reporter. On June 13, 1971, the *Times* began publishing excerpts. The Nixon administration immediately sued to stop publication, claiming potential damage to national security. The administration also had a political agenda, fearing that the already eroding public support for the war would crumble even more. On June 30 the Supreme Court ruled 6 to 3 against the Nixon administration. The Court did not totally disregard the national-security justification but ruled that the standard had not been met in this case, and that therefore First Amendment freedom of the press rights took precedence.[63] The *Times* continued its stories on the Pentagon Papers, as did other newspapers.*

Freedom of the press and national-security issues also have been heated in the struggle against terrorism, as we will see in Chapter 8.

## The Nature and Influence of Public Opinion

With respect to public opinion and foreign policy, our concern is with two principal questions: (1) What is the nature of public opinion? (2) How much influence does it have?

*It was in reaction to the Pentagon Papers leak that President Nixon set up the special White House unit known as the "plumbers" to "plug" any further leaks. Among the operations carried out by the "plumbers" was an illegal break-in to the offices of Daniel Ellsberg's psychiatrist, seeking information with which to discredit Ellsberg, and the 1972 June break-in at the headquarters of the Democratic National Committee in the Watergate building. These events and actions, and others later uncovered, ultimately led to an impeachment investigation against Nixon and on August 9, 1974, his resignation as president.

## *Ignorant or Sensible? The Nature of Public Opinion about Foreign Policy*



To read some of the commentaries on American public opinion and foreign policy, one would think that Americans believe much more in government *for* the people than in government *by* and *of* the people (Reading 2.3). Walter Lippmann, the leading U.S. foreign-affairs journalist of the first half of the twentieth century, disparaged public opinion as "destructively wrong at critical junctures . . . a dangerous master of decision when the stakes are life and death."[64] Nor was the traditional view taken by leading scholars any more positive. "The rational requirements of good foreign policy," wrote the eminent Realist Hans Morgenthau, "cannot from the outset count upon the support of a public whose preferences are emotional rather than rational."[65] Gabriel Almond, in *The American People and Foreign Policy,* a 1950 study long considered a classic in the field, stressed the "inattentiveness" of the vast majority of the public to foreign policy, an inattentiveness he attributed to the lack of "intellectual structure and factual content." [66] Others took this opinion even further, positing a historical pattern of reflexively alternating "moods" of introversion and extroversion, a sort of societal biorhythm by which every two decades or so the public shifted between internationalism and isolationism.[67]

These criticisms are built around a basic distinction between the "mass public," susceptible to all of the above and more, and the better-informed, more thoughtful, and more sophisticated "elites." The general public consistently has shown very little knowledge about foreign affairs. The following facts illustrate general public ignorance:

- In 1964, only 58 percent of the public knew that the United States was a member of NATO, and 38 percent thought the Soviet Union was.[68]
- Only four months after the dramatic ceremony held on September 13, 1993, on the White House lawn with President Clinton, the Israeli prime minister Yitzhak Rabin, and the Palestine Liberation Organization leader Yasir Arafat, 56 percent of Americans could not identify the group that Arafat headed.[69]
- In 2006, three years into the Iraq war, only 37 percent of young adults could locate Iraq on a map.[70]

Other critics point to overreactive tendencies in the mass public. Take the "rally 'round the flag" pattern in times of crisis. On the one hand this reaction can be quite positive in helping build consensus and national solidarity when the nation faces a serious threat. It also can be politically helpful to presidents whose popularity gets boosted as part of the rallying effect. But often it becomes blind "followership," and in extremes can pose dangers to democracy by adding to the forces equating dissent with disloyalty.

An alternative view sees the public as much more sensible about foreign policy than it gets credit for. Elmo Roper, who founded a trailblazing public-opinion-polling firm, observed back in 1942 that "during my eight years of asking the common man questions about what he thinks and what he wants . . . I have often been surprised and elated to discover that, despite his lack of information, the common man's native intelligence generally brings him to a sound conclusion."[71]

Those who share the "sensible public" view stress two key points. One is that rather than being wildly and whimsically fluctuating, public opinion has been quite stable over time. Take, for example, basic attitudes toward isolationism ("stay out of world affairs") vs. internationalism ("play an active role"). For the entire period from the end of World War II to the end of the Cold War (1945–90), as illustrated in Figure 2.1, despite some ups and downs the overall pro-internationalism pattern held. The same figure shows internationalism fluctuating a bit but staying robust in the 1990s, then surging up in the wake of 9/11 (81 percent support). Even when support for the Iraq war dropped dramatically (hovering around 30 percent), the public did not generalize this to an overall retreat from international affairs (still 69 percent in 2006). By the end

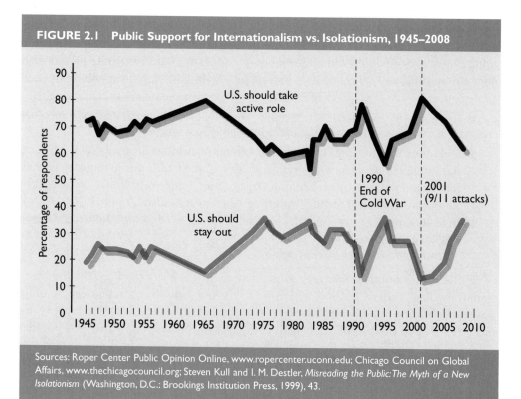

**FIGURE 2.1 Public Support for Internationalism vs. Isolationism, 1945–2008**

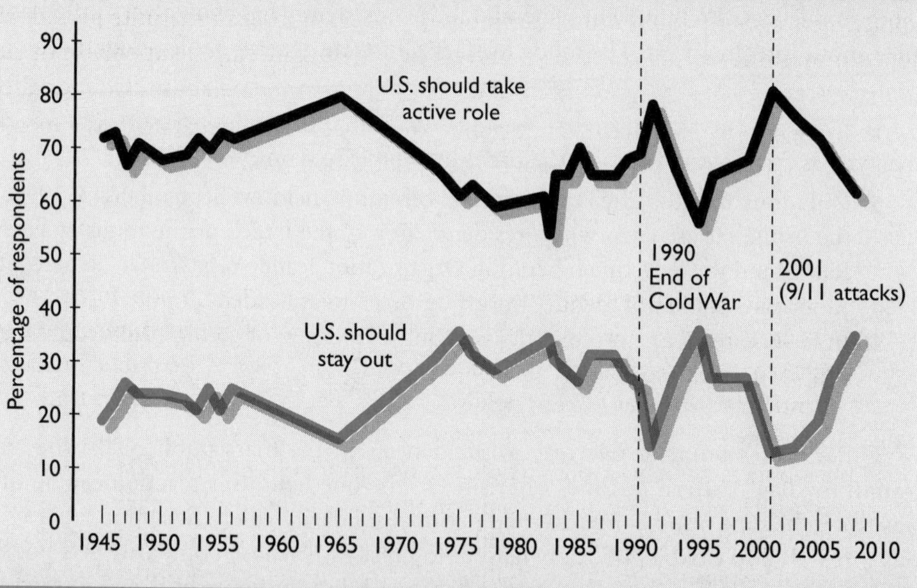


Sources: Roper Center Public Opinion Online, www.ropercenter.uconn.edu; Chicago Council on Global Affairs, www.thechicagocouncil.org; Steven Kull and I. M. Destler, *Misreading the Public: The Myth of a New Isolationism* (Washington, D.C.: Brookings Institution Press, 1999), 43.

of the George W. Bush administration, though, the combination of the strain of Iraq and other foreign policy problems, along with the economic and financial crisis, brought the pro and con internationalism figures down to 63 percent and up to 36 percent, respectively.

The second point made by those who view public opinion positively is that to the extent that public views on foreign policy have changed over time, it has been less a matter of moodiness and much more a rational process. A study of the fifty-year period 1935–85 concludes that "virtually all the rapid shifts [in public opinion] . . . were related to political and economic circumstances or to significant events which sensible citizens would take into account. In particular, most abrupt foreign policy changes took place in connection with wars, confrontations or crises in which major policy changes in the actions of the United States or other nations quite naturally affect preference about what policies to pursue."[72] This is termed an "event-driven" process; that is to say, when the threats facing the United States or other aspects of the international situation have changed, in an altogether rational way so too has public opinion.

What, for example, was so feckless about the public's turning against the Vietnam War when many people believed at the time, and former defense secretary Robert McNamara's memoirs confirmed, that even those at the highest levels did not believe the war could be won? "It is difficult to fault the American people," wrote the army major Andrew F. Krepinevich, Jr., "when, after that long a period of active engagement, the Joint Chiefs of Staff could only offer more of the same for an indefinite period with no assurance of eventual success."[73] Indeed, had the public stayed supportive of such an ill-conceived war effort, we might *then* really have wondered about its rationality.

We thus get two very different views of the nature of public opinion. The analytic challenge is that neither holds all the time, and both hold some of the time.

## *The Influence of Public Opinion on Foreign Policy*

The political scientist Bruce Russett characterizes the basic public opinion–foreign policy dynamic as an *interactive* one. Leaders do not control the public; they cannot "persuade the populace to support whatever the leaders wish to do." Nor is the public in control, having so much impact that foreign policy basically "obeys [its] dictates." Instead, "each influences the other."[74]

Public opinion influences foreign policy in five principal ways. The first is by *parameter setting*, which means that public opinion imposes limits on the range of the president's policy options via assessments made by presidential advisers of which options have any chance of being made to "fly" with the public and which are "nonstarters." A good example is U.S. policy toward Saddam Hussein in the 1980s, the period before he became Public Enemy No. 1 during the Persian Gulf War. During Saddam's war with Iran, which lasted from 1980 to 1988, the Reagan administration gave Iraq extensive support on the grounds that "the enemy of my enemy is my friend." Once the Iran-Iraq War was over, and Saddam attacked the Iraqi Kurds with chemical weapons and showed other signs of aggression in the region, some in the State Department began to question whether the United States should continue aiding Iraq. But with the Iran-contra affair still in the political air, the Reagan administration flatly ruled out any shift from the pro-Saddam policy on the grounds that it risked being seen by the public as "soft on Iran." Consequently, when the internal State Department paper proposing such a shift in policy was leaked to the press, Secretary of State George Shultz "called a meeting in his office, angrily demanding to know who was responsible for the paper. . . . [The paper] was dismissed less by any analytic refutation of its strategic logic than on political grounds. . . . On the cover page, in big letters, [Shultz] had written 'NO.'"[75]

A second way that public opinion influences policy is through *centripetal pull* toward the center on presidents who need to build supportive coalitions. This centering pull has worked both on presidents whose tendencies were too far to the left and on those too far to the right to gain sufficient political support. With President Jimmy Carter, whose foreign policy reputation generally raised doubts as to whether he was "tough" enough, the public sought to balance this concern by expressing low levels of approval of Carter's Soviet policy when it was in its conciliatory phases (1977–78, most of 1979), and higher levels of support when Carter got tough (mid-1978, 1979–80). President Ronald Reagan's foreign policy reputation, in contrast, was plenty tough but raised concerns among a substantial segment of the public as to whether it was reckless and risked war. Thus, public approval of Reagan's Soviet policy fell when it was most strident and confrontational (1981–83), and then increased in late 1985 once it started to become more genuinely open to cooperation, peaking at 65 percent following Reagan's first summit with the Soviet leader Mikhail Gorbachev in November 1985.[76]

The third influence of public opinion is its *impact on Congress*. Congress is very sensitive, arguably too sensitive, to public opinion on foreign policy. It responds both to polls on specific issues and to more general assessments of whether the public really cares much about foreign policy at all. Often this translates into Congress's paying the most attention to the groups that are the most vocal and are the most politically potent, and caring less about broader opinion-poll trends. The late senator Hubert H. Humphrey, a leading figure from the late 1940s to his death in 1978, excoriated many of his colleagues for being "POPPs," or what he called "public opinion poll politicians," on foreign policy.[77]

Fourth, public opinion can *affect diplomatic negotiations*. Public opinion does not come into play merely once a treaty or other diplomatic agreement is reached; it also can effect the actual diplomatic negotiations themselves, because U.S. diplomats need to know, while still at the table, what terms of agreement are politically viable back home.[78] This kind of influence is not necessarily a bad thing. It can be, to the extent that it ties the negotiators' hands in ways that are politically popular but unsound in policy terms. But public opinion also can strengthen negotiators' hands as part of a "good cop–bad cop" dynamic. "I'd be more than willing to consider your proposal," a U.S. negotiator might say to his Japanese or Russian counterpart, "but the American public would never accept it."

The fifth avenue for public opinion's influence is *through presidential elections.* Voting analysts identify three factors as key to attributing significant electoral impact to a foreign policy issue: the issue must be demonstrated through survey questions to be highly salient; there must be significant differences between the positions of the Republican and Democratic candidates; and the public's awareness of these differences must be evident.[79] Cold War–era examples of the strong impact of foreign policy issues on elections were in the 1952 (Dwight Eisenhower vs. Adlai Stevenson), 1972 (Richard Nixon vs. George McGovern), and 1980 (Jimmy Carter vs. Ronald Reagan) presidential contests.[80] In other instances the public has focused less on a specific issue than on a general sense of which candidate generally seems to be a strong leader, or which seems too "soft" to stand up to foreign enemies and otherwise be entrusted with the nation's security. Admittedly these are highly subjective assessments, and harder for pollsters and political scientists to measure precisely. But experience has shown that these difficulties don't make such opinions any less important.

## Summary

Foreign policy politics is the *process* by which the choices of foreign policy strategy are made. It is much more complex than the conventional wisdom depicts; as we have seen in this chapter, politics' stopping "at the water's edge" has been more the exception than the rule. The basic patterns are of both consensus and conflict, with positive and negative variations of each in terms of their effects on policy.

Table 2.4 summarizes the basic framework this chapter has laid out for foreign policy politics. The framework is a structural one, focusing on the roles of the principal political institutions involved in the making of foreign policy (the president, Congress, and the ex-

**TABLE 2.4 Foreign Policy Politics and the Process of Choice**

| | |
|---|---|
| President and Congress | Pennsylvania Avenue diplomacy |
| Executive-branch politics | Advisory process, decision making |
| Interest groups | Lobbying, other strategies of influence |
| News media | Traditional and new media |
| Public opinion | Its content and influence |

ecutive branch) and the major societal influences (interest groups, the news media, and public opinion).

In Chapters 3 through 5, we will see how the dynamics of foreign policy politics and the process of choice, as well as Chapter 1's foreign policy strategy and the essence of choice, have played out historically. We then come back to this framework in Part II, applying it to the Obama administration and key foreign policy politics cases in Chapters 6–11.

## *American Foreign Policy* Online Student StudySpace

- What is the media's main mode of influence on public opinion?
- What are some examples of civil liberties taking precedent over national security?
- What is the difference between intrabranch politics and interbranch politics?

For these and other study questions, as well as other features, check out the Chapter 2 section of the *American Foreign Policy* Online Student StudySpace at wwnorton.com/studyspace.

## Notes

[1]Joseph Marion Jones, *The Fifteen Weeks (February 21–June 5, 1947)* (New York: Harcourt Brace and World, 1955), 8.

[2]James M. McCormick, *American Foreign Policy and Process* (Itasca, Ill.: Peacock, 1992), 478.

[3]Quoted in Bruce W. Jentleson, "American Diplomacy: Around the World and Along Pennsylvania Avenue," in *A Question of Balance: The President, the Congress and Foreign Policy*, Thomas E. Mann, ed. (Washington, D.C.: Brookings Institution Press, 1990), 184.

[4]Edward S. Corwin, *The President: Office and Powers, 1787–1957*, 4th rev. ed. (New York: New York University Press, 1957), 171.

[5]Richard E. Neustadt, *Presidential Power: The Politics of Leadership* (New York: Wiley, 1976), 101.

[6]Cited in Arthur M. Schlesinger, Jr., *The Imperial Presidency* (New York: Atlantic Monthly Press, 1974), 17.

[7]Terry L. Deibel, "The Death of a Treaty," *Foreign Affairs* 81.5 (September/October 2002): 142–61.

[8]Deibel, "Death of a Treaty," 147.

[9]Deibel, "Death of a Treaty," 158.

[10]Deibel, "Death of a Treaty," 158.

[11]"Text of Lake's Sharply Worded Letter Withdrawing as the CIA Nominee," *New York Times*, March 18, 1997, B6.

[12]Quoted in Suzanne Nossel, "Bracing for Bolton," Center for American Progress, March 8, 2005 www.americanprogress.org/issues/2005/03/b413729.html (accessed 5/28/09).

[13]Excellent books on the executive-legislative politics of trade policy are I. M. Destler, *American Trade Politics*, 4th ed. (Washington, D.C.: Institute for International Economics, 2005); and Robert A. Pastor, *Congress and the Politics of Foreign Economic Policy, 1929–1976* (Berkeley: University of California Press, 1980).

[14]Destler, *American Trade Politics*, 37.

[15]James M. Lindsay, *Congress and the Politics of U.S. Foreign Policy* (Baltimore: Johns Hopkins University Press, 1994), 90.

[16]Cited in McCormick, *American Foreign Policy and Process,* 268.

[17]Lindsay, *Congress and the Politics of U.S. Foreign Policy,* chaps. 4 and 5.

[18]Lindsay, *Congress and the Politics of U.S. Foreign Policy,* 99.

[19]Linday, *Congress and the Politics of U.S. Foreign Policy,* 102–3.

[20]*United States v. Curtiss-Wright Export Corp.* 299 U.S. 304 (1936), quoted in *Foreign Relations and National Security Law: Cases, Materials and Simulations,* Thomas M. Franck and Michael J. Glennon, eds. (St. Paul: West Publishing, 1987), 32–37.

[21]*Youngstown Sheet and Tube Co. v. Sawyer,* 103 F. Supp. 569 (1952) [the *Steel Seizure* case], quoted in *Foreign Relations and National Security Law,* Franck and Glennon, eds., 5–28.

[22]One of these cases was *Goldwater et al. v. Carter* (1979), in which Republican senator Barry Goldwater led a suit challenging the constitutionality of President Carter's decision to terminate the Mutual Defense Treaty with Taiwan as part of his policy of normalizing relations with the People's Republic of China. The others were four suits brought by Democratic members of Congress in the Reagan and Bush administrations on war powers issues: *Crockett v. Reagan* (1984), on U.S. military aid and advisers in El Salvador; *Conyers v. Reagan* (1985), over the 1983 invasion of Grenada; *Lowry v. Reagan* (1987), over the naval operations in the Persian Gulf during the Iran-Iraq War; and *Dellums v. Bush* (1990), over the initial Operation Desert Shield deployment following the Iraqi invasion of Kuwait.

[23]Alexander L. George, *Presidential Decisionmaking in Foreign Policy: The Effective Use of Information and Advice* (Boulder, Colo.: Westview, 1980), 10.

[24]Elizabeth Drew, *On the Edge: The Clinton Presidency* (New York: Simon & Schuster, 1994), 158, 283.

[25]John E. Rielly, ed., *American Public Opinion and U.S. Foreign Policy 1999* (Chicago: Council on Foreign Relations, 1999), 35.

[26]Robert Jervis, *Perception and Misperception in International Politics* (Princeton: Princeton University Press, 1976), 28.

[27]For a thorough analysis of the role of the national security adviser, see Ivo H. Daalder and I. M. Destler, *In the Shadow of the Oval Office: Profiles of the National Security Advisers and the Presidents They Served, from JFK to George W. Bush* (New York: Simon & Schuster, 2009).

[28]See Irving L. Janis, *Groupthink: Psychological Studies of Policy Decisions and Fiascos* (Boston: Houghton Mifflin, 1982).

[29]Larry Berman and Bruce Jentleson, "Bush and the Post–Cold War World: Challenges for American Leadership," in *The Bush Presidency: First Appraisals,* Colin Campbell and Bert A. Rockman, eds. (Chatham, N.J.: Chatham House Publishers, 1991), 106–07.

[30]Quoted in Berman and Jentleson, "Bush and the Post–Cold War World," 103.

[31]Elaine Sciolino, "Berger Manages a Welter of Crises in the Post–Cold War White House," *New York Times,* May 18, 1998, A9.

[32]Jane Perlez, "Bush Team's Counsel Is Divided on Foreign Policy," *New York Times,* March 27, 2001, A1.

[33]Francis Fukuyama, *America at the Crossroads: Democracy, Power, and the Neoconservative Legacy* (New Haven: Yale University Press, 2006), 61.

[34]Graham T. Allison, *Essence of Decision: Explaining the Cuban Missile Crisis* (Boston: Little, Brown, 1971), 144; see also his "Conceptual Models and the Cuban Missile Crisis," *American Political Science Review* 63 (September 1969): 689–718.

[35]Larry Berman and Bruce Murphy, *Approaching Democracy* (Englewood Cliffs, N.J.: Prentice-Hall, 1996), 408.

[36]Quoted in Pastor, *Congress and the Politics of Foreign Economic Policy,* 79.

[37]Figures for 1920 from U.S. Census Bureau, as reported in the *Washington Post,* May 25, 1998, A1; 2005 figures are for legal immigrants, from "Where Do Immigrants Come From?" *Raleigh News and Observer,* June 4, 2006, 22A.

[38]For a differing view see John J. Mearsheimer and Stephen M. Walt, *The Israel Lobby and U.S. Foreign Policy* (New York: Farrar, Straus and Giroux, 2007).

[39]Earl H. Fry, *The Expanding Role of State and Local Governments in U.S. Foreign Policy* (New York: Council on Foreign Relations Press, 1998); also Chadwick Alger, "The World Relations of Cities: Closing the Gap between Social Science Paradigms and Everyday Human Experience," *International Studies Quarterly* 34.4 (1990): 493–518; and Michael H. Shuman, "Dateline Main Street: Local Foreign Policies," *Foreign Policy* 65 (1986/87): 154–74.

[40]Pat Choate, *Agents of Influence: How Japan's Lobbyists in the United States Manipulate America's Political and Economic System* (New York: Knopf, 1990), xiv.

[41]Jessica Mathews, "Power Shift," *Foreign Affairs* 76.1 (January–February 1997): 63.

[42]Alexander Cooley and James Ron, "The NGO Scramble: Organizational Insecurity and the Political Economy of Transnational Action," *International Security* 27 (Summer 2002): 5–39.

[43]Theodore J. Lowi, *The End of Liberalism: Ideology, Policy, and the Crisis in Public Authority* (New York: Norton, 1969).

[44]Mancur Olson, *The Rise and Decline of Nations: Economic Growth, Stagflation, and Social Rigidities* (New Haven: Yale University Press, 1982).

[45]Dwight D. Eisenhower, "Farewell Address," January 1961, *Public Papers of the Presidents of the United States, Dwight D. Eisenhower* (Washington, D.C.: U.S. Government Printing Office, 1962), 8: 1035–41.

[46]Sidney Lens, *The Military-Industrial Complex* (Philadelphia: Pilgrim, 1970), 12.

[47]Charles W. Kegley, Jr., and Eugene R. Wittkopf, *American Foreign Policy: Pattern and Process,* 5th ed. (New York: St. Martin's, 1996), 302.

[48]"The B-1: When Pentagon, Politicians Join Hands," *U.S. News and World Report,* July 1, 1983, 34. See also Nick Kotz, *Wild Blue Yonder: Money, Politics and the B-1 Bomber* (New York: Pantheon, 1988).

[49]David Skidmore and Valerie M. Hudson, eds., *The Limits of State Authority: Societal Groups and Foreign Policy Formation* (Boulder, Colo.: Westview, 1992), 36–38.

[50]James Madison, *Federalist 10,* in *The Federalist Papers,* Clinton Rossiter, ed. (New York: New American Library, 1961), 78.

[51]Theodore J. Lowi and Benjamin Ginsberg, *American Government: Freedom and Power,* 3d ed. (New York: Norton, 1993), 540.

[52]Quoted in Will Friedman, "Presidential Rhetoric, the News Media and the Use of Force in the Post–Cold War Era," paper presented to the Annual Conference of the American Political Science Association, New York, September 1994.

[53]Clayton R. Koppes and Gregory D. Black, *Hollywood Goes to War: How Politics, Profits and Propaganda Shaped World War II Movies* (New York: Free Press, 1987), vii.

[54]Bernard C. Cohen, *The Press and Foreign Policy* (Princeton: Princeton University Press, 1963), cited in Kegley and Wittkopf, *American Foreign Policy,* 310.

[55]See Shanto Iyengar, *Is Anyone Responsible? How Television Frames Political Issues* (Chicago: University of Chicago Press, 1991); and Shanto Iyengar and Donald R. Kinder, *News That Matters: Television and American Opinion* (Chicago: University of Chicago Press, 1987).

[56]Framing is defined as "selecting and highlighting some facets of events or issues, and making the connections among them so as to promote a particular interpretation, evaluation and/or solution." Robert M. Entman, "Cascading Activation: Contesting the White House's Frame After 9/11," *Political Communication* 20 (2003): 417.

[57]Quoted in Alan B. Krueger, "Fair? Balanced? A Study Finds It Does Not Matter," *New York Times,* August 18, 2005.

[58]Compare Eric Alterman, *What Liberal Media? The Truth about Bias and the News* (New York: Basic Books, 2003), and Bernard Goldberg, *Bias: A CBS Insider Exposes How the Media Distort the News* (Washington, D.C.: Regnery Publishing, 2002).

[59]Quoted in Richard A. Posner, "Bad News," *New York Times*, July 31, 2005.

[60]Quoted in Krueger, "Fair? Balanced?"

[61]James Aronson, *The Press and the Cold War* (New York: Bobbs Merrill, 1970), chap. 11.

[62]Michael R. Beschloss, *Presidents, Television, and Foreign Crises* (Washington, D.C.: Annenberg Washington Program, 1993).

[63]*New York Times Co. v. United States* (1971), cited in Franck and Glennon, eds., *Foreign Relations and National Security Law*, 863–78.

[64]Walter Lippmann, *Essays in the Public Philosophy* (Boston: Little, Brown, 1955), 20.

[65]Hans J. Morgenthau, *Politics among Nations: The Struggle for Power and Peace* (New York: Knopf, 1955), 20.

[66]Gabriel Almond, *The American People and Foreign Policy* (New York: Harcourt, Brace, 1950), 69.

[67]Frank L. Klingberg, "The Historical Alternation of Moods in American Foreign Policy," *World Politics* 4.2 (January 1952): 239–73.

[68]Lloyd A. Free and Hadley Cantril, *The Political Beliefs of Americans* (New York: Simon & Schuster, 1968), 60.

[69]Kegley and Wittkopf, *American Foreign Policy*, 265.

[70]National Geographic–Roper, "2006 Survey of Geographic Literacy." Available at www.nationalgeographic.com/roper2006/findings.html (accessed 6/2/09).

[71]Cited in Miroslav Nincic, *Democracy and Foreign Policy: The Fallacy of Political Realism* (New York: Columbia University Press, 1992), 48.

[72]Benjamin I. Page and Robert Y. Shapiro, "Changes in Americans' Policy Preferences, 1935–1979," *Public Opinion Quarterly* 46.1 (1982): 34.

[73]Andrew F. Krepinevich, Jr., *The Army and Vietnam* (Baltimore: John Hopkins University Press, 1986), 270.

[74]Bruce M. Russett, *Controlling the Sword* (Cambridge, Mass.: Harvard University Press, 1990), chap. 4.

[75]Bruce W. Jentleson, *With Friends Like These: Reagan, Bush and Saddam, 1982–1990* (New York: Norton, 1994), 90–91.

[76]Miroslav Nincic, "The United States, the Soviet Union and the Politics of Opposites," *World Politics* 40.4 (July 1988): 452–75.

[77]Interview by author, July 20 and 22, 1977, published in Bruce W. Jentleson, ed., *Perspectives 1979* (Washington, D.C.: Close Up Foundation, 1979), 273–79.

[78]Robert Putnam, "Diplomacy and Domestic Politics: The Logic of Two-Level Games," *International Organization* 42.3 (Summer 1988): 427–60.

[79]John H. Aldrich, John L. Sullivan, and Eugene Borgida, "Foreign Affairs and Issue Voting: Do Presidential Candidates 'Waltz Before a Blind Audience'?" *American Political Science Review* 83 (March 1989): 123–42.

[80]In the 1952 election, with the Korean War mired in stalemate, the public had much more confidence in the Republican candidate, General Dwight D. Eisenhower, the triumphant World War II commander of U.S. forces in Europe, than in the Democratic candidate, Illinois governor Adlai Stevenson. In the 1972 election, foreign policy was crucial in the Democratic presidential nomination process; Senator George McGovern (D–S.D.) won the nomination largely on the basis of being the candidate most strongly opposed to the Vietnam War. But McGovern lost to President Richard Nixon in the general election. Although the Vietnam War was highly unpopular, McGovern was seen as too "dovish," whereas Nixon countered some of the sense of his responsibility for the war with announcements in the month before the election that "peace [was] at hand." In the 1980 election, data show that whereas only 38.3 percent of the public could articulate the differences between Jimmy Carter and Ronald Reagan on inflation and unemployment, 63.5 percent could on defense spending and 58.8 percent could on relations with the Soviet Union. Moreover, the taking of American hostages in Iran was for many Americans "a powerful symbol of American weakness and humiliation," and, whether fairly or unfairly, the dominant view was "that an inability to bring the hostages home reflected directly on [Carter's] competence." Samuel L. Popkin, *The Reasoning Voter* (Chicago: University of Chicago Press, 1991), 111.

CHAPTER

# 3 The Historical Context: Great Debates in American Foreign Policy, 1789–1945

## Introduction: "The Past Is Prologue"

The words "The past is prologue" are inscribed on the base of the National Archives in Washington, D.C. For all the ways that today's world is new and different, we can learn much from history. The particular choices debated for U.S. foreign policy in the twenty-first century clearly differ in many ways from past agendas. But for all the changes, we still wrestle with many of the same core questions of foreign policy strategy and foreign policy politics that have been debated for more than two hundred years of American history.

To provide part of this important historical context, this chapter examines recurring "great debates" from pre–Cold War history (1789–1945) that are most relevant to U.S. foreign policy in the post–Cold War era. Six of these "great debates" deal with foreign policy strategy:

- the overarching debate over isolationism vs. internationalism, encompassing considerations of Power, Peace, Principles, and Prosperity
- Power and Peace debates over how big a military the United States should have and how much to spend on defense
- how true U.S. foreign policy has been to its democratic Principles
- whether U.S. foreign policy has been imperialistic (Prosperity)
- relations with Latin America as a key case exemplifying the competing tensions among the "4 Ps'
- U.S. emergence as a Pacific power and its relations with the countries of Asia as another key case

Three others deal with foreign policy politics:

- recurring "Pennsylvania Avenue diplomacy" struggles between the president and Congress over going to war
- tensions between considerations of national security and the constitutional guarantees of civil liberties
- interest-group pressures and other political battles over free trade vs. protectionism

## Brief Historical Chronology

Before getting to the great debates as analytic history, we present a brief chronology of key events and actions in American foreign policy from 1776 to 1945. The following section lays out a timeline of major events and their foreign policy significance traced through five historical periods: the Revolutionary War and the consolidation of independence, 1776–1800; expansion and preservation, 1801–65; global emergence, 1865–1919; isolationist retreat, 1919–41; and World War II, 1941–45.[1]

### *The Revolutionary War and the Consolidation of Independence, 1776–1800*

The first major ally the new nation had was France. Many historians think the American Revolution would have failed had it not been for the support—money, supplies, and army and navy units—that the French king Louis XVI provided. Why did France do this? The main factor was the "enemy of my enemy is my friend" calculation stemming from French-British wars and rivalry.

Independence did not guarantee security for the newly minted United States of America. Tensions with Britain continued. The Jay Treaty managed to avoid another war with Britain but had other controversial provisions, as discussed in Chapter 2. Relations with France also had become tense amid the upheaval of the French Revolution. It was with these and other issues in mind that George Washington urged isolationism from Europe's conflicts as he left office in 1796.

Tensions grew worse with France during John Adams's presidency, coming close to war and prompting the passage of the Alien and Sedition Acts. Although these laws protected against subversive activities by the French and their sympathizers they were also quite repressive of civil liberties.

| Date | Event | Foreign Policy Significance |
|---|---|---|
| 1776 | Declaration of Independence | Revolutionary War, support from France |
| 1781 | Articles of Confederation | Failed effort at creating a union |
| 1783 | Treaty of Paris | Britain defeated |
| 1787 | Constitution ratified | United States of America created |
| 1789 | George Washington, first president | Thomas Jefferson, first secretary of state |
| 1796 | Jay Treaty | United States avoids another war with Britain, but other provisions controversial |
| 1796 | Washington's Farewell Address | Warns against entangling alliances |
| 1798 | Alien and Sedition Acts | National security–civil liberties tension |

## *Expansion and Preservation, 1801–65*

On the one hand, this was a period of expansion of the size of the United States: The ***Louisiana Purchase,*** negotiated with France, capitalizing on Napoleon's need for money to finance his effort to conquer Europe, doubled the size of the country. The 1846–48 war with Mexico led to the annexation of Texas and the acquisition of California and other western territories. Numerous wars were fought with the Native Americans. The prevailing view of the times was that this territorial expansion was the United States' "manifest destiny," an expression coined in 1845.

This era also saw the expansion of American influence beyond territorial acquisitions. President Thomas Jefferson dispatched the navy against the Barbary pirates, who had been attacking American commercial shipping in the Mediterranean Sea. Although such forays into European affairs still were limited, the United States became more assertive within the Western Hemisphere. The Monroe Doctrine warned European powers to stay out in terms that, though affirming the independence of other nations, also were used to justify American dominance and numerous military interventions.

But for all this expansion the very existence of the nation was twice threatened. The British came close to winning the War of 1812, even invading the nation's capital, Washington, D.C., and burning the White House. When the election of Abraham Lincoln as president brought the issue of slavery to a head, civil war ensued. With some leverage from its cotton trade, the Confederacy tried to get Britain on its side. France tried to take advantage by invading Mexico and installing a new monarch, Emperor Napoleon III. The Civil War ended in 1865, and the Union was preserved.

| Date | Event | Foreign Policy Significance |
|---|---|---|
| **1803** | Louisiana Purchase from France | Doubles size of the United States |
| **1803–5** | Military action against Barbary pirates in Mediterranean | Early presidential use of force |
| **1812–14** | War of 1812 vs. Great Britain | Aug. 24–25, 1814: Washington, D.C. burned, White House included |
| **1823** | Monroe Doctrine proclaimed | U.S. hegemony in Wester Hemisphere |
| **1845** | Manifest destiny proclaimed | Basis for U.S. expansion across the continent |
| **1846–48** | War with Mexico | Texas, other territories annexed |
| **1853–54** | Commodore Perry's voyage to Japan | Some commercial and other relations |
| **1860** | Abraham Lincoln elected president | Southern states secede, form Confederacy, seek European support and recognition |

| Date | Event | Foreign Policy Significance |
|---|---|---|
| 1861–65 | Civil War | |
| 1863 | France conquers Mexico | Seeks foothold in North America |
| 1865 | Civil War ends | United States reunited |

## *Global Emergence, 1865–1919*

Post–Civil War Reconstruction as well as economic cycles of booms and busts engendered some further isolationism. Additional restrictions were imposed on immigration, on Asians in particular. Trade policy was largely protectionist, as with the 1890 tariff, which we discuss in the free trade-protectionism great debate later in the chapter.

3.2

Victory in the ***Spanish-American War*** left the United States with what the historian Walter LaFeber called a "new empire" (Reading 3.2). American forces, sent in part to "liberate" Cuba, stayed to occupy it over almost three decades. The Philippines was acquired as the first U.S. colony. As noted in Chapter 2, the United States took a number of actions to build further on its efforts to dominate Latin America (Panama Canal, Roosevelt Corollary, Nicaragua and Haiti occupations, interventions in the Mexican Revolution). The "Open Door policy" was a major foray into China, followed by "Dollar Diplomacy" and other efforts.

World War I began in 1914, but the United States did not enter until 1917, when the threat became sufficiently direct to overcome isolationism. American forces made substantial contributions to the Allied victory. President Woodrow Wilson played a lead role in the peace agreements, including creation of the League of Nations.

The ***Russian Revolution*** occurred in 1917, bringing the communists (Bolsheviks) to power and creating the Union of Soviet Socialist Republics (USSR).

| Date | Event | Foreign Policy Significance |
|---|---|---|
| 1882 | Chinese Exclusion Act passed | Severely limits Chinese immigration |
| 1890 | McKinley tariff passed | Protectionism |

| Date | Event | Foreign Policy Significance |
|---|---|---|
| 1898 | Spanish-American War | United States occupies Cuba, maintains occupation until 1922<br>Philippines becomes U.S. colony<br>Other Pacific territories acquired from Spain |
| 1899 | Secretary of State Hay's "Open Door" policy | United States competes with European powers for access and influence in China |
| 1903 | Panama Canal construction begins | President Theodore Roosevelt supports Panamanian independence from Colombia, strikes deal on canal |
| 1904 | Roosevelt Corollary | Reassertion of Monroe Doctrine including claim of right to intervene militarily |
| 1905 | Roosevelt's diplomacy helps end Russo-Japanese War | Roosevelt wins Nobel Peace Prize |
| 1909 | Occupation of Nicaragua | Maintained for most of period until 1933 |
| 1909–12 | President Taft's "Dollar Diplomacy" | Emphasis on economic interests in Latin America and China |
| 1910–17 | Mexican Revolution | U.S. involvement includes occupation of Veracruz, military pursuit of Pancho Villa |
| 1914 | World War I begins; Britain and France vs. Germany and Austria-Hungary | United States declares neutrality |

| Date | Event | Foreign Policy Significance |
|---|---|---|
| 1915 | United States occupies Haiti | Maintains until 1934 |
| 1916 | United States occupies Dominican Republic | Maintains until 1924 |
| 1917 | German hostilities against United States increase, including submarine warfare and pursuing alliance with Mexico | President Wilson proposes and Congress approves declaration of war, joins Britain-France alliance |
| 1917 | Bolshevik (Communist) revolution in Russia | Union of Soviet Socialist Republics (USSR) formed |
| 1918 | United States part of anti-Bolshevik military intervention in Russia | Intervention fails |
| 1918 | World War I ends | |
| 1919 | Paris peace conference, Treaty of Versailles | President Wilson plays lead role, including creation of League of Nations |

## *Isolationist Retreat, 1919–41*

These decades were dominated by a retreat back into isolationism. The U.S. Senate rejected membership in the League of Nations. Fears of communism and Soviet influence were exploited in the Red Scare violations of civil liberties. Efforts were made to guarantee security by passing a treaty, the Kellogg-Briand Pact, simply outlawing war.

The 1929 stock market crash set off the ***Great Depression,*** the nation's worst economic crisis up to that point. One of the more counterproductive reactions was the passage of the Smoot-Hawley Tariff, worsening the Depression at home and furthering its spread globally.

Although the Depression was his main concern on being elected president, Franklin Delano Roosevelt took some early diplomatic initiatives to improve relations with Latin

America and to initiate diplomatic relations with the USSR. His efforts to focus on the rise of Adolf Hitler and Nazism in Germany, though, were constrained by the Neutrality Acts passed by Congress.

World War II began with the German invasion of Poland in September 1939. Even when Hitler attacked Britain and conquered France the next year, isolationism still prevailed in the United States. FDR sought to change this attitude with his Four Freedoms speech and the Atlantic Charter he signed with Prime Minister Winston Churchill of Britain. But it took the Japanese attack on Pearl Harbor for political support finally to be sufficient for the United States to enter World War II.

| Date | Event | Foreign Policy Significance |
|---|---|---|
| **1919** | U.S. Senate rejects Versailles Treaty | League of Nations membership rejected, Wilson's global leadership discredited |
| **1920** | Palmer raids, anticommunist "Red Scare" | National security–civil liberties tension |
| **1921–22** | Washington Conference limiting navies | United States, Great Britain, France, Italy, Japan involved |
| **1928** | Kellogg-Briand Pact outlawing war | France-U.S.–led mix of diplomacy and isolationism |
| **1929** | U.S. stock market crash | Great Depression |
| **1930** | Smoot-Hawley Tariff | Imposes high tariffs and protectionism; exacerbates Great Depression |
| **1933** | Good Neighbor policy set by President Franklin Delano Roosevelt | Major shift toward Latin America, including ending most military occupations |
| **1933** | Diplomatic recognition of USSR | Another FDR initiative |

| Date | Event | Foreign Policy Significance |
|---|---|---|
| 1933 | Adolf Hitler and Nazi party come to power in Germany | Road to World War II |
| 1935 | Congress imposes Neutrality Acts | Tensions rising in Europe, but acts are passed despite FDR objections |
| 1936 | Spanish Civil War | Francsico Franco comes to power; rules as dictator for almost forty years |
| 1938 | Munich Agreement with Hitler signed by Britain and France | Appeasement of Hitler; fails and sets precedent constraining diplomacy |
| 1939 | World War II begins with Hitler's invasion of Poland | United States stays out of the war |
| 1940 | Britain under massive air attacks, "blitz" | United States stays out of the war |
| 1940 | Hitler conquers France | United States stays out of the war |
| 1940 | Lend-Lease and other aid to Britain, USSR | Some assistance to the allies against Hitler |
| 1940 | Congress approves military draft | First peacetime draft in U.S. history |
| 1940 | FDR elected to third term | |
| 1941 | FDR inaugural address; "Four Freedoms" | Addresses global U.S. role based on core values and principles |
| 1941 | FDR and British Prime Minster Winston Churchill issue Atlantic Charter | Solidifies U.S.-British alliance and vision for world order |

| Date | Event | Foreign Policy Significance |
|---|---|---|
| **December 7, 1941** | Japan attacks Pearl Harbor | Congress declares war the next day |
| **December 11, 1941** | Germany declares war on United States | United States now fully enters World War II |

## *World War II, 1941–45*

With isolationism having so constrained the nation's preparation for war and the Pearl Harbor attack having so devastated the naval fleet, America faced enormous challenges. Overcoming them took the collective efforts of government, the military, business, and ordinary people. No wonder many refer to World War II as the "good war." It did, though, have aspects that brought shame, such as the internment of over one hundred thousand Japanese Americans in camps on allegations of questionable loyalty based solely on their ethnicity.

Along with winning the war, initiatives were taken to build the peace that would follow. A new international economic system was designed, seeking to avoid protectionism and other impediments to global prosperity. The United Nations was created as a basis for global security. The Big Three—FDR, Britain's Winston Churchill, and the Soviet leader Josef Stalin—negotiated territorial and other issues in a mix of cooperation and seeds of the tensions that would become the Cold War.

| Date | Event | Foreign Policy Significance |
|---|---|---|
| **1942** | Initial Japanese victories in the Pacific | General Douglas MacArthur forced to flee the Philippines |
| **1942** | Internment in the United States of over one hundred thousand Japanese Americans | National security–civil liberties tension |
| **1942** | Battle of Midway (June) | U.S. victory; starts to turn the tide |

| Date | Event | Foreign Policy Significance |
|---|---|---|
| 1942 | Manhattan Project stepped up | Development of the world's first atomic bomb |
| 1942 | Germany invades USSR (September) | In November, Soviets retake key city of Stalingrad |
| 1942 | U.S. and British troops land in North Africa against German occupation | Victory by May 1943 |
| 1943 | FDR and Churchill meet in Casablanca, Morocco | Wartime summit |
| 1943 | French General Charles de Gaulle forms Free French Forces | French resistance to Nazi occupation intensifies |
| 1943 | Italian dictator Benito Mussolini forced to resign, then executed | Hitler ally ousted |
| 1943 | FDR, Churchill, and the Soviet dictator Josef Stalin meet in Tehran, Iran | Wartime summit and postwar planning |
| 1944 | June 6, D-Day | Allied landing at Normandy pushes German forces back |
| 1944 | Bretton Woods (New Hampshire) conference, forty-four countries | Planning postwar international economic system |
| 1944 | FDR elected to fourth term | First time in U.S. history |
| 1945 | Yalta conference (FDR, Churchill, Stalin) | Postwar planning |
| 1945 | April 12, FDR dies | Vice President Harry Truman becomes president |

| Date | Events | Foreign Policy Significance |
|---|---|---|
| 1945 | May 8, V-E day | Victory in Europe |
| 1945 | Germany divided into four occupation zones | United States, British, French, Soviet |
| 1945 | United Nations created | U.S. leadership role in creating the UN |
| 1945 | August 6–9, United States drops atomic bombs on Japanese cities Hiroshima and Nagasaki | First uses of nuclear weapons |
| 1945 | August 15, V-J day | Japan surrenders |

## Great Debates over Foreign Policy Strategy

### *Isolationism vs. Internationalism*

Should the United States seek to minimize its involvement in world affairs, to isolate itself from the rest of the world? Or should it take an active, internationalist role? Which strategy would best serve the national interest in all of its "4 Ps" components?

Contrary to many traditional histories, the United States never really was fully ***isolationist.*** From the very beginning the founders knew that this new nation needed a foreign policy, needed to find foreign support where it could, needed to be able to trade, and generally needed to have at least some involvement in the world. Their strategy, though, was to stay out of the "Old World" European rivalries, machinations, and wars. This was what President George Washington articulated in his famous 1796 farewell address. "Steer clear of permanent alliances with any portion of the foreign world," he urged the young nation as he left office and handed the reins to President John Adams (see "At the Source," p. 85). Temporary alliances were fine—Washington knew how important the alliance with France had been to winning the Revolutionary War against Britain. French loans had kept the new nation solvent, and French military support was so extensive that at the decisive battle of Yorktown there actually were more French soldiers than Americans fighting against the British. But the best way for the United States to preserve its own peace, according to its first president, was to avoid getting "entangled" in the affairs of Europe. "Europe has a set of primary interests which to us have none or a very remote relation," Washington stated. Those interests lead its nations to "be engaged in frequent controversies, the causes of which are essentially foreign to our concerns." Moreover, "foreign influence is one of the most baneful foes of republican government," Washington cautioned with regard to the impact on the principles of the nascent American democracy. So the United States should take advantage of its "detached and distant situation" across the Atlantic Ocean, which made it physically possible to avoid such entanglements.

As far as foreign trade was concerned, Washington and his successors pursued it to the extent that it contributed to Prosperity, but to develop these commercial relations with as little political connection as possible. In his first inaugural address in 1801, President Thomas Jefferson reaffirmed "entangling alliances with none" while also calling for "peace, commerce and honest friendship with all nations." The goal was to extend commercial relations more than political ones. About 70 percent of the treaties and other international agreements the United States signed in the nineteenth century were on matters related to trade and commerce.[2] Nor did isolationism preclude assertions of U.S. power and interests in its own hemisphere, as through the Monroe Doctrine. What isolationism did mean most essentially was staying out of the various wars Europe fought in the nineteenth century.

Many view the Spanish-American War of 1898 as marking the beginning of the emergence of the United States as a world power. The Americans won the war, defeating a European power, and for the first time gained a far-flung colony of their own: the Philippines. Theodore Roosevelt, as a "Rough Rider" during the Spanish-American War and as president from 1901 to 1908, embodied the new and more muscular spirit of internationalism. Isolationism was no longer in the national interest, as Roosevelt saw it. "The increasing interdependence and complexity of international political and economic relations," he explained, "render it incumbent on all civilized and orderly powers to insist on the proper policing of the world."[3]

President Woodrow Wilson also was inclined to internationalism, although his emphasis was more on Principles than on Power. Yet the old tradition of noninvolvement in Europe's wars was still strong enough that when ***World War I*** broke out in Europe, the Wilson administration tried to stay out. Even the usually sober *New York Times* editorialized as to how the nations of Europe had "reverted to the condition of savage tribes roaming the forests and falling upon each other in a fury of blood and carnage to achieve the ambitious designs of chieftains clad in skins and drunk with mead."[4] It was only after the threat to U.S. interests became undeniably direct that the futility of trying to stay isolated became evident. When the "Zimmermann telegram," a secret German message to Mexico in early 1917 proposing an alliance against the United States, was intercepted, the United States learned that the Germans were offering to help Mexico "reconquer the lost [Mexican] territory in Texas, New Mexico and Arizona." And German

## AT THE SOURCE

AT THE SOURCE

### GEORGE WASHINGTON'S FAREWELL ADDRESS

"History and experience prove that foreign influence is one of the most baneful foes of republican government. . . . Excessive partiality for one foreign nation and excessive dislike of another cause those whom they actuate to see danger only on one side and serve to veil and even second the arts of influence on the other. . . .

The great rule of conduct for us in regard to foreign nations is, in extending our commercial relations to have as little political connection as possible. So far as we have already formed engagements let them be fulfilled with perfect good faith. Here let us stop.

Europe has a set of primary interests which to us have none or a very remote relation. Hence she must be engaged in frequent controversies, the causes of which are essentially foreign to our concerns. Hence, therefore, it must be unwise for us to implicate ourselves by artificial ties in the ordinary vicissitudes of her politics or the ordinary combinations and collisions of her friendships or enmities.

Our detached and distant situation invites and enables us to pursue a different course. . . . Why forego the advantages of so peculiar a situation? . . . Why, by interweaving our destiny with that of any part of Europe, estrange our peace and prosperity in the toils of European ambition, rivalship, interest, humor or caprice?

It is our true policy to steer clear of permanent alliances with any portion of the foreign world, so far, I mean, as we are at liberty to do it. . . .

Taking care always to keep ourselves to suitable establishments on a respectable defensive posture, we may safely trust to temporary alliances for extraordinary emergencies. . . .

There can be no greater error than to expect or calculate upon real favors from nation to nation. It is an illusion which experience must cure, which a just pride ought to discard. . . ."

Source: George Washington, "Farewell Address," September 17, 1796, reprinted in *Congressional Record,* 106th Cong., 1st sess., February 22, 1999, S1673.

U-boats had opened up unrestricted submarine warfare and had sunk three U.S. merchant ships. Isolation no longer was possible; the world's war had come home to the United States.

However, immediately after the war, isolationism reasserted itself over what role the United States should play in building the peace. The League of Nations would create a "community of power" and provide a structure of peace, the internationalist President Wilson argued, with the collective security commitment embodied in Article X of the League Covenant destroying "the war-breeding alliance system and the bad old balance of power."[5] No, his isolationist opponents argued, it was precisely this kind of commitment that would obligate the United States to go to war to defend other League members and that would entangle Americans in other countries' problems. This was a time not "to make the world safe for democracy," as Wilson aspired, but for a "return to normalcy," back to the way things were before the war. The isolationists prevailed as the Senate refused to ratify U.S. membership in the League of Nations.

For the next two decades, Congress refused to budge from a strongly isolationist foreign policy. Interestingly, although their specific reasons for being isolationist differed, both the left and the right political wings feared the reverberations at home if the United States went to war again. As ***World War II*** brewed in Europe, conservatives such as Robert E. Wood, chairman of Sears, Roebuck and head of the America First Committee, argued that entry into the war against Hitler would give President Franklin Roosevelt the opportunity to "turn the New Deal into a permanent socialist dictatorship." At the other end of the political spectrum, socialists such as Norman Thomas feared that war would provide justification for repression that "would bring fascist dictatorship to America."[6] Congress even came very close to passing the ***Ludlow amendment,*** a proposed constitutional amendment that would have required a national referendum before any decision to go to war.

3.2

As our reading from Henry Kissinger's book *Diplomacy* recounts, FDR tried taking his case directly to the American people, as with his 1937 "quarantine of aggressor nations" speech:

> The very foundations of civilization are seriously threatened. . . . If those things come to pass in other parts of the world, let no one imagine that America will escape, that it will continue tranquilly and peacefully to carry on. . . . When an epidemic of physical disease starts to spread, the community approves and joins in a quarantine of the patients in order to protect the health of the community against the spread of the disease. . . . The peace-loving nations must make a concerted effort in opposition to those violations of treaties and those ignorings of humane instincts which today are creating a state of international anarchy and instability from which there is no escape through mere isolation or neutrality.

His appeal, however, fell flat. The public still did not see the connection between what was happening "over there" and American interests and security. A public-opinion poll taken the week *after* Hitler invaded Poland in September 1939 showed 94 percent of Americans opposed to declaring war.

In 1940, with FDR running for reelection to an unprecedented third term, even the fall of France to Hitler's armies was not enough to break through the isolationism of

American politics. With Britain also about to fall, and Prime Minister Winston Churchill urging the United States to provide support, FDR resorted to an "end run" around Congress to provide some support through the famous "destroyers-for-bases" deal.*[7]

FDR pushed again following his reelection. "This assault has blotted out the whole pattern of democratic life in an appalling number of independent nations, great and small," he told Congress and the American people in his January 1941 "Four Freedoms" speech, referring to Hitler's conquests in Europe. "And the assailants are still on the march, threatening other nations, great and small. Therefore, as your President, performing my constitutional duties to 'give to the Congress information on the state of the union,' I find it unhappily necessary to report that *the future of our country and our democracy are overwhelmingly involved in events far beyond our borders* [emphasis added]."[8] Still, it wasn't until December 7, 1941, when the Japanese launched a surprise attack on Pearl Harbor, that the politics changed and the United States joined the effort to restore world peace. The full national mobilization that ultimately occurred during World War II stands as a monumental example of what the United States is capable of achieving.

Even then, however, FDR worried during the closing months of the war that "anybody who thinks isolationism is dead in this country is crazy. As soon as this war is over, it may well be stronger than ever."[9] Indeed, once victory was achieved there was a rapid demobilization, another yearning to "bring the boys home" and get back to normal—only to be confronted by the threats of the Cold War.

## *Power, Peace: How Big a Military, How Much for Defense?*

For the United States to maximize its Power and to pursue Peace, how big a military is required? How much needs to be spent on defense? These issues have been hotly contested throughout American history.

This is evident even in the Constitution. On the one hand the Constitution provides for the creation of an army and a navy. On the other, it dedicates both the Second Amendment, the right of states to have their own militias, and the Third Amendment, the prohibition on "quartering" of troops in private homes without the owner's permission, to checks on the national military. Nor was much done initially with the constitutional provisions authorizing a standing army and navy. Building more than a few naval frigates was

*Under this agreement, the U.S. Navy provided the British navy with fifty destroyer warships in exchange for the rights to British military bases in the Western Hemisphere. The "end run" came from the deal's being made as an executive agreement not requiring any congressional approval.

too expensive for the young country. And when in 1790 President Washington proposed a permanent peacetime draft, Congress rejected it.

But the risks of a weak military were quickly made evident. By 1798 the United States was on the verge of war with its former ally and patron, France. President John Adams got Congress to authorize increases in the army and the navy, and George Washington came out of retirement to take command. War was avoided through a combination of successful diplomacy and displays of naval strength. Still, the British navy used its superiority over the next decade to harass American merchant ships with continual blockades and impressment (seizing) of sailors. Tensions escalated in the 1807 *Chesapeake* affair to an attack on an American naval ship. Secretary of the Treasury Albert Gallatin expressed the sense of vulnerability in these years, warning that the British "could land at Annapolis, march to the city [Washington, D.C.], and re-embark before the militia could be collected to repel [them]."[10] Gallatin's warning proved all too prophetic when, during the War of 1812, the British did march on Washington and burned down much of the capital city, the White House included. To fight the War of 1812, the U.S. Army had to be more than tripled in size from its standing level of about twelve thousand troops (see Table 3.1). Once the war was over, the army was rapidly demobilized.

The same pattern of low troop levels, massive mobilization, and rapid demobilization was played out even more dramatically during the Civil War. When the war broke out, the Union Army had only about sixteen thousand troops. President Abraham Lincoln mobilized the state militias and took unilateral action without prior budget approval from Congress to rapidly enlarge both the army and the navy. He also instituted the first military draft in U.S. history. Through these and other measures the Union forces grew to almost one million. Then, in the decade following the end of the Civil War in 1865, the Army went back down to twenty-five thousand troops.

**TABLE 3.1 Wartime Mobilization, Peacetime Demobilization**

| | Prewar troop levels | Wartime mobilization | Postwar demobilization |
|---|---|---|---|
| War of 1812 | 12,000 | 36,000 | n/a |
| Civil War, 1861–65 | 16,000 | 1,000,000 | 25,000 |
| World War I, 1917–18 | 130,000 | 2,000,000 | 265,000 |
| World War II, 1941–45 | 175,000 | 8,500,000 | 550,000 |

Note: Figures are for the army only and are approximate.

In the late nineteenth century, the main debate was over building up a larger and more modern navy. There was general consensus that the army could be kept small; another direct attack on the United States by Britain or another European power now seemed highly unlikely. The real competition with the Europeans was on the high seas. The greatness of a nation, argued the navy captain Alfred Thayer Mahan in his seminal book *The Influence of Sea Power upon History* (1890), depends on a strong navy capable not just of its own coastal defense but of command of the seas. Congress was sufficiently persuaded by Mahan and others to fund enough naval construction to make the U.S. Navy the seventh largest in the world by 1893. Yet there also were critics. Some objected to Mahan's naval buildup as draining resources from domestic priorities. Others warned that the new sense of power would make the pull toward the pursuit of empire irresistible.

When World War I came, because of the new navy buildup, the United States was better prepared on the seas than on land. The United States entered the war with only 130,000 soldiers in its Army. One of the first actions Congress took was passage of the Selective Service Act of 1917, reviving the military draft. At its World War I peak the army reached over two million soldiers.

Yet President Wilson also realized that "it is not [just] an army that we must shape and train for war, it is a nation"—including its economy. Indeed, during World War I Wilson requested and Congress approved powers over the economy that, in the view of the noted historians Samuel Eliot Morison and Henry Steele Commager, were "more extensive than those possessed by any other ruler in the Western world."[11] The president was empowered to seize and operate factories, to operate all systems of transportation and communication, to allocate food and fuel, to set industrial production schedules, and to fix prices. To exercise these vast and unprecedented economic regulatory powers, Wilson set up a host of new executive-branch agencies. The War Shipping Board was charged with keeping merchant shipping going and with building two ships for each one sunk by German U-boats. The Food Board supervised both food production and consumption, setting rules for "Wheatless Mondays" and "Meatless Tuesdays" to ensure enough food surplus to help feed the Allies. The War Industries Board regulated virtually every production and investment decision made by private companies, from the number of automobiles rolling off Henry Ford's assembly lines, to the number of colors on typewriter ribbons (reduced from 150 to 5 to free up carbon and other chemicals for the war effort), to cutting down the length of the upper parts of shoes (to save leather for uniforms and supplies). Wilson was even able to impose new taxes on consumption and to increase existing income, inheritance, and corporate taxes, all with relatively little political opposition.

Yet once the war ended, this vast governmental economic bureaucracy was disbanded, as was the military. The army came down to 265,000 troops by 1920. As part of the naval arms-control treaties signed at the 1921–22 Washington Naval Conference with the four other major naval powers (Britain, France, Italy, and Japan), the U.S. Navy scrapped, sank, or decommissioned about 2 million tons of ships, including thirty-one major warships.

The mobilization-demobilization pattern recurred with World War II. The army started at about 175,000 troops and grew to almost 8,500,000 by 1945. The navy amassed another 3,400,000 sailors in a fleet of 2,500 warships. President Roosevelt's wartime powers over the economy were even more extensive than his New Deal ones. He created the War Production Board (WPB), which mobilized and allocated industrial facilities and plants; the War Manpower Commission, which had sweeping authority to mobilize labor to meet the WPB's production goals; and the Office of Price Administration, which set prices and rationed goods even for such staples as meat, sugar, tires, and gasoline. The fiats these and other agencies could issue went so far as prohibiting the pleasure driving of automobiles, cutting the production of consumer durable goods by almost 30 percent, imposing wage and price controls, passing major tax increases, and taking other measures deemed necessary for "forging a war economy."[12]

The overall scope of the economic effort involved in World War II dwarfed that of any previous period in American history. The number of civilian employees of the federal government climbed from 1 million to 3.8 million. Annual budget expenditures soared from $9 billion to $98.4 billion. All told, the federal government spent nearly twice as much between 1940 and 1945 as it had in the preceding 150 years. The Manhattan Project, the program that developed the atomic bomb, itself involved expenditures of more than $2 billion, the employment of more than 150,000 people, and the building of new cities in Los Alamos, New Mexico; Oak Ridge, Tennessee; and Hanford, Washington—all with the utmost secrecy, so much so that little was known even by Vice President Harry Truman, let alone Congress.

Once Hitler was defeated and Japan had surrendered, however, the calculation of how big a military and how much for defense was made anew. By 1948 most of the wartime economic agencies had been dismantled. The army was down to 550,000 troops. The navy also was being scaled back. But then the Cold War raised yet again the how big, how much questions for ensuring the peace and maintaining U.S. power.

## *Principles: True to American Democratic Ideals?*

Theories of ***American exceptionalism,*** which hold that the United States has a uniqueness and special virtue that ground our foreign policy in Principles much more than the policies of other countries, can be traced back throughout American history (see "Theory in the World," p. 92).[13] The question, though, is whether American foreign policy has been as true to these values historically as it has claimed.

American exceptionalism was evoked early on in a poem by David Humphreys, a protégé of George Washington:

> All former empires rose, the work of guilt,
> On conquest, blood or usurpation built;
> But we, taught wisdom by their woes and crimes,
> Fraught with their lore, and born to better times;
> Our constitutions form'd on freedom's base,
> Which all the blessings of all lands embrace;
> Embrace humanity's extended cause,
> A world of our empire, for a world of our laws . . .[14]

Yes, America was to be an empire, but it would not be built like the Old World ones on "guilt, . . . conquest, blood or usurpation." It instead would serve "humanity's extended cause."

The same themes were developed further in the mid-nineteenth century in the concept of ***manifest destiny.*** As the term was originally coined in 1845, it referred to the "right" claimed for the United States "to overspread and to possess the whole continent which Providence has given us for the development of the great experiment of liberty and federated self government."[15] The immediate reference was to continental expansion and specific territorial disputes, including the immediate one with Mexico that resulted in the 1846–48 war and the annexation of Texas.

Again, though, manifest destiny was said not to be just typical self-interested expansionism, but rather based on principles and thus also in the interest of those over whom the United States was expanding, such as Native Americans and Mexicans. Toward the end of the nineteenth century, when the United States pretty much had finished its continental territorial expansion, manifest destiny was invoked in a similar spirit as part of the justification for the Spanish-American War and the acquisition of colonies and quasi colonies in the Pacific and the Caribbean.

For Woodrow Wilson, the main reason for fighting World War I was "to make the world safe for democracy." His message to Congress requesting a declaration of war was heavily laden with appeals to Principles (see "At the Source," p. 94). "Our motive will not be revenge or the victorious assertion of the physical might of the nation," Wilson proclaimed, "but only the vindication of right." And so too was the postwar order to be built on democratic principles and ideals.[16] Many of Wilson's Fourteen Points dealt with self-determination for various central and eastern European peoples and nations that had been subjugated in the Austro-Hungarian and Ottoman (Turkish) empires. Despite some compromises with Britain and France, which had little interest in dismantling their own empires, a "mandate" system was established under the League of Nations that was supposed

## THEORY IN THE WORLD

THEORY IN THE WORLD

### THEORIES OF AMERICAN EXCEPTIONALISM

We can trace the image of the United States as a ***city on the hill,*** often invoked by American leaders, back to the colonial days. It was John Winthrop, governor of the Massachusetts Bay Colony, who declared in 1630 that "wee shall be as a Citty upon a Hill, the eies of all people are upon us."* This image and related others evincing the theory that the United States was to play a highly principled role in the world that would be both good for us and good for others have had a long and influential history in American foreign policy.

Three important points about this link between theory and policy: First, the evidence of the theory-policy link is strong. American exceptionalism theory has had significant impact on American foreign policy over many years and under many presidents. We provide some historical examples in this chapter, and we will see the dynamic also in the Cold War (Chapters 4 and 5) as well as throughout Part II.

Second, the nature of the impact has varied, leading to a wide range of policies. Along the internationalism-isolationism dimension discussed earlier in this chapter, the exceptionalist self-image at times has fostered moralistic interventionism and at other times has fed retreat from those deemed less worthy. "American exceptionalism not only celebrates the uniqueness and special virtues of the United States, but also elevates America to a higher moral plane than other countries. . . . [E]xceptionalism can stimulate both crusading interventionism and complacent withdrawal from world affairs . . . the attendant American determination to spread American ideals around the world . . . [and] an excuse to remain smug and content in an isolationist cocoon, well protected from 'corrupt' or 'inferior' foreigners."†

Third is the normative analysis of whether actual policies have been consistent with the claims to virtue. We take this up in the discussion of consistency, contradictions, and cover stories.

*Cited in Loren Baritz, *City on a Hill: A History of Ideas and Myths in America* (New York: Wiley, 1964), 3.
†Tami R. Davis and Sean M. Lynn-Jones, "'Citty Upon a Hill,'" *Foreign Policy* (Spring 1987): 20–21.

to begin the process of decolonization in Africa, the Middle East, and Asia. Whatever the resistance of European leaders, as Strobe Talbott recounts, the European people hailed Wilson "as the most powerful and honored man on the earth."

> Placards . . . at every stop along Wilson's way through France, Britain and Italy proclaimed him "the Champion of the Rights of Man," "the Founder of the Society of Nations," "the God of Peace," "the Savior of Humanity," and "the Moses from Across the Atlantic." Crowds cheered and threw flowers as he passed. Streets and squares were renamed after him.[17]

As for World War II, the case for the values at stake in the war against Hitler and Nazism was about as incontrovertible as is possible. Underlying the political and strategic issues were what FDR called the ***Four Freedoms:*** freedom of religion, freedom of speech, freedom from fear, and freedom from want. The ***Atlantic Charter,*** a joint statement by FDR and Churchill even before the United States entered the war (August 1941), pledged to "respect the right of all peoples to choose the form of government under which they will live; and . . . to see sovereign rights and self-government restored to those who have been forcibly deprived of them."[18] The latter was a reference to those countries in Europe overrun by Hitler's Germany. The former was ostensibly about the colonial world and was something from which Churchill soon backed off. Although FDR was sincere at the time, with the onset of the Cold War the United States also did not fully or speedily follow through.

The basis for debate over how true to its Principles the United States historically has been is threefold: questions of consistency, of contradictions, and of cover stories. The question of consistency allows for acknowledgment that there has been some practicing of what is preached, but less than has been claimed. We saw this in the Mexican War, in which the U.S. claim to be liberating Texas was seen quite differently by Mexico. The condemnation by a Mexican leader of "the degenerate sons of Washington" for their "dissimulation, fraud, and the basest treachery" is a nineteenth-century echo of the "why do they hate us" question asked in the twenty-first-century in the wake of the September 11, 2001, terrorist attacks (see "International Perspectives," p. 96). Through much of the nineteenth and early twentieth centuries, the United States was more opposed to than supportive of social and political revolutions against undemocratic governments in Latin America. We will see this, for example, in the discussion later in this chapter of U.S. relations with Latin America. We can also see it in the case of the Philippines, where after gaining colonial control, 125,000 American troops fought to put down the pro-independence Filipino forces in what has been called "one of the ugliest wars in American history," in battles that took a death toll of more than five thousand Americans and two hundred thousand Filipinos.[19] The "Manifesto Protesting the United States' Claim of Sovereignty over the Philippines," issued in 1899 by Emilio Aguinaldo, leader of the Filipino independence movement, challenges the stated intentions of the United States in getting involved in the Philippine war in the first place.

## AT THE SOURCE

AT THE SOURCE

### MAKING THE WORLD SAFE FOR DEMOCRACY

"It is a war against all nations. . . . The challenge is to all mankind. Each nation must decide for itself how it will meet it. . . . We must put excited feeling away. Our motive will not be revenge or the physical might of the nation, but only the vindication of right, of human right, of which we are only a single champion. . . .

With a profound sense of the solemn and even tragical character of the step I am taking and of the grave responsibilities which it involves, but in unhesitating obedience to what I deem my constitutional duty, I advise the Congress to declare the recent course of the Imperial German Government to be in fact nothing less than war against the government and people of the United States. . . .

We are accepting this challenge of hostile purpose because we know that in such a government, following such methods, we can never have a friend; and that in the presence of its organized power, always lying in wait to accomplish we know not what purpose, there can be no assured security for the democratic governments of the world. . . . *The world must be made safe for democracy* [emphasis added]. . . .

It is a distressing and oppressive duty, Gentlemen of the Congress, which I have performed in thus addressing you. There are, it may be, many months of fiery trial and sacrifice ahead of us. . . . But the right is more precious than the peace, and we shall fight for the things we have always carried nearest our hearts—for democracy, for the rights and liberties of small nations, for a universal dominion of right by such a concert of free peoples as shall bring peace and safety to all nations and make the world itself at last free. To such a task we can dedicate our lives and our fortunes, everything that we are and everything that we have, with the pride of those who know that the day has come when America is privileged to spend her blood and her might for the principles that gave her birth and happiness and the peace which she has treasured. God helping her, she can do no other."

Source: Woodrow Wilson, "Address to Joint Session of Congress," April 2, 1917, reprinted in *Papers of Woodrow Wilson*, Arthur S. Link, ed. (Princeton: Princeton University Press, 1966), 41: 519–27.

Elements of racism found in a number of aspects of U.S. foreign policy also stand in contradiction to the ideals Americans espoused. This racism goes back to the African slave trade and the foreign policy importance given to protecting those trade routes. It also goes to the core of manifest destiny. "White Americans had not inherited the fabled empty continent," historian Michael Hunt writes with reference to what happened to Native Americans. "Rather, by their presence and policies, they had emptied it."[20] Similarly, the Mexican War was "fought with clear racial overtones."[21] These racial attitudes were captured by the poet James Russell Lowell: "Mexicans wor'nt human beans," just "the sort o'folks a chap could kill an' never dream on't after."[22] In another example, even if one were to concede a degree of benevolence in the paternalism, a sense of racial superiority was undeniable in President William McKinley's justification for making the Philippines a U.S. colony because "we could not leave [the Filipinos] to themselves—they were unfit for self-government, and they would soon have anarchy over there worse than Spain's was . . . [so] there was nothing left for us to do but take them all, and to educate the Filipinos and uplift and civilize them as our fellow-men."[23]

In addition, there have been times when principles have been less a genuine driving force than something of a cover story for other objectives. This was the case, for example, with Panama and the Panama Canal in the early years of the twentieth century. Until then, Panama had been a rebellious province of Colombia. And until then, U.S. efforts to acquire the rights to build a canal across the Panamanian isthmus had been stymied by the unwillingness of the Colombian government to agree to the terms the United States demanded. So although President Theodore Roosevelt could cite the historical basis for Panama's claim to independence, the landing of U.S. troops to support the revolt had far more to do with the willingness of the Panamanian leaders to make a deal for a canal. Less than a month after Panama had declared its independence, Teddy Roosevelt had a treaty with terms even more favorable to the United States than the one the Colombian legislature had rejected the year before.

## *Prosperity: U.S. Imperialism?*

Those who see U.S. foreign policy as historically imperialistic focus particularly on the late nineteenth and early twentieth centuries, a key period in what Walter LaFeber calls the "new empire" (see Reading 3.2). An 1898 editorial in the *Washington Post* evoked—indeed, lauded—the temper of the times: 3.2

> A new consciousness seems to have come upon us—the consciousness of strength—and with it a new appetite, the yearning to show our strength. . . . Ambition, interest, land hunger, pride, the mere joy of fighting, whatever it may be, we are animated by a new sensation. . . . The taste of Empire is in the mouth of the people. . . . It means an Imperial policy, the Republic, renascent, taking her place with the armed nations.[24]

One gets a different view, however, from Mark Twain's parody of the "Battle Hymn of the Republic":

> Mine eyes have seen the orgy of the launching of the sword;
> He is searching out the hoardings where the strangers' wealth is stored;
> He has loosed his fateful lightning, and with woe and death has scored;
> His lust is marching on.[25]

## INTERNATIONAL PERSPECTIVES

INTERNATIONAL PERSPECTIVES

### NINETEENTH-CENTURY CRITICS

#### Mexican War, 1846–48

"The annexation of the department of Texas to the United States, projected and consummated by the tortuous policy of the cabinet of the Union, does not yet satisfy the ambitious desires of the degenerate sons of Washington. The civilized world already has recognized in that act all the marks of injustice, iniquity, and the most scandalous violation of the rights of nations. Indelible is the stain which will forever darken the character for virtue falsely attributed to the people of the United States. . . . To the United States it has been reserved to put into practice dissimulation, fraud and the basest treachery, in order to obtain possession, in the midst of peace, of the territory of a friendly nation, which generously relied upon the faith of promises and the solemnity of treaties."

—Mexican general Francisco Mejia

#### Spanish-American War, 1898, and Philippine War, 1899–1902

"It is distinctly stated that the naval and field forces of the United States had come to give us our liberty, by subverting the bad Spanish Government. And I hereby protest against this unexpected act of the United States claiming sovereignty over these Islands. My relations with the United States did not bring me over here from Hong Kong to make war on the Spaniards for their benefit, but for the purpose of our own liberty and independence."

—Emilio Aguinaldo

Sources: Available at www.dmwv.org/mexwar/documents/mejia.htm; www.msc.edu.ph/centennial/ag 990105.html (accessed 6/6/09).

Consistent with theories of imperialism as examined in Chapter 1, the growing U.S. interest in foreign markets was in part a consequence of the severe economic crises of this period (there were depressions in 1873–78 and 1893–97), which set off the problems of underconsumption and overproduction. "We have advanced in manufactures, as in agriculture," Secretary of State William M. Evans stated in 1880, "until we are being forced outward by the irresistible pressure of our internal development." The United States needed new markets or, as an economist of the day warned, "we are certain to be smothered in our own grease."[26]

Those new markets were sought out principally in Latin America. U.S. exports to Latin America increased more than 150 percent between 1900 and 1914. Investments in plantations, mining, manufacturing, banking, and other industries shot up at an even faster pace. And the flag seemed to be following the dollar. As shown by the map on page 98, during this era the United States launched numerous military interventions in Latin America. In many instances these actions clearly were taken in defense of the foreign investments and other economic interests of American corporations and financiers. By 1913, for example, the United Fruit Company (UFCO) owned more than 130,000 acres of plantations (bananas and other fruits) in Central America—and it was in significant part to defend the economic interests of UFCO that the U.S. Marines went into Nicaragua (1909–10, 1912–25) and Honduras (1924–25). So too with other American corporations and the military interventions in Haiti (1915–34) and the Dominican Republic (1916–24).

In Cuba, "liberated" from Spain in the Spanish-American War only to be put under U.S. domination, the pattern was even more pronounced. Though formally allowing Cuba independence, the United States insisted that the ***Platt amendment*** be attached to the Cuban constitution, granting the United States the right to intervene to, among other things, protect the property of U.S. corporations.* And so the marines did on a number of occasions. The Platt amendment also gave the United States the power to veto treaties between Cuba and other governments as another way of giving U.S. interests special status. These measures made conditions as conducive as possible for American business: U.S. investments in Cuba increased from $50 million in 1896 to $220 million in 1913, and Cuban exports to the United States grew from $31 million in 1900 to $722 million in 1920.[27]

The other side of the debate, questioning the imperialist analysis, makes two principal arguments. One is based on counterexamples that are said to show that U.S. foreign policy has not consistently been geared to the defense of American capitalist interests. One such example is from early in the ***Mexican Revolution,*** when Woodrow Wilson refused to recognize the military government of General Victoriano Huerta despite pressures from U.S. corporations with some $1.5 billion in Mexican investments. "I . . . am not the servant of those who wish to enhance the value of their Mexican investments," Wilson declared.[28]

The other argument is based on alternative explanations. This argument doesn't deny that American foreign policy has had its expansionist dimension but attributes it less to Prosperity than to other factors, such as Power and Principles. For example, a Power-based alternative explanation of the U.S. military interventions in Latin America acknowledges that capitalist interests were well served, but emphasizes political and military

---

*This amendment was named for its principal congressional sponsor, Senator Orville Platt. This was not, however, a case of Congress's imposing something the executive branch didn't want. Secretary of War Elihu Root worked closely with Senator Platt in writing the amendment. Thomas G. Paterson, J. Gary Clifford, and Kenneth J. Hagan, *American Foreign Relations: A History to 1920,* Vol. 1 (Lexington, Mass.: Heath, 1995), 254–55.

**U.S. Military Interventions in Latin America, Early Twentieth Century**

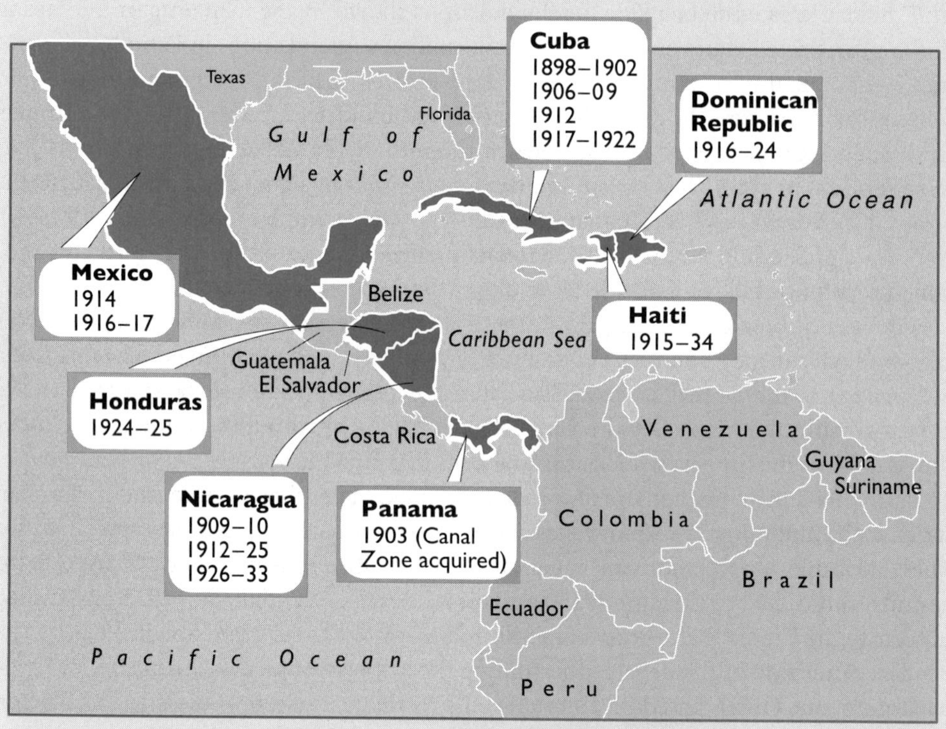


Source: Adapted from Thomas G. Paterson, J. Gary Clifford, and Kenneth J. Hagan, *American Foreign Relations: A History since 1895,* 4th ed. (Lexington, Mass.: Heath, 1995), 2: 55.

factors as the driving forces. Similarly, although the Panama Canal had unquestionable economic value, some would argue that what really motivated Teddy Roosevelt was linking up the Atlantic and Pacific fleets of the U.S. Navy and the confirmation of U.S. status as an emerging global power.

## *Key Case: U.S. Relations with Latin America—Good Neighbor or Regional Hegemon?*

U.S. relations with Latin America, which we have discussed above, warrant special focus as a historical case providing numerous examples of the competing tensions among the "4 Ps." As the richest and most powerful country in the Western Hemisphere, was the

United States to be the regional hegemon—the dominant country lording over its sphere of influence—exerting its Power largely as it saw fit, managing hemispheric Peace but on its own terms, and dominating economically for the sake of its own Prosperity? Or was the United States to be the good neighbor, true to its Principles, a benefactor to those in its hemispheric neighborhood who had less and were less powerful, promoting democracy and acting respectfully of their equal rights and privileges as sovereign nations?

For the most part the United States has played the role of regional hegemon. This role goes back to the Monroe Doctrine's warning to the European powers not to seek to recolonize or in other ways to "extend their system to any position of this hemisphere" (see "At the Source," p. 100). Initially, some Latin American countries saw this very positively as a U.S. pledge to help them maintain their independence, and even proposed "that the Doctrine be transformed into a binding inter-American alliance." But "[Secretary of State John Quincy] Adams said no. He emphasized that the Doctrine was a unilateral American statement and that any action taken under it would be for the United States alone to decide."[29] There was little altruism in this policy, or even straightforward good neighborliness; it was much more the self-interest of a regional power seeking to preserve its dominant position against outside challenges.

For the rest of the nineteenth century there were quite a few outside challenges from the European powers. Britain and the United States contested in the 1840s and 1850s for rights to build a transisthmian canal across Central America. In a particularly bold episode, amid the American Civil War, France sought to install its own hand-picked nobleman, Archduke Ferdinand Maximilian, as Napoleon III, emperor of Mexico. The Spanish-American War was in significant part about getting Spain not only out of Cuba but totally out of the hemisphere. Yet the U.S. support for Cuba's effort to end Spain's colonial rule was one thing, support for genuine Cuban independence quite another. U.S. troops stayed in Cuba for four years after the war (1898–1902) and then, as noted earlier, reintervened repeatedly in 1906–9, 1912, and 1917–22. And then there was the Platt amendment—what clearer manifestation of hegemony could there be than writing oneself into another country's constitution?

In 1904 President Theodore Roosevelt pronounced his corollary to the Monroe Doctrine (see "At the Source," p. 100). The ***Roosevelt Corollary*** claimed for the United States the "international police power" to intervene when instability within a Latin American country risked creating the pretext (e.g., to collect debts or protect property) for an Old World power to intervene. This policy became the basis for a host of interventions and extended military occupations in Cuba, the Dominican Republic, Haiti, Mexico, and Nicaragua. U.S. troops stayed in Haiti for almost twenty years, and in Cuba and Nicaragua on and off for twenty-five.

President Franklin Roosevelt sought to pursue a much different approach to Latin America than had his cousin Theodore and most of his other predecessors. A few years before becoming president, FDR had written an article in *Foreign Affairs* quite critical of

## AT THE SOURCE

AT THE SOURCE

### THE MONROE DOCTRINE (1823) AND THE ROOSEVELT COROLLARY (1904)

#### Monroe Doctrine

"The American continents, by the free and independent condition which they have assumed and maintained, are henceforth not to be considered as subjects for future colonization by any European powers. . . .

In the wars of the European powers in matters relating to themselves, we have never taken any part, not does it comport with our policy so to do. It is only when our rights are invaded or seriously menaced that we resent injuries or make preparations for our defense. With the movements in this hemisphere, we are of necessity more immediately connected, and by causes which must be obvious to all enlightened and impartial observers. . . .

We should consider any attempt on [the Europeans'] part to extend their system to any portion of this hemisphere as dangerous to our peace and safety. With the existing colonies or dependencies of any European power, we have not interfered and shall not interfere. But with the Governments who have declared their independence and maintained it, and whose independence we have, on great consideration and on just principles acknowledged, we could not view any interposition for the purpose of oppressing them, or controlling in any other manner their destiny, by any European power in any other light than as the manifestations of an unfriendly disposition toward the United States."

#### Roosevelt Corollary

"It is not true that the United States feels any land hunger or entertains any projects as regards the other nations of the Western Hemisphere save such as are for their welfare. All that this country desires is to see the neighboring countries stable, orderly and prosperous. Any country whose people conduct themselves well can count upon our hearty friendship. If a nation shows that it knows how to act with reasonable sufficiency and decency in social and political matters, if it keeps order and pays its obligations, it need fear no interference from the United States. Chronic wrongdoing, or an impotence which results in the general loosening of the ties of civilized society, may in America, as elsewhere, ultimately require intervention by some civilized nation, and in the Western Hemisphere the adherence of the United States to the Monroe Doctrine may force the United States, however reluctantly, in flagrant cases of such wrongdoing or impotence, to the exercise of an international police power. . . .

It is a mere truism to say that every nation, whether in America or anywhere else, which desires to maintain its freedom, its independence, must ultimately realize that the right of such independence can not be separated from the responsibility of making good use of it. . . .”

Sources: James Monroe, “Seventh Annual Message,” December 2, 1823, *The Writings of James Monroe* Stanislaus Murray Hamilton, ed. (New York: Putnam, 1912), 6:325–42; Theodore Roosevelt, “Fourth Annual Message,” December 16, 1904, *A Compilation of the Messages and Papers of the Presidents* (New York: Bureau of National Literature, 1923), 14: 6894–930.

U.S. interventionism in Latin America. “Never before in our history,” he wrote, “have we had fewer friends in the Western Hemisphere than we have today. . . . The time has come when we must accept not only certain facts but many new principles of a higher law, a newer and better standard in international relations. . . . [N]either from the argument of financial gain, nor from the sound reasoning of the Golden Rule, can our policy, or lack of policy, be approved.”[30] We want to be the “good neighbor,” FDR proclaimed once elected, “the neighbor who resolutely respects himself and because he does so, respects the rights of others—the neighbor who respects the sanctity of his agreements in and with a world of neighbors.”[31] To demonstrate this new approach, FDR repealed the Platt amendment, withdrew the marines from Nicaragua and Haiti, settled a long-standing oil dispute with Mexico, signed bilateral trade treaties as well as treaties of nonaggression and conciliation with a number of Latin American countries, and became the first U.S. president to visit South America. As World War II approached, FDR also struck a number of mutual security deals, including affirming a Monroe Doctrine–like commitment at the 1938 Pan-American Conference to resist any foreign intervention in the hemisphere.

Regional hegemon or good neighbor? Not only did the historical record feed this debate, but as we will see in the next chapter, the onset of the Cold War made it even more controversial.

## *Key Case: The United States as a Pacific Power*

Trade and commerce (Prosperity) first took the United States across the Pacific to Asia. In the 1840s American ships were sailing to China with cotton and returning with tea. The Treaty of Wangxia, the first trade treaty with China, was signed in 1844. Close to a decade later (1853) Commodore Matthew C. Perry sailed into Tokyo Harbor and "opened up" Japan. "Our steamships can go from California to Japan in eighteen days," President Millard Fillmore stated in the letter delivered to the Japanese rulers by Commodore Perry. "I am delighted that our two countries should trade with each other, for the benefit both of Japan and the United States."[32]

But it was never really just trade and commerce (Prosperity) that the United States was after. America's sense of moral mission (Principles) also was at work. Interestingly, it cut both ways. On the one hand was the U.S. desire to liberalize and democratize these societies. "The thirty millions of Japan," wrote one author at the time of Commodore Perry's expedition, "await the key of the western Democrat to open their prison to the sun-light of social interchange."[33] On the other hand were fear and animosity toward the Orient and its culture, the view that "there were in conflict two great types of civilization, . . . Eastern and Western, inferior and superior."[34]

The Power motive was also at work. The historian Thomas Paterson and his colleagues describe it thus: "Perry saw his Japanese expedition as but one step toward a U.S. empire in the Pacific. . . . Eventually, the commodore prophesied, the American people would 'extend their dominion and their power, until they shall have brought within their mighty embrace the Islands of the great Pacific, and place the Saxon race upon the eastern shores of Asia.'"[35] Asia was yet another region for competition with the Europeans, who had the advantage of colonies and experience but who lacked the U.S. geographic advantage of being a Pacific as well as an Atlantic country. The United States acquired Hawaii, Samoa, and other Pacific island territories in an effort to develop that advantage further, as later it acquired the Philippines. The United States also began maintaining a military presence in the region, thanks to Captain Mahan's "new Navy." The "***Open Door policy***" of the 1890s, contrary to self-justifying claims of being intended to help China against the encroachments of European colonialism, actually was a self-interested demand made on the major European powers that the United States not be closed out of spheres of trade and influence in China.

At the same time that the United States was extending its influence in Asia and the Pacific, so too was Japan. As but one example of the emerging rivalry, Japan initially refused to recognize the U.S. annexation of Hawaii, asserting its own claim based on the larger number of immigrants to Hawaii from Japan than from any other country. The antagonisms subsided somewhat when, in 1904 at the invitation of the Japanese government, President Theodore Roosevelt successfully mediated an end to the Russo-Japanese War.* Yet when the Japanese didn't get everything they wanted and for reasons of domestic politics and national honor blamed Roosevelt, the first anti-American demonstrations in

*For his efforts Roosevelt was awarded the 1905 Nobel Peace Prize; he was the first American president to win that esteemed recognition.

Japanese history broke out. Relations improved sufficiently by 1908 for the Root-Takahira Agreement to be signed, mutually recognizing the status quo in the Asia-Pacific region.

By World War I suspicions and tensions over commercial competition and naval rivalry again were running high. The wartime alliance against Germany superseded these tensions for a while, and the Washington Naval Conference of 1921–22 worked out naval arms-control agreements (also involving the European powers). But political forces at home were making Japan increasingly militaristic and expansionist. In 1931 it took the bold and provocative step of invading Manchuria, against which neither the United States nor the League of Nations responded effectively. U.S.-Japanese tensions mounted over the rest of the 1930s, culminating on December 7, 1941, in the attack on Pearl Harbor.

U.S. relations with China went through even more extreme fluctuations as China began what would become more than a half-century of revolution. The Chinese revolution in its various stages would be antiforeigner, prodemocracy, anti–indigenous warlords, anti–Japanese occupation, and Marxist. The United States had to grapple with how best to defend American interests and stand up for American ideals as its relationship with China shifted from friendship and even emulation to antipathy. In 1921 the Nationalist pro-republic revolutionary leader Sun Yat-sen appealed for assistance to the United States as "the champion of liberalism and righteousness, whose disinterested friendship and support of China in her hour of distress has been demonstrated to us more than once." Three years later, though, Sun expressed his disappointment not only in how little support had come, but in the United States's having joined with other foreign powers in yet another intervention in China over an economic dispute. "We might well have expected that an American Lafayette would fight on our side in this good cause. In the twelfth year of our struggle towards liberty there comes not a Lafayette but an American Admiral with more ships of war than any other nation in our waters."[36] The Nationalists soon thereafter struck their alliance with the communists of Mao Zedong. This alliance was short-lived and gave way to renewed civil war. But although the United States resumed its friendship with the Nationalists in 1928, the 1931 invasion of Manchuria by Japan made the limits of this support abundantly clear.

Thus by the time World War II broke out, American interests in Asia and the Pacific had been developing for close to a century.

## Great Debates in Foreign Policy Politics

### *Going to War*

Americans have a tendency to think that only since the trauma of the Vietnam War has the nation undergone political controversy and uncertainty regarding whether to go to war. Yet as we discussed in Chapter 2, no domain better fits the "invitation to struggle" characterization of the foreign policy provisions of the Constitution than war powers. A closer look at the historical record shows that decisions on going to war rarely have come easily or readily; time and again they have been the subject of intense political debate, in early versions of the contentious Pennsylvania Avenue diplomacy between the president and Congress.

In the ***War of 1812,*** for example, it took almost three weeks after President James Madison's request for a declaration of war for Congress to approve it. Even then, the votes were far from unanimous—79 to 49 in the House, 19 to 13 in the Senate—and closely followed party and regional lines. Opposition in the New England states was so strong that state leaders initially withheld both money and troops. Although myths later developed about the war's being a "glorious triumph," the historian Donald Hickey takes the view that "Mr. Madison's war" was a "futile and costly struggle in which the United States had barely escaped dismemberment and disunion." Hickey also quotes Thomas Jefferson that the War of 1812 "arrested the course of the most remarkable tide of prosperity any nation ever experienced."[37]

Controversy and interbranch maneuvering characterized the politics that led up to the ***Mexican War*** of 1846–48. The key issue in this war was the annexation of Texas, the "lone star republic," which in 1836 had declared its independence from Mexico. In the 1840s, knowing that Congress was divided on the issue and thus was not likely to authorize a troop commitment to defend the annexation against the Mexicans, President John Tyler sought to make war secretly. Word leaked, however, prompting Senator Thomas Hart Benton, a leading politician of the day, to denounce Tyler's actions as "a crime against God and man and our own Constitution . . . a piece of business which belonged to Congress and should have been referred to them." President Tyler next tried the treaty route, proposing a treaty of annexation to the Senate. But the ratification vote in the Senate fell short of the two-thirds margin needed. Tyler then pulled a deft legislative maneuver by which he reintroduced the annexation proposal in the form of a joint resolution. A joint resolution must be approved by both the House and the Senate but requires only a majority vote in each house. Although denounced as "an undisguised usurpation of power and violation of the Constitution," it worked—Texas was annexed as the twenty-eighth state.[38]

Mexico responded by breaking off diplomatic relations with the United States. The new president, James K. Polk, Jr., who had defeated Tyler in the 1844 elections, "stampeded Congress" into a declaration of war by sending American troops into an area of disputed land where "Mexican units who, operating no doubt on their own theory of defensive war, supposed themselves repelling an invasion of Mexico." Many in Congress "had the uneasy feeling that the President had put something over on them."[39] But political considerations then were no different than today: when forced to vote one way or the other, elected representatives were reluctant to go on record against declaring war on a country whose troops, however provoked, had fired on American troops.

Among those who had that uneasy feeling was a first-term representative from Illinois named Abraham Lincoln. "Allow the President to invade a neighboring nation, whenever he shall deem it necessary," Representative Lincoln wrote at the time, "and you allow him to make war at [his] pleasure. Study to see if you fix *any limit* to his power in this respect."[40] Many a member of Congress would invoke Lincoln's views a century and a quarter later in the context of the Vietnam War.

The Spanish-American War of 1898 began with quite a bit of fervor, especially among expansionists in Congress and as whipped up by the "yellow journalism" of the newspaper tycoon William Randolph Hearst. The primary precipitating incident was the bombing of the battleship U.S.S. *Maine,* allegedly by Spain, killing 266 Americans in Havana Harbor, Cuba. Spurred by rallying cries such as "Remember the *Maine,* To Hell with Spain," Congress declared war. Thousands of young men enlisted in what was dubbed "a splendid little war." But although it took only four months of fighting before Spain sued for peace, the death toll was much heavier than expected. For many, this was no more "splendid" than other wars, as movingly conveyed in a letter to the editor of the *San Francisco Examiner* from the widow of a fallen soldier:

> You men who clamored for war, did you know what it would mean to the women of our country, when strife and bloodshed should sweep o'er the land; when the shouts of victory would but ineffectually drown the moans of the women who mourned for the lives of those that were given to make that victory possible? . . .
>
> To you who will celebrate our nation's success, when your spirits are raised in triumph and your songs of thanksgiving are the loudest, remember that we, who sit and weep in our closed and darkened homes, have given our best gifts to our country and our flag.
>
> Patriotism, how many hearts are broken in thy cause?[41]

As we saw earlier in this chapter, U.S. entry into World War I came almost three years after the war had started, and only after German U-boats and other direct threats to U.S. security drove home the point that isolationism no longer was possible. Germany, as President Wilson made the case, had "thrust" war upon the United States. In this context of a clear and present danger the vote in Congress for approval of a declaration of war was by wide margins, 82 to 6 in the Senate and 373 to 50 in the House. The country pulled together, enlisting in droves under the rallying cry "Johnny Get Your Gun" and doing whatever was necessary for the war effort. Yet what was supposed to be "the war to end all wars" proved not to be so. More people died in this war than had in all the wars of all the world over the preceding century. The American death toll was 116,516, with more than twice that many wounded.

No wonder the pattern of going to war reluctantly repeated itself in World War II. It was only after the direct attack by Japan on ***Pearl Harbor***—a day of "infamy," as FDR called it—that the United States entered a war that already had been raging for more than two years in Europe and even longer than that in Asia. Some historians, noting that the initial declaration of war passed by Congress was only against Japan, still wonder whether the United States would have gone to war against Germany had Hitler not declared war against the United States a few days later.

Americans came to know World War II as the "good war," in the author Studs Terkel's phrase. But the "good war" took a heavy toll, including more than one million American soldiers killed or wounded. The belief in the justness and righteousness of the cause against Hitler and Nazism and against Japanese aggression—of Peace, Power, Principles, and Prosperity all being at stake—kept public support solid despite such high casualties. Compared with earlier and later wars, however, this one was very much the historical exception.

## *National Security vs. the Bill of Rights*

Another major recurring foreign-policy politics debate has been over the tension between the demands and exigencies of safeguarding the nation's security, and the guarantees of individual rights and civil liberties ensconced in the Bill of Rights. "Perhaps it is a universal truth," James Madison wrote in a letter to Thomas Jefferson in 1798, "that the loss of liberty at home is to be charged to provisions against danger, real or pretended, from abroad."[42] How far can the justification of national security be taken, even with respect to what Madison meant by "real" danger from abroad, let alone as a rationale for "pretended" ones?

Madison himself fought bitterly against the repressive ***Alien and Sedition Acts*** passed by Congress and signed by President John Adams in 1798. On their face these laws were protection against subversive activities by the French and their sympathizers at a time when the United States and France were on the verge of war. But in reality they were intended to silence the opponents of war—whose leaders were none other than Madison and Jefferson—by limiting their freedom of speech and of the press. The acts represented a "loss of liberty" in the name of a "danger from abroad" which, though not fully "pretended," also was not as real as it was made out to be.

In the name of saving the Union, over the course of the Civil War, President Lincoln took a number of actions that infringed on the Bill of Rights and other civil liberties. He suspended *habeas corpus* and claimed authority to arrest without warrant persons suspected of "disloyal" practices. He banned "treasonable" correspondence from being delivered by the U.S. Post Office. He censored newspapers. He seized property. He proclaimed martial law. To those who criticized such actions as going too far, Lincoln responded that "measures otherwise unconstitutional might become lawful by becoming indispensable to the preservation of the Constitution through the preservation of the Nation." Yet he also stressed that these must be temporary powers. "The Executive power itself would be greatly diminished," he stated in 1864, "by the cessation of actual war."[43]

The ***Espionage and Sedition Acts*** of 1917–18, passed during World War I, were "as extreme as any legislation of the kind anywhere in the world." They made it illegal to "willfully utter, print, write or publish any disloyal, profane, scurrilous or abusive language about the United States, its form of government, the Constitution, soldiers and sailors, the flag or uniform of the armed forces . . . or by word or act oppose the cause of the United States."[44] Quite the broad prohibition! Ads were placed in the *Saturday Evening Post* and other mass-circulation magazines urging readers to report to the government "the man who spreads pessimistic stories . . . cries for peace or belittles our effort to win the war."[45] The postmaster general refused to deliver any magazine that included critical views. Schools dropped German from their curricula. German books were taken off the shelves of public libraries. Some cities banned dachshunds from their streets. Restaurants and snack bars stopped serving sauerkraut and started calling hamburgers "liberty steaks." All told, about two thousand people were prosecuted and eight hundred convicted of violations of the Espionage and Sedition Acts. The most prominent was Eugene V. Debs, leader of the Socialist party, who as a candidate for president in 1912 had received about 6 percent of the vote. Debs was given a twenty-year prison sentence for giving a speech against the war—and while still in prison during the 1920 presidential election received nearly one million votes!

The Supreme Court justices Oliver Wendell Holmes and Louis Brandeis, two giants in the Court's history, wrestled with this balance between national security and civil liberties. Justice Holmes defended the constitutionality of the Espionage and Sedition Acts with a famous analogy: "The most stringent protection of free speech," Holmes wrote, "would not protect a man in falsely shouting 'fire' in a theater and causing a panic." Holmes argued that the same general principle applied but the key was to determine in any particular instance "whether the words are used in such circumstance and are of such a nature as to create a clear and present danger that they will bring about the substantive evils that Congress has a right to prevent." Something that might not meet the "clear and present danger" test in times of peace may meet it in times of war: "When a nation is at war many things that might be said in time of peace are such a hindrance to its effort that their utterance will not be endured so long as men fight." Justice Brandeis concurred in his opinion but expressed concerns that the clear and present danger test was too easy to pass. In one case in which a man was convicted for distributing pro-German press reports, Brandeis criticized what he saw as "an intolerant majority, swayed by passion or by fear, . . . prone . . . to stamp as disloyal opinions with which it disagrees." Holmes and Brandeis, however, were in the minority in qualifying their approval of the statutes with these concerns.[46]

World War I ended and the German enemy was defeated, but a new enemy had arisen with the 1917 Communist revolution in Russia. During the ***Red Scare*** of 1919–20, the Wilson administration, led by Attorney General A. Mitchell Palmer, grossly overreacted to fears of internal subversion linked to "world communism" with heavy-handed repression and blatant disregard for civil liberties. "The blaze of revolution," Palmer propounded, was "eating its way into the home of the American workman, its sharp tongues of revolutionary heat . . . licking the altars of churches, leaping into the belfry of the school bell, crawling into the sacred corners of American homes, burning up the foundations of society."[47] Claiming the wartime Sedition Act as authority, on the night of January 2, 1920, Palmer sent his agents sweeping into meeting halls, offices, and homes all over the country, arresting about four thousand people as alleged communists, many even without warrants. The "Palmer raids" were so extreme that Congress almost impeached the attorney general. But it didn't, and he kept up his anticommunist attacks. The Supreme Court largely supported these policies, although with strong dissents from Justice Brandeis. As his biographer recounts, Brandeis felt that restrictions on civil liberties made necessary by war "would be entirely inappropriate in peace . . . when the nation's survival was not at stake. . . . [D]uring a war 'all bets are off.' But not otherwise."[48]

Perhaps the most profound violation of civil liberties in the name of national security came during World War II with the internment of 120,000 Japanese Americans in prison camps. On February 19, 1942, about three months after the Japanese attack on Pearl Harbor, President Franklin Roosevelt issued Executive Order 9066, uprooting people of Japanese ethnicity from their homes, jobs, and communities and banishing them to fenced-in prison camps, in the name of the war effort. "A Jap's a Jap!" proclaimed one general. "It makes no difference whether he's an American or not." In reality, though, not only were the vast majority of Japanese Americans loyal and patriotic citizens of the United States, once they were allowed in 1943 to join the military more than seventeen thousand Japanese Americans volunteered. "Even though my older brother was living in Japan," one Japanese American stated, "I told my parents that I was going to enlist because America was my country."[49] One unit, the Japanese-American 442nd Regimental Combat Team, fought with such valor as to amass more than eighteen thousand individual decorations, more than any other unit of its size and duration.[50]

At the time of the ***Japanese-American internments,*** very few voices were raised in protest in government, the media, or society at large. The Supreme Court even ruled that FDR's executive order was constitutional.[51] Not until more than thirty years later was a law passed as an official apology, providing monetary compensation to those Japanese Americans who had been interned and to their families. Although this was an important act of repentance and retribution, it hardly made up for the thousands of lives damaged or destroyed. The Bill of Rights was trampled insofar as it pertained to Japanese Americans, in the name of national security.

Thus, repeatedly, between 1789 and 1945 tensions arose between considerations of national security and fundamental guarantees provided in the Bill of Rights. Repeatedly, the latter were overtaken by the former. And, repeatedly, the criticisms and outrage that followed were severe. Yet, as we will see in the next chapter, the pattern was repeated during the Cold War and, as we will see in Chapter 8, is repeating again in the context of the war on terrorism.

## *Free Trade vs. Protectionism*

A member of Congress from Detroit smashing a Toyota with a sledgehammer in a photo opportunity in front of the Capitol dome in the late 1970s; Ross Perot warning in 1992–93 of the "giant sucking sound" that passage of NAFTA (the North American Free Trade Agreement) would set off; outcries in 2006 over an Arab company's running some U.S. seaports: recent years have been full of controversies over trade and other international economic policies. But although it is true that this recent discord contrasts with the prevailing pro–free trade consensus of 1945–71, most of the rest of American history has seen extensive interest-group pressure and other political conflict over ***free trade*** vs. ***protectionism.***

In the first half of the nineteenth century, divisions over the tariff issue largely followed regional lines. Northern industrialists seeking protection from foreign competition for their "infant industries" and northern and western farmers who produced primarily for the domestic market favored high tariffs on imported goods. Northeastern merchants, whose economic interests lay in import and export businesses, and Southern plantation owners, whose cotton and tobacco crops were in high demand in Europe, favored low tariffs in order to facilitate international trade. Indeed, although slavery clearly was the most contentious issue, the Civil War also was fed by these fundamental differences over trade policy.

In the late nineteenth century not only was the tariff the primary foreign policy issue of the day, tariff policy was one of the defining differences between the Democratic and Republican parties. In those days the Democrats were predominately in support of free trade, and the Republicans were so protectionist as to proclaim high tariffs as one of the "plain and natural rights of Americans."[52] When President Grover Cleveland, a Democrat, managed to get a tariff reduction bill through the House, the Republican-controlled Senate killed it. The Republicans rode their protectionist position to a major victory in the 1888 elections, with Benjamin Harrison defeating Cleveland for president and Republicans winning majorities in both the House and the Senate.

Yet the Republican-controlled Congress and the new Republican president also fought over trade issues. They did agree on higher tariffs and passed these in the McKinley Tariff Act (named for William McKinley, then the chair of the House Ways and Means Committee). The most significant battle centered on the Harrison administration's proposal for authority to negotiate reciprocity treaties. A reciprocity treaty involves an agreement with another country for mutual reductions in tariffs. The Senate was willing to go along with this since it still would be a player through its treaty-ratification authority. But the House, which has no constitutional authority over treaties, was concerned about being left out of the ball game. It took extensive negotiations—seven days of Republican party caucuses, according to the leading historian of the period—to get the House to agree even to a compromise version.[53]

Politics in those days was extremely volatile. Democrats took control of both the House and the Senate in the 1890 midterm elections, and Grover Cleveland won back the White House in 1892, becoming the only president ever to win two nonconsecutive terms. Since Democratic victories were in large part attributable to the political pendulum's having swung back toward antitariff sentiment, Cleveland made major tariff reductions one of his highest priorities. But with special interests exerting extensive pressure, by the time his antitariff bill passed the Senate it had 634 amendments. It still reduced tariffs, but by much less than the president had wanted.

In 1896, in yet another swing of the political pendulum, Republican William McKinley was elected president and the Republicans regained control of Congress. Ironically, President McKinley now pushed for an even greater congressional delegation of authority to negotiate trade treaties than that which Representative McKinley had opposed as inimical to the Constitution. McKinley won the authority, but although he and his successors would use this authority to negotiate eleven trade treaties over the next decade, not a single one was ever ratified.[54] In 1909 Congress took back the reciprocal trade treaty authority and did not regrant it to the president for another quarter-century, until after the 1930 ***Smoot-Hawley*** protectionist tariff had worked its disastrous effects, including contributing to the Great Depression.

With these lessons in mind, Congress ceded much of its authority to set tariffs to the president in the ***Reciprocal Trade Agreements Act*** (RTAA) of 1934. The RTAA, called "a revolution in tariff making" by one historian,[55] delegated to the president authority to cut tariffs on his own by as much as 50 percent if he could negotiate reciprocal cuts with other countries. This laid the basis for a fundamental shift away from protectionism and toward free trade, a shift that was further manifested following World War II, when the United States played a key role in setting up the General Agreement on Tariffs and Trade as the basis for an international system of free trade.

## Summary

In studying history, we see that change often is more readily apparent than continuity. In so many ways the twenty-first century and its foreign policy challenges are vastly different from those of even the recent past, let alone those of the eighteenth, nineteenth, and early twentieth centuries. Yet many of the foreign policy choices we debate today are, at their core, about the same fundamental questions that have been debated over two centuries of U.S. history.

Can the United States best fulfill its national interest in all its components through isolationism or internationalism? How big a military and how much defense spending are needed to ensure U.S. Power and ensure the Peace? How true to its democratic

Principles does U.S. foreign policy need to be? Are those who criticize U.S. foreign policy as imperialistic right? How are we to assess the record of relations in such major regions as Latin America and Asia? Every one of these questions of foreign policy strategy has a long history that provides important context for current foreign policy choices.

The same is true with regard to the three historical debates over foreign policy politics examined in this chapter. Struggles between the president and Congress over decisions to go to war are hardly just a post-Vietnam matter; they go back a long way in U.S. history. The profoundly difficult trade-offs between the demands of national security and the constitutional guarantees of civil liberties have been demonstrated all too many times in U.S. history. The interest-group pressures over free trade vs. protectionism were at least as intense in the late nineteenth century as in the late twentieth century.

It is therefore crucial that as we consider the foreign policy challenges today, we not only seek to understand what is new about our world, but also seek to learn from the prologue that is the past.

In the next chapter we will look at the Cold War and the more recent historical context it provides to our analysis of today's challenges.

## *American Foreign Policy* Online Student StudySpace

- Isolationism vs. internationalism: which has been better for the United States historically?
- How true have we been to our claims of American exceptionalism?
- We wrestle with the balance between national security and civil liberties here in the twenty-first-century: How well has it been struck in prior eras?

For these and other study questions, as well as other features, check out Chapter 3 on the *American Foreign Policy* Online Student StudySpace at wwnorton.com/studyspace.

## Notes

[1]For a fuller diplomatic history, see such authors as Walter LaFeber, *The American Age: U.S. Foreign Policy at Home and Abroad, 1750–Present.* (New York: Norton, 1996); Walter A. McDougall, *Promised Land, Crusader State: The American Encounter with the World since 1776* (Boston: Houghton Mifflin, 1997); Walter Russell Mead, *Special Providence: American Foreign Policy and How It Changed the World* (New York: Knopf, 2001); Thomas G. Paterson, J. Gary Clifford, and Kenneth J. Hagan, *American Foreign Relations: A History Since 1895* (Lexington, Mass.: D.C. Health, 1995); also the timelines in Bruce W. Jentleson and Thomas G. Paterson, *Encyclopedia of U.S. Foreign Relations,* Appendix 1: Chronology of U.S. Foreign Relations (compiled by Kurk

Dorsey), vol. 4 (New York; Oxford University Press, 1997), and Knowledge Rush, www.knowledgerush.com/kr/encyclopedia/Timeline_of_United-States_diplomatic_history.

[2]James M. McCormick, *American Foreign Policy and Process* (Itasca, Ill.: Peacock, 1992), 15–16.

[3]Cited in John Gerard Ruggie, "The Past as Prologue? Interests, Identity and American Foreign Policy," *International Security* 21.4 (Spring 1997): 89–90.

[4]Richard J. Barnet, *The Rockets' Red Glare: War, Politics and the American Presidency* (New York: Simon & Schuster, 1990), 142.

[5]Woodrow Wilson, "An Address to a Joint Session of Congress," in Ray Stannard Baker and William E. Dodd, eds., *The Public Papers of Woodrow Wilson,* (New York: Harper and Brothers, 1927), 5: 6–16.

[6]Both cited in Barnet, *Rockets' Red Glare,* 200.

[7]Robert Shogan, *Hard Bargain: How FDR Twisted Churchill's Arm, Evaded the Law, and Changed the Role of the American Presidency* (New York: Scribner's, 1995).

[8]Franklin D. Roosevelt, 1941 State of the Union Address, www.americanrhetoric.com/speeches/fdrthefourfreedoms.htm (accessed 6/6/09).

[9]Arthur M. Schlesinger, Jr., "Back to the Womb? Isolationism's Renewed Threat," *Foreign Affairs* 74.4 (July/August 1995): 4.

[10]Quoted in Paul A. Varg, *Foreign Policies of the Founding Fathers* (Baltimore: Penguin, 1970), 192.

[11]Samuel Eliot Morison and Henry Steele Commager, *The Growth of the American Republic* (New York: Oxford University Press, 1940), 2:471.

[12]Richard Polenberg, *War and Society: The United States, 1941–1945* (New York: Lippincott, 1972), 5.

[13]There are also domestic-policy versions of American exceptionalism. See Seymour Martin Lipset, *American Exceptionalism: A Double-Edged Sword* (New York: Norton, 1996).

[14]Cited in Anders Stephanson, *Manifest Destiny: American Expansionism and the Empire of Right* (New York: Hill and Wang, 1995), 19.

[15]The term was first used by John L. O'Sullivan, editor of the *Democratic Review.* O'Sullivan was an interesting character, the descendant of "a long line of Irish adventurers and mercenaries," known among other things for being involved in failed plots to annex Cuba, and said by his friend, the writer Nathaniel Hawthorne, to be a "bizarre" fellow. Stephanson, *Manifest Destiny,* xi–xii.

[16]Woodrow Wilson, "Address to Joint Session of Congress," April 2, 1917, reprinted in Arthur S. Link, ed., *Papers of Woodrow Wilson* (Princeton: Princeton University Press, 1966), 519–27.

[17]Strobe Talbott, *The Great Experiment: The Story of Ancient Empires, Modern States and the Quest for a Global Nation* (New York: Simon & Schuster, 2008), 151.

[18]Atlantic Charter, joint statement by President Roosevelt and Prime Minister Churchill, August 14, 1941, in U.S. Department of State, *Foreign Relations of the United States: 1941, Vol. 1: General, the Soviet Union* (Washington, D.C.: U.S. Government Printing Office, 1958), 367–69.

[19]Thomas G. Paterson, J. Gary Clifford, and Kenneth J. Hagan, *American Foreign Relations: A History to 1920* (Lexington, Mass.: Heath, 1995), 233.

[20]Michael Hunt, *Ideology and U.S. Foreign Policy* (New Haven: Yale University Press, 1987), 53.

[21]Thomas Bortelsmann, "Race and Racism," in *Encyclopedia of U.S. Foreign Relations,* Bruce W. Jentleson and Thomas G. Paterson, eds. (New York: Oxford University Press, 1997), 3:451–52.

[22]Cited in Alexander DeConde, "Ethnic Groups," in *Encyclopedia of U.S. Foreign Relations,* Jentleson and Paterson, eds., 2: 111.

[23]Cited in Walter LaFeber, *The American Age: United States Foreign Policy at Home and Abroad,* 2d ed. (New York: Norton, 1994), 213.

[24]Cited in Morison and Commager, *Growth of the American Republic,* 324.

[25]Cited in Paterson, Clifford, and Hagan, *American Foreign Relations,* 229, from Hugh Deane, *Good Deeds and*

*Gunboats* (San Francisco: China Books and Periodicals, 1990), 65.

[26]Both cited in Paterson, Clifford, and Hagan, *American Foreign Relations,* 175.

[27]Paterson, Clifford, and Hagan, *American Foreign Relations,* 254–57.

[28]Quoted in Paterson, Clifford, and Hagan, *American Foreign Relations,* 262–63.

[29]Gaddis Smith, "Monroe Doctrine," in *Encyclopedia of U.S. Foreign Relations,* Jentleson and Paterson, eds., 3: 159–67.

[30]Franklin D. Roosevelt, "Our Foreign Policy: A Democratic View," *Foreign Affairs* 6.4 (July 1928): 584.

[31]Cited in Peter W. Rodman, *More Precious Than Peace: The Cold War and the Struggle for the Third World* (New York: Scribner's 1994), 38.

[32]Quoted in Paterson, Clifford, and Hagan, *American Foreign Relations,* 133.

[33]Quoted in Akira Iriye, *Across the Pacific: An Inner History of American–East Asian Relations* (New York: Harcourt, Brace, 1967), 23.

[34]Iriye, *Across the Pacific,* 60.

[35]Paterson, Clifford, and Hagan, *American Foreign Relations,* 135.

[36]Both quotes given in Iriye, *Across the Pacific,* 147–48.

[37]Donald R. Hickey, *The War of 1812: A Forgotten Conflict* (Urbana: University of Illinois Press, 1989), 305, 309.

[38]Arthur M. Schlesinger, Jr., *The Imperial Presidency* (New York: Atlantic Monthly Press, 1974), 51–52.

[39]Schlesinger, *The Imperial Presidency,* 53.

[40]Schlesinger, *The Imperial Presidency,* 54 (emphasis in original).

[41]The letter is from Mrs. Pauline O'Neill, wife of Captain William "Bucky" O'Neill. Captain O'Neill had been the mayor of Prescott in the territory of Arizona. Hailed in a newspaper of the day as "the most many-sided man Arizona had produced," he joined Teddy Roosevelt's fabled "Rough Riders" and was killed in the battle for Kettle Hill, outside Santiago, Cuba. Pauline O'Neill, letter published in the *San Francisco Examiner,* August 7, 1897, in the collection of the Sharlott Hall Museum, Prescott, Arizona.

[42]S. Padover, ed., *The Complete Madison* (New York: Harper, 1953), 258.

[43]Quoted in Schlesinger, *The Imperial Presidency,* 71, 75.

[44]Morison and Commager, *Growth of the American Republic,* 478.

[45]Cited in Barnet, *Rockets' Red Glare,* 158.

[46]Lewis J. Paper, *Brandeis* (Englewood Cliffs, N.J.: Prentice-Hall, 1983), 282–83.

[47]Paterson, Clifford, and Hagan, *American Foreign Relations,* 324.

[48]Paper, *Brandeis,* 283. On these cases Justice Holmes was much less supportive of Brandeis.

[49]Both quoted in Jerel A. Rosati, *The Politics of United States Foreign Policy* (New York: Harcourt, Brace, 1993), 476–78.

[50]Ronald Smothers, "Japanese-Americans Recall War Service," *New York Times,* June 19, 1995, A8.

[51]*Korematsu v. United States* (1944), cited in Thomas M. Franck and Michael J. Glennon, eds., *Foreign Relations and National Security Law: Cases, Materials and Simulations* (St. Paul, Minn.: West, 1987), 43–53.

[52]Tom E. Terrill, *The Tariff, Politics and American Foreign Policy, 1874–1901* (Westport, Conn.: Greenwood, 1973), 199.

[53]Terrill, *The Tariff,* 172

[54]Robert A. Pastor, *Congress and the Politics of Foreign Economic Policy, 1929–1976* (Berkeley: University of California Press, 1980), 75.

[55]Sidney Ratner, cited in Pastor, *Congress and the Politics of Foreign Economic Policy,* 92.

CHAPTER 4

# The Cold War Context: Origins and First Stages

## Introduction: "Present at the Creation"

"Present at the Creation" is how Dean Acheson, secretary of state in the early days of the Cold War, titled his memoirs. At the outset of the Cold War, Americans felt they were facing threats as dangerous and challenges as profound as any they had ever before faced in history. Moreover, the United States was no longer merely pursuing its own foreign policy; it was being looked to as a world leader, a "superpower." It had been a leader in World War II, but only after overcoming isolationism, and even then only for a period that, as dire as it was, lasted less than four years. The Cold War, though, would go on for more than four decades. And so it was that, when years later Acheson wrote his memoirs, he chose a title that reflected his generation's sense of having created its own new era.[1]

During World War II the United States and the Soviet Union had been allies. President Franklin D. Roosevelt, the British prime minister Winston Churchill, and the Soviet leader Josef Stalin were known as the Big Three. The Soviets were second only to the British as beneficiaries of American Lend-Lease economic assistance during the war, receiving more than $9 billion worth of food, equipment, and other aid. Even Stalin's image as a ruthless dictator who viciously purged his own people in the 1930s was "spun" more favorably to the more amiable "Uncle Joe." Yet fundamentally, the American-Soviet wartime alliance was based on the age-old maxim that "the enemy of my enemy is my friend." "I can't take communism," was how FDR put it, "but to cross this bridge I'd hold hands with the Devil."[2] After the war was over and the common enemy, Nazi Germany, had been vanquished, would the alliance continue? Should it?

Different views on these questions are reflected in the debate over the origins of the ***Cold War***. This debate is marked by two main schools of thought, the orthodox and the revisionist. The *orthodox* view puts principal responsibility squarely on the shoulders of Josef Stalin and the Soviet Union.[3] This view has been strengthened by revelations in recent years from Soviet and other archives. "We now know," the historian John Lewis Gaddis contends, that "as long as Stalin was running the Soviet Union, a cold war was unavoidable." The Soviets used the Red Army to make Eastern Europe their own sphere of influence. They sought to subvert governments in Western Europe. They blockaded West Berlin in an effort to force the United States, France, and Britain out. In Asia they supported the Chinese communists and helped start the Korean War. They supported communist parties in Southeast Asia and Latin America, and within African anticolonial movements; indeed, one of the fundamental tenets of Soviet communist ideology was to aid revolution everywhere. And in the United States they ran a major spy ring trying, among other things, to steal the secret of the atomic bomb.

In the *revisionist* view of the origins of the Cold War, as represented in Reading 4.1, the United States bears its own significant share of the responsibility.[4] Some revisionists see the United States as seeking its own empire, for reasons of both Power and Prosperity. Its methods may have been less direct and more subtle, but its objectives nevertheless were domination to serve American grand ambitions. In citing evidence for U.S. neo-imperialist ambitions, these critics point as far back as the 1918–19 U.S. "expeditionary force" that, along with European forces, intervened in Russia to try to reverse the Russian Revolution. Other revisionists see the problem more as one of U.S. miscalculation. They maintain that the Soviets were seeking little more than to ensure their own security by preserving Poland and Eastern Europe as a *cordon sanitaire* to prevent future invasions of Soviet soil. What transpired in those early post–World War II years, these revisionists argue, was akin to the classic "security dilemma," often present in international politics, in which each side is motivated less by aggression than by the fear that the other side cannot be trusted, and thus sees its own actions as defensive while the other side sees them as offensive. Had U.S. policy been more one of reassurance and cooperation, rather than deterrence and containment, there might not have been a Cold War.

4.1

With this debate in mind, in this chapter and the next we analyze the dynamics of foreign policy choice for the United States as played out during the Cold War, with regard to both foreign policy strategy and foreign policy politics. In so doing we will gain a deeper understanding of the Cold War itself and provide the contemporary context to go with the historical one (from Chapter 3) for the challenges and choices that face the United States in the post–Cold War era.

## Peace: International Institutionalism and the United Nations

Work on the United Nations (UN) was begun well before World War II was over. One of the primary reasons that World War I had not turned out to be "the war to end all wars," as Woodrow Wilson and other leaders had hoped, was the weakness of the League of Nations. Franklin Roosevelt and other world leaders felt they had learned from that experience, and this time intended to create a stronger global body as the basis for a stable peace.

### *The Original Vision of the United Nations*

The grand hope for the ***United Nations,*** as articulated by FDR's secretary of state, Cordell Hull, was that "there would no longer be need for spheres of influence, for alliances, for balance of power, or any other special arrangements through which, in the unhappy past, nations strove to safeguard their security or promote their interests." Their vision was of "one world" and a peace that was broad and enduring.

This was quintessential ***International Institutionalism,*** a vision of international relations in which the national interest of the United States, as well as the national interests of other nations, would be served best by multilateral cooperation through international institutions—a world that could be, in the metaphors cited back in Chapter 1, the "cultivable garden" of peace, not necessarily the "global jungle" of power. The United States, more than any other country, saw the world in these terms and pushed for the creation of the UN. It was in San Francisco on June 26, 1945, that the UN Charter was signed (with fifty-one original signatories). New York City was chosen as the location for UN headquarters.

The lesson drawn from the failure of the ***League of Nations*** was not that the International Institutionalist strategy was inherently flawed, but that the post–World War I version of it had two crucial errors. One was U.S. nonmembership. FDR knew that American membership was key to the UN and that the UN was necessary in order that the United States not revert to isolationism. U.S. membership in the UN thus was "an institutional tripwire," as John Ruggie calls it, "that would force American policymakers to take positions on potential threats to international peace and security . . . not simply to look the other way, as they had done in the 1930s."[5] FDR was determined not to make the same political mistakes that Woodrow Wilson had made. Roosevelt worked closely with Congress, including giving a major role in the U.S. delegation to the San Francisco Conference to senior Republicans such as Senator Arthur Vandenberg of Michigan. He also used his "fireside chats" and other political techniques to ensure that public opinion supported the UN. All this work paid off: the Senate vote on U.S. membership in the UN was 89–2, and public-opinion polls showed that 66 percent of Americans favored U.S. membership and only 3 percent were opposed (31 percent were uncertain).

Following the second lesson drawn from the interwar years, world leaders strove to ensure that the UN would be a stronger institution than the League had been. Having the United States as a member was part of this plan, but so was institutional design. The League had allocated roughly equal powers to its Assembly, comprising all member nations, and to its Council, made up of permanent seats for the four "great powers" that were League members (Britain, France, Italy, and Japan) and four seats to be rotated among other member nations; all seats on the Council were equally powerful. In contrast, the UN gave its Security Council much greater authority than its General Assembly. The UN Security Council could authorize the use of military force, order the severance of diplomatic relations, impose economic sanctions, and take other actions and make them binding on member states. And the five permanent members of the Security Council—the United States, the Soviet Union, Britain, France, and China—were made particularly powerful, being given the power to veto any Security Council action.

The UN Charter even envisioned a standing UN military force. Article 43 of the charter had called on "all Members . . . to make available to the Security Council, on its call and with special agreement or agreements . . . [to be] negotiated as soon as possible . . . armed force, assistance and facilities . . . necessary for the purpose of maintaining international peace and security." This standing force was to be directed by a Military Staff Committee, consisting of the chiefs of staff of the armed forces of the permanent members of the Security Council. The Military Staff Committee would directly advise the Security Council and be in operational charge of the military forces. No Article 43 agreements were ever concluded, however. Over the years the UN has raised temporary military forces for particular missions such as peacekeeping, but it has never had a permanent standing military of its own. In this and other respects, although making important contributions, the UN did not prove able to provide the institutional infrastructure for a "one world" peace.

### *The Scaled-Back Reality*

One reason the UN was unable to ensure peace was the political ambivalence of a number of countries, including the United States, that wanted an international institution strong enough to help keep the peace but not so strong as to threaten nation-state supremacy or sovereignty. Although Roosevelt and Truman administration officials had helped write the Article 43 provision into the UN Charter, many in Congress saw it as a step too far toward "world government." They supported the UN, but not that much, and had the power of the purse and other legislative authority to ensure that no American troops would be put under any sort of permanent UN command. Congress demonstrated similar reticence with the Genocide Convention ("convention" is used here as a synonym for treaty) and the Universal Declaration of Human Rights (UDHR). The goals of preventing genocide and promoting human rights obviously were nonobjectionable. But the U.S. Senate refused for years to ratify the Genocide Convention and gave only selective recognition to the UDHR because these documents ostensibly risked giving the UN and international courts jurisdiction over American domestic affairs in a manner that threatened American sovereignty. We will come back to this issue of international institutions versus national sovereignty in Part II of this book, for it has resurfaced as a major debate in post–Cold War foreign policy. The point here is that this issue was present even in the original grand vision of the UN.

The other, more important reason that the UN fell short of its original vision was the onset of the Cold War and the resultant priority given to considerations of Power. Even before the UN Charter was signed, U.S.-Soviet tensions had flared over the future of Poland and other states of Eastern Europe. It also was only weeks after the signing of the UN Charter that the United States dropped the world's first atomic bombs on Japan. President Harry Truman defended his A-bomb decision as the only alternative to a major and risky invasion, but some critics believed it was less about getting Japan to surrender and establishing peace than about demonstrating American military might so as to intimidate the Soviet Union.[6] Whichever interpretation one took, the tensions that arose during this time demonstrated the limits of the UN for managing key international events and actions. This weakness was confirmed by the controversy in 1946 over the ***Baruch Plan.*** Named for Truman's adviser Bernard Baruch, the plan was a U.S. proposal to the UN Atomic Energy Commission for establishing international control of nuclear weapons. The Soviet Union rejected the Baruch Plan. Some cited this as evidence of Stalin's non-peaceful intentions. Others assessed the Baruch Plan as one sided and actually intended to spur a rejection.[7]

In other ways as well, instead of a unifying institution the UN became yet another forum for the competition between the United States and the Soviet Union and their respective allies. They differed over who should be secretary-general. They disagreed on which countries would be admitted to the General Assembly. Each used its veto so many times that the Security Council was effectively paralyzed. At one point, following the October 1949 communist triumph in the Chinese civil war, the Soviets boycotted the Security Council in protest against its decision to allow Jiang Jei-shi (Chiang Kai-shek) and his anticommunist Nationalist government, which had fled to the island of Taiwan, to continue to hold China's UN seat. In fact, one of the few times the Security Council did act decisively in these early years was in June 1950, when communist North Korea invaded South Korea, setting off the Korean War: The United States took advantage of the Soviet boycott of the Security Council to get a resolution passed creating a UN-sponsored military force to defend South Korea.

Americans often view the United Nations as more hostile than friendly. In later chapters, we address this idea as it pertains to the contemporary era. During the early Cold War era, though, as the table in "International Perspectives" on page 119 shows, the UN was quite supportive of American foreign policy. Even so, as an international institution it

INTERNATIONAL PERSPECTIVES
INTERNATIONAL PERSPECTIVES

### SUPPORT FOR THE UNITED STATES IN THE UN GENERAL ASSEMBLY, 1946–60

This table compares U.S. and Soviet success rates on votes in the UN General Assembly from 1946 to 1960. Two sets of issues are disaggregated: Cold War issues and other international affairs issues. On Cold War issues the American position was supported in 94.3 percent of General Assembly votes, compared with only 6.1 percent for the Soviet position. On other issues the margin was closer but still favored the United States, 55.1 percent to 50.3 percent for successes and the even larger margin of only 28.6 percent of votes that passed the General Assembly despite U.S. opposition but 40 percent for the Soviets (this takes abstentions into account). The overall scores were 60.3 percent success and 25.3 percent failure for the United States, and 44.5 percent success and 47.2 percent failure for the Soviets.

**Percentage of votes in the UN General Assembly, 1946–60***

| | UNITED STATES | | SOVIET UNION | |
|---|---|---|---|---|
| | Success | Failure | Success | Failure |
| Cold War issues | 94.3% | 3.2% | 6.1% | 91.4% |
| Other issues | 55.1 | 28.6 | 50.3 | 40.0 |
| All issues | 60.3 | 25.3 | 44.5 | 47.2 |

*Differences from 100 percent are votes in which the United States and the Soviet Union abstained.
Source: Edward T. Rowe, "The United States, the United Nations and the Cold War," *International Organization* 25.1 (Winter 1971): 62.

was not strong enough to end the global game of "spheres of influence . . . alliances . . . balance of power" and make the break with that "unhappy past" envisioned by Secretary of State Hull and other UN founders. This was not the peace that was supposed to be.

## Power: Nuclear Deterrence and Containment

A "one world" peace had its attractions, but was unrealistic—power had to be met with power. Some argued that this should have been foreseen even before World War II was over, and that FDR had conceded too much at the Yalta summit on issues such as the future

UNIVERSITY OF WINCHESTER
LIBRARY

of Poland. Now more than ever, in the classic Realist dictum presented back in Chapter 1, American foreign policy had to be based on interests defined in terms of power.

For all the other differences that emerged over the course of the Cold War, two basic doctrines of Power that developed in these early years remained the core of U.S. foreign policy. One was ***nuclear deterrence.*** Bernard Brodie's *Strategy in the Missile Age* (Reading 4.2) was one of the first and most influential books developing nuclear deterrence doctrine. The standard definition of deterrence is the prevention of attack through the fear of retaliation. On the one hand, deterrence is more than just the capacity to defend oneself sufficiently to prevent defeat. On the other hand, it is less than ***compellence,*** which means getting another state to take a particular action that it otherwise would not.[8] Although the use of deterrence strategy goes far back in history, the nuclear age gave it greater centrality. As devastating as the 1941 Japanese attack on Pearl Harbor had been, the United States managed to absorb it and recover from it. But nuclear weapons, so much more destructive than anything the world had ever seen, changed the world's security landscape. The single atomic bomb (A-bomb) dropped on Hiroshima instantly killed 130,000 people, one-third of the city's population; another 70,000 died later of radiation poisoning and other injuries. As the United States thought about its own national security in the nuclear age, its leaders realized that a strong and resilient defense, though still necessary, no longer was sufficient. Any attack with nuclear weapons or that could lead to the use of nuclear weapons had to be deterred before it began. This capacity for deterrence required a strong military, and especially nuclear weapons superiority, and also had political, psychological, and perceptual dimensions. The deterrence "formula" was a combination of capabilities and intentions, both the capacity to retaliate and the will to do so. The requisites for meeting this nuclear deterrence formula changed over time, but the basic strategy of preventing attack through fear of retaliation stayed the same. Its development is a striking example of theory shaping policy, as we elaborate in "Theory in the World."

4.2

***Containment*** was the other basic doctrine developed during the early Cold War. In February 1946, George F. Kennan, then a high-ranking U.S. diplomat in Moscow, sent a "long telegram" back to Washington, in which he sounded the alarm about the Soviet Union. A version of the long telegram later appeared in the prestigious journal *Foreign Affairs* as "The Sources of Soviet Conduct," with authorship attributed to an anonymous "X" (Reading 4.3). Kennan's analysis of Stalin and his Soviet Union was that "there can never be on Moscow's side any sincere assumption of a community of interests between the Soviet Union and powers which are regarded as capitalist." American strategy therefore had to seek the "patient but firm and vigilant containment of Russian expansive tendencies." The Soviet Union was seeking "to make sure that it has filled every nook and cranny available to it in the basin of world power." Kennan recommended a policy of "containment," whereby the United States would counter any attempt by the Soviets to expand their sphere of influence or to spread communism beyond their own borders. Only sustained containment had a chance of bringing about "the gradual mellowing of

4.3

THEORY IN THE WORLD

THEORY IN THE WORLD

## THE "WIZARDS OF ARMAGEDDON" AND COLD WAR NUCLEAR DETERRENCE

Cold War nuclear deterrence doctrine is a particularly strong example of theory shaping policy. Its development involved a "small group of theorists [who] would devise and help implement a set of ideas that would change the shape of American defense policy," and with the highest stakes of possibly meaning "the difference between peace and total war." These theorists were seen as "the wizards of Armageddon," a group impressive in its intellect, developing sophisticated and mysterious theories and strategies, geared to avoiding the horrors of nuclear war.*

The nuclear age changed the nature of deterrence. Whereas in the past, countries could strategize to win wars if deterrence failed, nuclear war could not be won. Scholars and strategists who had studied naval fleets, armies, and even air power now had to develop theories and policies geared more to deterring than to winning wars. "Total nuclear war is to be avoided at all costs," Bernard Brodie wrote. "[S]uch a war, even if we were extraordinarily lucky, would be too big, too all-consuming to permit the survival even of those final values, like personal freedom, for which alone one could think of waging it."†

Brodie and his colleagues were a colorful group. Brodie had been a political science professor at Yale; he "hardly seemed the type to become the pioneer of nuclear strategy . . . short, with glasses . . . awkward . . . badly dressed." Then there was Albert Wohlstetter, a mathematician, up until then "a rather otherworldly figure," in the home-building business for a while. He later would become a professor at the University of Chicago, where among his students would be Paul Wolfowitz, a leading neoconservative in the George W. Bush administration.‡ Wohlstetter's main work was on the need for assured second-strike capabilities, that is, ensuring that even in a case of surprise attack or other Soviet first strike, the surviving American nuclear forces would still be sufficient to credibly threaten retaliation severe enough to destroy the Soviet Union. This was less actually to fight a nuclear war than to strengthen deterrence through fear of retaliation even as a second strike.

Most colorful of all was Herman Kahn, a physicist, "brazenly theatrical, long-winded, overflowing with a thousand and one ideas."§ Kahn's concern was whether the threat to retaliate ever could be sufficiently credible to convince the other side that America would do it even at the risk of annihilating the human race. He speculated on whether the United States needed a "Doomsday machine" that would be programmed

(*Continued*)

(*Continued*)

for automatic massive nuclear retaliation without the human factor, the president or anyone else, coming back into the decision. He too argued that this would strengthen deterrence, make nuclear war less likely. The Doomsday machine and Kahn became the basis for the 1962 movie *Dr. Strangelove,* directed by Stanley Kubrick and starring Peter Sellers, controversial at the time and later a film classic.

The leading think tank for these and other nuclear theoretician-strategists was the RAND Corporation. RAND was the Pentagon's main semi-outside think tank. Its location near the beaches of Santa Monica, California, provided a setting at once conducive to big thinking yet also in its serenity starkly contrasting with scenarios of nuclear war and deterrence. RAND had extensive influence in every administration in this era, especially the Kennedy administration, when Defense Secretary Robert S. McNamara brought RAND scholars into government as part of his team of "defense intellectuals." The wizards now had responsibility for helping avoid Armageddon.

*Fred Kaplan, *The Wizards of Armageddon* (New York: Simon & Schuster, 1983), 11.
†See Reading 4.2.
‡Kaplan, *Wizards of Armageddon,* 11–12, 94.
§Kaplan, *Wizards of Armageddon,* 220.

Soviet power," Kennan argued; it might even reveal the internal contradictions of their system to the point that the Soviet Union would "break up."[9]

## The Formative Period, 1947–50

Both deterrence and containment were evident in Truman administration foreign policies. The ***Truman Doctrine,*** proclaimed in March 1947, was essentially a U.S. commitment to aid Greece and Turkey against Soviet and Soviet-assisted threats. The U.S. aid was economic, not military, and it totaled only about $400 million. But the significance, as President Truman stressed in his historic speech to Congress and the nation, was much more sweeping (see "At the Source," p. 123). This was not just another foreign policy issue involving a couple of important but minor countries. It was a defining moment in history with significance for the fate of the entire post–World War II world. And the United States was the only country that could provide the necessary leadership.

A few months later the ***Marshall Plan*** was announced in a commencement speech at Harvard University by Secretary of State George Marshall (see "At the Source," p. 123). Most of Western Europe still had not recovered economically from the devastation of World War II. In France, Italy, and elsewhere, communist parties were gaining support by

## AT THE SOURCE

AT THE SOURCE

### THE TRUMAN DOCTRINE AND THE MARSHALL PLAN

#### Truman Doctrine

"At the present moment in world history nearly every nation must choose between alternative ways of life. The choice too often is not a free one.

One way of life is based upon the will of the majority, and is distinguished by free institutions, representative government, free elections, guaranties of individual liberty, freedom of speech and religion, and freedom from political oppression.

The second way of life is based upon the will of a minority forcibly imposed upon the majority. It relies upon terror and oppression, a controlled press and radio, fixed elections, and the suppression of personal freedoms.

I believe that it must be the policy of the United States to support free peoples who are resisting attempted subjugation by armed minorities or by outside pressures. . . .

Should we fail to aid Greece and Turkey in this fateful hour, the effect will be far-reaching to the West as well as to the East. . . ."

#### Marshall Plan

"In considering the requirements for the rehabilitation of Europe, the physical loss of life, the visible destruction of cities, factories, mines and railroads was correctly estimated, but it has become obvious during recent months that this visible destruction was probably less serious than the dislocation of the entire fabric of European economy.

The truth of the matter is that Europe's requirements for the next three or four years of foreign food and other essential products—principally from America—are so much greater than her present ability to pay that she must have substantial additional help or face economic, social, and political deterioration of a very grave character. The remedy lies in breaking the vicious circle and restoring the confidence of the European people in the economic future of their own countries and of Europe as a whole. . . .

It is logical that the United States should do whatever it is able to do to assist in the return of normal economic health in the world, without which there can be no

(*Continued*)

(*Continued*)

political stability and no assured peace. Our policy is directed not against any country or doctrine but against hunger, poverty, desperation, and chaos. Its purpose should be the revival of a working economy in the world so as to permit the emergence of political and social conditions in which free institutions can exist. ”

Sources: Harry Truman, "Special Message to the Congress on Greece and Turkey: The Truman Doctrine," March 12, 1947, in *Documents on American Foreign Relations* (Princeton: Princeton University Press for the World Peace Foundation, 1947), 19: 6–7; George Marshall, "European Initiative Essential to Economic Recovery," speech made June 5, 1947, at Harvard University, reprinted in *Department of State Bulletin* 16 (June 15, 1947), 1159.

capitalizing on economic discontent. To meet this threat to containment, the Marshall Plan pledged enormous amounts of money, the equivalent of over $60 billion today, as U.S. economic assistance to the countries of Western Europe. Thus began the first major U.S. Cold War foreign-aid program.

The creation of the ***North Atlantic Treaty Organization (NATO)*** in 1949 marked the first peacetime military alliance in American history. To the Truman Doctrine's political-diplomatic commitments and the Marshall Plan's economic assistance, NATO added the military commitment to keep U.S. troops in Europe and the *collective defense* pledge that the United States would defend its European allies if they were attacked. Article 5 of the NATO treaty affirmed this pledge of collective defense: "The Parties agree that an armed attack against one or more of them in Europe or North America shall be considered an attack against them all" (see "At the Source," p. 125). This included the commitment to use nuclear weapons against the Soviet Union, even if the attack was on Europe but not directly on the United States. All this was quite a change from earlier American foreign policy, such as George Washington's "beware entangling alliances" and 1930s isolationism. The 82–13 Senate vote ratifying the NATO treaty made clear that this was a consensual change.

Yet within months the Soviet threat became even more formidable. Reports emerged in August 1949 that the Soviet Union now also had nuclear weapons. This came as a surprise to the American public and even to the Truman administration. Could the Soviets really have achieved this on their own? Were spies at work stealing America's nuclear secrets? Although the answers to these questions were unclear at the time, what was certain was that the U.S. nuclear monopoly was broken, and thus the requirements of nuclear deterrence were going to have to be recalculated.

At virtually the same time the threat to containment grew worse as the Cold War was extended from Europe to Asia. On October 1, 1949, the People's Republic of China was proclaimed by the Chinese communists, led by Mao Zedong and Zhou Enlai, who had

## AT THE SOURCE

### THE NORTH ATLANTIC TREATY

"The Parties to this Treaty . . . seek to promote stability and well-being in the North Atlantic area. . . .

*Art. 3.* In order more effectively to achieve the objectives of this Treaty, the Parties, separately and jointly, by means of continuous and effective self-help and mutual aid, will maintain and develop their individual and collective capacity to resist armed attack. . . .

*Art. 5.* The Parties agree that an armed attack against one or more of them in Europe or North America shall be considered an attack against them all; and consequently they agree that, if such an armed attack occurs, each of them, in exercise of the right of individual or collective self-defense recognized by Article 51 of the Charter of the United Nations, will assist the Party or Parties, [taking] such actions as it deems necessary, including the use of armed force, to restore and maintain the security of the North Atlantic area. . . ."

*Signed in 1949 by twelve founding members: Belgium, Canada, Denmark, France, Iceland, Italy, Luxembourg, the Netherlands, Norway, Portugal, the United Kingdom, and the United States.*

Source: *Department of State Bulletin* 20.507 (March 20, 1949).

won China's civil war. Now China, the world's most populous country, joined the Soviet Union, the world's largest, as communism's giant powers. "Red China," for many Americans, seemed an even more ominous enemy than the Soviet Union.

These developments prompted a reassessment of U.S. strategy. ***NSC-68,*** a seminal security-planning paper developed in early 1950 by President Truman's National Security Council, called for three important shifts in U.S. strategy (see "At the Source," p. 126). First, there needed to be a *globalization* of containment. The threat was not just in Europe and Asia, but everywhere: "the assault on free institutions is world-wide now."[10] This meant that U.S. commitments had to be extended to span the globe. Allies needed to be defended, vital sea lanes protected, and access to strategic raw materials maintained. Part of the rationale was also psychological: the concern that a communist gain anywhere would be perceived more generally as the tide turning in their favor and thus would hurt American credibility.

Second, NSC-68 proposed a *militarization* of containment. The Truman Doctrine and the Marshall Plan were largely diplomatic and economic measures. What was needed

## AT THE SOURCE

### NSC-68

"The fundamental design of those who control the Soviet Union and the international communist movement . . . calls for the complete subversion or forcible destruction of the machinery of government and structure of society in the countries of the non-Soviet world and their replacement by an apparatus and structure subservient to and controlled from the Kremlin. To that end Soviet efforts are now directed toward the domination of the Eurasian land mass. The United States, as the principal center of power in the non-Soviet world and bulwark of opposition to Soviet expansion, is the principal enemy whose integrity and vitality must be subverted or destroyed by one means or another if the Kremlin is to achieve its fundamental design.

The Soviet Union is developing the military capacity to support its design for world domination. . . .

A more rapid build-up of political, economic, and military strength and thereby of confidence in the free world than is now contemplated is the only course which is consistent with progress toward achieving our fundamental purpose. The frustration of the Kremlin design requires the free world to develop a successfully functioning political and economic system and a vigorous political offensive against the Soviet Union. These, in turn, require an adequate military shield under which they can develop. It is necessary to have the military power to deter, if possible, Soviet expansion, and to defeat, if necessary, aggressive Soviet or Soviet-directed actions of a limited or total character. . . . Unless our combined strength is rapidly increased, our allies will tend to become increasingly reluctant to support a firm foreign policy on our part and increasingly anxious to seek other solutions, even though they are aware that appeasement means defeat. . . .

The whole success of the proposed program hangs ultimately on recognition by this Government, the American people, and all free peoples, that the cold war is in fact a real war in which the survival of the free world is at stake."

Source: Text of memorandum no. NSC-68, from U.S. Department of State, *Foreign Relations of the United States 1950*, 1: 237–39.

now was a broad and extensive military buildup: a global ring of overseas military bases, military alliances beyond NATO, and a substantial increase in defense spending. The latter had to be pursued, the NSC-68 strategists stressed, even if it meant federal budget deficits and higher taxes.

The third step called for by NSC-68 was the development of the ***hydrogen bomb***. As destructive as the atomic bomb was, a hydrogen bomb (or H-bomb) would be vastly more destructive. Now that the Soviets had developed the A-bomb much sooner than anticipated, the development of the H-bomb was deemed necessary to maintain nuclear deterrence. Some policy makers believed that the United States should pursue nuclear arms–control agreements with the Soviet Union before crossing this next threshold of a nuclear arms race. But NSC-68 dismissed the prospect of the Soviets' being serious about arms-control negotiations.

NSC-68 was never formally approved. Its recommendations were tough, both strategically and politically, and thus stirred debate within the Truman administration. All that debate became largely moot, though, when a few months later the Korean War broke out. There now could be little doubt that, as President Truman stated it, "communism was acting in Korea just as Hitler, Mussolini, and the Japanese had acted 10, 15, and 20 years earlier."[11] The Korean War lasted three years and ended largely in stalemate. Its lessons were mixed, on the one hand reinforcing the view of the communist threat as globalized, while on the other showing the difficulties of land wars in Asia. It was also during this time that the United States first began getting involved in another part of Asia, Vietnam, sending aid to the French as they sought to maintain their colonial control against nationalist-communist independence forces led by Ho Chi Minh.

## *Intensification, 1950s to the Early 1960s*

Over the rest of the 1950s and into the 1960s the Cold War intensified in virtually every global region. In Europe, West Germany was brought into NATO, not only to strengthen the NATO alliance, but also to address concerns rooted deep in European historical memories about Germany's rising again. In addition to "keeping the Americans in" and "the Soviets out," by integrating Germany into the U.S.-dominated alliance, NATO also was intended, with World Wars I and II in mind, to "keep the Germans down."[12] The Soviets' response, though, was to formalize their military alliance in Eastern Europe through the Warsaw Pact. The Soviets also demonstrated their determination to maintain their bloc when in 1956 they invaded Hungary to put down a political revolution that threatened communist control. The Soviet invasion left thousands dead and even more imprisoned. Despite much rhetoric from Secretary of State John Foster Dulles about not just the containment but the "rollback" of communism, NATO and the United States did nothing significant to aid the Hungarian freedom fighters.

In 1952 the United States ended the military occupation it had maintained in Japan since the end of World War II. Defense agreements were signed for U.S. troops and bases to be maintained there, both to help defend Japan and as part of the overall containment strategy in Asia. Japan had by then begun functioning as a democracy under a constitution written largely by U.S. officials and including provisions that renounced war and that permanently limited the size and scope of the Japanese military to "self-defense forces." Thus as with Germany, the U.S. strategy in Japan was to finish the business of World War II and start the business of the Cold War, in which these former U.S. enemies were now U.S. allies against the Soviet Union, China, and world communism.

As mentioned in the preceding section, this period was also when the United States began its involvement in Vietnam. The United States provided some aid to the French, for whom Vietnam was still a colony, and then stepped up its involvement following the French defeat in 1954. The American concern was not only Vietnam itself: Vietnam was the original case on which the domino theory was based. "You have a row of dominoes set up," as President Eisenhower stated at a 1954 press conference. "You knock over the first one, and what will happen to the last one is the certainty that it will go over very quickly. So you could have a beginning of a disintegration that would have the most profound influences."[13] Throughout this period the United States got more and more involved in Vietnam. Also in Asia, the United States and its allies created the Southeast Asia Treaty Organization (SEATO), somewhat modeled after NATO, to be the Asian link in the chain of alliances with which Eisenhower and Dulles sought to ring the globe.

In the Middle East, the Baghdad Pact was set up in 1955; within a year it included Iran, Iraq, Pakistan, Turkey, and Great Britain, with the United States as a de facto but not a formal member. Iraq withdrew from the group in 1958 following a radical coup against its monarchy; the rest of the alliance continued, albeit weakened, under the title Central Treaty Organization (CENTO). Containment was also manifested in Iran in 1953 in the U.S.-led covert action to bring the shah of Iran back to power and depose Prime Minister Mohammed Mossadegh, and in Lebanon in 1958 with the intervention of U.S. Marines in support of the pro-American government against its more radical domestic foes. The Lebanon case was made into a more general precedent, under the rubric of the Eisenhower Doctrine, of U.S. willingness to provide military support to any state in the Middle East against "overt armed aggression from any nation controlled by international communism."[14]

In Latin America, Cold War opposition to Soviet influence was cast as the contemporary follow-up to the Monroe Doctrine. The major challenge came in Cuba in 1958–59 with the revolution led by Fidel Castro. As in Vietnam and elsewhere, the Cuban revolution was a mix of nationalism, anti-imperialism, and communism. Historians continue to debate whether the absolute antagonism that developed between Castro's Cuba and the United States was inevitable, or whether some modus vivendi could have been worked out. Whatever chance there may have been for something other than adversarial relations was gone after the disastrous 1961 Bay of Pigs invasion. The Eisenhower administration planned and the Kennedy administration launched this covert project, in which the United States trained, supplied, and assisted Cuban exiles in an attempted invasion of Cuba aimed at overthrowing Castro. The invasion failed miserably, embarrassing the United States, leaving Castro in power, and intensifying hatreds and fears on both sides.*

As for nuclear-deterrence doctrine, this period saw a number of developments. For a while the Eisenhower administration pursued the doctrine of ***massive retaliation,*** by which it threatened to resort to nuclear weapons to counter any Soviet challenge anywhere of any kind. This doctrine was not very credible, though: If a threat was made and delivered on, there would be nuclear war; if a threat was made and not delivered on, its credibility would be undermined, as in the case of the boy who cried wolf. It also was quite risky, especially as the Soviets kept pace with and even seemed poised to overtake the U.S. nuclear program. The Soviets beat the Americans into space in 1957 with the launching of the *Sputnik* satellite. That same year they also tested their first intercontinental ballistic missile (ICBM), which meant that they now had the capacity to overcome large distances and reach U.S. territory with a nuclear attack. This led to great fears of a "missile gap," a Soviet advantage in nuclear weapons, and prompted a massive U.S. nuclear buildup during the Kennedy administration.

In October 1962 the Cuban missile crisis brought the United States and the Soviet Union to the brink of nuclear war.[15] The Soviet decision to base nuclear missiles in Cuba was a daring and by most accounts reckless move. The Soviets defended it as an attempt to equalize the imbalance caused by the massive U.S. nuclear buildup under Kennedy and by the stationing of U.S. nuclear forces close to Soviet borders at bases in Turkey and other NATO countries in Europe. For its part, Cuba saw this new Soviet commitment as a way to guarantee that there would not be another Bay of Pigs invasion. Whatever the claims, the effect was to take the world dangerously close to nuclear war.

In the end the crisis was managed effectively.† Nuclear war was averted. And by most assessments, especially at the time, it was the Soviets who backed down, the United States that "won." But the world had come so close—too close—to nuclear war. Thus, although many saw in the Cuban and Soviet actions that started the crisis confirmation of U.S. global-containment and nuclear-deterrence doctrines, the dangerous dynamics of a situation that could have had catastrophic consequences drove home, as never before, the risks of the Cold War.

---

*See p. 139 for further discussion of the Bay of Pigs as an example of flawed foreign policy decision-making.

†See p. 140 for further discussion of the Cuban Missile Crisis.

## Principles: Ideological Bipolarity and the Third World "ABC" Approach

One of the primary differences between the Cold War and other historical great-power struggles was that the Cold War was not just between rival nations but also between opposing ideologies. This "ideological bipolarity" can be seen in the Truman Doctrine, the Marshall Plan, and many other official pronouncements. There was not much doubt then, and there is even less now, about the evils of communism. Almost immediately after World War II, the Soviets had shown in Poland and elsewhere in Eastern Europe that they had little interest in allowing democracy. In this respect containment was consistent with American principles. The controversy, though, was less about what the United States opposed than whom it supported, and how it did so.

This wasn't so much a problem in Western Europe, where genuinely democratic leaders and political parties emerged (although in countries such as Italy, where the Communist party had major electoral strength, the CIA did covertly seek to manipulate elections). But quite a few Third World dictators garbed themselves in the rhetoric of freedom and democracy, though they really fitted only an "ABC" definition of democracy—"anything but communism." One doesn't have to be so naive as to expect the United States to support only regimes good at heart and pure in practice. But the ABC rationale was used repeatedly as if there could be only two options, the communists or the other guy, whoever he might be and whatever his political practices. Moreover, the criteria by which leaders, parties, and movements were deemed communist were often quite subjective, if not manipulative.

### *Support for "ABC Democrats"*

Vietnam is a good example of the U.S. support for an "ABC" leadership. There is much historical debate over whether a relationship could have been worked out with Ho Chi Minh, the Vietnamese leader who was both nationalist and communist. Ho had worked with the Allies during World War II against the Japanese occupation of Vietnam, even receiving arms and aid from the United States. After the war he made appeals to Washington for help, based on America's professed anticolonialism, against France's effort to reestablish its own colonial rule. He even cited the American Declaration of Independence in proclaiming Vietnam's independence in 1945. There was no question that Ho was a communist; he believed in social revolution at home and received support from the Soviet Union and the Chinese communists. Yet when some experts suggested that as a nationalist, and like Tito in Yugoslavia,* Ho would not inevitably make his country a mere communist satellite, such thinking was summarily rejected. It wasn't so much that there was evidence to the contrary as that, as put in a 1949 State Department cable to the U.S. consulate in Hanoi, the "question of whether Ho was as much nationalist as Commie was irrelevant."[16] His communism was all that mattered. Indeed, much later, Melvin Laird, who had been ardently pro-war while a Republican congressman in the 1960s and as secretary of defense in the Nixon administration, acknowledged that "had we understood the depth of his [Ho Chi Minh's] nationalism, we might have been able to derail his communism early on."[17]

Thus the United States threw its support to one Vietnamese "ABC democrat" after another. In 1949, as their alternative to Ho Chi Minh, the French reinstalled Emperor Bao Dai. He was neither a democrat (he bore the title "emperor") nor a nationalist (having sat on the throne during the Japanese occupation in World War II) and he had little credibility with his own people. Internal State Department documents showed that Bao Dai was recognized as a French colonial puppet, but U.S. support for him was rationalized as the only alternative to "Commie domination."[18]

In 1954 the Vietnamese had won their war for independence and the French were forced to withdraw. Two nations, North and South Vietnam, were established, with Ho and the communists in control of the north and the anticommunists in control of the south. This partition was supposed to be temporary, with unification and general elections to be held within a few years. In searching for someone who could be built up as a nationalist alternative to Ho, the Eisenhower administration came up with Ngo Dinh Diem. Diem was not communist, but his "nationalist" credentials were more made in America than earned in the Vietnamese colonial struggles. He also was a Catholic in a largely Buddhist country. Diem's rule was highly authoritarian—opposing political parties were abolished, press censorship strictly enforced, Buddhists brutally repressed. He gave extensive power to his brother Ngo Dinh Nhu, by most accounts a shadowy and sinister figure. When a seventy-three-year-old Buddhist monk set himself on fire to protest the regime's repression, Nhu's wife made a sneering remark about Buddhist "barbecues."[19] Indeed, by 1963 Diem was so unpopular that the Kennedy administration had a hand in the coup that brought him down and killed him. Thus, in this case the cycle of contradicting principles ran its course—support an ally in the name of democracy who is at best an ABC democrat, but kill him off when he clearly is not the solution, and may even be part of the problem.

*Josip Broz, better known as Tito, was a communist who led the Yugoslav partisans against Nazi Germany and who became Yugoslavia's dictator after the war. In 1948, Tito broke with Stalin and the other members of the Warsaw Pact and began to develop independent ties to the West.

In Latin America generally, U.S. policy in the early Cold War was summed up in the comment about support for the Nicaraguan dictator Anastasio Somoza: "He may be an S.O.B., but he's our S.O.B."[20] The ***Alliance for Progress,*** established in 1961 by the Kennedy administration, initially was heralded as a shift away from this approach and toward promotion of democracy. "Our Alliance for Progress is an alliance of free governments," President Kennedy proclaimed, "and it must work to eliminate tyranny from a hemisphere in which it has no rightful place."[21] While JFK was pointing his rhetorical finger at Cuba and Fidel Castro, the social and economic elites and the militaries in much of the rest of Latin America, seeing their own oligarchic interests threatened by political and economic reforms, undermined "la Alianza." Military coups ousted reformist governments in the early 1960s in Argentina, Brazil, Ecuador, Honduras, and elsewhere. Although the coup makers invoked anticommunism and containment, in most cases this was a transparent rationalization. Yet the United States largely bought it. In fact, in the case of Brazil, U.S. "enthusiasm" for the coup "was so palpable that Washington sent its congratulations even before the new regime could be installed."[22] The pro-American (Power) stance of these regimes was more important than their being nondemocratic (Principles).

To be sure, there were those who genuinely believed that communism was so bad that support for "anybody but a communist" and "anything but communism" was consistent with American principles, at least in relative terms and given an imperfect world. One of the problems with this defense, however, was the inclusion of more moderate socialists and nationalists in the "irredeemable communists" category. This attitude no doubt was due in part to the intolerance of ideological biopolarity: it recognized no third way. The ABC attitude also reflected a calculation that, in the event of conflicts between Power and Principles in the U.S. national interest, Principles were to give way.

## CIA Covert Action

Questions about consistency with Principles also were raised by CIA covert action seeking the overthrow of anti-American governments, including democratically chosen ones. A commission established by President Eisenhower provided the following recommendation: "Another important requirement is an aggressive covert psychological, political and paramilitary organization more effective, more unique, and if necessary, more ruthless than that employed by the enemy. No one should be permitted to stand in the way of the prompt, efficient and secure accomplishment of this mission. It is now clear that we are facing an implacable enemy. . . . There are no rules in such a game. Hitherto acceptable norms of human conduct do not apply."[23]

One of the cases in which this strategy was applied, in Guatemala in 1954, was discussed in Chapter 1 as an example of "4 Ps" tensions and trade-offs. Another case was that of Iran in 1953. In this case, as we saw earlier in this chapter, the target was the Iranian prime minister Mohammed Mossadegh, who had begun both to nationalize foreign-owned oil companies (Prosperity) and to develop closer relations with the Soviet Union (Power). The United States supported the exiled shah, and the CIA assisted royalist forces in a plot to return the shah to power. The plot succeeded, albeit with a "wave of repression" and "a purge of the armed forces and government bureaucracy" that "continued for more than a year, silencing all sources of opposition to the new regime." In the years following the coup the CIA helped establish and train the shah's new secret police, known as SAVAK. Over the next twenty to twenty-five years, SAVAK "became not just an externally directed intelligence agency but also a powerful, feared and hated instrument of domestic repression"—not exactly a practitioner of democratic principles.[24]

## Prosperity: Creation of the Liberal International Economic Order

Along with the dangers of isolationism and appeasement, one of the other lessons that U.S. leaders had learned from the 1920s and 1930s concerned the dangers of trade protectionism and other "beggar-my-neighbor" economic policies. These policies hurt global prosperity as well as that of the United States. They also contributed to the political instabilities that ultimately led to World War II. Thus one of the other major components of postwar U.S. policy was the creation of the ***liberal international economic order (LIEO).*** The term "liberal" as used in this context means a relatively open, market-based, free-trade system with a minimum of tariffs and other government-initiated trade barriers, and with international economic relations worked out through negotiations. The opposite of liberalism in this context is not conservatism, as in the domestic-policy context, but protectionism.

### *The Major International Economic Institutions*

As set up in the 1940s, the LIEO had three principal components: (1) a free trade system under the rubric of the ***General Agreement on Tariffs and Trade (GATT);*** (2) an international monetary system, based on fixed exchange rates and the gold standard, and overseen by the ***International Monetary Fund (IMF);*** and (3) an international lending and aid system under the International Bank for Reconstruction and Development, also known as the ***World Bank.***

The establishment of GATT did not bring about instantaneous free trade. Exceptions were made—for example, for agriculture, which for political and other reasons was much harder to open up to free trade. There were loopholes, as for labor-intensive industries such as shoes and textiles, which were allowed some, albeit not total, protection. And trade disputes continued. The success of GATT was in keeping the arrow pointed in the direction of free trade, in providing a mechanism for managing trade disputes so as to prevent their escalation to trade wars, and in moving the world gradually toward freer trade through periodic "rounds" of negotiations.

Protectionism had generated another insidious practice: the competitive manipulations of currencies. The fixed exchange rates of the IMF system sought to eliminate this form of destructive economic competition and help provide the monetary stability essential for global economic growth. The basic gold-standard exchange rate was set at $36 per ounce of gold. Countries whose international payments were not in balance (i.e., they imported more than they exported) could get some assistance from the IMF but also had to meet stringent IMF guidelines called "conditionalities" for economic and other reforms in order to get that assistance.

The World Bank later would grow into a major source of development aid for Third World countries, but initially it was focused more on European reconstruction. As of 1955, even though the U.S. Marshall Plan had ceased, about half of World Bank loans were going to industrialized countries; by 1965 this was down to one-fourth, and by 1967 virtually all lending was going to Third World development projects. The World Bank itself was chartered to lend only to governments, but over time it added an affiliate, the International Finance Corporation, that made loans to private enterprises involved in development projects.

## *Critiques: Economic Hegemony? Neo-Imperialism?*

Although in these and other respects the LIEO did provide broad economic benefits internationally, critics point out that it largely reinforced American economic dominance, or *economic hegemony.* Voting rights in both the IMF and the World Bank were proportional to capital contributions, which meant that, as the largest contributor of funds, the United States had a correspondingly large voting share. In GATT negotiations, American positions prevailed more often than not. Indeed, the emphasis on free markets, open trade, and minimal government intervention in the economy also fitted American laissez-faire economic ideology. And with Europe and Japan still recovering and rebuilding from World War II, the United States dominated the world economy. Thus, even though other countries benefited from the LIEO, it did also help maintain American economic hegemony to go with American diplomatic dominance and military superiority.

Another critique points to corporate interests as driving U.S. policy. This point is often stressed by revisionists in the debate over the origins of the Cold War. Critics cite cases such as Guatemala, where U.S. policy followed the interests of the United Fruit Company, and Iran, where big oil companies were eager to see the shah restored to power, knowing he would return property to them that had been nationalized under Mossadegh. Even in the case of Vietnam, where intrinsic U.S. economic interests were more limited, the fear was said to be of the succession of communist "dominoes" whose fall would undermine global capitalism. So, too, the Marshall Plan is explained as an effort to rebuild European markets in order to generate demand for American exports and investments, thereby overcoming the underconsumption-overproduction dilemma and averting a depression. The deciding factor in the formation of U.S. foreign policy, in this view, was the private interests of multinational corporations, big banks, and the other captains of global capitalism.

## Foreign Policy Politics and the Cold War Consensus

The main pattern in U.S. foreign policy politics during this period was the "Cold War consensus." This consensus was marked by three fundamental components: presidential dominance over Congress, a vast expansion of the executive-branch foreign and defense policy bureaucracy, and a fervent anticommunism pervading public opinion, culminating in the scourge of McCarthyism.

### *Pennsylvania Avenue Diplomacy: A One-Way Street*

The term *spirit of bipartisanship* was coined during this period to describe the strong support for the foreign policies of President Truman, a Democrat, from the Republican-majority Congress, led by the Senate Foreign Relations Committee chair, Arthur Vandenberg. What made this support especially striking was the extent of the foreign commitments being made—declaring U.S. willingness "to support free peoples everywhere" (the Truman Doctrine), spending billions of dollars in foreign aid (the Marshall Plan), joining a military alliance during peacetime for the first time in U.S. history (NATO)—all as a matter of consensus and presidential-congressional cooperation.

Before crumbling over the Vietnam War in the Johnson and Nixon administrations, this foreign policy bipartisanship lasted through almost every conceivable Pennsylvania Avenue combination: a Democratic president supported by a Republican Congress (Truman, 1947–48), a Republican president supported by a Democratic Congress (Eisenhower, 1955–60), a Republican president and a Republican Congress (Eisenhower, 1953–54), and Democratic presidents and Democratic Congresses (Truman 1949–52, Kennedy 1961–63, and Johnson 1963 to about 1966). One prominent theory of the day spoke of "one President but two presidencies": the domestic policy one, in which the president succeeded in getting his proposals through Congress only 40 percent of the time, and the foreign policy one, in which the president's success rate was 70 percent.[25]

One of the reasons for this presidential dominance was that, although the Cold War was not a war per se, the fearsome nature of the Soviet threat and the overhanging danger of nuclear war were seen as the functional and moral equivalents of war. Given these exigencies, the presidency had the greater institutional capacity to conduct foreign affairs.

Only the presidency possessed the information and expertise necessary for understanding the world, could move with the necessary speed and decisiveness in making key decisions, and had the will and the capacity to guard secrecy. Almost everywhere the president went, the "button" (the code box for ordering a nuclear attack) went with him—and it was conceivable that he would have less time to make a decision about whether to press it than it typically takes Congress just to have a quorum call. For its part, Congress was seen as too parochial to pay sufficient attention to world affairs, too amateur to understand them, and too slow and unwieldy in its procedures to respond with the necessary dispatch. Even its own foreign policy leaders had expressed strong doubts about its foreign policy competence. Congress "has served us well in our internal life," wrote Senator J. William Fulbright, the longest-serving chair of the Senate Foreign Relations Committee in American history, but "the source of an effective foreign policy under our system is Presidential power." Fulbright went on to propose that the president be given "a measure of power in the conduct of our foreign affairs that we [i.e., the Congress] have hitherto jealously withheld."[26] Fulbright's counterpart, House Foreign Affairs Committee Chair Thomas (Doc) Morgan, went even further, saying that he had a "blanket, all-purpose decision rule: support all executive branch proposals."[27]

Three areas of foreign policy show how in the basic relationship of separate institutions sharing powers, the presidency now had the much larger share.

WAR POWERS In the Korean War, Truman never asked Congress for a declaration of war. He claimed that the resolution passed by the UN Security Council for "urgent military measures . . . to repel the attack" provided him with sufficient authority to commit U.S. troops. Moreover, this wasn't really a war, Truman asserted, just "a police action." There is little doubt that Congress would have supported the president with a declaration of war if it had been asked. But in not asking, Truman set a new precedent for presidential assertion of war powers. This "police action" lasted three years, involved a full-scale military mobilization, incurred more than fifty thousand American casualties, and ended in stalemate.

In January 1951 Truman announced his intention to send the first divisions of U.S. ground troops to be stationed in Europe as part of NATO. Here he argued that he was merely fulfilling international responsibilities that Congress had previously approved (in this instance by Senate ratification in 1949 of the NATO treaty) and thus did not need any further congressional approval. Congressional opposition to the NATO deployment was greater than in the Korean War case but still was not strong enough to pass anything more than a nonbinding resolution urging, but not requiring, the president to obtain congressional approval for future NATO deployments.

The trend continued under President Eisenhower, although with some interesting twists. In 1955 a crisis was brewing over threats by China against Taiwan. Unlike Truman, Eisenhower did go to Congress for formal legislative authorization, but he did so with a very open-ended and highly discretionary resolution authorizing him to use military force if and when he deemed it necessary as the situation developed. This kind of anticipatory authorization was very different from declaring war or taking other military action against a specific country. Yet Eisenhower's request was approved by overwhelming margins, 83–3 in the Senate and 410–3 in the House. House Speaker Sam Rayburn (D-Texas) even remarked, "If the President had done what is proposed here without consulting Congress, he would have had no criticism from me."[28]

In 1957 Eisenhower requested and got a very similar anticipatory authorization for a potential crisis in the Middle East. Here the concern was Soviet gains of influence amid increasing radicalism and instability in a number of Arab countries. Yet once again by lopsided votes, Congress authorized the president "to employ the armed forces of the United States as he deems necessary . . . [against] international communism."[29]

COVERT ACTION We find scattered examples of covert action throughout U.S. history. In 1819, for example, President James Monroe took covert action aimed against Spain in the Spanish territory of Florida and kept it secret from Congress. In World War II the Office of Strategic Services (OSS) played a key role in the war effort. But it was only with the onset of the Cold War that the CIA was created as the first permanent intelligence agency in U.S. history and that covert action was undertaken on a sustained, systematic basis.

Here we see another pattern of disproportionate power sharing, and again as much because of congressional abdication as because of presidential usurpation. It was Congress that created the CIA as part of the National Security Act of 1947 and the Central Intelligence Agency Act of 1949. The latter legislation included a provision authorizing the CIA to "perform such other functions and duties related to intelligence affecting the national security"—i.e., covert operations. The members of congressional oversight committees were charged with responsibility for keeping an eye on these covert operations. But most senators and representatives who served on these committees during the early Cold War saw themselves more as boosters and protectors than as checkers and balancers. The "black budget" procedure, whereby funds are appropriated to the CIA without its having to provide virtually any details of its programs and its accounts, was set up with a congressional wink and nod.

INTERNATIONAL COMMITMENTS Another manifestation of presidential dominance was the much greater use of ***executive agreements*** rather than treaties for making significant international commitments.[30] If we compare 1789 to 1945 with the first three post–World War II decades (1945–76), we see two major trends. One is a huge overall increase in U.S. international commitments, from 2,335 in the one-hundred-fifty-plus-year period to 7,420 in the thirty-plus-year period, for annual averages of 15 before 1945 and 239 after. This skyrocketing overall number demonstrates how much more extensive U.S. international involvements had become. Second, a trend within these numbers shows more and more frequent use of executive agreements rather than treaties. Whereas the 1789–1945 breakdown is 843 treaties and 1,492 executive agreements (i.e., executive agreements as 64 percent of the total), for 1945–76 it was 437 and 6,983 respectively (94 percent).[31] This increase in the proportion of U.S. commitments represented by executive agreements shows how much presidents were trying to reduce Congress's role in the making of foreign policy.[32]

We do need to note that many executive agreements dealt with technicalities and details of relations and were pursuant to statutes passed by Congress, and thus some of the statistical difference is accounted for simply by the sheer increase in technicalities and details that had to be worked out. But some of the pattern is due to the fact that, the greater the policy significance of the issue, the more likely were Cold War–era presidents to use executive agreements rather than treaties. Military and diplomatic matters, for example, were more than 50 percent more likely to take the form of executive agreements than were economic, transportation, communications, or cultural-technical matters. Among the significant political-military commitments made by executive agreements were the placement of U.S. troops in Guatemala (1947) and in mainland China in support of Jiang Jei-shi (1948); the establishment of U.S. bases in the Philippines (1947); the sending of military missions to Honduras (1950) and El Salvador (1957); security pledges to Turkey, Pakistan, and Iran (1959); and an expanded security commitment to Thailand (1962).[33]

In sum, Pennsylvania Avenue had pretty much become a one-way street in terms of foreign policy politics during the first half of the Cold War. The arrow pointed down the avenue, away from Capitol Hill and toward the White House.

## *Executive-Branch Politics and the Creation of the "National Security State"*

To exercise his expanded powers the president needed larger, stronger, and more numerous executive-branch departments and agencies. Again, we can draw a parallel with the expansions of the executive branch during World Wars I and II. But this time the expansion was even farther reaching and longer lasting; it created the "national security state."[34]

One of the first steps in this process was the formation in 1947 of the ***National Security Council (NSC).*** The original purpose of the NSC was to provide a formal mechanism for bringing together the president's principal foreign policy advisers.* The NSC originally had only a small staff, and the national security adviser was a low-profile position.

*The standing members of the NSC were the president, the vice president, the secretary of state, and the secretary of defense. The national security adviser, the CIA director, and the chair of the Joint Chiefs of Staff were technically defined as advisers. Depending on the issue at hand, other Cabinet officials such as the attorney general and the secretary of the treasury may also be included in NSC meetings. The same has been true for political officials such as the White House chief of staff.

Few people can even name Truman's or Eisenhower's national security advisers. But beginning in the Kennedy administration, and peaking with Henry Kissinger in the Nixon administration, the national security adviser became even more powerful and prominent than the secretary of state in the making of U.S. foreign policy.

The ***Department of Defense (DOD)*** was created in 1949 to combine the formerly separate Departments of War (created in 1789) and the Navy (separated from the Department of War in 1798). During World War II, the Joint Chiefs of Staff had been set up to coordinate the military services. In 1947 the position of secretary of defense was created, but each military service still had its own Cabinet-level secretary. But even this proved to be inadequate coordination and consolidation, and the DOD was established with the army, navy, and air force and a newly created chair of the ***Joint Chiefs of Staff*** all reporting to the secretary of defense, who by law had to be a civilian. Measured in terms of both personnel and budget, DOD was and is the largest Cabinet department. And its building, the Pentagon, is the largest government office building.

The Central Intelligence Agency (CIA) was also created during this period, as noted earlier in this chapter. In addition, a number of other intelligence agencies were created, including the National Security Agency (1952) and the Defense Intelligence Agency (1961).

The State Department itself was vastly expanded. It grew from pre–World War II levels of about one thousand employees in Washington and two thousand overseas to about seven thousand and twenty-three thousand, respectively. It also added new bureaus and functions, notably the Policy Planning Staff established in 1949 with George Kennan ("X") as its first director, charged with strategic planning.

A number of other foreign-policy-related agencies were also created during this time: the Economic Cooperation Administration to administer the Marshall Plan; the Agency for International Development (AID), in charge of distributing foreign aid; the Arms Control and Disarmament Agency (ACDA) to monitor and negotiate arms-control agreements; the U.S. Information Agency (USIA) to represent U.S. policies abroad; the U.S. Trade Representative (USTR) to conduct international trade negotiations; and others.

It again is important to stress that this vast expansion of the executive branch was made largely with the consent of Congress. Some presidents did exploit, manipulate, and exceed the intended congressional mandates. But to appreciate fully the politics of the Cold War era, we need to take into account both seizings by presidential usurpation and cedings by congressional abdication.

**Flawed Executive-Branch Decision Making: The Bay of Pigs, 1961** The 1961 ***Bay of Pigs*** debacle is one of the most often cited cases of flawed executive-branch decision making.[35] It involved a U.S.-engineered invasion of Cuba by exiled forces seeking to overthrow Fidel Castro. (The Bay of Pigs was where they landed on the Cuban coast.) Not only did the invasion fail miserably, but major questions were raised about how the Kennedy administration could have believed that it had any chance of succeeding. Many of the assumptions on which the plan was based were exceedingly weak: for example, the cover story that the United States played no role in the invasion had already been contradicted by press reports that anti-Castro rebels were being trained by the CIA; and the planners asserted that the Cuban people were ready to rise up, even though it was less than two years since Castro had come to power and he was still widely seen by his people as a great liberator. Despite these obvious warning signs, a groupthink dynamic dominated the policy-making process. Arthur Schlesinger, Jr., a noted historian and at the time a special assistant to President Kennedy, later explained that he felt that "a course of objection would have accomplished little save to gain me a name as a nuisance."[36]

CIA intelligence failures also contributed to the Bay of Pigs fiasco. A report by the CIA's own inspector general, written in the immediate aftermath but declassified only in 1998, stressed the agency's "failure to subject the project, especially in its latter frenzied stages, to a cold and objective appraisal. . . . Timely and objective appraisal of the operation in the months before the invasion, including study of all available intelligence, would have demonstrated to agency officials that the clandestine paramilitary operation had almost totally failed." The report also criticized the "failure to advise the President, at an appropriate time, that success had become dubious and to recommend that the operation be therefore cancelled."[37] President Kennedy's own comment summed it up best: "How could I have been so stupid to let them go ahead?"[38]

SUCCESSFUL CRISIS DECISION MAKING: THE CUBAN MISSILE CRISIS, 1962 On the other hand, the case most often cited as a model of effective decision making is the 1962 ***Cuban missile crisis.***[39] Having learned from the Bay of Pigs, President Kennedy set up a process and structure that were more deliberate in their pace and deliberative in their consideration of options. He went outside normal bureaucratic channels and established a special crisis decision-making team, called ExCom, with members drawn from his own Cabinet and former high-ranking foreign policy officials of previous administrations, such as Dean Acheson, secretary of state under Truman. Robert Kennedy also was a key player, an unusual foreign policy crisis role for an attorney general, but a logical one for the brother of the president.

In one sense the reason that the decision-making process worked so well in this case was that formal structures were adapted and modified. The ExCom process gets much of the credit for bringing the superpowers back from the brink of nuclear war and for the successful resolution of the crisis. President Kennedy himself also gets an important share of the credit: no structure like ExCom can be established, no decision-making process function effectively, unless the president provides the mandate and the leadership.

It also was out of the Cuban missile crisis that bureaucratic politics and other important theories of intra-executive-branch politics were developed. Much of this was based on Graham Allison's 1971 book, *The Essence of Decision: Explaining the Cuban Missile Crisis.*[40] As recounted and analyzed by Allison and others who followed, much of what transpired during the Cuban missile crisis was quite inconsistent with the traditional rational-actor model (described in Chapter 2 and Reading 2.2) of hierarchical, orderly, and structured decision making and policy implementation. Further research has raised doubts about a number of the case "facts" first stated by Allison.[41] However, as Richard Betts notes, "other chilling examples have turned up" of dangerously dysfunctional bureaucratic politics during this crisis.[42] Bureaucratic problems still were there, even if they were not so bad as originally depicted and were ultimately transcended by the effectiveness of the ExCom structure and presidential leadership.

## *Interest Groups, the Media, and Public Opinion: Benefits and Dangers of Consensus*

On the one hand there clearly are benefits when presidents are able to count on public, interest-group, and even media support for their foreign policies. But consensus, when taken too far, also poses dangers and has disadvantages.

THE MEDIA AS CHEERLEADERS The news media largely carried over their role as uncritical supporters, even cheerleaders, for official policy from World War II to the Cold War. To the extent that there was media criticism and pressure, it was for the president to take a tougher stand. Indeed, the news media played a significant role in the shaping of Cold War attitudes. Many give credit for coining the term "Cold War" to Walter Lippmann, the leading newspaper columnist of the day. Henry Luce, owner and publisher of *Time* and *Life,* the two leading newsmagazines, personally championed South Vietnamese president Diem and ensured favorable, even laudatory coverage for him. Even the *New York Times* followed suit, as in a 1957 editorial titled "Diem on Democracy" in which the editors hailed Diem for being so true to democracy that "Thomas Jefferson would have no quarrel."[43]

In the Bay of Pigs case, the media actually had prior information about the planned invasion but for the most part refrained from publishing it. Most of what appeared in the media about the plan was "designed not to alert the American public to the potentially disastrous course of its own government, but to advance the universally accepted propaganda line that Cuba under Castro was courting disaster."[44] Although some of the postmortems were self-critical, others were more "expressions of sadness that the job was 'bungled,' that it did not 'succeed'—and that a well-meaning President *got caught* and got a 'bloody nose.'"[45] A few weeks after the Bay of Pigs, and despite his other acknowledgements of responsibility, President Kennedy delivered a very strong speech to the American Newspaper Publishers Association broadly construing the national security rationale as a constraint on freedom of the press (see "At the Source," p. 142).

## AT THE SOURCE

AT THE SOURCE

### "IS IT NEWS?" OR "IS IT IN THE INTEREST OF NATIONAL SECURITY?"

**Excerpts from a Speech by President John F. Kennedy**

"I do ask every publisher, every editor, and every newsman in the nation to reexamine his own standards, and to recognize the nature of our country's peril. In time of war, the Government and the press have customarily joined in an effort, based largely on self-discipline, to prevent unauthorized disclosure to the enemy. In times of clear and present danger, the courts have held that even the privileged rights of the First Amendment must yield to the public's need for national security.

Today no war has been declared—and however fierce the struggle may be, it may never be declared in the traditional fashion. Our way of life is under attack. . . .

If the press is awaiting a declaration of war before it imposes the self-discipline of combat conditions, then I can only say that no war has ever imposed a greater threat to our security. If you are awaiting a finding of 'clear and present danger,' then I can only say that the danger has never been more clear and its presence has never been more imminent. . . .

It requires a change in outlook, a change in tactics, a change in mission by the Government, by the people, by every businessman and labor leader, and by every newspaper. For we are opposed around the world by a monolithic and ruthless conspiracy that relies primarily on covert means for expanding its sphere of influence—on infiltration instead of invasion, on subversion instead of elections, on intimidation instead of free choice, on guerrillas by night instead of armies by day. . . .

The facts of the matter are that this nation's foes have openly boasted of acquiring through our newspapers information they would otherwise hire agents to acquire through theft, bribery or espionage; that details of this nation's covert preparations to counter the enemy's covert operations have been available to every newspaper reader, friend and foe alike; that the size, the strength, the location, and the nature of our forces and weapons, and our plans and strategy for their use, have all been pinpointed in the press and other news media to a degree sufficient enough to satisfy any foreign power. . . .

The newspapers which printed these stories were loyal, patriotic, responsible and well-meaning. Had we been engaged in open warfare, they undoubtedly would not have published such items. But in the absence of open warfare, they recognized only the tests of journalism and not the tests of national security. And my question tonight is whether additional tests should not now be adopted. . . .

I am asking the members of the newspaper profession and the industry in this country to reexamine their own responsibilities—to consider the degree and nature of the present danger—and to heed the duty of self-restraint which that danger imposes upon all of us.

Every newspaper now asks itself with respect to every story: 'Is it news?' All I suggest is that you add the question: 'Is it in the interest of national security?' ”

Source: John F. Kennedy, speech to the American Newspaper Publishers Association, April 27, 1961, from *Public Papers of the Presidents, John F. Kennedy, 1961* (Washington, D.C.: U.S. Government Printing Office, 1962), 334–38.

Interest Groups Foreign policy interest groups were relatively few in number and mostly supportive during the early Cold War. There were some protest movements, such as the nuclear disarmament movement in the late 1950s. But more common, and more influential, were groups in favor of Cold War policies.

If anything, some of these groups were more assertive and more anticommunist than official policy. The "China lobby" strongly sided with Jiang Jei-shi and Taiwan, criticizing various administrations for not "unleashing" Jiang to retake mainland China. Another example hails from the early 1960s when, in the wake of the Cuban missile crisis, Kennedy explored a "mini-détente" with the Soviets. He was attacked quite stridently when he gave a June 1963 commencement speech at American University proposing that the United States "re-examine our attitude" toward the Soviet Union. He continued that the United States should "not be blind to our differences—but let us also direct our attention to our common interests and to the means by which those differences can be resolved."[46] When later that year Kennedy announced a $250 million sale of grain to the Soviet Union, even agricultural interest groups were unwilling to breach their anticommunism. "We oppose this action," ten Republican members of the House Agriculture Committee stated, "because we believe the vast majority of American farmers, like the vast majority of all Americans, are unwilling to sell out a high moral principle, even for solid gold."[47] At the same time a group called the Committee to Warn of the Arrival of Communist Merchandise on the Local Business Scene was operating in forty-seven states, harassing merchants who dared to sell Polish hams or other "commie" products.[48]

PUBLIC OPINION Public opinion was grounded firmly in the Cold War consensus. Internationalism prevailed over isolationism—65 percent to 8 percent in a typical poll. Eighty percent of Americans expressed support for NATO. Containment was ranked second by the public among all national objectives, domestic policy included.

Consensus, though, when taken too far, can breed intolerance, suspicion, and repression. This is what happened during the late 1940s and early 1950s. First, the revealingly named House Un-American Activities Committee (HUAC) launched a series of investigations claiming that communists had infiltrated American government and society. It would be affirmed much later, after the fall of the Soviet Union and the opening of Soviet archives, that some of these allegations in fact were true. Soviet spies did steal secrets for building the atomic bomb. They also operated within the State Department and other U.S. government agencies.[49] But the manner in which early Cold War anti-communism was pursued, the wide net cast, and the arbitrariness of so many of the accusations made took a profound toll on civil liberties and created an environment inimical to the openness of a democratic society. The standards for the "clear and present danger" test set by Justices Holmes and Brandeis (see Chapter 3) did not require the danger to be all that clear or all that present for national security to be invoked as the basis for limiting—indeed, violating—civil liberties. This was especially the case with McCarthyism.

Senator Joseph McCarthy, until then the relatively unknown junior Republican senator from Wisconsin, became the most rabid spokesperson and instigator in the hunt for "reds under the bed." The essence of the appeal of ***McCarthyism*** comes through in a speech the senator gave in Wheeling, West Virginia, in February 1950 (see "At the Source," p. 145). "The chips are down," McCarthy warned, not because communists were superior in any way, but because of "traitorous actions" by Americans. He pointed his finger right at the State Department—"the bright young men who are born with silver spoons in their mouths," this heart of America's foreign policy "thoroughly infested with Communists." Nor did McCarthy and his cohort stop there. One member of Congress even charged Secretary of State Dean Acheson with being "on Stalin's payroll." No less a figure than George Marshall—General Marshall, the World War II hero, former secretary of state, former secretary of defense—was accused by one reckless senator of being "a front man for traitors, a living lie."[50]

Nor was it only government that was being purged. Accusations were hurled all over American society. Hollywood blacklisted writers, actors, and directors accused of being communists even though they had not been convicted. Universities fired professors. Scientists who held jobs requiring security clearances lost their positions. The country was consumed with paranoia. Ironically, many of the accusations that were true were discredited by the broader sense of injustice and illegitimacy. And from a foreign policy perspec-

## AT THE SOURCE

AT THE SOURCE

### McCARTHYISM

#### Excerpts from a Speech by Senator Joseph McCarthy

"Today we are engaged in a final, all-out battle between Communistic atheism and Christianity. The modern champions of Communism have selected this as the time. And, ladies and gentlemen, the chips are down—they are truly down. . . .

Ladies and gentlemen, can there be anyone here tonight who is so blind as to say that the war is not on? Can there be anyone who fails to realize that the Communist world has said, 'The time is now'—that this is the time for the show-down between the democratic Christian world and the Communistic atheistic world?

The reason why we find ourselves in a position of impotency is not because our only powerful potential enemy has sent men to invade our shores, but rather because of the traitorous actions of those who have been treated so well by this Nation. It has not been the less fortunate or members of minority groups who have been selling this Nation out, but rather those who have had all the benefits that the wealthiest nation on earth has had to offer—the finest homes, the finest college education, and the finest jobs in Government we can give. This is glaringly true in the State Department. There the bright young men who are born with silver spoons in their mouths are the ones who have been worst. . . .

In my opinion the State Department, which is one of the most important government departments, is thoroughly infested with Communists.

I have in my hand 57 cases of individuals who would appear to be either card carrying members or certainly loyal to the Communist Party, but who nevertheless are still helping to shape our foreign policy. . . .

However the morals of our people have not been destroyed. They still exist. This cloak of numbness and apathy has only needed a spark to rekindle them. Happily, this spark has finally been supplied."

Source: Senator Joseph McCarthy, speech given February 9, 1950, in Wheeling, W.V., from *Congressional Record,* 81st Cong., 2nd sess., February 20, 1954, 58–61.

tive, McCarthyism's equation of dissent with disloyalty had a chilling effect on those both within government and outside it who might have provided constructive criticisms, alternative policy ideas, and the like. The kind of self-examination that is essential for any successful policy process thus was closed off.

## Summary

The early Cold War years were a period of crucial choices for American foreign policy. The policies pursued in these years not only addressed the immediate issues but also became the foundations and framework for the pursuit of the "4 Ps" in the decades that followed. Containment and nuclear deterrence were the central foreign policy doctrines by which American power was exercised. The United Nations was the main political-diplomatic institutional structure for the pursuit of peace. The LIEO was the main institutional structure for the international economy and the pursuit of prosperity. Anticommunism was the dominant set of beliefs by which American principles were said to be manifested. And foreign policy politics was marked by a strong consensus, even as American political institutions underwent major changes in their structure and interrelationship.

A number of questions were raised, however, both at the time and in retrospect. Although Cold War strategy proponents stressed the complementarity among the four core national-interest objectives, critics pointed out tensions and trade-offs that pitted one objective against another: for example, strengthening the United Nations vs. maximizing American power; pursuing containment vs. being true to principles. Concerns also were raised about the domestic political consensus, which, for all its benefits, also had a downside in the expansion of presidential power and violation of civil liberties.

These and other issues would become more difficult and more controversial beginning in the late 1960s and continuing through the 1980s.

## *American Foreign Policy* Online Student StudySpace

- What were the key elements of deterrence and containment?
- How well did they work?
- Is there something to the revisionist views of the origins of the Cold War?

For these and other study questions, as well as other features, check out Chapter 4 on the *American Foreign Policy* Online Student StudySpace at wwnorton.com/studyspace.

## Notes

[1]Dean G. Acheson, *Present at the Creation: My Years at the State Department* (New York: Norton, 1969).

[2]Winston Churchill put it in very similar terms: "If Hitler invaded hell, I should at least make a favorable reference to the Devil in the House of Commons." Both quotes cited in Stephen M. Walt, *The Origins of Alliances* (Ithaca, N.Y.: Cornell University Press, 1987), 38.

[3]See, for example, Adam B. Ulam, *The Rivals: America and Russia since World War II* (New York: Viking, 1971); Arthur M. Schlesinger, Jr., "Origins of the Cold War," *Foreign Affairs* 46.1 (October 1967); John Spanier, *American Foreign Policy since World War II* (New York: Praeger, 1968).

[4]See, for example, Walter LaFeber, *America in the Cold War* (New York: Wiley, 1969); Thomas G. Paterson, *Meeting the Communist Threat: From Truman to Reagan* (New York: Oxford University Press, 1988); Melvyn P. Leffler, *A Preponderance of Power: National Security, the Truman Administration, and the Cold War* (Stanford: Stanford University Press, 1992).

[5]John Gerard Ruggie, "The Past as Prologue? Interests, Identity and American Foreign Policy," *International Security* 21.4 (Spring 1997): 100.

[6]Gar Alperovitz, *Atomic Diplomacy: Hiroshima and Potsdam* (New York: Simon & Schuster, 1965); Martin J. Sherwin, "The Atomic Bomb and the Origins of the Cold War: U.S. Atomic Energy Policy and Diplomacy," *American Historical Review* 78.4 (October 1973): 945–68.

[7]Martin J. Sherwin, "Baruch, Bernard Mannes," in *Encyclopedia of U.S. Foreign Relations*, Bruce W. Jentleson and Thomas G. Paterson, eds. (New York: Oxford University Press, 1997), 1:135–36.

[8]Patrick M. Morgan, "Deterrence," in *Encyclopedia of U.S. Foreign Relations*, Jentleson and Paterson, eds., 3:10–16; Thomas Schelling, *The Strategy of Conflict* (Cambridge, Mass.: Harvard University Press, 1960); Alexander L. George, "Coercive Diplomacy: Definition and Characteristics," in *The Limits of Coercive Diplomacy*, 2d ed., Alexander L. George et al. (Boulder, Colo.: Westview, 1994), 7–12.

[9]X [George F. Kennan], "The Sources of Soviet Conduct," *Foreign Affairs* 25.4 (July 1947): 572, 575, 582.

[10]"NSC-68, A Report to the President Pursuant to the President's Directive of January 31, 1950," in U.S. Department of State, *Foreign Relations of the United States: 1950* (Washington, D.C.: U.S. Government Printing Office, 1977), 1:240.

[11]Cited in Thomas G. Paterson, "Korean War," in *Encyclopedia of U.S. Foreign Relations*, Jentleson and Paterson, eds., 3:30.

[12]Quote from Lord Ismay, cited in David S. Yost, *NATO Transformed: The Alliance's New Role in International Security* (Washington, D.C.: U.S. Institute of Peace Press, 1998), 52.

[13]Jonathan Nashel, "Domino Theory," in *Encyclopedia of U.S. Foreign Relations*, Jentleson and Paterson, eds., 2:32–33.

[14]Text of the legislation as passed by Congress, cited in Seyom Brown, *The Faces of Power: Constancy and Change in United States Foreign Policy from Truman to Reagan* (New York: Columbia University Press, 1983), 124.

[15]Graham Allison, *The Essence of Decision: Explaining the Cuban Missile Crisis* (Boston: Little, Brown, 1971); Robert F. Kennedy, *Thirteen Days: A Memoir of the Cuban Missile Crisis* (New York: Norton, 1969); James Blight and David Welch, eds., *On the Brink: Americans and Soviets Re-examine the Cuban Missile Crisis* (New York: Hill and Wang, 1989); Don Munton and David A. Welch, *The Cuban Missile Crisis: A Concise History* (New York: Oxford University Press, 2007).

[16]"Telegram, Secretary of State to the Consulate at Hanoi, May 20, 1949," in U.S. Department of State, *Foreign Relations of the United States: 1949* (Washington, D.C.: U.S. Government Printing Office, 1973), 7:29–30.

[17]Melvin R. Laird, "Iraq: Learning the Lessons of Vietnam," *Foreign Affairs* 84.6 (November/December 2005): 31.

[18]Secretary of State Dean Acheson, cited in Thomas G. Paterson, J. Gary Clifford, and Kenneth J. Hagan, *American Foreign Relations: A History since 1895* (Lexington, Mass.: Heath, 1995), 369.

[19]Cited in Paterson, Clifford, and Hagan, *American Foreign Relations*, 405.

[20]Many attribute this quotation to President Franklin Roosevelt. Although there are doubts as to whether he actually said it, few doubt that the statement captures the essence of U.S. policy. See Robert A. Pastor, *Condemned to Repetition: The United States and Nicaragua* (Princeton: Princeton University Press, 1987), 3.

[21]"Address at a White House Reception for Members of Congress and for the Diplomatic Corps of the Latin American Republics, March 13, 1961," in *Public Papers of the Presidents: John F. Kennedy, 1961* (Washington, D. C.: U.S. Government Printing Office, 1962), 170–75.

[22]Abraham F. Lowenthal, *Partners in Conflict: The United States and Latin America* (Baltimore: Johns Hopkins University Press, 1987), 30.

[23]Report of the Hoover Commission, cited in "Get Personal," *New Republic*, September 14 and 21, 1998, 11.

[24]Mark J. Gasiorowski, "Iran," in *Encyclopedia of U.S. Foreign Relations*, Jentleson and Paterson, eds., 2:415–16. See also James A. Bill, *The Eagle and the Lion: The Tragedy of American-Iranian Relations* (New Haven: Yale University Press, 1988); Bruce R. Kuniholm, *The Origins of the Cold War in the Near East* (Princeton: Princeton University Press, 1980); Kermit Roosevelt, *Countercoup: The Struggle for the Control of Iran* (New York: McGraw-Hill, 1979); Stephen Kinzer, *All the Shah's Men: An American Coup and the Roots of Middle East Terror* (New York: Wiley, 2003); and Kinzer, *Overthrow: America's Century of Regime Change from Hawaii to Iraq* (New York: Times Books, 2006).

[25]Aaron Wildavsky, "The Two Presidencies," *Trans-action* 3 (December 1966): 8.

[26]Senator Fulbright titled the article quoted here "American Foreign Policy in the 20th Century under an 18th-Century Constitution" (*Cornell Law Quarterly* 47 [Fall 1961]). He wrote further: "The question we face is whether our basic constitutional machinery, admirably suited to the needs of a remote agrarian republic in the eighteenth century, is adequate for the formulation and conduct of the foreign policy of a twentieth-century nation, preeminent in political and military power and burdened with all the enormous responsibilities that accompany such power. . . . My question, then, is whether we have any choice but to modify, and perhaps overhaul, the eighteenth-century procedures that govern the formulation and conduct of American foreign policy" (1–2).

[27]Richard F. Fenno, Jr., *Congressmen in Committees* (Boston: Little, Brown, 1973), 71.

[28]Cited in James M. Lindsay, *Congress and the Politics of U.S. Foreign Policy* (Baltimore: Johns Hopkins University Press, 1994), 22.

[29]Text of the legislation as passed by Congress, cited in Brown, *Faces of Power*, 124.

[30]The main precedent for the use of executive agreements rather than treaties as a way of getting around Congress had actually been set by Franklin Roosevelt in 1940 with the "destroyers-for-bases" deal with Britain (mentioned in Chapter 3). Even among those who agreed with Roosevelt's objectives, there was some concern at the time about the precedent being set. This also was the view taken in a 1969 report by the Senate Foreign Relations Committee: "Had the president publicly acknowledged his incursion on the Senate's treaty power and explained it as an emergency measure, a damaging constitutional precedent would have been averted. Instead, a spurious claim of constitutionality was made, compounding the incursion on the Senate's authority into a precedent for future incursions." Cited in Loch K. Johnson, *America as a World Power: Foreign Policy in a Constitutional Framework* (New York: McGraw-Hill, 1991), 108–9.

[31]Based on data from Michael Nelson, ed., *Congressional Quarterly's Guide to the Presidency* (Washington, D.C.: Congressional Quarterly Press, 1989), 1104.

[32]There actually was one major effort in the early 1950s to rein in executive agreements. This was the Bricker Amendment, named for its principal sponsor, Senator John W. Bricker (R-Ohio), which would have amended the Constitution to require congressional approval of all executive agreements. Support for the Bricker Amendment was in part a reflection of McCarthyite distrust of the executive branch, and it too faded with the overall discrediting of McCarthyism. Indeed, until the late 1960s little was heard even about the executive's taking full advantage of the lack of any deadline in the requirement that executive agreements be reported to Congress, reporting very few of these agreements—and even those in a not particularly timely manner.

[33]Loch K. Johnson and James M. McCormick, "Foreign Policy by Executive Fiat," *Foreign Policy* 28 (Fall 1977): 121.

[34]Daniel Yergin, *Shattered Peace: The Origins of the Cold War and the National Security State* (Boston: Houghton Mifflin, 1977).

[35]See, for example, James G. Blight and Peter Kornbluh, eds., *Politics of Illusion: The Bay of Pigs Invasion Reexamined* (Boulder, Colo.: Lynne Rienner, 1997); "A Perfect Failure: The Bay of Pigs," in *Groupthink: Psychological Studies of Policy Decisions and Fiascoes,* 2d ed., Irving L. Janis (Boston: Houghton Mifflin, 1982), 14–47; Peter Wyden, *Bay of Pigs: The Untold Story* (New York: Simon & Schuster, 1979).

[36]Cited in Janis, *Groupthink,* 39.

[37]Peter Kornbluh, ed., *Bay of Pigs Declassified: The Secret CIA Report on the Invasion of Cuba* (New York: Norton, 1998).

[38]Cited in Janis, *Groupthink,* 16.

[39]Allison, *Essence of Decision;* Blight and Welch, *On the Brink;* Munton and Welch, *Cuban Missile Crisis.*

[40]Allison, *Essence of Decision;* Morton H. Halperin, *Bureaucratic Politics and Foreign Policy* (Washington, D.C.: Brookings Institution Press, 1974); Morton H. Halperin and Arnold Kanter, eds., *Readings in American Foreign Policy: A Bureaucratic Perspective* (Boston: Little, Brown, 1973); David C. Kozak and James M. Keagle, *Bureaucratic Politics and National Security: Theory and Practice* (Boulder, Colo.: Lynne Rienner, 1988). The movie *Thirteen Days,* released in 2000, had some inaccuracies but did provide a clear and vivid portrayal of the strong leadership President Kennedy provided. The movie was based on a book by the same name written by Attorney General Robert F. Kennedy, the president's brother and his main confidante during the Cuban missile crisis. See Robert F. Kennedy, *Thirteen Days* (New York: Norton, 1971).

[41]Dan Caldwell, "A Research Note on the Quarantine of Cuba, 1962," *International Studies Quarterly* 21.2 (December 1978): 625–33; Joseph F. Bouchard, *Command in Crisis: Four Case Studies* (New York: Columbia University Press, 1991); Richard K. Betts, *Soldiers, Statesmen, and Cold War Crises,* 2d ed. (New York: Columbia University Press, 1991); Scott D. Sagan, "Nuclear Alerts and Crisis Management," *International Security* 9.4 (Spring 1985): 99–139; Ernest R. May and Philip D. Zelikow, eds., *The Kennedy Tapes: Inside the White House During the Cuban Missile Crisis* (Cambridge, Mass.: Harvard University Press, 1997); Sheldon M. Stern, *The Week the World Stood Still: Inside the Secret Cuban Missile Crisis* (Stanford: Stanford University Press, 2005); and Graham T. Allison and Philip Zelikow, *Essence of Decision: Explaining the Cuban Missile Crisis,* 2d ed. (New York: Longman, 1999).

[42]Richard K. Betts, "Is Strategy an Illusion?" *International Security* 25.2 (Fall 2000): 34–35; Scott D. Sagan, *The Limits of Safety: Organizations, Accidents, and Nuclear Weapons* (Princeton: Princeton University Press, 1993), chaps. 2–3.

[43]James Aronson, *The Press and the Cold War* (New York: Bobbs Merrill, 1970), 186.

[44]Aronson, *The Press and the Cold War,* 159.

[45]Aronson, *The Press and the Cold War,* 159–60.

[46]"Commencement Address at American University in Washington," June 10, 1963, in *Public Papers of the Presidents: John F. Kennedy, 1963* (Washington, D.C.: U.S. Government Printing Office, 1964), 459–64.

[47]Quoted in Bruce W. Jentleson, *Pipeline Politics: The Complex Political Economy of East-West Energy Trade* (Ithaca, N.Y.: Cornell University Press, 1986), 129.

[48]Jentleson, *Pipeline Politics,* 100.

[49]Harvey Klehr, John Earl Haynes, and Kyrill M. Anderson, *The Soviet World of American Communism* (New Haven: Yale University Press, 1998); Ronald Radosh and Joyce Milton, *The Rosenberg File* (New Haven: Yale University Press, 1997).

[50]Cited in Jerel A. Rosati, *The Politics of United States Foreign Policy* (New York: Harcourt, Brace, 1993), 285.

CHAPTER

# 5 The Cold War Context: Lessons and Legacies

## Introduction: Turbulent Decades

The 1960s, 1970s, and 1980s were turbulent decades for the United States. Foreign policy was not the only reason—the civil rights movement, the counterculture, economic change, and other forces and factors also were at work. But the setbacks, shifts, and shocks endured by American foreign policy clearly were major factors.

The Vietnam War was the most profound setback American foreign policy had suffered since the beginning of the Cold War. Many saw it as the first war the United States had ever lost. The reasons were hotly debated—and still are. But the profundity of the loss as it affected both foreign policy strategy and foreign policy politics was undeniable.

The fate of détente with the Soviet Union—first its rise and then its fall—marked major shifts. The rise of détente challenged the dominant belief of the first quarter-century of the Cold War that minimal U.S.-Soviet cooperation was possible. This challenge was especially significant since the switch to détente was led by President Richard Nixon, who had built his political career on staunch anticommunist credentials. Yet although détente had some successes, its hopes and promises went largely unfulfilled. It engendered major political controversy at home. And when the Soviets invaded Afghanistan in December 1979, détente was pronounced dead.

The United States also endured tremendous economic shocks during the 1970s. Although not so bad as the Great Depression, these shocks were historically unique, for they arose from the international economy. In 1971, for the first time since 1893, the American merchandise trade balance was in deficit. Then came the oil embargo and price hikes by the Organization of Petroleum Exporting Countries (OPEC), first in 1973 and again in 1979. The assumption of cheap and reliable supplies of oil, in some respects no less part of the bedrock of the post–World War II order than anticommunism, was being called into question. Third World countries tried to capitalize on OPEC's success in bringing the industrialized West to its knees by trying to shift the defining axis of the international system from East-West to North-South. Another major economic blow fell when Japan, the country the United States defeated and occupied after World War II, became America's main economic competitor.

The 1980s thus began amid great foreign policy uncertainty, and it, too, proved a turbulent decade. Initially, following the demise of détente and the election of Ronald Reagan, the Cold War resurged. Policies on both sides grew increasingly confrontational, the rhetoric highly antagonistic. Fears of war, even nuclear war, were rising. In 1985 the Soviets selected a new leader, Mikhail Gorbachev, who made dramatic changes in Soviet foreign policy. By the end of the decade the Cold War was over. How much credit for the end of the Cold War goes to Gorbachev, how much to Reagan, and how much to other actors and factors has been and continues to be debated. The Cold War did end, though, and it ended peacefully.

In this chapter we examine these and other developments in U.S. foreign policy during the second half of the Cold War, with an eye to the lessons and legacies of the Cold War.

## The Vietnam War: A Profound Foreign Policy Setback

In 1995 Robert McNamara, secretary of defense under Presidents Kennedy and Johnson and one of the officials most closely associated with the ***Vietnam War,*** published his startling mea culpa memoir, *In Retrospect.* For almost thirty years McNamara had refused to talk about Vietnam. He had left government and had gone on to be president of the World Bank and to work during the 1980s for nuclear arms control, but he stayed mum on Vietnam. Now, though, he laid out his view of the reasons for the U.S. failure in Vietnam:

- We underestimated the power of nationalism to motivate a people (in this case, the North Vietnamese and Vietcong) to fight and die for their beliefs and values. . . .
- Our misjudgments of friend and foe alike reflected our profound ignorance of the history, culture, and politics of the people in the area and the personalities and habits of their leaders.
- We failed then—as we have since—to recognize the limitations of modern, high-technology military equipment, forces, and doctrine in confronting unconventional, highly motivated people's movements.
- We failed to draw Congress and the American people into a full and frank discussion and debate of the pros and cons of a large-scale U.S. military involvement in Southeast Asia before we initiated the action. . . .

- Underlying many of these errors lay our failure to organize the top echelons of the executive branch to deal effectively with the extraordinarily complex range of political and military issues, involving the great risks and costs—including above all else, loss of life—associated with the application of military force under substantial constraints over a long period of time.[1]

McNamara was not the only former high-level government official to express such doubts about and criticisms of Vietnam. The former secretary of state Dean Acheson later acknowledged receiving advice that there was "real danger that our efforts would fail," but nevertheless deciding that "having put our hand to the plow, we would not look back."[2] Dwight Eisenhower wrote of being "convinced that the French could not win" the 1945–54 colonial war, but that nevertheless "the decision to give this aid was almost compulsory. The United States had no real alternative."[3] John Kennedy was said to be "skeptical of the extent of our involvement in Vietnam but unwilling to abandon his predecessor's pledge."[4] And during Lyndon Johnson's "Americanization" of the war, Vice President Hubert Humphrey, Undersecretary of State George Ball, Senator J. William Fulbright, the journalist Walter Lippmann, and all other proponents of alternative options were closed out of the decision-making process because of their misgivings. Henry Kissinger himself later described "Vietnamization," the centerpiece of his own policy, as "the operation, conceived in doubt and assailed by skepticism [that] proceeded in confusion"—but proceeded nevertheless.[5]

Some critics argued that Vietnam was a war that should not have been fought, could not have been won, and could and should have been halted at several key junctures. Others vehemently contended that it was right to have fought it, and that it could have been won through tougher policies and more commitment by U.S. policy makers. Leslie Gelb makes a provocative and counterintuitive argument that "the system worked" (see Reading 5.1). The one point of consensus is that Vietnam was the most profound foreign policy setback the United States suffered during the Cold War era. For American foreign policy strategy, it amounted to failure on all counts: peace was not served, power was eroded, principles were violated, prosperity was damaged. In American foreign policy politics, the Cold War consensus was shattered, in terms of both its institutional structures and its societal underpinnings.

5.1

## *Foreign Policy Strategy: Failure on All Counts*

PEACE American casualities in Vietnam numbered more than two hundred thousand, including almost sixty thousand deaths. Vietnamese casualties were over 3 million. And the war failed to keep the dominoes from falling: communism came to Vietnam, got stronger in Laos, and spread to Cambodia.

Whether peace was achievable through the war effort is one of the main debates between the contending schools noted above. Secretary McNamara believed not, in part because of the inherent "limitations" of modern high-technology warfare when pitted against "the power of nationalism to motivate a people to fight and die for their beliefs and values."[6] Others faulted what was not done more than what was; one general wrote that American strategy violated two of the "time-honored principles of war. . . . We lacked a clear objective and an attainable strategy of a decisive nature."[7]

The sense of the war's unwinnability was not just retrospective. Even while he was intensifying American bombing of the Vietnamese, President Nixon privately acknowledged that "there's no way to win the war. But we can't say that, of course. In fact, we have to seem to say the opposite, just to keep some bargaining leverage." At the peace negotiations with the North Vietnamese in Paris, the ultimate objective was not to win but, as Kissinger stated it, to be able "to withdraw as an expression of policy and not as a collapse."[8] This approach continued after the Treaty of Paris had been signed in 1973. The Ford administration pushed for retaliation against North Vietnamese treaty violations. But it did so less to ensure a peace than to gain a "decent interval" that might convince the global audience that the United States had not lost.[9]

POWER All along, the main factor driving U.S. involvement in Vietnam was the belief that the credibility of American power was being tested there. A 1952 State Department memorandum delineated three reasons for "the strategic importance of Indochina": "its geographic position as key to the defense of mainland Southeast Asia," a somewhat dubious proposition; "its economic importance as a potential large-scale exporter of rice," an interest much closer to trivial than vital; and *"as an example of Western resistance to Communist expansion"* (emphasis added).[10] In 1965, when the decision finally was made to send in American troops, President Johnson quite explicitly articulated the need to demonstrate American credibility, as it pertained to global allies and adversaries alike: "Around the globe, from Berlin to Thailand, are people whose well-being rests, in part, on the belief that they can count on us if they are attacked. To leave Vietnam to its fate would shake the confidence of all these people in the value of an American commitment and in the value of America's word."[11]

This same precept carried over into the Nixon and Ford administrations. Kissinger stated unequivocally that "the commitment of 500,000 Americans has settled the issue of the importance of Vietnam. For what is involved now is confidence in American promises."[12] If the United States failed this test, President Nixon claimed, it would be perceived as "a pitiful, helpless giant" and "the forces of totalitarianism and anarchy will threaten free nations around the world."[13] On the eve of the American evacuation of Saigon in 1975, President Ford beseeched Congress in similar terms not to cut off aid, arguing that to do so "would draw into question the reliability of the United States and encourage the belief that aggression pays."[14]

The ***Munich analogy,*** from World War II and the failed appeasement of Adolf Hitler, was implicit and at times explicit in the thinking of American leaders (see "Historical Perspectives," p. 155). Ironically, though, nothing damaged the perception of American power more than these very policies, which were supposed to preserve it. No less a figure than Hans Morgenthau, whose books were cited in our discussion of the Realist paradigm in Chapter 1, had opposed the Vietnam War as early as 1967, precisely because he believed it would be damaging to American power. The interests at stake were not worth the commitments needed. On the contrary, as Morgenthau himself argued, U.S. power could best be served by developing a relationship with Ho Chi Minh that, even without converting him from communism, would "prevent such a communist revolution from turning against the interests of the United States."[15]

PRINCIPLES During the late 1950s, then senator John Kennedy tried to make the moral case for American responsibility: "If we are not the parents of little Vietnam, then surely we are the godparents."[16] When American troops were first sent to these distant jungles, LBJ described the action as necessary because "we remain fixed on the pursuit of freedom as a deep and moral obligation that will not let us go."[17] President Nixon turned the principles argument inward with his rebuttal to the antiwar movement: if we withdrew from Vietnam, Nixon claimed, "we would lose confidence in ourselves. . . . North Vietnam cannot defeat or humiliate the United States. Only Americans can do that."[18]

Yet nowhere did Americans feel that their foreign policy violated their principles more than in Vietnam. It needs to be acknowledged that among much of the antiwar movement there was a great deal of naiveté, wishful thinking, and rationalization. Ho Chi Minh and the Vietcong were hardly strictly freedom fighters, Jeffersonians, or the like. The horrors that the communist Khmer Rouge inflicted against their own people when they came to power in Cambodia shocked the world. But only according to the Cold War "ABC" definition did the likes of Presidents Ngo Dinh Diem and Nguyen Van Thieu in Vietnam, and Prime Minister Lon Nol in Cambodia, each of whom received staunch U.S. support, qualify as democrats. Moreover, the scenes of peasant villagers fleeing American aircraft spreading napalm, and of incidents such as the 1968 My Lai massacre, in which U.S. soldiers killed more than five hundred innocent Vietnamese villagers, were deeply disturbing to the American national conscience.

PROSPERITY Theorists of the military-industrial complex claim that the raging appetite of an economy in which defense industries were so central was a key factor leading to Vietnam. Whether or not that analysis is true, from the more general perspective of the overall American economy, the effects of the war were quite damaging to prosperity. LBJ calculated that cutting domestic spending to finance the war would only further weaken political support, but his ***guns and butter strategy*** of trying to keep spending up in both

## HISTORICAL PERSPECTIVES

HISTORICAL PERSPECTIVES

### THE MUNICH ANALOGY AND VIETNAM

*Policy makers often reason from history, usually through analogies between current issues and seemingly similar historical ones. One of the most striking examples of such reasoning is the "Munich analogy," from World War II, which greatly influenced U.S. policy in Vietnam.*

*The Munich analogy generally refers to negotiations held in Munich, Germany, in September 1938 at which the British prime minister Neville Chamberlain and the French prime minister Edouard Daladier agreed to Adolf Hitler's annexation of part of Czechoslovakia to Nazi Germany in the hope that it would satisfy Hitler's expansionism. It didn't. Six months later Hitler annexed all of Czechoslovakia. His invasion of Poland soon followed, and World War II was on us. The lesson of history that many policy makers have drawn from this, including with regard to Vietnam, is the need to confront dictators and aggressors, using force if necessary, rather than make concessions and pursue "appeasement."*

Everything I know about history told me that if I got out of Vietnam and let Ho Chi Minh run through the streets of Saigon, then I'd be doing exactly what Chamberlain did in WWII. I'd be giving a big fat reward for aggression.

—President Lyndon B. Johnson

The clearest lesson of the 1930s and '40s is that aggression feeds on aggression. I am aware that Mao and Ho Chi Minh are not Hitler and Mussolini. But we should not forget what we learned about the anatomy and physiology of aggression. We ought to know better than to ignore the aggressor's openly proclaimed intentions or to fall victim to the notion that he will stop if you let him have just one more bit or speak to him a little more gently.

—Secretary of State Dean Rusk

There are those who will say that this picture is much too dark. Like Neville Chamberlain, who in 1938 described Czechoslovakia as a little-known and faraway country, they deride the importance of South Vietnam and scoff at the suggestion that to lose one more major segment of Asia means to lose it all. Such optimists contend that we should reach an agreement with our adversaries—as Chamberlain reached an agreement with Hitler in Munich in 1938.

—President Richard M. Nixon

(*Continued*)

(*Continued*)

In 1938 the Munich agreement made Chamberlain widely popular and cast Churchill in the role of alarmist troublemaker; eighteen months later Chamberlain was finished because the Munich agreement was discredited. With the Vietnam War the problem was more complex. Rightly or wrongly—I am still thoroughly convinced rightly—we thought that capitulation or steps that amounted to it would usher in a period of disintegrating American credibility that could only accelerate the world's instability.

—National Security Advisor and Secretary of State Henry Kissinger

But looking back we think, as I am sure many of you do, that it is wise to stop aggression before the aggressor becomes strong and swollen with ambition from small successes. We think the world might have been spared enormous misfortunes if Japan had not been permitted to succeed in Manchuria, or Mussolini in Ethiopia, or Hitler in Czechoslovakia or in the Rhineland. And we think that our sacrifices in this dirty war in little Vietnam will make a dirtier and bigger war less likely.

—Senator Henry M. Jackson (D-Washington)

*Sources:* Johnson: Jeffrey P. Kimball, *To Reason Why: The Debate about the Causes of U.S. Involvement in the Vietnam War* (Philadelphia: Temple University Press, 1990), 43.
Rusk: Kimball, *To Reason Why,* 67.
Nixon: Richard Nixon, "Needed in Vietnam: The Will to Win," *Reader's Digest,* August 1964, 39.
Kissinger: Jeffrey Record, *Making War, Thinking History: Munich to Vietnam and Presidential Uses of Force from Korea to Vietnam* (Annapolis: Naval Institute Press, 2002), 71.
Jackson: Kimball, *To Reason Why,* 66.

areas backfired. The federal budget deficit grew. "Stagflation"—simultaneous high unemployment and high inflation—set in. For the first time since 1893, the trade balance went into deficit. The economic situation got so bad that President Nixon, a Republican, imposed wage and price controls and other stringent measures typically identified with liberal, Democratic politicians. But these moves only made the economic situation worse.

## *Foreign Policy Politics: Shattering the Cold War Consensus*

As for politics, here too the effects were paradoxical. "If I did not go into Vietnam," LBJ reflected, "there would follow in this country an endless national debate—a mean and destructive debate—that would shatter my Presidency, kill my administration, and damage our democracy. I knew that Harry Truman and Dean Acheson had lost their effectiveness from the day that the Communists took over China. I believed that the loss of China had played a large role in the rise of Joe McCarthy. And I knew that all these problems, taken together, were chickenshit compared with what might happen if we lost Vietnam."[19] The last part of this statement at least was right, but because LBJ went in, not because he stayed out.

PRESIDENTIAL-CONGRESSIONAL RELATIONS Recall Senator Fulbright's 1961 statement, cited in Chapter 4, about the need to give the president more power. It was the same Senator Fulbright who, as chairman of the Senate Foreign Relations Committee, became one of the leading opponents of the war. More sweepingly he now warned of "presidential dictatorship in foreign affairs. . . . I believe that the presidency has become a dangerously powerful office, more urgently in need of reform than any other institution in government."[20] Similarly, the historian and former Kennedy aide Arthur Schlesinger, Jr., attacked "the imperial presidency . . . out of control and badly in need of new definition and restraint."[21]

Now Congress was urged to be more assertive and less deferential. Some of its most ardent supporters even proclaimed the 1970s to be an age of "foreign policy *by* Congress."[22] Many of its members were now less parochial and more worldly, some having served earlier in their careers as State or Defense Department officials, as Peace Corps volunteers, or even as political science and international relations professors. Greater expertise also was available from the expanded and more professional staffs of congressional committees. For example, between 1960 and 1975, the staff of the Senate Foreign Relations Committee increased from 25 to 62 members, and the House Foreign Affairs Committee staff grew from 14 to 54.[23] Moreover, as Senator Fulbright wrote, only partially in jest, "whatever may be said against Congress . . . there is one thing to be said for it: It poses no threat to the liberties of the American people."[24]

Congress relied heavily on procedural legislation (defined in Chapter 2) in seeking to redress the imbalance of foreign policy powers. The ***War Powers Resolution (WPR) of 1973*** was among the most central and controversial of these procedural initiatives. No declaration of war had ever been passed for the military action in Vietnam. Presidents Johnson and Nixon both justified their actions on the basis of the 1964 ***Gulf of Tonkin Resolution,*** which Congress did pass by overwhelming margins, with an open-ended authorization to use military force.* For Vietnam itself Congress tried a number of ways to end the war, eventually

*It later was revealed that at least one of the two alleged North Vietnamese attacks on U.S. naval ships, the ostensible bases for the Gulf of Tonkin Resolution, never actually occurred. See Scott Shane, "Doubts Cast on Vietnam Incident, But Secret Study Stays Classified," *New York Times,* October 31, 2005; National Security Agency, Central Security Service, "Gulf of Tonkin—11/30/2005 and 5/30/2006," www.nsa.gov/public_info/declass/gulf_of_tonkin/index.shtml (accessed 6/7/09).

using the power of the purse to cut off funds. The WPR was intended to increase Congress's share of the war powers for the next Vietnam. Nixon vetoed the WPR, claiming it was unconstitutional as an infringement of his presidential powers as commander in chief. But with Republicans joining Democrats in a show of bipartisanship, the necessary two-thirds margin was reached in both the House and the Senate to override his veto.

The WPR limited presidential power through two sets of provisions. One set sought to tighten up requirements for the president to consult with Congress before, or at least soon after, committing U.S. troops in any situation other than a genuine national emergency. This stipulation was intended to give Congress more say in whether initial troop commitments would be made. The other established the "sixty-day clock," by which time the president would have to withdraw U.S. forces unless Congress explicitly allowed an extension. As things have turned out in practice, the WPR has not worked very well, as we will discuss later in this chapter. But at the time it seemed like a significant rebalancing of the war powers.

Congress also tried to stake a claim to a larger share of other aspects of shared foreign policy powers. With respect to treaties and other international commitments, it passed legislation to clamp down on the excessive use of executive agreements. It used its investigative and supervisory powers to tighten the reins on executive-branch departments and agencies, most notably on the CIA. It made frequent use of the legislative veto in policy areas such as arms sales, nuclear nonproliferation, foreign aid, and trade. All in all, the 1970s were a period in which Congress was trying to make Pennsylvania Avenue more of a two-way street.

EXECUTIVE-BRANCH POLITICS It was from Vietnam that the ***credibility gap*** arose. The Johnson and Nixon administrations kept trying to put the best face on the war by holding back from the public some information and distorting other information, and by outright lying. The public was left doubting the credibility of its leaders. Not only did this sense of skepticism, if not cynicism, cause the public to lose faith in the truthfulness of its leaders about Vietnam, but also it was applied increasingly to all high-level officials in all arenas of government, and thus developed into the more generalized problem of the credibility gap.

SHATTERING THE COLD WAR CONSENSUS During the early Cold War a few protest movements had emerged, but none that had any significant impact. The anti–Vietnam War movement marked a major change in this pattern. Hundreds of thousands of demonstrators marched on Washington, not just once but repeatedly. "Teach-ins" spread on college campuses, as did sit-ins and in some instances more violent demonstrations. In one particularly tragic incident in the spring of 1970, National Guard troops fired on antiwar protesters at Kent State University in Ohio, killing four students. Although some of its excesses worked against its very goals, overall the antiwar movement was an important influence on U.S. policy in Vietnam.

As for the news media, the old "cheerleader" role that had prevailed for much of the early Cold War was supplanted by the media as "critics." This, too, was born in Vietnam, where it was the media that first brought home to Americans news of how badly the war was going and how much of a credibility gap there was between official accounts and the reality on the ground. In one telling encounter a reporter posed a tough question to an American official at a press conference. The official asked the reporter his name. "Malcolm Browne of the Associated Press," he said. "So you're Browne," the official responded, revealing a knowledge of Browne's critical reporting. "Why don't you get on the team?"[25]

The ***Watergate*** scandal took media-government antagonism further. President Johnson and his administration had done quite a bit of shading of the truth, but Watergate revealed that President Nixon and his cronies had lied, covered up, and even committed crimes. Had it not been for the media, none of this might have been known. Moreover, even though Watergate wasn't a foreign policy scandal per se, among its revelations was Nixon's "enemies list," which included some journalists as well as leaders of the antiwar movement.

Table 5.1 shows the sharp contrasts in public opinion between the Cold War consensus and the mindset of the "Vietnam trauma." Whereas only 24 percent considered

**TABLE 5.1 Public Opinion from Cold War Consensus to Vietnam Trauma**

| | Cold War consensus | Vietnam trauma |
|---|---|---|
| Support internationalism | 65 percent | 41 percent |
| Support isolationism | 8 percent | 21 percent |
| Rank of containment as a national objective | 2nd | 7th |
| Supporting troops to defend Western Europe | 80 percent | 39 percent |
| Supporting troops to defend the Western Hemisphere | 73 percent | 31 percent |
| Vietnam War a mistake | 24 percent | 61 percent |

Sources: William Watts and Potomac Associates, presented in Charles W. Kegley, Jr., and Eugene R. Wittkopf, *American Foreign Policy: Pattern and Process,* 3d ed. (New York: St. Martin's, 1987), 292; Lloyd A. Free and Hadley Cantril, *The Political Beliefs of Americans* (New York: Simon & Schuster, 1968), 52; Michael Mandelbaum and William Schneider, "The New Internationalisms: Public Opinion and American Foreign Policy," in *Eagle Entangled: U.S. Foreign Policy in a Complex World,* Kenneth A. Oye, Donald Rothchild, and Robert J. Lieber, eds. (New York: Longman, 1979), 41–42; Eugene R. Wittkopf, "Elites and Masses: Another Look at Attitudes toward America's World Role," *International Studies Quarterly* 31.7 (June 1987): 131–59; Mandelbaum and Schneider, "New Internationalisms," 82; Wittkopf, "Elites and Masses"; Barry B. Hughes, *The Domestic Context of American Foreign Policy* (San Francisco: Freeman, 1978), 38–40.

involvement in Vietnam a mistake when the United States first sent troops in 1965, by 1971 61 percent did. More generally, the public had become much less internationalist and much more isolationist, as can be seen in its low ranking of the importance of containment as a national objective and its reduced willingness to use American troops to defend non-American territory, even in Western Europe.

Clearly, a lot had changed. The shift wasn't just because of Vietnam; there were other issues as well on which questions were increasingly being asked about foreign policy strategy and in foreign policy politics. But Vietnam in particular stood as a profound setback for American Cold War strategy and shattered the political patterns of the Cold War.

## The Rise and Fall of Détente: Major Foreign Policy Shifts

***Détente*** literally means a "relaxation of tensions." It was the principal term used to characterize efforts in the 1970s to break out of the Cold War and improve relations between the United States and the Soviet Union. But whereas at the beginning of the decade détente was heralded as the dawn of a new era, by the end of the decade these hopes had been dashed and the Cold War had resumed.

### *Nixon, Kissinger, and the Rise of Détente*

The principal architects of détente were President Nixon and Henry Kissinger. Kissinger served as national security advisor (1969–75) and secretary of state (1973–77). A former Harvard professor, Kissinger drew much of his strategy for détente from balance-of-power theory based on nineteenth-century Europe and the diplomacy led by Prince Metternich, the foreign minister of Austria (see "Theory in the World," p. 161).

What made the rise of détente possible were shifts in all "4 Ps", as well as in foreign policy politics.

5.2 Peace was a driving force behind détente for both the Americans and the Soviets. Reading 5.2, by Alexander George of Stanford University, provides an overview of the key aspects of this search for a "constructive" relationship. Both sides shared interests in stabilizing Europe, where the Cold War had originated and where it had been waged for nearly a quarter-century. It thus was important both substantively and symbolically that one of the first détente agreements achieved (1971) was on Berlin, the divided German city that had been the locus of recurring Cold War crises. Berlin's status as a divided city was not ended, but new agreements did allow increased contact between West and East Berlin, and West and East Germany more generally.

## THEORY IN THE WORLD

THEORY IN THE WORLD

### KISSINGER'S DÉTENTE AND BALANCE-OF-POWER THEORY

The first book Henry Kissinger wrote (and the subject of his Ph.D. dissertation at Harvard) was on Prince Klemens von Metternich, the Austrian foreign minister during the first half of the nineteenth century. His diplomacy was widely credited with the peace that prevailed among the major European powers of that era (Britain, France, Russia, Prussia [most of which later became Germany], and Austria).* It is instructive to see how much Kissinger's diplomacy of détente drew on Metternich. Following are two examples:

Metternich's strategy focused on maintaining sufficient balance of power to ensure system stability rather than trying to defeat a specific foe. Metternich was a "statesman of the equilibrium, seeking security in a balance of forces," Kissinger wrote. "This was the basis of Metternich's diplomacy throughout his life. Freedom of action, the consciousness of having a greater range of choice than any possible opponent. . . ."[†] We see this in détente in the triangulation of improving relations with China at the same time that tough negotiations were being pursued with the Soviet Union. "We moved toward China," Kissinger wrote of his own diplomacy, "to shape a global equilibrium. It was not to collude against the Soviet Union but to give us a balancing position for constructive ends—to give each Communist power a stake in better relations with us."[‡] The overarching goal of détente was stability, not defeating either of the communist foes.

Kissinger also drew from Metternich the Realpolitik approach of focusing on relations between countries more than on domestic policies. "Metternich was the last diplomat of the great tradition of the eighteenth century, a 'scientist' of politics, coolly and unemotionally arranging his combinations in an age increasingly conducting policy by causes. . . . He permitted no sentimental attachments to interfere with his measures."[§] Metternich's context was the prodemocratic revolutions then gaining force in many European countries. In his own time, despite such issues as Soviet abuse of human rights, Kissinger believed that "diplomacy should be divorced . . . from a moralistic and meddlesome concern with the internal policies of other nations. Stability is the prime goal of diplomacy. . . . [I]t is threatened when nations embark on ideological or moral crusades."**

*Henry Kissinger, *A World Restored: Metternich, Castlereagh and the Problems of Peace* (New York: Houghton Mifflin, 1957).

[†]Kissinger, *A World Restored,* 270, 319.

[‡]Cited in Walter Isaacson, *Kissinger: A Biography* (New York: Simon & Schuster, 1992), 336.

[§]Kissinger, *A World Restored,* 319.

**Isaacson, *Kissinger,* 75.

Other important agreements created the Conference on Security and Cooperation in Europe (CSCE) and led to the adoption of the ***Helsinki Accords of 1975.*** The CSCE was the first major international organization other than the UN to include countries of both Eastern and Western Europe, both NATO allies (including the United States and Canada) and Warsaw Pact members; it also included neutral countries such as Sweden and Switzerland. The Helsinki Accords were something of a trade-off. On the one hand they gave the Soviets the recognition they long had wanted of territorial borders in central and Eastern Europe as drawn after World War II. On the other hand they established human rights and other democratic values as basic tenets that CSCE members agreed to respect. Although this provision was not fully binding on Moscow or other communist governments, it provided a degree of legitimization and protection for dissidents that, as we will see, nurtured the seeds of what would become the anticommunist revolutions of 1989.

The United States and the Soviet Union also increasingly had come to recognize, especially in the wake of the Cuban missile crisis, their shared interest in working together to reduce the risks of nuclear war. This interest was clearly stated in the Basic Principles of Relations, a charterlike document signed by Nixon and the Soviet leader Leonid Brezhnev at their 1972 summit (see "At the Source," p. 163). Underlying this recognition was an important shift in nuclear deterrence doctrine (Power). One of the reasons noted in Chapter 4 that the Soviets put nuclear missiles in Cuba was to pose a threat close to American territory as a counterweight to America's overall nuclear superiority. Even though this didn't succeed—or, arguably, precisely because it didn't succeed—the Soviets came out of the Cuban missile crisis determined to close the nuclear-weapons gap. The nuclear arms race thus got another kick upward. On the U.S. side, the rising costs of maintaining nuclear superiority, especially on top of the costs of the Vietnam War, were becoming more burdensome. Moreover, even if nuclear superiority were maintained, the Soviets had increased their own nuclear firepower sufficiently that security would not be assured. The dilemma was laid out in a 1967 speech by Defense Secretary McNamara: "In the larger equation of security, our 'superiority' is of limited significance. . . . Even with our current superiority, or indeed with any numerical superiority realistically attainable, the blunt inescapable fact remains that the Soviet Union could still—with its present forces—effectively destroy the United States, even after absorbing the full weight of an American first strike."[26]

The strategic situation he was describing was one of ***mutually assured destruction,*** or MAD, as it became known in a fitting acronym. Yet as paradoxical as it might sound, MAD was seen as potentially stabilizing. Since neither side could launch a "first strike" without risking getting devastated itself in a "second strike"—that is, with destruction assured to be mutual—the chances were slim that either side would resort to using nuclear weapons. Trying to break out of this situation could make the arms race endless. Both sides thus had an interest in nuclear arms control.

## AT THE SOURCE

AT THE SOURCE

### U.S.-SOVIET DÉTENTE

"The United States of America and the Union of Soviet Socialist Republics . . . have agreed as follows:

*First.* They will proceed from the common determination that in the nuclear age there is no alternative to conducting their mutual relations on the basis of peaceful coexistence. Differences in ideology and in the social systems of the USA and the USSR are not obstacles to the bilateral development of normal relations based on the principles of sovereignty, equality, non-interference in internal affairs and mutual advantage.

*Second.* The USA and the USSR attach major importance to preventing the development of situations capable of causing a dangerous exacerbation of their relations. Therefore, they will do their utmost to avoid military confrontations and to prevent the outbreak of nuclear war. They will always exercise restraint in their mutual relations, and will be prepared to negotiate and settle differences by peaceful means. Discussions and negotiations on outstanding issues will be conducted in a spirit of reciprocity, mutual accommodation and mutual benefit.

Both sides recognize that efforts to obtain unilateral advantage at the expense of the other, directly or indirectly, are inconsistent with these objectives. The prerequisites for maintaining and strengthening peaceful relations between the USA and the USSR are the recognition of the security interests of the Parties based on the principle of equality and the renunciation of the use or threat of force. . . .

*Sixth.* The Parties will continue their efforts to limit armaments on a bilateral as well as on a multilateral basis. They will continue to make special efforts to limit strategic armaments. Whenever possible, they will conclude concrete agreements aimed at achieving these purposes.

The USA and the USSR regard as the ultimate objective of their efforts the achievement of general and complete disarmament and the establishment of an effective system of international security in accordance with the purposes and principles of the United Nations.

*Seventh.* The USA and the USSR regard commercial and economic ties as an important and necessary element in the strengthening of their bilateral relations and thus will actively promote the growth of such ties. . . .

*Ninth.* The two sides reaffirm their intention to deepen cultural ties with one another and to encourage fuller familiarization with each other's cultural values. They will promote improved conditions for cultural exchanges and tourism."

Source: Basic Principles of Relations, signed by the United States and the Soviet Union, May 1972, in *American Foreign Relations, 1972: A Documentary Record* (New York: New York University Press for the Council on Foreign Relations, 1976), 75–78.

Prior to the détente era there had been only a few U.S.–Soviet nuclear arms-control agreements.* Thus the signing in 1972 of the first ***Strategic Arms Limitation Treaty (SALT I)*** was highly significant as recognition that peace and stability were not achievable only through arms but also required arms control. SALT I set limits on strategic nuclear weapons according to a formula known as "essential equivalence," whereby the Soviets were allowed a larger quantity of missiles because the United States had technological advantages that allowed it to put more bombs on each missile.† The idea was that if the Soviets had a quantitative edge and the United States a qualitative one, both would be assured of deterrence. SALT I also severely limited ***anti–ballistic missile (ABM) defense systems,*** on the grounds that such defensive systems were destabilizing: if one side knew it could defend itself against nuclear attack, then mutual destruction no longer would be assured and that side might be more likely to launch a first strike.

Trade was also a major component of détente, both for economic reasons (Prosperity) and because of its utility for Peace and Power objectives. With respect to the latter two, as stated in one Nixon administration report, "our purpose is to build in both countries a vested economic interest in the maintenance of a harmonious and enduring relationship. . . . If we can create a situation in which the use of military force would jeopardize a mutually profitable relationship, I think it can be argued that security will have been enhanced."[27] The linkages between Prosperity and Peace and Power were evident both in the grain deal the United States offered the Soviets in 1971 at cut-rate prices, in part to induce them to agree to SALT I, and in the pressure the Soviets put on North Vietnam in late 1972 to sign the Paris peace treaty in order to keep U.S. trade flowing.‡

In terms of economic benefits for the United States, interests were strongest in two sectors. One was agriculture. Until the 1970s, the Soviets had been largely self-sufficient in grain. The only prior major grain deal with the United States was in 1963.

---

*One was the Antarctic Treaty of 1959, prohibiting the testing or deployment of nuclear weapons in the South Pole area. Another was the Limited Test Ban Treaty of 1963, with Great Britain and France also signees, prohibiting nuclear-weapons testing in the atmosphere, under water, or in outer space, and imposing some limits on underground testing.

†The technical term is MIRVs, or multiple independently targeted re-entry vehicles. Think of missiles as delivery vehicles on which nuclear bombs are loaded. A MIRVed missile is one that can hold multiple bombs, each aimed at its own target.

‡According to the *Wall Street Journal,* when President Nixon announced stepped-up bombing of North Vietnam and mining of its harbors, the Soviet trade minister, Nikolai Patolichev, was meeting with the U.S. commerce secretary, Peter G. Peterson. "After hearing Mr. Nixon's tough words, he [Patolichev] turned to his host [Peterson] and said: 'Well, let's get back to business.' And a couple of days later he posed happily with the President, a clear signal to Hanoi that Moscow put its own interests first." Cited in Bruce W. Jentleson, "The Political Basis for Trade in U.S.–Soviet Relations," *Millennium: Journal of International Studies* 15 (Spring 1986): 31.

But because of bad weather and bad planning, Soviet grain harvests now were falling far short of their needs. Ironically, their first purchases of American grain were so huge and transacted through such clever manipulation of the markets that they garnered low prices for themselves while leaving U.S. domestic grain markets with short supplies and high inflation. The Nixon and Ford administrations worked out trade agreements for future purchases that tried to lock in the export benefits from the grain sales while insulating American markets from further inflationary effects. By 1980, American exporters supplied 80 percent of Soviet grain imports.

The other key sector was energy. The Soviet Union was second only to Saudi Arabia in the size of its oil reserves, and it was first in the world in natural-gas reserves. Even before the OPEC shocks hit in late 1973, the Nixon administration assessed that "with the tremendous increases that are projected in our energy requirements by the end of this century, it may be very much in our interest to explore seriously the possibility of gaining access to, and in fact to aid in the development of energy fields as rich as those possessed by the Soviet Union."[28] After the OPEC crisis there was even more basis for this economic calculus, not least because while supporting the OPEC embargo against the United States and the Netherlands in their rhetoric, the Soviets had undercut it by quietly providing both countries with some additional oil.

The role of Principles in promoting détente was mixed. The Nixon-Kissinger approach was to give limited emphasis in their "high politics" to Soviet political and human rights dissidents and other such issues. "The domestic practices of the Soviet Union are not necessarily related to détente," which was primarily related to foreign policy, Kissinger stated in testimony to Congress. Such a position was not "moral callousness" but rather a recognition of the "limits on our ability to produce internal change in foreign countries."[29] A particularly contentious issue in this regard was the linkage between most-favored-nation (MFN) status and other trade benefits for the Soviet Union and U.S. pressures for increased emigration rights for Soviet Jews. In keeping with his view of détente as mainly about Soviet foreign policy, Kissinger preferred to leave the Soviet Jewry issue to "quiet diplomacy." Congress, however, saw it differently, and in 1974 passed the ***Jackson-Vanik Amendment,*** linking MFN status to a prescribed increase in emigration visas for Soviet Jews.

The Carter administration put much more emphasis on human rights in its détente strategy, in two respects. One was directly vis-à-vis the Soviet Union, as when President Carter met with Aleksandr Solzhenitsyn, the renowned Soviet author and dissident who had been exiled in 1974 after decades in prison camps (gulags), and with whom President Ford and Secretary Kissinger had refused to meet. Also in a radical departure from the policies of his predecessors, Carter championed human rights with respect to the Third World. Declaring in his 1977 inaugural address that "our commitment to human rights must be absolute," Carter cut or withdrew support from such traditional "ABC" allies as the Somozas in Nicaragua and the shah of Iran.[30]

As for foreign policy politics, initially it seemed that détente might provide the basis for a new consensus. It may have appeared ironic that Richard Nixon, who had launched his political career as a staunch anticommunist, was now the one both to pursue détente with the Soviet Union and to visit "Red" China. But there was a political logic to this seeming reversal, because someone with impeccable anticommunist credentials could be insulated from charges of being soft on communism. In any case, the public was captivated by images of President Nixon in China sharing Champagne toasts with Mao Zedong, and of Soviet leader Leonid Brezhnev donning a cowboy hat and giving a bear hug to the star of a popular American television series.

Even so, détente encountered some opposition from both ends of the political spectrum. Liberals supported its overall thrust but criticized the Nixon-Kissinger de-emphasis of human rights. Conservatives, though Nixon's longtime political comrades, were not yet ready to admit that anything other than confrontation was possible with the Soviets. They were skeptical of arms control in general and of SALT I in particular. Their main criticism of SALT I was that it gave the Soviets a potential advantage once they developed MIRV technology, breaking out of essential equivalence and gaining true superiority. And on China, Mao was still the subversive who wrote that "little red book," the most famous collection of communist principles since Lenin's "What is to be Done," and conservatives' real passion was to stop the "abandonment" of Taiwan.

Executive-branch politics was marked more by the personality of Henry Kissinger than by the policy of détente. Kissinger's biographers paint a picture of a man whose ego often got in the way of his brilliance.[31] Many examples can be drawn of Kissinger's penchant for bureaucratic warfare. As President Nixon's national security adviser, he tried to confine Secretary of State William Rogers only to minor issues. When Nixon in his second term made Kissinger secretary of state, he allowed him to keep the national security adviser title as well. When Kissinger did give up the NSC post once Gerald Ford became president, he ensured that the position went to his former deputy Brent Scowcroft. Kissinger also fought major bureaucratic battles with Defense Secretary James Schlesinger, who tended to be more hawkish on arms control and defense issues. To be sure, Kissinger won more rounds of executive-branch politics than he lost. And there is something to be said for a take-charge approach that avoids bureaucratic bogs. But some of the flaws in his policies were due to his resistance to input from other top officials, and some of the enemies he made engendered political problems that in turn hampered his effectiveness.

Executive-branch politics during this period was also marred by a number of scandals. The CIA was especially hard hit, both in congressional hearings and in the media, with revelations and allegations ranging from assassination plots concocted against Fidel Castro and other foreign leaders to illegal spying on U.S. citizens at home, including monitoring and intercepting the mail of members of Congress. Covert actions, in the words of the Senate Select Committee on Intelligence Activities (known as the Church Committee after its chair, Senator Frank Church, a Democrat from Idaho), had been intended only as "exceptional instruments used only in rare instances," but "presidents and administrations have made excessive, and at times self-defeating, use of covert action."[32]

No doubt the greatest political scandal during these years was Watergate. The Watergate break-in occurred in June 1972, only a little more than a month after President Nixon's first major summit in Moscow. As it built up over the next two years, the Watergate scandal dominated the media and public opinion, crowding out most other news stories. And it precluded any chance Nixon had of converting his 1972 landslide reelection victory into a mandate for foreign or domestic policy. Ultimately, on August 9, 1974, it led to Nixon's resignation. Although Nixon didn't take détente down with him, his political self-destruction surely added to the problems détente faced.

## *Reasons for the Fall of Détente*

John Lewis Gaddis argues that détente was more about stabilizing than ending American-Soviet competition. "Its purpose was not to end [the Cold War conflict] but rather to establish rules by which it would be conducted."[33] There were tensions all along, which largely were managed, until the December 1979 Soviet invasion of Afghanistan. The Soviet invasion of Afghanistan is the event most often cited as marking the end of détente. President Carter called it "a clear threat to peace" and warned the Soviets that unless they withdrew, "this [would] inevitably jeopardize the course of United States–Soviet relations throughout the world."[34] The U.S. government's main concern, even more than the Soviet presence in Afghanistan, was that the Soviets would not stop in Afghanistan but would continue on into the oil-rich Persian Gulf region. The ***Carter Doctrine,*** proclaimed in January 1980, echoed the Truman Doctrine and other cornerstones of the early Cold War: "Let our position be clear," Carter declared. "An attempt by any outside force to gain control of the Persian Gulf region will be regarded as an assault on the vital interests of the United States of America, and such an assault will be repelled by any means necessary, including military force."[35] This was much tougher talk and a more centrist policy than Carter had originally articulated and pursued.

Yet Afghanistan wasn't solely responsible for détente's fall. There were two deeper reasons. One was that all along, and for both sides, the relaxation of tensions and increased cooperation of détente did not put an end to continued competition and rivalry. Though the 1972 Basic Principles of Relations agreement (see "At the Source," p. 161) stated that "both sides recognize that efforts to obtain unilateral advantage at the expense of the other, directly or indirectly, are inconsistent" with the objectives of détente, this statement was an example of papering over rather than resolving fundamental differences. The differences are well stated by Raymond Garthoff, a scholar and former State Department official:

> The U.S. conception of détente . . . called for U.S. manipulation of incentives and penalties in bilateral relations in order to serve other policy interests . . . a strategy for managing the emer-

> gence of Soviet power by drawing the Soviet Union into the existing world order through acceptance of a code of conduct for competition that favored the United States.
>
> The Soviet conception of détente was one of peaceful coexistence, which would set aside direct conflict between the two superpowers, in order to allow socialist and anti-imperialist forces a free hand. The Soviet leadership thus saw their task as maneuvering the United States into a world no longer marked by U.S. predominance.
>
> This discrepancy led to increasing friction.[36]

For both sides the main objective still was Power much more than Peace. This fact was evident in the different ways in which each side tried to use its relations with China as leverage in great-power politics. The Soviets were trying to get U.S. support in their split with China. The Soviet-Chinese split long had been much worse than generally was realized in the United States. In 1969 military skirmishes took place along the Soviet-Chinese border. The Soviets even tried to find out what the U.S. reaction would be if they went to war with China. Not only was this inquiry rebuffed, but one of the strategic calculations for Nixon and Kissinger in their surprise opening to China (see "At the Source," p. 169) was to use this new relationship as leverage in U.S.-Soviet relations. They were "playing the China card," as it was dubbed, beginning the "careful search for a new relationship" and shifting emphasis from the twenty-odd most recent years of animosity to the longer "history of friendship" between the Chinese and American people. Nor were Nixon and Kissinger particularly subtle in playing the China card: it was no coincidence that their trip to China came a few months earlier in 1972 than their trip to Moscow.

The clashing conceptions of the purposes of détente also were evident in the limits of what was achieved through arms control. The best that could be said for SALT I and ***SALT II*** (the follow-up agreement) was that they somewhat limited the growth of nuclear arsenals. No cuts were made by either side, just limits on future growth, and there was plenty of room within those limits for new and more destructive weapons. In addition, the Soviets were discovered to have cheated in certain areas. It took seven years after SALT I was signed until Carter and Brezhnev signed SALT II. American conservatives were strongly opposed to the new treaty, and they raised the specter of the Soviets' gaining nuclear superiority and the United States' facing a "window of vulnerability." Liberals were more supportive, although some only grudgingly so, as they did not think the treaty went far enough. SALT II never was ratified by the Senate, because Carter withdrew it in response to the Soviet invasion of Afghanistan.

Nor was it just in Afghanistan that U.S.-Soviet Third World rivalries intensified and expanded. The U.S. expectation had been that détente meant Soviet acceptance of containment, that the Soviets would step back from spreading Marxist-Leninist revolution. The Soviets, though, as Garthoff indicated, saw détente mainly as a way to avoid superpower conflict while continuing global geopolitical competition. Thus in Vietnam the Soviets pressured North Vietnam to sign the 1973 Paris peace treaty, but then aided the North's military victory and takeover of the South in 1975. They also became much

## AT THE SOURCE

AT THE SOURCE

### THE OPENING OF RELATIONS WITH CHINA

**Excerpts from a Speech by President Richard Nixon**

"The following considerations shaped this Administration's approach to the People's Republic of China.

- Peace in Asia and peace in the world require that we exchange views, not so much despite our differences as because of them. A clearer grasp of each other's purposes is essential in an age of turmoil and nuclear weapons.
- It is in America's interest, and the world's interest, that the People's Republic of China play its appropriate role in shaping international arrangements that affect its concerns. Only then will that great nation have a stake in such arrangements; only then will they endure.
- No one nation shall be the sole voice for a bloc of states. We will deal with all countries on the basis of specific issues and external behavior, not abstract theory.
- Both Chinese and American policies could be much less rigid if we had no need to consider each other permanent enemies. Over the longer term there need be no clashes between our fundamental national concerns.
- China and the United States share many parallel interests and can do much together to enrich the lives of our peoples. It is no accident that the Chinese and American peoples have such a long history of friendship.

On this basis we decided that a careful search for a new relationship should be undertaken."

Source: Richard M. Nixon, "U.S. Foreign Policy for the 1970s: The Emerging Structure of Peace," report to Congress, February 9, 1972, reprinted in *Department of State Bulletin* 66.1707 (March 13, 1972): 327.

more active in Africa, supporting Marxist coups and guerrilla wars in places such as Angola and Ethiopia.

U.S. Third World policy was still mired in confusion and contradiction. On the one hand, the Nixon and Ford administrations were still intent on containment. In Chile, for example, the CIA was heavily involved in 1970–73 efforts to overthrow the socialist (but freely elected) president Salvador Allende.[37] In Angola, CIA and military aid were started for the pro-American faction battling the pro-Soviet one, but then Congress passed legislation prohibiting further aid. On these and other issues, the essence of the debate was over which "lessons of Vietnam" were the right ones: Did communism really have to be contained? Or would such efforts end up as costly quagmires?

Another, related part of the debate was over President Carter's emphasis on human rights. In Nicaragua, where the dictatorship of the Somoza family had a long record of human rights violations, the Carter administration cut back support and brought pressure for reform. Although this had some positive effects, the ensuing revolution that deposed Anastasio Somoza brought to power the Sandinistas, who initially were a mix of nationalists, socialists, Marxist-Leninists, and anti-Americans. Even though the history of U.S. imperialist domination was more the cause of the revolution than was the Carter human rights policy, the Carter policy got much of the blame. The same dynamic played out in Iran, with the fall of the shah to the virulently anti-American Islamic fundamentalist revolution led by Ayatollah Ruhollah Khomeini. Not only did the United States lose a strategically located ally when the shah fell, but the whole American psyche was deeply shaken by the November 1979 seizure of the U.S. embassy in Tehran and the taking of more than seventy Americans as hostages. Ayatollah Khomeini justified the hostage taking as action against "this great Satan—America." These developments were traumatic for Americans, unaccustomed to the sense of vulnerability that the Iranian hostage crisis evoked. Those shock waves—strategic, political, and psychological—were still being felt when barely a month later the Soviets invaded Afghanistan.

Amid all this, domestic politics grew more and more divisive. President Carter had a Democratic Congress, but that helped only marginally in getting congressional support. His executive branch was stricken by bitter internal politics, with National Security Adviser Zbigniew Brzezinski and Secretary of State Cyrus Vance waging their own bureaucratic war. Conservatives, now led by an organization called the Committee on the Present Danger, became increasingly active in opposition to détente. Carter also felt pressure from agricultural interest groups when he imposed grain sanctions as part of his response to the Soviet invasion of Afghanistan. General public opinion was deeply split, and increasingly confused.

Disparagements of "the decade of so-called détente" were staples of candidate Ronald Reagan's speeches. "We are blind to reality," he said on the campaign trail, "if we refuse to recognize that détente's usefulness to the Soviets is only as a cover for their traditional and basic strategy for aggression."[38] In November 1980 Reagan was elected president. The Cold War would be renewed, and then ultimately start to end, during the Reagan presidency.

## 1970s Economic Shocks

The 1970s were the decade during which the myth of assured prosperity was shattered. The American economy, and the economic psyche of the American people, endured a series of shocks that recast the international economy and the U.S. position in it as less hegemonic and more uncertain than it had been in generations. Some of the fundamental sources of these new economic problems actually were rooted in U.S. domestic and economic policies such as LBJ's "***guns and butter***" and the stagflation that ensued, and President Nixon's overstimulation of the economy as part of his 1972 reelection strategy. But the focus was more on external (foreign) sources.

## The Nixon Shock, 1971

On August 15, 1971, with the value of the dollar at its lowest point since World War II, President Nixon announced that the United States was unilaterally devaluing the dollar, suspending its convertibility to gold, and imposing a 10 percent special tariff on imports. These moves, which came to be known as the ***Nixon shock,*** were targeted principally at Europe and Japan, which were still strategic allies, but increasingly had also become economic competitors. "Foreigners are out to screw us," Treasury Secretary John Connally rather indelicately put it, "and it's our job to screw them first."[39]

In more analytical terms the principal significance was threefold. First, whereas for the previous quarter-century the United States had been willing to grant economic concessions to its allies to help them with their economic reconstruction and ensure their political stability as part of containment, now it was projecting onto them responsibility for its own economic problems. The United States was coming close, as Kissinger and others warned, to economic war with its own allies.

Second, one of the key pillars of the liberal international economic order (LIEO), the international monetary system based on fixed exchange rates and the gold standard, had crumbled with the U.S. abandonment of the gold standard. The world risked descending back into competitive devaluations and other monetary manipulations. Some efforts were made to prevent such moves, with a system first of "floating" exchange rates and then of "flexible" ones, but the new reality fell well short of the stability and multilateralism of the old system.

Third, the free trade versus protectionism debate was reopened in U.S. domestic politics. Labor unions such as the AFL-CIO had generally supported free trade during the 1950s and 1960s. They had lobbied for loopholes for industries facing the toughest competition from imports (textiles, for instance) but had supported most free-trade bills. As long as the United States was running a trade surplus, more jobs were being created by exports than were being lost to imports. But with the United States running a merchandise trade deficit for the first time since 1893, labor unions shifted their politics accordingly, becoming much more protectionist.

## The OPEC Shocks, 1973 and 1979

The American automobile culture was built on a steady and inexpensive supply of oil. American suburban families and college students alike took it for granted that they could drive to a nearby gas station and fill up at prices of about thirty-three cents per gallon. That all changed in October 1973, when Americans had to learn a new acronym: ***OPEC (Organization of the Petroleum Exporting Countries).***

OPEC, founded in 1960, had tried oil embargoes and oil price hikes before, but they hadn't succeeded. In 1967, during the Arab-Israeli Six-Day War, two factors undermined the embargo that OPEC instituted to weaken international support for Israel. One was that some of OPEC's non-Arab members, such as Iran (a Muslim but non-Arab country) and Venezuela, didn't go along, and even stepped up their oil production. The other was that the United States at that time was still the world's largest oil producer and was able to compensate by increasing its own production by a million barrels per day. In 1973, though, the cartel held together, with all OPEC members agreeing to 25 percent production cuts, full oil embargoes targeted at the United States and the Netherlands for their support of Israel in the Yom Kippur War, and a worldwide price increase of 325 percent. U.S. oil production had been falling since 1970, and this time only a meager increase of one hundred thousand barrels per day could be mustered.

Economically the OPEC embargo was, as they say, like pouring fuel onto a fire. The stagflation, the trade imbalance, and other economic problems plaguing the American economy were made much worse. No commodity was so central to industry as oil, and no commodity was so essential to the consumer culture. Moreover, beyond the material impact, the psychological shocks were highly disorienting. The easy-in, easy-out gas stations gave way to miles-long lines. For a while gas was rationed, with fill-ups alternated daily for even-numbered and odd-numbered license plates. The ultimate insult was that it wasn't even the Soviet Union or a European power that was revealing American vulnerabilities—it was weaker, less-developed, not even "modern" countries of sheiks and shahs. Though we may condemn that type of thinking as arrogant, it is important to acknowledge it in order to understand the trauma of the OPEC oil shock.

If there were doubts or hopes that this was a one-time thing, they were shattered when the second OPEC oil shock hit in 1979 with the Iranian Revolution. Oil supplies again were disrupted. Prices were hiked. Gas lines returned, unemployment was fed, inflation skyrocketed, interest rates hit double digits, trade deficits shot up. By the mid-1980s, oil prices actually started to come down in real terms, but the marks left by the OPEC shocks were permanent.

## *The North-South Conflict and Demands for an "NIEO"*

Despite having 74 percent of the world's population, as of the early 1970s Third World countries accounted for only 17 percent of the global gross national product (GNP). So when OPEC was so successful in bringing the industrialized world to heel, many Third World countries saw an opportunity to redefine international economic relations toward greater equity and justice for the developing-world "South" against the industrialized "North." They criticized the LIEO for giving inadequate attention to issues of development and for perpetuating inequalities in the global distribution of wealth. The General Agreement on Tariffs and Trade may have opened markets, but the terms of trade tended to favor the industrial exports of the developed countries over the raw materials and foodstuffs exported by the developing world. The IMF and the "conditionalities" it attached to its loans (i.e., economic, social, and other policy changes required of Third World debtor countries in exchange for receiving IMF financial assistance) were under so much fire as to be the targets of protests and riots in Third World cities. So, too, with foreign aid, which was criticized as too little and not the right kind of development assistance.

In May 1974, at a special session of the UN General Assembly, the South put forward a "Declaration of a New International Economic Order" (see "International Perspectives," p. 174). This NIEO was intended to replace the LIEO. For the United States, this proposal threatened both its economic interests and its free-market ideology. The American economy depended on cheap commodities and raw materials, yet the NIEO demanded higher prices for raw materials and commodities in the name of "justice and equity." American multinational corporations had substantial investments in the Third World, yet the NIEO called for some form of international "regulation and supervision." The NIEO even demanded that modern science and technology be "given" to developing countries. Among proposals for "special measures in favor of the least developed" and the "full and equal participation" of developing countries in setting international economic policy were direct and indirect accusations that the United States was the source of much that was wrong with the international economy.

The NIEO declaration was formally adopted by the UN General Assembly, and some of its measures were initiated. However, it was a mostly symbolic vote. Actual economic changes were limited, and many Third World countries fell even further behind economically. For the United States, though, here was yet another external source of disruption and challenge. Anti-UN, anti–foreign aid, and anti–Third World sentiments grew ever stronger in the U.S. Congress and among the American public.

## *Trade with Japan and the Rest of the World*

In the 1950s and 1960s, an American child whose parent came back from a business trip might be told, "I got you just a little something as a present; it's a toy made in Japan." By the 1970s and 1980s, though, any child told that a present had come from Japan would think it was a stereo, or television, or VCR—not exactly a "little" something. And his or her parents might be thinking "automobile."

In 1960 Japan's per capita income was only 30 percent of the U.S. level, about equal to that of Mexico. But between 1960 and 1970 its real gross national product (GNP) grew an average of more than 10 percent per year. Its merchandise exports grew even faster, and its share of world exports doubled between the mid-1960s and the mid-1980s. U.S. trade

## INTERNATIONAL PERSPECTIVES

INTERNATIONAL PERSPECTIVES

### THE DECLARATION OF A NEW INTERNATIONAL ECONOMIC ORDER (NIEO)

"*We, the Members of the United Nations,*
Having convened a special session of the General Assembly to study for the first time the problems of raw materials and development, devoted to the consideration of the most important economic problems facing the world community. . .

Solemnly proclaim our united determination to work urgently for the establishment of a new international economic order based on equity, sovereign equality, interdependence, common interest and co-operation among all States, irrespective of their economic and social systems which shall correct inequalities and redress existing injustices, make it possible to eliminate the widening gap between the developed and the developing countries and ensure steadily accelerating economic and social development and peace and justice for present and future generations, and to that end declare . . .

It has proved impossible to achieve an even and balanced development of the international community under the existing international economic order. The gap between the developed and the developing countries continues to widen in a system which was established at a time when most of the developing countries did not even exist as independent States and which perpetuates inequality. . . .

The developing world has become a powerful factor felt in all fields of international activity. These irreversible changes in the relationship of forces in the world necessitate the active, full and equal participation of the developing countries in the formulation and application of all decisions that concern the international community. . . .

The prosperity of the international community as a whole depends upon the prosperity of its constituent parts. International co-operation for development is the shared goal and common duty of all countries. Thus the political, economic and social well-being of present and future generations depends more than ever on co-operation between all members of the international community on the basis of sovereign equality and the removal of the disequilibrium that exists between them.

The new international economic order should be founded on full respect for the following principles: . . .

The broadest co-operation of all the State members of the international community, based on equity, whereby the prevailing disparities in the world may be banished and prosperity secured for all; . . .

The necessity to ensure the accelerated development of all the developing countries, while devoting particular attention to the adoption of special measures in favour of the least developed. . . .

The right [of] every country to adopt the economic and social system that it deems to be the most appropriate for its own development and not to be subjected to discrimination of any kind as a result; . . .

Regulation and supervision of the activities of transnational corporations by taking measures in the interest of the national economies of the countries where such transnational corporations operate on the basis of the full sovereignty of those countries; . . .

Just and equitable relationship between the prices of raw materials, primary products, manufactured and semi-manufactured goods exported by developing countries and the prices of raw materials, primary commodities, manufactures, capital goods and equipment imported by them with the aim of bringing about sustained improvement in their unsatisfactory terms of trade and the expansion of the world economy; . . .

Giving to the developing countries access to the achievements of modern science and technology, and promoting the transfer of technology and the creation of indigenous technology for the benefit of the developing countries in forms and in accordance with procedures which are suited to their economies. ”

Source: "Declaration on Establishment of a New International Economic Order," *Annual Review of UN Affairs 1974* (New York: Oceana Publications, 1976), 208–12.

with Japan went from surplus to deficit. Indeed, the deficit with Japan was the single largest component of the overall U.S. trade deficit.

The United States had had trade disputes with allies before. In the 1960s, for example, it fought "chicken wars" and "pasta wars" with the Europeans. But the trade tensions with Japan threatened to rise to an even more intense level. Some of the criticism of Japan was little more than protectionism. Some was more legitimate, as Japan did have higher trade barriers and more unfair trade practices than the United States did. The two sets of issues that these discrepancies generated, closing U.S. import markets to Japanese exports and opening Japanese markets to U.S. exports, were distinct but interconnected, especially in their politics.

Things started to come to a head in the late 1970s over the issue of Japanese auto imports. Toyota, Nissan, and other Japanese car companies were beating Ford, General Motors, and Chrysler in both price and reputation for quality. Chrysler was losing so much money that the Carter administration and Congress put together a bail-out package for the company. However, when the American auto companies and unions took their case to the ***International Trade Commission (ITC),*** the main U.S. regulatory agency on import-relief cases, the ITC ruled that the main problem was of the Big Three's own creation and denied the requests to restrict Japanese auto imports. Pressure nevertheless continued in Congress. Numerous protectionist and retaliatory bills were introduced. Some members of Congress even smashed a Toyota with a sledgehammer in front of the Capitol. In 1981 the Reagan administration negotiated a "voluntary" agreement with Japan for some limits on Japanese auto imports. "Voluntary" is in quotes because, in reality, Japan had little choice.

In part as a reflection of Japan's more prominent position in world trade, the 1970s round of GATT global trade negotiations was initiated in Tokyo, Japan's capital. Like the previous six GATT rounds of negotiations, going back to 1945, the ***Tokyo Round*** was intended to promote free trade. It went further than its predecessors, however, not only lowering tariffs but also bringing down "nontariff barriers"—various governmental policies and practices that discriminated against imports and thus impeded free trade. Examples of nontariff barriers include government procurement regulations requiring that purchases be made only from domestic suppliers, or government subsidies (such as aid and tax breaks) to exporters to make their products more competitive in global markets. Such policies were not just limited to the United States; many other countries had nontariff barriers higher than those of the United States, Japan in particular. As with all GATT agreements, the strategy in the Tokyo Round was to set new rules for the whole international economic system, with all countries both making their own concessions and benefiting from those of others.

Because trade politics became so much more contentious at home over the course of the 1970s, a new U.S. legislative mechanism called ***fast-track*** was developed to help ensure passage of the Tokyo Round. In Chapter 2 we saw that the Constitution was unusually explicit in granting authority over trade to Congress, with presidential trade authority heavily subject to the limits of what Congress chooses to delegate. Fast-track authority gets its name from the guarantee that any trade agreements the president negotiates and submits to Congress will receive expedited legislative consideration within ninety days, and under a special procedural rule the vote on that agreement will be "up or down," yea or nay, with no amendments allowed. In this way Congress could allow free trade to go forward while "protecting itself," as Professor I. M. Destler insightfully put it, from the pressure of interest groups demanding special protection.[40] With fast-track authority, representatives or senators could avoid having to respond to particular concerns from lobbyists, because Congress can deal only with the package as a whole. Such concerns would therefore be deflected on to the president—and become the president's potential political liability. This worked for the Tokyo Round, which Congress passed in 1979 with large majorities in both the House and the Senate. By the mid-1990s, though, as we'll see in Chapter 10, fast-track authority unraveled amid the increased pressures of trade politics.

## Reagan, Gorbachev, and the End of the Cold War

### *The "4 Ps" under Reagan*

Ronald Reagan came into office firmly believing that American foreign policy had to be reasserted along all four dimensions of the national interest.

PEACE Not only had détente failed to bring about peace, but as far as President Reagan and his supporters were concerned the Soviets had used it "as a cover for their traditional and basic strategy of aggression." Reagan pulled few rhetorical punches: the Soviets "lie and cheat"; they had been "unrelenting" in their military buildup; indeed, "the Soviet Union underlies all the unrest that is going on. If they weren't engaged in this game of dominoes, there wouldn't be any hot spots in the world."[41] The reference to the early Cold War domino theory was intentional, and it was telling. The Soviets hadn't changed one iota as far as Reagan was concerned. Democrats such as President Carter, and even Republicans such as Nixon, Ford, and Kissinger, had been deluding themselves, and endangering the country, in thinking the Soviets had changed.

With Reagan, then, peace was not going to be achieved through negotiations. It could be achieved only through strength. "Peace through strength" was the Reagan motto.

POWER American power had to be reasserted, in a big way, and in all its aspects. The ***Reagan Doctrine*** was developed as the basis not only for taking a harder line on global containment, but also for going further than ever before toward rollback—that is, ousting communists who had come to power. Unlike Secretary of State John Foster Dulles, who failed to deliver on rollback against the 1956 Soviet invasion of Hungary, the Reagan administration provided extensive military aid, weapons, and covert action for the Afghan mujahideen fighting against the Soviets and the puppet government they set up in the Afghan capital, Kabul. The struggle was a protracted one, as Afghanistan became the Soviets' Vietnam. They suffered their own decade of defeat and demoralization, and in 1989 were forced to withdraw from Afghanistan.

Another Reagan Doctrine target was Nicaragua, where the communist-nationalist Sandinistas had triumphed. They were being opposed by the Nicaraguan contras (in Spanish, "those against"), to whom the Reagan administration supplied extensive military aid, CIA assistance, and other support. For the Reagan administration the Nicaragua issue embodied all that was wrong with the Vietnam syndrome and Carterite moralism. The Sandinistas professed Marxism-Leninism as their ideology. They were Soviet and Cuban allies. They were running guns to comrades in El Salvador and other neighboring countries. Their heritage as a movement was rooted in anti-American songs, slogans, and versions of history. But even more than that, their very existence was deemed a challenge to the credibility of American power. "If the United States cannot respond to a threat near our own borders," Reagan asked, "why should Europeans or Asians believe that we are seriously concerned about threats to them? . . . Our credibility would collapse, our alliances would crumble."[42]

Opponents of the Reagan Nicaragua policy also invoked analogies to Vietnam, but as a quagmire to be avoided, not a syndrome to be overcome. They did not necessarily embrace the Sandinistas or deny that the United States had vital interests in the region; instead they stressed the possibilities for a negotiated settlement establishing viable terms for coexistence. As for the credibility issue, they saw this as a matter more of judgment than of resolve; what would truly be impressive would be a demonstration that the United States could distinguish a test from a trap.

The Reagan administration also had to contend with its disastrous 1982–84 military intervention in Lebanon. American troops were sent to Lebanon as part of a multilateral peacekeeping force following the June 1982 Israeli military invasion of that country. Although some initial success was achieved in stabilizing the situation, the United States increasingly was pulled into the still-raging Lebanese civil war. In October 1983 an Islamic fundamentalist terrorist group bombed the barracks in which the U.S. Marine Corps was stationed in Beirut, killing 241 Marines and other personnel. Within months the Reagan administration withdrew the remaining American troops. "Redeployment offshore" was the euphemism used in official pronouncements, but this could not mask the reality of retreat.

The Lebanon failure prompted Defense Secretary Caspar Weinberger in November 1984 to give a speech laying out six criteria that needed to be met for future uses of U.S. military force ("At the Source," p. 179). The ***Weinberger criteria*** set a high threshold for when and how to use military force. The lesson being drawn from Lebanon, and indeed going back to Vietnam, was that these failures resulted because too many military commitments had been made too half-heartedly with objectives that were too vague and with too little political support, or that in other ways were inconsistent with the criteria Weinberger laid out. The pronouncement of this new doctrine brought on some intrabranch tension, with Secretary of State George Shultz arguing for a more flexible approach and still being willing in certain situations to use force on a more limited basis. The Weinberger approach, though, largely prevailed. It also was the basis for the doctrine of "decisive force" developed in 1990–91 by Colin Powell, then chair of the Joint Chiefs of Staff, for U.S. strategy in the Persian Gulf War following Iraq's invasion of Kuwait (see Chapter 8).

Power considerations also were the basis for the Reagan nuclear buildup. The "window of vulnerability" that the Reaganites believed had opened up because of the combined effects of the Soviet nuclear buildup and the Carter "defense neglect" needed to be closed,

## AT THE SOURCE

AT THE SOURCE

### THE "WEINBERGER CRITERIA" FOR THE USE OF MILITARY FORCE (1984)

"Under what circumstances, and by what means, does a great democracy such as ours reach the painful decision that the use of military force is necessary to protect our interests or to carry out our national policy? . . .

Some reject entirely the question of whether any force can be used abroad. They want to avoid grappling with a complex issue because, despite clever rhetoric disguising their purpose, these people are in fact advocating a return to post–World War I isolationism. While they may maintain in principle that military force has a role in foreign policy, they are never willing to name the circumstances or the place where it would apply.

On the other side, some theorists argue that military force can be brought to bear in any crisis. Some of the proponents of force are eager to advocate its use even in limited amounts simply because they believe that if there are American forces of *any* size present they will somehow solve the problem.

Neither of these two extremes offers us any lasting or satisfying solutions. The first—undue reserve—would lead us ultimately to withdraw from international events that require free nations to defend their interests from the aggressive use of force. . . .

The second alternative—employing our forces almost indiscriminately and as a regular and customary part of our diplomatic efforts—would surely plunge us headlong into the sort of domestic turmoil we experienced during the Vietnam War, without accomplishing the goal for which we committed our forces. . . .

I believe the postwar period has taught us several lessons, and from them I have developed *six* major tests to be applied when we are weighing the use of U.S. combat forces abroad. . . .

*First,* the United States should not commit forces to *combat* overseas unless the particular engagement or occasion is deemed vital to our national interest or that of our allies. . . .

*Second,* if we decide it *is* necessary to put *combat* troops into a given situation, we should do so wholeheartedly, and with the clear intention of winning. If we are *un*willing to commit the forces or resources necessary to achieve our objectives, we should not commit them at all. . . .

*Third,* if we *do* decide to commit to combat overseas, we should have clearly defined political and military objectives. And we should know precisely how our forces

(*Continued*)

(*Continued*)

can accomplish those clearly defined objectives. And we should have and send the forces needed to do just that. . . .

*Fourth,* the relationship between our objectives and the forces we have committed—their size, composition and disposition—must be continually reassessed and adjusted if necessary. Conditions and objectives invariably change during the course of a conflict. When they do change, so must our combat requirements. . . .

*Fifth,* before the U.S. commits combat forces abroad, there must be some reasonable assurance that we will have the support of the American people and their elected representatives in Congress. . . .

*Finally,* the commitment of U.S. forces to combat should be a last resort. ”

Source: Speech by Secretary of Defense Caspar Weinberger to the National Press Club, November 28, 1984, included in Richard N. Haass, *Intervention: The Use of American Military Force in the Post–Cold War Era* (Washington, D.C.: Carnegie Endowment for International Peace Press, 1994), App. C, 173–81.

and quickly. Overall defense spending went up 16 percent in 1981, and another 14 percent in 1982. Major new nuclear-weapons systems, such as the B-1 bomber, the Trident submarine, and the MX missile, whose development had been slowed by President Carter, were revived and accelerated. The go-ahead was given for deployment in Europe of the Pershing and cruise missiles, modern and more capable intermediate-range nuclear missiles. And with great fanfare the ***Strategic Defense Initiative (SDI),*** also known as "Star Wars," was announced as an effort to build a nationwide defense umbrella against nuclear attack.

Guiding the Reagan nuclear buildup were two main shifts in *nuclear deterrence* doctrine. First, this administration was much more skeptical of arms control than were the Nixon, Ford, or Carter administrations. Security had to be guaranteed principally by one's own defense capabilities, the Reaganites believed. They did not write off arms-control prospects totally, but at minimum they wanted more bargaining chips to bring to the table. Second, they doubted the security and stability of the MAD (mutual assured destruction) doctrine. Thus they advocated replacing MAD with NUTS(!), which stood for ***nuclear utilization targeting strategy*** and which constituted a nuclear war-fighting capability. Only if the United States had the capacity to fight a "limited" nuclear war would deterrence be strengthened—and would the United States be in a position to "win" should it come to that. Their defensive strategy involved SDI, which reopened the question, supposedly settled with SALT I and the ABM Treaty, of the desirability and feasibility of building a defensive shield against nuclear attacks.

However, just as a president perceived as pursuing Peace at the expense of Power (Carter) was pulled from the left toward the center, now a president perceived as excessively risking Peace in pursuit of Power (Reagan) was pulled from the right back toward the center.[43] In the early 1980s the ***nuclear freeze movement*** gathered strength. A 1982 rally in New York City attracted some seven hundred thousand people. Large demonstrations also were held in Western Europe, protesting Pershing and cruise missile deployments there. *The Day After,* a made-for-television movie about a nuclear war, was both indicative of and a further contributor to a widespread fear that the buildup was going too far and that things might be careening out of control. These developments slowed the Reagan nuclear buildup, but they did not stop it.

PRINCIPLES They were "the focus of evil in the modern world," headed for "the ash bin of history." President Reagan didn't mince words in describing how he saw the Soviet Union (see "At the Source," p. 182). In a television debate during his 1984 reelection campaign, he accused his Democratic opponent, Walter Mondale, of being so misguided as to believe that the "Soviets were just people like ourselves." Reagan matched this view of the enemy as demonic with classic American exceptionalism. America was "a shining city on a hill," the "nation of destiny," the "last best hope of mankind." Even the Vietnam War (especially the Vietnam War) had been "a noble cause."[44]

In Nicaragua and elsewhere, the ostensibly principled human rights policies of the Carter administration came in for scathing attacks as having their own "double standards." Jeane Kirkpatrick, then a political science professor, wrote an article in 1979 strongly making this argument, which led to her appointment as Reagan's UN ambassador. How morally defensible was it, she questioned, to have cut support for Somoza in Nicaragua and the shah in Iran when the regimes that came to power in their wake (the Marxist-Leninist Sandinistas, Ayatollah Khomeini and his Islamic fundamentalists) were not just authoritarian but totalitarian? Although authoritarians weren't democratic, at least they largely limited their repression to the political sphere; totalitarian regimes sought "total" domination of the personal as well as the political spheres of life. Therefore, Kirkpatrick contended, there *was* a moral basis to the "ABC" rule, as communists were often far more repressive than other leaders, however imperfect those others may be. This argument resquared the circle, casting Principles and Power as complementary once again. The contras were freedom fighters, nothing less than the "moral equal of our Founding Fathers."[45]

This view was hard to reconcile, though, with U.S. support for the military regime in El Salvador, which tacitly supported the mass murder of its citizens. The Salvadoran "death squads" were brutal in their tactics and sweeping in whom they defined as a communist—as but one example, they assassinated the Roman Catholic archbishop Oscar Romero in his cathedral while he was saying Mass. It was Congress, over Reagan administration objections, that attached human rights conditions to U.S. aid to El Salvador. A few years later the Salvadoran defense minister conceded that Congress's insistence on these human rights conditions made the Salvadoran military realize that "in order to receive U.S. aid, we had to do certain things."[46] Among those "certain things" was cracking down on the death squads.

## AT THE SOURCE

AT THE SOURCE

### FREEDOM VS. "TOTALITARIAN EVIL"

#### Excerpts from a 1982 Speech by President Ronald Reagan

"We're approaching the end of a bloody century plagued by a terrible political invention—totalitarianism. Optimism comes less easily today, not because democracy is less vigorous, but because democracy's enemies have refined their instruments of repression. Yet optimism is in order, because day by day democracy is proving itself to be a not-at-all fragile flower. From Stettin on the Baltic to Varna on the Black Sea, the regimes planted by totalitarianism have had more than 30 years to establish their legitimacy. But none—not one regime—has yet been able to risk free elections. . . .

The decay of the Soviet experiment should come as no surprise to us. Wherever the comparisons have been made between free and closed societies—West Germany and East Germany, Austria and Czechoslovakia, Malaysia and Vietnam—it is the democratic countries that are prosperous and responsive to the needs of their people. And one of the simple but overwhelming facts of our time is this: Of all the millions of refugees we've seen in the modern world, their flight is always away from, not toward the Communist world. Today on the NATO front line our forces face east to prevent a possible invasion. On the other side of the line, the Soviet forces also face east to prevent their people from leaving. . . .

The objective I propose is quite simple to state: to foster the infrastructure of democracy, the system of a free press, unions, political parties, universities, which allows a people to choose their own way to develop their own culture, to reconcile their differences through peaceful means. . . .

No, democracy is not a fragile flower. Still it needs cultivating. If the rest of this century is to witness the gradual growth of freedom and democratic ideals, we must take action to assist the campaign for democracy. . . .

This is not cultural imperialism, it is providing the means for genuine self-determination and protection for diversity. Democracy already flourishes in countries with very different cultures and historical experiences. It would be cultural condescension, or worse, to say that any people prefer dictatorship to democracy. Who would voluntarily choose not to have the right to vote, decide to purchase government propaganda handouts instead of independent newspapers, prefer government to worker-controlled unions, opt for land to be owned by the state instead of

> those who till it, want government repression of religious liberty, a single political party instead of a free choice, a rigid cultural orthodoxy instead of democratic tolerance and diversity? ”
>
> Source: Ronald Reagan, "Address to Members of the British Parliament," June 8, 1982, *Public Papers of the Presidents: Ronald Reagan, 1982* (Washington, D.C.: U.S. Government Printing Office, 1983), 742–48.

PROSPERITY It often is forgotten that during the early 1980s the American economy was so mired in the deepest recession since the Great Depression that Ronald Reagan's popularity fell as low as 35 percent. Also forgotten is the fact that for all the attacks on Democrats for deficit spending, the Reagan administration ran up greater budget deficits during its eight years than the total deficits of every previous president from George Washington to Jimmy Carter combined. And the U.S. trade deficit, which had caused alarm in the 1970s when it was running around $30 billion, went over $100 billion in 1984, and over $150 billion in 1986.

Nevertheless the Reagan years became prosperous ones. Inflation was tamed, brought down from more than 20 percent in 1979 to less than 10 percent in 1982. The economy boomed at growth rates of over 7 percent per year. The increases in defense spending were in part responsible for this prosperity. One of candidate Reagan's most effective lines in the 1980 presidential campaign was the question posed in his closing statement in a debate with President Carter: "Are you better off now than you were four years ago?" With inflation and unemployment both running so high, most Americans answered "no." In 1984, with the economic recovery racing along, voters seemed to answer "we are now," as the revived prosperity contributed significantly to Reagan's landslide reelection victory.

## *Confrontational Foreign Policy Politics*

Pennsylvania Avenue diplomacy really broke down during the Reagan years. The dominant pattern of presidential-congressional relations was confrontational.

CONTRA AID The politics of aid to the contras and other aspects of the Nicaragua issue were the most glaring example. The debate was extremely bitter. The National Conservative Political Action Committee circulated a letter to all senators before one crucial vote on aid to the contras, threatening that "should you vote against Contra aid, we intend to see that a permanent record is made—a roll of dishonor, a list of shame, for all to see—of your failure of resolve and vision at this crucial hour."[47] For their part, liberal groups had no less harsh words for contra supporters, making for a virulent and vitriolic debate.

The contra-aid issue also got caught in "backward" institutional power-sharing arrangements. Each branch coveted the policy instruments of the other. The policy instrument the executive branch needed most—money—was controlled by Congress. The Reagan administration did get Congress to appropriate contra aid in 1983. But the aid was defeated in 1984, then passed again in 1985 but with restrictions, increased and de-restricted in 1986, cut back and re-restricted in 1987, and cut back and restricted further in 1988.

On the other side, for its preferred policy objective of a negotiated regional peace plan, Congress needed diplomatic authority and negotiating instruments of its own. But that remained the nearly exclusive authority of the executive branch, and the Reagan administration preferred more to appear to support peace negotiations than seriously to pursue them. At one point House Speaker Jim Wright actually launched his own "alternative-track diplomacy," meeting with the Nicaraguan president, Daniel Ortega. Irrespective of the ends being pursued, this was a serious breach, for the costs and risks are substantial when any member of Congress tries to circumvent the president and become an alternative negotiating partner for a foreign leader.

The greatest breach of all was the ***Iran-contra scandal,*** which combined the Nicaragua issue with U.S. Middle East policy, particularly the problem of the American hostages taken by Iranian-supported fundamentalist terrorists in Lebanon. The basic deal, as worked out by the National Security Council aide Colonel Oliver North and other Reagan administration officials, was that the United States would provide arms to Iran in exchange for Iran's help in getting the American hostages in Lebanon released; the profits from the arms sales would be used to fund the Nicaraguan contras, thereby circumventing congressional prohibitions. The scheme fell apart for a number of reasons, not the least of which was that at its core it was an illegal and unconstitutional effort to get around Congress. When the cover was broken and the scheme was revealed, Congress launched its most significant investigation since Watergate. "Secrecy, deception and disdain for the law" were among the findings of the congressional investigative committees. "The United States Constitution specifies the processes by which laws and policies are to be made and executed. Constitutional process is the essence of our democracy and our democratic form of Government is the basis of our strength. . . . The Committees find that the scheme, taken as a whole . . . violated cardinal principles of the Constitution. . . . Administration officials holding no elected office repeatedly evidenced disrespect for Congress' efforts to perform its constitutional oversight role in foreign policy."[48]

WAR POWERS The failings of the 1973 War Powers Resolution (WPR) also became increasingly apparent. As discussed earlier in this chapter, when originally passed with an override of President Nixon's veto, the WPR was regarded as finally settling the war powers issue. In practice, though, the resolution ended up being ignored far more than invoked. This was true in the Ford and Carter administrations, although the cases then were few and minor, such as the 1975 ***Mayaguez incident*** involving the limited use of force against Cambodia to rescue an American merchant ship and its crew, and the 1980 attempt to rescue American hostages in Iran. It was especially true in the Reagan administration, when uses of force were more frequent and of greater magnitude. In addition to the 1982–84 Lebanon case, these included the 1983 invasion of Grenada, which the Reagan administration defined as a rescue mission to protect American medical students but which congressional critics claimed was an effort to overthrow the island's Marxist government; the 1986 bombing of Libya in retaliation for Libyan leader Muammar Qaddafi's involvement in terrorism against Americans; and the 1987–88 naval operations in the Persian Gulf during the Iran-Iraq War to protect Kuwait, help Iraq, and maintain safe passage for oil tankers.

One of the problems inherent in the WPR that these cases made more apparent was that it ran against institutionally rooted attitudes in both branches. For presidents, opposition to the WPR has been almost an institutionally instinctual response. The WPR's very existence, let alone its specific provisions, has been seen as an infringement on the role of the commander in chief and other aspects of the presidency's constitutional share of war powers. This was true for presidents Ford and Carter but was especially so for President Reagan, who took a generally more assertive approach to the presidency.

The WPR's fundamental problem lies in the ambiguity of its legal and legislative language. Take the 1987–88 Persian Gulf naval operation as an example. The mission of the U.S. Navy in that case was defined as a defensive one: protecting oil tankers. This was not strictly a neutral act, however; it was taking the side of Kuwait and Iraq against Iran. Sure enough, Iran launched a series of attacks, and the American naval forces counterattacked. More than just one incident occurred, and there were casualties on both sides. Section 2 of the WPR, the law's statement of purpose, states that it is to apply to situations in which "imminent involvement in hostilities is clearly indicated." Yet there is no clear definition in the law of what level of attack was necessary to be considered not just "skirmishes" but actual "hostilities." Thus Congress had no definitive basis for challenging the Reagan administration's claim that the Kuwaiti reflagging operation was below the threshold of "hostilities," and thus did not fall under the strictures of the WPR.

Ambiguity also is inherent in Section 3 of the WPR and its provision for consultation with Congress "in every possible instance . . . before introducing U.S. armed forces into hostilities or into situations where imminent involvement in such is clearly indicated." When is consultation "possible"? Does it meet the requirement of being "before" if, as in 1986 when attacks were launched against Libya, congressional leaders are called in once the planes are on their way, but before they have dropped their bombs?

One doesn't have to be a linguist or a lawyer to see the problems that arise when these terms are left open to interpretation. It is true that the option was there when the law was written in 1973–74, and is there today for those who would rewrite it, to use tighter and more precise language. One could, for example, define "hostilities" as the firing of any first shot at a U.S. soldier, or "imminent involvement" as a U.S. soldier's being within range of an enemy's weapon—say 50 feet for a gun, 10 miles for a bomb, 100 miles for a missile. Clearly, though, such language tightening can present its own problems by taking too much discretion away from a president, straitjacketing the president's ability to formulate strategy.

With the WPR not resolving much, members of Congress resorted to lawsuits as a means of trying to rein the president in. In 1982 eleven House members filed suit, claiming that the commitment of U.S. military advisers to El Salvador without congressional consent violated the Constitution. A similar claim was made about the 1983 Grenada intervention. A third suit involved the 1987–88 Persian Gulf naval operation case. Yet in all three cases the courts refused to rule and dismissed the suits. These were some of the cases referred to in Chapter 2 as falling under the "political question" doctrine and therefore being "nonjusticiable," meaning that they involved political differences between the executive and legislative branches more than constitutional issues, and thus required a political resolution directly between those two branches rather than a judicial remedy. In other words, the courts were telling the president and Congress to go work the issues out themselves.

There were other issues on which President Reagan and Congress had less conflict, and some on which they even cooperated. The number of these common-ground issues increased in the second Reagan term, especially as the Cold War began to thaw.

## *The End of the Cold War: Why Did the Cold War End, and End Peacefully?*

Just as we can't say precisely when the Cold War began, neither can we pinpoint a specific date for its end. The year 1989 was truly revolutionary, as one East European Soviet-satellite regime after another fell (see Table 5.2). Some point to November 9, 1989, the day the Berlin Wall came down, as the Cold War's end. Others cite December 25, 1991, the day the Soviet Union officially was disbanded. Others place it on other dates.

But whatever the day, few if any academics, policy makers, intelligence analysts, journalists, or other "experts" predicted that the Cold War would end when it did, or as peacefully as it did. As with the origins of the Cold War, different theories have been put forward to explain its end.[49] Here we group them into two principal categories.

U.S. TRIUMPHALISM This theory gives the United States, and particularly President Reagan, the credit for having pursued a tough and assertive foreign policy that pushed

**TABLE 5.2 1989: Eastern Europe's Year of Revolution**

| Date | Event |
|---|---|
| January 11 | Hungarian parliament permits independent political parties for the first time under communist rule |
| April 5 | Ban repealed on Solidarity movement in Poland |
| May 2 | Hungary takes major steps to further open its borders with Austria, providing a route for thousands of East Germans to emigrate to West Germany |
| June 3 | Solidarity candidates for Parliament win by huge margin in Poland |
| July 21 | General Wojciech Jaruzelski, who had led the imposition of martial law in Poland in 1981, has no choice but to invite Solidarity to form a coalition government |
| October 18 | Hungary adopts a new constitution for multiparty democracy |
| October 18 | Longtime East German communist leader Erich Honecker is forced to resign, and is replaced by another, much weaker, Communist |
| November 3 | Czechoslovakia opens border for East Germans seeking to go to the West |
| November 9 | Amid mounting protests, East Germany opens the Berlin Wall and promises free elections in 1990 |
| November 10 | Unrest in Bulgaria forces resignation of Communist Party leader Todor Zhivkov |
| November 24 | Peaceful mass protests, dubbed the "velvet revolution" and led by the former political prisoner Vaclav Havel, overthrow the communist government of Czechoslovakia |
| December 6 | East German government resigns |
| December 22–25 | Protests turn violent in Romania, leading to execution of the communist leader Nicolae Ceausescu and his wife |



the Soviets into collapse (see Reading 5.3). In one sense, the credit is shared by every administration from President Truman's on; they all sustained deterrence and containment and generally pursued tough Cold War strategies (albeit some administrations more than others). The cumulative effects of those policies over the decades laid the groundwork. The pressure ratcheted up by the Reagan administration in the 1980s turned the tide. In this view, the domestic and foreign policy changes undertaken by Mikhail Gorbachev, who became the leader of the Soviet Union in 1985, were more reactions to the limited options the Reagan policies left him than bold new peace initiatives of his own.

The Soviets simply couldn't match American power as rebuilt and reasserted by Reagan. SDI was a good example. For all the questioning by critics within the United States of whether it was technologically feasible, SDI sure worried the Soviets. The Kremlin feared that the Soviet economy couldn't finance the huge expenditures necessary to keep up and doubted its scientists could master the new technologies needed. So when Gorbachev showed new interest in arms control, it was less because of his heralded "new thinking" than because he finally had to admit that his country couldn't win an arms race with the United States. So too with the Intermediate Nuclear Forces Treaty in 1987, eliminating major arsenals of nuclear weapons stationed in Europe.* This was the first U.S.–Soviet arms control treaty that ever actually reduced nuclear weapons, not just limiting their future growth (as did the SALT treaties). Yet in the triumphalist view, the INF treaty never would have happened if the Reagan administration had not withstood the political pressures of the nuclear freeze movement at home and the peace movements in Western Europe and gone ahead with the Pershing and cruise missile deployments.

The Reagan Doctrine, with its rollback as well as its containment components, stopped the tide of Soviet geopolitical gains in the Third World. In Nicaragua the Sandinistas were forced to agree to elections as part of a peace plan; sure enough, when elections were held in 1990 they lost. In El Salvador a peace accord was reached that included elections, and the pro-American side also won these elections. Most of all, the Red Army was forced to beat a retreat out of Afghanistan, with politically wrenching and demoralizing consequences back in the Soviet Union.

The triumph also was one of American principles. The fall of communism in Eastern Europe was a revolution from below, brought about by masses of people who wanted freedom and democracy. When Vaclav Havel, a playwright who had been a human rights activist and political prisoner under the communists in Czechoslovakia, became the new democratically elected president of that country, he quoted Thomas Jefferson in his inaugural speech. Lech Walesa, the courageous Polish shipyard worker and leader of the Solidarity movement, who was arrested when martial law was imposed in 1981 at Moscow's behest, now was elected president of Poland. Throughout most of the former Soviet bloc, and ultimately in most of the former Soviet Union itself, new constitutions were written, free elections held, an independent and free press established, and civil societies fostered. The "campaign for democracy" that Reagan had heralded in his 1982 speech (see "At the Source," p. 182) had been successful; "man's instinctive drive for freedom and self-determination," which throughout history "surfaces again and again" had done so, again.

---

*Intermediate-range nuclear missiles were those with attack ranges of between 500 and 5,500 kilometers (311 to 3,418 miles). This included most of the nuclear missiles stationed in NATO countries and those in the Soviet Union that could attack Western Europe. It did not include either long-range missiles that the United States and the Soviets had aimed at each other or shorter-range and battlefield nuclear weapons in the European theater.

Capitalism and its perceived promise of prosperity also were part of the appeal. Back in the late 1950s when Soviet leader Nikita Khrushchev had threatened the West that "we will bury you," he was speaking in part about economic competition and the sense that socialism was in the process of demonstrating its superiority. The Soviet system at that time had piled up impressive rates of economic growth. But this simply reflected the suitability of command economies for the initial stages of industrialization concentrated in heavy industries such as steel; over the ensuing three decades the inefficiencies of the Soviet economy both in itself and as a model had become glaringly clear. Meanwhile, for all its economic problems in the 1970s, capitalism was on the rebound in the 1980s. The postcommunist governments were quick to start selling off state enterprises, opening their economies to Western foreign investment, and taking other measures to hang out the sign "open for business," capitalist style. The results were not uniformly positive—growth rates were lower than expected, unemployment was higher, and corruption was more rampant in a number of countries. But there was no going back to communist economic systems.

Overall this view confirms the validity of the U.S. Cold War position and policies. The Soviets and their leaders really did bear most of the responsibility for the Cold War. Stalin *was* an evil megalomaniac with aspirations to global domination. Marxism-Leninism *was* an ideology whose limited appeal that declined even more over time. The Soviet Union was "a state uniquely configured to the Cold War—and it has become a good deal more difficult, now that that conflict has ended, to see how it could have done so without the Soviet Union itself having passed from the scene."[50]

Reagan also had the domestic political credibility within American foreign policy politics to counter pressures from remaining Cold Warriors. As when Nixon went to China, Reagan had sufficient standing as a hard-liner to make nuclear arms-control agreements and pursue other policies that emphasized engagement over confrontation. Although his first-term policies as well as much of his political advocacy in the 1970s fueled dangerous escalation of the Cold War, Reagan, as the historian John Patrick Diggins concludes, "turned from escalation to negotiation," from seeking to win the Cold War to seeking to end it.[51]

GORBACHEV'S LEADERSHIP AND REVISIONIST THEORIES Just as revisionist theories of the origins of the Cold War put more blame on the United States, revisionist theories of the end of the Cold War give the United States less credit. Much more credit in these explanations goes to Gorbachev. In 1982, after eighteen years in power, the Soviet leader Leonid Brezhnev died. He was replaced first by Yuri Andropov, the former head of the KGB (the Soviet spy agency), but Andropov died in 1984. His successor, Konstantin Chernenko, an old *apparatchik* (party bureaucrat) in the Brezhnev mold, was ill most of the time he was leader and died barely a year later. Gorbachev was a relative unknown when he came to power in 1985 but immediately was billed by no less a figure than the conservative British prime minister Margaret Thatcher as "a man we can do business with." And she didn't just mean business deals, she meant the whole foreign policy agenda.

5.4

At age fifty-one, Gorbachev was of a different generation than his predecessors (see Reading 5.4). He quickly proclaimed a "new thinking" based on ***glasnost (openness)*** and ***perestroika (restructuring).*** In terms of Soviet domestic policy *glasnost* meant greater political freedoms, including a degree of freedom of the press, the release of such leading dissidents as Andrei Sakharov,* and an end to the Communist party's "leading role" in society. *Perestroika* meant changes in the Soviet economy, allowing for more open markets with some private enterprise and foreign investment. In Soviet foreign policy the "new thinking" was manifest in numerous initiatives aimed at reducing tensions and promoting cooperation. Gorbachev saw possibilities for mutual security rather than just continued zero-sum East-West geopolitical competition. The British scholar Archie Brown argues that if another leader had been selected, he likely would not have pursued the policies that Gorbachev did, and the Cold War thus would not have ended when it did.[52] Under Gorbachev the Soviets became much more amenable to arms control. They signed the INF treaty in 1987 and moved forward with negotiations in the Strategic Arms Reduction Talks (START), which were the successor to SALT. Although there were doubts as to whether it was more than rhetoric, Gorbachev declared the goal of eliminating all nuclear weapons by 2000. It was also Gorbachev who agreed in 1988 to the UN-mediated accord under which the Soviets withdrew their military forces from Afghanistan. And whereas Nikita Khrushchev had crushed the 1956 Hungarian Revolution and Brezhnev had done the same to the "Prague Spring" in Czechoslovakia in 1968, Gorbachev did not send a single tank into any East European country as the people in one country after another overthrew their communist governments.

So at least part of the answer to the question of why the Cold War ended when it did, and especially to the question of why it ended peacefully, is Gorbachev. Whereas the triumphalists contend that U.S. pressures and strengths left Gorbachev with little choice other than to do what he did, revisionists argue that this is too simplistic. How many other times in history have leaders responded to crises at home and declining strength abroad by choosing repression and aggression? The central concept of foreign policy choice that frames our entire discussion of U.S. foreign policy in this book also applies to other countries. Gorbachev had choices: he could have sought to put down the rebellions in Eastern

*Andrei Sakharov was known around the world for his courageous opposition to the Soviet regime. He actually was the physicist who, earlier in his career, had developed the Soviet hydrogen bomb. But he became a leading advocate of arms control and, later, of human rights and political freedom. He was awarded the Nobel Peace Prize in 1973, but was denied permission to go to Stockholm, Sweden, to receive it. He was harassed by the KGB and, following his opposition to the Soviet invasion of Afghanistan, was put under house arrest. That was where and how he was forced to stay until Gorbachev freed him in 1986.

Europe. This might not have worked, but he could have tried it. The popular revolutions still might have prevailed, and the Cold War still might have come to an end—but it would have been a much less peaceful end. The same argument applies to many other aspects of the Gorbachev foreign policy. The choices he made were not the only ones he had. Gorbachev not only received the Nobel Peace Prize but was deemed by one leading American scholar "the most deserving recipient in the history of the award."[53]

Nor was it only Gorbachev. Revisionists also give credit to American and European peace movements.[54] They tempered Reagan's hard-line policies, keeping him, for example, from spending even more on SDI and possibly from a direct military intervention in Nicaragua. With the Reagan policies moved back toward the center, there was more of a basis for finding common ground with the Soviets. Peace activists had also built relationships over many years with intellectuals, activists, scientists, and others within the Soviet Union. Even in some of the dark days of the early 1980s, Reagan's "evil empire" rhetoric notwithstanding, various groups kept up efforts to exchange ideas, maintain communications, and try to find common ground with colleagues, counterparts, and friends within the Soviet Union. Many of these counterparts came into positions of influence under Gorbachev; even those who did not were important as sources of support and expertise for Gorbachev's liberalizing policies.[55]

Other international actors also deserve some of the credit. We have already mentioned the Polish dissident Lech Walesa and the Czech dissident Vaclav Havel, whose courage inspired and mobilized their peoples. So too did the courage of Pope John Paul II, the "Polish pope," whose influence was so great that the Soviets actually played a role in trying to assassinate him. A number of Western European leaders for many years had pushed more strongly for détente than the United States wanted. The West German chancellor Helmut Kohl was instrumental in the reunification of Germany following the fall of the Berlin Wall. The United Nations played such a key role in helping bring peace in Afghanistan and elsewhere that its peacekeeping units won the 1988 Nobel Peace Prize. Another Nobel Peace Prize went to Oscar Arias, the president of Costa Rica, whose peace plan was the basis for the settlements in Nicaragua and El Salvador. Principal focus on the two superpowers is warranted, but the roles of these other key international actors should not be ignored.

A further point concerns nuclear weapons and nuclear deterrence. Some revisionists take issue with any suggestion that nuclear weapons ultimately were part of the solution to the Cold War, seeing them more as a major part of the problem, causing close calls like the Cuban missile crisis and the overhanging specter of the arms race. Others give some credit to nuclear deterrence as having ensured the avoidance of a major-power war, but still argue that the ratcheting up of the nuclear arms race to ever higher levels prolonged the Cold War.

A final point distinguishes between the Soviets' having lost the Cold War and the United States' having "won." The assessment of the victory needs to be more nuanced, or we could draw the wrong lessons. Containment in Europe can be assessed as a successful policy, whereas aspects of Third World containment, such as the Vietnam War and support for the Nicaraguan contras, were misguided and failed. So too were various CIA covert actions, which even when they accomplished their objectives in the field had some dangerous domestic political reverberations. And some short-term successes turned out to have longer-term negative consequences—for example, in "failed states" such as Somalia and Zaire, where corrupt dictators took advantage of their "ABC" credentials to rob and repress their people, knowing that U.S. support would continue in the name of global containment; or in Afghanistan, where the void left by the Soviet defeat and the American decision to disengage once the Soviets had left was filled by the Taliban and by Osama bin Laden and his Al Qaeda terrorist organization.[56]

This is one of those debates that has no single right answer. And just as we still debate the origins of the Cold War, so too we will continue to debate its end.

What we must acknowledge is how humbling the end was, or should have been, for "experts." It was not uncommon in the mid-1980s for professors to assume that any student who imagined a post–Cold War world was just young, naive, and idealistic. The Cold War was with us and, students were told, likely to have its ups and downs, its thaws and freezes, but it was not about to go away. Yet it did.

We need to bear this lack of certainty in mind as we consider the twenty-first century and think about what the possibilities may be.

## Summary

Table 5.3 summarizes the main characteristics of U.S. foreign policy strategy in the early Cold War period, the Vietnam-détente-economic shocks period, and the Reagan-Gorbachev period. We can see elements of both continuity and change in the emphasis placed on and the strategies chosen for each of the "4 Ps:"

- *Peace:* pursued first principally by creating the multilateral structure of the United Nations, then during the 1970s through the bilateral superpower diplomacy of détente, then under President Reagan by reverting more to unilateral assertion of peace through strength.
- *Power:* containment starting in Europe and then extending to Asia and more globally, the 1970s dominated by the debate over the lessons of Vietnam, the 1980s pushing for rollback through the Reagan Doctrine; deterrence first seen as a matter of U.S. nuclear superiority to be maintained by winning the arms race, then to be ensured through arms control, then requiring a renewed arms race as a prerequisite to more effective arms control.

**TABLE 5.3 U.S. Cold War Foreign Policy Strategy**

| | Early Cold War | Vietnam, détente, economic shocks | Reagan-Gorbachev era |
|---|---|---|---|
| Peace | United Nations | Détente | Peace through strength |
| Power | Containment, arms race | Lessons of Vietnam, arms control | Reagan doctrine, arms race–arms control |
| Principles | Ideological bipolarity, Third World "ABC" | Human rights | "Evil empire," "ABC" |
| Prosperity | LIEO | OPEC, NIEO, Japan shock | Boom and deficits |

- *Principles:* the original conception of the Cold War as not simply typical great-power politics but also deeply ideological, and the attendant equation of "ABC" with democracy in the Third World; the 1970s shift to human rights and questioning of the ABC rationale; the 1980s "evil empire" ideological warfare and reversion to ABC.
- *Prosperity:* to be assured by the LIEO; then shaken by OPEC, the NIEO, and other 1970s economic shocks; and restored in the 1980s boom, albeit amid massive trade and budget deficits.

We also see varying patterns in the foreign policy politics of the different subperiods (Table 5.4). As long as the Cold War consensus held, Pennsylvania Avenue was largely a one-way street in the White House's favor, making for an imperial presidency. This was as much because of congressional deference as presidential usurpation. The executive branch grew dramatically in the size, scope, and number of foreign and defense policy agencies. Societal influences were limited and mostly supportive of official policy, the media included; they also included the extremism of McCarthyism. But the consensus was shattered by the Vietnam War. Other issues and factors also came into play, with the net effect of more conflictual Pennsylvania Avenue diplomacy, with a more assertive Congress, in the eyes of some a less imperial and more imperiled presidency, more divisive intra-executive-branch politics, more interest-group pressures, much more critical media, and more "dissensus" than consensus in public opinion. Foreign policy politics in the 1980s became even more contentious, to the point where many questioned whether, as one prominent book put it, we had become "our own worst enemy."[57]

UNIVERSITY OF WINCHESTER
LIBRARY

**TABLE 5.4 U.S. Cold War Foreign Policy Politics**

| | Early Cold War | Vietnam, détente, economic shocks | Reagan-Gorbachev era |
|---|---|---|---|
| Presidency | Imperial | Imperiled | Resurgent |
| Congress | Deferential | Assertive | Confrontational |
| Executive branch | Expanding | Bureaucratic warfare | Bureaucratic warfare |
| Interest groups | Supportive | Oppositional | Proliferating |
| News media | Cheerleaders | Critics | Critics |
| Public opinion | Consensus, McCarthyism | "Dissensus" | Polarized |

We now have a picture of the dynamics of foreign policy choice during the entire Cold War era, both the foreign policy strategy choices that were its essence (drawing on the Chapter 1 framework) and the foreign policy politics that were its process (Chapter 2). Chapter 3 gave us the historical context. And looking toward Part II, Chapters 4 and 5 have provided us with the contemporary context for the foreign policy choices that the United States faces in the post–Cold War era.

## *American Foreign Policy* Online Student StudySpace

- More insights into debates over the Vietnam war? Use the Internet exercises and videos on this chapter's *StudySpace.*
- Trying to pin down key facts and other details about détente? The web quiz can help.
- Want to get a fuller sense of what made some people call Ronald Reagan "the great communicator?" Go to a site that has one of his major speeches.

For these and other study questions, as well as other features, check out Chapter 5 on the *American Foreign Policy* Online Student StudySpace at wwnorton.com/studyspace.

## Notes

[1]Robert S. McNamara, *In Retrospect: The Tragedy and Lessons of Vietnam* (New York: Times Books, 1995), 321–33.

[2]Dean G. Acheson, *Present at the Creation: My Years at the State Department* (New York: Norton, 1969), 674.

[3]Dwight D. Eisenhower, *Mandate for Change* (New York: Doubleday, 1963), 372–73.

[4]Theodore C. Sorensen, *Kennedy* (New York: Harper and Row, 1965), 639.

[5]Cited in Stanley Karnow, *Vietnam: A History* (New York: Viking, 1983), 629.

[6]McNamara, *In Retrospect*, 322.

[7]Statement by General Bruce Palmer, Jr., cited in Bruce W. Jentleson, "American Commitments in the Third World: Theory vs. Practice," *International Organization* 41.4 (Autumn 1987): 696.

[8]Both cited in Col. Harry G. Summers, Jr., "How We Lost," *New Republic*, April 29, 1985, 22.

[9]Frank Snepp, *Decent Interval: An Insider's Account of Saigon's Indecent End* (New York: Random House, 1977); Arnold Isaacs, *Without Honor: Defeat in Vietnam and Cambodia* (Baltimore: Johns Hopkins University Press, 1983).

[10]William Appleman Williams, Thomas McCormick, Lloyd Gardner, and Walter LaFeber, *America in Vietnam: A Documentary History* (Garden City, N.Y.: Anchor Books, 1985), 122.

[11]Lyndon B. Johnson, Address at Johns Hopkins University: Peace Without Conquest, April 7, 1965, *Public Papers of the Presidents: Lyndon B. Johnson, 1965* (Washington, D.C.: U.S. Government Printing Office, 1966) 1: 395.

[12]Henry A. Kissinger, "The Vietnam Negotiations," *Foreign Affairs* 47.2 (January 1969): 218–19.

[13]Richard M. Nixon, Address to the Nation on the Situation in Southeast Asia, *Public Papers of the Presidents: Richard M. Nixon, 1970* (Washington, D.C.: U.S. Government Printing Office, 1971), 409.

[14]Cited in Snepp, *Decent Interval*, 175.

[15]Hans J. Morgenthau, "To Intervene or Not Intervene," *Foreign Affairs* 45.3 (April 1967): 434.

[16]Cited in James A. Nathan and James K. Oliver, *United States Foreign Policy and World Order*, 2d ed. (Boston: Little, Brown, 1981), 322.

[17]Lyndon B. Johnson, Telephone Remarks to the Delegates to the AFL-CIO Convention, December 9, 1965, *Public Papers of the Presidents: Lyndon B. Johnson, 1965* (Washington, D.C.: U.S. Government Printing Office, 1966) 2: 1149.

[18]Richard M. Nixon, Address to the Nation on the War in Vietnam, November 3, 1969, *Public Papers of the Presidents: Richard M. Nixon, 1969* (Washington, D.C.: U.S. Government Printing Office, 1970), 908–9.

[19]Cited in Doris Kearns, *Lyndon Johnson and the American Dream* (New York: New American Library, 1976), 264. See also Larry Berman, *Planning a Tragedy: The Americanization of the War in Vietnam* (New York: Norton, 1982); and Berman, *Lyndon Johnson's War* (New York: Norton, 1989).

[20]J. William Fulbright, "Congress and Foreign Policy," in Murphy Commission, *Organization of the Government for the Conduct of Foreign Policy* (Washington, D.C.: U.S. Government Printing Office, 1975), Vol. 5, App. L, 59.

[21]Arthur M. Schlesinger, Jr., *The Imperial Presidency* (New York: Atlantic Monthly Press, 1974), 11–12.

[22]Thomas M. Franck and Edward Weisband, *Foreign Policy by Congress* (New York: Oxford University Press, 1979).

[23]I. M. Destler, Leslie H. Gelb, and Anthony Lake, *Our Own Worst Enemy: The Unmaking of American Foreign Policy* (New York: Simon & Schuster, 1984), 137.

[24]Fulbright, "Congress and Foreign Policy," 60.

[25]James Aronson, *The Press and the Cold War* (New York: Bobbs-Merrill, 1970), 195.

[26]Speech by Secretary of Defense Robert S. McNamara, October 1967, reprinted in Bruce W. Jentleson, *Documents in American Foreign Policy: A Reader* (Davis, Ca.: University of California at Davis, 1984), 48–53.

[27]Peter G. Peterson, *U.S.-Soviet Commercial Relations in a New Era* (Washington, D.C.: U.S. Government Printing Office, 1972), 3–4.

[28]Peterson, *U.S.-Soviet Commercial Relations*, 14.

[29]Cited in Bruce W. Jentleson, *Pipeline Politics: The Complex Political Economy of East-West Energy Trade* (Ithaca, N.Y.: Cornell University Press, 1986), 142.

[30]Jimmy Carter, Inaugural Address, January 20, 1977, in *Public Papers of the Presidents: Jimmy Carter, 1977* (Washington, D.C.: U.S. Government Printing Office, 1977), 1–4.

[31]Walter Isaacson, *Kissinger: A Biography* (New York: Simon & Schuster, 1992). See also the three volumes of Kissinger's memoirs: *White House Years* (Boston: Little, Brown, 1979); *Years of Upheaval* (Boston: Little, Brown, 1982); and *Years of Renewal* (New York: Simon & Schuster, 1999).

[32]Cited in James M. McCormick, *American Foreign Policy and Process,* 2d ed. (Itasca, Ill.: Peacock, 1992), 414.

[33]John Lewis Gaddis, *The Cold War: A New History* (New York: Penguin, 2005), 198.

[34]Quoted in Gaddis Smith, *Morality, Reason and Power: American Diplomacy in the Carter Years* (New York: Hill and Wang, 1986), 223.

[35]Jimmy Carter, State of the Union Address, January 23, 1980, *Public Papers of the Presidents: Jimmy Carter, 1980–1981* (Washington, D.C.: U.S. Government Printing Office, 1981), 194–200.

[36]Raymond L. Garthoff, "Détente," in *Encyclopedia of U.S. Foreign Relations,* Bruce W. Jentleson and Thomas G. Paterson, eds. (New York: Oxford University Press, 1997), 2: 10–11.

[37]See the recently declassified documents, "New Kissinger 'Telcons' Reveal Chile Plotting at Highest Levels of U.S. Government," National Security Archive Electronic Briefing Book No. 255, www.gwu.edu/~nsarchiv/NSAEBB/NSAEBB255/index.htm (accessed 6/8/09).

[38]Cited in Bruce W. Jentleson, "Discrepant Responses to Falling Dictators: Presidential Belief Systems and the Mediating Effects of the Senior Advisory Process," *Political Psychology* 11.2 (June 1990): 371.

[39]Quoted in Seymour Hersh, *The Price of Power: Kissinger in the Nixon White House* (New York: Summit Books, 1983), 462.

[40]I. M. Destler, *American Trade Politics,* 2d ed. (Washington, D.C.: Institute of International Economics, 1992).

[41]Cited in Jentleson, "Discrepant Responses to Falling Dictators," 371.

[42]Cited in Bruce W. Jentleson, "American Diplomacy: Around the World and Along Pennsylvania Avenue," in *A Question of Balance: The President, the Congress and Foreign Policy,* Thomas E. Mann, ed. (Washington, D.C.: Brookings Institution Press, 1990), 149.

[43]Miroslav Nincic, "The United States, the Soviet Union and the Politics of Opposites," *World Politics* 40.4 (July 1988): 452–75.

[44]Cited in Jentleson, "Discrepant Responses," 372.

[45]Jentleson, "Discrepant Responses," 372.

[46]Cited in Jentleson, "American Diplomacy," 179.

[47]Cited in Jentleson, "American Diplomacy," 151.

[48]U.S. Congress, *Report of the Congressional Committees Investigating the Iran-Contra Affair,* 100th Congr., 1st sess., November 1987, 11, 411, 19.

[49]See, for example, Richard Ned Lebow and Thomas Risse-Kappen, eds., *International Relations Theory and the End of the Cold War* (New York: Columbia University Press, 1995); Richard K. Betts, ed., *Conflicts after the Cold War: Arguments on Causes of War and Peace* (New York: Macmillan, 1994); Raymond L. Garthoff, *The Great Transition: American-Soviet Relations and the End of the Cold War* (Washington, D.C.: Brookings Institution Press, 1994); and Jay Winik, *On the Brink: The Dramatic Saga of How the Reagan Administration Changed the Course of History and Won the Cold War* (New York: Simon & Schuster, 1997).

[50]John Lewis Gaddis, "The New Cold War History," lecture published by Foreign Policy Research Institute, *Footnotes* 5 (June 1998): 1–2. See also John Lewis Gaddis, *We Now Know: Rethinking Cold War History* (New York: Oxford University Press, 1997).

[51]John Patrick Diggins, "How Reagan Beat the Neocons," *New York Times,* June 11, 2004, A27.

[52]Archie Brown, "Gorbachev and the End of the Cold War," in *Ending the Cold War: Interpretations, Causation, and the Study of International Relations,* Richard K. Herrmann and Richard Ned Lebow, ed. (New York: Palgrave Macmillan, 2004), 31–57.

[53]Michael Mandelbaum, *The Ideas That Conquered the World* (New York: Public Affairs, 2002), 121.

[54]Thomas Risse-Kappen, "Did 'Peace through Strength' End the Cold War?" *International Security* 16.1 (Summer 1991): 162–88.

[55]Matthew Evangelista, *Unarmed Forces: The Transnational Movement to End the Cold War* (Ithaca, N.Y.: Cornell University Press, 1999).

[56]See Odd Arne Westad, *The Global Cold War* (Cambridge: Cambridge University Press, 2007).

[57]Destler, Gelb, and Lake, *Our Own Worst Enemy.*

# *Readings for Part I The Context of U.S. Foreign Policy: Theory and History*

# Power

1.1

HANS J. MORGENTHAU

## The Mainsprings of American Foreign Policy

Wherever American foreign policy has operated, political thought has been divorced from political action. Even where our long-range policies reflect faithfully, as they do in the Americas and in Europe, the true interests of the United States, we think about them in terms that have at best but a tenuous connection with the actual character of the policies pursued. We have acted on the international scene, as all nations must, in power-political terms; but we have tended to conceive of our actions in non-political, moralistic terms. This aversion to seeing problems of international politics as they are, and the inclination to view them in non-political and moralistic terms, can be attributed both to certain misunderstood peculiarities of the American experience in foreign affairs and to the general climate of opinion in the Western world during the better part of the nineteenth and the first decades of the twentieth centuries. Three of these peculiarities of the American experience stand out: the uniqueness of the American experiment; the actual isolation, during the nineteenth century, of the United States from the centers of world conflict; and the humanitarian pacifism and anti-imperialism of American ideology.

* * *

The fundamental error that has thwarted American foreign policy in thought and action is the antithesis of national interest and moral principles. The equation of political moralizing with morality and of political realism with immorality is itself untenable. The choice is not between moral principles and the national interest, devoid of moral dignity, but between one set of moral principles divorced from political reality, and another set of moral principles derived from political reality.

The moralistic detractors of the national interest are guilty of both intellectual error and moral perversion. The nature of the intellectual error must be obvious from what has been said thus far, as it is from the record of history: a foreign policy guided by moral abstractions, without consideration of the national interest, is bound to fail; for it accepts a standard of action alien to the nature of the action itself. All the successful statesmen of modern times from [Cardinal] Richelieu to [Winston] Churchill

---

From *In Defense of the National Interest* (New York: Knopf, 1951), chaps. 1 and 8.

have made the national interest the ultimate standard of their policies, and none of the great moralists in international affairs has attained his goals.

The perversion of the moralizing approach to foreign policy is threefold. That approach operates with a false concept of morality, developed by national societies but unsuited to the conditions of international society. In the process of its realization, it is bound to destroy the very moral values it sets out to promote. Finally, it is derived from a false antithesis between morality and power politics, thus arrogating to itself all moral values and placing the stigma of immorality upon the theory and practice of power politics.

There is a profound and neglected truth hidden in [Thomas] Hobbes's extreme dictum that the state creates morality as well as law and that there is neither morality nor law outside the state. Universal moral principles, such as justice or equality, are capable of guiding political action only to the extent that they have been given concrete content and have been related to political situations by society. What justice means in the United States can within wide limits be objectively ascertained; for interests and convictions, experiences of life and institutionalized traditions have in large measure created a consensus concerning what justice means under the conditions of American society. No such consensus exists in the relations between nations. For above the national societies there exists no international society so integrated as to be able to define for them the concrete meaning of justice or equality, as national societies do for their individual members. In consequence, the appeal to moral principles by the representative of a nation vis-à-vis another nation signifies something fundamentally different from a verbally identical appeal made by an individual in his relations to another individual member of the same national society. The appeal to moral principles in the international sphere has no concrete universal meaning. It is either so vague as to have no concrete meaning that could provide rational guidance for political action, or it will be nothing but the reflection of the moral preconceptions of a particular nation and will by that same token be unable to gain the universal recognition it pretends to deserve.

Whenever the appeal to moral principles provides guidance for political action in international affairs, it destroys the very moral principles it intends to realize. It can do so in three different ways. Universal moral principles can serve as a mere pretext for the pursuit of national policies. In other words, they fulfill the functions of those ideological rationalizations and justifications to which we have referred before. They are mere means to the ends of national policies, bestowing upon the national interest the false dignity of universal moral principles. The performance of such a function is hypocrisy and abuse and carries a negative moral connotation.

The appeal to moral principles may also guide political action to that political failure which we have mentioned above. The extreme instance of political failure on the international plane is national suicide. It may well be said that a foreign policy guided by universal moral principles, by definition relegating the national interest to the background, is under contemporary conditions of foreign policy and warfare a policy of national suicide, actual or potential. Within a national society the individual can at times afford, and may even be required, to subordinate his interests and even to sacrifice his very existence to a supra-individual moral principle—for in national societies such principles exist, capable of providing concrete standards for individual action. What is more important still, national societies take it upon themselves within certain limits to protect and promote the interests of the individual and, in particular, to guard his existence against violent attack. National societies of this kind can exist and fulfill their functions only if their individual members are willing to subordinate their individual interests in a certain measure to the common good of society. Altruism and self-sacrifice are in that measure morally required.

The mutual relations of national societies are fundamentally different. These relations are not controlled by universal moral principles concrete enough to guide the political actions of individual nations. What again is more important, no agency is able to promote and protect the interests of individual nations and to guard their existence—and that is emphatically true of the great powers—but the individual nations themselves. To ask, then, a nation to embark upon altruistic policies oblivious of the national interest is really to ask something immoral. For such disregard of the individual interest, on the part of nations as of individuals, can be morally justified only by the existence of social institutions, the embodiment of concrete moral principles, which are able to do what otherwise the individual would have to do. In the absence of such institutions it would be both foolish and morally wrong to ask a nation to forego its national interests not for the good of a society with a superior moral claim but for a chimera. Morally speaking, national egotism is not the same as individual egotism because the functions of the international society are not identical with those of a national society.

The immorality of a politically effective appeal to moral abstractions in foreign policy is consummated in the contemporary phenomenon of the moral crusade. The crusading moralist, unable in the absence of an integrated national society to transcend the limits of national moral values and political interests, identifies the national interest with the manifestation of moral principles, which is, as we have seen, the typical function of ideology. Yet the crusader goes one step farther. He projects the national moral standards onto the international scene not only with the legitimate claim of reflecting the national interest, but with the politically and morally unfounded claim of providing moral standards for all mankind to conform to in concrete political action. Through the intermediary of the universal moral appeal the national and the universal interest become one and the same thing. What is good for the crusading country is by definition good for all mankind, and if the rest of mankind refuses to accept such claims to universal recognition, it must be converted with fire and sword.

There is already an inkling of this ultimate degeneration of international moralism in [Woodrow] Wilson's crusade to make the world safe for democracy. We see it in full bloom in the universal aspirations of Bolshevism. Yet to the extent that the West, too, is persuaded that it has a holy mission, in the name of whatever moral principle, first to save the world and then to remake it, it has itself fallen victim to the moral disease of the crusading spirit in politics. If that disease should become general, as well it might, the age of political moralizing would issue in one or a series of religious world wars. The fanaticism of political religions would, then, justify all those abominations unknown to less moralistic but more politically-minded ages and for which in times past the fanaticism of other-worldly religions provided a convenient cloak.

In order to understand fully what these intellectual and moral aberrations of a moralizing in foreign policy imply, and how the moral and political problems to which that philosophy has given rise can be solved, we must recall that from the day of Machiavelli onward the controversy has been fought on the assumption that there was morality on one side and immorality on the other. Yet the antithesis that equates political moralizing with morality and political realism with immorality is erroneous.

* * *

In our time the United States is groping toward a reason of state of its own—one that expresses our national interest. The history of American foreign policy since the end of the Second World War is the story of the encounter of the American mind with a new political world. That mind was weakened in its understanding of foreign policy by half a century of ever more complete intoxication with moral abstractions. Even a mind less weakened would have found it hard to face with adequate understanding and successful action the unprecedented novelty and magnitude of the new political world. American foreign policy in that period presents itself as a slow, painful, and incomplete process of emancipation from deeply ingrained error, and of rediscovery of long-forgotten truths.

* * *

FORGET AND REMEMBER!

FORGET *the sentimental notion that foreign policy is a struggle between virtue and vice, with virtue bound to win.*

FORGET *the utopian notion that a brave new world without power politics will follow the unconditional surrender of wicked nations.*

FORGET *the crusading notion that any nation, however virtuous and powerful, can have the mission to make the world over in its own image.*

REMEMBER *that the golden age of isolated normalcy is gone forever and that no effort, however great, and no action, however radical, will bring it back.*

REMEMBER *that diplomacy without power is feeble, and power without diplomacy is destructive and blind.*

REMEMBER *that no nation's power is without limits, and hence that its policies must respect the power and interests of others.*

REMEMBER *that the American people have shown throughout their history that they are able to face the truth and act upon it with courage and resourcefulness in war, with common sense and moral determination in peace.*

*And, above all, remember always that it is not only a political necessity but also a moral duty for a nation to follow in its dealings with other nations but one guiding star, one standard for thought, one rule for action:*

THE NATIONAL INTEREST.

# *Peace*

1.2

ROBERT O. KEOHANE

## Governance in a Partially Globalized World

Talk of globalization is common today in the press and increasingly in political science. Broadly speaking, globalization means the shrinkage of distance on a world scale through the emergence and thickening of networks of connections—environmental and social as well as economic (Held et al. 1999; Keohane and Nye [1977] 2001). Forms of limited globalization have existed for centuries, as exemplified by the Silk Road. Globalization took place during the last decades of the nineteenth century, only to be reversed sharply during the thirty years after World War I. It has returned even more strongly recently, although it remains far from complete. We live in a partially globalized world.

Globalization depends on effective governance, now as in the past. Effective governance is not inevitable. If it occurs, it is more likely to take place through interstate cooperation and transnational networks than through a world state. But even if national states retain many of their present functions, effective governance of a partially—and increasingly—globalized world will require more extensive international institutions. Governance arrangements to promote cooperation and help resolve conflict must be developed if globalization is not to stall or go into reverse. . . . To make a partially globalized world benign, we need not just effective governance but the *right kind* of governance.

### DESIRABLE INSTITUTIONS FOR A PARTIALLY GLOBALIZED WORLD

. . . What political institutions would be appropriate for a partially globalized world? Political institutions are persistent and connected sets of formal and informal rules within which attempts at influence take place. In evaluating institutions, I am interested in their *consequences, functions, and procedures.* On all three dimensions, it would be quixotic to expect global governance to reach the standard of modern democracies or polyarchies, which

From "Governance in a Partially Globalized World: Presidential Address, American Political Science Association, 2000," *American Political Science Review* 95.1 (March 2001): 1–13.

Dahl (1989) has analyzed so thoroughly. Instead, we should aspire to a more loosely coupled system at the global level that attains the major objectives for which liberal democracy is designed at the national level.

## Consequences

We can think of outcomes in terms of how global governance affects the life situations of individuals. In outlining these outcome-related objectives, I combine Amartya Sen's concept of capabilities with Rawls's conception of justice. Sen (1999, 75) begins with the Aristotelian concept of "human functioning." . . . [A] person's "capability set represents the freedom to achieve: the alternative functioning combinations from which this person can choose" (p. 75). Governance should enhance the capability sets of the people being governed, leading to enhancements in their personal security, freedom to make choices, and welfare as measured by such indices as the UN Human Development Index. And it should do so in a just way, which I think of in the terms made famous by Rawls (1971). Behind the "veil of ignorance," not knowing one's future situation, people should regard the arrangements for determining the distribution of capabilities as just. As a summary of indicators, J. Roland Pennock's (1966) list holds up quite well: security, liberty, welfare, and justice.

## Functions

The world for which we need to design institutions will be culturally and politically so diverse that most functions of governance should be performed at local and national levels, on the principle familiar to students of federalism or of the European Union's notion of "subsidiarity." Five key functions, however, should be handled at least to some extent by regional or global institutions.

The first of these functions is to limit the use of large-scale violence. Warfare has been endemic in modern world politics, and modern "total warfare" all but obliterates the distinction between combatants and noncombatants, rendering the "hard shell" of the state permeable (Herz 1959). All plans for global governance, from the incremental to the utopian, begin with the determination, in the opening words of the United Nations Charter (1945), "to save succeeding generations from the scourge of war."

The second function is a generalization of the first. Institutions for global governance will need to limit the negative externalities of decentralized action. A major implication of interdependence is that it provides opportunities for actors to externalize the costs of their actions onto others. Examples include "beggar thy neighbor" monetary policies, air pollution by upwind countries, and the harboring of transnational criminals, terrorists, or former dictators. Much international conflict and discord can be interpreted as resulting from such negative externalities; much international cooperation takes the form of mutual adjustment of policy to reduce these externalities or internalize some of their costs (Keohane 1984). . . .

The third function of governance institutions is to provide *focal points* in coordination games. . . . In situations with a clear focal point, no one has an incentive to defect. Great efficiency gains can be made by agreeing on a single standard. . . . Actors may find it difficult, for distributional reasons, to reach such an agreement, but after an institutionalized solution has been found, it will be self-enforcing.

The fourth major function of governance institutions for a partially globalized world is to deal with system disruptions. As global networks have become tighter and more complex, they have generated systemic effects that are often unanticipated (Jervis 1997). Examples include the Great Depression (Kindleberger 1978); global climate change; the world financial crisis of 1997–98, with its various panics culminating in the panic of August 1998 following the Russian devaluation; and the Melissa and Lovebug viruses that hit the Internet in 2000. Some of these systemic effects arise from situations that have the structure of collaboration games in which incentives exist for defection. In the future, biotechnology, genetic manipulation, and powerful technologies of which we are as yet unaware may, like market capitalism, combine great opportunity with systemic risk.

The fifth major function of global governance is to provide a guarantee against the worst forms of abuse, particularly involving violence and deprivation, so that people can use their capabilities for productive purposes. Tyrants who murder their own people may need to be restrained or removed by outsiders. Global inequality leads to differences in capabilities that are so great as to be morally indefensible and to which concerted international action is an appropriate response. Yet, the effects of globalization on inequality are much more complicated than they are often portrayed. Whereas average per-capita income has vastly increased during the last forty years, cross-national inequality in such income does not seem to have changed dramatically during the same period, although some countries have become enormously more wealthy, and others have become poorer (Firebaugh 1999). Meanwhile, inequality within countries varies enormously. Some globalizing societies have a relatively egalitarian income distribution, whereas in others it is highly unequal. Inequality seems to be complex and conditional on many features of politics and society other than degree of globalization, and effective action to enhance human functioning will require domestic as well as international efforts.

* * *

## *Procedures*

Liberal democrats are concerned not only with outcomes but also with procedures. I will put forward three procedural criteria for an acceptable global governance system. The first is *accountability*: Publics need to have ways to hold elites accountable for their actions. The second is *participation*: Democratic principles require that some level of participation in making collective decisions be open to all competent adults in the society. The third is *persuasion*, facilitated by the existence of institutionalized procedures for communication, insulated to a significant extent from the use and threats of force and sanctions, and sufficiently open to hinder manipulation.

Our standards of accountability, participation, and persuasion will have to be quite minimal to be realistic in a polity of perhaps ten billion people. Because I assume the maintenance of national societies and state or state-like governance arrangements, I do not presume that global governance will benefit from consensus on deep substantive principles. Global governance will have to be limited and somewhat shallow if it is to be sustainable. Overly ambitious attempts at global governance would necessarily rely too much on material sanctions and coercion. The degree of consensus on principles—even procedural principles, such as those of accountability, participation, and persuasion—would be too weak to support decisions that reach deeply into people's lives and the meanings that they construct for themselves. The point of presenting ideal criteria is to portray a *direction*, not a blueprint. . . .

## *Accountability*

The partially globalized world that I imagine would not be governed by a representative electoral democracy. States will remain important; and one state/one vote is not a democratic principle. National identities are unlikely to dissolve into the sense of a larger community that is necessary for democracy to thrive.

Accountability, however, can be indirectly linked to elections without a global representative democracy. . . . Nonelectoral dimensions of accountability also exist. . . . Global governance, combined with modern communications technology (including technologies for linguistic translations), can begin to generate a public space in which some people communicate with one another about public policy without regard to distance. Criticism, heard and responded to in a public space, can help generate accountability. Professional standards comprise another form of nonelectoral accountability. . . . In devising acceptable institutions for global governance, accountability needs to be built into the mechanisms of rule making and rule implementation. . . .

Meaningful collective participation in global governance in a world of perhaps ten billion people will surely have to occur through smaller units, but these may not need to be geographically based. In the partially globalized world that I am imagining, participation will occur in the first instance among people who can understand one another, although they may be dispersed around the world in "disaporic public spheres," which Arjun Appuradai (1996, 22) calls "the crucibles of a postnational political order."

Whatever the geographical quality of the units that emerge, democratic legitimacy for such a governance system will depend on the democratic character of these smaller units of governance. It will also depend on the maintenance of sufficient autonomy and authority for these units, if participation at this level is to remain meaningful.

## *Persuasion and Institutions*

Since the global institutions that I imagine do not have superior coercive force to that of states, the influence processes that they authorize will have to be legitimate. . . . To understand the potential for legitimate governance in a partially globalized world, we need to understand how institutions can facilitate rational persuasion. How do we design institutions of governance so as to increase the scope for reflection and persuasion, as opposed to force, material incentives, and fraud?

* * *

Insofar as the consequences and functions of institutions are not seriously degraded, institutions that encourage reflection and persuasion are normatively desirable and should be fostered.

## Conclusion

The stakes in the mission I propose are high, for the world and for political science. If global institutions are designed well, they will promote human welfare. But if we bungle the job, the results could be disastrous. Either oppression or ineptitude would likely lead to conflict and a renewed fragmentation of global politics. Effective and humane global governance arrangements are not inevitable. They will depend on human effort and on deep thinking about politics.

As we face globalization, our challenge resembles that of the founders of this country: how to design working institutions for a polity of unprecedented size and diversity. Only if we rise to that challenge will we be doing our part to ensure Lincoln's "rebirth of freedom" on a world—and human—scale.

## References

Firebaugh, Glen. 1999. "Empirics of World Income Inequality." *American Journal of Sociology* 104 (May): 1597–1631.

Held, David, et. al. 1999. *Global Transformation: Politics, Economic and Culture.* Stanford, CA: Stanford University Press.

Herz, John H. 1959. *International Politics in the Atomic Age.* New York: Columbia University Press.

Jervis, Robert. 1997. *System Effects: Complexity in Political and Social Life.* Princeton: Princeton University Press.

Keohane, Robert O. 1984. *After Hegemony; Cooperation and Discord in the World Political Economy.* Princeton: Princeton University Press.

Keohane, Robert O., and Joseph S. Nye, Jr. [1977] 2001. *Power and Interdependence.* 3rd ed. New York: Addison-Wesley.

Kindleberger, Charles P. 1973. *The World in Depresssion, 1929–1939.* Berkeley: University of California Press.

Pennock, J. Roland. 1966. "Political Development, Political Systems and Political Goods." *World Politics* 18 (April): 415–34.

Rawls, John. 1971. *A Theory of Justice.* Cambridge, MA: Harvard University Press.

Sen, Amartya K. 1999. *Development as Freedom.* New York: Knopf.

# *Prosperity*

1.3

GABRIEL KOLKO

## The United States and World Economic Power

* * *

To understand the unique economic interests and aspirations of the United States in the world, and the degree to which it benefits or loses within the existing distribution and structure of power and the world economy, is to define a crucial basis for comprehending as well as predicting its role overseas.

* * *

### The United States and Raw Materials

The role of raw materials is qualitative rather than merely quantitative, and neither volume nor price can measure their ultimate significance and consequences. The economies and technologies of the advanced industrial nations, the United States in particular, are so intricate that the removal of even a small part, as in a watch, can stop the mechanism. The steel industry must add approximately thirteen pounds of manganese to each ton of steel, and though the weight and value of the increase is a tiny fraction of the total, a modern diversified steel industry *must* have manganese. The same analogy is true of the entire relationship between the industrial and so-called developing nations: The nations of the Third World may be poor, but in the last analysis the industrial world needs their resources more than these nations need the West, for poverty is nothing new to peasantry cut off from export sectors, and trading with industrial states has not ended their subsistence living standards. In case of a total rupture between the industrial and supplier nations, it is the population of the industrial world that proportionately will suffer the most.

* * *

It is extraordinarily difficult to estimate the potential role and value of these scarce minerals to the United States, but certain approximate definitions are quite sufficient to make the point that the future of American economic

From *The Roots of American Foreign Policy* (Boston: Beacon Press, 1969), chap. 3.

power is too deeply involved for this nation to permit the rest of the world to take its own political and revolutionary course in a manner that imperils the American freedom to use them. Suffice it to say, the ultimate significance of the importation of certain critical raw materials is not their cost to American business but rather the end value of the industries that *must* employ these materials, even in small quantities, or pass out of existence. And in the larger sense, confident access to raw materials is a necessary precondition for industrial expansion into new or existing fields of technology, without the fear of limiting shortages which the United States' sole reliance on its national resources would entail. Intangibly, it is really the political and psychological assurance of total freedom of development of national economic power that is vital to American economic growth. Beyond this, United States profits abroad are made on overseas investments in local export industries, giving the Americans the profits of the suppliers as well as the consumer. An isolated America would lose all this, and much more.

* * *

## World Trade and World Misery

If the postwar experience is any indication, the nonsocialist developing nations have precious little reason to hope that they can terminate the vast misery of their masses. For in reality the industrialized nations have increased their advantages over them in the world economy by almost any standard one might care to use.

The terms of trade—the unit value or cost of goods a region imports compared to its exports—have consistently disfavored the developing nations since 1958, ignoring altogether the fact that the world prices of raw materials prior to that time were never a measure of equity. Using 1958 as a base year, by 1966 the value of the exports of developing areas had fallen to 97, those of the industrial nations had risen to 104. Using the most extreme example of this shift, from 1954 to 1962 the terms of trade deteriorated 38 percent against the developing nations, for an income loss in 1962 of about $11 billion, or 30 percent more than the financial aid the Third World received that year. Even during 1961–66, when the terms of trade remained almost constant, their loss in potential income was $13.4 billion, wiping away 38 percent of the income from official foreign aid plans of every sort.

* * *

In fact, whether intended or otherwise, low prices and economic stagnation in the Third World directly benefit the industrialized nations. Should the developing nations ever industrialize to the extent that they begin consuming a significant portion of their own oil and mineral output, they would reduce the available supply to the United States and prices would rise. And there has never been any question that conservative American studies of the subject have treated the inability of the Third World to industrialize seriously as a cause for optimism in raw materials planning. Their optimism is fully warranted, since nations dependent on the world market for the capital to industrialize are unlikely to succeed, for when prices of raw materials are high they tend to concentrate on selling more raw materials, and when prices are low their earnings are insufficient to raise capital for diversification. The United States especially gears its investments, private and public, to increasing the output of exportable minerals and agricultural commodities, instead of balanced economic development. With relatively high capital-labor intensive investment and feeding transport facilities to port areas rather than to the population, such investments hardly scratch the living standards of the great majority of the local peasantry or make possible the large increases in agricultural output that are a precondition of a sustained industrial expansion.

* * *

## United States Investment and Trade

* * *

American foreign investments are unusually parasitic, not merely in the manner in which they use a minimum amount of dollars to mobilize maximum foreign resources, but also because of the United States' crucial position in the world raw-materials price structure both as consumer and exporter. This is especially true in the developing regions, where extractive industries and cheap labor result in the smallest permanent foreign contributions to national wealth. In Latin America in 1957, for example, 36 percent of United States manufacturing investments, as opposed to 56 percent in Europe and 78 percent in Canada, went for plant and equipment. And wages as a percentage of operating costs in United States manufacturing investments are far lower in Third World nations than Europe or Canada.[1]

* * *

Seen in this light, United States foreign aid has been a tool for penetrating and making lucrative the Third World in particular and the entire nonsocialist world in general. The small price for saving European capitalism made possible later vast dividends, the expansion of American capitalism, and ever greater power and profits. It is this broader capability eventually to expand and realize the ultimate potential of a region that we must recall when short-term cost accounting and a narrow view make costly American commitments to a nation or region inexplicable. Quite apart from profits on investments, during 1950–60 the United States allocated $27.3 billion in nonmilitary grants, including the agricultural disposal program. During that same period it exported $166 billion in goods on a commercial basis, and imported materials essential to the very operation of the American economy.[2] It is these vast flows of goods, profits, and wealth that set the fundamental context for the implementation and direction of United States foreign policy in the world.

## The United States and the Price of Stability

Under conditions in which the United States has been the major beneficiary of a world economy geared to serve it, the continued, invariable American opposition to basic innovations and reforms in world economic relations is entirely predictable. Not merely resistance to stabilizing commodity and price agreements, or non-tied grants and loans, but to every imperatively needed structural change has characterized United States policy toward the Third World. In short, the United States is today the bastion of the *ancient regime,* of stagnation and continued poverty for the Third World.

* * *

The numerous American interventions to protect its investors throughout the world, and the United States ability to use foreign aid and loans as a lever to extract required conformity and concessions, have been more significant as a measure of its practice. The instances of this are too plentiful to detail here, but the remarkable relationship between American complaints on this score and the demise of objectionable local political leaders deserves more than passing reference.

* * *

In today's context, we should regard United States political and strategic intervention as a rational overhead charge for its present and future freedom to act and expand. One must also point out that however high that cost may appear today, in the history of United States diplomacy specific American economic interests in a country or region have often defined the national interest on the assumption that the nation can identify its welfare with the profits of some of its citizens—whether in oil, cotton, or bananas. The costs to the state as a whole are less consequential than the desires and profits of specific class strata and their need to operate everywhere in a manner that, collectively, brings vast prosperity to the United States and its rulers.

Today it is a fact that capitalism in one country is a long-term physical and economic impossibility without a drastic shift in the distribution of the world's income. Isolated, the United States would face those domestic backlogged economic and social problems and weaknesses it has deferred confronting for over two decades, and its disappearing strength in a global context would soon open the door to the internal dynamics which might jeopardize the very existence of liberal corporate capitalism at home.

The existing global political and economic structure, with all its stagnation and misery, has not only brought the United States billions but has made possible, above all, a vast power that requires total world economic integration not on the basis of equality but of domination. And to preserve this form of world is vital to the men who run the American economy and politics at the highest levels.

## Notes

[1]Department of Commerce, *U.S. Business Investments,* 43, 65–66; *The Economist,* July 10, 1965, 167; Allan W. Johnstone, *United States Direct Investment in France* (Cambridge, 1965), 48–49; *Le Monde,* January 14–15, July 23, 1968; *Wall Street Journal,* December 12, 1967; Committee on Foreign Relations, *United States–Latin American Relations,* 388; *New York Times,* April 16, 1968.

[2]Department of Commerce, *Balance of Payments,* 120, 150–51.

# *Principles*

1.4

TONY SMITH

## The United States and the Global Struggle for Democracy: Early 1990s Perspective

If the United States had never existed, what would be the status in world affairs of democracy today? Would its forces based in France, Britain, the Low Countries, and Scandinavia have survived the assaults of fascism and communism, or would one of these rival forms of mass political mobilization have instead emerged triumphant at the end of the twentieth century?

The answer is self-evident: we can have no confidence that, without the United States, democracy would have survived. To be sure, London prepared the way for Washington in charting the course of liberal internationalism; and the United States was slow to leave isolationism after 1939, while the Red Army deserves primary praise for the defeat of Nazi Germany. Yet it is difficult to escape the conclusion that since World War I, the fortunes of democracy worldwide have largely depended on American power.

The decisive period of the century, so far as the eventual fate of democracy was concerned, came with the defeat of fascism in 1945 and the American-sponsored conversion of Germany and Japan to democracy and a much greater degree of economic liberalism. Here were the glory days of American liberal democratic internationalism (and not the 1980s, however remarkable that decade, as some believe). American leadership of the international economy—thanks to the institutions created at Bretton Woods in 1944, its strong backing for European integration with the Marshall Plan in 1947 and support for the Schuman Plan thereafter, the formation of NATO in 1949, the stability of Japanese political institutions after 1947 and that country's economic dynamism after 1950 (both dependent in good measure on American power)—created the economic, cultural, military, and political momentum that enabled liberal democracy to triumph over Soviet communism. Except perhaps for NATO, all of these developments were the product of the tenets of thinking first brought together in modern form by Woodrow Wilson, before

From *America's Mission: The United States and the Worldwide Struggle for Democracy in the 20th Century* (Princeton: Princeton University Press, 1994), chap. 1 and appendix.

being adapted to the world of the 1940s by the Roosevelt and Truman administrations.

In the moment of triumph, it should not be forgotten that for most of this century, the faith in the future expansion of democracy that had marked progressive thinking in Europe and America at the turn of the century seemed exceedingly naive. By the 1930s, democracy appeared to many to be unable to provide the unity and direction of its totalitarian rivals. Indeed, again in the 1970s, there was a resurgence of literature predicting democracy's imminent demise: its materialism, its individualism, its proceduralism (that is, the elaborate sets of rules and institutions needed to make it function), its tolerance, not to say its permissiveness—the list could be extended indefinitely—seemed to deprive it of the toughness and confidence necessary to survive in a harsh world of belligerent, ideologically driven fascist and communist states.

Fascism was essentially undone by its militarism and its racism; Soviet communism by its overcentralized economic planning and its failure to provide a political apparatus capable of dealing with the tensions of nationalism not only within the Soviet empire but inside the Soviet Union itself. By contrast, however varied the forms of government may be that rightly call themselves democratic, they have demonstrated a relative ability to accommodate class, gender, and ethnic diversity domestically through complicated institutional forms centering on competitive party systems and representative governments. As importantly, the democracies have shown an ability to cooperate internationally with one another through a variety of regimes managing the complex issues of their interdependence, despite the centrifugal force of rival state interests and nationalism. Hence, at the end of the twentieth century, democracy is unparalleled for its political flexibility, stability, legitimacy, and ability to cooperate internationally.

* * *

The most important statement on the uniqueness of American liberalism remains Alexis de Toqueville's *Democracy in America* published in 1835 (a second volume appeared in 1840). Commenting that the United States was "born free," that "the social state of the Americans is eminently democratic . . . even the seeds of aristocracy were never planted," Toqueville continues:

> There society acts by and for itself. There are no authorities except within itself; one can hardly meet anybody who would dare to conceive, much less to suggest, seeking power elsewhere. The people take part in the making of the laws by choosing the lawgivers, and they share in their application by electing the agents of the executive power; one might say that they govern themselves, so feeble and restricted is the part left to the administration, so vividly is that administration aware of its popular origin, and obedient to the fount of power. The people reign over the American political world as God rules over the universe. It is the cause and the end of all things; everything rises out of it and is absorbed back into it.[1]

Toqueville was correct to see how democratic the United States was by contrast with other countries in the 1830s, for with Andrew Jackson's election in 1828 it could rightfully call itself the first modern democracy. Yet it should be recalled that at the time of American independence there were property qualifications for the vote and that certain religious denominations, as well as women and slaves, were disfranchised. Had Toqueville arrived a decade earlier, his account might not have been so perspicacious.

* * *

It is inevitable that the meaning of liberal democracy in domestic American life should deeply mark the conduct of its foreign policy. When their policy intends to promote democracy abroad, Americans rather naturally tend to think in terms of a weak state relative to society. The result for others is a paradoxical form of "conservative radicalism": radical in that for many countries, democracy has meant an abrupt and basic political change away from the narrow-based authoritarian governments with which these people are familiar; conservative in that in fundamental ways, the Americans have not meant to disturb the traditional social power relations based on property ownership.

Here was the genius, and also the tragedy, of the American sponsorship of democracy abroad: it was genuinely innovative politically, but it was not profoundly upsetting socioeconomically. The genius of the approach was that it could be attractive to established elites abroad (provided that they had the wit to try to adapt), for whatever the hazards of introducing democracy, it promised to modernize and stabilize those regimes that could reform enough to be called democratic. The tragedy, especially in lands that were predominantly agrarian, was that these political changes (where they were accepted) were often not enough to create the cultural, economic, and social circumstances that could reinforce a democratic political order. As a result, American efforts either failed completely (as in Central America and the Caribbean during Wilson's presidency) or created narrowly based and highly corrupt elitist forms of democracy (as in the Philippines or more recently in the Dominican Republic).

It was different when the United States occupied Japan and Germany to promote democracy in 1945. But the men and women who undertook this mission were not liberal democrats of the traditional American sort. Instead, many of them were New Dealers, for whom the prerequisites of democracy included strong labor unions, land reform, welfare legislation, notions of racial equality, and government intervention in the economy. Moreover, they had the good fortune to be working with societies that already had centralized political institutions, diversified industrial economies, and (at least in Germany) many convinced democrats awaiting deliverance from fascism and communism alike. The Americans who conceived of the Alliance for Progress in Latin America were for the most part cut of the same cloth as the New Dealers. But their power in Latin America was not nearly so great as their predecessors' had been in Germany and Japan, and the socioeconomic structures of South and Central America lacked the inherent advantages for democratizers that the former fascist powers possessed. Hence the Alliance's failure.

This New Deal outlook was not typical of the Americans who took the Philippines in 1898 or who were in power under what was deservedly called the "progressive" presidency of Woodrow Wilson. These Franklin Roosevelt Democrats were also different from liberal reformers like Jimmy Carter, who favored a strictly human-rights approach to democratization. The most interesting contrast comes with Ronald Reagan, however, whose insistence on the contribution free markets could make to democratic government shared with the New Dealers the notion that political life depends in good measure on the structure of power socioeconomically (even if the two approaches differed on the need for governmental regulation and social redistribution).

As these cases suggest, American liberal democratic internationalism varied in its agenda over time. The continuity was such, however, that we can speak of a tradition in American foreign policy, one with an agenda for action abroad tied to a firm notion of the national interest that was to have momentous consequences for world affairs in the twentieth century.

* * *

In different countries, American influence has counted in different ways. For example, Czechs and Slovaks today often gratefully acknowledge the American contribution to the establishment of their democracy in 1918–9 and consider Woodrow Wilson to be virtually a founding father of their republic. Nevertheless, Czechoslovak democracy during the interwar period was almost entirely the doing of its own people. So too, Germany might well have become a democracy even without the American occupation after 1945, though the character of its political order without Allied supervision might have made it less liberal than it is today, and the pace of European economic integration might have been altogether slower, with dramatic consequences for political stability on the continent. By contrast, Japanese democracy bears a more indelible American mark due to General Douglas MacArthur's assertive role in the establishment of its postwar order.

When we turn to the pre-industrial world, the impact of American policy changes dramatically. Thus, the Philippines is a fragile democracy, the American-inspired political institutions not having resolved fundamental issues of class power in this predominately agrarian country. So too in Latin America, the American contribution to democracy has been problematic, as in the case of Chile, or decidedly negative, as in Guatemala or in the Dominican Republic (before 1978, when for the first time a positive intervention occurred). Indeed, whatever its intentions, American policy on balance may have done substantially more to shore up dictatorships in the region than to advance the cause of democracy: the emergence of the Somoza and Trujillo tyrannies as the fruits of American interventions beginning with Wilson illustrates this clearly.

However, country studies alone do not tell us enough. After both the First and Second world wars, and again today in the aftermath of the cold war, America has formulated frameworks for world order in which the promotion of democracy plays a conspicuous role. The emphasis on global security, the world market, and international law and organizations figure prominently alongside the call for national, democratic self-determination. The administrations of Wilson, Roosevelt, Truman, and Reagan emerge as particularly important in this context, where the focus is on the ability of democratic countries to cooperate internationally.

Historical watersheds, such as we are now passing through, are moments when the study of the past is especially invigorating. The past is now securely the past: the actors and the consequences of their policies have less claim on the present and so can be studied with some dispassion. Simultaneously, the present is in search of its future and must take stock of how it arrived at its current position.

As Americans ponder the challenges of world affairs at the end of the cold war, they may think back to other times when Washington's decisions were critical: not only to the end of the world wars in 1918 and 1945, but to the end of the Spanish-American War in 1898 and the Civil War in 1865 as well. What they will find is that in the aftermath of victory, Washington determined to win the peace by promoting a concept of national security calling ultimately for democratic government among those with whom the United States would work most closely.

Just how to achieve this end was never a clear matter, to be sure. As the North debated what to do with its victory over the South in 1865, so in 1898 American leaders were somewhat unsure what to do with their new role in the Far East and the Caribbean. The national debate in 1918–9 over Wilson's vision of a "peace without victory" so as "to make the world safe for democracy" was likewise raucous and uncertain. Only in the 1940s, in its planning for the postwar order, did Washington appear relatively clear in its thinking (and here too there were debates, contradictions, improvisations, and accidents aplenty as policy was made). Thus, when President Clinton, like Presidents Bush and Reagan before him, speaks of his conviction that no feature of U.S. foreign policy is more critical at the end of the cold war than helping the democratic forces in Russia, he may often be at a loss on how best to proceed. But he is articulating his concerns for peace in a recognizable way that stretches back across the generations, to American leaders in other times who have speculated on what to do in the aftermath of victory and who rightly concluded that the answer consisted in promoting the fortunes of democracy for others for the sake of American national security.

* * *

## Notes

[1]Alexis de Toqueville, *Democracy in America* (New York: Harper and Row, 1966), pt. 1, chaps. 2–3. For a modern restatement of Toqueville's insistence on American egalitarianism, see Gordon S. Wood, *The Radicalism of the American Revolution* (New York: Knopf, 1992).

# The President and Congress

2.1

ARTHUR M. SCHLESINGER, JR.

## What the Founding Fathers Intended

* * *

In drafting the Constitution, [the Founders] were, of course, concerned to correct the deficiencies of the Articles of Confederation, under which the rebellious colonies had been governed during the Revolution. The Articles had bestowed executive as well as legislative authority on Congress, establishing in effect parliamentary government without a prime minister. Article VI gave Congress control over the conduct of foreign affairs, and Article IX gave it "the sole and exclusive right and power of determining on peace and war." But the Constitution was founded on the opposite principle of the separation of power. The men of Philadelphia therefore had to work out a division of authority between the legislative and executive branches. In domestic policy, this division was reasonably clear. In foreign affairs, it was often cryptic, ambiguous and incomplete.

Their experience under the Articles led the Founding Fathers to favor more centralization of executive authority than they had known in the Confederation. Many of them probably agreed with [Alexander] Hamilton's statement in the 70th Federalist [paper] that "energy in the Executive is a leading character in the definition of good government." Those who disagreed were reassured by the expectation that Washington would be the first head of state. At the same time, their experience under the British crown led the Founding Fathers to favor less centralization of authority than they perceived in the British monarchy. As victims of what they considered a tyrannical royal prerogative, they were determined to fashion for themselves a Presidency that would be strong but still limited.

Nothing was more crucial for the new nation than the successful conduct of its external relations. There was broad agreement that national safety could best be assured through the development of equal trading relations with the states of Europe. America's "plan is commerce," Thomas Paine wrote in *Common Sense,* "and that, well attended to, will secure us the peace and friendship of all Europe, because it is the interest of all Europe to have America as a free port."[1] Washington summed up the policy in his Farewell Address: "The great rule of conduct for us in regard to foreign nations is, in extending our commercial relations to have with them as little political connection as possible." Given the clear priority the Founding Fathers

---

From *The Imperial Presidency* (Boston: Houghton Mifflin, 1973), chap. 1.

assigned to commercial over political relations, it is significant that the Constitution vested control over this primary aspect of foreign policy in Congress, assigning it the definite and unqualified power "to regulate Commerce with foreign Nations."

The Constitution also brought Congress into the treaty-making process, withholding from the President the exclusive authority enjoyed by European monarchs to make treaties. Where the British King, for example, could conclude treaties on his own, the American President was required to win the consent of two-thirds of the Senate. "The one can do alone," said Hamilton, "what the other can do only with the concurrence of a branch of the legislature."[2] And Congress received other weighty powers related to the conduct of foreign affairs: the power to make appropriations, to raise and maintain the armed forces and make rules for their government and regulation, to control naturalization and immigration, to impose tariffs, to define and punish offenses against the law of nations and, above all, "to declare War, grant Letters of Marque and Reprisal, and make Rules concerning Captures on Land and Water."

## II

This last clause—in Article I, Section 8, of the Constitution—was of prime importance. The Founders were determined to deny the American President what Blackstone had assigned to the British King—"the sole prerogative of making war and peace."[3] Even Hamilton, the most consistent advocate of executive centralization, proposed in the [Constitutional] Convention that the Senate "have the sole power of declaring war" with the executive to "have the direction of war when authorized or begun."[4]

In an early draft, the Constitution gave Congress the power to "make" war. Every scholar knows the successful intervention by [James] Madison and [Elbridge] Gerry—

> M.^r^ MADISON and M.^r^ GERRY Moved to insert "*declare*," striking out "*make*" war; leaving to the Executive the power to repel sudden attacks.

—but no one really quite knows what this exchange meant.

* * *

What does seem clear is that no one wanted either to deny the President the power to respond to surprise attack or to give the President general power to initiate hostilities. The first aspect—the acknowledgment that Presidents must on occasion begin defensive war without recourse to Congress—represented the potential breach in the congressional position and would have the most significance in the future. But the second aspect gained the most attention and brought the most comfort at the time. James Wilson, next to Madison the most penetrating political thinker at the Convention, thus portrayed the constitutional solution: this system "will not hurry us into war; it is calculated to guard against it. It will not be in the power of a single man, or a single body of men, to involve us in such distress."[5]

The Founding Fathers did not have to give unconditional power to declare war to Congress. They might have said, in language they used elsewhere in the Constitution, that war could be declared by the President with the advice and consent of Congress, or by Congress on the recommendation of the President.[6] But they chose not to mention the President at all in connection with the war-making power. Nor was this because they lacked realism about the problems of national security. In a famous passage in the 23rd Federalist [paper], Hamilton said that the powers of national self-defense must "exist without limitation, *because it is impossible to foresee or define the extent and variety of national exigencies.* . . . The circumstances that endanger the safety of nations are infinite, and for this reason no constitutional shackles can wisely be imposed on the power to which the care of it is committed. This power ought to be co-extensive with all the possible combinations of such circumstances." The Founding Fathers were determined that the national government should have all the authority required to defend the nation. But Hamilton was not asserting these unlimited powers for the Presidency, as careless commentators have assumed. He was asserting them for the national government *as a whole*—for, that is, Congress and the Presidency combined.

The resistance to giving a "single man," even if he were President of the United States, the unilateral authority to decide on war pervaded the contemporaneous literature. Hamilton's observations on the treaty-making power applied all the more forcibly to the war-making power: "The history of human conduct does not warrant that exalted opinion of human virtue which would make it wise to commit interests of so delicate and momentous a kind, as those which concern its intercourse with the rest of the world, to the sole disposal of a magistrate created and circumstanced as would be a President of the United States."[7] As Madison put it in a letter to [Thomas] Jefferson in 1798: "The constitution supposes, what the History of all Govts demonstrates, that the Ex. is the branch of power most interested in war, & most prone to it. It has accordingly with studied care vested the question of war in the Legisl."[8]

## III

At the same time, the Constitution vested the command of the Army and Navy in the President, which meant that, once Congress had authorized war, the President as Commander in Chief had full power to conduct military operations. "Of all the cares or concerns of government," said the Federalist, "the direction of war most peculiarly demands those qualities which distinguish the exercise of power by a single hand."[9] The designation of the President as Commander in Chief also sprang from a concern to assure civilian control of the military establishment. By making the Commander in Chief a civilian who would be subject to recall after four years, the Founders doubtless hoped to spare American tribulations of the sort that the unfettered command and consequent political power of a Duke of Marlborough had brought to England.

There is no evidence that anyone supposed that his office as Commander in Chief endowed the President with an independent source of authority. Even with Washington in prospect, the Founders emphasized their narrow and military definition of this presidential role. As Hamilton carefully explained in the 69th Federalist [paper], the President's power as Commander in Chief

> would be nominally the same with that of the king of Great Britain, but in substance much inferior to it. It would amount to nothing more than the supreme command and direction of the military and naval forces . . . while that of the British king extends to the *declaring* of war and to the *raising* and *regulating* of fleets and armies,—all which, by the constitution under consideration, would appertain to the legislature.

As Commander in Chief the President had no more authority than the first general of the army or the first admiral of the navy would have had as professional military men. The President's power as Commander in Chief, in short, was simply the power to issue orders to the armed forces within a framework established by Congress. And even Congress was denied the power to make appropriations for the support of the armed forces for a longer term than two years.

In addition to the command of the armed forces, the Constitution gave the President the power to receive foreign envoys and, with the advice and consent of the Senate, to appoint ambassadors as well as to make treaties. Beyond this, it had nothing specific to say about his authority in foreign affairs. However, Article II gave him general executive power; and, as the 64th and 75th Federalist Papers emphasized, the structural characteristics of the Presidency—unity, secrecy, decision, dispatch, superior sources of information—were deemed especially advantageous to the conduct of diplomacy.

The result was, as Madison said, "a partial mixture of powers." Madison indeed argued that such mingling was indispensable to the system, for unless the branches of government "be so far connected and blended as to give to each a constitutional control over the others, the degree of separation which the maxim requires, as essential to a free government, can never in practice be duly maintained." Particularly in the case of war and peace—the war-making and treaty-making powers—it was really a matter, in Hamilton's phrase, of "joint possession."[10]

In these areas the two branches had interwoven responsibilities and competing opportunities. Moreover, each had an undefined residuum of authority on which to draw—the President through the executive power and the constitutional injunction that "he shall take Care that the Laws be faithfully executed," Congress through the constitutional authorization "to make all Laws which shall be necessary and proper for carrying into Execution . . . all . . . Powers vested by this Constitution in the Government of the United States." In addition, the Constitution itself was silent on certain issues of import to the conduct of foreign affairs: among them, the recognition of foreign governments, the authority to proclaim neutrality, the role of executive agreements, the control of information essential to intelligent decision. The result, as Edward S. Corwin remarked 40 years ago, was to make of the Constitution "an invitation to struggle for the privilege of directing American foreign policy."[11]

## IV

One further consideration lingered behind the words of the Constitution and the debates of the Convention. This was the question of emergency. For the Founding Fathers were more influenced by Locke than by any other political philosopher; and, as students of Locke, they were well acquainted with Chapter 14, "Of Prerogative," in the *Second Treatise of Government.* Prerogative was the critical exception in Locke's rendition of the social contract. In general, the contract—the reciprocal obligation of ruler and ruled within the frame of law—was to prevail. In general, the authority of government was to be limited. But in emergency, Locke argued, responsible rulers could resort to exceptional power. Legislatures were too large, unwieldy and slow to cope with crisis; moreover, they were not able "to foresee, and so by laws to provide for, all accidents and necessities." Indeed, on occasion "a strict and rigid observation of the laws may do harm." This meant that there could be times when "the laws themselves should . . . give way to the executive power, or rather to this fundamental law of nature and government, viz., that, as much as may be, all the members of society are to be preserved."

Prerogative therefore was the exercise of the law of self-preservation. It was "the people's permitting their rulers to do several things of their own free choice, where the law was silent, and sometimes, too, against the direct letter of the law, for the public good, and their acquiescing in it when so done." The executive, Locke contended, must have the reserve power "to act according to discretion for the public good, without the prescription of law and sometimes even against it." If emergency prerogative were abused, the people would rebel; but, used for the good of the society, it would be accepted. "If there comes to be a question between the executive power and the people about a thing claimed as prerogative, the tendency of the exercise of such prerogative to the good or hurt of the people will easily decide that question."[12]

Locke's argument, restated in more democratic terms, was that, when the executive perceived what he deemed an emergency, he could initiate extralegal or even illegal action, but that he would be sustained and vindicated in that action only if his perception of the emergency were shared by the legislature and by the people. Though prerogative enabled the executive to act on his individual finding of emergency, whether or not his finding was right and this was a true emergency was to be determined not by the executive but by the community.

The idea of prerogative was *not* part of presidential power as defined in the Constitution. The Founding Fathers had lived with emergency, but they made no provision in the Constitution, except in relation to *habeas corpus*, for the suspension of law in the case of necessity (and even here they did not specify whether the power of suspension belonged to the executive). The argument of the Federalist Papers, in the words of Clinton Rossiter, was in effect that the Constitution was "equal to any emergency."[13]

Yet there is reason to believe that the doctrine that crisis might require the executive to act outside the Constitution in order to save the Constitution remained in the back of their minds. Even in the Federalist Papers Hamilton wrote of "that original right of self-defence which is paramount to all positive forms of government" and Madison thought it "vain to oppose constitutional barriers to the impulse of self-preservation."[14]

* * *

## Notes

[1]Felix Gilbert, *The Beginnings of American Foreign Policy: To the Farewell Address* (Harper Torchbook, 1965), 42–43.

[2]69th Federalist.

[3]E. S. Corwin, *The President* (New York, 1940), 154.

[4]C. C. Tansill, ed., *Documents . . . of the Formation of the Union of the American States* (Washington, 1927), 224.

[5]Charles A. Lofgren, "War-Making Under the Constitution: The Original Understanding," *Yale Law Review*, March 1972 (81 Yale L.J.), 685.

[6]Cf. James Grafton Rogers, *World Policing and the Constitution* (Boston, 1945), 21.

[7]75th Federalist.

[8]Madison to Jefferson, April 2, 1798, Madison, *Writings*, Gaillard Hunt, ed. (New York, 1906), VI, 312–13.

[9]73rd Federalist.

[10]The quotations are from the 47th, 48th, and 75th Federalist Papers.

[11]Corwin, *President*, 200.

[12]John Locke, *Second Treatise of Government*, Ch. 14.

[13]Clinton Rossiter, *Constitutional Dictatorship* (Princeton, 1948), 212.

[14]28th and 41st Federalist Papers.

# *Bureaucratic Politics*

2.2

GRAHAM T. ALLISON

## Conceptual Models and the Cuban Missile Crisis

Most analysts explain (and predict) the behavior of national governments in terms of various forms of one basic conceptual model, here entitled the Rational Policy Model (Model I). In terms of this conceptual model, analysts attempt to understand happenings as the more or less purposive acts of unified national governments. For these analysts, the point of an explanation is to show how the nation or government could have chosen the action in question, given the strategic problem that it faced.

* * *

For some purposes, governmental behavior can be usefully summarized as action chosen by a unitary, rational decisionmaker: centrally controlled, conpletely informed, and value maximizing. But this simplification must not be allowed to conceal the fact that a "government" consists of a conglomerate of semi-feudal, loosely allied organizations, each with a substantial life of its own. Government leaders do sit formally, and to some extent in fact, on top of this conglomerate. But governments perceive problems through organizational sensors. Governments define alternatives and estimate consequences as organizations process information. Governments act as these organizations enact routines. Government behavior can therefore be understood according to a second conceptual model, less as deliberate choices of leaders and more as *outputs* of large organizations functioning according to standard patterns of behavior.

* * *

### MODEL III: BUREAUCRATIC POLITICS

The leaders who sit on top of organizations are not a monolithic group. Rather, each is, in his own right, a player in a central, competitive game. The name of the game is bureaucratic politics: bargaining along regularized channels among players positioned hierarchically within the government. Government behavior can thus be understood according to a third conceptual model, not as organizational outputs, but as outcomes of bargaining games. In contrast with Model I, the bureaucratic politics model sees no unitary actor but rather many actors as players who focus not on a single strategic issue but on many diverse intra-national problems as well, in terms of no consistent set of strategic objectives but rather ac-

From *American Political Science Review* 62.3 (September 1969).

cording to various conceptions of national, organizational, and personal goals, making government decisions not by rational choice but by the pulling and hauling that is politics.

* * *

The concept of national security policy as political outcome contradicts both public imagery and academic orthodoxy. Issues vital to national security, it is said, are too important to be settled by political games. They must be "above" politics. To accuse someone of "playing politics with national security" is a most serious charge. What public conviction demands, the academic penchant for intellectual elegance reinforces. Internal politics is messy; moreover, according to prevailing doctrine, politicking lacks intellectual content. As such, it constitutes gossip for journalists rather than a subject for serious investigation. Occasional memoirs, anecdotes in historical accounts, and several detailed case studies to the contrary, most of the literature of foreign policy avoids bureaucratic politics. The gap between academic literature and the experience of participants in government is nowhere wider than at this point.

* * *

*Players in Positions.* The actor is neither a unitary nation, nor a conglomerate of organizations, but rather a number of individual players. Groups of these players constitute the agent for particular government decisions and actions. Players are men in jobs. . . . Positions define what players both may and must do. The advantages and handicaps with which each player can enter and play in various games stem from his position. So does a cluster of obligations for the performance of certain tasks. . . .

*Action as Politics.* Government decisions are made and government actions emerge neither as the calculated choice of a unified group, nor as a formal summary of leaders' preferences. Rather the context of shared power but separate judgments concerning important choices determines that politics is the mechanism of choice. Note the *environment* in which the game is played: inordinate uncertainty about what must be done, the necessity that something be done, and crucial consequences of whatever is done. These features force responsible men to become active players. The *pace of the game*—hundreds of issues, numerous games, and multiple channels—compels players to fight to "get other's attention," to make them "see the facts," to assure that they "take time to think seriously about the broader issue." The *structure of the game*—power shared by individuals with separate responsibilities—validates each player's feeling that "others don't see my problem," and "others must be persuaded to look at the issue from a less parochial perspective." The *rules of the game*—he who hesitates loses his chance to play at that point, and he who is uncertain about his recommendation is overpowered by others who are sure—pressures players to come down on one side of a 51–49 issue and play. The *rewards of the game*—effectiveness, i.e., impact on outcomes, as the immediate measure of performance—encourages hard play. Thus, most players come to fight to "make the government do what is right." The strategies and tactics employed are quite similar to those formalized by theorists of international relations. . . .

*Where you stand depends on where you sit.* Horizontally, the diverse demands upon each player shape his priorities, perceptions, and issues. For large classes of issues, e.g., budgets and procurement decisions, the stance of a particular player can be predicted with high reliability from information concerning his seat.

* * *

# *Public Opinion*

2.3

OLE R. HOLSTI

## Public Opinion and Foreign Policy: Challenges to the Almond-Lippmann Consensus

* * *

### The Post–World War II Consensus

The availability after World War II of growing sets of polling data and the institution of systematic studies of voting behavior, combined with the assumption of a leadership role in world affairs by the United States, served to stimulate a growth industry in analyses of public opinion. The consensus view that developed during this period of some fifteen or twenty years after the end of World War II and just prior to the Vietnam escalation centered on three major propositions:

- Public opinion is highly volatile and thus it provides very dubious foundations for a sound foreign policy.
- Public attitudes on foreign affairs are so lacking in structure and coherence that they might best be described as "non-attitudes."
- At the end of the day, however, public opinion has a very limited impact on the conduct of foreign policy.

#### *Public Opinion Is Volatile*

As noted earlier, Walter Lippmann's books of the interwar period described the mass public as neither sufficiently interested nor informed to play the pivotal role assigned to it by classical democratic theory. At the height of the Cold War thirty years later, Lippmann had become even more alarmed, depicting the mass public as not merely uninterested and uninformed, but as a powerful force that was so out of synch with reality as to constitute a massive and potentially fatal threat to effective government and policies.

> The unhappy truth is that the prevailing public opinion has been destructively wrong at the critical junctures. The people have impressed a

From *International Studies Quarterly* 36.4 (December 1992).

> critical veto upon the judgments of informed and responsible officials. They have compelled the government, which usually knew what would have been wiser, or was necessary, or what was more expedient, to be too late with too little, or too long with too much, too pacifist in peace and too bellicose in war, too neutralist or appeasing in negotiations or too intransigent. Mass opinion has acquired mounting power in this country. It has shown itself to be a dangerous master of decision when the stakes are life and death.[1]

Similarly pessimistic conclusions and dire warnings were emerging from disparate other quarters as well. Drawing on a growing body of polling data and fearing that the American public might relapse into a mindless isolationism, because only a thin veneer of postwar internationalism covered a thick bedrock of indifference to the world, Gabriel Almond depicted public opinion as a volatile and mood-driven constraint upon foreign policy: "The undertow of withdrawal is still very powerful. Deeply ingrained habits do not die easy deaths. The world outside is still very remote for most Americans; and the tragic lessons of the last decades have not been fully digested."[2] Consequently, "Perhaps the gravest general problem confronting policy-makers is that of the instability of mass moods, the cyclical fluctuations which stand in the way of policy stability."[3]

* * *

Further support for the critics and skeptics emerged from the growing body of polling data which yielded ample evidence of the public's limited store of factual knowledge about foreign affairs. Innumerable surveys revealed such stunning gaps in information as: X percent of the American public are unaware that there is a communist government in China, Y percent believe that the Soviet Union is a member of NATO, or Z percent cannot identify a single nation bordering on the Pacific Ocean. Such data reinforced the case of the critics and led some of them to propose measures to reduce the influence of the public. Thus, Lippmann called for stronger executive prerogatives in foreign affairs, and Bailey wondered whether the requirements of an effective foreign policy might make it necessary for the executive deliberately to mislead the public.[4]

## *Public Opinion Lacks Structure and Coherence*

A growing volume of data on public opinion and voting behavior, as well as increasingly sophisticated methodologies, enabled analysts not only to describe aggregate results and trends, but also to delve into the structure of political beliefs. Owing to immediate policy concerns about the U.S. role in the postwar era, many of the early studies were largely descriptive, focusing on such issues as participation in international organizations and alliances, the deployment of troops abroad, security commitments, foreign aid, trade and protectionism, and the like. The underlying premise was that a single internationalist-isolationist dimension would serve to structure foreign policy beliefs, much in the way that a liberal-conservative dimension was assumed to provide coherence to preferences on domestic issues.

In a classic study based on data from the late 1950s and early 1960s, Philip Converse concluded that the political beliefs of the mass public lack a real structure or coherence.[5] Comparing responses across several domestic and foreign policy issues, he found little if any "constraint" or underlying ideological structure that might provide some coherence to political thinking. In contrast, his analyses of elites—congressional candidates—revealed substantially higher correlations among responses to various issues. Moreover, Converse found that both mass and elite attitudes on a given issue had a short half-life. Responses in 1956 only modestly predicted responses two years later, much less in 1960. These findings led him to conclude that mass political beliefs are best described as "non-attitudes." Although Converse's findings were later to become the center of an active debate, it should be emphasized that his was not a lone voice in the wilderness. His data were drawn from the National Election Studies [NES] at the University of Michigan, and his findings were only the most widely quoted of a series of studies from the NES that came to essentially the same conclusion about the absence of structure, coherence, or persistence in the political beliefs of the mass public—especially on foreign affairs.[6]

### *Public Opinion Has Limited Impact on Foreign Policy*

The driving force behind much of the post–World War II attention to public opinion on foreign policy issues was the fear that an ill-informed and emotional mass public would serve as a powerful constraint on the conduct of American diplomacy, establishing unwise limits on policy makers, creating unrealistic expectations about what was feasible in foreign affairs, otherwise doing serious mischief to American diplomacy and, given the American role in the world, perhaps even to international stability. As Bernard Cohen demonstrated in a critical survey of the literature, however, the constraining role of public opinion was often asserted but rarely demonstrated—or even put to a systematic test.[7]

By the middle of the 1960s a consensus in fact seemed to emerge on a third point: Public opinion has little if any real impact on policy. Or, as the point was made most pithily by one State Department official: "To hell with public opinion. . . . We should lead, and not follow."[8] The weight of research evidence cast doubt on the potency of public opinion as a driving force behind, or even a significant constraint upon, foreign policy-making. For example, a classic study of the public-legislator relationship revealed that constituents' attitudes on foreign policy had less impact on members of the House of Representatives than did their views on domestic issues.[9] Cohen's research on the foreign policy bureaucracy indicated that State Department officials had a rather modest interest in public opinion, and to the extent that they even thought about the public, it was as an entity to be "educated" rather than a lodestar by which to be guided.[10] The proposition that the president has "almost a free hand" in the conduct of foreign affairs received support from other analysis, including Lipset, LaFeber, Levering, Paterson, and Graebner.[11]

* * *

## The Renaissance of Interest in Public Opinion and Foreign Policy

Just as World War II and fears of postwar isolationism among the mass public gave rise to concern about public opinion and its impact on foreign policy, the war in Vietnam was the impetus for a renewed interest in the subject. It was a major catalyst in stimulating a reexamination of the consensus that had emerged during the two decades after World War II. * * * [D]uring the past two decades analysts have begun to challenge important aspects of the consensus described above.

* * *

[J. E.] Mueller's study of public opinion toward the Korean and Vietnam wars posed [a] challenge to the thesis of mindless changes in public attitudes. To be sure, public support for the U.S. war effort in both conflicts eventually changed, but in ways that seemed explicable and rational, rather than random and mindless. More specifically, he found that increasing public opposition to the conflicts traced out a pattern that fit a curve of rising battle deaths, suggesting that the public used an understandable, if simple, heuristic to assess American policy.[12]

The most comprehensive challenge to the Almond-Lippmann thesis has emerged from studies conducted by Benjamin Page and Robert Shapiro. Their evidence includes all questions that have been posed by major polling organizations since the inception of systematic surveys in the 1930s. Of the more than 6000 questions, almost 20 percent have been asked at least twice, providing Page and Shapiro with a large data set to assess the degree of stability and change in mass public attitudes. Employing a cutoff point of a difference of 6 percent from one survey to another to distinguish between continuity and change, they found that mass opinion in the aggregate is in fact characterized by a good deal of stability and that this is no less true of foreign policy than on domestic issues.[13] More important, when attitude shifts take place, they seem to be neither random nor 180 degrees removed from the true state of world affairs. Rather, changes appear to be "reasonable, event driven" reactions to the real world, even if the information upon which they are based is marginally adequate at best. They concluded that

> virtually all the rapid shifts [in public opinion] we found were related to political and economic circumstances or to significant events which sensible citizens would take into account. In particular, most abrupt foreign policy changes took place in connection with wars, confrontations, or crises in which major changes in the actions of the United States or other nations quite naturally affect preferences about what policies to pursue.[14]

* * *

Similar conclusions, supporting Page and Shapiro and casting doubt on the Almond-Lippmann thesis, have also emerged from other studies. Jentleson found that during the post-Vietnam era, variations in public support for the use of force are best explained by differences between force to coerce foreign policy restraint by others, and force to influence or impose internal political changes within another state; the former goal has received much stronger support than the latter.[15]

An interesting variant of the "rational public" thesis stipulates that the public attempts to moderate American behavior toward the USSR by expressing preferences for a conciliatory stance from hawkish administrations while supporting more assertive policies from dovish ones.[16] To the extent that one can generalize from this study focusing on the Carter and Reagan administrations to other periods or other aspects of foreign policy, it further challenges the Almond-Lippmann thesis—indeed, it turns that proposition on its head—for it identifies the public as a source of moderation and continuity rather than of instability and unpredictability.

It is important to emphasize that none of these challenges to the Almond-Lippmann thesis is based on some newly found evidence that the public is in fact well informed about foreign affairs. Not only do polls repeatedly reveal that the mass public has a very thin veneer of factual knowledge about politics, economics, and geography; they also reveal that it is poorly informed about the specifics of conflicts, treaties, negotiations with other nations, characteristics of weapons systems, foreign leaders, and the like. Because the modest factual basis upon which the mass public reacts to international affairs remains an unchallenged—and unchallengable—fact, we are faced with a puzzle: If a generally poorly informed mass public does indeed react to international affairs in an events-driven, rational manner, what are the means that permit it to do so? Recall that a not-insignificant body of research evidence indicated that mass public attitudes lack the kind of ideological structure that would provide some coherence across specific issues and persistence through time.

* * *

## *Challenge #2: Do Public Attitudes Lack Structure and Coherence?*

* * *

Although the more recent research literature has yet to create a consensus on all aspects of the question, there does appear to be a considerable convergence of findings on two general points relating to belief structures:

1. Even though the general public may be rather poorly informed, attitudes about foreign affairs are in fact structured in at least moderately coherent ways. Indeed, low information and an ambiguous foreign policy environment are actually likely to motivate rather than preclude some type of attitude structure.
2. A single isolationist-to-internationalist dimension inadequately describes the main dimensions of public opinion on international affairs.

An early study, based on the first of the quadrennial Chicago Council on Foreign Relations (CCFR) surveys, employed factor analysis and other methods to uncover three foreign policy outlooks: "liberal internationalism," "conservative internationalism," and "non-internationalism."[17] A comparable trichotomy ("three-headed eagle") emerged from early analyses of the data on opinion leaders generated by the Foreign Policy Leadership Project (FPLP).[18]

Others have questioned the division of foreign policy attitudes into three *types* rather than *dimensions*, and they have offered compelling evidence in support of their critiques. Chittick and Billingsley have undertaken both original and secondary analyses which indicated the need for three *dimensions*, including one that taps unilateralist-multilateralist sentiments, not three *types*, to describe adequately the foreign policy beliefs of both the mass public and leaders.[19]

A major set of contributions to the debate about how best to describe foreign policy attitudes has come from Wittkopf's exemplary secondary analyses of the CCFR surveys of both the general public and leaders.[20] His results, developed inductively from the first four CCFR surveys, revealed that with a single exception, two dimensions are necessary to describe foreign policy attitudes: "support-oppose militant internationalism" (MI) and "support-oppose cooperative internationalism" (CI). Dichotomizing and crossing these dimensions yields four types, with the quadrants labeled as *hard-liners* (support MI, oppose CI), *internationalists* (support MI, support CI), *isolationists* (oppose MI, oppose CI), and *accommodationists* (oppose MI, support CI).

Support for Wittkopf's MI/CI scheme also emerges from a reanalysis of the FPLP data on American opinion leaders.[21] That study put the MI/CI scheme to a demanding test because of three major differences in the data sets: (1) The CCFR surveys were undertaken in 1974, 1978, 1982, and 1986, whereas the four FPLP studies followed two years later in each case; (2) the two sets of surveys have only a few questionnaire items in common; and (3) the MI/CI scheme was developed largely from data on the mass public, whereas the FPLP surveys focused solely on opinion leaders.

* * *

## *Challenge #3: Is Public Opinion Really Impotent?*

* * *

Several recent quantitative studies have challenged some important foundations of the theory that, at least on foreign and defense issues, the public is virtually impotent. One element of that thesis is that policy makers are relatively free agents on foreign policy questions because these issues pose few dangers of electoral retribution by voters: elections are said to be decided by domestic questions, especially those sometimes described as "pocketbook" or "bread and butter" issues. However, a systematic study of presidential campaigns between 1952 and 1984 revealed that in five of the nine elections during the period, foreign policy issues had "large effects." Or, as the authors put it, when presidential candidates devote campaign time and other resources to foreign policy issues, they are not merely "waltzing before a blind audience."[22]

Recent research on voting behavior has also emphasized the importance of retrospective evaluations of performance on voter choice among candidates, especially when one of them is an incumbent.[23] Because voters are perceived as punishing incumbent candidates or parties for foreign policy failures (for example, the Iran hostage episode) or rewarding them for successes (for example, the invasion of Panama to capture General Noriega), decisions by foreign policy leaders may be made in anticipation of public reactions and the probabilities of success or failure.

* * *

Finally, two major studies have measured the congruence between changes in public preferences and a broad range of policies over extended periods. The first, a study of public opinion and policy outcomes spanning the years 1960–1974, revealed that in almost two-thirds of 222 cases, policy outcomes corresponded to public preferences. The consistency was especially high (92%) on foreign policy issues. Monroe offers three possible explanations for his findings: Foreign policy issues permit more decision-making by the executive, are likely to be the object of relatively less interest and influence by organized interest groups, and are especially susceptible to elite manipulation.[24] The second study covered an even longer span—1935 to 1979—which included 357 significant changes of public preferences.[25] Of the 231 instances of subsequent policy changes, 153 (66%) were congruent with changes in public preferences. There was little difference in the level of congruence for domestic (70%) and foreign policy (62%) issues.

* * *

Among the more difficult cases are those dealing with public opinion as a possible constraint on action. During the 1980s, the Reagan administration undertook a massive public relations campaign of dubious legality to generate public support for assistance to the "contra" rebels in Nicaragua,[26] but a careful analysis of surveys on the issue revealed that a majority of the public opposed American military involvement in Central America.[27] Would the Reagan administration have intervened more directly or massively in Nicaragua or El Salvador in the absence of such attitudes? Solid evidence about contemporary non-events is, to understate the case, rather hard to come by. Case studies seem to be the only way to address such questions, although even this approach is not wholly free of potential problems. Does an absence of documentary references to public opinion indicate a lack of interest by decision-makers? Alternatively, was attention to public attitudes so deeply ingrained in their working habits that it was unnecessary to make constant references to it? Are frequent references to public opinion an indication of a significant impact on decisions—or of a desire on the part of officials to be "on record" as having paid attention to public sentiments?

* * *

## Conclusion

The consensus of the mid-1960s on the nature, structure, and impact of public opinion has clearly come under vigorous challenge during the past quarter century. The Vietnam War, while not the sole causal factor in the reexamination of the conventional wisdom, was certainly a catalyst. If a new consensus has yet to emerge on all of the issues discussed above, at least it seems safe to state that the field is marked by innovative research and active debates on the implications of the results.

* * *

## Notes

1Walter Lippmann, *Essays in the Public Philosophy* (Boston: Little, Brown, 1955), 20.

2Gabriel Almond, *The American People and Foreign Policy* (New York: Praeger, 1950), 85.

3Almond, *The American People*, 239. Almond's use of the term "mood" differs from that of Frank Klingberg. Almond refers to sudden shifts of interest and preferences, whereas Klingberg has used the term to explain American foreign policy in terms of generation-long societal swings between introversion and extraversion.

4Lippman, *Essays;* T. A. Bailey, *The Man in the Street: The Impact of American Public Opinion on Foreign Policy* (New York: Macmillan, 1948), 13.

5Philip E. Converse, "The Nature of Belief Systems in Mass Publics," in D. E. Apter, ed., *Ideology and Discontent* (New York: Free Press, 1964).

6A. Campbell, P. E. Converse, W. E. Miller, and D. E. Stokes, *The American Voter* (New York: Wiley, 1964).

[7]Bernard Cohen, *The Public's Impact on Foreign Policy* (Boston: Little, Brown, 1973).

[8]Quoted in Cohen, *The Public's Impact,* 62.

[9]W. E. Miller and D. E. Stokes, "Constituency Influence in Congress," *American Political Science Review* 57 (1963), 45–46.

[10]Cohen, *The Public's Impact.*

[11]S. M. Lipset, "The President, Polls, and Vietnam," *Transaction,* September/October 1966, 10–24. W. LaFeber, "American Policy-Makers, Public Opinion, and the Outbreak of Cold War, 1945–1950," in Y. Nagai and A. Inye, eds., *The Origins of Cold War in Asia* (New York: Columbia University Press, 1977); R. B. Levering, *The Public and American Foreign Policy, 1918–1978* (New York: Morrow, 1978); T. G. Paterson, "Presidential Foreign Policy, Public Opinion, and Congress: The Truman Years," *Diplomatic History* 3 (1979), 1–18; and N. A. Graebner, "Public Opinion and Foreign Policy: A Pragmatic View," in D. C. Piper and R. J. Tercheck, eds., *Interaction: Foreign Policy and Public Policy* (Washington, D.C.: American Enterprise Institute, 1983).

[12]J. E. Mueller, *War, Presidents, and Public Opinion* (New York: Wiley, 1973). During the summer of 1965, as the Johnson administration was moving toward fateful decisions regarding Vietnam, George Ball warned: "We can't win," he said, his deep voice dominating the Cabinet Room. "The war will be long and protracted, with heavy casualties. The most we can hope for is a messy conclusion. We must measure this long-term price against the short-term loss that will result from withdrawal." Producing a chart that correlated public opinion with American casualties in Korea, Ball predicted that the American public would not support a long and inconclusive war. * * *

[13]Benjamin Page and Robert Shapiro, "Foreign Policy and the Rational Public," *Journal of Conflict Resolution* 32 (1988), 211–470.

[14]Benjamin Page and Robert Shapiro, "Changes in Americans' Policy Preferences, 1935–1979," *Public Opinion Quarterly* 46 (1982), 24–42.

[15]B. W. Jentleson, "The Pretty Prudent Public: Post-Post Vietnam American Opinion on the Use of Military Force," *International Studies Quarterly* 36 (1992) 48–73.

[16]M. Nincie, "The United States, the Soviet Union, and the Politics of Opposites," *World Politics* 40 (1988), 452–750.

[17]M. Mandelbaum and W. Schneider, "The New Internationalisms," in K. A. Oye et al., eds., *Eagle Entangled: U.S. Foreign Policy in a Complex World* (New York: Longman, 1979).

[18]O. R. Holsti, "The Three-Headed Eagle: The United States and the System Change," *International Studies Quarterly* 23 (1979), 339–59; O. R. Holsti and J. N. Rosenau, "Vietnam, Consensus, and the Belief Systems of American Leaders," *World Politics* 32 (1979), 1–56; O. R. Holsti and J. N. Rosenau, *American Leadership in World Affairs: Vietnam and the Breakdown of Consensus* (London: Allen and Unwin, 1984).

[19]W. Chittick and K. R. Billingsley, "The Structure of Elite Foreign Policy Beliefs," *Western Political Quarterly* 42 (1989), 201–24. See also B. A. Barde and R. Oldendick, "Beyond Internationalism: The Case for Multiple Dimensions in Foreign Policy Attitudes," *Social Science Quarterly* 59 (1978), 732–42; and W. Chittick, K. R. Billingsly, and R. Travis, "Persistence and Change in Elite and Mass Attitudes toward U.S. Foreign Policy," *Political Psychology* 11 (1990), 385–402.

[20]E. R. Wittkopf, "On the Foreign Policy Beliefs of the American People: A Critique and Some Evidence," *International Studies Quarterly* 30 (1986), 425–45; E. R. Wittkopf, *Faces of Internationalism: Public Opinion and Foreign Policy* (Durham: Duke University Press, 1990).

[21]O. R. Holsti and J. N. Rosenau, "The Structure of Foreign Policy Attitudes among American Leaders," *Journal of Politics* 52 (1990), 94–125.

[22]J. H. Aldrich, J. I. Sullivan, and E. Bordiga, "Foreign Affairs and Issue Voting: Do Presidential Candidates 'Waltz before a Blind Audience?'" *American Political Science Review* 83 (1989), 123–41.

[23]M. Fiorina, *Retrospective Voting in American National Elections* (New Haven: Yale University Press, 1981); P. Abramson, J. H. Aldrich, and J. Rhode, *Change and Continuity in the 1988 Election* (Washington, D.C.: Congressional Quarterly, 1990).

[24]A. D. Monroe, "Consistency between Public Preferences and National Policy Decisions," *American Politics Quarterly* 7 (1979), 3–19.

[25]Benjamin Page and Robert Shapiro, "Effects of Public Opinion on Policy," *American Political Science Review* 77 (1983), 175–90.

[26]R. Parry and P. Kornbluh, "Iran-Contra's Untold Story," *Foreign Policy* 72 (1988), 3–30.

[27]R. Sobel, "Public Opinion about United States Intervention in El Salvador and Nicaragua," *Public Opinion Quarterly* 53 (1989), 114–28. See also R. H. Hinckley, *People, Polls, and Policy-Makers* (New York: Lexington, 1992).

# *Isolationism vs. Internationalism*

3.1

HENRY KISSINGER

## Franklin D. Roosevelt and the Coming of World War II

For contemporary political leaders governing by public opinion polls, Roosevelt's role in moving his isolationist people toward participation in the war serves as an object lesson on the scope of leadership in a democracy. Sooner or later, the threat to the European balance of power would have forced the United States to intervene in order to stop Germany's drive for world domination. The sheer, and growing, strength of America was bound to propel it eventually into the center of the international arena. That this happened with such speed and so decisively was the achievement of Franklin Delano Roosevelt.

All great leaders walk alone. Their singularity springs from their ability to discern challenges that are not yet apparent to their contemporaries. Roosevelt took an isolationist people into a war between countries whose conflicts had only a few years earlier been widely considered inconsistent with American values and irrelevant to American security. After 1940, Roosevelt convinced the Congress, which had overwhelmingly passed a series of Neutrality Acts just a few years before, to authorize ever-increasing American assistance to Great Britain, stopping just short of outright belligerency and occasionally even crossing that line. Finally, Japan's attack on Pearl Harbor removed America's last hesitations. Roosevelt was able to persuade a society which had for two centuries treasured its invulnerability of the dire perils of an Axis victory. And he saw to it that, this time, America's involvement would mark a first step toward permanent international engagement. During the war, his leadership held the alliance together and shaped the multilateral institutions which continue to serve the international community to this day.

No president, with the possible exception of Abraham Lincoln, has made a more decisive difference in American history. Roosevelt took the oath of office at a time of national uncertainty, when America's faith in the New World's infinite capacity for progress had been severely shaken by the Great Depression. All around him, democracies seemed to be faltering and anti-democratic governments on both the Left and the Right were gaining ground.

---

From *Diplomacy* (New York: Simon & Schuster, 1994), chap. 15.

* * *

America's journey from involvement in the First World War to active participation in the Second proved to be a long one—interrupted as it was by the nation's about-face to isolationism. The depth of America's revulsion toward international affairs illustrates the magnitude of Roosevelt's achievement. A brief sketch of the historical backdrop against which Roosevelt conducted his policies is therefore necessary.

In the 1920s, America's mood was ambivalent, oscillating between a willingness to assert principles of universal applicability and a need to justify them on behalf of an isolationist foreign policy. Americans took to reciting the traditional themes of their foreign policy with even greater emphasis: the uniqueness of America's mission as the exemplar of liberty, the moral superiority of democratic foreign policy, the seamless relationship between personal and international morality, the importance of open diplomacy, and the replacement of the balance of power by international consensus as expressed in the League of Nations.

All of these presumably universal principles were enlisted on behalf of American isolationism. Americans were still incapable of believing that anything outside the Western Hemisphere could possibly affect their security. The America of the 1920s and 1930s rejected even its own doctrine of collective security lest it lead to involvement in the quarrels of distant, bellicose societies. The provisions of the Treaty of Versailles were interpreted as vindictive, and reparations as self-defeating. When the French occupied the Ruhr, America used the occasion to withdraw its remaining occupying forces from the Rhineland. That Wilsonian exceptionalism had established criteria no international order could fulfill, made disillusionment a part of its very essence.

Disillusionment with the results of the war erased to a considerable extent the distinctions between the internationalists and the isolationists. Not even the most liberal internationalists any longer discerned an American interest in sustaining a flawed postwar settlement. No significant group had a good word to say about the balance of power. What passed for internationalism was being identified with membership in the League of Nations rather than with day-to-day participation in international diplomacy. And even the most dedicated internationalists insisted that the Monroe Doctrine superseded the League of Nations, and recoiled before the idea of America's joining League enforcement measures, even economic ones.

* * *

The Kellogg-Briand Pact turned into another example of America's tendency to treat principles as self-implementing. Although American leaders enthusiastically proclaimed the historic nature of the treaty because sixty-two nations had renounced war as an instrument of national policy, they adamantly refused to endorse any machinery for applying it, much less for enforcing it. President Calvin Coolidge, waxing effusive before the Congress in December 1928, asserted: "Observance of this Covenant . . . promises more for the peace of the world than any other agreement ever negotiated among the nations."[1]

Yet how was this utopia to be achieved? Coolidge's passionate defense of the Kellogg-Briand Pact spurred internationalists and supporters of the League to argue, quite reasonably, that, war having been outlawed, the concept of neutrality had lost all meaning. In their view, since the League had been designed to identify aggressors, the international community was obliged to punish them appropriately. "Does anyone believe," asked one of the proponents of this view, "that the aggressive designs of Mussolini could be checked merely by the good faith of the Italian people and the power of public opinion?"[2]

The prescience of this question did not enhance its acceptability. Even while the treaty bearing his name was still in the process of being debated, Secretary of State Kellogg, in an address before the Council on Foreign Relations, stressed that force would never be used to elicit compliance. Reliance on force, he argued, would turn what had been intended as a long stride toward peace into precisely the sort of military alliance that was so in need of being abolished.

* * *

To prevent America from once again being lured into war, the Congress passed three so-called Neutrality Acts between 1935 and 1937. Prompted by the Nye Report, these laws prohibited loans and any other financial assistance to belligerents (whatever the cause of war) and imposed an arms embargo on all parties (regardless of who the victim was). Purchases of nonmilitary goods for cash were allowed only if they were transported in non-American ships.[3] The Congress was not abjuring profits so much as it was rejecting risks. As the aggressors bestrode Europe, America abolished the distinction between aggressor and victim by legislating a single set of restrictions on both.

* * *

After his landslide electoral victory of 1936, Roosevelt went far beyond the existing framework. In fact, he demonstrated that, though preoccupied with the Depression, he had grasped the essence of the dictators' challenge better than any European leader except Churchill. At first, he sought merely to enunciate America's moral commitment to the cause of the democracies. Roosevelt began this educational process with the so-called Quarantine Speech, which he delivered in Chicago on October 5, 1937. It was his first warning to America of the approaching peril, and his first public statement that America might have to assume some responsibilities with respect to it. Japan's renewed military aggression in China, coupled with the previous year's announcement of the Berlin-Rome Axis, provided the backdrop, giving Roosevelt's concerns a global dimension:

> The peace, the freedom and the security of ninety percent of the population of the world is being jeopardized by the remaining ten percent who are threatening a breakdown of all international order and law. . . . It seems to be unfortunately true that the epidemic of world lawlessness is spreading. When an epidemic of physical disease starts to spread, the community approves and joins in a quarantine of the patients in order to protect the health of the community against the spread of the disease.[4]

Roosevelt was careful not to spell out what he meant by "quarantine" and what, if any, specific measures he might have in mind. Had the speech implied any kind of action, it would have been inconsistent with the Neutrality Acts, which the Congress had overwhelmingly approved and the President had recently signed.

Not surprisingly, the Quarantine Speech was attacked by isolationists, who demanded clarification of the President's intentions. They argued passionately that the distinction between "peace-loving" and "warlike" nations implied an American value judgment which, in turn, would lead to the abandonment of the policy of nonintervention, to which both Roosevelt and the Congress had pledged themselves. Two years later, Roosevelt described the uproar that resulted from the speech as follows: "Unfortunately, this suggestion fell upon deaf ears—even hostile and resentful ears. . . . It was hailed as war mongering; it was condemned as attempted intervention in foreign affairs; it was even ridiculed as a nervous search 'under the bed' for dangers of war which did not exist."[5]

Roosevelt could have ended the controversy by simply denying the intentions being ascribed to him. Yet, despite the critical onslaught, Roosevelt spoke ambiguously enough at a news conference to keep open the option of collective defense of some kind. According to the journalistic practice of the day, the President always met with the press off-the-record, which meant that he could neither be quoted nor identified, and these rules were respected.

* * *

Munich seems to have been the turning point which impelled Roosevelt to align America with the European democracies, at first politically but gradually materially as well. From then on, his commitment to thwarting the dictators was inexorable, culminating three years later in America's entry into a second world war. The interplay between leaders and their publics in a democracy is always complex. A leader who confines himself to the experience of his people in a period of upheaval purchases temporary popularity at the price of condemnation by posterity, whose claims he is neglecting. A leader who gets too far ahead of his society will become irrelevant. A great leader must be an educator, bridging the gap between his visions and the familiar. But he must also be willing to walk alone to enable his society to follow the path he has selected.

There is inevitably in every great leader an element of guile which simplifies, sometimes the objectives, sometimes the magnitude, of the task. But his ultimate test is whether he incarnates the truth of his society's values and the essence of its challenges. These qualities Roosevelt possessed to an unusual degree. He deeply believed in America; he was convinced that Nazism was both evil and a threat to American security, and he was extraordinarily guileful. And he was prepared to shoulder the burden of lonely decisions. Like a tightrope walker, he had to move, step by careful, anguishing step, across the chasm between his goal and his society's reality in demonstrating to it that the far shore was in fact safer than the familiar promontory.

On October 26, 1938, less than four weeks after the Munich Pact, Roosevelt returned to the theme of his Quarantine Speech. In a radio address to the Herald-Tribune Forum, he warned against unnamed but easily identifiable aggressors whose "national policy adopts as a deliberate instrument the threat of war."[6] Next, while upholding disarmament in principle, Roosevelt also called for strengthening America's defenses:

> . . . we have consistently pointed out that neither we, nor any nation, will accept disarmament while neighbor nations arm to the teeth. If there is not general disarmament, we our-

> selves must continue to arm. It is a step we do not like to take, and do not wish to take. But, until there is general abandonment of weapons capable of aggression, ordinary rules of national prudence and common sense require that we be prepared.[7]

In secret, Roosevelt went much further. At the end of October 1938, in separate conversations with the British air minister and also with a personal friend of Prime Minister Neville Chamberlain, he put forward a project designed to circumvent the Neutrality Acts. Proposing an outright evasion of legislation he had only recently signed, Roosevelt suggested setting up British and French airplane-assembly plants in Canada, near the American border. The United States would supply all the components, leaving only the final assembly to Great Britain and France. This arrangement would technically permit the project to stay within the letter of the Neutrality Acts, presumably on the ground that the component parts were civilian goods. Roosevelt told Chamberlain's emissary that, "in the event of war with the dictators, he had the industrial resources of the American nation behind him."[8]

Roosevelt's scheme for helping the democracies restore their air power collapsed, as it was bound to, if only because of the sheer logistical impossibility of undertaking an effort on such a scale in secret. But from then on, Roosevelt's support for Britain and France was limited only when the Congress and public opinion could neither be circumvented nor overcome.

* * *

Isolationists observing Roosevelt's actions were deeply disturbed. In February 1939, before the outbreak of the war, Senator Arthur Vandenberg had eloquently put forward the isolationist case:

> True, we do live in a foreshortened world in which, compared with Washington's day, time and space are relatively annihilated. But I still thank God for two insulating oceans; and even though they be foreshortened, they are still our supreme benediction if they be widely and prudently used. . . .
>
> We all have our sympathies and our natural emotions in behalf of the victims of national or international outrage all around the globe; but we are not, we cannot be, the world's protector or the world's policeman.[9]

When, in response to the German invasion of Poland, Great Britain declared war on September 3, 1939, Roosevelt had no choice but to invoke the Neutrality Acts. At the same time, he moved rapidly to modify the legislation to permit Great Britain and France to purchase American arms.

* * *

Roosevelt had for many months been acting on the premise that America might have to enter the war. In September 1940, he had devised an ingenious arrangement to give Great Britain fifty allegedly over-age destroyers in exchange for the right to set up American bases on eight British possessions, from Newfoundland to the South American mainland. Winston Churchill later called it a "decidedly unneutral act," for the destroyers were far more important to Great Britain than the bases were to America. Most of them were quite remote from any conceivable theater of operations, and some even duplicated existing American bases. More than anything, the destroyer deal represented a pretext based on a legal opinion by Roosevelt's own appointee, Attorney General Francis Biddle—hardly an objective observer.

Roosevelt sought neither Congressional approval nor modification of the Neutrality Acts for his destroyer-for-bases deal. Nor was he challenged, as inconceivable as that seems in the light of contemporary practice. It was the measure of Roosevelt's concern about a possible Nazi victory and of his commitment to bolstering British morale, that he took this step as a presidential election campaign was just beginning. (It was fortunate for Great Britain and for the cause of American unity that the foreign policy views of his opponent, Wendell Willkie, were not significantly different from Roosevelt's.)

Concurrently, Roosevelt vastly increased the American defense budget and, in 1940, induced the Congress to introduce peacetime conscription. So strong was lingering isolationist sentiment that conscription was renewed by only one vote in the House of Representatives in the summer of 1941, less than four months before the outbreak of the war.

* * *

Few American presidents have been as sensitive and perspicacious as Franklin Delano Roosevelt was in his grasp of the psychology of his people. Roosevelt understood that only a threat to their security could motivate them to support military preparedness. But to take them into a war, he knew he needed to appeal to their idealism in much the same way that Wilson had. In Roosevelt's view, America's security needs might well be met by control of the Atlantic, but its war aims required some vision of a new world order. Thus "balance of power" was not a term ever found in Roosevelt's pronouncements, except when he used it disparagingly. What he sought was to bring about a world community compatible with America's democratic and social ideals as the best guarantee of peace.

In this atmosphere, the president of a technically neutral United States and Great Britain's quintessential wartime leader, Winston Churchill, met in August 1941 on a cruiser off the coast of Newfoundland. Great Britain's position had improved somewhat when Hitler invaded the Soviet Union in June, but England was far from assured of victory. Nevertheless, the joint statement these two leaders issued reflected not a statement of traditional war aims but the design of a totally new world bearing America's imprimatur. The Atlantic Charter proclaimed a set of "common principles" on which the President and Prime Minister based "their hopes for a better future for the world."[10] These principles enlarged upon Roosevelt's original Four Freedoms by incorporating equal access to raw materials and cooperative efforts to improve social conditions around the world.

* * *

When the Atlantic Charter was proclaimed, German armies were approaching Moscow and Japanese forces were preparing to move into Southeast Asia. Churchill was above all concerned with removing the obstacles to America's participation in the war. For he understood very well that, by itself, Great Britain would not be able to achieve a decisive victory, even with Soviet participation in the war and American material support. In addition, the Soviet Union might collapse and some compromise between Hitler and Stalin was always a possibility, threatening Great Britain with renewed isolation. Churchill saw no point in debating postwar structure before he could even be certain that there would be one.

In September 1941, the United States crossed the line into belligerency. Roosevelt's order that the position of German submarines be reported to the British Navy had made it inevitable that, sooner or later, some clash would occur. On September 4, 1941, the American destroyer *Greer* was torpedoed while signaling the location of a German submarine to British airplanes. On September 11, without describing the circumstances, Roosevelt denounced German "piracy." Comparing German submarines to a rattlesnake coiled to strike, he ordered the United States Navy to sink "on sight" any German or Italian submarines discovered in the previously established American defense area extending all the way to Iceland. To all practical purposes, America was at war on the sea with the Axis powers.[11]

Simultaneously, Roosevelt took up the challenge of Japan. In response to Japan's occupation of Indochina in July 1941, he abrogated America's commercial treaty with Japan, forbade the sale of scrap metal to it, and encouraged the Dutch government-in-exile to stop oil exports to Japan from the Dutch East Indies (present-day Indonesia). These pressures led to negotiations with Japan, which began in October 1941. Roosevelt instructed the American negotiators to demand that Japan relinquish all of its conquests, including Manchuria, by invoking America's previous refusal to "recognize" these acts.

Roosevelt must have known that there was no possibility that Japan would accept. On December 7, 1941, following the pattern of the Russo-Japanese War, Japan launched a surprise attack on Pearl Harbor and destroyed a significant part of America's Pacific fleet. On December 11, Hitler honored his treaty with Tokyo by declaring war on the United States. Why Hitler thus freed Roosevelt to concentrate America's war effort on the country Roosevelt had always considered to be the principal enemy has never been satisfactorily explained.

America's entry into the war marked the culmination of a great and daring leader's extraordinary diplomatic enterprise. In less than three years, Roosevelt had taken his staunchly isolationist people into a global war. As late as May 1940, 64 percent of Americans had considered the preservation of peace more important than the defeat of the Nazis. Eighteen months later, in December 1941, just before the attack on Pearl Harbor, the proportions had been reversed—only 32 percent favored peace over preventing triumph.[12]

Roosevelt had achieved his goal patiently and inexorably, educating his people one step at a time about the necessities before them. His audiences filtered his words through their own preconceptions and did not always understand that his ultimate destination was war, though they could not have doubted that it was confrontation. In fact, Roosevelt was not so much bent on war as on defeating the Nazis; it was simply that, as time passed, the Nazis could only be defeated if America entered the war.

That their entry into the war should have seemed so sudden to the American people was due to three factors: Americans had had no experience with going to war for security concerns outside the Western Hemisphere; many believed that the European democracies could prevail on their own, while few understood the nature of the diplomacy that had preceded Japan's attack on Pearl Harbor or Hitler's rash declaration of war on the United States. It was a measure of the United States' deep-seated isolationism that it had to be bombed at Pearl Harbor before it would enter the war in the Pacific; and that, in Europe, it was Hitler who would ultimately declare war on the United States rather than the other way around.

By initiating hostilities, the Axis powers had solved Roosevelt's lingering dilemma about how to move the American people into the war. Had Japan focused its attack on Southeast Asia and Hitler not declared war against the United States, Roosevelt's task of steering his people toward his views would have been much more complicated. In light of Roosevelt's proclaimed moral and strategic convictions, there can be little doubt that, in the end, he would have somehow managed to enlist America in the struggle he considered so decisive to both the future of freedom and to American security.

Subsequent generations of Americans have placed a greater premium on total candor by their chief executive. Yet, like Lincoln, Roosevelt sensed that the survival of his country and its values was at stake, and that history itself would hold him responsible for the results of his solitary initiatives. And, as was the case with Lincoln, it is a measure of the debt free peoples owe to Franklin Delano Roosevelt that the wisdom of his solitary passage is now, quite simply, taken for granted.

## *Notes*

[1]Selig Adler, *The Isolationist Impulse, Its Twentieth-Century Reaction* (New York: Free Press; London: Collier-Macmillan, 1957), 214.

[2]Quoted in Adler, *The Isolationist Impulse,* 216.

[3]Ruhl J. Bartlett, ed., *The Record of American Diplomacy* (New York: Knopf, 1956), 572–77. The First Neutrality Act, signed by FDR on August 31, 1935: arms embargo; Americans not permitted to travel on ships of belligerents. The Second Neutrality Act, signed by FDR on February 29, 1936 (a week before the reoccupation of the Rhineland on March 7): extended the First Act through May 1, 1936, and added a prohibition against loans or credits to belligerents. The Third Neutrality Act, signed by FDR on May 1, 1937: extended previous acts due to expire at midnight plus "cash and carry" provisions for certain nonmilitary goods.

[4]Address in Chicago, October 5, 1937, in Franklin Roosevelt, *Public Papers* (New York: Macmillan, 1941), 1937 vol., 410.

[5]Introduction, in Roosevelt, *Public Papers,* 1939 vol., xxviii.

[6]Radio address to the Herald-Tribune Forum, October 26, 1938, in Roosevelt, *Public Papers,* 1938 vol., 564.

[7]Radio address, 565.

[8]Donald Cameron Watt, *How War Came: The Immediate Origins of the Second World War, 1938–1939* (London: William Heinemann, 1989), 130.

[9]Vandenberg speech in the Senate, "It Is Not Cowardice to Think of America First," February 27, 1939, in *Vital Speeches of the Day,* vol. v, no. 12 (April 1, 1939), 356–57.

[10]The Atlantic Charter: Official Statement on Meeting Between the President and Prime Minister Churchill, August 14, 1941, in Roosevelt, *Public Papers,* 1941 vol., 314.

[11]Fireside Chat to the Nation, September 11, 1941, in Roosevelt, *Public Papers,* 1941 vol., 384–92.

[12]Adler, *The Isolationist Impulse,* 257.

# *Imperialism*

WALTER LAFEBER

## The American "New Empire"

Some intellectuals speak only for themselves. Theirs is often the later glory, but seldom the present power. Some, however, speak not only for themselves but for the guiding forces of their society. Discovering such men at crucial junctures in history, if such a discovery can be made, is of importance and value. These figures uncover the premises, reveal the approaches, provide the details, and often coherently arrange the ideas which are implicit in the dominant thought of their time and society.

The ordered, articulate writings of Frederick Jackson Turner, Josiah Strong, Brooks Adams, and Alfred Thayer Mahan typified the expansive tendencies of their generation. Little evidence exists that Turner and Strong directly influenced expansionists in the business community or the State Department during the 1890's, but their writings best exemplify certain beliefs which determined the nature of American foreign policy. Adams and Mahan participated more directly in the shaping of expansionist programs. It is, of course, impossible to estimate the number of Americans who accepted the arguments of these four men. What cannot be controverted is that the writings of these men typified and in some specific instances directly influenced the thought of American policy makers who created the new empire.[1]

### Frederick Jackson Turner and the American Frontier

* * *

The importance of the frontier will be associated with the name of Frederick Jackson Turner as long as historians are able to indent footnotes. Yet as Theodore Roosevelt told Turner in a letter of admiration in 1894, "I think you . . . have put into definite shape a good deal of thought which has been floating around rather loosely." As has been amply shown by several scholars, a number of observers warned of the frontier's disappearance and the possible consequences of this disappearance long before Turner's epochal paper. The accelerating communication and transportation revolution, growing agrarian unrest,

From *The New Empire: An Interpretation of American Expansion, 1860–1898* (Ithaca, N.Y.: Cornell University Press, 1963), chaps. 2 and 7.

violent labor strikes, and the problems arising from increasing numbers of immigrants broke upon puzzled and frightened Americans in a relatively short span of time. Many of them clutched the belief of the closing or closed frontier in order to explain their dilemma.[2]

Turner rested the central part of his frontier thesis on the economic power represented by free land. American individualism, nationalism, political institutions, and democracy depended on this power: "So long as free land exists, the opportunity for a competency exists, and economic power secures political power." Stated in these terms, landed expansion became the central factor, the dynamic of American progress. Without the economic power generated by expansion across free lands, American political institutions could stagnate.[3]

Such an analysis could be extremely meaningful to those persons who sought an explanation for the political and social troubles of the period. Few disputed that the social upheavals in both the urban and agrarian areas of the nation stemmed from economic troubles in the international grain markets, from the frequent industrial depressions, or, as the Populists averred, from the failure of the currency to match the pace of ever increasing productivity. This economic interpretation also fitted in nicely with the contemporary measurement of success in terms of material achievement. Perhaps most important, the frontier thesis not only defined the dilemma, but did so in tangible, concrete terms. It offered the hope that Americans could do something about their problems. Given the assumption that expansion across the western frontier explained past American successes, the solution for the present crisis now became apparent: either radically readjust the political institutions to a nonexpanding society or find new areas for expansion. When Americans seized the second alternative, the meaning for foreign policy became apparent—and immense.

With the appearance and definition of the fundamental problems in the 1880's and 1890's, these decades assumed vast importance. They became not a watershed of American history, but *the* watershed. Many writers emphasized the supremely critical nature of the 1890's, but no one did it better than Turner when he penned the dramatic final sentence of his 1893 paper: "And now, four centuries from the discovery of America, at the end of a hundred years of life under the Constitution, the frontier has gone, and with its going has closed the first period of American history." The American West no longer offered a unique escape from the intractable problems of a closed society. As another writer stated it four years after Turner's announcement in Chicago, "we are no longer a country exceptional and apart." History had finally caught up with the United States.[4]

The first solution that came to some minds suggested the opening of new landed frontiers in Latin America or Canada. Yet was further expansion in a landed sense the answer? Top policy makers, such as Secretaries of State James G. Blaine, Thomas F. Bayard, and Walter Quintin Gresham, opposed the addition of noncontiguous territory to the Union. Some Americans interpreted the labor violence of 1877, 1886, and 1894 as indications that the federal government could no longer harmonize and control the far-flung reaches of the continental empire. Labor and agrarian groups discovered they could not command the necessary political power to solve their mushrooming problems. The sprouting of such factions as the Molly Maguires, Populists, Eugene Debs' Railroad Union, and several varieties of Socialist parties raised doubts in many minds about the ameliorating and controlling qualities which had formerly been a part of the American system.

* * *

Expansion in the form of trade instead of landed settlement ultimately offered the answer to this dilemma. This solution, embodied in the open-door philosophy of American foreign policy, ameliorated the economic stagnation (which by Turner's reasoning led to the political discontent), but it did not pile new colonial areas on an already overburdened governmental structure. It provided the perfect answer to the problems of the 1890's.

* * *

## Alfred Thayer Mahan

* * *

The austere, scholarly, arm-chair sailor-turned-prophet constructed a tightly knit historical justification of why and how his country could expand beyond its continental limits.

Mahan grounded his thesis on the central characteristic of the United States of his time: it was an industrial complex which produced, or would soon be capable of producing, vast surpluses. In the first paragraph of his classic, *The Influence of Sea Power upon History, 1660–1783,* Mahan explained how this industrial expansion led to a rivalry for markets and sources of raw materials and would ultimately result in the need for sea power. He summarized his theory in a postulate: "In these [two] things—production, with the necessity of exchanging products, shipping, whereby the exchange is carried on, and colonies . . .—is to be found the key to much of the history, as well as of the policy, of nations bordering upon the sea." The order is all-important. Production leads to a need for shipping, which in turn creates the need for colonies.[5]

Mahan's neat postulate was peculiarly applicable to his own time, for he clearly understood the United States of the 1890's. His concern, stated in 1890, that ever increasing production would soon make necessary wider trade and markets, anticipated the somber, depression-ridden years of post-1893. Writing three years before Frederick Jackson Turner analyzed the disappearance of the American frontier, Mahan hinted its disappearance and pointed out the implications for America's future economic and political structure. He observed that the policies of the American government since 1865 had been "directed solely to what has been called the first link in the chain which makes sea power." But "the increase of home consumption . . . did not keep up with the increase of forth-putting and facility of distribution offered by steam." The United States would thus have to embark upon a new frontier, for "whether they will or no, Americans must now begin to look outward. The growing production of the country demands it. An increasing volume of public sentiment demands it." The theoretical and actual had met; the productive capacity of the United States, having finally grown too great for its continental container and having lost its landed frontier, had to turn to the sea, its omnipresent frontier. The mercantilists had viewed production as a faculty to be stimulated and consolidated in order to develop its full capabilities of pulling wealth into the country. But Mahan dealt with a productive complex which had been stimulated by the government for years and had been centralized and coordinated by corporate managers. He was now concerned with the problem of keeping this society ongoing without the problems of underemployment and resulting social upheavals.[6]

Reversing the traditional American idea of the oceans as a barrier against European intrigue, Mahan compared the sea to "a great highway; or better, perhaps . . . a wide common, over which men pass in all directions."

* * *

To Mahan, William McKinley, Theodore Roosevelt, and Henry Cabot Lodge, colonial possessions, as these men defined such possessions, served as stepping stones to the two great prizes: the Latin-American and Asian markets. This policy much less resembled traditional colonialism than it did the new financial and industrial expansion of the 1850–1914 period. These men did not envision "colonizing" either Latin America or Asia. They did want both to exploit these areas economically and give them (especially Asia) the benefits of western, Christian civilization. To do this, these expansionists needed strategic bases from which shipping lanes and interior interests in Asia and Latin America could be protected.

* * *

## President William McKinley and the Spanish-American War of 1898

* * *

The President [McKinley] did not want war; he had been sincere and tireless in his efforts to maintain the peace. By mid-March, however, he was beginning to discover that, although he did not want war, he did want what only a war could provide: the disappearance of the terrible uncertainty in American political and economic life, and a solid basis from which to resume the building of the new American commercial empire. When the President made his demands, therefore, he made the ultimate demands; as far as he was concerned, a six-month period of negotiations would not serve to temper the political and economic problems in the United States, but only exacerbate them.

To say this is to raise another question: why did McKinley arrive at this position during mid-March? What were the factors which limited the President's freedom of choice and policies at this particular time? The standard interpretations of the war's causes emphasize the yellow journals and a belligerent Congress. These were doubtlessly crucial factors in shaping the course of American entry into the conflict, but they must be used carefully.

Influences other than the yellow press or congressional belligerence were more important in shaping McKinley's position of April 11. Perhaps most important was the transformation of the opinion of many spokesmen for the business community who had formerly opposed war. If, as one journal declared, the McKinley administration, "more than any that have preceded it, sustains . . . close relations to the business interests of the country," then this change of business sentiment should not be discounted.[7] This transformation brought important financial spokesmen, especially from the Northeast, into much the same position that had long been occupied by pro-interventionist business groups and journals in the trans-Appalachian area. McKinley's decision to intervene placated many of the same business spokesmen whom he had satisfied throughout 1897 and January and February of 1898 by his refusal to declare war.

Five factors may be delineated which shaped this interventionist sentiment of the business community. First, some business journals emphasized the material advantages to be gained should Cuba become a part of the world in which the United States would enjoy, in the words of the New York *Commercial Advertiser,* "full freedom of development in the whole world's interest." The *Banker's Magazine* noted that "so many of our citizens are so involved in the commerce and productions of the island, that to protect these interests . . . the United States will have eventually to force the establishment of fair and reasonable government." The material damage suffered by investors in Cuba and by many merchants, manufacturers, exporters, and importers, as, for example, the groups which presented the February 10 petition to McKinley, forced these interests to advocate a solution which could be obtained only through force.[8]

A second reason was the uncertainty that plagued the business community in mid-March. This uncertainty was increased by [Senator Redfield] Proctor's powerful and influential speech and by the news that a Spanish torpedo-boat flotilla was sailing from Cadiz to Cuba. The uncertainty was exemplified by the sudden stagnation of trade on the New York Stock Exchange after March 17. Such an unpredictable economic basis could not provide the spring board for the type of overseas commercial empire that McKinley and numerous business spokesmen envisioned.

Third, by March many businessmen who had deprecated war on the ground that the United States Treasury did not possess adequate gold reserves began to realize that they had been arguing from false assumptions. The heavy exports of 1897 and the discoveries of gold in Alaska and Australia brought the yellow metal into the country in an ever widening stream. Private bankers had been preparing for war since 1897. *Banker's Magazine* summarized these developments: "Therefore, while not desiring war, it is apparent that the country now has an ample coin basis for sustaining the credit operations which a conflict would probably make necessary. In such a crisis the gold standard will prove a bulwark of confidence."[9]

Fourth, antiwar sentiment lost much strength when the nation realized that it had nothing to fear from European intervention on the side of Spain. France and Russia, who were most sympathetic to the Spanish monarchy, were forced to devote their attention to the Far East. Neither of these nations wished to alienate the United States on the Cuban issue. More important, Americans happily realized that they had the support of Great Britain. The *rapprochement* which had occurred since the Venezuelan incident now paid dividends. On an official level, the British Foreign Office assured the State Department that nothing would be accomplished in the way of European intervention unless the United States requested such intervention. The British attitude made it easy for McKinley to deal with a joint European note of April 6 which asked for American moderation toward Spain. The President brushed off the request firmly but politely. On an unofficial level, American periodicals expressed appreciation of the British policy on Cuba, and some of the journals noted that a common Anglo-American approach was also desirable in Asia.[10] The European reaction is interesting insofar as it evinces the continental powers' growing realization that the United States was rapidly becoming a major force in the world. But the European governments set no limits on American dealings with Spain. McKinley could take the initiative and make his demands with little concern for European reactions.

Finally, opposition to war melted away in some degree when the administration began to emphasize that the United States enjoyed military power much superior to that of Spain. One possible reason for McKinley's policies during the first two months of 1898 might have been his fear that the nation was not adequately prepared. As late as the weekend of March 25 the President worried over this inadequacy. But in late February and early March, especially after the $50,000,000 appropriation by Congress, the country's military strength developed rapidly. On March 13 the Philadelphia *Press* proclaimed that American naval power greatly exceeded that of the Spanish forces. By early April those who feared a Spanish bombardment of New York City were in the small minority. More representative were the views of Winthrop Chanler who wrote Lodge that if Spanish troops invaded New York "they would all be absorbed in the population . . . and engaged in selling oranges before they got as far as 14th Street."[11]

As the words of McKinley's war message flew across the wires to Madrid, many business spokesmen who had opposed war had recently changed their minds, American military forces were rapidly growing more powerful, banks and the United States Treasury had secured themselves against the initial shocks of war, and the European powers were divided among themselves and preoccupied in the Far East. Business boomed after McKinley signed the declaration of war. "With a hesitation so slight as to amount almost to indifference," *Bradstreet's* reported on April 30, "the business community, relieved from the tension caused by the incubus of doubt and uncertainty which so long controlled it, has stepped confidently forward to accept the situation confronting it owing to the changed conditions. Unfavorable circumstances . . . have hardly excited remark, while the stimulating effects have been so numerous and important as to surprise all but the most optimistic," this journal concluded.[12] A new type of American empire, temporarily clothed in armor, stepped out on the international stage after a half century of preparation to make its claim as one of the great world powers.

* * *

By 1899 the United States had forged a new empire. American policy makers and businessmen had created it amid much debate and with conscious purpose. The empire progressed from a continental base in 1861 to assured pre-eminence in the Western Hemisphere in 1895. Three years later it was rescued from a growing economic and political dilemma by the declaration of war against Spain. During and after this conflict the empire moved past Hawaii into the Philippines, and, with the issuance of the Open-Door Notes, enunciated its principles in Asia. The movement of this empire could not be hurried. Harrison discovered this to his regret in 1893. But under the impetus of the effects of the industrial revolution and, most important, *because of the implications for foreign policy which policy makers and businessmen believed to be logical corollaries of this economic change*, the new empire reached its climax in the 1890's. At this point those who possessed a sense of historical perspective could pause with Henry Adams and observe that one hundred and fifty years of American history had suddenly fallen into place. Those who preferred to peer into the dim future of the twentieth century could be certain only that the United States now dominated its own hemisphere and, as [William] Seward had so passionately hoped, was entering as a major power into Asia, "the chief theatre of events in the world's great hereafter."

## Notes

[1]One of the weakest sections in the history of ideas is the relationship between the new intellectual currents and American overseas expansion during the last half of the nineteenth century. The background and some of the general factors may be found in Alfred Kazin, *On Native Grounds: An Interpretation of Modern American Prose Literature* (Garden City, N.Y., 1942, 1956); Henry Steele Commager, *The American Mind: An Interpretation of American Thought and Character since the 1880's* (New Haven, 1950, 1959); Weinberg, *Manifest Destiny;* Julius W. Pratt, "The Ideology of American Expansion," *Essays in Honor of William E. Dodd . . .*, edited by Avery Craven (Chicago, 1935).

[2]See especially Fulmer Mood, "The Concept of the Frontier, 1871–1898," *Agricultural History,* XIX (January, 1945), 24–31; Lee Benson, "The Historical Background of Turner's Frontier Essay," *Agricultural History,* XXV (April, 1951), 59–82; Herman Clarence Nixon, "The Precursors of Turner in the Interpretation of the American Frontier," *South Atlantic Quarterly,* XXVIII (January, 1929), 83–89. For the Roosevelt letter, see *The Letters of Theodore Roosevelt,* selected and edited by Elting E. Morison *et al.* (Cambridge, Mass., 1951), I, 363.

[3]Frederick Jackson Turner, *The Frontier in American History* (New York, 1947), 32, 30; see also Per Sveaas Andersen, *Westward Is the Course of Empires: A Study in the Shaping of an American Idea: Frederick Jackson Turner's Frontier* (Oslo, Norway, 1956), 20–21; Henry Nash Smith, *Virgin Land: The American West as Symbol and Myth* (New York, 1959), 240.

[4]Turner, *Frontier in American History,* 38; Eugene V. Smalley, "What Are Normal Times?" *The Forum,* XXIII (March, 1897), 98–99; see also Turner, *Frontier in American History,* 311–312. For a brilliant criticism of Turner's closed-space concepts, see James C. Malin, *The Contriving Brain and the Skillful Hand in the United States . . .* (Lawrence, Kan., 1955), the entire essay, but especially ch. xi.

[5]A. T. Mahan, *The Influence of Sea Power upon History, 1660–1783* (Boston, 1890), 53, 28. This postulate is mentioned two more times in the famous first chapter, pages 70 and 83–84.

[6]*Ibid.,* 83–84; Mahan, "A Twentieth-Century Outlook," *The Interest of America in Sea Power, Present and Future* (Boston, 1897), 220–222; Mahan, "The United States Looking Outward," *ibid.,* 21–22. In their work which traces this centralization movement, Thomas C. Cochran and William Miller call the result the "corporate society" (*The Age of Enterprise: A Social History of Industrial America* [New York, 1942], 331).

[7]Chicago *Times-Herald* quoted in Cincinnati *Commercial Tribune,* Dec. 28, 1897, 6:2. The Chicago paper was particularly close to the administration through its publisher's friendship with McKinley. The publisher was H. H. Kohlsaat. Ernest May remarks, regarding McKinley's antiwar position in 1897 and early 1898, "It was simply out of the question for him [McKinley] to embark on a policy unless virtually certain that Republican businessmen would back him" (*Imperial Democracy: The Emergence of America as a Great Power* [New York, 1961], 118). The same comment doubtlessly applies also to McKinley's actions in March and April.

[8]*Commercial Advertiser,* March 10, 1898, 6:3; *Bankers' Magazine,* LVI (April, 1898), 519–520.

[9]*Bankers' Magazine,* LVI (March, 1898), 347–348; LVI (April, 1898), 520; *Pittsburgh Press,* April 8, 1898, 4:1; *Commercial and Financial Chronicle,* April 23, 1898, 786.

[10]Dugdale, *German Documents,* II, 500–502; Porter to Sherman, April 8, 1898, France, Despatches, and Hay to Sherman, March 26, 28, 29, April 1, Great Britain, Despatches, NA, RG 59; *Public Opinion,* March 24, 1898, 360–361.

[11]Margaret Leech, *In the Days of McKinley* (New York, 1969), 176; *Philadelphia Press,* March 13, 1898, 8:3; Garraty, *Lodge,* 191.

[12]*Bradstreet's,* April 9, 1898, 234, also April 30, 1898, 272, 282.

# *Cold War Revisionist Critique*

4.1

MELVYN P. LEFFLER

## The American Conception of National Security and the Beginnings of the Cold War, 1945–48

* * *

In an interview with Henry Kissinger in 1978 on "The Lessons of the Past," Walter Laqueur observed that during the Second World War "few if any people thought . . . of the structure of peace that would follow the war except perhaps in the most general terms of friendship, mutual trust, and the other noble sentiments mentioned in wartime programmatic speeches about the United Nations and related topics." Kissinger concurred, noting that no statesman, except perhaps Winston Churchill, "gave any attention to what would happen after the war." Americans, Kissinger stressed, "were determined that we were going to base the postwar period on good faith and getting along with everybody."[1]

That two such astute and knowledgeable observers of international politics were so uninformed about American planning at the end of the Second World War is testimony to the enduring mythology of American idealism and innocence in the world of *realpolitik.* * * * American assessments of the Soviet threat were less a consequence of expanding Soviet military capabilities and of Soviet diplomatic demands than a result of growing apprehension about the vulnerability of American strategic and economic interests in a world of unprecedented turmoil and upheaval. Viewed from this perspective, the Cold War assumed many of its most enduring characteristics during 1947–8, when American officials sought to cope with an array of challenges by implementing their own concepts of national security.

* * *

The need to predominate throughout the western hemisphere was not a result of deteriorating Soviet-American relations but a natural evolution of the Monroe Doctrine, accentuated by Axis aggression and new technological imperatives.[2] Patterson, Forrestal, and Army Chief of Staff Dwight D. Eisenhower initially were impelled less by reports of Soviet espionage, propaganda, and infiltration in Latin America than by accounts of British efforts to sell cruisers and aircraft to Chile and Ecuador; Swedish sales of anti-aircraft artillery to Argentina; and

From *American Historical Review* 89 (April 1984).

French offers to build cruisers and destroyers for both Argentina and Brazil.[3] To foreclose all foreign influence and to ensure US strategic hegemony, military officers and the civilian Secretaries of the War and Navy Departments argued for an extensive system of US bases, expansion of commercial airline facilities throughout Latin America, negotiation of a regional defense pact, curtailment of all foreign military aid and foreign military sales, training of Latin American military officers in the United States, outfitting of Latin American armies with US military equipment, and implementation of a comprehensive military assistance program.[4]

* * *

From the closing days of the Second World War, American defense officials believed that they could not allow any prospective adversary to control the Eurasian land mass. This was the lesson taught by two world wars. Strategic thinkers and military analysts insisted that any power or powers attempting to dominate Eurasia must be regarded as potentially hostile to the United States.[5] * * * Concern over the consequences of Russian domination of Eurasia helps explain why in July 1945 the joint chiefs decided to oppose a Soviet request for bases in the Dardanelles; why during March and April 1946 they supported a firm stand against Russia in Iran, Turkey, and Tripolitania; and why in the summer of 1946 Clark Clifford and George Elsey, two White House aides, argued that Soviet incorporation of any parts of Western Europe, the Middle East, China, or Japan into a Communist orbit was incompatible with American national security.[6]

Economic considerations also made defense officials determined to retain American access to Eurasia as well as to deny Soviet predominance over it. Stimson, Patterson, McCloy, and Assistant Secretary Howard C. Peterson agreed with Forrestal that long-term American prosperity required open markets, unhindered access to raw materials, and the rehabilitation of much—if not all—of Eurasia along liberal capitalist lines. * * * But American economic interests in Eurasia were not limited to Western Europe, Germany, and the Middle East. Military planners and intelligence officers in both the army and navy expressed considerable interest in the raw materials of Southeast Asia, wanted to maintain access to those resources, and sought to deny them to a prospective enemy.[7]

* * *

During 1946 and 1947, defense officials witnessed a dramatic unravelling of the geopolitical foundations and socioeconomic structure of international affairs. Britain's economic weakness and withdrawal from the eastern Mediterranean, India's independence movement, civil war in China, nationalist insurgencies in Indo-China and the Dutch East Indies, Zionist claims to Palestine and Arab resentment, German and Japanese economic paralysis, Communist inroads in France and Italy—all were ominous developments. Defense officials recognized that the Soviet Union had not created these circumstances but believed that Soviet leaders would exploit them. Should Communists take power, even without direct Russian intervention, the Soviet Union would gain predominant control of the resources of these areas because of the postulated subservience of Communist parties everywhere to the Kremlin. Should nationalist uprisings persist, Communists seize power in underdeveloped countries, or Arabs revolt against American support of a Jewish state, the petroleum and raw materials of critical areas might be denied the West. The imminent possibility existed that, even without Soviet military aggression, the resources of Eurasia could fall under Russian control. With these resources, the Soviet Union would be able to overcome its chronic economic weaknesses, achieve defense in depth, and challenge American power—perhaps even by military force.[8]

In this frightening postwar environment American assessments of Soviet long-term intentions were transformed. Spurred by the "long telegram" written by George F. Kennan, the US chargé d'affaires in Moscow, it soon became commonplace for policy makers, military officials, and intelligence analysts to state that the ultimate aim of Soviet foreign policy was Russian domination of a Communist world.[9] There was, of course, plentiful evidence for this appraisal of Soviet ambitions—the Soviet consolidation of a sphere of influence in Eastern Europe; Soviet violation of the agreement to withdraw troops from Iran; Soviet relinquishment of Japanese arms to the Chinese Communists; the Soviet mode of extracting reparations from the Russian zone in Germany; Soviet diplomatic overtures for bases in the Dardanelles, Tripolitania, and the Dodecanese; Soviet requests for a role in the occupation of Japan; and the Kremlin's renewed emphasis on Marxist-Leninist doctrine, the vulnerability of capitalist economies, and the inevitability of conflict.

Yet these assessments did not seriously grapple with contradictory evidence. They disregarded numerous signs of Soviet weakness, moderation, and circumspection. During 1946 and 1947 intelligence analysts described the withdrawal of Russian troops from northern Norway, Manchuria, Bornholm, and Iran (from the latter under pressure, of course). Numerous intelligence sources reported the reduction of Russian troops in Eastern Europe and the extensive demobilization going on within the Soviet Union. In October 1947 the Joint Intelligence Committee forecast a Soviet army troop strength during 1948 and 1949 of less than 2 million men. Other reports dealt with the inadequacies of Soviet transportation and bridging equipment and the moderation of Soviet military expenditures. And, as already noted, assessments of the Soviet economy revealed persistent problems likely to restrict Soviet adventurism.[10]

Experience suggested that the Soviet Union was by no means uniformly hostile or unwilling to negotiate with the United States. In April 1946 Ambassador [Gerard C.] Smith reminded the State Department that the Soviet press was not unalterably critical of the United States, that the Russians had withdrawn from Bornholm, that Stalin had given a moderate speech on the United Nations, and that Soviet demobilization continued apace. The next month General Lincoln acknowledged that the Soviets had been willing to make numerous concessions regarding Tripolitania, the Dodecanese, and Italian reparations. In the spring of 1946, General Echols, General Clay, and Secretary Patterson again maintained that the French constituted the major impediment to an agreement on united control of Germany. In early 1947 central intelligence delineated more than a half-dozen instances of Soviet moderation or concessions. In April the Military Intelligence Division noted that the Soviets had limited their involvement in the

Middle East, diminished their ideological rhetoric, and given only moderate support to Chinese Communists.[11]

In their overall assessments of Soviet long-term intentions, however, military planners dismissed all evidence of Soviet moderation, circumspection, and restraint. In fact, as 1946 progressed, these planners seemed to spend less time analyzing Soviet intentions and more time estimating Soviet capabilities.[12] They no longer explored ways of accommodating a potential adversary's legitimate strategic requirements or pondered how American initiatives might influence the Soviet Union's definition of its objectives.[13] Information not confirming prevailing assumptions either was ignored in overall assessments of Soviet intentions or was used to illustrate that the Soviets were shifting tactics but not altering objectives. A report from the Joint Chiefs of Staff to the President in July 1946, for example, deleted sections from previous studies that had outlined Soviet weaknesses. A memorandum sent by Secretary [Robert P.] Patterson to the President at the same time was designed to answer questions about relations with the Soviet Union "without ambiguity." Truman, Clark Clifford observed many years later, liked things in black and white.[14]

* * *

The dynamics of the Cold War after 1948 are easier to comprehend when one grasps the breadth of the American conception of national security that had emerged between 1945 and 1948. This conception included a strategic sphere of influence within the western hemisphere, domination of the Atlantic and Pacific oceans, an extensive system of outlying bases to enlarge the strategic frontier and project American power, an even more extensive system of transit rights to facilitate the conversion of commercial air bases to military use, access to the resources and markets of most of Eurasia, denial of those resources to a prospective enemy, and the maintenance of nuclear superiority. Not every one of these ingredients, it must be emphasized, was considered vital. Hence, American officials could acquiesce, however grudgingly, to a Soviet sphere in Eastern Europe and could avoid direct intervention in China. But cumulative challenges to these concepts of national security were certain to provoke a firm American response. This occurred initially in 1947–8 when decisions were made in favor of the Truman Doctrine, the Marshall Plan, military assistance, the Atlantic alliance, and German and Japanese rehabilitation. Soon thereafter, the "loss" of China, the Soviet detonation of an atomic bomb, and the North Korean attack on South Korea intensified the perception of threat to prevailing concepts of national security. The Truman administration responded with military assistance to Southeast Asia, a decision to build the hydrogen bomb, direct military intervention in Korea, a commitment to station troops permanently in Europe, expansion of the American alliance system, and a massive rearmament program in the United States. Postulating a long-term Soviet intention to gain world domination, the American conception of national security, based on geopolitical and economic imperatives, could not allow for additional losses in Eurasia, could not risk a challenge to its nuclear supremacy, and could not permit any infringement on its ability to defend in depth or to project American force from areas in close proximity to the Soviet homeland.

To say this, is neither to exculpate the Soviet government for its inhumane treatment of its own citizens nor to suggest that Soviet foreign policy was idle or benign. Indeed, Soviet behavior in Eastern Europe was often deplorable; the Soviets sought opportunities in the Dardanelles, northern Iran, and Manchuria; the Soviets hoped to orient Germany and Austria toward the East; and the Soviets sometimes endeavored to use Communist parties to expand Soviet influence in areas beyond the periphery of Russian military power. But, then again, the Soviet Union had lost 20 million dead during the war, had experienced the destruction of 1,700 towns, 31,000 factories, and 100,000 collective farms, and had witnessed the devastation of the rural economy with the Nazi slaughter of 20 million hogs and 17 million head of cattle. What is remarkable is that after 1946 these monumental losses received so little attention when American defense analysts studied the motives and intentions of Soviet policy; indeed, defense officials did little to analyze the threat perceived by the Soviets. Yet these same officials had absolutely no doubt that the wartime experiences and sacrifices of the United States, though much less devastating than those of Soviet Russia, demonstrated the need for and entitled the United States to oversee the resuscitation of the industrial heartlands of Germany and Japan, establish a viable balance of power in Eurasia, and militarily dominate the Eurasian rimlands, thereby safeguarding American access to raw materials and control over all sea and air approaches to North America.[15]

To suggest a double standard is important only in so far as it raises fundamental questions about the conceptualization and implementation of American national security policy. If Soviet policy was aggressive, bellicose, and ideological, perhaps America's reliance on overseas bases, air power, atomic weapons, military alliances, and the rehabilitation of Germany and Japan was the best course to follow, even if the effect may have been to exacerbate Soviet anxieties and suspicions. But even when one attributes the worst intentions to the Soviet Union, one might still ask whether American presuppositions and apprehensions about the benefits that would accrue to the Soviet Union as a result of Communist (and even revolutionary nationalist) gains anywhere in Eurasia tended to simplify international realities, magnify the breadth of American interests, engender commitments beyond American capabilities, and dissipate the nation's strength and credibility. And, perhaps even more importantly, if Soviet foreign policies tended to be opportunist, reactive, nationalistic, and contradictory, as some recent writers have claimed and as some contemporary analysts suggested, then one might also wonder whether America's own conception of national security tended, perhaps unintentionally, to engender anxieties and to provoke countermeasures from a proud, suspicious, insecure, and cruel government that was at the same time legitimately apprehensive about the long-term implications arising from the rehabilitation of traditional enemies and the development of foreign bases on the periphery of the Soviet homeland. To raise such issues anew seems essential if we are to unravel the complex origins of the Cold War.

## Notes

[1]Henry Kissinger, *For the Record: Selected Statements, 1977–80* (Boston, MA, 1980), 123–4.

[2]This evaluation accords with the views of Chester J. Pach, Jr; see his "The Containment of United States Military

Aid to Latin America, 1944–1949," *Diplomatic History,* 6 (1982): 232–4.

[3]For fears of foreign influence, see, for example, [no signature] "Military Political Cooperation with the Other American Republics," June 24, 1946, RG 18, 092 (International Affairs), box 567; Patterson to the Secretary of State, July 31, 1946, RG 353, SWNCC, box 76; Eisenhower to Patterson, November 26, 1946, RG 107, HCPP, general decimal file, box 1 (top secret); S. J. Chamberlin to Eisenhower, November 26, 1946, ibid.; Minutes of the meeting of the Secretaries of State, War, and Navy, December 11, 1946, ibid., RPPP, safe file, box 3; and Director of Intelligence to Director of P&O, February 26, 1947, RG 319, P&O, 091 France. For reports on Soviet espionage, see, for example, Military Intelligence Service [hereafter MIS], "Soviet-Communist Penetration in Latin America," March 24, 1945, RG 165, OPD 336 (top secret).

[4]See, for example, Craig, "Summary," January 5, 1945; JPS, "Military Arrangements Deriving from the Act of Chapultepec Pertaining to Bases," January 14, 1946, RG 218, ser. CCS 092 (9-10-45), JPS 761/3; Patterson to Byrnes, December 18, 1946; and P&O, "Strategic Importance of Inter-American Military Cooperation" [January 20, 1947].

[5]This view was most explicitly presented in an army paper examining the State Department's expostulation of US foreign policy. See S. F. Giffin, "Draft of Proposed Comments for the Assistant Secretary of War on 'Foreign Policy'" [early February 1946], RG 107, HCPP 092 international affairs (classified). The extent to which this concern with Eurasia shaped American military attitudes is illustrated at greater length below. Here I should note that in March 1945 several of the nation's most prominent civilian experts (Frederick S. Dunn, Edward M. Earle, William T. R. Fox, Grayson L. Kirk, David N. Rowe, Harold Sprout, and Arnold Wolfers) prepared a study, "A Security Policy for Postwar America," in which they argued that the United States had to prevent any one power or coalition of powers from gaining control of Eurasia. America could not, they insisted, withstand attack by any power that had first subdued the whole of Europe or of Eurasia; see Frederick S. Dunn *et al.,* "A Security Policy for Postwar America," NHC, SPD, ser. 14, box 194, A1–2.

The postwar concept of Eurasia developed out of the revival of geopolitical thinking in the United States, stimulated by Axis aggression and strategic decisionmaking. See, for example, the reissued work of Sir Halford F. Mackinder: *Democratic Ideals and Reality* (1919; reprint edn, New York, 1942), and "The Round World and the Winning of Peace," *Foreign Affairs,* 21 (1943): 598–605. Mackinder's ideas were modified and widely disseminated in the United States, especially by intellectuals such as Nicholas John Spykman, Hans W. Weigert, Robert Strausz-Hupé, and Isaiah Bowman.

[6]For the decision on the Dardanelles, see the attachments to JCS, "United States Policy concerning the Dardanelles and Kiel Canal" [July 1945], RG 218, ser. CCS 092 (7-10-45), JCS 1418/1; for the joint chiefs' position on Iran, Turkey, and Tripolitania, see JCS, "U.S. Security Interests in the Eastern Mediterranean," March 1946, ibid., ser. CCS 092 USSR (3-27-45). JCS 1641 series; and Lincoln, Memorandum for the Record, April 16, 1946, RG 165, ser. ABC 336 Russia (8-22-43); and, for the Clifford memorandum, see Arthur Krock, *Memoirs: Sixty Years on the Firing Line* (New York, 1968), 477–82.

[7]Strategy Section, OPD, "Post-War Base Requirements in the Phillipines," April 23, 195, RG 165, OPD 336 (top secret); MID, "Positive US Action Required to Restore Normal Conditions in Southeast Asia," July 3, 1947, RG 319, P&O, 092 (top secret); and Lauris Norstad to the Director of Intelligence, July 10, 1947, ibid.

[8]See, for example, JCS, "Presidential Request for Certain Facts and Information Regarding the Soviet Union," July 25, 1946, RG 218, ser. CCS 092 USSR (3-27-45), JCS 1696; P&O, "Strategic Study of Western and Northern Europe," May 21, 1947, RG 319, P&O, 092 (top secret); and Wooldridge to the General Board, April 30, 1948.

[9]For Kennan's "long telegram," see *FRUS, 1946* (Washington, DC, 1970), Vol. 4: 696–709; for ominous interpretations of Soviet intentions and capabilities, also see JCS, "Political Estimate of Soviet Policy for Use in Connection with Military Studies," April 5, 1946, RG 218, ser. CCS 092 USSR (3-27-45), JCS 1641/4; and JCS, "Presidential Request for Certain Facts and Information Regarding the Soviet Union," July 25, 1946.

[10]For the withdrawal of Soviet troops, see, for example, MID, "Soviet Intentions and Capabilities in Scandinavia as of 1 July 1946," April 25, 1946, RG 319, P&O, 350.05 (top secret). For reports on reductions of Russian troops in Eastern Europe and demobilization within the Soviet Union, see MID, "Review of Europe, Russia, and the Middle East," December 26, 1945, RG 165, OPD, 350.05 (top secret); Carl Espe, weekly calculations of Soviet troops, May–September 1946, NHC, SPD, ser. 5,

box 106, A8; and JIC, "Soviet Military Objectives and Capabilities," October 27, 1947. For references to Soviet military expenditures, see Patterson to Julius Adler, November 2, 1946, RG 107, RPPP, safe file, box 5; and for the Soviet transport system, see R. F. Ennis, Memorandum for the P&O Division, June 24, 1946, RG 165, ser. ABC 336 (8-22-43); Op-32 to the General Board, April 28, 1948, NHC, General Board 425 (ser. 315).

[11]Smith to the Secretary of State, April 11, 1946, RG 165, Records of the Chief of Staff, 091 Russia; and, for Soviet negotiating concessions, see Lincoln, Memorandum for the Chief of Staff, May 20, 1946, USMA; GLP War Dept/files. For the situation in Germany, see OPD and CAD, "Analysis of Certain Political Problems Confronting Military Occupation Authorities in Germany," April 10, 1946, RG 107, HCPP 091 Germany (classified); Patterson to Truman, June 11, 1946, RG 165, Records of the Chief of Staff, 091 Germany. For Clay's references to French obstructionism, see, for example, Smith, *Papers of General Lucius D. Clay*, Vol. 1: 84–5, 88–9, 151–2, 189–90, 212–17, 235–6. For overall intelligence assessments, see Central Intelligence Group [hereafter CIG], "Revised Soviet Tactics in International Affairs," January 6, 1947, HTL, HSTP, PSF, box 254, MID, "World Political Developments Affecting the Security of the United States during the Next Ten Years," April 14, 1947.

[12]My assessment is based primarily on my analysis of the materials in RG 218, ser. CCS.092 USSR (3-27-45); ser. CCS 381 USSR (3-2-46); RG 319, P&O, 350.05 (top secret); and NHC, SPD, central files, 1946–8, A8.

[13]During 1946 it became a fundamental tenet of American policy makers that Soviet policy objectives were a function of developments within the Soviet Union and not related to American actions. See, for example, Kennan's "long telegram," in *FRUS, 1946*, Vol. 4: 696–709; JCS, "Political Estimate of Soviet Policy," April 5, 1946.

[14]Norstad, memorandum, July 25, 1946, RG 319, P&O, 092 (top secret). For references to shifting tactics and constant objectives, see Vandenberg, Memorandum for the President, September 27, 1946, HTL, HSTP, PSF, box 249; CIG, "Revised Soviet Tactics," January 6, 1947; and, for the JCS report to the President, compare JCS 1696 with JIC 250/12. Both studies may be found in RG 218, ser. CCS 092 USSR (3-27-45). For Clifford's recollection, Clark Clifford, HTL, oral history, 170.

[15]For Soviet losses, see Nicholas V. Riasanovsky, *A History of Russia* (3rd edn, New York, 1977), 584–5. While Russian dead totaled almost 20 million and while approximately 25 percent of the reproducible wealth of the Soviet Union was destroyed, American battlefield casualties were 300,000 dead, the index of industrial production in the United States rose from 100 to 196, and the gross national product increased from $91 billion to $166 billion. See Gordon Wright, *The Ordeal of Total War* (New York, 1968), 264–5.

# *Nuclear Deterrence Doctrine*

4.2

BERNARD BRODIE

## Strategy in the Missile Age

* * *

We shall be talking about the strategy of deterrence of general war, and about the complementary principle of limiting to tolerable proportions whatever conflicts become inevitable. These ideas spring from the conviction that total nuclear war is to be avoided at almost any cost. This follows from the assumption that such a war, even if we were extraordinarily lucky, would be too big, too all-consuming to permit the survival even of those final values, like personal freedom, for which alone one could think of waging it. It need not be certain that it would turn out so badly; it is enough that there is a large chance that it would.

The conceptions of deterrence and of limited war also take account of the fact that the United States is, and has long been, a status quo power. We are uninterested in acquiring new territories or areas of influence or in accepting great hazard in order to rescue or reform those areas of the world which now have political systems radically different from our own. On the other hand, as a status quo power, we are also determined to keep what we have, including existence in a world of which half or more is friendly, or at least not sharply and perennially hostile. In other words, our minimum security objectives include not only our own national independence but also that of many other countries, especially those which cherish democratic political institutions. Among the latter are those nations with which we have a special cultural affinity, that is, the countries of western Europe.

* * *

### Deterrence Old and New

Deterrence as an element in national strategy or diplomacy is nothing new. Since the development of nuclear weapons, however, the term has acquired not only a special emphasis but also a distinctive connotation. It is usually the new and distinctive connotation that we have in mind when we speak nowadays of the "strategy of deterrence."

From *Strategy in the Missile Age* (Princeton: Princeton University Press, 1965), chap. 8.

The threat of war, open or implied, has always been an instrument of diplomacy by which one state deterred another from doing something of a military or political nature which the former deemed undesirable. Frequently the threat was completely latent, the position of the monitoring state being so obvious and so strong that no one thought of challenging it. Governments, like individuals, were usually aware of hazard in provoking powerful neighbors and governed themselves accordingly. Because avoidance of wars and even of crises hardly makes good copy for historians, we may infer that the past successes of some nations in deterring unwanted action by others add up to much more than one might gather from a casual reading of history. Nevertheless the large number of wars that have occurred in modern times prove that the threat to use force, even what sometimes looked like superior force, has often failed to deter.

We should notice, however, the positive function played by the failures. The very frequency with which wars occurred contributed importantly to the credibility inherent in any threat. In diplomatic correspondence, the statement that a specified kind of conduct would be deemed "an unfriendly act" was regarded as tantamount to an ultimatum and to be taken without question as seriously intended.

Bluffing, in the sense of deliberately trying to sound more determined or bellicose than one actually felt, was by no means as common a phenomenon in diplomacy as latter-day journalistic interpretations of events would have one believe. In any case, it tended to be confined to the more implicit kinds of threat. In short, the operation of deterrence was dynamic; it acquired relevance and strength from its failures as well as its successes.

Today, however, the policy of deterrence in relation to all-out war is markedly different in several respects. For one thing, it uses a kind of threat which we feel must be absolutely effective, allowing for no breakdowns ever. The sanction is, to say the least, not designed for repeating action. One use of it will be fatally too many. Deterrence now means something as a strategic policy only when we are fairly confident that the retaliatory instrument upon which it relies will not be called upon to function at all. Nevertheless, that instrument has to be maintained at a high pitch of efficiency and readiness and constantly improved, which can be done only at high cost to the community and great dedication on the part of the personnel directly involved. In short, we expect the system to be always ready to spring while going permanently unused. Surely there is something almost unreal about all this.

## The Problem of Credibility

The unreality is minimal when we are talking about what we shall henceforward call "*basic deterrence*," that is, deterrence of direct, strategic, nuclear attack upon targets within the home territories of the United States. In that instance there is little or no problem of credibility as concerns our reactions, for the enemy has little reason to doubt that if he strikes us we will try to hit back. But the great and terrible apparatus which we must set up to fulfill our needs for basic deterrence and the state of readiness at which we have to maintain it create a condition of almost embarrassing availability of huge power. The problem of linking this power to a reasonable conception of its utility has thus far proved a considerable strain.

* * *

On the other hand, it would be tactically and factually wrong to assure the enemy in advance (as we tend to do by constantly assuring ourselves) that we would in no case move against him until we had already felt some bombs on our cities and airfields. We have, as we have seen, treaty obligations which forbid so far-reaching a commitment to restraint. It is also impossible for us to predict with absolute assurance our own behavior in extremely tense and provocative circumstances. If we make the wrong prediction about ourselves, we encourage the enemy also to make the wrong prediction about us. The outbreak of war in Korea in 1950 followed exactly that pattern. The wrong kind of prediction in this regard might precipitate that total nuclear war which too many persons have lightly concluded is now impossible.

## Deterrence Strategy versus Win-the-War Strategies: The Sliding Scale of Deterrence

To return now to the simpler problem of basic deterrence. The capacity to deter is usually confused with the capacity to win a war. At present, capacity to win a total or unrestricted war requires either a decisive and *completely secure* superiority in strategic air power or success in seizing the initiative. Inasmuch as mere superiority in numbers of vehicles looks like a good thing to have anyway, the confusion between deterring and winning has method in it. But deterrence *per se* does not depend on superiority.

* * *

Now that we are in a nuclear age, the potential deterrence value of an admittedly inferior force may be sharply greater than it has ever been before. Let us assume that a menaced small nation could threaten the Soviet Union with only a single thermonuclear bomb, which, however, it could and would certainly deliver on Moscow if attacked. This would be a retaliatory capability sufficient to give the Soviet government pause. Certainly they would not provoke the destruction of Moscow for trivial gains, even if warning enabled the people of the city to save themselves by evacuation or resort to shelters. Naturally, the effect is greater if warning can be ruled out.

Ten such missiles aimed at ten major cities would be even more effective, and fifty aimed at that number of different cities would no doubt work still greater deterrent effect, though of course the cities diminish in size as the number included goes up. However, even when we make allowance for the latter fact, it is a fair surmise that the increase in deterrent effect is less than proportional to the increase in magnitude of potential destruction. We make that surmise on the basis of our everyday experience with human beings and their responses to punishment or deprivation. The human imagination can encompass just so much pain, anguish, or horror. The intrusion of numbers by which to multiply given sums of such feelings is likely to have on the average human mind a rather dull effect—except insofar as the increase in the threatened amount of harm affects the individual's statistical expectation of himself being involved in it.

Governments, it may be suggested, do not think like ordinary human beings, and one has to concede that the *maximum possible deterrence* which can be attained by the threat of retaliatory damage must involve a power which guarantees not only vast losses but also utter defeat. On the other hand, governments, including communistic ones, also comprise human beings, whose departure from the mold of ordinary mortals is not markedly in the direction of greater intellectualism or detachment. It is therefore likely that considerably less retaliatory destruction than that conceived under "maximum possible deterrence" will buy only slightly less deterrence. If we wish to visualize the situation graphically, we will think of a curve of "deterrence effect" in which each unit of additional damage threatened brings progressively diminishing increments of deterrence. Obviously and unfortunately, we lack all the data which would enable us to fill in the values for such a curve and thus to draw it.

If our surmises are in general correct, we are underlining the sharp differences in character between a deterrence capability and strategy on the one hand, and a win-the-war strategy and capability on the other. We have to remember too that since the winning of a war presupposes certain limitations on the quantity of destruction to one's own country and especially to one's population, a win-the-war strategy could quite conceivably be an utter impossibility to a nation striking second, and is by no means guaranteed to a nation striking first. Too much depends on what the other fellow does—how accessible or inaccessible he makes his own retaliatory force and how he makes his attack if he decides to launch one. However much we dislike the thought, a win-the-war strategy may be impossible because of circumstances outside our control.

Lest we conclude from these remarks that we can be content with a modest retaliatory capability—what some have called "minimum deterrence"—we have to mention at once four qualifying considerations, which we shall amplify later: (a) it may require a large force in hand to guarantee even a modest retaliation; (b) deterrence must always be conceived as a relative thing, which is to say it must be adequate to the variable but generally high degree of motivation which the enemy feels for our destruction; (c) if deterrence fails we shall want enough forces to fight a total war effectively; and (d) our retaliatory force must also be capable of striking first, and if it does so its attack had better be, as nearly as possible, overwhelming to the enemy's retaliatory force. Finally, we have to bear in mind that in their responses to threat or menace, people (including heads of government) do not spontaneously act according to a scrupulous weighing of objective facts. Large forces look more impressive than small ones—for reasons which are by no means entirely irrational—and in some circumstances such impressiveness may be important to us. Human beings, differing widely as they do in temperamental and psychic make-up, nevertheless generally have in common the fact that they make their most momentous decisions by what is fundamentally intuition.

* * *

## The Problem of Guaranteeing Strong Retaliation

It should be obvious that what counts in basic deterrence is not so much the size and efficiency of one's striking force before it is hit as the size and condition to which the enemy thinks he can reduce it by a surprise attack—as well as his confidence in the correctness of his predictions. The degree to which the automaticity of our retaliation has been taken for granted by the public, unfortunately including most leaders of opinion and even military officers, is for those who have any knowledge of the facts both incredible and dangerous. The general idea is that if the enemy hits us, we will kill him.

* * *

## Deterrence and Armaments Control

We come finally to the question of the political environment favoring the functioning of a deterrence strategy, especially with respect to the much abused and belabored subject of international control of armaments. There is a long and dismal history of confusion and frustration on this subject. Those who have been most passionate in urging disarmament have often refused to look unpleasant facts in the face; on the other hand, the government officials responsible for actual negotiations have usually been extremely rigid in their attitudes, tending to become more preoccupied with winning marginal and ephemeral advantages from the negotiations than in making real progress toward the presumed objective. There has also been confusion concerning both the objective and the degree of risk warranted by that objective.

Here we can take up only the last point. One must first ask what degree of arms control is a reasonable or sensible objective. It seems by now abundantly clear that total nuclear disarmament is not a reasonable objective. Violation would be too easy for the Communists, and the risks to the non-violator would be enormous. But it should also be obvious that the kind of bitter, relentless race in nuclear weapons and missiles that has been going on since the end of World War II has its own intrinsic dangers.

* * *

The kind of measures in which we ought to be especially interested are those which could seriously reduce on all sides the dangers of surprise attack. Such a policy would be entirely compatible with our basic national commitment to a strategy of deterrence. The best way to reduce the danger of surprise attack is to reduce on all sides the incentives to such attack, an end which is furthered by promoting measures that enhance deterrent rather than aggressive posture—where the two can be distinguished, which, if one is looking for the chance to do so, is probably pretty often. It also helps greatly to reduce the danger of accidental outbreak of total war if each side takes it upon itself to do the opposite of "keeping the enemy guessing" concerning its pacific intentions. This is accomplished not through reiterated declaration of pacific intent, which is for this purpose a worn and useless tactic, but through finding procedures where each side can assure the other through the latter's own eyes that deliberate attack is not being prepared against him.

* * *

Our over-riding interest, for the enhancement of our deterrence posture, is of course in the security of our own retaliatory force. But that does not mean that we especially desire the other side's retaliatory force to be insecure. If the opponent feels insecure, we suffer the hazard of his being more trigger-happy.

* * *

Stability is achieved when each nation believes that the strategic advantage of striking first is overshadowed by the tremendous cost of doing so. If, for example, retaliatory weapons are in the future so well protected that it takes more than one missile to destroy an enemy missile, the chances for stability become quite good. Under such circumstances striking first brings no advantage unless one has enormous numerical superiority. But such a situation is the very opposite of the more familiar one where both sides rely wholly or predominately on unprotected aircraft.

Technological progress could, however, push us rapidly towards a position of almost intolerable mutual menace. Unless something is done politically to alter the environment, each side before many years will have thousands of missiles accurately pointed at targets in the other's territory ready to be fired at a moment's notice. Whether or not we call it "push-button" war is a matter of our taste in phraseology, but there is no use in telling ourselves that the time for it is remote. Well before that time arrives, aircraft depending for their safety on being in the air in time will be operating according to so-called "airborne alert" and "fail-safe" patterns. Nothing which has any promise of obviating or alleviating the tensions of such situations should be overlooked.

# *The Sources of Containment*

4.3

## Mr. X [George Kennan]

## The Sources of Soviet Conduct

The political personality of Soviet power as we know it today is the product of ideology and circumstances: ideology inherited by the present Soviet leaders from the movement in which they had their political origin, and circumstances of the power which they now have exercised for nearly three decades in Russia. There can be few tasks of psychological analysis more difficult than to try to trace the interaction of these two forces and the relative rôle of each in the determination of official Soviet conduct.

* * *

[T]remendous emphasis has been placed on the original Communist thesis of a basic antagonism between the capitalist and Socialist worlds. It is clear, from many indications, that this emphasis is not founded in reality. The real facts concerning it have been confused by the existence abroad of genuine resentment provoked by Soviet philosophy and tactics and occasionally by the existence of great centers of military power, notably the Nazi régime in Germany and the Japanese Government of the late 1930's, which did indeed have aggressive designs against the Soviet Union. But there is ample evidence that the stress laid in Moscow on the menace confronting Soviet society from the world outside its borders is founded not in the realities of foreign antagonism but in the necessity of explaining away the maintenance of dictatorial authority at home.

Now the maintenance of this pattern of Soviet power, namely, the pursuit of unlimited authority domestically, accompanied by the cultivation of the semi-myth of implacable foreign hostility, has gone far to shape the actual machinery of Soviet power as we know it today. Internal organs of administration which did not serve this purpose withered on the vine. Organs which did serve this purpose became vastly swollen. The security of Soviet power came to rest on the iron discipline of the party, on the severity and ubiquity of the secret police, and on the uncompromising economic monopolism of the state. The "organs of suppression," in which the Soviet leaders had sought security from rival forces, became in large measure the masters of those whom they were designed to serve. Today the major part of the structure of Soviet power is committed to the perfection of the dictatorship and to the maintenance of the concept of Russia as in a state of siege, with the enemy lowering beyond the walls. And the millions of human beings who form that part of the structure of power must defend at all costs

From *Foreign Affairs* (July 1947).

this concept of Russia's position, for without it they are themselves superfluous.

As things stand today, the rulers can no longer dream of parting with these organs of suppression. The quest for absolute power, pursued now for nearly three decades with a ruthlessness unparalleled (in scope at least) in modern times, has again produced internally, as it did externally, its own reaction. The excesses of the police apparatus have fanned the potential opposition to the régime into something far greater and more dangerous than it could have been before those excesses began.

But least of all can the rulers dispense with the fiction by which the maintenance of dictatorial power has been defended. For this fiction has been canonized in Soviet philosophy by the excesses already committed in its name; and it is now anchored in the Soviet structure of thought by bonds far greater than those of mere ideology.

## II

So much for the historical background. What does it spell in terms of the political personality of Soviet power as we know it today?

Of the original ideology, nothing has been officially junked. Belief is maintained in the basic badness of capitalism, in the inevitability of its destruction, in the obligation of the proletariat to assist in that destruction and to take power into its own hands. But stress has come to be laid primarily on those concepts which relate most specifically to the Soviet regime itself: to its position as the sole truly Socialist régime in a dark and misguided world, and to the relationships of power within it.

The first of these concepts is that of the innate antagonism between capitalism and Socialism. We have seen how deeply that concept has become imbedded in foundations of Soviet power. It has profound implications for Russia's conduct as a member of international society. It means that there can never be on Moscow's side any sincere assumption of a community of aims between the Soviet Union and powers which are regarded as capitalist. It must invariably be assumed in Moscow that the aims of the capitalist world are antagonistic to the Soviet régime, and therefore to the interests of the peoples it controls. If the Soviet Government occasionally sets its signature to documents which would indicate the contrary, this is to be regarded as a tactical manœuvre permissible in dealing with the enemy (who is without honor) and should be taken in the spirit of *caveat emptor*. Basically, the antagonism remains. It is postulated. And from it flow many of the phenomena which we find disturbing in the Kremlin's conduct of foreign policy: the secretiveness, the lack of frankness, the duplicity, the wary suspiciousness, and the basic unfriendliness of purpose. These phenomena are there to stay, for the foreseeable future. There can be variations of degree and of emphasis. When there is something the Russians want from us, one or the other of these features of their policy may be thrust temporarily into the background; and when that happens there will always be Americans who will leap forward with gleeful announcements that "the Russians have changed," and some who will even try to take credit for having brought about such "changes." But we should not be misled by tactical manœuvres. These characteristics of Soviet policy, like the postulate from which they flow, are basic to the internal nature of Soviet power, and will be with us whether in the foreground or the background, until the internal nature of Soviet power is changed.

* * *

These considerations make Soviet diplomacy at once easier and more difficult to deal with than the diplomacy of individual aggressive leaders like Napoleon and Hitler. On the one hand it is more sensitive to contrary force, more ready to yield on individual sectors of the diplomatic front when that force is felt to be too strong, and thus more rational in the logic and rhetoric of power. On the other hand it cannot be easily defeated or discouraged by a single victory on the part of its opponents. And the patient persistence by which it is animated means that it can be effectively countered not by sporadic acts which represent the momentary whims of democratic opinion but only by intelligent long-range policies on the part of Russia's adversaries—policies no less steady in their purpose, and no less variegated and resourceful in their application, than those of the Soviet Union itself.

In these circumstances it is clear that the main element of any United States policy toward the Soviet Union must be that of a long-term, patient but firm and vigilant containment of Russian expansive tendencies. It is important to note, however, that such a policy has nothing to do with outward histrionics: with threats or blustering or superfluous gestures of outward "toughness." While the Kremlin is basically flexible in its reaction to political realities, it is by no means unamenable to considerations of prestige. Like almost any other government, it can be placed by tactless and threatening gestures in a position where it cannot afford to yield even though this might be dictated by its sense of realism. The Russian leaders are keen judges of human psychology, and as such they are highly conscious that loss of temper and of self-control is never a source of strength in political affairs. They are quick to exploit such evidences of weakness. For these reasons, it is a *sine qua non* of successful dealing with Russia that the foreign government in question should remain at all times cool and collected and that its demands on Russian policy should be put forward in such a manner as to leave the way open for a compliance not too detrimental to Russian prestige.

* * *

## IV

It is clear that the United States cannot expect in the foreseeable future to enjoy political intimacy with the Soviet régime. It must continue to regard the Soviet Union as a rival, not a partner, in the political arena. It must continue to expect that Soviet policies will reflect no abstract love of peace and stability, no real faith in the possibility of a permanent happy coexistence of the Socialist and capitalist worlds, but rather a cautious, persistent pressure toward the disruption and weakening of all rival influence and rival power.

Balanced against this are the facts that Russia, as opposed to the western world in general, is still by far the weaker party, that Soviet policy is highly flexible, and that Soviet society may well contain deficiencies which will eventually weaken its own total potential. This would of itself warrant the United States entering with reasonable confidence upon a policy of firm containment, designed to confront the Russians with unalterable counterforce at every point where they show signs of encroaching upon the interests of a peaceful and stable world.

But in actuality the possibilities for American policy are by no means limited to holding the line and hoping for the best. It is entirely possible for the United States to influence by its actions the internal developments, both within

Russia and throughout the international Communist movement, by which Russian policy is largely determined. This is not only a question of the modest measure of informational activity which this government can conduct in the Soviet Union and elsewhere, although that, too, is important. It is rather a question of the degree to which the United States can create among the peoples of the world generally the impression of a country which knows what it wants, which is coping successfully with the problems of its internal life and with the responsibilities of a World Power, and which has a spiritual vitality capable of holding its own among the major ideological currents of the time. To the extent that such an impression can be created and maintained, the aims of Russian Communism must appear sterile and quixotic, the hopes and enthusiasm of Moscow's supporters must wane, and added strain must be imposed on the Kremlin's foreign policies. For the palsied decrepitude of the capitalist world is the keystone of Communist philosophy. Even the failure of the United States to experience the early economic depression which the ravens of the Red Square have been predicting with such complacent confidence since hostilities ceased would have deep and important repercussions throughout the Communist world.

By the same token, exhibitions of indecision, disunity and internal disintegration within this country have an exhilarating effect on the whole Communist movement. At each evidence of these tendencies, a thrill of hope and excitement goes through the Communist world; a new jauntiness can be noted in the Moscow tread; new groups of foreign supporters climb on to what they can only view as the band wagon of international politics, and Russian pressure increases all along the line in international affairs.

It would be an exaggeration to say that American behavior unassisted and alone could exercise a power of life and death over the Communist movement and bring about the early fall of Soviet power in Russia. But the United States has it in its power to increase enormously the strains under which Soviet policy must operate, to force upon the Kremlin a far greater degree of moderation and circumspection than it has had to observe in recent years, and in this way to promote tendencies which must eventually find their outlet in either the break-up or the gradual mellowing of Soviet power. For no mystical, Messianic movement—and particularly not that of the Kremlin—can face frustration indefinitely without eventually adjusting itself in one way or another to the logic of that state of affairs.

Thus the decision will really fall in large measure in this country itself. The issue of Soviet-American relations is in essence a test of the over-all worth of the United States as a nation among nations. To avoid destruction the United States need only measure up to its own best traditions and prove itself worthy of preservation as a great nation.

Surely, there was never a fairer test of national quality than this. In the light of these circumstances, the thoughtful observer of Russian-American relations will find no cause for complaint in the Kremlin's challenge to American society. He will rather experience a certain gratitude to a Providence which, by providing the American people with this implacable challenge, has made their entire security as a nation dependent on their pulling themselves together and accepting the responsibilities of moral and political leadership that history plainly intended them to bear.

# *Vietnam*

5.1

Leslie H. Gelb

## Vietnam: The System Worked

The story of United States policy toward Vietnam is either far better or far worse than generally supposed. Our Presidents and most of those who influenced their decisions did not stumble step by step into Vietnam, unaware of the quagmire. U.S. involvement did not stem from a failure to foresee consequences.

Vietnam was indeed a quagmire, but most of our leaders knew it. Of course there were optimists and periods where many were genuinely optimistic. But those periods were infrequent and short-lived and were invariably followed by periods of deep pessimism. Very few, to be sure, envisioned what the Vietnam situation would be like by 1968. Most realized, however, that "the light at the end of the tunnel" was very far away—if not finally unreachable. Nevertheless, our Presidents persevered. Given international compulsions to "keep our word" and "save face," domestic prohibitions against "losing," and their personal stakes, our leaders did "what was necessary," did it about the way they wanted, were prepared to pay the costs, and plowed on with a mixture of hope and doom. They "saw" no acceptable alternative.

Three propositions suggest why the United States became involved in Vietnam, why the process was gradual, and what the real expectations of our leaders were:

*First,* U.S. involvement in Vietnam is not mainly or mostly a story of step by step, inadvertent descent into unforeseen quicksand. It is primarily a story of why U.S. leaders considered that it was vital not to lose Vietnam by force to Communism. Our leaders believed Vietnam to be vital not for itself, but for what they thought its "loss" would mean internationally and domestically. Previous involvement made further involvement more unavoidable, and, to this extent, commitments were inherited. But judgments of Vietnam's "vitalness"—beginning with the Korean War—were sufficient in themselves to set the course for escalation.

*Second,* our Presidents were never actually seeking a military victory in Vietnam. They were doing only what they thought was minimally

---

From *Foreign Policy* 3 (Summer 1971): 140–67.

necessary at each stage to keep Indochina, and later South Vietnam, out of Communist hands. This forced our Presidents to be brakemen, to do less than those who were urging military victory and to reject proposals for disengagement. It also meant that our Presidents wanted a negotiated settlement without fully realizing (though realizing more than their critics) that a civil war cannot be ended by political compromise.

*Third,* our Presidents and most of their lieutenants were not deluded by optimistic reports of progress and did not proceed on the basis of wishful thinking about winning a military victory in South Vietnam. They recognized that the steps they were taking were not adequate to win the war and that unless Hanoi relented, they would have to do more and more. Their strategy was to persevere in the hope that their will to continue—if not the practical effects of their actions—would cause the Communists to relent.

Each of these propositions is explored below.

## I. Ends: "We Can't Afford to Lose"

Those who led the United States into Vietnam did so with their eyes open, knowing why, and believing they had the will to succeed. The deepening involvement was not inadvertent, but mainly deductive. It flowed with sureness from the perceived stakes and attendant high objectives. U.S. policy displayed remarkable continuity. There were not dozens of likely "turning points." Each post-war President inherited previous commitments. Each extended these commitments. Each administration from 1947 to 1969 believed that it was necessary to prevent the loss of Vietnam and, after 1954, South Vietnam by force to the Communists. The reasons for this varied from person to person, from bureaucracy to bureaucracy, over time and in emphasis. For the most part, however, they had little to do with Vietnam itself. A few men argued that Vietnam had intrinsic strategic military and economic importance, but this view never prevailed. The reasons rested on broader international, domestic, and bureaucratic considerations.

* * *

The *domestic* repercussions of "losing" Vietnam probably were equally important in Presidential minds. Letting Vietnam "go Communist" was undoubtedly seen as:

- opening the floodgates to domestic criticism and attack for being "soft on Communism" or just plain soft;
- dissipating Presidential influence by having to answer these charges;
- alienating conservative leadership in the Congress and thereby endangering the President's legislative program;
- jeopardizing election prospects for the President and his party;
- undercutting domestic support for a "responsible" U.S. world role; and
- enlarging the prospects for a right-wing reaction—the nightmare of a McCarthyite garrison state.

* * *

## II. Means: "Take the Minimal Necessary Steps"

None of our Presidents was seeking total victory over the Vietnamese Communists. War critics who wanted victory always knew this. Those who wanted the U.S. to get out never believed it. Each President was essentially doing what he thought was minimally necessary to prevent a Communist victory during his tenure in office. Each, of course, sought to strengthen the anti-Communist Vietnamese forces, but with the aim of a negotiated settlement. Part of the tragedy of Vietnam was that the compromises our Presidents were prepared to offer could never lead to an end of the war. These preferred compromises only served to reinforce the conviction of both Communist and anti-Communist Vietnamese that they had to fight to the finish in their civil war. And so, more minimal steps were always necessary.

* * *

Our Presidents reacted to the pressures as brakemen, pulling the switch against both the advocates of "decisive escalation" and the advocates of disengagement. The politics of the Presidency largely dictated this role, but the personalities of the Presidents were also important. None were as ideological as many persons around them. All were basically centrist politicians.

Their immediate aim was always to prevent a Communist takeover. The actions they approved were usually only what was minimally necessary to that aim. Each President determined the "minimal necessity" by trial and error and his own judgment. They might have done more and done it more rapidly if they were convinced that: (1) the threat of a Communist takeover were more immediate, (2) U.S. domestic politics would have been more permissive, (3) the government of South Vietnam had the requisite political stability and military potential for effective use and (4) the job really would have gotten done. After 1965, however, the minimal necessity became the maximum they could get given the same domestic and international constraints.

* * *

## III. Expectations: "We Must Persevere"

Each new step was taken not because of wishful thinking or optimism about its leading to a victory in South Vietnam. Few of our leaders thought that they could win the war in a conventional sense or that the Communists would be decimated to a point that they would simply fade away. Even as new and further steps were taken, coupled with expressions of optimism, many of our leaders realized that more—and still more—would have to be done. Few of these men felt confident about how it would all end or when. After 1965, however, they allowed the impression of "winnability" to grow in order to justify their already heavy investment and domestic support for the war.

The strategy always was to persevere. Perseverance, it seemed, was the only way to avoid or postpone having to pay the domestic political costs of failure. Finally, perseverance, it was hoped, would convince the Communists that our will to continue was firm. Perhaps, then, with domestic support for perseverance, with bombing North Vietnam, and with inflicting heavy casualties in the South, the Communists would relent. Perhaps, then, a compromise could be negotiated to save the Communists' face without giving them South Vietnam.

* * *

Most of our leaders saw the Vietnam quagmire for what it was. Optimism was, by and large, put in perspective. This means that many knew that each step would be followed by another. Most seemed to have understood that more assistance would be required either to improve the relative position of our Vietnamese allies or simply to prevent a deterioration of their position. Almost each year and often several times a year, key decisions had to be made to prevent deterioration or collapse. These decisions were made with hard bargaining, but rapidly enough for us now to perceive a preconceived consensus to go on. Sometimes several new steps were decided at once, but announced and implemented piecemeal. The whole pattern conveyed the feeling of more to come.

With a tragic sense of "no exit," our leaders stayed their course. They seemed to hope more than expect that something would "give." The hope was to convince the Vietnamese Communists through perseverance that the U.S. would stay in South Vietnam until they abandoned their struggle. The hope, in a sense, was the product of disbelief. How could a tiny, backward Asian country *not* have a breaking point when opposed by the might of the United States? How could they not relent and negotiate with the U.S.?

And yet, few could answer two questions with any confidence: Why should the Communists abandon tomorrow the goals they had been paying so dear a price to obtain yesterday? What was there really to negotiate? No one seemed to be able to develop a persuasive scenario on how the war could end by peaceful means.

Our Presidents, given their politics and thinking, had nothing to do but persevere. But the Communists' strategy was also to persevere, to make the U.S. go home. It was and is a civil war for national independence. It was and is a Greek tragedy.

* * *

# *Détente*

5.2

Alexander L. George

## Détente: The Search for a "Constructive" Relationship

* * *

This relationship [détente] did not occur accidentally; it was the result of developments in world politics that U.S. and Soviet leaders recognized and to which they attempted to adapt. Détente—whatever it was intended to be—emerged as a result of policy choices made by the two leaderships, and it was shaped by the way in which they concerted efforts in an attempt to define a new relationship that would replace the acute hostility of the cold war, moderate the conflict potential inherent in their competition, and strengthen cooperation in issue areas in which they believed their interests converged. A mutual desire to move in the direction of détente had been powerfully stimulated by the brush with thermonuclear disaster during the Cuban missile crisis in 1962. Important steps to develop a new relationship were taken during the remainder of the decade of the sixties, but détente was given stronger impetus and moved more steadily in the early seventies during President Nixon's first administration.

It is important to recognize that while both [Richard] Nixon and [Leonid] Brezhnev wanted to develop a more constructive relationship between their countries, they came to the task from different starting points and with expectations that differed in important respects. Soviet leaders wanted to formalize their relationship with the United States in such a way as to encourage that country to accept the emergence of the Soviet Union as a co-equal, with all that they hoped this status would imply for the future. Nixon and [Henry] Kissinger, on the other hand, wanted to draw the Soviet Union into a new relationship that would enable the United States to maintain as much of its declining world position as possible. They were very much aware of changes in the arena of world politics that were eroding the predominant position that the United States had enjoyed during the cold war. As Nixon put it in his annual foreign policy report to Congress of February 25, 1971: "The postwar order in international relations—the configuration of power that emerged from the Second World War—is gone. With it are gone the conditions which have determined the assumptions and practices of United States foreign policy since 1945."[1]

---

From *Managing U.S.-Soviet Rivalry: Problems of Crisis Prevention* (Boulder, Colo.: Westview, 1983), chap. 2.

Nixon had in mind the many important changes that had taken place in the international and domestic environments in which U.S. foreign policy had to operate—and to which it had to adjust. Many of the nations that had suffered severe losses and dislocation from World War II had now substantially recovered. New nations had emerged as the major European powers divested themselves of or were deprived of their colonies. Many of these new states displayed an increasing ability to maintain their independence and to avoid becoming battlegrounds for the cold war. U.S. leaders were experiencing increasing limits on the ability of their policies to influence world developments unilaterally (of this limitation, the Vietnam War was only the most obvious and tragic example). U.S. strategic military superiority was giving way to the achievement of strategic parity by the Soviet Union. But, at the same time, the nature of the Communist challenge to the free world had changed with the passing of Moscow's near-monolithic control of the international communist movement and the emergence of competing centers of communist doctrine, power, and practice. In this regard, particularly, the Sino-Soviet split seemed to offer new opportunities for the United States to benefit from the possible emergence of a tripolar balance of power. Finally, U.S. foreign policy had to adjust to the growing constraints on resources available to support the ambitious global role the United States had assumed during the cold war and to the increasing domestic unwillingness in the United States to continue support of costly commitments abroad.

Accordingly, Nixon and Kissinger sought to introduce a web of incentives into the relationship with the Soviet Union that would give the USSR a stake in a more stable world order and induce it to operate with greater restraint. Thereby, a measure of *self*-containment on the part of Soviet leaders would be introduced that would reduce the need for the United States to rely exclusively on deterrence, as it had in the cold war, to contain the Soviet Union. In time, it was hoped, the new positive relationship with the Soviet Union would become part of a new, more stable international system.

Nixon and Kissinger were intrigued by the possibility of establishing a tripolar balance of power among the United States, the Soviet Union, and the People's Republic of China (PRC). By developing a measure of friendly relations with both of these archrivals, the United States could hope to reduce potential threats to its interests from either side and to induce each to a greater measure of cooperation with U.S. policy. By using its unique middle position in such a triangular relationship, Washington could tilt or threaten to tilt in favor of one or the other of the two Communist rivals, as the situation required, to promote its own interests. Thus, Nixon and Kissinger believed the United States could compensate for the decline of U.S. power by presiding over a tripolar system that, if delicately managed by Washington, would give the United States additional leverage with which to protect and enhance its interests. The immediate, indeed urgent, U.S. objective to be realized by employing this neo-Bismarckian strategy was, of course, to induce both the PRC and the Soviet Union to influence North Vietnam to end the war in Southeast Asia on terms acceptable to the United States.

This is not to say that Nixon and Kissinger viewed the PRC in the same terms as they did the Soviet Union. The major potential threat to U.S. security and worldwide interests was perceived to emanate from the growing power of the USSR. The People's Republic was not a superpower and would not become one for many years. And so the major incentive behind Nixon's improving relations with the PRC was to obtain leverage for developing a more satisfactory relationship with the Soviet Union. The threat of a positive development of U.S. relations with the PRC was supposed to be part of the "stick" that, coupled with the "carrot" of various positive inducements held out to Soviet leaders, would draw the USSR into a more constructive relationship with the United States, one in which the Soviets would restrain themselves from employing the growing power and new global reach of their military forces to make advances at the expense of U.S. interests and the interests of its allies. In seeking an improved relationship with the Soviet Union Nixon and Kissinger did not expect to eliminate competition but merely to moderate it in order to reduce its dangerous potential. What, then, was the grand strategy for achieving the important long-range objective? It had at least four major components.

First, there was Nixon's willingness to acknowledge that the Soviet Union was entitled to the same status of superpower that the United States enjoyed. Aware of the importance that Soviet leaders attached to achieving equality of status, Nixon was willing to recognize this equality symbolically in various ways, via summit meetings and in rhetorical statements. What "equality" was to mean in practice, however, was left undefined and was soon to become a source of fundamental friction in the détente relationship.

A second element in the strategy was Nixon's conditional willingness to recognize and legitimize, as it were, the changes in Eastern Europe that had taken place following World War II. Nixon agreed to go along with the long-standing Soviet desire for a formal document, signed by all European countries as well as by the United States, that would recognize existing borders in Europe and thereby tacitly confirm the dominant role of the Soviet Union in Eastern Europe. This recognition of borders was part of the Helsinki Declaration that finally emerged in 1975 from the Conference on Security and Cooperation in Europe. Nixon agreed to move in this direction at the first summit meeting held in Moscow in May 1972, coupling his acquiescence with a Soviet agreement to regularize the status of West Berlin and to engage in discussions for mutual and balanced force reductions in Europe.

A third element of the strategy called for a variety of formal agreements with the Soviet Union to further mutual cooperation and interdependence. Most important in this connection were to be agreements for limiting the strategic arms race. In this respect the two sides were initially successful, and SALT I [the first Strategic Arms Limitation Treaty] was signed at the Moscow summit in May 1972. In addition, Nixon offered the prospect of important, continuing economic and technical assistance to the Soviet Union as a major inducement for giving Soviet leaders a strong stake in the evolving constructive relationship. Nixon's willingness to move in this direction was part of the set of understandings developed at the Moscow summit. The trade agreement signed in October, however, was to encounter unexpected difficulties in the Senate and was never carried out, a failure that dealt a major blow to the further development of détente.

The fourth element of their strategy was particularly important to Nixon and

Kissinger, even though they recognized its difficulty and elusive character. They hoped that the momentum of détente would lead in time to the development of a new set of norms and rules for regulating and moderating the global competition and rivalry between the two superpowers. A start was made in this direction with some of the provisions of the Basic Principles Agreement (BPA) that Nixon and Brezhnev signed at the Moscow summit. These provisions were characterized as an agreement by the United States and the Soviet Union to cooperate in "crisis prevention," as compared to "crisis management." But neither the objective of crisis prevention nor the means for attempting to achieve it were conceptualized in any useful detail. In fact, the agreement to cooperate in order to prevent dangerous crises contained important ambiguities and unresolved disagreements that were to become a major source of friction.

The Basic Principles Agreement included much more than a vague commitment to crisis prevention. It was described by U.S. and Soviet leaders as a sort of charter for détente. In the document the two sides agreed to adopt the practice of periodical high-level meetings, to continue efforts to limit armaments, and to develop economic, scientific, and cultural ties between their two countries on a long-term basis in order to strengthen their relationship. Nixon tried to clarify the nature of the Basic Principles Agreement for the U.S. public by referring to it as a road map. But terms such as "charter" and "road map" were inadequate designations for what had been accomplished and agreed to in Moscow. So far as the analogy of a road map is concerned, the Basic Principles Agreement was certainly not a Cooks Tour itinerary for a voyage that the two parties had decided to embark upon together; it was more in the nature of Lewis and Clark's rough description of uncharted territory. Perhaps a more apt way of characterizing the Basic Principles Agreement would be to explain it as a contractual arrangement of a very loose and general character, the specifics of which remained to be filled in over time. In the parlance of nineteenth-century European diplomacy, the BPA (together with associated agreements and understandings arrived at in the Moscow summit) was in the nature of a rapprochement (i.e., an arrangement in which both sides express a desire to search for agreements on various issues) but went beyond that to an entente (in which the two sides recognize a similarity of views and interests that, however, are limited to certain issues). In other words, as George Breslauer puts it, U.S. and Soviet leaders set out to develop a new relationship of restrained "collaborative competition" to replace the "confrontational competition" of the cold war. However, important aspects of the collaborative competition, including what has been called the "rules" of détente, remained to be worked out.

* * *

## Domestic Constraints on Foreign Policy: The Need for Policy Legitimacy

* * *

To conduct a long-range foreign policy of this kind, a president must find ways of dealing with the special requirements for democratic control of foreign policy. Public opinion, Congress, the media, and powerful interest groups often assert themselves in ways that seriously complicate and jeopardize the ability of an administration to pursue long-range foreign policy objectives in a coherent, consistent manner.

* * *

Policy legitimacy for détente was necessary also in the Soviet Union but, of course, the problem of domestic constraints on the conduct of a long-range foreign policy of this kind arises in a less acute form in a nondemocratic political system. Nixon and Kissinger were acutely aware of the dimensions of the challenge they faced in obtaining and maintaining sufficient domestic support for their détente policy. In his earlier scholarly study of the Concert of Europe system, Kissinger noted the failure of statesmen of that era to maintain domestic support for their policies. "The acid test of a policy," Kissinger emphasized, ". . . is its ability to obtain domestic support. This has two aspects: the problem of legitimizing a policy within the governmental apparatus . . . and that of harmonizing it with the national experience."[2]

Ironically, in the end Kissinger and the two presidents he served also failed to meet the "acid test" of their policy of détente. The problems they encountered in this respect are sobering and have been discussed elsewhere.[3] Suffice it to say that the erosion of domestic support for their complex détente policy increasingly burdened and eventually crippled the effort to develop détente with the Soviet Union. Critical in this respect was the perception that détente was not effective in dissuading Soviet leaders from embarking on an increasingly assertive policy in third areas. In response to this turn of events, President Ford and Kissinger were forced into making a belated effort to define the rules of détente in such a way as to label assertive Soviet actions as violations or, at least, as contrary to the spirit of détente. . . .

Gradually, as the initial promise of détente proved elusive and concern with Soviet policy in third areas mounted, Kissinger began to redefine détente's objectives. In his major defense of détente in September 1974 he had emphasized, still hopefully, that it entailed "the search for a more *constructive relationship* with the Soviet Union. . . ." Almost a year later, in July 1975, as William Hyland notes, Kissinger's emphasis was shifting: "We consider détente a means to regulate a *competitive relationship. . . .*"[4] With a further erosion of domestic support for détente that extended to important elements of the Ford administration and the Republican party, the themes of balance of power and containment began to reappear and to assume new prominence in Kissinger's statements regarding the objectives of the administration's foreign policy. While it would be too much to say that détente foundered on the inability of the two superpowers to manage their rivalry in third areas, the increasingly assertive character of Soviet foreign policy in the mid-seventies contributed to erosion of the legitimacy of the détente policy and became a major issue in the presidential election of 1976, first in the contest for the Republican nomination, in which Reagan mounted a strong challenge to President Ford, and then in the presidential contest between Ford and Carter.

President Carter attempted to retain and strengthen what remained of the détente relationship, but the efforts of his administration in this direction were handicapped by inadequate conceptualization of a comprehensive policy toward the Soviet Union, poor policy implementation, and divided counsels at the highest policymaking level. If Carter had a clear notion of the type of relationship with the Soviet Union that U.S. policy should seek to bring about, that conception was not accompanied by a well-developed idea of grand strategy or consistently implemented with appropriate tactics. Carter never succeeded in gaining policy legitimacy and stable domestic support for his policy toward the Soviet Union. Soviet activities in third areas continued to be of concern in Washington and further eroded domestic support for what remained of détente, a trend that developments in Poland accentuated at the beginning of President Reagan's administration.

## Notes

[1]Richard M. Nixon, *U.S. Foreign Policy for the 1970's: Building for Peace* (Washington, D.C.: Government Printing Office, February 25, 1971), p. 3.

[2]Henry Kissinger, *A World Restored* (New York: Houghton Mifflin, 1957), p. 327.

[3]Alexander L. George, "Domestic Constraints on Regime Change in U.S. Foreign Policy: The Need for Policy Legitimacy," in *Change in the International System*, ed. Ole R. Holsti, Randolph M. Siverson, and Alexander L. George (Boulder, Colo.: Westview Press, 1980), pp. 233–262.

[4]Henry Kissinger, "Détente with the Soviet Union," address given September 19, 1974 (*Department of State Bulletin*, October 14, 1974); Kissinger, "The Moral Foundations of Foreign Policy," address given July 15, 1975 (*Department of State Bulletin*, August 4, 1975), as quoted in William G. Hyland, *Soviet-American Relations: A New Cold War?* (Santa Monica, Calif.: RAND Corp., May 1981), pp. 31–32. (Italics added.)

# *The End of the Cold War*



JOHN LEWIS GADDIS

## The Unexpected Ronald Reagan

* * *

It is difficult, now, to recall how far Soviet-American relations had deteriorated at the time Ronald Reagan entered the White House. Some of the responsibility for this rested with Jimmy Carter: at a time when defeat in Vietnam had severely shaken American self-confidence, when the energy crisis appeared to be demonstrating American impotence, when the military balance seemed to be shifting in the Russians' favor, and when the domestic consensus in favor of detente was rapidly dissolving, he had chosen to launch an unprecedented effort to shift the entire basis of foreign policy from power to principle.[1] Carter's timing was terrible; his implementation was haphazard and inconsistent; only his intentions were praiseworthy, and in the climate of the late 1970s, that was not enough.

But the primary responsibility for the decline of detente must rest with the Soviet Union itself, and its increasingly senescent leader, Leonid Brezhnev. Given the long-term economic and social problems that confronted it, the Kremlin needed detente even more than Washington did. And yet, Brezhnev failed to see that he had, in Carter, an American counterpart who sincerely shared that objective; instead he chose to view the administration's fumbling earnestness as a sinister plot directed against Soviet interests. As if to compound this error, Brezhnev also allowed Soviet foreign policy to get caught up in a pattern of imperial overextension like the one that had afflicted the United States in the 1950s and 1960s. For just as the Americans had felt obliged, during those years, to prevent the coming to power of Third World Marxist governments, so the Russians now believed it necessary to sustain such governments, whatever the effect on the Soviet economy, on relations with the West, or on Moscow's overall reputation in world affairs. By equating expansionism with defense, the Soviet leader made the same mistake Stalin had made in the late 1940s: he brought about what he must have most feared. Brezhnev cannot have found it reassuring to know, as he approached the end of his life, that the invasion of Afghanistan had tarnished the Soviet image in the Third World; that a new American military buildup was under way with widespread domestic support; that an unusually

From *The United States and the End of the Cold War* (New York: Oxford University Press, 1992), chap. 7.

determined NATO alliance had decided to deploy a new generation of missiles capable of striking Moscow itself; that detente was dead; and, most unsettling of all, that Ronald Reagan had become president of the United States.

* * *

The record of the Reagan years suggests the need to avoid the common error of trying to predict outcomes from attributes.[2] There is no question that the President and his advisers came into office with an ideological view of the world that appeared to allow for no compromise with the Russians; but ideology has a way of evolving to accommodate reality, especially in the hands of skillful political leadership. Indeed a good working definition of leadership might be just this—the ability to accommodate ideology to practical reality—and by that standard, Reagan's achievements in relations with the Soviet Union will certainly compare favorably with, and perhaps even surpass, those of Richard Nixon and Henry Kissinger.

Did President Reagan intend for things to come out this way? That question is, of course, more difficult to determine, given our lack of access to the archives. But a careful reading of the public record would, I think, show that the President was expressing hopes for an improvement in Soviet-American relations from the moment he entered the White House, and that he began shifting American policy in that direction as early as the first months of 1983, almost two years before Mikhail Gorbachev came to power.[3] Gorbachev's extraordinary receptiveness to such initiatives—as distinct from the literally moribund responses of his predecessors—greatly accelerated the improvement in relations, but it would be a mistake to credit him solely with the responsibility for what happened: Ronald Reagan deserves a great deal of the credit as well.

Critics have raised the question, though, of whether President Reagan was responsible for, or even aware of, the direction administration policy was taking.[4] This argument is, I think, both incorrect and unfair. Reagan's opponents have been quick enough to hold him personally responsible for the failures of his administration; they should be equally prepared to acknowledge his successes. And there are points, even with the limited sources now available, where we can see that the President himself had a decisive impact upon the course of events. They include, among others: the Strategic Defense Initiative, which may have had its problems as a missile shield but which certainly worked in unsettling the Russians; endorsement of the "zero option" in the INF [Intermediate-Range Nuclear Forces] talks and real reductions in START [the Strategic Arms Reduction Talks]; the rapidity with which the President entered into, and thereby legitimized, serious negotiations with Gorbachev once he came into office; and, most remarkably of all, his eagerness to contemplate alternatives to the nuclear arms race in a way no previous president had been willing to do.[5]

Now, it may be objected that these were simple, unsophisticated, and, as people are given to saying these days, imperfectly "nuanced" ideas. I would not argue with that proposition. But it is important to remember that while complexity, sophistication, and nuance may be prerequisites for intellectual leadership, they are not necessarily so for political leadership, and can at times actually get in the way. President Reagan generally meant precisely what he said: when he came out in favor of negotiations from strength, or for strategic arms reductions as opposed to limitations, or even for making nuclear weapons ultimately irrelevant and obsolete, he did not do so in the "killer amendment" spirit favored by geopolitical sophisticates on the right; the President may have been conservative but he was never devious. The lesson here ought to be to beware of excessive convolution and subtlety in strategy, for sometimes simple-mindedness wins out, especially if it occurs in high places.

Finally, President Reagan also understood something that many geopolitical sophisticates on the left have not understood: that although toughness may or may not be a prerequisite for successful negotiations with the Russians—there are arguments for both propositions—it is absolutely essential if the American people are to lend their support, over time, to what has been negotiated. Others may have seen in the doctrine of "negotiation from strength" a way of avoiding negotiations altogether, but it now seems clear that the President saw in that approach the means of constructing a domestic political base without which agreements with the Russians would almost certainly have foundered, as indeed many of them did in the 1970s. For unless one can sustain domestic support—and one does not do that by appearing weak—then it is hardly likely that whatever one has arranged with any adversary will actually come to anything.

There is one last irony to all of this: it is that it fell to Ronald Reagan to preside over the belated but decisive success of the strategy of containment George F. Kennan had first proposed more than four decades earlier. For what were Gorbachev's reforms if not the long-delayed "mellowing" of Soviet society that Kennan had said would take place with the passage of time? The Stalinist system that had required outside adversaries to justify its own existence now seemed at last to have passed from the scene; Gorbachev appeared to have concluded that the Soviet Union could continue to be a great power in world affairs only through the introduction of something approximating a market economy, democratic political institutions, official accountability, and respect for the rule of law at home.[6] And that, in turn, suggested an even more remarkable conclusion: that the very survival of the ideology Lenin had imposed on Russia in 1917 now required infiltration—perhaps even subversion—by precisely the ideology the great revolutionary had sworn to overthrow.

I have some reason to suspect that Professor Kennan is not entirely comfortable with the suggestion that Ronald Reagan successfully completed the execution of the strategy he originated. But as Kennan the historian would be the first to acknowledge, history is full of ironies, and this one, surely, will not rank among the least of them.

## *Notes*

[1]The best overall treatment of Carter administration foreign policy is Gaddis Smith, *Morality, Reason, and Power: American Diplomacy in the Carter Years* (New York: Hill and Wang, 1986).

[2]See, on this point, Kenneth N. Waltz, *Theory of International Relations* (New York: Random House, 1979), p. 61.

[3]See Lou Cannon's account of a secret Reagan meeting with Soviet Ambassador Anatolii Dobrynin in February, 1983, in *President Reagan: The Role of a Lifetime* (New York: Simon and Schuster, 1991), pp. 311–12.

[4]A typical example is Garry Wills, "Mr. Magoo Remembers," *New York Review of Books*, XXXVII (December 20, 1990), 3–4.

[5]Reagan's most perceptive biographer has pointed out that he was guided "both by extraordinary vision and by remarkable ignorance." [Cannon, *President Reagan*, p. 290]. The implication is that the ignorance may have made possible the vision.

[6]Or so it appeared at the time. Whether these principles will survive the pressures that now threaten to break up the Soviet Union remains to be seen.

# *The End of the Cold War*

5.4

MIKHAIL GORBACHEV

## The Soviet Union's Crucial Role

* * *

If at the first phase of the invasion into Afghanistan, Soviet leaders could nourish hopes for a favorable outcome, it became clear after two to three years that we would be stuck for a long time without any chances of resolving the matter in our favor. As the United States generously supplied the anti-Kabul opposition groups with money and weapons, Afghanistan turned into a whirlpool, sucking in and crushing our manpower and making the related huge expenditures increasingly unbearable for our country. In general, this war was one of the causes for the economic and political crisis that necessitated *perestroika*.

The situation was further worsened by our society's silent and humble reconciliation with this years-long adventure. Unlike the case of Vietnam for the United States, no strong antiwar movement appeared in the USSR. The reason was not only that the lack of *glasnost* and hard-line political pressure ruled out any massive protest. Our public was not aware of the scale of our spending and losses since it received the strictly rationed and propaganda-processed information on actions of the so-called limited contingent of Soviet troops, "the international assistance to the friendly people of Afghanistan," and so on. Of course, rumors were bringing news about the growing number of zinc coffins with the repatriated remains of Soviet soldiers. But the public reacted limply, without emotions, as if paralyzed by some narcotic.

* * *

### German Unification and the Fall of Eastern European Communism

First, let me say that unification did not proceed according to a predesigned plan and following predetermined methods and pace. A lot happened spontaneously. As always, history took its own course, frustrating the designs of politicians and diplomats. However,

From *Essays on Leadership* (Washington, D.C.: Carnegie Commission on Preventing Deadly Conflict, 1998).

there was an understanding, or, more precisely, a sense of historical inevitability in the course of events. This grew organically from the transformations that were dictated by the new thinking.

Proceeding from the growing interdependence of countries and peoples and from the fact that a universal disaster can be avoided only through collective efforts that require the balancing of interests, we placed a conscious emphasis on the removal of the military-political bloc confrontation, elimination of the Iron Curtain, and integration of the Soviet Union into European and international economic and political structures. This process was inevitably to result in the change of the political arrangement known as the Yalta agreement, which existed on our continent for half a century. Under the new conditions, East European states gained the possibility for self-determination, and it was logical to assume that sooner or later Germans would use this chance to end the half-century of national division.

Therefore, there are no bases for contending that I did not foresee Germany's unification and the collapse of the Warsaw Pact treaty, that all of that fell upon us unexpectedly, and that the Soviet leadership had to simply reconcile itself since it had neither the power nor the possibility to impede such developments.

This is false. In reality, my colleagues and I were aware of the remote consequences of our actions. Having had sufficiently complete information about the situation in our allied states of East and Central Europe—about their difficulties and the growing influence of the opposition forces—it was not hard to imagine that the weakening of the bloc's discipline and of the political control from the "flagship" would lead to a change in power and then in foreign policy. Under these conditions, it seemed logical for us not to run counter to the inevitable, but to do all we could for the process to take place without huge disturbances and to protect to the maximum the interests of our country.

By the way, to this day, traditionalists fiercely blame me for betrayal, saying that I gave away Poland, Czechoslovakia, Hungary, etc. I always reply with a question: "Gave to whom? Poland to the Poles, Czechoslovakia to the Czechs and Slovaks. . . ." Peoples gained the possibility to decide their own destiny. For us, this was a chance to right a historical wrong and to atone for our attempts to keep these countries forcibly in the orbit of our influence (i.e., the suppression of disturbances in the German Democratic Republic [GDR] and Poland in 1953, the uprising of Hungarians in 1956, the Prague Spring of 1968, and finally, the building of the Berlin Wall, which came to symbolize the division of Europe and of the world).

I repeat, we were not naive simpletons caught in the net of our own speeches advocating the new thinking. It was not incidentally or as a result of failures and mistakes, but by intention that we gave the possibility to our allied countries to make a free choice. This was not at all easy. There were plenty of people in the Soviet Union who considered it necessary to use any means in order not to lose the fruits of the victory in the Second World War. These voices were heard not only at home. Ceaucescu was persistently addressing me and the other leaders of the Warsaw Pact countries with a demand to undertake an armed invasion into Poland to prevent the removal of the Communist party from power. One needs only to imagine the consequences of one such punitive expedition in the late 1980s to appreciate the significance of the new thinking and the foreign policy course then taken by Moscow.

* * *

Looking back, one can see blemishes and mistakes that could have been avoided. But as the saying goes, "one doesn't shake fists after the fight is over." With all the criticism deserved for the actions of the parties involved in that process, it should be acknowledged that most importantly, they withstood the test. They managed to evade bloodshed, which would have been quite possible under the circumstances, managed not to hamper the new strategic nuclear disarmament, and did not push the world back into the Cold War.

The position of the Soviet Union then played a crucial role.

* * *

# PART II

# *American Foreign Policy in the Twenty-First Century: Choices and Challenges*

CHAPTER

# 6 Foreign Policy Strategy and Foreign Policy Politics in a New Era

## Introduction: 11/9 and 9/11—Crumbling Wall and Crashing Towers

What times these are. We have seen soaring highs such as the crumbling of the Berlin Wall, an event that many had hoped for but that few believed would come about peacefully. Yet so it did on that fateful evening of November 9, 1989. We have also seen traumatic lows such as the crashing down of the World Trade Center's twin towers after a terrorist attack that shocked America and much of the rest of the world on the morning of September 11, 2001. 11/9 and 9/11, and so much else, uplifting and depressing, foreign policy successes and foreign policy failures, causes for gratification and celebration and for criticism and mourning.

Ours are truly times of historic transition. Their frequent labeling as the "post–Cold War era" is very telling: we know more about what they are not than about what they are. One system has ended; another one is in the process of emerging. A number of major global forces are at work, creating a new context and posing new challenges for American foreign policy.

In the second part of this book we turn to key issues that American foreign policy faces in this new era and this new century. Our framework again encompasses both foreign policy strategy and foreign policy politics—the *essence of choice* as it pertains to the core national interest goals of Peace, Power, Prosperity, and Principles, and the *process of choice* in the domestic politics of American foreign policy in each of these issue areas. What is the mix of conflict and cooperation in U.S. relations with the other major powers: China, Russia, Western Europe, Japan, and such rising powers as India, and what are the key issues in each of the major regions (Chapter 7)? With so many issues in the Middle East, Chapter 8 provides a more in-depth focus: What are the key issues there amid the wars in Iraq and Afghanistan, terrorism, Iran, and the Arab-Israeli conflict? What are the major policy challenges posed by ethnic conflict, genocide, and humanitarian intervention (Chapter 9)? What are the key economic, social, environmental, public-health, and other policy challenges in this age of globalization (Chapter 10)? Will the twenty-first century be a democratic one, an era in which principles play ever greater roles in American foreign policy (Chapter 11)? Our study of these questions will take us into many new issues and debates while staying grounded in the theoretical and historical contexts established in Part I. We will see how the "4 Ps" framework (Power, Peace, Prosperity, and Principles) sets the context for the policy choices within each of these issue areas. We also include pertinent cases of foreign policy politics in each chapter.

The first section of this chapter provides the strategy overview of key overarching debates about American foreign policy. The second section takes an initial look at foreign policy politics in the Obama administration.

## Foreign Policy Strategy for a New Era

Our initial overview focuses on seven broad debates over U.S. foreign policy strategy: unilateralism versus multilateralism as a particularly prominent debate during the Clinton and George W. Bush administrations; the defining characteristics of the international system in these initial years of the Obama administration; broad strategies and guiding doctrines for balancing force and diplomacy; the role of the United Nations; the particular challenges posed by nuclear weapons and other weapons of mass destruction (WMD); security threats posed by nonstate actors; and the broad strategic challenges of the international economy, energy security, and the global environment.

### *The Unilateralism versus Multilateralism Debate in the Clinton and Bush Years*

The debate about the U.S. role in this changing world is often cast in terms of unilateralism versus multilateralism. ***Unilateralism*** can be defined as an approach to foreign policy that emphasizes actions that a nation takes largely on its own, or acting with others but largely on its own terms. ***Multilateralism*** emphasizes acting with other nations (three or more is what distinguishes *multi*lateral from *bi*lateral) through processes that are more consultative and consensual as structured by international institutions, alliances, and coalitions. Although the distinction is one of degree and not a strict dichotomy, this contrast helps frame the debate over how to define the U.S. role in the world.

The contrast is also apparent when we compare the foreign policies of the Clinton and George W. Bush administrations. As a general pattern, the Clinton approach was largely multilateralist whenever possible and unilateral only when necessary. In contrast, the Bush approach, especially in the first term, was largely unilateralist whenever possible and multilateral only when necessary.

THE CASE FOR UNILATERALISM The unilateralist foreign policy strategy is based on six main points.

6.1

**Unipolarity** With the end of the Cold War, the bipolar system also came to an end. The United States won; the Soviet Union didn't just lose, it collapsed. The United States was left as the sole surviving superpower. Its military superiority was vast. Its economy drove globalization. Its ideology was spreading around the world. It was, in Charles Krauthammer's classic phrase, the "unipolar moment."[1] The scholars Stephen Brooks and William Wohlforth concurred: "There has never been a system of sovereign states that contained one state with that degree of domination."[2] Comparisons were being drawn with nothing less than ancient Rome at its height—indeed, some even openly referred to an American empire.

Richard Perle, a former Reagan administration official and a prominent adviser to the second Bush administration, argued for a largely unilateral approach to the war on terrorism because "the price you end up paying for an alliance is collective judgment, collective decision-making." Perle went on to question whether in this case, and indeed more generally, "the source of enthusiasm for the coalition . . . is a strong desire on the part of those who are promoting the coalition to see the United States restrained."[3] Perle's speech was titled "Next Stop, Iraq." He gave it in November 2001, almost a year and a half before the war with Iraq began.

**Power** "Power matters," wrote Condoleezza Rice during the 2000 presidential campaign. Of the components of the national interest, it is the most important. The problem, though, as Rice and other Bush strategists saw it, has been that "many in the United States are (and always have been) uncomfortable with the notions of power politics, great powers, and power balances."[4] Multilateralists in general and the Clinton administration in particular were the implied targets of this critique. The Bush team billed itself as having no such discomfort. Indeed, now more than ever, it felt American foreign policy makers should not have such concerns. The "inescapable reality" of today's world, the neoconservatives William Kristol and Robert Kagan asserted, is "American power in its many forms."[5] American foreign policy should be geared to maintaining this ***primacy,*** as some theorists call it, or ***preponderance,*** as others call it.[6] For as we have known since the time of the ancient Greek historian Thucydides, "the strong do what they have the power to do, and the weak accept what they have to accept."[7]

Although some Realists strongly opposed many of the Bush policies, particularly the war in Iraq, as diverting from and distorting power politics logic, they held to the view that power politics remains the way of the world. Foreign policy competition is an inherently stronger dynamic than is foreign policy cooperation. In John Mearsheimer's view, states always have sought and always will seek "opportunities to take advantage of one another" as well as to "work to insure that other states do not take advantage of them."[8] This is why, as Stephen Walt puts it as both an analytic point and a criticism of the Bush foreign policy, the United States does need to seek to maintain its primacy, but must do so "in ways that make its position of primacy acceptable to others."[9]

**Benevolent Hegemony** The United States is a benign superpower, or benevolent hegemon, committed to using its power to preserve peace and promote democratic values. This vision was posed in the Bush 2002 National Security Strategy as promoting "a balance of power that favors freedom": "The United States possesses unprecedented—and unequaled—strength and influence in the world. . . . [T]his position comes with unparalleled responsibilities, obligations and opportunity. The great strength of this nation must be used to promote a balance of power that favors freedom."[10] Thus, only those who oppose peace and freedom should fear American power and dominance.

This outlook reflects in part the Realist view that international order is most possible with a dominant ***hegemon.*** It also is rooted in part in the self-conception of ***American exceptionalism,*** the view that the United States is different from classical great powers in that it pursues peace and principles as well as power. "The United States would lead the civilized world," as one scholar captures this view, "in the expansion and consolidation of a liberal world order."[11] It thus is in everyone's interest, or at least in the interest of the peace loving and democratic spirited, for the United States to assert its power and to maintain its freedom of action with minimal impingements from treaties and other multilateral obligations. It is in this sense that the argument is said to be "hard-headed," not hard-hearted—in effect, American unilateralism is multilateral in function even if not in form.[12]

This strong linking of Power and Principles has been a defining feature of ***neoconservatism.*** As one author summarizes the main tenets of neoconservatism, "History had singled out the United States to play a unique role as the chief instrument for securing the advance of freedom. . . . American ideals defined America's purpose, to be achieved through the exercise of superior American power."[13] Neoconservatives such as Paul Wolfowitz held top foreign policy posts in the Bush administration, while others such as Charles Krauthammer and William Kristol and Robert Kagan and Joshua Muravcik exercised influence through the media and think tanks.

**National, Not Global, Interests** Unilateralists stress the distinction between the U.S. national interest and global interests. They criticize multilateralists for thinking too much in terms of "humanitarian interests" and the "international community," and too little in terms of the national interest. "There is nothing wrong with doing something that benefits all humanity," wrote Rice, "but that is, in a sense, a second-order effect" of pursuing the national interest.[14] That is to say, what is good for the world is not a sufficient goal in itself for U.S. foreign policy. Global interests may be satisfied by the pursuit of the national interest but are not in themselves a justification for major foreign policy commitments and undertakings.

It was along these lines that unilateralists criticized the Clinton administration for its position on international commitments such as the Comprehensive Test Ban Treaty, the International Criminal Court, and the Kyoto global-warming treaty as being "so anxious to find multilateral solutions to problems that it has signed agreements that are not in America's interest."[15] This also was the essence of the pre-Iraq critique by the Bush administration and others of humanitarian military interventions as "social work," and not in most cases a sufficiently vital U.S. national interest to warrant the use of force, or especially the commitment of U.S. troops.[16]

**Inefficacy of Multilateralism** In addition to all these points about the positives of unilateralism are the negatives of multilateralism. A major negative is said to be the loss of freedom of action the United States incurs in making key foreign policy decisions subject to multilateral approval. "Subcontracting to the UN" or "giving the UN a veto over *our* foreign policy" are the stump-speech political rhetoric expressions of this point. ***Prerogative encroachment*** is the more analytic term; that is, acting through the UN and other multilateral institutions encroach on the prerogatives of American power.

Moreover, unilateralists contend, multilateralism just doesn't work very well. They grant some acknowledgment to the role of international institutions such as the United Nations and the possibilities of international cooperation, but only as partial constraints on international competition and the potential for conflict. This was Mearsheimer's point when he said that "international institutions have minimal influence on state behavior, and thus hold little promise for promoting stability in the post–Cold War world."[17] It also was a principal reason that the Bush administration chose the unilateral route for the Iraq war.

The inherent problems are those of both process and impact. The process problem arises when so many countries with so many national interests try to act jointly. Making decisions and building consensus among such a large number of states with such disparate interests may hinder prompt action or dilute policies that need to be clear and firm. Moreover, if decisions are made on a one-country, one-vote basis, the United States is left with the same voting weight as Ecuador, Burkina Faso, Luxembourg, and other small countries. Procedures such as the veto power wielded by the United States on the UN Security Council only partially alleviate this problem.

The problem of impact is rooted in a view of international law, as expressed by the former undersecretary of state and later UN ambassador John Bolton, as "deeply and perhaps irrevocably flawed."[18] Unilateralists have specific critiques of particular institutions and particular treaties. But even beyond these individual instances, unilateralists are highly skeptical even of best-case scenarios of the role of multilateral institutions and treaties in keeping international order and their value for American foreign policy.

**Conservative Domestic Politics** Unilateralists raise the specter of America's own constitutional democracy being undermined by the impingements of multilateral institutions, agreements, and other aspects of global governance. This debate over safeguarding American sovereignty against multilateralism, "fought out at the confluence of constitutional theory and foreign policy," to quote Bolton again, "is *the* decisive issue facing the United States internationally."[19] On issues such as the jurisdiction of the ***International Criminal Court*** over American soldiers and other citizens, or U.S. troops under foreign command in UN peacekeeping operations, the debate is said to be a constitutional one, not just a foreign policy one.

Domestic politics also bring more baldly electoral considerations. The noted historian Arthur Schlesinger, Jr., a strong supporter of multilateralism and particularly of the UN, nevertheless notes that "there is no older American tradition in the conduct of foreign affairs" than unilateralism.[20] Unilateralism taps the self-concept of American exceptionalism in ways that have political appeal even if, as in Schlesinger's view, exceptionalism is a form of hubris that is bad for the United States as well as for the world. Unilateralists are well positioned politically because they can claim to be more concerned than their multilateralist opponents with "what's good for America" and play to fears and prejudices about the outside world. UN-bashing in particular has great appeal for these groups, many of which are especially influential in the conservative wing of the Republican party. Right-wing militia groups adhere to an extreme version of this view, with their paranoid theories that the UN is seeking to take over and even invade the United States.

THE CASE FOR MULTILATERALISM Multilateralism has its own case to make, which also can be summarized in six main points.

**International Institutionalism** Multilateralism is grounded in the International Institutionalist paradigm. The essence of this paradigm, as laid out in Chapter 1, is an emphasis on the building of a system of international institutions, organizations, and regimes that provide the basis for cooperation among states to resolve tensions, settle disputes, and work together in ways that are mutually beneficial and, above all, to avoid war.[21] With reference to the relatively peaceful end of the Cold War, International Institutionalist scholars such as John Ruggie contend that "there seems little doubt that multilateral norms and institutions have helped stabilize [the] international consequences." And as for the post–Cold War world, "such norms and institutions appear to be playing a significant role in the management of a broad array of regional and global changes in the world system today."[22] We entered the post–Cold War era, in this view, with international institutions that, although not without their weaknesses, are quite strong and have the potential to be made stronger.

6.2

International Institutionalists lay claim to a "realism" of their own. Their realism takes the system as it is, not as it used to be. The United States is unquestionably the strongest country, but it is neither in the U.S. interest, nor even within the realm of achievability, for the United States to try to maintain peace and security on its own. It often does need to be the lead actor, and at times it needs to act unilaterally, but the greatest power is the power of numbers that comes with effective multilateralism. Reading 6.2, from the Millennium Report of then–UN Secretary-General Kofi Annan, gives a sense of what is meant by "we the peoples" of the world.

With regard to the United Nations, rather than concerns about prerogative encroachment, the emphasis is on ***policy enhancement.*** The freedom of action the United States gives up by acting multilaterally tends to be outweighed by the capacity gained to achieve shared objectives. Part of that gain is a political version of the international trade principle of comparative advantage, whereby different nations as well as relevant international institutions and nongovernmental organizations (NGOs) all bring to bear their complementary expertises based on their own historical experiences, traditional relationships, and policy emphases. Also gained is a sharing of the burdens in ways that can help with both the politics and finances of sustaining commitments over time. Another gain is the legitimacy that can come only from a broadly multilateral effort. International norms surely "do not determine action," as Martha Finnemore aptly puts it, but they do "create permissive conditions for action."[23] Achieving broadly multilateral efforts has its obstacles and pitfalls, but the potential advantages are there in ways that any nation, even the United States, cannot achieve when acting alone or even largely on its own.

This line of thinking characterized much of the Clinton administration's foreign policy:

> International cooperation will be vital for building security in the next century because many of the challenges America faces cannot be addressed by a single nation. Many U.S. security objectives are best achieved—or can only be achieved—by leveraging our influence and capabilities through international organizations, our alliances, or as a leader [*sic*] of an ad hoc coalition formed around a specific objective. Leadership in the United Nations and other international organizations, and durable relationships with allies and friendly nations, are critical to our security.[24]

This viewpoint also came through in the thinking of the "Powell faction" within the Bush administration. Richard Haass, who as director of the State Department's policy planning staff was a top aide to Secretary of State Colin Powell, laid out a "doctrine of integration" and a strategy of shifting from "a balance of power to a pooling of power":

> In the twenty-first century, the principal aim of American foreign policy is to integrate other countries and organizations into arrangements that will sustain a world consistent with U.S.

> interests and values, and thereby promote peace, prosperity and justice as widely as possible.... Integration is about bringing nations together and then building frameworks of cooperation and, when feasible, institutions that reinforce and sustain them even more.... With war between great powers almost unthinkable, we can turn our efforts from containment and deterrence to consultation and cooperation. We can move from a balance of power to a pooling of power.[25]

Haass and others claimed that their multilateralism was more "hard-headed" than the Clinton version, but they seemed to share as much if not more with their predecessors than with the unilateralists within their own administration. Even the *Economist*, which usually took pro-American views, editorialized, "Has George Bush ever met a treaty that he liked? . . . It is hard to avoid the suspicion that it is the very idea of multilateral cooperation that Mr. Bush objects to."[26]

**Power-Influence Conversion** Second is the distinction between power and influence in measuring international leadership, position, and system structure. Multilateralists acknowledge the military and economic power advantages the United States has. But they are less likely to speak of unipolarity, preponderance, and primacy because of their greater emphasis on the difficulties of converting power to influence. In the multilateralists' view, the unilateralists are too quick to assume that the possession of power brings the exertion of influence. It is one thing to have more power than another country, but quite another to get that country to do what you want it to do, and to ensure that the outcomes will be what you want them to be. The "conversion" of power to influence quite often involves persuasion and the use of what the Harvard professor Joseph Nye calls ***soft power.*** Although coercion and "hard power" remain a key currency in the realm of international politics, persuasion and soft power often can be more effective tools. As Nye wrote:

> Military power remains crucial in certain situations, but it is a mistake to focus too narrowly on the military dimensions of American power.... Soft power is also more than persuasion or the ability to move people by argument. It is the ability to entice and attract. And attraction often leads to acquiescence or imitation.... If I can get you to *want* to do what I want, then I do not have to force you to do what you do *not* want to do.[27]

Thus, achieving foreign policy objectives is not so simple as Thucydides' dictum about the powerful doing what they want makes it sound. Advantages in military and economic power clearly help but do not always suffice. Moreover, if hard power is wielded in ways that exacerbate tensions or antagonize others, it can be even more difficult to achieve the influence that is key to effective leadership. This more nuanced view of the nature of power and the dynamics of influence is something that, as Nye put it, "unilateralists forget at their and our peril."[28]

**Not-So-Benign Hegemony** Third is a questioning of whether other nations generally share the "benevolent hegemon" view that unilateralists claim for the United States. The essence of U.S. Cold War leadership, particularly among Western European and other allies, was the overriding sense that they generally did benefit from America's pursuit of its own national interest. It wasn't just that the United States claimed that its hegemony was benign; these others generally saw it that way as well. With the Bush foreign policy, though, on a number of issues, other countries—including many U.S. allies—saw their interests as being hurt rather than helped by the U.S. pursuit of its own interests. The Bush administration deemed it in America's interest to use military force unilaterally, even preemptively, when necessary. Other nations and the UN not only disagreed on specific cases but were also concerned about the broader destabilizing effects, such as the undermining of international norms of nonintervention. The Bush administration opposed the Kyoto global-warming treaty as not in U.S. interests. The countries that had signed this treaty saw their interests as hurt by the unwillingness of the world's largest producer of the emissions that are causing the problem to be part of the treaty. The Bush administration unilaterally imposed tariffs on steel imports in 2002 and claimed to be acting in accord with the World Trade Organization (WTO) system. Those nations whose steel industries bore the costs saw this as U.S. exploitation of its economic power and as contrary to the WTO's multilateral rules. Although the general critique stops short of casting the United States as a malevolent hegemon, it does see America as not so benign.

**National and Global Interests** Multilateralists tend to agree that if a choice has to be made, the national interest must come first. But they see the national and global interests as much more interconnected than unilateralists do. So many of the foreign policy issues the United States faces today simply cannot be solved by one nation acting alone. Even the best national environmental policies would not be sufficient to deal with global warming; global policies are needed for a global problem. Even the tightest homeland security would not be enough to guarantee against the global threat of terrorism; as many countries as possible must cooperate against terrorists, wherever they may be. It is basic logic that if the scope of the problem reaches beyond national boundaries, the policy strategies for dealing with it must have comparable reach. The national and global interests are more complementary and less competitive than unilateralists claim. Whatever freedom of action is given up, it is outweighed by the capacity gained to achieve shared objectives and serve national interests in ways that are less possible unilaterally. Where unilateralists tally losses of prerogative encroachment, multilateralists see gains of policy enhancement. "American citizens are safer and more secure," Princeton's John Ikenberry wrote on the America Abroad blog, "when the country's outside political environment is stable and ruly—in the same way that citizens are safer and more secure when their towns and cities and the country itself is thusly organized. To get a congenial international environment, the U.S. has to make commitments—but in many cases this is a very attractive trade-off."[29]

**Correct, Not Reject** Yes, the United Nations and other multilateral institutions have problems. But the optimal strategy is to correct them, not reject them. Professors Robert Keohane and Lisa Martin lay out in functional terms the theoretical basis for why international institutions develop: "Institutions can provide information, reduce transaction costs, make commitments more credible, establish focal points for coordination and, in general, facilitate the operation of reciprocity."[30] In so doing, international institutions help states overcome the difficulties of collective action, which as discussed earlier, can persist even when states have common interests. This is a very rational argument, much more pragmatically grounded than classical Wilsonian idealism. The world it envisions is not entirely free of tensions and conflicts. But it is one in which the prospects for achieving cooperation and the policy benefits of doing so are greater than unilateralists are willing to acknowledge. Substantial progress has been made in recent years in reforming the UN; more needs to be done and can be done if people would just get past bashing the institution. The Kyoto treaty did have its flaws, but the debate should have been about amending it, not discarding it. So too with the International Criminal Court, arms-control treaties and organizations, and other multilateral measures—correct them, don't reject them.

**Liberal Domestic Politics** Multilateralism has broader but less intense domestic political support than does unilateralism. Public-opinion polls show, for example, that support for the United Nations averages around 60 percent. Generally, though, pro-UN groups are less likely to make this their "single-issue vote" than are anti-UN groups.

Unilateralists often accuse multilateralists of being "one-worlders," with notions of a world government superseding national governments. This is a distortion, albeit one that sells politically. Multilateralists do see the value of greater capacity for global governance in terms of structures and processes for governments to work together, which is very different from being supplanted or superseded. Indeed, multilateralists can make their own claim to American exceptionalism with a vision of the United States as a leader in efforts to bring nations together in common purpose and for common values.

These are main points in the unilateralism-multilateralism debate. As we stressed earlier, although this debate is not a strict dichotomy in terms of either theory or policy, the differences are significant in the relative priority given to Power, Peace, Prosperity, and Principles as well as in how each is defined and what strategies are optimal for achieving them.

## The Emergence of a Global Era

As the Obama administration came to office, along with debates over the successes and failures of the Bush foreign policy, the broader "big picture" debate continued among scholars as well as in policy circles. It had elements of the long-standing "-isms" debate among Realism, Liberal Internationalism, and other theories, as our "Theory in the World" feature (p. 291) illustrates.

Although not using the unilateralist or unipolar terminology, Realists such as Stephen Brooks and William Wohlforth stress American power as still supreme. John Ikenberry sees liberal internationalism changing from prior forms but still potentially prevailing. Others stress how much the world has changed and continues to change in what Fareed Zakaria calls the "rise of the rest" and Kishore Mahbubani sees as the shift of global power to Asia. I characterize it as the emergence of a "global era," emphasizing four fundamental features.[31]

"POSTPOLAR" SYSTEM STRUCTURE Typically, the structure of the international system is defined by counting the poles of power. The nineteenth century was the multipolarity of the major European powers. They had the power to divide up the world—this colony for us and that one for you. They established the rules of the game—when to compete and when to collude against shared enemies. They controlled the global economy in classic center-periphery terms. The system didn't always work and ultimately fell apart during World War I, but the point was the same in peace or war: that world politics were largely determined by the multipoles.

The Cold War was the ***bipolarity*** of the two superpowers. There were efforts to loosen this grip, as with the 1950s' Non-Aligned Movement, but overall the ties within each bloc (volitional or coercive) were binding. The conflict and competition between the United States and the Soviet Union, manifested in their global containment and international solidarity strategies respectively, divided the world. The division was ideological and economic as well as geopolitical. Some leaders and states sought to escape from the bipolar structure, or at least bend it, but never broke it. Other issues came up, other dynamics played out, but world politics was largely determined by the bipoles.

Some see the current era as a twenty-first-century version of ***multipolarity.*** But although this idea captures the emergence of new powers such as China, India, and Brazil, it still doesn't sufficiently get at the dynamics of today's world. Regionalism is strengthening and deepening, not only as a matter of economic relations but also through regional security institutions. Many of the 190-plus nations in the world finally emerging on the global stage after long histories of colonialism and superpower dominance are more assertive in putting forth their own interests and identities. Nonstate actors are playing more significant roles, for better (the Gates Foundation Global Health Program) and worse (Al Qaeda). So although some states and other actors still matter more than others, more mat-

## THEORY IN THE WORLD

THEORY IN THE WORLD

### CONCEPTUALIZING THE TWENTY-FIRST CENTURY

"That the United States weighs more on the traditional scales of world power than has any other state in modern history is as true now as it was when the commentator Charles Krauthammer proclaimed the advent of a 'unipolar moment'. . . . The United States continues to account for about half of the world's defense spending and one-quarter of its economic output. Some of the reasons for bearishness concern public policy problems that can be fixed (expensive health care, for example), whereas many of the reasons for bullishness are more fundamental (such as the greater demographic challenges faced by the United States' potential rivals)."

—Stephen Brooks and William Wohlforth

"Over the past century, the liberal international 'project' has evolved and periodically reinvented itself. The liberal international ideas championed by Woodrow Wilson were extended and reworked by Franklin Roosevelt and Harry Truman. Today's liberal internationalist agenda is evolving yet again. . . . The ways in which liberal order evolves will hinge in important respects on the United States—and its willingness and ability to make new commitments to rules and institutions while simultaneously reducing its rights and privileges within the order. . . . American power may rise or fall and its foreign policy ideology may wax and wane between multilateral and imperial impulses—but the wider and deeper liberal global order is now a reality that America itself must accommodate to."

—G. John Ikenberry

"For most of the last century, the United States has dominated global economics, politics, science and culture. For the last twenty years, that dominance has been unrivaled, a phenomenon unprecedented in modern history. We are now living through . . . "the rise of the rest." . . . For the first time ever, we are witnessing genuinely global growth. This is creating an international system in which countries in all parts of the world are no longer objects or observers but players in their own right. It is the birth of a truly global order. . . . We are moving into a *post-American world*, one defined and directed from many places and by many people."

—Fareed Zakaria

(*Continued*)

(*Continued*)

"The rise of the West transformed the world. The rise of Asia will bring about an equally significant transformation. . . . Asia and the West have yet to reach a common understanding about the nature of this new world. The need to develop one has never been greater. . . . [T]he mental maps of the leading minds of the world, especially in the West, are trapped in the past, reluctant or unable to conceive of the possibility that they may have to change their world-view. But unless they do, they will make strategic mistakes, perhaps on a disastrous scale."

—Kishore Mahbubani

*Sources:* Stephen G. Brooks and William C. Wohlforth, "Reshaping the World Order," *Foreign Affairs* 88.2 (March/April 2009): 54; G. John Ikenberry, "Liberal Internationalism 3.0: America and the Dilemmas of Liberal World Order," *Perspectives on Politics* 7.1 (March 2009): 71, 84; Fareed Zakaria, *The Post-American World* (New York: Norton, 2008), 2–5; Kishore Mahbubani, *The New Asian Hemisphere: The Irresistible Shift of Global Power to the East* (New York: Public Affairs, 2008), 1–5.

ter more than ever before. This makes for a system that is much less tightly and hierarchically structured than pole counting conveys.

The "alphabet soup" of twenty-first-century alliances and associations gives a sense of this variety. There are the BRICs: Brazil, Russia, India, and China; IBSA: India, Brazil, South Africa; SCO, the Shanghai Cooperation Organization, with Russia, China, and the Central Asian countries Kyrgyzstan, Kazakhstan, Tajikistan, and Uzbekistan as members; UNASUR, the Union of South American Nations; the OIC, Organization of Islamic Countries; and others. The United States is not a member of any of these groups. Although that does not mean that they are necessarily anti-American, they do indicate some geopolitical balancing.

"THREE DS" THREATS Historically, states seeking *dominance* over each other have been the central security dynamic in international affairs: Britain-France for centuries, Spain-Britain during the maritime colonial era, World Wars I and II, the Cold War. This type of threat still exists and must be defended and deterred against. But although today's major powers have their differences and conflicts, they are not seeking dominance over each other. Tensions between the West and Russia have grown worse, but more as a "cold shower" than a new "cold war."[32] Questions remain about how peaceful China's rise will be, but most indications are more of competition than confrontation. Even the Middle East, rhetoric notwithstanding, is less about conquest than before.

Two other types of threats have become much more foreboding than in prior eras. One is *disruption,* transnational forces with major disruptive effects both internationally and penetrating within domestic societies. 9/11 demonstrated how a relatively small group operating from caves in a state deemed too far away and too unimportant to worry about could shake the sense of security of the world's most powerful country. The 1997 global financial crisis, set off by a minor currency in a small country (the Thai bhat), shook stock markets everywhere, cracked many a family nest egg, and left a foreboding sense of what could happen if next time the catalyst came from a major economy—confirmed in spades in 2008 with the worldwide effects of the U.S. financial collapse. Threats of cyberwarfare are not just about Pentagon computer systems but could potentially disrupt water supplies, electricity generation, home computers, personal cell phones, and other systems on which daily life so heavily relies.

Of even greater concern are the multiple "MD" (mass destruction, not medical doctoring) threats. We long have lived with the threat of weapons of mass destruction (WMD). For a while we could find solace in having done better than the world of twenty or more nuclear powers that John Kennedy warned against. Of late, though, more states have acquired or seek to acquire nuclear weapons, and terrorists threaten to gain access to chemical and biological as well as nuclear weapons. Then there is the "DMD" (diseases of mass destruction) threat, as with a possible avian flu pandemic for which estimates of deaths run into the millions and economic costs into the billions. "EMD," environmental mass destruction, could be even more devastating than some WMD and could be more imminent than had been more conveniently assumed. And identities of mass destruction ("IMD"), genocides and ethnic cleansings, kill hundreds of thousands, again and again, despite the "never again" pledged after World War II and the Holocaust.

GLOBALIZATION AND THE GLOBAL GOVERNANCE GAP The interconnectedness of globalization, whatever its other benefits, poses its own strategic challenges. Economics has gone global. Communications have gone global. People flows—whether of businesspeople, tourists, refugees, or terrorists—have gone global. But politics and policy are way behind. This has left a "global governance gap" between the scope of the forces driving globalization and the international community's limited policy capacity for coordination, cooperation, and collective action. Some issues still can be dealt with primarily or even exclusively on a national basis—but fewer can today than yesterday, and even fewer tomorrow.

In this respect, multilateralism is more important than unilateralists acknowledge but has been less successful than multilateralists claim. Although the unilateralist critique goes too far, multilateralism's record is stronger on process than performance. There certainly are success stories, important in their own right and with broader implications. But overall, multilateralism has done more to establish its desirability than its doability.

This is in part about the United Nations and other international organizations, as we will see below. But closing the global governance gap is not just about the UN and formal international institutions. It also entails state-to-state collaboration as well as roles for the private sector and NGOs in public-private-nonprofit partnerships as well as more informal networks. It is in this respect that we use the term *global governance* and not *world government.*

THE "VEGAS DILEMMA" According to a popular television commercial, "What happens in Vegas stays in Vegas." That may be true for Vegas, but what happens in states doesn't stay in states.

Not viruses like swine flu, which started in Mexico but spread to the United States and then around the globe. Not political instability in Pakistan, which not only has affected neighboring Afghanistan but, with the specter of the first nuclear-armed failed state, threatened the world. Not the long-failed Somali state, whence marauders turn from local violence to piracy on the high seas.

In these and other cases, the "Vegas dilemma" is that the weakness of states poses as great a threat—perhaps greater—than the strength of states. The nation-state is still the main building block unit in the international system. States still need to provide basic governance capacity. Yet one major index found one in four states in danger of failing, and within that number one in seven warranting major alerts.[33] Globalization has been accentuating rather than overriding the systemic effects of weak states. Whether it is safe havens providing refuge for terrorists, internal conflicts spreading to neighboring states, inadequate public health capacity failing to prevent disease outbreaks from becoming pandemics, or other transmittals of threat and instability, globalization's interconnectedness means that there are few if any states whose weakness or failure stay their own business. Among other issues this interconnectedness has been raising fundamental questions about state sovereignty as both control and authority, and whether states have too little or too much.

## *Force and Diplomacy: Striking A Balance*

One of the great international dilemmas, in our contemporary era no less than at other times, is how to balance force and diplomacy. We may reach a point at which diplomacy in the classical sense—defined by Sir Harold Nicolson as "the management of international relations by negotiation"—fully suffices for international peace, national security, and humanitarian justice.[34] But we are not there yet. Indeed, we are much further from it than we thought amid the immediate post–Cold War euphoria. The end of the Cold War has not meant the end of war—not for ethnic conflicts and genocides as in Bosnia and

Darfur; nor for September 11, Afghanistan, and Iraq. Thus we need to continue to seek how the United States can best strike the balance between force and diplomacy, given both the threats and opportunities of the contemporary era.

DEFENSE SPENDING: HOW MUCH IS ENOUGH? WHICH PRIORITIES? One of the historical "great debates" (Chapter 3) and a recurring controversy during the Cold War, the question of defense spending levels is still with us. Defense budget cuts were the trend for the first decade or so of the post–Cold War era. From a peak of $304 billion in fiscal year 1989, the defense budget fell to $270 billion in fiscal year 1998, a 12 percent decline. Corrected for inflation, the drop was even sharper, at 30 percent. Over the last years of the Clinton administration, the trend line shifted as defense spending started increasing again, although by small amounts. It was September 11 and the war on terrorism that first brought major increases. The fiscal-year 2003 defense budget reached $405 billion. The Iraq war then pushed it up even higher, to over $530 billion in FY 2006. It has kept going up from there.

Part of the debate is over how to interpret statistics such as these. By some measures spending seems too high, by others arguably too low. Two comparisons on the "more than enough" side: one is with Cold War defense budgets. The 2003 defense budget of $405 billion was more than double the defense budget in the early Reagan years ($185 billion in fiscal year 1982), one of the tensest times of the Cold War. We can also compare America's defense budget with those of other major powers. When it reached $454 billion in FY 2004, it was higher than the defense spending of the next twenty-three nations combined. China, for example, was spending $65 billion, Russia $50 billion.[35]

Those on the "not enough" side have their own statistical interpretations. The Cold War comparisons need first of all to be corrected for inflation. When that is done, fiscal year 2003 spending is only 9 percent more than that of 1982, and 2007 spending is just 14 percent more than that of 1960. A further measurement supporting this view is defense spending as a percentage of the total federal budget and of the gross domestic product (GDP). Here we see actual declines: the fiscal year 1982 figures, for example, are 25 percent of the federal budget and 5.7 percent of GDP, whereas the fiscal year 2003 figures amount to only 18 percent of the federal budget and 3.5 percent of GDP.

Another part of the debate concerns setting priorities. The FY 2010 defense budget, the first one submitted by the Obama administration, sought to make a major shift to greater emphasis on irregular warfare and counterinsurgency. Even with some increases in overall spending, this meant less money for many traditional weapons systems such as bombers, large naval ships, and certain army combat vehicles systems, and more for intelligence and surveillance equipment, special forces, countering cyber warfare, and training foreign military units. "This budget moves the needle closer to irregular warfare and counterinsurgency," a Pentagon spokesman said. But "it is not an abandonment of the need to prepare for conventional conflicts."[36] Where exactly that needle should be—Had it gone too far toward irregular warfare? Not far enough?—continues to be contested in strategic terms as well as on political grounds.

***Cyber warfare*** is another area getting increased attention. With day-to-day operations of public utilities, transportation, communications, banking, schools, and businesses large and small computerized and operating in cyberspace, society has become increasingly vulnerable to "weapons of mass disruption." Attacks could come from a range of sources—terrorists, other states, thrill-seeking hackers. How to provide cybersecurity, and how to do so while not violating citizens' rights to privacy or imposing undue costs and obstacles on normal cyber activity raises challenging issues.

Whatever the defense budget issue, pork-barrel politics often intrudes. One member of Congress slipped $250,000 into the defense budget for a study of a caffeinated chewing gum that might help sleep-deprived troops—and that is manufactured by a company in his district. Another added $5 million for retrofitting locks used on classified documents to meet stricter specifications—as manufactured by (you guessed it!) a company in his district.[37]

A further dimension of the debate is over whether fewer dollars should be spent on defense and more on diplomacy. As of 2008, more musicians were in military bands than diplomats in the foreign service. The seven thousand additional soldiers that the army was estimated to add was more personnel than the entire existing foreign service. More than eleven hundred additional foreign service officers could be hired for the cost of one C-17 military cargo plane.[38] Secretary of Defense Robert Gates acknowledged the discrepancy:

> My message today is not about the defense budget or military power. My message is that if we are to meet the myriad challenges around the world in the coming decades, this country must strengthen other important elements of national power both institutionally and financially, and create the capability to integrate and apply all of the elements of national power to problems and challenges abroad.[39]

Admiral Michael Mullen, the chairman of the Joint Chiefs of Staff, called for

> a whole-of-government approach to solving modern problems; that we need to reallocate roles and resources in a way that places our military as an equal among many in government. . . . If we are truly to cut oxygen from the fire of violent extremism, we must leverage every single aspect of national power—soft and hard. . . . [We need] a comprehensive approach, from diplomacy, to foreign assistance, to building partnership capacity, to building partners.[40]

However, notwithstanding such statements, the DOD budget has continued to be more than ten times greater than the State Department's.

Various proposals have been made for putting more emphasis on diplomacy and increasing civilian capacity. "At the Source" (p. 298) provides some recommendations made by various think tanks, NGOs, and others.

USE OF FORCE Two principal strategies for the threat or use of force prevailed as the Cold War ended: ***deterrence,*** the credible threat of retaliatory force that had been a key factor in avoiding nuclear war and maintaining containment in Europe; and the ***Powell Doctrine,*** the decisive use of force, as in the 1990–91 Persian Gulf war. Three sets of issues raise questions about their sufficiency in this new era.

First, starting in the 1990s with conflicts in such places as Somalia, where state authority had collapsed, ethnic cleansing in Bosnia, and genocide in Rwanda, *humanitarian intervention* and *peace operations* posed challenges that could not be met through the Powell Doctrine. We focus on these in Chapter 9.

Second, 9/11 raised doubts as to whether deterrence would work against Al Qaeda and other terrorist networks. Since terrorists did not have capital cities, other major population centers, or regular military installations against which to threaten retaliation, could deterrence work against them? The Bush administration developed a doctrine of ***preemption,*** of first and early military strikes (see Chapter 8).

Third was a shift from containment to *regime change.* Iraq became the principal case, which we also address in Chapter 8.

DIPLOMACY: OBAMA'S "ENGAGEMENT" STRATEGY President Obama and his foreign policy team came into office believing that diplomacy needed both to play a larger role in U.S. foreign policy strategy and to be exercised differently than in the Bush administration. As the "International Perspectives" box (p. 300) shows, global public opinion on U.S. foreign policy became quite negative during the Bush years. As of 1999–2000, majorities held favorable views of the United States in thirteen of fifteen countries polled. Support remained strong in the wake of 9/11 (2002 polls) in Europe, Asia, Latin America, and Africa; in Russia it rose from 37 percent to 61 percent, in Nigeria 46 percent to 76 percent. In the Middle East, though, support levels were low: 25 percent in Jordan, 36 percent in Lebanon, down from 52 percent to 30 percent in Turkey. But the Iraq war made the big difference. Support fell sharply in Europe (Germany from 60 percent to 38 percent, France from 62 percent to 37 percent, Spain from 50 percent to 23 percent) and Latin America (Brazil 56 percent to 35 percent, Argentina 50 percent to 16 percent). It plunged to deep lows of 1 percent in Jordan, and 9 percent in Turkey. Asian countries had some but less decline. There were some fluctuations in ensuing years, as with increased support in Indonesia following U.S. aid for recovery from the 2004 tsunami (up from 15 percent in 2003) and in Lebanon in response to U.S. support after the assassination of the former prime minister Rafiq Hariri. Still, all told, as the Bush administration ended, in only nine of twenty-three countries were there pro-U.S. majorities.

## AT THE SOURCE

AT THE SOURCE

### ENHANCING DIPLOMACY AND BUILDING CIVILIAN CAPACITY

*A number of think thanks, NGOs, and others have made proposals for additional emphasis on diplomacy and civilian capacity for international affairs. The Center for U.S. Global Engagement, a Washington-based NGO, issued a report summarizing key proposals from over twenty other reports. Some of those proposals are excerpted below.*

**Increase Substantially Resources for Civilian-Led Agencies and Programs, Especially through USAID and the State Department.**
U.S. civilian agencies are gravely underfunded and understaffed relative to the challenges of the 21st century. . . . USAID (Agency for International Development) has roughly half the number of staff compared to 1980 during the height of the Cold War. . . . Both military and nonmilitary experts repeatedly stress that America must prioritize rebuilding civilian agencies and programs to augment our national security and achieve greater aid effectiveness.

**Leading recommendations:**

- **Rebuild Human Capacity.** The majority of the reports call for substantially increasing human resources, especially for the Foreign Service, Civil Service, and USAID. . . .
- **Increase Development Assistance Funds.** Most of the reports called for increasing overall development funding. . . . The most ambitious recommendation was for doubling official U.S. development assistance to $44 billion in FY 2010.
- **Ensure Adequate Funding for Emergencies.** Many of the reports focused on the need for additional resources for emergency funding. As one example, to permit ambassadors to respond more effectively to humanitarian and political emergencies, two reports called for increase in funding by $125 million in FY 2010 and $75 million annually.
- **Invest in Training and Professional Incentives.** Nearly half of the reports call for increasing resources to provide training and professional development opportunities for State Department and AID staff.

* * *

**Integrate Civilian and Military Instruments to Deal with Weak and Fragile States.**
. . . Both military and civilian-led capabilities are necessary to respond to situations in such fragile environments, but their specific roles and points of intervention will vary depending on the political and security situation, scope of the crisis and humanitarian needs. . . .

**Leading recommendations:**

- **Civilian Surge Capacity.** . . . [T]he U.S. needs to establish a civilian surge capacity to respond to humanitarian emergencies. . . .
- **Inter-Agency Crisis Coordination.** Create a mechanism that will improve inter-agency coordination in crisis situations. . . .
- **Target Assistance to Secure Weak and Fragile States.** Increase the amount of development assistance we provide to the world's weakest states and target development programs to address unique performance gaps in these countries.

* * *

**Strengthen U.S. Support for International Organizations and Other Tools of International Cooperation.**
America must strengthen its partnerships with other nations by working through international institutions to enhance global security and prosperity. Working through multilateral channels wherever possible will serve the important goal of burden sharing and making each U.S. aid dollar go further by aligning and leveraging our monies with those of other donors. In addition, re-engaging on a multilateral basis will build the trust and support of our allies and partners abroad. . . .

*Source:* Center for U.S. Global Engagement, "Report on Reports: Putting 'Smart Power' to Work; An Action Agenda for the Obama Administration and the 11th Congress," 2009, pp. 5–6, 8–9, 10, www.usglobalengagement.org/Portals/16/ftp/Putting_Smart_Power_to_Work.pdf (accessed 6/22/09).

The very election of Barack Obama had a strong initial positive effect on America's reputation. Election-night celebrations were held in many cities around the world. That an African American had become president was a strong statement about the country and its political system. Obama himself had global roots from his Kenyan father and spent some of his childhood in Indonesia. On his first trips as president he was greeted by enthusiastic

## INTERNATIONAL PERSPECTIVES

INTERNATIONAL PERSPECTIVES

### GLOBAL PUBLIC OPINION ON THE UNITED STATES, 1999–2008

| | Favorable Views of the United States (%) | | | | | | | |
|---|---|---|---|---|---|---|---|---|
| | 1999/2000 | 2002 | 2003 | 2004 | 2005 | 2006 | 2007 | 2008 |
| Britain | 83 | 75 | 70 | 58 | 55 | 56 | 51 | 53 |
| France | 62 | 62 | 42 | 37 | 43 | 39 | 39 | 42 |
| Spain | 50 | — | 38 | — | 41 | 23 | 34 | 33 |
| Germany | 78 | 60 | 45 | 38 | 42 | 37 | 30 | 31 |
| Poland | 86 | 79 | — | — | 62 | — | 61 | 68 |
| Russia | 37 | 61 | 37 | 46 | 52 | 43 | 41 | 46 |
| Turkey | 52 | 30 | 15 | 30 | 23 | 12 | 9 | 12 |
| Lebanon | — | 36 | 27 | — | 42 | — | 47 | 51 |
| Egypt | — | — | — | — | — | 30 | 21 | 22 |
| Jordan | — | 25 | 1 | 5 | 21 | 15 | 20 | 19 |
| South Korea | 58 | 52 | 46 | — | — | — | 58 | 70 |
| India | — | 66 | — | — | 71 | 56 | 59 | 66 |
| Japan | 77 | 72 | — | — | — | 63 | 61 | 50 |
| Australia | — | — | 59 | — | — | — | — | 46 |
| China | — | — | — | — | 42 | 47 | 34 | 41 |
| Indonesia | 75 | 61 | 15 | — | 38 | 30 | 29 | 37 |
| Pakistan | 23 | 10 | 13 | 21 | 23 | 27 | 15 | 19 |
| Brazil | 56 | 51 | 35 | — | — | — | 44 | 47 |
| Mexico | 68 | 64 | — | — | — | — | 56 | 47 |
| Argentina | 50 | 34 | — | — | — | — | 16 | 22 |
| Tanzania | — | 53 | — | — | — | — | 46 | 65 |
| Nigeria | 46 | 76 | 61 | — | — | 62 | 70 | 64 |
| South Africa | — | 65 | — | — | — | — | — | 60 |

Note: 1999/2000 trends provided by the Office of Research, U.S. Department of State.

Source: Pew Global Attitudes Project, "Global Public Opinion in the Bush Years," p. 3, http://pewglobal.org/reports/pdf/263.pdf (accessed 6/22/09).

crowds in Europe, Turkey, Latin America, Egypt, and elsewhere. Secretary of State Hillary Clinton was also received very positively in Asia as well as other early destinations.

The overarching Obama diplomatic strategy has been frequently characterized as *engagement.* Six main elements can be identified.

**Build on the Strengths of Long-Standing Alliances and Friendships** The American commitment to NATO, Japan, Latin America, and other long-standing allies was reaffirmed. Emphasis was still on U.S. leadership but with a degree of collaboration and collegiality that recognized that others have particular strengths and strategies that in certain ways can give them comparative advantages for sharing or even taking the lead.

**Build Up Newer Partnerships and Relationships** Some new partners are former adversaries with whom America still has differences, such as Russia and China. Others are states with which America hadn't had much of a relationship, such as India, or others with which our relations are in transition, such as Brazil. Shared interests are to be worked on while differences are worked out.

**Talk with Adversaries** Whether with Iran, Cuba, Syria, or others, talking is more likely to succeed than not talking or setting too many preconditions. Talk tough if need be, but talk. This is not about apologizing to assuage someone else's hurt feelings; it's about being smart enough to assess when a policy is not working and self-confident enough to be able to say so. It's also shrewd strategically to make America less of a target and eliminate the easy point scoring by those who exploit America bashing, leaving them to make their case on its own merits—or not.

**Renew America's Peace-Brokering Role** The United States needs to resume an active and sustained role as a peace broker in major conflicts. This role goes back over a century, as we saw in earlier chapters, to the role President Theodore Roosevelt played in 1906 in ending the war between Russia and Japan (for which he won the Nobel Peace Prize). The Cold War era had numerous examples, including Secretary of State Henry Kissinger's "shuttle diplomacy" in the Middle East and President Jimmy Carter's Camp David accord between Israel and Egypt. The Clinton administration negotiated the Dayton Accords ending the Bosnia war. It didn't get to a final Arab-Israeli settlement, but it did help bring about an Israel-Jordan peace treaty and some Israeli-Palestinian agreements. The Bush administration's Middle East efforts were not much more than drive-by diplomacy.

**Use All the Tools in the Toolkit** As the earlier quotes from Defense Secretary Gates and Joint Chief of Staff Chairman Admiral Mullen stress, military power is rarely the only and not always the preferable alternative. The United States needs to draw on all the instruments that can be effective to meet threats and capitalize on opportunities. The key is "smart power," as Secretary Clinton put it in her confirmation hearing, "the full range of tools at our disposal—diplomatic, economic, political, military, legal, and cultural—picking the right tool, or combination of tools, for each situation."[41]

**Work with, Not Around, International Institutions** Working through international institutions enhances U.S. capacity to achieve key policy objectives, given the global realities noted above. A win-win dynamic is possible, whereby the UN and other international institutions are shown to be essential, and the United States in turn is shown to be essential to their being essential. Reforms are needed, for which the United States should stop being the foil and start being the fulcrum leveraging the kind of reform that helps the UN and other international institutions achieve the effectiveness America needs them to have.

From the start this strategy has had its critics. Some are on the right, including former Bush administration officials and supporters. Some have been on the left. Among the points made and questions raised:

Will it let allies off the hook for doing their share: for example, NATO allies in Afghanistan?
What kind of partnership is possible with a Russia that invades its neighbor, Georgia?
Will we sacrifice human rights principles to get China's cooperation on other issues?
Will Obama's foreign policy embolden adversaries? Talking with adversaries without preconditions risks being seen as weakness.
"Smart power," like "soft power," at most is a supplement. Isn't hard power still what it's all about?

As with containment in the Cold War, the Bush war on terrorism, and other such debates, this one will continue at the level of general doctrine and strategy and as well as over specific key issues.

## *The United Nations*

The only way to study the United Nations effectively is to get beyond both the idealized views and the caricatures. At the UN's founding in 1945, Secretary of State Cordell Hull declared that cooperative and harmonious world government would alleviate "the need for spheres of influence, alliances, balances of power," freeing the world from its "unhappy past." Such sweeping visions never were very realistic.[42] On the other hand, right-wing conspiratorial views of the UN as plotting to take over the United States, including supposed sightings of UN "black helicopters" on secret maneuvers in the U.S. hinterland, are even more far out.

UN proponents stress the institution's three unique strengths. First is its *near-global membership.* At the UN's founding in 1945, the General Assembly had only fifty-one members. As of 2009 there are 192. The first major wave of growth came with decolonization and independence for the former European colonies in Africa. Between 1960 and 1962, the UN took in twenty-eight new members, twenty-three of which were from Africa. Another surge came in the 1990s, a manifestation of the many new nations formed after the breakups of the Soviet Union (one state became fifteen), Yugoslavia (one became five), and Czechoslovakia (which divided into two states). Its inclusive membership makes the UN the one place where representatives of all the world's states regularly meet. As Gareth Evans, a former Australian foreign minister, put it, "[T]he world needs a center. . . . The United Nations is the only credible candidate."[43]

Second, the UN Security Council (UNSC) is vested, by the terms of the UN Charter, with "primary responsibility for the maintenance of international peace and security." Even though the UNSC does not always have the actual power to enforce its resolutions, these resolutions carry a *normative legitimacy* that no other institution can convey. The UNSC holds the international community's ultimate "seals of approval and disapproval."[44] Its resolutions are particularly important in legitimizing and mobilizing broad support for coercive measures against aggressors, human rights violators, or other offending states. This role is evident in the use of economic sanctions, which have the greatest chance of getting multilateral support when the UNSC authorizes them. Post–Cold War cases include the sanctions against Libya, Haiti, Serbia, and Afghanistan. The UNSC's leadership role is especially evident in justifying the use of military force, both for major wars (the Korean War, the Persian Gulf War, the 2001 Afghanistan war) and for peace operations (Somalia, Haiti, Bosnia). The 2002–2003 debate over war with Iraq, in which the United States challenged the Security Council's role and went to war without full and final Security Council approval, was among the most contentious and divisive cases in UN history.

Third is the *scope of UN programs, geared to the full global agenda,* including not only peace but also economic development, the environment, human rights, and public health. Although crises such as those in Somalia, Bosnia, and Iraq get the most publicity, arguably the most meaningful work the UN does is in seeking, as stated in its Charter, "to employ international machinery for the promotion of the economic and social advancement of all peoples." It does this through specialized agencies and programs, such as UNICEF (the United Nations International Children's Emergency Fund), the WHO (World Health Organization) and the UNHCR (Office of the United Nations High Commissioner for Refugees).

Critics counter each of these points. They see the benefits of the UN's near global membership as offset by the difficulties of getting things done. They see the Security Council as more often than not falling short of the international peace and security responsibilities with which the UN Charter endowed it. They emphasize the programs that don't work, such as the Human Rights Council, which gives seats to countries that are among the most egregious violators of human rights. These criticisms come not just from neoconservatives but also from such world-respected human rights leaders as Vaclav Havel, the first president of postcommunist Czechoslovakia and a leading dissident during communist rule. "Countries must express solidarity with the victims of human rights abuses," Havel urged in 2009, "and reclaim the [Human Rights] Council by simply refusing to vote for human rights abusers."[45] Havel's view did not prevail.

Susan E. Rice, the Obama administration's UN ambassador, sought to strike a balance in calling the UN

> an indispensable, if imperfect, institution. [Its diplomacy] can be slow, frustrating, complex and imperfect. . . . The UN is not a cure-all; we must be clear-eyed about the problems, challenges and frustrations of the institution. But it is a global institution that can address a tremendous range of critical American and global interests. . . . Around the world, the United Nations is performing vital, and in many areas life-saving, services. . . . Achieving the backing of an institution that represents every country in the world can give added legitimacy and leverage to our actions and facilitate our efforts to garner broad support for our policy objectives."[46]

In later chapters, we will explore the UN's role in particular issues such as the Persian Gulf and Iraq wars (Chapter 8), humanitarian intervention and peacekeeping (Chapter 9), global AIDS and pandemic prevention (Chapter 10), and human rights (Chapter 11). Here we focus on the debate over expanding the membership of the UN Security Council.

UN SECURITY COUNCIL EXPANSION Expansion of the Security Council has been one of the most controversial and complex reform issues.[47] The structure of the UNSC reflects the global balance of power at the end of World War II. The five permanent members are the United States, Russia (formerly the Soviet Union), Britain, France, and China (the Republic of China on Taiwan until 1971, and since then the People's Republic). In addition to their permanent seats, these states also have the power to veto any UNSC action. Ten other UNSC seats rotate among countries for two-year terms and do not carry the veto.

In recent years questions have been raised as to whether this World War II–era structure was outdated. Brian Urquhart, the former undersecretary general of the United Nations, called for a UNSC which "represent[s] the world as it is...not the world as it was in 1945."[48] Three main issues have been raised: Should the Security Council enlarge and add more member states? If so, which states? How many new permanent and/or nonpermanent members should be added? Which new members, if any, should have veto rights?

Positions have been wide ranging. To "make that body [the Security Council] more democratic, legitimate and representative," President Luiz Inácio Lula da Silva of Brazil contended, "the expansion of the Security Council must envisage the entry of developing countries as permanent members."[49] With his country's substantial financial contributions in mind, Prime Minister Junichiro Koizumi of Japan argued, "We believe that the role that Japan has played provides a solid basis for its assumption of permanent membership on the Security Council."[50] Prime Minister Manmohan Singh of India has argued his country's case on the basis of India's large population, saying that "the voice of the world's largest democracy surely cannot be left unheard on the Security Council when the United Nations is being restructured."[51] Aminu Bashir Wali, Nigeria's UN ambassador, argued, "We [Nigeria] have a track record [of doing] a lot in terms of peace and security, and we have exhibited our own commitment to the peace and security in the world. . . . Nigeria is definitely qualified."[52] Ahmed Aboul Gheit, Egypt's foreign minister, argued that appointing Egypt would increase cultural representation. "Egypt's regional and international contributions—in African, Arab, Islamic circles, in the Middle East and among developing countries and blooming economies . . . qualifies her to bear the responsibility of new membership in the expanded Security Council," he said.[53]

In 2005 a task force that included prominent members from the United States and other existing UNSC members as well as from many candidate countries was asked to come up with a proposal to put to the full UN membership. Yet even the task force could not settle on one proposal. It put forward a "model A" and a "model B." Model A would create six new permanent seats, none having veto power, and three new nonpermanent seats elected to two-year, renewable terms. The total membership would be expanded to twenty-four states, and each region would have six representatives. Model B would not establish any new permanent members, instead creating an entirely new category of eight seats with four-year renewable terms and one new, nonpermanent seat with a nonrenewable two-year term. As in model A, total membership would be expanded to twenty-four states and each region would have six representatives.

Neither model gained sufficient support to prevail. One problem was the "who" of the expansion: Even if a number could be agreed to, there were differences over who should get the seats. As Brent Scowcroft, the U.S. national security advisor under presidents Gerald Ford and George H. W. Bush and a UN task force member, put it, "for every country that people think yes, this is a power that should get it...Japan, Brazil, India and so forth, there are those around it who think no, it shouldn't get in."[54] Japan, for example, has had the conditional support of the United States, but China and South Korea strongly oppose its bid. Pakistan is vehemently against Indian ascension to the UNSC. In Europe, Spain and the Netherlands oppose a seat for Germany. In Latin America, Argentina and Mexico are against Brazil. And in Africa, along with the claims made by Nigeria and Egypt, the South African ambassador, D. S. Kumalo, pressed for South Africa by saying, "[M]y country is ready to serve as a Permanent Member of a restructured and expanded Security Council."[55]

Another aspect of the issue is whether expansion would make the Security Council more effective. As put by Michael Doyle, a former advisor to Kofi Annan and a professor at Columbia University, "[T]he more members you've got of a committee, often the harder it is to get a decision." Recalling the fundamental purpose of the Council, he said the real need is for "an effective Security Council, not just a larger one, not even just a more representative one."[56] Professor Thomas Weiss, a noted authority on the UN, assesses many of the problems facing the Security Council as political rather than institutional. He believes that adding more members will not make the body any more likely to reach consensus on divisive issues.[57]

Ambassador Rice stated that "the United States believes that the long-term legitimacy and viability of the United Nations Security Council depends on its reflecting the world of the 21st century."[58] Thus, the United States is committed to a "serious, deliberate effort, working with partners and allies, to find a way forward."[59] But while this is the official position, the issue has yet to become a priority. This is another issue to follow.

### *WMD Proliferation*

Consider the following possible scenario, set in 2013:

> Less than three months after assuming office on January 20, 2013, President Martin Simmons faces perhaps the greatest threat to America's security since the 1962 Cuban Missile Crisis. . . . [T]he dramatic events of the last eight weeks, which began with the assassination of Pakistan's president on February 24, are now coming to a head. . . . Of greatest concern is the disposition of Pakistan's arsenal of nuclear weapons, estimated to number 80 to 120, each of which is capable of causing greater destruction than the atomic bombs that destroyed the Japanese cities of Hiroshima and Nagasaki at the end of World War II. . . . Both U.S. and other national intelligence services have concluded that sympathetic elements of the ISI [Pakistan's National Intelligence Service] have provided Islamist officers leading the breakaway army units with the activation codes needed to arm the nuclear weapons under their control. If so, there may be little to prevent these weapons from being used.[60]

This future-oriented scenario may not happen. But it is sufficiently plausible as to underline how the ***proliferation*** of ***weapons of mass destruction (WMD)***—nuclear, chemical, and biological—poses an even greater security challenge today than in the past.

"In a strange turn of history," as President Obama observed, "the threat of global nuclear war has gone down, but the risk of a nuclear attack has gone up."[61] What he meant was that with the end of the Cold War the threat of war between the two nuclear superpowers was much smaller. Cuts in existing nuclear weapon arsenals still is a major issue between the United States and Russia (Chapter 7). But the WMD threat was now much greater in four principal potential ways: a WMD attack directly on the United States; an attack on U.S. forces overseas; an attack on U.S. allies; and the general threat to international peace and stability. Threats along any of these dimensions may come from other states and/or from nonstate actors such as terrorists.

Some make the argument that at least some nuclear proliferation could strengthen peace.[62] One of the factors that kept the United States and the Soviet Union from engaging in direct conflict during the Cold War was the possibility of escalation to nuclear war. Following such reasoning, we might conclude that war between India and Pakistan is less likely now that both have nuclear weapons—although another Kashmir crisis might move them to the brink, the specter of escalation to the nuclear level would give them added incentive to de-escalate. Although a number of prominent scholars make this type of argument, the prevailing view stresses the risks and dangers of nuclear proliferation. For example, in its report "World at Risk," the Commission on the Prevention of Weapons of Mass Destruction and Terrorism, warned that the world is "imperiled by a new era of proliferation." With more states and nonstate actors having access to WMD technology and materials, among the grave risks is that "it is more likely than not that a weapon of mass destruction will be used in a terrorist attack somewhere in the world by the end of 2013 unless the issue is treated effectively soon."[63] In "At the Source," (p. 308), an excerpt from this report shows some of the analysis on which this warning was based.

Another part of the debate concerns ***counterproliferation*** strategies that draw on American military power and technological capabilities. ***National missile defense (NMD)*** has been a big part of this.

The Bush administration made NMD its first national security priority on coming into office. "Unlike the Cold War," President Bush stated in a May 2001 speech at the National Defense University, "today's most urgent threats stem not from thousands of ballistic missiles in Soviet hands, but from a small number of missiles in the hands of [the world's least responsible] states—states for whom terror and blackmail are a way of life."[64] The Obama administration has been less supportive of NMD but has maintained some of the programs.

Three issues define the debate over NMD. One is technological effectiveness. Will the system work? There isn't much margin for misses—even "just" one nuclear weapon getting through would wreak mass destruction. Tests have been mixed at best.

Second is cost. According to a February 2009 study by the Government Accountability Office (GAO), about $56 billion already has been spent, with an additional $50 billion projected through 2013.

Third is strategic effectiveness. Even if the system works technologically, will it contribute to security? On the affirming side are arguments along the lines noted earlier about the unreliability of traditional nuclear deterrence doctrine against leaders such as North Korea's Kim Jong-il or by terrorists. On the doubting side are arguments about countermeasures that likely would be pursued to get around whatever protection NMD provided.

"Bunker-busting" tactical nuclear weapons have been another controversial counterproliferation strategy. Because North Korea and Iran have reportedly built deep and well-fortified bunkers for command centers and WMD arsenals, a new generation of nuclear

UNIVERSITY OF WINCHESTER
LIBRARY

## AT THE SOURCE

AT THE SOURCE

### THREATS FROM WMD PROLIFERATION

#### Nuclear Proliferation and Terrorism

The number of states that are armed with nuclear weapons or are seeking to develop them is increasing. Terrorist organizations are intent on acquiring nuclear weapons or the material and expertise needed to build them. Trafficking in nuclear materials and technology is a serious, relentless, and multidimensional problem.

Yet nuclear terrorism is still a preventable catastrophe. The world must move with new urgency to halt the proliferation of nuclear weapons nations—and the United States must increase its global leadership efforts to stop the proliferation of nuclear weapons and safeguard nuclear material before it falls into the hands of terrorists. The new administration must move to revitalize the Nuclear Nonproliferation Treaty (NPT).

The nonproliferation regime embodied in the NPT has been eroded and the International Atomic Energy Agency's [IAEA] financial resources fall far short of its existing and expanding mandate. The amount of safeguarded nuclear bomb-making material has grown by a factor of 6 to 10 over the past 20 years, while the agency's safeguards budget has not kept pace and the number of IAEA inspections per facility has actually declined. . . .

#### Biological Proliferation and Terrorism

Since terrorists attacked the United States on September 11, 2001, the U.S. government had addressed the risk of biological proliferation and terrorism with policies rooted in a far different mind-set than the one that guides its policies towards nuclear weapons. While U.S. strategies to combat nuclear terrorism focus on securing the world's stock of fissile materials before terrorists can steal or buy enough on the black market to build a nuclear bomb, the government's approach to bioterrorism has placed too little emphasis on prevention. The Commission believes that the United States must place a greater emphasis on the prevention side of the equation.

To date the U.S. government has invested the largest portion of its nonproliferation efforts and diplomatic capital in preventing nuclear terrorism. Only by elevating the priority of preventing bioterrorism will it be possible to substantially improve U.S. and global biosecurity.

The nuclear age began with a mushroom cloud—and, from that moment on, all those who worked in the nuclear industry in any capacity, military or civilian, understood they must work and live under a clear and undeniable security mandate.

But the life sciences community has never experienced a comparable iconic event. As a result, security awareness has grown slowly, lagging behind the emergence of biological risks and threats. . . .

The cornerstone of international efforts to prevent biological weapons proliferation and terrorism is the 1972 Biological Weapons Convention (BWC). The treaty bans the development, production and acquisition of biological and toxin weapons and the delivery systems specifically designed for their dispersal. But because biological activities, equipment and technology can be used for good as well as harm, BW-related activities are exceedingly difficult to detect, rendering traditional verification measures ineffective. In addition, the globalization of the life sciences and technology has created new risks of misuses by states and terrorists. The BWC has been undercut by serious violations, which went undetected for years, and by its failure to gain universal membership. Moreover, the treaty is not supported at the international level by an overarching strategy for preventing biological weapons proliferation and terrorism. . . .

Source: Commission on the Prevention of Weapons of Mass Destruction and Terrorism, *World at Risk*, December 2, 2008, http://documents.scribd.com/docs/2avb51ejt0uadzxm2wpt.pdf (accessed 9/1/09).

weapons is said to be needed as the offensive complement to NMD. Critics contend that this weaponry will be destabilizing, not stabilizing. Those against whom it is to be targeted will see it as an offensive threat, not just a defensive capacity. Critics also see the nuclear-war-fighting scenario against proliferators as just as unrealistic as the nuclear-war-fighting scenarios of the Cold War.

Counterproliferation also includes less controversial measures such as protection suits and masks against chemical weapons for soldiers in combat theaters where chemical weapons use is a significant risk, and anthrax, smallpox, and other vaccination programs against biological weapons.

Even in optimistic scenarios, though, counterproliferation strategies based on American Power can only accomplish so much. Multilateral treaties and institutions establishing the international regimes and norms, rules and verification, and enforcement mechanisms—the structures of Peace—also are key.

NUCLEAR NONPROLIFERATION REGIME The first multilateral treaties preventing the proliferation of nuclear weapons began during the Cold War. In 1957 the ***International Atomic Energy Agency (IAEA)*** was created to ensure that, as nations develop nuclear energy, it would be used only for peaceful purposes such as nuclear power plants. In

1968 the UN General Assembly approved the ***Nuclear Nonproliferation Treaty (NPT).*** The NPT allowed the five states that already had nuclear weapons—the United States, the Soviet Union, Britain, France, and China—to keep them. These states pledged to reduce their nuclear arsenals through arms control agreements. All other states were prohibited from acquiring or developing nuclear weapons.

The NPT has had some success. Nearly 190 countries have signed it. But some countries have refused to sign it and have developed nuclear weapons. Among those, India and Pakistan successfully tested their nuclear weapons in 1998. Israel is widely believed to have nuclear weapons, although it has never officially stated so. Several other countries signed it but have cheated on their commitments. Iraq, North Korea, Libya, and Iran have been among the chief cases. We discuss Iraq and Iran in Chapter 8. Here we look at North Korea and Libya.

NORTH KOREA Intelligence reports in the early 1990s indicated that North Korea was diverting its ostensibly peaceful nuclear energy program to develop nuclear weapons, despite having signed the NPT. The prospect of a nuclear-armed North Korea threatened not just South Korea but also Japan, other U.S. allies in the region, and U.S. troops stationed in these countries. Concern also arose that North Korea would sell nuclear weapons to other anti-U.S. ***rogue states.*** The Clinton administration pursued a strategy toward North Korea that emphasized negotiations but backed them with measures that threatened military action. The combination helped achieve a crisis-defusing agreement, called the Agreed Framework, in 1994.

In October 2002, new revelations indicated that North Korea had been cheating on the 1994 Agreed Framework and had continued nuclear weapons development. North Korea reportedly now possessed more than the one or two actual nuclear weapons that it had when the 1994 agreement imposed its freeze and was very close to being able to get production lines going that would generate more. North Korea was quite provocative in its reactions, expelling IAEA inspectors, firing up a nuclear reactor that could produce more plutonium (a key material for nuclear bombs), and renouncing the NPT. Some saw North Korea as reacting to George W. Bush's inclusion of it in the "axis of evil" and Bush administration threats of regime change. Still, most experts doubted North Korea's trustworthiness and felt quite sure that another crisis was developing. "Six-party talks" were initiated in 2003, with China as the host and also involving Russia, Japan, and South Korea as well as the United States and North Korea. Some diplomatic progress was made, including a September 2005 agreement on joint principles. But the crisis heated up again when North Korea conducted a series of missile tests in July 2006 and then tested an actual nuclear weapon in October.

Coercive diplomacy was ratcheted up. Condemnations came not only from the United States but in stronger-than-usual terms from China and others. The UN Security Council imposed targeted economic sanctions and threatened additional sanctions and other measures. China, the key economic linchpin, reportedly applied some sanctions to energy supplies and financial relationships. The incentives of expanded aid and trade also remained on the table. The strategy seemed to be having some effect when after some ups and downs a Six-party agreement was reached in February 2007 on next steps.

Over the course of 2007, some actions were taken, but some key deadlines were missed. This continued into 2008. By mid-year enough progress had been made that Secretary of State Condoleeza Rice agreed to meet directly with her North Korean counterpart. "We didn't get into specific timetables, but the spirit was good," Secretary Rice stated, "because people believe we have made progress."[65] That optimism did not last long amid border incidents and other rising tensions between North and South Korea, and an apparent serious illness suffered by North Korea's leader Kim Jong-il. And the debate continued. The former U.S. ambassador to the United Nations and arch-neoconservative John Bolton called for a more stringent U.S. stance toward North Korea. "They're in the classic North Korean role of deception," Bolton said in an interview. "It's like Groundhog Day; we've lived through this before."[66] In contrast, Ambassador Christopher Hill, the lead U.S. negotiator, argued that "multilateral efforts have had a stabilizing effect. . . . Without that process we could have seen a much more dangerous counter-reaction in the region."[67]

In May 2009 events reached another crisis point when North Korea conducted another nuclear test. The UN Security Council voted unanimously to impose another round of sanctions. Tensions were further compounded when two young American journalists, Laura Ling and Euna Lee, were sentenced to 12 years hard labor for allegedly crossing the North Korean border illegally. Meanwhile, reports of Kim Jong-il's illness continued with the added speculation that he had anointed one of his sons, Kim Jong-un, as his successor. Over the next few months the pendulum swung somewhat toward a reduction of tensions. Former President Bill Clinton made a surprise mission to North Korea and brought the two journalists home. The content of his meeting with Kim Jong-il was not revealed, but photos did seem to show the North Korean leader in less dire health than rumored. Over the next few months, North Korean-South Korean relations warmed a bit, including resumption of family visits.

While the Six Party Talks had not yet resumed as of October 2009, the prospects seemed better than they had in a while—then again, there have been more ups and downs on this issue than on almost any other in recent years.

LIBYA Although the term *rogue state* did not come into common usage until the 1990s, it aptly describes Libya, given its foreign policy—particularly its pursuit of weapons of mass destruction and its involvement in terrorism—for most of the period following the 1969 coup against the pro–U.S. King Idris that brought Muammar Qaddafi to power.[68] Even though Libya had signed the Nuclear Nonproliferation Treaty shortly before the coup, and Qaddafi's government ratified it five years later, within his first year in power the Libyan leader was seeking a nuclear capability. He continued to do so, and also to seek chemical and biological weapons, for over thirty years. Yet on December 19, 2003, in an announcement that caught most of the world by surprise, following extensive secret diplomacy with the United States and Britain, Qaddafi agreed to full WMD disarmament.

The debate over why Libya made such dramatic policy changes has been politically lively and analytically challenging. Vice President Dick Cheney cast Libya's concessions on WMD as "one of the great by-products . . . of what we did in Iraq and Afghanistan," stressing that just "five days after we captured Saddam Hussein, Muammar Qaddafi came forward and announced that he was going to surrender all of his nuclear materials to the United States."[69] Others found this timing less significant and gave more credit to diplomacy. These included such key Clinton officials as the former assistant secretary of state Martin Indyk, who led the secret talks started with Libya in 1999–2000 and contended that "Libyan disarmament did not require a war with Iraq"; Bush administration officials such as Deputy Secretary of State Richard Armitage, for whom Saddam's capture "didn't have anything to do" with Libya's concessions; and the British prime minister Tony Blair, who stressed that "problems of proliferation can, with good will, be tackled through discussion and engagement" and that "countries can abandon programs voluntarily and peacefully."[70] The Libyan prime minister Shukri Ghanem asserted that his government based its decision on an independent assessment of its national interests, on "a careful study of the country's future in all its domains . . . conforming to the aspirations of the Libyan leadership and people." Qaddafi's son Seif el-Islam Qaddafi said that the December 19 agreement was a "win-win deal" for both sides: "[Our] leader believed that if this problem were solved, Libya would emerge from the international isolation and become a negotiator and work with the big powers to change the Arab situation."[71]

The timing of the December 19, 2003, agreement, six days after the capture of Saddam Hussein, would seem to support the Bush administration's position that the Qaddafi regime's decisions were products of U.S. military force. As with many strong correlations, though, causality is more complicated. In one sense, Qaddafi could have interpreted the Iraq war, which overextended the U.S. military and generated intense international opposition, as reducing any threat the United States could pose to his regime. It is far from clear that Qaddafi believed that after Hussein, he would be next. Still, as one key U.S. official stressed, the use of force in Iraq (and Afghanistan) had a "demonstration effect" that could not be dismissed.

Force was not the only factor, though, and probably not the most important one. A fuller analysis shows the greater importance of diplomacy, both American and multilateral. First the Clinton administration and then the Bush administration conducted secret talks along with the British that worked through various issues over a number of years. The United Nations also played a role through multilateral sanctions imposed in 1992 and 1993. These and other measures interacted with internal political and economic pressures on Qaddafi to make for an agreement. Although not perfect, it achieved much more at much less cost and less risk than in the Iraq or North Korea cases.

One of the most important lessons of the Libya case was that it was possible even for a charter rogue to make a major policy change. The nature of the regime clearly was a factor, but it was not determinative. Qaddafi's principal motivation remained the same: staying in power. The means for doing so, though, proved more functionally flexible than ideologically fixed. The combination of internal pressures and coercive diplomacy strategy helped bring Qaddafi to a point where his hold on power was better served by global engagement than by global radicalism. By 2006, the United States and Libya had resumed diplomatic relations. They still had their differences, including over democracy and human rights. But the WMD issue had been settled.

COMPREHENSIVE TEST BAN TREATY (CTBT) The ***Comprehensive Test Ban Treaty (CTBT)*** is another key component of the nuclear nonproliferation regime. Efforts to limit nuclear testing began during the Cold War, most notably with the 1963 Limited Nuclear Test Ban Treaty. Negotiated by the United States, the Soviet Union, and the United Kingdom, and later signed on to by many other states, the Limited Test Ban Treaty prohibited nuclear testing in the atmosphere, underwater, and in outer space. These types of tests created the most radioactive fallout. The ban was limited, though, still allowing underground testing and other exemptions. The CTBT is an effort to move further toward a total ban on nuclear testing.

As we discussed in Chapter 2, the failure of the Senate to ratify the CTBT in 1998 after President Clinton had signed it was among the worst foreign policy politics defeats since the rejection of Woodrow Wilson's Versailles treaty. President Obama committed early on to reviving the CTBT as part of his overall nuclear nonproliferation agenda. U.S. ratification of the CTBT was part of a "basic bargain" by which countries with nuclear weapons will move towards disarmament, countries without nuclear weapons will not acquire them, and all countries can access peaceful nuclear energy."[72] Although opposition to the CTBT remained, three factors may decrease it. One is the further technological advances that alleviate many of the earlier concerns. Second is the stronger linkage made by other countries between U.S. CTBT ratification and their willingness to support renewal and strengthening of the NPT. Third is the endorsement of a distinguished bipartisan group, including the former secretaries of state Henry Kissinger and George P. Shultz, the former secretary of defense William Perry, and the former Senate Armed Services Committee chairman Sam Nunn. In a widely cited op-ed piece in the *Wall Street Journal,* they stressed their concern about "a new nuclear era that will be more precarious, psychologically disorienting, and economically even more costly than was Cold War deterrence."[73] CTBT ratification wasn't the only measure needed, but it was an important one, and one that the United States could do on its own.

Other international actors also have been pushing hard. The International Commission on Nuclear Nonproliferation was formed by the leaders of Japan, Australia, and a number of countries for "reinvigorating, at a high political level, awareness of the global need for nuclear non-proliferation and disarmament, in the context of the 2010 Nuclear Non-Proliferation Treaty (NPT) Review Conference and beyond."[74] Global Zero, an international group of one hundred political, military, business, religious, and civic leaders from across political lines, set out to help achieve nonproliferation by combining high-level policy work and global public outreach.[75] Mohamed El Baradei, the head of the International Atomic Energy Agency (IAEA) for a number of years, including when it won the Nobel Peace Prize, proposed a five-point plan to eliminate nuclear weapons. The British government issued its own plan. With the major NPT Review Conference scheduled for 2010, this is another issue on which to watch what develops.

CHEMICAL AND BIOLOGICAL WEAPONS Many view chemical and biological weapons as even scarier than nuclear ones. One reason is that chemical and biological weapons are less expensive to produce—the "poor man's nuclear weapon," some call them. Another is that the level of technology and military capability required for their use is much less sophisticated, and thus they are more accessible to terrorists. Americans experienced this in the weeks after the September 11 terrorist attacks, when anthrax-laden letters made people fearful of even opening their mail. Even before this, in Japan in 1995 a cult called Aum Shinrikyo unleashed a chemical-weapons attack on a busy subway train in Tokyo. The cult had intended to kill millions of people. Although the actual death toll was limited, as a *New York Times* headline put it, the "Japanese Cult's Failed Germ Warfare Succeeded in Alerting the World."[76] Investigation of the cult found a veritable arsenal of chemical weapons, as well as labs equipped to produce lethal germs and bacteria for biological weapons.

The first major anti-chemical-weapons treaty, the Geneva Protocol, was negotiated in 1925. Its impetus was the battlefield use of chemical weapons (CW) in World War I by both sides. The Geneva Protocol prohibited the use of chemical weapons, although it did not prohibit their production or possession. Even so, chemical weapons were used subsequently—by Japan in Manchuria in the 1930s, by Italy in Ethiopia in 1935, by Egypt in Yemen in the 1960s, by both Iran and Iraq in their 1980–88 war, possibly by the Soviets in Afghanistan in their 1979–88 war, and by Iraq against its own Kurdish population in 1988. Over the course of the Cold War, both the United States and the Soviet Union built up large CW stockpiles. By the 1990s an estimated twenty other countries were believed to have chemical weapons.

The need for a new and stronger CW nonproliferation treaty was quite clear. The crucial step came with the Chemical Weapons Convention (CWC). After many years of negotiations, the CWC was completed in 1993 and came into force in 1997. As of early 2009, 188 states were party to the CWC, and another two had signed but not yet ratified. The CWC bans the development, production, acquisition, stockpiling, trade, and use of chemical weapons; it calls, in effect, for the total elimination of chemical weapons. As such it has been called "the most ambitious treaty in the history of arms control."[77] It is farther-reaching than the NPT in three important respects. First, it applies to all states—no exceptions. No previous possessors are grandfathered in, as were the five major-power nuclear-weapons states in the NPT. All states are required to destroy all their chemical weapons. Second, it has tougher and more intrusive enforcement provisions. It mandates short-notice, anytime, anywhere "challenge inspections" of sites where cheating is believed to be taking place. The Organization for the Prohibition of Chemical Weapons (OPCW) is the CWC's version of the IAEA, but has greater authority. Third, states that do not join the treaty face automatic trade sanctions. This was a primary reason that most of the U.S. chemical industry, though not overly welcoming to the additional regulations imposed by the CWC, calculated that American companies had more to lose if the United States was not part of the treaty and therefore supported it during the Senate ratification debate.

The key test of the CWC lies in whether these tough provisions work in practice. A number of countries still are suspected of retaining undeclared chemical weapons stockpiles, including China, Egypt, Iran, Israel, North Korea, and Syria. Questions still remain as to whether Russia will fully follow through with eliminating its arsenal of 40,000 metric tons of chemical weapons. As with Russian "loose nukes," the concern is not only about official Russian policy but also about terrorists and others getting access to the weapons complex. The United States, which had had the world's second-largest chemical weapons stockpile, had destroyed about half of it as of mid-2008.

There also are doubts about the effectiveness of the OPCW. Challenge inspections, as innovative as they are with the right they give to the OPCW to demand entry and access for inspections in a country suspected of violating the treaty, have stayed largely on paper. At least three factors have impeded their application. First, for all the high-minded rhetoric at the CWC signing ceremonies, member states have not followed through in meeting their budget commitments. Insufficient funding translates to inadequate technical and other professional expertise to ensure strong enforcement and verification. Second, the OPCW has had its own bureaucratic politics and inefficiencies, with some allegations of corruption and incompetence against its original director. Although each of these issues is fixable by management, the third issue is the continuing ambivalence about challenge inspections as an abridgment of traditional conceptions of state sovereignty. As with human rights and other issues, strict sovereigntists raise concerns about abuses of this authority, whereas those stressing the responsibilities of states and the priority of international peace and security see such authority as essential for the CWC to have teeth and for the OPCW to be effective as a monitoring, verification, and enforcement organization. Moreover, like the NPT, the CWC deals with states but not with terrorists and other non-state actors. They pose their own quite serious challenges.

Biological weapons (also called germ warfare) have met with even less nonproliferation progress. The Biological and Toxin Weapons Convention of 1972 purported to ban them totally (development, production, stockpiling, acquisition, trade, use). It has been agreed to by 155 countries; another sixteen have signed but not yet ratified; twenty-three have not signed. But it has been a very weak treaty. Its monitoring, verification, and enforcement provisions and mechanisms are much weaker than those of the CWC/OPCW and the NPT/IAEA.

Efforts to strengthen the BW treaty have not made much progress. In mid-2001, negotiations broke up over whether the proposed changes in verification would be effective. The Bush administration contended that the treaty proposals would end up violating the confidentiality of the American pharmaceutical and biotechnology industries while doing little to detect treaty violations by states that were determined to develop BW. The debate in part reflected the even greater difficulties of dual-use distinctions—it can be tough to distinguish pharmaceutical or bioagricultural research from development of biological weapons. Negotiations held in 2006 went better. Some concrete measures strengthening implementation were agreed to. The treaty, one lead diplomat claimed, "is alive and well . . . and remains effective as the fundamental legal norm against biological weapons."[78] Others were less sanguine. The BioWeapons Prevention Project, an NGO, assessed the gains as less significant than claimed, acknowledging that a final report was agreed to, but with text that "does not move the convention much beyond what had already been agreed ten years earlier at the 4th Review Conference."[79]

Biological WMD issues are tough ones. Blame for the lack of progress can be spread widely. Proposals for how to do better can be debated. Just as long as we keep in mind that after months of research, interviews, and site visits, the Commission on the Prevention of Weapons of Mass Destruction assessed biological weapons to be even more of a threat than nuclear ones.[80]

## *Security Threats from Nonstate Actors*

Most attention regarding security threats from ***nonstate actors*** focuses on terrorism and terrorists (see Chapter 8). Here we address three other security threats posed by nonstate actors.

PIRACY When in April 2009 pirates off the coast of Somalia seized the American merchant ship *Maersk Alabama* and held Captain Richard Phillips hostage, the incident got full-bore media attention. But piracy had stopped being a thing of the past and of Hollywood movies well before that. In early 2009 alone there already had been 66 pirate attacks, with 14 ships and 260 crew members held hostage. Many of these attacks have been in the Gulf of Aden, the waters off the coasts of Somalia and Yemen through which many ships pass on their way to and from the Suez Canal. Many other attacks have occurred off Nigeria and other parts of the west coast of Africa, as well as in the waters off Southeast Asia.

The economic toll has been severe. Piracy "flourishes at the seams of globalization," as two authors cogently put it. The combination of ransoms, lost and delayed cargoes, soaring insurance rates, and other costs has been estimated at $13–15 billion annually. On top of this is the shock to oil markets: twenty thousand ships per year carrying 12 percent of the world's daily oil supply pass through the Gulf of Aden, which has the highest risk of piracy in the world.[81]

Military measures can have some impact. The U.S. Navy freed Captain Phillips, although less because of its "big boats" than because of its skilled sharpshooters. Other navies also are involved, from countries in the European Union, China, India, Iran, and Malaysia. But whereas sixty-one naval ships are estimated to be needed to control the Gulf of Aden, as of mid-2009 the international flotilla only had about twelve to sixteen naval vessels on patrol at any one time. And the Gulf of Aden is just a fraction of the 1.1 million square miles where the pirates have been operating.[82]

International law and multilateral organizations provide some, but also limited, policy options. Although piracy is illegal according to the Law of the Sea and other international laws, the lines between national jurisdictions over territorial waters and international jurisdiction over the high seas beyond are unclear. UN agencies such as the International Maritime Organization (IMO) have been working to strengthen the necessary coalition. The UN Security Council has also gotten involved by passing resolutions that allow foreign navies to enter Somali territorial waters in pursuit of pirates and to attack on shore if necessary. These measures have made a dent but not much more.

Root causes for piracy can be found on land. Professor Ken Menkhaus, a leading expert on Somalia, traces the rise of piracy there back to the early 1990s, "when the state first collapsed and warlords sought new ways to parlay their firepower into profit."[83] Another study found 98.4 percent of all pirate attacks occurred off the coasts of states that are considered failed states.[84] These states combine terrible economic conditions that motivate ransom seeking with political institutions and authorities so weak as to be unable and/or unwilling to enforce order. What Menkhaus says about Somalia is also more broadly pertinent:

> The Somali piracy epidemic is unquestionably an on-shore crisis demanding on-shore solution. Naval operations to interdict and apprehend pirates will help, but cannot possibly halt the daily quest of over a thousand gunmen in such vast waters when the risks are so low, the rewards so high and alternatives so bleak.[85]

DRUG RINGS To the extent that the measure of a security threat is its impact on the everyday lives of the American people, illegal narcotics rank quite high. They have penetrated the nation's cities, schools, workplaces, and families. Although the war against drugs does have a "demand-side" domestic policy component, the "supply side" is largely a foreign policy problem. It tends to focus on Latin America, particularly Mexico, Colombia, Panama, Peru, and Bolivia. But the problem is virtually global: the "golden triangle" of Burma, Thailand, and Laos in Southeast Asia; Afghanistan and Pakistan; former Soviet republics in central Asia; Lebanon and Syria; and Nigeria. "When law enforcement somewhere rises from its torpor," one expert writes, "the traffickers switch to alternative routes. . . . The number of players has grown, their activities have decentralized, and they have become smarter and more financially savvy.[86]

The United States has pursued three principal strategies to fight the international narcotics trade, with only mixed results all around. One strategy, of course, has been to try to use diplomacy. The State Department has a special bureau dealing with international narcotics ("drugs and thugs," some call it). The White House has its "drug czar," who coordinates efforts both within the U.S. government and with other countries. Diplomatic efforts go on all the time at working levels, and on occasion even at the head-of-state level. Such efforts include programs to provide assistance for drug eradication, crop substitution, and police training. One problem, though, has been concern about the reliability of diplomatic partners. In Mexico in 1997, the army general who headed the national drug-fighting agency was himself arrested for being on the payroll of the drug cartels. Another problem arises when diplomacy degenerates to finger-pointing, as with American accusations that Mexico or Colombia or some other supplier country isn't doing enough to stop the flow of drugs, and their countercharges that the United States isn't doing enough to curtail demand.

Another strategy is a form of economic sanctions known as *decertification*. Every year the State Department presents to Congress reports on every country known to be a source of drugs. If a country is deemed not to be doing enough against drugs, it can be "decertified," which means that it loses eligibility for a number of U.S. economic and trade-assistance programs. In some instances this coercive pressure has been effective, prompting countries to step up their antidrug efforts to avoid decertification and motivating countries that have been decertified to do more to regain eligibility for U.S. assistance. Some countries have reacted nationalistically against the whole process, seeing it as another demonstration of American arrogance. To some the very term *decertification* means the United States is putting itself in an overlord position. This also has led to charadelike, credibility-weakening situations in which the State Department has certified a country to avoid a diplomatic dispute even though its antidrug record was highly questionable.

A third strategy has been military. It is not just rhetoric to speak of "drug wars." Some of the largest post–Cold War U.S. military-assistance programs have gone to the Colombian and other Latin American militaries for antidrug operations. American military personnel have been stationed in Colombia, Peru, and elsewhere, in small but still significant numbers. There have even been U.S. military casualties. "This is not a one-night stand," said General Charles E. Wilhelm, the commander of U.S. military forces in Latin America and the Caribbean. "This is a marriage for life."[87] Others, however, warn that these military commitments risk drawing the United States deeper into these countries' internal political conflicts. Colombia, where American military involvement has been extensive, has been a particular concern because of the interweaving of the drug war with a long-festering guerrilla war, and because of the Colombian military's history of human rights violations and other undemocratic practices that make it a questionable partner. Mexico also has become a major concern (Chapter 7). Afghanistan, where poppy growing and the opium trade have increased markedly since the U.S. military intervention in 2001, is another (Chapter 8).

GLOBAL CRIME SYNDICATES "Most Americans still refuse to believe just how well organized global crime has become," wrote Senator John Kerry in 1997, while he was a senior member of the Senate's main anticrime subcommittee. "The new global criminal axis is composed of five principal powers in league with a host of lesser ones. The Big Five are the Italian Mafia, the Russian mobs, the Japanese *yakuza*, the Chinese triads and the Colombian cartels. They coordinate with smaller but highly organized gangs with distinct specialties in such countries as Nigeria, Poland, Jamaica and Panama." The threats have become so severe that they go well beyond "being exclusively in the realm of law enforcement; they also become a matter of national security."[88]

However many benefits globalization has brought, it also has an underside that has empowered criminals and at the very same time weakened the agencies in charge of fighting them:

> Criminal networks thrive on international mobility and their ability to take advantage of the opportunities that flow from the separation of marketplaces into sovereign states with borders. For criminals, frontiers create business opportunities and convenient shields. But for the government officials chasing the criminals, borders are often insurmountable obstacles. The privileges of national sovereignty are turning into burdens and constraints on governments. Because of this asymmetry, in the global clash between governments and criminals, governments are systematically losing. Everywhere.[89]

Among the consequences is that, as Senator Kerry quoted a former head of the CIA, "international organized crime can threaten the stability of regions and the very viability of nations."[90] The annual income of many of these global crime rings exceeds the GDP of many a country; the United Nations estimates that international crime costs $750 billion a year. This gives criminals enormous economic power. Among other things, they can finance major weapons purchases for building formidable military arsenals of their own and provide plenty of money in bribes and kickbacks to public officials. So much of the global arms trade has gone underground that it's become like a "weapons Wal-Mart, or maybe even an eBay: a supermarket that knows no borders, and in which virtually anything can be procured for virtually anyone, so long as the buyer is prepared to pay the price."[91] International crime follows the same basic pattern as with terrorists and drug lords: money and guns, both critical power resources, are more and more in the hands of nonstate actors.

Another reason for heightened concern is that, although U.S. "domestic" crime has long had international dimensions, as with the Mafia, the international-domestic interconnection has become more pervasive. In years past the FBI's "Ten Most Wanted" list consisted mostly of bank robbers, big-city racketeers, and kidnappers. By 1997 eight of the ten fugitives on it were international criminals who had committed crimes in the United States, and this was before terrorists such as Osama bin Laden were put at the top of the list.

## *The International Economy, Energy Security, and the Global Environment*

"The primary near-term security concern of the United States is the global economic crisis and its geopolitical implications," the director of national intelligence, Dennis Blair, told Congress in February 2009.[92] Although there's always some year-to-year shifting in such rankings, there can be little doubt that economics is a strategic issue affecting Power and Peace, not only Prosperity.

The statistics on the economic crisis that began in 2008 have been staggering. The overall global economy contracted for the first time since World War II. The drop in global trade was the steepest since the Great Depression. No region or country escaped. Not booming economies like China and India. Not export leaders like Japan and Germany. Not anywhere in Europe, west or east. Not oil exporters such as OPEC and Russia. Not countries in Africa, Asia, and Latin America that are still mired in poverty. And surely not the United States.

Four main factors have been making the economic crisis a strategic issue as well. One is the political instability being caused. DNI Blair estimated that by early 2009, economic shock waves already had set off political instability in about one quarter of the countries in the world—and there have been more since. Second is worsening global poverty. The World Bank estimated that an additional 192,000 children would die because of the toll taken by the global economic crisis. That's 22 children per hour, every day—and that's the "best"-case scenario, with some estimates fearing a rate more than double.[93]

Third is the calling into question of the overall international economic system. The ***Bretton Woods system*** set up after World War II (Chapter 4)—based on the International Monetary Fund; the GATT and its successor, the World Trade Organization; and the World Bank—had endured a number of crises, adapting to varying degrees but largely persisting as the basis of the international political economy. The current crisis has spurred more than the usual calls for fundamental change. China, for example, has proposed moving away from the U.S. dollar as the principal reserve currency. China and such other emerging economies as India and Brazil have been pushing for larger roles in institutional decision making, including opening up the top positions at the IMF and World Bank to non-Europeans and non-Americans.

Fourth is a fundamental questioning of the American model itself. Whereas in the past the American economy had helped pull others out of economic crises, this time the American economy was the epicenter of the global economic crisis. Many saw the Wall Street meltdown as not merely a cyclical downturn but a demonstration of the excesses inherent in the American version of capitalism. In the twentieth century capitalism had demonstrated its superiority to socialism. But in the twenty-first century the debate now concerns which form of capitalism is better—the heavily laissez-faire American form or the more state-directed form that had evolved in a number of countries including China, India, Brazil, and some OPEC countries. Does the market need the state as much as the state needs the market?[94]

We discuss the international economy further in Chapter 10. We focus on two other issues there as well, but it is important to mention them here as part of the overall strategic context. They are energy and the environment.

When oil prices skyrocketed in the summer of 2008, hitting close to $150 a barrel on global markets and around $5 a gallon at the pump, ***energy security*** once again became more than a fringe issue. We say "once again" with the 1973 OPEC embargo and price hike, the 1979 Iranian Islamist revolution, and other recent oil-markets crises in mind. When oil and gasoline prices started falling a few months later, their political salience once again declined with them. But given that the next oil crisis is less a question of if than of when, there has been some continued effort for policy changes. "The lack of sustained attention to energy issues," a bipartisan task force chaired by two former secretaries of energy stressed, "is undercutting U.S. foreign policy and national security."[95]

As in the past, part of the concern is on the supply side, whether from deliberate price hikes by the OPEC cartel or from another war or further political instability. Now, though, a big part of the problem also is on the demand side, "keeping pace with the voracious global demand for energy."[96] The very economic progress that is seen as a positive in other respects also means more demand for gasoline for cars, fuel for factories, and power for homes. Between 1977 and 1995, the total worldwide demand for oil grew from 60 million barrels per day (b/d) to 70 million b/d. From 1995 to 2003, an eight-year period compared with the previous eighteen, global demand grew another 10 million b/d. Though temporarily slowed by the economic crisis, the trajectory still points toward rapid demand growth. Only OPEC countries have the reserves to meet this growth—the very countries of most concern for supply-side disruptions.

In considering energy security, though, it is important not to equate it with "energy independence." This is one of those politically resonant but policy-distorting terms. Whether the United States should increase domestic oil production can be debated. But production could never be sufficient to eliminate the need for oil imports. Interdependence is a fundamental, twenty-first-century reality. Being independent of foreign suppliers of oil is as unrealistic as being independent of any other area of international trade. What is realistic is reducing energy vulnerability by diversifying the sources of oil imports, shifting to alternative energy sources (wind, solar, nuclear), and other measures.

The global environment is of concern for many reasons. Some are moral and ethical. Some are economic. Some are about security threats. Global warming and associated climate change could pose threats of the "EMD" magnitude noted earlier. This possibility is not merely in forecasts by academic futurists or environmental activists. "The [Intelligence Community] judges global climate change will have important and extensive implications for US national security interests over the next 20 years," to quote DNI Blair again.[97] Nor is it just future forecasts. We already have seen how resource shortages and environmental degradation have been contributing to wars and other deadly conflicts, as in Darfur.

The global environment is also an important issue within the overall Obama engagement strategy of going from what many view as the laggard to the leader in efforts to forge cooperative multilateral policies. No country has a "clean" record: China has become an even greater emitter of carbon dioxide than the United States; European Union countries have set some admirable goals but largely have fallen short. Were the United States to shift its own policies, there could be a real opportunity for leadership.

We would do well to bear in mind the warning from Jared Diamond in his book *Collapse: How Societies Choose to Fail or Succeed.* Looking back through history at societies that inflicted so much environmental degradation that they brought about their own collapse, Diamond asks, "How could a society fail to have seen the dangers that seem so clear in retrospect?" Moreover, today the risks are even greater than when Easter Island or Norse Greenland collapsed centuries ago because "globalization makes it impossible for societies to collapse in isolation."[98]

These are some of the key overarching debates about American foreign policy strategy in the twenty-first century. Individually and collectively they manifest some of the tensions and trade-offs in the choices to be made about setting priorities among and devising strategies for Power, Peace, Prosperity, and Principles. We will explore these choices more specifically in key issue areas in the chapters that follow.

## Foreign Policy Politics: Diplomacy Begins at Home

"We are about to do a terrible thing to you," a Soviet official quipped toward the end of the Cold War. "We are going to deprive you of an enemy."[99] The Soviet official's remark was an astute observation of U.S. foreign policy politics. Despite all the other dangers that the Soviet Union posed, having an Enemy (capital letter intentional) helped American presidents garner the domestic political support necessary for a strong and active foreign policy. Without the Soviet threat—indeed, without a Soviet Union at all—the U.S. foreign policy debate split wide open.

Some wanted to heed the cry, Come home, America. Who needs foreign policy anyway? these neo-isolationists asked. Why not just take advantage of the opportunity provided by the end of the Cold War to "put America first"? Reduce America's international commitments, and as for those commitments the United States does keep, make them more self-centered. Get beyond the old debate about whether politics should "stop at the water's edge"; just stay on America's side of the water.

Yet the paradox of the post–Cold War era is that international affairs affect America and Americans at least as much, if not more than, during the Cold War. This was true even before the September 11, 2001 terrorist attacks on the United States. Recall the five major reasons stated at the outset of this book for the continued importance of foreign policy, reasons that were first laid out in our first edition, published before September 11:

- The United States still faces significant potential threats to its national security.
- The U.S. economy is more internationalized than ever before.
- Many other areas of policy that used to be considered "domestic" also have been internationalized.
- The increasing diversity of the American people—in race, ethnicity, religion, nationality, and heritage—makes for a larger number and wider range of groups with personal bases for interest in foreign affairs.
- It is hard for the United States to claim to be true to its most basic values if it ignores their violation around the world.

Prior to September 11, none of these rationales resonated in tones anything close to the clarion calls of the Truman Doctrine, JFK's 1961 inaugural "Ask not," or Reagan's "tear down this wall." Especially in the immediate aftermath of 9/11, there was a strong sense of Osama bin Laden and Al Qaeda as capital-E enemies. But as is evident from the fuller foreign policy agenda, the threats and opportunities posed by this global era go well beyond terrorism.

This new era thus is characterized by a mix of foreign policy politics with and without an Enemy. In the rest of this chapter, drawing on parts of the analytic framework laid out in Chapter 2, we examine President Obama as a foreign policy leader and the politics in his administration both interbranch ("Pennsylvania Avenue diplomacy") and intra–executive branch; the changing nature of the media including the impact of the Internet and blogs; and broad trends in public opinion. We then move on to the politics of specific foreign policy issues in each of the succeeding chapters: U.S.-China relations (Chapter 7); the Iraq War and terrorism (Chapter 8); humanitarian intervention (Chapter 9); trade and other globalization issues (Chapter 10); and global democratization and human rights (Chapter 11).

## *President Barack Obama and the Obama Administration*

BARACK OBAMA AS FOREIGN POLICY LEADER Here we focus in on the two main personal factors identified in Chapter 2—prior experience and political-psychological belief systems—that affect how well presidents fulfill their roles as foreign policy leaders.

Barack Obama came to the presidency with limited foreign policy experience. Most of his political career had been at the state and local level, as a community organizer in Chicago and a state senator in the Illinois legislature. He was elected to the U.S. Senate in 2004, and had been in that position for only about two years before hitting the campaign trail as a presidential candidate. During the Democratic primaries, Hillary Clinton, then his principal opponent, attacked Obama on this point, particularly in the "3 AM Red Phone" television ad. This ad depicted the crisis hotline ringing in the middle of the night while an ominous voice questioned whether Obama had the experience needed to "protect your children."[100] The Republican presidential candidate, John McCain, himself a Vietnam War hero, pushed this attack even harder. During the campaign, Obama took a trip to Iraq, the Middle East, and Europe to show his capacity for statesmanship. He and his supporters stressed his extensive knowledge and sound judgment as qualities not strictly dependent on experience.

The belief-systems framework that Obama brought to his presidency can be understood in terms of the same three factors applied to those of other presidents. First, Obama's conception of the international system recognizes America's central role but within a more multilateral context. America seeks a "common security for our common humanity," he stated. The world is such that "America cannot meet the threats of this century alone, and the world cannot meet them without America. We can neither retreat from the world nor try to bully it into submission. We must lead the world, by deed and by example."[101]

Second, though including all four "Ps" in his national interest hierarchy, Obama differentiates in a couple of ways. He acknowledges the importance of Power: "The American moment is not over, but it must be seized anew. To see American power in terminal decline is to ignore America's great promise and historic purpose in the world."[102] But he also stresses that "our power alone cannot protect us, nor does it entitle us to do as we please . . . Our power grows through its prudent use, our security emanates from the justness of our cause, the force of our example, the tempering qualities of our humility and restraint."[103] He sees American Principles as a set of ideals that "speak to aspirations shared by all people: that we can live free from fear and free from want; that we can speak our minds and assemble with whomever we choose and worship as we please."[104] Along with the immediate demands of the national and international economic crisis, Prosperity requires that "we must build on the wealth that open markets have created, and share its benefits more equitably. Trade has been a cornerstone of our growth and global development. But we will not be able to sustain this growth if it favors the few, and not the many."[105]

Obama's overarching strategy is based on two main elements. First is "using all elements of American power to keep us safe, and prosperous, and free."[106] This starts with the military and diplomatic but does not end there. Also included are halting global climate change, achieving greater energy security, reducing global poverty, and dealing with failed and failing states. Second is that "America is strongest when we act alongside strong partners."[107] Cooperation with other countries is to be more the norm, for pragmatic, not altruistic, reasons.

OBAMA AND CONGRESS The period from 2003 to 2006, with George W. Bush as president and the Republicans controlling Congress, was the longest period since 1980 without the divided government of one party controlling the White House and the other Capitol Hill. The 2006 midterm congressional election, which gave Democrats majorities in both the House and Senate, redivided government.

The 2008 election of the Democrat Barack Obama as president and the gaining of larger Democratic majorities in both chambers of Congress put that party in charge of both ends of Pennsylvania Avenue for the first time since 1994. But as we've seen before—the isolationist Congress FDR faced was a Democratic one, and conservative Republicans opposed Nixon's détente—interbranch politics on foreign policy is not just about partisanship. Two foreign policy issues in particular bring out fissures within the Democratic Party. One is trade policy, on which Democrats vary along the protectionism–free trade spectrum. The other is the defense budget, in which cuts and changing priorities can hurt some pet projects and constituent interests.

President Obama's enormous initial popularity gave him standing that he could use as political capital to win over members of Congress who might not agree on a particular issue but did not want to be seen as opposing a popular president. Conversely, when Obama's popularity has declined, this political capital has been less useful. Indeed, political gains can be made by taking on an unpopular president, even one of the same party.

THE OBAMA FOREIGN POLICY TEAM We also have stressed looking at intra–executive branch bureaucratic politics and organizational dynamics. Table 6.1 identifies the key players on the Obama foreign policy team at the outset of this new administration. Vice President Joseph Biden has extensive foreign policy experience, including as chairman of the Senate Foreign Relations Committee. The big three appointees were Hillary Rodham Clinton as secretary of state, General James Jones as national security adviser, and Robert Gates as secretary of defense. Also included are the ambassador to the United Nations, Susan Rice, whose position has been reelevated to Cabinet rank; Janet Napolitano, secretary of Homeland Security; Admiral Michael Mullen, chairman of the Joint Chiefs of

**TABLE 6.1 The Obama Foreign Policy Team (initial)**

| | |
|---|---|
| Vice President | Joseph Biden |
| National Security Advisor | James Jones |
| Secretary of State | Hillary Rodham Clinton |
| Secretary of Defense | Robert Gates |
| Chair, Joint Chiefs of Staff | Admiral Michael Mullen |
| Ambassador to the United Nations | Susan Rice |
| Director of National Intelligence | Dennis Blair |
| Director of the CIA | Leon Panetta |
| Secretary of Homeland Security | Janet Napolitano |
| Secretary of the Treasury | Timothy Geithner |
| U.S. Trade Representative | Ron Kirk |
| Director of the National Economic Council | Lawrence Summers |
| Secretary of Commerce | Gary Locke |

Staff; Dennis Blair, Director of National Intelligence; Leon Panetta, CIA director; and those with principal responsibility for international economic policy: Timothy Geithner, secretary of the treasury; Gary Locke, secretary of commerce; Ron Kirk, U.S. trade representative; and Lawrence Summers, director of the National Economic Council.

Which pattern will the Obama team follow? Some questions to keep in mind:

With the appointment of former political rival Hillary Clinton as Secretary of State, will this be a "team of rivals" in the constructive sense, or will old tensions carry over?

Following two vice presidents—Al Gore and Dick Cheney—who had active foreign policy roles, what role will Vice President Joseph Biden play?

What kind of national security advisor will the former marine general James Jones be?

Robert Gates replaced Donald Rumsfeld as Secretary of Defense in the last two years of the Bush administration. For reasons both of political bipartisanship and policy continuity, he was reappointed to that position. How has this worked out?

Amid the international financial crisis and with international economic issues more important than ever, what advisory and decision-making structures will best integrate and coordinate the political-military-diplomatic and international economic agendas?

INTELLIGENCE AGENCIES The CIA, FBI, and other intelligence agencies have been beset by a series of problems. In the latter days of the Cold War, both the CIA and the FBI had internal spy scandals. Reports also came out about the unsavory relationships the CIA maintained during the Cold War with some of its "ABC" (anything but communist) partners.

Then came 9/11. Among the many specific points made by the 9/11 Commission (known formally as the National Commission on Terrorist Attacks Upon the United States), a core one was that the CIA and others still were too rooted in Cold War threats and scenarios.[108] The 9/11 Commission proposed a number of reforms. Some were organizational, such as the creation of an overall "czar," or National Intelligence Director, with authority to coordinate and manage the CIA, FBI, and other intelligence agencies. Others concerned strategy and the need to commit greater resources and priority to Al Qaeda and other major threats from Islamist terrorism. Others were about mindsets, questions asked, thinking ahead of the curve, and other aspects of high-quality intelligence work that are analytic and not just organizational or budgetary.

Professor Loch Johnson of the University of Georgia, a leading authority on U.S. intelligence agencies, gives a sense of the dilemmas involved in providing high quality intelligence while operating within democratic principles and laws. On the one hand, standing oversight mechanisms such as the congressional intelligence committees as well as special investigations responding to scandals "can prove useful, leading to critical reforms, stronger oversight and, perhaps most important, changed attitudes about the CIA and other intelligence agencies." Still, though, as Johnson writes based not only on his scholarly work but also having served as a staff member to the Church committee CIA investigations in the mid-1970s (Chapter 5), "I've also learned that high-profile investigations will not transform human nature, turning intelligence officials—or the presidents and White House aides who direct them—into angels, unsusceptible to zeal and folly."[109] The particular incident he was responding to was the decision by Obama administration Attorney General Eric Holder to appoint a special prosecutor to investigate CIA prisoner abuses in the Iraq War. Controversy over this decision not only swirled on Capitol Hill and in the media, but also opened up splits within the Obama administration. Among other things this issue made it clear that while (George W.) Bush policies exacerbated controversies about the intelligence agencies, the Obama administration had its own challenges.

## *The Internet, Blogs, and the Changing Media*

The nature of the media has been undergoing profound change. More and more people are getting their news on the Internet, and at an accelerating rate. A December 2008 study found 40 percent of Americans getting "most of their news about national and international issues from the internet," a substantial number in its own right and a dramatic jump from the 24 percent found in a September 2007 study.[110] Among youth, the pattern is even more striking. Fifty-nine percent of Americans younger than thirty say they get most of their national and international news online; an identical percentage cites television. Comparatively, in September 2007, twice as many young people said they relied mostly on television for news as mentioned the internet (68 percent vs. 34 percent).[111]

The other side of this trend is reflected in the drop in daily newspaper readership from 52.6 percent of adults in 1990 to 37.5 percent in 2000, and with an even steeper drop among twenty- to forty-nine-year-olds.[112] More recent data show further drops. Measured as sales across the industry, the decrease was almost 3 percent in 2007, compared with 2006, and another 2.6 percent in 2008.[113] In 2009 the decline was even steeper, more than 10 percent, leaving the newspaper business facing "the greatest threat since the Depression."[114] The situation may not be so dire for newspaper readership as a whole, though. An independent study of eighty-eight newspapers showed that in the last two years, about half had seen no significant change in *combined print and online readership, or showed an increase.*[115] This may indicate that although individuals are getting more and more of their news on line, they still use traditional sources (that is, on line versions of newspapers).

The Internet also has substantially enhanced the capacity of NGOs, think tanks, and other organizations to become independent sources of information, analysis, and advocacy. Nik Gowing, a journalist with the BBC, calls this development a breaking of the "information dominance" of governments, whether they are repressive regimes that would prefer to cut their people off from outside communication or democratic governments that must respond to the new dynamics of pressure.[116] And Gowing was writing well before the explosive growth of the "blogosphere." In 1999 the total number of blogs was estimated at about fifty; by 2004 estimates were of 2.4 million to 4.1 million; by 2005 this was up to over 14 million, with a growth rate doubling every five to six months.[117] A March 2008 social media study by the marketing firm Universal McCann suggests that 346 million people worldwide read blogs. The 2008 edition of the State of the Blogosphere, published by Technorati on its Web site, had respondents from six continents.[118]

Meanwhile the "MSM" (mainstream media) have been cutting back their international coverage. Whereas in 1988 each of the major television networks spent about two thousand minutes covering international news over the course of the year, this total had declined by the year 2000 to between eleven hundred and twelve hundred minutes. This amounted to only about 9 percent of each evening news broadcast.[119]

The print media also have been undergoing major changes. By the early 1990s cutbacks were so extensive that only twenty-five of the top one hundred newspapers had at least one full-time foreign correspondent.[120] "Before September 11," wrote the *Washington Post* editors Leonard Downie and Robert Kaiser, "most of the American news media gave scant coverage to the fact that the United States was the key participant in an interdependent global society, or that our economic well-being depended on foreigners, or that our population includes millions of people born in foreign lands, more every year."[121] A

*Los Angeles Times* reporter expressed his concern that "you don't have editors and staff members who are conversant with the issues and with the world beyond our borders, so foreign news is easy to ignore a lot of the time."[122] Nor was this an isolated view. In a 2002 survey of newspaper editors' own views, nearly two-thirds rated post–September 11 foreign news coverage as only fair or poor.[123]

These trends have intensified, as indicated in a 2008 Pew Research Center study that found almost two-thirds of American newspapers publishing less foreign news than even just three years before. Only 10 percent of editors surveyed saw foreign news as "very essential" to their newspapers. "It's really concerning when we have two wars overseas, our economy is more global, we're competing with economies that are growing faster than ours, and our dependence on foreign oil is one of the biggest stories," commented a top Pew official.[124] Major regional newspapers such as the *Boston Globe*, the *Philadelphia Inquirer*, and the *Baltimore Sun* shut down their foreign bureaus. Even coverage of Washington has been hit hard, with many major newspapers shutting down their D.C. bureaus and others cutting way back. For example, the number of newspapers accredited to cover Congress has fallen two-thirds since 1980.[125]

## *Public Opinion: Continuity, Change, and Uncertainty*

What does the public think about foreign policy these days? As befits a period of historic transition, we find a mix of continuity with previous patterns, change from them, and uncertainty about priorities and preferences. In later chapters we will look at public opinion on some specific issues; here our focus is on some general patterns.

INTERNATIONALISM-ISOLATIONISM The long-term trends in ***internationalism-isolationism*** (Chapter 2) showed consistent preferences for internationalism with some fluctuations, including some recent narrowing of the gap. The 36 percent saying "stay out of world affairs" in the 2008 Chicago Council on Global Affairs was the highest in many years, but still substantially lower than the 63 percent saying "take an active part." That the gap was not narrower, given opposition to the Iraq war and the economic crisis, shows that the American public learned the lessons of the twentieth century: of how both world wars inevitably pulled the United States in, and the crucial contributions the United States made to both victories; of the folly of isolationist moves such as not joining the League of Nations and passing the 1929 Smoot-Hawley protectionist tariff; of the indispensable role the United States played in the Cold War; of oil crises and the interdependence of the American economy with the global economy. The public fundamentally understands that the United States has become so interconnected in so many ways with the rest of the world that isolationism is not just undesirable—it simply is not possible.

The debate has had two dimensions within the pro-internationalist general sentiment. One is over the importance of different issues and objectives. Figure 6.1 shows

**FIGURE 6.1 Foreign Policy Goals**

*Percentage who think the following should be very, somewhat, or not important foreign policy goals of the United States.*

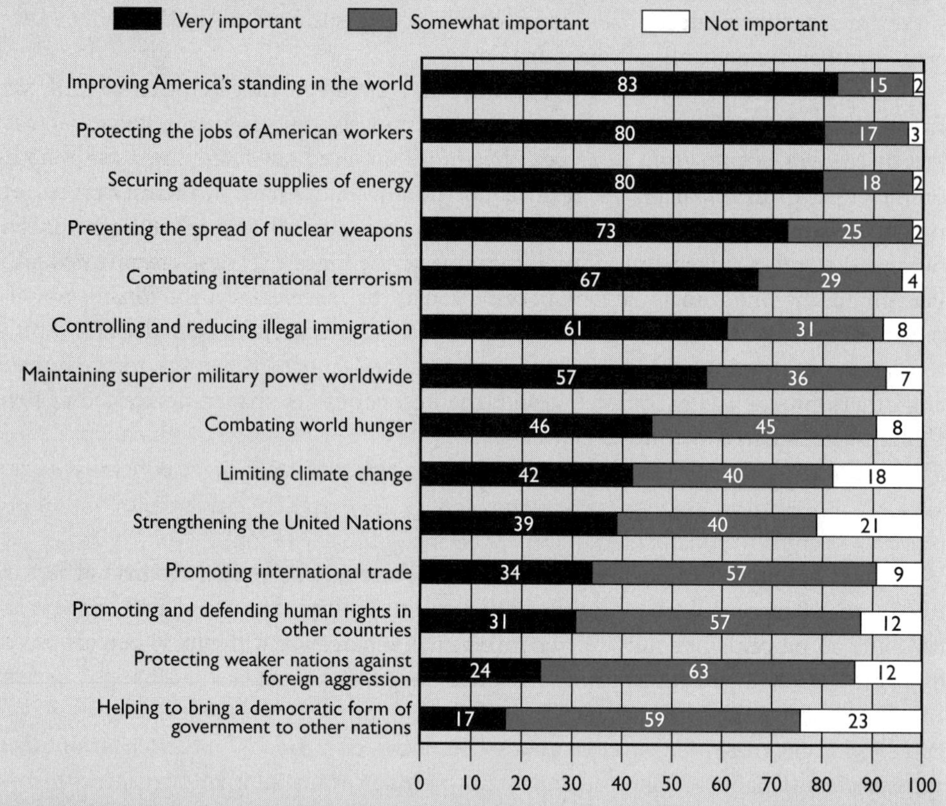


Source: Chicago Council on World Affairs, "Troubled by Loss of Standing in the World, Americans Support Major Foreign Policy Changes," 2008, p. 1, www.thechicagocouncil.org/UserFiles/File/POS_Topline%20Reports/POS%202008/2008%20Public%20Opinion_Foreign%20Policy.pdf (accessed 6/29/09).

rankings of different foreign policy goals from the 2008 Chicago Council survey. Along with straightforward observations about each ranking, some interesting patterns can be discerned. First is a reflection of the unpopularity of the Bush foreign policy in the highest "very important" rating (83 percent) given to improving America's standing in the world. Second is that four of the next five highest goals—protecting the jobs of American workers (80 percent), securing adequate supplies of energy (80 percent), combating international terrorism (67 percent) and controlling and reducing illegal immigration (61 percent)—were those with the greatest impact on Americans at home. Third is that less than one in three of those surveyed considered promoting and defending human rights, protecting weaker nations against foreign aggression, and democracy promotion very important. Fourth is an indication of the free trade–protectionism debate in the much greater support for protecting jobs than for promoting international trade.

The other dimension has been debate over conservative and liberal internationalisms, roughly tracking with the earlier discussion of unilateralism and multilateralism. Disapproval of the Bush foreign policy had shifted the public toward liberal internationalism. Seventy-three percent agreed that "a positive image of America around the world is necessary to achieve our national security goals"; 68 percent that "America's security is best promoted by working through diplomacy, alliances and international institutions." But 57 percent also agreed that military force is the most effective strategy against terrorism, and 51 percent that "we must do whatever is necessary to protect America from terrorism, even if it means restricting civil liberties or engaging in methods some might consider torture."[126]

An early round of polling showed strong support for the Obama foreign policy. Obama's approval ratings for his overall handling of international affairs was 67 percent; of Iraq, 71 percent; of Afghanistan, 63 percent; of global warming, 61 percent; and of engagement with adversaries, 71 percent. His numbers also were high as being a strong leader (77 percent) and being trusted in a crisis (73 percent). As commander in chief it was 56 percent, still a majority but lower than the other assessments.[127]

These numbers fell over the course of Obama's first year, some more than others. By October 2009, approval for his handling of Afghanistan was down to the 40s, in one poll as low as 42 percent. Overall approval ratings still were relatively high: 58 percent in one poll, and, while 48 percent in another, only 28 percent were opposed in that poll and the rest were uncertain.[128] PollingReport.com, from which we drew these numbers, is a good source for following future fluctuations.

VIEWS OF THE UNITED NATIONS Views of the United Nations bring out a particular aspect of the above debate. Figure 6.2 shows how strong U.S. public support was for the UN from the 1950s through the 1960s. This is consistent with the policy enhancement–prerogative encroachment analysis earlier in this chapter. In those years the American public viewed the UN's role as enhancing U.S. foreign policy. The UN generally supported U.S. positions during the Cold War. The strongest example of this support was during the Korean War. On the very same day that North Korea invaded South Korea, the UN Security Council ordered it to cease and withdraw, and then made the defense of South Korea a UN operation led by the United States and with troops from other UN member countries. On many other issues as well, a pro-U.S. tilt generally characterized UN decisions. Furthermore, people felt that the UN largely was effective in achieving its programmatic goals.

The "good job"/"poor job" lines first cross in the early 1970s. The "poor job" view dominated public opinion through the mid-1980s. During this period, votes in the Gen-

**FIGURE 6.2 American Public Opinion on the United Nations, 1953–2007**

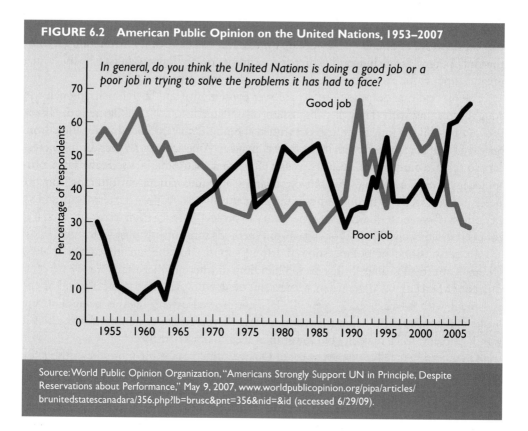

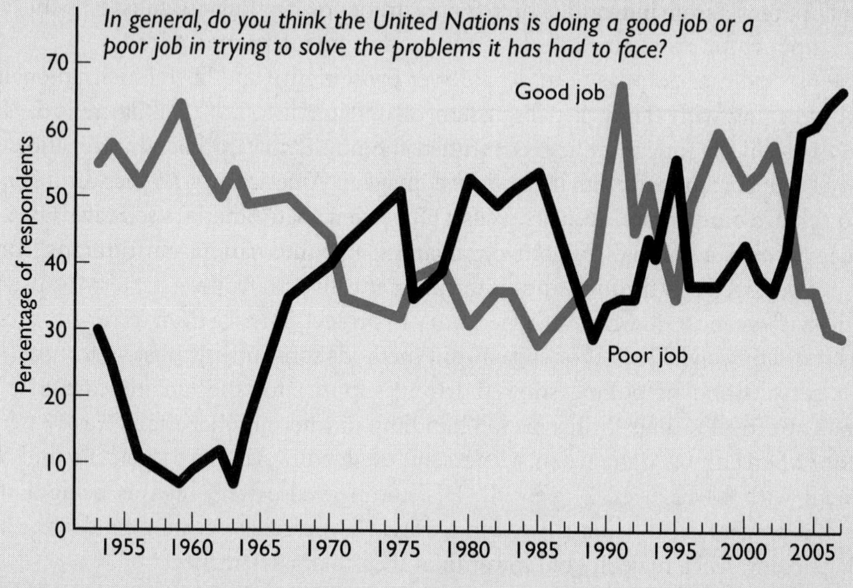


Source: World Public Opinion Organization, "Americans Strongly Support UN in Principle, Despite Reservations about Performance," May 9, 2007, www.worldpublicopinion.org/pipa/articles/brunitedstatescanadara/356.php?lb=brusc&pnt=356&nid=&id (accessed 6/29/09).

eral Assembly often were critical of U.S. foreign policy, and criticisms of UN inefficiencies and corruption mounted. The turnaround of the late 1980s and early 1990s was prompted initially by peacekeeping successes in Afghanistan and elsewhere, and then especially by the 1990–91 Persian Gulf War.

The "poor job" gap reopened in reaction to Somalia and Bosnia. In August 1995, only 35 percent of Americans rated the UN positively, whereas 56 percent rated it negatively. Polls began to even out again in 1996 as the situation in Bosnia improved and the UN got credit at least for agreeing to let NATO take charge. Other factors, such as internal reforms and the election of a new secretary-general, Kofi Annan, also helped the "good job" rating recapture a majority.

American public opinion stayed steadily supportive of the UN until the controversies of the 2003 Iraq war. Still, UN supporters took some solace in responses to a differently phrased question about what role the UN should play in setting global policy. Sixty-eight percent said either "leading" (26 percent) or "major" (42 percent), and only 28 percent "minor." All told, as one analyst said, the American public "doesn't appear too fond of the UN these days" but also is not "giving up on the idea of the UN . . . a strong supporter of the UN's potential role in world affairs, but a strong critic of its current role."[129]

POST–SEPTEMBER 11 PATRIOTISM Overall, the domestic consensus in the wake of September 11 was broader and stronger than at any point since the end of the Cold War. It was, once again, foreign policy politics with an Enemy. Bush's popularity, which had been dipping over the summer of 2001, soared to over 80 percent. Whereas in 1999 only 7 percent cited foreign policy as one of the biggest problems the United States faces, now 41 percent did. A new sense of patriotism flourished, a sense for many of "recapturing the flag" well portrayed by the journalist George Packer:

> Among the things destroyed with the twin towers was the notion, held by certain Americans ever since Vietnam, that to be stirred by national identity, carry a flag and feel grateful toward someone in uniform ought to be a source of embarrassment. The force of the blows woke us up to the fact that we are a part of a national community. This heightened awareness could be the disaster's greatest legacy.

Packer also warned, though, about the underside:

> Patriotism is as volatile as any emotion; once released, it can assume ugly forms. "I'm a patriot," said Frank Roque after being arrested for murdering a Sikh in Arizona. But in the past decade, our national disorder has been narcissism, not hysteria. Anyone who wants reform should figure out how to harness the civic passion that rose from the smoking debris. Like jet fuel, it can be used for good or ill.[130]

This new consensus has its foreign policy benefits, just as it did during the Cold War and other periods in U.S. history. It also has negative aspects for foreign policy politics, just as in the past, raising issues such as the tension between national security and civil liberties and the narrowing of the parameters of policy debate. And just as the Vietnam War shattered the Cold War consensus, so did the Iraq war have a similar impact on the September 11 consensus (Chapter 8).

USE OF MILITARY FORCE During the early Cold War, the public generally was willing to support the use of military force. In Chapter 5 we saw how, as part of the "Vietnam trauma," public support for the use of force became extremely weak. Starting in the 1980s, the pattern became more mixed, with public support consistently greater for the use of force for certain policy objectives than others. The picture we get is of a public that is neither as trigger happy as sometimes during the Cold War nor as gun shy as in the wake of Vietnam. The American public has become "pretty prudent."[131]

Behind these trends we can see three general patterns. First, public support tends to be greatest when the principal policy objective for which force is being used is to coerce *foreign policy restraint* on an aggressor threatening the United States, its citizens, or its interests. Second, the public tends to be least supportive of military force when the principal objective is to engineer *internal political change* in another country's government. Third are *humanitarian interventions,* for which public support tends to fall between.

This basic pattern has an underlying logic based on conceptions of legitimacy and calculations of efficacy. On the first point, using force to restrain aggression has a much stronger normative claim than does trying to remake governments. Humanitarian intervention falls in between, with some situations so dire that claims to legitimacy can be made even if the intervention is within a state and without the consent of that state's government. As for prospects for effectiveness, foreign policy restraint objectives have the inherent advantage of being more readily translatable into an operational military plan. Internal political change objectives, however, tend to require strategies more political in nature and less suitable to an operational military plan. Humanitarian interventions fall in between on this point as well; they usually have discrete missions and objectives but are difficult to keep from crossing over into state building.

Other factors, may also come into play in any particular case. Multilateral support and burden sharing is one; the public often wants to know that other countries are also bearing some of the risks and costs. The reactions of congressional leaders, newspaper editorialists, television pundits, and other elites are also a factor. Fundamentally, though, the American public is hardly eager to use military force, but is not invariably opposed to it. It still lacks lots of information, and may not even be able to find the relevant places on a map, but it manages to show "good judgment in the use of resources" and "caution and circumspection as to danger and risk"—exactly how the dictionary defines "prudence."

In ensuing chapters, we will see how this pattern plays out in such cases as the Iraq war (Chapter 8) and ethnic conflicts and genocides in Somalia, Bosnia, and Darfur (Chapter 9).

## Summary

This chapter has provided an overview of U.S. foreign policy strategy and foreign policy politics in this new era. Seven broad foreign policy strategy debates have been addressed: unilateralism vs. multilateralism; the nature and dynamics of the emerging global era; key issues in striking a balance between force and diplomacy; the role of the United Nations; WMD proliferation; threats from nonstate actors; and the international economy, energy security, and the global environment. Individually and collectively, they manifest some of the tensions and trade-offs in the choices to be made about setting priorities among and forming strategies for Power, Peace, Prosperity, and Principles—choices that we explore more specifically in key issue areas in the chapters that follow.

Although foreign policy politics in this new era has its own dynamics, it is structured by the same key domestic political institutions and processes as in earlier eras. Along with the foreign policy politics case studies in the chapters that follow, here our focus has been on President Obama and his administration, the foreign policy impact of the changing media, and broad trends in public opinion. All in all, we should not forget that disagreements over issues as important and complex as foreign policy are to be expected. It is precisely because foreign policy issues so often raise such vital concerns and pose choices between core American values that they take on such political importance.

Working through debates such as these is what diplomacy is all about—at home as well as abroad.

## *American Foreign Policy* Online Student StudySpace

- What are the key points in the unilateralism-multilateralism debate?
- What makes the emerging twenty-first century international landscape different from the twentieth century?
- Where and why have we succeeded in preventing WMD proliferation? Where and why haven't we?
- How can we meet the international economic, global environmental, and energy security challenges better than we have in the past?
- How have the new electronic media been impacting foreign policy strategy and foreign policy politics?

For these and other study questions, as well as other features, check out Chapter 6 on the *American Foreign Policy* Online Student StudySpace at wwnorton.com/studyspace.

## Notes

[1]Charles Krauthammer, "The Unipolar Moment," *Foreign Affairs* 70 (1990); Krauthammer, "The Unipolar Moment Revisited," *The National Interest* 70 (Winter 2002–2003): 5–17.

[2]Stephen G. Brooks and William Wohlforth, "American Primacy in Perpective," *Foreign Affairs* 81.4 (July–August 2002): 23.

[3]Richard Perle, "Next Stop, Iraq," speech at the Foreign Policy Research Institute, Philadelphia, November 30, 2001, www.fpri.org/enotes/americawar.20011130.perle.nextstopiraq.html (accessed 6/30/09).

[4]Condoleezza Rice, "Promoting the National Interest," *Foreign Affairs* 79.1 (January–February 2000): 47.

[5]William Kristol and Robert Kagan, "The Present Danger," *National Interest* 59 (Spring 2000): 67.

[6]Christopher Layne, "From Preponderance to Offshore Balancing: America's Future Grand Strategy after the Cold War," *International Security* 22.1 (Summer 1997): 86–124.

[7]Thucydides, *History of the Peloponnesian War,* R. Warner, trans. (New York: Penguin, 1972), 402.

[8]John J. Mearsheimer, "The False Promise of International Institutions," *International Security* 19.3 (Winter 1994–95): 12.

[9]Stephen M. Walt, *Taming American Power: The Global Response to Primacy* (New York: Norton, 2005), 217.

[10]George W. Bush, "The National Security Strategy of the United States of America," September 17, 2002, www.informationclearinghouse.info/article2320.htm (accessed 6/30/09).

[11]Richard K. Betts, "The Soft Underbelly of American Primacy: Tactical Advantages of Terrorism," *Political Science Quarterly* 117.1 (2002): 21.

[12]Richard N. Haass, "Multilateralism for a Global Era," speech at Carnegie Endowment for International Peace/Center on International Cooperation Conference, Washington, D.C., November 14, 2001, http://164.109.48.103/s/p/rem/6134.htm (accessed 6/30/09).

[13]Andrew J. Bacevich, *The New American Militarism: How Americans Are Seduced by War* (New York: Oxford University Press, 2005), 75. See also Stefan Halper and Jonathan Clarke, *America Alone: The Neo-Conservatives and the Global Order* (Cambridge: Cambridge University Press, 2004); and James Mann, *Rise of the Vulcans: The History of Bush's War Cabinet* (New York: Viking, 2004).

[14]Rice, "Promoting the National Interest," 47.

[15]Rice, "Promoting the National Interest," 48.

[16]Michael Mandelbaum, "Foreign Policy as Social Work," *Foreign Affairs* 75.1 (January/February 1996): 16–32.

[17]Mearsheimer, "False Promise of International Institutions," 7.

[18]John R. Bolton, "Unilateralism Is Not Isolationism," in *Understanding Unilateralism in American Foreign Relations,* Gwyn Prins, ed. (London: Royal Institute of International Affairs, 2000), 81.

[19]John R. Bolton, "Should We Take Global Governance Seriously?" paper presented at the American Enterprise Institute conference, "Trends in Global Governance: Do They Threaten American Sovereignty?" April 4–5, 2000, Washington, D.C. (italics in original).

[20]Arthur M. Schlesinger, Jr., "Unilateralism in Historical Perspective," in Prins, *Understanding Unilateralism in American Foreign Relations,* 18.

[21]Among the major works are Robert O. Keohane, *International Institutions and State Power: Essays in International Relations Theory* (Boulder, Colo.: Westview Press, 1989); Robert O. Keohane and Lisa L. Martin, "The Promise of Institutionalist Theory," *International Security* 20.1 (Summer 1995): 39–51; John Gerard Ruggie, *Winning the Peace: America and World Order in the New Era* (New York: Columbia University Press, 1996); and Stephen D. Krasner, ed. "International Regimes," special edition of *International Organization* 26.2 (Spring 1982).

[22]John Gerard Ruggie, "Multilateralism: The Anatomy of an Institution," *International Organization* 46.3 (Summer 1992): 561–98.

[23]Martha Finnemore, "Constructing Norms of Humanitarian Intervention," in *The Culture of National Security,* Peter J. Katzenstein, ed. (New York: Columbia University Press, 1996), 158.

[24]Bill Clinton, *A National Security Strategy for a New Century* (Washington, D.C.: U.S. Government Printing Office, 1998), 3.

[25]Richard N. Haass, "Defining U.S. Foreign Policy in a Post Post–Cold War World," speech to the Foreign Policy Association, April 22, 2002, www.fpa.org/topics_info2414/topics_info_show.htm?doc_id=108768 (accessed 6/30/09). See also his book written after he left the Bush administration, *The Opportunity: America's Moment to Alter History's Course* (New York: Public Affairs, 2005).

[26]"Stop the World, I Want to Get Off," *Economist,* July 28, 2001, cited in Walt, *Taming American Power,* 58.

[27]Joseph S. Nye, Jr., *The Paradox of American Power: Why the World's Only Superpower Can't Go It Alone* (New York: Oxford University Press, 2002), 8–9 (italics in original).

[28]Nye, *The Paradox of American Power,* 10.

[29]G. John Ikenberry, "America and Global Rules," October 23, 2005, America Abroad, TPM Café, http://tpmcafe.talkingpointsmemo.com/2005/10/23/america_and_global_rules/ (accessed 6/30/09).

[30]Keohane and Martin, "Promise of Institutionalist Theory," 42.

[31]This section draws on my article "America's Global Role after Bush," *Survival: Global Politics and Strategy* 49.3 (September 2007): 179–200.

[32]Neil Buckley and Hugh Williamson, "Russia and U.S. Play Down Missile Dispute," *Financial Times,* February 23, 2007.

[33]*Foreign Policy* magazine and Fund for Peace, "The Failed States Index," *Foreign Policy,* May/June 2006.

[34]Harold Nicolson, *Diplomacy* (New York: Oxford University Press, 1980; first edition 1939), 4.

[35]Globalsecurity.org, "World Wide Military Expenditures," www.globalsecurity.org/military/world/spending.htm (accessed 6/30/09).

[36]Greg Jaffe, "Short '06 Lebanon War Stokes Pentagon Debate," *Washington Post,* April 6, 2009.

[37]Charles R. Babcock, "Pentagon Budget's Stealth Spending," *Washington Post,* October 13, 1998, A1, A4.

[38]Nicholas Kristof, "Make Diplomacy, Not War," *New York Times,* August 9, 2008.

[39]Robert Gates, "Long-Term Success against Security Challenges Depends on Many Elements," Landon Lecture, Kansas State University, November 26, 2007, www.america.gov/st/texttrans-english/2007/November/20071206191908bpuh0.9181177.html (accessed 6/30/09).

[40]John J. Kruzel, "Mullen Urges Emphasis on 'Soft Power,'" DefenseLINK, January 13, 2009, www.defenselink.mil/News/newsarticle.aspx?id=52664 (accessed 6/30/09).

[41]Statement of Senator Hillary Rodham Clinton, Nominee for Secretary of State, Senate Foreign Relations Committee, January 13, 2009, http://foreign.senate.gov/testimony/2009/ClintonTestimony090113a.pdf (accessed 6/30/09).

[42]Quoted in Thomas J. Paterson, J. Gary Clifford, and Kenneth J. Hagan, *American Foreign Relations: A History since 1895* (Lexington, Mass.: Heath, 1995), 243–44.

[43]Quoted in Michael N. Barnett, "Bringing in the New World Order: Liberalism, Legitimacy, and the United Nations," *World Politics* 49.4 (July 1997): 541.

[44]Barnett, "Bringing in the New World Order," 543.

[45]Vaclav Havel, "A Table for Tyrants," *New York Times,* May 11, 2009.

[46]Council on Foreign Relations, Susan Rice's Confirmation Statement, January 15, 2009, www.cfr.org/publication/18321/susan_rices_confirmation_hearing_statement.html (accessed 6/30/09).

[47]Particular thanks to Jessica Wirth, my research assistant in 2008–2009, for her work on a case study on which this section draws.

[48]Andre de Nesnera, "UN Security Council Reform May Shadow Annan's Legacy," Voice of America, November 1, 2006, www.voanews.com/english/archive/2006-11/2006-11-01-voa46.cfm?CFID=277905610&CFTOKEN=77677347&jsessionid=0030ca1239a2eecf238a7b1225544517077a (accessed 9/1/09).

[49]Statement by H. E. Mr. Luiz Inácio Lula da Silva at the General Debate of the 61st Session of the United Nations General Assembly, September 19, 2006, www.un.org/webcast/ga/61/pdfs/brasil-e.pdf (accessed 6/30/09).

[50]Ministry of Foreign Affairs (Japan), "Reform of the UN Security Council: Why Japan Should Become a Member," March 2005, www.mofa.go.jp/policy/un/reform/pamph0503.pdf (accessed 6/30/09).

[51]Address by Prime Minister Manmohan Singh of India to a joint session of the U.S. Congress, Washington D.C., July 21, 2005, www.nriol.com/content/articles/article87.asp (accessed 6/30/09).

[52]Aminu Bashir Wali, "Is Makeup of Security Council About to Change?" *Diplomatic License,* Richard Roth, host, New York, October 15, 2004, http://edition.cnn.com/TRANSCRIPTS/0410/15/i_dl.01.html (accessed 6/30/09).

[53]"Egypt Seeks Permanent Seat on Expanded U.N. Security Council," *San Diego Union-Tribune,* September 12, 2004.

[54]de Nesnera, "UN Security Council Reform May Shadow Annan's Legacy."

[55]Statement by Ambassador D. S. Kumalo to the General Assembly on the Question of Equitable Representation on and Increase in the Membership of the Security Council and Related Matters, October 11, 2004, www.southafrica-newyork.net/pmun/ (accessed 6/30/09).

[56]de Nesnera, "UN Security Council Reform May Shadow Annan's Legacy."

[57]Thomas G. Weiss, "Overcoming the Security Council Reform Impasse: The Implausible versus the Plausible," Friedrich Ebert Stiftung, Berlin, 2005, Occasional Paper no. 14.

[58]Bill Varner, "Security Council Expansion Talks at UN Get New Boost From Obama," Bloomberg.com, February 19, 2009, www.bloomberg.com/apps/news?pid=20601085&sid=aEpKLbSnxkOI&refer=europe (accessed 6/30/09).

[59]Varner, "Security Council Expansion Talks at UN Get New Boost."

[60]Andrew F. Krepinevich, *7 Deadly Scenarios: A Military Futurist Explores War in the 21st Century* (New York: Bantam Books, 2009), 30, 33.

[61]Philip Taubman, "The Trouble with Zero," *New York Times,* May 10, 2009.

[62]See Scott D. Sagan and Kenneth N. Waltz, *The Spread of Nuclear Weapons: A Debate* (New York: Norton, 1995).

[63]Commission on the Prevention of Weapons of Mass Destruction and Terrrorism, *World at Risk,* December 2, 2008, xi, xv, http://documents.scribd.com/docs/2avb51ejt0uadzxm2wpt.pdf (accessed 9/1/09).

[64]George W. Bush, speech at the National Defense University, Washington, D.C., May 1, 2001, www.nti.org/e_research/official_docs/pres/5101pres.pdf (accessed 7/1/09).

[65]Helene Cooper, "In First Meeting, Rice Presses North Korea on Nuclear Effort," *New York Times,* July 24, 2008.

[66]John R. Bolton, quoted in Helene Cooper, "U.S. Sees Stalling by North Korea on Nuclear Pact," *New York Times,* January 19, 2008.

[67]Christopher R. Hill, Statement before the House Foreign Relations Committee: North Korea and the Status of the Six-Party Talks, February 28, 2007, http://merln.ndu.edu/archivepdf/northkorea/state/81204.pdf (accessed 7/1/09).

[68]This section draws on Bruce W. Jentleson and Christopher A. Whytock, "Who 'Won' Libya? The Force-Diplomacy Debate and Its Implications for Theory and Policy," *International Security* 30.4 (Winter 2005–06): 47–86.

[69]Cheney made his comments in the vice presidential debate with John Edwards. David Ignatius, "A Gaddafi Cover-up," *Washington Post,* October 26, 2004. See also Andrew Gumbel, "Libya Weapons Deal: U.S. Neoconservatives Jubilant over WMD Agreement," *Independent* (London), December 22, 2003; and Tod Lindberg, "A Policy of Prevention: The Administration's Strategy against WMD Is Working," *Washington Times,* December 30, 2003.

[70]Martin S. Indyk, "The Iraq War Did Not Force Gaddafi's Hand," *Financial Times* (London), March 9, 2004; Indyk, "Was Kadafi Scared Straight? The Record Says No," *Los Angeles Times,* March 28, 2004; Richard Armitage, interview with Juan Williams, National Public Radio, December 24, 2003, www.npr.org/templates/story/story.php?storyId=1568912 (accessed 7/1/09); Flynt Leverett, "Why Libya Gave Up on the Bomb," *New York Times,* January 23, 2004; and Tony Blair, statement on Libya, December 19, 2003, http://news.bbc.co.uk/2/hi/uk_news/politics/3336073.stm (accessed 7/1/09). See also Joseph Cirincione, "The World Just Got Safer: Give Diplomacy the Credit," *Washington Post,* January 11, 2004.

[71]"Libyan Prime Minister Says Weapons Decision Motivated by Economy, Oil," *Al-Hayat,* December 24, 2003, translated and reported by BBC Monitoring; Khaled al-Deeb, "Libya: No Coercion in Weapons Agreement," Associated Press Online, December 20, 2003; "Libyan WMD: Tripoli's Statement in Full," BBC News, December 20, 2003, http://news.bbc.co.uk/go/pr/fr/-/1/hi/world/africa/3336139.stm (accessed

7/1/09); interview with Seif el-Islam Qaddafi, *Al-Hayat*, March 10, 2004, translated and reported by BBC Monitoring. See also Ronald Bruce St. John, "'Libya Is Not Iraq': Preemptive Strikes, WMD, and Diplomacy," *Middle East Journal* 58.3 (Summer 2004): 386–402; Diederik Vandewalle, "The Origins and Parameters of Libya's Recent Actions," *Arab Reform Bulletin* 2.3 (March 2004), www.carnegieendowment.org/arb/?fa=downloadArticlePDF&article=21304 (accessed 7/1/09).

[72]Barack Obama, Remarks, Hradcany Square, Prague, Czech Republic, April 5, 2009, www.whitehouse.gov/the_press_office/Remarks-By-President-Barack-Obama-In-Prague-As-Delivered/ (accessed 9/1/09).

[73]George P. Shultz, William J. Perry, Henry A. Kissinger, and Sam Nunn, "A World Free of Nuclear Weapons," *Wall Street Journal*, January 4, 2007, p. A15. Their statement was endorsed by more than two-thirds of the still-living former secretaries of defense and state.

[74]Joint Statement by Gareth Evans and Yoriko Kawaguchi, New York, September 25, 2008, www.icnnd.org/news/releases/080925_js_evans_kawaguchi.html (accessed 7/1/09).

[75]Global Zero Website, About the Campaign, www.globalzero.org/en/about-campaign (accessed 7/1/09).

[76]*New York Times*, May 26, 1998, A1.

[77]Joseph Cirincione, *Deadly Arsenals: Tracking Weapons of Mass Destruction* (Washington, D.C.: Carnegie Endowment for International Peace, 2002), 396.

[78]The United Nations Office at Geneva, Disarmament: Sixth Review Conference, www.unog.ch/80256EE600585943/(httpPages)/3496CA1347FBF664C12571860036433l?OpenDocument (accessed 7/1/09).

[79]BioWeapons Prevention Project, 6th Review Conference of the Biological and Toxin Weapons Convention, www.bwpp.org/6RevCon/6thRevConResources.html (accessed 7/1/09).

[80]Commission on the Prevention of Weapons of Mass Destruction and Terrrorism, *World at Risk*, xv.

[81]James Kraska and Brian Wilson, "Fighting Pirates: the Pen and the Sword," *World Policy Journal*, 25.4 (Winter 2008–2009): 42–52.

[82]Anne Gearan, "U.S. Options Limited to Prevent, Fight Somali Piracy," Associated Press, April 9, 2009.

[83]Ken Menkhaus, "Dangerous Waters," *Survival: Global Politics and Strategy* 51.1 (February–March 2009): 22.

[84]Donna Nincic, "State Failure and the Re-emergence of Maritime Piracy in Africa," paper delivered at the International Studies Association 49th Annual Convention, San Francisco, March 2008, www.allacademic.com//meta/p_mla_apa_research_citation/2/5/4/3/2/pages254325/p254325-1.php (accessed 7/1/09).

[85]Menkhaus, "Dangerous Waters," 22.

[86]Moises Naim, *Illicit: How Smugglers, Traffickers, and Copycats Are Hijacking the Global Economy* (New York: Doubleday, 2005), 73, 77.

[87]Diana Jean Schemo, "Bogota Aid: To Fight Drugs or Rebels?" *New York Times*, June 2, 1998, A1, A12.

[88]Senator John Kerry, "Organized Crime Goes Global While the United States Stays Home," *Washington Post*, May 1, 1997, C1.

[89]Naim, *Illicit*, 13.

[90]Kerry, "Organized Crime."

[91]Naim, *Illicit*, 57.

[92]Dennis C. Blair, "Annual Threat Assessment of the Intelligence Community for the Senate Select Committee on Intelligence," February 12, 2009, http://intelligence.senate.gov/090212/blair.pdf (accessed 7/2/09).

[93]Nicholas D. Kristof, "At Stake Are More than Banks," *New York Times*, April 2, 2009.

[94]Bruce W. Jentleson and Steven Weber, "America's Hard Sell," *Foreign Policy* 169 (November/December 2008), 42–49.

[95]Council on Foreign Relations, "National Security Consequences of U.S. Oil Dependency," October 2006, www.cfr.org/publication/11683/ (accessed 7/2/09).

[96]Suzanne Maloney, "The Gulf's Renewed Oil Wealth: Getting It Right This Time?" *Survival: Global Politics and Strategy* 50.6 (December 2008), 132.

[97]Blair, "Annual Threat Assessment," 42.

[98]Jared Diamond, *Collapse: How Societies Choose to Fail or Succeed* (New York: Viking, 2005), 23.

[99]Quoted in Thomas McCormick, *America's Half-Century: United States Foreign Policy in the Cold War* (Baltimore: Johns Hopkins University Press, 1989), 232.

[100]See this ad on YouTube, www.youtube.com/watch?v=kddX7LqgCvc (accessed 7/2/09).

[101]Barack Obama, "Renewing American Leadership," *Foreign Affairs* 4.86 (July/August 2007): 2.

[102]Obama, "Renewing American Leadership," 4.

[103]Barack Obama, Inaugural Address, January 20, 2009, www.nytimes.com/2009/01/20/us/politics/20text-obama.html?_r=2 (accessed 7/2/09).

[104]Barack Obama, "A World That Stands as One," Berlin, Germany, July 24, 2008, www.americanrhetoric.com/speeches/barackobamaberlinspeech.htm (accessed 7/2/09).

[105]Obama, "A World That Stands as One."

[106]Barack Obama, "A New Strategy for a New World," Washington, D.C., July 15, 2008, www.barackobama.com/2008/07/15/remarks_of_senator_barack_obam_96.php (accessed 7/2/09).

[107]Obama, "A New Strategy for a New World."

[108]National Commission on Terrorist Attacks Upon the United States, *9/11 Commission Report* (New York: Norton, 2004).

[109]Loch K. Johnson, "It's Never a Quick Fix at the CIA," *Washington Post*, August 30, 2009, www.washingtonpost.com/wp-dyn/content/article/2009/08/28/AR2009082802097.html.

[110]Pew Research Center of the People and the Press, "Internet Overtakes Newspapers as News Outlet," December 23, 2008, http://people-press.org/report/479/internet-overtakes-newspapers-as-news-source (accessed 9/3/09).

[111]Pew Research Center of the People and the Press, "Internet Overtakes Newspapers as News Outlet."

[112]Richard A. Posner, "Bad News," *New York Times*, July 31, 2005.

[113]Richard Pérez-Peña, "More Readers Trading Newspapers for Web Sites," *New York Times*, November 6, 2007. See also Scarborough Research, "Newspaper Audience Ratings Report 2008," www.scarborough.com/press_releases/SNARR%20FINAL%20A%204.30.08.pdf (accessed 7/2/09), referred to in Pérez-Peña, "More Readers Trading Newspapers for Web Sites."

[114]Richard Perez-Pena, "Newspaper Circulation Falls By More Than 10%, *New York Times*, October 27, 2009, B3.

[115]Scarborough Research, "Newspaper Audience Ratings Report 2008."

[116]Nik Gowing, presentation at Managing Information Chaos, conference held at the United States Institute of Peace, Washington, D.C., March 12, 1999.

[117]Daniel W. Drezner and Henry Farrell, "Web of Influence," *Foreign Policy* 145 (November–December 2004): 32–40; Editorial, "Measuring the Blogosphere," *New York Times*, August 5, 2005.

[118]Technorati, "State of the Blogosphere 2008, Day 1: Who Are the Bloggers?" http://technorati.com/blogging/state-of-the-blogosphere/who-are-the-bloggers/ (accessed7/2/09).

[119]Ken Auletta, "Annals of Communications: Battle Stations," *New Yorker*, December 10, 2001, 60–61.

[120]Auletta, "Annals of Communications," 61.

[121]Leonard Downie, Jr., and Robert G. Kaiser, *The News about the News: American Journalism in Peril* (New York: Knopf, 2002), 241.

[122]Cited in Downie and Kaiser, *The News about the News*, 241.

[123]Howard Kurtz, "Despite Sept. 11, Interest Still Low in Foreign News," *Washington Post*, June 10, 2002, A13.

[124]Quoted in Richard Pérez-Peña, "As Papers Struggle, News Is Cut and the Focus Turns Local," *New York Times*, July 21, 2008.

[125]Richard Pérez-Peña, "Big News in Washington, But Far Fewer Cover It," *New York Times,* December 18, 2008. Presentation by Phillip Bennett, former managing editor, *Washington Post,* Terry Sanford Institute of Public Policy, Duke University, February 16, 2009.

[126]John Halpin and Karl Agne, State of American Political Ideology 2009: A National Study of Political Values and Beliefs, Center for American Progress, March 2009, www.americanprogress.org/issues/2009/03/political_ideology.html (accessed 7/2/09).

[127]Washington Post–ABC News Poll, April 30, 2009, /www.washingtonpost.com/wpsrv/politics/polls/postpoll_042609.html (accessed 10/30/09).

[128]PollingReport.com, www.pollingreport.com/obama_ad.htm (accessed October 26, 2009)

[129]Ruy Teixeria, "The UN: Good Idea, Bad Execution," *DonkeyRising,* March 16, 2006, www.emerging-democraticmajorityweblog.com/donkeyrising/archives/001406.php (accessed 7/2/09).

[130]George Packer, "Recapturing the Flag," *New York Times Magazine*, September 30, 2001, 15–16.

[131]This section draws on Bruce W. Jentleson, "The Pretty Prudent Public: Post Post-Vietnam American Public Opinion on the Use of Military Force," *International Studies Quarterly* 36.1 (March 1992): 49–74; and Bruce W. Jentleson and Rebecca L. Britton, "Still Pretty Prudent: Post–Cold War American Opinion on the Use of Military Force," *Journal of Conflict Resolution* 42.4 (August 1998): 395–417. See also Richard C. Eichenberg, "Victory Has Many Friends: U.S. Public Opinion and the Use of Military Force," *International Security* 30.1 (Summer 2005): 140–77.

CHAPTER

# 7 Post–Cold War Geopolitics: Major Powers and Regions

The end of the Cold War closed one geopolitical era and opened the way for another. From the late 1940s, when the Cold War began, until the late 1980s and early 1990s, when the fall of the Berlin Wall and then the dissolution of the Soviet Union brought it to an end, U.S. relations with most other countries in the world were structured by the bipolarity of the international system. The United States was at one pole and the Soviet Union at the other. With the end of the Cold War, the alignments and dynamics of major power geopolitics were put in flux. This has been true for relations with the former adversaries Russia and China, with the long-standing major allies Western Europe and Japan, with emerging powers such as India, and in regional security balances.

There is some good news here. War between or among the major world powers seems less likely today than in almost any prior historical period. Most scholars would agree with the basic proposition, as stated by the George W. Bush administration, that "today, the international community has the best chance since the rise of the nation-state in the seventeenth century to build a world where great powers compete in peace instead of continually prepare for war."[1] Still, post–Cold War geopolitics poses tough choices for American foreign policy strategy and the balancing of the "4 Ps" elements of the national interest:

- *Power:* What is the scope of American power? What are its limits? How can the United States best shape, sustain, and use that power?
- *Peace:* What are the prospects for integrating the other major powers, especially China, into international institutions that are key to system stability? Are new or significantly changed institutions needed?
- *Prosperity:* What weight should be given to, and what policies should be pursued, on trade and other economic issues in relations with the other major powers?

- *Principles:* What priority should be given to the advocacy of democracy and human rights in relations with Russia and China?

In this chapter we examine U.S. relations with other major powers and in key regions, including the role of regional multilateral organizations. (The Middle East is kept for Chapter 8.) The foreign policy politics section focuses on a case study of the "China lobbies" and their quest to influence U.S. policy from the early Cold War to the present.

## Major Powers Geopolitics

In every era, the geopolitics of relations among major powers has been a key factor determining international relations. This is no less true today.

In March 1992 a Pentagon planning document addressing the "fundamentally new situation which has been created by the collapse of the Soviet Union" was leaked to the press. The strategy it proposed was geared to ensuring that the United States would remain the dominant world power: "Our strategy must now refocus on precluding the emergence of any potential future global competitor." Part of the leadership task would be convincing other major powers that their interests would be taken care of, that the United States would "establish and protect a new order that holds the promise of convincing potential competitors that they need not aspire to a greater role or pursue a more aggressive posture to protect their legitimate interests." Lest this strategy sound too altruistic, the Pentagon also emphasized maintaining and asserting American Power in ways that would make it clear that even if other countries were not convinced of this benevolence, there wasn't a lot they could do about it: "We must maintain the mechanisms for deterring potential competitors from *even aspiring* to a larger regional or global role."[2]

The leak of this document, which was written while Dick Cheney was the secretary of defense, stirred controversy both within the United States and internationally. It fitted with readings of history that stressed the risks of war amid "power transitions" when an existing great power was challenged by a rising one. It also fit Realist international relations theories stressing ***primacy.*** "The maintenance of *primacy*—preponderance in the economic, military, technological, and cultural dimensions of power—is in the national interest. And although the very fact of predominance can be a source of foreign resentment, a large disparity of power is more likely to deter challenges by other would-be powers than to provoke them." Unipolarity, primacy theorists contend, makes for a stable world.[3]

Michael Mandelbaum poses this as "the case for Goliath"(Reading 7.1). He sees American power as "the defining feature of world affairs." It is a Goliath, but "a benign 7.1

one." Other countries may not always want to acknowledge it explicitly, but the American role in the world has their "tacit consent." This or that issue may come up as a bone of contention, but the overall arrangement provides the degree of order that the world needs. No other major power either is ready to play this role or, if it were, would do so in a manner so much in the collective interest.

Another Realist, Stephen Walt, contends that American power has had a boomerang effect of prompting others to seek to "tame" it. He reviews a series of strategies—balancing, balking, binding, blackmail, delegitimation—that manifest "the true paradox of American primacy: Instead of enabling the United States to act however it wishes, America's dominant position encourages other states to fear our unchecked power and look for ways to constrain it."

Some observers express particular concern about the rise of China. History and international relations theory show that tensions and war are often associated with the rise of a new great power. Professor A. F. K. Organski has written about the dangers of ***power transitions,*** when whether through intention or miscalculation a rising power and the existing dominant power may end up going beyond competition to conflict.[4] The main historical example is Germany's rise in the 1870–1914 period, when it challenged Great Britain's dominance through rivalry and an arms race, a challenge that ultimately led to World War I. The alternative view, with its own basis in history and theory, sees competition but not necessarily major conflict in what another expert has called a "peaceful contestation" by which China will pursue its own interests but largely within the rules of the game and open to cooperation with the United States.[5] Chinese leaders use terms such as "peaceful rise," by which they mean that China will seek to increase its role in the world but will do so without threatening the United States or other countries.

International institutionalists stress an *integration* strategy—bringing others in rather than keeping them down. As John Ikenberry argues, and as elaborated in this chapter's Historical Perspective box: "Power and Peace over the Centuries," (p. 345) peace has been most durable when the victors in war and the most powerful states have used their position and power to foster international order based on shared interests. When they have sought only to dominate—keep others down—their power has brought some gains but not very stable or sustainable ones. This is what Joseph Nye calls "the paradox of American
7.2 can power," expanded on in the excerpt from his book in Reading 7.2.

Add to these complications the fact that, to a greater extent than during any prior historical period, the issues that nations face in the contemporary era make integration and cooperation more in the interests of the major powers than strict competition or even balance of power. Increasing the stakes of the other major powers in a stable, peaceful international system, and enhancing their role in and responsibility for maintaining and strengthening it, is strategically sounder than efforts premised on American primacy or hegemony.

This debate frames our focus on U.S. relations with each of the other major powers.

## HISTORICAL PERSPECTIVES

HISTORICAL PERSPECTIVES

### POWER AND PEACE OVER THE CENTURIES

As we face another era of major global transition, what lessons can we learn from other historical periods?

One historical perspective sees Power as the key.* Great-power politics always has been and always will be a competition for Power. This was true of Spain in the sixteenth century, of Britain and France in the seventeenth and eighteenth centuries, and of Germany and Japan, going back to their rise in the nineteenth century and through World War II. It was true of the Soviet Union in the Cold War. Some believe it was true of the United States, both earlier in its history and in the Cold War. Great-power competition is hard wired into the international system. Peace is inherently uncertain, a product of maintaining sufficient power to ensure one's own security and dominate others as and when necessary.

An alternative perspective sees this great-power competition as likely but not inevitable, with history showing that Peace can be achieved when the most powerful states use their power to build order through institutions and other forms of cooperation.† This was achieved somewhat following the Napoleonic wars, starting with the 1815 Congress of Vienna and its agreements among the major European powers to limit their competition. The peace broke down with World War I, although after lasting almost one hundred years. The post–World War I peace, of which President Woodrow Wilson was the principal architect, was notable in its ambition and vision but flawed in its construction. The League of Nations was too weak an institution on which to build order, especially when the United States opted out because of isolationist domestic politics. The post–World War II system, with its more numerous and stronger international institutions backed by formidable yet self-restrained American Power, proved "distinctive and unprecedented," a durable Peace that transitioned into a new era through the collapse without war of the Soviet Union and its empire.‡

*See, for example, John J. Mearsheimer, *The Tragedy of Great Power Politics* (New York: Norton, 2001).

†See, for example, G. John Ikenberry, *After Victory: Institutions, Strategic Restraint, and the Rebuilding of Order after Major Wars* (Princeton: Princeton University Press, 2001).

‡Ikenberry, *After Victory,* 210.

## Europe

### *Western Europe, the European Union (EU), and NATO*

At first glance it might seem that the United States and western Europe have so much in common that even with the end of the Cold War, relations between the two would still be strong. They are a community of democracies. Their economies are highly interdependent. They still face common threats, including global terrorism. ***NATO*** is the most successful peacetime alliance in history. Yet transatlantic geopolitics also has had to make adjustments.

Even before the Iraq war, Robert Kagan, a conservative American analyst and columnist, postulated a deep and fundamental European-American divergence: "It is time to stop pretending that Americans and Europeans share a common view of the world," he wrote. "On major strategic and international questions Americans are from Mars and Europeans from Venus: They agree on little and understand one another less and less."[6] Kagan put most of the blame on the Europeans for their naiveté about the continuing need for power and force in international affairs, for lapsing further into military weakness, and for not pulling their weight in NATO, especially on global security threats.

Many Europeans saw the problems quite differently. In their view the United States had fallen into a "cult of unilateralism," characterized by an "instinctive refusal to admit to any political restraint on its action . . . placing itself above international law, norms and restraints when they do not suit its objectives." There was some acknowledgment of "European legalistic fervour" as going too far in its own right, and of both sides' contributing to "a dialogue of the deaf."[7] But the driving dynamic was seen as emanating from the United States' side of the Atlantic.

Whatever one's view of the causes, it was clear by 2001–2002 that the list of issues on which the United States and Western Europe were in conflict had been growing longer. The list included the Kyoto global warming treaty, the International Criminal Court, the multilateral land mines treaty, relations with Iran, the Israeli-Palestinian conflict, and a number of international trade issues. And then came the Iraq war, over which tensions ran extremely high and conflicts cut quite deep. Britain was front and center in supporting the United States, as were some other European countries. But France, Germany, and others were strongly opposed. The foreign minister of France, Dominique de Villepin, went so far as to threaten to use France's veto in the UN Security Council to try to block U.S. military action against Iraq.

These intra-European differences partly fitted with earlier patterns of relations with the United States and partly manifested transitions to post–Cold War foreign policy identities. British-American relations, though not the "special relationship" of Roosevelt and Churchill during World War II, had been close under Clinton as well as George H. W. Bush. In the Persian Gulf War, the "no-fly zone" 1990s containment strategy against Iraq, the Kosovo war, the Afghanistan war, and especially the Iraq war, British and American interests were sufficiently shared to provide the basis for joint military action. The British prime minister Tony Blair was the key ally for the George W. Bush administration during the Iraq war. In Blair's view, on Iraq and more broadly, "There never has been a time when the power of America was so necessary; or so misunderstood." Europe and America needed partnership, not rivalry, "a common will and a shared purpose in the face of a common threat. . . . [I]f we split, all the rest will play around, play us off and nothing but mischief will be the result of it. . . . We should not minimize the differences. But we should not let them confound us either."[8]

Although the U.S.-French conflict over Iraq was particularly intense, tensions in this relationship were hardly new. It was right in the middle of the Cold War that President Charles de Gaulle took France out of the NATO military command. U.S. leaders often see France as an irksome ally, a country that hasn't come to grips with its faded imperial status. The French, in turn, often view the United States as both naïve and arrogant. "For my part," Foreign Minister Hubert Vedrine stated, "I believe that since 1992 the word 'superpower' is no longer sufficient to describe the United States. That's why I use the term 'hyperpower.' . . . We cannot accept either a politically unipolar world, nor a culturally uniform world, nor the unilateralism of a single hyperpower. And that is why we are fighting for a multipolar, diversified and multilateral world."[9] Still, despite such views and the differences over Iraq, there has been significant French-American cooperation on some issues, such as some major covert action operations in the war on terrorism.[10]

As for Germany, one of the old sayings about NATO as cited earlier was that, in addition to keeping the Russians out of Europe and the Americans in, its tacit purpose was also to keep the Germans down. Germany's "traumatic past" and the determination "never again to allow German militarism and nationalism to threaten European stability" defined the parameters of Germany's foreign policy as that of a "civilian power."[11] The toughest post–Cold War issues for Germany have involved military intervention. The United States and other NATO countries deployed peacekeeping forces in Bosnia and then fought the war in Kosovo, but the former Yugoslavia had been an area of Nazi brutalization during World War II. In light of this, how would Germany balance historical memory and its present alliance obligation in deciding what role its military should take on? German troops did join in the Bosnia peacekeeping effort, and the German air force participated in the Kosovo war in ways that struck a balance and marked an evolution of, but not a departure from, the "civilian power" role. This issue came up again during the 2001 Afghanistan war, when Chancellor Gerhard Schroeder proposed committing almost four thousand German troops to the war effort. The sensitivity and complexity of the issue was evidenced in the fact that the bill authorizing the participation of the Bundeswehr (German army) passed the Bundestag (German parliament) by only two votes. When the

Iraq war loomed, Schroeder was in the midst of a tough reelection campaign. Along with his foreign policy differences, he seized on the issue of Iraq as a way of gaining support from those German voters who had become the most anti-American. This was a striking contrast with how pro-American positions had been good politics in Germany for decades.

American-European relations improved during the Bush second term, but only partially. Whereas in 2002 64 percent of Europeans had viewed U.S. leadership as desirable, in 2008 only 36 percent did. Approval of President Bush's handling of international affairs was at 18 percent. Some saw the tensions as having become even more fundamental. As one group of scholars writes in *The End of the West? Crisis and Change in the Atlantic Order,* issues of "the logic and character of the Atlantic political order and its future" run deeper than just who is the American President. Indeed, whether we are *Growing Apart?*—as another book on the subject was titled—is a matter not just of the particulars of the foreign policy agenda but of social forces and other dynamics within European and American political systems and overall societies.[12]

For Europe the debate also has been about the role of the European Union (EU). Efforts by the EU to develop further a "common foreign and security policy" (CFSP) are also a factor. The EU's goal is to establish itself as a stronger and more independent foreign policy player in its own right. The CFSP, however, has been slower to develop than EU economic collaboration. Although most European countries have adopted the euro, the common European currency that began replacing national currencies in 2002, foreign policy is still made primarily in individual national capitals such as London, Paris, and Berlin rather than at EU headquarters in Brussels. "The idea that the European Union should speak with one voice in world affairs is as old as the European integration process itself. But," the EU acknowledges on its own Web site, "the Union has made less progress in forging a common foreign and security policy over the years than in creating a single market and a single currency."[13] The defeat of the new EU constitution in 2005, which was supposed to strengthen collective action in this and other areas, raised even further doubts about the future of CFSP. Even now that the EU constitution has passed, it's unlikely that the EU foreign minister would fully supplant the British, French, and German foreign ministers anytime soon.

## *The Future of NATO*

Time and again during the Cold War and at its end, pundits sounded warnings about the decline and possible death of NATO. But when the Berlin Wall fell, the Warsaw Pact was torn up, and the Soviet Union came asunder, NATO was still standing. Its central goal—to "safeguard the freedom, common heritage and civilization of [its] peoples, founded on the principles of democracy, individual liberty and the rule of law"—had been achieved, without a single shot having been fired in anger. No wonder NATO has been touted as the most successful peacetime alliance in history.

The ensuing question has been whether NATO's very success would lead to its demise. "Alliances are against, and only derivatively for, someone or something," according to an old international relations axiom.[14] With the Soviet enemy gone, did NATO really have a strong enough reason to continue? Given budgetary costs and other factors, should it just be showered with testimonials, given its "gold watch," and sent into retirement? All these questions boil down to two issues about NATO's future: its membership and its mission.

THE EXPANSION OF NATO MEMBERSHIP At the end of the Cold War, NATO faced a problem that was the fruit of its success: its former adversaries had been defeated. Indeed, their major alliance, the Warsaw Pact, had fallen apart; their major empire, the Soviet Union, had crumbled. Confrontation had ended, and cooperation was now possible. The challenge for NATO now was how to build new cooperative relationships with these former adversaries, and with Russia in particular.

The initial transitional strategy, started by the first Bush administration and furthered by the Clinton administration, was to create new institutional mechanisms linked to NATO but not fully part of it. In 1991 all of the former Soviet and Soviet-bloc states were invited to join the North Atlantic Cooperation Council, later renamed the European-Atlantic Partnership Council. This was to be a mechanism for consultation on political and security issues. In 1994 the Partnership for Peace (PFP) was created, also involving most Soviet and Soviet-bloc states and geared toward building cooperation among the members' militaries and defense establishments. The PFP also made possible participation in actual NATO operations; for example, thirteen PFP members sent troops to Bosnia as part of the NATO peacekeeping force there. Although these institutional linkages confer the right to consult with NATO if a state feels its security is threatened, this is not the same as the "Article 5" collective-security guarantee that full NATO members give each other. Article 5 of the NATO treaty defines an attack on one state as an attack on all and pledges members to come to each other's defense.

In 1998, the first three ex–Warsaw Pact countries were brought into NATO: Poland, Hungary, and the Czech Republic (see Table 7.1). The expansion process for the second group of prospective members began in late 2002. This group included additional ex-Soviet-bloc countries (Bulgaria, Romania, and Slovakia), part of the former Yugoslavia (Slovenia), and—for the first time—countries that had been part of the Soviet Union itself (the Baltic states of Estonia, Latvia, and Lithuania). Two more countries, Albania and Croatia, joined in 2009. Others may follow according to the official NATO policy statement of "an open door policy on enlargement. Any European country in a position to further the principles of the North Atlantic Treaty and contribute to the security in the Euro-Atlantic area can become a member of the Alliance, when invited to do so by the existing member countries."[15] Most controversial are Ukraine and Georgia, two former Soviet republics that have had major tensions with Russia, including Moscow's interference in the 2004 Ukrainian election and the 2008 Russia-Georgia war.

**TABLE 7.1 NATO: Its Evolution, Cold War to Post–Cold War**

| Charter Members | Joined during the Cold War | Joined after the Cold War |
|---|---|---|
| Belgium | Greece (1952) | Czech Republic (1999)‡ |
| Canada | Turkey (1952) | Hungary (1999)‡ |
| Denmark | Federal Republic of Germany (1955)† | Poland (1999)‡ |
| France* | Spain (1982) | Bulgaria (2004)‡ |
| Iceland | | Estonia (2004)§ |
| Italy | | Latvia (2004)§ |
| Luxembourg | | Lithuania (2004)§ |
| Netherlands | | Romania (2004)‡ |
| Norway | | Slovakia (2004)‡ |
| Portugal | | Slovenia (2004)¶ |
| United Kingdom | | Albania (2009)‡ |
| United States | | Croatia (2009)¶ |

*Withdrew from NATO military command in 1965 but maintained political membership; it rejoined the NATO military command in 2009.
†As a condition of German reunification in 1990, NATO agreed not to station military forces in the territory of the former German Democratic Republic (East Germany).
‡Former Warsaw Pact members.
§Formerly part of the Soviet Union.
¶Part of the former Yugoslavia.

Three principal arguments are made in favor of ***NATO expansion.*** The first is based on the concept of a ***security community,*** defined as an area "in which strategic rivalries are attenuated and the use of force within the group is highly unlikely."[16] NATO expansion has enlarged the area of Europe in which this sense of security and stability prevails. Once a country is a member of NATO, it gives the assurance that it will not threaten the security of other members, and it gets the assurance that other countries in the security community will help ensure its security.

Second is the reinforcement of democratization. Free elections and the building of other democratic political institutions and practices, including civilian control of the military, are prerequisites to NATO membership. This provides an incentive to choose and then stay on the democratic path. The Czech president Vaclav Havel, who spent years in prison as a dissident during the communist era, took this concept further, stressing the political, cultural, and even psychological benefits for the countries of Eastern Europe once they finally became genuine and full members of the Western community.

The third pro-expansion argument stresses the continued, albeit changed, need for deterrence. NATO doctrine still calls for a deterrence posture to ensure collective security against a potential aggressor. The main concern, mostly left implicit, is a resurgent Russia. It is not so much a fear that the Soviet Union may be reconstituted, although this possibility is not totally dismissed. The more salient concerns about Russia run deeper historically—Russia does have a precommunist history of regional expansionism—and grow out of the uncertainties and instabilities of Russia's own postcommunist transition and the possibility of more aggressively nationalist leaders coming to power.

Critics of NATO expansion stress two chief points. One is that NATO still has not figured out what to do about Russia. The first round of NATO expansion to former Soviet-bloc countries included an agreement for closer NATO-Russia consultation. Russia was to be given a voice in NATO, but not such a strong voice as to be a veto. This agreement was heralded at the time but did not prove very meaningful in actual practice. A similar agreement was reached in 2002 in the prelude to the next round of NATO expansion. It too was vague as to what it meant to have a voice and not a veto, and what it meant to be in a special relationship but not a member of the alliance. The 2008 Russia-Georgia war left both sides in the NATO-expansion debate claiming validation. Russia remains expansionist and aggressive, proponents say, not ready to live in peace with its neighbors. Now more than ever Georgia and Ukraine need to be brought into NATO. NATO's own credibility is even more at stake. No, NATO expansion opponents contend, we've ended up with the self-fulfilling prophecy we warned about. NATO expansion did not strengthen deterrence so much as provoke Russia. The Russians expressed their concerns all along, and now that they have recovered economically and these issues are hitting closer to home, what analysts are seeing is less of a shift than a culmination in what had been building all along as NATO expanded.[17]

Second is the concern that adding new members will dilute the cohesion that has made NATO function so effectively. This is less a criticism of any specific new members than a basic organizational precept: as the number of members goes up, making decisions and carrying out policies becomes that much harder. "If one country after another is admitted," a former U.S. ambassador to NATO argued, "it will no longer be today's functioning and cohesive NATO that the new members will be joining but rather a diluted entity, a sort of league of nations."[18] The intra-alliance tensions brought out during the Kosovo war could be even worse with even more members. A bigger NATO may not be a better NATO if we take seriously the importance of being able to function effectively first and foremost as a military alliance.

NATO'S POST–COLD WAR MISSION During the Cold War, NATO focused on deterring and defending against the threat posed by the Soviet Union and the Warsaw Pact. Its central mission was to meet this threat with the necessary forces, weapons, and doctrine. Post–Cold War NATO doctrine recognized that security threats are less likely to come from "classical territorial aggression" than from "the adverse consequences that may arise from the serious economic, social, and political difficulties, including ethnic rivalries and territorial disputes, which are faced by many countries in Central and Eastern Europe."[19] This meant both that deterrence strategy needed to be reformulated and that peace operations needed to be a new and major part of NATO's mission.

The wars in the former Yugoslavia posed the first test of how well NATO would handle this new mission of peace operations. These wars—first in Croatia and Bosnia, and then in Kosovo—posed a number of difficult issues for NATO, and the results were decidedly mixed. The former Yugoslavia was "out of area" in terms of the North Atlantic Treaty's provisions pertaining to attacks on or within the territory of member countries. On the other hand, the underlying purpose of the alliance was to keep the peace in Europe, and these were the most gruesome and destructive wars in Europe since World War II. They also were a different type of conflict than NATO had been formed to fight. NATO doctrine, training, deployments, battle plans, and equipment were geared to conventional warfare against the Warsaw Pact forces—armies against armies, along demarcated battle lines, relying on technology and classical strategy. In Bosnia and Kosovo, though, the wars were marked by ethnic passion more than by military professionalism, and they were driven by ethnic "cleansing," not classical invasion.

From 1992 until late 1995, while the Bosnia war raged, the United States and western Europe mostly hurled accusations and counteraccusations across the Atlantic—"three years of collective buck-passing," as Joseph Lepgold put it.[20] NATO finally did intervene in Bosnia following the signing of the Dayton accord in December 1995. It did so with a sixty-thousand-troop Implementation Force (IFOR), which was followed about a year later by a somewhat smaller Stabilization Force (SFOR). IFOR and SFOR succeeded in restoring stability to Bosnia, demonstrating that NATO could play an important peacekeeping role. Both operated much more efficiently and conveyed much more of a deterrent threat than had the crazy-quilt UN force that had preceded them. They also were noteworthy in including Russian and other former Soviet-bloc troops.

Yet what was the lesson? That NATO would intervene only late in such conflicts, only after ethnic "cleansings" had run their horrific course? What about initiating earlier peacemaking and peace-enforcing operations, which might have prevented so many lives from being lost, so many rapes from being committed, so many villages from being plundered? The decision to intervene in Kosovo was made more quickly, but still only after much of the ethnic "cleansing" had been inflicted. In 2001, when Macedonia, another part of the former Yugoslavia, began sliding into its own ethnic violence, NATO did act sooner and was able to prevent the conflict from escalating or spreading. But it left NATO with the burden of maintaining three simultaneous peacekeeping missions in the former Yugoslavia.

Terrorism has been posing yet another set of issues about NATO's mission. When the United States was attacked on September 11, 2001, its NATO allies invoked Article 5 of the North Atlantic Treaty and came to its defense with a number of military measures. This was the first time that Article 5 actually has been invoked, and it was by the allies to help the United States rather than the reverse. NATO's action reflected the new reality of terrorism as a shared threat.

Within that general threat perception, though, lie other differences over how best to deal with terrorism. The United States originally chose to conduct the war in Afghanistan with some assistance from European allies in their individual national capacities, but outside of NATO, in order to have greater control over wartime command and strategy than it had during the Kosovo war. It later turned to NATO to take over the International Security Assistance Force (ISAF) and its peacekeeping mission in Afghanistan. This not only was a further instance of NATO's new mission of peacekeeping; it also was the first time that NATO had taken on a major ongoing mission outside the Euro-Atlantic geographic area. In the Iraq war the Bush administration again opted to fight outside NATO. The ad hoc coalition included some NATO members in their individual national capacities. (Britain again was the main partner, along with Poland, the Czech Republic, and some others.) Unlike with Afghanistan, though, there were major policy differences and open and intense confrontations with France and Germany.

A personal anecdote: In February 2003, on the eve of the Iraq war, I was at a major conference in Germany. One evening I was talking with an American military officer stationed with NATO. Although he steered clear of a position on Iraq, his concern was that the bitter intra-NATO conflicts over Iraq not spill over to other areas in the fight against terrorism in which NATO cooperation was working well. Areas such as intelligence sharing, force transformation, and small counterterrorism operations needed to be kept going, as they had their own crucial roles to play in the overall strategy. The overall objective, as reflected in a NATO policy statement, was "a far-reaching transformation of its forces and capabilities to better deter and defend against terrorism[. NATO] is working closely with partner countries and organizations to ensure broad cooperation in the fight against terrorism."[21]

The Afghanistan war has continued to bring out intra-alliance differences. The Bush administration wanted greater commitments from allies. But only a few countries—Britain, France, Canada, the Netherlands—were willing to make substantial troop commitments. Others such as Germany constrained their personnel from being assigned to the riskiest areas. Some of this reluctance reflected genuine differences over strategy and how best to balance the military operations with civil society building, economic assistance, and other components of the overall strategy. Some also reflected differing domestic politics. Polls showed similar views in Europe and America on some dimensions of the mission. For example, 73 percent of Americans and 79 percent of Europeans were in favor of providing security for economic reconstruction projects, 76 percent and 68 percent were in favor of assisting training of Afghan police and military forces, and 70 percent and 76 percent were in favor of antinarcotics measures. But on conducting combat operations, support diverged between 76 percent of Americans and 43 percent of Europeans.[22] Some countries, such as Canada, had made substantial troop commitments. But their own domestic political pressures to cut back have increased to the extent that other NATO countries have been reluctant to share more of the burden. The intra-NATO debate carried over into the Obama administration.

Beyond Afghanistan, proposals have been made for NATO to take on even more of a global role. One such proposal for a "global NATO" was made in a 2006 article by Ivo Daalder, who has since become the Obama administration's ambassador to NATO.[23] Others have proposed a NATO role in a peacekeeping force as part of an Israeli-Palestinian agreement (Chapter 8); others want NATO to have a role in a humanitarian intervention in Darfur (Chapter 9). All told, although some answers about NATO's post–Cold War mission have been worked out, many questions remain.

## *Russia*

The great uncertainty about Russia and its future should not surprise us. Think about it: Russia has not gone through a change just of policy, or of leadership, or of ruling party. The Union of Soviet Socialist Republics, heralded in 1922 by Vladimir Ilyich Lenin as a new and revolutionary empire that would transform the entire world, collapsed and fell apart in 1991. Democracy was proclaimed, capitalism replaced socialism: change swept through every part of Russian society. The first free elections in Russian history were held. A stock market opened in Moscow. Cultural freedom came out of the shadows. Western influences were let in, including even the Rolling Stones, who played a live concert in Moscow in the summer of 1998.

The Russian economy's transition to its form of capitalism has had three principal characteristics. One is a boom-and-bust pattern. The Russian economy shrank by almost 40 percent in the first post-Soviet years and underwent a major financial crisis in 1998. The economy recovered over the ensuing decade, particularly as world oil prices soared and Russian oil exports brought in unprecedented revenues. Then Russia too was hit hard by the 2008 global economic crisis. Export earnings fell nearly 50 percent. The stock market plummeted 80 percent from its peak. What had been $600 billion in foreign-exchange reserves were depleted by about one-third. The World Bank raised concerns that the recent global financial crisis could push another 5.8 million Russians into poverty.

Second, the Russian economy is heavily petro based. Russia's oil reserves are the world's eighth largest, its oil exports the second largest. Natural gas reserves and natural gas exports both are the largest in the world. At the peak price of the 2008 oil boom, Russia was taking in $1.25 billion *a day* in energy export revenue. These windfalls also strengthened prime minister Vladimir Putin's geopolitical hand for an "energypolitik" foreign policy, making Russia much more assertive regionally and globally.

Third is the amassing of huge fortunes by a relatively small number of individuals through varying combinations of entrepreneurship and political connections. At one point Moscow had more billionaires than any other city in the world. Yet about one-quarter of the population, close to 37 million people, still live near the poverty line.

Fundamentally, no matter the particular nature or pace of ups and downs, the central post–Cold War issue for Russia has been, as Stanford University's Gail Lapidus posed it, "defining a new Russian identity and place in the world after the Soviet collapse."[24] Russia "was attempting to come to grips with a profound and traumatic set of losses." It had lost territory, its alliance system, much of its power, and even its superpower status:

> The sudden transformation of a country that had once controlled the fate of millions to a country that perceived itself to have lost control of its own fate created a radical sense of vulnerability that deeply influenced the ongoing Russian struggle to define its identity and place in the post–Cold War international system. How to manage the fundamental asymmetry of power, interests, and priorities had become and would long remain the central challenge of the Russian-American bilateral relationship.[25]

The key question in the U.S.-Russian relationship is, Which of three scenarios will prevail as time goes on: friend, competitor, or adversary? Will relations improve to the point that Russia genuinely could be considered a friend or even an ally? Does U.S.-Russian cooperation have limits based on differences in national interests and other factors that may lead even a noncommunist, non-Soviet Russia to reemerge as a great-power competitor of the United States? Or might foreign policy differences become so great, or might Russian domestic politics take such a turn, that the two end up again as adversaries?

**Russia as Friend** "Ron and Mikhail," "Bill and Boris," "George and Vladimir"—the end of the Cold War brought quite a bit of chumminess between American and Soviet/Russian leaders. There was much mutual praise, lots of amiable photo ops, plenty of pledges to work together. Andrei Kozyrev, Boris Yeltsin's first foreign minister, spoke in 1992 of Russia's becoming "a reliable partner in the community of civilized nations."[26] Warren Christopher, President Clinton's first secretary of state, reciprocated with numerous affirmations of his own about the new Russian-American friendship. The administration of George W. Bush initially was much harsher in its rhetoric and approach, but President Bush left his first summit with Russian president Vladimir Putin speaking of a newfound friend. "I looked the man in the eye," Bush went so far as to say. "I found him to be very straightforward and trustworthy. . . . I was able to get a sense of his soul."[27]

A number of genuine and substantive areas of foreign policy cooperation did emerge in the post–Cold War Russian-American relationship.

**U.S. Foreign Aid to Russia and the Other Ex-Soviet States** American aid to Russia and the other ex-Soviet states exceeded $13 billion during the 1990s. These programs included food aid, medical and health care aid, business development, a first-time Peace Corps presence, funding for the development of the rule of law and other democratization initiatives, military cooperation, and even the construction of housing for former Soviet troops returning from East Germany and elsewhere in Eastern Europe. All this was quite a change from the preceding half-century, when the Soviet threat was the principal rationale for U.S. foreign aid programs to other states. It was somewhat reminiscent of World War II, when as part of the anti-Hitler alliance, Russia was second only to the United Kingdom as a beneficiary of Lend-Lease and other U.S. aid programs.

**Nuclear Arms Control** The first of the post–Cold War U.S.-Soviet nuclear arms-control agreements, known as ***START*** (the Strategic Arms Reduction Treaty), was signed in 1991 by President George H. W. Bush and the Russian president, Mikhail Gorbachev. It cut strategic nuclear weapons from Cold War levels of 13,000 U.S. and 11,000 Soviet warheads to 6,000 on each side. START I was ratified by both the U.S. Senate and the Russian Duma. START II, mandating further cuts of about 50 percent, was signed in 1993 and ratified by the U.S. Senate in 1996 but not by the Russian Duma until 2000. The third major treaty, the Moscow Treaty on Strategic Offensive Reductions, was signed by Presidents George W. Bush and Vladimir Putin in May 2002. It superseded START II with deeper cuts, 1,700 to 2,200 on each side by 2012.

Among the consequences of the breakup of the Soviet Union into numerous independent countries was that where there had been a single nuclear-weapons power, there now were four: Russia, Ukraine, Belarus, and Kazakhstan. As the principal successor state to the Soviet Union, Russia had the principal claim to Soviet nuclear weapons. Deals were struck with Belarus and Kazakhstan to give up the old Soviet nuclear weapons left on their territories. But Ukraine was more reluctant. This was a good example, as detailed in this chapter's "Theory in the World" (p. 358), of how the United States played a key peace-broker role in getting Ukraine also to agree to give up its nuclear weapons to Russia.

The momentum toward further nuclear arms–control negotiations slowed amid other Russian-American tensions during the Bush-Putin years. Each side fingered the other for principal responsibility for the slowdown, Russia blaming such Bush policies as missile defense and Iraq and the United States blaming the Russia-Georgia war and other Putin policies. President Obama and the Russian president, Dmitri Medvedev, reinitiated negotiations. At their July 2009 summit they agreed to reduce strategic warheads to between 1,500 and 1,675 within seven years, a significant cut from the 2,200 set in the prior treaty as a goal to be reached by 2012. Intercontinental missiles and other delivery vehicles (submarines, bombers) were to be cut from the prior target of 1,600 to between 500 and 1,100.

**Cooperative Threat Reduction** Many analysts stress the threat from Russian ***"loose nukes."*** Given Russia's economic instability and broader societal dislocation, these analysts have expressed great concerns about the safety and security of the country's remaining nuclear weapons, of the plutonium and other components from dismantled weapons, and from Russian weapons scientists who might be tempted to sell their expertise on the "WMD market" to rogue states or terrorists. The Nunn-Lugar Cooperative Threat Reduction program was named for its key congressional bipartisan sponsors, Senators Sam Nunn (D-Georgia) and Richard Lugar (R-Indiana). Originally established in 1991, it has provided U.S. funds, expertise, and other assistance on a cooperative basis with the Russian government to reduce these dangers. Its inventory is quite impressive: over 7,000 strategic nuclear warheads deactivated, over 700 intercontinental ballistic missiles (ICBMs) destroyed, over 30 submarines capable of launching ballistic missiles destroyed, upgraded security at 17 nuclear weapons storage sites. To put it into perspective, the Nunn-Lugar program has dismantled more nuclear weaponry than Great Britain, France, and China currently possess combined. From another viewpoint, though, few if any experts believe that the program has sufficed to ensure that terrorists or others don't get their hands on ex-Soviet loose nukes.

**Terrorism** Then president Vladimir Putin was the first foreign leader to phone President Bush with condolences and support following the September 11 terrorist attacks. Russian cooperation was especially important in the initial war in Afghanistan against the Taliban and Al Qaeda. It included Russian aid to the anti-Taliban Northern Alliance, and agreement not to oppose U.S. military bases set up in the former Soviet republics of Uzbekistan, Tajikistan, and Kyrgyzstan. The significance of Russian consent to an American military presence in these former Soviet republics is not to be underestimated, given the more competitive dynamics on other issues involving the Russian "near abroad," discussed below. In part, Russia agreed to the U.S. military presence in anticipation of at least a tacit quid pro quo whereby Washington would not actually oppose Russia's effort to quell the separatist insurgency in Chechnya, a largely Muslim part of the Russian Federation, an effort that the Russian government portrays as its own war on terrorism.

However, cooperation waned amid other tensions. In 2008–2009, Russia pressured Kyrgyzstan not to renew the American base agreement. The Kyrgyz did eventually renew it, although with adroit bargaining that upped the U.S. rent by over 250 percent while also working out a deal with the Russians. At the 2009 Obama-Medvedev summit, Russia also agreed to allow U.S. aircraft to travel through Russian airspace en route to Afghanistan. This was indicative of the underlying shared interest in working against a reradicalized Afghanistan, along with the continuing competition for power and influence.

RUSSIA AS GEOPOLITICAL COMPETITOR One of the axioms of international relations is that major powers often seek to balance against whichever state is the most

## THEORY IN THE WORLD

THEORY IN THE WORLD

### THE RUSSIA-UKRAINE NUCLEAR ARMS DEAL AND AMERICAN PEACE BROKERING

Ukraine had a number of reasons for its reluctance to give up its Soviet-era nuclear weapons to Russia. Ukraine and Russia had a long history of rivalry and hostility. Ukraine had briefly been an independent nation (1917–19) before the Soviets forcibly absorbed it into the USSR. Now independent again, Ukraine was contesting a number of military and security issues with Russia in addition to the nuclear-weapons problem. Moreover, Ukraine was the second largest Soviet successor state, and was bigger and only slightly less populous than Britain or France, Europe's other nuclear powers.

As has been true in other cases, historical and contemporary, American peace-brokering is most successful when three conditions are present: U.S. recognition of its leadership responsibilities, acceptability of a major U.S. role to the parties in conflict, and significant U.S. interests being at stake. This theoretical framework helps explain why and how the Clinton administration succeeded in helping broker the 1994 treaty by which Ukraine overcame its differences with Russia and agreed to give up the nuclear weapons left on its territory following the breakup of the Soviet Union.

#### U.S. Interests

Fear of a "Yugoslavia with nukes"—of a country's breaking up and potentially becoming embroiled in ethnic and other conflicts, only this time with nuclear weapons present—was high on everyone's list. Even without that, the START I and II arms-control treaties were at risk of being undermined. So, too, possibly was the global nonproliferation treaty (NPT), for if ex-Soviet republics other than Russia retained nuclear weapons, the case against other countries elsewhere doing so would be weakened.

#### Leadership and Acceptability to the Parties

Only the United States had the prestige and leverage to act as broker on such a major issue between such major countries. Although not willing to grant the full security guarantees Ukraine wanted, the Clinton administration did provide some security assurances and took a number of steps to develop closer U.S.–Ukrainian bilateral relations, including substantial sums of foreign aid and special initiatives to promote American trade with and investment in Ukraine. Clinton also helped get Russia to pledge to respect Ukraine's sovereignty and security.

In January 1994, after much negotiation, the trilateral agreement among the United States, Russia, and Ukraine was signed by Presidents Clinton, Yeltsin, and Kravchuk. And on June 1, 1996, the last nuclear weapon was removed from Ukraine. As Clinton said that day, "In 1991 there were more than 4,000 strategic and tactical nuclear warheads in Ukraine. Today there are none . . . [a] historic contribution in reducing the nuclear threat."* U.S. peace-brokering had worked well.

*James E. Goodby, "Preventive Diplomacy for Nuclear Nonproliferation in the Former Soviet Union," in *Opportunities Missed, Opportunities Seized: Preventive Diplomacy in the Post–Cold War World*, Bruce W. Jentleson, ed. (Lanham, Md.: Rowman and Littlefield, 1999).

powerful in the international system. Even as Russia was being weighed down with economic and other problems, many analysts felt that its sheer size, resource endowments (especially oil and natural gas), geography, and history ensured that it again would be a great power. Even when the Russian-American friendship was at its peak in the early 1990s, it had a degree of geopolitical competition and even conflict. This was evident on the U.S. side in the 1992 Pentagon "primacy" document cited earlier. On the Russian side, it comes through in the 2000 National Security Concept, which delineated two potential future directions. One direction was the cooperative one of "the strengthened economic and political positions of a significant number of states and their integrative associations and in improved mechanisms for multilateral management of international processes." The other direction was the more competitive one of "attempting to create an international relations structure based on domination by developed Western countries in the international community, under U.S. leadership and designed for unilateral solutions." Such "attempts to ignore Russia's interests . . . are capable of undermining international security, stability, and the positive changes achieved in international relations."[28]

Whereas the Clinton administration was split between the friend and competitor approaches, the Bush administration brought the latter approach to office. "In some ways," Secretary of State Colin Powell stated, "the approach to Russia shouldn't be terribly different than the very realistic approach we had to the old Soviet Union in the late '80s. We told them what bothered us. We told them where we could engage on things. We tried to convince them of the power of our values and our system. They argued back."[29] Others in the administration were even more caustic. Secretary of Defense Donald Rumsfeld accused Russia of being "an active proliferator . . . helping Iran and others develop nuclear and other weapons of mass destruction." Paul Wolfowitz, the deputy secretary of defense (and a lead author of the 1992 primacy strategy), was even blunter, saying that the Russians "seem to be willing to sell anything to anyone for money." The Russian response to such statements was to accuse the Bush administration of reverting to "the spirit of the Cold War."[30]

"It's time to press the reset button," Vice President Joe Biden suggested in a speech early in the Obama administration, "and to revisit the many areas where we can and should be working together with Russia." Biden acknowledged that "we will not agree with Russia on everything."[31] Given history, geography, and other factors, the two countries still would have different interests. The competition could be kept limited, but it still would be there, on a number of issues, as it has been thus far.

**The 1990s Balkan Wars** As fellow Slavs and for their own geopolitical reasons, Russia and Serbia historically have had close relations. Serbia thus had pretty solid Russian support in its aggressive struggle for dominance as Yugoslavia was breaking up. During the war in Bosnia and Herzegovina (1992–95), the United States sided with the Bosnian Muslims, and Russia sided with the Orthodox Serbs. These differences were bridged following the 1995 Dayton accord, which ended the Bosnian war. The Russian military was even brought into the NATO-led peacekeeping effort that followed.

The 1999 Kosovo war, though, was a much greater source of tension. Again, Russian sympathies and political allegiances were with the Serbs; the United States and NATO sided with the Muslim Kosovars. This time, the United States and NATO actually intervened militarily in the conflict, not just after the fact as a peacekeeping force. Although U.S.–NATO intervened in reaction to Serbian aggression, from the Russian perspective the key issues were that the military action was taken against a sovereign state (whereas Bosnia was an independent state, Kosovo was a province of Serbia) and without UN Security Council authorization. This "fed into an already heightened sense of Russia's own vulnerability and fueled highly implausible anxieties about Kosovo as a precedent for possible Western intervention in Russia's internal affairs, particularly in Chechnya."[32] When the war reached the point when NATO was about to move from air strikes to ground troops, Russia assisted with the diplomacy, helping convince the Serbian leader Slobodan Milosevic to concede and withdraw. Even then, though, Russia's peacekeeping cooperation was much less than in Bosnia. U.S.–Russian tensions over the Balkans persisted, as did broader multilateral issues of sovereignty and intervention. When in 2008 Kosovo declared its independence, the United States and most of western Europe recognized the new nation, but Russia did not.

**Chechnya** Russia's wars and antiterrorism against Chechnya have posed a Power-Principles tension between, on the one hand, American strategic interests in maintaining good relations with Russia, and, on the other, the atrocities and other blatant human rights violations that Russian troops have committed in Chechnya. In 1996, during the first Chechen war, Bill Clinton drew stinging criticism from human rights advocates and others for drawing an analogy to the U.S. Civil War, with Russian president Boris Yeltsin as Russia's Abraham Lincoln seeking to preserve the Union. The Clinton administration was a bit more critical of the Russians in the Chechnya war that began in 1999. So too was the Bush administration, initially. But after September 11, the Russians cast Chechnya as their own war on terrorism. The Russian national security adviser, Sergei Ivanov, went so far as to declare that the Russian war in Chechnya was in the West's interest, with Russia serving as "a front-line warrior fighting international terrorism . . . saving the civilized world [from] the terrorist plague in the same way as it used to save Europe from the Tatar-Mongol invasions in the twelfth century."[33] The Chechens, too, definitely have been guilty of atrocities. In the 2002 siege of a theater in Moscow, insurgents took more than eight hundred people hostage. In the 2004 seizure of a schoolhouse in the town of Beslan, hundreds of children and adults died. But many analysts also blame Putin for botched rescue attempts that increased the casualties in both incidents, for brutal policies in Chechnya that have fed support for the insurgents and the terrorists, and for making Chechnya a magnet and a rallying cry for Al Qaeda and other global terrorist groups. This view sees American interests and not just American principles as threatened by Russia's Chechnya policies. The Chechnya issue has continued, albeit with less visibility and prominence. Russian troops have remained in Chechnya. Moscow has continued to choose Chechnyan presidents. Human rights groups have continued to report killings and repression. Kidnappings were up 80 percent in the first half of 2009. In July 2009, Natalia Estemirova, a leading human rights activist and critic of the Russian role in Chechnya, was murdered.

**The Russian Near Abroad** The "near abroad" is the term Russia uses to refer to the other former Soviet republics. To Russia this is its traditional sphere of influence, an area in which it claims a right to exert political pressure and even to intervene militarily to protect its interests, as it already has done in Georgia, Estonia, Moldova, Tajikistan, Armenia, and Azerbaijan. Putin drew his own precedent from the Bush administration's doctrine of preemption for asserting Russia's right to intervene in other states if it determines that terrorism or some other serious threat exists. In the case of Ukraine, Russia intervened not militarily but politically and covertly in an effort to rig the 2004 presidential election in favor of the pro-Russian but highly unpopular presidential candidate Viktor Yanukovich over the reformist Viktor Yushchenko. This attempt backfired and sparked the "orange revolution" of mass protests by Ukrainians demanding a fair election, which Yushchenko won. Although vast credit goes to the brave Ukrainian people, American and European NGOs also played a helpful role in providing funds and support for the democratization movement.

**NATO Expansion** As noted before, although proponents of expanding NATO to include former Soviet allies and then former Soviet republics claimed that this would strengthen Peace, Russia saw it as strengthening American Power. As Richard K. Betts writes, "One need not be an apologist for the regime in Moscow or its behavior, or sympathetic to Russia's national interests, to empathize with its resentments of this revolutionary overturning of the balance of power. . . . Washington, and with its prodding other NATO governments, succumbed to victory and kept kicking Russia while it was down."[34] NATO and Russia did reach their own agreements for consultation that defused tensions but did not eliminate them, particularly as NATO began considering major former Soviet republics such as Ukraine and Georgia for membership. Putin went so far as to say that admitting the Ukraine into the alliance would put Russia's security at risk and that "one can't theoretically exclude the possibility that Russia will have to point its warheads at Ukrainian territory."[35] Vice President Dick Cheney countered, "At times it appears Russian policy is based upon the desire to impose its will on countries it once dominated, . . . [T]he enlargment of NATO will continue as and where the Allies decide."[36]

**Russia-Georgia 2008 War** In Georgia, things went past a war of words to outright war. Georgia had been one of the closest U.S. allies among the former Soviet republics. It received U.S. military aid. It sent troops to Iraq. In 2004 it elected a charismatic and strongly pro-U.S. and anti-Russia president, Mikhail Saakashvili. In 2005 George W. Bush, the first U.S. leader to visit Georgia, proclaimed it a "beacon of liberty" and pledged continued U.S. support.[37] Since independence, though, Georgia had experienced tensions and violence with South Ossetia and Abkhazia, two regions with ethnic and cultural differences whose peoples had been pushing first for greater autonomy and then for independence. Both were getting support from Russia, especially after Saakashvili was elected.

When war did break out in August 2008, each side has its own version of how much of the responsibility lay with Russian aggression and how much with Georgian provocation. Russian actions, Secretary of State Condoleezza Rice stated, were unprovoked and aggressive: "[W]e have to deny Russian strategic objectives, which were clearly to undermine Georgia's democracy, to use its military capability to damage, and in some cases, destroy Georgian infrastructure, and to try and weaken the Georgian state."[38] Russia's foreign minister, Sergei Lavrov, argued that Russia was responding to atrocities committed by Georgian troops against its citizens and peacekeepers in the region, saying, "[T]he Georgian leadership gave an order which led to an act of genocide, which resulted in war crimes, ethnic cleansing. And this, of course, cannot go unanswered."[39]

The fighting lasted about two weeks. A ceasefire was worked out, requiring an end to military action, a pull back to prewar positions, and access for humanitarian and monitoring missions from the United Nations and the Organization for Security and Cooperation in Europe (OSCE). The ceasefire, though, was a tenuous one. Russia did not comply with the troop withdrawal provisions. It used its UN Security Council veto to blow renewal of the UN observer mission. It also pressed for ending the OSCE mission. The claims to independence by Abkhazia and South Ossetia were recognized only by Russia and a few other countries such as Hugo Chávez's Venezuela. Meanwhile, NATO deferred the issue of Georgian and Ukrainian membership rather than resolving it, keeping their candidacies on the agenda but not taking significant steps toward acting on them.

**The Middle East and the Persian Gulf** During the Cold War, U.S.-Soviet rivalry was deep and recurring in these regions. In this context, the Russian-American cooperation that was achieved in the early 1990s was quite significant. During the 1990–91 Persian Gulf War, although Russia did not join the U.S.-led military coalition, it did give unprecedented diplomatic cooperation to the war effort. Russia and the United States cochaired the Middle East multilateral peace negotiations of the 1990s, involving Israel and most Arab countries, on issues ranging from arms control and regional security to regional economic cooperation, water, and the environment. This cooperation continued through the "Quartet" of the United States, Russia, the European Union, and the United Nations, which sought to get the Israeli-Palestinian peace process back on track after the renewed violence of 2000–2002 through a peace plan called the "road map."

Iraq, though, was a very divisive issue. Throughout the 1990s, Russia had been a consistent opponent within the UN Security Council of U.S. efforts to tighten economic sanctions and get UN weapons inspectors back into Iraq. In 2002–2003, when the Bush administration moved toward war, Russia joined France in threatening to use its UN Security Council veto to try to block American military action. Putin labeled the war "some new form of colonialism."[40] Russian motivations were in part economic: the $7 billion debt Saddam owed Russia, plus the stakes the rising Russian oil industry had in potential investment opportunities in Iraq. They also were geopolitical, in two respects. One was in the Middle East–Persian Gulf as this crucial region entered yet another period of historic transformation. The other was in the broader global context. "The future international security architecture must be based on a multipolar world," Putin stressed during the Iraq debate. "I am absolutely confident that the world will be predictable and stable only if it is multipolar."[41]

The Iran issue has been a mix of cooperation and competition. Russia's official position has been opposition to Iranian nuclear proliferation: "We are categorically opposed to the enlargement of the club of nuclear states," Putin stated.[42] Russia supported the imposition of three sets of economic sanctions by the UN Security Council in 2006–08, but less stringent ones than those originally proposed by the United States. It continued nonsanctioned trade with Iran, including some arms sales.

The impact of any further sanctions has continued to depend heavily on Russian support. Also as part of the "P5 + 1" negotiations with Iran (all five permanent members of the UN Security Council plus Germany), and through some specific proposals seeking to work out how to ensure Iran's rights to peaceful nuclear energy while ending the proliferation threat, Russia has had a key role in the overall diplomacy.

Russia as Adversary In a third possible scenario, Russia could become an adversary. The Columbia University scholar Robert Legvold has raised concern about an "alienated and combative Russia. . . . It would take only a mishandling of the mounting issues in contention between the United States and Russia to turn Russia into the odd man out among great powers, a spoiler in the sphere of great power cooperation, and a state with a grudge looking for ways to inflict damage on U.S. interests."[43]

Russia could become an adversary in one of two ways. One would be through the rise of a nationalist leader who might go beyond the normal great-power competition, seeking to rebuild an empire and regain global influence through an aggressive and militaristic foreign policy. Expansionism is rooted deep in Russian history, some historians argue; it did not just start with Lenin and the communists. Moreover, the instabilities of Russian politics raise concerns that, as with Hitler in Weimar Germany during the 1930s, an aggressively nationalist leader could rise to power by promising to restore the motherland's greatness. The extremist Vladimir Zhirinovsky, with promises to restore the old Russian empire (including taking back Alaska!), caused a scare with the gains he and his party made in the December 1993 Duma elections. The communist Gennadi Zyuganov raised new fears with the political support he received during the 1996 presidential campaign. Neither prevailed, but that hasn't alleviated the concern that they or others like them may come to power, whether through elections or through nondemocratic means such as a military coup.

The other scenario involves Russia's becoming a major threat out of weakness rather than out of strength—for example, if Russia is less and less able to govern itself effectively. As Legvold also observed, "Russia alone among the great powers ends [the twentieth] century with unanswered questions about its ability to avoid a basic breakdown of its domestic order and maybe even its demise as a state."[44] This specter of societal disorder has many aspects, perhaps most significantly (from a U.S. perspective) the "loose nukes" issue raised earlier: an accidental launching after a false alarm that is not checked out properly amid the breakdown of discipline or of equipment; an intentional but unauthorized launching by disgruntled officers; a terrorist group's stealing or buying a nuclear weapon. Such scenarios have been depicted in Hollywood movies and Tom Clancy novels, but any one of them could become all too real.

RUSSIAN DEMOCRATIZATION What Russia has achieved in its transition from almost a century of authoritarian communism to democracy should not be underestimated. Very few people anywhere predicted that the change would have been so peaceful. A bicameral representative legislature was put in place, and the Duma (the lower house of the legislature) in particular was given a major role in governing. Russia's new constitution has held up despite a number of crises. Free elections have been held at the local, provincial, and national level, including the election in 2000 of Vladimir Putin as the new president succeeding Boris Yeltsin—the first democratic succession in Russian history.

Still, Russia's road has been anything but straight and smooth. It has faced the challenge of moving from the initiation of democracy toward its consolidation and institutionalization.

An early and graphic example of this challenge occurred in October 1993. Boris Yeltsin, who led the anti-Soviet revolution and became the first president of Russia, was pushing hard for political and economic reform. His main opposition came from the Duma, where the communists and other hard-line and antireform political parties had sufficient strength to block many of these reforms. Amid political deadlock Yeltsin resorted to a military attack on the parliament building. The image of the man who in August 1991 defiantly stood on a Soviet army tank, personifying the democratic revolution, now commanding Russian army tanks in an attack on the national legislature, captured the dilemmas of democratization. This posed a difficult policy choice for the Clinton administration: Although Clinton strongly supported Yeltsin, a military attack on an elected legislature was not exactly an exemplary practice of democracy.

Nor did the political tensions subside. The communists and other hard-liners kept posing challenges. They gained additional seats in the Duma in the December 1993 elections, and in 1995 won the largest block of seats of any political party. In the 1996 presidential elections Yeltsin was reelected, but the communist candidate Zyuganov made a strong showing.

Yeltsin also faced growing discontent arising from the deepening economic crisis. The transition from the Soviet command economy to market-based capitalism initially proved to be a "great leap backward."[45] The Russian GDP fell below those of Mexico, Brazil, and Indonesia. The standard of living for the average Russian was lower in 2000 than it had been in 1990, with 40 percent of the population living below the poverty line. Government employees, Russian soldiers, and others went months without receiving paychecks. Social services were cut back dramatically in the name of fiscal responsibility. Corruption was rampant, with "robber-baron capitalism" creating a new economic elite of billionaires. In 1998 the Russian government defaulted on its debt, setting off a major financial crisis. The ruble (Russian unit of currency) collapsed, and investment plummeted.

Yeltsin's own behavior added to the problems. He always had been mercurial, but now he became even more unpredictable and unstable. He resorted to means of questionable constitutionality, did not govern very effectively, and periodically lapsed from the scene for health problems (some related to his alcoholism). On December 31, 1999, Yeltsin announced his resignation as president and appointed Putin as his successor. At first this appointment was provisional, but in March 2000 Putin was elected with slightly over 50 percent of the vote. (The communist Zyuganov again was the leading challenger, with 29 percent.)

Putin mitigated some of the drift of Yeltsin's last years by strengthening the state in ways that, as reported in the *New York Times*, "managed to produce a measure of order and even modest prosperity that his embattled predecessor [Yeltsin] could only dream of."[46] Yet the question, as the *Times* went on to say, "is where a strong state ends and a strongman begins." Putin himself is a former agent of the KGB (the Soviet spy agency). As president he strengthened the KGB's successor agencies, reversing the breakup into separate departments that Yeltsin began. He gave their leaders more power within the Kremlin and a mandate for stepping up internal security measures. "I see only one aim in reuniting all the security services into one large monster," stated the noted dissident Sergei Kovalev, "the creation of a more authoritarian state."[47] Newspapers and television stations were shut down for criticizing the Putin government. Their owners were arrested and forced into exile. In 2000, sixteen journalists were killed and seventy-three attacked, many of them badly beaten. The Committee to Protect Journalists, a major free-press NGO, named Putin to its list of the "ten worst enemies of the press" in 2001.[48] In 2003 the government shut down Russia's last independent national television network, replacing it with a state-run sports channel.

Putin won reelection in 2004 with 71 percent of the vote. Part of his appeal was having gotten the economy going again, with a 6.5 percent annual economic growth rate. Still, the election observer group from the Organization for Security and Cooperation in Europe (OSCE) gave the election a mixed assessment as not fixed but also not fully fair. The OSCE observers cited heavily biased media coverage and suspiciously high voter turnout. One of the issues was the arrest of the oil billionaire Mikhail Khodorkovsky on trumped-up charges. Some issues had been raised as to whether Khodorkovsky made his fortune fully legally, but Putin's main concern was that Khodorkovsky was shifting to politics and might mount a serious political challenge.

Legislative elections were held in 2007, but their legitimacy was questioned on a number of counts including that, according to the Council of Europe, "the media showed strong bias in favour of President Putin and the ruling United Russia party. The new election code makes it extremely difficult for new and smaller parties to develop and compete effectively. There were widespread reports of harassment of opposition parties."[49]

In this and other ways, Putin did much to personalize power around himself and his small circle, prompting questions about whether he would abide by the two-term limit in the Russian constitution and not run again in 2008. He did abide by the two-term limit, at least technically. His hand-picked candidate, Dmitri Medvedev, was elected president while Putin became prime minister. All told, as a Council on Foreign Relations study concludes, "The political balance sheet of the past five years is extremely negative. The practices and institutions that have developed over this period have become far less open, [less] pluralistic, [less] subject to the rule of law, and vulnerable to the criticism and counterbalancing of a vigorous opposition or independent media."[50]

Thus, although we should not dismiss the democratization that Russia has achieved, questions remain about its sustainability. Elections have been held, but the overall pattern has been "electoralism with authoritarian institutions and values; democratic consolidation remains a distant goal."[51] Although this description may sound abstract, assassinations, including those of leading human rights activists and prominent journalists, make it all too concrete. Broader questions also remain as to whether, if political and economic conditions do not get better, the Russian people may turn to a "strongman" leader, whether a military man, an ultranationalist, or some other antidemocrat.

## *Organization for Security and Cooperation in Europe (OSCE)*

The Conference on Security and Cooperation in Europe (CSCE) was established in 1975 during détente as the only European institution with full East-West regional membership. With thirty-five members drawn from NATO, the Warsaw Pact, and the neutral states of Europe, the conference made its principal impact through the Helsinki Final Act, whose most important sections established norms and principles for human rights within and peaceful conflict resolution among member countries. For the most part the CSCE was just that—a conference that met from time to time as a forum for consultation and discussion. But when the East European revolutions came in 1989, it became clear in retrospect how important the CSCE had been in providing a political platform and moral support for the champions of democratic change, such as Solidarity in Poland and Charter 77 in Czechoslovakia, that brought communism down.

In the post–Cold War era, the CSCE expanded its membership to fifty-six states, enhanced its role, and changed its name. The name change, made in 1994 to the ***Organization for Security and Cooperation in Europe (OSCE),*** was intended to imply greater institutionalization. The rationale for the larger role lay in increased recognition of the link between regional security and the peaceful resolution of ethnic and other internal conflicts. On this basis the OSCE has taken on a greater role in preventive diplomacy and other types of political and diplomatic conflict management and in conflict resolution. It does so through structures such as its Office for Democratic Institutions and Human Rights, which monitors elections, provides assistance in the drafting of constitutions and other laws, and promotes the development of civil society; the High Commissioner on National Minorities, which seeks to protect the rights of ethnic minorities through human rights monitors and other measures; and third-party mediators to help resolve conflicts.

The OSCE's record has been a mixed one. One major study concludes that it has the most success "in relatively low-level situations."[52] These tend to be cases in which tensions have not yet crossed the Rubicon of widespread violence: Estonia and Latvia in the early 1990s, over the withdrawal of Russian troops along with human rights protections for Russian ethnic minorities; and Macedonia, like Bosnia a former Yugoslav republic with deep ethnic splits but which has managed to limit ethnic violence. But in cases such as Bosnia, Croatia, Kosovo, and Nagorno-Karabakh (an enclave with a large Armenian population that is geographically separate from but ruled by Azerbaijan), the conflicts ran too deep and had degenerated too much for the limited tools of the OSCE.

## Asia

One major U.S. task force argued for more of an "Asia-centric grand strategy:" "The shifting distribution of power in Asia is one of the largest, if not the largest, geopolitical events confronting the United States in the next two decades. Although this power shift has many components it is largely defined by the rise of China." The authors go even further, contending that "the rise of China may be the most complex of all the challenges posed to the United States since it became a player in great power politics"—that is, a larger challenge than both World War II and the Cold War.[53] Although that may be a touch hyperbolic, U.S. policy toward China in particular and Asia in general does present a host of new and complex issues.

### *China*

China's emergence as a global power is measured by various indicators:

*Economic:* By 2003 the People's Republic of China (PRC) had grown to be the world's third largest economy, by 2005 the world's third largest trading country, and also that year the number one destination of foreign direct investment. Its 9 percent average annual economic growth rate, maintained over many years, was astounding. Its economic relations spanned the world. Trade with Latin America was growing rapidly; for example, China had become Brazil's second largest trading partner. Trade with Africa was up over 500 percent. China struck numerous oil and natural-gas deals in the Middle East, seeking to lock up the energy supplies it needed to fuel its economic growth.

*Diplomatic:* China has been active on many diplomatic fronts. It improved relations with Russia, after decades of tensions going back to the Sino-Soviet split of the 1950s. It also improved relations with India, with which it had fought a war in the 1960s. It forged a more positive identity within the East Asia region through what one American Sinologist (China expert) called "remarkably adept and nuanced diplomacy, earning praise around the region."[54] Relations with Europe, as characterized by China's own foreign ministry, "never have been more dynamic and more productive."[55] China also became more of a geopolitical player in the Middle East, especially in pursuit of its oil interests. In Africa and Latin America, enhanced diplomatic relations accompanied the growth in economic relations.

*Military:* China's military power and reach are growing. Its spending on the military increased to become the third largest in the world, behind only the United States and Russia. This included modernization of its forces and more advanced technology. China both strengthened its regional military presence and created for the first time a "blue-water navy" capacity, giving it more of a global military presence.

*Size:* At 1.3 billion people, China remains the world's most populous country. With 3.7 million square miles, it is the fourth largest in territory.

That China is rising is a fact. The question is, What does it mean for U.S. foreign policy? Should the emphasis be on China as assertive geopolitical challenger, cooperation with which has significant limits and which must be contained? Or is the optimal strategy to engage China in a web of relations and institutions, seeking to ensure that its greater global and regional emergence will be along more cooperative lines? Not only are these questions complex as policy matters, but relations with China long have engendered contentious domestic politics. The "China lobbies" are the focus of our foreign policy politics case study later in this chapter.

The debate initially was defined as posing two principal options for U.S. policy, generally defined as containment and engagement. *Containment* is a variation, albeit milder and more limited, of the Cold War strategy toward the Soviet Union. The strategy that follows from this analysis is short of confrontational but is firm, cautious, and attentive to threats and relative power—that is, geared to containment. It rests on the same logic as George Kennan's original 1947 formulation of containment of the Soviet Union (see Chapter 4): that the internal changes needed to make China both less of a threat and more of a democracy are more likely to occur if the country's external ambitions are contained and the system is thus forced to fall on its own contradictions. Summits are acceptable, as they were for Henry Kissinger with the Soviets, but the U.S. posture should be kept strong. China may not have an inherently expansionist ideology, as did the Soviet Union, but it does have its own strong nationalism and historical sense of itself as the "middle kingdom" at the figurative center of the world. It also has been expanding its influence globally. It initiated the ***Shanghai Cooperation Organization (SCO)*** as a quasi alliance with Russia and a number of Central Asian countries to balance against American power. It has been expanding trade and other relations in Africa as well as Latin America. Its profile is rising in the Middle East. We know for sure it is rising; whether it will be a peaceful rise is less clear.

Those who support *engagement* take a different view of China, although not the polar opposite view. They are wary about Chinese regional interests but assess them as less threatening. China wants the role in the Asia-Pacific region to which, because of its size and history, it feels entitled. This does create tensions, and the United States must stand by its allies and its interests, but these issues can be worked out through diplomacy and negotiations. Besides, the Chinese military doesn't come close to matching that of the United States, even with its recent advances. Henry Kissinger warns that the United States "must not mesmerize itself with the Chinese military build-up. . . . Even at its highest estimate, the Chinese military budget is less than 20 percent of America's."[56] Taiwan is acknowledged to be a more contentious issue, although policy makers are cautioned to be careful that the Taiwanese don't exploit U.S. support as a provocation. The emphasis in engagement is on integration and diplomacy. China needs to be brought into more multilateral organizations, as it was with the World Trade Organization. This integration will provide structured, peaceful mechanisms for dealing with China's own concerns, and will also encourage China to adopt international norms and to abide by international rules. On a bilateral basis, the United States should continue with periodic summits in diplomacy, trade, and other areas of engagement. Human rights issues and democratization are not to be ignored, and other approaches should be pursued, but options besides economic sanctions are preferred.

Whereas the Clinton administration leaned more toward engagement, initially the second Bush administration tilted more toward containment. From the outset, it drew the distinction between the Clinton view of the relationship as a "strategic partnership" and its own view of "strategic competition." This changed outlook was revealed in Secretary of State Colin Powell's first statement on China: "Our challenge with China is to do what we can that is constructive, that is helpful and that is in our interest. . . . A *strategic partner* China is not, but neither is China our inevitable and implacable foe. China is a *competitor,* a potential regional rival but also a trading partner willing to cooperate in areas where our strategic interests overlap. . . . China is all of these things, but China is not an enemy, and our challenge is to keep it that way."[57] During the second Bush term, "responsible stakeholder" became more of a core concept. On the one hand this idea recognized China's increased power and position as a stakeholder in most major global issues; on the other, it was a push for China to be what the United States considered more responsible in playing that role.

The Obama China policy began with more elements of continuity with prior Bush policies than on many other issues. In his Senate confirmation hearing, Assistant Secretary of State for East Asian and Pacific Affairs Kurt M. Campbell spoke of "the Administration's objective to expand the cooperative aspects of the bilateral relationship in a way that parallels the complex and comprehensive nature of our engagement with China while further facilitating China's integration into the international system."[58] Among the issues that continue to be key parts of U.S.-China relations are:

TAIWAN From 1949, when the Chinese communist revolution triumphed, until 1971 and the Nixon-Kissinger opening to the People's Republic of China (PRC), the United States was allied to the government of Jiang Jeishi (Chiang Kai-shek) on the island of Taiwan. As part of the détente, Nixon and Kissinger established the ***"one China" policy,*** by which American policy supported the peaceful reunification of China. The reunification part of the policy meant that the United States ended its diplomatic recognition of Taiwan as an independent state; the peaceful part, that it maintained its commitment to defend Taiwan if the PRC attacked. With only a few variations this has been the policy of every president, Democratic and Republican, since Nixon. Yet it has been a difficult balance to strike, with recurring crises along the way. One of these crises came in 1995–96 when China targeted missile tests close to Taiwan as a show of force. The Clinton administration responded by deploying U.S. naval forces to deter possible Chinese aggression.[59] Another came in 2001 over the issue of arms sales to Taiwan. According to agreements going back to the 1970s and 1980s for the normalization of U.S.-China relations, the United States would continue to sell Taiwan defensive weapons but not offensive ones. Often, the line between what is defensive (and therefore stabilizing) and what is offensive (and thus risks destabilization) is not inherently clear in the nature of a weapons system. Moreover, not only the particulars of the weapons system but perceptions of intent and message affect assessments of its potential use. In this instance the Bush administration sought to strike a balance by selling some weapons to Taiwan, but not those most objectionable to China. The arms sale issue came up again late in the Bush presidency, and likely will in the Obama presidency as well.

Concern is increasing that although this balancing act has worked for many years, it may be becoming more tenuous. Pro-independence sentiment on Taiwan has grown and could lead to stronger pushes toward independence, with risks of provoking PRC retaliation. For its part, even the younger generation in the PRC, which did not live through the 1930–40s civil war, is strikingly nationalistic on reunification. Taiwan-PRC economic ties have increased, exerting some influence for a cooperative resolution. But whether over another arms sales package to Taiwan or another crisis like that of 1995–96, the Taiwan issue is likely to continue to pose problems for U.S.-China relations. U.S. domestic politics also play in, as we discuss in the foreign policy politics case study later in this chapter.

THE CHINESE MILITARY China has been increasing its military spending, modernizing its forces, and developing new capabilities. The debate has been over how much and what this means for U.S. interests.

The military budget published by the Chinese government in 2009 equaled $70.3 billion. A Pentagon analysis put the figure much higher, between $105 and $150 billion. Other studies, such as those by the RAND Corporation and the Swedish think tank SIPRI, put the figure higher than the official Chinese one but lower than the Pentagon estimate. Whatever the figure, it has been increasing in recent years and makes China the second or third largest military spender, though it still lags well behind the U.S. defense budget of over $530 billion.

China defends its increased military spending as catching up for past weaknesses and as necessary for its own legitimate national defense. It vows that it will "unswervingly" pursue a foreign policy centered on ensuring "peace" and a "national defense policy solely aimed at protecting its territory and people," and that it will never seek hegemony or engage in military expansion now or in the future.[60] The U.S.-China Economic and Security Commission, a bipartisan body albeit with a strong conservative containment leaning, stressed concern that China's "development of impressive but disturbing capabilities for military use of space and cyber warfare, and its demonstrated employment of these capabilities, suggest China is intent on expanding its sphere of control." It urged the United States to "watch these trends closely and act to protect its interests where they are threatened.[61] The Pentagon also issued its own annual report, warning that "China's leaders have yet to explain in detail the purposes and objectives of the PLA's [People's Liberation Army's] modernizing military capabilities. . . . China continues to promulgate incomplete defense expenditure figures, and engage in actions that appear inconsistent with its declaratory policies."[62] This debate also applies to strategic weaponry and whether China's increase in its nuclear weapons is a mounting threat to be checked by missile defense and other measures or is still sufficiently inferior to U.S. capacity as to leave deterrence intact.

"Hedging" is one much-discussed U.S. strategy. On the one hand, hedging has appeal as a cautious strategy amid the uncertainties of Chinese military capabilities and geopolitical intentions. On the other hand, if perceived by the other side as threatening in its own right, it may precipitate the very trends it was intended to check.

China's increasing military exchanges and cooperation raise similar ambivalence and uncertainty. It has established military ties with over 150 countries and has military attaché offices in 109 countries. In 2007–2008, senior PLA delegations visited more than forty countries, and defense ministers and chiefs of general staff from more than sixty countries visited China. China has held over twenty joint military exercises or joint training exercises. No doubt some greater influence comes with these activities and relationships. But they also have some security-enhancing aspects of shared regional and international benefit. For example, the Chinese and Indian armies have conducted joint counterterrorism exercises; the Chinese and Japanese navies have exchanged port calls.

Direct relations between the Chinese and American militaries have had their ups and downs. In April 2001 an American intelligence-gathering plane flying in international airspace off the coast of China collided with a Chinese air force jet in an accident that most analysts attributed to recklessness on the part of the Chinese pilot. The American plane made an emergency landing on a Chinese island. The crew members were held for ten days until negotiations secured their release. Other incidents have occurred at sea. Such incidents reflect the presence of tensions between the two nations. The capacity to manage them has positive implications as does the initiation of direct military-to-military cooperation, including the first exchange of naval commanding officers and some joint naval exercises.

EAST ASIAN–PACIFIC REGIONAL SECURITY During the Cold War, security in the East Asian–Pacific region was based on the U.S. military presence, which protected Japan, the Philippines, South Korea, and other states from the Russian and Chinese communist threats. The end of the Cold War meant the end of these threats. But China's increasing economic and military strength has raised additional issues for the regional balance of power. China's regional diplomacy has helped provide some reassurance and shared interests with its neighbors. But concerns and sources of tension persist, particularly in China-Japan relations. For China the historical legacies of Japan's invasion during the 1930s and World War II remain vibrant, especially when memories are fomented intentionally by the Chinese government, as has happened in recent years. Japan has both security and economic concerns about China's growing power, as well as its own unresolved political-cultural issues of how to deal with its imperial past. In this relationship and others, the United States is challenged to adjust its regional role in ways that continue to protect American interests in the region and provide security and reassurance to American allies while also approaching China less as a regional adversary than as a combination partner and competitor. Part of this strategic balance involves the relative roles of various regional multilateral organizations, which are discussed below.

NORTH KOREA The 1950–53 Korean War brought the PRC in on one side and the United States on the other, and came dangerously close to an American invasion of China. China and North Korea remained close allies over the course of the Cold War and largely since. In recent years, the United States and China have both been involved with the nuclear proliferation threat by North Korea. There has been a mix of cooperation, as in the ***Six-Party Talks*** and UN Security Council; economic sanctions; and differences of interests, as discussed in Chapter 6.

TERRORISM The impact on Sino-American relations of the war on terrorism has also been mixed. The bullish view was articulated in early 2002 by Richard Holbrooke, who was the UN ambassador during the Clinton administration and assistant secretary of state for East Asia during the Carter administration. Holbrooke posited a "unique opportunity offered by the fact that China and the United States once again share a common strategic concern—terrorism—on which a revitalized relationship can be based."[63] China joined the antiterrorism coalition and has cooperated with the United States in a number of ways. A more skeptical view, though, sees this cooperation as limited in scope and significance. As the Princeton professor and former Bush administration official Aaron Friedberg argued, "It was not the result of a convergence of basic strategic visions or fundamental values, but rather the product of special circumstances that permitted what will likely prove to have been a partial and fleeting confluence of interests." Friedberg and others further question whether, like Russia on Chechnya, China has been especially interested in justifying under the antiterrorism umbrella its conflicts with the Uighurs, a largely Muslim group of about 9 million people in the far western province of Xinjiang.[64]

MIDDLE EAST AND OIL China did not support the United States in the Iraq war, but its opposition had a lower profile than that of France, Germany, or Russia. It also has developed its own relations with Israel, even to the point of some Israeli arms and military technology sales to China that the United States found objectionable. Overall Chinese interests in the

Middle East have concerned both oil and geopolitics. China has needed more and more oil to fuel its economic growth. About one-third of the growth in world oil consumption in recent years is due to China. Almost 60 percent of China's oil imports come from the Middle East. Iran is one of its main suppliers, hence China's reluctance to support stringent sanctions on the nuclear proliferation issue. Another main supplier is Sudan, whose government has been committing genocide in its Darfur region but which also has been supplying China with oil and buying its arms exports.

U.S.-CHINA ECONOMIC RELATIONS In 1989, when the Tiananmen Square massacre was perpetrated against Chinese students and other pro-democracy demonstrators in Beijing, the main issue in U.S.-China relations was human rights. This case was examined back in Chapter 1 as an example of "4 Ps" tensions. The first Bush administration opted to give priority to Power over Principles and imposed only limited economic sanctions. The Clinton administration came into office after heavily criticizing its predecessor for not championing democracy and human rights, but it too stopped short of serious sanctions against China. Its motivation was more Prosperity than Power, given its interest in rapidly growing investment in and trade with China.

Trade between the United States and China has grown, bringing its own issues. By 2005, the U.S. trade deficit with China was over $200 billion. This was a huge imbalance, indeed the largest bilateral trade deficit the United States has ever run with any country. The specific issues included limits on Chinese textile exports, a crackdown on the pirating of American recordings, movies, and other intellectual property, and a revaluation of the Chinese currency (the yuan). Trade with China has replaced trade with Japan as a contentious foreign policy politics issue, as we will see later in this chapter.

The shifts in financial power as the United States has run up huge debt and China has amassed financial reserves have both strategic and economic consequences. China has been a principal purchaser of the Treasury bonds the United States has needed to sell to finance its huge trade and budget deficits. Although such sales have served some mutual interests, they have strengthened China as a global financial power. Its foreign exchange reserves exceed $2 trillion; compare to U.S. reserves of only about $70 billion. The 2008 global economic crisis exacerbated these shifts. In 2006 China did not have any banks among the world's top twenty and the United States had seven, including the top two. By 2009 the top three banks were Chinese. Only three U.S. banks even made the list. These shifts in global financial power underlie the greater role China has been playing in the G20 as well as its proposals for major changes in the international financial system (Chapter 10).

THE GLOBAL ENVIRONMENT China and the United States are the two largest producers of greenhouses gases in the world. Their roles are crucial to dealing with global climate change, as we discuss further in Chapter 10.

### Democratization, Human Rights, and Chinese Political Stability

Whereas Russia exemplifies the problems involved in the transition from communism to democracy, China's problems are associated with seeking to maintain communism and resist the transition to democracy. It is, as Professor Edward Friedman put it, "the only major surviving communist dictatorship."[65]

The overall dilemma China faces is how to combine economic liberalization, modernization, and opening to the global economy with continuation of a closed, repressive, nondemocratic political system. Since China began its economic opening over twenty years ago under the leadership of Deng Xiaoping, the strategy has been based on the populace's being sufficiently satisfied with the economic benefits that it remains politically quiescent. This tacit bargain, though, has not fully worked out. High economic growth rates have not brought political quiescence. Even by the official statistics of the Chinese government, there were 74,000 mass protests involving 3.76 million people in 2004; in 2005 the number of mass protests increased to 87,000, the next year to 94,000.[66] Some of these protests have been in rural areas, where the peasantry has been largely left out of the economic boom. Some factory workers in urban areas have protested, dissatisfied with their meager wages and benefits. Some protests have been over environmental issues. China has come to have six of the world's ten most polluted cities. Five of its largest rivers have become too polluted even to touch, let alone to support village fishing industries.[67] Even before the 2003 SARS (severe acute respiratory syndrome) epidemic, China's health system was ranked 144th in the world by the World Health Organization. Its incidence of AIDS has been mounting at alarming rates, leading some experts to warn about a crisis equal to or even worse than the one that has occurred in Africa.[68]

Further, although the technologies that U.S. and other foreign investment have brought into the country have been essential to economic growth and modernization, some such as the Internet also have aspects that bring pressure for political opening. Indicative of its fear of how the Internet was undermining its monopoly on the flow of politically relevant information, the Chinese government arrested a young computer whiz while he was "on his way back from his grandmothers's funeral," without any apparent cause other than that he was known to have the skills to be able to "run circles around Beijing's Internet fire walls."[69] Soho.com, China's main Internet portal, posted the notice that "topics which damage the reputation of the state" are forbidden. It went on to warn that "if you are a Chinese national and willingly choose to break these laws, Soho.com is legally obliged to report you to the Public Security Bureau."[70]

Should American computer, software, and Internet firms comply with Chinese regulations? One U.S. congressman accused firms such as Google, Yahoo, Cisco, and Microsoft of "compromising the integrity of their product and their duties as corporate citizens . . . aiding and abetting the Chinese regime . . . and supporting the secret police in a number of ways, including surveillance and invasion of privacy." A Microsoft executive countered that his firm and others "are having a major positive impact despite the effort by various agencies of the Chinese government to control certain kinds of political content." Similarly, a Google executive stated "our conviction that expanding access to information will make our world a better, more informed and freer place."[71]

Human rights pressures also have been increasing. Amnesty International and Human Rights Watch, the two major human rights NGOs, both rate China as among the world's worst human rights violators. These groups cite numerous cases involving individual dissidents, as well as the Falun Gong, a partly religious and partly political movement.

Another set of issues involves national and ethnic groups that seek greater autonomy from the central government in Beijing and possibly secession from China itself. March 2008 saw the largest protests in ***Tibet*** against Chinese military rule and denial of autonomy or independence since 1989. The protests, of particular concern at a time when China sought to present a "harmonious image" to the rest of world at the 2008 Beijing Olympics, were squelched through violent clashes between protestors and Chinese security forces and the imposition of martial law. The global running of the Olympic torch was met with pro-Tibet protests in many American and other cities. With the Dalai Lama aging and questions of succession imminent, the issue may become even more contentious.

In July 2009 riots exploded in Xinjiang Province between the ***Uighurs*** and the Han, China's ethnic majority. Tensions have deep roots in this area, where the mix of ethnic and religious groups dates back centuries. This area borders eight countries and once was a hub of trade along the Silk Road. Xinjiang contains thirteen principal ethnic groups, of which the Uighurs are the largest. They are Turkic by ethnicity and Muslim by religion. The Han Chinese population has increased through Beijing's efforts to "Chinesify" the area. The 2009 riots began as a clash between Uighur and Han Chinese factory workers. They intensified as retaliations and backlash spiraled between the Uighurs and Chinese security forces and between the Uighurs and the Han Chinese. With close to two hundred people dead and two thousand injured, these were the most violent clashes in China in decades.

Given these and other issues, as with Russia, China's weaknesses even more than its strength may become a concern to the United States and others in the international community.

## *Japan*

The end of the Cold War has raised new issues and dynamics for U.S.-Japan relations. The old security concern of a Soviet invasion no longer pertains; Russia and Japan still have some outstanding issues, including territorial disputes dating from World War II, but their relations now are well within the bounds of diplomacy. Nevertheless, the U.S.-Japan security alliance has continued into the post–Cold War era as, to quote the State Department, "it is the cornerstone of U.S. security interests in Asia and is fundamental to regional stability and prosperity."[72] A new U.S.-Japan defense agreement was signed in 1997 and another in 2005. About fifty thousand American troops continue to be based in Japan. American-Japanese cooperation also has continued on Taiwan, North Korea, and missile defense.

Within this basic alliance, however, there are some tensions. One is over trade and other economic issues. The trade disputes that began in the 1970s and grew especially heated in the 1980s were tempered as Japan's economic problems in the 1990s eroded its image as an economic powerhouse. Still, the recent bilateral U.S.-Japan trade deficit was $73 billion, second only to the deficit with China. As long as U.S.-Japanese trade continues to run sharp imbalances, trade will continue to be a point of contention. So too will banking and financial issues. The Japanese government's weakness in dealing with its own economic problems exacerbated the overall Asian financial crisis of the late 1990s. The 2008 U.S.-induced financial crisis hurt Japan along with the rest of the world, and with far greater impact than the decade-earlier Asian financial crisis.

A second issue concerns, to borrow from the title of a popular Japanese book, "The Japan That Can Say No"—say "no," that is, to the United States, a sentiment that reflects resentments on that side of the Pacific that mirror the Japan bashing on this side. Whereas some in the United States have felt that Japan takes advantage of American support, some in Japan feel that the United States is domineering and that Japan needs to show that its support for the United States can't be taken for granted. An issue on which these sentiments have been especially strong has been the presence of U.S. military bases in Japan, especially on the island of Okinawa. Tensions over the continued existence of the Okinawa bases have been exacerbated by incidents in which American soldiers stationed there have been charged with rape and other sexual offenses. Partly in response to such incidents, some U.S. troops are being transferred to Guam. Another incident involved a tragic accident off Hawaii in early 2001, in which a U.S. submarine crashed into a Japanese fishing boat that had families and young children aboard, killing nine Japanese and injuring many more. Although these are incidents and not policy, they tap deep roots of Japanese political opinion.

Third is Japan's post–Cold War military role. The "peace constitution" written for Japan by the United States during the post–World War II occupation limited Japan's military forces strictly to self-defense. The question now is whether those limits should be loosened somewhat. As with Germany, this question reflects pressures for Japan to become a more "normal" major power amid a historical legacy of aggression and militarism. During the 1990–91 Persian Gulf War, this historical legacy was sufficiently strong that the Japanese Diet (the Parliament) rejected even a bill calling for a limited, noncombat role for the Japanese military in the war; instead, Japan confined its role to providing financial assistance. Some shift came during the 1990s as the Diet passed the International Peace Cooperation Law, which allows Japanese military units to serve in some UN peacekeeping missions, albeit in limited roles. In 2001 the war on terrorism posed further challenges. This time the Diet passed a bill permitting Japan to deploy a naval task force as offshore noncombat support for the United States in Afghanistan. As reported at the time,

> Flying the Rising Sun flag, a destroyer, a minesweeper and a supply ship left Japanese naval bases Sunday headed for the Indian Ocean. . . . Only a few dozen protesters gathered at the Japanese ports with anti-war banners as the ships departed following patriotic speeches from politicians and tearful families waving goodbye. But in a demonstration that not all of the old restrictions have been cast off, Japan decided against deploying a destroyer with an Aegis missile-hunting system after some lawmakers argued that to do so would violate the constitution.[73]

In the Iraq war, Japan went further, sending about eight hundred troops as part of a reconstruction and humanitarian mission—still not combat troops but for the first time since World War II a ground military presence outside its own borders.[74] Japan has taken on other military missions, as when its navy joined an international antipiracy deployment off the coast of Somalia.

Polls show the Japanese public is split on whether to change the constitution to allow for a greater military role. One former prime minister stressed that "Japan's role in international society has largely changed from 60 years ago. We are expected, and have a responsibility, to play a greater role, and we can contribute to achieving global peace and stability by living up to that expectation."[75] The Diet set up committees to review draft amendments and to draw up procedures for a national referendum regarding changing the constitution. The United States backs the constitutional change so that Japan can play a larger military role as part of their security alliance. "We hope and expect Japan will choose to accept more global security responsibilities in the years ahead," said Secretary of Defense Robert Gates.[76] Conservative opinion further holds that promoting a strong, secure Japan to counterbalance China is conducive to U.S. interests in the region.[77]

Another aspect of this debate concerns nuclear weapons. Japanese anti-nuclearism has been driven not just by the fears of others; it stems also from the experiences of Hiroshima and Nagasaki, the two Japanese cities on which the United States dropped nuclear bombs in 1945 in the last stages of World War II. Japan's foreign policy had held to three non-nuclear principles: never to own, produce, or permit nuclear weapons on Japanese territory. But with China's military growing stronger, in part through its advanced nuclear weapons programs; with North Korea as an unstable and now nuclear-armed neighbor; with the risks of Russian "loose nukes"; and amid concerns about the long-term reliability of U.S. security guarantees, some are asking whether it still is in Japan's interest to be a non-nuclear nation. "You have to wonder," one analyst said, "how long Japan can remain the only non-nuclear power among the major countries in the region."[78]

In 2006 Taro Aso, then the foreign minister and in 2008 the prime minister, suggested that it might be prudent for Japan to develop nuclear capability. He said, "The reality is that it is only Japan that has not discussed possessing nuclear weapons, and all other countries have been discussing it."[79] He later clarified, noting that "Japan is capable of producing nuclear weapons. . . . But we are not saying we have plans to possess nuclear weapons." In the same speech, however, he made the argument that Japan's pacifist constitution does not forbid possession of an atomic bomb for defense.[80] The U.S. response to this shift was and remains the promise to act as Japan's nuclear shield. Then secretary of state Condoleezza Rice publicly pledged that the United States would retaliate swiftly and massively against aggression toward Japan, using nuclear weapons if necessary.[81] Further questions arose when the Democratic Party of Japan (DPJ) won the August 2009 national elections. This was only the second time since Japan became a democracy in 1955 that the Liberal Democratic Party (LDP) was out of power. Although economic and other domestic issues were a big part of the campaign, Yukio Hatoyama, the DPJ leader and the new prime minister, also called for greater foreign policy independence from the United States. His proposals included reconsideration of American military bases and reorientation of Japanese foreign policy toward Asia.

These issues are of concern not just for the United States but also for Japan's regional neighbors. Americans often don't appreciate the extent to which anti-Japan sentiments and fears persist in China, South Korea, the Philippines, and elsewhere in the region. These fears draw not only on the World War II experience, but go back further in history and have been stirred up recently in both politics and culture.[82] With its memories of hundreds of thousands killed during the Japanese occupation of China in the 1930s and through World War II, China reacted very negatively to visits by the Japanese prime minister Junichiro Koizumi to the Yakasuni war memorial in Tokyo. South Koreans still remember the oppression of Japanese colonial rule from 1910 to 1945. Moreover, in terms of current interests, Japan and its neighbors have a number of issues that are a mix of cooperation and competition. China and Japan are increasingly competing globally for energy supplies, yet they also have enjoyed a booming two-way trade, with China surpassing the United States as Japan's top trade partner. South Korea and Japan continue military cooperation under the U.S. security umbrella yet have their own differences, including lingering territorial disputes over two islands. East Asian–Pacific regional stability thus has uncertainties that involve Japan as well as China, and that bear substantially on American interests.

### *The Korean Peninsula*

Like Germany, Korea was split into two countries at the end of World War II. North Korea was communist and allied with the Soviet Union and later with China. South Korea was noncommunist, democratic but also for periods ruled by the military, and allied with the United States.

Unlike East and West Germany, however, North and South Korea went to war. The war began in 1950 when the North invaded the South. The United States came to South Korea's defense with endorsement by the UN and support from the militaries of a number of other countries. The war lasted three years and ended without either side able to claim victory. An armistice was signed, but not a full peace treaty. A demilitarized zone

(DMZ) was created, separating the two countries. American soldiers have been stationed at the DMZ and on bases in South Korea on an ongoing basis ever since. Even after the end of the Cold War, about thirty-seven thousand American troops have remained in South Korea.

Efforts to improve relations between South and North Korea have had numerous ups and downs over the past two decades. At times trade has started to develop and borders opened for family reunification visits, only to be followed by increased tensions and retightening of relations. Other countries in the region also are affected, notably Japan. In the past, North Korea kidnapped some Japanese citizens and fired missiles in Japan's vicinity. China, which shares a border with North Korea, fears, among other things, a massive refugee flow. Food shortages, malnutrition, and starvation in North Korea—in significant part due to government policies—have stirred global humanitarian concerns. Human rights violations also have been a major issue. Control of North Korea has been handed down from father (Kim Il-sung) to son (Kim Jong-il) and perhaps soon to grandson (Kim Jung-un). These and other issues—in addition to North Korean nuclear weapons, on which we focused in Chapter 6—have kept the Korean peninsula a major regional hotspot.

### *India*

The continuing tensions between India and Pakistan raise one set of concerns. India and Pakistan have fought three wars and endured numerous crises since their independence from British colonial rule in 1947. India was created as a largely Hindu country, Pakistan as a largely Muslim country. In setting the boundaries, though, both sides claimed sovereignty over the state of Kashmir. Pakistan's claim was based on Kashmir's largely Muslim population, India's on the decision by the maharaja (prince) of Kashmir (a Hindu) to unite with India. Two of the India-Pakistan wars, one at independence in 1947 and the other in 1965, were fought in part over Kashmir. Both of these wars ended with cease-fires and peace plans, but neither solved the underlying conflict.

In 1999 India and Pakistan went to the brink of another war over Kashmir. This time, the crisis was compounded because both countries had become nuclear weapons powers. Pakistan had responded to India's nuclear weapons tests in May 1998 with tests of its own, affirming what many had suspected—that both countries had been secretly developing nuclear weapons for many years. This situation gave the conflict over Kashmir much broader regional and global implications. The risk now was not just another conventional India-Pakistan war but possibly a nuclear war. The 1999 crisis was defused when the Clinton administration played an important peace-brokering role.

The United States traditionally had had much closer relations with Pakistan than with India. During the Cold War, India was a leader of the Third World "nonaligned movement" and also had close ties with the Soviet Union. Pakistan was part of the U.S. Cold

War alliance system, first as a member of the Central Treaty Organization during the 1950s and then through a number of bilateral agreements. Pakistan also was a key ally in the U.S.-supported 1979–88 insurgency against the Soviet invasion of Afghanistan. The principal strains in U.S.-Pakistani relations were due to human rights and democracy concerns prompted by Pakistani military coups. A bill passed by Congress in 1985 cut off economic and military aid unless Pakistan ended its nuclear weapons program. The United States also opposed India's nuclear weapons program, but since it didn't give India foreign aid it couldn't impose comparable nonproliferation pressure.

The war on terrorism pushed the United States and Pakistan closer together once again. Pakistan was the crucial front-line state for launching the 2001 war in Afghanistan. Within days of the September 11 attacks, General Pervez Musharraf, who became the leader of Pakistan in an October 1999 coup that the United States opposed, pledged to help the United States openly and covertly against the Taliban and Al Qaeda.

Yet in the middle of the war in Afghanistan, Kashmir heated up again. The violence intensified in and around Kashmir, then spread to Delhi, the Indian capital, where terrorists attacked the Indian parliament, killing thirteen people. India accused Pakistan of directly supporting these attacks. Pakistan responded by blaming India for its army's attacks on Pakistani soldiers along the border. Both sides began talking of and making military movements toward war. Neither side was willing to say it would not escalate to nuclear war. For a period in early 2002 the world feared the worst. A nuclear war seemed closer than at any point since the 1962 Cuban missile crisis. The Bush administration engaged in diplomacy and played an important role in bringing the crisis under control.

In November 2008, Lashkar-e-Taiba, a Pakistani terrorist group, attacked the Indian city of Mumbai (formerly known as Bombay), killing over 160 people in a three-day siege. Although the Pakistani government was not directly implicated, it long had had close ties to Lashkar, Pakistan's military having worked with it as a guerrilla force in Kashmir. Lashkar also had ties to Al Qaeda, as reflected in statements by Osama bin Laden. He put India in the same camp as the United States and Israel, accusing them of a "Crusader-Zionist-Hindu war against Muslims."[83] Kashmir thus wasn't the only issue in the mix, but once again was a major part of tensions that brought further death and destruction and risked further escalation. Some new diplomatic overtures followed, lifting hopes that a lasting solution may be found. The possibility of another India-Pakistan crisis, though, cannot be dismissed.

Beyond Kashmir, overall American-Indian relations have come to reflect India's status as an emerging world power. Four factors make India stand out.

First is its size. India is the world's second most populous country, with over 1.1 billion people, amounting to about 15 percent of the world population. This makes it the world's largest democracy. It also is interesting to note that although it is a Hindu majority country, India has the second largest Muslim population in the world (144 million, behind only Indonesia and more than Pakistan).

Second is India's place in globalization. You may have first-hand experience with this if you have called a 1-800 phone number in the United States and gotten a call center operator with an Indian accent. India's place in globalization goes well beyond such semi-skilled outsourcing, as it has become a major center of technological innovation in its own right. Trade with the United States, only $14.3 billion in 2000, increased to $43.4 billion by 2008. In recent years the Indian economy has had one of the world's fastest growth rates. Although this has made for substantial prosperity, economic inequality remains sharp: India now has over one hundred thousand millionaires, but the majority still lives on 50 cents a day. Rates of child malnutrition are comparable to those of Bangladesh and Ethiopia.

Third is its possession of nuclear weapons. India had been developing nuclear weapons for many years. The culminating event was its 1998 major nuclear weapons test. The Clinton administration imposed trade sanctions, but with little effect. The Bush administration lifted these sanctions in the wake of September 11, in large part because of the priority it gave to the war on terrorism and the partnership role India could play. In 2005, President Bush and the Indian prime minister Manmohan Singh signed an agreement whereby the United States gave de facto recognition to India's status as a nuclear weapons state. Technically, the agreement allowed trade and cooperation on civil nuclear energy, which was supposed to be prohibited to countries that had tested nuclear weapons in violation of the ***Nuclear Nonproliferation Treaty (NPT).*** Supporters argued that as a democracy India could be trusted more than others not to use its nuclear weapons aggressively. They also stressed the economic benefits for U.S. exports and investment in a lucrative market and the geopolitical gains from closer U.S.-India ties. Opponents contended that the NPT regime would be further weakened by the precedent that other nuclear weapons nations—for example, Pakistan, Israel—could cite. The deal did go through, winning approval of the U.S. Congress and the Indian parliament.

Fourth, India has been playing an increasingly significant global diplomatic role. The first UN peacekeeping force sent to the former Yugoslavia in the early 1990s was headed by an Indian general. Many also see India as first in line for a new permanent seat on the UN Security Council. American and Indian officials now refer to their relationship as a "strategic partnership." This includes extensive defense and security cooperation as well as economic relations, joint efforts on HIV/AIDS prevention, and other initiatives. Yet the United States and India disagree on some issues. On Iran, for example, India went ahead with negotiations on a major energy deal at a time when the United States was pressuring for economic sanctions. When the Bush administration reprimanded India, New Delhi replied by releasing a statement saying, "India and Iran are ancient civilizations whose relations span centuries. Both nations are perfectly capable of managing all aspects of their relationship with the appropriate degree of care and attention. . . . Neither country needs any guidance on the future conduct of bilateral relations. . . ."[84] India is a very nationalistic country with a strong sense of its own interests and aspirations for its own global role. "Our policy," as Prime Minister Singh stated, "seeks to . . . give us strategic autonomy in the world. Independence of our foreign policy enables us to pursue mutually beneficial cooperation with all major countries of the world."[85]

### *Asian Regional Organizations*

Regional organizations traditionally have been less prominent in Asia than Europe. Although this is still true, they have been growing in both roles and numbers in recent years.

The ***Association of Southeast Asian Nations (ASEAN)*** was established in 1967 largely to promote economic cooperation among its members, which at that time were Indonesia, Malaysia, the Philippines, Singapore, and Thailand. Security threats mostly arose from Cold War politics, and since most countries in ASEAN were U.S. allies, the United States took care of the region's security. Today ASEAN includes five other nations as full members—Brunei, Burma (Myanmar), Cambodia, Laos, and Vietnam. Whereas ASEAN held only three summit meetings in its first twenty-five years, it has held twelve in its next eighteen years. It also created the ASEAN Regional Forum (ARF) with twenty-seven members, including the United States, China, Japan, North and South Korea, Australia, Russia, and the European Union. The ARF deals more with regional security issues than economic ones. Then there is ASEAN Plus Three—China, Japan, South Korea—for more focused efforts at regional security. The East Asian Summit is another recently created regional organization, this one including only East Asian countries and not the United States.

Asia also has numerous regional organizations that focus more exclusively on economic matters, for example, Asia-Pacific Economic Cooperation (APEC). All told, none of these organizations are comparable to NATO in the security realm, OSCE in the political-diplomatic realm, or the EU in economic matters. Still, the intra-region trend over time has been toward greater regional multilateralism.

## Latin America

Historically the United States has been more dominant in Latin America than any other region. U.S. military interventions were frequent in the nineteenth and early twentieth centuries (Chapter 3). FDR's Good Neighbor policy of the 1930s decreased interventionism, although even then relations were not conducted as among equals. Latin America was a major front in the Cold War: Castro's revolution in Cuba, the Cuban missile crisis, the revolutionary icon Che Guevara in Bolivia, the Sandinistas in Nicaragua (see Chapters 4, 5). Relations improved somewhat in the 1990s with the passage of NAFTA (North American Free Trade Agreement) and the spread of democracy and embrace of globalization in most of the region. But the heralded ***Summits of the Americas*** haven't produced very much. And even before the 2008 global crisis, disillusionment with globalization according to the "Washington consensus" on free markets was spreading. Bushian unilateralism and the Iraq war alienated the region further, as did rising anti-immigration sentiment, directed largely at Hispanics. As the Obama administration came into office, the sense was that, as the Latin America expert Julia E. Sweig captured it, "For the first time in nearly two centuries, the United States will find a Latin America that has unapologetically dropped the region's deference to U.S. power. . . . Simply put, the U.S. government no longer has the cachet, influence or political weight it exercised during much of the nineteenth and twentieth centuries."[86]

## *Cuba*

Cuba is almost the last bastion of the Cold War. It's been over a half-century since Fidel Castro came to power. For nearly all that time, U.S. policy has sought to oppose and at times overthrow the Castro regime. So many economic sanctions have been imposed that their statutes and regulations fill numerous three-ring binders. The Castro regime (headed by Fidel, and since his illness in 2006 by his brother Raúl) has ruled repressively. The Cuban economy has suffered. But the regime has remained in power. Efforts to shift U.S. policy have kept running into the vehemently anti-Castro Cuban lobby.

Recently there have been some signs of possible change. Seeking dialogue rather than isolation fits within the Obama engagement strategy. Some sanctions were lifted early in the Obama administration. Members of Congress from both parties have become more supportive of policy change. A diverse coalition is emerging, including the U.S. Chamber of Commerce and agricultural groups, both traditionally conservative groups but with economic interests at stake, and liberal groups, such as Human Rights Watch, concerned about human rights violations but believing that these can be better effected through engagement. Senator Robert Menendez (D-New Jersey), a Cuban American, spoke for those still opposed: "Let's know who's for democracy and human rights and who wants to sell their stuff no matter how many people are in prison." But polls show shifts even in the Cuban American community. Whereas in 2003 53 percent of Cuban Americans opposed American citizens being able to travel to Cuba and 61 percent supported continuing the embargo, in 2009 the numbers were down to 29 percent and 42 percent, respectively. The demographics were especially interesting: the 2009 numbers for the younger Cuban American generation (ages eighteen to forty-nine) were 22 percent and 33 percent.[87]

## *Mexico*

The Bush administration began with much fanfare about improved U.S.-Mexican relations. The Mexican president, Vicente Fox, a businessman whose party was roughly equivalent to the Republican party, was the first foreign leader Bush met with after his election. But promised immigration reforms first ran into post–9/11 priority for greater border security and then to anti-immigration politics that Bush did try to counter but unsuccessfully. Immigration carried over into the Obama administration as a major issue in U.S.-Mexican relations.

The future of NAFTA is another major issue. The ***North American Free Trade Agreement (NAFTA),*** approved in 1993, created a free-trade area among the three North American countries: Canada, Mexico, and the United States. Proponents have stressed the value of creating the world's largest free-trade area, linking 444 million people producing $17 trillion worth of goods and services. American exports to its NAFTA partners nearly tripled in the first fifteen years. Critics differ on a number of points, particularly on attributing job losses in the United States to factories moving to Mexico. The debate was intense when NAFTA was up for approval in 1993 and has remained so since. During the 2008 Democratic presidential primaries in Ohio and Pennsylvania, both Barack Obama and Hillary Clinton stressed their opposition to, more than their support for, NAFTA.

Mexico also has been having its own debate about NAFTA's cost-benefit balance. Mexican exports have quintupled under NAFTA. The Mexican economy went from fifteenth largest in the world to ninth. Per capita income rose 24 percent to just over $4,000. But real wages for most Mexicans are lower. Small farmers have been particularly hard hit. Although factors other than NAFTA are part of the problem, this still is a reason that support for NAFTA fell from 68 percent in 1993 to 45 percent in 2003. Mexicans also cite particular disputes, such as U.S. barriers to Mexican long-haul trucks, a ban said to be on safety grounds but seen by many as protectionism.

The Mexican drug wars began getting a great deal of attention in late 2008 and 2009. Over six thousand people were killed in Mexico in 2008 in confrontations between the drug cartels and the Mexican government. Kidnappings, less than one hundred a decade earlier, were now close to four hundred. The drug cartels were armed like paramilitaries with platoon-size units, antitank rockets, heavy machine guns, encrypted communications, and fleets of helicopters and submarines. Law enforcement not only was exceedingly difficult against such forces; webs of corruption problems reached into the Mexican police, army, and government. Human rights groups also flagged abuses the government committed in the name of combating the drug cartels.

Some studies warned that Mexico was heading toward being a failed state. Although this idea was overly alarmist, the drug wars already were having immediate and tangible effects within the United States. In Tucson, Arizona, three-quarters of the two hundred home invasions investigated by the police were linked to the drug trade. Violent incidents even farther from the border in Atlanta, Georgia, and Shelby County, Alabama, were linked to the Mexican drug cartels. The Drug Enforcement Administration (DEA) arrested over seven hundred people linked to Mexican cartels in one hundred and twenty American cities. In early 2009, the State Department issued a travel alert warning of the risks of travel to Mexico— its timing geared in no small part to college students about to head out on spring break.

The United States, though, has not just been the bearer of consequences. Its policies, such as lax gun control and societal habits that create much of the demand for illegal drugs, are part of the problem. "Our insatiable demand for illegal drugs fuels the drug trade," Secretary of State Hillary Clinton stated. "Our inability to prevent weapons from being illegally smuggled across the border to arm these criminals causes the death of police officers, soldiers and civilians."[88] Secretary of Homeland Security Janet Napolitano increased the Border Patrol and Immigration and Customs Enforcement (ICE) agents along the border. More sophisticated equipment was provided. There even was some talk of joint military operations. Although these actions can help, as can Mexico's own efforts, the roots of the problem, as noted by Secretary Clinton, also need to be addressed.

## *Brazil*

When emerging powers are discussed, Brazil is one of those most often included. It's the "B" in BRICs (Brazil, Russia, India, China). Its land mass covers more than half of South America. Two of its cities are among the world's most populous—Sao Paulo (18 million) and Rio de Janeiro (11 million). Its leader, President Luiz Inácio Lula da Silva, has gained increased prestige regionally and globally. So, too, did the country as a whole, as evidenced by its winning bid for the 2016 Olympics.

As with much of Latin America, U.S. relations with Brazil have had a mixed history. The United States had a hand in the 1964 military coup, and then supported the military regime for most of its two-plus decades. When Lula was first elected president in 2002, his left-leaning ideas and his role as a labor leader were looked on suspiciously by the Bush administration. Relations did improve somewhat and have continued to do so in the Obama administration. But even without major disputes, Brazil has been moving toward a more independent foreign policy, measured less by whether it is pro- or anti-U.S. than by its desire to get its own seat at the table and pursue its own interests.

In trade, for example, China became Brazil's largest trade partner. The two countries also agreed to shift from the dollar to their own currencies, China's yuan and Brazil's real, as the main media of exchange in their bilateral trade. This was in part a reaction to the U.S.-induced global financial crisis, as well as part of the broader effort to make the international financial system less dominated by the dollar. The $10 billion loan China made to Brazil for development of its newly discovered oil fields, from which quantities of oil will be exported to China, reflects the further growth likely in China-Brazil economic relations. U.S.-Brazil trade still is substantial and has its own dynamics for possible growth; it's just no longer the dominant relationship.

Brazil's rising diplomatic position is evident globally and regionally. It is a member of the G20. It is on the short list for new permanent seats should the UN Security Council expand. It has been playing a lead role in development of the Union of South American Nations (UNASUR), a new regional organization that excludes the United States. It has been building up its own military and pursuing discussions with other countries about the creation of a South American defense council. These initiatives, too, are less about opposition to the United States than lessened dependence on it. Relations could become more problematic, but even if they don't Brazil's trend is toward a more independent foreign policy.

## *Venezuela*

Hugo Chávez has stirred more recent controversy than any other Latin American leader. In 1992 as a lieutenant colonel in the Venezuelan military, he had been involved in a military coup attempt against President Carlos Andres Pérez. The coup sought to capitalize on unrest sown by economic decline, corruption, and repression. Although it failed, and Chávez went to prison for two years, popular dissatisfaction remained. Chávez motivated and mobilized this dissatisfaction with a blend of classical Latin American populism and Bolivarianism, evoking the country's founder Simon Bolívar. He won the 1998 presidential election with 56 percent of the vote. Although Chávez delivered on some promised social programs, once in power his rule became increasingly repressive politically and had very mixed economic results. Foreign-policy clashes with any U.S. administration likely were inevitable.

Opposition to Chávez within Venezuela reached the point of a coup attempt in April 2002. Whether or not the Bush administration actively or explicitly supported the coup is a matter of debate; even if it did not, it certainly did nothing to oppose it and appeared to welcome it. Though only a few Latin American leaders were pro-Chávez, most also were not pro-Bush and were concerned about the antidemocratic precedent that a coup would set.

Over the rest of the Bush administration, U.S.-Venezuelan relations worsened. Some stayed at the level of rhetoric, some more tangible as with a military cooperation deal Chávez signed with Russia. Chávez was the moving force behind the creation of ALBA, the Bolivarian Alternative for the Americas, bringing together the more left-leaning countries such as Cuba, Nicaragua, Ecuador, and Bolivia. The Obama administration has been trying to avoid playing into Chávez's hands by being too negative and confrontational, while feeling out prospects for meaningful engagement.

## *Organization of American States (OAS)*

During the Cold War virtually all of U.S. policy toward Latin America, including the creation of the ***Organization of American States (OAS)*** in 1948, was geared to the global containment strategy. The OAS largely was seen as being under the U.S. thumb. It dutifully supported the 1954 U.S. covert action in Guatemala and the 1965 military intervention in the Dominican Republic, as well as the expulsion of Cuba following Fidel Castro's revolution in 1959. With so many military dictatorships among its members, the OAS could be seen as pro-democracy only if one accepted the "ABC" (anything but communism) definition of democracy.

With the Cold War over and anticommunism no longer the Western Hemisphere's organizing principle, and with all of its member states now democracies (albeit some quite limited ones), in June 1991 the OAS adopted a resolution on its "Commitment to Democracy and the Renewal of the Inter-American System," also called the Santiago Resolution. (The meeting took place in Santiago, Chile.) Though including qualifiers about "due respect for the principle of nonintervention," it legitimized as grounds for an OAS response "the sudden or irregular interruption of the democratic political institutional process, or of the legitimate exercise of power by the democratically elected government in any of the Organization's member states." In 2001—coincidentally on September 11—the new Inter-American Democratic Charter was approved, building on the Santiago Resolution to further firm up the member countries' shared commitment to defending democracy.

When the first test came a few months later in Haiti, the OAS took only limited action. It authorized some trade sanctions, but not even comprehensive ones. Memories of past U.S. interventions in Latin America were still too strong for authorizing military force even against the brutal Haitian military regime. Later, after the 1994 U.S. military intervention and a period of UN peacekeeping, the OAS did send a peacekeeping force to help provide order and recovery in Haiti.

When in 1996 the Paraguayan military attempted a coup, the OAS joined the Clinton administration in threatening diplomatic and economic sanctions, and it did so immediately and comprehensively. The joint U.S.-OAS action helped block the coup, providing an example of how effective regional cooperation can be. In the 2002 coup attempt in Venezuela, with the Bush administration's apparent involvement stoking historical memories, the OAS issued a condemnation of this "alteration of the constitutional order." Some saw in this resolution a demonstration of the OAS's greater willingness to assert itself against U.S. policy.

Another issue is whether to readmit Cuba to the OAS. The issue was raised in 2009 but not approved.

### *Honduras*

The latest challenge to Latin American democracy came in this small Central American country in June 2009 when the military ousted Honduran President Manuel Zelaya. Photos showing Zelaya being taken from the presidential residence in his pajamas and put on a plane leaving the country seemed like a classic Latin American coup. Anti-Zelaya forces claimed this was not a coup, that it was upholding the constitution and in particular the provision prohibiting presidents from being reelected against Zelaya's efforts to engineer his own reelection later in the year. Zelaya's close relations with Venezuela's Hugo Chávez also were part of the context.

Opposition to the coup was widespread. The Obama administration condemned it as illegal and setting a dangerous regional precedent. The UN General Assembly called on member states to recognize only the Zelaya government. The OAS suspended Honduras. It sought to provide the diplomacy to resolve the conflict through the efforts of its

## INTERNATIONAL PERSPECTIVES

INTERNATIONAL PERSPECTIVES

### AFRICAN LEADERS' VIEWS

The following quotes from major African leaders reflect views of U.S. policy and more broadly of international affairs.

*Kwame Nkrumah was the first president of Ghana, one of the first African countries to gain independence. This excerpt is from a 1960 speech to the United Nations in which Nkrumah addressed anticolonialism, opposition to the Cold War, and belief in the UN.*

The flowing tide of African nationalism . . . constitutes a challenge to the colonial powers to make a just restitution for the years of injustice and crime committed against our continent. . . . For years and years Africa has been the foot-stool of colonialism and imperialism, exploitation and degradation. From the north to the south, the east to the west, her sons languished in the chains of slavery and humiliation. . . . Those days are gone and gone forever, and now I, an African, stand before this august Assembly of the United Nations and speak with a voice of peace and freedom, proclaiming to the world the dawn of a new era. . . .

[P]reoccupation with armaments prevents the big powers from perceiving what are the real forces in the world today. If world population continues to grow, and if inequality between the so-called developed and under-developed countries is allowed to remain . . . then however great the armaments piled up, an international explosion cannot in my view be averted. . . .

[I]t is essential that we on the African continent take positive steps to isolate ourselves as far as is possible from the effects of nuclear warfare. One of the first and most practical steps which could be taken in this regard is to prevent any state having nuclear weapons from possessing military bases on the African continent. . . .

The responsibility for keeping the Cold War out of Africa rests squarely on the United Nations.

*Julius Nyerere, president of Tanzania from 1961 to 1985, was a leading proponent of African continental unity.*

[T]he requirements of African Unity necessitate the establishment of a new international entity to replace the present small international entities which now exist in our continent. Until we have achieved that we shall not be in a position to utilize the resources of Africa for the people of Africa, and we shall not be free from fear

(*Continued*)

(*Continued*)

of the rest of the world. A continent-wide state, single and indivisible, must be established. . . .

And it must be quite clear to everyone that the achievement of unity will not itself solve the problems of Africa. It will merely enable them to be solved by Africa. At the beginning, the effectiveness of the All-African government will be limited; it will have more responsibility than power. It will have to inch forward, organizing and arguing every step of the way, and gradually growing in stature—just as the federal government of the United States is still growing in relation to the states' governments because of the necessities of the people and the world. . . .

These preliminary steps need not be day-dreaming. If we have courage and intelligence they can become reality in the immediate future. And certainly they are essential if the ordinary African citizen is ever really to overcome the poverty which at present grips him and if he is to increase his degree of personal safety. For this is, and must be, the purpose of greater unity in Africa and elsewhere. Not size for its own sake, but strength and power used to defend the real freedoms of the ordinary man and to help him progress in his freedom.

*Nelson Mandela came to Washington to address the U.S. Congress in 1990. This was after he had been released as a political prisoner but before he became president of South Africa. Although the United States had supported apartheid for many years, it shifted to opposing it in the mid-1980s.*

We have come here to tell you, and through you, your own people, who are equally noble and heroic, of the troubles and trials, the fond hopes and aspirations, of the people from whom we originate. . . .

Our people demand democracy. Our country, which continues to bleed and suffer pain, needs democracy. It cries out for the situation where the law will decree that the freedom to speak of freedom constitutes the very essence of legality and the very thing that makes for the legitimacy of the constitutional order. . . .

To deny people their human rights is to challenge their very humanity. To impose on them a wretched life of hunger and deprivation is to dehumanise them. But such has been the terrible fate of all black persons in our country under the system of apartheid. The extent of the deprivation of millions of people has to be seen to be believed. The injury is made that more intolerable by the opulence of our white compatriots and the deliberate distortion of the economy to feed that opulence. . . .

> The stand you took established the understanding among the millions of our people that here we have friends, here we have fighters against racism who feel hurt because we are hurt, who seek our success because they too seek the victory of democracy over tyranny. And here I speak not only about you the members of the United States Congress, but also of the millions of people throughout this great land who stood up and engaged the apartheid system in struggle. . . .
>
> We could not have made an acquaintance through literature with human giants such as George Washington, Abraham Lincoln and Thomas Jefferson and not been moved to act as they were moved to act. We could not have heard of and admired John Brown, Sojourner Truth, Frederick Douglass, W.E.B. DuBois, Marcus Garvey, Martin Luther King Jr. and others, and not be moved to act as they were moved to act. We could not have known of your Declaration of Independence and not elected to join in the struggle to guarantee the people life, liberty and the pursuit of happiness.
>
> Sources: Nkrumah, www.nkrumah.net/un-1960/kn-at-un-1960-cvrfrn.htm; Nyerere, www.worldbeyondborders.org/africanunity.htm; Mandela, www.anc.org.za/ancdocs/history/mandela/1990/sp900626.html.

secretary-general and former Costa Rican President Oscar Arias, appointed as a special representative. The Obama administration supported this regional diplomacy while making a tactical decision to keep a relatively low profile. At one point it stepped up its diplomacy and claimed to have achieved a breakthrough. This quickly fell apart, though. When the administration then shifted toward accepting that Zelaya would not be restored to the presidency, even symbolically, prior to the November 2009 election, it was criticized for its inconsistency and taking the pressure off. The election was held and a new president chosen. But Honduras' underlying political and socioeconomic tensions remained, as did concerns about whether a broader precedent may have been set for other Latin American coups.

## Africa

Our "International Perspectives" box (p. 389) gives a sense of the views African leaders have had of U.S. policy and international affairs more broadly over the years. During the Cold War most attention was paid to parts of the continent where the United States and the Soviet Union were in direct geopolitical competition, such as the Congo-Zaire (1960s) and Angola (1970s–1980s). During the 1990s, ethnic conflicts and civil wars ravaged many countries, notably Somalia and Rwanda. In 1992–1993, the Bush and Clinton administrations undertook humanitarian military intervention in Somalia. In 1994 genocide swept through Rwanda while the United States and the rest of the international community did little to nothing. Following 9/11, antiterrorism became a principal priority, leading among other things to the creation of Africom, a new regional command structure for an expanded U.S. military presence on the continent.

The Obama administration has pledged to make Africa a higher priority and to base policy less heavily on Power and more on Principles, Prosperity, and Peace. "I do not see the countries and peoples of Africa as a world apart," President Obama declared in a speech in Ghana during his first trip to Africa. "I see Africa as a fundamental part of our interconnected world—as partners with America on behalf of the future that we want for all our children."[89] The fact that both President Obama and Secretary of State Clinton went to Africa during the first year of their administration—the first time this has ever happened—provided initial substantiation for the claim of higher priority. Enduring assessments, though, will depend on ongoing policy.

## *Somalia*

Somalia remains a major issue for some of the same reasons as in the past and some newer ones. The 1992–94 humanitarian intervention, discussed in Chapter 9, failed to help create stability; indeed, in the decades since then, Somalia has become even more of a failed state. Humanitarian crises recur amid food shortages, disease outbreaks, pervasive unemployment, and the absence of law and order. Various Islamic fundamentalist groups have fed off such turmoil. In 2006 one such group, the Islamic Courts, came to power. A few months later Ethiopia invaded Somalia, ousting the Islamic Courts government. Ethiopia claimed to be acting in its own national defense as a largely Christian country against which the Islamist regime was issuing threats as well as in the interest of the Somali people. The United States supported the Ethiopian invasion with intelligence and some military cooperation. A little over two years later, though, Ethiopia was forced to withdraw amid military losses and failure to impose stability, leaving behind what the NGO Refugees International called the world's worst humanitarian crisis. Even more radical Islamist groups grew stronger. It also was during the Ethiopian intervention that some Somali Americans living in Minneapolis returned to their homeland to join the ***jihad,*** or holy war.

Somalia also has been the principal locus for piracy. Although piracy occurs at sea, it is, as stated by an expert cited in our discussion in Chapter 6, "an onshore crisis demanding onshore solutions," driven by economic deprivation and societal disorder.

## *Darfur*

Ethnic conflicts and civil wars continue to tear many African countries and regions apart. Darfur, part of Sudan, is not the only one. There are all too many others, as in the Democratic Republic of Congo and Uganda. But only in Darfur has the current situation been deemed a genocide. We focus on it in Chapter 9.

## *South Africa*

The United States was slow to end its support for apartheid. The few links Nelson Mandela and the African National Congress party had to the communists were deemed sufficient during the Cold War for another "ABC" rationale justifying U.S. support for the white, apartheid regime. The policy shifts that finally did occur in the mid-1980s, including the imposition of economic sanctions, helped bring apartheid to an end. The South African transition to black majority rule was peaceful and democratic, wisely and ably led by Nelson Mandela.

South Africa has gone quickly from global pariah to continental leader. It is on the short list for a possible African seat if the UN Security Council expands. It is part of the G20 as well as the G5 (along with Brazil, India, China, and Mexico). Its neighbors have turned to it for leadership on key regional issues. But its heralded status has been tarnished since Mandela left office. Thabo Mbeki, Mandela's successor as president, confounded other leaders as well as the public-health community with his opposition to science-based AIDS policies. The next president, Jacob Zuma, came to power amid ethics scandals. Meanwhile, the South African economy has been hit by high unemployment and other economic problems even worse than those in many other countries in the region. Whether South Africa will play the global and regional leadership role it took on during the Mandela years, or again become a problem in its own right, remains to be seen.

## *Good Governance, Economic Development, AIDS*

In his July 2009 Ghana speech, besides pledging shifts in U.S. Africa policy, President Obama delivered a "tough love" message about what Africans needed to do in their own politics and societies:

> Development depends on good governance. That is the ingredient which has been missing in far too many places, for far too long. That is the change that can unlock Africa's potential. And that is a responsibility that can only be met by Africans. . . .
>
> Africa doesn't need strongmen, it needs strong institutions. . . .
>
> [I]t is still far too easy for those without conscience to manipulate whole communities into fighting among faiths and tribes.
>
> These conflicts are a millstone around Africa's neck. We all have many identities—of tribe and ethnicity; of religion and nationality. But defining oneself in opposition to someone who belongs to a different tribe, or who worships a different prophet, has no place in the 21st century. Africa's diversity should be a source of strength, not a cause for division.[90]

These were not totally new themes. The Bush administration had more closely linked U.S. foreign aid to good-governance practices. The World Bank had developed good-governance criteria. Various studies had shown a strong relationship between good governance and economic development, although with debate about sequencing and causal direction. Although most of these studies were global in scope, applying across regions, Africa was a principal focus.

AIDS has many aspects of concern. It is a human tragedy. It carries enormous economic costs. It can destabilize whole societies. We come back to these problems in Chapter 10.

### *African Union (AU)*

The Organization for African Unity (OAU) was established in 1963 as part of the struggle for decolonization. It originally had thirty-two members. Membership grew as more African nations became independent, and as secessionist movements created additional states. By 2002, when the OAU was replaced by the ***African Union (AU),*** there were fifty-three member states. Membership remains at that level today.

The OAU-AU change was a conscious effort by African leaders to strengthen their regional organization. The AU charter went further than the OAU's had in establishing the right to intervene in member states in cases of genocide, war crimes, or gross violations of human rights. The "Mechanism for Conflict Prevention and Resolution" is intended to provide a basis for military as well as diplomatic action. Like the OAS's Santiago Resolution, the AU's "Mechanism" had significant qualifiers about "respect of sovereignty" and functioning "on the basis of consent and the cooperation of the parties to a conflict." In practice these qualifiers have proven more potent than the broader statements. On Darfur, the AU has largely sided with the Sudanese government's claims of sovereignty even in the face of UN Security Council resolutions authorizing peace operations forces. It has condemned but not acted against the dictator Robert Mugabe's brutal rule over Zimbabwe.

"Africa Must Unite" is the slogan that flashes on the AU's Web site: "An Efficient and Effective African Union for a New Africa." How, though, should efficiency and effectiveness be defined?

## Foreign Policy Politics: A Case Study

### *The China Lobbies*

During the Cold War, the People's Republic of China (PRC) was commonly referred to in the American political debate as "Red China." It was generally depicted as more evil and in many respects more dangerous than even the Soviet Union. The U.S. ally Jiang Jeishi (Chiang Kai-shek) fled mainland China for the island of Taiwan in 1949 after he was defeated in the Chinese civil war by Mao Zedong and the Chinese communists. The Truman administration refused to recognize Mao's new government and stayed allied to Jiang and Taiwan. The Korean War (1950–53) came close to escalating to a direct war between the United States and the PRC.

The fervent anticommunism of McCarthyism, which had such a profound impact on foreign policy politics, was especially targeted at those said to be sympathetic, or worse, to Red China. For not extending the Korean War to China, Senator Joseph McCarthy attacked President Truman as "a rather sinister monster."[91] Secretary of State Dean Acheson was accused of appeasement. The State Department Foreign Service was purged of its "China hands." Their alleged crimes included using their expertise to warn that Jiang Jeishi was going to lose, an assessment that McCarthy twisted into having plotted to defeat Jiang.

Even after Senator McCarthy was censured by the Senate, the ***"China lobby"*** kept the domestic political pressure on. Many viewed the China lobby as among the most powerful foreign policy interest groups of the Cold War era. It included strong supporters of Jiang Jeishi, missionaries of sects whose proselytizing in China went back to the nineteenth century, business leaders, journalists, various anticommunist groups such as the Committee to Defend America by Aiding Anti-Communist China, and numerous members of Congress. The China lobby urged maintaining a close alliance with Taiwan, keeping the PRC out of the United Nations and the China seat on the Security Council in Taiwan's hands, and nipping in the bud policy proposals that might seek improved relations with the PRC.

It seemed ironic that Richard Nixon, a key member of the China lobby at the start of his political career, as president initiated the "opening" to Red China. But it made political sense. Nixon's staunch anticommunist credentials made him harder to attack as "soft." So when Nixon went to Beijing in 1972 for an official summit with Mao and Zhou Enlai, preceded by secret talks led by the National Security Advisor Henry Kissinger, he and his administration were more protected politically than more liberal politicians would have been. Nixon and Kissinger also stressed the "strategic triangle" rationale—that good relations with China would give the United States more leverage with the Soviet Union.

Still, the China lobby was strong enough to inhibit the fuller development of U.S.-PRC relations until 1979, when President Jimmy Carter announced the normalization of relations and the establishment of diplomatic relations. The China lobby was not able to stop normalization, but it did manage to get guarantees that the United States would continue to supply Taiwan with defensive arms and other assistance. In the years since, it has continued to press for Taiwan's interests.

Beyond the Taiwan issue, the end of the Cold War changed the U.S. domestic politics of relations with China. Without a Soviet Union, the geopolitical rationale was less compelling. Issues such as human rights, which had been superceded by geopolitics, were given greater priority, especially after the May 1989 Tiananmen Square massacre. Other human rights issues also were raised, such as the use of forced prison labor, the treatment of the Dalai Lama and of Tibet, and China's "one child" policy and forced sterilizations and abortions. These made for an interesting coalition of conservatives from the long-standing China lobby, liberal human rights groups such as Human Rights Watch, and the AFL-CIO and other labor unions pushing for linkages to trade. On the other side were business interests, for which the attractiveness of the China market for exports as well as investments was rapidly increasing. Individual companies lobbied, as did associations such as the U.S. Chamber of Commerce, the National Association of Manufacturers, and the Business Coalition for U.S.-China Trade.

The politics played out within both Congress and the executive branch. In Congress the splits did not strictly follow party lines. Among those on the pro–human rights side were Congresswoman Nancy Pelosi, a staunchly liberal Democrat from California who later became Speaker of the House, and Senator Jesse Helms, a staunchly conservative Republican from North Carolina. Bureaucratic politics divisions were evident in the executive branch. Within the State Department itself a rift grew between the Bureau of East Asian Affairs, which was concerned that trade–human rights linkages would disrupt overall U.S.-China relations, and the Bureau of Democracy, Labor and Human Rights, which was concerned that U.S. credibility on human rights around the world would be damaged if America didn't stand by Principles against China. Although the presidential candidate Bill Clinton had been very tough in criticizing President George H. W. Bush for coddling "the butchers of Beijing," President Clinton opted for a compromise that provided for some linkage through annual human rights reviews, but largely tilted toward the pro-trade side.

In the years since, trade and other economic relations with China have continued to cause contention in American politics. In 2000 the issue was whether to establish normal trade relations with China on a permanent basis rather than continue the annual human rights reviews. The various China lobbies again clashed. Human rights supporters wanted the annual reviews as a way of keeping some pressure on; pro-trade groups argued that American exporters were being handicapped because other countries did not have annual human rights reviews. The pro-trade side again prevailed. The following year the issue was China's membership in the World Trade Organization (WTO). Again intense political debate arose, again on whether to seek human rights leverage through economic linkages, and again with an outcome more about Prosperity than Principles.

Implicit in this debate was the calculation that the United States was the economically stronger party and could use this advantage as leverage with political issues. But by 2005 much of the talk was about how economically powerful China had become. China was the one with the huge favorable balance of trade; indeed, the U.S. trade deficit with China made that with Japan pale in comparison. Once again, talk about a "red scare" in American politics arose, but this time, it was about the red ink of the bilateral trade deficit. When China tried to buy a U.S. oil company, protests abounded about dangers to U.S. national security. Numerous bills were introduced in Congress targeted at Chinese trade policies on such issues as its currency exchange rate, pirating of computer software and other violations of intellectual property rights, and unfair labor practices. The issue of Chinese workers' rights, Thea Lee of the AFL-CIO testified to Congress, "is both a moral and economic issue, impacting the lives of Chinese workers, and the quality and composition of American jobs."[92]

Some also traced the trade imbalance to China's policy of keeping the value of its currency, the yuan or renminbi (RMB), artificially low. "Alone among the world's major economies," one report stated, "China refuses to allow the *renminbi* (RMB), its currency, to respond to free market movements. China's leaders instead keep the currency trading at an artificially low level in order to suppress export prices—a deliberate violation of the rules of the International Monetary Fund, of which it is a member."[93] One Senate bill proposed an offsetting 27.5 percent tax on Chinese products. Some opponents disputed the analysis of the currency-valuation issue. Others claimed that the proposed remedy would ratchet up prices and hurt American consumers and businesses. The tax was not approved, but the issue continued to stir debate.

Security issues also have engendered a number of controversies. In 1996, reports indicated that China had been helping Pakistan develop its nuclear weapons. Policy makers on both sides acknowledged that weapons proliferation was an issue, especially China's transfer of missile and chemical-weapons technology. The debate primarily revolved around whether to use economic sanctions to punish China for this behavior, with arguments similar to those on the human rights issue being invoked. Opponents of sanctions stressed working cooperatively within the nonproliferation treaties signed by China, whereas supporters of sanctions pointed to China's breaches of those conventions. Because their exports were the particular target, American high-technology companies led the antisanctions lobby.

An even politically hotter issue involved allegations that China had been using contacts developed through military, scientific, and economic cooperation to steal secrets about American nuclear weapons design and development. Congress launched a major investigation into alleged Chinese espionage. A congressional report stated that China had acquired key data on seven of the most advanced nuclear warheads in the U.S. arsenal, as well as other military and high technology secrets. Focus fell on Wen Ho Lee, a Taiwanese-American scientist working at Los Alamos National Laboratory. Lee was arrested and held without bail in solitary confinement for almost a year. He did plead guilty in a plea bargain to a lesser charge, but denied any involvement in espionage. Lee eventually won a $1.6 million settlement against the federal government and with media organizations that had run major stories on the espionage accusations.

Nevertheless, concerns remained about China's military power, as noted earlier. Congress established the U.S.-China Economic and Security Review Commission, with a mandate to evaluate the national security effects of bilateral trade and economic relations. Though bipartisan, it has tended to lean toward the conservative containment perspective.

Meanwhile human rights groups have continued to raise their concerns. Tibet's cause has received added attention from the involvement of actors such as Richard Gere, groups such as Students for a Free Tibet, and the series of Free Tibet concerts. In 2009 in her first major speech regarding Asia, Secretary of State Hillary Clinton said little regarding Tibet other than the United States believes that "Tibetans . . . can enjoy religious freedom without fear of persecution."[94] This position disappointed advocates of a free Tibet, who remembered the strong stance Clinton took on the issue as first lady and hoped the United States might once more actively pressure China.[95] Instead, Secretary Clinton publicly espoused limiting the priority given to Tibet and other human rights issues, particularly publicly, if those issues would block consensus on climate change, nonproliferation, and rebuilding the international economy. Organizations such as Amnesty International and Human Rights Watch urged Clinton to "tell Chinese officials that China's relationship with the United States 'will depend in part on whether it lives by universally accepted human rights norms.' "[96]

And then there's ***Taiwan.*** Still. In 2008 the United States and China did reach an agreement on opposing efforts for an independence referendum in Taiwan. Secretary of State Condoleezza Rice warned Taiwan not to provoke China, stating that "this referendum is not going to help anyone, and, in fact, it shouldn't be held."[97] On additional arms sales, though, traditional differences reemerged. The Bush administration had been considering a major arms sale for a number of years. Intra-administration bureaucratic politics included some opposition to it. In Congress, though, the Taiwan lobby asserted itself. More than one-third of all House members were part of the Congressional Taiwan Caucus, drawn from both parties.[98] HR 6646, a bipartisan resolution, was introduced to require the executive branch to provide detailed briefings to Congress on the state of Taiwanese arms sales. A Democrat, Representative David Scott (D-Georgia), said that U.S. policy toward Taiwan was clear: "The United States is obligated to provide defensive military equipment to Taiwan, not just because it is right to aid our democratic friends, but also because it is the law of the land under the Taiwan Relations Act." A Republican, Ed Royce (R-California), added that "the People's Republic of China continues to expand its military capabilities, amassing hundreds of short-range missiles pointed across the strait," he said. "Now they're pointed at Taiwan."[99] Notably, the *Congressional Record* did not register any representatives as speaking out against the resolution. In October 2008, the White House moved ahead and offered Taiwan a $6 billion dollar package. Then-candidate Barack Obama objected to some parts of the package but supported the rest as consistent with the 1970s agreements on normalization. China responded to the arms sale by suspending military-to-military exchanges and nonproliferation talks, resuming them a few months later.

These politics are not just a matter of the Chinese government and the U.S. government. "K Street" lobbyists (nicknamed for the D.C. street where many lobbyists have their offices) and public-relations firms are involved on both sides. As early as the 1990s, China began a public relations campaign to promote a benign and peaceful image in the United States and around the world.[100] As part of China's political strategy for gaining approval of permanent trade partner status, Fortune 500 companies such as Boeing, AT&T, General Motors, and General Electric—all of which sought to expand their operations into the rapidly growing Chinese market—bankrolled a successful million-dollar "China Normalization Initiative" campaign.[101] In addition, China's State Council Information Office and its Ministry of Culture launched a $7 million campaign, also partly underwritten by American corporations with large investments in China, to bring a positive image of China to the United States through a traveling display of Chinese culture.[102] During the 2007 food- and product-safety scares, China put together a string of lobbyists who were "practically living on Capitol Hill." In Beijing, the government sought advice from the American public-relations giants Ogilvy and Edelman on how to convince Americans that Chinese goods were as safe as their own.[103]

On the other side of the lobbying street, Taiwan long has operated a sophisticated, well-financed public relations machine in the United States.[104] The U.S.-China Economic and Security Commission has called the rivalry nothing less than "public opinion warfare." Citing the example of Chinese attempts to reform its image in the aftermath of the Tibetan protests just before the 2008 Olympics, the commission reported that the "Chinese press published articles vigorously denouncing the actions of sympathizers for Tibet and trying to reframe the issue as an attempt by Tibetan separatists to destabilize China prior to the Olympics." It also noted that PR efforts are not confined to conventional forms of media. They include "comments to the press by Chinese officials, . . . advertisements purchased in domestic or foreign publications, and actions of Chinese representatives at various international venues, including UN gatherings."[105]

With this history and with the array of issues on the agenda, U.S.-China relations may stir even more lobbying and greater political debate in the years ahead.

## Summary

The end of the Cold War put the alignments and dynamics of major-power geopolitics into flux. Realists, international institutionalists, and other theorists and policy intellectuals present various alternative strategies. U.S. relations with Russia have improved substantially since the end of the Cold War, but uncertainties remain as to which scenario—Russia as friend, as great-power competitor, or as adversary—will prevail in the future. Relations with China also pose many uncertainties and encompass a wide range of issues, with debate manifesting different assessments of the mix of common and competing interests. Relations with Cold War–era allies in Western Europe and Japan remain generally positive but are going through their own transitions. So are relations with India, Brazil, and other emerging powers. Regional geopolitics also shows shifts from

Cold War patterns. All told, post–Cold War geopolitics is providing both opportunities and challenges across the "4 Ps" objectives of Power, Peace, Prosperity, and Principles. Foreign policy politics in these issue areas has been a mix of continuity with and change from past patterns. Relations with China continue to bring influential lobbies into play in ways that provide an instructive case study.

## *American Foreign Policy* Online Student StudySpace

- How are major power geopolitics playing out?
- Is East Asia going to be a zone of stability or conflict?
- Does NATO have a future?
- What is the status of relations within our own hemisphere with Latin America?
- What are the politics of U.S.-China relations?

For these and other study questions, as well as other features, check out Chapter 7 on the *American Foreign Policy* Online Student StudySpace at wwnorton.com/studyspace.

## Notes

[1]George W. Bush, The National Security Strategy of the United States of America, September 2002, www.acq.osd.mil/ncbdp/nm/docs/Relevant%20Docs/national_security_strategy.pdf (accessed 8/13/09).

[2]Excerpts from "Pentagon's Plan: 'Prevent the Re-Emergence of a New Rival,'" *New York Times*, March 8, 1992 (emphasis added).

[3]Robert J. Lieber, *The American Era: Power and Strategy for the 21st Century* (New York: Cambridge University Press, 2005), 5. See also William Wohlforth, "The Stability of a Unipolar World," *International Security* 24.1 (Summer 1999): 5–41, and Stephen Brooks and William Wohlforth, "American Primacy in Perspective," *Foreign Affairs* 82.4 (July/August 2002): 20–33.

[4]A. F. K. Organski, *World Politics*, 2d ed. (New York: Knopf, 1968); Organski and Jacek Kugler, *The War Ledger* (Chicago: University of Chicago Press, 1981); Robert Gilpin, *War and Change in World Politics* (New York: Cambridge University Press, 1983); John J. Mearsheimer, *The Tragedy of Great Power Politics* (New York: Norton, 2001).

[5]Alistair Iaian Johnston, "Is China a Status Quo Power?" *International Security* 27.4 (Spring 2003): 5–56.

[6]Robert Kagan, "Power and Weakness," *Policy Review* 113 (June 2002): 1.

[7]Nicole Gnesotto, "Reacting to America," *Survival: Global Politics and Strategy* 44.4 (Winter 2002–2003): 100, 102.

[8]Tony Blair, speech to the U.S. Congress, July 18, 2003, www.number10.gov.uk/Page4220 (accessed 8/13/09).

[9]Craig R. Whitney, "France Presses for a Power Independent of the U.S.," *New York Times*, November 7, 1999, Section 1, p. 9.

[10]Dana Priest, "Help From France Key in Covert Operations," *Washington Post*, July 3, 2005, A1.

[11]Hans W. Maull, "Germany and the Use of Force: Still a 'Civilian Power'?" *Survival: Global Politics and Strategy* 42.2 (Summer 2000): 56–80.

[12]Jeffrey Anderson, G. John Ikenberry, and Thomas Risse, eds., *The End of the West? Crisis and Change in the Atlantic Order* (Ithaca, N.Y.: Cornell University Press, 2008). See also Dana H. Allin, Gilles Andreani, Philippe Errera, and Gary Samore, *Repairing the Damage: Possibilities and Limits of Transatlantic Consensus*, Adelphi Paper 389 (London: International Institute for Strategic Studies, 2007); Jeffrey Kopstein and Sven Steinmo, eds., *Growing Apart? America and Europe in the Twenty-First Century* (New York: Cambridge University Press, 2008).

[13]European Union, Activities of the European Union, Foreign and Security Policy, http://europa.eu/pol/cfsp/index_en.htm (accessed 9/17/09).

[14]George Liska, *Nations in Alliance: The Limits of Interdependence* (Baltimore: Johns Hopkins University Press, 1962), 12.

[15]NATO, "Enlargement." Available at www.nato.int/issues/enlargement/index.html (accessed 8/13/09).

[16]Joseph Lepgold, "NATO's Post–Cold War Collective Action Problem," *International Security* 23 (Summer 1998): 84–85.

[17]Bruce W. Jentleson, "The Atlantic Alliance in a Post-American World," *Journal of Transatlantic Studies* 7.1 (March 2009): 61–72.

[18]David Abshire, "A Debate for 16 Parliaments," *Washington Post*, February 19, 1997, A21.

[19]Lepgold, "NATO's Post–Cold War Collective Action Problem," 81.

[20]Lepgold, "NATO's Post–Cold War Collective Action Problem," 91.

[21]NATO, "NATO and the Fight Against Terrorism," www.nato.int/issues/terrorism/index.html (accessed 8/14/09).

[22]*Transatlantic Trends Report: Key Findings 2008*, 4, www.eliamep.gr/wp-content/uploads/2008/10/trans-atlantic-trends-2008.pdf (accessed 9/17/09).

[23]Ivo Daalder and James Goldgeier, "Global NATO," *Foreign Affairs* 85.5 (September/October 2006): 105–13.

[24]Gail W. Lapidus, "Transforming Russia: American Policy in the 1990s," in *Eagle Rules? Foreign Policy and American Primacy in the Twenty-First Century*, Robert J. Lieber, ed. (Upper Saddle River, N.J.: Prentice-Hall, 2002), 108.

[25]Lapidus, "Transforming Russia," 108–09.

[26]Andrei Kozyrev, "Russia: A Chance for Survival," *Foreign Affairs* 71.2 (March/April 1992): 9–10.

[27]Press Conference by President Bush and Russian Federation president Putin, Brdo Castle, Brdo Pri Kranju, Slovenia, June 16, 2001, http://georgewbush-whitehouse.archives.gov/news/releases/2001/06/20010618.html (accessed 8/14/09).

[28]"Russia's National Security Concept," *Arms Control Today* (January/February 2000). Available at www.armscontrol.org/act/2000_01-02/docjf00 (accessed 8/14/09).

[29]Jane Perlez, "U.S. Scolds Russia for Plans to Resume Arms Sales to Iran," *New York Times*, March 15, 2001, A15.

[30]Patrick E. Tyler, "Moscow Says Remarks by U.S. Resurrect 'Spirit of Cold War,'" *New York Times*, March 21, 2001.

[31]Remarks by Vice President Biden at 45th Munich Conference on Security Policy, Munich, Germany, February 7, 2009, www.whitehouse.gov/the_press_office/RemarksbyVicePresidentBidenat45thMunichConferenceonSecurityPolicy/ (accessed 8/14/09).

[32]Lapidus, "Transforming Russia," 126.

[33]Sergei Ivanov, speech at the Wehrkunde Security Conference, Munich, Germany, February 4, 2001.

[34]Richard K. Betts, "The Three Faces of NATO," *National Interest Online*, April 10, 2009, www.nationalinterest.org/Article.aspx?id=20944 (accessed 8/14/09).

[35]"Bush Supports Ukraine's NATO Dream," *Russia Today*, April 1, 2008, www.russiatoday.com/news/news/22852?gclid=CIr7wa6I3JUCFQtZHgodhQhgXw (accessed 8/14/09).

[36]Vice President's Remarks at the Ambrosetti Forum, Cernobbio, Italy, September 6, 2008, http://georgewbush-whitehouse.archives.gov/news/releases/2008/09/20080906-1.html (accessed 8/14/09).

[37]Bush Addresses Tens of Thousands in Georgia's Freedom Square, Tbilisi, May 10, 2005, www.america.gov/st/washfile-english/2005/May/20050510114027btruevecer0.9125635.html (accessed 8/14/09).

[38]Condoleezza Rice, Remarks en Route to Brussels, Belgium, August 18, 2008, http://sarajevo.usembassy.gov/georgia_20080818.html (accessed 8/14/09).

[39]BBC News Europe, "Russia and Georgia Agree on a Truce," August 13, 2008, http://news.bbc.co.uk/2/hi/europe/7557457.stm (accessed 8/14/09).

[40]Jim Hoagland, "Three Miscreants," *Washington Post*, April 13, 2003, B7.

[41]Cited in Stephen M. Walt, *Taming American Power: The Global Response to U.S. Primacy* (New York: Norton, 2005), 111.

[42]Putin: "Iran Does Not Need Nuclear Weapons," Globalsecurity.org, September 25, 2004, www.globalsecurity.org/wmd/library/news/iran/2004/iran-040925-irna01.htm (accessed 8/14/09).

[43]Robert Legvold, "The Three Russias: Decline, Revolution and Reconstruction," in *A Century's Journey: How the Great Powers Shape the World*, Robert A. Pastor, ed. (New York: Basic Books, 1999), 188–89.

[44]Legvold, "The Three Russias," 189.

[45]Lapidus, "Transforming Russia," 120.

[46]Michael Wines, "Russia's Latest Dictator Goes by the Name of Law," *New York Times*, January 21, 2001, Section 4, p. 3.

[47]Mark Franchetti, "Putin Resurrects Spectre of KGB," *Sunday Times* (London), February 4, 2001.

[48]Ellen Mickiewicz, *Changing Channels: Television and the Struggle for Power in Russia* (New York: Oxford University Press, 1997); Kathy Lally, "Battle over Free Press Intensifies in Russia," *Baltimore Sun*, February 3, 2001, 1A; "A Moscow Media Magnate Urges a Definition of Limits for Russia," *New York Times*, May 4, 2001.

[49]Council of Europe, Russian Duma Elections "'Not Held on a Level Playing Field,' Say Parliamentary Observers," December 3, 2007, https://wcd.coe.int/ViewDoc.jsp?id=1221469&Site=DC&BackColorInternet=F5CA75&BackColorIntranet=F5CA75&BackColorLogged=A9BACE (accessed 8/14/09).

[50]Council on Foreign Relations, "Russia's Wrong Direction: What the United States Can and Should Do," March 2006, www.cfr.org/publication/9997 (accessed 8/14/09).

[51]Lapidus, "Transforming Russia," 117.

[52]Abram Chayes and Antonia Handler Chayes, *Preventing Conflict in the Post-Communist World: Mobilizing International and Regional Organizations* (Washington, D.C.: Brookings Institution Press, 1996), 10.

[53]Francis Fukuyama and G. John Ikenberry, "Report of the Working Group on Grand Strategic Choices," Princeton Project on National Security, September 2005, 3, 14–15.

[54]David Shambaugh, "China Engages Asia: Reshaping the Regional Order," *International Security* 29.3 (Winter 2004/05): 64.

[55]Ministry of Foreign Affairs, Department of Policy Planning, *China's Foreign Affairs, 2005 Edition* (Beijing: World Affairs Press, 2005), 352.

[56]Henry A. Kissinger, "China: Containment Won't Work," *Washington Post*, June 13, 2005, A19.

[57]Confirmation Hearing by Secretary of State-Designate Colin L. Powell, January 17, 2001, http://2001-2009.state.gov/secretary/former/powell/remarks/2001/443.htm (accessed 8/14/09).

[58]Kurt M. Campbell, Senate Foreign Relations Committee Confirmation Hearing Statement, June 10, 2009, http://foreign.senate.gov/testimony/2009/CampbellTestimony090610a.pdf (accessed 8/14/09).

[59]Robert S. Ross, "The 1995–96 Taiwan Straits Confrontation: Coercion, Credibility and the Use of Force," in *The United States and Coercive Diplomacy*, Robert J. Art and Patrick M. Cronin, eds. (Washington, D.C.: U.S. Institute of Peace Press, 2003), 225–73.

[60]Information Office of the State Council of the People's Republic of China, "China's National Defense in 2008," Information Office of the State Council of China, January 20, 2009, 2, http://news.xinhuanet.com/english/2009-01/20/content_10688124.htm (accessed 8/14/09).

[61]U.S.-China Economic and Security Review Commission, *2008 Report to Congress,* November 2008, 7, www.uscc.gov/annual_report/2008/annual_report_full_08.pdf (accessed 8/14/09).

[62]U.S. Department of Defense, Annual Report to Congress, *Military Power of the People's Republic of China 2008,* March 3, 2008, I, www.defenselink.mil/pubs/pdfs/China_Military_Report_08.pdf (accessed 8/14/09).

[63]Richard Holbrooke, "A Defining Moment with China," *Washington Post,* January 2, 2002, A13.

[64]Aaron L. Friedberg, "11 September and the Future of Sino-American Relations," *Survival: Global Politics and Strategy* 44.1 (Spring 2002): 36; Craig S. Smith, "China, in Harsh Crackdown, Executes Muslim Separatists," *New York Times,* December 16, 2001, 1.

[65]Edward Friedman, "Lone Eagle, Lone Dragon? How the Cold War Did Not End," in *Eagle Rules? Foreign Policy and American Primacy in the Twenty-First Century,* Robert Lieber, ed. (Upper Saddle River, NJ: Prentice Hall, 2001), 195.

[66]Edward Cody, "China Grows More Wary Over Rash of Protests," *Washington Post,* August 10, 2005, p. A11; Joseph Kahn, "Pace and Scope of Protest in China Accelerated in '05," *New York Times,* January 20, 2006, A10; Bruce Einhorn, "In China, a Winter of Discontent," *BusinessWeek,* January 30, 2008, www.businessweek.com/globalbiz/content/jan2008/gb20080130_195483.htm?chan=globalbiz_asia+index+page_top+stories (accessed 8/14/09).

[67]Elizabeth C. Economy, *The River Runs Black* (Ithaca, N.Y.: Cornell University Press, 2004).

[68]Minxin Pei, "Future Shock: The WTO and Political Change in China," *Policy Brief* 3 (February 2001), Washington, D.C.: Carnegie Endowment for International Peace, www.carnegieendowment.org/files/dem.PolBrief3.pdf (accessed 8/14/09).

[69]Elisabeth Rosenthal, "China Detains and Isolates Liberal Computer Whiz," *New York Times,* April 21, 2001, A3.

[70]Tom Malinowski, "China's Willing Censors," *Washington Post,* April 20, 2001, A25.

[71]Elliot Schrage, statement for joint hearing on "The Internet in China: A Tool for Freedom or Suppression?" before the Subcommittee on Africa, Global Human Rights and International Operations and the Subcommittee on Asia and the Pacific, Committee on International Relations, U.S. House of Representatives, February 15, 2006, 136, http://commdocs.house.gov/committees/intlrel/hfa26075.000/hfa26075_0f.htm (accessed 9/14/09), cited in "The Great Firewall: Globalization, China and the Internet," case study prepared by Jake Palley for my course Globalization and Governance.

[72]U.S. Department of State, Bureau of East Asian and Pacific Affairs, "Background Note: Japan," June 2006, www.state.gov/r/pa/ei/bgn/4142.htm (accessed 8/14/09).

[73]Peter Finn and Kathryn Tolbert, "Ex-Axis Powers Recast Foreign Military Roles," *Washington Post,* November 30, 2001, A34.

[74]Christopher W. Hughes, *Japan's Re-Emergence as a "Normal" Military Power,* International Institute for Strategic Studies, Adelphi Paper 368–69 (London: Oxford University Press, 2004); Akio Watanabe, "A Continuum of Change," *Washington Quarterly* 27.4 (Autumn 2004): 137–46.

[75]Justin McCury, "Japan Moves Towards Amending Pacifist Constitution," *The Guardian, UK,* May 14, 2007, www.guardian.co.uk/world/2007/may/14/japan.justinmccurry (accessed 8/14/09).

[76]Thom Shanker, "Gates Urges More Japanese Action on Global Security," *New York Times,* November 9, 2007.

[77]Bruce Klingner, "Forging a New Era in the U.S.–Japan Alliance," Heritage Foundation, October 9, 2008, www.heritage.org/Research/AsiaandthePacific/bg2196.cfm (accessed 8/14/09).

[78]Howard W. French, "Taboo against Nuclear Arms Is Being Challenged in Japan," *New York Times,* June 9, 2002, 1.

[79]Thom Shanker and Norimitsu Onishi, "Japan Tells Rice It Will Not Seek Nuclear Weapons," *New York Times,* October 18, 2008.

[80]"Japan's Nuclear Envoy says Six Party Talk on N Korea Still Possible This Year," *International Herald Tribune,* November 29, 2006.

[81]Thom Shanker and Norimitsu Onishi, "Japan Tells Rice It Will Not Seek Nuclear Weapons."

[82]See, for example, Norimitsu Onishi, "Ugly Images of Asian Rivals Become Best Sellers in Japan," *New York Times,* November 19, 2005, A1.

[83]Tim Weiner, "The Kashmir Connection: A Puzzle," *New York Times,* December 7, 2008.

[84]Madhur Singh, "India and Iran: Getting Friendly?" *Time,* April 24, 2008, www.time.com/time/world/article/0,8599,1734777,00.html (accessed 8/15/09).

[85]Christopher Bodeen, "India: Foreign Policy to Stay Independent," Associated Press, January 15, 2008, www.foxnews.com/wires/2008Jan15/0,4670,ChinaIndia,00.html (accessed 8/15/09).

[86]Julia E. Sweig, "The Hemispheric Divide," *National Interest* 100 (March/April 2009), 48–49.

[87]Menendez quote in Shailagh Murray and Karen DeYoung, "Momentum Grows for Relaxing Cuba Policy," *Washington Post,* March 30, 2009, A1; poll was published April 21, 2009 in the *New York Times.*

[88]Mark Landler, "Clinton Says U.S. Feeds Mexico Drug Trade," *New York Times,* March 26, 2009.

[89]Barack Obama, Remarks by the President to the Ghanaian Parliament, July 11, 2009, www.whitehouse.gov/the_press_office/Remarks-by-the-President-to-the-Ghanaian-Parliament/ (accessed 8/15/09).

[90]Obama, Remarks to the Ghanaian Parliament.

[91]*Congressional Record* XCVII (April 19, 1951), 4261.

[92]"Human Rights in China: Improving or Deteriorating Conditions?" Testimony of Thea M. Lee, Policy Director, AFL-CIO, before the House Committee on International Relations, Subcommittee on Africa, Global Human Rights and International Operations, April 19, 2006, www.aflcio.org/issues/jobseconomy/manufacturing/iuc/upload/lee_04192006.pdf (accessed 8/15/09).

[93]U.S.-China Economic and Security Review Commission, *2008 Report to Congress, 2.*

[94]Hillary Clinton, "U.S.-Asia Relations: Indispensable to Our Future," remarks at the Asia Society, New York, February 13, 2009, www.state.gov/secretary/rm/2009a/02/117333.htm# (accessed 8/15/09).

[95]Matthew Lee, "Human Rights Not Focus of Clinton's China talks," *Independent,* February 21, 2009, www.independent.co.uk/news/world/asia/human-rights-not-focus-of-clinton8217s-china-talks-1628258.html (accessed 8/15/09).

[96]Glenn Kessler, "Clinton Criticized for Not Trying to Force China's Hand," *Washington Post,* February 21, 2009.

[97]Edward Wong, "Taiwan's Independence Movement Likely to Wane," *New York Times,* March 12, 2008.

[98]Scott L. Kastner and Douglas R. Grob, "Legislative Foundations of U.S.-Taiwan Relations: A New Look at the Congressional Taiwan Caucus," *Foreign Policy Analysis* 5:1 (January 2009): 57–72.

[99]U.S. House of Representatives, Requiring Consultations On U.S.-Taiwan Arms Sales Talks, *Congressional Record,* September 23, 2008, http://thomas.loc.gov/cgi-bin/query/z?r110:H23SE8-0049: (accessed 8/15/09).

[100]Xu Wu, "The New 'China Lobby?' China's Government PR Effort in the U.S.," paper presented at the National Communication Association, 94th Annual Convention, November 21–24, 2008, San Diego, www.allacademic.com/meta/p258233_index.html (accessed 8/15/09).

[101]"Doing Business with Strongmen," *BusinessWeek Online,* April 22, 1996, www.businessweek.com/archives/1996/b3472069.arc.htm (accessed 8/15/09).

[102]Elisabeth Rosenthal, "China's U.S. Road Show, Aimed at Making Friends," *New York Times,* August 23, 2000.

[103]Ariana Eunjung Cha, "After Silence, China Mounts Product Safety PR Offensive," *Washington Post,* July 14, 2007.

[104]U.S.-China Economic and Security Review Commission, *2008 Report to Congress,* 154.

[105]U.S.-China Economic and Security Review Commission, *2008 Report to Congress,* 154.

CHAPTER 8

# The Middle East: A Special Focus

## Introduction: September 13, 1993, to September 11, 2001: From Hope to Tragedy

In the early 1990s, things seemed to be going well for American foreign policy in the Middle East. The end of the Cold War meant the end of the Soviet threat in this geopolitically and economically crucial region. The 1990–91 Persian Gulf War, which reversed Saddam Hussein's invasion of Kuwait, was a major victory for American military power and American diplomatic leadership. Even the Arab-Israeli conflict seemed to have gotten on a path to peace. On September 13, 1993, following secret talks held in Norway, the Israeli prime minister Yitzhak Rabin and the Palestine Liberation Organization (PLO) chairman Yasir Arafat shook hands on the White House lawn. With President Bill Clinton as witness, they signed an initial peace agreement.

The day of the Rabin-Arafat handshake was a beautiful late summer day: sunny, with a blue sky, full of hope and promise. Eight years later, another late summer day that started out just as beautifully—September 11, 2001—didn't end that way.

Most of us will always remember where we were when we first heard the news, when we first saw the images, when we first felt the fear. The shock of the crashing World Trade Center towers and the gashes in the walls of the Pentagon—symbols of American economic and military strength—were seared deeply into the American psyche.

More than ever before in its modern history, the United States was proven vulnerable right at home. Foreign policy usually had been about U.S. involvements "over there"—in the Middle East, in the developing world, in Europe, in Asia. Now the threat was "here," on the American side of the oceans. Not since the bloodiest battles of the U.S. Civil War (1861–65) had so many Americans been killed in conflict on a single day. Not since the War of 1812, when the British attacked Washington, D.C., and set fire to the White House,

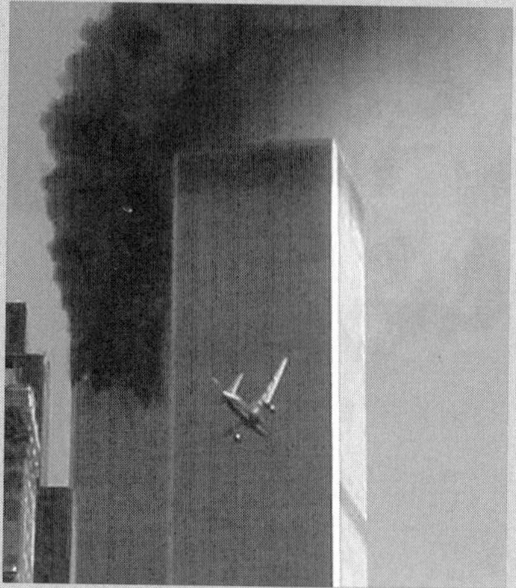

9/13/93, 9/11/01: Peacemaking, Terrorism (*AP/Wide World Photos; AP Photo*)

had America's own capital been attacked. Even Pearl Harbor was an attack on a military base, not on cities and civilian populations. For Americans, the sense of threat was greater than at any time since the end of the Cold War.

President George W. Bush declared ***a war on terrorism.*** Within the month, the United States retaliated, leading an invasion of Afghanistan seeking to kill or capture Osama bin Laden, destroy his Al Qaeda terrorist network, and topple the Taliban regime that governed Afghanistan and gave bin Laden safe haven. This was just a start: The war on terrorism "will not end," Bush declared, "until every terrorist group of global reach has been found, stopped and defeated." Less than two years later, the Bush administration took the United States to war in Iraq, a war that proved to be the most controversial U.S. foreign policy issue since the Vietnam war.

Other regions of the world grew in their own importance, but the Middle East became ever more central. Wars in Iraq and Afghanistan, and Al Qaeda displaced and damaged but not destroyed or defeated, raised questions about whether American *Power* has been strengthened or weakened. Hopes of *Peace* were dashed amid the breakdown of the 1990s Arab-Israeli peace process, the 2006 Israel-Lebanon war, and the 2008–2009 Israel-Hamas war. Tensions heightened with Iran over nuclear proliferation and other issues. Pakistan verged on being a failed state. *Principles* were called into question by inconsistencies in support for democracy and alliances with authoritarian governments that risked replacing the Cold War "ABC" (anybody but communists) with "ABT" (anybody but terrorists). *Prosperity* was shaken by $140 per barrel oil in 2008 and continued threats to stability of supply. Even more foreboding Middle East scenarios may face us in the future. We thus make the Middle East the special focus of this chapter.

Policies in this region also have raised key *foreign policy politics* issues. This chapter's foreign policy politics section focuses on the war on terrorism's version of the national security–civil liberties "great debate" and the domestic politics of the Iraq war, particularly regarding presidential-congressional war powers and intra–executive branch decision making.

## Operations Desert Shield and Desert Storm: The 1990–91 Persian Gulf War

On August 2, 1990, the Iraqi armies of Saddam Hussein invaded neighboring Kuwait. Although Iraq and Kuwait had a border dispute as well as some other issues, the real issue was Saddam Hussein's desire to become the dominant power in the Persian Gulf region. Indeed, his forces were poised to keep going straight into Saudi Arabia, an even more strategic country and a close U.S. ally.

The threat to vital American interests was deemed so serious that it was met by the most rapid buildup of U.S. military forces since World War II, first as a "desert shield" to protect Saudi Arabia and then as a "desert storm" to drive Saddam back out of Kuwait. Deployments for ***Operation Desert Shield*** were begun of what would be nearly 400,000 American troops. "This will not stand," President George H. W. Bush declared about Saddam's invasions of Kuwait. A twenty-seven-nation coalition was built, including most of Western Europe, Japan, and much of the Arab world, and with some support even from the Soviet Union. The UN Security Council (UNSC) moved swiftly to impose economic sanctions and issue diplomatic condemnations of Iraq. As the crisis wore on and Saddam remained intransigent, the UNSC passed a resolution authorizing "all necessary means" to get Iraqi troops out of Kuwait, including the use of military force. The UN set a deadline of January 15 for Iraqi withdrawal from Kuwait. When the deadline wasn't met, the multinational military force that had been assembled under the command of General Norman Schwarzkopf of the U.S. Army went to war.

***Operation Desert Storm*** proved a formidable military victory. In little more than a month, Iraqi forces were defeated and forced to withdraw from Kuwait. This was achieved with few American and coalition casualties. There was some debate about whether to keep going to Baghdad and overthrow Saddam at this moment of weakness, but President Bush decided against it. Instead he worked through the UN to punish and contain Iraq, including through the creation of the UN Special Commission on Iraq (UNSCOM), which was mandated to go into Iraq and inspect and destroy Saddam's weapons-of-mass-destruction (WMD) complex.

In Chapter 1 we cited the 1990–91 Persian Gulf War as a major example of complementarity among the "4 Ps" of American foreign policy. Here we draw a number of more specific policy lessons from this war. The most immediate was that aggression was still a fact of international life. Troops marched and tanks rolled as Iraq took over Kuwait, its smaller and militarily weaker neighbor.

Second was the value of working through the UN. This case was a strong example of the policy-enhancement argument made in Chapter 6 about how American foreign policy objectives are more likely to be achieved by working through the UN. Operation Desert Shield had both the benefits of UNSC legitimization and the burden sharing of the broad multilateral coalition, which sent troops, footed the bill, and provided other assistance. Being able to make this not just George H. W. Bush versus Saddam Hussein but a coalition of the world's major nations, including some of Saddam's Arab brethren, forged under U.N. auspices, made the U.S. position that much stronger. Yet both the military command for fighting the war and the diplomatic initiative for negotiating the terms of the peace were left to the United States.

The third lesson was that the military victory left no doubts about American military power. It is important to recall how dire many of the predictions were of the risks that going to war might bring. But these predictions did not come to pass, and with the help of CNN the whole world watched the vivid images of American military might, particularly of American air power. Bombers took out most Iraqi air defenses and hit targets with a new generation of highly accurate precision-guided munitions. These were part of the heralded ***revolution in military affairs (RMA),*** through which mastery of electronic and information technologies gave the United States unprecedented conventional military capabilities. Later studies indicated that the precision was not so great as was claimed at the time. Still, the dominant sense was of a new age in which the U.S. military had superiority in the air.

The fourth lesson was an affirmation of the ***Powell doctrine*** of decisive force. Named for General Colin Powell, who at the time was chair of the Joint Chiefs of Staff, this doctrine advocated that when military force is to be used, it should be used overwhelmingly and decisively. This was a major lesson that General Powell and others drew from the Vietnam War and its incremental approach to the use of force.

There were, however, some limits and negatives to the Gulf War's significance. As a military operation, for all the technological innovations the U.S. military displayed, it was fundamentally a classical strategy of armed forces against armed forces on the battlefield. But the nature of this war would prove to be more the exception than the rule. Somalia, Bosnia, Haiti, Kosovo, and the other ethnic conflicts and internal wars in which the United States became involved in the 1990s were much more politically based uses of military force, and much less battlefield based—more like Vietnam than Desert Storm, and thus presenting different challenges for the use of military force. The 2003 Iraq war started out seemingly like Desert Storm, but winning the peace was a very different challenge from winning the war.

Another limitation on the significance of the Gulf War was that it left Saddam in power in Baghdad. A number of factors went into the decision to stop the ground war after only one hundred hours, before potentially reaching Saddam himself. As understandable as this decision was, the succeeding years would show the problems and threats Saddam still could cause. One of these was his attempted assassination of former president Bush during a visit to Kuwait in 1993.

The UN coalition also frayed over the course of the 1990s. Economic sanctions were kept on the books but violated in practice. They also were manipulated by Saddam so that the Iraqi people were hit hard and humanitarian concerns aroused, but the regime maneuvered around them. Saddam kicked out the UN WMD inspectors, but the UNSC did little more than protest. Despite all these flaws, many felt Iraq was being effectively contained. Still, neoconservatives were stepping up the pressure even before 9/11 to shift from containment to regime change.

Finally, there were the lessons of the period leading up to Saddam's invasion of Kuwait, during which the United States had tilted toward Iraq in its 1980–88 war with Iran.[1] The policy was based on the greater threat posed by Iran's Islamic fundamentalists and the deep animosity of its anti-American leader, Ayatollah Ruhollah Khomeini. But the Reagan and first Bush administrations failed to see past the old adage ***"the enemy of my enemy is my friend."*** Indeed, the enemy of my enemy *may be* my friend, but he also may be my enemy, too. Thus it was one thing to feed the Iraqi population while it was at war with Iran, or to provide some industrial equipment, or even to share military intelligence and bolster Iraqi defensive military capabilities. It was quite another matter to loosen controls on technology and equipment with "dual uses" (both commercial and military applications). The United States did this to a degree that, along with Europe and on top of Soviet aid, significantly and substantially contributed to Iraqi development of offensive military capabilities, especially its nuclear, biological, and chemical weapons.

Some argued that these prewar mistakes really didn't matter, since the U.S.-led forces won the war. Some even argued that the United States and the world in general were better off because the war had been fought. At best this was a cold power-politics calculus that too readily dismissed the death toll, other human suffering, economic costs, environmental destruction, and further consequences of the war. Yet over time, as the conflicts with Iraq persisted and ultimately led to another war twelve years later, even this strategic logic came into question. Thus, along with the military lessons to be learned from how the war was fought, there were important lessons to be learned about why the war occurred.

## 9/11 and the Bush War on Terrorism

Before September 11, 2001, the post–Cold War foreign policy agenda had a long list of issues, but no single defining one, as anticommunism had been during the Cold War. The war on terrorism became that defining issue for the George W. Bush administration's foreign policy.

Osama bin Laden and his ***Al Qaeda*** terrorist network emerged during the 1990s. They were responsible for a number of terrorist attacks on the U.S. presence abroad, including the August 1998 bombings of the American embassies in Kenya and Tanzania and the October 2000 bombing of the naval warship USS *Cole* in a harbor in Yemen. Indeed, even before the September 11 attacks, arguments were being made that terrorism had to be given higher priority in U.S. foreign policy. Consider, for example, the report of the National Commission on Terrorism, issued in June 2000:

> Terrorists attack American targets more often than those of any other country. America's preeminent role in the world guarantees that this will continue to be the case, and the threat of attacks creating massive casualties is growing. If the United States is to protect itself, if it is to remain a world leader, this nation must develop and continuously refine sound counterterrorism policies appropriate to the rapidly changing world around us.
>
> International terrorists once threatened Americans only when they were outside the country. Today, international terrorists attack us on our own soil. . . .
>
> Terrorist attacks are becoming more lethal. Most terrorist organizations active in the 1970s and 1980s had clear political objectives. They tried to calibrate their attacks to produce just enough bloodshed to get attention for their cause, but not so much as to alienate public support. . . . Now, a growing percentage of terrorist attacks are designed to kill as many people as possible.[2]

This analysis and others like it were based in part on intelligence about bin Laden and Al Qaeda and other terrorists, as well as being grounded in three broader dynamics. First was terrorism as the "underside" of globalization. For all the benefits of the rapid and widespread movement of people, money, technology, and ideas, these trends also facilitated the operation of terrorists. They too could move from one corner of the globe to another. They too could communicate through the Internet. They too could visit various readily accessible Web sites and download information on various technologies, including WMD. They too could move their money around electronically. Terrorists operated in other eras, but globalization was part of what makes the terrorist threat that much greater today.

Second was the advantage that comes with being on the offensive and having the element of surprise on one's side. Terrorism's "tactical advantages," as the national security expert Richard Betts puts it, target "the soft underbelly of American primacy." In some situations, depending on the balance of forces and the nature of the warfare, the defense has the advantage. But with terrorism, the advantage is often with the attacker. They have the "capacity for strategic judo, the turning of the West's strength against itself. . . . Nineteen men from technologically backward societies did not have to rely on homegrown instruments to devastate the Pentagon and World Trade Center. They used computers and modern financial procedures with facility, and they forcibly appropriated the aviation technology of the West and used it as a weapon."[3] The openness of American society further complicates this, as we will see later in this chapter in the discussion of foreign policy politics and tensions between national security and civil liberties.

Third was the interconnection with many aspects of U.S. policy in the Middle East and more broadly toward the Islamic world. These areas and relationships had been conflict-ridden for the United States for many years. Iran since the 1979 Islamic fundamentalist revolution; Iraq since the 1990–91 Persian Gulf War; relations with Arab governments such as Saudi Arabia and Egypt, which largely supported U.S. foreign policy but had their own instabilities and opposition (bin Laden is Saudi, and his top lieutenant Egyptian); Islamic fundamentalism as it spread in many countries, including Pakistan and Lebanon; the failure to stay engaged in Afghanistan after the defeat of the Soviets in 1988; the Arab-Israeli conflict: these and other issues fed terrorism and turned it increasingly toward the United States as a principal target, while making strategizing against it an especially complicated task.

Still, it took the 9/11 attacks on the World Trade Center and the Pentagon for the shift from *a* problem to *the* problem to occur. "We are at war," President George W. Bush told the nation in announcing the military action against the Taliban regime and the Al Qaeda terrorist network in Afghanistan. And he didn't just mean Afghanistan; the struggle was global, and it was for the long term. It was not a classical war, but it was a war nevertheless. Other foreign policy issues had to be dealt with, but there was no higher priority for the Bush administration than the war on terrorism.

## The Afghanistan War under Bush

The initial war in Afghanistan was as internationally consensual as wars get. The U.S. claim to be acting in self-defense was strong. The Taliban regime had been denied its country's seat in the United Nations, and only two countries in the world had granted it diplomatic recognition. It was among the world's worst repressors of women and worst offenders against human rights. Some aspects of the U.S. strategy were debated, but the right to use force in this situation was widely accepted by the international community. The United Nations Security Council supported it, and over 170 nations joined the broader U.S.-led global coalition against terrorism.

Militarily, in its initial October–December 2001 phase, the ***Afghanistan war*** showed that American military power had reached even more dominant levels than demonstrated in the Kosovo and Persian Gulf wars. A vast new array of technologies was displayed. JDAMs (joint direct-action munitions) were satellite-guided bombs. Predators were unmanned drones equipped with high-tech sensors and real-time streaming video that enabled commanders to direct warplanes to targets around the clock and with unprecedented precision. Special Operations forces, consisting of Green Berets, other elite units, and CIA agents, infiltrated enemy areas, often riding on horseback in the rugged terrain yet technologically equipped to identify targets and communicate the enemy's exact location to bombers overhead. One U.S. Air Force officer called this basic equation of technology on horseback "21st-century air and space power combined with 16th-century land forces." Looking ahead, one report referred to plans for 2020 or earlier in which "pilotless planes and driverless buggies will direct remote-controlled bombers toward targets; pilotless helicopters will coordinate driverless convoys, and unmanned submarines will clear mines and launch cruise missiles. . . . In years to come, once targets are found, chances are good that they will be destroyed by weapons from pilotless vehicles that can distinguish friends from foes without consulting humans."[4]

For all the technological sophistication, though, the Afghan war strategy did have its shortcomings. One was the reliance on local forces as a way of limiting the ground forces that the United States itself had to commit. The Afghan Northern Alliance, the main anti-Taliban group, was a valuable ally in many respects, but not in all. As long as its interests were consistent with those of the United States, it proved a reliable ally. But when it had its own interests, it went its own way. An example came in the key battle of Tora Bora in December 2001. Many Al Qaeda leaders, possibly including bin Laden, were holed up in caves in this mountainous region but still managed to escape because the attacks on the caves by the Northern Alliance were poorly executed. The Northern Alliance had achieved its main objective—toppling the Taliban. Capturing Al Qaeda was less important to it than to the United States, so it was less inclined to run the risks inherent in the Tora Bora mission.

Of course, one of the reasons the United States relied on the Northern Alliance rather than its own ground forces was consternation over the U.S. domestic political impact of significant casualties. Ground troops were used more in Afghanistan than in Kosovo, but politics still kicked in to self-constrain U.S. military strategy. Here too it was an overcompensation, but the point is that even amid the broad consensus on the Afghanistan war, domestic politics was a constraining factor.

Human error also was a problem. Some of this was bureaucratic. One report cited at least ten instances within six weeks at the height of the war in which commanders believed they had top Taliban and Al Qaeda leaders "in [the] cross hairs" but were delayed in getting the attack clearances necessary from U.S. Central Command and the Pentagon.[5] Some errors were simply the fog of war, which even the best technology cannot preclude. On occasion bombs were misguided because of mistakes in identifying targets; such bombs could become "friendly fire," hitting their intended targets—except that the targets were not the enemy. In one incident in December 2001, three U.S. Green Beret soldiers and five Afghan allied fighters were killed. In another, rifle shots fired in celebration at a wedding ceremony in a small village were mistaken for enemy fire, and bombs were brought down on the wedding party, killing a number of people, including the bride.

Finally, the initial victory proved inconclusive. An FBI-CIA report leaked to the press in June 2002 "concluded that the war in Afghanistan failed to diminish the threat to the United States. . . . Instead the war might have complicated counterterrorism efforts by dispersing potential attackers across a wider geographic area."[6] A few months later, Lt. General Dan McNeil, the U.S. commander in Afghanistan, forecast that it would take up to two more years to eliminate Al Qaeda and build an Afghan army strong enough to deny terrorists a future safe haven.[7] Even this prediction proved much too optimistic. "'The Taliban and Al Qaeda are everywhere,' a shopkeeper told an American general in May 2006. The arrival of large numbers of Taliban in the villages, flush with money and weapons, has dealt a blow to public confidence in the Afghan government, already undermined by lack of tangible progress and frustration with corrupt and ineffective leaders."[8] The Afghan army's capacity remained questionable, with only about 27,000 trained soldiers, though the goal was 70,000. With economic reconstruction and development also proceeding slowly and marked by corruption, opium production was one of the few "booming" areas of the Afghan economy, so much so that 90 percent of the global opiate supply was now coming from Afghanistan. As the Bush administration left office, the situation was so bad that Admiral Mike Mullen, the chairman of the Joint Chiefs of Staff, warned that the United States was "running out of time" in Afghanistan.[9]

## Overall Bush War on Terrorism Strategy

The broader strategy of the Bush global war on terrorism was based on five principal elements.

**Destroy, Disrupt, Defeat** The overarching goal was to destroy, disrupt, and defeat Al Qaeda and other terrorists threatening U.S. security wherever they could be found. "Every day," Defense Secretary Donald Rumsfeld stated in 2003, we need to ask ourselves, "are we capturing, killing, or deterring and dissuading more terrorists than the radical clerics and madrassas are recruiting, training and deploying against us?"[10] Defeating the Taliban and forcing bin Laden out of his safe haven in Afghanistan, capturing other Al Qaeda leaders and operatives, deposing Saddam Hussein and ending his horrific rule, and preventing another major terrorist attack on its watch are among the achievements that the Bush administration claimed for its policy.

**The Bush Doctrine on Preemption** As discussed in Chapter 6, the "Bush doctrine" put increased emphasis on the need, in the post–September 11 world, to use military force preemptively. President Bush made an initial statement of this doctrine in a June 2002 speech at West Point:

> For much of the last century, America's defense relied on the Cold War doctrines of deterrence and containment. In some cases, those strategies still apply. But new threats also require new thinking. Deterrence—the promise of massive retaliation against nations—means nothing

> against shadowy terrorist networks with no nation or citizens to defend. Containment is not possible when unbalanced dictators with weapons of mass destruction can deliver those weapons on missiles or secretly provide them to terrorist allies.[11]

The U.S. doctrine on using force, therefore, would have to shift from relying on after-the-incident retaliation to preemptive action. "If we wait for threats to fully materialize, we will have waited too long. . . . [O]ur security will require all Americans to be forward-looking and resolute, to be ready for preemptive action when necessary to defend our liberty and to defend our lives."[12] This new doctrine was elaborated in the president's National Security Strategy of the United States, issued in September 2002 (see Reading 8.1), and was manifested six months later in the Iraq war.

8.1

COALITIONS OF THE WILLING The Bush administration recognized that no matter how preponderant American power was, some aspects of the antiterrorism strategy could not be achieved without the cooperation of other nations. It wanted to be sure, though, that no international institution, no alliance, and no other country constrained American freedom of action. It wanted the collective action, legitimization, and other benefits that multilateralism brings without any impediments on the U.S. capacity to act unilaterally. It thus put principal emphasis on assembling "coalitions of the willing" rather than working through formal institutional and alliance structures.

The global coalition initially forged after September 11 numbered over 170 countries. Not all joined the war effort in Afghanistan, but most if not all provided some form of support for some aspect of the war on terrorism. In addition, the Bush administration forged a new set of global military commitments on a more bilateral basis. The post–Cold War trend had been toward reducing U.S. overseas military bases and military aid programs. Here, too, the war on terrorism caused a major policy shift. Afghanistan was Al Qaeda's principal base but not its only one; it had developed a global network of cells. Other terrorist groups not formally affiliated but sharing goals, tactics, and enemies were also operating in countries around the world. American military commitments were made to a number of these countries where the threat was deemed the greatest: the South and Central Asian front-line states surrounding Afghanistan (Pakistan, Uzbekistan, Tajikistan, and Kyrgyzstan), Southeast Asian states with large Muslim populations and known active Al Qaeda cells and similar groups (Indonesia, Malaysia, and the Philippines), Yemen (where the October 2000 Al Qaeda attack on the USS *Cole* had occurred), Qatar (where bases were built up for attacking Iraq) and other Middle Eastern states, and Georgia (the ex-Soviet state in the Caucasus, near where Al Qaeda operatives were active in Chechnya). This also has included Africa, both Muslim northern Africa (e.g., Morocco, Tunisia, and even the former adversary Libya) and such sub-Saharan African countries as Nigeria, Mali, and Senegal.

PRINCIPLES The war on terrorism is not just about security; it also claims higher purposes. It is said to be about Principles as well as Power. Just as the United States fought the Cold War to ensure democracy's triumph over the communist "evil empire," so it now must fight the war on terrorism to ensure the triumph of freedom over this era's forces of evil. From the beginning President Bush frequently used the language of "good," "evil," and "freedom." Bin Laden and the other terrorists were, in his words, "evildoers." Iraq, Iran, and North Korea were named in Bush's 2002 State of the Union speech as the three principal points on the ***"axis of evil."*** The war on terrorism in all its aspects was being fought to defeat evil and defend freedom: freedom for Afghan women, who had been so brutally repressed by the Taliban; freedom for the Iraqi people, who needed to be liberated from Saddam Hussein; freedom for Americans to be able to live without the fear of terrorist attack; freedom for people everywhere to live without repression and fear.

Numerous political initiatives were taken to try to answer the "Why do they hate us?" question. A "public diplomacy" strategy was premised on the belief that the problem was principally a communications one. The American "message" was solid, it just needed to get out more accurately and more widely. Charlotte Beers, a prominent advertising executive, was appointed undersecretary of state for public diplomacy and public affairs to take up this task. Karen Hughes, one of Bush's top campaign and political aides, later took this job. Among the initiatives to get the American message out were a new Arabic-language radio station, more engagement with moderate Islamic religious leaders, and other efforts to fare better in "the battle of ideas" that underlay and fed into much of the fundamentalism and anti-Americanism around the world.

HOMELAND SECURITY Ensuring the security of the American homeland became a crucial issue, and an extremely complex one at that. Airport security was an obvious area for improvement. The anthrax letters that followed the World Trade Center attacks showed that anyone could be at risk in simply opening a letter at home. The United States has nearly 600,000 bridges, 170,000 water systems, 2,800 power plants (104 of them nuclear), 190,000 miles of interstate natural-gas pipelines, 463 skyscrapers, and innumerable shopping malls and sports stadiums that could become terrorist targets.[13] And nuclear waste sites. And harbors that every day receive millions of tons of shipping containers. And thousands of miles of border to patrol.

In his last foreign policy speech as president, delivered at West Point, George W. Bush stressed the success his terrorism strategy had had. Among his points:

> We have severely weakened the terrorists. We've disrupted plots to attack our homeland. We have captured or killed hundreds of al Qaeda leaders and operatives in more than two dozen countries—including the man who mastermind the 9/11 attacks, Khalid Sheikh Mohammed. . . .

> We've helped key partners and allies strengthen their capabilities in the fight against the terrorists. We've increased intelligence-sharing with friends and allies around the world. We've provided training and support to counterterrorism partners like the Philippines, and Indonesia, and Jordan, and Saudi Arabia. . . .
>
> America recognized the only way to defeat the terrorists in the long run is to present an alternative to their hateful ideology. So when we overthrew the dictators in Afghanistan and Iraq, we refused to take the easy option and instill friendly strongmen in their place. Instead, we're doing the tough work of helping democratic societies emerge as examples for people all across the Middle East.[14]

Critics of the Bush strategy come to a different assessment. In their view, the credits the Bush administration claimed for its war on terrorism are classic single-column accounting. The debits column also has many entries, arguably more: the thousands of deaths in Iraq of Americans, other foreigners, and Iraqi civilians; the tripling of terrorist attacks in 2004 over 2003, reaching the highest number since the State Department started compiling these data over twenty years ago, only to be followed by further major attacks, including those in Spain in 2004, London and Amman (Jordan) in 2005, Egypt in 2006, and Israel throughout this period; the growth of new terrorist groups and networks; and the further growth of anti-Americanism, fed by Bush policies. In a June 2006 survey that asked national security experts whether the United States was winning the war on terrorism, 83 percent said no. And although it is true that there had not been another major attack on the United States, it could be that none was intended, at least not yet, as Al Qaeda focused on other fronts and waited for the right opportunity.

In support of their assessment, critics make their own five main points:

PLAYING INTO AL QAEDA'S HANDS Although Al Qaeda underestimated the effectiveness of the immediate U.S. retaliation for 9/11 that drove them out of Afghanistan, much of the rest of the Bush strategy played right into their hands. The Al Qaeda strategy, as one terrorism expert put it, was "fundamentally one of bleeding the United States to exhaustion, while simultaneously using U.S. reaction to incite a mass uprising within the Islamic world."[15] The U.S. was not fully exhausted but it did get quite overextended, with major tolls on its military, economy, and international reputation. And although unrest in the Islamic world fell short of a mass uprising, anti-Americanism did reach unprecedented levels. Western intervention, as another military expert put it, was serving "as al-Qaeda's [sic] best recruiting tool."[16]

8.2 BUSH DOCTRINE DANGERS John Ikenberry is among those who argue that the Bush Doctrine on preemption made us less, not more, secure and the world more, not less, dangerous (Reading 8.2). Part of the argument sees preemption as a violation of international law and norms. Article 51 of the UN Charter acknowledges the inherent right of states to act in self-defense but only "if an armed act occurs" and until the UN Security Council acts. Some would extend this to include situations in which the threat is so imminent as to be virtually certain, so long as the decision is made by the UN, not just an individual country. But the Bush preemption doctrine does not hold even to this standard of evidence and is unilateral in its decision making and action. The argument against the Bush Doctrine, then, is in part ethical and juridical—about what is right and legal—and in part pragmatic—about how the weakening of laws and norms concerning the use of force in the name of today's security concern can become tomorrow's insecurity.

Besides legal and normative points are questions about whether preemptive strikes can be counted on to work. To use force decisively when using it preemptively imposes an especially demanding requirement for reliable intelligence and especially careful planning for enemy countermoves and other contingencies, including the enemy's own possible decision to act "pre-preemptively" and attack before you do. Although some then would argue "I told you so" and claim justification, the net effect could end up being a self-fulfilling prophecy in which the targeted regime ends up defeated or removed, but only after the threat that was to be prevented has already wreaked its havoc, perhaps with WMD. Then there is the dangerous precedent set. As the British scholar Lawrence Freedman writes, "The ambiguity about situations in which it [military force] might be justified means that elevating this notion [preemption] to a security doctrine rather than an occasional stratagem by the USA creates opportunities for states that might use new-fangled notions of preemption as rationalization when embarking on old-fashioned aggression."[17] If the United States can take preemptive action in the name of its own security and on the basis of its own threat assessments and its own decision making, then why can't other countries? Why can't India or Pakistan in their conflict? Israel or the Arab states in theirs? Russia with its near abroad? China against Taiwan? In any one of these or other cases, a state may genuinely see preemptive action as necessary in security terms, or even if not could still seize on the Bush Doctrine as a convenient rationalization, laying claim to the precedent for political cover. Either way, the world could end up a more dangerous place.

MORE MULTILATERAL, LESS UNILATERAL Many critics concur with a degree of unilateralism in American strategy. The balance they seek, though, has a stronger multilateral component. This in part is a matter of pragmatism: just as the terrorist threat has global reach, so too must the strategy used against it. The United States cannot on its own gather the intelligence needed, disrupt financial transactions, block WMD acquisition, break up cells of operatives, establish surveillance over borders and the oceans, pay the expenses of winning the peace, and share other burdens and solve other problems central to the overall counterterrorism strategy. The coalitions can be flexible, with different nations playing varying roles, but they need to be strong and meaningful coalitions, to which the United

States must be genuinely committed if it expects others to be. On this point many critics felt the Iraq war reinforced their position.

PRINCIPLES: FROM "ABC" TO "ABT" Although acknowledging that some of its new allies did not have very good human rights records themselves, the Bush administration maintained back in 2002 that improved human rights performance would be "an important byproduct of our alliance with them."[18] On the contrary, the new wave of global military commitments may be more part of the problem than the solution. The "ABT" (anybody but terrorists) rationale for alliances and commitments risks giving the United States bedfellows as strange as those brought out by the "ABC" (anything but communism) rationale used during the Cold War. Many of the governments now receiving military aid and hosting American bases in the name of the war on terrorism have very poor human rights records. Does this not contradict the principles-based claim of fighting the war on terrorism in the name of freedom? "America has a serious image problem," as a Council on Foreign Relations (CFR) task force concluded. "The credibility of an American message will be enhanced when it does not appear unilateral, and when international legitimacy and consensus are sought for the principles being defended."[19]

HOMELAND SECURITY The Bush administration's record fell well short of its rhetoric. Numerous studies have pointed to vulnerabilities in ***homeland security.*** Of course the criterion cannot be 100 percent invulnerability, but we can hope for reduced vulnerability. Yet a study by the Government Accountability Office (GAO) showed that despite expenditures of about $800 million, protections against smuggling a nuclear weapon into the United States still were dangerously inadequate. "Nationally, less than a quarter of the radiation detection devices needed to check all goods crossing the borders have been installed, federal officials said. In New York, for example, none of the cargo that moves through the largest ship terminal or goods leaving the port by rail or barge are [sic] inspected for radiation," Bethany Rooney, manager of security for the Port Authority of New York and New Jersey, testified.[20] The report card issued by the 9/11 Commission on whether its overall homeland security recommendations had been implemented awarded mostly Cs, Ds, and Fs.[21]

There also was the lag in recruiting translators of Arabic and other languages in which Al Qaeda and other terrorists typically communicate. The FBI's backlog of untranslated terrorism intelligence was twice as great in 2005 as in 2004, from 4,086 hours to 8,354. In addition, the FBI was slow to modernize its computer systems for better searching and for organizing files related to terrorism. "It sounds to me very much like business as usual," stated Lee Hamilton (the former chairman of the House Foreign Affairs Committee while in Congress and then co-chairman of the 9/11 Commission), "and business as usual is unacceptable."[22]

## The Iraq War

As noted earlier, despite all of the ways in which the 1990–91 Persian Gulf War was a major victory, Saddam Hussein's Iraq continued to pose challenges to the United States and the United Nations.[23] The issue came to a head in 2002–2003, when the Bush administration decided Iraq was to be the first application of the Bush doctrine on preemption. The administration debated internally whether to go to the UN Security Council for support. Those who favored doing so, such as Secretary of State Powell, in effect made the policy enhancement argument that having UNSC support would provide normative legitimacy as well as a broader coalition for burden sharing. Vice President Dick Cheney and Secretary of Defense Donald Rumsfeld opposed requesting UNSC support because of what they viewed as the greater downside risks of prerogative encroachment. President Bush initially did go the UN route, getting a unanimous UNSC vote in November 2002 to pressure Iraq to comply with the UN weapons of mass destruction inspections and threatening military action if it did not. This consensus proved fleeting, though. Over the ensuing four months, tensions within the UNSC reached extraordinary levels as France, Russia, and others pushed back against the Bush administration's pressures for UNSC support for moving on to military action. The Bush administration ultimately decided to go to war without another UNSC vote. In part it claimed actually to have sufficient legitimacy based on past UNSC resolutions. In part it claimed it did not really need UNSC support, since it viewed military action as an act of self-defense within the Bush doctrine of preemption. The administration also knew it faced a veto by France and likely Russia in the Security Council.

Some analysts felt this actually was the way the Bush administration wanted it all along. In this view the administration had gone to the UN in the summer and fall of 2002 just to "check off the box," calculating that the basis for taking unilateral military action would be strengthened after it had at least tried the multilateral route. "We told you so," said those who all along had been skeptics of the UN and for whom the lack of action was not a surprise.

Whichever analysis was more accurate, on March 19, 2003, President George W. Bush went on television from the Oval Office: "My fellow citizens, at this hour, American and coalition forces are in the early stages of military operations to disarm Iraq, to free its people and to defend the world from grave danger."[24] The ***Iraq War*** coalition had about forty countries; the main partner was Great Britain, led by Prime Minister Tony Blair. It thus was not strictly a unilateral war, but the multilateral coalition was not nearly so strong as it was for the 1990–91 Persian Gulf War or Afghanistan. France, Germany, Russia, and Egypt were among those opposed. The "International Perspectives" box on page 420 gives a sense of the global debate.

## INTERNATIONAL PERSPECTIVES

INTERNATIONAL PERSPECTIVES

### SUPPORT FOR AND OPPOSITION TO THE IRAQ WAR

#### Support

*Prime Minister Tony Blair, Great Britain:* "The brutality of the repression—the death and torture camps, the barbaric prisons for political opponents, the routine beatings for anyone or their families suspected of disloyalty—are well documented. . . . We take our freedom for granted. But imagine not to be able to speak or discuss or debate or even question the society you live in. To see friends and family taken away and never daring to complain. To suffer the humility of failing courage in face of pitiless terror. That is how the Iraqi people live. Leave Saddam in place and that is how they will continue to live. We must face the consequences of the actions we advocate. For me, that means all the dangers of war. But for others, opposed to this course, it means—let us be clear—that the Iraqi people, whose only true hope of liberation lies in the removal of Saddam, for them, the darkness will close back over them again; and he will be free to take his revenge upon those he must know wish him gone."

*Prime Minister Silvio Berlusconi, Italy:* "I'm here today to help my friend President Bush to convince everybody that this is in the interest of everybody. And if we are all united, the European Union, the United States, the Federation of Russia, everybody, all the other states under the United Nations, then Saddam Hussein will understand that he will have no other option but to reveal the arms and to destroy them."

*Prime Minister John Howard, Australia:* "Of course our alliance with the United States is also a factor, unapologetically so. . . . Alliances are two-way processes and our alliance with the United States is no exception and Australians should always remember that no nation is more important to our long-term security than that of [sic] the United States."

#### Opposition

*President Jacques Chirac, France:* "Whether it concerns the necessary disarmament of Iraq or the desirable change of the regime in this country, there is no justification for a unilateral decision to resort to force. . . . No matter how events evolve now, this ultimatum challenges our view of international relations. It puts the future of a people, the future of a region and world stability at stake."

*President Vladimir Putin, Russian Federation:* "[The Iraq War will be a] mistake fraught with the gravest consequences which may result in casualties and destabilize the international situation in general."

*Crown Prince Abdullah bin Abdulaziz, Saudi Arabia:* "Under no circumstances will the Kingdom participate in the war against the brotherly nation of Iraq; nor will its armed forces by any means trespass by one inch into Iraqi territory."

*President Hosni Mubarak, Egypt:* "When it is over, if it is over, this war will have horrible consequences: There will be more terrorism and a terror organization will become united. Instead of having one (Osama) bin Laden, we will have one hundred bin Ladens."

*President Vicente Fox, Mexico:* "Mexico reiterates its support for the multilateral route to solve conflicts and regrets the path to war. . . . The world has to continue pushing solutions that comply with the letter and spirit of the UN Charter, which establishes that the use of force should be the last and exceptional recourse, justified only when other methods have failed."

Note: The Saudi crown prince's address is no longer available on the Web in English.

Sources: "Full Text: Tony Blair's Speech," *Guardian,* March 18, 2003, www.guardian.co.uk/politics/2003/mar/18/foreignpolicy.iraq1 (accessed 7/10/09); Bush, Italy's Berlusconi Warn Saddam to Disarm, January 30, 2003, www.america.gov/st/washfile-english/2003/January/20030130145138jthomas@pd.state.gov0.1734735.html (accessed 7/10/09); John Howard, Address to the National Press Club, Great Hall, Parliament House, March 14, 2003, http://pandora.nla.gov.au/pan/10052/20030521-0000/www.pm.gov.au/news/speeches/2003/speech2185.htm (accessed 7/10/09); Jacques Chirac, quoted in "In Quotes: Reaction to Bush Ultimatum," March 18, 2003, http://news.bbc.co.uk/2/hi/middle_east/2859485.stm (accessed 7/10/09); Vladimir Putin, quoted in Ron Hutcheson and Martin Merzer, "Bush Gives Saddam, Sons 48 Hours to Leave Iraq," *Stars and Stripes,* European edition, March 18, 2003, http://cndyorks.gn.apc.org/caab/articles/bushgives48hrs.htm (accessed 7/10/09); Abdullah bin Abdulaziz, "Crown Prince Addresses Nation in Crisis," Royal Embassy of Saudi Arabia Newsroom, March 18, 2003; "President Mubarak Gives Warning," April 1, 2003, http://transcripts.cnn.com/TRANSCRIPTS/0304/01/se.06.html (accessed 7/10/09); Vicente Fox, quoted in "In Quotes: Reaction to Bush Ultimatum," March 18, 2003, http://news.bbc.co.uk/2/hi/middle_east/2859485.stm (accessed 7/10/09).

Within a month, American and coalition military forces had prevailed. On April 10, 2003, Bush sent a message to the Iraqi people: "This is George W. Bush, the President of the United States. At this moment, the regime of Saddam Hussein is being removed from power, and a long era of fear and cruelty is ending. American and coalition forces are now operating inside Baghdad—and we will not stop until Saddam's corrupt gang is gone. The government of Iraq, and the future of your country, will soon belong to you."[25] The war was an overwhelming military victory. It took just three weeks, less than half as long as the 1991 Persian Gulf War. It achieved victory with about one-third as many troops as the 1991 war. And it did what that war stopped short of attempting: it removed Saddam Hussein from power.

"Shock and awe" was the term coined for this military strategy. The idea was to bring so much military power to bear so quickly, inflicting such heavy destruction on enemy forces as to shock and intimidate them, leaving them so materially weakened and psychologically in awe as to undermine their will to keep fighting. The 1991 war's doctrine of decisive and overwhelming force had proceeded sequentially, with six weeks of air power before moving into the ground war. The 2003 war strategy was simultaneous rather than sequential, with special operations and ground forces coordinated with and in some cases even preceding the air war, geared to what was called a "rapid dominance" strategy of achieving the overwhelming levels of force much more quickly.

The war demonstrated the extraordinary levels American military technology had reached. In the 1991 war only one in five combat aircraft could drop a bomb sighted by a laser; in this war all could. In the 1991 war only 9 percent of the attacks used precision-guided munitions; in this war it was close to 70 percent. In the 1991 war, often two days elapsed between the time a reconnaissance aircraft photographed a target and the target was struck; now with streaming video these events often happened nearly instantaneously. The ground-air coordination of spotters helping to target air attacks, which drew so many kudos in Afghanistan, was even more sophisticated and widespread less than two years later in Iraq. Unmanned aircraft such as the Predator drone were used much more extensively than ever before. Real-time data flowed by the "trillions of megabytes" to command centers both in the region (in Doha, the capital of neighboring Qatar) and back at the Pentagon. All this had one military expert speculating that "it's possible that in our lifetime we will be able to run a conflict without ever leaving the United States."[26]

The image that most conveyed the sense of great victory was that of President Bush flying onto the aircraft carrier USS *Abraham Lincoln* on May 1, "arriving in the co-pilot's seat of a Navy S-3B Viking after making two fly-bys of the carrier." The account on CNN continued:

> It was the first time a sitting president has arrived on the deck of an aircraft carrier by plane. The jet made what is known as a "tailhook" landing, with the plane, traveling about 150 mph, hooking onto the last of four steel wires across the flight deck and coming to a complete stop in less than 400 feet. The exterior of the four-seat Navy S-3B Viking was marked with "Navy 1"

> in the back and "George W. Bush Commander-in-Chief" just below the cockpit window. . . . Moments after the landing, the president, wearing a green flight suit and holding a white helmet, got off the plane, saluted those on the flight deck and shook hands with them. Above him, the tower was adorned with a big sign that read, "Mission Accomplished."[27]

But the sense of victory did not last. Opponents raised three main sets of issues about the Iraq war: the validity and honesty of the rationale for going to war, the results on the ground of having won the war but perhaps not the peace, and the broader ramifications for American foreign policy.

## *Rationale for Going to War: Validity? Honesty?*

Of the various reasons that the Bush administration cited for going to war against Iraq when and how it did, two received the most emphasis and were deemed the most important. One was the WMD threat—that Saddam Hussein had weapons of mass destruction. The other was the terrorism coalition link between Al Qaeda and Saddam. Putting the two together, if Iraq were to supply WMD to Al Qaeda, "then the attacks of September the 11th would be a prelude to far greater horrors."[28] But neither of these claims proved to be true.

The WMD claim was a staple of administration speeches in the buildup to the war:

> *Vice President Cheney:* "There is no doubt that [Saddam Hussein] is amassing [WMD] to use against our friends, against our allies, and against us."[29]

> *President Bush:* "Evidence indicates that Iraq is reconstituting its nuclear weapons program. . . . Iraq has attempted to purchase high-strength aluminum tubes and other equipment needed for gas centrifuges, which are used to enrich uranium for nuclear weapons."[30]

> *President Bush:* "The United States of America will not permit the world's most dangerous regimes to threaten us with the world's most destructive weapons. . . . The British government has learned that Saddam Hussein recently sought significant quantities of uranium from Africa."[31]

> *CIA Director George Tenet on the strength of the WMD evidence:* "Tenet, a basketball fan who attended as many home games of his alma mater Georgetown as possible, leaned forward and threw his arms up again, 'Don't worry, it's a slam dunk!'"[32]

> *National Security Adviser Condoleezza Rice:* "We know that he has the infrastructure, nuclear scientists, to make a nuclear weapon. . . . The problem here is that there will always be some uncertainty about how quickly he can acquire nuclear weapons. But we don't want the smoking gun to be a mushroom cloud."[33]

> *Secretary of State Colin Powell at the UN:* "The facts and Iraq's behavior show that Saddam Hussein and his regime are concealing their efforts to produce more weapons of mass destruc-

> tion. . . . Everything we have seen and heard indicates that, instead of cooperating actively with the inspectors to ensure the success of their mission, Saddam Hussein and his regime are busy doing all they possibly can to ensure that inspectors succeed in finding absolutely nothing. My colleagues, every statement I make today is backed up by sources, solid sources. These are not assertions. What we're giving you are facts and conclusions based on solid intelligence."[34]

The evidence, though, did not bear out these claims. No WMD were found. No nuclear weapons. And no significant nuclear program was left of what UN inspectors had dismantled in the 1990s and sanctions had continued to block. No significant traces of the alleged 100 to 500 tons of chemical weapons agents, enough to fill 16,000 battlefield rockets. The mobile lab said to be a production facility for biological weapons was more likely used for manufacturing hydrogen for military weather balloons. Far from being a "slam dunk," the WMD claims were "riddled with errors," as even a commission appointed by President Bush reported back to him.[35] Others were much harsher.

The Bush administration also was very assertive regarding the Saddam–Al Qaeda terrorism link. "We've learned," President Bush stated, "that Iraq has trained Al Qaeda members in bomb making and poisons and gases."[36] The former top antiterrorism official Richard Clarke describes a conversation with Bush on September 12, 2001:

> "Look," he told us, "I know you have a lot to do and all . . . but I want you, as soon as you can, to go back over everything, everything. See if Saddam did this. See if he's linked in any way. . . ."
>
> I was once again taken aback, incredulous, and it showed. "But, Mr. President, al Qaeda did this."
>
> "I know, I know, but . . . see if Saddam was involved. Just look. I want to know any shred. . . ."
>
> "Absolutely, we will look . . . again." I was trying to be more respectful, more responsive. "But, you know, we have looked several times for state sponsorship of al Qaeda and not found any real linkages to Iraq. Iran plays a little, as does Pakistan, and Saudi Arabia, Yemen."
>
> "Look into Iraq, Saddam," the President said testily and left us.[37]

Three years later the 9/11 Commission was unequivocal in its conclusion that no evidence existed of a "collaborative operational relationship" between Saddam and Al Qaeda generally. Most especially, "We have no credible evidence that Iraq was supporting al Qaeda."[38]

Other rationales for war against Iraq also were cited. Saddam Hussein truly was among the worst of the worst dictators. He had used chemical weapons against his own people. He had murdered thousands, tortured thousands more. He had started two wars against his neighbors. Many who supported the war did so in the name of liberating the Iraqi people. The most compelling reasons for going beyond containment to war, though, were WMD and terrorism. Yet neither proved valid. To the extent that the Bush administration acknowledged any error (and it only partially did so), it claimed inherent uncertainties and the need to err on the side of caution when faced with such threats. It referred to the Bush doctrine on preemption, as in National Security Adviser Rice's image of the smoking gun being the mushroom cloud. Even at the time many questioned the claim of unknowability and instead saw flawed policy analysis and decision making. Many raised questions of honesty. Did the Bush administration intentionally misrepresent the intelligence? Did it manipulate the press for political ends? Did it break its own rules against leaks in going after critics? We delve deeper into some of these questions in the foreign policy politics section at the end of this chapter. Here the main point is that the rationales for the war were called into serious question, at the same time that the results of the war were raising their own questions.

## *Results: Winning the Peace?*

Vice President Cheney said American forces "will be greeted as liberators." "I can't say if the use of force would last five days or five weeks or five months," Defense Secretary Rumsfeld stated, "but it certainly isn't going to last any longer than that." Kenneth Adelman, a leading neoconservative commentator, predicted a "cakewalk."[39] Other Bush administration officials and supporters were no less bullish. Reality proved quite different.

One problem was security. Before the war, Army Chief of Staff General Eric Shinseki had recommended that several hundred thousand troops would be needed for stabilization and security once Saddam had been overthrown. Deputy Defense Secretary Paul Wolfowitz called this "wildly off the mark."[40] Wolfowitz's criticism was more about politics than strategy. He was trying to keep the numbers low so that the public and others would be more likely to believe that the war could be won with limited commitments. Yet events showed Shinseki's number to be all too near the mark. Chaos broke out after Saddam's fall, and American forces were far too insufficient to respond. General Shinseki was reprimanded and forced to retire. The security situation was made worse by Ambassador L. Paul Bremer III, the head of the governing structure the United States set up (the Coalitional Provisional Authority). Bremer disbanded the entire Iraqi army on the grounds that they might still be loyal to Saddam. This had the doubly negative effects of enlarging the security vacuum while idling masses of former army officers and soldiers, who still had their weapons and now had an additional motivation to turn to terrorism, insurgency, and criminal violence.

For the first two or so years, the major security threat was from Sunni and foreign terrorists. The Iraqi population largely comprises three groups: Sunnis and Shiites—both Arab peoples but following historically conflicting branches of Islam—and Kurds, also Muslim but ethnically distinct from Iraqi Arabs and concentrated in the northern part of the country. Saddam was a Sunni; he favored the Sunnis (a minority) while repressing and at times slaughtering Shiites and Kurds. After Saddam's fall, the Shiites and Kurds gained dominance. Some Sunnis turned to terrorism against rival Iraqi groups as well as against American and other coalition forces. With the Iraqi borders exceedingly porous, in part because of the limited American forces, foreign jihadist terrorists joined the fray.

Some success stories emerged where American troops, working with Iraqi forces and political leaders, enhanced security in key cities and villages. But by early 2006 the situation was increasingly recognized as a civil war. Sunnis attacked Shiites. Shiites attacked Sunnis. Shiite factions and militias were fighting each other. Kurds also were in the picture. American casualties climbed. Iraqi casualties climbed higher. During the six weeks of full warfare, only 140 Americans died, but over 2,000 died in the three years following. Whereas only 1,300 Iraqi police and soldiers had been killed before 2005, over 2,500 died that year. Civilian casualties in 2005 were over 5,600, and almost triple that in 2006.[41]

The political dimension of democratic institutionalization saw some notable achievements. Since Saddam's fall, Iraq has had more and freer elections than any other Arab country. A constitution was approved. A government was elected. At each such watershed, hopes surged that democracy was taking root and political order was being established. We should not forget that many Iraqi citizens have been striving to build a better life for themselves and their families and that American soldiers, NGO workers, and others from the international community have helped, often at the risk of their own lives.

Sufficiently consolidating such progress, though, in the face of violence, disorder, and flawed policies proved difficult. Soon after each election was held and other political milestones reached, limits were evident, disappointment set in, and violence increased. Could the Sunnis, Shiites, and Kurds reach enough of a compromise for political stability? How could they share power? One of the main issues in this regard has been the militias that each group maintains as its own private army at the same time that an Iraqi national army is supposed to be built.[42] Creating a national army while allowing separate sectarian armed forces outside the formal structure of this new state fundamentally contradicts a cardinal principle for any state, a principle first formulated by the nineteenth-century European political philosopher Max Weber—a state *must* have authoritative control of the means of legitimate violence in its society. Where is an example of a state that stayed stable, peaceful, and just while allowing private armies to roam and ruin in the name of their own subgroups? These questions have been difficult in other nation-building and humanitarian intervention cases, as we'll see in a later chapter. In Iraq they have been especially so.

The economic aspects of reconstruction also have been problematic. During the prewar debate Lawrence Lindsey, then the top Bush administration economic adviser, predicted costs as much as $200 billion. This was the economic equivalent of General Shinseki's point about troop underestimation. Lindsey lost his job, too. Official cost projections were much lower, including the claim by Deputy Defense Secretary Wolfowitz that much would be paid for by Iraqi oil revenues. In reality, by early 2006 U.S. military operations in Iraq had cost $220 billion and Iraqi reconstruction another $29 billion, with projections for substantial increases in both. A report by the nonpartisan Congressional Research Service put the possible long-term cost as high as $2 trillion.[43] Iraqi oil exports were only 1.1 million barrels per day, less than half of what the Bush administration claimed they would be.[44]

The 2004 Abu Ghraib prison scandal, with its graphic photos and accounts of torture by American forces, did profound damage to the credibility of American claims to the moral high ground, also a crucial asset for winning the peace. One didn't have to go so far as those who claimed moral equivalence between the Abu Ghraib torture of suspected terrorists and the terrorists' killing of innocent civilians. Claims about the ends justifying the means didn't work either, though. American abuses were disillusioning and alienating for many in Iraq as well as in many other countries. Even close to two years after the Abu Ghraib revelations, conditions at the prison still were so bad that some American officers "expressed concern that [it] has become a breeding ground for extremist leaders and a school for terrorist foot soldiers."[45] Then in early 2006 came revelations of rapes and wanton killings by American soldiers of Iraqi civilians, including women and children, in the Iraqi city of Haditha. The Haditha killings had occurred in late 2005. Attempts were made to conceal them, but the press uncovered the story.

Such atrocities notwithstanding, the American military largely fulfilled its responsibilities with courage and commitment. Yet it was being stretched to and possibly beyond the limit. By spring 2006, nearly every active-duty combat unit had been deployed to Iraq twice, with little if any time back home with friends and families. A *Military Times* poll in January 2006 found high morale but declining support for Bush and the war effort. Only 54 percent of soldiers polled supported President Bush's Iraq policy, and only 40 percent felt the Defense Department civilian leaders "have my best interests at heart."[46] Some military officers became outspoken. Marine Lt. General Greg Newbold, who had been the director of operations for the Joint Chiefs of Staff and retired in part because of his opposition to the Iraq war, called it "an unnecessary war" brought about "by the missteps and misjudgments of the White House and the Pentagon." He went further: "I am driven to action now . . . by many painful visits to our military hospitals. In those places, I have been both inspired and shaken by the broken bodies but unbroken spirits of soldiers, Marines and corpsmen returning from this war. The cost of flawed leadership continues to be paid in blood. The willingness of our forces to shoulder such a load should make it a sacred obligation for civilian and military leaders to get our defense policy right."[47]

The National Guard and reserves were being drawn on for an unprecedented 40 percent of the forces in Iraq. One top general testified to Congress that this was sending the guard and reserves into "meltdown."[48] Hurricane Katrina revealed some immediate consequences. Over three thousand Louisiana guardsmen as well as high-water trucks, fuel trucks, satellite phones, and much other emergency equipment were overseas in Iraq.[49]

Additionally, the international coalition, never as strong as the coalitions during the 1990–91 Persian Gulf War and in Afghanistan, was eroding. The combination of the toll of the war, terrorist retaliations, and domestic opposition led a number of coalition members to pull out. Spain withdrew its military forces following the 2004 terrorist attack in Madrid and the election of a new government in part on an anti-Iraq platform. Italy and Japan withdrew in 2006. South Korea and Australia stayed in but at reduced troops levels. Ukraine, Hungary, the Philippines, and Nicaragua were among those that withdrew fully.

At home, support was weakening as well. Whereas in late 2003 nearly six in ten Americans surveyed saw the Iraq war as worth the cost, by March 2006 only 42 percent took this view. Approval of the Bush policy, which had been as high as 75 percent in the "mission accomplished" days, fell to 36 percent in late 2005. Indeed, discontent over Iraq was so deep and widespread as to be the major issue in the Democratic victory in the 2006 midterm congressional elections. It was unusual for a foreign policy issue to be so decisive in congressional elections. It also was unusual, at least in recent years, for the public to favor Democrats over Republicans on a major foreign policy issue. But all this was the case in 2006, fueling the voting that for the first time since 1994 gave the Democrats majorities in both the Senate and the House.

Rather than withdrawing from Iraq, the Bush administration made a major shift in strategy. Dubbed the ***surge,*** it involved a buildup of another thirty thousand troops combined with a revised counterinsurgency strategy led by General David Petraeus. As President Bush explained in a televised speech in early 2007, "Our past efforts to secure Baghdad failed for two principal reasons: There were not enough Iraqi and American troops to secure neighborhoods that had been cleared of terrorists and insurgents . . . and there were too many restrictions on the troops we did have."[50] Another key element was building some common cause with leaders of Sunni tribes who had been opposing the U.S. presence in Iraq but who had grown disillusioned with the violence, radicalism, and competition for power from Al Qaeda in Iraq (AQI). The "enemy of my enemy is my friend" calculus of shared security interests was a part of this; so too was money, as many of the Sunnis who changed sides were put on the U.S. payroll.

Proponents of the surge such as the Heritage Foundation defended it as "while risky, present[ing] the best chance for moving forward in Iraq and should be given the chance to prove its mettle." Moreover, they contended, "the alternative policy advocated by many opponents of Bush's New Way Forward is far worse: an immediate troop withdrawal that would swiftly lead to a strategic, moral, and humanitarian catastrophe not only for Iraq but for the entire region, as refugees, terrorism, political instability, and sectarian conflict spill over into surrounding countries."[51]

Debate continues over whether the surge worked. Fred Kagan, a military historian who was one of the principal strategists behind the surge, stressed that "violence and American casualties have dropped remarkably since the surge began last year" and that the "basic reality" the surge has created is that "Iraq is an independent, sovereign state able to negotiate on an equal basis with the United States."[52] The casualty data backed him up. U.S. soldier deaths were down almost two-thirds in 2008, compared with 2007; Iraqi civilian casualties about 60 percent. The number of enemy-initiated attacks fell from almost 1,500 per week to about 150; the number of foreign militants crossing into Iraq to support the insurgency fell from eighty to ninety per week to ten to twenty. The size of Iraq's own security forces grew from 323,000 to 589,000.[53] Anbar Province, which had been the site of the largest number of U.S. casualties two years earlier, was now sufficiently stable to be handed back to Iraqi control. Some political progress also had been made with additional rounds of elections, some Shiite-Sunni-Kurd power sharing, and some other steps toward national reconciliation.

Although criticisms of the surge were not as searing as of the earlier war effort, significant questions were raised about the claims of success. Lawrence Korb of the Center for American Progress wrote that although the surge may have removed Iraq from the front page of the newspapers, it did not resolve the underlying tension. "Despite recent security gains in Iraq," he said, "the surge of over 30,000 troops there has failed to meet its strategic objective—meaningful national reconciliation. The war in Afghanistan meanwhile continues to drift."[54] Political progress continued to lag, as indicated by such unmet benchmarks as disbanding militias, fulfilling the promised reintegration of Sunnis, resolving territorial and autonomy issues with the Kurds, and sharing oil revenues. Economic progress also was slow, including such basic measures as the provision of electricity to homes, lowering unemployment, and raising oil production.[55]

As a candidate Barack Obama had been strongly opposed to the war and made much of a pledge to end the war within sixteen months of taking office. He also stressed that although in his view the war had been started irresponsibly, it still needed to be ended responsibly. In one of his first foreign policy speeches, given in February 2009 at Camp Lejeune in North Carolina, he announced an eighteen-month timeline in which all U.S. combat troops would be out of Iraqi cities by July 2009 and largely out of Iraq by August 2010. Some troops with counterterrorism, training, and related missions would remain until the end of 2011, which was the date set for a full U.S. military withdrawal in the Status of Forces Agreement signed with the Iraqi government in the last months of the Bush administration. The Obama plan, with its core goal "to end the war in Iraq through a transition to full Iraqi responsibility," thus was consistent with this official U.S.–Iraqi agreement.[56] The president also stressed more sustained diplomacy at the global level with the other major powers (Europe, Russia, China) and the United Nations to garner support for Iraqi stabilization and reconstruction; at the regional level with key parties including Iran, Jordan, Saudi Arabia, Syria, and Turkey for nonintervention and cooperative regional security initiatives; and within Iraq with Shia, Sunnis, and Kurds for greater political reconciliation. Time would tell how successful the Obama strategy would be.

Thus, although much remains to be seen, what is clear is that winning the peace has been much more problematic than winning the war.

## Ramifications: Iraq and the "4 Ps"

One point that proponents and critics agree on is that the Iraq war has never been about just Iraq. As "Theory in the World" (p. 431) illustrates, the issues have been more broadly about America's role in the world and, in this book's terms, all "4 Ps" of the national interest. For the Bush administration and its supporters, the Iraq war was to be a "4 Ps" complementarity case. For Iraq war critics, it is riven with "4 Ps" contradictions.

Consider the points that the Bush administration and other Iraq war supporters made:

POWER The demonstration of American military might strengthened American power. Iraq was what the Bush administration called "the central front" in the war on terror:

> Terrorists want to defeat America in Iraq and force us to abandon our allies. . . . The terrorists believe they would then have proven that the United States is a waning power and an unreliable friend. In the chaos of a broken Iraq the terrorists believe they would be able to establish a safe haven like they had in Afghanistan, only this time in the heart of a geopolitically vital region. Surrendering to the terrorists would likewise hand them a powerful recruiting tool: the perception that they are the vanguard of history. When the Iraqi Government, supported by the Coalition, defeats the terrorists, terrorism will be dealt a critical blow.[57]

The message would go out throughout the Middle East that the United States has the capabilities and the will to defend its interests and security when and how it sees fit. In the rest of the world, whatever doubts may still have been out there about American primacy would be dispelled. The United States was number 1. It would lead. Others needed to follow or get out of the way.

PEACE The elimination of Saddam Hussein enhanced the prospects for peace in a region that has known too little of it. Saddam had launched wars against his neighbors (Iran, Kuwait). He had threatened Israel repeatedly, even attacking it during the 1991 Gulf War, and led efforts to block peace when Arab leaders such as Anwar Sadat had forged ahead. The United States may not have been able to find WMD, but he had them before and would have sought them again: "with the elimination of Saddam's regime, this threat has been addressed, once and for all."[58] And although defying the United Nations in the moment, America's willingness to do what needed to be done (and which the UN kept refusing to do), including fully enforcing its own multiple resolutions, would be good for the world body in the long run.

THEORY IN THE WORLD

THEORY IN THE WORLD

## INTERNATIONAL RELATIONS THEORY AND THE IRAQ WAR

*What positions did different international relations theorists take on the Iraq war?*

Neoconservatives were the strongest supporters. The Iraq war was "the right war for the right reasons," Robert Kagan and William Kristol still argued in 2004:

> It is fashionable to sneer at the moral case for liberating an Iraqi people long brutalized by Saddam's rule. Critics insist mere oppression was not sufficient reason for war, and in any case that it was not Bush's reason. In fact, of course, it was one of Bush's reasons, and the moral and humanitarian purpose provided a compelling reason for a war to remove Saddam Hussein. . . . Such a rationale is not merely "moral." As is often the case in international affairs, there was no separating the nature of Saddam's rule at home from the kinds of policies he conducted abroad. Saddam's regime terrorized his own people, but it also posed a threat to the region, and to us. The moral case for war was linked to strategic considerations related to the peace and security of the Middle East. . . . It will continue to be the case that the war was worth fighting, and that it was necessary.

Support also came from "liberal interventionists," such as Michael Ignatieff, then a leading scholar and journalist and now a political leader in Canada:

> Some of the immediate consequences of the Iraq intervention have been good indeed: a totalitarian regime is no longer terrorizing Iraqis; Shiites marching in the hundred of thousands to celebrate at their shrine at Karbala, along with professors, policemen, and office workers demonstrating in the streets of Baghdad are tasting freedom for the first time; Iraqis as a whole are discovering the truth about the torture chambers, mass graves and other squalid secrets of more than two decades of tyranny. . . . If the consequence of intervention is a rights-respecting Iraq in a decade or so, who cares whether the intentions that led to it were mixed at best? . . . A lot of people who would call themselves defenders of human rights opposed intervention in Iraq for sound, prudential reasons—too risky, too costly, not likely to make America safer—but prudence also amounted to a vote for the status quo in the Middle East, and that status quo had at its heart a regime that tortured its citizens, used poison gas against its own population and executed people for the free exercise of religious faith.

The historian John Lewis Gaddis took a mixed view. He praised what he saw as

> a *grand* strategy. What appeared at first to be a lack of clarity about who was deterrable and who wasn't turned out to be a plan for transforming the entire Muslim Middle

(*Continued*)

(*Continued*)

> East: for bringing it, once and for all, into the modern world. There'd been nothing like this in boldness, sweep and vision since Americans took it upon themselves, more than a half century ago, to democratize Germany and Japan, thus setting in motion processes that stopped short of only a few places on earth, one of which was the Muslim Middle East.

Yet he also acknowledged that "within a little more than a year and a half, the United States exchanged its long-established reputation as the principal *stabilizer* of the international system for one as its chief *destabilizer*. This was a heavy price to pay to sustain momentum, however great the need for it may have been."

Among the strongest critics were such Realist scholars as John Mearsheimer and Stephen Walt, who argued on the eve of the war:

> Both logic and historical evidence suggest a policy of vigilant containment would work, both now and in the event Iraq acquires a nuclear arsenal. . . . If the United States is, or soon will be, at war with Iraq, Americans should understand that a compelling strategic rationale is absent. This war would be one the Bush administration chose to fight but did not have to fight. . . . None of the nightmare scenarios invoked by preventive-war advocates are likely to happen. Consider the claim that Saddam would employ nuclear blackmail against his adversaries. To force another state to make concessions, a blackmailer must make clear that he would use nuclear weapons against the target state if he does not get his way. But this strategy is feasible only if the blackmailer has nuclear weapons but neither the target state nor its allies do. If the blackmailer and the target state both have nuclear weapons, however, the blackmailer's threat is an empty one because the blackmailer cannot carry out the threat without triggering his own destruction. This logic explains why the Soviet Union, which had a vast nuclear arsenal for much of the Cold War, was never able to blackmail the United States or its allies and did not even try.

Francis Fukuyama, one of the original neoconservatives, became another major critic of the Iraq war. In his view it was "very doubtful . . . that history will judge the Iraq war kindly." In his assessment the effect on the overall war on terrorism was net negative: "Iraq has now replaced Afghanistan as a magnet, training ground, and operational base for jihadist terrorists." He also stressed the "enormous costs," including the strategic consequence that "preoccupation with Iraq limits Washington's options in other parts of the world and has distracted the attention of senior policy makers from other regions such as Asia that in the long run are likely to present greater strategic challenges." He went so far as to characterize the Bush administration's emphasis on regime change as "almost obsessive."

Joseph Nye, best known for his theories of "soft power" (see Chapter 11), also stressed the counterproductiveness of the Iraq war to the struggle against Al Qaeda:

> Mounting a military campaign against Iraq at this point poses a significant problem for our war on terrorism. Right now, according to recent testimony by CIA Director George Tenet, the clear and present danger is posed by the al Qaeda network, which has cells in some 50 countries. We have probably destroyed only 20% to 30% of the network, and our military prowess is not the most effective way to deal with what remains. We are not about to bomb Hamburg [Germany], Jakarta [Indonesia] or Kuala Lumpur [Malaysia]. Wrapping up al Qaeda will require painstaking civilian cooperation across borders among intelligence, law enforcement, financial, customs and immigration agencies. Unilateral military operations against Iraq that divert our attention and weaken the willingness of others to work with us would be counterproductive.

The historian Lloyd Gardner crystallized some of the more sweeping critiques:

> The Bush administration succeeded in using WMD to scare the nation into giving it a green light to bring down Saddam Hussein's dictatorship. . . . The real issue was never the disarmament of Iraq, but fulfilling the long-term goal of finding a "friendly" government to carry out the American global mission. . . . To get to the point where the neocons wanted to take the United States, the road led through Baghdad. . . . This ideology is married to a political economy that simply ignores—at its peril, we are discovering—any limits on the sacrifice of its own citizenry to be able to place high-tech centurions around the globe. It was all going to be so easy.

Sources: Robert Kagan and William Kristol, "The Right War for the Right Reasons," in *The Right War? The Conservative Debate on Iraq,* Gary Rosen ed. (New York: Cambridge University Press, 2005), 18–19, 35; Michael Ignatieff, "Why Are We in Iraq? (And Liberia? And Afghanistan?)," *New York Times Magazine,* September 7, 2003, pp. 71–72; John Lewis Gaddis, *Surprise, Security and the American Experience* (Cambridge, Mass: Harvard University Press, 2004), 94, 101 (italics in original); John J. Mearsheimer and Stephen M. Walt, "An Unnecessary War," *Foreign Policy* 134 (January–February 2003): 59, 56–57; Francis Fukuyama, *America at the Crossroads: Democracy, Power and the Neoconservative Legacy* (New Haven: Yale University Press, 2006), 2; Joseph Nye, "Attacking Iraq Now Would Harm War on Terror," *Wall Street Journal,* May 12, 2002, A26; Lloyd C. Gardner, "Present at the Culmination: An Empire of Righteousness," in *The New American Empire: A 21st-Century Teach-In on U.S. Foreign Policy,* Lloyd C. Gardner and Marilyn R. Young, eds. (New York: New Press, 2005), 3, 5, 21, 27.

PROSPERITY No commodity is more economically crucial than oil. American as well as global prosperity would be served by making world oil supplies more secure. The United States would build a new economy for Iraqis based on free enterprise and opportunity. American companies would gain new investment opportunities that would also benefit average Iraqis. The new Iraqi economy would be a model for others in the region to move away from state-based to market-based systems.

PRINCIPLES American principles were manifested in the liberation of the Iraqi people. As Kagan and Kristol argue ("Theory in the World"), "It is fashionable to sneer at the moral case for liberating an Iraqi people long brutalized by Saddam's rule. Critics insist mere oppression was not sufficient reason for war, and in any case that it was not Bush's reason. In fact, of course, it was one of Bush's reasons, and the moral and humanitarian purpose provided a compelling reason for a war to remove Saddam Hussein." The Bush administration had proclaimed the overarching foreign policy goal of bringing democracy to the Middle East. Positive effects could be seen in smaller but still significant moves toward democratization in Saudi Arabia, Egypt, and elsewhere.

Here are some counterarguments:

POWER The Bush administration was right about one thing. Iraq had a demonstration effect—largely, though, the opposite of what was intended. It has shown the limits of American power. It has left American leadership in tatters. Francis Fukuyama, one of the original neoconservatives but a strong opponent of the Iraq war, sees it as "very doubtful . . . that history will judge the Iraq war kindly." A main reason is that it has been net negative on terrorism: "Iraq has now replaced Afghanistan as a magnet, training ground, and operational base for jihadist terrorists." Fukuyama goes on to stress the "enormous costs," including the strategic consequence that "preoccupation with Iraq limits Washington's options in other parts of the world and has distracted the attention of senior policy makers from other regions such as Asia that in the long run are likely to present greater strategic challenges." John Lewis Gaddis speaks of the broader strategic consequence that "within a little more than a year and a half, the United States exchanged its long-established reputation as the principal *stabilizer* of the international system for one as its chief *destabilizer.*"

PEACE As critics warned all along, the line between being a liberating force and an occupying one proved to be a lot harder to walk than the Bush administration wanted Americans to believe. Terrorism was strengthened both within Iraq and globally. America's reputation and credibility were dramatically diminished in many countries, particularly in the Arab world. In the global context, many of the international norms and institutions that the United States worked for over fifty years to build up as structures of international peace and stability were severely damaged.

PROSPERITY The Bush administration manipulated the budget numbers; the White House's leading economic advisor was fired for saying so.[59] The American economy was weakened by the hundreds of billions added to the federal budget deficit. Some estimates projected the costs of the Iraq war as high as $3 trillion. The further instability in Iraq added to the forces pushing global oil prices, and especially the price at the pump for the average American, higher and higher. And the Iraqi people suffered through even worse economic conditions than before Saddam fell.

PRINCIPLES The Iraqi people's thirst for democracy, as shown in their participation in their first free elections, deserves praise and admiration. But all in all, American principles have been more undermined than reinforced. The Abu Ghraib and Haditha scandals resonated around the world. So too have revelations of the mistreatment of prisoners at the Guantánamo Bay prison and elsewhere in violation of the Geneva Conventions on torture. The Bush administration's claims that Iraq set off a positive democratizing domino effect on the Middle East were much overstated. The 2005 Lebanon case was a rejection of foreign occupation (Syria) rather than of internal democratization—and even that was achieved more because the United States worked with France and through the UN Security Council than because of Iraq. The basic trust that the United States built up with so much of the world—what one astute foreign observer has called the "huge reservoirs of goodwill towards America among the six billion other inhabitants of this earth"—was being called into question not just by those on the side of "evil" but also by those who have looked to the United States for hope, inspiration, and leadership.[60]

## Key Issues and Initial Obama Strategies

More than in any other region, the Obama administration sought to separate from Bush policies in the Middle East. This did not mean a total break with the past. American foreign policy has always been a mix of change and continuity. But both generally and on specific key issues, the Obama administration set out early to establish its distinctiveness.

One main shift was in tone. "To the Muslim world," President Obama stated in his inaugural address, "we seek a new way forward, based on mutual interest and mutual respect."[61] He reinforced and elaborated on this message in his speech to the Turkish Parliament a little more than two months later: "We will bridge misunderstandings, and seek common ground. We will be respectful, even when we do not agree. We will convey our deep appreciation for the Islamic faith"—and, with the most emphasis—"[t]he United States is not, and never will be, at war with Islam."[62] President Bush made disclaimers of his own, but they had not stuck. Foreign policy is about the music as well as the words, and the Obama team's assessment was that a new tone had to be struck.

This new tone came through especially in President Obama's June 2009 speech in Cairo. He called for "a new beginning between the United States and Muslims around the world." For much of U.S. history this relationship had been defined more by differences than by what was shared or what could be shared. "America and Islam are not exclusive, and need not be in competition," Obama stressed. "Instead, they overlap, and share common principles." "At the Source" (p. 437) includes further excerpts from the Cairo speech.

A second major shift was from seeking to isolate adversaries to engaging them. During the presidential campaign, Obama had stressed engagement as a key part of his effort to strengthen and revitalize U.S. diplomacy. Differences were to be addressed. America could talk tough, but America should talk. The Middle East was not the exclusive focus for this strategy, but it was the principal one, particularly with regard to countries like Iran and Syria, as is further discussed below.

Within this broad strategic approach, particular policies were defined on key issues.

## *"Af-Pak"*

The Obama administration made Afghanistan and Pakistan—dubbed "Af-Pak" in recognition that they were "two countries but one challenge"—the focus of one of its earliest major policy reviews.[63] As noted earlier in this chapter, by the end of the Bush administration, the war in Afghanistan was in deep trouble. The Taliban was coming back. U.S. casualties were now higher in Afghanistan than in Iraq. Afghan civilian casualties were up 40 percent. Some NGOs had to pull out because of attacks on their workers despite their humanitarian mission. The drug trade had grown to a $4 billion business, compared with the Afghan government's budget of just over $700 million. President Hamid Karzai and his government were growing less and less popular amid mounting evidence that the government was "shot through with corruption and graft" as well as persisting ethnic tensions. The on-the-ground reality was that the central government was exerting less and less control beyond the capital city of Kabul.[64]

The objective in Afghanistan was "to disrupt, dismantle and defeat al Qaeda and its safe havens." This was a scaling back from Bush-era notions of democracy building. Some criticized this objective as abandoning Principles. The administration defined it as "clear, concise, attainable."[65] An initial commitment was quickly made to increase troops

AT THE SOURCE
AT THE SOURCE

## OBAMA'S SPEECH TO THE ARAB AND MUSLIM WORLDS

Cairo, Egypt, June 4, 2009

We meet at a time of great tension between the United States and Muslims around the world—tension rooted in historical forces that go beyond any current policy debate. The relationship between Islam and the West includes centuries of coexistence and cooperation, but also conflict and religious wars. More recently, tension has been fed by colonialism that denied rights and opportunities to many Muslims, and a Cold War in which Muslim-majority countries were too often treated as proxies without regard to their own aspirations. Moreover, the sweeping change brought by modernity and globalization led many Muslims to view the West as hostile to the traditions of Islam.

Violent extremists have exploited these tensions in a small but potent minority of Muslims. The attacks of September 11, 2001 and the continued efforts of these extremists to engage in violence against civilians has led some in my country to view Islam as inevitably hostile not only to America and Western countries, but also to human rights. All this has bred more fear and more mistrust.

So long as our relationship is defined by our differences, we will empower those who sow hatred rather than peace, those who promote conflict rather than the cooperation that can help all of our people achieve justice and prosperity. And this cycle of suspicion and discord must end.

I've come here to Cairo to seek a new beginning between the United States and Muslims around the world, one based on mutual interest and mutual respect, and one based upon the truth that America and Islam are not exclusive and need not be in competition. Instead, they overlap, and share common principles—principles of justice and progress; tolerance and the dignity of all human beings. . . .

The first issue that we have to confront is violent extremism in all of its forms.

In Ankara, I made clear that America is not—and never will be—at war with Islam. We will, however, relentlessly confront violent extremists who pose a grave threat to our security—because we reject the same thing that people of all faiths reject: the

(*Continued*)

(*Continued*)

killing of innocent men, women, and children. And it is my first duty as President to protect the American people. . . .

The second major source of tension that we need to discuss is the situation between Israelis, Palestinians and the Arab world.

America's strong bonds with Israel are well known. This bond is unbreakable. It is based upon cultural and historical ties, and the recognition that the aspiration for a Jewish homeland is rooted in a tragic history that cannot be denied. . . .

On the other hand, it is also undeniable that the Palestinian people—Muslims and Christians—have suffered in pursuit of a homeland. . . . The situation for the Palestinian people is intolerable. And America will not turn our backs on the legitimate Palestinian aspiration for dignity, opportunity, and a state of their own. . . .

The fourth issue that I will address is democracy. . . .

Each nation gives life to this principle in its own way, grounded in the traditions of its own people. America does not presume to know what is best for everyone, just as we would not presume to pick the outcome of a peaceful election. But I do have an unyielding belief that all people yearn for certain things: the ability to speak your mind and have a say in how you are governed; confidence in the rule of law and the equal administration of justice; government that is transparent and doesn't steal from the people; the freedom to live as you choose. These are not just American ideas; they are human rights. And that is why we will support them everywhere. . . .

The sixth issue—the sixth issue that I want to address is women's rights. . . .

I am convinced that our daughters can contribute just as much to society as our sons. Our common prosperity will be advanced by allowing all humanity—men and women—to reach their full potential. . . .

I know there are many—Muslim and non-Muslim—who question whether we can forge this new beginning. Some are eager to stoke the flames of division, and to stand in the way of progress. Some suggest that it isn't worth the effort—that we are fated to disagree, and civilizations are doomed to clash. Many more are simply skeptical that real change can occur. There's so much fear, so much mistrust that has built up over the years. But if we choose to be bound by the past, we will never move forward. And I want to particularly say this to young people of every faith, in every country—you, more than anyone, have the ability to reimagine the world, to remake this world. . . .

Source: Barack Obama, Remarks by the President on a New Beginning, Cairo University, Cairo, Egypt, June 4, 2009, www.whitehouse.gov/the_press_office/Remarks-by-the-President-at-Cairo-University-6-04-09/ (accessed 9/1/09).

in both the U.S. force and the NATO force. The Iraq "surge" strategy, with its emphasis on building cooperative relations with civilian populaces, training indigenous security forces, and taking a comprehensive approach with more resources for economic support, was adapted to Afghan politics and geography. Economic and other civilian assistance was increased. "We can't kill our way to victory," as Joint Chiefs of Staff Chairman Admiral Mike Mullen put it. Economic development, including alternative crops to poppy and basic services such as electricity as well as social benefits such as health care and political reform, were "the keys to success."[66] Other elements included making foreign aid more effective, providing security for elections and ensuring that they were free and fair, and increasing international support and engagement including from NATO, the UN, and regional countries.

Doubts about the Karzai government were accentuated by widespread fraud in the August 2009 election. For this and other reasons, American public opinion began to question whether the Afghan war was worth fighting further. Leaks indicated splits within the Obama administration over how many troops to add, indeed, whether to add any at all. On December 1, 2009, in a speech delivered at West Point and televised in prime time, the President laid out his policy. Its main component was a major troop build-up of another 30,000 U.S. troops (bringing the total to about 100,000) to be deployed quickly to gain military momentum against the Taliban and step up training of Afghan military and policy. The President set a July 2011 semi-flexible deadline for achieving key objectives and then starting to draw down. Other key aspects of the policy were diplomatic efforts to get NATO allies to increase their troops, increased economic and civil society assistance to the Afghan people, more concerted pressure on the Karzai government for political reform, and broader global and regional diplomacy for support and complementary efforts by Europe, Russia, China, India, and other states with significant interests at stake.

Although there was general consensus that the old strategy was not working, there was doubt as to whether the new one would. Was the troop increase enough, some asked? On the other hand, was increasing troop numbers the wrong way to go? Would this strategy land America in another quagmire, Obama's Vietnam or Iraq?

At the same time there was increasing recognition that Pakistan, which was supposed to be part of the solution for stabilizing Afghanistan, had become part of the problem. The Bush administration's support for the Pakistan president, Pervez Musharraf, including over $10 billion in aid, had not produced the cooperation promised. Pakistan had become a safe haven where the Taliban rebuilt and rearmed and from which it launched attacks back into Afghanistan. It wasn't only that Pakistan had tried but had been unable to counter the Taliban. The evidence was quite strong that President Musharraf; the military; and the ISI, Pakistan's intelligence agency, had been "playing both sides of the war, the American side and the Taliban side. In return for the American billions, Pakistani forces or intelligence operatives occasionally picked off a few al Qaeda leaders (though even that had slowed to a trickle). But they were actively supporting the Taliban and even some of the militants in the tribal regions."[67]

Indeed, Pakistan itself had become more unstable. Musharraf was driven from power by popular unrest.* The former prime minister Benazir Bhutto was assassinated on her return from exile. Her widower, Asif Ali Zardari, was elected president, but he brought with him his own past of having been convicted of corruption and showed limited skill at governing. Meanwhile Islamist fundamentalism was winning a foothold. Pakistan's own Taliban was gaining power, as reported by the *New York Times* journalist David Sanger:

> The country is turning a blind eye as fundamentalism is taught in the schools—not just in the religious madrassas, but in the public and private schools that educate the rest of the population. . . . Take the word *collision,* which is pronounced *tay* in Urdu. The illustration [in a widely used textbook]: A picture of two airplanes flying into a burning World Trade Center. "Of all the pictures of a collision that you could find," Hoodhboy [a Pakistani critic] told me, "it's curious that they use that one in the textbook. . . . And the problem is not limited to basic readers for first-graders. Leafing through today's high school textbooks . . . [reveals that they] say little about Afghanistan or the brutal rule of the Taliban.[68]

The objectives in Pakistan were to provide sufficient political stability, economic progress and security cooperation to contribute to the anti–Al Qaeda three d's (disrupt, dismantle, defeat) and more broadly ensure that Pakistan did not become the first failed state possessing nuclear weapons. Economic aid was substantially increased on the basis of a plan originally developed by Vice President Biden while he was still a senator, in

---

*See Chapter 11 for a discussion of democratization issues in Pakistan.

conjunction with Republican Senator Richard Lugar (Indiana). Conditions on military aid were tightened to try to ensure that the aid went toward the counterterrorism and counterinsurgency missions.

Would this be enough? Were Pakistan's internal political problems correctable, or at least manageable, through a shift in U.S. policy? Or did they run so deep, with so many of their own rivalries, with such weak political institutions, and such profound economic problems that major impact was beyond the reach of even an improved U.S. policy?

For a while the Pakistani strategy was to make concessions to the Taliban, even ceding parts of the country such as the Swat Valley to their control. When this appeared to be exacerbating rather than alleviating the threats, the Pakistani military stepped up its efforts to retake the Swat Valley and other areas. Yet the fighting forced over one million people to flee their homes, creating a massive refugee crisis. Thus even when the Taliban was pushed back on the ground, the refugee situation fostered resentment and radicalization that became yet another source of instability.

As if these challenges were not tough enough, there also was the contentious issue of U.S. military action inside Pakistan to attack Al Qaeda and related targets. In its last months, the Bush administration had authorized using drones—unpiloted aircraft that could be operated remotely from as far away as the United States—to attack Al Qaeda and related targets inside Pakistan. The Obama administration continued this policy, even stepping up the number of attacks. There also were reports of some special operations forces crossing over from Afghanistan into Pakistan on quick, targeted missions.

These incursions raised a number of issues. Was such action justified? Defenders traced its legitimacy back to the original 2001 retaliation against Al Qaeda for 9/11. They also viewed it as akin to "hot pursuit" tactics employed against terrorists and other fighters who had crossed over into Afghanistan to attack U.S. and NATO forces and then crossed back into Pakistan. Opponents saw the incursions as invading an ally, which violated international law and norms.

Were the incursions effective? This part of the debate was framed as decapitation versus destabilization, pitting the benefits of killing Al Qaeda leaders (nine of the top twenty were said to have been killed by early 2009) against the risks of feeding anti-Americanism and fueling radicalization.

A third, less explicitly discussed but potentially more monumental question is: If Pakistan does end up a failed state, or if radical Islamists come to power—perhaps even through their penetration of the military—with the risk that Pakistan's nuclear arsenal would fall into their hands, what would, should, and could the Untied States do? This could be, as the military strategist Andrew Krepinevich describes the possibility, "the century's greatest crisis."[69]

## Terrorism

Besides reaching out to the Muslim world in his inaugural address, President Obama had this message for terrorists: "We will not apologize for our way of life, nor will we waver in its defense, and for those who seek to advance their aims by inducing terror and slaughtering innocents, we say to you now that our spirit is stronger and cannot be broken; you cannot outlast us, and we will defeat you." Terrorism remained a top priority. But the strategy was changing.

The term "global war on terrorism" would no longer be used. "The Administration has stopped using the phrase, and I think that speaks for itself," Secretary of State Hillary Clinton stated.[70] This was in part a matter of political communication, given the negatives that "global war on terrorism" engendered. Many at home and abroad associated it with the Iraq war, the Guantánamo Bay detention camps, torture, and other Bush policies. Dropping this term reflected substantive strategy changes.

This shift in strategy had its source in a different analysis of the principal sources of terrorism.[71] The Bush administration had leaned heavily toward the "clash of civilizations" view of Samuel Huntington. "The great divisions among humankind and the dominating source of conflict will be cultural," Huntington wrote in his widely cited article. "The clash of civilizations will dominate global politics. . . . Civilizations are differentiated from each other by history, culture, tradition and, most important, religion. The people of different civilizations have different views of God and man, the individual and the group, the citizen and the state, parents and children, and husband and wife, as well as differing views of the relative importance of rights and responsibilities, liberty and authority, equality and hierarchy."[72] Although Huntington posed the conflict as being between "the West and the Rest," the emphasis came to be especially on the Arab and Islamic world.

One of the main criticisms of the Huntington thesis is that the actual clash is less one *of* civilizations than one *within* the Arab-Islamic world. This view was not new to the Obama administration; indeed, it was articulated in the ***9/11 Commission Report*** (Reading 8.3). Al Qaeda embodied a ***jihadism*** targeted not only against the West but also toward transforming the Arab and Islamic world. Its fundamentalism pushed a vision of a new caliphate (Islamic theocracy) ruling according to *sharia* (religious law based on the Koran). At one level, the clash was with governments such as the Saudi and Egyptian ones, which, frankly, were vulnerable to charges of corruption and poor governance. At a deeper level, it was a clash with all those in the Arab and Islamic world who sought reform and moderation, a third way between the status quo and jihadist fundamentalism. As put by Mohammed Sayed Tantawi, the grand imam of Egypt's al-Azhar mosque, "Do not commit aggression, for verily Allah does not love aggressors. . . . Killing civilians is a horrific, hideous act that no religion can condone."[73]

8.3

The impact of poverty and other economic factors as the sources of terrorism is less straightforward than often assumed. For example, Mohamed Atta, the leader of the 9/11 terrorists, was college educated and from the middle class. A study of the biographies of 172 Al Qaeda members found two-thirds to be from upper- or middle-class families; over 60 percent had gone to college.[74] Bin Laden himself is from a very wealthy Saudi family. A study of Palestinian terrorists concluded that "any connection between poverty, education and terrorism is indirect, complicated and probably quite weak."[75] But although poverty is not a major motivation for the particular individuals who become terrorists, it does have significance as part of the context in which terrorism gains acceptance and even support among broader groups. "Justice and prosperity for the poor and dispossessed" are critical, as the former British prime minister Tony Blair put it, "so that people everywhere can see the chance of a better future through the hard work and creative power of the free citizen, not the violence and savagery of the fanatic."[76]

The Palestinian issue is another factor. It is likely true that even if the Camp David talks in 2000 had brought about a full Israeli-Palestinian peace agreement, bin Laden and Al Qaeda still would have launched the September 11 attacks. They are opposed to Israel's very existence, not just to the terms of a deal but to any deal at all. Still, the plight of the Palestinians does add to the support base for terrorism.

National issues also are a factor. During the Cold War, as discussed in Chapters 4 and 5, one of the major U.S. mistakes was lumping together Third World guerrilla groups and revolutionary movements as part of global communism, not taking their national identities sufficiently into account. Similarly, although terrorist groups today do have global links, many also have national identities. Hezbollah in Lebanon, for example, has been closely linked to Iran for arms and training. But it also grew in the Lebanese social, historical and cultural context and has goals geared to Lebanese politics. The same is true of groups in East Asia such as Abu Sayyaf in the Philippines and Jemaah Islamiyah in Indonesia, which have links to but are not merely extensions of Al Qaeda. This analysis does not necessarily make any of these groups less dangerous. The point is rather that the sources of the threat need to be accurately assessed if the policy to deal with it is to have a chance of success.

These interwoven dynamics also have been part of the rising terrorism within the West. Some attacks, such as that in Madrid, Spain, in March 2004, have had strong operational links back to Al Qaeda. The July 2005 bombings in the London subway ("tube") and on buses and the August 2006 plot to blow up airplanes headed from London to the United States had some Al Qaeda links but were mostly homegrown, carried out by Muslims disaffected from British society and radicalized by jihadism as an ideology. So too were others, such as the plot broken up in Canada in June 2006 that involved students and others whose plans included the beheading of the Canadian prime minister. The Internet also played a role: the Canadian group's radicalization was fed by militant Web sites and online advice from an Islamic extremist Webmaster based in Britain who called himself "Terrorist 007."[77]

A series of public opinion polls conducted in mid-2008 in a number of Arab and other Islamic countries provided interesting data.[78] Views of the United States were quite negative. Only 12 percent on average said "the U.S. mostly shows respect to the Islamic world." Asked to rank how well the United States fulfills its world role on a 0 (very poorly) to 10 (very well) scale, ratings were as low as 1.4 (Egypt) and not higher than 4.2 (Indonesia and Pakistan). Opposition to U.S. military presence in Muslim countries was very high. Belief that the United States is genuinely pursuing democracy was low. So too was confidence that the United States was committed to a Palestinian state. But when asked whether they approved, disapproved, or had mixed feelings about attacks on civilians in the United States, majorities as high as 84 percent and no lower than 59 percent said no. "Bombings and assassinations that are carried out to achieve political or religious goals" are rejected as "not justified at all" by large majorities ranging from 67 to 89 percent.

Al Qaeda's personal attacks on Barack Obama right after he was elected indicated concern that the anti-Americanism they had been feeding off would diminish. Ayman al-Zawahiri, the number two leader to bin Laden, called Obama "a hypocrite," "enemy of Muslims," and even "a house Negro." Many jihadist Web sites had been hoping that John McCain would win the election, seeing him "as the man most likely to continue Bush administration policies and, it was hoped, drive the United States more deeply into a prolonged guerrilla war." The vitriolic personal attacks on Obama were interpreted by terrorism experts as "a deliberate, even desperate propaganda campaign against a president who appears to have gotten under [their] skin."[79]

Although the benefits of the Obama persona were helpful, the ongoing key would be the actual strategy and policies. Obama brought significant change but also a degree of continuity. Military force remained a core component, with greater efforts to adapt military strategy better to fit counterterrorism missions. For example, the first Obama defense budget made substantial shifts in resources toward counterterrorism, counterinsurgency, and other irregular methods of warfare. The initial dismissal of deterrence by the Bush administration and others is being reassessed. History does show that some terrorist movements end without having been defeated militarily, for example, by the loss of popular support, unsuccessful generational succession, or a transition into nonviolent national political processes. Differentiated analyses are starting to synchronize particular counterstrategies more closely to what strategy terrorists are pursuing—for example, whether they are goading the United States to overreact, or seeking to intimidate, in which case there is greater need to show resolve.[80]

The Obama strategy also has been seeking to do more to integrate diplomatic, political, economic, and other instruments of power and influence. This approach is based on its analysis of the sources of terrorism and the importance of addressing the broader dynamics of the Middle East by supporting socioeconomic reform and development, strengthening political alternatives to oppressive autocracy or radical theocracy, and improving public diplomacy and other strategic communications efforts. This has meant increased roles for the State Department and the U.S. Agency for International Development (AID).

At the same time, preventing ***catastrophic terrorism***—the use of nuclear, chemical, or other weapons of mass destruction (WMD)—has remained the highest priority. This goal entails working in cooperation with other nations to prevent WMD acquisition by Al Qaeda or other terrorists. One such preventive program is the Nunn-Lugar Cooperative Threat Reduction program with Russia, intended to safeguard against "loose nukes." It also includes efforts by the Department of Homeland Security, the FBI, the Coast Guard, and other agencies closer to home both to maximize prevention and to ensure resilience if an attack should occur.

All of these strategies and policies were to be consistent with the rule of law and the principles of both American democracy and the rules-based international order that the United States long has championed. The Obama administration made the closing of the Guantánamo Bay detention center and the renunciation of torture two of its early initiatives. Civil libertarians and other critics have been questioning whether the administration was living up to these pledges. We discuss these and other issues that have involved tensions between national security and civil liberties in the foreign policy politics section later in this chapter.

## *Iran*

During the Cold War, as discussed in Part I, the shah of Iran was a major U.S. ally. But after he was overthrown in 1979 by the Islamist revolution led by Ayatollah Ruhollah Khomeini, U.S.-Iranian relations had been tense, to say the least. The seizure of the American embassy and the taking of American hostages in November 1979 led the Carter administration to break off diplomatic relations. The Reagan administration tilted toward Iraq in the 1980–88 Iran-Iraq war, although it did also have an ill-fated arms for hostages deal with Iran. The Bush administration continued the tilt toward Iraq right up until Saddam Hussein's invasion of Kuwait; even as it turned against Iraq it did not turn toward Iran.[81] Economic sanctions were ratcheted up during the Clinton administration. Relations with Iran became even tenser during the George W. Bush administration, with its "axis of evil" formulation and its threat of regime change, the Iraq war, and revelations that Iran appeared to be developing nuclear weapons in violation of its commitments under the Nonproliferation Treaty (NPT).

Iran insisted that its nuclear energy programs were for peaceful uses only, and that these were both consistent with the NPT and within its sovereign rights. However, not only the Bush administration but also many in Europe and at the International Atomic Energy Agency (IAEA), the principal enforcer of the NPT, had suspicions. In late 2003 the "EU-3"—Britain, France, and Germany—took the lead in negotiations with Iran along with the IAEA to get it to abide by the NPT and not build nuclear weapons. Some initial compromises and partial agreements were achieved over the next two years. The EU-3 strategy was carrot-and-stick diplomacy: economic sanctions and other penalties for noncooperation and economic and political incentives if Iran did cooperate. But a full deal was elusive. In mid-2006, the Bush administration partially shifted its position, becoming somewhat more supportive of the EU-3 and IAEA but still unwilling to directly negotiate with Iran. It set the precondition for even having negotiations that Iran first suspend the enrichment and reprocessing programs that were suspected of being most geared to nuclear weapons development. The administration was concerned that once the talks started, Iran would stretch them out inconclusively while buying time for its nuclear weapons programs to go forward.

Tensions increased as Mahmoud Ahmadenijad, the new Iranian president, stoked things up with calls for the destruction of Israel, denials that the Nazi Holocaust had occurred, and other inflammatory rhetoric. He also was more defiant of the EU-3 and the IAEA on the nuclear issue. One uncertainty was how long it would take Iran to develop a nuclear weapon. In 2005 the CIA revised its estimate from five more years to ten. Two years later, the U.S. intelligence assessment was that although uranium-enrichment programs were continuing, Iran had halted its actual nuclear weapons programs back in 2003. Which estimate was the most reliable? On the one hand, Iraq's WMD had been grossly overestimated. On the other, India's successful test of a nuclear weapon in 1998 caught American intelligence by surprise.

In late 2006 and early 2007, the UN Security Council passed two resolutions with a number of measures seeking to persuade and pressure Iran into compliance with the NPT, including some economic sanctions. The strategic significance of the sanctions was twofold. First, as a unanimous decision of the UN Security Council—including Russia and China, which lined up with Europe and the United States—such action could send a strong, credible geopolitical message of international unity. Second, the Iranian economy was vulnerable amid high unemployment and high inflation, along with investment and technology shortages in the oil and gas sector. But the fact that agreement could be achieved only on limited rather than comprehensive sanctions tempered the credibility of the geopolitical message. And the boom in oil prices, which hit $140 per barrel in mid-2008, took some of the edge off the economic impact. A third round of UNSC sanctions was imposed in 2008, as were additional unilateral U.S. sanctions, including financial ones that made it harder for banks to lend to Iran. These did add somewhat to Iran's costs but still did not resolve the diplomatic deadlock over the nuclear issue.

Some called for military strikes. "Iran is right at the top of the list," Vice President Cheney told the radio host Don Imus in January 2005.[82] Analogies were drawn to the 1981 Israeli attack on Iraq's main nuclear weapons development site at Osirak. But Iran had numerous suspected sites, not just one, and many were hardened and protected in other ways. One expert effort to "war game" the military options was not optimistic.[83] Iranian counterstrategies, particularly terrorism by Iran's own networks or others in solidarity, warranted particular concern.

Other issues also were sources of tensions. One was Iraq. Iran had its own ambivalence about the Iraq War. On the one hand, Iran regarded the U.S. invasion of Iraq, along with the "axis of evil" rhetoric and its implication that Iran could be next, as a threat to its own security. On the other hand, once Saddam was toppled and the Sunni minority lost power, Iran, as the leading Shia state, benefited from the ascendance of the Iraqi Shiites. Over the course of the war evidence emerged of direct Iranian involvement training and arming Shia militias in Iraq and of Iranian-supplied weapons that were used against American soldiers.

Iran's support for Hezbollah in Lebanon and Hamas in Palestine also was a contentious issue. Hezbollah, the main Shiite force in Lebanon, was a major contender for political power in Lebanon against factions the United States supported. It also squared off against Israel in the 2006 war. The military aid as well as other support that came from Iran was a key part of Hezbollah's strength and strategy. Hamas also received arms, training, and other support from Iran.

Iran has been a crucial test case for the Obama administration's engagement strategy. As in other efforts to build cooperation with adversaries, common interests such as "the enemy of my enemy is my friend" can be a starting point. Early on, three key elements of this strategy emerged. One was to seek to work with Iran on Afghanistan. Iran had long been opposed to the Taliban, with its Sunni heritage and its fundamentalism, and whose repressive rule was even more extreme than Iran's own. Evidence was substantial that in the wake of 9/11, Iran had offered to cooperate with the United States against the Taliban but was rebuffed by the Bush administration, which instead opted for the axis of evil–regime change route.[84]

Second was President Obama's own personal diplomacy. Iran was among those nations to which he directed his inaugural address offer to "extend a hand if you are willing to unclench your fist." His video message on the occasion of Nowruz, the celebration of the beginning of spring and a new year among Iranians and other Shiite Muslims, was called "a new beginning" and spoke of mutual respect and moving forward.[85]

A few months later, though, Iranian politics changed dramatically when the June 12 presidential election was hotly disputed over substantial evidence of fraud in Ahmadinejad's claim to victory. Iranians protested in numbers not seen since the fall of the Shah, rallying in what became known as the "Green Movement" (for the official color of opposition presidential candidate Mir Hossein Musavi). The Ahmadinejad regime and the Supreme (religious) Leader Ayatollah Ali Khamenei responded with brutal repression, yet protests continued. Calculating that speaking out too much would play into the regime's effort to blame the unrest on the United States and other foreigners, the Obama administration was initially restrained in its support for the Green Movement. This strategy was supported by some as pragmatic, criticized by others as weak and not true to American principles.

The third element in the Obama administration's Iran strategy has been "bigger carrots and bigger sticks:" greater economic and security incentives for cooperation, further sanctions and possibly other measures if not. In October 2009 the administration opened more direct negotiations with Iran than the Bush administration had been willing to do. These were within the "P-5 + 1" framework involving the other permanent members of the UN Security Council (Britain, France, China, and Russia) plus Germany, which had been involved in the EU-Iran negotiations and which had major trade ties with Iran. Some U.S.-Iranian bilateral meetings were also held along the "margins" of the full group. The multilateral dimension reflected the need for broad cooperation if sanctions were to be imposed; the bilateral dimension was that U.S.-Iranian tensions were at the core of this and other issues.

Will the engagement strategy succeed? How long should it be given to work? Is the United States offering too much? Too little? Should military force be used if negotiations fail and Iran gets closer to nuclear weapons—by the United States? By Israel? What of the Green Movement or other possible major political change within Iran? These and other questions are likely to continue to press on us. About the only point of agreement in this debate is the importance of US-Iranian relations. It has been and is likely to continue to be a "high synergy" issue. For 30 plus years we've seen the negative synergy side of bilateral conflict and tension as major problems in their own right as well as feeding into and exacerbating other problem issues and hot spots in the Middle East and globally. This could get worse. On the other hand, were relations to improve, there could be a positive synergy with benefits for other issues in the Middle East, i.e., weakening of Hamas in Palestine and Hezbollah in Lebanon. The stakes are high, the optimal policies uncertain—another issue to watch and on which the *American Foreign Policy* Online StudySpace will provide updates.

## The Arab-Israeli Conflict

This chapter's "Historical Perspectives" box (pp. 449–51) provides a summary historical timeline of the Arab-Israeli conflict, 1947–2008. One could of course go much further back in history, even to biblical times. We focus on the period since the founding of the state of Israel.

As the timeline shows, the Arab-Israeli conflict has gone through four major regional wars (1948, 1956, 1967, 1973), two Palestinian ***intifadas*** (1987–93 and 2000–2004), two Israeli-Lebanon wars (1982, 2006), the Israel-Gaza war (2008) and other violence and instability. The core issue has been "land for peace," meaning recognition by the Arabs of

## HISTORICAL PERSPECTIVES

HISTORICAL PERSPECTIVES

### ARAB-ISRAELI CONFLICT: SUMMARY TIMELINE, 1947–2008

| Dates | Developments |
|---|---|
| 1947 | Motivated in significant part by the Nazi Holocaust killing of 6 million Jews, the United Nations approves a partition plan for a Jewish state and an Arab state in Palestine |
| 1948 | Israel declares independence; Arab states (Egypt, Jordan, Syria, Iraq, Lebanon, Saudi Arabia) declare war |
| 1956 | Suez War: Israel, supported by Britain and France, attacks Egypt; Eisenhower pressure helps end war |
| 1964 | Palestine Liberation Organization (PLO) established with Yasir Arafat as head |
| 1967 | Six-Day War: Israel defeats Arab states, takes Sinai, West Bank, Gaza Strip, Golan Heights; UN Security Council Resolution 242 calls for "land for peace" |
| 1970 | Civil war in Jordan between King Hussein and PLO-led Palestinians |
| 1973 | Yom Kippur War: surprise attack on Israel; OPEC oil embargo and price hike |
| 1974 | Secretary of State Henry Kissinger's "shuttle diplomacy" on cease-fire and other partial agreements |
| 1976 | Syria invades Lebanon, begins military occupation that lasts over thirty years |

| Dates | Developments |
|---|---|
| 1977 | Egyptian President Anwar Sadat makes historic visit to Israel |
| 1978–79 | With President Jimmy Carter as main diplomat, Egyptian president Sadat and Israeli prime minister Menachem Begin sign Camp David peace treaties |
| 1981 | Israel attacks Iraqi nuclear reactor at Osirak, sets back Saddam Hussein's nuclear weapons program |
| 1981 | Egyptian President Sadat assassinated by Islamic fundamentalists |
| 1982–84 | Israel invades Lebanon, going beyond earlier military incursions; eventually forced to withdraw. |
| 1983 | Over two hundred Americans, part of Lebanon peacekeeping force, killed in terrorist bombing of their barracks in Beirut |
| 1987 | The first *intifada,* a Palestinian popular uprising against Isareli occupation of the West Bank and Gaza |
| 1991 | With end of Cold War and following U.S.-led victory in Persian Gulf War, Madrid peace process negotiations between Israel and numerous Arab states, with George H. W. Bush administration in lead role |
| 1993 | First Israeli-Palestinian peace agreement, signed by PLO leader Arafat and Israeli prime minister Yitzhak Rabin, called the "Oslo agreement" because started by Norwegian diplomats, with Clinton administration then taking on lead role |
| 1994 | Palestinian Authority established in Gaza and West Bank with some limited governing authority. Jordan and Israel sign peace treaty |

| Dates | Developments |
|---|---|
| 1995 | Prime Minster Rabin assassinated by right-wing Israeli opponent of peace |
| 1993–2000 | Various partial peace agreements but fall short of comprehensive peace for Israel-Palestinians and Israel-Syria |
| 2000 | Violence increases with second *initfada* and Israeli military action |
| 2001–2004 | Ariel Sharon elected Israeli prime minister. Palestinian suicide bombings, Israeli military reoccupation, little progress in peace process |
| 2005 | After Arafat's death in 2004, Mahmoud Abbas elected president of Palestinian Authority. Shift in Sharon policy, withdraws from Gaza |
| 2006 | Sharon incapacitated by stroke; Ehud Olmert becomes Israeli prime minister |
| 2006 | Hamas, which is on U.S. list of terrorist organizations, wins Palestinian legislative election. Clashes with President Abbas and his Fatah party as well as with Israelis |
| 2006 | Israel-Lebanon war prompted by border clashes and Hezbollah kidnapping of Israeli soldiers. Generally seen as setback for Israel |
| 2007 | Fatah and Hamas form Palestinian unity government, but doesn't last. In June, Hamas takes control of Gaza |
| 2007 | Annapolis peace conference convened by Bush administration. Makes little progress |
| 2008 | Responding to Hamas attacks on Israeli towns, Israel invades Gaza. Achieves some military objectives, but widely criticized for civilian casualties; overall security situation still uncertain |

Israel's right to exist and a genuine commitment to peaceful coexistence with Israel, Israel's return of territories captured in the 1967 war, and creation of a Palestinian state. Intensive U.S. peace brokering in the Middle East goes back at least to Secretary of State Henry Kissinger's ***shuttle diplomacy*** during and following the 1973 Arab-Israeli war, working out cease-fires and other agreements among Israel, Egypt, Jordan, Syria, and others in the region. The main breakthrough came in the 1979 ***Camp David Accord*** between Egypt and Israel, negotiated by the Egyptian president Anwar Sadat, the Israeli prime minister Menachem Begin, and the U.S. president Jimmy Carter. Egypt became the first Arab state to make peace with Israel, and consistent with the land-for-peace formula, it regained territories such as the Sinai Peninsula, lost in the 1967 war.

One of the main reasons the Middle East peace process took off in the early 1990s was the transformed regional context caused by the double-barrelled effects of the end of the Cold War and the U.S.-led victory in the Gulf War. Without the Soviet Union, Middle East "rejectionists" (those who reject peace with Israel) such as the PLO were bereft of a superpower patron. In contrast, with its profound political victory in the Cold War and overwhelming military victory in the Gulf War, U.S. prestige was at an all-time high. Seeking to capitalize on this, the first Bush administration called a Middle East peace conference for October 1991, held in Madrid, Spain.[86]

The major breakthrough came in 1993 with the Israeli-Palestinian Declaration of Principles (DOP), signed by Israel's prime minister Yitzhak Rabin and the Palestine Liberation Organization (PLO) leader Yasir Arafat alongside President Bill Clinton. "It is time to put an end to decades of confrontation and conflict," the DOP stated, "and strive to live in peaceful coexistence and mutual dignity and security and achieve a just, lasting and comprehensive peace." The negotiations for this agreement actually had been conducted during secret talks in Oslo, Norway. This led some to see the ***"Oslo agreement"*** as evidence that the U.S. role as Middle East peace broker had diminished. But this was too superficial an analysis. The personal role of the Norwegian foreign minister Johan Jorgen Holst, who had built trust with both sides, definitely was an important factor in the decision to hold the talks in Oslo, and a good reminder that Americans do not have a monopoly on peace brokering. Another factor was the need to conduct the talks where they would be out of the limelight, which would have been nearly impossible in the United States. Once the talks were completed, though, the signing ceremony took place in Washington. The United States played the major diplomatic role in ensuing years in brokering the follow-up agreements, including the 1994 Israel-Jordan treaty, and in trying to move the process along toward a comprehensive peace.

Prior to 1993 Arafat and the PLO considered the United States an enemy, and the United States condemned and opposed them as terrorists. But for a number of reasons those views changed. For Arafat, although other world leaders had received him for many years, the invitation to the White House conferred a degree of legitimacy and status that could come only from Washington. The United States also was the key to unlocking international economic assistance, for example with the two Donors Conferences. The first was convened at the State Department within weeks of the 1993 DOP; $2.2 billion in economic assistance was pledged to the Palestinians by more than forty nations and international institutions such as the World Bank. The second was held in December 1998 shortly after the Israeli-Palestinian Wye River agreement (its name coming from the area in eastern Maryland where the final negotiations were held); an additional $3 billion to $4 billion in aid was pledged to the Palestinians. Arafat also knew that if there ever was to be peace and independence for his people, only the United States could provide the combination of reassurance, persuasion, and pressure for Israel to agree.

The 1993 DOP had set a five-year timetable for final status agreement on a just, lasting, and comprehensive peace. The Wye River accord and other agreements were only small steps in this process. The Clinton administration called its own Camp David summit in July 2000, bringing together the Israeli prime minister Ehud Barak and the Palestinian Authority president Arafat. This Camp David summit broke up in disarray. A last-ditch effort was tried in January 2001, just before President Clinton left office, with negotiations in Taba, Egypt. Although no agreement was reached, many believe that when a final status agreement ultimately is signed, it probably will look a lot like the Taba draft.[87]

On the ground, violence again raged. The Palestinians launched a second *intifada* marked by suicide bombings and other terrorist acts. The Israeli military, with Ariel Sharon as prime minister, reoccupied many parts of the West Bank and Gaza. The Bush administration refused to meet with Yasir Arafat and struck common chords with Sharon about fights against terrorism. A peace plan known as the "road map" was proposed by the "quartet" of the United States, the European Union, Russia, and the United Nations. But it did not have much impact.

Some progress was made in 2004–2005. In late 2004, Yasir Arafat died. Many attributed to Arafat a major part of the responsibility for the breakdown of the peace process. Arafat also had been losing standing with the Palestinian people because of corruption and human rights violations. He was succeeded by Mahmoud Abbas, the new leader of Arafat's political organization Fatah, and generally viewed as more pragmatic. On the Israeli side Prime Minister Sharon was shifting his approach and his strategy. Sharon had been elected on a platform of peace with security. Yet he too saw that although there was no guarantee that peace would bring security, Israel could never have real security without peace. In 2005 Sharon took the bold step of unilaterally withdrawing from Gaza, meaning both pulling out the Israeli military and disbanding Israeli settlements. He ran for reelection on a much more pro-peace platform than he'd originally been elected on, including withdrawals and settlement disbandment in the West Bank.

In January 2006, however, two things happened that halted whatever momentum had been building. Ariel Sharon had an incapacitating stroke. He was replaced by Ehud Olmert, whose positions on key issues were largely the same as Sharon's but who lacked

Sharon's personal credibility. On the Palestinian side, parliamentary elections were held. The winner was Hamas, an Islamic fundamentalist group that had been a major perpetrator of terrorism and a staunch opponent of peace, but which also had been gaining popular support through its domestic agenda of fighting corruption and providing social services to the Palestinian people. Outside observers deemed the elections free and fair.

This posed a dilemma for the Bush administration. It had been strongly advocating democracy in the Arab world, yet in this election the winner was a group that was on the U.S. terrorism list and whose charter called for the destruction of Israel. The Bush policy, and also that of much of Europe, was to suspend financial aid to the Hamas government to pressure it to moderate. How could the United States support a government that was led by terrorists and that was sworn to the destruction of an American ally? On the other hand, the financial pinch from the aid suspension added to the instability and reinforced Hamas's hard line. Tensions increased, not only between the Palestinians and Israelis but also between Hamas and Fatah. Violence, both Israeli-Palestinian and Palestinian-Palestinian, was again on the rise.

In late June 2006, Israeli-Hamas clashes in Gaza intensified with the kidnapping of an Israeli soldier. But it was on the northern front where the next crisis broke out. In mid-July, Hezbollah, the Lebanese Islamic terrorist and political force closely allied with Iran, crossed the border and kidnapped two more Israeli soldiers. Over the next month, war intensified between Israel and Hezbollah. In one sense, everyone lost. Hezbollah and Lebanon suffered massive damage, many lives were lost, and much of the Lebanese economy and infrastructure, which had been reconstructed after decades of war, was again in ruins. Israel not only suffered damage to several northern cities and a relatively large number of deaths for such a small population, but also experienced further erosion of its security. Its military, which had been formidable in many previous wars, performed poorly. Part of the problem could be traced to failures in planning and execution. Much had to do with the difference between the more conventional combat methods of taking on Arab state armies and air forces, which the Israelis were well equipped and trained for, and the asymmetric warfare required against an enemy such as Hezbollah. This problem was similar to that encountered by U.S. forces in Iraq and Afghanistan. Notwithstanding the damage the Israeli armed forces did inflict, Hezbollah ended up with greater political power within Lebanon and enhanced prestige in the Arab world for having stood up to Israel.

In late December 2008, the Gaza war broke out. Citing increased rocket attacks by Hamas on Israeli populations in nearby towns, Israel invaded Gaza. This war was even more controversial than the 2006 Lebanon war. On the one hand, Israelis felt they had a stronger claim to acting in self-defense, given Hamas' attacks on Israeli towns. Israel also received a degree of tacit support, or at least less overt opposition and criticism, from such surrounding Arab states as Egypt, Jordan, and Saudi Arabia, which were concerned about Hamas's fundamentalism and links to Iran. On the other hand, numerous reports of civilian causalities and humanitarian emergencies among the Gazan people, including some accusations of war crimes, had damaging international political effects and raised ethical questions. Assessments of the war's impact on the ground varied. Some saw Israeli success in the killing or capture of some Hamas leaders and members and the Israeli military's demonstration of its will and capacity to respond. Others questioned whether even this degree of military success left Israel more secure in a sustainable way, considering the political damage done by the humanitarian consequences.

The Gaza war came amid the Bush-Obama transition. If the Obama transition team had any doubt about the need to engage quickly in Arab-Israeli diplomacy, the Gaza war dispelled it. George Mitchell, a former Senate majority leader as well as the key U.S. negotiator in the 1990s settlement of the Protestant-Catholic conflict in Northern Ireland, was appointed as the lead diplomat for the Arab-Israeli conflict. This was a shift from the Bush policy, which had relegated the Arab-Israeli peace process to a lower priority.

Through much of the first year of the Obama administration, U.S.-Israeli relations were tense. Benjamin Netanyahu had come back into office as the Israeli prime minister, leading a largely right-wing coalition. Netanyahu and Obama clashed over the issue of Israeli settlements. The Obama administration pushed hard for a full freeze on settlements. The Netanyahu government resisted. Amidst this and other issues, Israeli public opinion polls showed Obama's approval at below 10 percent. On the U.S. side, controversies over the "Israeli lobby" were exacerbated. Still, cooperation continued on a number of fronts including joint military exercises, continued diplomatic consultations, and President Obama's reiteration that policy differences were one thing, but U.S. support for Israel's security and survival remained firm.

On the Palestinian side, along with and interrelated to the peace process with Israel were the economic and security challenges crucial to moving toward a viable state. In June 2009, along with colleagues from a number of other American universities, I met in Ramallah with Palestinian Prime Minister Salam Fayyad. While we discussed the peace process, most of the focus was on Palestinian economic and security policies geared to making life better for their own people. There was recognition that while economic and security progress could not go past a certain point unless peace was achieved, making that progress would help progress toward peace. Such progress would also strengthen Fatah in its internal competition with Hamas and other forces.

Syria remains another key part of the Middle East peace equation. In January 2009, this author had the opportunity to be part of a delegation from two Washington think tanks to meet with Syrian President Bashar Asad. Our meeting ran over two hours and included Iraq, Iran, Lebanon, Israel, U.S. economic sanctions, and a range of other issues. Our sense was of both differences remaining on some issues but opportunities to improve cooperation on numerous others. Developments since then have borne both aspects out. The Obama administration shifted from Bush efforts to isolate Syria and perhaps precipitate regime change to reengage it. The Bush administration had withdrawn the U.S. admbassador; the Obama administration agreed to send one back. It continued some economic sanctions but lifted others. The American and Syrian militaries started cooperating on intercepting terrorists crossing the Iraq-Syria border in both directions. Some progress was made toward an Israeli-Syrian peace. Yet plenty of other issues remained in contention, including Syrian-Iranian relations and Syria's support for Hezbollah in Lebanon and for Hamas. Time would tell whether progress would continue or not.

Amid these and other uncertainties, two things are clear. One is that as difficult as peace is today, it will be even more difficult tomorrow. More children on both sides will grow up socialized into hatred. More violence will be perpetrated. More distrust will build up. More windows of opportunity will slam shut.

The other is that American interests will continue to be significantly affected. The particular strategies for peace brokering are not necessarily the same as those used by Secretary of State Kissinger after the 1973 war, or by President Carter at Camp David, or by President Clinton in the Oslo process. But the history of recent decades has been that progress in Middle East peace requires a central role for the United States.

## Foreign Policy Politics: Terrorism and the Iraq War

September 11, 2001, transformed foreign policy politics no less than foreign policy strategy. For the first time since the end of the Cold War, there was an Enemy. Not just a number of small-e enemies, or the possibility that a major one might emerge down the road: Osama bin Laden, Al Qaeda, and terrorism writ large together constituted a capital-e Enemy.

The stakes now also were higher than perhaps at any point since the nuclear-war scare of the Cuban missile crisis in 1962. The threat was here at home, not just out there. The terrorists could target average citizens in their daily lives, anywhere, anytime. As bad as the September 11 attack was, the next one could be much worse.

Initially, consistent with the historical pattern of "politics stopping at the water's edge" during crises and times of war, foreign policy politics again was characterized by broad domestic consensus. Congress overwhelmingly voted to support the Afghanistan war. The 2001 USA PATRIOT Act* was passed by near unanimous votes. The Department of Homeland Security (DHS) was created. Congress voted in support of the Iraq war.

But although this new political consensus had its foreign policy benefits, it also raised difficult issues, just as previous consensuses had in the past. Moreover, the consensus began to crack over some issues of the war on terrorism and especially over the Iraq war.

*USA PATRIOT Act was the cleverly derived acronym for *U*niting and *S*trengthening *A*merica (USA) by *P*roviding *A*ppropriate *T*ools *R*equired to *I*ntercept and *O*bstruct *T*errorism (PATRIOT) Act of 2001. The USA PATRIOT Act was reauthorized with some changes in 2006.

## *National Security, the Bill of Rights, and the War on Terrorism*

As in the past, one of the toughest balances to strike is between national security and the Bill of Rights. How can the United States make security against terrorism a priority in this new and threatening age while safeguarding the freedoms and rights on which it was founded and that have been fundamental to American democracy for more than two hundred years?

These debates did not just split along standard liberal and conservative, Democratic and Republican lines. For example, William Safire, a noted conservative columnist and outspoken hawk on national security issues, warned about the dangers of greater government surveillance: "Is this the kind of world we want? The promise is greater safety; the tradeoff is government control of individual lives. Personal security may or may not be enhanced by this all-seeing eye and ear, but personal freedom will surely be sharply curtailed."[88] Yet Democrats in Congress voted in overwhelming numbers for the USA PATRIOT Act and other laws that gave priority to the national security objective over the civil liberties one.

Two fundamental sets of questions lie at the heart of the various national security–civil liberties issues. First, what should the scope of governmental and especially presidential powers be? How much power is justified in the name of national security? Second, how is accountability in the exercise of those powers to be ensured? How can checks and balances, provisions for judicial review, freedom of the press, and other political mechanisms be ensured?

DOMESTIC POWERS OF THE MILITARY AND INTELLIGENCE AGENCIES In the aftermath of September 11, Americans began hearing much about a law called the Posse Comitatus Act of 1878. This law was passed during the Reconstruction era in reaction to President Ulysses S. Grant's use of federal troops to monitor elections in the former Confederate states. It prohibited the armed forces from engaging in police activities such as search, seizure, and arrest within the borders of the United States. In the century and a half since, this issue had rarely arisen. Even during World War II, domestic security against German and Japanese espionage and infiltration was maintained within these bounds. Now, though, given the nature of the terrorist threat, genuine debate arose about the military's role in homeland security.

One step was the creation of the Northern Command. The American military is organized globally into regional commands: the Southern Command covers Latin America, the European Command covers NATO and Europe, the Central Command covers the Middle East and Central Asia, the African Command covers Africa, and the Pacific Command covers South and East Asia. Never before had there been a command structure to cover the United States or the rest of North America. As an organizational issue, the creation of the Northern Command generally was seen as necessary and enhancing national defense. What role, though, would it play and what powers would it exercise? Could it fulfill its mission within the no-policing restrictions of the Posse Comitatus law? Should this law be changed?

Even more than for the military, debate intensified over the roles of the CIA, the FBI, and the rest of the intelligence community. One of the main controversies was over a secret Bush program through which the ***National Security Agency (NSA)*** monitored the international phone calls and e-mails of "hundreds, perhaps thousands, of people inside the United States to search for evidence of terrorist activity without the court-approved warrants ordinarily required for domestic spying."[89] The Bush administration claimed that this domestic surveillance program was necessary to track down possible terrorists linked to Al Qaeda. According to President Bush, "one of the ways to protect the American people is to understand the intentions of the enemy. . . . If they're making phone calls into the United States, we need to know why."[90] The administration also argued that the domestic surveillance program was legal, citing two principal sources of authority: the president's inherent authority under Article II of the Constitution as the commander in chief of the military, and implicit authority in the post–9/11 bill passed by Congress authorizing the president "to use all necessary and appropriate force against those nations, organizations, or persons he determines planned, authorized, committed, or aided the terrorist attacks that occurred on September 11, 2001, or harbored such organizations or persons, in order to prevent any future acts of international terrorism against the United States by such nations, organizations or persons."

Critics saw the NSA program as a major threat to the Fourth Amendment prohibition of unreasonable searches and seizures, applied here to wiretaps and other forms of electronic eavesdropping. Before a search, the government is required to show probable cause that the items being searched for are connected with criminal activity and will be found in the place being searched—mere suspicion is not enough. With certain exceptions, a warrant must be issued by a neutral and detached magistrate before a search is conducted, and notice of the search must be given. Because it did not go through this process of oversight by the courts, the Bush NSA program raised concerns that citizens might be monitored even if they had no connection to terrorism or other criminal activity. Part of these concerns was the Bush administration's own track record and part the historical abuses by U.S. intelligence agencies during the 1960s (spying on civil rights groups and protesters against the Vietnam War). Indeed, FBI counterterrorism agents were reported to have "conducted numerous surveillance and intelligence-gathering operations that involved, at least indirectly, groups active in causes as diverse as the environment, animal cruelty, and poverty relief"—although officials said that investigators have no interest in monitoring political or social activities and that if these investigations touched on advocacy groups, they were based on evidence of criminal or violent activity at public protests or in other settings.[91]

The program's counterterrorism effectiveness also has been debated. Supporters cited cases such as breaking up a planned bombing of the New York City subway system in

2004 in part through electronic surveillance. In a 2006 Canada case, the terrorist suspects were tracked through Internet chat rooms, e-mail, and telephone communications. But critics saw investigators being swamped by a "vacuum cleaner approach" that brought in much information that "led to dead ends or innocent Americans. . . . 'We'd chase a number, find it's a schoolteacher with no indication they've ever been involved in international terrorism,' said one former FBI official, who was aware of the program and the data it generated for the bureau. 'After you get a thousand numbers and not one is turning up anything, you get some frustration.'"[92]

In July 2009 a joint report critical of the surveillance program was issued by the inspectors general (IGs) of the Departments of Justice and Defense as well as the IGs of the CIA, the Director of National Intelligence, and the NSA itself. The IGs function as largely independent legal voices within government agencies, designed to provide checkpoints and accountability. In their view the legal basis claimed by the Bush administration for the warrantless surveillance program had serious deficiencies.

Seeking to strike a better balance between national security and civil liberties, Congress made some changes in 2008. Still, the controversies continue into the Obama administration. In April 2009, the press reported e-mail and phone call intercepts "that went beyond the broad legal limits." The NSA responded that its operations were "in strict accordance with U.S. laws and regulations." The director of national intelligence raised the possibility that some mistakes may have been made "inadvertently" and if so, were being corrected.[93] Congress had its own further investigations under way, and the Justice Department a policy review.

## *Torture*

The debate over torture has focused on two main issues: Did the United States torture? If so, was torture justified?

The debate over whether torture has been conducted has revolved around how torture gets defined. This involves interpretations of both the U.S. Constitution and the Geneva Conventions and other international law. President George W. Bush, Vice President Dick Cheney, and other key administration officials contended that their methods, though harsh, were not torture. The "torture memos" written by the Bush Justice Department delineated such practices as forced nudity, slamming detainees into walls, prolonged sleep deprivation, and dousing with ice-cold water but claimed that these "enhanced techniques" were short of torture and thus consistent with U.S. and international law.[94] They also claimed that the information gained had been vital to both getting the 9/11 perpetrators and preventing another terrorist attack on the United States. This was how America captured Khalid Sheikh Mohammed, the leader of the 9/11 planning. Other examples have been kept classified but show "the success of the effort," as former vice president Cheney argued.[95]

Critics disagreed, strongly so. How could the administration claim that waterboarding was not torture when the United States had held it to be when Japanese soldiers inflicted it on American prisoners during World War II? Was putting a suspect known to be afraid of insects in a small enclosed box with insects crawling over him not torture? What about shackling a suspect to a chair for two to three weeks? Some critics acknowledged that valuable security information had been gained, but still objected on legal and ethical grounds. Others questioned the claims of security gains. According to a former FBI agent, the information from and about Khalid Sheikh Mohammed was gained through "traditional interrogation methods . . . before the harsh techniques were introduced." Other confessions made under torture were inaccurate, even intentionally deceptive, a gambit by the tortured to tell the torturers what they wanted to hear so that the torture would stop.[96]

This debate continued into the Obama administration. Views differed within the Cabinet on whether to release the "torture memos." There also was the question of how far to take further investigations, and whether to consider prosecuting any of those associated with the policy. "We don't torture," President Obama firmly stated. Would his administration stick to this? If it did, and there was a major terrorist strike, how much would it be criticized for doing so?

JUDICIAL PROCESSES A number of issues have arisen regarding due process of the law.

**Secrecy in the Courts** Individuals suspected of terrorism have been arrested on immigration charges, and others have been arrested and detained as potential witnesses. Some of the detentions were indefinite, and the cases were heard in secret. "The courtroom must be closed for these cases," said Judge Michael J. Creppy, the nation's top immigration judge. "No visitors, no family and no press." This secrecy even included "confirming or denying whether such a case is on the docket." Judge Gladys Kessler of the Federal District Court in Washington, D.C., saw it differently: "The court fully understands and appreciates that the first priority of the executive branch in a time of crisis is to ensure the physical security of its citizens. By the same token, the first priority of the judicial branch must be to ensure that our government always operates within the statutory and constitutional constraints which distinguish a democracy from a dictatorship."[97] Another district court made a different ruling, saying the press and public do not have a First Amendment right to have access to "special interest" deportation proceedings. "Since the primary national policy must be self-preservation, it seems elementary that, to the extent open deportation hearings might impair national security, that security" must be taken into account, the ruling stated.[98]

**Guantánamo and Military Tribunals** Despite conflicts with Cuba, the United States has maintained a military base at Guantánamo Bay for over one hundred years. Since September 11, the Guantánamo base was used as a prison for hundreds of suspected terrorists. Since Guantánamo was not within the United States, the Bush administration claimed that prisoners held there were not protected by the right of *habeas corpus* and other constitutional provisions that applied within America's own borders. They also claimed limited applicability of international laws, such as the 1949 Geneva Conventions protecting prisoners of war. Human rights groups condemned the Guantánamo "legal black hole."[99] International criticism also has been widespread, even from Great Britain. The Supreme Court made a number of rulings during the latter years of the Bush administration that ran counter to the administration's legal claims and practices. These somewhat constrained the use of military tribunals and affirmed *habeas corpus* rights for detainees. Candidate Barack Obama had campaigned on a pledge to close the prisons and detention centers at Guantánamo. Soon after his inauguration, he announced a plan for doing so within a year. This has been proving harder to do than originally thought. Would it be risky to release the most dangerous prisoners? Where to send prisoners still retained? Some prisoners came from home countries that might have their own reasons for releasing them, including some of the more dangerous ones. Some American communities launched "not in the prisons near us" campaigns. These and other issues have been difficult to work out.

PRESIDENTIAL POWERS The Supreme Court also had addressed the broad question of presidential powers in the post-9/11 world in 2004 in an earlier Guantánamo case, *Hamdi v. Rumsfeld.* The majority opinion, written by Justice Sandra Day O'Connor, was strong in its statement that even a state of war "is not a blank check for the President when it comes to the rights of the Nation's citizens." Citing the 1952 *Youngstown Steel* case, in which the Court had restrained powers being exercised by President Truman during the Korean War (see Chapter 2), Justice O'Connor continued: "Whatever power the United States Constitution envisions for the Executive in its exchanges with other nations or with enemy organizations in times of conflict, it most assuredly envisions a role for all three branches when individual liberties are at stake."[100]

FREEDOM OF THE PRESS The freedom of the press questions raised by coverage within the United States of aspects of the war on terrorism were in many respects even more complex and difficult than war-reporting issues have been (see pp. 470–71). The Persian Gulf, Afghanistan, and Iraq wars largely stayed "over there." World War II had an "in here" dimension because of German and Japanese espionage. But the sense of penetration of American society by the enemy in the war on terrorism is much greater. It can be exaggerated and misplaced, but it also is a very real concern. Should the press be restricted, for example, from breaking a story about an FBI operation aimed at an Al Qaeda cell in the United States? Perhaps such a cell planning to launch a biological weapons attack might escape or evade capture if it knew it was under surveillance. Yet what if the FBI were wrong and the suspects were innocent people? Breaking a story in such a situation could ensure that civil liberties are not violated, nor other unwarranted consequences inflicted on individuals and their families.

**DISTORTIONS OF DOMESTIC POLITICS** We've seen a number of times in American history the distorting effects on domestic politics when national security concerns run high. The national security rationale sometimes gets invoked to justify policy choices for which its application is a real stretch. Take, for example, the claim made by President Bush that agricultural subsidies paid to American farmers to keep prices up were not just a farm policy or budget policy issue but a matter of national security: "This nation has got to eat," President Bush told a cheering crowd at the annual convention of the National Cattlemen's Beef Association in Denver, Colorado, at a time when Congress was considering a bill that would provide $172 billion in farm subsidies over ten years. "It's in our national security interests that we be able to feed ourselves. Thank goodness, we don't have to rely on somebody else's meat to make sure our people are healthy and well-fed."[101] Bush's political strategy aimed to trump the economic and budgetary arguments by invoking the national security rationale as a superseding justification. This is tried-and-true politics, but is it good policy? If eating beef is a matter of national security, then what isn't?

Another version of this pattern was the "pork-barreling" by Congress during the Iraq war of a bill intended primarily to pay for the war. The scene was described by a reporter: "The hour was late, the war in Iraq was raging, and members of the Senate simply wanted to pass the $80 billion bill to pay for the war and go home for the night." Before going home, though, various senators (Democrats and Republicans alike) inserted into the bill such pork-barrel projects and other special interest provisions as $3.3 million to fix a leaky dam in Vermont, a provision benefiting the Alaska salmon industry by allowing wild salmon to be labeled organic, $10 million in additional funds for a science research station at the South Pole, and $5 million for new police radio systems in Kentucky.[102]

When the domestic consensus is too restrictive, a distorting effect that cuts even deeper to fundamental questions about democracy is the equating of dissent with disloyalty. Manifesting national solidarity is one thing, the delegitimization of debate and dissent quite another. The war on terrorism has not produced repressive trends as dangerous to democracy as 1950s McCarthyism, but it has produced some worrisome political dynamics. In the immediate aftermath of the September 11 attacks, Attorney General John Ashcroft accused critics of his domestic security policies of using tactics that "aid terrorists" and "give ammunition to America's enemies" by "erod[ing] our national unity."[103] A few months later, after the Senate Democratic leader Tom Daschle criticized some of the Bush administration's antiterrorism policies, even in the context of saying that some policies had been successful but others less so, he was attacked by the Senate Republican leader Trent Lott: "*How dare* Senator Daschle criticize President Bush while we are fighting our war on terrorism, especially when we have troops in the field? He should not be trying to divide our country."[104] Had Senator Lott given specific substantive rebuttals of the Daschle criticisms, that would have been legitimate policy and political debate. It was the "how dare" notion that equated dissent with disloyalty.

**Open Society** In a certain sense the openness of American society is a source of vulnerability. The very values that Americans have cherished for so long, the freedoms that come with being a democracy, are creating opportunities for terrorism. An Al Qaeda manual told its operatives that they could find much of the information and equipment they needed in libraries, magazines, shopping malls, and other everyday parts of American life. The September 11 hijackers visited the World Trade Center a number of times, going up with the throngs of tourists to the observation deck. They bought portable global-positioning-system equipment in electronics stores. They bought videotapes of the instrument panels of the jets they would hijack from toll-free phone numbers. They took their flight lessons in American flight schools.

But how can the vulnerabilities of openness be reduced without threatening the essence of American democracy and freedom? The war on terrorism has been called a war to preserve freedom. How is it to be fought so that freedom at home is not compromised, or worse? This is the essence of the tension between national security and the Bill of Rights, one that we have seen before in American history but that may well now pose even greater dilemmas and challenges.

## *Domestic Politics of the Iraq War*

The Iraq War proved to be the most contentious foreign policy politics issue since Vietnam.

**Bush, Congress, and War Powers** It is instructive to compare the war powers politics of the two Iraq wars. In 1990–91, when Saddam Hussein's forces invaded Kuwait, President George H. W. Bush proposed the initial deployment of American forces in Operation Desert Shield as "consistent with," and not as required by, the 1973 War Powers Resolution (WPR). His report denied that hostilities were imminent. The same language game was played a few weeks later, when the deployed troops got higher salaries according to the Pentagon's pay rate for personnel placed in "imminent danger," not that for "hostilities," even though the Pentagon was busily drawing up war plans and Bush likened Saddam to Hitler. Still, responding to Bush's televised speech to the nation, the House majority leader Richard Gephardt (D–Missouri) declared, "In this crisis we are not Republicans or Democrats. We are only proudly Americans. The President has asked for our support. He has it." Even traditional liberals, such as the Senate Foreign Relations Committee chairman Claiborne Pell (D–Rhode Island), initially took the position that to invoke the WPR "would upset the applecart." Instead, in early October both chambers overwhelmingly passed resolutions outside the WPR supporting Operation Desert Shield, 380–29 in the House and 96–3 in the Senate.[105]

Greater tensions with Congress emerged on November 8, when Bush announced a doubling of U.S. forces to over four hundred thousand troops and a shift in strategy to mounting "an adequate offensive military option." The issue came to a head in early January 1991. The Bush administration had won support in the UN Security Council for a resolution setting January 15 as the deadline for Iraqi withdrawal from Kuwait and authorizing any member state to use "all necessary means" after that date. Bush claimed that, just as Truman had claimed in 1950 that the UN resolution authorizing war against North Korea after its invasion of South Korea precluded the need for a formal declaration of war by the U.S. Congress, so his UN resolution provided comparable authorization. Bush indicated that he had no intention of invoking the WPR or asking for congressional approval before moving to war. Some in his administration, however, felt it was politically risky not go to Congress at all. Bush agreed to a nonbinding resolution outside of the WPR, stating up front that even if it was defeated, he would proceed as planned.

For its part, Congress faced criticism for being politically spineless for not taking a position one way or the other. For the Democrats in Congress, the political dilemma was a particularly tough one. Did economic sanctions really still have a chance to get Iraq out of Kuwait? And, politically, should the Democrats again take a stand against the use of force and as "the party of peace?" Or did they risk further reinforcing their post-Vietnam "wimp" image?

On January 11 and 12, both chambers of Congress voted on identical resolutions "to authorize the use of United States Armed Forces pursuant to United Nations Security Council Resolution 678." The resolutions passed, although by much closer votes than the earlier ones: 250–183 in the House, 52–47 in the Senate.

On January 16, 1991, Operation Desert Storm was launched. The war against Iraq was on. We will never know whether the political coalition would have held together had the war not gone as well as it did. It wasn't politically difficult to stand behind a war with so few American casualties and such a quick and overwhelming military victory. So although consensual foreign policy politics held firm for the moment, the core constitutional issues that the 1973 WPR had claimed to resolve—who had what share of the war power—once again were left unresolved.

Three days after September 11, Congress overwhelmingly approved a resolution authorizing President Bush to use military force against those responsible for the terrorist attacks. The Senate approved it 98–0, the House 420–1. "I am gratified that the Congress has united so powerfully by taking this action," President Bush stated. "It sends a clear message—our people are together, and we will prevail."[106] A few weeks later this resolution became the basis for the war in Afghanistan, though it, too, was kept outside the WPR.

Congress voted for the Iraq war by smaller but still very large margins, 77–23 in the Senate and 296–133 in the House. These margins included virtually all Republicans and most Democrats. The consensus had policy, process, and political bases. The post–September 11 context of terrorism and Saddam Hussein's track record—going back to his 1990 invasion of Kuwait, his 1987–88 gassing of the Kurds, and other aggression and brutality—raised concerns about the threats that Saddam posed, especially given the intelligence reports coming from the Bush administration that he possessed weapons of mass destruction (WMD). The Bush congressional relations strategy was to hold extensive consultations with the congressional leadership and key members, providing them with some input but mostly a sense of inclusion. The White House also exploited the fear of being seen as "soft." During the Cold War this had been the specter of being "soft on communism." After September 11 it was "soft on terrorism." This was a key factor, for example, in why the three Democratic members of Congress who ran for president in 2004 (Senators John Kerry and John Edwards and House Minority Leader Richard Gephardt) and one who would run in 2008 (Senator Hillary Rodham Clinton) all voted for the Iraq war resolution.

As the war went bad, the interbranch consensus began to crack. "I was wrong," the former Senator John Edwards wrote in an op-ed column in November 2005, intending to run for president again in 2008. "It was a mistake to vote for this war in 2002."[107] Edwards cited the flawed WMD and other intelligence the Bush administration had provided. As we discuss below, many came to see these flaws as not just mistakes but intentional deceptions and manipulation. Representative John Murtha (D-Pennsylvania), a leading House military expert and himself a former marine, spoke out during the same month against this "flawed policy wrapped in illusion. . . . Our military is suffering. The future of our country is at risk." Murtha called for a withdrawal of American troops: "It is time to bring them home."[108] With the Democrats in the majority following the 2006 congressional elections, and with more and more Republicans in both the House and the Senate becoming Iraq war critics, and with Senator Barack Obama making his Iraq war opposition a main part of his presidential candidacy, the debate intensified.

The debate was not just about Iraq, but also, on an overall and continuing basis, about the war powers issue. Senator Robert C. Byrd (D-West Virginia) had tried to take the debate over the October 2002 Iraq use of force resolution back to constitutional principles:

> Nobody will support this country in war any more strongly than will I. But here today we are being tested . . . This is my fiftieth year in Congress. I never would have thought I would find a Senate which would lack the backbone to stand up against the stampede, this rush to war, this rush to give to the President of the United States, whatever President he is, whatever party, this rush to give a President, to put in his hands alone, to let him determine alone when he will send the sons and daughters of the American people into war, let him have control of the military forces. He will not only make war, but he will declare war. That flies in the face of this Constitution.[109]

Senator Byrd's critique concerned both presidential usurpation and congressional abdication. The president came under criticism from Byrd and others for the flawed and manipulated intelligence and more generally for looking for ways to bypass the formal constitutional process of asking for a declaration of war. But the debate wasn't just about what the president took, it also was what the Congress gave up. Congress did not "assert its rights and take political responsibility," Leslie Gelb (president of the Council on Foreign Relations) and Anne-Marie Slaughter (dean of the Woodrow Wilson School at Princeton) wrote.[110] As a Constitution Project report suggested, Congress "should not wait for the president to ask its judgment on initiating a use of force. Instead, it should involve itself early in the decision-making process, demand and acquire relevant information, and reach a collective judgment by a roll call vote after full and public debate."[111]

One of the most prominent sets of proposals for war powers reform came from a bipartisan group chaired by two former secretaries of state, James Baker and Warren Christopher, called the National War Powers Commission. "Few would dispute," the group's report accurately stated, "that the most important decisions our leaders make involve war. Yet after more than 200 years of constitutional history, what powers the respective branches of government possess in making such decisions is still heavily debated." The common thread running among the particular proposals the commission made was the "importance of getting the President and Congress to consult meaningfully and deliberate before committing the nation to war." The goal was to tap the "unique competencies and bases of support" that each branch has. Among the proposals made was that meaningful consultation should occur before any "significant armed conflict," defined as a combat operation lasting or anticipated to last more than one week. Another was for creation of a joint congressional consultation committee consisting of key congressional leaders from both parties and the most relevant legislative committees. This committee would meet with the president and his top foreign policy team regularly, not just during crises.[112]

The commission urged that this reform be taken up in the first one hundred days of the Obama administration, before the next war powers crisis struck. That didn't happen. The ideas, as well as those of others, are still out there.

The one point of consensus is that the 1973 War Powers Resolution has not solved the problem. In Iraq as in Vietnam, Americans found themselves questioning not just the foreign policy strategy but the foreign policy politics that got them into this war and how to reform the process so that perhaps it would not happen again.

INTRA–BUSH ADMINISTRATION POLITICS The intra–Bush administration politics over Iraq illustrate the presidential belief systems, bureaucratic politics, and groupthink patterns we identified in Chapter 2 and have seen in some other administrations. Here we focus on three executive-branch decision-making issues: the WMD threat, Saddam–Al Qaeda links, and strategies for winning the peace.

**Did Saddam Have WMD?** Although the Bush administration stressed many reasons for going to war, its main reason, as noted earlier, was the allegation that Saddam Hussein's Iraq possessed weapons of mass destruction. The administration repeatedly and unequivocally claimed that this allegation was true. President Bush cited two main pieces of evidence: one was the attempted purchase of "high-strength aluminum tubes and other equipment needed for gas centrifuges, which are used to enrich uranium for nuclear weapons"; the other, that "Saddam Hussein recently sought significant quantities of uranium from Africa."[113] In fact, though, as also noted earlier, Saddam did not have WMD. The various U.S. and UN military and inspection teams that went in after Saddam fell searched the country and found little to nothing. The bipartisan commission appointed directly by President Bush reported that the WMD assessments were "riddled with errors." The assessment that "Iraq was reconstituting its nuclear weapons program and was actively pursuing a nuclear device . . . was almost completely wrong." The assessment on biological weapons "was wrong"; that on chemical weapons "was also wrong."[114]

Why and how were the intelligence assessments so wrong? We do need to acknowledge the inherent element of uncertainty in getting accurate information about a secretive regime. But the chief explanation lies in the politicization of the policy process that made this case a glaring example of how bureaucratic politics and groupthink distort effective policy making.

The October 2002 ***National Intelligence Estimate (NIE)*** exemplifies this pattern. The official definition of an NIE is "the coordinated judgments of the Intelligence Community regarding the likely course of future events," written with the goal of providing "policymakers with the best, unvarnished and unbiased information—regardless of whether analytic judgments conform to US policy."[115] The October 2002 Iraq NIE stated that Saddam had chemical and biological weapons and that although he might not yet have nuclear weapons, he likely would within a few years.[116] But this assessment was based on some very suspect sources—for example, an Iraqi defector code-named "Curveball," who was known to have had a nervous breakdown and drinking problems yet who was the principal source that the NIE relied on for the biological weapons intelligence.[117] Moreover, dissenting analyses largely were ignored. For example, the State Department Bureau of Intelligence and Research (INR) found that the claims of Iraqi purchases of uranium in Africa were "highly dubious"; INR and the Energy Department found that the aluminum tubes said to be for uranium enrichment "most likely are intended for conventional weapons use (artillery shells)."[118]

Some of the responsibility lies with the CIA and other intelligence agencies for failing at their basic tradecraft. A Senate committee report attributed this not just to inherent limits of discoverable information but also to groupthink:

> The Intelligence Community (IC) has long struggled with the need for analysts to overcome analytic biases, that is, to resist the tendency to see what they would expect to see in the intel-

> ligence reporting. In the case of Iraq's weapons of mass destruction (WMD) capabilities, the Committee found that intelligence analysts, in many cases, based their analysis more on their expectations than on objective evaluation of the information in the intelligence reporting. Analysts expected to see evidence that Iraq has retained prohibited weapons and that Iraq would resume prohibited WMD activities once United Nations' (UN) inspections ended. This bias that pervaded both the IC's analytic and collection communities represents "group think" . . . examining few alternatives, selective gathering of information, pressure to conform within the group or withhold criticism, and collective rationalization.[119]

But the distortions and failures also occurred at the political level of top White House and Cabinet decision-makers. How could President Bush and Vice President Cheney make their unequivocal claims when the NIE and other intelligence agencies raised doubts? Why didn't they push tough questions about the credibility of sources such as Curveball? It didn't seem to matter to the president or vice president that, as the journalist George Packer writes, "there was no strong evidence to back up the doomsday prognosis. . . . The campaign of persuasion proceeded by rhetorical hyperbole, by the deliberate slanting of ambiguous facts in one direction, and by a wink-and-nod suggestion that the administration knew more than it could reveal."[120] Packer also recounts an effort by Richard Haass, State Department Policy Planning Director, to raise concerns about going to war. "Save your breath," he was told by National Security Adviser Rice in June 2002. "The president has already made up his mind."[121]

**Saddam–Al Qaeda Links** Although the administration also based its rationale for war on this claim, it was not true either. This claim also was based on questionable sources, including an Al Qaeda prisoner who had been "identified as a likely fabricator" by both the CIA and the Defense Intelligence Agency. But the Office of Special Plans—set up within the Pentagon by Defense Secretary Donald Rumsfeld and sheltered under a nondescript title as a bastion for neoconservative appointees to provide their own intelligence analysis—kept insisting that the link existed. They approached the issue not to test a question but "to prove an assumption." They took as a given that the Saddam–Al Qaeda link was there: "the premise was true" by definition; "facts would be found to confirm it." The Pentagon neoconservatives, along with others in Vice President Cheney's office and still others "dispersed on key islands across the national security archipelago allowed the intelligence 'product' and its effects on policy to circumvent the normal interagency process, in which the unconverted would have been among the participants and might have raised objections."[122] A former army major who was a psychiatrist assigned to interrogating prisoners at Guantánamo Bay told army investigators that "a large part of the time we were focused on trying to establish a link between Al Qaeda and Iraq and we were not being successful." This was, he testified, a factor in the resort to torture: as the higher-ups grew more "frustrated," pressure increased "to resort to measures" that might get the desired answers, valid or not.[123]

**Winning the Peace** At a June 2003 conference outside Washington, I gave a talk in which I criticized the lack of a strategy, already becoming apparent, for how to move from having won the war to winning the peace. A colleague who worked in the government as a distinguished career national security expert berated me. "Don't assume we didn't plan," she said. A few months later when stories about "the 'Future of Iraq' project" broke in the press, I realized what she meant.[124] In fact, the State Department had led an extensive process to plan postwar strategy, producing a four-volume set of memos, background analyses, and strategy papers called "The Future of Iraq." State had set up seventeen working groups on issues including the economy, the justice system, and political institutions, coordinating with over two hundred Iraqi lawyers, engineers, businesspeople, and other Iraqi nationals, as well as leading American policy experts. One of the conclusions they reached was to "prepare for a messy aftermath." Another was that Iraq "would not provide fertile ground for democracy. . . . that a foreign occupying force would itself be the target of resentment and attacks—including guerrilla warfare."[125] Those running the Iraq policy, mostly a small group of officials surrounding Defense Secretary Rumsfeld and Vice President Cheney, simply ignored this report and other parts of the Future of Iraq study. Studies conducted by leading think tanks—including the Council on Foreign Relations, the Center for Strategic and International Studies, the RAND Corporation, and the U.S. Institute of Peace—met the same fate. It is one thing to study a study and then reject it on the basis of contrary analysis and information. That's the nature of policy choice. It's quite another, though, to dismiss studies largely because the conclusions they reach and the recommendations they make complicate or perhaps contradict what the policy already has been decided to be.

Both groupthink and bureaucratic politics were at work on postwar strategies as well. The dominant mindset within top decision-making circles assumed postwar stability in Iraq rather than analyzing its requisites. "There was little discussion in Washington of the aftermath of military action," the head of British intelligence reported back to Prime Minister Tony Blair after a round of meetings in Washington. As George Packer writes, on the basis of his sources within the Bush administration, "Plan A was that the Iraqi government would be quickly decapitated, security would be turned over to remnants of the Iraqi police and army, international troops would soon arrive, and most American forces would leave within a few months. There was no Plan B."[126] The Bush administration got trapped in the illogic of its own logic. "Because detailed planning for the postwar situation meant facing costs and potential problems, it weakened the case for a 'war of choice,' and was seen by the war's proponents as an 'antiwar' undertaking."[127] As a result, accounts surfaced of American officials once in Iraq having to rely on a Lonely Planet guidebook to help identify key sites that needed to be safeguarded. In another instance a national guardsman from a small town in Rhode Island charged with organizing an Iraqi police force was given so little to work with that he sent home for his town's police manual.

The bureaucratic politics vested control principally in the Defense Department and Vice President Cheney's office. That Defense would control the military forces in Iraq was a given. But many felt the State Department should have controlled the political and diplomatic presence. Secretary of State Powell lost one bureaucratic battle after another to what his former chief of staff called "a secretive, little-known cabal . . . made up of a very small group of people led by Vice President Dick Cheney and Defense Secretary Donald Rumsfeld."[128] A number of others involved in the Iraq policy have made similar points both about who won and who lost in the bureaucratic politics and how these dynamics led to the policy flaws that contributed to the difficulties in winning the peace.[129]

Along with these criticisms, the shift to the "surge" strategy showed some benefits from the Bush-Cheney determination to stay the course. By late 2006, with the Democrats having gained control of Congress partly because of the public's opposition to the Iraq War and amid increased calls for withdrawal from Iraq, the Bush administration conducted an extensive strategy review. This was a "gamble," as the journalist Tom Ricks titled his book.[130] "The question is whether our new strategy will bring us closer to success," President Bush told the nation. "I believe that it will."[131] Although the surge had its critics and, as discussed earlier in this chapter, the sustainability of its impact remains to be seen, the success it achieved in the immediate term did improve a situation many believed already lost. In this instance, some of the same qualities that had been problematic for the Bush administration's Iraq War decision making had a more positive effect.

ROLE OF THE MEDIA The "cheerleader or critic" framing applicable in earlier periods fits here as well. During the 1990–91 Persian Gulf war, the White House and the military sought to manage the news coverage with two principal goals: to limit the independence of the media coverage and to shape it to be as positive as possible. War correspondents were confined to "pools" of limited numbers and restricted to designated locations. Film footage released for TV was carefully screened so as to give the impression of a near-flawless bombing campaign—"smart" bombs going through ventilation shafts, high "target-kill" ratios, very few civilian sites hit. General Norman Schwarzkopf, the commanding officer of the U.S. and allied forces in the Persian Gulf, proved to be not only an excellent military strategist but also a whiz at media briefings and TV communication, and became a new folk hero.

The media protested that, although certain restrictions were understandable during war, the measures taken to control the coverage "go far beyond what is required to protect troop safety and mission security."[132] *Newsweek* called it "the propaganda war. . . . In theory, reporters in democratic societies work independent of propaganda. In practice they are treated during war as simply more pieces of military hardware to be deployed."[133] The military essentially was saying to the media, With the nation at war, our intention is to limit and direct your role to the cheerleader one, not the critic one. In pursuit of cheerleader coverage, the military limited the amount and accuracy of information provided to the media. It was later learned that in fact the air campaign had not been nearly as successful as portrayed. Information revealed that only 7 percent of the bombs were precision-guided munitions, and although these did hit their targets 90 percent of the time, more than 90 percent of the bombs were "dumb" conventional ones that missed their targets 75 percent of the time. Data such as these sharply contrasted with "the high-tech, never-miss image that the Pentagon carefully cultivated during the war."[134]

Media coverage during the 2003 Iraq War was even more intensive and instantaneous. The pools were replaced by a new policy of "embedding" journalists within military units, putting them directly in the field and on the march with the combat troops. The six hundred "embeds" included reporters not only from the *New York Times* and the *Washington Post,* but also from *People* magazine, MTV, and local news stations; some were also foreign correspondents. Equipped with the latest in satellite phones and other advanced communications technology, the embeds could air their live television broadcasts and file their stories on the spot and in the moment.

Two main questions have been debated about Iraq war journalism. One is whether it was too critical or too uncritical. Both arguments have been made. Those who thought the reporting was too uncritical question whether journalistic perspective might have been constrained by the natural empathy that developed between the embedded journalists and the troops with whom they were stationed, troops who became their immediate community and also their protectors. Those who thought the reporting was too critical accused the press of overdoing the bad news, whether to keep filling the "news hole" created by 24/7 coverage or from doubts about the war policy.

The other main question has been about the quality of press coverage. Even though journalists were on the spot, some critics felt that the coverage was like "looking through a straw," with the viewer able to see only what was within a reporter's defined and delimited field of vision. And although they were outfitted with the latest technologies, the instantaneity of reporting did not leave journalists the time they needed for reflection and insight. They were providing a huge amount of information, but they were giving much less emphasis—especially in television coverage—to its context, to whether its importance was brief or of more enduring significance, and to how different pieces of the story fitted together.

Howard Kurtz, the noted media critic for the *Washington Post,* summarized the key questions: "What did the media accomplish during the most intensively and instantaneously covered war in history? Did the presence of all those journalists capture the harsh realities of war or simply breed a new generation of Scud studs? Were readers and viewers well served or deluged with confusing information? And what does it portend for future wars?"[135]

**Public Opinion** Public opinion on the Iraq war has been consistent with the "pretty prudent" public framework for explaining patterns in support of the use of force (see Chapter 2). The claims about WMD and Al Qaeda, on top of Saddam's track record of aggression, framed the principal objective for the use of force as foreign policy restraint. In the months of buildup to the war, the American public supported threatening to use force, although as late as January 2003 it continued to favor acting through the UN. A poll showed 56 percent agreed that the United States "should not invade unless a new UN vote authorizes action," and only 39 percent favored invading without UN authorization. But spurred by the rally 'round the flag effect of President Bush's 2003 State of the Union speech and fed by the increasing perception that France and other countries were more intent on obstructing American power than on offering a viable alternative, public opinion began shifting toward strong support for the unilateralist option. For example, in polls conducted the night before military action began, 75 percent disapproved of "the way the UN is handling the situation with Iraq and Saddam," and 65 percent said that the president was right not to wait for "[UN] approval before issuing tonight's [March 17, 2003] ultimatum."[136]

An April 30, 2003, poll, on the eve of President Bush's "mission accomplished" speech, showed 75 percent approval of how the president was handling Iraq. The public saw the war as being principally about restraining aggression, and the public was supportive. But this proved to be the high point. The first *Washington Post*–ABC poll to show majority disapproval was on October 29, 2003, 47 to 51 percent. Support went back up to 60 percent approval following the capture of Saddam Hussein in December 2003. But as the problems of winning the peace compounded, and as the public began to see the principal objective as having become internal political change, its support declined. By May 2006 only 32 percent approved and 66 disapproved of the Bush Iraq policy. And whereas in April 2003, 81 percent said "the United States did the right thing in going to war in Iraq," now only 40 percent held this view.[137] Although some credit was given to the surge strategy, *Washington Post*–ABC polls toward the end of the Bush administration found only 25 percent approving Bush's overall Iraq policy. And only 39 percent felt that Iraq had been worth fighting. A June 2008 *Newsweek* poll asking about troop withdrawals had 45 percent saying bring them home now or in less than one year, 20 percent saying within one to two years, 4 percent saying three to five years and 26 percent saying as long as it takes to achieve U.S. goals.

It also is worth noting that even during the early days of the war, when all seemed to be going well for the United States, when asked "who should take the leading role in rebuilding Iraq and helping its people set up a new government," 61 percent of Americans surveyed said the UN; only 31 percent the United States.[138] Later polls showed 63 percent saying the UN, not the United States, "should have the most say in establishing a stable government in Iraq," and 72 percent favoring "turning over some authority" to the UN.[139] So even on Iraq the swing toward unilateralism was limited and temporary, with the American public showing a preference for multilateralism for a long time in the period leading up to the war and then coming back to it rather quickly as the war continued.

## Summary

The war on terrorism and the Iraq war were the Bush administration's most defining issues. Terrorism was *an* issue before September 11, 2001, but afterward, it became *the* central issue of American foreign policy. The Bush administration developed a multifaceted strategy, including a doctrine for the preemptive use of force and the most extensive expansion of American global military commitments since the early days of the Cold War. Both within the United States and around the world debates raged over the Bush strategy.

The Iraq war has been the most controversial foreign policy issue since Vietnam. Among the issues it has raised are the rationales for going to war, the results of the war, and its broader ramifications.

The Middle East has continued to be a crucial region for the Obama administration. The wars in Afghanistan and Iraq carried over, as did relations with Iran and other key issues. The Obama Middle East policy has had some continuity along with distinctive changes.

The hopes of the early 1990s for Arab-Israeli peace gave way to intensified conflict between Israel and the Palestinians, and wars between Israel and Lebanon and Israel and Hamas. The U.S. role continues to be central to any prospects for peace.

Thus, as we look to the coming years, no region is likely to have greater geopolitical importance than the Middle East (Power). It has endured more wars than any other region since 1945 (Peace). Its oil remains crucial to America's economy (Prosperity). Its issues test America's Principles.

The foreign policy politics issues raised by September 11 and Iraq have been highly contentious. They manifest some of the toughest recurring debates the American democracy has seen, particularly over the balance between national security and civil liberties and over presidential-congressional war powers. Executive-branch decision making on Iraq has shown signs of the problems of groupthink and bureaucratic politics. The role of the media and the impact of public opinion also have been major components of the domestic politics of the Iraq war.

## *American Foreign Policy* Online Student StudySpace

- What are the differences between the two Iraq wars?
- How do you see the lasting lessons of 9/11?
- What do you think is the solution to the Israeli-Palestinian conflict?
- How do you assess how the Afghanistan war is going?
- Should Iran be engaged?
- How best to strike the balance between national security and civil liberties?

For these and other study questions, as well as other features, check out Chapter 8 on the *American Foreign Policy* Online Student StudySpace at wwnorton.com/studyspace.

## Notes

[1]Bruce W. Jentleson, *With Friends Like These: Reagan, Bush, and Saddam, 1982–1990* (New York: Norton, 1994).

[2]National Commission on Terrorism, *Countering the Changing Threat of International Terrorism,* report issued in 2001. Available at www.gpo.gov/fdsys/pkg/CHRG-106shrg867/pdf/CHRG-106shrg867.pdf (accessed 7/20/09). On Osama bin Laden and other Islamic terrorist groups, see the "Holy Warriors" three-part series published by the *New York Times,* January 14–16, 2001.

[3]Richard K. Betts, "The Soft Underbelly of American Primacy: Tactical Advantages of Terror," *Political Science Quarterly* 117.1 (Spring 2002): 25.

[4]Keith B. Richburg and William Branigin, "Attacks from Out of the Blue," *Washington Post,* November 18, 2001, A24; James Dao and Andrew C. Revkin, "A Revolution in Warfare," *New York Times,* April 16, 2002, D1, 4.

[5]Thomas E. Ricks, "Target Approval Delays Cost Air Force Key Hits," *Washington Post,* November 18, 2001, A1.

[6]David Johnston, Don Van Natta, Jr., and Judith Miller, "Qaeda's New Links Increase Threats from Global Sites," *New York Times,* June 16, 2002, A1.

[7]Drew Brown, "Commander: Afghan Mission May Last 2 Years," *Durham Herald-Sun,* September 21, 2002, A7.

[8]Carlotta Gall, "Taliban Threat Is Said to Grow in Afghan South," *New York Times,* May 3, 2006.

[9]Cited in editorial, "Running Out of Time," *New York Times,* September 22, 2008.

[10]Fred Kaplan, "Rumsfeld's Pentagon Papers: His Leaked Memo Is the Most Astonishing Document of This War So Far," *Slate,* October 23, 2003, www.slate.com/id/2090250/ (accessed 7/20/09).

[11]George W. Bush, Commencement Address, U.S. Military Academy, West Point, New York, June 1, 2002, www.nytimes.com/2002/06/01/international/02PTEX-WEB.html (accessed 7/20/09).

[12]Bush, West Point speech, June 1, 2002.

[13]Betts, "Soft Underbelly of American Primacy," 30.

[14]George W. Bush, Commencement Address, U.S. Military Academy, West Point, New York, December 9, 2008, www.clipsandcomment.com/2008/12/10/transcript-bush-delivers-defenseterrorism-speech-at-west-point-december-9/ (accessed 7/20/09).

[15]David Kilcullen, an Australian terrorism expert who served as an advisor to the Bush administration in 2006–2008, cited in review of his book *The Accidental Guerrilla: Fighting Small Wars in the Midst of a Big One,* in Andrew Bacevich, "Raising Jihad," *National Interest* 100 (March/April 2009), 95.

[16]Bacevich, "Raising Jihad," Bacevich's own statement, 95.

[17]Lawrence Freedman, *Deterrence* (Cambridge: Polity Press, 2004), 4.

[18]Peter Slevin, "Some War Allies Show Poor Rights Records," *Washington Post,* March 5, 2002, A13.

[19]Peter G. Peterson, "Public Diplomacy and the War on Terrorism," *Foreign Affairs* 81.5 (September/October 2002): 76; Finding America's Voice: A Strategy for Reinvigorating U.S. Public Diplomacy, Council on Foreign Relations, 2003, www.cfr.org/content/publications/attachments/public_diplomacy.pdf (accessed 7/20/09).

[20]Eric Lipton, "U.S. Borders Vulnerable, Witnesses Say," *New York Times,* June 22, 2005.

[21]9/11 Public Discourse Project, "Final Report on 9/11 Recommendations," December 5, 2005, www.9-11pdp.org/press/2005-12-05_report.pdf (accessed 7/20/09).

[22]Eric Lichtblau, "F.B.I.'s Translation Backlog Grows," *New York Times,* July 28, 2005.

[23]See, for example, George Packer, *The Assassins' Gate: America in Iraq* (New York: Farrar, Straus and Giroux, 2005); Michael R. Gordon and General Bernard E. Trainor, *Cobra II: The Inside Story of the Invasion and Occupation of Iraq* (New York: Pantheon Books, 2006); Larry Diamond, *Squandered Victory: The American Occupation and the Bungled Effort to Bring Democracy to Iraq* (New York: Times Books, 2005); Gen. Tommy Franks, *American Soldier* (New York: HarperCollins, 2004); Hans Blix, *Disarming Iraq* (New York: Pantheon Books, 2004); Bob Woodward, *Plan of Attack* (New York: Simon & Schuster, 2004) and *State of Denial* (New York: Simon & Schuster, 2006); Philip H. Gordon and Jeremy Shapiro, *Allies at War: America, Europe and the*

*Crisis Over Iraq* (Washington, D.C.: Brookings Institution Press, 2004); Gary Rosen, ed., *The Right War: The Conservative Debate on Iraq* (New York: Cambridge University Press, 2005); David L. Phillips, *Losing Iraq: Inside the Postwar Reconstruction Fiasco* (Boulder, Colo.: Westview Press, 2005); and Thomas E. Ricks, *Fiasco: The American Military Adventure in Iraq* (New York: Penguin, 2006).

[24]George W. Bush, War Message, Washington, D.C., March 19, 2003, www.presidentialrhetoric.com/speeches/03.19.03.html (accessed 7/20/09).

[25]"President Bush's Message to the Iraqi People," April 10, 2003, www.gpo.gov/fdsys/pkg/WCPD-2003-04-14/pdf/WCPD-2003-04-14-Pg424-2.pdf (accessed 7/20/09).

[26]Matthew Brzezinski, "The Unmanned Army," *New York Times Magazine*, April 20, 2003, 38, 41.

[27]"Commander-in-Chief Lands on *USS Lincoln*," May 2, 2003. Available at www.cnn.com/2003/ALLPOLITICS/05/01/bush.carrier.landing/ (accessed 7/20/09).

[28]George W. Bush, remarks at the United Nations General Assembly, September 12, 2002, www.presidential-rhetoric.com/speeches/09.12.02.html (accessed 7/20/09).

[29]Dick Cheney, Remarks by the Vice President to the Veterans of Foreign Wars 103rd National Convention, August 27, 2002, www.nationalreview.com/document/document082702.asp (accessed 7/20/09).

[30]George W. Bush, Remarks on Iraq at Cincinnati Museum Center–Cincinnati Union Terminal, Cincinnati, Ohio, October 7, 2002, www.presidentialrhetoric.com/speeches/10.7.02.html (accessed 7/20/09).

[31]George W. Bush, State of the Union Address, January 28, 2003, www.presidentialrhetoric.com/speeches/01.28.03.html (accessed 7/20/09).

[32]Woodward, *Plan of Attack*, 249.

[33]Quoted from a September 8, 2002, interview in Wolf Blitzer, "Search for the 'Smoking Gun,'" January 10, 2003, www.cnn.com/2003/US/01/10/wbr.smoking.gun/ (accessed 7/20/09).

[34]Transcript of Colin Powell's U.N. Presentation, February 6, 2003, www.cnn.com/2003/US/02/05/sprj.irq.powell.transcript/index.html (accessed 7/20/09).

[35]Commission on the Intelligence Capabilities of the United States Regarding Weapons of Mass Destruction [Robb-Silberman Commission], *Report to the President of the United States*, March 31, 2005, www.gpoaccess.gov/wmd/pdf/full_wmd_report.pdf (accessed 7/20/09); See also U.S. Senate, Select Committee on Intelligence, *Report on Whether Public Statements Regarding Iraq by U.S. Government Officials Were Substantiated by Intelligence Information, Together with Additional and Minority Views*, July 9, 2004, http://intelligence.senate.gov/080605/phase2a.pdf (accessed 7/20/09); Central Intelligence Agency, *Comprehensive Revised Report with Addendums on Iraq's Weapons of Mass Destruction* (Duelfer Report), rev. ed., September 2004, www.gpoaccess.gov/duelfer/index.html (accessed 7/20/09); Douglas Jehl and David E. Sanger, "The Struggle for Iraq: Intelligence; Powell's Case, a Year Later: Gaps in Picture of Iraq Arms," *New York Times*, February 1, 2004, 1.

[36]Bush, Remarks on Iraq at Cincinnati Museum Center.

[37]Richard A. Clarke, *Against All Enemies: Inside America's War in Terror* (New York: Free Press, 2004), 32.

[38]Walter Pincus and Dana Milbank, "Al Qaeda–Hussein Link is Dismissed," *Washington Post*, June 17, 2004, A1.

[39]Cheney statement on March 16, 2003, videotape shown and discussed on *Meet the Press*, September 14, 2003, www.msnbc.msn.com/id/3080244 (accessed 7/21/09); Rumsfeld cited in Bob Herbert, "The Army's Hard Sell," *New York Times*, June 27, 2005; Ken Adelman, "Cakewalk in Iraq," *Washington Post*, February 13, 2002, A27.

[40]Packer, *The Assassins' Gate*, 114; Gordon and Trainor, *Cobra II*, 102–3.

[41]Iraq Coalition Casualty Count, http://icasualties.org/Iraq/index.aspx (accessed 7/21/09).

[42]I raised concerns on this issue back in August 2005 as part of the debate over the Iraqi constitution. Bruce W. Jentleson, "Get It Done, Get It Right?" http://tpmcafe.talkingpointsmemo.com/2005/08/22/get_it_done_get_it_right/ (accessed 7/21/09). See also Dexter Filkins, "Armed Groups Propel Iraq Towards Chaos," *New York Times*, May 24, 2006, A1.

[43]Kevin G. Hall, "Reports Estimate Ultimate Price of Iraq War: $2 Trillion," *Arizona Republic,* January 14, 2006, A8.

[44]Steven M. Kosiak, "Iraqi Reconstruction: Without Additional Funding, Progress Likely to Fall Short, Undermining War Effort," Center for Strategic and Budgetary Assessments, February 27, 2006. See also the Brookings Iraq Index, a statistical compilation of economic, public opinion, and security data seeking to benchmark security and reconstruction, www.brookings.edu/saban/iraq-index.aspx (accessed 7/21/09).

[45]Thom Shanker, "Abu Ghraib Called Incubator for Terrorists," *New York Times,* February 15, 2006, A12.

[46]Gordon Trowbridge, "Troops Sound Off: Military Times Poll Finds High Morale, But Less Support for Bush, War Effort," *Military Times,* January 5, 2006, www.militarycity.com/polls/2005_main.php (accessed 7/21/09).

[47]Lt. Gen. Greg Newbold (ret.), "Why Iraq Was a Mistake," *Time,* April 17, 2006.

[48]Gen. Barry McCaffrey (ret.), cited in Mark Danner, "The War on Terror: Four Years On; Taking Stock of the Forever War," *New York Times Magazine,* September 11, 2005, 45.

[49]Scott Shane and Thom Shanker, "When Storm Hit, National Guard Was Deluged Too," *New York Times,* September 28, 2005.

[50]George W. Bush, "The New Strategy in Iraq," address to the nation, January 10, 2007, www.presidentialrhetoric.com/speeches/01.10.07.html (accessed 7/21/09).

[51]Mackenzie Eaglen and James Phillips, "The President's New Military Strategy in Iraq," Heritage Foundation, January 31, 2007, www.heritage.org/Research/Iraq/wm1333.cfm (accessed 7/21/09); James Phillips, "President Bush's New Way Forward in Iraq," Heritage Foundation, January 11, 2007, www.heritage.org/Research/Iraq/wm1304.cfm (accessed 7/21/09).

[52]Frederick W. Kagan, "Out of Conflict, A Partnership," *New York Times,* November 22, 2008.

[53]Brookings Institution, "Iraq Index."

[54]Lawrence J, Korb and Sean Duggan, "A Very Quiet Surge," *Guardian,* September 9, 2008.

[55]Brookings Institution, "Iraq Index."

[56]Barack Obama, remarks on "responsibly ending the war in Iraq," Camp Lejeune, North Carolina, February 27, 2009, www.cfr.org/publication/18657/ (accessed 7/21/09).

[57]George W. Bush, The National Security Strategy, March 2006, 12–13, http://georgewbush-whitehouse.archives.gov/nsc/nss/2006/ (accessed 7/21/09).

[58]National Security Strategy (2006), 23.

[59]Packer, *The Assassins' Gate,* 116.

[60]Kishore Mahbubani, *Beyond the Age of Innocence: Rebuilding Trust Between America and the World* (New York: Public Affairs, 2005), xvii.

[61]Barack Obama, Inaugural Address, January 20, 2009, www.whitehouse.gov/the_press_office/President_Barack_Obamas_Inaugural_Address/ (accessed 7/21/09).

[62]Barack Obama, remarks to the Turkish Parliament, April 6, 2009, www.whitehouse.gov/the_press_office/Remarks-By-President-Obama-To-The-Turkish-Parliament/ (accessed 7/21/09).

[63]*White Paper of the Interagency Policy Group's Report on U.S. Policy toward Afghanistan and Pakistan,* March 27, 2009, www.whitehouse.gov/assets/documents/afghanistan_pakistan_white_paper_final.pdf (accessed 7/21/09).

[64]Dexter Filkins, "Bribes Corrode Afghans' Trust in Government," *New York Times,* January 2, 2009.

[65]"What's New in the Strategy for Afghanistan and Pakistan," March 27, 2009, www.whitehouse.gov/the_press_office/Whats-New-in-the-Strategy-for-Afghanistan-and-Pakistan/ (accessed 7/21/09).

[66]Bing West, "Afghan Awakening," *National Interest* 98 (November–December 2008), 24.

[67]David E. Sanger, *The Inheritance: The World Obama Confronts and the Challenges to American Power* (New York: Harmony Books, 2009), 245.

[68]Sanger, *The Inheritance,* 213–14.

[69]Andrew F. Krepinevich, "The Collapse of Pakistan," in *7 Deadly Scenarios: A Military Futurist Explores War in the 21st Century* (New York: Bantam Books, 2009), 30–62.

[70]Elise Labott, "Global War on Terror—No More," *AC360°*, March 30, 2009, http://ac360.blogs.cnn.com/2009/03/30/global-war-on-terror-no-more/ (accessed 7/21/09).

[71]See, for example, Daniel Benjamin and Steven Simon, *The Age of Sacred Terror: Radical Islam's War Against America* (New York: Random House, 2002); Benjamin and Simon, *The Next Attack: The Failure of the War on Terror and a Strategy for Getting It Right* (New York: Times Books, 2005); Bruce Hoffman, *Inside Terrorism* (New York: Columbia University Press, 1998); Gilles Kepel, *Jihad: The Trail of Political Islam* (Cambridge, Mass.: Harvard University Press, 2002); Martha Crenshaw, ed., *Terrorism in Context* (University Park, Pa.: Penn State Press, 1995); Jessica Stern, *Terror in the Name of God: Why Religious Militants Kill* (New York: HarperCollins, 2003); Olivier Roy, *Globalized Islam* (New York: Columbia University Press, 2004); Marc Sageman, *Leaderless Jihad: Terror Networks in the Twenty-First Century* (Philadelphia: University of Pennsylvania Press, 2008); Alan B. Krueger, *What Makes a Terrorist: Economics and the Roots of Terrorism* (Princeton: Princeton University Press, 2007); Seth G. Jones and Martin C. Libicki, *How Terrorist Groups End: Lessons for Countering al Qa'ida* (Santa Monica, Calif.: RAND Corporation, 2008).

[72]Samuel P. Huntington, "The Clash of Civilizations?" *Foreign Affairs* 72.3 (Summer 1993), 22–49.

[73]James Reston, Jr., "Seeking Meaning From a Grand Imam," *Washington Post*, March 31, 2002, B4.

[74]Marc Sageman, *Understanding Terror Networks* (Philadelphia: University of Pennsylvania Press, 2004).

[75]Alan B. Krueger and Jitka Maleckova, "The Economics and the Education of Suicide Bombers: Does Poverty Cause Terrorism?" *New Republic Online*, June 24, 2002.

[76]Tony Blair, "Building a Strong International Community," October 2, 2001, www.guardian.co.uk/politics/2001/oct/02/labourconference.labour6 and www.guardian.co.uk/politics/2001/oct/02/labourconference.labour7 (accessed 7/21/09).

[77]Paul Cruickshank and Mohamed Hage Ali, "Jihadist of Mass Destruction," *Washington Post*, June 11, 2006, B2.

[78]World Public Opinion.org, Public Opinion in the Islamic World on Terrorism, al Qaeda, and US Policies, February 25, 2009, www.worldpublicopinion.org/pipa/pdf/feb09/STARTII_Feb09_rpt.pdf (accessed 7/21/09); "Muslim Publics Oppose Al Qaeda's Terrorism, But Agree with Its Goal of Driving US Forces Out," February 24, 2009, www.worldpublicopinion.org/pipa/articles/brmiddleeastnafricara/591.php?nid=&id=&pnt=591 (accessed 7/21/09).

[79]Joby Warrick, "To Combat Obama, Al Qaeda Hurls Insults," *Washington Post*, January 25, 2009, A1.

[80]See, for example, Lawrence Freedman, *Deterrence* (Cambridge: Polity Press, 2004); Robert F. Trager and Dessislava P. Zagorcheva, "Deterring Terrorism: It Can Be Done," *International Security* 30.3 (Winter 2005/06): 87–123; Audrey Kurth Cronin, *How Terrorism Ends: Understanding the Decline and Demise of Terrorist Campaigns*, (Princeton: Princeton University Press, 2009); Andrew H. Kydd and Barbara F. Walter, "The Strategies of Terrorism," *International Security* 31.1 (Summer 2006): 49–80; Bruce W. Jentleson, "Military Force against Terrorism: Questions of Legitimacy and Efficacy," in *Beyond Preemption: Force and Legitimacy in a Changing World*, Ivo H. Daalder, ed., 40–58 (Washington, D.C.: Brookings Institution, 2007).

[81]Bruce W. Jentleson, *With Friends Like These: Reagan, Bush and Saddam, 1982–1990* (New York: Norton, 1994).

[82]Joseph Cirincione, "Bombs Won't 'Solve' Iran," Issue Brief, *Washington Post*, May 11, 2005.

[83]James Fallows, "Will Iran Be Next?" *Atlantic* 294.5 (December 2004): 97–110; Sam Gardiner, *The End of the "Summer of Diplomacy": Assessing U.S. Military Options on Iran* (New York: Century Foundation, 2006).

[84]Flynt Leverett and Hillary Mann, "Opportunity Knocked," *National Interest Online*, July 23, 2008, www.nationalinterest.org/Article.aspx?id=19440 (accessed 7/21/09).

[85]Barack Obama, "A New Year, a New Beginning," March 19, 2009, www.whitehouse.gov/Nowruz/ (accessed 7/21/09).

[86]The venue was symbolic because both Jews and Muslims (Moors) had been driven out of Spain in the fifteenth century during the Spanish Inquisition.

[87]Dennis Ross, *The Missing Peace: The Inside Story of the Fight for Middle East Peace* (New York: Farrar, Straus and Giroux, 2004).

[88]William Safire, "The Great Unwatched," *New York Times,* February 18, 2002, A19.

[89]James Risen and Eric Lichtblau, "Bush Lets U.S. Spy on Callers without Courts." *New York Times,* December 16, 2005, A1. Risen and Lichtblau were awarded the Pulitzer Prize for this and related articles.

[90]George W. Bush, "The War on Terror: At Home and Abroad," Kansas State University, Manhattan, Kansas, January 23, 2006, www.presidentialrhetoric.com/speeches/01.23.06.html (accessed 7/21/09).

[91]Eric Lichtblau, "F.B.I. Watched Activist Groups, New Files Show," *New York Times,* December 20, 2005, A1.

[92]Lowell Bergman, Eric Lichtblau, Scott Shane, and Don Van Natta Jr., "Spy Agency Data After Sept. 11 Led FBI to Dead Ends," *New York Times,* January 17, 2006, A1.

[93]Eric Lichtblau and James Risen, "N.S.A.'s Intercepts Exceed Limits Set by Congress," *New York Times,* April 16, 2009, A1.

[94]"Justice Department Torture Memos," redacted text, *New York Times,* April 16, 2009, http://documents.nytimes.com/justice-department-memos-on-interrogation-techniques#p=1 (accessed 7/22/09).

[95]Mark Silva, "Cheney: Torture Memos Miss 'Success,'" *The Swamp,* April 20, 2009, www.swamppolitics.com/news/politics/blog/2009/04/cheney_torture_memos_miss_succ.html (accessed 7/22/09).

[96]Ali Soufan, "My Tortured Decision," *New York Times,* April 23, 2009; Peter Finn and Joby Warrick, "Detainee's Harsh Treatment Foiled No Plots," *Washington Post,* March 29, 2009, A1.

[97]Adam Liptak, Neil A. Lewis, and Benjamin Weiser, "After September 11, A Legal Battle on the Limits of Civil Liberty," *New York Times,* August 4, 2002, 1, 16; Linda Greenhouse, "The Imperial Presidency vs. the Imperial Judiciary," *New York Times,* September 8, 2002, WK 3.

[98]*North Jersey Media Group, Inc., v. Ashcroft,* 308 F.3d 198 (3rd Cir. 2002).

[99]Amnesty International, "Guantánamo Bay—A Human Rights Scandal," www.amnestyusa.org/war-on-terror/guantanamo-bay---a-human-rights-scandal/page.do?id=1108202 (accessed 7/22/09).

[100]*Hamdi v. Rumsfeld,* 542 U.S. 507, 536 (2004).

[101]Mike Allen, "Bush Calls Farm Subsidies a National Security Issue," *Washington Post,* February 9, 2002, A4. The article also notes that the rural areas and business interests that stood to benefit the most from the farm subsidies were key Bush supporters in the 2000 presidential election.

[102]David Firestone, "Senate Rolls a Pork Barrel into War Bill," *New York Times,* April 9, 2002, A12.

[103]Neil A. Lewis, "Ashcroft Defends Antiterrorism Plans and Says Criticism May Aid Foes," *New York Times,* December 7, 2001, A1.

[104]Todd S. Purdum, "Democratic Leader Questions War Aims," *San Francisco Chronicle,* February 28, 2002, A20; Audrey Hudson, "Daschle Hits Execution of War," *Washington Times,* March 1, 2002, A1.

[105]Bruce W. Jentleson, "The Domestic Politics of Desert Shield: Should We Go to War? Who Should Decide?" *Brookings Review* 9 (Winter 1990–91): 22–28.

[106]"Congress Approves Resolution Authorizing Force," CNN, September 14, 2001. Available at http://archives.cnn.com/2001/US/09/15/congress.terrorism/ (accessed 7/22/09).

[107]John Edwards, "The Right Way in Iraq," *Washington Post,* November 13, 2005, B7.

[108]John P. Murtha, "War in Iraq," November 17, 2005, www.wagingpeace.org/articles/2005/11/17_murtha-its-time-to-bring-the-troops-home.htm (accessed 7/22/09).

[109]Robert C. Byrd, remarks in the U.S. Senate, Oct. 10, 2002, *Congressional Record,* October 10, 2002, S10233 (Washington, D.C.: Government Printing Office, 2002).

[110]Leslie H. Gelb and Anne-Marie Slaughter, "No More Blank-Check Wars," *Washington Post,* November 8, 2005, A19; Gelb and Slaughter, "Declare War," *Atlantic Monthly,* November 2005, 54–56.

[111]Constitution Project, *Deciding to Use Force Abroad: War Powers in a System of Checks and Balances,* June 29, 2005, 37, www.constitutionproject.org/pdf/War_Powers_Deciding_To_Use_Force_Abroad.pdf (accessed 7/22/09).

[112]James A. Baker III and Warren Christopher, co-chairs, *National War Powers Commission Report* (Miller Cen-

ter for Public Affairs, University of Virginia, 2008), http://millercenter.org/policy/commissions/warpowers/report (accessed 7/22/09).

[113]Bush, remarks on Iraq at Cincinnati Museum Center and 2003 State of the Union address.

[114]Robb-Silberman Commission, 8–9; see also Duelfer Report.

[115]National Intelligence Council, "NIC Mission," www.dni.gov/nic/NIC_about.html (accessed 7/22/09).

[116]Woodward, *Plan of Attack*, 194–99.

[117]Bob Drogin and John Goetz, "The Curveball Saga: How U.S. Fell Under the Spell of 'Curveball,'" *Los Angeles Times*, November 20, 2005, A1.

[118]Murray Waas, "What Bush Was Told About Iraq," *National Journal*, March 2, 2006; Waas, "Insulating Bush," *National Journal*, March 30, 2006.

[119]Senate Select Committee on Intelligence, 18.

[120]Packer, *The Assassins' Gate*, 62.

[121]Packer, *The Assassins' Gate*, 45.

[122]Packer, *The Assassins' Gate*, 107.

[123]Cited in Frank Rich, "The Banality of Bush White House Evil," *New York Times*, April 26, 2009; see also Jonathan S. Landay, "Report: Abusive Tactics Used to Seek Iraq–al Qaida Link," McClatchy Washington Bureau, April 22, 2009, www.mcclatchydc.com/227/v-print/story/66622.html (accessed 7/22/09).

[124]Eric Schmitt and Joel Brinkley, "The Struggle for Iraq: Planning; State Dept. Study Foresaw Trouble Now Plaguing Iraq," *New York Times*, October 19, 2003, 1.

[125]Statements by Paul R. Pillar, CIA National Intelligence Officer for the Near East and South Asia, cited in Walter Pincus, "Ex-CIA Official Faults Use of Data on Iraq," *Washington Post*, February 10, 2006, A1.

[126]Packer, *The Assassins' Gate*, 118.

[127]James Fallows, "Blind into Baghdad," *Atlantic Monthly* (January/February 2004), 57.

[128]Lawrence B. Wilkerson, "The White House Cabal," *Los Angeles Times*, October 25, 2005, B1.

[129]See, for example, Phillips, *Losing Iraq;* Diamond, *Squandered Victory;* Packer, *The Assassins' Gate;* Gordon and Trainor, *Cobra II.*

[130]Thomas E. Ricks, *The Gamble: General David Petraeus and the American Military Adventure in Iraq, 2006–2008* (New York: Penguin, 2009). Ricks's book on the earlier period of the Iraq war was titled *Fiasco: The American Military Adventure in Iraq* (New York: Penguin, 2006).

[131]George W. Bush, "The New Strategy in Iraq," prime time address to the nation, Washington, D.C., January 10, 2007, www.presidentialrhetoric.com/speeches/01.10.07.html (accessed 7/22/09).

[132]John T. Rourke, Ralph G. Carter, and Mark A. Boyer, *Making American Foreign Policy*, 2d ed. (Dubuque, Iowa: Brown and Benchmark, 1996), 362.

[133]"The Propaganda War," *Newsweek*, February 25, 1991, 38.

[134]Jerel A. Rosati, *The Politics of United States Foreign Policy* (New York: Harcourt, Brace, 1993), 507.

[135]Howard Kurtz, "For Media after Iraq, a Case of Shell Shock," *Washington Post*, April 28, 2003, A1.

[136]Polls cited in Bruce W. Jentleson, "Tough Love Multilateralism, *Washington Quarterly* 27.1 (Winter 2002–2003): 20.

[137]ABC News–*Washington Post* polls: "Do you approve or disapprove of the way Bush is handling the situation in Iraq?" May 11–15, 2006, www.washingtonpost.com/wp-srv/politics/polls/postpoll_051606.htm (accessed 7/22/09).

[138]Jentleson, "Tough Love Multilateralism," 20–21.

[139]Pew Research Center poll, September 17–22, 2003, http://people-press.org/reports/pdf/194.pdf (accessed 7/22/09); *Newsweek* poll, September 25–28, 2003.

CHAPTER

# 9 Never Again or Yet Again? Genocide and Other Mass Atrocities

## Introduction: Success and Failure, Hope and Despair

The mood at the end of the Cold War in 1989 was almost euphoric. President George H. W. Bush spoke of "a new world order where diverse nations are drawn together in common cause to achieve the universal aspirations of mankind."[1] He and other world leaders, gathering in January 1992 at the United Nations for its first-ever heads of state summit meeting, called for enhancement of the UN's role "for preventive diplomacy, for peacemaking and for peacekeeping."[2] The Clinton administration picked up these themes with its emphasis on the need for "a new diplomacy that can anticipate and prevent crises . . . rather than simply manage them."[3] There was a real sense that the end of the Cold War could mean the end of war. And then, long before September 11, came Somalia, Bosnia, Rwanda, and Kosovo.

In Somalia, the United States intervened with twenty-seven thousand troops (***Operation Restore Hope***) in the largely humanitarian mission of helping restore order and get food to the Somali people. This mission, launched by the Bush administration in December 1992 and continued by the Clinton administration, ended disastrously when the United States abruptly withdrew following the October 1993 killing of eighteen U.S. soldiers in urban battles in the capital city of Mogadishu. Today, over a decade later, Somalia still is a failed state, with continuing humanitarian crises as well as security concerns about its use as a haven for terrorists and other issues.

The war in Bosnia (1992–95) left close to a million people dead or wounded, and almost 2 million displaced and added a new term, ***ethnic "cleansing,"*** to the lexicon of warfare. These were the most massive killings in Europe since the Nazi Holocaust in World War II. Yet for over three years, under George H. W. Bush and then Bill Clinton, the United States did not intervene, leaving the United Nations and the European Union to lead the multilateral peacekeeping forces. But these forces proved unable to prevent the ethnic "cleansing," most graphically in the mass killings of more than seven thousand Bosnian Muslims in the supposed safe haven of the town of Srebrenica. When the Clinton administration finally stepped in, the United States played the crucial peace-broker role in sponsoring the 1995 Dayton accord ending the war, but only after enormous death and destruction.

In Rwanda the horrors that transpired in 1994 were more than ethnic "cleansing"—they were ***genocide.*** "In one hundred days," as reported by Samantha Power in her Pulitzer Prize–winning book, *"A Problem From Hell:" America and the Age of Genocide*, "some eight hundred thousand Tutsi and politically moderate Hutu were murdered. . . . The Rwandan genocide would prove to be the fastest, most efficient killing spree of the twentieth century." Yet, Ms. Power continues, "the United States did almost nothing to try to stop it."[4] Nor did the UN, or Europe, or any other major actor in the international community.

In Kosovo, the United States and NATO did intervene in 1999 to stop the ethnic "cleansing" that Serbia was perpetrating against this heavily Muslim province. The United States and NATO won, but they "won ugly."[5] Success came only after extensive killings, only after scores of villages were ravaged, only after thousands were left refugees. The conflict was contained and reduced, but it had not been prevented.

Thus, even before September 11, it was all too clear that the end of the Cold War had not meant the end of war. *Whereas much of the Cold War had been driven by differences in ideology, the post–Cold War world was being driven by differences in identity.* Following World War II and the Nazi Holocaust killing of more than 6 million Jews, other minorities, and homosexuals, the United States and much of the rest of the world pledged "never again" to permit genocide or other horrific crimes against humanity. But the "politics of identity" was sparking deadly conflicts that were "yet again," not never again.

September 11 had a mixed impact. On the one hand, it prompted the Bush administration to be less skeptical of nation building and humanitarian intervention—"the 82nd

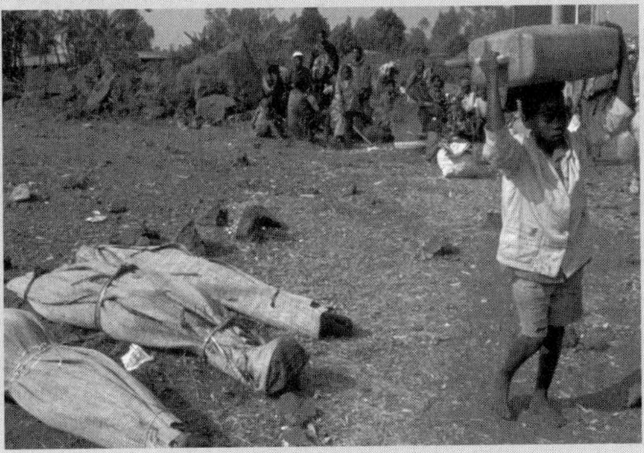

A Rwandan boy passes the bodies of those killed in the violent clashes between the Hutu and Tutsi ethnic groups. (*Betty Press/Woodfin Camp/PNI*)

Airborne escorting kids to kindergarten," as the Bush team had disparagingly termed these operations during the 2000 presidential election campaign.[6] In the wake of September 11, the Bush administration did at least partially rethink this attitude, with attempts at nation building first in Afghanistan and then in Iraq. The 2002 Bush National Security Strategy articulated the broader strategic argument of tracing some of the roots of terrorism back to weak states, poverty, and related suffering.

On the other hand, September 11 put "hard" security issues back at the top of the U.S. foreign policy agenda. Although there are some connections between humanitarian crises and terrorism, they tend to be insufficiently integral to be principal drivers behind decisions on what commitments to make, what resources to allocate, and what priorities to set. Making such connections can even work against the solving of humanitarian crises that have their own moral imperatives and interest-based rationales but are not linked to terrorism as, for example, in Darfur, a region of Sudan, where starting in 2003 yet another genocide occurred while the United States, the UN, and the rest of the international community once again did too little too late. Moreover, with the Iraq war so dominating attention and resources during the Bush years, there was little of either left for these issues.

In late 2008, amid the transition from the Bush to the Obama administration, a report was issued by the bipartisan Genocide Prevention Task Force, co-chaired by the former secretary of state Madeleine K. Albright and the former secretary of defense William S. Cohen. "We are convinced," the co-chairs wrote, "that the U.S. government can and must do more to prevent genocide, a crime that threatens not only our values, but our national interests." Their report made a series of policy recommendations, acknowledging that although not all mass atrocities could be prevented, "we must do better."[7]

For those who would throw up their hands, thinking that little if anything can be done about these conflicts, there is some basis for encouragement. The *2005 Human Security Report* shows the trend lines for some measures of conflict moving downward. More wars stopped than started; though still disturbingly high, death tolls are lower than a decade ago; so are the numbers of refugees.[8] A 2008 follow-up study confirmed these trends.[9] The biggest reason for this decrease is the increased willingness and capacity of the United States, the United Nations, and others in the international community to get involved with preventive diplomacy, humanitarian intervention, and other policies. The record thus is one of both success and failure, of both hope and tragedy. The challenge for the United States and the international community is how to have more success and more hope, and less failure and less tragedy in preventing genocide and mass atrocities—how to get to "never again" rather than "yet again."

In this chapter we review recent cases (including Somalia, Rwanda, Haiti, Bosnia, Kosovo, Macedonia, East Timor, Democratic Republic of Congo, Burma, and Darfur) and address future policy with regard to seven core questions. Is the U.S. national interest at stake in genocides and other mass atrocities? What are the driving forces of these wars of identity? What about claims of national sovereignty against intervention by the United States, the United Nations, and other international actors? Which "preventive diplomacy" strategies are most effective? When should military force be used? Who decides on military intervention? What are the best ways to end conflicts and build peace through diplomatic and/or military means? We then look at the genocide in Darfur, which raises many of these questions. In the final section we focus on key issues and patterns in the U.S. foreign policy politics as seen across various recent cases.[10]

## Is the U.S. National Interest at Stake?

While our focus is on recent cases, an historical perspective is also important. The historical record, we must acknowledge, is not one to be proud of (see "Historical Perspectives," p. 484). "The United States had never in its history intervened to stop genocide and had in fact rarely even made a point of condemning it as it occurred." Samantha Power makes that searing indictment in *A Problem From Hell.* Time and again "we all have been bystanders to genocide."[11] The prevailing view each time was that preventing genocide was not sufficiently in the U.S. national interest to warrant the necessary action.

Thus when Secretary of State James Baker offhandedly explained the first Bush administration's inaction as the killing mounted in the former Yugoslavia, by saying, "We don't have a dog in that fight," he was, however perversely, being consistent with past U.S. foreign policy.[12] As for Somalia, it was, as a former U.S. ambassador put it, "not a critical piece of real estate for anybody in the post–Cold War world."[13] Principles come most to mind when we question such national-interest assessments. But the other "Ps"—Power, Peace, Prosperity—also can come into play. The argument was well framed in the "Mother Teresa" exchange of articles in *Foreign Affairs* by Michael Mandelbaum and Stanley Hoffmann. Mandelbaum argued that giving national-interest weight to humanitarian concerns is being "too much like Mother Teresa" and turns foreign policy into "social work." Hoffmann countered that the very distinction between interests and values is "largely fallacious," in that "a great power has an 'interest' in world order that goes beyond strict national security concerns and its definition of world order is largely shaped by its values."[14]

Professor Hoffman's argument taps the Peace component of the American national interest. He emphasizes the overall macroglobal level and the intangible yet still potent ways that failures to defend basic values and confront genocide and other crimes against humanity, no matter where they occur, undermine the sense as well as the structures of international community. Moreover, and more tangible, these conflicts do not just feed on themselves but spread to other areas. This occurs through varying combinations of direct "contagion" (the actual physical movement of refugees and weapons to neighboring countries in a region), "demonstration effects" that even without direct contact activate and es-

## HISTORICAL PERSPECTIVES

HISTORICAL PERSPECTIVES

### "GENOCIDE IN THE TWENTIETH CENTURY"

It wasn't until the early 1940s that the word *genocide* appeared in *Webster's New International Dictionary.* Derived from the Greek *geno*, meaning "race" or "tribe," with the Latin *cide*, meaning "killing," it was first used to characterize Hitler's horrors against German and other European Jews.* Over 6 million Jews were killed by Hitler and the Nazis in gas chambers and other horrific ways in what came to be known as the Holocaust. The United States eventually did enter World War II as leader of the Allies, but not until more than two years after the war had started. And even then, despite information about the Nazi concentration camps, the war strategy did not give much priority to stopping the genocide.†

Earlier in the twentieth century, during World War I, nearly 1 million Armenians were killed by the Turks. The word did not exist yet, but the actions constituted genocide. Nor was this secret or without warning. "800,000 Armenians counted destroyed," was the headline in the October 17, 1915 *Times of London.* Henry Morgenthau Sr., U.S. Ambassador to Turkey, cabled back to Washington about the "race murder" going on. But neither the United States nor Great Britain nor any other country took serious action.‡

Amid these horrors a hero emerged. Raphael Lemkin did more than any other individual to try to generate outrage about and action against genocide. A Polish Jew, Lemkin started working on the issue in the 1920s while still a college student in his native Poland and then as a young lawyer in the 1930s. When the Nazis invaded Poland, he was forced to flee and ended up in the United States as a law professor at Duke University. Lemkin not only coined the term *genocide* but also was the moving force behind the 1948 Convention on the Prevention and Punishment of the Crime of Genocide. This was the very first human rights treaty approved by the United Nations. Its purpose, as stated in its preamble, "recognizing that at all periods of history genocide has inflicted great losses on humanity," was "to liberate mankind from such an odious scourge." This was part of the "never again" pledge so many made in so many ways after the Nazi Holocaust.

Yet it would be almost forty years before the United States signed and ratified the Genocide Convention. No one "supported" genocide of course, but opponents of the treaty claimed that it would infringe on America's own sovereignty and bind American foreign policy to commitments that the United States might not want to make. Meanwhile more cases of genocide piled up: in the "killing fields" of Cambodia, where radical communists who came to power after the defeat of the U.S.-

backed government killed 2 million of their own people between 1975 and 1978; in Iraq, where Saddam Hussein used chemical weapons in 1987-88 against Iraqi Kurds.[§] And then in the 1990s we have the cases we will discuss in this chapter, including Bosnia, Rwanda, and Kosovo, as well as the more recent case of Darfur.

In none of these cases, historical or contemporary, was the problem a lack of information or options. "I have found," Samantha Power writes, "that in fact U.S. policymakers knew a great deal about the crimes being perpetrated. . . . And the United States did have countless opportunities to mitigate and prevent slaughter. But time and again, decent men and women chose to look away. . . . The crucial question is why."[**]

That question, perhaps more than any other, is worth pondering.

*Samantha Power, *"A Problem from Hell": America and the Age of Genocide* (New York: Basic Books, 2002) 42, 44.

†David S. Wyman, *The Abandonment of the Jews: America and the Holocaust, 1941–1945* (New York: Pantheon Books, 1984).

‡Power, *"A Problem from Hell,"* 9, 6.

§*The Killing Fields,* a powerful movie about Cambodia, was nominated for a Best Picture Oscar in 1984. On the Iraqi Kurds, see chapter 2 in Bruce W. Jentleson, *With Friends Like These: Reagan, Bush and Saddam, 1982–1990* (New York: Norton, 1994).

**Power, *"A Problem from Hell,"* xvi–xvii.

calate other conflicts, and other modes of conflict diffusion.[15] This is what happened in Africa with the spread of the Rwandan conflict to Zaire (now Democratic Republic of Congo), as well as in the former Yugoslavia with the connections between the wars in Croatia, Bosnia, and Kosovo. As a Clinton Pentagon report stated, "These events can threaten U.S. interests because they may spread beyond the parties initially involved, incur intervention by outside powers, or put at risk the safety and well-being of American citizens in the region."[16] The 2002 Bush National Security Strategy made its own assessment at least somewhat along these lines: "[W]eak states, like Afghanistan, can pose as great a danger to our national interests as strong states. Poverty does not make poor people into terrorists and murderers. Yet poverty, weak institutions and corruption can make weak states vulnerable to terrorist networks and drug cartels within their borders."[17] Chester Crocker, the assistant secretary of state for Africa under President Reagan, made the point even more strongly, arguing that it simply "is not possible to compartmentalize the globe and wall off the strategic slums. Regional crises exist, they worsen when left unattended, and they have a way of imposing themselves on the Western agenda."[18]

American Power also is more at risk than the Mandelbaum view claims. As discussed frequently in this book, power depends heavily on credibility. Weak action or inaction in the face of humanitarian crises undermines American credibility. No matter how much the no-dog-in-this-fight claim is made, American inaction is a factor. If aggressors calculate a military advantage over their internal opponents, so long as those opponents cannot count on international assistance for balance and buttressing, it should be no wonder that they choose war and violence. That is what the Serbian leader Slobodan Milosevic did in Bosnia, and because the United States, the UN, and Europe did so little for so long to support his victims, it was what he did again in Kosovo. Credibility rests on the combination of judgment and resolve. When they are brought into question by inaction in the face of humanitarian horrors, a fundamental basis of power is undermined. As Professor Donald Rothchild pointedly puts it, "Inaction in the face of genocide involves costs in terms of purpose and self-esteem on the part of a great power and its people that must not be underestimated."[19]

Policy makers have had a similar tendency to underestimate the economic stakes. In a sense, policy makers are no different from most people in putting greater weight on immediate costs than on anticipated ones. It often seems easier to pay tomorrow rather than today—hence the success of credit cards, hence the failures of conflict prevention. It is only human to hope that perhaps the costs won't have to be paid, the bill won't come due, if the issue peters out or at least self-limits. But the bills have been coming due, with the equivalent of exorbitant interest and late fees. "The costs of remedying a situation once it gets out of control," as Sir David Hannay, the British ambassador to the United Nations stated, "is infinitely greater than the costs of . . . international efforts to head off such disasters before they occur."[20]

This situation is not even new. In 1951, when the United Nations High Commission on Refugees was established, there were about 1.5 million refugees in the world; by 1980 this number was up to 8.2 million; by 1996 it was up to 14.5 million. The number declined to about 10 million by 2005 but was back up to 11.4 million by 2007. The numbers of internally displaced persons (refugees within their own country) rose even more sharply, to 26 million, reflecting how many wars were now intrastate.[21] In 1971 the total expenditure by refugee, disaster, and humanitarian relief agencies was $200 million; in 1994 it was $8 billion. Even with overall U.S. foreign aid levels falling, the annual amount going to relief agencies increased from $300 million to $1.3 billion.[22] At one point the peacekeeping force in the former Yugoslavia was costing $1.6 billion per year, accounting for half of the UN's total peacekeeping budget. Yet in Macedonia, also a part of the former Yugoslavia but one of the few cases in which early preventive action was taken (1993), the entire cost of the peacekeeping force was *less* than the annual budget for only the Bosnia war crimes tribunal, set up for after-the-fact pursuit of justice.[23] Another study estimated that the costs to the United States and other outside powers of conflict prevention in

Bosnia would have been $33.3 billion, compared with the $54 billion spent just by 1999 for conflict management and postconflict reconstruction.[24]

As for Principles, it is hard to think of a more compelling purpose than prevention of genocide. In Kosovo, where the United States led the NATO intervention in 1999, Principles and Power were largely complementary. The intervention was intended both to stop ethnic "cleansing" and to ensure stability in Europe (a vital region) and the credibility of NATO (a vital alliance). Are values alone, then, not a sufficient basis for U.S. intervention or other concerted action? That position has the strength of avoiding overcommitment or always being called on as the "global 911." But it qualifies, if not undermines, the claim that the United States genuinely and consistently stands for Principles. This trade-off can be debated, but it cannot be denied.

All "4 P's" are clear in the 2008 Genocide Prevention Task Force Report "making the case" why genocide and mass atrocities "threaten core U.S. national interests":

> Genocide and mass atrocities are a direct assault on universal human values. . . . Genocide fuels instability, usually in weak, undemocratic and corrupt states. It is in these same types of states that we find terrorist recruitment and training, human trafficking, and civil strife, all of which have damaging spillover effects for the entire world. . . .
>
> Refugee flows start in bordering countries but often spread. Humanitarian needs grow, often exceeding the capacities and resources of a generous world. . . . And the longer we wait, the more exorbitant the price tag. . . .
>
> America's standing in the world—and our ability to lead—is eroded when we are perceived as bystanders to genocide. . . .
>
> No matter how one calculates U.S. interests, the reality of our world today is that national borders provide little sanctuary from international problems. Left unchecked, genocide will undermine American security.[25]

## What Are the Driving Forces of Wars of Identity?

"It's really a tragic problem," Secretary of State Warren Christopher stated in early 1993 amid the horrors of ethnic "cleansing" in Bosnia. "The hatred between all these groups—the Bosnians and the Serbs and the Croatians—is . . . centuries old. That really is a problem from hell."[26] If this were true, then, whatever the stakes, both American foreign policy and the United Nations really had little chance of having much impact. But there was reason to doubt whether the problem was as intractable as the secretary portrayed it.

The debate here is between ***primordialist*** and ***purposive*** theories of the sources of ethnic conflict. The primordialist view sees ethnicity as a fixed and inherently conflictual historical identity; thus the 1990s conflicts were primarily continuations of ones going back hundreds of years—"Balkan ghosts" going back to the fourteenth century, Somali clan rivalries dating from the precolonial pastoral period, the medieval *buhake* agricultural caste system of Tutsi dominance over Hutu in what is now Rwanda.

The histories, though, are not nearly so deterministic. A number of studies have shown that ethnic identities are much less fixed over time, and the frequency and intensity of ethnic conflict much more varied over both time and place, than primordialist theory would have it. In Bosnia, for example, the ethnic intermarriage rate in 1991 was around 25 percent, and there were very few ethnically "pure" urban residents or ethnically homogeneous smaller communities. As a Bosnian Muslim schoolteacher put it, "We never, until the war, thought of ourselves as Muslims. We were Yugoslavs. But when we began to be murdered because we are Muslims things changed. The definition of who we are today has been determined by our killing."[27]

An alternative explanation of the sources of ethnic conflict is the "purposive" view. This view acknowledges the deep-seated nature of ethnic identifications and the corresponding animosities and unfinished agendas of vengeance that persist as historical legacies. But the purposive view takes a much less deterministic view of how, why, and if these identity-rooted tensions become deadly conflicts. Historically shaped, yes; historically determined, no. The focus is on forces and factors that intensify and activate historical animosities into actions and policies reflecting conscious and deliberate choices for war and violence. In Rwanda, notwithstanding the deep historical roots of Hutu-Tutsi tensions, the genocide was not primordialistic "mindless violence" but all too purposive: "planned . . . fully prepared . . . to retain political power and all that went with it."[28] The driving forces in this and so many other cases have not been the playing out of historical inevitability but, as another author put it, "the purposeful actions of political actors who actively create violent conflict" to serve their own domestic political agendas by "selectively drawing on history in order to portray [events] as historically inevitable."[29]

Nor were these forces so subtle that the killings came as surprises to the outside world. Even amid what intelligence analysts call sorting out "the signal" from "the noise," there was ample credible "early warning." In Somalia, going back over a decade, "the international community witnessed visible signs of a worsening political crisis. . . . [T]here was no shortage of information warning of a deteriorating political situation."[30] In Rwanda, "information about the possibility of an oncoming genocide—or at any rate, civil violence on a scale that would undermine the peace process—was 'in the system' in ample quantity."[31] In Bosnia "there was plenty of early warning."[32]

We cannot know for sure that conflict could have been prevented; this is what is called a ***counterfactual argument,*** and we must acknowledge its limits. Such arguments must be based on what genuinely was known and possible *at the time,* not just in retrospect—otherwise they would be vulnerable to the charge of "Monday-morning quarterbacking."

Nevertheless the evidence in virtually every case is that different policies were possible, and such policies had plausible chances of positive impact.

In Somalia, for example, although "no amount of preventive diplomacy could have completely pre-empted some level of conflict," there is solid evidence of "a virtual litany of missed opportunities" implying "that timely diplomatic interventions at several key junctures might have significantly reduced, defused and contained that violence." In Rwanda, Major General Romeo Dallaire, the Canadian commander of the small and limited UN peacekeeping force already on the ground, sounded the warning bell but got little response or support from the UN, the United States, or Europe when "forces appropriately trained, equipped, and commanded, and introduced in a timely manner, could have stemmed the violence in and around the capital, prevented its spread to the countryside, and created conditions conducive to the cessation of the civil war."[33]

In sum, these conflicts were not strictly centuries-old "problems from hell." They were fed by, shaped by, and turned toward the purposes of leaders and others whose interests were served by manipulating identity politics. Some conflict and killing probably were inevitable, but there is a huge difference between "some" killing and what actually occurred.

## What about National Sovereignty?

A further question concerns whether international norms, laws, and practices justify intervention. Central to this question is the debate over "state sovereignty" and the balance between the *rights* conferred on states and the *responsibilities* expected of them. The "Theory in the World" box on page 490 provides context for a debate that has become especially acute, given the intrastate nature of many of the conflicts we face today and the fact that perpetrators of genocide and other mass killings against their own peoples invoke state sovereignty as a normative barrier behind which to hide their aggression.

The concept of sovereignty as responsibility came through very strongly in the 2001 report *The Responsibility to Protect,* issued by the International Commission on Intervention and State Sovereignty (ICISS) and from which Reading 9.1 is an excerpt. The core conception of the ***responsibility to protect (R2P)*** reflects the sense that individuals must be protected from mass killings and other gross violations of their rights, and that the state that is sovereign over the territory in which they reside has primary but not exclusive responsibility. If the state does not live up to that responsibility, "then coercive intervention for human protection purposes, including ultimately military intervention, by others in the international community may be warranted in extreme cases."[34] To answer the concern that this could simply open the way for big powers to go on doing what they want to do, the commission was careful to distinguish its conception of the responsibility to protect from a "right to intervene." Although acknowledging the historical roots of such 9.1

## THEORY IN THE WORLD

### SOVEREIGNTY AS RIGHTS VS. SOVEREIGNTY AS RESPONSIBILITY

We learn in introductory international relations courses that state sovereignty is one of the bedrock principles of the international system. This is traced back to the 1648 Treaty of Westphalia, which established the sovereignty of states. As Robert Art and Robert Jervis write, "No agency exists above the individual states with authority and power to make laws and settle disputes." The strong emphasis is on the rights that come with sovereignty, "the complete autonomy of the state to act as it chooses," as Abram and Antonia Handler Chayes put it. More particularly, in a classic dictum from Max Weber, "the state is a human community that successfully claims the monopoly of the legitimate use of physical force within a given territory." Not only is this an absolute conception, it is seen as fixed historically. "The logic of sovereignty is inherent in the nature of the state," wrote the eminent British scholar F. H. Hinsley, "and it has become and is likely to remain the defining principle in the political organization of the world."*

But has sovereignty remained the defining principle? Should it? Defenders of the Westphalian theory of sovereignty point to Article 2, Section 7 of the UN Charter as the embodiment of sovereignty as the rights of states: "Nothing contained in the present Charter shall authorize the United Nations to intervene in matters which are essentially within the domestic jurisdiction of any state." Others, though, including the former secretary-general Kofi Annan, stress that the UN Charter "was issued in the name of 'the peoples,' not the governments of the United Nations. . . . The Charter protects the sovereignty of peoples. It was never meant as a license for governments to trample on human rights and human dignity. Sovereignty implies responsibility, not just power." This sense of *sovereignty as responsibility not just rights* also comes through in other provisions of the UN Charter. Article 3 affirms that "everyone has the right to life, liberty and the security of person." Article 55 commits the UN to "promote . . . universal respect for, and observance of, human rights and fundamental freedoms." Article 56 pledges all members "to take joint and separate action" toward this end. Even Article 2(7) needs to be qualified, according to Mr. Annan: "Even national sovereignty can be set aside if it stands in the way of the Security Council's overriding duty to preserve international peace and security."† Further affirmations are manifested in the Genocide Convention, the Universal Declaration of Human Rights, and other international covenants that make no distinction as to whether the offender is a foreign invader or one's own government.

This is the theoretical and historical context for the current policy debate over how to balance the rights that states possess as sovereign bodies with the responsibilities that come with those rights. Scholars as well as policy makers have written much on where this balance lies.‡ Although this debate bears on a number of policy areas, it is especially acute for humanitarian intervention, as we see in this chapter.

*Robert J. Art and Robert Jervis, *International Politics: Enduring Concepts and Contemporary Issues* (New York: Harper Collins, 1992), 2; Abram Chayes and Antonia Handler Chayes, eds., *Preventing Conflict in the Post–Cold War World: Mobilizing International and Regional Organizations* (Washington, D.C.: Brookings Institution Press, 1996), 60; Joseph A. Camilleri and Jim Falk, *The End of Sovereignty? The Politics of a Shrinking and Fragmented World* (Brookfield, Vt.: Elgar, 1992), 24.

†"Secretary-General Reflects on 'Intervention' in Thirty-fifth Annual Ditchley Foundation Lecture," Press Release SG/SM/6613, June 26, 1998, www.un.org/News/Press/docs/1998/19980626.sgsm6613.html (accessed 7/23/09). See "United Nations Report of the Secretary-General on the Work of the Organization," 54th sess., supp. No. 1 (A/54/1), August 31, 1999, 4, www.un.org/Docs/SG/Report99/toc.htm (accessed 9/8/09).

‡See, for example, J. L. Holzgrefe and Robert O. Keohane, eds., *Humanitarian Intervention: Ethical, Legal and Political Dilemmas* (New York: Cambridge University Press, 2003); Nicholas J. Wheeler, *Saving Strangers: Humanitarian Intervention in International Society* (New York: Oxford University Press, 2000); Simon Chesterman, *Just War or Just Peace? Humanitarian Intervention and International Law* (New York: Oxford University Press, 2001); International Commission on Intervention and State Sovereignty (ICISS), *The Responsibility to Protect* (Ottawa: International Development Research Centre, 2001).

fears in colonialism and the Cold War, the commission was unwilling to allow such arguments to be too easily invoked as rationalizations distracting from its core concern about ethnic "cleansings," genocides, and other mass killings: "What is at stake here is not making the world safe for big powers, or trampling over the sovereign rights of small ones, but delivering practical protection for ordinary people at risk of their lives, because their states are unwilling or unable to protect them."[35]

Especially if sovereignty was to be less sacrosanct, establishing criteria for justifiable intervention was all the more important. These efforts tapped heavily into the ***just war*** tradition. Though differing in some particulars, the commission generally stressed four factors:

1. just cause, in terms of an "extreme humanitarian emergency" or comparably dire situation and a credible claim that the United States or other intervener is acting for these humanitarian motivations more than out of particularistic self-interest

2. proportionality of the military means, which should be only enough to achieve the humanitarian objective
3. a strong probability of success, taking into account collateral damage, civilian casualties, and avoidance of "destroying the village in order to save it"
4. force as a last resort[36]

These criteria left obvious room for interpretation and contestation. Thomas Weiss, who served as ICISS research director, observes that "the 'just cause threshold' is higher than many would have hoped."[37] Others still bristled at any sovereignty-abridging justification. The debate thus hardly was settled, but it was advanced.

The Iraq war further complicated this debate in a number of ways. One was the George W. Bush administration's invocation of humanitarianism as part of its rationale for going to war. This "had the effect," as the British scholar Adam Roberts observes, "of reinforcing fears both of U.S. dominance and of the chaos that could ensue if what is sauce for the U.S. goose were to become sauce for many other would-be interventionist ganders."[38] Moreover, the fact that humanitarian rationales were invoked as part of the potpourri of *causus belli* made it even worse, demonstrating "the danger of abuse":

> If all wars can be "humanitarian," then the humanitarian exception itself ceases to have meaning. . . . The danger with accepting the legal and moral arguments for war with Iraq is that it will undermine the veracity of those arguments: Security Council resolutions can be interpreted so broadly as to mean anything and nothing; pre-emptive self-defense blurs into aggression; humanitarian wars become the norm, but selectivity on the basis of the "national interests" of the interveners remains.[39]

When the UN took the sovereignty issue up as part of its 2004–2005 reform process, it did adopt the "responsibility to protect" norm, although with some watering down from the 2001 ICISS Report. The official UN 2005 World Summit Fact Sheet claims that there was "clear and unambiguous acceptance by all governments of the collective international responsibility to protect populations from genocide, war crimes, ethnic cleansing and crimes against humanity."[40] Yet as Edward Luck, a noted scholar serving as special adviser to UN Secretary-General Ban Ki-moon, notes, "UN member states are united in their support for the goals of R2P but less so on how to achieve them."[41] Even more crucial was the question of whether statements would lead to action. The actual UN summit final document couched the responsibility to protect as the responsibility of "each individual state." The role of the international community was no more than to "encourage and help States to exercise this responsibility."[42] What if states don't exercise that responsibility? What if international encouragement and help are not enough? Answers to these and other questions were left to actual policy cases.

The humanitarian emergency created by Cyclone Nargis in Burma/Myanmar in May 2008 raised the sovereignty issue in the context of a natural disaster rather than a civil war. The cyclone left over 130,000 dead and thousands at risk from disease, starvation, and exposure. Many in the international community—the UN, the United States, Asian nations, NGOs—were prepared to provide disaster relief. But the Burmese military government, considered among the world's most repressive, resisted allowing international actors to enter the country. With aid kept to a regime-controlled trickle, the situation on the ground deteriorated further and further as more people died and disease spread. Was the Burmese government acting within its sovereign rights? Or was this a case of sovereignty as responsibility? If so, would military intervention to help deliver humanitarian relief have been legitimate? No such intervention occurred. Eventually, some aid was allowed in, but very little, very late. Thus Burma was another case in which the sovereignty as rights versus responsibilities debate was raised but not resolved.

## *Which Types of Preventive Diplomacy Strategies Can Be Most Effective?*

Saving more people from dying than already have is, of course, a worthy goal. Even more worthy is to prevent conflicts from reaching the point of mass killings through ***preventive diplomacy.*** The basic logic of preventive diplomacy seems unassailable. Act early to prevent disputes from escalating or problems from worsening.[43] Reduce tensions that if intensified could lead to war. Deal with today's conflicts before they become tomorrow's crises. Preventive statecraft follows the same logic as preventive medicine: Don't wait until the cancer has spread or the arteries are fully clogged. Or, as the auto mechanic says in a familiar television commercial, as he holds an oil filter in one hand and points to a seized-up car engine with the other, "Pay me now or pay me later."

In one sense preventive diplomacy involves getting at problems at the root of violent conflict. Economic development is one possible strategy. It is going too far to say that poverty is consistently a main cause of violent conflict. "If it were," as Gareth Evans writes, "the world, with a billion people still living on around a dollar a day, would be much more alarmingly violent than it is now." But, Evans continues, "there is every reason to accept that economic decline, low income and high unemployment are contributing conditions, either directly by fueling grievances among particular disadvantaged or excluded groups, or indirectly by reducing the relevant opportunity costs of joining a violent rebellion—or quite probably both."[44]

Similar points pertain to environmental degradation. In instances where arable land, water supply and other resources are depleted, environmental issues contribute to violent conflict; Darfur is an example, as we discuss later in this chapter. In other instances, environmental issues are less of a factor in violent conflict, although of concern in their own right, as we will see in Chapter 10.

Promoting good governance is another preventive diplomacy strategy. This may be equated with democracy promotion. It also may involve achieving greater accountability and capacity within traditional governing structures that are not elections based. Either way, "achieving good governance in all its manifestations—representative, responsive, accountable and capable—is at the heart of effective long-term conflict and mass atrocity prevention strategies."[45] These include improving rule of law, strengthening civil society organizations, police and security sector reform, public official training programs, and a range of other good-governance initiatives.

In some instances, membership in international organizations has been linked to good governance. The preventive logic is twofold: The lure of membership and its benefits can be an incentive for avoiding mass violence; and once a member, a country would be socialized and assisted into better domestic governance practices. This strategy has been most effective in Europe, where first the prospect and then the practice of membership in the European Union, NATO, and other organizations has helped countries such as Latvia, Hungary, and Romania manage their ethnic tensions short of mass violence.[46]

At the local level, community reconciliation programs also can be important for getting at long-standing ethnic and other identity-based tensions. As we stressed earlier, history does not determine, but it does shape. To the extent that programs can assist groups and facilitate peaceful mechanisms for reducing and managing tensions, violence can have less appeal. NGOs often play particularly important roles in such programs.

9.2 The 2008 Genocide Prevention Task Force addressed these and other preventive diplomacy strategies in its recommendations. We excerpt some of these in Reading 9.2.

To be sure, all of these policies have difficulties. None come with guarantees. But as difficult as preventive diplomacy is, the onset of mass violence transforms the nature of a conflict. A Rubicon is crossed, on the other side of which resolution and even limitation of the conflict are that much more difficult. A former Croatian militiaman who later turned himself in reflected on his own killing of seventy-two civilians and command of a death camp. "The most difficult thing is to ignite a house or kill a man for the first time," he stated, "but afterward even this becomes routine."[47] Adding revenge and retribution to other sources of tension plunges a conflict situation to a fundamentally different and more difficult depth. None of these conflicts would ever have been easy to resolve, but after all the killings, the rapes, the other war crimes, the tasks were vastly harder.

Another aspect of preventive action is that certain international strategies that may have been effective at lower levels of conflict are less likely to be so amid intensified violence. One reason for this is the classic problem of statecraft is that the more extensive the objectives, the greater and usually more coercive are the strategies needed to achieve them. Consistent with both Thomas Schelling's deterrence/compellence distinction and Alexander George's work on coercive diplomacy, preventing a conflict from escalating to violence is a more limited objective than ending violence once it has begun.[48] The violence can become so indiscriminate that even humanitarian-aid NGOs are in danger. In

2008, 260 aid workers were attacked and 122 killed while trying to carry out their work, with the highest rates in Somalia, Afghanistan, and Sudan. In this very crucial sense, options do *not* necessarily stay open. A problem can get harder down the road. When you wait, you may see a much more difficult problem than you did at first.

This point also has implications for the theory of ***"ripeness."*** As developed by William Zartman and others, this is an important and powerful theory.[49] The central idea is that at certain points in the life cycle of conflicts, they are more conducive to possible resolution than at others. When a situation is not "ripe," as determined in large part by the extent to which the parties to the conflict are disposed even to consider an agreement seriously, international strategies have much less chance of succeeding. But although ripeness theory is helpful in counseling prudent assessments of when and where to engage so as not to overestimate the chances of success, it sometimes gets interpreted and applied in ways that underestimate the risks and costs of waiting. Natural processes do not work in only one direction; they can move toward ripening but also toward "rotting." The crops can be left in the fields too long, as well as harvested too early; intervention may come too early, but a conflict also can deteriorate over time, grow worse, become too far advanced.

Putting severely shattered societies back together again is enormously difficult, hugely expensive, very risky—and, very possibly, just not possible. It is a problem, to draw again on Bill Zartman's expressive language, of "putting Humpty-Dumpty together again."[50] We have seen this situation in Somalia, where almost twenty years after the UN and U.S. interventions, governments keep falling; in Haiti where extreme poverty and political instability persist; in Bosnia, where almost fifteen years after the 1995 Dayton Accords ended the war, ethnic tensions still ran high and stability was shaky; and in the Democratic Republic of Congo (DRC), where death tolls mounted even higher than in Rwanda as a consequence of both its own conflicts and the spillover from Rwanda.

Even providing the basic relief of humanitarian aid to war-torn societies can be difficult and dangerous. The Rwandan case illustrates how food distribution and other humanitarian assistance risk becoming politicized, feeding the conflict rather than the people. Relief agencies allowed the exiled Hutu government to reconstitute itself in the camps, thinking that it would help with food distribution and maintenance of order. Instead, though, the militants made their own people their hostages and used their control of food and other relief supplies as weapons in the continuing struggle. Another glaring case was the murder of six International Red Cross workers in Chechnya while they slept in their beds in a hospital—the worst atrocity against the Red Cross in its more than 130-year history. In March 1998, the Red Cross withdrew its workers from Kosovo because of death threats. Overall, an estimated several hundred relief workers are killed worldwide every year.

And these wars have been economically devastating as well. At the time of the signing of the Dayton accord, industrial output in Bosnia and Herzegovina was only 5 percent of its 1990 level. The former World Bank chairman James D. Wolfensohn summarized the situation: "A quarter of a million men, women and children killed; another 200,000 wounded; a third of all health facilities damaged . . . [as well as] half of all educational facilities and two-thirds of all housing . . . 9 out of 10 people dependent on humanitarian assistance."[51]

## When Should Military Force Be Used?

Early preventive action is hard enough for diplomatic strategies; it poses even tougher issues for the use of military force. Noninterventionism had largely served the post–World War II international system well. The constraints on the major powers had helped maintain order and security. The protection for small countries and newly independent states emerging from colonialism had buttressed (albeit not guaranteed) self-determination, freedom, and justice. Force was to be a last resort and a highly restricted one at that. But Bosnia, Rwanda, and related conflicts exposed deep and disturbing contradictions between the limits of the traditional noninterventionist regime and the very norms and values of peace, justice, and humanitarianism on which the UN system claimed to rest.

Take Rwanda. The 1994 genocide in Rwanda, in which mass murders were carried out while the United States and the rest of the international community did very little, was "a failure of international will—of civic courage—at the highest level."[52] Professor Michael Barnett, who then was working at the U.S. Mission to the United Nations, pulls no punches in his account:

> In one hundred days, between April 6 and July 19, 1994, [Hutu extremists] murdered roughly eight hundred thousand individuals [Tutsis, who were the rival ethnic group, and Hutu moderates]. . . . And unlike the Nazis, who used modern industrial technology to accomplish the most primitive of ends, the perpetrators of the Rwandan genocide employed primarily low-tech and physically demanding instruments of death that required an intimacy with their victims. The genocide was executed with a brutality and sadism that defy imagination. Eyewitnesses were in denial. They believed that the high-pitched screams they were hearing were wind gusts, that the packs of dogs at the roadside were feeding on animal remains and not dismembered corpses, that the smells enveloping them emanated from spoiled food and not decomposing bodies.[53]

Yet despite knowing the horrors that were unfolding, neither the United States nor the United Nations nor any other country or international institution took any significant action.

A strong argument can be made that a more credible and robust, and earlier military strategy could have prevented the Rwandan conflict from reaching a genocidal scale. This argument has three distinct components. First is the failure to deter the Hutu extremists effectively because of the weaknesses of the United Nations Mission in Rwanda

(UNAMIR). Astri Suhrke and Bruce Jones see the formation and deployment of UNAMIR as a "critical juncture" that was not taken advantage of. Instead, because of its small size, inadequate equipment, narrow mission, and highly circumscribed mandate, UNAMIR became counterproductive. This not only left it in a very poor position to do anything once the genocide was unleashed on April 6, but also made it a very weak deterrent against the planning in the preceding months. "A more decisive and robust demonstration of international force at that time [UNAMIR's initial formation]," Suhrke and Jones contend, "might have restrained the extremist forces directly, and at any rate sent signals to the effect that the international community was fully behind the peace accords."[54]

Second is the failure to act on the warning that UNAMIR picked up in January 1994 from a Hutu informant about the mass killings being planned and the arms being stockpiled by Hutu extremists. Not only was the information borne out by later events, but the level of detail and other aspects of the information made it highly credible at the time. The UNAMIR commander, General Romeo Dallaire, passed it back to UN headquarters in a coded cable including his plan to raid the arms caches and break up the genocide planning. He was not asking for additional troops. He was not even asking for permission. He saw this action as consistent with the existing UNAMIR peacekeeping mandate, and was doing what he thought was responsible in informing UN headquarters. UN headquarters turned him down. General Dallaire repeated his requests the next month but again was turned down.

This was a crucial moment for possibly preventing the Rwandan genocide. "At the Source" (p. 498) provides General Dallaire's account. It is important testimony on what was proposed in real time and what could have been done. Although we cannot be certain that these actions would have prevented the Rwandan genocide, that's true of any "what if"—and the case General Dallaire makes is a credible one.

Then there was the response to the April 1994 crisis. Again General Dallaire sent requests for strengthening UNAMIR, but again they were rebuffed, with the blame shared by key UN officials and the United States and other Security Council members.[55] A study by the Carnegie Commission sets the last week of April as the closing of the window of opportunity for an emergency intervention short of massive force. By that time mass violence had spread to the countryside.[56] Yet one of the reasons that the Hutu "crisis committee" decided to expand the massacre to the countryside was "the failure of the international community to respond forcefully to the initial killings in Kigali and other regions." Choices and calculations were being made. Violence was not spreading just by its own momentum. The evidence of divisions within the Hutu military as cited by Suhrke and Jones suggests that "a more determined international response against the extremists would have found allies within."[57]

The Clinton administration had a large part in this pattern of inaction. Although others, including the UN and major European nations, also bore responsibility, had the

## AT THE SOURCE

AT THE SOURCE

### "SAVE US FROM CATASTROPHE"

General Romeo Dallaire,
Force Commander, United Nations Assistance Mission in Rwanda (UNAMIR)

Late in the afternoon of January 10, Faustin [a Rwandan government official] came to my office and insisted on a private meeting. He was shaking with excitement and fear. I took him out onto the balcony where we could talk without being overheard. Almost breathlessly, he told me that he was in contact with someone inside the Interahamwe [a Hutu paramilitary organization] who had information he wanted to pass on to UNAMIR. I had a moment of wild exhilaration as I realized we might finally have a window on the mysterious third force, the shadowy collection of extremists that had been growing in strength ever since I had arrived in Rwanda. . . .

He [Jean-Pierre, the code name for the informer] and others like him were ordered to have the cells under their command make lists of the Tutsis in their various communes. Jean-Pierre suspected that these lists were being made so that, when the time came, the Tutsis, or the *Inyenzi* as Rwandan hate radio called them—the word means "cockroaches" in Kinyarwanda—could easily be rounded up and exterminated. Jean-Pierre said he hated the RPF [the Tutsi Rwandan Patriotic Front] and saw them as the enemy of Rwanda, but he was horrified that he had been drawn into a plan to create a series of highly efficient death squads that, when turned loose on the population, could kill a thousand Tutsis in Kigali within twenty minutes of receiving the order. He described in detail how the Interahamwe were being trained at army bases and by army instructors in several locations around the country, and that on a weekly basis a number of young men would be collected and transported for a three-week weapons and paramilitary training course that placed special emphasis on killing techniques. Then the young men were returned to their communes and ordered to make lists of Tutsis and await the call to arms.

I was silent, hit by the depth and reality of this information. It was as if the informant, Jean-Pierre, had opened the floodgates on the hidden world of the extremist third force, which until this point had been a presence we could sense but couldn't grasp.

Luc [a UN peacekeeping force officer] told us that until now the only weapons the Interahamwe possessed were traditional spears, clubs and machetes, but Jean-Pierre had claimed that the army had recently transferred four large shipments of AK-47s, ammunition and grenades to the militia. These weapons were stored in four separate arms caches in Kigali. He offered to show us one of the caches to confirm the information he was giving us. . . .

Jean-Pierre warned that the leadership was about to make a decision to distribute the arms caches to every Interahamwe cell in Kigali. If that happened, he said, there would be no way to stop the slaughter.

I made the decision to go after the weapons caches. I had to catch these guys off guard, send them a signal that I knew who they were and what they were up to, and that I fully intended to shut them down. . . .

After Luc left, I decided to inform the SRSG [Special Representative of the UN Secretary-General] first thing in the morning. . . .

I needed New York [UN headquarters] to realize that, even though I wanted to move quickly, I was not blind to the possibility that this could be a well-laid trap to force UNAMIR onto the offensive and jeopardize our role as keepers of a fragile peace. I also wanted to make it clear in the cable that I was not asking permission to raid the caches but was informing New York of my intentions, as was my responsibility as force commander. I was finally going to be able to wrest the initiative from the hard-liners. . . .

When I woke up the next morning after a few fitful hours of sleep, I was convinced that we were on the verge of regaining the initiative or at least of throwing the extremists off-balance, making them vulnerable to defections, to panic, to making foolish mistakes. Little did I realize as I waved to the local kids on the side of the dirt road on my way to work, that New York was already shooting my plan of action out of the water. . . .

Something had to be done to save us from catastrophe. For the rest of the week, I made phone call after phone call to New York, arguing over the necessity of raiding the arms caches. During these exchanges, I got the feeling that New York now saw me as a loose cannon and not as an aggressive but careful force commander.

* * *

My failure to persuade New York to act on Jean-Pierre's information still haunts me. . . . I was presenting a reasonable, carefully laid-out plan that was consistent with the approach I had adopted from the very beginning: to maximize our rules of engagement in order to ensure the atmosphere of security demanded by the peace agreement. . . . In my view the inside information offered us by Jean-Pierre represented a real chance to pull Rwanda out of the fire. The DPKO's [UN Department of Peacekeeping Operations] response whipped the ground out from under me. . . .

The genocide in Rwanda was a failure of humanity that could easily happen again.

Source: General Romeo Dallaire, *Shake Hands with the Devil: The Failure of Humanity in Rwanda* (New York: Carroll and Graf, 2003), 141–147, xxv.

United States spoken out and pushed for action it is likely that the UN would have acted or that, as in other cases, a coalition of nations could have been put together. But the Rwanda crisis came just months after the October 1993 debacle in Somalia, and the Clinton administration balked at confronting potential domestic political opposition. It expressed its empathy, but largely contended that the U.S. national interest was not sufficiently at stake. Indeed, people working in the State Department at the time recall being told to be sure not to use the word *genocide* because doing so could invoke obligations under the international genocide treaty to take action, and the Clinton administration did not want to get significantly involved.

In addition to failures such as Rwanda that could have been successes, other cases very possibly could have become deadly conflicts, but preventive statecraft worked. The former Yugoslav republic of Macedonia, which had its own quite significant ethnic tensions and vulnerabilities in the wake of the breakup of Yugoslavia but did not fall into mass violence, is a good example.[58] The Macedonia case had two phases. The first was in 1993–95, in which analysts credit the maintenance of peace to the fact that an international presence was established on the ground early. The Conference on Security and Cooperation in Europe (CSCE) sent an observer mission headed by a skilled American diplomat and with a broadly defined mandate. A number of nongovernmental organizations also established themselves in Macedonia, both providing an early-warning system and helping establish conflict-resolution mechanisms and other multiethnic programs. Most significant was the actual deployment of a multinational military force before significant violence had been unleashed. This force included U.S. troops, which, despite their small number and their confinement to low-risk duties, "carry weight," as Macedonian president Kiro Gligorov stressed. "It is a signal to all those who want to destabilize this region."[59] The second phase in Macedonia came in 2001, when ethnic violence had begun to break out, but a NATO force was deployed, and U.S. and European diplomacy worked to prevent escalation.

With cases such as these very much in mind, the 2001 ICISS Report cautiously but significantly acknowledged that from a humanitarian perspective military force may need to be something other than an absolute last resort. As passages in Reading 9.1 show, the ICISS Report defined "last resort" to include military force "as an *anticipatory* measure in response to clear evidence of likely large scale killing." Every other option did not have to be tried first, but "there must be *reasonable grounds for believing that, in all the circumstances, if the measure had been attempted it would not have succeeded.*"[60] Though couched in diplomatic language, the thrust was that force should not be a first resort, but its threat or use did need to be possibly an early and not just a last resort.

This is the humanitarian-intervention version of the debate over preemptive use of force. Indeed, this debate already was going on before the Bush Doctrine and the Iraq case drew so much attention. Liberal internationalists made the "force as an early resort" argument. For example, Stanley Hoffmann wrote that "there are situations in which a quick, early use of force may well be the best method, and the only one capable of preventing a further aggravation of the [humanitarian] crisis."[61] In a study written in 2000 for the U.S. Institute of Peace, I argued strongly for "coercive prevention" to act early and prevent mass killings, not just respond to them, as both more realist and more humanitarian.[62]

One of the lessons of cases such as Bosnia and Rwanda was that it was extremely unrealistic to believe that vicious demagogues such as Milosevic in the former Yugoslavia and the Hutu extremists in Rwanda will agree to peaceful methods of conflict resolution if they think they can achieve their goals by force at costs they deem acceptable. Each situation will have to be analyzed to assess whether and how preventive military action or the threat thereof is likely to deter and not exacerbate oppression, but "preserving force as a last resort implies a lockstep sequencing of the means to achieve foreign policy objectives that is unduly inflexible and relegates the use of force to *in extremis* efforts to salvage a faltering foreign policy."[63] The message "I'll do this only if I absolutely have to" does not convey much credibility. It also cedes the initiative to the aggressor, who knows that time is available before noncompliance may have major consequences.

In the Bosnia case, credit is due to the U.S.-led NATO peacekeeping mission begun in late 1995. About one-third of the sixty thousand NATO troops first sent to enforce the Dayton accord were American. And for all the killing that took place between 1991 and 1995, there has been very little in Bosnia since. Still, it seemed that the United States acted only when forced to do so, when most if not all other options had been exhausted, and only when the aggressor's defiance and disregard for the West had reached the brazen extremes that the Serbs' did. If it was then and only then that the United States would commit its military forces, this was not a very credibility-enhancing example in the long run.

In Kosovo, the United States and NATO acted sooner than they had in Bosnia, but still not soon or effectively enough to prevent massive killings and other violence. The threat of air strikes was made only in late 1998, many months after the first wave of Serbian aggression against the Kosovar Albanians and despite numerous warnings and calls for earlier preventive action. When the air campaign was launched in March 1999, despite the massive tonnage dropped, the many sorties flown, and the number of physical targets hit, it was too little and too late to stop much of the ethnic "cleansing" of Kosovo.

Ideally, force will not have to be used. Concerns remain about force being used too often and too early. Diplomatic strategies are generally preferable. But sometimes they are more effective if combined with, rather than preceding, threats and the use of force. Moreover, if the threshold for intervention is that the bodies have started to pile up, intervention is hardly humanitarian—perhaps less inhumanitarian than not acting at all, but that's not exactly a high standard or one very consistent with American Principles.

## Who Decides on Military Intervention?

In a later section, we discuss this question as an issue within American domestic politics. Here the focus is on the international sphere. Who in the international community should be able to decide to use military force for humanitarian interventions? Can the United States and other major countries make this decision on their own or through alliances such as NATO? Or must it be a decision of the UN Security Council (UNSC)?

The Kosovo case came to a head when Chinese and Russian opposition prevented UNSC action and the United States and NATO decided on their own to intervene. Secretary-General Kofi Annan criticized the U.S.-NATO action on the grounds that the UNSC is "the sole source of legitimacy on the use of force." Yet he also acknowledged the failure of the Security Council to act as it should have in this crisis, noting that it did not "unite around the aim of confronting massive human rights violations and crimes against humanity on the scale of Kosovo," thereby "betray[ing] the very ideals that inspired the founding of the United Nations."[64] For all the invocations of Serbian sovereignty and claims of principle that Russia and China made as reasons for opposing intervention in Kosovo, their positions were based more on their concerns about precedents with Chechnya, Russia's rebellious Muslim area, and Taiwan and Tibet for China.[65] Kosovo also led to an unusual distinction when an independent international commission called the U.S.-NATO intervention illegal in the sense of not having followed the letter of the UN Charter but legitimate in being consistent with the norms and principles that the charter embodies.[66]

The ICISS report answered the "who decides" question with a strong but not unqualified answer of "the UN." It conveyed the sense that any answer other than a UN-centric one has problems of political viability. Military interventions outside UN auspices "do not—it would be an understatement to say—find wide favour. . . . As a matter of political reality, it would be impossible to find consensus, in the Commission's view, around any set of proposals for military intervention which acknowledge the validity of any intervention not authorized by the Security Council or General Assembly." But the report then continued, with its own ambivalence: "But that may still leave circumstances when the Security Council fails to discharge what this Commission would regard as its responsibility to protect, in a conscience-shocking situation crying out for action. It is a real question in these circumstances where lies the most harm: in the damage to international order if the Security Council is bypassed or in the damage to that order if human beings are slaughtered while the Security Council stands by."[67]

And here is where the commission delivered its tough-love message to the UNSC. The first part of this message is that if the UNSC doesn't act, others will. One cannot expect otherwise "in conscience-shocking situations crying out for action." One shouldn't, in the name of the responsibility to protect. Such interventions may end up not being done for the right reasons or in the right ways, but the fault will not be only with the interveners, but also with the UNSC for not acting. Second, if the intervention actually is carried out in a normatively appropriate manner and also is successful, "this may have enduringly serious consequences for the stature and credibility of the UN itself."

The Fall 2005 UN World Summit, though, stuck more strictly to the UNSC as the exclusive, not just the preferred, decision maker. As stated in the report of the Secretary-General's High-Level Panel (HLP) on Threats, Challenges and Change, "the task is not to find alternatives to the Security Council as a source of authority but to make the Council work better than it has."[68] Others were not willing to be this exclusive and continued to argue for the potential legitimacy of the United States' and NATO's deciding to intervene as they did in Kosovo. Although no other body or international actor can claim comparable legitimacy for establishing global norms and for authorizing action in their name, by its very nature the United Nations also is often constrained from acting in ways that best serve those norms. Therefore the UN Security Council is to be the preferred but not the exclusive source of legitimate authority. Similarly, a study conducted by the Fund for Peace of regional views on humanitarian intervention found general agreement on the UN as "the preferred authorizing body," but also of "the UN's limits in both addressing conflicts before they become emergencies and coming to the rescue once a humanitarian crisis is clear." The balance proposed was that regional and subregional organizations should "be seen as having legitimacy both to authorize and organize a response with the provision that UN approval be sought, ex post facto if necessary."[69]

## How to End Conflicts and Build Peace?

This has been an issue for both diplomatic and military strategies, not only for the United States but also for the UN and for others in the international community taking lead roles. Bosnia and Kosovo are useful cases for examining U.S. strategy in the 1990s. We then look at two key aspects of the UNs' role, UN peacekeeping and the International Criminal Court.

### *Bosnia*

Even before the Bosnia war started in 1992, the breakup of Yugoslavia had led to war in Croatia. The Bush policy was "no dog in that fight," according to Secretary of State James Baker, quoted earlier. These conflicts were largely seen as a European problem, and the Europeans should take the lead along with the UN. During the 1992 presidential campaign, candidate Bill Clinton was harshly critical of the Bush policy and promised to be more assertive by, among other things, lifting the arms embargo against the Bosnian Muslims and launching air strikes against the Bosnian Serbs ("lift and strike"). But once in office, Clinton backed off, showing indecisiveness and succumbing to political concerns about the risks involved.

By mid-1995 the urgency of the situation no longer could be denied. The Bosnian Serbs had become so brash as to take several hundred UN peacekeepers hostage. Congress was threatening to cut off aid to the UN peacekeeping mission. This not only endangered what was left of any semblance of peacekeeping and humanitarian assistance, but also threatened a crisis within NATO, because British and French troops were among the UN forces such abandonment would endanger. Then three top American officials were killed in Bosnia when their jeep hit a land mine. Realizing that it no longer had much of a middle option, that the choices now were give up or get serious, the Clinton administration finally asserted American leadership. NATO air strikes were launched against Bosnian Serbs, and with more firepower than the earlier "pinprick" strikes. Military support was given to the Croatian army for a major offensive against the Serbs. Economic sanctions were ratcheted up. And diplomacy was stepped up, culminating in the peace conference convened in Dayton, Ohio.

The United States had been the principal Western supporter of the Bosnian Muslims, so their leader, Alija Izetbegovic, was more receptive to negotiations led by the United States than by others. So, too, with Croatia, which also had been receiving significant American military aid and assistance. U.S. relations with Serbia and its president, Slobodan Milosevic, had been more conflictual, but Milosevic knew that only Washington could lift the sanctions ravaging the Serbian economy and turn off the NATO air strikes against the Bosnian Serbs. The parties to the conflict knew that they needed to deal with the only country that could deliver.

Skilled peace brokering by President Clinton and his lead diplomat, Richard Holbrooke, helped the negotiations succeed. The warring parties signed the Dayton Accord in November 1995. The agreement ended the war and established terms for a political settlement. NATO was mandated to provide a peacekeeping force, and the Organization on Cooperation and Security in Europe (OSCE, formerly the CSCE) was given principal responsibility for establishing free and fair elections and other political measures.

The original NATO force had about sixty thousand troops, of which about twenty thousand were American. By 2004, the peacekeeping mission was handed over to the European Union, with only a few U.S. troops remaining to hunt war-crimes suspects and help train the Bosnian army. Elections were held on numerous occasions, generally meeting the criteria of free and fair. Still, almost fifteen years later, tensions remained high and stability uncertain. Concerns still were being expressed that Bosnia could lapse into "a severe crisis."[70] Among other things, Bosnia showed that even in a case in which much had been done to build postconflict peace, the toll that war and mass atrocities had taken persisted.

## *Kosovo*

In the 1999 Kosovo war, the United States and NATO were victorious, but with mixed lessons. The Serbian leader Slobodan Milosevic and his forces were defeated and forced to withdraw from Kosovo, but not until ethnic violence against the Albanian minority had taken a heavy toll. One of the points critics raise is that Operation Allied Force could have prevailed more quickly, more overwhelmingly, and with less ethnic killing had the United States been willing to send in ground troops as well as launching air strikes. Concerned that "casualty phobia" would undermine American public support, however, President Clinton had stated from the start that ground troops were "off the table." At a minimum, critics argue, the ground-troops option should have been left open as a threat for ratcheting up the war effort that could have coerced Milosevic into surrendering sooner.

Similarly mixed lessons came from Kosovo as a case of "war by alliance." This was the first time NATO had fought a war. It had trained, prepared, positioned, and formulated strategies for war throughout the Cold War, but had never had to actually fight one. To its credit, NATO did hold together politically and did carry out generally well-coordinated and effectively executed military operations in Kosovo. But this did not happen without political pulling and tugging. As the British scholar Michael Cox put it, "Friends were politically necessary but militarily problematic."[71] Within a general consensus of common interests in defending Kosovo, different NATO members had different particular interests at stake. Yet NATO decision-making rules required unanimity, or at least no dissenting votes. (Some states might choose to abstain.) Some in the United States saw the internal NATO politics as bothersome and cumbersome, getting in the way of military planning. So the dominant lesson of Kosovo was that although NATO did succeed in its first war, that success did have its qualifiers.

Some saw a "Clinton Doctrine" emerging from the Kosovo war when in a June 1999 speech the president asserted that "if somebody comes after innocent civilians and tries to kill them, en masse, because of their race, ethnic background, or religion, and it's within our power to stop it, we will stop it."[72] But this wasn't really tested during the remainder of Clinton's term. Major studies were initiated, such as the interagency one on Managing Complex Contingency Operations (PDD [Presidential Decision Directive] 56), seeking to coordinate more effectively the range of actors involved (civilian, military, NGO). But these principally concerned after-the-fact interventions and postconflict reconstruction, and did not take on the tougher issues of prevention and deterrence.

In Kosovo itself, as in Bosnia, the peacekeeping force set up at the end of the war was NATO led with a UN mandate. Elections were held and other peace-building measures taken. But there were some substantial outbreaks of violence, as in March 2004, when unfounded reports that Serbs had drowned Albanian children set off riots that killed nineteen and injured nine hundred. UN-authorized peace negotiations led by Martti Ahtisaari, the

UNIVERSITY OF WINCHESTER
LIBRARY

former prime minister of Finland, led to independence for Kosovo in February 2008.* The United States and most member states of the European Union were supportive, as were over fifty countries that granted Kosovo diplomatic recognition. Serbia, as well as Russia and some others, was opposed. The situation remained sufficiently tense that the UN peacekeeping force and the EU political delegation stayed in Kosovo. Here, too, the peace has remained tenuous.

## *UN Peace Operations*

As for the United Nations, it has a long history of peacekeeping and humanitarian intervention that reaches back to 1948 and includes cases in the Middle East, India and Pakistan, the Congo, Cyprus, the 1980s Iran-Iraq War, and the 1988–90 Soviet withdrawal from Afghanistan. Amid the controversies over more recent cases such as Somalia and Bosnia, the UN's peacekeeping successes are often forgotten. Indeed, the record was so strong that the UN Peacekeeping Forces received the 1988 Nobel Peace Prize. Whereas the UN had undertaken only thirteen peacekeeping missions prior to 1988, since then more than forty-five new missions had been initiated. The number of UN peacekeeping troops shot up from 9,570 in 1988 to 73,393 in 1994. These numbers dropped for a few years as some peacekeeping missions were brought to a close. But they have again been climbing, to over 90,000 peacekeepers in fifteen missions in 2009. Similarly, UN peacekeeping budgets, as low as $230 million in the late 1980s, were close to $8 billion twenty years later. These huge and simultaneous increases of operations made for an enormous agenda, especially for an institution with so little of the military infrastructure of command and control, communications, intelligence, training, and logistics. Furthermore, the structure of decision-making authority often proved too slow and indecisive either to carry out complex and speedy military operations or to convey credibility to an aggressor.

Additionally, all of these ***peace operations*** involved soldiers assembled on a temporary basis from the national armies of UN member countries. The original idea that the UN would have its own standing army of troops and officers assigned to it on an ongoing basis was never realized, as we discussed in Chapter 4. Each time there is need for a UN peace operation, it is necessary to assemble a new force. This adds to the problems of timely response, unit cohesiveness, and effective training. "International Perspectives" (p. 507), lists some of the countries these forces come from.

The more fundamental problem has been the difference in missions between ***peacekeeping*** and ***peace enforcing.*** Most of the "first-generation" UN successes had been peacekeeping missions. In these situations the UN forces are brought in after the parties have agreed to the terms of peace, and with the consent of those parties, to ensure

*Ahtisaari won the 2008 Nobel Peace Prize for his role in Kosovo as well as for other diplomacy.

## INTERNATIONAL PERSPECTIVES

INTERNATIONAL PERSPECTIVES

### WHO PROVIDES TROOPS FOR UN PEACE OPERATIONS?

With all those peacekeeping and related missions around the world, who is it that is providing the troops? Contrary to what many believe, the United States ranks sixty-seventh in the number of military troops and police provided for UN peacekeeping missions. Of the 91,382 military troops and police deployed in the sixteen UN peace operations (as of January 2009), only 90 were American. The top 10 countries:

| | |
|---|---|
| Pakistan | 10,989 |
| Bangladesh | 9,424 |
| India | 8,640 |
| Nigeria | 6,001 |
| Nepal | 3,924 |
| Rwanda | 3,635 |
| Ghana | 3,283 |
| Jordan | 3,109 |
| Italy | 2,565 |
| Uruguay | 2,538 |

A total of 120 countries contribute forces to UN peace operations.

Sources: United Nations, Peacekeeping, List of Operations, www.un.org/Depts/dpko/list/list.pdf (accessed 7/24/09); Ranking of Military and Police Contributions to UN Operations, www.un.org/Depts/dpko/dpko/contributors/2009/jan09_2.pdf (accessed 7/24/09).

and facilitate the keeping of that peace. The peacekeepers' rules of engagement are neutral and impartial: to use force only for their own self-defense, and not to interfere in the internal affairs of the parties.

The UN had some further successes in the late 1980s and early 1990s in Namibia, Mozambique, El Salvador, and Cambodia in "second-generation peacekeeping," intrastate cases that involved elections and other aspects of nation building. Cases such as Bosnia, though, were much more about peace*making* and peace *enforcing* in that the conflicts were still raging or at best under tenuous cease-fires, conditions in which traditional stratagems of impartiality and limited mission were not sufficient. *There was no peace to be kept; it had to be imposed and enforced.* To the extent that the parties had reached any agreements, they were but partial ones—holding actions, gambits, even outright deceptions. In such situations the UN's limited rules of engagement do not work very well; neutrality and impartiality can let aggressors off the hook. Even a Nobel laureate's method will not succeed when applied to purposes as fundamentally different as peacekeeping, peacemaking, and peace enforcing. By late 1995 even UN Secretary-General Boutros Boutros-Ghali was acknowledging that "[peace] enforcement is beyond the power of the UN. . . . In the future, if peace enforcement is needed it should be conducted by countries with the will to do it."[73] Along these lines, one recent study of major 1990s cases showed that "interventions that directly challenge the perpetrator or aid the target of the brutal policy are the only effective type of military responses, increasing the probability that the magnitude of the slaughter can be slowed or stopped."[74]

Even given these problems, the UN has been more successful than it is often given credit for. A study by the RAND Corporation, a think tank with close links to the Pentagon, shows that the UN was more effective in some respects than the United States.[75] Other studies qualify this finding. The UN's capacity varies according to the scope of the mission. Peacekeeping is more doable than peace enforcement. As one study put it, "the UN is both structurally ill equipped and unlikely to ever obtain the requisite political support to undertake—that is, to plan, mount, direct and sustain—enforcement operations."[76] Another factor is the actual peacekeeping strategy. Are the forces well trained and properly equipped? One study found that 24 percent of military, 33 percent of police, and 81 percent of civilians deployed in UN forces did not receive premission training.

Lately, concern also has been mounting about overextension in the sheer number of missions on the UN docket, with the lessons of the early 1990s overload in numbers as well as types of missions in mind.[77] Along with some long-standing missions that still are ongoing, two new missions were undertaken in 2004 (Côte d'Ivoire, Haiti), one in 2005 (Sudan), another in 2006 (Timor-Leste), and three more in 2007 in Darfur and neighboring Chad and the Central African Republic.

INTERNATIONAL CRIMINAL COURT (ICC) Following World War II, special international war-crimes tribunals were created to prosecute the Nazis (the Nuremberg trials) and Japanese military leaders. At various times since then, the UN General Assembly has considered creating a permanent international criminal court, but no such action has been taken. Nuremberg-like temporary war-crimes tribunals were set up in the 1990s to deal with atrocities committed during civil wars and ethnic conflicts in the former Yugoslavia and in Rwanda. In their wake, proposals to create a permanent ***International Criminal Court (ICC)*** gained increasing support.

The ICC was approved at a UN conference held in Rome in mid-1998. Very few countries voted against it, but the United States was one of them. Originally the Clinton administration had supported the idea of an ICC, in large part because a permanent international court would potentially enhance U.S. foreign policy in cases against aggressors, gross violators of human rights, and rogue states. It backed off, though, in part for substantive reasons but mostly for political ones. The ICC struck the chords of antimultilateralism and leeriness about international law in American politics. The treaty would have to be ratified by the U.S. Senate, and the anticipated vote count came up well short of the two-thirds majority needed. In December 2000, just before leaving office, Clinton finally did sign the Rome Treaty, albeit far too late for him to begin a ratification process in the Senate.

The George W. Bush administration was clear, quick, and blunt in its opposition to the ICC. Soon after taking office it announced that it was holding the treaty back and not sending it to the Senate. Then in May 2002 it officially rescinded the U.S. signature. The timing was deliberate: the previous month, the sixtieth country in the world had ratified the ICC treaty, the number necessary for the treaty to enter into force.

ICC proponents make three main arguments. First is that the ICC is the "missing link" in the international justice system that will help achieve "justice for all," and especially deal with perpetrators of genocide, war crimes, and other crimes against humanity. The existing International Court of Justice in The Hague deals only with cases between states, not individuals. The ad hoc tribunals have had some impact but are subject to delays, uncertainties, and other deficiencies. The ICC also claims jurisdiction when national criminal-justice institutions are unwilling or unable to act. "In the prospect of an international criminal court," stated then Secretary-General Annan, "lies the promise of universal justice."[78] It was the ICC that was conducting the trial of the former Serbian leader Slobodan Milosevic for his war crimes in Bosnia and Kosovo, until Milosevic died in 2006 while the trial was in progress.

Second, the ICC can help strengthen peace processes and promote conflict resolution. Negotiators have at their disposal an array of policy instruments and incentives and disincentives in seeking cease-fires and peace settlements for conflicts that already are raging. Their hand will be strengthened if they can provide assurances for all sides that once they have laid down their arms, justice will be even handed. This means both prosecuting those whose actions warrant it and protecting the innocent from vengeful and other politically charged prosecutions. Ideally, states should be able to create their own process of justice. In war-torn situations, though, that ideal often is not achievable, at least in the near term. As an international body the ICC has the standing and credibility to provide the necessary assurances and thus help move peace processes along.

Third, the existence of the ICC will deter future war criminals and other aggressors. To quote the UN: "Most perpetrators of such atrocities have believed that their crimes would go unpunished. . . . Once it is clear that the international community will no longer tolerate such monstrous acts without assigning responsibility and meting out appropriate punishment—to heads of State and commanding officers as well as to the lowliest soldiers in the field or militia recruits—it is hoped that those who would incite a genocide; embark on a campaign of ethnic cleansing; murder, rape and brutalize civilians caught in armed conflict; or use children for barbarous medical experiments will no longer find willing helpers. . . . Effective deterrence is a primary objective of the International Criminal Court."[79]

Opponents make their own three main points. The first rejects the ICC's claim to jurisdiction over Americans on U.S. constitutional grounds. They argue that the U.S. Constitution prohibits the U.S. government from consenting to judicial proceedings against American citizens by any courts other than American ones. As stated by John Negroponte, then the Bush administration's ambassador to the United Nations, "An American judge [has] the legal and moral right, founded in our Constitution and in democratic procedures, to jail an American. But the International Criminal Court does not operate in the same democratic and constitutional context, and therefore does not have that right to deprive Americans of their freedom."[80]

Second is the concern that U.S. soldiers and diplomats, NGO workers, and others would be subjected to politically motivated charges and prosecutions. "We're the ones who respond when the world dials 911," another opponent stated, "and if you want us to keep responding you should accommodate our views."[81] The Bush administration pushed legislation through Congress linking American military aid to recipient countries that agreed to sign an exemption from ICC jurisdiction for American soldiers. Many countries resisted signing such agreements as a matter of principle, even at the risk of losing their military aid. Yet the issue remained a fundamental one for ICC opponents.

Third, some question the claim to deterrence for the ICC. When so many perpetrators of ethnic cleansing and genocide are never charged, and when the prosecution of others takes so long, how strong a deterrent effect can the ICC have? To deter those who would commit war crimes, the potential consequences of such actions have to be severe and probable. In the eyes of opponents, the ad hoc tribunals have not measured up, and the ICC is not likely to, either. They cite the Milosevic trial, questioning whether he ever would have been convicted if he had not died.

Debate about the ICC went from the general to the specific when in March 2009 the ICC indicted the Sudanese president, Omar Hassan al-Bashir, for crimes against humanity in Darfur. Darfur has been the most important case on which the genocide prevention debate has focused in recent years. It is to this case that we now turn.

## Darfur: "Yet Again"

As many as 400,000 dead. Around 4 million in internal refugee camps and across the border in Chad. Countless villages burned or otherwise devastated. Like so many other cases, although not fully preventable, Darfur was containable well short of the tragic dimensions it reached.

Darfur is a region in the western part of the country of Sudan. It is large, about the size of France. Historically there have been tensions with the central government. There also are ethnic differences. Much of Darfur's population is Muslim but is ethnically distinct from the dominant Arab population. These tensions were exacerbated by the devastating 1980s drought, which left the various tribal and religious groups competing for shrinking resources of water, grassland, and arable soil. But what turned this economic-ecological limited conflict into mass killings were the "Arabization" policies of the Khartoum government. These policies intensified and radicalized parts of the antigovernment insurgency in Darfur, which did pose a threat. Mostly, though, the insurgency provided an excuse for the Sudanese government to team up with Arab tribesmen. The tribesmen were dubbed ***Janjaweed*** from an old epithet of "devils on horseback." Documents captured by the African Union peacekeeping force showed the direct complicity of the Sudanese government. As reported by the *New York Times* columnist Nicholas Kristof, one document directed to regional commanders and security officials calls for the "'execution of all directives from the president of the republic. . . . Change the demography of Darfur and make it void of African tribes . . . [by] killing, burning villages and farms, terrorizing people, confiscating property from members of African tribes and forcing them from Darfur.'"[82]

Although some details surfaced only over time, the first warning went back to early 2003, when Darfur refugees escaping to Chad reported the scorched-earth attacks of the Sudanese army and the Janjaweed.[83] By December 2003, close to 100,000 refugees were in Chad. When UN agencies, NGOs, and journalists finally were able to get into Darfur in early 2004, the scope and scale of the conflict were very heavily reported.[84] After seeing for themselves, both Secretary-General Annan and Secretary of State Colin Powell used the term *genocide.* So did President Bush in his own statement and the U.S. Congress in a condemnatory resolution. But the Janjaweed militias continued to kill, rape, and destroy with the Sudanese government's support and complicity.

The international community did little, and what it did do was too weak to be effective. An opportunity came when Chad led negotiations in 2003 to apply pressure on Khartoum. But attention was concentrated almost entirely on humanitarian relief and not the underlying political issues fueling the crisis.[85] The UN Security Council did pass a number of resolutions, but they were weak and their deadlines were not enforced. UNSC 1547 (June 11, 2004) focused mostly on southern Sudan, with only brief mention of Darfur. UNSC 1556 (July 30) was tough in its rhetoric, giving Khartoum thirty days to disarm the Janjaweed and invoking a Chapter VII mandate to intervene, based on threats to international peace and security. But the resolution was more words than action. The UN was more than happy to delegate, encouraging the African Union, which was pushing for an "African solution to an African problem," to take the lead on a peacekeeping force. The Security Council authorized the African Union Mission in Sudan (AMIS), but with too limited a mandate to be effective. Nor did the UNSC invoke economic sanctions, saying only that it would "consider further actions." When the thirty-day deadline was not met, the UN Special Envoy signed on to a "plan of action" with Khartoum that lacked solid benchmarks and to some observers looked "more like an escape route than a discipline upon the government."[86]

UNSC 1564 (September 18) established a commission of inquiry but once again did little more than reiterate possible future action. UNSC 1574 (November 19) authorized an increase in the size of AMIS and some extension of its mandate, but again failed to demand specific actions, imposed no deadlines, and made no explicit or specific threats of consequences. UNSC 1591 (March 29, 2005) again deplored and again demanded, but again took limited action, in this instance no more than targeted sanctions such as banning travel by and freezing assets of key perpetrators (once of course a commission that would meet over the ensuing months decided who they were). Yet an International Crisis Group report showed continued Sudanese government financing of the Janjaweed, and a UN High Commissioner for Refugees report documented rape and gang rape being perpetrated by Sudanese armed forces and law-enforcement agencies.[87]

The message to aggressors is in the limits, not the scope, of such actions. They know what they are doing, what conditions they are not complying with, what deadlines they are not meeting. Opponents may claim to be sending a tough or toughening message, but the message as received is devoid of credibility.

Opposition from Russia and China was a principal reason for the limits and weaknesses of UN action. Their positions in part reflected similar strict constructionism regarding sovereignty as over Kosovo and in part their economic interests. Russia actually completed a sale of military aircraft, the same aircraft that were being used to bomb villages in Darfur, "even as Security Council members deliberated over how to address the crisis."[88] For China the issue was Sudanese oil. Sudan was part of China's "global hunt for energy."[89] As of 2004, Sudan was supplying 6 percent of China's oil needs, with projections very much on an upward curve. China also had approximately $3 billion invested in Sudan's oil sector, had been awarded hundreds of millions of dollars in additional contracts for the construction of pipelines and port facilities, and was the principal financer of a $200 million hydroelectric plant.[90] It also has been Sudan's largest arms supplier. To get China even to abstain, the UNSC resolutions had to be watered down.

Even the limited pledges of humanitarian assistance that had been made were going unfulfilled. The UN appeal for $693 million in the first half of 2005 brought in only $358 million. The United States was the largest donor at $252 million, plus another $100 million for relief efforts elsewhere in Sudan. Britain was second at $36 million, plus another $50 million for the rest of Sudan. Japan gave only $7.9 million, Germany $4.2 million, France $1.8 million. Only two fellow Muslim countries even made the list of the top eighteen donors.[91] The Arab League saw fit to hold its March 2006 summit in Khartoum, at which it once again showed more support for, than outrage against, the Sudanese government.[92] Osama bin Laden called for *jihadists* to go to Sudan to fight any effort the West might make to stop this mass killing of Muslims. By this "logic," the *jihadists* would be killing other Muslims—based on other UN peace operations, most of the troops likely will be from Bangladesh, Pakistan, India, and Jordan—who are seeking to protect the Muslim people who've already suffered over 400,000 deaths.[93]

Although the African Union deserves credit for taking on the humanitarian mission, its role has reflected three of the major dilemmas in many humanitarian intervention cases. First is the discrepancy between the nature of the mission and the mandate and resources for achieving it. AMIS started in April 2004 as only a cease-fire monitoring mission, not an enforcement one, and with only 120 monitors spread across a vast territory. It became a troop presence later that year, building up to about 7,700 by October 2005, with a goal of 12,300 by spring 2006. But it wasn't able to build capacity to that level. Moreover, its mandate remained largely one of monitoring and forcing self-protection. The aid, training, and support pledged by the United States, Western Europe, and others materialized slowly and only partially. Sensing this weakness, and calculating that aggression against the existing AMIS forces would deter more than foster expanded deployments, the Sudanese government and Janjaweed forces ambushed AMIS forces on October 8, 2005, killing six. The next day an entire AMIS patrol of eighteen was kidnapped, and then a rescue mission of twenty was also captured.

Second has been the AU's own ambivalence to step up fully to its own charter's commitment to collective intervention. The final communiqué of its October 2004 minisummit reaffirmed support for Sudan's sovereignty, rejecting "any foreign intervention by any country, whatsoever."[94] This tension increased even further when Sudan was scheduled to rotate to the AU presidency in 2006. This move was blocked, but the tacit quid pro quo was an AU resolution that leaned much more toward the traditional conception of sovereignty and its restrictions on intervention than toward responsibility to protect.

Third has been the ways in which deferring to regional initiatives allows the international community to pass the buck. Although regional leadership has many benefits and rationales, it can have a perverse dynamic, making for what Susan Rice, then a Brookings Institution senior fellow who became the U.S. ambassador to the United Nations in the Obama administration, has called "a conspiracy of absolution" in which "the African Union has absolved reluctant Western countries of any responsibility to consider sending their own troops," for which the United States, the UN, and the EU "are "undoubtedly grateful."[95] The regional actor, the AU in this case, ends up being put in a position far beyond its feasible capacity and political will.

Bush administration policy showed some signs of focus and leadership but was uneven at best in its follow-through and substance. The United States did more than its share as a donor. The "g-word" was invoked, although with the caveat of a restrictive interpretation of the 1948 Genocide Convention that did not require concerted action.[96] Then secretary of State Condoleezza Rice made a dramatic visit in July 2005, making it a point to meet with rape victims. Back home, though, the administration was slow to break the congressional deadlock over the Darfur Peace and Accountability Act. The bill that finally passed included some tough measures such as targeted economic sanctions and training for AMIS, but was watered down from what had been originally proposed.

The problem has not been a shortage of ideas and alternatives. Numerous viable proposals for international action have been put forward at various junctures of the crisis, but time and again little has been done. Even with early warning and a strong rationale for action, the missed-opportunity argument also requires that the commitments entailed be measured and proportional and that the alternatives that were available at the time are not just products of hindsight. Both conditions have been met in the Darfur case. No one has talked about a need for Iraq-size forces or a U.S. presence as in Somalia. Indeed, just from one NGO, the International Crisis Group (ICG), many suggestions have come. In March 2004, ICG made a series of proposals to toughen diplomacy; in August it laid out an "international action plan"; in April, July, and October 2005, it announced updated versions; in March 2006, it proposed a plan for the hand-off of peacekeeping from the African Union to the UN.[97] These and other suggestions were measured, although as each opportunity was missed the next proposal had to be scaled up. In a dynamic we have seen so many other times, the problems grow worse over time and the scope and nature of the options needed become greater.

A peace agreement was reached in early May 2006. Its key provisions included rapid disarmament of the Janjaweed, some military and political integration of the rebel movements, and funds for economic reconstruction and refugee resettlement. Even at the time, the agreement was greeted with a note of caution. With some groups outside the agreement and the will of the parties that did sign still untested, the situation seemed susceptible to the "spoiler" problem as well as other factors that have undermined similar agreements.[98] "Unless the right spirit is there, the right attitude," said the Nigerian president Olusegun Obasanjo, who had been playing a key role in the negotiations, "this document will not be worth the paper it's written on."[99] Indeed, with the ink barely dry, the Sudanese government reinvoked the sovereignty rationale to try to ban UN peacekeepers. Some rebel groups that had not signed the agreement escalated their attacks. By July 2006 Oxfam felt it necessary to close some of its offices because of excessive risks to humanitarian workers. Over the next year, attacks on humanitarian workers rose 150 percent, including one hundred aid workers kidnapped, sixty-six assaulted or raped, and sixty aid convoys ambushed. These attacks were at the hands of both the Sudanese government and its allies as well as rebel groups opposed to the agreement. Rather than being places of refuge, refugee camps were "increasingly violent, with residents manipulated by all sides."[100] Spillover into Chad grew worse. In February 2008, Chadian rebels based in Sudan tried to overthrow Chad's government. Meanwhile, the peacekeeping force finally promised by the UN Security Council was slow to deploy and mounted in a piecemeal fashion, with insufficient troops and other resources. All told, "the conflict has mutated, the parties have splintered, and the confrontations have multiplied."[101]

In July 2008, the International Criminal Court (ICC) got more into the picture. UNSC 1593, passed in 2004, had referred the Darfur case to the ICC chief prosecutor, Luis Moreno-Ocampo. In July 2008, Moreno-Ocampo announced that he would seek an arrest warrant against the Sudanese president, Omar al-Bashir, for crimes against humanity and genocide. In March 2009 the ICC issued the arrest warrant. This was the first time it had taken such action against an incumbent head of state. President Bashir refused to comply, casting the ICC action as akin to colonialism and imperialism in a rallying cry to his people. He also retaliated by kicking out NGOs that had been providing food, medical care, and other humanitarian aid to the Darfuri people.

The international community response was not very firm. The Obama administration protested, but its cry was well less than full throated. China argued that the arrest warrant was making the situation more unstable. President Bashir went to neighboring Eritrea and then to an Arab League summit in Qatar with impunity. On this and other aspects of its Darfur policy, the Obama administration was criticized for not living up to commitments that seemed to be made during the campaign. Initial efforts to engage with the Sudanese government were not applying enough pressure in the view of ENOUGH and other Darfur activist groups. Press reports highlighted splits within the administration during its overall first year policy review over balancing pressures and incentives. When the policy was announced in October 2009, it appeared to strike a balance with firm statements about accountability for the genocide and other atrocities, benchmarks for measuring progress before trade and other incentives would kick in, and support for the referendum on self-determination scheduled for 2011. Questions remained as to whether the administration would stick to these policy parameters and whether they would have sufficient impact to make real progress on the issues. Multilateral support from China and others remained a challenge. So too was making the peace operations force, the United Nations Assistance Mission in Darfur (UNAMID), effective. By late 2009, it still was only partially deployed with about 15,000 of its authorized 20,000 troops and 3,800 of the authorized 6,400 police.

## Foreign Policy Politics Case Study: War Powers, Public Opinion, and Humanitarian Intervention

Three key issues in the U.S. foreign policy politics of ***humanitarian intervention*** have been war powers issues between the president and Congress, the role of the media, and American public opinion.

The politics of war powers in humanitarian intervention cases is both similar to and different from the politics of the two Iraq wars and the Afghanistan war, as discussed in the previous chapter.

SOMALIA Somalia was Bill Clinton's first war-powers issue, and it was a disaster. The original troop commitment had been made by President George H. W. Bush in December 1992, with the mission defined largely as a short-term humanitarian one of relief from starvation (Operation Provide Comfort). The troops were sent by executive action, outside the procedures of the War Powers Resolution (WPR), although with strong bipartisan support. The Clinton administration later would be criticized for keeping the troops in and taking on the broader mission of "nation building." Had it withdrawn the troops according to the original schedule, however, the risk of reversion to chaos was high. In this regard the administration's mistake may not have been taking on the broader mission per se but inattention to the requirements of a more effective strategy and insufficient consultation with Congress to bring it to having some "co-ownership" of the policy.

Once the policy started to go badly, and especially in October 1993 when eighteen American soldiers were killed, and one dead soldier was ignominiously dragged through the streets of the capital city, Mogadishu, a political firestorm erupted on Capitol Hill, on the airwaves, and with the general public. Within hours the president felt he had no choice but to get on television with a hastily prepared speech promising to withdraw the American troops. Whether this was the right decision, and whether the mistake was not having withdrawn the troops sooner or not having made a more concerted effort to accomplish the mission, the picture conveyed to the world was of an American political system still fumbling the war power. The Somalia intervention kicked off an intense political debate over whether U.S. troops should serve under foreign (i.e., non-American) command. The dominant perception in the United States of the Somalia debacle was that it was caused principally by the failures of UN commanders, and American soldiers paid the price with their lives. In fact, the decision to launch the commando operations that resulted in American deaths was made without the knowledge of the UN force commander. The political pressure after U.S. soldiers were killed was so great that the Clinton administration retreated, not only withdrawing U.S. troops from Somalia but also changing its policy on whether U.S. troops would serve under foreign command. Just a few months earlier the administration had been reported to be leaning toward putting American troops under UN commanders "on a regular basis." But in the wake of Somalia it issued a major policy statement that "the United States does not support a standing UN army nor will it earmark specific military units for participation in UN operations."[102]

Although there is plenty to debate on this issue, it is not true that U.S. troops have never served under foreign command. U.S. troops served under foreign command in World Wars I and II, and in some successful Cold War–era UN peacekeeping operations. They currently are doing so in Afghanistan under NATO command. It still can be argued that these were mostly exceptional situations, with vital U.S. interests at stake. But the record at least should be clear.

HAITI The September 1994 Haiti intervention went better, but actually was a close call. Clinton sent the high-level team of former president Jimmy Carter, former senator Sam Nunn, and former chairman of the Joint Chiefs of Staff Colin Powell on a last-minute negotiating mission. Had the Carter-Nunn-Powell mission not succeeded in persuading the Haitian military to step down, and had the invasion brought casualties, the outcry on Capitol Hill likely would have been deafening. Other than the Congressional Black Caucus and some other liberal Democrats who had been pushing for military action, most others in Congress were nonsupportive if not outright opposed to a Haiti intervention. Moreover, the Clinton administration had not bothered to come to Congress, despite the consultation clause of the WPR, not even for a resolution such as the one George H. W. Bush got for the Persian Gulf War.

The usual presidentialist claim of the demands of a crisis situation was not very convincing in this case, given all the advance planning and the fact that the Clinton administration had gone to the UN Security Council almost two months earlier for an "all necessary means" resolution authorizing the intervention. The real reason for not consulting Congress was that the administration was afraid it would lose. In the end, and yet again, the ambiguities of the War Powers Resolution and the reluctance of Congress to act on its own allowed the president to go his own way, with plenty of criticism but few biting procedural constraints.

BOSNIA The politics of the deployment of U.S. troops to Bosnia as part of the NATO force following the Dayton accord largely adhered to the same pattern. The president was not stopped from deploying the troops, but he was not exactly supported in doing so, either. The House did pass a resolution that was at best a mixed message; it stated support for the troops themselves but "disowned the deployment decision."[103] The Senate resolution was more supportive, but it too contained far more caveats, criticisms, and reservations than presidents usually get when putting American troops on the ground. Moreover, to get even this much Clinton had to state that the deployment was only for one year. Yet it was clear from the outset that this was an unrealistic timetable. Indeed, a year later the president announced that, although he would make some cuts in numbers, the American troops needed to stay in Bosnia another year. Another year later came yet another extension; this one was left more open ended. Congress criticized, and passed various measures affecting the deployment at the margins, but didn't stop them.

KOSOVO In the Kosovo case as well there was neither strong and explicit congressional support nor a concerted effort to stop the military action. Support did come from numerous congressional leaders, both political and foreign policy, Republican and Democrat. The Senate approved air strikes before hostilities began, but the House was "as confusing and irresolute as possible about where it stood."[104] It delayed voting on air strikes for over a month after they had begun, and then when it did vote, the result was a tie. Although the resolution was nonbinding, it did have a signaling effect. Signals were further mixed by approval of the president's funding request for the war and rejection of a resolution to end the war. President Clinton said that if the war were to move to a ground campaign, he would come to Congress for its support. We'll never know whether he would have, or what would have happened if he did, since the war ended without ground forces being deployed.

Some House members did try to go the judicial route with a case claiming that the president had violated the War Powers Resolution. But the courts dismissed the case on the nonjusticiability grounds cited in earlier cases (and in Chapter 2). In other words, the issue was not clearly presidential usurpation but also congressional abdication, and that the evidence did not show a "sufficiently genuine impasse between the legislative and executive branches."[105]

The pattern in these cases, and one likely to hold in other instances of humanitarian intervention, is of a Congress more divided and more critical of presidential action than in cases such as the 2001 Afghanistan and 2003 Iraq wars, in which there was a much stronger and more evident argument that America's own security was more directly threatened. Still, though, in all of these humanitarian intervention cases Congress stopped short of blocking presidential action. In Somalia it reacted to the Mogadishu debacle, as it likely would to other instances of apparent failed and flawed strategy. But there has yet to be a case in which Congress has voted down a president determined to make a commitment in the name of humanitarian intervention.

## *The Media and the "CNN Curve"*

Somalia and Bosnia were the two cases that most gave rise to theories of the ***CNN curve.*** On the front end, the klieg-light intensity that is focused on such humanitarian crises is said to raise public awareness of a crisis so much that it brings great pressure on officials, impelling them to precipitate military intervention too quickly and with too little fleshing out of strategy. On the back end, negative coverage of casualties or other major policy disasters can fuel a steep enough drop in public support to make the political pressure too much to bear without a withdrawal or other major shift in policy, even if such a move is premature or unwise as a matter of strategy.

9.3 Although the effect of CNN and other new telecommunications technologies should not be denied, it also should not be exaggerated. The journalist Warren Strobel provided one of the most insightful analyses of this dynamic (Reading 9.3). Strobel argued that the power of the media to influence a policy is inversely related to how well grounded the policy itself is:

> It is true that U.S. government policies and actions regarding international conflict are subject to more open public review than previously in history. But policy-makers retain great power to frame events and solicit public support—indeed, CNN at times increases this power. Put another way, if officials do not have a firm and well-considered policy or have failed to communicate their views in such a way as to garner the support of the American people, the news media will fill this vacuum (often by giving greater time and attention to the criticisms or policy preferences of its opponents).[106]

Strobel's research in Somalia and Bosnia included more than a hundred interviews with senior policy makers from both the first Bush and the Clinton administrations, military officers and spokespersons, journalists, and others. He acknowledges that "CNN and its brethren have made leadership more difficult," and that it is television's inherent nature as a visual medium to "feed on conflict, whether political or physical, emphasizing the challenge to policy." But "when policy is well grounded, it is less likely that the media will be able to shift officials' focus. When policy is clear, reasonably constant, and well communicated, the news media follow officials rather than lead them."[107]

## Public Opinion and Humanitarian Intervention

Public support for humanitarian intervention has been consistent with the "pretty prudent public" framework: lower than in cases where the principal policy objective for the use of military force is foreign policy restraint (the 1990–91 Persian Gulf War, the 2001 Afghanistan war, the initial 2003 invasion of Iraq), and higher than when the principal policy objective is internal political change (Nicaragua in the 1980s, Haiti in 1994, Iraq in the "winning the peace" mode).

In Somalia, for example, which started out as the archetypal "pure" humanitarian intervention case, initial polls showed 70 percent support or higher. However, as perceptions of the mission changed to "nation building"—i.e., internal political change—public support dropped to 47 percent, and then to 35 percent when the American soldiers were killed. This indicated much lower public tolerance for casualties when the objective was remaking governments rather than restraining aggression. Then when, six months later, the Rwandan genocide began, the "Somalia effect" worked against getting involved in a conflict that was strikingly similar and which to many seemed more protracted and dangerous. Bosnia was a particularly complex case, with elements of interstate aggression, intrastate civil war, and humanitarian crisis. The American public both feared a quagmire and felt moral outrage over ethnic "cleansing." For the most part, the polls averaged in the 40–45 percent support range. Consistent with the "pretty prudent public" framework, polling questions that cast the use of force in terms of humanitarian objectives received higher average support (56 percent) than those that linked the use of force to internal political change (34 percent). The humanitarian objective explains why support for the use of ground troops was higher than many expected in the early stages of the Kosovo war. The American public was not eager to send ground forces in, but it was willing to do so given the nature of the principal policy objectives. One poll found 54 percent support that it was "worth risking American soldiers' lives to demonstrate that Serbia should not get away with killing and forcing people from their homes." Another question, specifically about casualties—"If there was a ground war and up to 250 Americans were killed, would the war still be a right decision?"—registered 60 percent support and only 33 percent opposition.[108]

The Darfur issue has been less of a domestic U.S. political problem than often is the case for humanitarian intervention. In Congress a bipartisan coalition was led by then senators Barack Obama (D-Illinois) and Sam Brownback (R-Kansas). The Christian right, which had been very involved in the southern Sudan conflict in defense of the Sudanese Christians, also weighed in on Darfur. "Just because you've signed a peace deal with the South," Franklin Graham (son of Billy) told a White House aide, "doesn't mean you can wash your hands of Darfur."[109] On the left, various NGOs were generating at least a degree of attention and action. Socially entrepreneurial college students started the Genocide Intervention Fund and had raised $250,000 by late 2005.[110] A June 2005 public opinion poll showed strong and broad support for more U.S. leadership and tougher policies, albeit short of sending American ground forces.[111] The Rally to Stop Genocide, held on April 30, 2006, in Washington, D.C., featured a range of speakers rarely found on the same podium, including Richard Land, president of the Southern Baptist Convention; the actor George Clooney; the Holocaust survivor Elie Wiesel; and Paul Rusesabagina, made famous by the movie *Hotel Rwanda.* Although overall media attention was limited, Nicholas Kristof made Darfur a recurring focus, using a creative blend of his newspaper column and Internet resources, for which he received a 2006 Pulitzer Prize.

Recent surveys showed that, despite the toll of the war in Iraq, the American public still had humanitarian concerns. Asked in 2006 whether U.S. troops should intervene against genocide, 71 percent said yes. This was only 4 percent below those who said yes in a 2004 poll, a striking consistency given how badly things had gone in Iraq in the two years between the polls.[112] We noted above how in the Darfur case, both liberal and conservative groups pressured for UN and U.S. intervention. The aggregate percentages in another poll asking specifically about Darfur show significant support: 61 percent said the UN should intervene militarily, 71 percent favored a NATO role, and 54 percent favored the use of U.S. troops.[113]

This pattern held up in another set of polls conducted in 2008. Seventy-one percent favored creating an international marshals service empowered to arrest leaders responsible for genocide. Seventy percent supported instituting a standing UN peacekeeping force. Sixty-nine percent supported U.S. troops' being involved in stopping genocide as a general matter, and sixty-two percent did so when asked specifically about U.S. troops' being part of an international peacekeeping force for Darfur.[114]

## Summary

The end of the Cold War world did not mean the end of war. Whereas much of the Cold War world had been driven by differences in ideology, the post–Cold War world was driven by differences in identity. Following World War II and the Nazi Holocaust, the United States and much of the rest of the world pledged "never again" for genocide and other horrific crimes against humanity. But the "politics of identity" sparked deadly conflicts that were "yet again," not never again. These issues were on the agenda long before September 11, and since then have stayed there, jockeying for foreign policy attention and priority.

Who gets what share of the blame for recent atrocities can be debated. There's plenty of blame to go around. Although prevention of all mass killings is unrealistic, prevention of more of them than in the past is not.

The seven sets of issues that structured this chapter provide a framework for pursuing strategies that can get us closer to "never again." First, we've seen how the U.S. national interest often is at stake not only in terms of the Principles for which we stand but also in terms of Power, Peace, and Prosperity.

Second, political causality rather than historical determinism should be the analytic starting point for what drives these conflicts. Of course, the conflicts are historically shaped. "The past is never dead," as William Faulkner once wrote. "It's not even past."[115] But historical shaping is one thing; fixed determinism positing few if any options for international actors is quite another.

Third, the norm of the responsibility to protect needs to be strengthened as a legitimate basis for abridging state sovereignty and intervening in intrastate conflicts that cross the just-cause threshold. Given that over 95 percent of contemporary armed conflicts are intrastate, shifts away from classic noninterventionism are crucial to international peace, security, and justice.

Fourth, preventive diplomacy strategies pose challenges but also have had real impact. Some strategies are long term, geared to getting at the roots of conflicts. Others are more immediate, intended for negotiations and other methods of conflict management and resolution. They involve the United States as well as the UN and other international actors.

Fifth, unless force can be used as something more than a last resort, we will continue to pick up the pieces of societies torn asunder by mass deaths and other devastation. As hard as conflict prevention is, postconflict reconstruction is harder. To be sure, any and all debates about the use of force other than as a last resort are further complicated in the aftermath of Iraq. But as we stressed earlier, the debate about the threat of force having to be more than just a last resort for humanitarian interventions was already engaged before Iraq.

Sixth, on the question of who decides, the UN Security Council is to be the preferred but not the exclusive source of legitimate authority. Regional organizations provide a viable intermediate basis with potentially stronger claims to legitimacy than largely unilateral actors or ad hoc coalitions of the willing. It is worth bearing in mind the challenge of which is worse for the international community, "if the Security Council is bypassed or . . . the damage to that order if human beings are slaughtered while the Security Council stands by."[116]

Seventh, greater humanitarian intervention capacity must be created. Here there is real progress. But it will take shifts in U.S. diplomacy and defense strategy. The UN also needs to develop greater capacity, as do key regional organizations and other major powers such as the European Union.

Meeting these challenges is difficult. But it is possible—and, most of all, necessary if we are to have any chance of making the "never again" pledge reality and not just rhetoric.

## *American Foreign Policy* Online Student StudySpace

- How do we get from "yet again" to "never again"? What can the United States do? The United Nations? Others in the international community?
- Why do ethnic conflicts and other "politics of identity" occur?
- In which cases have there been success in preventing, or at least minimizing, deadly conflicts? What are the lessons of such successes?
- What are the strengths and weaknesses of the International Criminal Court?
- What do you think of the "Responsibility to Protect"?
- What are the similarities and differences in the war powers issues posed by humanitarian intervention compared to other uses of force?
- Where does the "pretty prudent public" come down on these conflicts?

For these and other study questions, as well as other features, check out Chapter 9 on the *American Foreign Policy* Online Student StudySpace at wwnorton.com/studyspace.

## Notes

[1]"President Bush's State of the Union Message to the Nation," *New York Times*, January 30, 1991, A8.

[2]United Nations Security Council Statement of the Heads of State and Government, January 31, 1992, cited in UN Secretary-General Boutros Boutros-Ghali, *An Agenda for Peace* (New York: United Nations, 1992), 1.

[3]David Binder and Barbara Crossette, "As Ethnic Wars Multiply, U.S. Strives for a Policy," *New York Times*, February 7, 1993.

[4]Samantha Power, *"A Problem from Hell": America and the Age of Genocide* (New York: Basic Books, 2002), 334.

[5]Ivo H. Daalder and Michael E. O'Hanlon, *Winning Ugly: NATO's War to Save Kosovo* (Washington, D.C.: Brookings Institution Press, 2000).

[6]Michael R. Gordon, "The 2000 Campaign: The Military: Bush Would Stop U.S. Peacekeeping in Balkan Fights," *New York Times*, October 21, 2000.

[7]Genocide Prevention Task Force, *Preventing Genocide: A Blueprint for U.S. Policymakers* (Washington, D.C.: U.S. Institute of Peace, 2008).

[8]Human Security Centre and Andrew Mack, *Human Security Report 2005: War and Peace in the 21st Century* (New York: Oxford University Press, 2005), 1.

[9]Human Security Report Project, *Mini Atlas of Human Security*, www.miniatlasofhumansecurity.info/en/access.html (accessed 7/28/09).

[10]This chapter draws on a number of my publications, including Bruce W. Jentleson, "Yet Again: Humanitarian Intervention and the Challenges of 'Never Again'," in *Leashing the Dogs of War: Conflict Management in a Divided World,* Chester A. Crocker, Fen O. Hampson, and Pamela Aall, eds. (Washington, D.C.: U.S. Institute of Peace Press, 2007); and Jentleson, *Opportunities Missed, Opportunities Seized: Preventive Diplomacy in the Post–Cold War World* (Lanham, Md.: Rowman and Litttlefield, 2000).

[11]Power, *"A Problem from Hell,"* xv, xvii.

[12]Power, *"A Problem from Hell,"* 267.

[13]Keith B. Richburg, "Somalia Slips Back to Bloodshed," *Washington Post,* September 4, 1994, A43.

[14] Michael Mandelbaum, "Foreign Policy as Social Work," *Foreign Affairs* 75.1 (January/February 1996): 16–32; Stanley Hoffman, "In Defense of Mother Theresa: Morality in Foreign Policy, *Foreign Affairs* 75.2 (March/April 1996): 172–75.

[15]Stuart Hill and Donald Rothchild, "The Contagion of Political Conflict in Africa and the World," *Journal of Conflict Resolution* 30 (December 1986): 716–35; Stuart Hill, Donald Rothchild, and Colin Cameron, "Tactical Information and the Diffusion of Peaceful Protests," in *The International Spread of Ethnic Conflict: Fear, Diffusion and Escalation,* David A. Lake and Donald Rothchild, eds. (Princeton: Princeton University Press, 1998), 61–88.

[16]William S. Cohen, *Annual Report to the President and the Congress,* January 2000, www.fas.org/man/docs/adr_01/index.html (accessed 7/28/09).

[17]George W. Bush, *National Security Strategy of the United States,* September 2002, http://georgewbush-whitehouse.archives.gov/nsc/nss/2002/index.html (accessed 7/28/09).

[18]Chester A. Crocker, "A Poor Case for Quitting: Mistaking Incompetence for Interventionism," *Foreign Affairs* 79 (January–February 2000), 184.

[19]Donald Rothchild, "The Logic of a Soft Intervention Strategy: The United States and Conflict Conciliation in Africa," *International Negotiation* 10 (2006): 327.

[20]Arthur M. Schlesinger, Jr., "America and the World: Isolationism Resurgent?" *Ethics and International Affairs* 10 (1996), 162–63.

[21]Alan Dowty and Gil Loescher, "Refugee Flows as Grounds for International Action," *International Security* 21 (Summer 1996): 307–08; *2007 United Nations High Commission on Refugees Statistical Yearbook,* 23, www.unhcr.org/4981b19d2.html (accessed 7/28/09).

[22]John Pomfret, "Aid Dilemma: Keeping It from the Oppressors," *Washington Post,* September 23, 1997, A1, A12–A13.

[23]"Bosnia and Herzegovina in the Balkans," *Peace Watch* (Washington, D.C.: U.S. Institute of Peace Press, 1998), 2.

[24]Michael E. Brown and Richard N. Rosecrance, eds., *The Costs of Conflict: Prevention and Cure in the Global Arena* (Boulder, Colo.: Rowman and Littlefield, 1999), 225.

[25]Genocide Prevention Task Force, *Preventing Genocide,* xx.

[26]Cited in Power, *"A Problem from Hell,"* xii.

[27]Chris Hedges, "War Turns Sarajevo Away from Europe," *New York Times,* July 28, 1995, A4.

[28]Astri Suhrke and Bruce Jones, "Preventive Diplomacy in Rwanda: Failure to Act or Failure of Actions?" in Jentleson, *Opportunities Missed, Opportunities Seized,* 241.

[29]V. P. Gagnon, "Ethnic Nationalism and International Conflict: The Case of Serbia," *International Security* 19.3 (Winter 1994–95). The Carnegie Commission for Preventing Deadly Conflict in its *Final Report* makes its own strong statement of the purposive view: "Mass violence invariably results from the deliberately violent response of determined leaders and their groups to a wide range of social, economic and political conditions that provide the environment for violent conflict, but usually do not independently spawn violence" (39).

[30]Kenneth Menkhaus and Louis Ortmayer, "Misread Crisis in Somalia," in Jentleson, *Opportunities Missed, Opportunities Seized,* 220.

[31]Suhrke and Jones, "Preventive Diplomacy in Rwanda," 254.

[32]Susan L. Woodward, *Balkan Tragedy: Chaos and Dissolution after the Cold War* (Washington, D.C.: Brookings Institution, 1995), 396.

[33]Menkhaus and Ortmayer, "Somalia: Missed Crises and Missed Opportunities," 259; Scott R. Feil, *Preventing Genocide: How the Early Use of Force Might Have Succeeded in Rwanda* (Washington, D.C.: Carnegie Commission on Preventing Deadly Conflict, 1998), 3.

[34]International Commission on Intervention and State Sovereignty (ICISS), *The Responsibility to Protect* (Ottowa: International Development Research Centre, 2001), 69.

[35]ICISS, *The Responsibility to Protect,* 11.

[36]Michael Walzer, *Just and Unjust Wars: A Moral Argument with Historical Illustrations* (New York: Basic Books, 1977); ICISS, *The Responsibility to Protect;* Simon Chesterman, *Just War or Just Peace? Humanitarian Intervention and International Law* (New York: Oxford University Press, 2003).

[37]Thomas G. Weiss, "The Sunset of Humanitarian Intervention? The Responsibility to Protect in a Unipolar Era," *Security Dialogue* 35.2 (June 2004): 139.

[38]Cited in Weiss, "The Sunset of Humanitarian Intervention?" 143.

[39]Alex J. Bellamy, "Ethics and Intervention: The 'Humanitarian Exception' and the Problem of Abuse in the Case of Iraq," *Journal of Peace Research* 41.2 (March 2004): 145.

[40]United Nations Department of Public Information, *Fact Sheet: 2005 World Summit,* September 2005, www.un.org/summit2005/presskit/fact_sheet.pdf (accessed 7/28/09).

[41]Edward C. Luck, *The United Nations and the Responsibility to Protect,* Stanley Foundation Policy Analysis Brief, August 2008, www.stanleyfoundation.org/resources.cfm?id=345 (accessed 7/28/09). See also Gareth Evans, *The Responsibility to Protect: Ending Mass Atrocity Crimes Once and For All* (Washington, D.C.: Brookings Institution Press, 2008).

[42]United Nations General Assembly, *2005 World Summit Outcome,* A/RES/60/1, September 20, 2005, paragraph 138, www.un.org/summit2005/documents.html (accessed 7/28/09).

[43]This section draws especially on Bruce W. Jentleson, *Coercive Prevention: Normative, Political, and Policy Dilemmas,* Peaceworks 35 (Washington, D.C.: U.S. Institute of Peace Press, 2000).

[44]Evans, *The Responsibility to Protect,* 91.

[45]Evans, *The Responsibility to Protect,* 88.

[46]Judith Kelley, *Ethnic Politics in Europe: The Power of Norms and Incentives* (Princeton: Princeton University Press, 2004).

[47]Chris Hedges, "Croatian's Confession Describes Torture and Killing on a Vast Scale," *New York Times,* September 5, 1997, A1.

[48]Thomas C. Schelling, *Arms and Influence* (New Haven: Yale University Press, 1966); Alexander L. George and William E. Simmons, eds., *The Limits of Coercive Diplomacy,* 2nd ed. (Boulder, Colo.: Westview, 1994); Alexander L. George, *Forceful Persuasion* (Washington, D.C.: U.S. Institute of Peace Press, 1992).

[49]I. William Zartman, *Ripe for Resolution: Conflict and Intervention in Africa* (New York: Oxford University Press, 1989); Richard N. Haass, *Conflicts Unending: The United States and Regional Disputes* (New Haven: Yale University Press, 1992).

[50]I. William Zartman, "Putting Humpty-Dumpty Together Again," in Lake and Rothchild, eds., *International Spread of Ethnic Conflict.*

[51]Fred Barbash, "Diplomats, Aid Officials Grapple with Plans for Rebuilding Bosnia and Herzegovina," *Washington Post,* December 2, 1995. A32.

[52]ICISS, *The Responsibility to Protect,* 1.

[53]Michael Barnett, *Eyewitness to a Genocide: The United States and Rwanda* (Ithaca, N.Y.: Cornell University Press, 2002), 1. See also Power, *"A Problem from Hell,"* ch. 10.

[54]Suhrke and Jones, "Preventive Diplomacy in Rwanda," 247.

[55]Suhrke and Jones, "Preventive Diplomacy in Rwanda," 257–58; Charles Truehart, "UN Alerted to Plans for Rwanda Bloodbath," *Washington Post,* September 25, 1997, A1, A28; Philip Gourevitch, *We Wish to Inform You That Tomorrow We Will Be Killed with Our Families: Stories from Rwanda* (New York: Farrar, Straus, and Giroux, 1998).

[56]Feil, *Preventing Genocide,* 22.

[57]Suhrke and Jones, "Preventive Diplomacy in Rwanda," 259. See also Alison Des Forges, *Leave None to Tell the Story* (New York: Human Rights Watch, 1999). The viability of a late intervention is questioned by Alan J. Kuperman, "Rwanda in Retrospect," *Foreign Affairs* 79 (January–February 2000): 94–118. Kuperman argues that even a force of 13,500 troops could have reduced the death toll by only 25 percent. Even if his analysis is accurate regarding what a late intervention could have achieved, the first two points made herein remain on the inadequacy of the earlier coercive measures; in this respect, Kuperman's argument further underscores the importance of acting early and steadily.

[58]Michael Lund, "Preventive Diplomacy for Macedonia, 1992–1998: From Containment to Nation-Building," in Jentleson, ed., *Opportunities Missed, Opportunities Seized,* 173–208.

[59]Michael G. Roskin, "Macedonia and Albania: The Missing Alliance," *Parameters* (Winter 1993–94): 98.

[60]ICISS, *The Responsibility to Protect,* 33, 36, emphasis added.

[61]Stanley Hoffmann, *World Disorders: Troubled Peace in the Post–Cold War Era* (Lanham, Md.: Rowman and Littlefield, 1998), 170.

[62]Jentleson, *Coercive Prevention.*

[63]Jane E. Holl, "We the People Here Don't Want No War: Executive Branch Perspectives on the Use of Force," in *The United States and the Use of Force in the Post–Cold War Era: A Report by the Aspen Strategy Group* (Queenstown, Md.: Aspen Institute Press, 1995), 124.

[64]United Nations, "Secretary-General Says Renewal of Effectiveness and Relevance of Security council Must Be Cornerstone of Efforts to Promote Peace in Next Century," United Nations Press Release SG/SM/6997, May 18, 1999.

[65]Statement by H. E. Mr. Tang Jiaxuan, Minister of Foreign Affairs of the People's Republic of China at the 54th Session of the UN General Assembly, September 22, 1999, www.fmprc.gov.cn/eng/wjdt/zyjh/t24963.htm (accessed 7/28/09); Bates Gill and James Reilly, "Sovereignty, Intervention and Peacekeeping: The View from Beijing," *Survival: Global Politics and Strategy* 42.3 (Autumn 2000): 41–59.

[66]Independent International Commission on Kosovo, *The Kosovo Report: Conflict, International Response, Lessons Learned* (Oxford: Oxford University Press, 2000).

[67]ICISS, *The Responsibility to Protect,* 54–55.

[68]Secretary-General's High-Level Panel on Threats, Challenges and Change, *A More Secure World: Our Shared Responsibility* (United Nations, 2004), 63.

[69]Fund for Peace, *Neighbors on Alert: Regional Views on Humanitarian Action,* Summary Report of the Regional Response to Internal War Program, October 2003. See also Alex J. Bellamy and Paul D. Williams, "Who's Keeping the Peace? Regionalization and Contemporary Peace Operations," *International Security* 29.4 (Spring 2005): 166.

[70]International Crisis Group, *Bosnia's Incomplete Transition: Between Dayton and Europe,* Europe Report No. 198, March 9, 2009, 3, www.crisisgroup.org/library/documents/europe/balkans/198_bosnias_incomplete_transition___between_dayton_and_europe.pdf (accessed 7/28/09).

[71]Michael Cox, "American Power Before and After September 11: Dizzy with Success?" *International Affairs* 78.2 (2002): 290.

[72]Seyom Brown, *The Illusion of Control: Force and Foreign Policy in the 21st Century* (Washington, D.C.: Brookings Institution Press, 2003), 36.

[73]John M. Goshko, "Balkan Peacekeeping Exposes Limits of UN, Boutros-Ghali Says," *Washington Post,* October 10, 1995, A21.

[74]Matthew Krain, "International Intervention and the Severity of Genocides and Policides," *International Studies Quarterly* 49.3 (September 2005): 363.

[75]James Dobbins et al., *The UN's Role in Nation-Building: From the Congo to Iraq* (Santa Monica: Rand, 2005); James Dobbins et al., *America's Role in Nation-Building: From Germany to Iraq* (Santa Monica: Rand, 2003).

[76]Mats Berdal, "The UN Security Council: Ineffective but Indispensable," *Survival: Global Politics and Strategy* 45.2 (Summer 2003): 24.

[77]As of June 2004 the number of UN peacekeeping forces authorized was 74,478, but only 56,261 actually had been provided; Paul D. Williams and Alex J. Bellamy, "The Responsibility to Protect and the Crisis in Darfur," *Security Dialogue* 36.1 (March 2005): 43.

[78]Kofi Annan, statement at the opening of the Preparatory Commission for the International Criminal Court, New York, February 16, 1999, www.ngos.net/un/icc.html (accessed 9/10/09).

[79]"Rome Statute of the International Criminal Court: Overview."

[80]Statement by John D. Negroponte, U.S. Ambassador to the United Nations, July 12, 2002, www.amicc.org/docs/Negroponte_1422.pdf (accessed 7/28/09).

[81]Thomas W. Lippman, "America Avoids the Stand," *Washington Post,* July 26, 1998, C1, C4.

[82]Nicholas Kristof, "The Secret Genocide Archive", *New York Times,* February 23, 2005. See also Human Rights Watch, *Entrenching Impunity: Government Responsibility for International Crimes in Darfur,* December 2005, www.hrw.org/en/reports/2005/12/08/entrenching-impunity (accessed 7/28/09).

[83]Scott Anderson, "How Did Darfur Happen?" *New York Times Magazine,* October 17, 2004; International Crisis Group (ICG), *Darfur Rising: Sudan's New Crisis,* ICG Africa Report No. 76, March 25, 2004; Amnesty International, "Sudan: Crisis In Darfur—Urgent Need For International Commission Of Inquiry And Monitoring," press release, April 28, 2003, www.amnesty.org/en/library/asset/AFR54/026/2003/en/094fac27-d6f9-11dd-b0cc-1f0860013475/afr540262003en.html (accessed 7/28/09).

[84]See, for example, the numerous columns by Nicholas Kristof in the *New York Times.*

[85]ICG, *Darfur Rising,* 23.

[86]International Crisis Group, *Darfur Deadline: A New International Action Plan,* August 23, 2004, ICG Africa Report No. 83, 4.

[87]Joel Brinkley, "Sudan Still Paying Militias Harassing Darfur, U.S. Says," *New York Times,* July 21, 2005; Warren Hoge, "UN Charges Sudan Ignores Rapes in Darfur by Military and Police," *New York Times,* July 30, 2005.

[88]Cheryl O. Igiri and Princeton Lyman, *Giving Meaning to "Never Again": Seeking an Effective Response to the Crisis in Darfur and Beyond,* Council on Foreign Relations, CSR No. 5, September 2004, 24.

[89]David Zweig and Bi Jianhi, "China's Global Hunt for Energy," *Foreign Affairs* 84.5 (September/October 2005): 25–38.

[90]Gerald Butt, "Thirst for Crude Pulling China Into Sudan," *Daily Star,* August 17, 2004; U.S. Department of Energy, Energy Information Administration, *Sudan: Country Analysis Brief,* March 2005, www.eia.doe.gov/emeu/cabs/Sudan/Background.html (accessed 7/29/09).

[91]"The Donors and Darfur," editorial, *Washington Post,* June 20, 2005, A14.

[92]"Shameful and hypocritical," wrote one Muslim commentator in the Lebanese newspaper *The Daily Star.* Fatema Abdul Rasul, "Arab, Muslim Silence on Darfur Conflict Is Deafening," *Daily Star,* April 10, 2006.

[93]Bruce W. Jentleson, "Bin Laden Supports Genocide Against Muslims," *America Abroad,* April 24, 2006, http://tpmcafe.talkingpointsmemo.com/2006/04/24/bin_laden_supports_genocide_ag/ (accessed 7/29/09).

[94]Williams and Bellamy, "The Responsibility to Protect and the Crisis in Darfur," 43. See also International

Crisis Group, *The AU's Mission in Darfur: Bridging the Gaps,* Africa Briefing No. 28, July 6, 2005, www.crisisgroup.org/home/index.cfm?id=3547&1=1 (accessed 7/29/09).

[95]Susan E. Rice, "Why Darfur Can't Be Left to Africa," *Washington Post,* August 7, 2005.

[96]Williams and Bellamy, "The Responsibility to Protect and Darfur," 31.

[97]International Crisis Group, *Darfur Rising; Darfur Deadline; A New Sudan Action Plan,* Africa Briefing No. 24, April 26, 2005; *The AU's Mission in Darfur; Unifying Darfur's Rebels: A Prerequisite for Peace,* Africa Briefing No. 32, October 6, 2005; *To Save Darfur,* Africa Report No. 105, March 17, 2006.

[98]Stephen J. Stedman, "Spoiler Problems in Peace Processes," *International Security* 2.2 (Fall 1997): 5–53; Philip G. Roeder and Donald Rothchild, eds., *Sustainable Peace: Power and Democracy after Civil Wars* (Ithaca, N.Y.: Cornell University Press, 2005).

[99]Glenn Kessler and Emily Wax, "Sudan, Main Rebel Groups Sign Peace Deal," *Washington Post,* May 5, 2006.

[100]International Crisis Group, *Crisis in Darfur,* updated March 2009, www.crisisgroup.org/home/index.cfm?id=3060 (accessed 7/29/09).

[101]International Crisis Group, *Crisis in Darfur.*

[102]Cited in Bruce W. Jentleson, "Who, Why, What and How: Debates over Post–Cold War Military Intervention," in *Eagle Adrift: American Foreign Policy at the End of the Century,* Robert J. Lieber, ed. (New York: Longman, 1997), 62–63.

[103]Pat Towell and Donna Cassata, "Congress Takes Symbolic Stand on Troop Deployment," *Congressional Quarterly Weekly Report,* December 16, 1995, 3817.

[104]Daalder and O'Hanlon, *Winning Ugly,* 161.

[105]Daalder and O'Hanlon, *Winning Ugly,* 162.

[106]Warren P. Strobel, "The Media and U.S. Policies toward Intervention: A Closer Look at the 'CNN Effect'," in *Managing Global Chaos,* Chester A. Crocker and Fen Osler Hampson with Pamela Aall, eds. (Washington, D.C.: U.S. Institute of Peace Press, 1996), 358.

[107]Strobel, "The Media and U.S. Policies," 373–74.

[108]Cited in Jentleson, *Coercive Prevention,* Table 2, 26.

[109]Samantha Power, "Dying in Darfur," *New Yorker,* August 30, 2004.

[110]Nicholas Kristof, "Walking the Talk," *New York Times,* October 9, 2005; www.genocideinterventionfund.org.

[111]International Crisis Group, *Do Americans Care About Darfur? An International Crisis Group/Zogby International Opinion Survey,* Africa Briefing No. 26, June 1, 2005.

[112]Chicago Council on Global Affairs, *The United States and the Rise of China and India: Results of a 2006 Multination Survey of Public Opinion,* 22; www.thechicagocouncil.org/UserFiles/File/POS_Topline%20Reports/POS%202006/2006%20Full%20POS%20Report.pdf (accessed 7/29/09); Chicago Council on Foreign Relations, *Global Views 2004,* www.thechicagocouncil.org/UserFiles/File/POS_Topline%20Reports/POS%202004/US%20Public%20Opinion%20Global_Views_2004_US.pdf (accessed 7/29/09).

[113]Globescan-Program on International Policy Attitudes (PIPA), *The Darfur Crisis: African and American Public Opinion,* June 29, 2005, 4–5, www.pipa.org/OnlineReports/Africa/Darfur_Jun05/Darfur_Jun05_rpt.pdf (accessed 7/29/09).

[114]Chicago Council on Global Affairs, "Troubled by Loss of Standing in the World, Americans Support Major Foreign Policy Changes," *Global Views 2008,* 5, 6, www.thechicagocouncil.org/UserFiles/File/POS_Topline%20Reports/POS%202008/2008%20Public%20Opinion_Foreign%20Policy.pdf (accessed 7/29/09).

[115]William Faulkner, *Requiem for a Nun,* I, iii, www.mcsr.olemiss.edu/~egjbp/faulkner/faulkner.html (accessed 7/29/09).

[116]ICISS, *The Responsibility to Protect,* 54–55.

CHAPTER

# 10 The Globalization Agenda

## Introduction: American Foreign Policy in an Era of Globalization

"If you want to understand the post–Cold War world," wrote Thomas Friedman, the Pulitzer Prize–winning columnist for the *New York Times,* in the 1990s, "you have to start by understanding that a new international system has succeeded it—globalization. Globalization is not the only thing influencing events in the world today, but to the extent that there is a North Star and a worldwide shaping force, it is this system."[1] Recent events, particularly the global economic crisis that began in 2008, show how interconnected our twenty-first-century world is. Profound changes in the international political economy join the end of Cold War bipolarity, terrorism, the politics of identity that cause ethnic and related wars, and the struggles to spread democracy as driving forces of this new era. Our focus in this chapter is on the challenges U.S. foreign policy faces amid the complex and powerful forces of globalization:

- *Prosperity:* The American economy is increasingly interconnected with the international economy. Our prosperity depends on the prosperity of others. And their prosperity depends on ours. Indeed whereas other recent economic crises began in other countries and then spread to the American economy, the 2008 one largely began in the United States and spread globally.
- *Power:* As important as military might continues to be, American Power increasingly depends on America's international economic position and leadership on the range of issues on the globalization agenda.
- *Peace:* Economic conflict and competition have caused war before. They could do so again. Also, global poverty continues to be a major factor affecting peace and

stability in many states and regions. Moreover, concerns are increasing about the instability and conflict caused by global public health crises such as AIDS and possible pandemics such as swine flu, as well as about resource scarcity, climate change, and other global environmental problems.

- *Principles:* The millions of people still living in grinding poverty raise fundamental normative and ethical questions. Mass poverty also makes stable democracy much more difficult to achieve.

The first section of this chapter looks at the overall debate on globalization as it has developed over the past two decades as well as at the issues raised by the recent international economic crisis and other factors that even earlier were beginning to reshape the international political economy. Next are issue areas of major importance to American foreign policy: international trade and the World Trade Organization; international finance and the International Monetary Fund; sustainable development and global poverty; AIDS and other global public health issues; and global environmental issues. The foreign policy politics section includes two subsections, one on the role of nongovernmental organizations (NGOs) and other aspects of the politics of globalization, and one on the making of U.S. trade policy.

## The Globalization Debate

So what is ***globalization*** anyway? What's so new and different about it? Is it a good thing or a bad thing? We can address these and related questions initially in terms of the dynamics, dimensions, and dilemmas of globalization.

### *Defining Globalization: Dynamics, Dimensions, Dilemmas*

The basic *dynamic* of globalization is the increasing interconnectedness of the world across nation-state boundaries—an interconnectedness that affects governments, businesses, communities, and people in a wide range of policy areas. This is not totally new. As we will see in "Historical Perspectives," on page 530, past eras also had their global dimensions. What makes the dynamic driving contemporary globalization unique is that it is "wider," "deeper," and "faster." By "wider" we mean that it stretches beyond just the largest and richest countries of North America, Europe, and Asia increasingly to include countries and peoples in all corners of the globe. By "deeper" we stress the "thickness" of networks of interaction: that economic, cultural, and other interactions are not just individualized exchanges of goods, ideas, and the like but are more ongoing and interwoven with a greater "density" of interrelationship. The speed with which these interactions hap-

## HISTORICAL PERSPECTIVES
HISTORICAL PERSPECTIVES

### HOW "NEW" IS GLOBALIZATION?

So much is new about our current era of globalization that sometimes we lose sight of ways in which past eras also had their global dimensions. This broader historical perspective is helpful in differentiating what is and isn't unique about the twenty-first century, and for drawing lessons from the past. Here are three examples.

#### International Finance

Wall Street giants such as Goldman Sachs have their global financial networks today, but so did the Fuggers, a prominent German family in the Middle Ages. As Professor Stephen Krasner recounts: "The Fuggers controlled mines in central Europe and the Alps; had correspondents in Venice; were the dominant firm in Antwerp, the most important financial center of the time; and had branches in Portugal, Spain, Chile, Fiume, and Dubrovnik. They had agents in India and China by the end of the sixteenth century. Braudel [a leading historian] suggests that 'the empire of this huge firm was vaster than the mighty empire of Charles V and Philip II, on which as we know the sun never set.'"*

#### Global Public Health

As severe as today's threats of global disease pandemics are, the 1918–19 Spanish flu epidemic killed at least 50 million people, possibly even double that. Here is part of an account from Laurie Garrett, a global public health expert at the Council on Foreign Relations:

> Nearly half of all deaths in the United States in 1918 were flu-related. Some 675,000 Americans—about six percent of the population of 105 million and the equivalent of 2 million American deaths today—perished from the Spanish flu . . . The highest death tolls were among young adults, ages 20–35. . . . Many deaths were never included in the pandemic's official death toll—such as the majority of victims in Africa, Latin America, Indonesia, the Pacific Islands and Russia. . . . The official estimate of 40–50 million total deaths is believed to be a conservative extrapolation of European and American records. In fact, many historians and biologists believe that nearly a third of all humans suffered from influenza in 1918–19—and that of these, 100 million died.†

#### Immigration to the United States

The 2000 census showed that 56 million Americans, equal to about 20 percent of the entire U.S. population, either had been born in a foreign country or had at least one parent who had been. This was far and away the highest number ever. In 1970, it was about 33 million. The previous historic high was 40 million in 1930, following a major post–World War I wave of immigration. But as a percentage of the total U.S. population, the 2000 figure was only about 20 percent, whereas the figures for 1890 to 1930 all were above 30 percent.

The following graph shows how here too globalization was not a totally new phenomenon.

**Percentage of Americans Born in a Foreign Country or Having at Least One Parent Who Was**

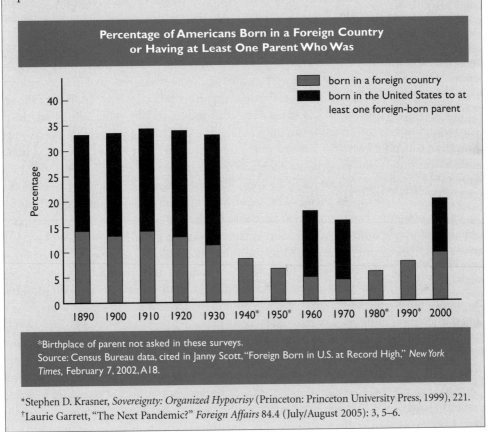

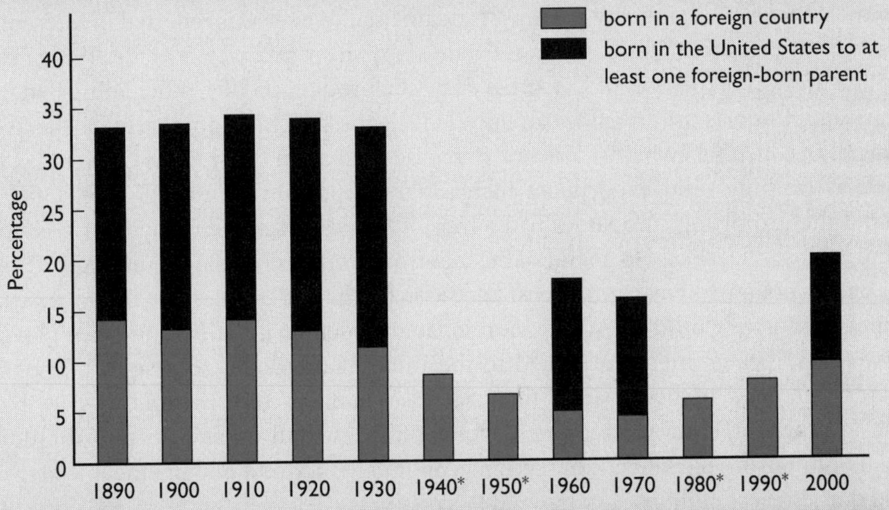


*Birthplace of parent not asked in these surveys.
Source: Census Bureau data, cited in Janny Scott, "Foreign Born in U.S. at Record High," *New York Times*, February 7, 2002, A18.

*Stephen D. Krasner, *Sovereignty: Organized Hypocrisy* (Princeton: Princeton University Press, 1999), 221.
†Laurie Garrett, "The Next Pandemic?" *Foreign Affairs* 84.4 (July/August 2005): 3, 5–6.

pen is remarkable, whether it involves a few computer keystrokes that move billions of dollars from one side of the world to the other, or the instantaneous movement of news via cable and satellite telecommunications.

Thomas Friedman captured this mix of historical precedent and contemporary uniqueness in his influential book, *The Lexus and the Olive Tree:*

> While there are a lot of similarities in kind between the previous era of globalization and the one we are now in, what is new today is the degree and intensity with which the world is being tied together into a single globalized marketplace. What is also new is the sheer number of people and countries able to partake of this process and be affected by it. . . . This new era of globalization, compared to the one before World War I, is turbocharged.[2]

A similar sense is conveyed in a report by the United Nations:

> Globalization is not new. Recall the early sixteenth century and the late nineteenth. . . . But the present era has distinctive features. Shrinking space, shrinking time and disappearing borders are linking people's lives more deeply, more intensely, more immediately than ever before.[3]

What also makes today's era of globalization unique is its many *dimensions*. The economic dimension is arguably the most fundamental. We see this reflected in international trade in two respects. One is its extensiveness, the sheer quantity of trade. Trade now accounts for over 30 percent of U.S. gross domestic product (GDP), much more than thirty years ago. Imports are much more prevalent in the purchasing patterns of the average American consumer, whether a major purchase such as an automobile or everyday items such as clothing. And exports are increasingly important sources of jobs. One study found that exporting companies had almost 20 percent faster employment growth and were 9 percent less likely to go out of business than companies that did not export.[4] As for monetary policy, whereas in the past decisions by the Federal Reserve Board were based almost exclusively on domestic economic factors such as inflation and unemployment, now much greater attention is paid to the value of the dollar relative to that of other major currencies, to the impact of financial crises in other countries on U.S. growth rates, and to other international economic factors. In these and other ways globalization has been both raising the salience of foreign economic policy and making the line between it and domestic economic policy less and less distinct.

The other key pattern in international trade is its organization and nature. "It is not just how much countries trade with each other that is important," one globalization expert wrote, "but also the way in which this trade is structured: what goods and services are traded, and between whom they are traded."[5] About one-fourth to one-third of world trade is *intrafirm*—i.e., between divisions of the same global corporation located in different countries, rather than between different companies in different countries. As an example, truck axles are shipped from a General Motors (GM) plant in Detroit to a GM affiliate in Brazil. This counts as a trade transaction between the two countries (U.S. export, Brazilian import), yet "the goods never leave the corporate 'boundaries' of GM."[6] The trade is between countries yet within a corporation that is organized on a global basis. For the United States, intrafirm trade accounts for about one-third of total trade. Another large component of trade takes place on an *intraindustry* basis—i.e., within the same industry even if not within the same firm. Computers are an example: U.S.-based companies such as Dell contract with companies in India, Taiwan, Mexico, and elsewhere to produce parts and software. They are not part of the same firm, but they are part of the same industry. This facet of international trade is not totally new, but its extent is much greater than in the past, making for depth and thickness of globalized economic relationships that are qualitatively different from past trade patterns.[7] Thus the trade policy challenges posed in this new era are even more complex than in earlier eras.

A similar dynamic is evident in international finance. In the late 1990s, one prominent investment banker drew attention to the widening gap between the "awesome force of the global financial marketplace" and the more limited reach of the policies of national governments and international institutions such as the International Monetary Fund (IMF).[8] With many more countries having market economies than ever before, and given how drastically new technology has reduced intracorporate costs of running distant operations, major multinational corporations (MNCs) have a much wider range of choices about where to build a new factory or make other foreign direct investments. Bankers, money managers, stockbrokers, and other international financiers don't have only Wall Street, London, Frankfurt, and Tokyo, but also Hong Kong, Moscow, Brasília, and many other of the world's proliferated stock markets, currency markets, and other investment exchanges from which to choose. Whatever their choices, it takes just one click of a computer mouse to move huge sums of money instantly—often over $2 trillion going from one country to another in a single day. Although market-based principles dictate that private investors should be free to make such decisions, one of the main purposes both of U.S. policy and of international economic institutions has been to provide a degree of governance against instabilities, inequities, and other imperfections.

Another key dimension of globalization involves telecommunications technology. News regularly moves instantaneously, 24/7, from one end of the world to the other, whether through the BBC (British Broadcasting Company), CNN (Cable News Network), the Arab satellite network Al Jazeera, or others in this growth industry. The Internet provides an especially widespread communications network that, even in the developing world, which is much less networked, is putting all types of information at the fingertips of more and more people. The Internet also demonstrates how globalization can be both a positive force and a negative one. The openness it provides and the way in which it undermines governmental monopolies on information can impose a check against dictators, who might be more likely to repress their people if they knew they could keep it quiet. Yet the Internet also facilitates such problems as terrorism: the terrorists who plotted the World Trade Center attacks communicated with each other from Internet cafés around the world and even from American public libraries.

Globalization also has an important social and cultural dimension involving the flow of ideas, customs, and people. This flow is more multidirectional than many Americans realize. American products, music, movies, and other cultural influences can be found in almost every corner of the globe. Want a McDonald's hamburger? You'll find one in almost every major city in the world. Walk around a small village in Latin America or the Middle East and you'll see people wearing Michael Jordan T-shirts or New York Yankees baseball caps or other American clothing. In turn, American culture is much more diverse than ever before. A walk through almost any American city reveals how many more ethnic restaurants there are today than existed twenty years ago. More and more foreign-language movies are available through Netflix and other sources. School calendars for the high school my children went to in the Washington, D.C. area are written in Spanish and Vietnamese as well as in English.

Although driven in part by economics and communications, this cultural dimension especially reflects immigration patterns. It is the movement of peoples that in the long run may be the most profound dimension of globalization. Immigration into the United States has been increasing in both numbers and diversity. The most dramatic shifts have come from Latin America (which accounted for 4 percent of total immigration in 1920, but 41 percent in 2007) and from Asia (which grew from 1 percent to 36 percent), whereas European immigrants fell from 87 percent to 12 percent. Western Europe itself is also becoming much more ethnically heterogeneous due to increased immigration, especially from Africa, South Asia, and the Arab world. Other parts of the world have also seen substantial population shifts, as in Africa, where they have been largely the consequence of refugees fleeing ethnic wars and famines.

All of this poses a number of major policy *dilemmas.* Although each of these policy dilemmas has its own details and specific issues, in the broadest sense all are manifestations of the challenges of "governance" amid globalization. The interconnectedness of globalization has outpaced policy capacities, creating a gap between globalization and global governance. Closing this ***global governance gap*** is one of the major challenges that American foreign policy and, more broadly, the international community face. Global governance is not the same thing as global government. The latter term usually refers to ideas about making the United Nations and other international institutions into full governing structures, along with some sort of global constitution. Such withering of the nation-state is highly unlikely. ***Global governance*** is a broader and more flexible concept:

> Governance does not mean mere government. It means the framework of rules, institutions and established practices that set limits and give incentives for the behavior of individuals, organizations and firms.
>
> Governance signifies a diverse range of cooperative problem-solving arrangements, state and nonstate, to manage collective affairs. . . . It takes place through "laws, norms and architectures," not necessarily the field of action of governments alone but rather in association with one another, with multinational bodies, with corporate and sometimes academic research entities and NGOs. Such collective activity, structured or improvised, produces governance, sometimes without governmental activity.[9]

Even with this distinction between global governance and global government, these new arrangements raise the issue of ***sovereignty.*** Although sensitive and controversial, this issue is unavoidable. The complex dynamics and multiple dimensions of globalization lay bare the ways in which states are not so insulated or self-contained as traditional conceptions of state sovereignty presume. Whereas in Chapter 9 the issue was how much the international community could choose to intervene militarily and diplomatically in states without violating their sovereignty, here it is less a matter of intervention by other countries or international institutions than penetration of states by economic and other globalized forces. Prognostications about the "withering of the nation-state" are overstated, but the powerful forces of globalization belie traditional conceptions of state sovereignty.

For a while in the 1990s there was a sense that the global governance agenda really was not that complex, that a ready and largely standard formula could be followed to maximize international trade and stabilize international finance for the benefit of all, and that the rest of the globalization agenda would benefit accordingly. Dubbed the ***Washington consensus,**** the basic formula held that countries should give the highest priority to reducing barriers to international trade and investment, cutting their own government spending, reducing government regulations, promoting privatization, and taking other steps to gain the greater economic efficiency and competitiveness that would promote economic growth. Joseph Stiglitz, a former top Clinton administration and World Bank official and a co-winner of the 2001 Nobel Prize in economics, defined the Washington consensus as follows:

> According to the Washington consensus, growth occurs through liberalization, "freeing up" markets. Privatization, liberalization and macrostability are supposed to create a climate to attract investment, including from abroad. This investment creates growth. Foreign business brings with it technical expertise and access to foreign markets, creating new employment possibilities. Foreign companies also have access to sources of finance, especially important in those developing countries where local financial institutions are weak.[10]

This strategy relied largely on the "magic of the marketplace," which we can trace back to Adam Smith and his conception of the "invisible hand" by which growth would be maximized and all would benefit accordingly. In practice, though, the magic was not there so much or for so many as advertised. In the United States and other industrialized countries, labor groups and others saw themselves as "losers," whereas others were "winners." In many developing countries, both intrasocietal inequalities and the North-South income gap in the international system were seen as widening; worse, as the boom of the

---

*So called because of its ideological and programmatic roots in both the Clinton administration and two Washington D.C.–based international economic institutions, the International Monetary Fund (IMF) and the World Bank.

1990s faded, a number of countries plunged into deep economic crises. This led to calls for "globalization with a human face":

> Inequality between countries has increased. The income gap between the fifth of the world's people living in the richest countries and the fifth in the poorest was 74 to 1 in 1997, up from 60 to 1 in 1990 and 30 to 1 in 1960. . . . Markets are neither the first nor the last word in human development. Many activities and goods that are critical to human development are provided outside the market—but these are being squeezed by the pressures of global competition. . . . When the market goes too far in dominating social and political outcomes, the opportunities and rewards of globalization spread unequally and inequitably—concentrating power and wealth in a select group of people, nations and corporations, marginalizing the others.[11]

The statistic that the 500 richest people in the world earn more money than the 416,000,000 poorest is particularly telling.[12]

The "democratic deficit" has posed another dilemma in global governance institutions and processes. Do institutions such as the World Trade Organization (WTO) and the International Monetary Fund (IMF) have too much power? Are they too unrepresentative? Should NGOs have larger roles in key policy processes? We will take these issues up in the sections that follow.

Another global governance challenge has been from globalization's "underside," the ways in which the very interconnectedness that globalization has brought also has enhanced the capacity of drug traffickers, arms merchants, human traffickers, money launderers, and others involved in illegal and illicit trade and other activities. In his book *Illicit,* Moises Naim argues that these kinds of economic activities are "*transforming the international system,* upending the rules, creating new players, and reconfiguring power in international politics and economics."[13] The global arms trade is a "supermarket that knows no borders and in which virtually anything can be procured for virtually anyone, so long as the buyer is prepared to pay the price." Sex slavery and other human trafficking is "booming . . . [at a] furious pace of growth." Money laundering may be as high as 10 percent of world GDP, facilitated by financial markets that have ended up "expand[ing] the flexibility of traffickers to invest the profits and the range of uses they can give to their capital, as well as generat[ing] many new instruments with which to move funds across the globe." Organ trade—kidneys, livers, and more—is fed by "forcible donations" for transplants.[14]

In sum, globalization is neither wholly positive nor wholly negative. It simply *is.* Policies can shape it, but they cannot stop or reverse it. The world is too interconnected to be disconnected. The issues thus are how to close the global governance–globalization gap in ways that best work with its dynamics, address all its dimensions, and deal with the dilemmas posed for international trade, international finance, sustainable development, and other key related policy areas.

## *The 2008 Global Economic Crisis*

When the 2008 economic crisis hit, the globalization debate became even more intense. The overall global economy contracted for the first time since World War II. The drop in global trade was the steepest since the Great Depression. No region or country escaped. Not booming economies such as in China and India. Not export leaders such as Japan and Germany. Not countries in Europe, west or east. Not oil exporters such as ***OPEC (Organization of Petroleum Exporting Countries)*** and Russia. Not countries in Africa, Asia, and Latin America, still mired in poverty. And definitely not the United States.

Would globalization collapse? That was "absolutely possible," as the noted economist Jeffrey Sachs reflected in a view also held by others. "It happened in the twentieth century in the wake of World War I and the Great Depression, and could happen again. Nationalism is rising and our political systems are inward looking, the more so in times of crisis."[15] Indeed, though stopping short of heavy-handed protectionism, many countries were shifting toward less open policies. They had learned sufficient lessons from the 1930s to contain protectionist measures. But two principal debates intensified.

Did global governance institutions need major reforms? Immediate attention focused on the role of the "G" groupings. Back in the mid-1970s, the ***G7 (Group of Seven)*** had been created by the United States and other advanced industrial states (Canada, Britain, France, Germany, Italy, Japan) for consultation and coordination on international economic issues. The G7 was an informal institution but an influential one, given that it included the major economic and political powers of the day. It became the ***G8*** when Russia was added after the Cold War. Another institution, the ***G20,*** which included China, India, and a number of other developing countries, had been created in 1999, but had had a less prominent role. Yet when the 2008 global economic crisis struck, the broader inclusiveness of the G20 made it the principal forum. An initial emergency meeting was held in Washington in November 2008, a second in London in April 2009. Although American and other Western leaders still had major roles, so too did others. Leaders such as China's prime minister, Hu Jintao, and Brazil's president, Luis Inácio Lula da Silva, played much greater roles than developing country leaders had ever played before at a major international economic summit. They and others brought their own perspectives, as can be seen in the excerpts from news accounts around the world in the "International Perspectives" box (p. 538).

This greater assertiveness reflected the underlying economics. Even before the 2008 crisis hit, the original G7's share of world output, still at 65 percent as of 2003, was projected to fall to 37 percent by 2030. The major emerging economies were increasing their share from 7 percent to 32 percent. In this respect the pressure for greater representativeness was quite logical. Broader representativeness, though, did not ensure more effective global governance capacity. With even more parties at the table, an even wider range of positions came into play. Policy preferences still were largely based on national strategies

## INTERNATIONAL PERSPECTIVES

INTERNATIONAL PERSPECTIVES

### VIEWS ON THE 2008-2009 GLOBAL ECONOMIC CRISIS

#### China

"America is the culprit and epicenter of the financial crisis, and now the world looks to China, hoping for the best and praying against the worst. Whether or not it will be able to heave a sigh of relief is directly related to China's economic growth this year. China is America's greatest creditor and before the summit meeting Wen Jia-Bao twice expressed concern over America's credit, forcing Obama to take a stand and reply.... China is the world's third great economic entity, and a steadying weight in the world economy, but she still knows how to stamp her feet."

#### India

"Was it because of the increasing economic clout of India or the personality of Manmohan Singh that prompted *Financial Times* [sic] to carry a full-page interview of the Indian Prime Minister yesterday with his colour picture? Only the newspaper editor has the answer....

"But Indians here are certainly feeling proud that their Prime Minister is attracting headlines in the British newspapers for the first time. Never in the past has any Indian leader been given so much of a space in a British newspaper....

"As world leaders grapple with differences on how to overcome the economic crisis, Prime Minister Manmohan Singh has asked the industrialised nations not to 'repeat past mistakes' of resorting to protectionism and favoured sharing information [sic] and bringing tax havens and non-cooperating jurisdictions under close scrutiny.

"'An issue of vital concern to developing countries is the rise of protectionist sentiment in the industrialised world. This phenomenon is not surprising, given the downturn in economic activity and the rise in unemployment,' Singh said."

#### Saudi Arabia

"[B]ehind the hype of these new-found resource commitments to the IMF is a potentially divisive power struggle looming between the old developed economies led by the US, UK, EU and Japan and the emerging new tiger economies led by China, India, Brazil and Saudi Arabia. ... [T]he IMF is in need of radical change and an image makeover."

**South Africa**

"The recent meeting of the G20 summit dispelled some of this negativity because a total of 1.1-trillion was pledged to restore a bruised and battered global economy. The meeting had a profound effect—causing markets to rally as risk appetite suddenly returned. . . . The change in sentiment bodes well for South Africa, because the increase in risk appetite leads to increased investment flows into emerging markets."

**Brazil**

"President Luiz Inacio Lula da Silva said Thursday he wants to be the first Brazilian leader whose administration will lend money to the International Monetary Fund. . . .

"Lula recalled during the press conference that Brazil used to borrow from the IMF not too long ago. He also said that he had previously participated in protests against the IMF.

"'Don't you find it very chic that Brazil is lending to the IMF? I spent part of my youth carrying banners against the IMF in downtown Sao Paulo,' he said. . . .

"Lula said the G20 meeting was the first in which he saw developed and emerging nations negotiating as equals. To him, the London summit is a great step toward a new economic reality in the world."

Sources: Shen Pei-Jun, "As China Sits, America Stands Off to the Side," *United Daily News*, April 8, 2009, John Yu, trans., http://watchingamerica.com/News/25220/as-china-sits-america-stands-off-to-the-side/ (accessed 7/30/09); Ashok Tuteja, "PM Fully Booked"; "Don't Repeat Mistakes: PM" (PTI [Press Trust of India), *Tribune*, online edition, April 3, 2009, www.tribuneindia.com/2009/20090403/world.htm#4 (accessed 7/30/09); Mushtak Parker, "Will IMF Prove Global Fund of Last Resort?" *Arab News*, April 9, 2009, www.arabnews.com/?page=6&section=0&article=121360&d=9&m=4&y=2009 (accessed 7/30/09); Rushil Jaga, "Cautious Optimism After G20 Perks up Markets," *The Times*, April 18, 2009, www.thetimes.co.za/News/Article.aspx?id=982942 (accessed 7/30/09); "Brazilian President Happy to Lend Money to IMF," *China View*, April 2, 2009, http://news.xinhuanet.com/english/2009-04/03/content_1126744.htm (accessed 7/30/09).

and domestic politics. Those still left out pushed for a G20-plus. The gap between globalization and global governance capacity was at best simply narrowed a bit.

Within the broader critique of the overall system, the main issue was U.S. dominance. Whereas in the past the American economy had helped pull others out of economic crises, in the 2008 economic crisis the American economy was the epicenter from which the shock waves went out. Though not the only cause of the crisis, American economic policies and practices were the principal one. After all, at a time when the United States had become a major debtor, the four ***BRIC*** countries (Brazil, Russia, India, China) held 40 percent of global gold and currency reserves. China alone was financing close to $2 trillion in American debt. The term *BRICs* had been around for a while, actually having been coined by a Goldman Sachs economist in 2001. Though not constituting a formal alliance or bloc, the BRICs started holding summit meetings in June 2009. "The world economy should not remain entangled, so directly and unnecessarily, in the vicissitudes of a single great world power," said Roberto Mangabeira Unger, Brazil's minister for strategic affairs.[16]

Was the American model one that other countries should emulate? Many analysts, commentators, and policy makers saw the Wall Street meltdown as not merely a cyclical downturn but as a demonstration of the inherent excesses of the American version of capitalism. They saw the failure of GM as exemplifying the loss of the innovative entrepreneurialism that had been a key part of past American economic success. Yes, in the twentieth century capitalism had demonstrated its superiority to socialism. But in the twenty-first century the debate was between different forms of capitalism, the heavily laissez-faire American version and the state-directed versions that had evolved in a number of countries, including China, India, Brazil and some OPEC members. Does the market need the state as much as the state needs the market?[17] Indeed, even in the United States the state was playing a larger role in the economy than it traditionally had, at least in the immediate term.

All told, the forces driving change in the international economic system preceded the current crisis and will remain even if the crisis is effectively managed. The system is under pressure to change. America's twenty-first-century role and position will be different than in the twentieth century. And irrespective of who plays what role, the fundamental challenge will continue to be closing the globalization–global governance gap.

## International Trade

The year 1971 was the first since 1893 in which the United States ran a balance-of-payments deficit (see Table 10.1). Since then the American trade balance has been in surplus only twice, in 1973 and 1975. The trade deficit first exceeded $100 billion in 1984. Since 1998 the trade deficit has shot up to record levels. In 2000 it was over $377 billion; in 2004, over $611 billion; in 2008, almost $700 billion.

The ***trade deficit*** goes up when the growth in the value of American exports does not keep up with the growth in the value of American imports. A number of factors contribute to this dynamic. Export growth is principally affected by four of these: economic growth rates in other countries and their consequent overall demand for goods and services, in-

**TABLE 10.1 The U.S. Trade Balance, 1960–2008 (in millions of dollars)**

| | Exports | Imports | Trade balance |
|---|---|---|---|
| 1960 | 25,940 | 22,432 | 3,508 |
| 1970 | 56,640 | 54,386 | 2,254 |
| 1971 | 59,677 | 60,979 | −1,302 |
| 1980 | 271,834 | 291,241 | −19,407 |
| 1985 | 289,070 | 410,950 | −121,880 |
| 1990 | 535,233 | 616,097 | −80,864 |
| 1995 | 794,387 | 890,771 | −96,384 |
| 1996 | 851,602 | 955,667 | −104,065 |
| 1997 | 934,453 | 1,042,402 | −107,949 |
| 1998 | 933,174 | 1,097,780 | −164,606 |
| 1999 | 965,884 | 1,229,170 | −263,286 |
| 2000 | 1,070,597 | 1,448,156 | −377,559 |
| 2001 | 1,004,896 | 1,367,691 | −362,795 |
| 2002 | 974,721 | 1,395,789 | −421,067 |
| 2003 | 1,016,096 | 1,510,993 | −494,897 |
| 2004 | 1,151,942 | 1,763,238 | −611,296 |
| 2005 | 1,275,245 | 1,991,975 | −716,370 |
| 2006 | 1,451,685 | 2,212,044 | 760,359 |
| 2007 | 1,643,168 | 2,344,590 | 701,423 |
| 2008 | 1,826,590 | 2,522,532 | 695,937 |

Source: U.S. Census Bureau, "U.S. Trade in Goods and Services—Balance of Payments (BOP) Basis," www.census.gov/foreign-trade/statistics/historical/gands.pdf (accessed 7/30/09).

cluding for American exports; the openness of other countries' markets; currency exchange rates and the international value of the dollar; and the overall competitiveness of American exporters against foreign domestic producers and other exporters. Import growth is affected by its own four factors: U.S. economic growth rates and the consequent overall demand for goods and services from both domestic and foreign producers; the openness of American markets; price patterns of imports, particularly oil; and the competitiveness of American domestic producers against foreign producers selling in American markets. Thus, for example, the 1997–2000 jump in the U.S. trade deficit was driven in large part by the discrepancy between the global recession that followed the 1997 Asian financial crisis and the continuing American domestic economic boom. The drop in the trade deficit in 2001 came about despite a decline in U.S. exports, because of a larger decline in U.S. imports due to recession at home. In 2002 imports went up, but exports kept going down. The trade defict thus increased by almost 90 percent in the first five years of the Bush administration. The big jumps in 2004 and 2005 were largely due to major increases in imports as the American economy recovered from recession. The weaker dollar, which made American exports less expensive, combined with slower rates of import growth amid the emerging domestic economic problems to bring the trade deficit down in 2007 and 2008, albeit only by a little.

Two of the principal components of this deficit are trade with China and oil imports. In 2008 the bilateral trade deficit with China was $266 billion. This amounted to 38 percent of the total deficit. It was three times greater than the next-largest bilateral deficit, which was with Japan. Some of the deficit was due to China's manipulation of its exchange rate in ways some considered an unfair trade practice. Overall it reflected the heavy investments made by American manufacturing companies in China for lower-wage, lower-priced consumer goods for the market back home, and the corresponding profits companies made.

The oil import bill in 2008, the year oil prices went up to over $140 per barrel and gasoline to four to five dollars per gallon, was almost $342 billion. This was over $100 billion more than the previous year, even though the actual volume of oil imports was lower. Nor was this the first time for such a differential. In 2005 the cost was one-third more than in 2004, even though the volume was about 2 percent less. America's "oil addiction" had been causing trade problems, along with environmental and other ones, at least since 1973, the year that the first OPEC oil crisis hit. The 1979 Iranian revolution set off another oil crisis, the 1990–91 Persian Gulf War another, the 2003 Iraq War another, although less severe, one. All of these crises resulted from a combination of supply-driven and OPEC cartel decisions to raise prices. The 2008 crisis was much more demand driven, reflecting the entry into the global marketplace of India, China, and other rapidly growing countries. Although global demand slowed amid the 2008–2009 economic crisis, there was little doubt that it would rise again.

Over the years there had been numerous calls to action to reduce oil dependence from various U.S. administrations: from President Nixon after the 1973 OPEC crisis, President Carter after the 1979 OPEC crisis, from President George W. Bush about America's "oil addiction," and from President Obama. With only 4 percent of world population, the United States accounts for 25 percent of world oil consumption. About 70 percent of this is in the transportation sector. American fuel efficiency standards for cars lag far behind not only Europe's and Japan's but also China's. Reducing vulnerability to that next oil crisis is as much if not more about domestic policy than foreign policy. Will U.S. policy be more concerted and serious than in the past?

## *The World Trade Organization (WTO)*

The 1994 Uruguay Round trade agreement was the transition from the General Agreement on Tariffs and Trade (GATT) discussed in Chapter 4 to the ***World Trade Organization (WTO).**** The WTO was designed as a significantly stronger multilateral institution

*Like previous rounds of multilateral trade negotiations, the Uruguay Round Table agreement was named for the locale (country or city) in which the negotiations were initiated.

than the GATT had been. One aspect of this strengthening is the WTO's formalization as an institution. Whereas the GATT always was more of a set of agreements than an international institution per se, the WTO has full legal standing and is very much a formal organization, with more than five hundred employees at its headquarters in Geneva, Switzerland. The WTO is also more inclusive than was its predecessor. As of 2008, 153 countries were members of the WTO (accounting for over 97 percent of world trade), with many other countries in the process of applying for membership.

The Uruguay Round agreement extended free-trade policies to additional economic sectors. Whereas the GATT principally had covered trade in industrial and manufactured goods, the Uruguay Round also included agreements on trade in services (e.g., banking, insurance, some investment areas), intellectual property (e.g., movies, books, computer software, other inventions), and other areas. The term *GATT* still is used to refer to the trade agreements covering industrial goods; it has now been supplemented by the GATS, General Agreement on Trade in Services; TRIPS, Trade Related Aspects of Intellectual Property Rights; and TRIMs, Trade Related Investment Measures. In the years since the Uruguay Round, additional agreements have been reached covering telecommunications and information technology equipment as well as further liberalization of financial services.

One of the general issues that has been the most controversial within the United States has been the greater regulatory authority given to the WTO. In the past the GATT secretariat could play an advisory and facilitative role in resolving trade disputes, but it lacked authority to impose a settlement. The WTO, by contrast, has been given ***dispute-settlement authority*** that is binding. Initial rulings by its panels can be appealed, at which point the final decision is made by a vote of the full membership. Each country has one vote, irrespective of its size. This structure is like the UN General Assembly, and quite different from other international economic institutions such as the IMF and the World Bank, where voting is proportional to a country's financial contribution. For the United States this means that, whereas it gets about a 17 percent vote in the IMF and the World Bank, in the WTO its vote counts no more than that of any other country.

In general, proponents of a strong dispute-settlement process believe that in the end it is beneficial because it adds to the sense of order that is critical for the growth of global trade. If American exporters are being treated unfairly, they now have a better chance of making their case on its merits to the WTO (a neutral third party) and having the dispute resolved in their favor. However, critics fear that any such benefits are outweighed by other countries' using and abusing the system against the United States, taking advantage of a forum in which the rules provide power in numbers. These critics would prefer the older way of doing things, whereby American power and status could be brought to bear, whether explicitly or implicitly, to help resolve trade disputes in the United States' favor. Proponents, on the other hand, see the WTO as a needed administrative and regulatory body for an age of such extensive trade interdependence.

THE DOHA ROUND In late 2001, two years after an earlier effort to begin a new round of global trade negotiations failed amid massive antiglobalization protests at the WTO summit in Seattle, the ***Doha Round*** of trade negotiations (named for the capital of Qatar) was launched. The Doha Declaration, released at the first meeting, stressed the overall free trade goal of "maintain[ing] the process of reform and liberalization of trade policies." Within that goal it pledged "to ensure that developing countries, and especially the least developed among them, secure a share of the growth of world trade commensurate with their needs of economic development." It was dubbed the "Doha Development Round," reflecting the greater emphasis than in past rounds on the issues most affecting developing countries. The particulars of the Doha negotiating agenda picked up where the 1994 Uruguay Round had left off: further reductions in tariffs and non-tariff barriers, further liberalization of trade in services (GATS), follow-up work on TRIMs, some key TRIPs measures including on pharmaceuticals and the global AIDS crisis, and issues involving trade and the environment, electronic commerce, technology transfer, and agriculture among others. January 1, 2005, was set as the deadline for reaching agreement. But that deadline has long since passed.

The George W. Bush administration came into office trumpeting its strong support of free trade, but its record on this issue was mixed. On the one hand, it made a proposal for the elimination of tariffs on manufactured goods by 2015. On the other hand, in 2002 the administration raised tariffs on steel to protect the American steel industry against imports from the European Union, Russia, Brazil, East Asia, and other lower-cost producers. Unquestionably, the American steel industry had been hit hard: more than one-third of the companies in the U.S. steel industry had gone into bankruptcy, 20 percent of domestic steel production capacity had been shut down, and more than seventy thousand workers had lost their jobs. But questions arose about whether higher tariffs were the optimal policy response, whether they were allowable under WTO rules, and whether such actions amounted to hypocrisy on the part of the free-trade-preaching United States.

Similar debate arose over agricultural trade. In 2002 the Bush administration and Congress increased subsidies to American agriculture by $180 billion over the next decade. Although proponents claim that these subsidies fulfill a necessary economic need on the part of American farmers, critics see subsidies as a major hit on the U.S. budget deficit and a significant barrier to developing countries' efforts to compete in global markets. To be sure, the United States is far from the only offender. The European Union, Japan, and other developed countries have their own agricultural protectionism. All told, the developed world pays out over $300 billion a year in agricultural subsidies, which is seven times more than what it gives out in foreign aid for economic development. By one estimate, a 40 percent reduction in agricultural protectionism on the part of developed countries would increase the world's real income by $60 billion per year.[18] This is why agricultural trade has been such a big issue in the Doha Round.

As noted earlier, though not leading to total abandonment of the free-trade system, the 2008 global economic crisis did set off additional protectionism. One study found that fifty-five of seventy-seven trade measures enacted in various countries in the months after the economic crisis hit were trade restrictive.[19] France conditioned its aid to its auto industry on using French-made parts and relocating factories from Eastern Europe back home. British banks being bailed out were required to make loans to British companies and individuals the priority. Russia added import barriers on cars and farm machinery. Indonesia told civil servants to consume food, clothing, shoes, and other products made only in Indonesia. Malaysia expelled foreign workers. Argentina imposed discriminatory licensing requirements. India and Brazil raised tariffs on steel. China tightened standards that discriminated against imports. "Buy American" provisions restricted chunks of the $787 billion stimulus package to American firms.

## *Western Hemisphere Free Trade Agreements*

The ***North American Free Trade Agreement (NAFTA),*** approved in 1993, created a free-trade area among the three North American countries: Canada, Mexico, and the United States. Proponents have stressed the value of creating the world's largest free-trade area, linking 444 million people producing $17 trillion worth of goods and services. American exports to its NAFTA partners nearly tripled in the first fifteen years. Canada and Mexico also are said to have benefited. Critics differ on a number of points, particularly on attributing job loss in the United States to factories moving to Mexico. The debate not only was intense when NAFTA was up for approval in 1993, but has remained so. During the 2008 Democratic presidential primaries in Ohio and Pennsylvania, both candidates Barack Obama and Hillary Clinton stressed their opposition to more than their support for NAFTA.

In the late Clinton and early Bush years there were efforts to create a hemisphere-wide Free Trade Area of the Americas (FTAA). FTAA supporters claimed that it "would open a spectrum of new economic opportunities for the United States and every other nation of the hemisphere."[20] Their main argument was the regional version of free trade theory and strategy: free trade promotes growth; growth benefits all. Opponents' main arguments were the regional version of the free trade critique: labor unions and others within the United States feared that jobs would be lost as manufacturing and other industries increasingly move to lower-wage Latin American countries; some within Latin America feared domination by large U.S. corporations and local elites without significant reduction of economic inequality; and environmental groups pressed for stronger regionwide standards to protect the environment. The FTAA had the same January 2005 deadline as the WTO Doha Round. It too did not come close to meeting its deadline.

The ***Central American Free Trade Agreement (CAFTA)*** encapsulated this debate. An intermediate step between NAFTA and FTAA, CAFTA was negotiated in 2003–2004 among the United States, Guatemala, Honduras, Nicaragua, El Salvador and the Dominican Republic. It came to the U.S. Congress for approval in 2005. After extensive debate, largely along the lines noted above, it was approved by the Congress with a comfortable margin in the Senate (54–45) but in a very close vote in the House (217–215). Moreover, any expectation that CAFTA's approval would catalyze momentum on FTAA was dashed at the hemispheric summit later that year in Argentina, when President Bush was greeted with massive protests in the streets and no significant agreement could be reached among the leaders.

Bilateral free trade agreements have been signed and entered into force with Chile and Peru. The Colombia free-trade agreement was signed, but its approval by the U.S. Congress was caught up in human rights concerns and other issues. The Panama free-trade agreement also was signed but has not yet been fully approved.

## International Finance

U.S. goals for the international financial system remain fundamentally the same as when the system was set up at the end of World War II: help provide the monetary and financial stability necessary for global economic growth and particularly for the growth of international trade; avoid the monetary versions of economic nationalism and protectionism that lead countries to compete more than they cooperate; and in these and other ways contribute to international peace and stability. The system as designed has been grounded in free-market principles but with sufficient international management and regulation to prevent or at least correct the imperfections of market forces. This management has been carried out primarily through the multilateral institutional structure of the ***International Monetary Fund (IMF),*** with the United States in a lead role, and with Japan and western Europe also playing key roles.

However, the 2008 global economic crisis, on top of the smaller but still substantial financial crises in the 1990s, has called these arrangements into question.

### *1990s Financial Crises*

Beginning in the mid-1990s, the world economy was wracked by a chain of financial crises in Asia and Latin America. The first of these crises hit Mexico in 1995. The Mexican peso collapsed, losing almost half its value in less than a month. In this crisis as well as the others, primary responsibility lay with the national government itself.

A key additional factor that made the crisis so severe was the problem of "hot money"—short-term investments in stocks, bonds, and currencies for quick returns. Such investments are held by investors ready and able to shift these funds from one country to another at the slightest doubt about the rate of return. Hot money had been surging into Mexico, so much so that it was second only to China in the amount of foreign investment entering the country between 1990 and 1994. When the worse-than-expected economic news broke on top of concerns about political stability, both Mexican and foreign investors rushed their funds out of Mexican financial markets.

The Mexican crisis hit home in the United States. The success of NAFTA was at stake, just a year after the hard-fought political battle to pass the agreement. Concern arose about "contagion" effects spreading to other countries in the Western Hemisphere. In putting together a financial rescue package, the Clinton administration faced substantial congressional opposition, which claimed that the proposed rescue plan would misuse American taxpayers' money to "bail out" Mexico and Wall Street. The administration therefore resorted to a bit of an end-run to provide much-needed aid to Mexico by drawing on the president's discretionary authority to meet an economic emergency without additional congressional legislation. Working with the IMF, the administration put together a package of credits worth $50 billion, of which about $20 billion came from the United States.

The ***Asian financial crisis*** that struck in mid-1997 involved not just one country but a number of them. It started in Thailand and spread to Indonesia and South Korea. These "Asian tigers" had been success stories, exemplars of the newly industrialized countries that the United States hailed in the 1970s and 1980s as proof that capitalism worked better than socialism or other forms of statism. But the underside of East Asian capitalism—its speculative investments, cronyism and corruption, overconsumption of imports, and excessive debt—now burst the bubbles. This crisis proved much less controllable than the Mexican one. In the second half of 1997 the Thai, Korean, and Indonesian stock markets fell by 33 to 45 percent. Their currencies (the baht, won, and rupiah, respectively) fell by even larger percentages. In all three cases, the overall GDP shrank, meaning that their economies were shrinking and massive numbers of working- and middle-class families were losing their jobs and most of their savings.

U.S. interests were affected in a number of ways by this crisis. American banks and mutual funds had invested heavily in Asian markets. American companies had factories, fast-food restaurants, computer programming, and other major investments at risk. American exporters lost some of their fastest-growing markets, accounting for a big chunk of the rise in the 1998–2000 trade deficit. And all three countries were political allies of the United States. In Indonesia the government of President Suharto fell; this was a potentially positive change, given Suharto's thirty-two-year-long corrupt and authoritarian rule, but the immediate effects were more chaos and rising political violence. There also was continuing concern about the spread of the crisis to Japan, already having serious economic problems. If worsened, these problems could make the crisis spiral dangerously downward.

Then two other major countries, Russia and Brazil, joined the list of financial crisis victims. The Russian crisis hit in late 1998; the ruble had tumbled by 282 percent by December 1998 and 324 percent by May 1999. Even though less foreign investment was at stake in Russia than in the Mexican and Asian cases, the Russian crisis had a "last straw" effect on investor psychology and set off a sharp drop on Wall Street. The Dow Jones industrial average plummeted more than 20 percent. This crisis also affected average Americans, who watched their retirement funds, college savings for their children, and other nest eggs shrink with each passing day. The stock market restabilized later in 1998, only to have Brazil—another heralded economic success story, the world's eighth-largest economy, and a potential source of contagion to other parts of Latin America—go into financial crisis in early 1999. Two years later it was Argentina, albeit not so much because of a direct contagion from Brazil as a manifestation of its own extensive fiscal and financial problems.

In the Asian, Russian, Brazilian, and Argentinean crises, IMF rescue packages were put together, but they were less effective than in the Mexican case. There were a number of reasons for this, among which were greater doubts than before about both U.S. and IMF policy.

## *Policy Debates over the IMF*

When a country faces financial crisis, the IMF usually makes credits and other support available, but also insists that the recipient state agree to tight fiscal policies, outright austerity measures, and economic reforms as a condition of receiving the IMF assistance. From the IMF's point of view, overspending, inefficiency, corruption, and other forms of economic ineptitude are what get countries into financial fixes, and unless major reforms are put in place any added money likely will be wasted. In the 1995 Mexican peso crisis, for example, the IMF made its financing conditional on Mexican agreement to implement stringent fiscal and monetary policies and take other steps to stabilize the exchange rate and reform the economy. This is the financial piece of the Washington consensus discussed earlier. According to the Washington consensus, too much government regulation and spending are the problem, and greater deregulation of banks and other financial markets are key to the solution. These and other policy guidelines are established as "conditionalities" that must be met for a country to receive IMF loans and credits. The IMF then disburses the financing in "tranches" at designated intervals, conditional on compliance and performance.

Two quite different critiques were offered of the IMF formula. One was that the Washington consensus had it wrong.[21] It overvalued the benefits of freeing markets up and overassumed that what was good for capital would be good for developing world economies. It relied too much on "one size fits all" solutions and did not tailor strategies to different national political and economic contexts and structures. Its emphasis on "structual adjustment" policies, with their fiscal austerity, cut deeply into employment, health, and other government services that provided a safety net for those most in need. In these and other ways, the medicine was too harsh; in the name of saving the patient it risked killing him. In countries already in serious crisis, the immediate effect of IMF austerity was to ratchet up unemployment, push up the prices of food and other staples, and cut way back on the social safety net governments could provide. There had to be a better way to get reform, these critics argued, a more graduated approach that still had room for necessary social services.

The other critique held that the IMF's readiness to bail countries out when they got in financial trouble created a version of the classic problem of "moral hazard." This means that in the name of providing help, incentives for the very behavior and actions that are to be encouraged are in fact reduced because the IMF demonstrates that, if things get bad enough, someone else will step in to reduce the risks and lower the costs. Might the very success of the 1995 bailout of Mexico have led the Thai, Korean, and Indonesian governments to think that they could continue in their profligate and corrupt ways, for if real trouble hit, the IMF would be there for them, too? Perhaps U.S. banks and mutual funds felt the same false sense of security. States and others in similar situations are more likely to learn and change their ways, this argument claims, if they have to pay the price for their mistakes.

Another level of the debate touched on the very viability of the IMF as the principal multilateral institution for managing the international financial system. Here, too, we got two quite contrasting sets of arguments. One view was that the IMF is not powerful enough, and that a much stronger international financial institution needs to be created, possibly a global central bank modeled after the U.S. Federal Reserve. International rules and norms also need to be changed to allow countries, as a French official put it, "to bring the Frankenstein of deregulated global financial markets under control."[22] Doing so could include policies such as capital controls, long prohibited as inconsistent with free markets and unfettered capital flows, but now advocated by some in at least their partial form as a necessary check on the extraordinary power that markets wield.

Other critics, such as the former treasury secretary Robert Rubin, concurred on the need for change but questioned whether such sweeping new proposals would not end up creating a host of their own problems. Instead they pushed for reforms to strengthen the IMF in a more step-by-step manner. Among their proposals were policies requiring greater "transparency," that is, more disclosure of financial information to the IMF both by banks and other private-sector actors and by national governments; new powers for the IMF to act preventively before a full financial crisis hits; and increases in the funds available to the IMF.

Further compounding this debate were the beginnings of broader shifts in international monetary power. As Joan Spero and Jeffrey Hart write, "although the United States is still necessary, it is not sufficiently powerful to fulfill its earlier role. . . . In a world in which monetary power is more widely dispersed, management will depend not on the preferences of a dominant power but on the negotiations of several key powers."[23] When

Spero and Hart wrote this in 1997, they were principally referring to Europe and the development of the ***euro*** as a common currency. Now in the wake of the 2008 global financial crisis, it also—and arguably even more so—means China and others.

## *Shifts in International Financial Power?*

Consider the Chinese position: You hold almost $2 trillion in hard currency reserves. You are the world's largest creditor. The United States has become the world's largest debtor. You view the 2008 global financial crisis, as do many others around the world, as largely due to American financial irresponsibility, both on Wall Street and in Washington. Your own economy has been damaged by this American profligacy. Why should the system continue to operate with most of the power to set the rules still in U.S. hands?

Even taking into account that China and other countries also contributed to their own economic problems through their own policies, the core argument cannot be summarily dismissed. Other countries are making it, too, as are some analysts and policy makers within the U.S. debate. And it both feeds into and is fed by the broader power shifts of this global era, as we discussed back in Chapter 6.

One issue is whether the dollar should remain the principal currency for financial reserves and trade exchanges. In early 2009 China proposed giving a larger role to IMF "special drawing rights" (SDRs). SDRs are not actual currency you can put in your wallet, but a unit of accounting administered by the IMF that is usable for various international transactions. Its value is based on a "basket" of currencies, of which the dollar represents over 40 percent and the rest are European and Japanese currencies. SDRs have been around since 1969 but have not been used very much. In April 2009, though, for the first time in almost thirty years, the IMF issued over $250 billion in SDRs, more than 800 percent more than the prior *cumulative* total. At the June 2009 BRICs summit, India, Russia, and Brazil joined China in advocating a shift towards SDRs and other steps for a "more diversified" global monetary system. Although the economics are such that it is not in the interest of the BRICs and most other countries to reduce the role of the dollar too much too quickly, this may be the beginning of one of the most significant changes in the international financial system since Bretton Woods.[24]

The BRICs's communiqué also called for a "greater voice" for themselves and other developing countries in international financial institutions. Along with the currencies issue, this call is directed at such intra-IMF issues as the requirement that the IMF director be a European and the distribution of voting rights. Why shouldn't developing-world experts also be eligible? Voting rights have been based on percentage contributions to the IMF budget. At one time this was over 40 percent for the United States; it now is about 17 percent. Although this is not enough to prevail on a vote on its own, this share is much greater than that of any other country: Japan is at 6.1 percent, the United Kingdom 4.9 percent, China 3.7 percent. In 2008, the IMF did alter the formula slightly so that developing countries' votes were slightly larger than their actual budget contributions. We may not contribute as much money, the argument ran, but we are heavily affected by IMF policies. The BRICs's position is based on both increasing their budget contributions and the "who is affected" argument.

Amid this debate about the IMF's future, the institution also has been turned to for immediate steps. Of the $1.1 trillion in additional support for the global economy pledged at the April 2009 G20 summit, $575 billion was to be new IMF lending commitments and credit guarantees. Among the countries with new IMF packages were Pakistan, Ukraine, Hungary, Turkey, Iceland, and El Salvador. By June 2009 the IMF already had committed more money to Africa than in all of 2008, and 2008 was a record year. This has rekindled debates about conditionalities, the balance between overly restrictive requirements and too little accountability, and other aspects of the IMF role.

It is an interesting question whether these power shifts and policies are in the U.S. national interest. The dollar's role as the principal reserve currency has had benefits for the United States, including less pressure than other countries face to balance its budget and trade accounts. But it also has had costs, including in some respects enabling rather than checking huge deficits. Some still want to maximize U.S. centrality in the IMF, as with most other considerations of power. Others see forces of change as inherent to this global era and resisting them as counterproductive. They think that working with and shaping these forces toward shared interests is a more useful strategy.

## Global Poverty and Sustainable Development

***Sustainable development*** has been defined as a policy approach that "meets the needs of the present without compromising the ability of future generations to meet their own needs." Its conception of "needs of the present" has two key elements: an emphasis on issues of global inequality and "the essential needs of the world's poor, to which [sic] overriding priority should be given"; and a broadening of the agenda beyond just the economic aspects of development to also include such issues of human development and human security as AIDS and other global public health crises, hunger and nutrition, and education and literacy. "The real wealth of a nation is its people," states a major UN report. "And the purpose of development is to create an enabling environment for people to enjoy long, healthy and creative lives. This simple but powerful truth is too often forgotten in the pursuit of material and financial wealth."[25]

The other key part of the definition of sustainable development is its reference to future generations—a reference that is particularly relevant to the global environment. Can it really be considered development in the positive sense of the term if the economic growth rates achieved today result from overexploitation and despoliation of natural resources that will impose major costs and serious risks on future generations? Just as the first part of the definition of sustainable development broadens our conception, this second part puts it in a longer-term time frame. All told, the conception calls for policy makers to look beyond immediate pocketbook concerns, to look down the road and across the planet: across the planet at poverty and the dire conditions in which billions of people live; down the road to future generations for whom we are but stewards of the environment and creators of policies that have lasting legacies.

## *Poverty and the Human Condition*

Despite some economic-development success stories during the Cold War, overall not a lot of progress was made in reducing Third World poverty, in either absolute or relative terms. One of the most telling absolute measures is the World Bank's "human development index," which quantifies the quality of life for people around the world by tabulating income data (per capita GDP), basic nutrition, access to clean water and health services, life expectancy, adult literacy rates, and other indicators of the human condition. As of 2008, of 126 developing countries, only 29 made the "high" human development category, whereas 75 were in the "medium" and 22 in the "low" category.[26] This is an improvement over the 2004 figures cited in this book's previous edition, when only 21 countries made the high category and 36 were in the low. Still, only 23 percent of developing countries have "high" human development.

The most telling relative measure is the widening of the income gap between North and South. Whereas in 1960 about 70 percent of global income went to the richest 20 percent of countries, by 1990 this was up to 83 percent. Put another way, the ratio of the richest to the poorest had gone from 30:1—itself enormously unequal—to 64:1. Despite the end of the Cold War and other developments that seemed propitious for progress against Third World poverty and social ills, this overall trend continues. For every country whose per capita income went up in the 1990s, almost three have seen it go down. The map on page 561, depicting regions and countries in proportion to income, shows how disproportional global income distribution continues to be.

Moreover, the intracountry income gap between the "haves" and the "have-nots" has been getting wider. In Latin America the income share of the richest 20 percent of the population grew to more than 50 percent, whereas the poorest 20 percent receive only about 8 percent of their nations' income. In Mexico, for example, about half the people live below the poverty line, defined as earning less than $4 per family member per day. The top 10 percent elite hold 45 percent of the wealth, a gap that NAFTA has done little to narrow.[27] Life expectancy data also show gross inequalities. In Nairobi, Kenya, for example, infant mortality was only 15 per 1,000 births in the wealthiest area but 254 per 1,000 births in a poor neighborhood. Worldwide average life expectancy was eighty-one years for the richest 10 percent but forty-six years for the poorest 10 percent.[28]

Various leaders on the world scene have raised their voices on behalf of the world's poor. The late Pope John Paul II, in a speech to the UN General Assembly, put much of the blame on the developed world—and by implication particularly the United States—for its "consumerist culture," its "unjust criteria in the distribution of resources and production," and its politics "to safeguard special interest groups." The former UN secretary-general Kofi Annan, in a speech to the World Economic Forum, a conclave of the world's leading government officials and international business leaders, warned that until and unless people in poor countries can gain confidence in the global economy, it "will be fragile and vulnerable—vulnerable to backlash from all the '-isms' of our post–Cold War world: protectionism, populism, nationalism, ethnic chauvinism, fanaticism and terrorism." The key to gaining that confidence, he stressed, is to break away from the idea that the choice is only "between a global market driven . . . by calculations of short-term profit and one which has a human face."[29]

Other research and analysis supports a critical view of the international trading system's effect on development and poverty. Oxfam, a leading NGO, calls the WTO system "rigged rules and double standards." Oxfam's position is not protectionist; rather, it pushes for fairer trade. "The great rewards of globalised trade," the Nobel economics laureate Amartya Sen states in a tempered but critical assessment, "have come to some but not to others. What is needed is to create conditions for a fuller and fairer sharing of the enormous benefits of trade."[30] Notwithstanding their finding about the benefits of openness to trade, Spero and Hart also support the argument about the declining terms of North-South trade with data showing that between 1965 and 1991, the average terms of trade deteriorated almost 50 percent for the poorest Third World countries and about 30 percent for those considered middle-income developing countries.[31] In other words, the poorest countries were getting half as much value for their exports to the developed world, in terms of the prices they could charge compared with the prices they had to pay; middle-income countries were getting only about 70 percent value compared with 1965.

On the other hand, the World Bank economist David Dollar contends that those developing countries that have been most open to trade have made the most progress in reducing their poverty.[32] His logic follows classical free trade theory: free trade leads to higher economic growth than protectionism; higher economic growth leads to lower poverty. His main examples are China and India, both of which have substantially opened their economies and which together have gone from about 1 billion living on $1 or less per day in the late 1970s to about 650 million by the late 1990s.[33] Spero and Hart also report a very strong correlation between economic growth rates and "outward" rather than "inward" national economic policies—that is, policies open to foreign trade and investment rather than closed off through import substitution, expropriation of foreign investment, and the like. The difference was almost twofold between the 8–9 percent average growth rate for those Third World countries most outwardly oriented, and 3–4 percent for those most inwardly oriented.[34] Developing countries also have to be concerned about attracting foreign private investment.

In 2000, at what was billed as its Millennium Summit, the UN established ***Millennium Development Goals (MDGs).*** Including the United States, 189 countries agreed to eight MDGs with twenty-one targets within them, to be achieved by 2015 or sooner (see "At the Source," p. 555). As a set the MDGs have four principal characteristics: (1) they most fundamentally are about ending poverty; (2) they are based on a broad conception of development as not just about economic growth but also about education, health, women's rights, and other factors; (3) they exemplify the strategy of sustainable development, particularly with regard to the environment; and (4) they are geared to provide a role for the private sector as well as the public sector and NGOs.

With 2015 approaching, and with some of the goals set for 2010 already at their targeted deadline, how much progress has been made? The UN secretary-general, Ban Ki-moon, acknowledged that although progress had been made, "We are not on track to fulfill our commitments." For example, on the one hand the overall goal of reducing poverty was "within reach for the world as a whole," but sub-Saharan Africa remained far behind. About 1.6 billion people had gained access to safe drinking water since 1990, but 2.5 billion, almost half the developing world's population, still did not have improved sanitation. The gender parity index in primary education was at 95 percent or higher in six of ten regions, but at least ninety-five countries were not expected to meet the goal.[35]

Although the MDG concerning gender equality and empowering women refers particularly to education, a number of studies as well as actual programs have shown that broader economic empowerment of women can contribute substantially to development across the board. Nicholas Kristof and Sheryl WuDunn invoke the Chinese saying "women hold up half the sky" to make the point that if nations underinvest in half the population, the prospects for progress on any formidable challenge are that much less. Ending forced female labor, including sexual servitude; reducing maternal mortality; targeting economic assistance to women entrepreneurs; and providing equal legal rights to ownership and inheritance are among the principal women's empowerment policies, along with those on education. Secretary of State Hillary Clinton and others in the Obama administration have taken a number of initiatives along these lines. So too have various NGOs, including the Hunger Project, CARE, and Kiva. Some in the private sector also have come around to the view that, as a Goldman Sachs report put it, "Gender inequality hurts economic growth."[36]

## U.S. Foreign Aid Policy

***Foreign aid*** has been an important part of U.S. foreign policy for many years. The Lend-Lease program provided aid during World War II to Britain and the Soviet Union.

## AT THE SOURCE

AT THE SOURCE

### MILLENNIUM DEVELOPMENT GOALS

The Millennium Development Goals were adopted by the Untied Nations in 2000. Unless otherwise indicated, 2015 is the target date for reaching these goals.

**1. Eradicate extreme poverty and hunger**
Cut by 50 percent the proportion of people whose income is less than $1 per day
Full and productive employment for all, including women and young people
Cut by 50 percent the proportion of people who suffer from hunger

**2. Achieve universal primary education**
All children, boys and girls alike, should be able to complete primary education

**3. Promote gender equality and empower women**
Eliminate gender disparity in primary and secondary education, preferably by 2005, and in all levels of education by 2015

**4. Reduce child mortality**
Reduce by two-thirds the under-five mortality rate

**5. Improve maternal health**
Reduce by 75 percent the maternal mortality rate
Universal access to reproductive health

**6. Combat HIV/AIDS, malaria, and other diseases**
Halt and begin to reverse the spread of HIV/AIDS
By 2010, universal access to HIV/AIDS treatment for all who need it
Halt and begin to reverse the incidence of malaria and other diseases

**7. Ensure environmental sustainability**
Integrate the principles of sustainable development into country policies and programs and reverse the loss of environmental resources
By 2010, significant reduction in biodiversity loss
Cut by 50 percent the proportion of population without safe drinking water and sanitation
By 2020, significant improvement in lives of at least 100 million slum dwellers

(*Continued*)

*(Continued)*

**8. Develop a global partnership for development**

Address the special needs of least-developed countries, landlocked countries, and small island developing states

Develop further an open, rule-based, predictable, nondiscriminatory trading and financial system

Deal comprehensively with developing countries' debt

In cooperation with pharmaceutical companies, provide access to affordable essential drugs in developing countries

In cooperation with the private sector, make available benefits of new technologies, especially information and communications

Source: United Nations Millennium Development Goals, www.un.org/millenniumgoals/global.shtml (accessed 8/4/09).

The Marshall Plan (Chapters 1 and 4), providing recovery and reconstruction aid to Western Europe, was a crucial part of the Cold War. Aid to developing countries started with President Truman's Point Four program. The Kennedy administration launched the Alliance for Progress to aid Latin America, created the Peace Corps, and established the Agency for International Development (AID), which is still the principal government agency for foreign aid.

These and other administrations since have wrestled with four principal questions regarding foreign aid: how much, to whom, in what form, and how effective?

*How much foreign aid should the United States provide?* The United States used the end of the Cold War as a rationale to cut back on, rather than reallocate, its foreign aid. In inflation-adjusted terms, the decline was close to 50 percent. U.S. aid to Central America, for example, fell from $226 million a year in the 1980s to $26 million in 1997. The politics here were predictable in some respects but paradoxical in others. One poll found that 75 percent of the American public believed that too much was spent on foreign aid, and only 4 percent thought that too little was spent (17 percent thought the amount was about right). But whereas most people thought that foreign aid accounted for 15 percent of the federal budget, the actual figure is less than 1 percent.[37] When the question was rephrased to ask whether a full 1 percent was too little, too much, or about right, 46 percent said "about right," and only 34 percent "too little."

Overall economic aid was lower (adjusted for inflation) at the end of the Clinton administration than at the beginning. The Bush administration did increase foreign aid, although the increase was more military than economic and the economic increase went heavily to Iraq. The Obama administration's first budget provided some increase but less than pledged during the campaign, in significant part because of the transformed budget landscape amid the economic crisis.

The debate over how the United States compares with other countries hinges on the question of what measures to use. On the one hand, the total amount of U.S. aid is the largest in the world. On the other hand, a widely referenced standard is foreign aid as 0.7 percent of national income. Although only a few countries reach this level—Sweden, Norway, Denmark, the Netherlands, Luxembourg—the average among developed nations is 0.28. At about 0.15 percent, the United States ranks last.

*To whom should foreign aid go?* Officially, of course, U.S. policy always has favored Third World economic development. But in reality, for virtually the entire Cold War, this goal was a much lower priority than global containment. This is evident when we consider who received the bulk of U.S. Cold War foreign aid: geopolitically strategic countries such as South Vietnam in the 1960s and 1970s, Israel and Egypt since the late 1970s, and El Salvador in the 1980s. Post-9/11 geopolitical considerations have made Iraq and Afghanistan priorities.

*What form should aid take?* The principal debate here is over economic versus military aid. Between the end of the Cold War and 9/11, military aid decreased from 31 percent of total aid to 21 percent. After 9/11 it went back up to over 30 percent. Even these numbers don't show the full picture, though, because military support to other countries also takes other forms than what is considered military aid. Another aspect of the debate is over long-term development versus humanitarian relief. The sad fact is that humanitarian crises constantly arise and must be responded to, often exceeding the amount budgeted for them. Yet as long as the total amount of aid does not increase significantly and substantial chunks go to military aid, humanitarian relief and economic development will be at least partially paired in a zero-sum calculation.

*Through which channels should foreign aid go? Bilateral (country to country) or multilateral (through the World Bank and other international organizations, such as NGOs)?* About 10 percent of U.S. aid is multilateral, whereas the average for other major donors is 33 percent. Bilateral aid can be more specifically tailored to political considerations. To the extent that basic human needs and development are the priority, multilateral aid tends to be freer from politics. The debate over which channels are preferable also is a long-standing one. In recent years the "which channels" question has taken another turn: Should AID and other government agencies be the sole administrators of their own programs? Or should they partner with NGOs? The budgetary savings of having fewer permanent staff members on the government payroll and the strengths that NGOs bring to the mission have resulted in a trend toward partnerships. Concerns have arisen, though, about ending up with too little in-house government expertise. AID has fallen to about one-third the staffing level it had in 1990. The foreign service also has experienced shortages of trained personnel.

*How effective is foreign aid?* It's actually more effective than it often gets credit for. Villages all over the world have water and sanitation that they would not have had; schools have been built, jobs created, businesses started, infrastructures built. Foreign aid does suffer from being susceptible to easy criticism. But few would argue that foreign aid is as effective as it could be and needs to be. Some critics, such as Jeffrey Sachs, argue that more money and better programs are needed. Some programs fail because they do not have sufficient funding and resources to be brought up to scale and to have the follow-up necessary for sustainability. He also wants to deemphasize the one-size-fits-all approach and program design by outside bureaucracies whether U.S. AID or the World Bank. Sachs would prefer more "clinical economics," a differential diagnosis for each country combined with more rigorous methods for monitoring and evaluation.[38] William Easterly is much more skeptical of how effective even improved foreign aid can be. *The White Man's Burden: How the West's Efforts to Aid the Rest Have Done So Much Ill and So Little Good* is the title of one of his most important books. After fifty years and over $2.3 trillion in aid, "there is shockingly little to show for it. . . . [T]he majority of places we have meddled [with] the most are in fact no better off or are even worse off than they were before."[39] Plenty of others, scholars and policy experts, have joined this debate, in the United States and worldwide.

## The World Bank

The **World Bank** continues to be the principal multilateral institution for fighting global poverty. Over the years it has achieved many successes but has also been plagued by a number of failures and controversies. In the current era, it faces a number of key policy dilemmas. As with the WTO and the IMF, many critics were disillusioned with the World Bank's advocacy of the Washington consensus. As one former World Bank official wrote: "To argue that developing countries need market-friendly policies, stable macroeconomic environments . . . open and transparent capital markets and equity-based corporate structures with attention to modern shareholder values is to say that you will be developed when you are developed. It is the old debate about inputs and outputs, where everything that development brings has become a necessary input to achieving it."[40]

Debate is also swirling over the World Bank's commitment to sustainable development. The bank long was seen by environmentalists as among the worst offenders, and much in need of "greening" in its policies and programs. Since the mid-1990s it has taken a number of steps in this direction. Critics have also pointed to the need to pay more attention to corruption, political repression, and other domestic political issues in recipient countries. Traditionally, the World Bank claimed that it was apolitical, that its decisions were economic ones based on economic criteria, and that its success was to be evaluated on the basis of growth rates and other hard economic data. By the mid-1990s, though, the

World Bank had begun to shift its stand, acknowledging the strong evidence that good government is a necessary part of sound economic development. This evidence was reinforced by cases such as Indonesia, a formerly vaunted success story that was then undermined in large part by massive corruption.

A further issue is the extent to which donor countries should be allowed to attach political conditions to their lending and voting.* In theory, as a multilateral economic development institution the World Bank is supposed to be detached from the politics of the international agenda. Yet the United States, its biggest donor, has also been the country most inclined to make political linkages and attach conditions to its funding. Some of these restrictions have been initiated by presidents, some imposed by Congress. Back when the U.S. voting share in the World Bank was over 40 percent, it was much easier for the United States to impose its position. But with its voting share less than 17 percent now and without the bloc strength of the Cold War alliances, other countries are both more willing and more able to oppose the United States on these issues. Moreover, the United States now also needs to be concerned about precedents; in the future other countries might also seek to impose political conditions on World Bank lending and be able to get 51 percent of the vote despite U.S. opposition.

Just as the IMF directorship has been reserved for a European, the World Bank president always has been an American. The push from emerging powers and developing countries for greater inclusiveness also includes opening this position up.

## *Overpopulation and World Hunger*

The *global population problem* has grown worse. World population is now around 7 billion. Population growth in the 1990s was the fastest in the 250 years that such measurements have been taken. In 1800, world population was 1 billion. It took 125 years to reach 2 billion (1925). It then took 35 years to reach 3 billion (1960). Since then the intervals have been 14 years (4 billion, 1974), 13 years (5 billion, 1987), and 12 years (6 billion, 1999). Projections for 2050 are of growth to 9.1 billion. Not only is the sheer size of these numbers a problem in itself, but more than 90 percent of this population growth is in the Third World. This includes tripling in some of the poorest of the poor countries, such as Burundi, Chad, Congo, Liberia, Niger, and Uganda.[41]

Take a look back at the standard world map at the front of this book. The map is based on country size as measured in its land mass. Now consider the alternative global maps on pages 560 and 561. One is drawn proportional to population size. China and India are much larger than in the standard map; so, too, are large-population countries

*As in the IMF but not in the UN General Assembly, voting in the World Bank is not "one country, one vote" but is proportional to the size of a country's financial contribution.

## ALTERNATIVE GLOBAL MAP

### Global Population Patterns

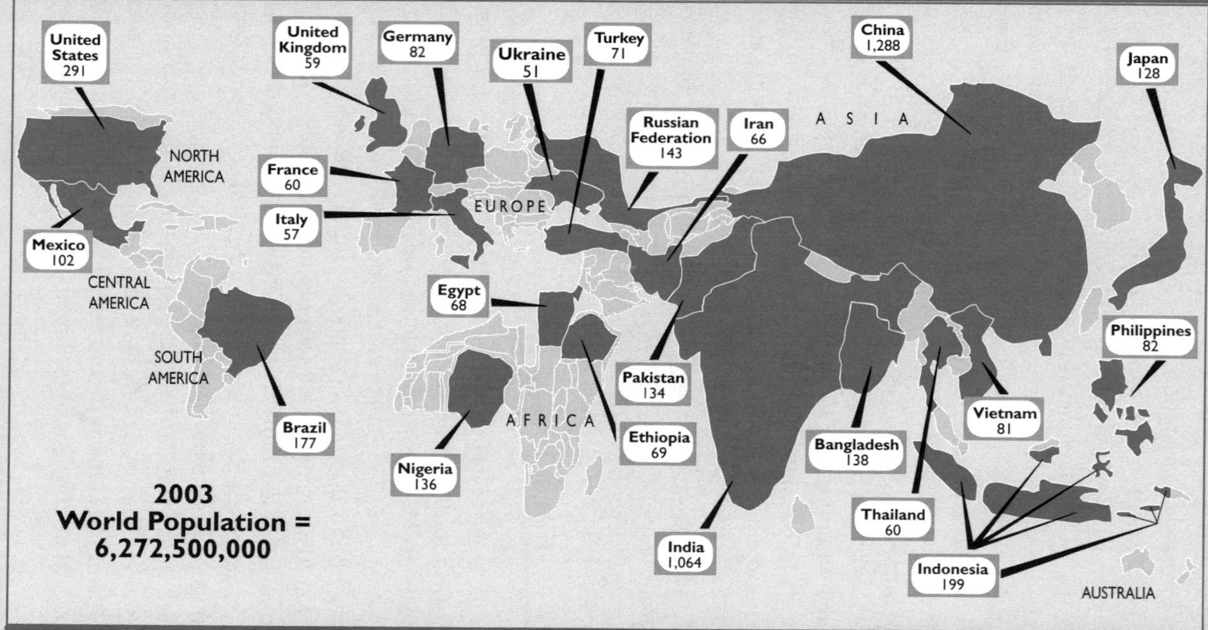


Note: All figures in millions

Source: *2005 World Development Indicators* (Washington, D.C.: World Bank, 2005)

## ALTERNATIVE GLOBAL MAP

### Global Income Distribution

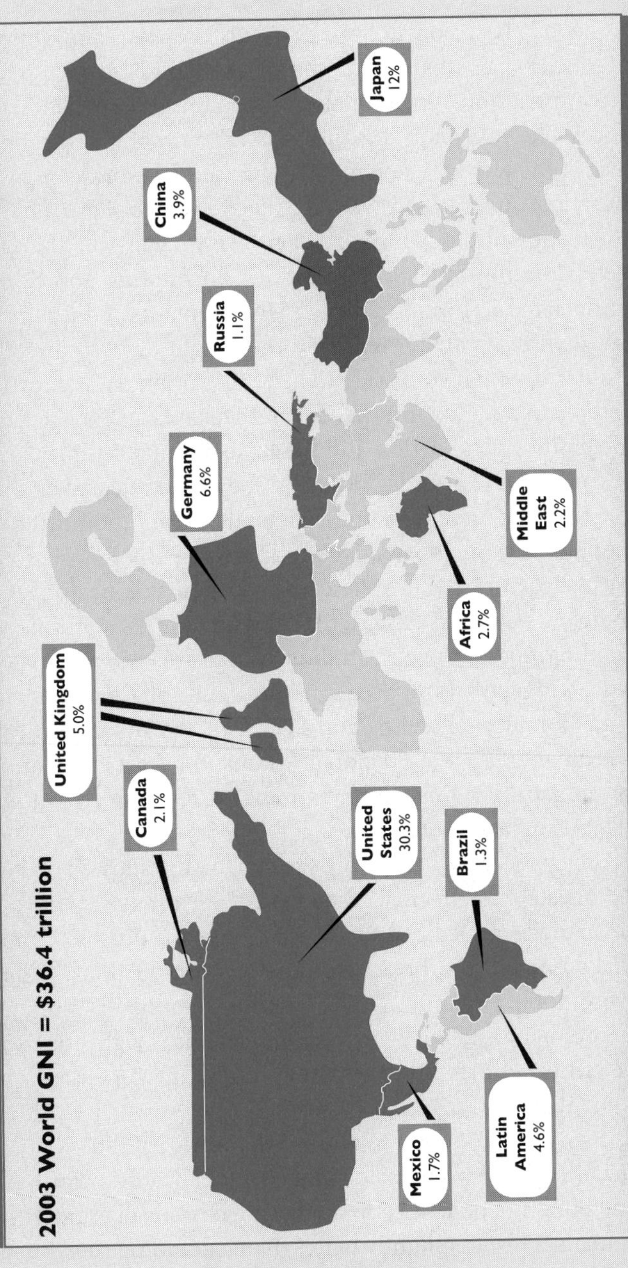


Source: *World Development Indicators,2003* (Washington, D.C: World Bank, 2004); John Allen, *Student Atlas of World Politics,* 7th ed. (New York: McGraw-Hill), 2006.

such as Nigeria, Indonesia, and Brazil as well as Africa as a whole. The United States is smaller, as is Europe.

Next consider the map based on global income distribution. The United States, Japan, and Germany are much bigger than in the population and land-area maps. Conversely, many of the large countries on the population map are small on the income map. Can you even find Africa? The two maps together provide a graphic indication of global inequality and a sense of the way in which many others see the world.

The second Bush administration reverted to the Reagan policy of making American aid to international population planning heavily contingent on the UN's and other multilateral agencies' abiding by U.S. prohibitions on funding abortion. Even though Congress had appropriated $34 million for the UN Population Fund, the Bush administration froze the money. It equated foreign aid that might be used directly or indirectly to support abortions in other countries to federal funding for abortion within the United States, the topic of a raging internal debate. This was an externalization of America's own domestic politics on abortion and the Bush administration's desire to support a key issue on the conservative agenda. Others in the world rejected as a matter of principle such an effort to apply one's own domestic policies (and politics) to the rest of the world. They also opposed it on substantive grounds. The UN Population Fund limited its work in China to provinces where the one-child policy is no longer enforced, and more generally audited its budget so as not to spend any American money on China programs. Yet the withholding of the $34 million, which was 13 percent of the agency's budget, threatened a wide global impact: "2 million unwanted pregnancies, 800,000 induced abortions, 4,700 maternal deaths and 77,000 infant and child deaths."[42] Similar issues arose in December 2002 at the regional Asian and Pacific Population Conference, where the Bush administration pushed its anti-abortion positions but was rebuffed by votes of 31–1 and 32–1 on key resolutions.[43]

Although U.S. policy was hardly the only cause, statistics showed 200 million women worldwide in need of safe and effective contarception. Estimates spoke of 70 to 80 million unwanted pregnancies annually and 150,000 maternal deaths.[44] In one of its first actions, the Obama administration rescinded the Bush restrictions. "They have undermined efforts to promote safe and effective voluntary family planning in developing countries," President Obama stated. "For these reasons, it is right for us to rescind this policy and restore critical efforts to protect and empower women and promote global economic development."[45]

*Hunger* also remains a huge problem around the world. A 2003 report by the ***World Health Organization (WHO)*** pointed to hunger as the leading cause of death in the world. Close to one billion people, it estimated, were chronically undernourished—one out of every six humans. This was slightly better than a decade earlier, but at a rate of improvement not nearly rapid enough to meet the Millennium Development Goal of a 50 percent reduction by 2015. The same was true for child malnutrition, which also had improved but only slightly, with 150 million children under the age of five in the developing world still malnourished. Since then the situation has grown even worse. First world food prices skyrocketed in 2007–2008, and then the full global economic crisis struck. In 2008 the number of those suffering from hunger increased by 40 million. Women and children suffered the most. More then 3.5 million mothers and children still die annually from malnutrition. About 13 million children are born severely underweight, and 178 million under five have stunted growth. Of these, 90 percent live in just thirty-six countries and constitute 46 percent of the total child population in those countries.[46]

## Global Public Health

In 2005 *Time* named as its "persons of the year" the rock star Bono and Bill and Melinda Gates. Bono was named for his overall work on global poverty, the Gateses particularly for their foundation's commitment of billions of dollars in support of improved ***global public health,*** especially in the developing world. Infectious diseases are the number one cause of death worldwide: ***HIV/AIDS,*** malaria, and tuberculosis alone are responsible for 25 percent of all worldwide deaths. Since 1973 over thirty new diseases have emerged, including SARS (severe acute respiratory syndrome), West Nile virus, and avian flu. Twenty old diseases, believed to have been wiped out, have reemerged. Although some of these diseases hit the United States directly, the greatest impact continues to be in the developing world. Among the most challenging policy questions these and other global public health issues raise is the "10/90" inequality: that is, that 90 percent of investments in health care go toward diseases that primarily affect the 10 percent of the world population in the richer and more developed countries, whereas only 10 percent of health care investments go toward diseases that primarily affect the other 90 percent in the world's poorer and less developed countries.

There are at least three major reasons why American foreign policy needs to be concerned about global public health. First is the humanitarian dimension. This is another issue area in which it is hard to maintain a strong claim to Principles if American foreign policy does not give priority to helping prevent and treat the diseases that ravage so much of humanity. Responsibility does not fall only on the United States, but as the richest, most powerful, and most medically advanced country in the world, America knows that it can make a significant difference.

Second is that global public health relates to the fight against global poverty (Prosperity). Three of the eight UN Millennium Development Goals are explicitly concerned with global public health. Even the most ambitious economic development strategies cannot succeed unless global public health is improved. Extensive research conducted at the village level in a number of developing countries by Professor Anirudh Krishna of Duke University shows that one of the key factors for families that escape from poverty is avoiding major health problems, and that one of the key factors for those who fall back into poverty is the onset of major health problems.[47] The poverty-health link is especially strong for HIV/AIDS, which may have as much as a 20 percent depressing effect on GDP growth rates over the next decade. From a U.S. national interest perspective, this is another instance of how American Prosperity interconnects with greater prosperity for the developing world.

Third is national security and considerations of Peace and Power. This point was made and concern raised about AIDS and other global infectious diseases in a landmark 2000 study by the Central Intelligence Agency:

> The persistent infectious disease burden is likely to aggravate and, in some cases, may even provoke economic decay, social fragmentation, and political destabilization in the hardest hit countries in the developing and former communist worlds. . . .
>
> The infectious disease burden will weaken the military capabilities of some countries—as well as international peacekeeping efforts—as their armies and recruitment pools experience HIV infection rates ranging from 10 to 60 percent. . . .
>
> Infectious diseases are likely to slow socioeconomic development in the hardest hit developing and former communist countries and regions. This will challenge democratic development and transitions and possibly contribute to humanitarian emergencies and civil conflicts.
>
> Infectious disease–related embargoes and restrictions on travel and immigration will cause friction among and between developed and developing countries.[48]

We take a closer look at three aspects of global health problems: HIV/AIDS, the role of the Gates Foundation, and swine flu and other possible pandemics.

### *Global AIDS*

10.1

The figures are staggering. As the 2008 UN Report lays out (Reading 10.1), in the nearly thirty years since the epidemic began, 25 million people have died of HIV/AIDS and 33 million are infected with it. Sub-Saharan Africa has the worst problem. In South Africa almost 6 million people are infected, which amounts to one in five adults. It is not, though, just an African problem. In India the total numbers are not so great, but the growth rate of new cases is alarmingly high. Russia also now has an alarmingly high AIDS growth rate, as does China. HIV/AIDS is truly, as the UN Joint Program on HIV/AIDS (UNAIDS) has called it, "a global epidemic." The twofold challenge is prevention and treatment. Those who have already contracted the disease must be provided with treatment. At the same time education and access to health care must be improved and other measures taken to prevent the further spread of AIDS.

The link to economic development, noted earlier, cannot be stressed strongly enough. How can a country succeed in economic development when it is losing such large numbers of citizens, often at the most productive stages of their working lives? As then UN secretary-general Kofi Annan stated in a speech to the African summit on HIV/AIDS:

> Disease, like war, is not only a product of underdevelopment. It is also one of the biggest obstacles preventing our societies from developing as they should. This is especially true of HIV/AIDS, which takes its biggest toll among young adults—the age group that normally produces most, and has the main responsibility for rearing the next generation. That is why AIDS has become not only the primary cause of death on this continent, but our biggest development challenge.[49]

Even more immediate are the added costs of dealing with the consequences; consider, for example, the 12 million children orphaned by AIDS in sub-Saharan Africa alone. HIV/AIDS also is a factor in worsening famines, having left so many farm workers unable to work the fields that the amount of cultivated land has declined by almost 70 percent in some countries.

Some progress has been made. Data in the 2008 UNAIDS Report showed the new HIV infection rate slowing in some countries. The overall death rate was down 10 percent, although this still amounted to about 2 million deaths per year. And new infection rates generally had not decreased substantially. Two lessons can be drawn from these data. One is that policies are having an impact; there was some real payoff for the 600 percent increase in global funding from $1.6 billion in 2001 to $10 billion in 2007. The other was that more impact and more funding were needed, with a target of a 50 percent further increase.

The Bush administration received credit for substantially increasing funding for combating global AIDS. The President's Emergency Plan for AIDS Relief (PEPFAR) increased funding from $2.3 billion in 2004 to $6 billion in 2008. The State Department billed this as "the largest international health initiative any nation has ever undertaken directed at a single disease."[50] A Stanford University Medical School study credited Bush's PEPFAR with reducing global AIDS death rates by 10 percent.[51] But although garnering praise, the Bush AIDS policy also was criticized for its overemphasis on abstinence. As with population control, this was seen as an extension of American domestic politics and counter to more effective global strategies. Obama's dropping the emphasis on abstinence was greeted positively by many global HIV/AIDS activists. His policy was criticized, though, for providing less increased funding than he pledged in his campaign.

Global HIV/AIDS is not just an issue for U.S. policy. It also involves the UN and other international institutions, other donor governments, the domestic policies of those countries most affected, the private sector, and NGOs. The UN is credited with making HIV/AIDS a priority, including making access to treatment universal by 2010 and halting the spread of the disease by 2015. But the 2010 goal has not been achieved, and progress on the 2015 one is lagging. Although responsibility rests with the full range of actors mentioned, UN efforts have had their own problems. The World Health

Organization, the principal UN agency dealing with HIV/AIDS as well as other global health issues, has achieved a great deal but also has had setbacks. So too has UNAIDS, the coordinating body established to try to bring together the efforts of the ten separate UN agencies involved in HIV/AIDS prevention and treatment. Although having so many entities bring their own specialized capacities to bear does demonstrate the priority given to the issue, it also has made for coordination problems that hamper effectiveness.

The South African government has come in for particular criticism, particularly under the former president Thabo Mbeki (1999–2008), for its resistance to science-based policies. One study estimated that 365,000 deaths could have been prevented if the Mbeki government had not refused to provide antiretroviral drugs to AIDS patients and other widely administered drugs to pregnant women at risk for infecting their babies. As a result, only 23 percent of those in need were reached compared with 85 percent in neighboring Botswana and 71 percent in Namibia.[52] The post-Mbeki government has been shifting toward more science-based policies.

A number of issues have arisen with regard to the role of the private sector. We have previously mentioned the "10/90" inequality of disease research and population. A more specific controversy for HIV/AIDS has been the high pricing and limited availability of antiretroviral and other drugs. This issue weighs drug companies' patents and intellectual property rights against the right of afflicted nations and peoples to affordable, life-saving health care. These have been major issues in the WTO Doha Round as well as in other areas of policy.

Many NGOs have been very involved with HIV/AIDS as well as other global health issues. We take a look at the role of the Gates Foundation as the most important NGO in this policy area.

## *Role of the Gates Foundation*

A few days before a WHO meeting in Geneva, a Swiss newspaper ran the headline "The Health of the World Depends More on Bill Gates than on the WHO."[53] Though an exaggeration, it made a point. The WHO's annual programmatic budget was just over $4 billion; as of early 2009 the ***Gates Foundation*** had committed nearly $10 billion to its global public health programs. Its endowment is greater than the GDPs of 70 percent of the world's nations. And the Gates Foundation has a lot less bureaucracy and a lot less politics impeding its efforts.

"Our role as a foundation," Bill Gates stated in his annual letter, "is to help make sure the new science is applied to the needs of the poor, because the marketplace doesn't respond when buyers have almost no money."[54] The foundation's global public health work includes HIV/AIDS as well as other diseases and health problems most afflicting the poorest countries of the world such as malaria, tuberculosis, diarrhea, polio, and maternal and child health. Particular emphasis across many of these areas is on vaccine development and the immunization of children. Over 20 percent of children do not have access to needed vaccines. This translates to 2.4 million deaths per year. Millions more who survive are left severely impaired. "The long-range effects of childhood illnesses hinder the ability of those who survive to become educated, work, or care for themselves or others. This puts a strain on their families and on the economies of developing countries."[55] The Global Alliance for Vaccination and Immunisation—a partnership of the Gates Foundation, other NGOs, the WHO, governments, and the private sector—has been making an impact through both research for vaccine development and on-the-ground immunization programs.

At the same time, the Gates Foundation has its critics. Some see it as too oriented to "techno-fix" solutions and discovery with insufficient focus on development and delivery. It has investments in companies whose business is in areas that seem to run counter to the goals of its public health programs. Some also are concerned that although its sheer size gives it some economies of scale, it can crowd out other NGOs. What is clear is that it is one of the key actors in global public health policy, with healthy debate about its optimal role.

## *Global Pandemics and the "DMD" Threat*

In addition to WMD, weapons of mass destruction, the world faces the threat of ***"DMD,"*** or ***diseases of mass destruction.*** As bad as the 1918–19 Spanish flu epidemic was (see "Historical Perspectives," p. 530), forecasts for the avian flu are even worse. In New York City, for example, where the Spanish flu killed about 33,000, avian flu estimates run as high as 2.8 million people potentially infected. At a possible 55 percent fatality rate, this could be close to 1.5 million deaths in New York City alone. Costs to the American economy could be as high as $600 billion. Questions still remain as to whether avian flu (the A/H5N1 strain in scientific terms) will transmit from human to human or will stay largely concentrated in birds and those who come in direct contact with them. But as with nuclear weapons and other WMD threats, the DMD policy challenge is to prevent, and if not prevent, contain, amid the uncertainties of the future. As the expert Laurie Garrett writes, "Nothing could happen . . . or doom may loom."[56]

Here too the challenges face both American foreign policy and, more broadly, the international community. This was evident in 2003, with the SARS (severe acute respiratory syndrome) outbreak. SARS was first detected in China. Initially, though, the Chinese government delayed providing the WHO access to its territory or even to its health information. Once reports leaked out through the international press and travelers, the WHO was able to respond more effectively. Also, other governments could then take action both to prevent the spread of SARS to their countries and to assist the WHO and China in containing and mitigating the outbreak.

The international challenge also was evident in 2009, with the swine flu (the H1N1 virus) outbreak, which began in Mexico and spread globally. Its impact was less than initially feared. One reason was that the flu strain was not so strong as it could have been. Another was the relatively rapid and well-coordinated response of the WHO, the U.S. ***Centers for Disease Control and Prevention (CDC),*** and other governments and their key public health agencies. The WHO was credited for recognizing early warning signs in March/April 2009 case data from Mexico as abnormally high for so late in the flu season. On April 21, the CDC alerted U.S. physicians about a possible pandemic. On April 25, the WHO delcared a health emergency of "international concern." On April 28, the United States declared a public emergency. By mid-July the WHO deemed H1N1 as the fastest-moving pandemic ever, abetted as it has been by the interconnectedness of globalization. Even with the early warning and other policy measures that helped control and mitigate the spread, there were over 250,000 cases worldwide, with deaths in Mexico, Brazil, Chile, Argentina, Spain, Britain, Ukraine, Austria, Afghanistan, Australia, Thailand, and the Phillippines, as well as the United States and numerous other countries. And new signs continued to appear of the risks of the much more lethal avian flu (H5N1).

Looking to the future, we can draw two important lessons. One is that global public health is another issue in which traditional Westphalian conceptions of state sovereignty collide with the interconnectedness of a global age. China's invocation of its rights of sovereignty in the SARS outbreak impeded the capacity of the international community to respond. The crisis could have been much worse if the Chinese government had stuck to this position. Unless the norm of sovereignty as responsibility and not just the rights of states continues to strengthen in general and with specific applicability to global public health, the risks of global pandemics will be all the greater. "After all," as Dr. Margaret Chan, the WHO's director general, stated, "it really is all humanity that is under threat during a pandemic."[57]

Second are the limits of any nation's domestic policies. The "Vegas dilemma," whereby what happens inside states doesn't stay inside states (see Chapter 6), pertains to pandemics as well. As with so many other globalization issues, a sound national policy is necessary but not sufficient. Avian flu and other global pandemics require global and not just national strategies. States where the outbreaks may occur need to have the capacity to deal with them in the early stages. Yet many of those states are developing countries with little public health capacity. Many therefore advocate U.S. policies that give more emphasis to building the preventive and early-detection capacities of other states, as well as the WHO's authority and resources as the fulcrum of global policy capacity.

## Global Environmental Issues

Are global environmental problems so bad as they are said to be? And even if they are, isn't the environment still an issue for the future, with so many pressing issues today? Not so, according to a recent think-tank study that attributed around 300,000 deaths, negative effects on another 325 million people, and economic losses of $125 billion each year to disasters related to climate change.[58] This reflects the "EMD" concern, potential environmental mass destruction.

Before getting into specific issues, we lay out an analytic framework for the policy challenges posed by global environmental issues.

## Analytic Framework

Global environmental issues pose six types of policy challenges. First, they constitute a classic problem of "public goods" and "collective action." The renowned economist Paul Samuelson defined public goods as "collective consumption goods . . . which all enjoy in common in the sense that each individual's consumption of such a good leads to no subtraction from any other individual's consumption of that good."[59] Collective-action problems are those in which all would benefit by taking joint action to deal with a problem, and all suffer from not doing so, but collective action is impeded by each waiting for the other to act first or by lack of agreement on what should be done. The old example was the grassy commons in a small nineteenth-century New England town. It was altogether rational for me to want to graze my cows there, and for you as well, but neither of us would be much concerned about overgrazing, which could ruin the commons for all of us. A current example is the global environment. It is the essence of interdependence that all countries will suffer if global warming, ozone depletion, and other global environmental problems grow worse, and that all countries therefore have an interest in ensuring that they do not. But it is the essence of the problem of global governance that taking such action is so difficult.

Second is the balance between environmental and economic priorities. Although the treaty establishing the WTO includes environmental protection and sustainable development as goals, there often are tensions between these goals and trade promotion. The WTO claims that it gives due consideration to the environment; many environmental NGOs strongly disagree.[60] Similarly, the IMF debate concerns whether the fiscal austerity and export-promotion emphases of its structural adjustment policies increase pressure to adopt environmentally damaging policies. In Indonesia, for example, pressure to generate foreign exchange to pay back foreign debt led to massive burnings of biologically rich tropical forests to clear land for export-oriented palm oil production. As part of its IMF austerity package, Russia slashed the budget for government-protected environmental areas 40 percent.

Third, issues of North-South equity further complicate global environmental negotiations. For example, on global warming, developing countries claim a right to higher ceilings on industrial emissions. They base their claim both on economic grounds that poor countries cannot afford more sophisticated emissions-scrubbing technologies, and on the historical-justice argument that developed countries did more than their share of polluting when they were developing during the nineteenth and early twentieth centuries. You had your turn, the argument goes; it's our turn now. Moreover, the developing countries argue, the problem is largely of the developed world's making.

Fourth is the problem of enforcement. As in other policy areas, once multilateral agreements are reached, norms affirmed, and actions mandated, how will fulfillment and compliance be ensured? Most treaties and other agreements do call for sanctions or other penalties and consequences for states that do not meet their obligations, but these are not always enforced. Special multilateral bodies can be created, but as a practical matter such bodies have very limited authority and power. For example, following the 1992 Earth Summit in Rio de Janeiro, Brazil, the UN created the Commission on Sustainable Development. Ten years later, though, at the Johannesburg, South Africa, World Summit on Sustainable Development, even the UN's own statements acknowledged how little this commission had achieved and how much it needed to be "recharged" and "revitalized."[61]

Fifth, the environment is also a peace and security issue. Not only environmentalists, but also the more traditional security establishment, the Pentagon included, have conducted numerous studies about the environment as a security issue. Environmental scarcity and degradation have been sources of conflict and violence in a number of wars, both recent and historical. Entire states, particularly island ones, risk being washed over and out by rising sea levels caused by global warming (see below). States that face "only" environmental degradation and not extinction risk destabilization. The Norwegian Nobel Committee recognized this in awarding the 2004 Peace Prize to Wangari Maathai, a Kenyan woman who started an environmental movement that among other things planted 30 million trees in Africa. "With this award," the Nobel committee chair stated, "we have expanded the term 'peace' to encompass environmental questions related to our beloved Earth. . . . Peace on Earth depends on our ability to secure our living environment."[62] The environment is also an issue for Russia, where for decades pollution standards for industries were close to nil, where entire bodies of water such as the Aral Sea were totally destroyed, where nuclear and other wastes were disposed of with much too little precaution. It also is an issue for China, five of whose largest cities are among the most polluted in the world, and where numerous other environmental problems continue to grow worse.

Sixth is the dilemma of prevention and the trade-off between immediate costs and future benefits. In his book *Collapse: How Societies Choose to Fail or Succeed*, the Pulitzer Prize–winning author Jared Diamond looks back through history at societies that inflicted so much environmental degradation that they brought about their own collapse. "How could a society," Diamond asks, "fail to have seen the dangers that seem so clear in retrospect?" Moreover, today the risks are even greater than when Easter Island or Norse Greenland collapsed centuries ago because "globalization makes it impossible for societies to collapse in isolation."[63] So much of politics is short term, today's issues filling the in-boxes, that little priority is given to tomorrow's problems. But tomorrow comes, and when it does the problems often are far past the tipping point at which the costs go up and the chances of impact go down. It is difficult to act preventively, but it is possible. The risk and the opportunity are expressed in the subtitle of Diamond's book; failure is not inevitable and success not guaranteed—both are dependent on the choices that societies make.

This analytic context helps explain both the scope and the limits of progress by the United States and the international community on global environmental issues. The 1972 Stockholm Conference that established the United Nations Commission on the Human Environment was an early sign that the environment was starting to move up on the global policy agenda. An infrastructure of treaties and other global environmental agreements began to be created. One example generally considered a success for global environmental policy was the 1987 Montréal Protocol dealing with ozone depletion. The ozone layer—that part of the upper atmosphere that shields the earth from ultraviolet rays and other dangers—was being thinned out by chlorofluorocarbons (CFCs) in spray cans, air-conditioning systems, and other common items. Through the ***Montréal Protocol*** and its follow-up agreements, nations acted collectively to address this problem. ***"Common but differentiated responsibility,"*** whereby all nations of the world agreed to make policy changes but those that were the largest sources of the problem accepted proportional responsibility, was a key part of the multilateral agreement. Technological innovations that helped reduce the costs of CFC substitutes helped make the agreement work economically. As with other policy areas, no one success is an absolute model for others, but the Montréal Protocol does show that policy success on global environmental issues is possible. It's helpful to bear this in mind as we consider global climate change, the most pressing issue today.

## *Global Climate Change*

How strong is the scientific evidence on ***global climate change?*** Most scientists and relevant policy analysts say quite strong. "Warming of the climate system," the Nobel Peace Prize–winning UN ***Intergovernmental Panel on Climate Change (IPCC)*** states, "is unequivocal." Yet the problem is getting worse. Eleven of the twelve years between 1997 and 2008 rank among the twelve warmest years of global surface temperatures since 1850. Unless major policy changes are implemented, chances are 50 percent that temperatures will rise another 5 degrees Celsius over this century—yet it has taken thousands of years since the last ice age for the world to become 5 degrees warmer. Even a 1-degree rise could irreversibly damage coral reef ecosystems and melt small glaciers. A 2- to 3-degree rise would melt major glaciers and the Greenland ice sheet and might cause 40 percent of animal species to become extinct. A 4-degree rise would have a major impact on global food production. A 5-degree rise could raise sea levels to the point of threatening such large coastal and river cities as London, Shanghai, New York, and Tokyo, and could even wipe out whole island nations.[64] In the United States, barrier islands such as those at Cape Hatteras, North Carolina, could be threatened. So, too, could U.S. coastal areas, including heavily populated sites on the east and west coasts as well as the Gulf of Mexico.

Additional studies have focused particularly on the melting of the world's glacial ice caps. "The seemingly indestructible snows of [Mount] Kilimanjaro that inspired Ernest Hemingway's famous short story," one *New York Times* lead editorial warned, "may well disappear in the next 15 years."[65] The seven hundred scientists who conducted the study issued an even more dire warning: "Projected climate changes during the 21st century have the potential to lead to future large-scale and possible irreversible changes in Earth systems resulting in impacts at continental and global scales."[66] For any Americans who might try to take comfort in this being relevant only to mountains in Asia or glaciers at the north and south poles, the report went on to stress how the interlinking chain of global climate also could increase droughts in the American Midwest and floods in the Pacific Northwest, and could have many other destructive effects on American life, the American economy, and the American environment.

Harmful emissions increased by 70 percent between 1970 and 2004. This put overall emissions concentrations in the atmosphere at levels vastly exceeding the natural range going back 650,000 years. This and other evidence shows that these climate problems are caused by humans. One of the disputes among scientists has been over how much of global warming and other climate change is attributable to natural processes, which may run through self-equilibrating cycles over time, and how much is the result of excessive use of oil and other fossil fuels, industrial pollution, wasteful consumption patterns, and other non-inevitable human and societal practices. The evidence is said to be stronger than ever that this is not happening *to* us but is being done *by* us. On a positive note, this also means that we can correct the problems we have been creating—but only through major policy shifts.

10.2 The former vice president Al Gore had a major impact on the debate through his 2006 movie and book, *An Inconvenient Truth.* Gore cast the issue as having a much broader sweep and magnitude than just another policy issue (Reading 10.2). "The relationship between human civilization and the Earth has been utterly transformed by a combination of factors, including the population explosion, the technological revolution, and a willingness to ignore the future consequences of our present actions. The underlying reality is that we are colliding with the planet's ecological system, and its most vulnerable components are crumbling as a result."[67]

Some observers disagree. The columnist George Will points repeatedly to scientific predictions of global cooling in the 1970s, saying the threat of global warming is just another instance of predictions that won't come true.[68] He believes much of the data that support the prediction of global warming are exaggerated or inaccurate. He contends that recent scientific data show that whatever warming trend may have been occurring recently has halted, and he questions the link between ***greenhouse gas*** production and warming. He considers climate change to be a "hypothetical calamity" that distracts us from focusing on "real calamities" such as the current economic situation. He refers to a report from the U.S. National Snow and Ice Data Center stating that defective satellite monitors underestimated the amount of Arctic sea ice by 193,000 square miles (about the area of California). In a February 2009 column titled "Dark Green Doomsayers," Will went into some detail on this:

> As global levels of sea ice declined last year, many experts said this was evidence of man-made global warming. Since September, however, the increase in sea ice has been the fastest change, either up or down, since 1979, when satellite record-keeping began. According to the University of Illinois' Arctic Climate Research Center, global sea ice levels now equal those of 1979.

But when this assertion generated much controversy, the *Washington Post* ombudsman fact-checked the article and found that although global sea-ice levels are about the same as in 1979, the Northern Hemisphere has lost about a million square miles of sea ice, about the area of California and Texas combined.

Other prominent critics include the economist Julian Simon and the Slovak president, Václav Klaus. Simon long disputed the accuracy of the evidence that scientists cited, as well as its policy implications. Species extinction was no more than one per year, he contended. "[T]he world was not being deforested, it was being reforested." The limits to growth claimed by today's environmentalists were going to be as wrong as Thomas Malthus was about the perils of population growth. Simon's writings also reflected a sense that whatever the problems, markets and technology would provide the fix.[69] Klaus has been more outspoken, calling global warming a "hysteria" and global environmentalism "the biggest threat to freedom, democracy, the market economy and prosperity." And "some people believe in irrational things and events—some of them in UFOs, some in witches, some in fairy-tales, some in omnipotent governments, some in global warming."[70]

In this debate, most people (including the vast majority of climate scientists) believe that the evidence does support concerns about global warming as a serious problem, indeed a crisis. What, then, should we do about it? The 1997 United Nations Framework on Climate Change, also known as the ***Kyoto treaty*** for the city in Japan where key negotiations were held, has been a key part of this debate. The Clinton administration signed the treaty but held back on submitting it to the Senate for ratification for fear that the treaty would not garner the two-thirds majority needed to pass—even with a Senate controlled by the Democrats, Clinton's own party. The dissension stemmed partly from interest-group and regional politics, with strong opposition coming from the auto and coal industries. Another issue was that China, India, and other rising developing countries were exempted. The principle of "common but differentiated responsibility" had been a key to the Montreal ozone treaty. Although it was included in the formal language of the Kyoto global warming treaty, it had the qualifier "taking into account . . . specific national and regional development priorities, objectives and circumstances." This in effect meant *no* required burdens, not just fewer. Kyoto proponents still pushed for ratification, arguing that it still was in the U.S. national interest, but to no avail.

The Bush administration flatly opposed the treaty. In early 2001 National Security Adviser Condoleezza Rice was reported to have told a meeting of European ambassadors that the Kyoto treaty was "dead on arrival."[71] President Bush described it as "fatally flawed," "unrealistic," and "not based on science."[72] Much of the world was highly critical of Bush's stance. Even some who agreed that countries such as China should have to meet some binding targets emphasized the United States was by far the world's largest greenhouse gas emitter, both in total quantity and on a per capita basis. Even compared with Europeans, the average American consumed twice as much energy. During the Bush years the U.S. ranking in the Environmental Performance Index went from bad to worse, from twenty-eighth in the world, behind most of Western Europe and Japan, to thirty-ninth in 2008.[73] Moreover, many saw the Bush administration's opposition to the Kyoto treaty as not just a quibble about the treaty's details but as a broader manifestation of Bush's antimultilateralism.

Despite American opposition, the Kyoto treaty went into effect in February 2005, when it met the requirement of ratification by at least fifty-five countries, which together account for at least 55 percent of global carbon dioxide emissions. Its record has been mixed. Many countries that did sign, such as Canada, Japan, and much of Europe, have not met their targets. Particular policies such as ***cap and trade,*** whereby companies and others agree to emission-cuts targets and can sell emissions permits to those who have trouble meeting their targets, were not working so well as projected. Still, many experts assess that the situation would have been even worse without the Kyoto treaty and that it provides a basis on which to build, particularly with studies indicating worsening climate conditions. A December 2008 study by the U.S. Geological Survey warned that climactic shifts may be even more dramatic over this century than previously predicted; so too did the UN IPCC, stressing the "vicious cycle of feedback" whereby how "higher temperatures are triggering self-reinforcing feedback mechanisms in global ecosystems."[74]

The Obama administration has been much more committed to global climate change than its predecessor. It approached the issue not just as a "green" one but also as a positive one on economic and security grounds. The economic argument posited the costs of reducing carbon emissions and other environmentally friendly measures as less than the jobs to be created, profits to be earned, and other economic benefits from developing globally competitive industries in this growing sector. The security argument was a combination of the direct risks to U.S. national security from remaining so vulnerable to foreign oil prices and supplies, and the more global risks from environmental degradation causing political instability and wars in various parts of the world.

But while pledging to make America more of a leader and less of a laggard in the next round of forging a global climate change treaty, the administration went to the December 2009 Copenhagen climate change summit having made only limited changes in U.S. policy. Some actions were taken through executive orders, but Congress had not passed any major new legislation. While other countries also bore responsibility for the Copenhagen summit making only limited progress, the U.S. share ran counter to the claim to global leadership on this issue.

## *Other Key Issues*

As challenging as climate change is, it isn't the only pressing global environmental issue. We discuss several others here.

THE WORLD'S OCEANS The world's oceans also are under threat from rising acidity. Oceans absorb about a quarter of carbon dioxide emissions. As this gas dissolves in sea water, it creates carbonic acid. The rising acidity threatens coral reefs, shellfish, and potentially the entire marine food web. Already shellfish have decreased in number, and growth of coral skeletons has been affected by this rising acidity. These problems, along with other patterns of pollution, have raised concerns of a "global collapse" of fish species.[75] Close to 30 percent of fish species are down to 10 percent of their previous levels. This drop in turn sets off a destructive cycle that leaves overall marine ecosystems more vulnerable to overfishing and less able to replenish. The world's fishing industry, both large-scale corporate level and small-scale village level, is at risk.

BIODIVERSITY Fish species are not the only ones threatened with reduction and even extinction. The overall number and variety of plant and animal species, which scientists call ***biodiversity,*** is at risk. One in four land mammals faces extinction, according to a study by the International Union for Conservation of Nature (IUCN).[76] Key factors are habitat loss to development, hunting, and climate change. Land mammals make up 1,141 of 5,487 species on the IUCN "red list"—and that excludes another 836 species for which there was insufficient data. By way of comparison, only 76 mammal species have become extinct since 1500. The good news was that 5 percent of currently threatened mammals for which conservation measures had been taken were showing signs of recovery in the wild. The message was the same for both the problem and the solution: policy matters.

One-third of U.S. bird species are also endangered.[77] The mix of causes here also included loss of habitat to development and climate change as well as to wildfires and disease. In this case too, the policy message cut both ways, with findings that herons, egrets, ducks, and other birds have benefited from wetlands conservation. Fish stocks have benefited from programs such as catch shares, initiated by the Environmental Defense Fund.

Poor communities bear a disproportionate burden in such ecosystem changes. Degradation and declining productivity of ecosystems threatens the survival of the 1.1 billion people who survive on less than $1 per day of income. Most of them are located in rural areas and are highly dependent on agriculture, grazing, and hunting for subsistence. Even among less poor populations, declining ecosystems are expected to lead to "[d]eclines in incomes, loss of culturally important natural resources, and increases in threats to health."[78]

DESERTIFICATION The United Nations Convention to Combat Desertification (UNCCD) defines ***desertification*** as "the degradation of land in arid, semi-arid and dry sub-humid areas. It is caused primarily by human activities and climatic variations. . . . It occurs because dryland ecosystems, which cover over one third of the world's land area, are extremely vulnerable to over-exploitation and inappropriate land use."[79] Each year, according to James "Gus" Speth, dean of the Yale School of Forestry and Environmental Studies, "desertification claims a Nebraska-sized area of productive capacity worldwide."[80] Costs are estimated at $40 billion annually on the global scale, not even including hidden costs such as the need for increased fertilizer, the loss of biodiversity, poor health, and malnutrition.[81] Over 250 million people are presently affected, and about 1 billion people in over one hundred countries are at risk of being so. The food and health crises associated with desertification predominantly affect the world's poorest, most marginalized, and politically weakest citizens.

DEFORESTATION ***Deforestation*** is the removal of trees in forested areas, primarily by logging and/or burning. Although deforestation meets some human needs, it also has profound local and global consequences, including social conflict, extinction of plants and animals, and climate change. The leading direct causes of tropical deforestation are agricultural expansion, high levels of wood extraction, and the extension of roads and other infrastructure into forested areas. Indirect causes include increasing economic activity and associated market failures; a wide range of policy and institutional weaknesses and failures; the effects of technological change; low public awareness of the importance of forest areas; and human demographic factors such as population growth, density, and migration.[82] Tropical forests are the most threatened.

Overall, more than 1.7 billion people live in the forty nations with critically low levels of forest cover, which in many cases hinders prospects for sustainable development. The number of people living in low-forest-cover nations is expected to triple by 2025 to 4.6 billion. Thirteen additional countries will experience forest-resource scarcity if deforestation continues at its current pace.[83]

AIR POLLUTION Every year, the American Lung Association publishes its "State of the Air" report on air quality in the United States. The 2009 report found that 61.7 percent of the United States population lives in counties that have unhealthful levels of air pollution. Moreover, more than 47 million U.S. residents live in areas where chronically poor levels of air quality are regularly a threat to their health.[84] Worldwide, the World Health Organization attributes 2 million premature deaths to air pollution each year. More than half of the burden from air pollution is borne by people in developing countries.

Since air is the classic example of knowing no national boundaries, mitigating the situation calls for concerted global efforts. The WHO estimates that if particulate matter pollution is reduced from 70 to 20 micrograms per cubic meter, air-quality-related deaths would diminish by around 15 percent. Moreover, reducing air-pollution levels also can help reduce the global burden of illness from respiratory infections, heart disease, and lung cancer.[85]

URBANIZATION The world is undergoing the largest wave of urban growth in history. In 2008, the United Nations Population Fund found that for the first time in history, more than half the entire human population—3.3 billion people—was living in urban areas. By 2030, this is expected to swell to almost 5 billion.[86] At the global level, all future population growth will thus be in towns and cities; most of this growth will be in developing countries. The urban population of Africa and Asia is expected to double between 2000 and 2030. Though urbanization has been a historical precursor for economic growth, cities tend to concentrate poverty, slum growth, environmental degradation, and social unrest.[87]

## Foreign Policy Politics: The New Politics of Globalization and the Old Politics of Trade

We see elements of both the old and the new in the foreign policy politics of issues focused on in this chapter. The new is manifested by the much expanded and more influential role that NGOs play; the old in the basic historical pattern of free trade versus protectionism being played out yet again in the making of U.S. trade policy.

### *NGOs and the Politics of Globalization*

The rise of ***nongovernmental organizations,*** or ***NGOs,*** has become a major part of foreign policy politics. As we have seen, NGOs usually are unofficial, nonprofit organizations whose "business" is some aspect of foreign policy. They have been particularly active in the politics of globalization.

Simply saying the word "Seattle" to a trade-policy specialist signifies the new politics of globalization. Seattle is not merely the city that is the home of Bill Gates, Microsoft, and Starbucks; Seattle is where antiglobalization protest politics first emerged as a major political force during the November 1999 WTO summit there. Whether we think this is a good thing or a bad thing, trade policy politics have been redefined since Seattle, both in the United States and globally. At many of the major international economic meetings since then, the antiglobalization movement has disrupted the proceedings and sought to redefine the agenda through mass demonstrations.

Three principal traits characterize the antiglobalization movement as a political force. One is the form of its political action. In the past, protest politics has been associated more with other areas of foreign policy—the anti-Vietnam movement of the 1970s, or the nuclear freeze and anti-apartheid movements of the 1980s. Traditional trade policy politics largely worked through legislative and executive-branch lobbying, and through election campaign contributions and support. Although these "insider" and campaign activities continue, taking to the streets in Seattle, Quebec, Hong Kong, and elsewhere is a new form of political action in the realm of trade policy.

Second, a host of new groups has gotten involved in the policy-making process. Labor unions, corporations, and other economic interest groups continue to play major roles, of course. But environmental groups, human rights groups, public health groups, and other political issue groups have become actively engaged to a much greater extent than in the past. Whereas in the past the main issues in trade negotiations were tariffs and nontariff barriers, the agenda now almost always includes labor standards, environmental impact, and other such issues; the broad social and political agenda has become increasingly interconnected with the international economic agenda.

Third, this trend is not exclusively an American phenomenon. Many of the NGOs involved are based in western Europe, in Russia and the former Soviet bloc countries, and in many developing countries. They use the Internet, cell phones, and social networking for communication, and apply professional media strategies and target prominent international meetings for maximum news coverage. They seek change not just on a national, policy-by-policy basis, but through multilateral forums and global agreements.

The political impact of the antiglobalization movement was evident at the 2001 Summit of the Americas. In his major speech at the summit, President Bush tempered his pure free-trade leanings with the additional statement that "our commitment to open trade must be matched by a strong commitment to protecting our environment and improving labor standards." Lori Wallach, a leader of the antiglobalization movement, remarked, "You could have dialed 911 when I heard what Bush said. I needed to be resuscitated"—although she added that although Bush's statement "show[ed] the political shift, now we've got to see the policy shift."[88]

The antiglobalization movement also has engendered negative reactions, and not just from purist free traders. The violence and vandalism that marred many of these protests, much of it precipitated by anarchists and related groups, had some discrediting effect. There also is a distinction, as a key Democratic member of Congress put it, between trying to "stop" globalization and trying to "shape" it. "Those who come across as trying to stop globalization aren't winning," said Representative Sander Levin (D-Michigan), whose district includes major auto plants and large numbers of auto workers. "But for those —and I'm among them—who think you must shape it, there is some progress."[89]

10.3 A study by the scholars Margaret Keck and Kathryn Sikkink has provided important insights into how NGOs work and what makes them effective (Reading 10.3).[90] Keck and Sikkink stress four sets of factors. First is "information politics" and the ability of NGOs to be alternative sources of credible information and to use the Internet and other information technologies for timely and targeted communication of that information. National governments and international institutions no longer have an exclusive position as the sources of the "facts" and other key information about the issues of the day. Many NGOs produce their own studies, issue their own policy papers, and conduct their own press briefings. The key for them is to safeguard their reputations for credibility and not overstate or misstate their case.

Second is "symbolic politics," meaning "the ability to call upon symbols, actions or stories that make sense of a situation that is frequently far away."[91] NGOs have mastered the art of politics as theater, and global politics as global theater. They have been adept at getting celebrity endorsements, staging events for the media that dramatize issues, and otherwise tapping symbols as well as the substance of issues.

Third is "leverage politics." In addition to generally using information and tapping into symbols, NGOs target the actors and institutions that are the greatest points of leverage on a particular issue. On some issues they aim for the United States; on other issues another country's government; on yet other issues, the UN, the WTO, the IMF, the World Bank, or other international institutions may be the ideal targets. The NGOs' own global networks can give them the reach and flexibility for exercising this leverage.

Fourth is "accountability politics." We have seen throughout this chapter the lag between the global extent of so many policy areas and the still-limited reach of political structures and processes for global governance. NGOs have positioned themselves as the voice of the people on many issues, as the ostensible vehicles for representing the interests and views of constituencies outside the global bureaucracies of the WTO and other international institutions or the board rooms of global corporations.

This claim to being the vehicle for accountability is one of the major reasons that NGOs often are seen as the "good guys" in the politics of globalization. Yet, although this often is true, it is not always the case. NGOs are not strictly high-minded, altruistic actors. They have their own interests, including competition with other NGOs for prominence or funding. One study showed that "organizational insecurity, competitive pressures, and fiscal uncertainty" have become increasingly common among NGOs.[92] Nor are NGOs always effective in carrying out the goals to which they claim to aspire. In some instances their impact has been counterproductive and opportunistic.

The politics of globalization, then, like politics in general, is all the more interesting when we analyze it, rather than just making assumptions about who has what impact for what reasons and in what ways.

## *Making U.S. Trade Policy: Process and Politics*

Trade policy has been among the more politically contentious issue areas of post–Cold War U.S. foreign policy. The old free-trade consensus is not dead, but it has eroded and fractured. Indeed, the long-standing consensus on free trade theory is being challenged more than ever before (see "Theory in the World," p. 580).

Politics arises in each of three key areas in the making of U.S. trade policy: executive-branch negotiation and congressional approval of treaties and other trade agreements;

## THEORY IN THE WORLD

THEORY IN THE WORLD

### DEBATES ABOUT FREE TRADE

Perhaps no theory in American foreign policy has had more support over the last sixty-plus years than free trade theory.

We saw in Chapter 3 how free trade versus protectionism has been one of the great debates in American history, with policy often coming down on the protectionist side. With the lesson in mind of how much worse the 1929 Smoot-Hawley protectionist tariff made the Great Depression, Americans entered the post–World War II period with a strong pro–free trade consensus. The United States organized the international economy largely consistent with free trade theory (Chapter 4). It was never pure free trade, as compromises and concessions were made to key domestic interest groups as well as for foreign policy considerations in relations with particular countries. But free trade policy was very much theory in practice—until recent years when not only particular policies but also the validity of the underlying theory of free trade have been challenged, with major impact on the domestic politics of U.S. trade policy.

Free trade theory long has held that there are more winners than losers. The basic proposition goes back to Adam Smith and David Ricardo: that the aggregate benefits from the competition and specialization that free trade encourages are greater than the costs imposed on those who lose jobs and businesses to import competition. This promotion is said to still hold. As the economist Douglas Irwin puts it, trade makes for improved resource allocation, higher productivity, and overall increases in wealth.* Exports accounted for more than one-fourth of U.S. economic growth in the 1990s. About 12 million jobs in the United States depend on exports of goods and services. These jobs pay 13 to 18 percent higher wages than the overall average.

Four principal arguments have been raised challenging free trade theory in ways that do not necessarily lapse into protectionism. One is *particularistic costs vs. diffuse benefits.* It is true that in net aggregate terms, the economic benefits of free trade are greater than its costs. But whereas the benefits are important but not central to people's livelihood (for example, lower car prices) and are spread throughout the population, costs such as lost jobs are felt by fewer people but in more fundamental ways. This makes for what Professor I. M. Destler calls "the root problem [of] political imbalance."† The number of people bearing the particularistic costs is less than the number of those getting the diffuse benefits, but they are more inclined to bring political pressure than those for whom the benefits are not so central.

Second is *the limited capacity of free markets to facilitate economic adjustment.*

The impact of factory closings on workers, families, and communities is intense and immediate. Jobs do get created in more globally competitive industries, but this takes time. Federal Trade Adjustment Assistance (TAA) programs provide special government assistance to companies, workers, and communities hurt by import competition. But this program has been more about the second A (Assistance) than the first (Adjustment): provisions such as unemployment compensation have helped with the short-term pain, but adjusting more permanently to greater global competitiveness has been much harder.

Third are *environmental issues, labor standards, and other broader social agenda issues* that are raised within U.S. politics as well as in the global arena. Critics fault free trade theory for leaving such factors out of its narrowly economic calculations of efficiency and wealth creation.

Fourth is the *fair trade argument,* questioning whether the playing field is level in terms of other countries being sufficiently committed to rules of openness. Fair trade supporters claim ground between free trade and protectionism, arguing that although fair trade is a less elegant theory, it is more consistent with political realities.

These arguments don't necessarily lead to a rejection of free trade theory. But they do pose questions and critiques about how well it works in practice.

*Douglas A. Irwin, *Free Trade under Fire* (Princeton: Princeton University Press, 2002), 3.
†I. M. Destler, *American Trade Politics,* 4th ed. (Washington, D.C.: Institute for International Economics, 2005).

the promotion of American exports and foreign investments; and the regulation of imports.

TRADE AGREEMENTS The executive-branch agency that takes the lead in conducting trade negotiations is the ***U.S. Trade Representative (USTR).*** The office of the USTR was first established in 1962 and in the years since has grown in importance; the USTR now holds the rank of ambassador and is a member of the president's Cabinet. Depending on the issue area, other executive-branch actors may also be part of the negotiating team: the Commerce Department on issues relating to industrial goods and technology, or the Agriculture Department on agricultural trade. The State Department may also be involved through its Bureau of Economics, Business, and Agricultural Affairs. On issues that may affect the environment, the Environmental Protection Agency (EPA) plays a role.

When trade agreements take the form of treaties, they require ratification by two-thirds of the Senate. Although the House of Representatives has no formal role in treaties, it usually finds a way to be involved—often through legislation providing the funds needed for treaty implementation, because the Constitution requires all appropriations bills to originate in the House. Trade agreements that are not formal treaties require approval by both chambers, although only by simple majority votes.

NAFTA was a major political test in U.S. trade policy, one that showed broader patterns in post–Cold War trade politics.[93] A big protectionist push was made by NAFTA opponents, led by the billionaire businessman Ross Perot, who at the time was riding high as an independent candidate in the 1992 presidential election and as a national protest figure. The liberal wing of the Democratic Party and the neo-isolationist wing of the Republican Party also were part of the anti-NAFTA coalition. As they saw it, jobs would be lost as U.S. companies closed American factories and moved south to Mexico for its cheap labor, weak environmental regulations, and other profit-enhancing benefits.

NAFTA was originally signed in 1992 by President George H. W. Bush. President Clinton pushed it through congressional approval, and did so with a coalition drawing much more support from Republicans than from Democrats. In the end, the margin of victory, 61–38 in the Senate and 234–200 in the House, was larger than expected. Although this amounted to a choice for free trade over protectionism, the decision was not based strictly on the policy merits of the case—there was plenty of wheeling and dealing, as senators and representatives linked their votes to related trade issues, to other pet projects, and even to invitations to White House dinners.

By 1997, though, trade policy politics had shifted sufficiently against trade agreements that the Clinton administration was unable to get Congress to renew its fast-track trade treaty–negotiating authority. ***Fast-track authority*** was first established in the 1970s (see Chapter 5) as a way of keeping trade agreements from being amended to death or unduly delayed in Congress. It got its name from the guarantee that any trade agreements the president negotiates and submits to Congress under this authority will receive expedited legislative consideration within ninety days, and that under the special procedural rule that the vote be "up or down," yea or nay—that is, no amendments are allowed. Proponents saw this special procedure as being key to the success of trade agreements over the previous two decades, as it prevented Congress from excessively delaying or amending agreements already negotiated with other countries. Opponents, though, claimed that without some amending, trade agreements go too far in picking winners and forsaking losers. The immediate effect of the loss of fast-track authority was to set back the Clinton administration's efforts to build from NAFTA to a hemispheric Free Trade Area of the Americas. The broader effect was to delay initiation of a new round of global trade talks, because the credibility of U.S. leadership was undermined when the president could not show sufficient political strength at home to regain fast-track authority.

In 2001–2002, the Bush administration and fast-track supporters mounted another effort to renew fast-track authority. Part of their strategy was a lesson in political semantics: "fast-track" authority became ***"trade promotion" authority.*** Whereas the original name, with its connotation of moving quickly and not getting bogged down, had once been an advantage, it now seemed to imply a process that moved too fast and allowed too little opportunity for input. "Trade promotion" seemed to convey something that more people could support, something seemingly less political. It passed this time, by a solid margin in the Senate but only by a very close vote in the House and only for two years. It was not renewed in 2007.

EXPORT PROMOTION The opening of markets through trade treaties and agreements does not ensure that American exporters will win the major sales. Nor is it purely a matter of economic competitiveness. All major industrial countries have government policies to promote the exports of their companies, although such efforts are subject to rules, established by the GATT and furthered by the WTO, as to what is permissible.

The key executive-branch actors in this policy area are the Export-Import Bank of the United States, which provides credit and other financing for foreign customers to buy American exports; the Trade and Development Agency, which helps American companies put together business plans and feasibility studies for new export opportunities; and the Overseas Private Investment Corporation, which provides insurance and financing for foreign investments by U.S. companies that will create jobs back home and increase exports. Even though agricultural exports account for less than 10 percent of American exports, the Agriculture Department gets more than 50 percent of the export-promotion budget, reflecting interest-group politics and the power of farm constituencies. The State Department also has increased its role in export promotion as part of its post–Cold War retooling. As part of their training before assuming their embassy posts, U.S. ambassadors now go through a course titled "Diplomacy for Global Competitiveness." Once in their posts, as described in *Newsweek,* the U.S. ambassador to South Korea "hosted an auto show on the front lawn of his residence, displaying Buicks and Mercurys like a local used-car huckster"; the U.S. ambassador to India "won a contract for Cogentrix, a U.S. power company, with what he calls 'a lot of hugging and kissing' of Indian officials"; and the U.S. ambassador to Argentina "called in Argentine reporters to inform them that he was there as the chief U.S. lobbyist for his nation's businesses."[94]

ADMINISTRATIVE TRADE REMEDIES Administrative trade remedies are actions by executive-branch agencies in cases in which relief from import competition is warranted under the rules of the international trading system. From early on GATT had an "escape clause" that allowed governments to provide temporary relief to industries seriously injured by import competition that resulted from lower tariffs. GATT also provides "antidumping" provisions against foreign suppliers that export goods at less than fair value. In such cases the importing country can impose an additional duty equal to the calculated difference between the asking price and the fair-market price. In cases involving unfair subsidies provided by a foreign government, the importing country can impose "countervailing duties," also according to an equalizing calculation. Some of these can activate

TAA programs for affected companies, workers, and communities. TAA programs are the province of the Department of Labor.

The U.S. agency that administers escape clause, antidumping, and countervailing duty cases is the ***International Trade Commission (ITC).*** The ITC is an independent regulatory agency with six members, evenly divided between Republicans and Democrats, all appointed by the president (subject to Senate confirmation). Its ability to decide its cases objectively rather than politically is further aided by the seven-year length of the members' terms. The Commerce Department is also involved in antidumping and countervailing duty cases. Headed as it is by a member of the president's Cabinet, it is more political, but unless the ITC concurs, Commerce alone cannot provide import relief.

These administrative trade remedies also provide a good example of how Congress can shape policy through legislative crafting. Take the escape clause remedies. The 1962 Trade Expansion Act set the criteria for escape clause relief as imports being the "major cause" of the injury suffered by an industry. This meant imports had to be *greater* than all the other causes combined, a difficult standard to meet. The 1974 Trade Act changed "major" to "substantial," which meant that the injury from imports now has only to be *equal* to any of the other individual factors, a much less stringent criterion on which the ITC must base its rulings.[95]

A reverse example involved the Federal Trade Commission (FTC), another independent regulatory agency, and a case involving the "Made in the U.S.A." label.* In 1997 the FTC announced that it was lowering the standard required for a product to be considered made in the United States from its being "all or virtually all" made of American parts by American labor to allowing the label when 75 percent of the product met these standards. Reaction was strong from labor unions and their congressional supporters, who saw this as taking away an incentive for industries to invest and create jobs at home. The FTC was forced to back down.

## Summary

Like the other main issue areas of U.S. foreign policy, the post–Cold War international political economy poses complex policy choices amid dynamic patterns of change. Globalization has many aspects, and as stressed at the outset of this chapter, it is not inherently or exclusively a positive or negative force. Three things are certain, however. One is that globalization has made foreign economic and social policy issues more salient than in the past: we now hear much less "low politics" denigration of foreign economic policy issues

*The FTC's name is a bit deceptive. It deals with fair advertising, consumer protection, economic competition, and other aspects of domestic commerce and "trade."

compared with political-military ones. Second is that achieving foreign economic and social policy objectives is more complex and difficult now than when the United States enjoyed greater international economic dominance. Third, American Prosperity is affected by the overall health, stability, and growth of the international economy, and increasingly globalization affects other components of the national interest as well. The "DMD" threat of global pandemics requires more than the military might of American Power. Global poverty can undermine Peace as well as democracy (Principles).

In trade, international finance, and development, the three principal multilateral institutions (the World Bank, the IMF, and the WTO) continue to play central roles. Each of these areas of policy poses challenges to them as well as to the United States. Free and fair trade is seen as ever more crucial to U.S. Prosperity. It needs to be achieved, though, in the dual context of the WTO at the international level and increasingly contentious domestic trade politics.

What are the lessons of the recent financial crises and other experiences that will help U.S. policy, the IMF, and others do a better job at financial crisis prevention and management? Even when global growth was going strong, its rising tide did not lift all boats: poverty deepened for billions of people. We know quite a bit about what doesn't work for development but still too little about what does, especially for sustainable development and responsible stewardship of the human condition and the global environment. At the same time, risks of global disease pandemics pose further challenges.

All told, the questions, issues, and policy choices posed by globalization are another area in which the twenty-first century presents both challenges and opportunities for U.S. foreign policy.

## *American Foreign Policy* Online Student StudySpace

- So what, really, is globalization all about?
- What are the key lessons to be drawn from the 2008–09 global financial crisis?
- Which strategies hold the most promise for the global millions living in grinding poverty?
- Is global warming a hoax or a crisis?
- How safe are we from a global pandemic "DMD" (disease of mass destruction)?
- How has the role of NGOs and other forces changed the politics of globalization?

For these and other study questions, as well as other features, check out Chapter 10 on the *American Foreign Policy* Online Student StudySpace at wwnorton.com/studyspace.

## Notes

[1]Thomas L. Friedman, *The Lexus and the Olive Tree: Understanding Globalization* (New York: Farrar, Straus, and Giroux, 1999), xviii.

[2]Friedman, *Lexus and the Olive Tree,* xv.

[3]United Nations Development Program (UNDP), *Human Development Report 1999* (New York: Oxford University Press, 1999), 1.

[4]J. David Richardson and Karin Rindal, *Why Exports Matter: More!* (Washington, D.C.: Institute of International Economics and the Manufacturing Institute, 1996), 1.

[5]Wolfgang E. Reinicke, *Global Public Policy: Governing without Government?* (Washington, D.C.: Brookings Institution Press, 1998), 24.

[6]Reinicke, *Global Public Policy,* 25.

[7]Robert Keohane and Joseph Nye use the term "thickness" in their Introduction in Joseph S. Nye, Jr. and John D. Donahue, *Governance in a Globalizing World* (Washington, D.C.: Brookings Institution Press, 2000), 1–41.

[8]Roger C. Altman, "The Nuke of the 1990s," *New York Times Magazine,* March 1, 1998, 34.

[9]UNDP, *Human Development Report 1999,* 276.

[10]Joseph Stiglitz, *Globalization and Its Discontents* (New York: Norton, 2002), 67.

[11]UNDP, *Human Development Report 1999,* 266–69.

[12]Nicholas D. Kristof, "At Stake Are More Than the Banks," *New York Times,* April 2, 2009.

[13]Moises Naim, *Illicit: How Smugglers, Traffickers and Copycats Are Hijacking the Global Economy* (New York: Doubleday, 2005), 5.

[14]Naim, *Illicit,* 57, 88, 22, 161–62.

[15]Anthony Faiola, "A Global Retreat as Economies Dry Up," *Washington Post,* March 5, 2009, A1.

[16]Clifford J. Levy, "Emerging Economic Powers Meet in Russia," *New York Times,* June 16, 2009.

[17]Bruce W. Jentleson and Steven Weber, "America's Hard Sell," *Foreign Policy* 169 (November/December 2008): 42–49.

[18]"The Hypocrisy of Farm Subsidies," *New York Times,* December 1, 2002, 8; "Plowing Up Subsidies," *Foreign Policy* 133 (November/December 2002): 30–32.

[19]Uri Dadush, "Resurgent Protectionism: Risks and Possible Remedies," Policy Outlook, March 2009, Carnegie Endowment for International Peace, www.carnegieendowment.org/publications/index.cfm?fa=view&id=22844&prog=zgp&proj=zted (accessed 8/6/09).

[20]Inter-American Dialogue, *Agenda for the Americas 2005: Report of the U.S. Policy Task Force of the Inter-American Dialogue,* March 2005, www.thedialogue.org/PublicationFiles/agenda_2005.pdf (accessed 8/6/09).

[21]See, for example, Stiglitz, *Globalization and Its Discontents.*

[22]Jean-Paul Fitoussi, quoted in Roger Cohen, "Redrawing the Free Market," *New York Times,* November 14, 1998, A17, A19.

[23]Joan E. Spero and Jeffrey A. Hart, *The Politics of International Economic Relations* (New York: St. Martin's, 1997), 44.

[24]Andrew E. Kramer, "Emerging Economies Meet in Russia," *New York Times,* June 17, 2009, A10.

[25]World Commission on Environment and Development, *Our Common Future* (New York: Oxford University Press, 1987), 43; UNDP, *Human Development Report 1999,* 265.

[26]World Bank, *Human Development 2004* (New York: Oxford University Press, 2005).

[27]James C. McKinley, Jr., "Mexico's Populist Tilts at a Privileged Elite," *New York Times,* June 17, 2006.

[28]Neil MacFarquhar, "Wider Disparity in Life Expectancy Is Found Between Rich and Poor," *New York Times,* October 17, 2008.

[29]Kofi Annan, "Markets for a Better World," World Economic Forum, Davos, Switzerland, January 31, 1998, www.unhchr.ch/huricane/huricane.nsf/view01/2C716C42373EC4F0C125662E00352F58?opendocument (accessed 8/6/09).

[30]*Rigged Rules and Double Standards: Trade, Globalization and the Fight Against Poverty*, foreword by Amartya Sen, March 2002, www.maketradefair.com/en/index.php?file=03042002121618.htm (accessed 8/6/09).

[31]Spero and Hart, *Politics of International Economic Relations*, 219.

[32]David Dollar, "Globalization, Poverty and Inequality," in *Globalization: What's New?* Michael M. Weinstein, ed. (New York: Columbia University Press, 2005), 96–129; Dollar and Aart Kraay, "Trade, Growth and Poverty," Policy Research Working Paper No. 2199 (Washington, D.C.: World Bank, 2001).

[33]Dollar, "Globalization, Poverty and Inequality," 108.

[34]Spero and Hart, *Politics of International Economic Relations*, 233.

[35]United Nations, *The Millennium Development Report 2008*, 3–4, www.un.org/millenniumgoals/pdf/The%20Millennium%20Development%20Goals%20Report%202008.pdf (accessed 8/6/09).

[36]Nicholas D. Kristof, "The Women's Crusade," *New York Times Magazine*, August 23, 2009, 28–39, as well as other articles in this issue of the magazine. See also Kristof and Sheryl WuDunn, *Half the Sky: Turning Oppression into Opportunity for Women Worldwide* (New York: Knopf, 2009).

[37]Steven Kull and I. M. Destler, *Misreading the Public: The Myth of a New Isolationism* (Washington, D.C.: Brookings Institution Press, 1999), 113–33.

[38]Jeffrey D. Sachs, *The End of Poverty: Economic Possibilities for Our Time* (New York: Penguin, 2005).

[39]William Easterly, *The White Man's Burden: How the West's Efforts to Aid the Rest Have Done So Much Ill and So Little Good* (New York: Penguin, 2006).

[40]Jessica Einhorn, "The World Bank's Mission Creep," *Foreign Affairs* 80.5 (September/October 2001): 31.

[41]United Nations, Department of Economic and Social Affairs, Population Division, "World Population to Increase by 2.6 Billion over Next 45 Years, With All Growth Occurring in Less Developed Regions," Press Release POP/918, February 2, 2005, www.un.org/News/Press/docs/2005/pop918.doc.htm (accessed 8/6/09).

[42]Barbara Crossette, "UN Agency on Population Blames U.S. for Cutbacks," *New York Times*, April 6, 2002, A8.

[43]James Dao, "Over U.S. Protest, Asian Group Approves Family Planning Goals," *New York Times*, December 18, 2002, A7.

[44]Nicholas D. Kristof, "Pregnant (Again) and Poor," *New York Times*, April 5, 2009.

[45]Barack Obama, Statement on Rescinding the Mexico City Policy, January 23, 2009, www.whitehouse.gov/the_press_office/StatementofPresidentBarackObamaonRescindingtheMexicoCityPolicy/ (accessed 8/6/09).

[46]*The Lancet's* Series on Maternal and Child Undernutrition: Executive Summary, January 2008, www-tc.iaea.org/tcweb/abouttc/tcseminar/Sem6-ExeSum.pdf (accessed 8/6/09).

[47]Anirudh Kirshna et al., "Why Growth Is Not Enough: Household Poverty Dynamics in Northeast Gujarat, India," *Journal of Development Studies* 41.7 (October 2005).

[48]Central Intelligence Agency, *The Global Infectious Disease Threat and Its Implications for the United States*, National Intelligence Estimate 99-17D, January 2000, www.fas.org/irp/threat/nie99-17d.htm (accessed 8/6/09).

[49]Kofi Annan, address to the African Summit on HIV/AIDS, Tuberculosis and Other Infectious Diseases, Abuja, Nigeria, April 26, 2001, www.un.org/News/Press/docs/2001/SGSM7779R1.doc.htm (accessed 8/6/09).

[50]U.S. Department of State, Office of the U.S. Global AIDS Coordinator, "Action Today, A Foundation For Tomorrow: Second Annual Report to Congress on PEPFAR (2006)," www.state.gov/s/gac/rl/c16742.htm# (accessed 8/6/09).

[51]Ali Gharib and Jim Lobe, "U.S.: Obama's Global Health Plan Disappoints Activists," May 5, 2009, http://ipsnews.net/news.asp?idnews=46734 (accessed 8/6/09).

[52]Celia W. Dugger, "Study Cites Toll of AIDS Policy in South Africa," *New York Times*, November 26, 2008.

[53]Michael Specter, "What Money Can Buy," *New Yorker,* October 24, 2005, 58.

[54]2009 Annual Letter from Bill Gates: Introduction, Bill and Melinda Gates Foundation, www.gatesfoundation.org/annual-letter/Pages/2009-annual-letter-introduction.aspx (accessed 8/6/09).

[55]Gates Foundation, "Vaccine-Preventable Diseases," www.gatesfoundation.org/topics/Pages/vaccine-preventable-diseases.aspx (accessed 8/6/09).

[56]Laurie Garrett, "The Next Pandemic?" *Foreign Affairs* 84.4 (July/August 2005): 3–4.

[57]Gardiner Harris and Lawrence K. Altman, "Managing a Flu Threat with Seasoned Urgency," *New York Times,* May 10, 2009.

[58]Global Humanitarian Forum, "Human Impact Report, Climate Change: The Anatomy of a Silent Crisis," May 2009, www.ghfgeneva.org/Portals/0/pdfs/human_impact_report.pdf (accessed 8/6/09).

[59]Paul A. Samuelson, "The Pure Theory of Public Expenditure," *Review of Economics and Statistics* 36 (November 1954): 387–89.

[60]See, for example, the WTO's "10 Common Misunderstandings about the WTO," www.wto.org/english/thewto_e/whatis_e/10mis_e/10m00_e.htm (accessed 8/6/09); Deborah James, "Free Trade and the Environment," Global Exchange, updated October 2007, www.globalexchange.org/campaigns/wto/Environment.html (accessed 8/6/09).

[61]"UN Taking First Steps towards Implementing Johannesburg Outcome," September 23, 2002. Available at www.un.org/jsummit/html/whats_new/feature_story40.html (accessed 10/20/06).

[62]Patrick E. Tyler, "Peace Prize Goes to Environmentalist in Kenya," *New York Times,* October 4, 2004, A1.

[63]Jared Diamond, *Collapse: How Societies Choose to Fail or Succeed* (New York: Viking, 2005), 23.

[64]Rajendra Pachauri, address to the World Economic Forum, Davos, Switzerland, opening session, January 23, 2008, UN Intergovernmental Panel on Climate Change, www.ipcc.ch/graphics/speeches/pachauri-davos-january-2008.pdf (accessed 8/6/09); Nicholas Stern, *The Economics of Climate Change* (Cambridge: Cambridge University Press, 2007).

[65]"A Global Warning to Mr. Bush," *New York Times,* February 26, 2001, A18.

[66]Eric Pianin, "UN Report Forecasts Crises Brought on by Global Warming," *Washington Post,* February 20, 2001, A6.

[67]Al Gore, *An Inconvenient Truth: The Planetary Emergency of Global Warming and What We Can Do About It* (New York: Rodale, 2006), 8.

[68]George F. Will, "Dark Green Doomsayers," *Washington Post,* February 15, 2009; Will, "Climate Science in a Tornado," *Washington Post,* February 27, 2009.

[69]Ed Regis, "The Doomslayer," *Wired,* February 1997, www.wired.com/wired/archive/5.02/ffsimon_pr.html (accessed 8/6/09).

[70]"Global Warming: Truth or Propaganda?" *Financial Times,* June 13, 2007, www.ft.com/cms/s/2/e9df7200-19c7-11dc-99c5-000b5df10621.html (accessed 8/6/09); Vaclav Klaus, "Freedom, Not Climate, Is at Risk," *Financial Times,* June 13, 2007, www.ft.com/cms/s/2/9deb730a-19ca-11dc-99c5-000b5df10621.html (accessed 8/6/09).

[71]Cited in Alan Sipress, "Aggravated Allies Waiting for U.S. to Change Its Tune," *Washington Post,* April 22, 2001, A4.

[72]Chris Woodford, "Global Warming," *World at Risk: A Global Issues Sourcebook* (Washington, D.C.: Congressional Quarterly Press, 2002), 261.

[73]Yale and Columbia Universities, Environmental Performance Index, 2008, http://epi.yale.edu/Home (accessed 8/7/09).

[74]Juliet Eilperin, "Faster Climate Change Feared: New Report Points to Accelerated Melting, Longer Drought," *Washington Post,* December 25, 2008, A2; Kari Lydersen, "Scientists: Pace of Climate Change Exceeds Estimates," *Washington Post,* February 15, 2009, A3.

[75]Cornelia Dean, "Study Sees 'Global Collapse' of Fish Species," *New York Times,* November 3, 2006.

[76]International Union for Conservation of Nature, "IUCN Red List Reveals World's Mammals in Crisis," October 6, 2008, www.iucn.org/about/work/programmes/species/red_list/?1695/IUCN-Red-List-reveals-worlds-mammals-in-crisis (accessed 8/7/09).

[77]The State of the Birds, 2009 report, March 2009, http://www.stateofthebirds.org/ (accessed 8/7/09).

[78]Millennium Ecosystem Assessment, *Current State and Trends Assessment,* Chapter 5, Marc Levy, Suresh Babu, and Kirk Hamilton, "Ecosystem Conditions and Human Well-being," 2005, www.millenniumassessment.org/documents/document.274.aspx.pdf (accessed 8/7/09).

[79]United Nations Convention to Combat Desertification, "The Problem of Land Degradation," www.unccd.int/convention/text/leaflet.php (accessed 8/7/09).

[80]"Environmental Failure: A Case for a New Green Politics," *Guardian,* October 17, 2008, www.guardian.co.uk/environment/2008/oct/21/network (accessed 8/7/09).

[81]UNCCD, "United Nations and Top US Universities Pair Up to Develop Land Degradation Strategy," press release, updated June 23, 2009, www.unccd.int/publicinfo/pressrel/showpressrel.php?pr=press24_02_09 (accessed 8/7/09).

[82]Millennium Ecosystem Assessment, *Current State and Trends Assessment,* Chapter 21, Anatoly Shvidenko, Charles Victor Barber, Reidar Persson, "Forest and Woodland Systems," 587, www.millenniumassessment.org/documents/document.290.aspx.pdf (accessed 8/7/09).

[83]Millennium Ecosystem Assessment, *Current State and Trends Assessment,* Chapter 21, 613, www.millenniumassessment.org/documents/document.274.aspx.pdf (accessed 8/7/09).

[84]American Lung Association, "State of the Air: 2009," www.stateoftheair.org/2009/key-findings/ (accessed 8/7/09).

[85]World Health Organization, "Air Quality and Health: Questions and Answers," www.who.int/phe/air_quality_q&a.pdf (accessed 8/7/09).

[86]The United Nations Population Fund, "State of World Population 2007 Report: Unleashing the Potential of Urban Growth," June 27, 2007. Available at: http://www.unfpa.org/swp/2007/english/chapter_1/index.html

[87]United Nations Population Fund, *State of World Population 2007 Report: Unleashing the Potential of Urban Growth,*" Chapter 1, "The Promise of Urban Growth," June 27, 2007, www.unfpa.org/swp/2007/english/introduction.html (accessed 8/7/09).

[88]Paul Blustein, "Protests a Success of Sorts," *Washington Post,* April 23, 2001, A11.

[89]Quoted in Blustein, "Protests a Success."

[90]Margaret E. Keck and Kathryn Sikkink, *Activists beyond Borders: Advocacy Networks in International Politics* (Ithaca, N.Y.: Cornell University Press, 1998).

[91]Keck and Sikkink, *Activists beyond Borders,* 16.

[92]Alexander Cooley and James Ron, "The NGO Scramble: Organizational Insecurity and the Political Economy of Transnational Action," *International Security* 27 (Summer 2002): 5–39.

[93]Frederick W. Mayer, *Interpreting NAFTA: The Science and Art of Political Analysis* (New York: Columbia University Press, 1998).

[94]Bruce Stokes, "Team Players," *National Journal,* January 7, 1995, 10–11.

[95]I. M. Destler, *American Trade Politics,* 2d ed. (Washington, D.C.: Institute of International Economics, 1992), 142–43.

CHAPTER

# 11 The Coming of a Democratic Century?

## Introduction: Democracy and the U.S. National Interest

Democracy was sweeping the world—at least it seemed that way in the heady days of the late 1980s and early 1990s. The Berlin Wall, one of the Cold War's starkest symbols, had fallen. The Soviet Union itself crumbled. Nelson Mandela, a political prisoner of apartheid for almost thirty years, was released from prison and within a few years was elected president of a post-apartheid South Africa. Military and Marxist governments fell in Latin America. How captivating was the drama, how exhilarating the joy, how inspiring the sense of hope of those amazing days that marked the beginning of the 1990s.

Amid these and other events there was a sense that the world was witnessing ***the end of history,*** as the scholar Francis Fukuyama termed it—not just the end of the Cold War but "the universalization of Western liberal democracy as the final form of human government":

> Western liberal democracy seems at [the close of the century] to be returning full circle to where it started: not to an "end of ideology" or a convergence between capitalism and socialism, as earlier predicted, but to an unabashed victory of economic and political liberalism. . . . The triumph of the West, of the Western *idea,* is evident . . . in the total exhaustion of viable systematic alternatives to Western liberalism.[1]

11.1

This excerpt captures the sweeping essence of Fukuyama's thesis (Reading 11.1). He didn't claim that all conflict was over, or that there wouldn't be a few communist "isolated true believers." But he did see the big issues of world affairs as having been settled once and for all.

As the 1990s went on, however, history came roaring back. In Bosnia, Rwanda, East Timor, Liberia, Sierra Leone, and elsewhere, the world witnessed horrors and inhumanity that many had hoped were part of the past. Politics was once again more about bullets than ballots—indeed, not just bullets but machetes and mass mutilations. In other countries, including China, where the 1989 Tiananmen Square protests were crushed with killings and mass arrests, human rights were trampled. In the Islamic world, although some progress was being made, there still was not a single country that could be pointed to as a full democracy.

11.2

A very different view from Fukuyama's was offered by Harvard's Samuel Huntington in his 1993 article "The Clash of Civilizations" (Reading 11.2). "It is my hypothesis," Huntington wrote,

> that the fundamental source of conflict in this new world will not be primarily ideological or primarily economic. The great divisions among humankind and the dominating source of conflict will be cultural. . . . [T]he principal conflicts of global politics will occur between nations and groups of different civilizations. The clash of civilizations will dominate global politics. The fault lines between civilizations will be the battle lines of the future. . . . [T]he paramount axis of world politics will be the relations between "the West and the Rest."

Huntington started with a definition of "civilization" and the reasons for attributing significant causality to it:

> Civilizations are differentiated from each other by history, language, culture, tradition and, most important, religion. The people of different civilizations have different views of God and man, the individual and the group, the citizen and the state, parents and children, husband and wife, as well as differing views of the relative importance of rights and responsibilities, liberty and authority, equality and hierarchy.

These differences, he argued, are even more fundamental than those over political ideologies or economic systems. They are "the product of centuries. They will not soon disappear."[2] Huntington's ***clash of civilizations*** theory received attention even before September 11, 2001, although afterward it became as widely known and as hotly debated as any recent international relations theory.

All told, as the world entered what had been proclaimed the "democratic century," the record was more mixed and the outlook less clear than it had seemed in those heady days. The policy choices facing the United States were more complicated than they had seemed. At one level the issue was how much priority to give to democracy promotion and human

Nelson Mandela raises his fist in triumph as he celebrates his release after twenty-seven years of imprisonment in South Africa. (*AP/Wide World Photos*)

rights protection in defining the U.S. national interest (that is, how much to favor Principles over the other "Ps"). Even to the extent that Principles were given priority, the next issue was how to ensure that policies aimed at democracy promotion and human rights protection were effective. The holding of free and fair elections in countries that had never or rarely held them before clearly was an important goal. But the consolidation and institutionalization of democracy and human rights were broader and longer-term challenges. As we will see, U.S. policies under all recent administrations have had a decidedly mixed record. We can learn much from both their successes and their failures.

In this chapter we first want to take stock of *the status and prospects of global democracy and human rights,* assessing both the progress that has been made and the problems that have arisen in regions and countries of particular concern to U.S. foreign policy. The next three sections involve relationships between Principles and the other three core national interest objectives: *Principles-Peace* and the debate over "democratic peace" theory and its claim that democracies do not fight wars against each other; *Principles-Power,* and the tensions and trade-offs often posed; and *Principles-Prosperity,* focusing on the use of economic sanctions.

We then assess the *policy strategies for promoting democracy and protecting human rights,* linking these to some of the literature on democratization and political development, and focusing on U.S. policy along with some discussion of the UN, other international actors, and nongovernmental organizations. The chapter's final section examines the foreign policy politics of democracy-promoting economic sanctions, as exemplified by the case of the anti-apartheid sanctions against South Africa.

## Global Democracy and Human Rights: Status and Prospects

As we survey the status of democracy and human rights in the world, we need to take into account the successes, the limits and setbacks, and the uncertainties that remain. It's also helpful to have a historical perspective on the four "waves" through which democratization has developed in the modern world (see "Historical Perspectives," p. 594).

### *Post–Cold War Democratic Success Stories*

Looking at the overall global democracy scorecard in Table 11.1 (p. 596), we can see how widespread democracy has become. Of 193 countries, 151 are ranked as democracies (78 percent). This is a much higher number and a much higher percentage than in the 1980s. Today's figures include 49 countries that have made a transition to democracy since 1989 (marked in Table 11.1 in **bold**), and only six countries that slipped from democracy to nondemocracy (marked in *italics*).*

Among the new democracies is much of the former Soviet bloc. Twelve of these countries—Croatia, the Czech Republic, Estonia, Hungary, Latvia, Lithuania, Poland, Romania, Serbia, Slovakia, Slovenia, and Ukraine—make it into the "free" category. Eight others—Albania, Armenia, Bosnia & Herzegovina, Georgia, Kyrgyzstan, Macedonia, Moldova, and Montenegro—are "partly free." Belarus, Kazakhstan, Tajikistan, Turkmenistan, and Uzbekistan are noncommunist but still not free. Russia, previously qualifying as "partly free," dropped into "not free."

Also included as democracies are all the countries of Latin America except Cuba. This, too, is a major historical shift. Going back to the 1980s, countries such as El Salvador, Panama, Nicaragua, Argentina, Chile, Brazil, Ecuador, Paraguay, and Peru were not democracies. Indeed, almost every Latin American country has had a military coup at least once in the twentieth century. For a number of years there were some signs that Latin American militaries had become more accepting of the principles of civilian control and the illegitimacy of an active role for the military in politics. A scene at the second Conference of Defense Ministers of the Americas held in Argentina in 1996 was illustrative: "The civilian cabinet ministers in their business suits were in the front row. Almost all of the generals with their epaulets and medals and gold trim were relegated to the back—a vivid reminder that the balance of power has clearly shifted to the civilians."[3]

---

*These data are based on surveys by Freedom House, a New York–based nongovernmental organization. The key criteria used as measures of democracy and freedom are political rights and civil liberties. Freedom House's definition of democracy is "a political system in which the people choose their authoritative leaders freely from among competing groups and individuals," freedom as "the opportunity to act spontaneously in a variety of fields outside the control of the government and other centers of potential domination."

## HISTORICAL PERSPECTIVES

HISTORICAL PERSPECTIVES

### "WAVES" OF DEMOCRATIZATION

Many political scientists and historians see democratization as having had a number of "waves" in the modern world.*

The first wave is dated roughly from 1776 to 1933. This "long, slow wave" starts with the American Revolution, runs through the nineteenth century and greater democratization in monarchical Europe, and then into the twentieth century, including the period just after World War I when Germany and parts of Eastern Europe (e.g., Czechoslovakia) briefly were democracies. The 1933–45 period was a major reversal as Nazism, other forms of fascism, and communism spread. Germany's democracy was taken over by Hitler, who went on to conquer much of Europe; Spain and Italy became fascist under Francisco Franco and Benito Mussolini, respectively. Russia, which ever so briefly had been a democracy for some months in 1917, became communist and brought with it most of its neighbors.

The second wave of democratization ran from 1945 to 1964. It included liberation and the restoration of democracy to much of Western Europe, the shift from military governments to democratic ones in many Latin American countries, and democracy in a number of newly independent African states. By 1964, though, key Latin American countries such as Brazil and Argentina underwent military coups, many of which were supported by the United States according to its "ABC" (anything but communism) strategy. In Chile, where the United States had substantial involvement, the socialist but democratically elected government of President Salvador Allende was overthrown in an especially violent coup. In Africa, one-man rule replaced many nascent democracies. And in Europe, a coup in 1967 installed a military government in Greece, the very birthplace of democracy. In 1973, of the 135 countries in the world, only 39 were democracies.

The third wave dates from 1974 to 1986. Greece, Spain, and Portugal, the three major Western European countries still ruled by the military, became democratic. Some other countries such as the Philippines (as we discuss in this chapter) also overthrew dictators and became democratic. On the other hand, countries such as Pakistan had military coups.

The fourth wave, starting in 1989, saw the end of communism and the emergence of democracy in much of the former Soviet Union and Soviet bloc. By 1992, 117 of 192 countries were democracies. This also included many Latin American countries where the decline in U.S. "ABC" support for authoritarian leaders removed a main barrier. This is the wave that Table 11.1 provides a further update on, including the reversals of democracy in Russia and some other ex-Soviet states.

Will there be a fifth wave? This question focuses especially on Africa and the Middle East, as we see in this chapter.

*See Larry Diamond, *Developing Democracy: Toward Consolidation* (Baltimore: Johns Hopkins University Press, 1997); Samuel P. Huntington, *The Third Wave: Democratization in the Late Twentieth Century* (Norman, Okla.: University of Oklahoma Press, 1991); Robert A. Dahl, *Polyarchy: Participation and Opposition* (New Haven: Yale University Press, 1971); Philippe C. Schmitter, "The International Context of Contemporary Democratization, " *Stanford Journal of International Affairs* 2.1 (1993): 1–34; Thomas Carothers, *Aiding Democracy Abroad: The Learning Curve* (Washington, D.C.: Carnegie Endowment for International Peace, 1999).

The 2009 coup in Honduras, as well as increasing instability in other Latin American countries, however, called into question just how strong the new norms and practices are.

Africa has been making some progress on democratization. Whereas in 2003 almost half of African countries were nondemocracies, the total now is less then one-third. Six countries—Burundi, Djibouti, Gambia, Kenya, Mauritania, and Togo—moved from nondemocracies to "partly free"; only two, Congo (Brazzaville) and Zimbabwe, went in the other direction. More also moved from "partly free" to "free" than the reverse. In Africa the most remarkable case is South Africa. The apartheid system had ensured the white minority's total control of the government and the economy, and had condemned the black majority to oppression, injustice, and poverty—indeed, later revelations pointed to torture and assassination plots ordered by government officials against black leaders. Yet by 1994 Nelson Mandela, a former political prisoner, had been elected president of South Africa. Black majority rule was established, with protections for white minority rights. The past was not forgotten, but Mandela limited retribution and focused on building the political institutions and norms needed for democracy. Although the transition to democracy is far from over, and not everything has gone perfectly, it is not hard to imagine a more violent and undemocratic path than South Africa has taken to this point.

## *Limits and Uncertainties*

Quite a few cases and countries, though, are on the other side of the scale: 42 countries in Table 11.1, or about 22 percent of the world. Although this is still many fewer than the democracies, 2007 and 2008 were the first two consecutive years since 1994 that saw a net decrease in democracies. Moreover, tremendous uncertainties remain as to whether

**TABLE 11.1 The Status of Global Democracy**

**Democracies (151)**

**(a) Free (89)**

- Andorra
- Antigua & Barbuda
- Argentina
- Australia
- Austria
- Bahamas
- Barbados
- Belgium
- Belize
- **Benin**
- Botswana
- Brazil
- **Bulgaria**
- Canada
- **Cape Verde**
- Chile
- Costa Rica
- **Croatia**
- Cyprus
- **Czech Republic**
- Denmark
- Dominica
- Dominican Republic
- El Salvador
- **Estonia**
- Finland
- France
- Germany
- Ghana
- Greece
- Grenada
- Guyana
- **Hungary**
- Iceland
- India
- Indonesia
- Ireland
- Israel
- Italy
- Jamaica
- Japan
- Kiribati
- Korea, South
- **Latvia**
- **Lesotho**
- Liechtenstein
- **Lithuania**
- Luxembourg
- Mali
- Malta
- Marshall Islands
- Mauritius
- Mexico
- Micronesia
- Monaco
- **Mongolia**
- Namibia
- Nauru
- Netherlands
- New Zealand
- Norway
- **Palau**
- **Panama**
- Peru
- **Poland**
- Portugal
- **Romania**
- Saint Kitts & Nevis
- Saint Lucia
- Saint Vincent & Grenadines
- Samoa
- San Marino
- **San Tome & Principe**
- **Serbia**
- **Slovakia**
- **Slovenia**
- South Africa
- Spain
- Suriname
- Sweden
- Switzerland
- Taiwan
- Trinidad & Tobago
- Tuvalu
- **Ukraine**
- United Kingdom
- United States
- Uruguay
- Vanuatu

**(b) Partly free (62)**

- **Albania**
- **Armenia**
- **Bahrain**
- Bangladesh
- **Bhutan**
- Bolivia
- **Bosnia & Herzegovina**
- **Burkina Faso**
- **Burundi**
- **Central African Republic**
- Colombia
- **Comoros**
- **Djibouti**
- **East Timor**
- Ecuador
- **Ethiopia**
- Fiji
- **Gabon**
- **Gambia**
- **Georgia**
- Guatemala
- **Guinea Bissau**
- Haiti
- Honduras
- Jordan
- **Kenya**
- **Kyrgyzstan**
- Kuwait
- **Lebanon**
- Liberia
- **Macedonia**
- Madagascar
- **Malawi**
- Malaysia
- **Maldives**
- **Moldova**
- **Montenegro**
- Morocco
- **Mozambique**
- Nepal
- **Nicaragua**
- **Niger**
- Nigeria
- Pakistan
- Papua New Guinea
- Paraguay
- Philippines
- Senegal
- **Seychelles**
- Sierra Leone
- Singapore

(*Continued*)

**TABLE 11.1 The Status of Global Democracy** *(Continued)*

**(b) Partly free** *(Continued)*

| | | | |
|---|---|---|---|
| Solomon Islands | Thailand | Turkey | **Yemen** |
| Sri Lanka | Togo | Uganda | Zambia |
| Tanzania | Tonga | Venezuela | |

**Nondemocracies (not free) (42)**

| | | | |
|---|---|---|---|
| Afghanistan | Congo (Kinshasa) | Laos | *Swaziland* |
| *Algeria* | *Côte d'Ivoire* | Libya | Syria |
| Angola | Cuba | Mauritania | Tajikistan |
| *Azerbaijan* | Egypt | Myanmar (Burma) | *Tunisia* |
| Belarus | Equatorial Guinea | Oman | Turkmenistan |
| Brunei | Eritrea | Qatar | United Arab Emirates |
| Cambodia | Guinea | Russia | Uzbekistan |
| Cameroon | Iran | Rwanda | Vietnam |
| Chad | Iraq | Saudi Arabia | *Zimbabwe* |
| China | Kazakhstan | Somalia | |
| Congo (Brazzaville) | Korea, North | Sudan | |

Note: ***Bold*** indicates post-1989 democracy. *Italic* indicates shift from democracy to nondemocracy since 1989.
Source: Freedom House, *Freedom in the World: The Annual Survey of Political Rights and Civil Liberties*, 2009, www.freedomhouse.org/template.cfm?page=475&year=2009 (accessed 9/14/09).

the gains made in many new democracies will be consolidated and institutionalized. History is replete with democratic revolutions that failed—the February 1917 revolution in Russia, for example, which was trumped by Vladimir Lenin and the Bolsheviks, or the Weimar Republic of the 1920s and thirties in Germany, which elected as chancellor one Adolf Hitler.

To be sure, the problems and setbacks that feed pessimism have to be kept in perspective—after all, who believed that the successes of the early 1990s would be possible even just a few years before they occurred? The lesson that endures despite the fading euphoria is that positive political change is always possible. This is a major reason that theories such as Huntington's clash of civilizations are too deterministic, as if states, their leaders, and their people can only play out the civilizational script as already inscribed over the centuries and cannot shape their societies, their political systems, and their values in an evolving way.

Yet so, too, Fukuyama's end-of-history optimism on the other side needs to be tempered. It takes nothing away from the successes achieved thus far to acknowledge that declaring democracy is not the same as consolidating and institutionalizing it. Democracy can be said to be consolidated and institutionalized when governing regimes can change, but the political system itself remains stable. The political change that does occur must be within the bounds of a constitutional order, and it must be peaceful, with little or limited political violence. This is the challenge facing so many of the newly democratic countries.

We discussed democratization in Russia and China in Chapter 7. Here we look at Africa, the Middle East, and Latin America.

AFRICA One principal pattern among African nondemocracies is domination by strongman leaders. Zimbabwe under President Robert Mugabe is an example. Mugabe has been president for over thirty years, and although at earlier points there were free elections, he increasingly has ruled dictatorially. Another pattern has been countries torn by civil wars and genocidal killings—for example, Angola, Somalia, Rwanda, the Democratic Republic of Congo (the former Zaire), and others. There is no doubt that some of Africa's problems are the legacies of the Cold War, when the United States readily supported dictators friendly to its cause, and the Soviet Union supported various Afro-Marxist-Leninist regimes. The European colonial powers (France, Britain, and Belgium, especially) also bear a substantial share of responsibility for their disregard of tribal and ethnic divisions in drawing national boundaries as they withdrew from their colonial empires. But to acknowledge the degree of Western responsibility is not to dismiss the responsibility of Africa's own leaders, whose rivalries, repression, and corruption have taken a significant toll on their own people.[4]

Concern has been increasing about post-Mandela South Africa. Would the African National Congress (ANC), which continued to dominate, remain a democratic force, or would South Africa become too much of a one-party state? One survey found 89 percent of South Africans believing corruption widespread in their government. Would the political system remain stable amid mounting socioeconomic problems? The gap between rich and poor has been widening. Unemployment was over 25 percent, and two to three times as high in the extremely poor townships. Crime rates have been very high. The HIV/AIDS crisis continues to tear at the social fabric of this nation, which has been such an inspiration to so much of the world.

THE MIDDLE EAST The high percentage (65 percent) of Arab-Muslim countries that are not free, with six partly free but none free, seems at least somewhat consistent with Huntington's "clash of civilizations" analysis. "Western ideas of individualism, liberalism, constitutionalism, human rights, equality, liberty, the rule of law, democracy, free markets, the separation of church and state, often have little resonance in Islamic societies," Huntington contends. Saudi Arabia and most of the other Persian Gulf Arab states are monarchies or sheikdoms. Others, such as Syria and Libya, are dictatorships. Egypt has elections, but not free ones, and Egypt's president, Hosni Mubarak, has been in power for almost three decades.

The relation of Islamic fundamentalism to human rights and democratization is particularly controversial. "Democracy is irrelevant to Islam and Islam is superior to democracy," is how one noted scholar assesses the political dogma common among Islamic fundamentalist leaders. "Their notion of the 'rule of law' refers to the unalterable law of Islam," hardly a basis for social tolerance or political pluralism.[5] In a number of instances where militants have come to power, domestic repression has been totalitarian in scope, seeking to regulate virtually all aspects of society and individual conduct in accordance with fundamentalist interpretations of the Koran. An "ends-justify-the-means" logic is often used to rationalize terrorism, assassinations, and other political violence.

Other scholars point to signs of nonfundamentalist ***political Islam*** emerging, "a new generation of Islamic thinkers and parties . . . seeking to harmonize imaginatively Islam's injunctions with democracy's imperatives."[6] Professor Mohammed Ayoob of Michigan State University stresses that "the assumption that political Islam is inherently violent cannot be farther from the truth. . . . Most mainstream Islamist movements operate peacefully within national boundaries and attempt to influence and transform their societies and polities largely through constitutional means, even when the constitutional and political cards are stacked against them."[7] Ayoob cites Turkey and Indonesia as examples of Muslim democracies. Although there are no Arab countries that as yet are democracies, some "Islamic perestroika" trends have been identified in Bahrain, Kuwait, Morocco, Jordan, and Qatar. How strong these trends will become and whether they will spread more broadly remain to be seen. But they are there, and too often missed in Western analyses that focus too singularly on Islamic fundamentalism.

Recent experience has demonstrated the complexity of these dynamics. On the one hand is a much stronger sense that unless paths to democratization are opened, fundamentalism may appear to be the only route to change for people dissatisfied with the status quo. On the other hand, when elections have been held, Islamic fundamentalist groups have proven quite competitive. In the 2006 Palestinian elections, Hamas, an Islamist group still committed to terrorism, was the victor. The Muslim Brotherhood did so well in Egypt's 2005 legislative elections that President Mubarak reneged on his pledge to change the constitution to allow for greater political competition. Saudi Arabia has made only very limited reforms.

Iran has been a particularly important case. The 1978–79 Islamic fundamentalist revolution led by Ayatollah Ruhollah Khomeini that overthrew the shah established a theocratic state. Elections were held in the years that followed, and a president and parliament were established, but the principal governing authority rested with the religious "supreme leader"—Khomeini until his death in 1989, and later Ayatollah Ali Khamenei, his successor. Then in 1997, in a surprise result, the presidential election was won by Mohammad Khatami, a more moderate pro-reform *mullah* (religious leader) over the candidate favored by the theocrats. Khatami's victory came about largely because of strong support among women and youth (the voting age is sixteen) and other groups within Iranian society favoring liberalization. Tensions between the moderates and the fundamentalists grew even more intense. Elections in early 2000 produced a strong reformist majority in the *majlis* (parliament), setting off a fundamentalist backlash that included shutting down newspapers and a wave of political killings. Khatami was reelected in 2001, but the fundamentalists stayed in control for the rest of his term.

In 2005 Mahmoud Ahmadinejad was elected president on a platform that combined appeals to economic discontent with fiery fundamentalist rhetoric, including threats to destroy Israel and strong anti-Americanism. Ahmadinejad did not deliver on his economic promises. Inflation and unemployment both ran high. Nor did the repressive measures he and Supreme Leader Khamenei pursue stomp out pushes for political reform. While it wasn't as neat as the reformists vs. Islamists depiction often portrayed in the United States, discontent with the status quo intensified and spread. When Ahmadinejad ran for reelection in June 2009, the political opposition rallied around the candidacy of Mir Hossein Musavi. When the government announced that Ahmadinejad had won with over 60 percent of the vote, accusations of fraud were widespread. Mass demonstrations protested the results. The government responded with brutal repression, killing some protesters, and jailing many others, with evidence of rape and torture. Opposition continued in what came to be known as the "green movement," named for the insignia color of Musavi supporters. Whereas in the past protests came mostly from groups such as students and journalists, this time there were deep splits within elites, including some in the religious establishment who, while still believing in an Islamic state, believed that Ahmadinejad and Supreme Leader Khamenei were violating core principles of how Islam and democracy could be compatible. While much was uncertain, it did seem that the existing regime had forfeited its legitimacy in ways that even severe repression would not compensate for over time.

LATIN AMERICA Any complacency brought on by the spread of democracy in the 1990s has been shaken by the instabilities of recent years. Argentina had musical-chair presidents, five in fewer than four years between 1999 and 2003. In Bolivia, one president was forced to resign in 2003; another tried to resign in early 2005 but had his resignation rejected by Congress and then was pressured by public protests to call early elections. In Ecuador, one president was forced to resign in 2000 and another in 2005. In Venezuela, Hugo Chavez survived coup attempts (including at least one with a Bush administration role) and rigged elections; his rule became increasingly autocratic. Honduras had a hotly disputed election in 2005. In Hounduras in June 2009, the military ousted Honduran President Manuel Zelaya in a contested coup, as discussed in Chapter 7.

As a general pattern, these instabilities have two principal sources. One is the continued weakness of political institutions. As assessed by one prominent analyst, "severe deficiencies mark political life—weak capacity and performance of government institutions, widespread corruption, irregular and often arbitrary rule of law, poorly developed patterns of representation and participation, and large numbers of marginalized citizens."[8] Because of both its economic impact of wasted resources and its political effects of delegitimization, corruption has been especially corrosive. A survey of eighteen countries by a Chilean public opinion firm found that the Latin American people see corruption as one of their most severe problems. The World Bank concurs, saying that "official graft and nepotism are so powerful that they are rotting governmental institutions and stunting economic growth." An American government analysis estimated "that official corruption might shave as much as 15 percent off annual growth in Latin America, as public funds are pilfered and wary foreign investors shy away."[9]

Second is the limits and failures of globalization. There is much debate, as discussed in Chapter 10, over the extent to which the recent economic problems of many developing countries are being caused by their own governments' policy blunders or are inherent in the dynamics of globalization. Whatever the case, Latin America has been hit hard. It long has been the region with the greatest inequalities in the distribution of wealth among social classes. Although the middle classes have seen some growth, Latin American economies still tend to be dominated by wealthy elites, with impoverished masses of urban poor and rural *campesinos* (peasants). Some 220 million people, equal to 43 percent of the region's population, still live in poverty. In Bolivia, for example, a lack of clean water contributes to the death of one in ten children before the age of five.[10] Indeed, a regionwide poll found that "a majority of Latin Americans would prefer a return to dictatorship if it would bring economic benefits." Fifty-eight percent agreed that leaders should go "beyond the law" if necessary for the social good. Fifty-six percent gave higher priority to economic development than to democracy.[11]

During the Cold War Latin America was one of the regions where socialism had its greatest appeal as a popular movement. Although socialism itself may not reemerge, the question remains whether other competing ideologies and political models may develop. In their fundamentals, socialism and communism were efforts to address the problem of social, political, and economic inequality. These particular remedies largely failed, and the core problem of inequality remains—indeed, income gaps and disparities in wealth have been growing wider in many societies around the world. If democracy and capitalism do not more effectively deal with these fundamental problems, it stands to reason that other ideologies will be articulated and other political models advanced with at least the promise of doing so. "The logic of the market does not resolve all problems," Chile's president Michelle Bachelet stated. "You need strong and powerful social policies by the state to resolve the problems of income and equality of opportunity."[12] The wave of electoral victories by left-of-center presidential candidates—Luiz Inácio Lula da Silva in Brazil, Rafael Correa in Ecuador, Daniel Ortega in Nicaragua, Evo Morales in Bolivia, and Alan García in Peru, along with Bachelet in Chile—demonstrated the political appeal of this "social market" approach.

It may well be that the recent trend to democracy will be durable. But given Latin America's history, the possibility of popular unrest pulling the military out of the barracks and back into politics in cases besides Honduras cannot be dismissed; in the early 1960s, for example, a democratizing wave then gaining force was swept away by a string of military coups.

Latin America is also plagued by its infamous drug cartels. In Colombia the drug cartels have assassinated government officials who sought to crack down on them, including supreme court justices and a popular presidential candidate; their leaders even continued to run their businesses from jail. Mexico and Panama are among the other Latin American countries that must cope with the reality that "narco-democracies" cannot remain democracies for very long.

GLOBAL HUMAN RIGHTS ***Amnesty International (AI)***, one of the leading human rights NGOs in the world, began its recent report with a stark assessment: "World leaders owe an apology for failing to deliver on the promise of justice and equality in the Universal Declaration of Human Rights (UDHR), adopted 60 years ago. In the past six decades, many governments have shown more interest in the abuse of power or in the pursuit of political self-interest, than in respecting the rights of those they lead."[13] The AI report went through country by country, region by region, with the kind of strong evidence and analysis that won it the 1977 Nobel Peace Prize. Some of its assessments:

*Africa:* "Economic and social rights remained illusory for millions of people. The internal armed conflicts that continued to ravage several states were accompanied by gross human rights abuses including unlawful killings and torture, including rape. In some countries all forms of dissent were suppressed, and in many freedom of expression was restricted and human rights defenders suffered intimidation and harassment. Women endured widespread discrimination and systematic human rights abuse. Throughout the continent, those responsible for human rights violations escaped being held to account."

*Latin America:* "The end of military rule and the return to civilian, constitutionally elected governments have seen an end to the pattern of widespread and systematic enforced disappearances, extrajudicial executions and torture of political opponents. However, the hopes that a new era of respect for human rights had arrived have in many cases proved unfounded. . . .

"The legacy of the authoritarian regimes of the past lives on in the institutional weaknesses. . . . Corruption, the absence of judicial independence, impunity for state officials, and weak governments have undermined confidence in state institutions. Equal protection may exist in law, but it is often denied in practice, particularly for those in disadvantaged communities."

*Asia-Pacific:* "On the face of it, 'freedom from want' appeared to find some vindication in Asia's subsequent, explosive emergence as a powerful economic force. . . . The challenge to match unbridled economic expansion with an increase in economic, social and cultural rights for the region's poor remains unmet.

"Ongoing conflicts and the growing violence perpetrated by armed groups have continued to generate grave abuses across the region, undermining the security of millions. . . . [I]n many countries security forces have enjoyed impunity for decades for human rights violations . . . in the name of 'national security.' Political instability and the reassertion of military authority—often via the imposition of states of emergency—have undermined institutions crucial for the protection of human rights, or stalled their reform, in several countries."

*Europe and Central Asia:* "Within and across Europe, women, men and children continue to be trafficked for exploitation in informal sectors such as domestic work, farming, manufacturing, construction, hospitality and forced sexual exploitation. Such trafficking was widespread, and thrived on poverty, corruption, lack of education and social breakdown. . . .

"Access to justice including redress, compensation, restitution and rehabilitation for the abuses was rare. Non-nationals without rights to residence in the country in which they were found were frequently deported without consideration of the risks that they may face on return, be they re-trafficking, retribution, or other violence."

*Middle East and North Africa:* "Governments in the region continue to focus on 'state security' and 'public safety' to the detriment of human rights, and the lives of their citizens. This has been exacerbated since the onset of the 'war on terror'. Grievous human rights abuses continue to be both widespread and firmly entrenched in many Middle Eastern and North African states. Despite talk of greater democracy, good governance and accountability, most power remains firmly in the grasp of small elites—the clerical oligarchy in Iran; civilians with close links to the military in Algeria, Egypt and Tunisia; religious minorities in the Gulf states; secular Ba'athists in Syria. All are largely unaccountable to those they govern.

"Throughout the region, state power is maintained, and dissenting voices or debate repressed, by all-powerful security and intelligence services."[14]

As serious as these problems are, the AI report is not all despair. It also gives many examples of "positive change" and the roles played by human rights activists, civil society groups, and governments. "Much has improved in many parts of the world. . . . More countries today provide constitutional and legal protection for human rights than ever before. . . .

"To a degree almost unimaginable in 1948, today there is a global citizens' movement that is demanding their leaders recommit themselves to upholding and promoting human rights. . . .

"A consciousness of human rights is sweeping the globe. World leaders ignore it at their peril."[15] So here too the message is both the scope of the problem and the possibilities of progress.

## Principles and Peace: The Democratic Peace Debate

According to the theory of the ***democratic peace,*** the United States should support the spread of democracy not just because it is the right thing to do, but also because history demonstrates that democracies do not fight wars against fellow democracies; thus it is in the U.S. interest to support democratization in order to reduce the risks of war. The theory does not claim that democracies don't go to war at all. They have, and they do—against nondemocracies. But they don't, and they won't, it is argued, against other democracies. This tenet of the democratic peace paradigm implies that right makes for might, that the world is a safer and a better place to the extent that democracy spreads. For American foreign policy, the promotion of democracy thus is said to have the added value of serving objectives of Peace as well as of Principles.

Democratic peace theory had a major influence on actual U.S. foreign policy in recent administrations (see "Theory in the World," p. 605). It is thus all the more important that we consider the theory's validity. We examine the main arguments and evidence first from proponents and then from critics of the theory.

### *Democratic Peace Theory*

Proponents of the democratic peace theory make the sweeping claim that "the absence of war between democratic states comes as close to [sic] anything we have to an empirical law in international relations."[16] The empirical evidence as they present it indeed is impressive:

- Democracies have not fought any wars against each other since 1815. This encompasses 71 interstate wars involving nearly 270 participants.
- Since the end of World War II, democracies have been only one-eighth as likely as nondemocracies to threaten to use military force against a democracy, and only one-tenth as likely to use even limited force against each other.
- Democracies have fought numerous wars against nondemocracies, however, including World War I, World War II, and many wars during the Cold War.[17]

The central tenets of the democratic peace paradigm and their logic and philosophical basis, although very often associated with President Woodrow Wilson in the history of U.S. foreign policy, can be traced all the way back to the eighteenth-century European political philosopher Immanuel Kant and his book *Perpetual Peace.* The basic argument has three components: the constraints imposed by democratic political systems, the internationalization of democratic norms, and the bonds built by trade.

## THEORY IN THE WORLD

THEORY IN THE WORLD

### DEMOCRATIC PEACE THEORY AND THE CLINTON AND BUSH FOREIGN POLICIES

Bill Clinton's 1994 State of the Union address sounded almost like an exact quote out of the political science literature on democratic peace theory. "Democracies don't attack each other," President Clinton declared, so therefore "ultimately the best strategy to ensure our security and to build a durable peace is to support the advance of democracy elsewhere."* Clinton's advisers coined the term "enlargement," playing off the old Cold War "containment," to refer to the spread of global democracy and the U.S. interests thus served. As laid out in a major Clinton administration policy statement, "all of America's strategic interests—from promoting prosperity at home to checking global threats abroad before they threaten our territory—are served by enlarging the community of democratic and free-market nations. Thus, working with new democratic states to help preserve them as democracies committed to free markets and respect for human rights is a key part of our national security strategy."[†] Ensuring the success of democracy was thus posed as a pragmatic and not just an idealistic goal, serving Peace as well as Principles.

The officials of the George W. Bush administration came into office as self-styled Realists who, though not opposed to democracy, did not make its global promotion a high priority. During the 2000 presidential campaign, while serving as then Governor Bush's senior foreign policy advisor, Condoleezza Rice laid out five priorities, none of which gave much weight to democracy promotion.[§] This started to change after September 11. The administration made democracy-promotion claims for the Iraq war, although many questioned whether this was after-the-fact rationalization and spin rather than genuine driving motivation in the first place.

Bush's 2005 inaugural address went much further in invoking democratic peace logic. So too did now Secretary of State Condoleezza Rice, including in an op-ed tellingly titled "The Promise of Democratic Peace." "Supporting the growth of democratic institutions in all nations is not some moralistic flight of fancy," Secretary Rice wrote. "It is the only realistic response to our present challenges." The reasoning: "Fundamental character of regimes matters more today than the international distribution of power. . . . Democracy is the only assurance of lasting peace and security between states, because it is the only guarantee of freedom and justice within states."[‡]

(*Continued*)

(*Continued*)

Clinton's 1994 State of the Union, Bush's 2005 inaugural, Rice's 2005 op-ed: the theory-policy links were so strong and so direct that we might even have asked for footnotes!

*Bill Clinton, State of the Union Address, *New York Times,* January 26, 1994, A17.
†"A National Security Strategy of Engagement and Enlargement," reprinted in *America's Strategic Choices,* Michael E. Brown et al., eds. (Cambridge, Mass.: MIT Press, 1997), 319.
§Condoleezza Rice, "Promoting the National Interest," *Foreign Affairs* 79.1 (January/February 2000): 45–62.
‡Rice, "The Promise of Democratic Peace," *Washington Post,* December 11, 2005, B7.

DOMESTIC POLITICAL CONSTRAINTS We already have seen how, historically, going to war has been one of the recurring great debates in American politics. Kant, who was writing before there even was a United States of America with its own constitution and foreign policy, made his argument with reference to democracies generally. If "the consent of the citizens is required in order to decide that war should be declared," he wrote,

> nothing is more natural than that they would be very cautious in commencing such a poor game. . . . Among the [calamities of war] would be: having to fight, having to pay the costs of war from their own resources, having painfully to repair the devastation war leaves behind, and, to fill up the measure of evils, load themselves with a heavy national debt that would embitter peace itself and that can never be liquidated on account of constant wars in the future. But, on the other hand, in a constitution which is not republican, and under which the subjects are not citizens, a declaration of war is the easiest thing to decide upon, because war does not require of the ruler . . . the least sacrifice of the pleasure of his table, the chase, his country houses, his court functions and the like.[18]

Kant also stressed, though, that these constraints were less likely in wars against nondemocracies, for which mass publics were more likely to be aroused by crusadelike appeals. Democracies' willingness to go to war against nondemocracies and their unwillingness to go to war against each other thus follow the same domestic political logic.

INTERNATIONALIZATION OF DEMOCRATIC NORMS All democracies, no matter what their particular representative structure, must practice compromise and consensus-building in their domestic politics and policy. Their watchwords need to be tolerance and trust, and the essence of a successful democratic system is managing if not resolving conflicts and tensions within society in lawful and peaceful ways. As Michael Doyle, whose articles were among the first to advance the democratic peace thesis, states, democracies, "which rest on consent, presume foreign republics to also be consensual, just, and therefore deserving of accommodation."[19] Nondemocracies, in contrast, as another author puts it, "are viewed *prima facie* as unreasonable, unpredictable."[20] There is a rational logic here, not just ideology. It makes sense not to go to war against a country that you are confident won't move quickly to war against you. But going to war may become the rational choice if you fear the other may seek to strike preemptively or by surprise.

BONDS OF TRADE The combination of this spirit of political commonality and the common tendency of democracies to have free-market economic systems also leads them to develop trade and other economic relations with each other. "The 'spirit of commerce,'" in Kant's term, in turn becomes another factor inhibiting war. The same idea also is found in the work of such other eminent political philosophers as Montesquieu, who wrote of "the natural effect" of trade "to bring about peace," and John Stuart Mill, who went even further in seeing the expansion of international trade in the mid-nineteenth century as "rapidly rendering war obsolete."[21] The basic ideas are that as trade develops countries have more to lose from going to war, and in any event that war would be against people who are no longer strangers. This is said to be especially true today, given how international interdependence now encompasses not just trade but investment, finance, and many of the other economic interconnections discussed in Chapter 10.

## *Critiques and Caveats*

Four principal arguments have been made by those who question the democratic peace theory.

SPURIOUS RELATIONSHIP? Some scholars question whether there really is a strong relationship between states' forms of government and the likelihood of their going to war against each other. These critics contend that on two counts the claim for this causal link is "spurious," meaning not valid because of methodological problems. One count is how both "democracy" and "war" are defined by democratic peace theorists, and the resulting criteria for including or excluding cases. These critics examined the empirical data going back to 1815 and cited a number of cases in which they say democratic peace proponents inaccurately excluded some conflicts that involved democracies vs. democracies, or miscategorized countries that fought wars as nondemocracies when they should be considered democracies.[22] Among the historical examples cited are the American Civil War and Finland's siding with the Axis powers in World War II. Applying the theory to the contemporary context is problematic: so many of today's wars are ethnic conflicts, civil wars, and other intrastate conflicts, yet the democratic peace theory principally addresses classical interstate wars.

A second methodological criticism is that democratic peace theorists confuse correlation with causality, mistakenly emphasizing the nature of the domestic political system as the cause of peaceful relations rather than a Realist calculation that cooperation served national interests better than conflict. For example, with regard to the claim that the United States, Western Europe, and Japan didn't fight wars with each other from 1945 to 1991 because they are democracies, critics argue that the more important factor was these countries' shared security interests, which were based on the Cold War and the common threat from the Soviet Union. In a number of historical cases of "near-miss" crises, democracies almost did go to war against each other, but refrained for reasons that had more to do with assessments of their interests than with the other side's being a democracy. These include two crises between the United States and Great Britain in the nineteenth century, as well as some others.[23]

TRADE AND PEACE? A second point raises doubts about how much trade actually inhibits war. On the eve of World War I, Sir Norman Angell, the foremost heir to the Kant-Montesquieu-Mill tradition, diagnosed war as "a failure of understanding" that could be corrected by the kind of mutual familiarity and interchange bred by international commerce. Yet the fact that Germany was Britain's second leading trade partner didn't stop the two countries from going to war. In other historical cases, high levels of economic interdependence did not prevent war. Moreover, high levels of trade surely do not prevent other political and diplomatic conflicts. U.S.-European and U.S.-Japanese relations provide numerous examples.

AGGRESSIVE TENDENCIES OF DEMOCRATIZING STATES Third, and more in the way of a qualifying caveat than outright criticism, is that even if we accept that mature democracies may not fight with each other, states that are still undergoing democratization and are not yet stable democracies may actually be even *more* aggressive and warlike than stable nondemocracies. These transition periods are notoriously unstable, as elites and other groups compete for political influence, and as the general public struggles with the economic difficulties of transitions, the disorientation of political change, and an uncertain future. They thus are quite susceptible to "belligerent nationalism" as a rallying cry and a diversion from domestic problems. As the political scientists Edward Mansfield
11.3 and Jack Snyder put it (Reading 11.3), "like the sorcerer's apprentice, these elites typically find that their mass allies, once mobilized, are difficult to control. When this happens, war can result from nationalist prestige strategies that hard-pressed leaders use to stay astride their unmanageable political coalitions."[24] Slobodan Milosevic in Serbia was one important example. Democratization in the Arab world, as discussed earlier, also offers examples.

DEMOCRACY AT THE END OF A BAYONET The fourth point is derived from the ways in which the George W. Bush administration's approach to global democratization differed from the Clinton administration's. The 2002 National Security Strategy reflected some democratic peace logic in committing to "extend the peace by encouraging free and open societies on every continent."[25] President Bush went further in his 2005 inaugural address, stating that "it is the policy of the United States to seek and support the growth of democratic movements and institutions in every nation and culture." But there is less confidence that democracy will succeed in key countries around the world without more direct American intervention than just building civil society and other political initiatives. This has included, as in Iraq, efforts to use American military power to overthrow dictators and then as military occupation—what many call democracy at the end of a bayonet.

## Principles and Power: Tensions and Trade-Offs

As we have seen throughout this book, American foreign policy repeatedly has been faced with tensions and trade-offs between considerations of Power and Principles. They were there in pre–Cold War history; they were there during the Cold War; and they are with us in this new era. Here we focus on the war on terrorism and the Principles-Power tension it has posed.

### *From ABC to ABT?*

During the Cold War American foreign policy sided with nondemocratic but anticommunist regimes, still claiming to be true to its principles through the "ABC" (anything but communist) definition of Third World democrats. In the contemporary context of the war on terrorism, are we moving towards an "ABT"—anybody but terrorists—definition?

Consider Pakistan, where General Pervez Musharraf came to power in a military coup in 1999. The Clinton administration opposed the Musharraf coup as a violation of democratic principles and imposed economic sanctions on the country. The Bush administration largely continued this policy until the September 11, 2001, terrorist attacks. At that point, power considerations strongly overrode principles; the United States needed close relations with Pakistan to fight the war in Afghanistan, to try to break up Al Qaeda, and to try to capture Osama bin Laden. The United States also came to see Musharraf as the best bet for blocking Islamic fundamentalists and other anti-American forces from gaining ground within Pakistan.

Although the government Musharraf forced out was democratic, independent analysts acknowledged that "Pakistanis broadly welcomed [Musharraf's] overthrow of what was widely perceived as a corrupt civilian government."[26] His own popularity, though, fell. When the first post-coup legislative elections were held in October 2002, opposition groups fared better than Musharraf's political party. Among the opposition groups that did well were Islamic fundamentalist parties that were anti-American and called for the imposition of Islamic law.

Some argued that the United States was actually feeding into anti-Americanism by being so supportive of Musharraf. His dictatorial rule had contributed to the political strength of his opponents. The previous spring he had called a referendum seeking support for his staying in power beyond the period he had promised at the time of his coup. He got the positive vote he wanted but by a smaller margin than expected and amid widespread accusations of a rigged referendum. Although he went ahead with the October 2002 legislative elections, he circumscribed them by maintaining his right as president to dismiss the legislature and amend the constitution. By being so pro-Musharraf, and by not pushing him to be more genuinely democratic, the United States both was inconsistent with its own principles and risked a boomerang effect against its power interests.

The counterargument saw the anti-American nature of much of the Pakistani opposition as all the more reason for supporting Musharraf. If the Islamic fundamentalist parties came to power, it was argued, they were unlikely to stick by democracy. Moreover, the security interests at stake could not be underestimated in the wake of September 11. This was the war on terrorism's theater of origin. If American power did not continue to be effectively asserted here, the whole war on terrorism could be lost and American security seriously endangered. From this perspective, therefore, the ABT case was seen as both consistent with Principles and also giving Power its due.

This debate grew even more intense as Musharraf became even more dictatorial and delivered even less on the anti-terrorism front. Facing pressure from the United States to move back toward democracy, in October 2007 Musharraf agreed to grant amnesty to Benazir Bhutto, a two-time former prime minister living in exile, and other politicians who had been accused of political corruption. However, shortly after Bhutto returned to Pakistan, Musharraf declared a state of emergency in the country. He suspended the Constitution, fired the Supreme Court, shut off independent and international news channels, and arrested many of his opponents.

The White House was forced to criticize one of its foremost allies and call on Musharraf to resign as army chief of staff and hold elections before January 2008. Musharraf gave no timeline as to when elections would be held or when the state of emergency would end. Pakistani police forces flooded the streets and barricaded opposition leaders, including Benazir Bhutto, in their homes so they could not stage protests. The opposition to Musharraf reached a tipping point when Ms. Bhutto was assassinated leaving a political rally on December 27, 2007. Although the assassination was perpetrated by Islamist extremists, the effects reverberated back against Musharraf.

Even before Bhutto's assassination, the state of emergency caused public opinion in Pakistan to turn further away from Musharraf. In a poll conducted by the U.S. International Republic Institute, about two-thirds of the Pakistani public was calling for Musharraf's resignation. Meanwhile, the U.S. began to doubt how effective Musharraf was as an ally in the fight against terrorism. In February 2008, Musharraf's party was voted out in the nation's parliamentary elections. On August 18, 2008, Musharraf announced his resignation as president of Pakistan. The head of the Pakistan People's Party—Benazir Bhutto's widower, Ali Asif Zardari—won the ensuing elections.

Not only were there doubts about Zardari and his political competence and honesty, but the political situation had deteriorated so much that Pakistan was verging on becoming a failed state and/or one controlled by Islamist extremists. This was the security situation discussed in Chapter 8 in which the Principles-for-Power trade-off had undermined the former without achieving the latter.

Pakistan is not the only country over which this debate has been playing out. The war on terrorism brought U.S. military aid and other forms of cooperation to a number of other governments with questionable democratic credentials and human rights records. Many of these are Central Asian states also bordering Afghanistan: Uzbekistan, Tajikistan, Turkmenistan, and Kyrgyzstan. All have their own Islamic fundamentalist movements known to be or suspected of being anti-American and linked to Al Qaeda or other global terrorist networks. Here, too, the Bush administration stressed the overriding importance of Power considerations and claimed a degree of consistency with Principles by making comparisons with the alternatives and by pointing to military-training programs and other cooperation as ways to help infuse greater respect for democracy and human rights. But the more repressive these regimes become, the weaker this argument gets. "You've got to find and nullify enemy leadership," one senior Bush administration official stated. "We are going to support any viable political actor that we think will help us with counterterrorism."[27] The Obama administration has also been wrestling with this dilemma.

In sum, just as the ABC debate was central to Cold War policies, so is the ABT debate central to our current era.

## *Principles as Power: Soft Power's Significance*

The term "soft power" captures how American principles encompass more than just idealism and altruism. *Soft power,* as defined by Professor Joseph Nye, is based less on coercion and traditional measures of power than on intangible assets such as cultural attraction, political values, and societal strengths that others admire.[28] This is not a strictly new phenomenon; historically the United States and other major powers always have tried to use their reputations and ideologies as sources of power. But it is more important in the post–Cold War world, when power has become "less fungible, less coercive and less tangible."[29] It is part of how "right" can make for "might," how principles can be a source of power.

The crucial policy choice from a soft-power perspective is not so much whether the United States still can claim to be truer to democratic values than other major powers, but whether it lives up to the standards to which it lays claim for itself. It is one thing to pursue a power-politics foreign policy if the state doing so makes only limited claims to standing for some set of values greater than self-interest. But if higher standards are claimed, then the situation is more problematic. The soft-power concept provides important perspective for understanding this issue not just as Democratic Idealism but also in terms of how Power may be less well served than often is claimed. The issue is not purity but contradiction.

The "International Perspectives" feature that begins on page 53 illustrates the range of views of the United States as a promoter of democracy. There is praise for the role the United States has played in some cases, and criticism in others. In 1990, on becoming the first president of postcommunist Czechoslovakia, Vaclav Havel quoted Thomas Jefferson as the inspiration for the ideals for which he stood, indeed, for which he had gone to jail as a political prisoner. The Ukrainian president Viktor Yushchenko, leader of the ***"Orange Revolution"*** that overturned old Soviet-style rigged elections in 2004, also invoked the crucial role the United States played for his country.

On the other side, the Venezuelan president Hugo Chávez has been a harsh critic. Although plenty of doubts have been raised about Chávez's own commitment to democracy, some of his accusations, as when he claims that the Bush administration had a hand in an attempted coup against him, are generally deemed credible. The other international perspective critical of the United States comes from an e-mail exchange between an Egyptian university student and an American one.

Emphasis on ***public diplomacy*** has increased. The challenge was well stated by Kristin Lord in her report, *Voices of America: U.S. Public Diplomacy for the 21st Century:*

> Public opinion holds more sway than [at] any previous time in history. Information and communication technologies are cheap and ubiquitous. A dense network of private companies, non-governmental organizations, and social movements exert ever more influence relative to governments. Vicious ideologies sustain violence that puts Americans and our allies in jeopardy both at home and around the globe. In this environment, our country needs new strategies, stronger institutions, and innovative methods.[30]

Numerous reports have been written and proposals made for how best to meet this challenge; Lord's report summarizes seventeen of these and includes numerous others in its bibliography. Improved communication methods and strategies for getting the American message out are part of the solution. But the issue concerns more than how the message is communicated, it also is what the message is, what the policies are, what the basic sense of trust and respect is. All of these things bring us back to policy—the what, not just the how, of communication, the substance about which soft power seeks to persuade.

Concerns about public diplomacy and soft power also point us to how U.S. domestic policy has indirect foreign policy effects. In 1957, when the segregationist governor of Arkansas was blocking integration of the public schools, President Eisenhower sent in

## INTERNATIONAL PERSPECTIVES

INTERNATIONAL PERSPECTIVES

### THE UNITED STATES AND DEMOCRACY PROMOTION

*International perspectives on the U.S. commitment to democracy promotion vary widely. Here is a sampling.*

#### Vaclav Havel, President of Czechoslovakia, 1990

*Havel, a political prisoner for many years under communist rule and Soviet domination, gave much credit to the United States for its policies and inspiration.*

Twice in this century, the world has been threatened by a catastrophe. Twice this catastrophe was born in Europe, and twice Americans, along with others, were called upon to save Europe, the whole world and yourselves. . . .

Thanks to the great support of your President Wilson, our first President, Tomas Garrigue Masaryk, was able to found a modern independent state. He founded it, as you know, on the same principles on which the United States of America had been founded, as Masaryk's manuscripts held by the Library of Congress testify. . . .

You have helped us to survive until today without a hot war this time, merely a cold one. . . . to enter . . . into an era in which all of us, large and small, former slaves and former masters, will be able to create what your great President Lincoln called "the family of man." . . .

When Thomas Jefferson wrote that "Governments are instituted among Men, deriving their just powers from the Consent of the Governed," it was a simple and important act of the human spirit.

What gave meaning to that act, however, was the fact that the author backed it up with his life. It was not just his words, it was his deeds as well.

#### Viktor Yushchenko, President of Ukraine, 2004

*Efforts to fix the 2004 elections to defeat Yushchenko were uncovered and overturned in the "Orange Revolution" (named for the color used by the mass protests as their symbol). The United States, along with Western Europe, provided crucial support.*

The American example of freedom has always been luring. Other regimes that have sought to suppress democracy in Ukraine would often endeavor to nurture anti-American phobias. But they would invariably fail.

Efforts of our American friends, who in the past so generously shared their democratic experience with us, enhanced the partnership between our two nations.

(*Continued*)

(*Continued*)

Many noble men and women on both sides of the Atlantic have always believed in Ukraine's democratic future. Our common belief came true in the days of the Orange Revolution.

We highly appreciate the message sent by your country's leadership before the elections and during the Orange Revolution. It was clear and unambiguous: The United States condemned fraud and upheld Ukraine's right to freely elect their government.

This message enhanced our partnership even stronger in the name of democracy. . . .

The United States and Ukraine have common strategic interests, and we have unity in one thing: everywhere where possible, we want to uphold freedom and democracy. We are prepared for such a responsibility because we know if somebody is deprived of freedom, this freedom has been taken away from us.

### Hugo Chávez, President of Venezuela

*Chávez has been a very outspoken critic of the United States. The following is taken from a press report.*

Venezuelan president Hugo Chavez denounced that the U.S. government is preparing [sic] "new aggressions" against him and against the Venezuelan people. "Before the world, before our people, before the Latin American people, and before the people of North America for whom we have respect, I accuse the government of the United States of continuing their aggressions against Venezuela," he said during his weekly live TV show.

"The U.S. government has crashed in Venezuela and will continue to crash as many times as they want," Chavez said in a reference to alleged past attempts by the U.S. to remove him from power.

The mercurial Venezuelan leader has repeatedly accused the U.S. government of trying to oust him. Scattered evidence has linked the U.S. government to the 2002 coup d'état against Chavez, and the U.S. financed opposition groups in Venezuela through the National Endowment for Democracy. Last August, twice-elected Chavez won a referendum on his rule, which was largely organized by groups that receive funds from the U.S. government.

### Views of an Egyptian University Student

*Here we draw from a fascinating e-mail dialogue in 2005 between an American university student, Benjamin B. Brandenburg, and an Egyptian university student, Mona Akil El-Kouedi, facilitated by IslamOnline.net.*

The dialogue starts out with the American student affirming the U.S. commitment to democracy. "While every nation on earth looks out for its own security and national interest, I would argue that none have had the same idealistic sense of mission since their inception." Ben acknowledges mistakes while supporting the Bush administration as having shifted toward being more prodemocracy especially in the Middle East.

Mona's initial response disputes the motivation even more than the content of the Bush policy. "People in the Middle East do think and believe that the U.S. administration is calling for democratization to expand America's hyperpower—and they have their reasons. Yes, the U.S. policies throughout the last years supported autocratic regimes in the Middle East, but this isn't only history; unfortunately, the United States is still supporting autocratic regimes."

Ben responds with a number of examples of democracy promotion in Egypt, Jordan, and elsewhere in the Middle East. It's not perfect, he says, but it's more than just rhetoric. "America's democracy campaign may be strategically tactful in some countries like Saudi Arabia or Pakistan, but for you, be assured, it's for real." He also rebuffs her criticisms of U.S. policy in Iraq: "Would you say that to one of the brave Iraqis who live in danger because they are working on the constitution that will give Iraqis liberty and freedom?"

Mona's response comes just a few days after Hurricane Katrina and starts with an empathetic message: "For you to know that you are having brother and sisters here in Egypt, united with you in humanity, I wanted to get across the deep condolences of all Egyptians for the families of the victims and for the American people." She goes on to take issue with Ben's depiction of U.S. policy as "extraordinarily angelic." She raises the Abu Ghraib torture scandal, asking, "Don't you think that the people of the Middle East have the right to doubt the U.S. intentions when American politicians speak about democratization?"

Their dialogue continues through other exchanges. The differences are real, the views intense—but so too is the respect they show one another. "Having some differences in opinion, I think, doesn't mean that we have to close the debate," Mona states. "On the contrary, I think it aims at having another starting point." From Ben, a thank you "for your sincere compassion for the victims of the Katrina disaster. It is a solemn reminder that all humans, even Americans, are subject to the laws of nature and in need of the comforts of a higher power." Part of his response on Abu Ghraib underlines that "all lives are precious, and deaths and sufferings will have consequences for generations to come." And, as he signs off, "Salam Aleikum."

Sources: Havel, address to the U.S. Congress, February 21, 1990, http://old.hrad.cz/president/Havel/speeches/1990/2102_uk.html (accessed 8/20/09); Yuschchenko, address to the U.S. Congress, April 6, 2005, www.america.gov/st/washfile-english/2005/April/20050406163828lCJsamohT0.3202631.html (accessed 8/20/09); Cleto A. Sojo, "Venezuela's Chavez Accuses U.S. Government of Considering His Assassination," Venezuelanalysis, February 20, 2005, www.venezuelanalysis.com/news/951 (accessed 8/20/09); "Letters of Understanding: US-Promoted Reform: Genuineness or Rhetoric?" www.islamonline.net/English/Views/2005/09/article03.shtml (accessed 8/20/09).

the National Guard partly out of concern about how the U.S. record of segregation would undermine the mantle of Principles in foreign policy. It was harder to sustain the claim of standing for freedom in foreign policy if the United States did not live up to it at home.

The Realist scholar Hans J. Morgenthau emphasized this point. The Cold War struggle ultimately will not be determined by military strength or diplomatic maneuvering, he wrote in 1967 with particular reference to Vietnam, but "by the visible virtues and vices of their [the U.S. and Soviet] respective political, economic and social systems. . . . It is at this point that foreign policy and domestic politics merge. . . . The United States ought to again concentrate its efforts upon creating a society at home which can again serve as a model for other nations to emulate."[31]

In a broad sense some of America's severe social problems also come into play when questions of soft power arises. "In most Asian eyes," Kishore Mahbubani of Singapore has written, "the evidence of real social decay in the United States is clear and palpable": a 560 percent increase in violent crime since 1960, and a total of 10,567 people killed by handguns in just one year (1990) compared with just 87 in Japan; increases since 1960 of greater than 400 percent in out-of-wedlock births, and more than 200 percent in teenage suicides; a 50 percent increase in hunger since 1985; schools where the chief problems have changed, according to a survey of teachers, from rather innocuous acts such as talking out of turn, chewing gum in class, and making noise to assault, robbery, rape, drug abuse, alcohol abuse, and pregnancy.[32] The American media are depicted as having become overly aggressive, too muckraking, and too sensationalist, and emanating a self-righteous self-image that leads them "to undermine public confidence in virtually every public institution, while leaving their own powers neither checked nor balanced by any countervailing institution." Overall, and quite provocatively, Mahbubani poses the question of whether "in working so hard to increase the scope of individual freedom within their society, Americans have progressively cut down the thick web of human relations and obligations that have produced social harmony in traditional societies. . . . Is there *too much freedom* in American society?" [emphasis added].[33]

In an incident along similar lines, I was struck by a conversation shortly after Hurricane Katrina with a distinguished diplomat and military officer from India. How can those of us who are friends of the United States and who so often have held your political system and society up as a model, he asked me, continue to do so when your government failed so miserably in responding to Hurricane Katrina? Helping people hit by natural disasters is one of the most fundamental functions any government has. What do we tell people in our part of the world, for whom tsunamis and other natural disasters hit plenty often, about Katrina?

Critiques such as these are more "tough love"than ideological America-bashing. Any nation that allows an increase of social problems risks having its claim to moral leadership increasingly questioned around the world.

## Principles and Prosperity: The Economic Sanctions Debate

One area in which Principles-Prosperity tensions and trade-offs have come up with great frequency in recent years has been the use of economic sanctions.[34] Though not the only purpose for which economic sanctions are used, democracy promotion and human rights protection have been among their main purposes. Therefore, policy makers must decide whether to impose limits on economic relations with other countries (trade, investment, loans, foreign aid) to try to force internal political changes.

### *Key Cases*

The case most often cited as a success was the 1980s anti-apartheid sanctions against South Africa, a mix of U.S., UN, and European measures. Other factors also contributed to ending apartheid, but sanctions get a substantial share of the credit. We will study this case in depth later in this chapter in our look at the U.S. domestic politics of sanctions.

CHINA, 1989 Back in Chapter 1 we highlighted the debate over economic sanctions against China following the 1989 ***Tiananmen Square*** massacre. Other issues came into play, but mostly this debate was about the tensions and trade-offs between, on the one hand, the economic interests at stake in trade with and investment in China, and, on the other, the defense of human rights as a fundamental American principle. The first Bush administration imposed only limited sanctions on China, stopping short of revoking China's main economic benefit, most favored nation (MFN) status. Despite Bill Clinton's harsh criticism of this policy during his 1992 presidential campaign as coddling "the butchers of Beijing," once in office the Clinton administration imposed only limited additional sanctions and also did not revoke MFN. Both administrations claimed that they were not abandoning Principles and that they were taking other pro–human rights steps, but most analysts and observers saw this as a choice of economic interests over principles.

In recent years one of the main Prosperity-Principles issues has involved Microsoft, Google, Yahoo, and other Internet service providers and conditions imposed by the Chinese government on their operations in China. Do these companies compromise American Principles in agreeing to restrictions on freedom of information? For example, using the unfiltered Google search engine returns more than two thousand images of the Dalai Lama. However, with the filters required by the Chinese government, that number drops to 161 and returns photos of the Dalai Lama meeting with Chinese officials more than fifty years ago, before the People's Liberation Army invaded Tibet. Representative Christopher Smith (R-New Jersey), then the chairman of a key House subcommittee with jurisdiction over human rights, voiced this concern:

> I believe that two of the most essential pillars that prop up totalitarian regimes are the secret police and propaganda. Yet for the sake of market share and profits, leading U.S. companies like Google, Yahoo, Cisco and Microsoft have compromised both the integrity of their product and their duties as responsible corporate citizens. They have aided and abetted the Chinese regime to prop up both of these pillars, propagating the message of the dictatorship unabated and supporting the secret police in a myriad of ways, including surveillance and invasion of privacy, in order to effectuate the massive crackdown on its citizens (2006).[35]

Or even with such restrictions, can the Internet still be a force for freedom and democracy? A Microsoft executive voiced this alternative view:

> Internet services like Microsoft MSN Spaces which host personal Web sites or "blogs" are having a major positive impact in China despite the effort by various agencies of the Chinese Government to control certain kinds of political content. In just the past few years, we have seen repeated examples in China of official responses to domestic developments that have been shaped for the better because of information provided and opinions expressed over the Internet. . . . Ultimately, we must ask ourselves, will the Chinese citizens be better off without access to our services? . . . We believe information is power. We also believe that the Internet is a positive force in China. It has revolutionized information access, helps create more open societies, and accelerates the gradual evolution toward a more outward-looking Chinese society.[36]

HAITI, 1991–94 In 1991 the Haitian military staged a coup, overthrowing the democratically elected government of President Jean-Bertrand Aristide. The first Bush administration again imposed only limited sanctions. The Clinton administration significantly increased the sanctions, including working through the UN for a multilateral oil embargo. The sanctions had limited efficacy, though, and it took a U.S. military intervention in September 1994 to bring Aristide back to power.

The Haiti case demonstrated the "political gain–civilian pain" dilemma, in which sanctions risk hurting most those they seek to help.[37] Sanctions hit Haiti so hard that per capita GDP fell 25 percent, unemployment leaped to 60 to 70 percent, and inflation rose to 60 percent, all in a country that already was the poorest in the Western Hemisphere. When sanctions were first imposed, the Haitian people generally supported them, showing a willingness to bear some costs in the expectation that the military regime and its supporters would be brought down. Instead, in large part because the sanctions were poorly enforced and targeted, the coup leaders bore so few of the costs that in Creole (the Haitian language), *anbago,* the word for "embargo," gave way to *anba gwo,* meaning "under the heels of the rich and powerful."[38]

As analysts we need to ask whether the Haiti case is proof that "sanctions don't work," as many critics contend as a general rule, or whether this is a "false negative" in which sanctions could have worked had they been implemented differently. The plausibility of the question is based primarily on the sanctions' having been imposed partially and incrementally rather than comprehensively and decisively. Haiti was the epitome of a target state vulnerable to economic sanctions: a small country with a weak economy, dependent on the United States for almost 70 percent of its trade, and pretty conducive to sanctions enforcement given its island geography. But the initial Bush administration sanctions were very limited. Even when the Clinton administration moved to more comprehensive sanctions, it did so in an on-off fashion. In June 1993 it stepped up the sanctions to include a ban from U.S. ports on all foreign ships doing business with Haiti, froze the financial assets in U.S. banks of the coup leaders, and pushed the oil embargo through the UN. The decision soon after by the coup leaders to agree to terms for ending the coup indicated that the stepped-up sanctions were working. But the Clinton administration moved too quickly to loosen the sanctions. Intended as a carrot, the easing of sanctions backfired, allowing the coup leaders to stockpile oil and take other steps to bolster their antisanctions defense, after which they abrogated the agreement. The noted sanctions analysts Kimberly Ann Elliott and Gary Hufbauer make the case that tighter and quicker sanctions, especially financial ones, could have worked. "Carefully crafted financial sanctions, swiftly applied, might have captured the attention of the economic elite, without whose support the military would not [have been] able to rule. The Haitian elite keeps little of its wealth in Haiti and enjoys spending time and money in the United States. A global assets freeze, coupled with a travel ban, would have hit primarily that class."[39]

IRAQ, 1990S The case of Iraq in the 1990s is another example of sanctions that did not work so well as intended, although the reasons for their ineffectiveness are more complicated. These sanctions had a broad range of objectives, including the military goals of preventing Saddam Hussein from importing technology and materials for building weapons of mass destruction, as well as the overall aim of trying to undermine Saddam's regime economically so as to bring about regime change without military intervention or covert action.

This case, too, poses the political gain–civilian pain dilemma. The Iraqi people suffered tremendously. In late 1996 UNICEF (the UN Children's Fund) estimated that 4,500 children under the age of five were dying in Iraq every month. A UN Food and Agriculture Organization report in 1997 found that food shortages and malnutrition in Iraq had become ever more "severe and chronic."[40] Yet all along, going back to the first UN sanctions against Iraq in 1990, provisions were offered to allow for humanitarian relief with the caveat that the UN would control the funds to ensure that Saddam Hussein did not divert them for weapons of mass destruction or other such purposes. Moreover, while blaming the United States and the international community for the suffering of the Iraqi people, Saddam kept managing to find funds to build and refurbish his multiple presidential palaces and to secretly import military equipment and technology. This does not relieve U.S. policy from concern for the humanitarian issues, but it does reveal the complexity of the policy choices and policy effects.

## Policy Strategies for Promoting Democracy and Protecting Human Rights

In this section we discuss the major international actors involved in ***democracy promotion*** and human rights protection, the strategies for achieving these objectives, and the effectiveness of those strategies.

### *Who: Key International Actors*

The array of actors involved in promoting democratization may be broader than in any other area of foreign policy.

U.S. GOVERNMENT The lead U.S. agency for democracy promotion is the Agency for International Development (AID). Since the end of the Cold War, AID has broadened its "development" mission increasingly to include political as well as economic development. AID runs some programs directly, and also provides funding to nongovernmental organizations (NGOs). The National Endowment for Democracy, a quasi-governmental agency, receives funds from Congress and AID and channels them principally to four NGOs (see the discussion of NGOs below).

The State Department is involved principally through its Bureau of Democracy, Human Rights, and Labor. It also manages the Fulbright scholarships and other educational and cultural-exchange programs. Almost every Cabinet department plays additional roles: the Pentagon works on civil-military relations, the Justice Department helps develop the rule of law, the Education Department conducts literacy training, the Commerce Department promotes free enterprise. The U.S. Congress also is involved, with its numerous legislative-exchange programs for legislators and their staffs from newly democratizing countries. Local governments participate, too, through programs such as "Sister Cities," linking people at the grassroots level across the United States to other cities around the world. Davis, California, for example, is a sister city with four foreign cities: Uman, Ukraine; Rutillo Grande, El Salvador; Qufu, China; and Inuyama, Japan. Some also take other initiatives, as did Dayton, Ohio, the city where the accord ending the Bosnian war was negotiated in 1995, in developing its own city-to-city contacts with Sarajevo, the capital of Bosnia.

INTERNATIONAL ORGANIZATIONS The United Nations is involved in promoting democracy in a number of ways. One of the first times the UN was given a role in monitoring elections and helping build democratic political institutions was in 1989 in Namibia, a territory in Africa previously under UN trusteeship. Since then the UN's electoral assistance and observer missions have been sent to numerous states. The International Court of Justice, based in The Hague in the Netherlands, exercises some capacity to enforce international law. The UN High Commissioner for Refugees (UNHCR) seeks to provide protection and relief for populations displaced by war, repression, or natural disasters.

Regional multilateral organizations also have been playing increasingly important roles. The Organization for Security and Cooperation in Europe (OSCE) has been the most active such organization. "We are convinced," one of the provisions in its charter reads, "that in order to strengthen peace and security among our states, the advancement of democracy and respect for and effective exercise of human rights are indispensable." The OSCE has sent election observers, conflict-resolution teams, and other missions to a number of member countries. The Organization of American States (OAS), which had tolerated if not condoned military coups in the past, amended its charter in 1992 to suspend member states whose democratic governments are overthrown. Its 2001 Inter-American Democratic Charter further strengthened the OAS's commitment to and role in protecting and promoting democracy. The new African Union (AU) has committed to playing a more active regional democracy role than had its predecessor, the Organization of African Unity.

OTHER GOVERNMENTS The European Union (EU) long has made democracy a precondition for membership. This created an incentive for countries such as Greece, Spain, and Portugal to democratize in the 1970s and 1980s and has created one over the past two decades for the former communist countries seeking EU membership. The EU also has programs similar to the AID ones to provide direct democracy assistance. A number of countries also run their own bilateral democracy programs. The Scandinavian countries are widely regarded as world leaders in this area.

NGOS NGOs often receive government or UN funding, but maintain significant independence in their democracy programs. In the United States, based on a model adapted from Germany, where each major political party has run international democracy-promotion programs since the 1950s, the four NGOs that get most of the National Endowment for Democracy funding are the Democratic Party's National Democratic Institute for International Affairs, the Republican Party's International Republican Institute, the AFL-CIO's Free Trade Union Institute, and the U.S. Chamber of Commerce's Center for International Private Enterprise. Similarly, Britain has the Westminster Foundation for Democracy, Canada its International Center for Human Rights and Democratic Development.

Other NGOs active in building and supporting democracy include private nonprofit foundations such as the Ford, Soros, and Asia Foundations; professional associations such as the American Bar Association and its Central and Eastern Europe Law Initiative (ABA-

CEELI); and groups with their own global networks of offices such as Amnesty International and Human Rights Watch.

## *How: Key Strategies*

Along with this identification of the "who" is the question of "how." To be sure, there is no single, one-size-fits-all strategy for democracy promotion. The foreign policy challenge for the United States as well as for other international actors is to determine the right fit and the right mix for different countries with different sets of problems, and to pursue those strategies with the right combination of international actors.

This generally involves five key objectives: facilitating free and fair elections; helping build strong and accountable political institutions; strengthening the rule of law; protecting human rights; and helping cultivate a robust civil society.

FACILITATING FREE AND FAIR ELECTIONS *International electoral assistance and monitoring* often provide the most reliable assurance that elections in newly democratizing countries will be free and fair. The mere presence of American and other international observers can deter electoral fraud or detect attempted fraud. One major example is the 1986 presidential election in the Philippines. The dictator Ferdinand Marcos tried to steal the election in order to keep himself in power. But a bipartisan U.S. congressional observer team was there as witness to the fraud. Marcos initially was able to convince President Reagan back in Washington that there was "fraud on both sides." But when Reagan made this statement, Senator Richard Lugar (R-Indiana), head of the U.S. observer team, was in a position to state that "the President was misinformed." Senator Lugar was able to come to his own conclusion in part because, since 1983, when Marcos had assassinated the opposition leader Benigno Aquino, some U.S. aid to the Philippines had been channeled to Catholic church and human rights groups for purchasing computers and other equipment that gave them the technical capacity to count the votes independently. Marcos ended up having no choice but to concede the election to Corazon Aquino, the widow of the assassinated opposition leader, and to flee the country.[41]

Another example is the February 1990 election in Nicaragua, the first free election in that country's history. An election-observer team, headed by the former president Jimmy Carter and including a number of Latin American former presidents, monitored the voting processes. As the election returns were coming in, and it became clear that the Sandinista president Daniel Ortega was going to lose to the challenger Violeta Chamorro, word spread in Managua that Ortega and the Sandinistas might not accept the results. Because of both his pro–human rights record as U.S. president and the conflict resolution and humanitarian assistance work he had been doing after leaving office, Jimmy Carter had a great deal of credibility with both sides in the Nicaraguan election and more generally in the eyes of the world. Carter shuttled between Ortega's headquarters and Chamorro's, and told Ortega in no uncertain terms that he would be declaring the elections as having been free and fair, and would oppose any move not to abide by their results. Ortega felt that he had little choice but to back off and accept the results. A crisis was averted, and Nicaragua started on the path to democracy.

Ukraine was another dramatic case, as mentioned earlier. In 2004 the reformist Viktor Yushchenko was running for president against the autocratic prime minister Viktor Yanukovych. Going well beyond "normal" dirty campaign tricks, Yanukovych supporters (including, many believed, Russia) poisoned Yushchenko. The dioxin did not kill him, although it might have had he not received medical attention outside Ukraine. When the election was first held on November 21, Yanukovych was declared the victor. But with thousands of people protesting (clad in orange t-shirts and waving orange banners, hence the term "Orange Revolution") and substantial evidence of fraud produced by international election monitors, the results were nullified. When the new election was held on December 26, with about twelve thousand international election observers deployed to monitor polling places, Yushchenko emerged victorious by a wide margin. Yushchenko campaign officials thanked their own people as well as the international monitors for ensuring that the election could not be "stolen" this time.[42]

On the other hand, a number of cases have been less successful. In Belarus, Azerbaijan, and Kazakhstan, three former Soviet republics, fraud occurred despite the presence of OSCE election-observer teams. The OSCE responded by not certifying the fairness of the elections, and OSCE member countries did impose some sanctions and penalties, but the results stood nevertheless. In Uganda, for many years considered a positive case of democracy in Africa, President Museveni pushed through a change in the constitutional limit of two terms. In 2006, he won in an election marred by "dirty tricks" such as trumped-up charges of treason and rape against the opposition leader. In Egypt, President Mubarak refused to allow foreign observers for the 2005 presidential election. In some cases, such as the parliamentary elections in Haiti in 1995 and in Cambodia in 1998, different observers came to different conclusions as to whether the elections were free and fair.[43]

Critical forms of electoral assistance also are provided prior to the actual election day. *Voter education programs* help prepare populaces that may rarely or never have had a genuinely free and fair election to participate effectively. In Namibia, for example, an NGO hosts a Web page (www.democracy.org.na/index.php) as part of a voter-education campaign that provides useful information on "democracy, democratic principles, government structure, human rights and freedoms, and the electoral process," and promotes an essay competition among schoolchildren on strengthening and improving democracy.

*Political parties* need to be built, either to fill the void or to replace old, undemocratic parties. Effective parties are essential for channeling and coalescing groups and individuals within society in ways that help make for organized and peaceful political processes. Helping countries create and strengthen democratic political parties involves everything from training in membership recruitment to fund raising, public-opinion polling, message development, candidate selection systems, grassroots organizing, and, yes, even making campaign commercials. The National Endowment for Democracy and its Democratic and Republican Party partners are very involved in this area, as are the German party-based democracy-promotion *Stiftungs* (combination think tanks/political activism institutions).

BUILDING STRONG AND ACCOUNTABLE POLITICAL INSTITUTIONS Although democratic revolutions often are personality driven, with people mobilizing around a charismatic leader, long-term stable democracy requires strong and accountable ***political institutions.*** The democratization literature stresses three principal sets of reasons that political institutionalization is important.[44] The first concerns maintaining political stability. Political systems that have built strong political institutions are less dependent on and less vulnerable to the fate or whims of a particular governing regime. The stronger the political institutions, the better they can withstand the ups and downs of a governing regime's popularity, and the better they can stand up to any extraconstitutional challenges that a leader or regime may attempt, particularly the threat or use of force and violence for political change. This is particularly important vis-à-vis the military, because democracies with strong democratic institutions are better able to resist coups and maintain civilian control of the military.

The second set of reasons concerns representativeness. Political systems with strong political institutions are more likely to convey a sense of genuine choice, competition, and accountability. People need to feel that the system has integrity irrespective of whether their favored candidates win an election. This means believing in the fairness of the electoral process and feeling assured that civil liberties and minority rights will be guaranteed. Strong institutions help ensure a level of confidence that the rules of the game will be fair.

Third is effective governance. The instability that comes with weak institutions makes the steadiness and follow-through that governing requires very difficult to achieve. In contrast, well-institutionalized democracies are more capable of governing effectively because, as the democracy scholar Larry Diamond writes, "they have more effective and stable structures for representing interests and because they are more likely to produce working legislative majorities or coalitions that can adopt and sustain policies."[45]

An important area for democratic institution building is strengthening *legislatures.* To fulfill their representative functions, legislatures must also develop other professional and institutional capacities to carry out such tasks as designing committee systems, developing the legal and technical expertise for drafting legislation, computerizing legislative operations, communicating and servicing constituencies, and building up research and library support systems. As have the parliaments and assemblies of a number of western European countries, the U.S. Congress has developed a number of training and exchange programs with legislatures in newly democratizing countries, including through the

House Democracy Assistance Commission, established in 2005 on a bipartisan basis. Its goal, according to Representative David Price (D–North Carolina), the commission chair (and a former professor of political science and public policy at Duke University), is "to give parliaments in emerging democracies the necessary advice and tools to set up their governments . . . to serve not just as a model, but as a partner in the effort to strengthen democracy across the globe."[46]

Another key area is ***civil-military relations.*** This is where the Pentagon has been playing a key role. An important example is the NATO Partnership for Peace (PFP) program. Its objective has been not only to foster military cooperation but also to have western NATO militaries inculcate in their ex-communist counterparts the principles of civilian control of the military. Related to this are various training and education programs for military officers, as at the George C. Marshall Center for Security Studies, linked to NATO and based in Germany, with what William J. Perry, the secretary of defense in the Clinton administration from 1994 to 1997, characterized as a "democratic defense management" curriculum.[47]

*Local government programs* are the focus of a number of AID initiatives. An official AID document stressed the reasons for this focus: "Decentralization shifts responsibility for decision-making to the leadership and the citizens most directly affected. Fiscal decentralization helps improve local finances, enabling local officials to better provide for their constituencies. Improvements in service delivery build public confidence in democratic processes. Accordingly, they reinforce citizen participation."[48] Among the programs cited were aid to a fishermen's association in the Philippines seeking to ban commercial trawlers from local waters, the creation of a national mayors's association in Bulgaria, and a petition drive in Mozambique to help small farmers get title to their lands.

Another crucial need has been for *anticorruption initiatives.* Corruption undermines democratization both by siphoning off scarce resources in largely poor countries, and in an even more fundamental sense by deeply delegitimizing those in power and potentially the political system itself. It is hard enough to convince a long-suffering people that the benefits of democratization will take time, that they must be patient and make individual sacrifices for the collective good. But if those who govern and their friends and associates are enriching themselves, the disillusionment and anger among the people are not hard to understand. In Russia, for example, corruption became so endemic in the 1990s that economic privatization was dubbed *prikhvatizatsiya* (literally, "grabification"). Few things can more quickly and widely delegitimize a new government than corruption. One NGO called Transparency International was formed for the express purpose of fighting corruption. Each year it issues a list ranking countries by their levels of corruption and uses these and other strategies to pressure countries into enacting anticorruption reforms. One of its projects is the "Corruption Fighters' Tool Kit," which includes a range of strategies for NGOs, civil society, governments, and others "to demand and promote accountable and responsive public administration."[49]

In this regard and in many others, the accountability provided by a *free press* is crucial. Yet democratizing countries have mostly limited experience in this area and are in need of outside assistance. The Vienna-based International Press Institute (IPI), another NGO, has played an important role in this effort. With membership of about two thousand leading editors, publishers, broadcasting executives, and journalists in more than 120 countries, the IPI runs training programs and conferences for journalists from ex-communist and other newly democratizing countries. It also publishes a monthly magazine and an annual report monitoring press freedom.[50] Journalists also need protection against repression and assassinations targeted against them. In 2007, according to the New York–based Committee to Protect Journalists, 65 journalists were killed, almost 40 percent more than just two years earlier, journalists "who died in the line of duty or were deliberately targeted for assassination because of their reporting or their affiliation with a news organization." Eight months into 2009, the annual total was 66. In addition, 127 journalists in twenty-four countries were jailed, with China being the worst offender, followed by Cuba, Eritrea, Iran, and Azerbaijan.[51]

STRENGTHENING THE RULE OF LAW The ***rule of law*** means that citizens are protected by a strong constitution and other legal guarantees against both arbitrary acts by the state and lawless acts by other citizens. A wide range of programs and initiatives are needed to strengthen the rule of law. They include assistance in the very drafting of a constitution, as well as in writing other legal codes. Courts may lack the most basic infrastructures of trained judicial reporters, computers for compiling jury lists, "bench books" for how to conduct jury trials, and the like. Law schools often need to have their curriculums overhauled. Police forces need to be trained. Special initiatives may be needed to help women, minorities, and the disadvantaged. Broad education programs on the very principle of the rule of law as the basis for justice need to be undertaken.

The American Bar Association's Central and East European Law Initiative (CEELI) is a good example. The ABA is the principal association of lawyers in the United States. Through CEELI it has been seeking to provide legal expertise to countries emerging from communism on constitutional law, judicial restructuring, criminal law, commercial law, environmental law, gender-related issues, and other legal areas. These programs cover quite a range of topics, including how trials by jury are supposed to work, advocacy training for defense lawyers, a resource manual for commercial law, consumer rights protection, legal ethics, sexual harassment, domestic violence, criminal legal procedures such as pretrial detention and plea bargaining, natural resource management, and bankruptcy law. CEELI also has created partnerships linking law schools in the region with American law schools.

Another challenge is reckoning with the past, or what is often called *transitional justice*.[52] Many newly democratizing societies are emerging from pasts that can only be characterized as horrific: El Salvador, with its decade of civil war, right-wing "death squads," and guerrilla violence; Cambodia, where the Khmer Rouge left hundreds of thousands dead in the "killing fields"; South Africa, with generations of discrimination, oppression, and killings under the apartheid system; Chile and Argentina, freed from the torture, arbitrary arrests, and cases of *desaparecidos* ("disappeared ones") under military dictatorships; Hungary, where property-rights claims must be adjudicated against confiscations made not only in the communist era but going back to the Nazi occupation.

The transitional-justice dilemma pulls between retribution and moving on.[53] Many countries have granted amnesty for past political crimes as part of a reconciliation process. In South Africa the government of Nelson Mandela set up a process stressing amnesty in return for truth about the past. The South African "truth commission" heard startling and disturbing revelations from former high-level government officials who admitted their roles in assassinations, attacks on unarmed protesters, and other heinous acts. Truth was being revealed, and overall it seemed that in the South African case it was contributing to national healing. In Guatemala, however, where the 1996 Law of National Reconciliation ending more than thirty years of civil war included a sweeping amnesty, some critics derided it as a "piñata of forgiving, of forgetting the human toll of the war they share responsibility for inciting."[54] And the human toll continued: in April 1998 a Roman Catholic bishop was bludgeoned to death in Guatemala City two days after issuing a scathing report on human rights abuses by the army, the government, and paramilitary units.

An interesting and precedent-challenging case arose in 1998–99 over charges of human rights violations by the former Chilean dictator General Augusto Pinochet. Pinochet's rule, which lasted from 1973 to 1990, was notorious for brutal human rights violations. Part of the transitional justice agreement made in 1990 when democratic rule was restored in Chile was amnesty for Pinochet; in fact, he was made a senator for life. But not only Chileans were killed, tortured, and abducted under Pinochet; some foreigners were as well. When Pinochet traveled to London in October 1998 for medical attention at a British hospital, a judge in Spain invoked international law to demand that he be extradited to Spain to face trial for the killing of Spanish citizens who had been residing in Chile. He wasn't extradited, but the British kept him under house arrest before releasing him on medical grounds to return to Chile. In Chile the case went back and forth, with Pinochet indicted on some charges but not others, until his death in December 2006.

The Pinochet affair's broader international effect has been a heightened debate over two related principles. One is *universal jurisdiction,* which contends that certain offenses are so severe that they constitute crimes against humanity that any nation's courts should be able to prosecute, not just those with home jurisdiction over the perpetrator or where the crimes were committed. The other key issue was whether ex-leaders still were protected by the principle of *sovereign immunity* from legal action in the courts of another country (as distinct from the jurisdiction of the International Criminal Court, discussed in Chapter 9). Chilean government officials argued that other governments should not interfere, that this was their business, part of their effort "to re-establish peace in a country where friends and former enemies can coexist." Samuel Pisar, a distinguished French international lawyer and a survivor of the Nazi death camps, hailed Pinochet's arrest as manifesting the "almost universal clamor today that those who commit crimes against humanity must be pursued to the ends of the world, wherever and whenever they can be found, and brought to justice."[55] The former U.S. secretary of state Henry Kissinger was among the staunchest critics, warning that we "must not allow legal principles to be used as weapons to settle political scores" and that "historically, the dictatorship of the virtuous has often led to inquisitions and even witch hunts."[56] The issue arose again more recently with efforts by a Spanish judge to apply universal jurisdiction to some Bush administration officials over Iraq and Guantánamo.

PROTECTING HUMAN RIGHTS Recent U.S. administrations' human rights policies have differed in the emphasis and focus they give to human rights violations. The Carter administration went further than its predecessors in focusing on human rights violations by leaders who, although pro-American, were authoritarian and repressive—for example, Antonio Somoza in Nicaragua and the shah of Iran. The Reagan administration put its focus on communist regimes such as the Soviet Union, Cuba, and post-Somoza Marxist Nicaragua. During the first Bush and the Clinton administrations, with the Cold War over and the war on terrorism not yet begun, there was less of a pattern along pro- or anti-American lines. The pattern was revived in the second Bush administration, though, with its emphasis on the "axis of evil" and other states that support terrorism. Other human rights violators were not ignored, but the emphasis was on those that link most closely to the anti-Americanism of global terrorism.

The Obama administration came into office pledging greater priority to human rights. In practice it has been seeking to strike its own balance. When, during her first trip to China, Secretary of State Hillary Clinton stated that human rights did not necessarily supersede other issues in U.S.-China relations, Human Rights Watch and others were quite critical. Was the Obama administration becoming a classically "Realist" one, focusing principally on the foreign, not the domestic, policies of other countries? The administration contended that this was in part a tactical shift to less "in-your-face" efforts to work the human rights issue. The administration also argued that it did have to weigh issues on which it was seeking China's cooperation, such as climate change, North Korea, and the global economic crisis. Similar "4 Ps" dynamics have come up on a number of other issues including relations with such nondemocratic Arab regimes as Saudi Arabia and Egypt.

The United Nations' commitment to human rights can also be called into question. On human rights issues, such as humanitarian intervention, the UN often is constrained by invocations of state sovereignty and noninterference in internal affairs. As stated in Article 2, Section 7, of the UN Charter, "nothing contained in the present Charter shall authorize the United Nations to intervene in matters which are essentially within the domestic jurisdiction of any state." Yet other portions of the UN Charter manifest the norm of the *universality* of the rights of individuals, irrespective of the state in which they reside or whether threats to those rights come from foreign forces or their own governments. Article 3 affirms that "everyone has the right to life, liberty and the security of person"; Article 55 commits the UN to "promote . . . universal respect for, and observance of, human rights and fundamental freedoms"; Article 56 pledges all members "to take joint and separate action toward this end." In addition, documents such as the Universal Declaration of Human Rights, adopted by the UN General Assembly in 1948 by a unanimous vote, provide a sweeping affirmation of the "equal and inalienable rights of all members of the human family."

The UN Commission on Human Rights, which drafted the Universal Declaration of Human Rights and other human rights covenants, long had been the principal UN forum in which human rights issues were raised. But it severely undermined the credibility of its own message by having such gross human rights violators as China, Cuba, Libya, Sudan, Syria, and Zimbabwe as members. Criticism came not just from the Bush administration; many NGOs were outraged over this "rogues' gallery of human rights abusers."[57] Secretary-General Kofi Annan also was a critic: "Too often states seek membership [on the Human Rights Commission] to insulate themselves from criticism or to criticize others, rather than to assist in the body's true task, which is to monitor and encourage the compliance of all states with their human rights obligations. The time has come for real reform."[58] Reforms were made, including changing the name to the Human Rights Council; real change, though, has been slow at best. A UN Human Rights Council that takes its mission seriously enough to say that you have to practice what you preach could have a real impact.

NGOs such as Amnesty International and Human Rights Watch play such an important role in human rights advocacy that they are often referred to as the "conscience" of governments. Unbound by trade-offs with other foreign policy objectives and less inhibited by the formalities of traditional diplomacy, human rights NGOs can be more vocal and assertive than governments or multilateral organizations. Their impact often is quite substantial in terms of both influencing official policy and initiating their own direct efforts. Indeed, Amnesty International won the Nobel Peace Prize in 1977. Since then, the Internet, cell phones, and other advanced communications methods have made it both more difficult for repressive governments to hide their human rights violations and easier for advocacy groups to communicate with their own global networks of activists. The NGO role in human rights advocacy has grown even more significant.

CULTIVATING CIVIL SOCIETY A strong ***civil society*** is one that has lots of what Harvard scholar Robert Putnam calls ***"social capital"***—a public-spiritedness and community involvement that goes beyond just voting. It entails other forms of civic engagement, a sense of "reciprocity and cooperation," and a shared ethic among citizens of being "helpful, respectful and trustful towards one another, even when they differ on matters of substance."[59] The statement of goals by Dialog, a community outreach NGO in Poland, captures well what is meant by civil society: "to encourage citizens to respond actively to problems that concern them; and, through such responses, to build—or rebuild—a civil society. A society in which ordinary citizens trust each other, organize voluntarily to achieve common ends, expect local government to respond to their needs, and participate generally in the public life of the community."[60]

In many newly democratizing societies, decades of dictatorship and even longer historical traditions of authoritarianism have left little basis on which to build such practices and values. Particularly in states recently torn by ethnic "cleansing," genocide, and other bitter and violent societal rending, conceptions of trust and common goals can seem altogether alien. Yet cultivation of the values and practices of civil society is all the more essential in these very cases, for as the British political scientist Richard Rose states, "the construction of trustworthy political institutions is more likely to happen from the bottom up than the top down."[61] Elections won't work, political institutions won't be stable, and the rule of law won't become established unless the basic civic values of nonviolent resolution of political differences, tolerance for societal differences, and commitment to some level of political engagement provide a societal foundation.

Thus, although policies geared to helping develop civil society are much less dramatic than election monitoring, much less visible than legislative exchanges, and much less noticeable than human rights advocacy, they are no less essential over the long term. Illustrative programs and policies include the National Endowment for Democracy's funding for training of newly elected village committee members on effective local governance in China, civic and voter education initiatives by youth NGOs in Slovakia, public-advocacy training and assistance for a local association of small farmers seeking formal title to their land in Mozambique, and training community leaders to become conflict mediators in Colombia.

The very importance of civil society programs is also why repressive regimes have tried to block them. In 2005 Russia began imposing choking controls on foreign NGOs, labeling civil society programs conducted outside government control "subversive." Thomas Carothers cites this civil society crackdown as one of the main signs of Russia's "dispiriting slide back toward authoritarianism." He also cites Zimbabwe, where the dictator Robert Mugabe "has driven out Western NGOs and forced the closure of many local groups that get external support, claiming that they are fronts through which Western 'colonial masters' subvert the government."[62]

## *What: Assessing Effectiveness*

Enough time has now passed that assessments of the effectiveness of post–Cold War democracy promotion are beginning to come in.[63] These assessments have been decidedly mixed. Some observers take a critical view. "The effects of democracy promotion programs," Thomas Carothers concludes, "are usually modestly positive, sometimes negligible and occasionally negative." He runs through many of the major program areas:

- Rule of law: "What stands out about U.S. rule-of-law assistance since the mid-1980s is how difficult and often disappointing such work is. . . . Most of the projects launched with enthusiasm—and large budgets—. . . have fallen far short of their goals."
- Legislative assistance: "The record is riddled with disappointment and failure. . . . All too often [programs] have barely scratched the surface in feckless, corrupt, patronage-ridden parliaments. . . ."
- Civil society: "Democracy promoters are starting to learn . . . just how inflated their expectations have been and how limited their capabilities to produce broad-scale change really are."[64]

In each of these areas Carothers does also make some positive points: that rule-of-law programs have "help[ed] push the issue onto the agenda of governments . . . [which] in the long run may prove an important contribution"; that in some important cases legislative aid "has helped make possible significant improvement" (citing Poland, the Czech Republic, Hungary, El Salvador, and the Philippines); and "various lines of positive evolution" and "more sophisticated programming" in civil society efforts. And in his conclusions he stresses that his analysis does not mean that "democracy aid does not work or is futile," that it is "a useful element of American foreign aid and foreign policy that is gradually gaining coherence, one that is rarely of decisive importance but usually more than a decorative add-on."[65]

Seven key lessons can be drawn from recent experience. First is that the difficulties of promoting democracy do not take away from the importance of doing so. The principles "P" is vital to the U.S. national interest both as a matter of being true to the values for which Americans claim to stand, and as a manifestation of "soft power" and the precept that right also can make for might. U.S. foreign policy needs to be more realistic and less romantic about what effective democracy promotion requires, to reassess but not to reduce the commitment to democracy promotion.

Second, the emphasis on consolidation and institutionalization is the right one. "American foreign policymakers should indeed view the democratic consolidation of post-transition countries as a legitimate foreign policy objective," the *Foreign Affairs* editor Gideon Rose argued, "and their most important democracy-related policy challenge over the next decade."[66] Free and fair elections remain crucial to this effort, but they are not enough by themselves. Many countries have managed to hold elections that qualify as free and fair, but only barely, without becoming "liberal democracies" in terms of also allowing civil liberties, a free press, and other basic freedoms and democratic practices.[67] Strong and accountable political institutions do need to be built; the rule of law does need to be strengthened; human rights do need to be protected; civil society does need to be cultivated—but by learning the lessons of what worked and what did not over the past decade, and why.

Third is the "no blueprints" caveat. The United States has transposed its model to too many places as if one size fits all. Any political system must have its local roots, connecting it to its nation's history, culture, economic system, and political dynamics. Indeed, the U.S. democratic political system succeeds in spite of many aspects of the model, not because of them. Lessons can be learned from other Western democracies, not just the United States. Strong criticisms have been launched at the consultants who fly in to a democratizing country, give their "made-in-America" PowerPoint presentations, and then head out to the next destination. Local ideas need to be tapped and local leaders need to be engaged in ways that adapt and apply general democratization strategies to particular national contexts.

Fourth is the importance of working with other countries and within international institutions whenever possible, including both the United Nations and regional multilateral organizations such as the OSCE and the OAS.

Fifth is the importance of long-term perspectives. The U.S. democratic system was not built in a few years or few decades; it is an ongoing process, and indeed still an imperfect one. So although impact has to be measurable, markers need to be set that allow for short- and medium-term assessment but also for a longer-term approach. One of the studies noted earlier points to the not fully tangible "enhancing [of] the resources, skills, techniques, ideas and legitimacy of civil society organizations, civic education efforts, the mass media" and other local actors as one of the main contributions of democracy-promotion programs.[68] Another concurs, stressing that "many of the most important results of democracy promotion are psychological, moral, subjective, indirect and time-delayed."[69]

Sixth is the need to start thinking again about democratization as not just a political dynamic but also an economic one. This partially harks back to the 1950s and 1960s, when democratization strategies were linked to socioeconomic development. In the 1990s, U.S. foreign aid for democracy promotion went up substantially, but in part at the cost of a decline in economic development aid. Yet to try to build democracy without tackling problems of poverty, the concentration of economic power, and related social inequalities is "to float on the surface of current politics, never affecting the broader structural tides beneath."[70] This economic factor is another example of continuity amid change as we look at American foreign policy over time, and as a link among the "4 Ps"—in this instance, Principles and Prosperity.

Finally, and most important, although our focus has been on U.S. and other international policies and strategies, ultimately the key to successful democratization and well-protected human rights lies with *the leaders and peoples themselves.* The example of Nelson Mandela in South Africa shines above all. Mandela was held as a political prisoner for twenty-seven years but did not do unto his old enemies as they had done unto him. As president, Mandela displayed extraordinary statesmanship and ruled in a spirit of reconciliation, not retribution. It is no wonder that Mandela won the Nobel Peace Prize, along with F. W. de Klerk, the white former president of South Africa, who led the move to bring apartheid down from within. Other cases are less historically dramatic but also involve leaders and groups opting for peaceful and democratic transitions over narrow self-interest. When the opposite choice is made, though, the effects are devastating. Ethnic conflict in recent years has resulted when leaders foment political violence, when they play to and play up the historical roots of hatreds, and when they seek to mobilize groups around these divisions rather than seek reconciliation.

Another important characteristic of leaders is their ability to make the often difficult transition from leading a revolutionary movement to leading a government. Revolutionary leaders need to inspire their people, lead them to the barricades with bold rhetoric and defiance, project a persona larger than life, and often keep political power highly concentrated in their own hands and those of a small inner circle. But governing requires creating political institutions, delivering services, building an economy, accepting accountability, and opening up processes for greater access and representation. The differences between the skills and dispositions required by each of these two roles are among the reasons that great revolutionary leaders often are less successful when it comes to governing. This was an issue for Yasir Arafat as the Israeli occupation of Gaza and the West Bank approached its end: Arafat had trouble making the transition from revolutionary and terrorist to president of an incipient independent state responsible for delivering on policies for the day-to-day betterment of his people and for leading the way in building Palestinian democracy. Boris Yeltsin, too, whose defiant leadership on top of the tanks facing down the August 1991 military coup was crucial, showed substantial limitations as president of Russia.

## Foreign Policy Politics: Economic Sanctions and the South Africa Case

Earlier in this chapter we discussed Prosperity-Principles tensions and other aspects of foreign policy strategy, with economic sanctions as a principal example. Here we focus on economic sanctions from the standpoint of foreign policy politics.

The baseline for presidential-congressional relations on cases of economic sanctions is the provision of the Constitution granting Congress the power "to regulate commerce with foreign nations." Sanctions are like tariffs in this respect. Although one is more politically motivated and the other more economically motivated, both constitute regulation of international trade. Presidents do have some powers to impose sanctions granted through the International Economic Emergency Powers Act and other legislation. Executive-branch politics is also often evident: different departments and agencies have different perspectives and interests at stake, for in bureaucratic politics, where you stand depends on where you sit.

All five types of interest groups in our interest group typology from Chapter 2 can exert pressure in sanctions cases: economic interest groups, motivated by their trade and investment interests; identity groups, motivated by their ethnic, racial, national, religious, and other links to targeted countries; political issue groups, including many NGOs engaged in democracy promotion and human rights protection; state and local governments, drawing on their purchasing power, pension funds, and other economic levers to pursue their own sanctions; and foreign governments, through contracts with Washington, D.C., law firms, public relations firms, and other lobbyists. The media may also be engaged, depending on the salience and drama of the case. The extent to which public opinion is activated varies in similar ways.

Of all the recent sanctions cases, the 1985–86 anti-apartheid sanctions against South Africa stand out as an example in which the foreign policy politics was especially intense and for our purposes very instructive.[71] Since 1948, South Africa had been governed by a system called "apartheid." Literally meaning "separatehood," apartheid gave the white minority power over the black African majority. The black majority was denied meaningful political participation, relegated to economic inequality, confined to living in designated areas, and repressed overall. The apartheid system was viewed as the most unequal and racist in the world.

Prior to the mid-1980s, the United States had done little to oppose or seek to change the apartheid system. The Kennedy administration had imposed an arms embargo (i.e., economic sanctions on military weapons). The Carter administration had signed on to the United Nations arms embargo and added some other selected sanctions. The Reagan administration shifted back in the other direction: Secretary of State Alexander Haig spoke of "old friends . . . who are getting together again."[72] By 1984 American exports of aircraft, computers, communications equipment, and other military-related goods had increased 100 percent over Carter administration levels.

But things grew worse in South Africa. ***Anti-apartheid*** protests so intensified that President P. W. Botha declared a state of emergency, cracking down against political demonstrations, school boycotts, labor stoppages, and rent strikes. His regime arrested key black leaders, including the leaders of the largest black political movement, the African National Congress (ANC). These leaders joined the imprisoned Nelson Mandela, the ANC leader who had been arrested and held in prison since the early 1960s. By late 1985, as the situation became increasingly violent, the reported death toll was more than three people every day.

The anti-apartheid movement in the United States responded to these events with a political impact greater than that of any protest movement since the Vietnam War. It was led by TransAfrica, a small political issue group that until then was not all that well known. TransAfrica came up with the very effective initial strategy of dramatizing the issue and demonstrating outrage by having political leaders and celebrities protest at the South African embassy in Washington, D.C., in ways that would intentionally get them arrested. By mid-December 1985 the "celebrity arrests" included American civil rights leaders, Hollywood movie stars, religious leaders of many faiths, and fifteen members of Congress. This public protest in turn led to greater press coverage; before long the average American "was gaining an unprecedented awareness of South Africa."[73] Public opinion was strongly opposed to apartheid. College campuses became seized with this issue. Teach-ins, demonstrations, and other manifestations of student activism were somewhat reminiscent of activities on campuses during the Vietnam era.

The principal policy issue was whether to impose economic sanctions and, if so, how comprehensive to make those sanctions. Some proposals included sanctioning all U.S. trade and investment in South Africa. American companies had extensive economic interests in South Africa. The United States was South Africa's leading trade partner, supplying 15 percent of its imports, including 70 percent of its computer equipment, 45 percent of its oil, and 33 percent of its cars. Imports from South Africa were only 8 percent of total U.S. imports but included 75 percent of the U.S. supply of chromium, vital for manufacturing stainless steel and aircraft engines; 67 percent of platinum, used in automobile catalytic converters, fertilizer, explosives, and purified glass; and $140 million in diamonds. In terms of investments, about 350 American firms had operations in South Africa, including fifty-seven of the Fortune 100 companies. American banks had about $7.5 million in loans out to South African companies. It thus was no surprise that most of the American business community opposed sanctions.

However, the strong support from Democrats in Congress for an anti-apartheid sanctions bill was no surprise either. The support that started to come from Republicans was. The Republican Reagan administration was opposed to sanctions, as Republicans in Congress long had been. But a group of young conservative House members saw this issue as one that could be politically beneficial in broadening the party's popular base. "South Africa has been able to depend on conservatives in the United States . . . to treat them with benign neglect," said Representative Vin Weber (R-Minnesota), a leader of this group. "We served notice that, with the emerging generation of conservative leadership, that is not going to be the case."[74] Senator Richard Lugar (R-Indiana), chair of the Senate Foreign Relations Committee, also became a supporter of at least some sanctions. Lugar was generally seen as a moderate on foreign policy issues, and was emerging through this and other issues as a more prominent foreign policy figure.

The Anti-Apartheid Act of 1985 was approved by huge margins, 380–48 in the House and 80–12 in the Senate, despite continued opposition from the Reagan administration. When the White House threatened to veto the bill, Weber and Lugar were among those warning the White House that on this issue the two-thirds majorities needed for veto override would be there, with many Republicans as part of them.

Congress still had to go through the final steps of a conference committee to work out differences between the House and Senate bills, and then bring that bill to final votes in both chambers. The Reagan administration took advantage of this delay to shift tactics. It issued an executive order imposing its own sanctions, which were more than it had previously favored but less than those mandated by the congressional bills. Party loyalty prevailed at that point, and the House and Senate Republicans blocked final passage of the congressional bills.

But the issue was taken up again the following year. In May 1986 Democrats in the House introduced a new bill, the Comprehensive Anti-Apartheid Sanctions Act, which called for even more extensive sanctions. This bill was approved on the floor with an amendment by Representative Ron Dellums (D-California), that not only prohibited new investments by American companies in South Africa but also required disinvestment (i.e., selling off of existing investments). The Senate then passed its own bill, which went further than the 1985 Reagan executive order but not so far as the House bill. Lugar kept the Senate coalition together amid opposition to any sanctions bill from conservatives such as Jesse Helms (R-North Carolina) and pressure from liberals such as Edward Kennedy (D-Massachusetts) to make the Senate bill as tough as the House one.

Largely on the basis of a commitment by Senator Lugar to stand by the bill even if President Reagan vetoed it, House Democratic leaders agreed to bypass the negotiations of a conference committee and accept the Senate version of the bill. President Reagan did veto it. But by votes of 313–83 in the House and 78–21 in the Senate, well beyond the necessary two-thirds majorities, the veto was overridden and the Comprehensive Anti-Apartheid Sanctions Act became law.

This was the first foreign policy veto override since President Richard Nixon's veto in 1973 of the War Powers Resolution. It showed how politically strong the anti-apartheid forces had become. All along, groups such as TransAfrica had been keeping up their pressure, as had businesses and other interests on the other side. State and local governments were coming out against apartheid, passing their own versions of sanctions through prohibitions on purchases from and investments in American companies doing business with South Africa. Public opinion showed ever larger majorities in favor of sanctions. Campuses stayed active. Meanwhile, the press and television kept covering the South African government's violent and repressive tactics.

In this case the foreign policy politics were strong enough to push the government to give priority to Principles over Prosperity. The anti-apartheid sanctions case offers lessons and implications helpful for understanding the foreign policy politics of other sanctions cases, as well as other democracy-promotion and human rights–protection cases.

## Summary

Will the twenty-first century be a democratic one? This is the question with which we began this chapter. The reasons that the answer still is uncertain should now be clear.

The fall of communism, apartheid, military dictatorships, and other forms of repression during the 1990s constituted historic progress in the spread of democracy and human rights around the world. Yet this progress had limits and uncertainties, especially in regions such as Africa and the Middle East, and a long list of human rights violations in all too many countries. The long-term trend depends on whether the political, social, economic, and other challenges to democratic consolidation and institutionalization are met.

This trend is important to the United States for a number of reasons. Democracy and individual freedom are the essence of the Principles to which American foreign policy has long laid claim. They also can further the U.S. interest in Peace. The relationship posited by the democratic peace theory is a strong one, albeit not so simple or unequivocal as often portrayed.

Democracy promotion and human rights protection also can create tensions and trade-offs with considerations of Power and Prosperity. This problem has come up repeatedly in our discussion, in this chapter and throughout the book, with other Power-Principles and Prosperity-Principles dilemmas. Yet the complementarities are more frequent and more significant than is often recognized.

Policies for promoting democracy and protecting human rights thus require serious and extensive attention. A number of other international actors and NGOs play key roles, but as partners with and complements to, not substitutes for, the United States. These policy strategies are varied; all require ongoing commitments. They pose a number of difficult policy choices for devising effective strategies and for providing sufficient funding and other resources.

The ancient Athenians, often credited with establishing one of the earliest democracies, chose as their patron the goddess Athena. Athena was said to have sprung forth, fully formed, from the head of Zeus, the god of gods. Democracy, however, cannot just spring forth. It must be built, painstakingly, continuously, by those who want it for their own political systems and by those whose foreign policy is served by its global spread.

## *American Foreign Policy* Online Student StudySpace

- Will this be a "democratic century?"
- How important should the Principles "P" be to American foreign policy?
- Is soft power really power . . . or just "soft"?
- What strategies are most effective at promoting democracy?
- Which countries do you think will be the big democracy success stories in the coming years? Which the major failures?

For these and other study questions, as well as other features, check out Chapter 11 on the *American Foreign Policy* Online Student StudySpace at wwnorton.com/studyspace.

## Notes

[1]Francis Fukuyama, "The End of History?" *National Interest* 16 (Summer 1989): 3.

[2]Samuel P. Huntington, "The Clash of Civilizations," *Foreign Affairs* 72.3 (Summer 1993): 22, 48, 25.

[3]Gabriel Escobar, "A Nod to Civilian Ascendancy," *Washington Post*, October 14, 1996, p. A23.

[4]See, for example, Donald Rothchild, *Managing Ethnic Conflict in Africa: Pressures and Incentives for Cooperation* (Washington, D.C.: Brookings Institution Press, 1997); David R. Smock, ed., *Making War and Waging Peace: Foreign Intervention in Africa* (Washington, D.C.: U.S. Institute of Peace Press, 1993); and Keith B. Richburg, *Out of America: A Black Man Confronts Africa* (New York: Basic Books, 1997).

[5]Martin Kramer, "Where Islam and Democracy Part Ways," in *Democracy in the Middle East: Defining the Challenge* Yehuda Mirsky and Matt Ahrens, eds. (Washington, D.C.: Washington Institute for Near East Policy, 1993), 32, 34.

[6]Ray Takeyh, "The Lineaments of Islamic Fundamentalism," *World Policy Journal* 18.4 (Winter 2001–2002): 59–67.

[7]Mohammed Ayoob, *The Many Faces of Political Islam: Religion and Politics in the Muslim World* (Ann Arbor: University of Michigan Press, 2008), 17.

[8]Thomas Carothers, "Democracy without Illusion," *Foreign Affairs* 76.1 (January/February 1997): 89.

[9]Larry Rohter and Juan Forero, "Unending Graft Is Threatening Latin America," *New York Times*, July 30, 2005, p. A1.

[10]Juan Forero, "Fiscal Growth in Latin Lands Fails to Fill Social Needs," *New York Times*, April 25, 2005, p. A4; Forero, "Latin America Fails to Deliver on Basic Needs," *New York Times*, February 22, 2005, p. A1.

[11]Rohter and Forero, "Unending Graft Is Threatening Latin America"; Warren Hoge, "Latin America Losing Hope in Democracy," *New York Times*, April 22, 2004, p. A3.

[12]Larry Rohter, "Visit to U.S. Isn't a First for Chile's First Female President," *New York Times*, June 8, 2006, p. A3.

[13]*Amnesty International Report 2008: State of the World's Human Rights*, Foreword: Broken Promises, 3, http://archive.amnesty.org/air2008/document/47.pdf (accessed 8/21/09).

[14]*Amnesty International Report 2008: State of the World's Human Rights*, 4,11–12, 19, 30–31, 34, http://archive.amnesty.org/air2008/document/101.pdf (accessed 8/21/09).

[15]*Amnesty International Report 2008: State of the World's Human Rights*, Foreword, 3, 15.

[16]Jack S. Levy, "Domestic Politics and War," in *The Origin and Prevention of Major Wars*, Robert I. Rotberg and Theodore K. Rabb, eds., (Cambridge: Cambridge University Press, 1989), 88.

[17]See, for example, Bruce Russett, *Grasping the Democratic Peace* (Princeton: Princeton University Press, 1993); John Owen, "How Liberalism Produces Democratic Peace," *International Security* 19.2 (Fall 1994): 87–125; Melvin Small and J. David Singer, "The War Proneness of Democratic Regimes," *Jerusalem Journal of International Relations* 1 (Summer 1976): 50–69.

[18]Immanuel Kant, "Perpetual Peace," cited in Michael W. Doyle, "Kant, Liberal Legacies, and Foreign Affairs," in *Debating the Democratic Peace*, Michael E. Brown et al., eds. (Cambridge, Mass.: MIT Press, 1997), 24–25.

[19]Doyle, "Kant, Liberal Legacies, and Foreign Affairs," 49.

[20]Owen, "How Liberalism Produces Democratic Peace," 96.

[21]Cited in Bruce W. Jentleson, "The Political Basis for Trade in U.S.-Soviet Relations," *Millennium: Journal of International Studies* 15 (Spring 1986): 27.

[22]David E. Spiro, "The Insignificance of the Liberal Peace," *International Security* 19.2 (Fall 1994): 50–86.

[23]Henry S. Farber and Joanne Gowa, "Politics and Peace," *International Security* 20.2 (Fall 1995): 123–46; Christopher Layne, "Kant or Cant: The Myth of the Democratic Peace," *International Security* 19.2 (Fall 1994): 5–49.

[24]Edward D. Mansfield and Jack Snyder, "Democratization and the Danger of War," *International Security* 20.1 (Summer 1995): 7; Mansfield and Snyder, *Electing to Fight: Why Emerging Democracies Go to War* (Cambridge, Mass.: MIT Press, 2005).

[25]George W. Bush, *National Security Strategy of the United States of America, 2002,* http://georgewbush-whitehouse.archives.gov/nsc/nss/2002/nss.pdf (accessed 8/21/09).

[26]David Rohde, "Pakistani Fundamentalists and Secular Opponents of Muhsarraf Do Well in Election," *New York Times,* October 11, 2002, p. A8.

[27]Mark Mazzetti, "Efforts by CIA Fail in Somalia, Officials Charge," *New York Times,* June 8, 2006, p. A1.

[28]Joseph S. Nye, Jr., *Bound to Lead: The Changing Nature of American Power* (New York: Basic Books, 1990); Nye, *The Paradox of American Power: Why the World's Only Superpower Can't Go It Alone* (New York: Oxford University Press, 2002).

[29]Nye, *Bound to Lead,* 188.

[30]Kristin M. Lord, *Voices of America: U.S. Public Diplomacy in the 21st Century* (Washington, D.C.: Brookings Institution, 2008).

[31]Hans J. Morgenthau, cited in Michael J. Smith, "Ethics and Intervention," *Ethics and International Affairs* 1989 (3): 8.

[32]Kishore Mahbubani, "The United States: 'Go East, Young Man,'" *Washington Quarterly* 17.2 (Spring 1994): 6 and *passim.*

[33]Mahbubani, "'Go East, Young Man,'" 7, 9.

[34]This section draws on a study I did for the National Academy of Sciences, National Research Council, Commission on Behavioral and Social Sciences and Education, Committee on International Conflict Resolution. See Bruce W. Jentleson, "Economic Sanctions and Post–Cold War Conflicts: Challenges for Theory and Policy," in *International Conflict Resolution after the Cold War,* Paul C. Stern and Daniel Druckman, eds. (Washington, D.C.: National Academy Press, 2000), 123–77.

[35]Christopher Smith, statement for joint hearing on "The Internet in China: A Tool for Freedom or Suppression?" before the Subcommittee on Africa, Global Human Rights and International Operations and the Subcommittee on Asia and the Pacific, Committee on International Relations, U.S. House of Representatives, February 15, 2006, 19, http://commdocs.house.gov/committees/intlrel/hfa26075.000/hfa26075_0f.htm (accessed 9/14/09), cited in "The Great Firewall: Globalization, China and the Internet," case study prepared by Jake Palley for my course Globalization and Governance.

[36]Jack Krumholtz, statement for joint hearing on "The Internet in China: A Tool for Freedom or Suppression?" before the Subcommittee on Africa, Global Human Rights and International Operations and the Subcommittee on Asia and the Pacific, Committee on International Relations, U.S. House of Representatives, February 15, 2006, 123, http://commdocs.house.gov/committees/intlrel/hfa26075.000/hfa26075_0f.htm (accessed 9/14/09), cited in "The Great Firewall: Globalization, China and the Internet," case study prepared by Jake Palley for my course Globalization and Governance.

[37]Thomas G. Weiss, David Cortright, George A. Lopez, and Larry Minear, eds., *Political Gain and Civilian Pain: Humanitarian Impact of Economic Sanctions* (Lanham, Md.: Rowman and Littlefield, 1997).

[38]Claudette Antoine Werleigh, "The Use of Sanctions in Haiti: Assessing the Economic Realities," in *Economic Sanctions: Panacea or Peacebuilding in the Post–Cold War World?* David Cortright and George Lopez, eds. (Boulder, Colo.: Westview, 1995), 169.

[39]Kimberley Ann Elliott and Gary Clyde Hufbauer, "'New' Approaches to Economic Sanctions," in *U.S. Intervention Policy for the Post–Cold War World,* Arnold Kanter and Linton F. Brooks, eds. (New York: Norton, 1994), 153–54.

[40]Eric Hoskins, "The Humanitarian Impact of Economic Sanctions and War in Iraq," in Weiss et al., *Political Gain and Civilian Pain.*

[41]Bruce W. Jentleson, "Discrepant Responses to Falling Dictators: Presidential Belief Systems and the Mediating Effects of the Senior Advisory Process," *Political Psychology* 11 (June 1990): 377–80.

[42]"Yushchenko Wins Ukraine Election," BBC News, December 27, 2004, http://news.bbc.co.uk/2/hi/europe/4127203.stm (accessed 8/21/09).

[43]Thanks to my colleague Professor Judith Kelley for sharing some of her research on election observer groups.

[44]Larry Diamond, *Promoting Democracy in the 1990s: Actors and Instruments, Issues and Imperatives* (Washington, D.C.: Carnegie Commission for Preventing Deadly Conflict, 1995), 40–48.

[45]Diamond, *Promoting Democracy in the 1990s,* 41.

[46]"Price Named Top Democrat on International Commission," http://price.house.gov/list/press/nc04_price/051805.shtml (accessed 8/21/09).

[47]William J. Perry, "Defense in an Age of Hope," *Foreign Affairs* 79.6 (November/December 1996): 69–70.

[48]AID, *Agency Performance Report 1997,* 42, www.usaid.gov/pubs/apr97/pnacb775.pdf (accessed 8/21/09).

[49]Transparency International, Corruption Fighters' Tool Kit, www.transparency.org/publications/tookit (accessed 8/21/09).

[50]Adam Feinstein, "Fighting for Press Freedom," *Journal of Democracy* 6 (January 1995): 159–68.

[51]Committee to Protect Journalists, "Journalists Killed in 2007: 66 Confirmed," www.cpj.org/deadly/killed07.html (accessed 8/21/09).

[52]Neil J. Kritz, ed., *Transitional Justice: How Emerging Democracies Reckon with Former Regimes* (Washington, D.C.: U.S. Institute of Peace Press, 1995).

[53]Among the sources on transitional justice see the three-volume study *Transitional Justice: How Emerging Democracies Reckon with Former Regimes* (Washington, D.C.: U.S. Institute of Peace Press, 1995).

[54]Francisco Goldman, "In Guatemala, All Is Forgotten," *New York Times,* December 23, 1996, A13.

[55]Genaro Arriagada, "Beyond Justice," *Washington Post,* October 25, 1998, C7; Charles Trueheart, "Pinochet Case Signifies Cries for Retribution," *Washington Post,* October 25, 1998, A21.

[56]Henry Kissinger, *Does America Need a Foreign Policy? Toward a Diplomacy for the 21st Century* (New York: Simon & Schuster, 2001), 273, 275. As secretary of state in the Nixon administration, Kissinger played a central role in U.S. policy toward Chile, including opposition to the Salvador Allende government and support for the Pinochet coup.

[57]Barbara Crossette, "For First Time U.S. Is Excluded from UN Human Rights Panel," *New York Times,* May 4, 2001, A1.

[58]Kofi Annan, "'In Larger Freedom': Decision Time at the UN," *Foreign Affairs* 84.3 (May/June 2005): 70.

[59]Robert D. Putnam, *Making Democracy Work: Civic Traditions in Modern Italy* (Princeton: Princeton University Press, 1993), 176. This section draws on an outstanding paper written by Sarah Schroeder, one of my students in Fall 1996, "How Should the United States Support Democracy Consolidation in Haiti? The Relationship between Civil Society and Political Institutions."

[60]Cited in Diamond, *Promoting Democracy in the 1990s,* 56–57.

[61]Richard Rose, "Rethinking Civil Society: Postcommunism and the Problem of Trust," *Journal of Democracy* 5 (July 1994): 29.

[62]Thomas Carothers, "The Backlash Against Democracy Promotion," *Foreign Affairs* 85.2 (March/April 2006).

[63]Gideon Rose, "Democracy Promotion and American Foreign Policy: A Review Essay," *International Security* 25.2 (Winter 2000–01): 186–203.

[64]Thomas Carothers, *Aiding Democracy Abroad: The Learning Curve* (Washington, D.C.: Carnegie Endowment for International Peace, 1999), 308, 171, 182, 251.

[65]Carothers, *Aiding Democracy Abroad,* 171, 182, 249–50, 347.

[66]Rose, "Democracy Promotion and American Foreign Policy," 198.

[67]Fareed Zakaria, *The Future of Freedom: Illiberal Democracy at Home and Abroad* (New York: Norton, 2003).

[68]Diamond, *Developing Democracy in the 1990s,* 272.

[69]Carothers, *Aiding Democracy Abroad,* 340.

[70]Rose, "Democracy Promotion and American Foreign Policy," 200.

[71]This section draws on Bruce W. Jentleson, "American Diplomacy: Around the World and Along Pennsylvania Avenue," in *A Question of Balance: The President, the Congress and Foreign Policy,* ed. Thomas E. Mann (Washington, D.C.: Brookings Institution Press, 1990), 146–200; and Jentleson, ed., *Perspectives on American Foreign Policy: Readings and Cases* (New York: Norton, 2000), chap. 2, and the Kennedy School of Government (Harvard University) case study, "The United States and South Africa: The Anti-Apartheid Sanctions Debate of 1985," by Pamela Varley for Gregory Treverton (1989).

[72]Cited in Jentleson, "American Diplomacy," 157.

[73]Jentleson, *Perspectives,* 42.

[74]Cited in Jentleson, *Perspectives,* 42.

# *Readings for Part II American Foreign Policy in the Twenty-First Century: Choices and Challenges*

# Unilateralism

6.1

CHARLES KRAUTHAMMER

## The Unipolar Moment Revisited

In late 1990, shortly before the collapse of the Soviet Union, it was clear that the world we had known for half a century was disappearing. The question was what would succeed it. I suggested then that we had already entered the "unipolar moment." The gap in power between the leading nation and all the others was so unprecedented as to yield an international structure unique to modern history: unipolarity.

* * *

### Unipolarity after September 11, 2001

There is little need to rehearse the acceleration of unipolarity in the 1990s. Japan, whose claim to power rested exclusively on economics, went into economic decline. Germany stagnated. The Soviet Union ceased to exist, contracting into a smaller, radically weakened Russia. The European Union turned inward toward the great project of integration and built a strong social infrastructure at the expense of military capacity. Only China grew in strength, but coming from so far behind it will be decades before it can challenge American primacy—and that assumes that its current growth continues unabated.

The result is the dominance of a single power unlike anything ever seen. Even at its height Britain could always be seriously challenged by the next greatest powers. Britain had a smaller army than the land powers of Europe and its navy was equaled by the next two navies combined. Today, American military spending exceeds that of the next *twenty* countries combined. Its navy, air force and space power are unrivaled. Its technology is irresistible. It is dominant by every measure: military, economic, technological, diplomatic, cultural, even linguistic, with a myriad of countries trying to fend off the inexorable march of Internet-fueled MTV English.

American dominance has not gone unnoticed. During the 1990s, it was mainly China and Russia that denounced unipolarity in their occasional joint communiqués. As the new century dawned it was on everyone's lips. A French foreign minister dubbed the United States not a

From *The National Interest* 70 (Winter 2002/03).

superpower but a hyperpower. The dominant concern of foreign policy establishments everywhere became understanding and living with the 800-pound American gorilla.

And then September 11 *heightened* the asymmetry. It did so in three ways. First, and most obviously, it led to a demonstration of heretofore latent American military power. Kosovo, the first war ever fought and won exclusively from the air, had given a hint of America's quantum leap in military power (and the enormous gap that had developed between American and European military capabilities). But it took September 11 for the United States to unleash with concentrated fury a fuller display of its power in Afghanistan. Being a relatively pacific, commercial republic, the United States does not go around looking for demonstration wars. This one was thrust upon it. In response, America showed that at a range of 7,000 miles and with but a handful of losses, it could destroy within weeks a hardened, fanatical regime favored by geography and climate in the "graveyard of empires." . . .

Second, September 11 demonstrated a new form of American strength. The center of its economy was struck, its aviation shut down, Congress brought to a halt, the government sent underground, the country paralyzed and fearful. Yet within days the markets reopened, the economy began its recovery, the president mobilized the nation, and a united Congress immediately underwrote a huge new worldwide campaign against terror. The Pentagon started planning the U.S. military response even as its demolished western façade still smoldered.

America had long been perceived as invulnerable. That illusion was shattered on September 11, 2001. But with a demonstration of its recuperative powers—an economy and political system so deeply rooted and fundamentally sound that it could spring back to life within days—that sense of invulnerability assumed a new character. It was transmuted from impermeability to resilience, the product of unrivaled human, technological and political reserves.

The third effect of September 11 was to accelerate the realignment of the current great powers, such as they are, behind the United States. In 1990, America's principal ally was NATO. A decade later, its alliance base had grown to include former members of the Warsaw Pact. Some of the major powers, however, remained uncommitted. Russia and China flirted with the idea of an "anti-hegemonic alliance." Russian leaders made ostentatious visits to pieces of the old Soviet empire such as Cuba and North Korea. India and Pakistan, frozen out by the United States because of their nuclear testing, remained focused mainly on one another. But after September 11, the bystanders came calling. Pakistan made an immediate strategic decision to join the American camp. India enlisted with equal alacrity, offering the United States basing, overflight rights and a level of cooperation unheard of during its half century of Nehruist genuflection to anti-American non-alignment. Russia's Putin, seeing both a coincidence of interests in the fight against Islamic radicalism and an opportunity to gain acceptance in the Western camp, dramatically realigned Russian foreign policy toward the United States. (Russia has already been rewarded with a larger role in NATO and tacit American recognition of Russia's interests in its "near abroad.") China remains more distant but, also having a coincidence of interests with the United States in fighting Islamic radicalism, it has cooperated with the war on terror and muted its competition with America in the Pacific.

* * *

The American hegemon has no great power enemies, an historical oddity of the first order. Yet it does face a serious threat to its dominance, indeed to its essential security. It comes from a source even more historically odd: an archipelago of rogue states (some connected with transnational terrorists) wielding weapons of mass destruction.

The threat is not trivial. It is the single greatest danger to the United States because, for all of America's dominance, and for all of its recently demonstrated resilience, there is one thing it might not survive: decapitation. The detonation of a dozen nuclear weapons in major American cities, or the spreading of smallpox or anthrax throughout the general population, is an existential threat. It is perhaps the only realistic threat to America as a functioning hegemon, perhaps even to America as a functioning modern society.

* * *

## The Crisis of Unipolarity

Accordingly, not one but a host of new doctrines have come tumbling out since September 11. First came the with-us-or-against-us ultimatum to any state aiding, abetting or harboring terrorists. Then, pre-emptive attack on any enemy state developing weapons of mass destruction. And now, regime change in any such state.

The boldness of these policies—or, as much of the world contends, their arrogance—is breathtaking. The American anti-terrorism ultimatum, it is said, is high-handed and permits the arbitrary application of American power everywhere. Pre-emption is said to violate traditional doctrines of just war. And regime change, as Henry Kissinger has argued, threatens 350 years of post-Westphalian international practice. Taken together, they amount to an unprecedented assertion of American freedom of action and a definitive statement of a new American unilateralism.

To be sure, these are not the first instances of American unilateralism. Before September 11, the George W. Bush Administration had acted unilaterally, but on more minor matters, such as the Kyoto Protocol and the Biological Weapons Convention, and with less bluntness, as in its protracted negotiations with Russia over the ABM treaty. The "axis of evil" speech of January 29, however, took unilateralism to a new level. Latent resentments about American willfulness are latent no more. American dominance, which had been tolerated if not welcomed, is now producing such irritation and hostility in once friendly quarters, such as Europe, that some suggest we have arrived at the end of the opposition-free grace period that America had enjoyed during the unipolar moment.[1]

* * *

## Realism and the New Unilateralism

The basic division between the two major foreign policy schools in America centers on the question of what is, and what should be, the fundamental basis of international relations:

paper or power. Liberal internationalism envisions a world order that, like domestic society, is governed by laws and not men. Realists see this vision as hopelessly utopian. The history of paper treaties—from the prewar Kellogg-Briand Pact and Munich to the post–Cold War Oslo accords and the 1994 Agreed Framework with North Korea—is a history of naiveté and cynicism, a combination both toxic and volatile that invariably ends badly. Trade agreements with Canada are one thing. Pieces of parchment to which existential enemies affix a signature are quite another. They are worse than worthless because they give a false sense of security and breed complacency. For the realist, the ultimate determinant of the most basic elements of international life—security, stability and peace—is power.

Which is why a realist would hardly forfeit the current unipolarity for the vain promise of goo-goo one-worldism. Nor, however, should a realist want to forfeit unipolarity for the familiarity of traditional multipolarity. Multipolarity is inherently fluid and unpredictable. Europe practiced multipolarity for centuries and found it so unstable and bloody, culminating in 1914 in the catastrophic collapse of delicately balanced alliance systems, that Europe sought its permanent abolition in political and economic union. Having abjured multipolarity for the region, it is odd in the extreme to then prefer multipolarity for the world.

Less can be said about the destiny of unipolarity. It is too new. Yet we do have the history of the last decade, our only modern experience with unipolarity, and it was a decade of unusual stability among all major powers. It would be foolish to project from just a ten-year experience, but that experience does call into question the basis for the claims that unipolarity is intrinsically unstable or impossible to sustain in a mass democracy.

I would argue that unipolarity, managed benignly, is far more likely to keep the peace. Benignity is, of course, in the eye of the beholder. But the American claim to benignity is not mere self-congratulation. We have a track record. Consider one of history's rare controlled experiments. In the 1940s, lines were drawn through three peoples—Germans, Koreans and Chinese—one side closely bound to the United States, the other to its adversary. It turned into a controlled experiment because both states in the divided lands shared a common culture. Fifty years later the results are in. Does anyone doubt the superiority, both moral and material, of West Germany vs. East Germany, South Korea vs. North Korea and Taiwan vs. China?

* * *

The form of realism that I am arguing for—call it the new unilateralism—is clear in its determination to self-consciously and confidently deploy American power in pursuit of those global ends. Note: global ends. There is a form of unilateralism that is devoted only to narrow American self-interest and it has a name, too: It is called isolationism. Critics of the new unilateralism often confuse it with isolationism because both are prepared to unashamedly exercise American power. But isolationists *oppose* America acting as a unipolar power not because they disagree with the unilateral means, but because they deem the ends far too broad. Isolationists would abandon the larger world and use American power exclusively for the narrowest of American interests: manning Fortress America by defending the American homeland and putting up barriers to trade and immigration.

The new unilateralism defines American interests far beyond narrow self-defense. In particular, it identifies two other major interests, both global: extending the peace by advancing democracy and preserving the peace by acting as balancer of last resort. Britain was the balancer in Europe, joining the weaker coalition against the stronger to create equilibrium. America's unique global power allows it to be the balancer in every region. We balanced Iraq by supporting its weaker neighbors in the Gulf War. We balance China by supporting the ring of smaller states at its periphery (from South Korea to Taiwan, even to Vietnam). Our role in the Balkans was essentially to create a microbalance: to support the weaker Bosnian Muslims against their more dominant neighbors, and subsequently to support the weaker Albanian Kosovars against the Serbs.

Of course, both of these tasks often advance American national interests as well. The promotion of democracy multiplies the number of nations likely to be friendly to the United States, and regional equilibria produce stability that benefits a commercial republic like the United States. America's (intended) exertions on behalf of pre-emptive non-proliferation, too, are clearly in the interest of both the United States and the international system as a whole.

* * *

When I first proposed the unipolar model in 1990, I suggested that we should accept both its burdens and opportunities and that, if America did not wreck its economy, unipolarity could last thirty or forty years. That seemed bold at the time. Today, it seems rather modest. The unipolar moment has become the unipolar era. It remains true, however, that its durability will be decided at home. It will depend largely on whether it is welcomed by Americans or seen as a burden to be shed—either because we are too good for the world (the isolationist critique) or because we are not worthy of it (the liberal internationalist critique).

The new unilateralism argues explicitly and unashamedly for maintaining unipolarity, for sustaining America's unrivaled dominance for the foreseeable future. It could be a long future, assuming we successfully manage the single greatest threat, namely, weapons of mass destruction in the hands of rogue states. This in itself will require the aggressive and confident application of unipolar power rather than falling back, as we did in the 1990s, on paralyzing multilateralism. The future of the unipolar era hinges on whether America is governed by those who wish to retain, augment and use unipolarity to advance not just American but global ends, or whether America is governed by those who wish to give it up—either by allowing unipolarity to decay as they retreat to Fortress America, or by passing on the burden by gradually transferring power to multilateral institutions as heirs to American hegemony. The challenge to unipolarity is not from the outside but from the inside. The choice is ours. To impiously paraphrase Benjamin Franklin: History has given you an empire, if you will keep it.

## Note

[1] A Sky News poll finds that even the British public considers George W. Bush a greater threat to world peace than Saddam Hussein. The poll was conducted September 2–6, 2002.

# *The United Nations*

6.2

Kofi A. Annan

## "We the Peoples"

We need to remind ourselves why the United Nations exists—for what, and for whom. We also need to ask ourselves what kind of United Nations the world's leaders are prepared to support, in deeds as well as words. Clear answers are necessary to energize and focus the Organization's work in the decades ahead. It is those answers that the Millennium Summit must provide.

Of course, the United Nations exists to serve its member States. It is the only body of its kind with universal membership and comprehensive scope, and encompassing so many areas of human endeavour. These features make it a uniquely useful forum—for sharing information, conducting negotiations, elaborating norms and voicing expectations, coordinating the behaviour of states and other actors, and pursuing common plans of action. We must ensure that the United Nations performs these functions as efficiently and effectively as possible.

The United Nations is more than a mere tool, however. As its Charter makes clear, the United Nations was intended to introduce new principles into international relations, making a qualitative difference to their day-to-day conduct. The Charter's very first Article defines our purposes: resolving disputes by peaceful means; devising cooperative solutions to economic, social, cultural and humanitarian problems; and broadly encouraging behaviour in conformity with the principles of justice and international law. In other words, quite apart from whatever practical tasks the United Nations is asked to perform, it has the avowed purpose of transforming relations among states, and the methods by which the world's affairs are managed.

Nor is that all. For even though the United Nations is an organization of states, the Charter is written in the name of "we the peoples". It reaffirms the dignity and worth of the human person, respect for human rights and the equal rights of men and women, and a commitment to social progress as measured by better standards of life, in freedom from want and fear alike. Ultimately, then, the United

From Millennium Report of the Secretary-General of the United Nations, *"We the Peoples:" The Role of the United Nations in the 21st Century,* September 2000, www.un.org/millennium/sg/report/full.htm (accessed 10/16/09).

Nations exists for, and must serve, the needs and hopes of people everywhere.

* * *

When it was created more than half a century ago, in the convulsive aftermath of world war, the United Nations reflected humanity's greatest hopes for a just and peaceful global community. It still embodies that dream. We remain the only global institution with the legitimacy and scope that derive from universal membership, and a mandate that encompasses development, security and human rights as well as the environment. In this sense, the United Nations is unique in world affairs.

We are an organization without independent military capability, and we dispose of relatively modest resources in the economic realm. Yet our influence and impact on the world is far greater than many believe to be the case—and often more than we ourselves realize. This influence derives not from any exercise of power, but from the force of the values we represent; our role in helping to establish and sustain global norms; our ability to stimulate global concern and action; and the trust we enjoy for the practical work we do on the ground to improve people's lives.

The importance of principles and norms is easily underestimated; but in the decades since the United Nations was created, the spreading acceptance of new norms has profoundly affected the lives of many millions of people. War was once a normal instrument of statecraft; it is now universally proscribed, except in very specific circumstances. Democracy, once challenged by authoritarianism in various guises, has not only prevailed in much of the world, but is now generally seen as the most legitimate and desirable form of government. The protection of fundamental human rights, once considered the province of sovereign states alone, is now a universal concern transcending both governments and borders.

* * *

The United Nations plays an equally important, but largely unsung, role in creating and sustaining the global rules without which modern societies simply could not function. * * * Indeed, it is impossible to imagine our globalized world without the principles and practice of multilateralism to underpin it. An open world economy, in the place of mercantilism; a gradual decrease in the importance of competitive military alliances coupled with a Security Council more often able to reach decisions; the General Assembly or great gatherings of states and civil society organizations addressing humanity's common concerns—these are some of the signs, partial and halting though they may be, of an indispensable multilateral system in action.

Taking a long-term view, the expansion of the rule of law has been the foundation of much of the social progress achieved in the last millennium. Of course, this remains an unfinished project, especially at the international level, and our efforts to deepen it continue. Support for the rule of law would be enhanced if countries signed and ratified international treaties and conventions. Some decline to do so for reasons of substance, but a far greater number simply lack the necessary expertise and resources, especially when national legislation is needed to give force to international instruments.

* * *

If the international community were to create a new United Nations tomorrow, its make-up would surely be different from the one we have. In 2000, our structure reflects decades of mandates conferred by Member States and, in some cases, the legacy of deep political disagreements. While there is widespread consensus on the need to make the United Nations a more modern and flexible organization, unless Member States are willing to contemplate **real structural reform,** there will continue to be severe limits to what we can achieve.

When the scope of our responsibilities and the hopes invested in us are measured against our resources, we confront a sobering truth. The budget for our core functions—the Secretariat operations in New York, Geneva, Nairobi, Vienna and five regional commissions—is just $1.25 billion a year. That is about 4 percent of New York City's annual budget—and nearly a billion dollars less than the annual cost of running Tokyo's Fire Department. Our resources simply are not commensurate with our global tasks.

* * *

The purposes and principles of the United Nations are set out clearly in the Charter, and in the Universal Declaration of Human Rights. Their relevance and capacity to inspire have in no way diminished. If anything they have increased, as peoples have become interconnected in new ways, and the need for collective responsibility at the global level has come to be more widely felt. The following values, which reflect the spirit of the Charter, are—I believe—shared by all nations, and are of particular importance for the age we are now entering:

### *Freedom*

Men and women have the right to live their lives and raise their children in dignity, free from hunger and squalor and from the fear of violence or oppression. These rights are best assured by representative government, based on the will of the people.

### *Equity and solidarity*

No individual and no nation must be denied the opportunity to benefit from globalization. Global risks must be managed in a way that shares the costs and burdens fairly. Those who suffer, or who benefit least, are entitled to help from those who benefit most.

### *Tolerance*

Human beings must respect each other, in all their diversity of faith, culture and language. Differences within and between societies should be neither feared nor repressed, but cherished.

### *Non-violence*

Disputes between and within nations should be resolved by peaceful means, except where use of force is authorized by the Charter.

### *Respect for nature*

Prudence should be shown in handling all living species and natural resources. Only so can the immeasurable riches we inherit from nature be preserved and passed on to our descendants.

### *Shared responsibility*

States must act together to maintain international peace and security, in accordance with the Charter. The management of risks and threats that affect all the world's peoples should be considered multilaterally.

• • •

In applying these values to the new century, our priorities must be clear.

**First, we must spare no effort to free our fellow men and women from the abject and dehumanizing poverty** in which more than 1 billion of them are currently confined. Let us resolve therefore:

- To halve, by the time this century is 15 years old, the proportion of the world's people (currently 22 percent) whose income is less than one dollar a day.
- To halve, by the same date, the proportion of people (currently 20 percent) who are unable to reach, or to afford, safe drinking water.
- That by the same date all children everywhere, boys and girls alike, will be able to complete a full course of primary schooling; and that girls and boys will have equal access to all levels of education.
- That by then we will have halted, and begun to reverse, the spread of HIV/AIDS.
- That, by 2020, we will have achieved significant improvement in the lives of at least 100 million slum dwellers around the world.
- To develop strategies that will give young people everywhere the chance of finding decent work.
- To ensure that the benefits of new technology, especially information technology, are available to all.
- That every national government will from now on commit itself to national policies and programmes directed specifically at reducing poverty, to be developed and applied in consultation with civil society.

At the international level, the more fortunate countries owe a duty of solidarity to the less fortunate. Let them resolve therefore:

- To grant free access to their markets for goods produced in poor countries—and, as a first step, to be prepared, at the Third United Nations Conference on the Least Developed Countries in March 2001, to adopt a policy of duty-free and quota-free access for essentially all exports from the least developed countries.
- To remove the shackles of debt which currently keep many of the poorest countries imprisoned in their poverty—and, as first steps, to implement the expansion of the debt relief programme for heavily indebted poor countries agreed last year without further delay, and to be prepared to cancel all official debts of the heavily

indebted poor countries, in return for those countries making demonstrable commitments to poverty reduction.

- To grant more generous development assistance, particularly to those countries which are genuinely applying their resources to poverty reduction.
- To work with the pharmaceutical industry and other partners to develop an effective and affordable vaccine against HIV; and to make HIV-related drugs more widely accessible in developing countries.

At both the national and international levels, private investment has an indispensable role to play. Let us resolve therefore:

- To develop strong partnerships with the private sector to combat poverty in all its aspects.

Extreme poverty in sub-Saharan Africa affects a higher proportion of the population than in any other region. It is compounded by a higher incidence of conflict, HIV/AIDS and many other ills. Let us resolve therefore:

- That in all our efforts we will make special provision for the needs of Africa, and give our full support to Africans in their struggle to overcome the continent's problems.

For my part, I have announced four new initiatives in the course of this report:

- A Health InterNetwork, to provide hospitals and clinics in developing countries with access to up-to-date medical information.
- A United Nations Information Technology Service (UNITeS), to train groups in developing countries in the uses and opportunities of information technology.
- A disaster response initiative, "First on the Ground", which will provide uninterrupted communications access to areas affected by natural disasters and emergencies.
- A global policy network to explore viable new approaches to the problem of youth employment.

**Second, we must spare no effort to free our fellow men and women from the scourge of war**—as the Charter requires us to do—and especially from the violence of civil conflict and the fear of weapons of mass destruction, which are the two great sources of terror in the present age. Let us resolve therefore:

- To strengthen respect for law, in international as in national affairs, in particular the agreed provisions of treaties on the control of armaments, and international humanitarian and human rights law. I invite all governments that have not done so to sign and ratify the various conventions, covenants and treaties which form the central corpus of international law.
- To make the United Nations more effective in its work of maintaining peace and security, notably by
  -Strengthening the capacity of the United Nations to conduct peace operations.

-Adopting measures to make economic sanctions adopted by the Security Council less harsh on innocent populations, and more effective in penalizing delinquent rulers.

- To take energetic action to curb the illegal traffic in small arms, notably by
  -Creating greater transparency in arms transfers.
  -Supporting regional disarmament measures, such as the moratorium on the importing, exporting or manufacturing of light weapons in West Africa.
  -Extending to other areas—especially post-conflict situations—the "weapons for goods" programmes that have worked well in Albania, El Salvador, Mozambique and Panama.
  -To examine the possibility of convening a major international conference to identify ways of eliminating nuclear dangers.

**Third, we must spare no effort to free our fellow men and women, and above all our children and grandchildren, from the danger of living on a planet irredeemably spoilt by human activities, and whose resources can no longer provide for their needs.** Given the extraordinary risks humanity confronts, let us resolve:

- To adopt a new ethic of conservation and stewardship; and, as first steps:
  -To adopt and ratify the Kyoto Protocol, so that it can enter into force by 2002, and to ensure that its goals are met, as a step towards reducing emissions of greenhouse gases.
  -To consider seriously incorporating the United Nations system of "green accounting" into national accounts.
  -To provide financial support for, and become actively engaged in, the Millennium Ecosystem Assessment.

**Finally, we must spare no effort to make the United Nations a more effective instrument in the hands of the world's peoples** for pursuing all three of these priorities—the fight against poverty, ignorance and disease; the fight against violence and terror; and the fight against the degradation and destruction of our common home. Let us resolve therefore:

- To reform the Security Council, in a way that both enables it to carry out its responsibilities more effectively and gives it greater legitimacy in the eyes of all the world's peoples.
- To ensure that the Organization is given the necessary resources to carry out its mandates.
- To ensure that the Secretariat makes best use of those resources in the interests of all Member States, by allowing it to adopt the best management practices and technologies available, and to concentrate on those tasks that reflect the current priorities of Member States.
- To give full opportunities to non-governmental organizations and other non-state actors to make their indispensable contribution to the Organization's work.

• • •

I believe that these priorities are clear, and that all these things are achievable if we have the will to achieve them. For many of the priorities, strategies have already been worked out, and are summarized in this report. For others, what is needed first is to apply our minds, our energies and our research budgets to an intensive quest for workable solutions.

No state and no organization can solve all these problems by acting alone. Nor however, should any state imagine that others will solve them for it, if its own government and citizens do not apply themselves wholeheartedly to the task. Building a twenty-first century safer and more equitable than the twentieth is a task that requires the determined efforts of every state and every individual. In inspiring and coordinating those efforts, a renewed United Nations will have a vital and exalting role to play.

# America as the World's Government

7.1

MICHAEL MANDELBAUM

## The Case for Goliath

When the Cold War ended, a question arose: What would succeed that great political, military, economic, and ideological conflict as the central issue in international relations? By the middle of the first decade of the twenty-first century, the question had been answered. The enormous power and pervasive influence of the United States was universally acknowledged to be the defining feature of world affairs.

In the eyes of many, American supremacy counted as a great misfortune. The foreign policy of the world's strongest country, in this account, resembled the conduct of a schoolyard bully who randomly assaults others, steals the lunch money of weaker students, and generally makes life unpleasant wherever he goes. The United States was seen as the world's Goliath. . . .

Although the United States looks like Goliath, however, in important ways the world's strongest power does not act like him. If America is a Goliath, it is a benign one. Unlike the case of Goliath, moreover, no David, or group of Davids, has stepped forward to confront the United States. This book explains other countries' acceptance of the American role in the world by painting a different and more benign picture of that role than the one implied by the comparison with Western civilization's archetypal bully. As portrayed in the pages that follow, it has something in common with the sun's relationship to the rest of the solar system. Both confer benefits on the entities with which they are in regular contact. The sun keeps the planets in their orbits by the force of gravity and radiates the heat and light that make life possible on one of them. Similarly, the United States furnishes services to other countries, the same services, as it happens, that governments provide within sovereign states to the people they govern. The United States therefore functions as the world's government. . . .

The United States performs, within the international system, the first duty of all governments: providing security. One of the principal American policies during the Cold War—deterrence—was transformed, in the wake of

From *The Case for Goliath: How America Acts as the World's Government in the Twenty-First Century* (New York: Public Affairs Press, 2006).

that conflict, into a related but distinct mission: reassurance. * * *

American foreign policies also correspond to the economic tasks that governments perform within sovereign states. One is the enforcement of contracts and the protection of property in their jurisdictions. America's international military deployments have these effects on transactions across borders. Governments also supply the power and water without which industrial economies cannot function. Similarly, the United States helps to assure global access to the economically indispensable mineral, oil. Governments supply the money used in economic transactions: The American dollar serves as the world's money. At the outset of the post–World War II period and thereafter, the United States fostered the conditions in which yet another major economic activity—trade—flourished and expanded. Finally, just as, in the twentieth century, governments took it upon themselves to sustain the level of consumption within their societies in order to support a high level of production and thus of employment, so the huge American appetite for consumer products has helped to sustain economic activity the world over, especially in East Asia. * * *

No early twenty-first-century version of imperial Japan and Nazi Germany is likely to appear: The twentieth-century ideologies of conquest—fascism and communism—have been discredited and no comparable set of ideas, whose adherents could seize control of a powerful state and thus menace the world, are in circulation. The militant Islam of the early twenty-first century does bear a resemblance to the twentieth century's totalitarian ideologies[1] but does not pose a threat of the same kind or of the same magnitude as fascism and communism did. The Islamist ideology lacks appeal in the world's most powerful countries and has had little success in gaining control of even less powerful, predominantly Muslim countries.

Still, the twenty-first century is not necessarily destined to be free of conflict involving the strongest members of the international system. At the start of the century, China loomed as a potential disturber of the peace by virtue of its size, its surging economic growth, and its long premodern history of cultural and political primacy in East Asia. Together, these national characteristics could fuel a drive for enhanced power and status. * * *

With 450 million people, an economic output larger than that of any other political unit, and members with glorious histories of scientific discovery, cultural achievement, and global power, the EU has reason to expect to play a leading role in the world of the twenty-first century. * * *

At least in the early years of the twenty-first century, however, Europe was likely to follow neither path. In important ways the EU has had, and will continue to have, powerful effects on other countries. But as a source of governmental services to the international system, Europe seems destined, in the short term, to be neither a counterweight nor a makeweight but instead a lightweight.[2] * * *

For all their criticisms of it, the American role in the world enjoys other countries' tacit consent. More important than what others say about it is what they do, or rather what they choose not to do. They have chosen not to mount serious opposition to what the United States does in the world, something that they would do if they considered the United States dangerous to their interests. * * *

Nor do the recipients and beneficiaries of these services manifest enthusiasm either for what the United States does for them or for the American power that makes the services possible. If anything, the American global presence is unpopular. * * *

Still, in the world outside the United States, the case for Goliath enjoys at least tacit support. For while others may consider that presence annoying, even infuriating, they do not, apparently, find it intolerable. They do tolerate it, and for the same reason that Americans are willing to pay for it. Americans and non-Americans, whatever their differences, find the American international role to be convenient. The world needs governance and the United States is in a position to supply it.

## Notes

[1]See Daniel Pipes, *Militant Islam Reaches America* (New York: Norton, 2002), Part I.

[2]For the contrary argument, that Europe will become a global rival to the United States, see Charles Kupchan, *The End of the American Era: U.S. Foreign Policy and the Geopolitics of the Twenty-first Century* (New York: Knopf, 2002), especially chap. 4.

# *Superpower—But Can't Go It Alone*

7.2

Joseph S. Nye, Jr.

## The Paradox of American Power

How should Americans set our priorities in a global information age? What grand strategy would allow us to steer between the "imperial overstretch" that would arise out of the role of global policeman while avoiding the mistake of thinking the country can be isolated in this global information age? The place to start is by understanding the relationship of American power to global public goods. On one hand, . . . American power is less effective than it might first appear. We cannot do everything. On the other hand, the United States is likely to remain the most powerful country well into this century, and this gives us an interest in maintaining a degree of international order. More concretely, there is a simple reason why Americans have a national interest beyond our borders. Events out there can hurt us, and we want to influence distant governments and organizations on a variety of issues such as proliferation of weapons of mass destruction, terrorism, drugs, trade, resources, and ecological damage. After the Cold War, we ignored Afghanistan, but we discovered that even a poor, remote country can harbor forces that can harm us.

To a large extent, international order is a public good—something everyone can consume without diminishing its availability to others.[1] A small country can benefit from peace in its region, freedom of the seas, suppression of terrorism, open trade, control of infectious diseases, or stability in financial markets at the same time that the United States does without diminishing the benefits to the United States or others. Of course, pure public goods are rare. And sometimes things that look good in our eyes may look bad in the eyes of others. Too narrow an appeal to public goods can become a self-serving ideology for the powerful. But these caveats are a reminder to consult with others, not a reason to discard an important strategic principle that helps us set priorities and reconcile our national interests with a broader global perspective.

If the largest beneficiary of a public good (like the United States) does not take the lead in providing disproportionate resources to-

From *The Paradox of American Power: Why the World's Only Superpower Can't Go It Alone* (New York: Oxford University Press, 2002).

ward its provision, the smaller beneficiaries are unlikely to be able to produce it because of the difficulties of organizing collective action when large numbers are involved.[2] While this responsibility of the largest often lets others become "free riders," the alternative is that the collective bus does not move at all. (And our compensation is that the largest tends to have more control of the steering wheel.) . . .

Our grand strategy must first ensure our survival, but then it must focus on providing *global* public goods. We gain doubly from such a strategy: from the public goods themselves, and from the way they legitimize our power in the eyes of others. That means we should give top priority to those aspects of the international system that, if not attended to properly, would have profound effects on the basic international order and therefore on the lives of large numbers of Americans as well as others. The United States can learn from the lesson of Great Britain in the nineteenth century, when it was also a preponderant power. Three public goods that Britain attended to were (1) maintaining the balance of power among the major states in Europe, (2) promoting an open international economic system, and (3) maintaining open international commons such as the freedom of the seas and the suppression of piracy. . . .

All three translate relatively well to the current American situation. Maintaining regional balances of power and dampening local incentives to use force to change borders provides a public good for many (but not all countries). The United States helps to "shape the environment" (in the words of the Pentagon's quadrennial defense review) in various regions, and that is why even in normal times we keep roughly a hundred thousand troops forward-based in Europe, the same number in Asia, and some twenty thousand near the Persian Gulf. The American role as a stabilizer and reassurance against aggression by aspiring hegemons in key regions is a blue chip issue. . . .

Promoting an open international economic system is good for American economic growth and is good for other countries as well. Openness of global markets is a necessary (though not sufficient) condition for alleviating poverty in poor countries even as it benefits the United States. In addition, in the long run economic growth is most likely to foster stable, democratic middle-class societies in other countries, though the time scale may be quite lengthy. . . .

The United States, like nineteenth-century Britain, has an interest in keeping international commons, such as the oceans, open to all. . . . Today, however, the international commons include new issues such as global climate change, preservation of endangered species, and the uses of outer space, as well as the virtual commons of cyberspace. . . .

These three classic public goods [balance of power, open international economic systems, and open international commons] enjoy a reasonable consensus in American public opinion, and some can be provided in part through unilateral actions. But there are also three new dimensions of global public goods in today's world. First, the United States should help develop and maintain international regimes of laws and institutions that organize international action in various domains—not just trade and environment, but weapons proliferation, peacekeeping, human rights, terrorism, and other concerns. . . .

We should also make international development a higher priority, for it is an important global public good as well. Much of the poor majority of the world is in turmoil, mired in vicious circles of disease, poverty, and political instability. Large-scale financial and scientific help from rich countries is important not only for humanitarian reasons but also, as Harvard economist Jeffrey Sachs has argued, "because even remote countries become outposts of disorder for the rest of the world."[3] . . .

As a preponderant power, the United States can provide an important public good by acting as a mediator. By using our good offices to mediate conflicts in places such as Northern Ireland, the Middle East, or the Aegean Sea, the United States can help in shaping international order in ways that are beneficial to us as well as to other nations. It is sometimes tempting to let intractable conflicts fester, and there are some situations where other countries can more effectively play the mediator's role. Even when we do not want to take the lead, our participation can be essential—witness our work with Europe to try to prevent civil war in Macedonia. But often the United States is the only country that can bring together mortal enemies as in the Middle East peace process. And when we are successful, we enhance our reputation and increase our soft power at the same time that we reduce a source of instability. . . .

The United States should aim to work with other nations on global problems in a multilateral manner whenever possible. I agree with the recent bipartisan commission on our national security, chaired by former senators Gary Hart and Warren Rudman, which concluded that "emerging powers—either singly or in coalition—will increasingly constrain U.S. options regionally and limit its strategic influence. As a result we will remain limited in our ability to impose our will, and we will be vulnerable to an increasing range of threats." Borders will become more porous, rapid advances in information and biotechnologies will create new vulnerabilities, the United States will become "increasingly vulnerable to hostile attack on the American homeland, and the U.S. military superiority will not entirely protect us."[4] This means we must develop multilateral laws and institutions that constrain others and provide a framework for cooperation. In the words of the Hart-Rudman Commission, "America cannot secure and advance its own interests in isolation."[5] As the terrorist attacks of September 11 showed, even a superpower needs friends. . . .

Multilateralism involves costs, but *in the larger picture,* they are outweighed by the benefits. International rules bind the United States and limit our freedom of action in the short term, but they also serve our interest by finding others as well. Americans should use our power now to shape institutions that will serve our long-term national interest in promoting international order. "Since there is little reason for believing that the means of policy will be increased, we are left to rely on the greater cooperation of others. But the greater cooperation of others will mean that our freedom of action is narrowed."[6] It is not just that excessive unilateralism can hurt us; multilateralism is often the best way to achieve our long-run objectives.

## Notes

[1]For a full discussion of the complexity and problems of definition, see Inge Kaul, Isabelle Grunberg, and Marc A. Stern, eds., *Global Public Goods: International Cooperation in the 21st Century* (New York: Oxford University Press, 1999). Strictly defined, public goods are nonrivalrous and nonexclusionary.

[2]Mancur Olson, *The Logic of Collective Action: Public Goods and the Theory of Groups* (Cambridge, MA: Harvard University Press, 1965).

[3]Jeffrey Sachs, "What's Good for the Poor Is Good for America," *The Economist*, July 14, 2001, 32–33.

[4]United States Commission on National Security in the Twenty-first Century, *New World Coming: American Security in the 21st Century* (Washington, D.C., 2000), 4.

[5]United States Commission on National Security in the Twenty-first Century, *Roadmap for National Security: Imperative for Change, Phase III Report* (Washington, D.C., 2001), 2, 5.

[6]Robert W. Tucker in "American Power—For What? A Symposium," *Commentary*, January 2000, 46.

# *Bush Doctrine on Pre-Emption*

8.1

George W. Bush

## Pre-Emption and National Security Strategy

For much of the last century, America's defense relied on the Cold War doctrines of deterrence and containment. In some cases, these strategies still apply. But new threats also require new thinking. Deterrence—the promise of massive retaliation against nations—means nothing against shadowy terrorist networks with no nation or citizens to defend. Containment is not possible when unbalanced dictators with weapons of mass destruction can deliver those weapons on missiles or secretly provide them to terrorist allies. * * *

If we wait for threats to fully materialize, we will have waited too long. * * * [O]ur security will require all Americans to be forward-looking and resolute, to be ready for pre-emptive action when necessary to defend our liberty and to defend our lives.

* * *

The great struggles of the twentieth century between liberty and totalitarianism ended with a decisive victory for the forces of freedom—and a single sustainable model for national success: freedom, democracy, and free enterprise. In the twenty-first century, only nations that share a commitment to protecting basic human rights and guaranteeing political and economic freedom will be able to unleash the potential of their people and assure their future prosperity. People everywhere want to be able to speak freely; choose who will govern them; worship as the please; educate their children—male and female; own property; and enjoy the benefits of their labor. These values of freedom are right and true for every person, in every society—and the duty of protecting these values against their enemies is the common calling of freedom-loving people across the globe and across the ages.

Today, the United States enjoys a position of unparalleled military strength and great economic and political influence. In keeping with our heritage and principles, we do not use our strength to press for unilateral advantage. We seek instead to create a balance of power that favors human freedom: conditions in which all nations and all societies can choose for them-

First two paragraphs are from George W. Bush, Commencement Address, U.S. Military Academy, West Point, New York, June 1, 2002, http://georgewbush-whitehouse.archives.gov/news/releases/2002/06/20020601-3.html (accessed 9/23/09); rest from George W. Bush, "The National Security Strategy of the United States of America," September 17, 2002, http://georgewbush-whitehouse.archives.gov/nsc/nss/2002/index.html (accessed 9/23/09).

selves the rewards and challenges of political and economic liberty. In a world that is safe, people will be able to make their own lives better. We will defend the peace by fighting terrorists and tyrants. We will preserve the peace by building good relations among the great powers. We will extend the peace by encouraging free and open societies on every continent.

Defending our nation against enemies is the first and fundamental commitment of the Federal Government. Today, that task has changed dramatically. Enemies in the past needed great armies and great industrial capabilities to endanger America. Now, shadowy networks of individuals can bring great chaos and suffering to our shores for less than it costs to purchase a single tank. Terrorists are organized to penetrate open societies and to turn the power of modern technologies against us.

To defeat this threat we must make use of every tool in our arsenal—military power, better homeland defenses, law enforcement, intelligence, and vigorous efforts to cut off terrorist financing. The war against terrorists of global reach is a global enterprise of uncertain duration. America will help nations that need our assistance in combating terror. And America will hold to account nations that are compromised by terror, including those who harbor terrorists—because the allies of terror are the enemies of civilization. The United States and countries cooperating with us must not allow the terrorists to develop new home bases. Together, we will seek to deny them sanctuary at every turn.

The gravest danger our nation faces lies at the crossroads of radicalism and technology. Our enemies have openly declared that they are seeking weapons of mass destruction, and evidence indicates that they are doing so with determination. The United States will not allow these efforts to succeed. We will build defenses against ballistic missiles and other means of delivery. We will cooperate with other nations to deny, contain, and curtail our enemies' efforts to acquire dangerous technologies. And, as a matter of common sense and self-defense, America will act against such emerging threats before they are fully formed. We cannot defend America and our friends by hoping for the best. So we must be prepared to defeat our enemies' plans, using the best intelligence and proceeding with deliberation. History will judge harshly those who saw this coming danger but failed to act. In the new world we have entered, the only path to peace and security is the path of action. * * *

The struggle against global terrorism is different from any other war in our history. It will be fought on many fronts against a particularly elusive enemy over an extended period of time. Progress will come through persistent accumulation of successes—some seen, some unseen. * * *

While the United States will constantly strive to enlist the support of the international community, we will not hesitate to act alone, if necessary, to exercise our right of self-defense by acting preemptively against such terrorists, to prevent them from doing harm against our people and our country. * * *

In the war against global terrorism, we will never forget that we are ultimately fighting for our democratic values and way of life. Freedom and fear are at war, and there will be no quick or easy end to this conflict. In leading the campaign against terrorism, we are forging new, productive international relationships and redefining existing ones in ways that meet the challenges of the twenty-first century.

# *Bush Doctrine Critique*

8.2

G. JOHN IKENBERRY

## America's Imperial Ambition

### The Lures of Preemption

In the shadows of the Bush administration's war on terrorism, sweeping new ideas are circulating about U.S. grand strategy and the restructuring of today's unipolar world. They call for American unilateral and preemptive, even preventive, use of force, facilitated if possible by coalitions of the willing—but ultimately unconstrained by the rules and norms of the international community. At the extreme, these notions form a neoimperial vision in which the United States arrogates to itself the global role of setting standards, determining threats, using force, and meting out justice. It is a vision in which sovereignty becomes more absolute for America even as it becomes more conditional for countries that challenge Washington's standards of internal and external behavior. It is a vision made necessary—at least in the eyes of its advocates—by the new and apocalyptic character of contemporary terrorist threats and by America's unprecedented global dominance. These radical strategic ideas and impulses could transform today's world order in a way that the end of the Cold War, strangely enough, did not.

* * *

### A New Grand Strategy

For the first time since the dawn of the Cold War, a new grand strategy is taking shape in Washington. It is advanced most directly as a response to terrorism, but it also constitutes a broader view about how the United States should wield power and organize world order. According to this new paradigm, America is to be less bound to its partners and to global rules and institutions while it steps forward to play a more unilateral and anticipatory role in attacking terrorist threats and confronting rogue states seeking WMD [weapons of mass destruction]. The United States will use its unrivaled military power to manage the global order.

* * *

From *Foreign Affairs* 81.5 (September–October 2002).

## Imperial Dangers

Pitfalls accompany this neoimperial grand strategy, however. Unchecked U.S. power, shorn of legitimacy and disentangled from the postwar norms and institutions of the international order, will usher in a more hostile international system, making it far harder to achieve American interests. The secret of the United States' long brilliant run as the world's leading state was its ability and willingness to exercise power within alliance and multinational frameworks, which made its power and agenda more acceptable to allies and other key states around the world. This achievement has now been put at risk by the administration's new thinking.

* * *

The specific doctrine of preemptive action poses a related problem: once the United States feels it can take such a course, nothing will stop other countries from doing the same. Does the United States want this doctrine in the hands of Pakistan, or even China or Russia? After all, it would not require the intervening state to first provide evidence for its actions. The United States argues that to wait until all the evidence is in, or until authoritative international bodies support action, is to wait too long. Yet that approach is the only basis that the United States can use if it needs to appeal for restraint in the actions of others. Moreover, and quite paradoxically, overwhelming American conventional military might, combined with a policy of preemptive strikes, could lead hostile states to accelerate programs to acquire their only possible deterrent to the United States: WMD. This is another version of the security dilemma, but one made worse by a neoimperial grand strategy.

Another problem follows. The use of force to eliminate WMD capabilities or overturn dangerous regimes is never simple, whether it is pursued unilaterally or by a concert of major states. After the military intervention is over, the target country has to be put back together. Peacekeeping and state building are inevitably required, as are long-term strategies that bring the UN, the World Bank, and the major powers together to orchestrate aid and other forms of assistance. This is not heroic work, but it is utterly necessary. Peacekeeping troops may be required for many years, even after a new regime is built. Regional conflicts inflamed by outside military intervention must also be calmed. This is the "long tail" of burdens and commitments that comes with every major military action.

When these costs and obligations are added to America's imperial military role, it becomes even more doubtful that the neoimperial strategy can be sustained at home over the long haul—the classic problem of imperial overstretch. The United States could keep its military predominance for decades if it is supported by a growing and increasingly productive economy. But the indirect burdens of cleaning up the political mess in terrorist-prone failed states levy a hidden cost. Peacekeeping and state building will require coalitions of states and multilateral agencies that can be brought into the process only if the initial decisions about military intervention are hammered out in consultation with other major states. America's older realist and liberal grand strategies suddenly become relevant again.

A third problem with an imperial grand strategy is that it cannot generate the cooperation needed to solve practical problems at the heart of the U.S. foreign policy agenda. In the fight on terrorism, the United States needs cooperation from European and Asian countries in intelligence, law enforcement, and logistics. Outside the security sphere, realizing U.S. objectives depends even more on a continuous stream of amicable working relations with major states around the world. It needs partners for trade liberalization, global financial stabilization, environmental protection, deterring transnational organized crime, managing the rise of China, and a host of other thorny challenges. But it is impossible to expect would-be partners to acquiesce to America's self-appointed global security protectorate and then pursue business as usual in all other domains.

The key policy tool for states confronting a unipolar and unilateral America is to withhold cooperation in day-to-day relations with the United States. One obvious means is trade policy; the European response to the recent American decision to impose tariffs on imported steel is explicable in these terms. This particular struggle concerns specific trade issues, but it is also a struggle over how Washington exercises power. The United States may be a unipolar military power, but economic and political power is more evenly distributed across the globe. The major states may not have much leverage in directly restraining American military policy, but they can make the United States pay a price in other areas.

Finally, the neoimperial grand strategy poses a wider problem for the maintenance of American unipolar power. It steps into the oldest trap of powerful imperial states: self-encirclement. When the most powerful state in the world throws its weight around, unconstrained by rules or norms of legitimacy, it risks a backlash. Other countries will bridle at an international order in which the United States plays only by its own rules. The proponents of the new grand strategy have assumed that the United States can single-handedly deploy military power abroad and not suffer untoward consequences; relations will be coarser with friends and allies, they believe, but such are the costs of leadership. But history shows that powerful states tend to trigger self-encirclement by their own overestimation of their power. Charles V, Louis XIV, Napoleon, and the leaders of post-Bismarck Germany sought to expand their imperial domains and impose a coercive order on others. Their imperial orders were all brought down when other countries decided they were not prepared to live in a world dominated by an overweening coercive state. America's imperial goals and modus operandi are much more limited and benign than were those of age-old emperors. But a hard-line imperial grand strategy runs the risk that history will repeat itself.

## Bring in the Old

Wars change world politics, and so too will America's war on terrorism. How great states fight wars, how they define the stakes, how they make the peace in its aftermath—all give lasting shape to the international system that emerges after the guns fall silent. In mobilizing their societies for battle, wartime leaders have tended to describe the military struggle as more than simply the defeat of an enemy. Woodrow Wilson sent U.S. troops to Europe not only to stop the kaiser's army but to destroy militarism and usher in a worldwide democratic revolution. Franklin Roosevelt saw the war with

Germany and Japan as a struggle to secure the "four great freedoms." The Atlantic Charter was a statement of war aims that called not just for the defeat of fascism but for a new dedication to social welfare and human rights within an open and stable world system. To advance these visions, Wilson and Roosevelt proposed new international rules and mechanisms of cooperation. Their message was clear: If you bear the burdens of war, we, your leaders, will use this dreadful conflict to usher in a more peaceful and decent order among states. Fighting the war had as much to do with building global relations as it did with vanquishing an enemy.

Bush has not fully articulated a vision of postwar international order, aside from defining the struggle as one between freedom and evil. The world has seen Washington take determined steps to fight terrorism, but it does not yet have a sense of Bush's larger, positive agenda for a strengthened and more decent international order.

This failure explains why the sympathy and goodwill generated around the world for the United States after September 11 quickly disappeared. Newspapers that once proclaimed, "We are all Americans," now express distrust toward America. The prevailing view is that the United States seems prepared to use its power to go after terrorists and evil regimes, but not to use it to help build a more stable and peaceful world order. The United States appears to be degrading the rules and institutions of international community, not enhancing them. To the rest of the world, neoimperial thinking has more to do with exercising power than with exercising leadership.

In contrast, America's older strategic orientations—balance-of-power realism and liberal multilateralism—suggest a mature world power that seeks stability and pursues its interests in ways that do not fundamentally threaten the positions of other states. They are strategies of co-option and reassurance. The new imperial grand strategy presents the United States very differently: a revisionist state seeking to parlay its momentary power advantages into a world order in which it runs the show. Unlike the hegemonic states of the past, the United States does not seek territory or outright political domination in Europe or Asia; "America has no empire to extend or utopia to establish," Bush noted in his West Point address. But the sheer power advantages that the United States possesses and the doctrines of preemption and counterterrorism that it is articulating do unsettle governments and people around the world. The costs could be high. The last thing the United States wants is for foreign diplomats and government leaders to ask, How can we work around, undermine, contain, and retaliate against U.S. power?

Rather than invent a new grand strategy, the United States should reinvigorate its older strategies, those based on the view that America's security partnerships are not simply instrumental tools but critical components of an American-led world political order that should be preserved. U.S. power is both leveraged and made more legitimate and user-friendly by these partnerships. The neoimperial thinkers are haunted by the specter of catastrophic terrorism and seek a radical reordering of America's role in the world. America's commanding unipolar power and the advent of frightening new terrorist threats feed this imperial temptation. But it is a grand strategic vision that, taken to the extreme, will leave the world more dangerous and divided—and the United States less secure.

# *A Global Strategy against Terrorism*

8.3

9/11 COMMISSION

## Final Report of the National Commission on Terrorist Attacks upon the United States

Three years after 9/11, Americans are still thinking and talking about how to protect our nation in this new era. The national debate continues.

Countering terrorism has become, beyond any doubt, the top national security priority for the United States. This shift has occurred with the full support of the Congress, both major political parties, the media, and the American people.

The nation has committed enormous resources to national security and to countering terrorism. Between fiscal year 2001, the last budget adopted before 9/11, and the present fiscal year 2004, total federal spending on defense (including expenditures on both Iraq and Afghanistan), homeland security, and international affairs rose more than 50 percent, from $354 billion to about $547 billion. The United States has not experienced such a rapid surge in national security spending since the Korean War.

This pattern has occurred before in American history. The United States faces a sudden crisis and summons a tremendous exertion of national energy. Then, as that surge transforms the landscape, comes a time for reflection and reevaluation. Some programs and even agencies are discarded; others are invented or redesigned. Private firms and engaged citizens redefine their relationships with government, working through the processes of the American republic.

Now is the time for that reflection and reevaluation. The United States should consider *what to do*—the shape and objectives of a strategy. Americans should also consider *how to do it*—organizing their government in a different way.

### Defining the Threat

In the post-9/11 world, threats are defined more by the fault lines within societies than by the territorial boundaries between them. From terrorism to global disease or environmental degradation, the challenges have become transnational rather than international.

From *Final Report of the National Commission on Terrorist Attacks upon the United States* (New York: Norton, 2004).

That is the defining quality of world politics in the twenty-first century.

National security used to be considered by studying foreign frontiers, weighing opposing groups of states, and measuring industrial might. To be dangerous, an enemy had to muster large armies. Threats emerged slowly, often visibly, as weapons were forged, armies conscripted, and units trained and moved into place. Because large states were more powerful, they also had more to lose. They could be deterred.

Now threats can emerge quickly. An organization like al Qaeda, headquartered in a country on the other side of the earth, in a region so poor that electricity or telephones were scarce, could nonetheless scheme to wield weapons of unprecedented destructive power in the largest cities of the United States.

In this sense, 9/11 has taught us that terrorism against American interests "over there" should be regarded just as we regard terrorism against America "over here." In this same sense, the American homeland is the planet.

But the enemy is not just "terrorism," some generic evil. This vagueness blurs the strategy. The catastrophic threat at this moment in history is more specific. It is the threat posed by *Islamist* terrorism—especially the al Qaeda network, its affiliates, and its ideology.

As we mentioned in chapter 2, Usama Bin Ladin and other Islamist terrorist leaders draw on a long tradition of extreme intolerance within one stream of Islam (a minority tradition), from at least Ibn Taimiyyah, through the founders of Wahhabism, through the Muslim Brotherhood, to Sayyid Qutb. That stream is motivated by religion and does not distinguish politics from religion, thus distorting both. It is further fed by grievances stressed by Bin Ladin and widely felt throughout the Muslim world—against the U.S. military presence in the Middle East, policies perceived as anti-Arab and anti-Muslim, and support of Israel. Bin Ladin and Islamist terrorists mean exactly what they say: to them America is the font of all evil, the "head of the snake," and it must be converted or destroyed.

It is not a position with which Americans can bargain or negotiate. With it there is no common ground—not even respect for life—on which to begin a dialogue. It can only be destroyed or utterly isolated.

Because the Muslim world has fallen behind the West politically, economically, and militarily for the past three centuries, and because few tolerant or secular Muslim democracies provide alternative models for the future, Bin Ladin's message finds receptive ears. It has attracted active support from thousands of disaffected young Muslims and resonates powerfully with a far larger number who do not actively support his methods. The resentment of America and the West is deep, even among leaders of relatively successful Muslim states.

Tolerance, the rule of law, political and economic openness, the extension of greater opportunities to women—these cures must come from within Muslim societies themselves. The United States must support such developments.

But this process is likely to be measured in decades, not years. It is a process that will be violently opposed by Islamist terrorist organizations, both inside Muslim countries and in attacks on the United States and other Western nations. The United States finds itself caught up in a clash *within* a civilization. That clash arises from particular conditions in the Muslim world, conditions that spill over into expatriate Muslim communities in non-Muslim countries.

Our enemy is twofold: al Qaeda, a stateless network of terrorists that struck us on 9/11; and a radical ideological movement in the Islamic world, inspired in part by al Qaeda, which has spawned terrorist groups and violence across the globe. The first enemy is weakened, but continues to pose a grave threat. The second enemy is gathering, and will menace Americans and American interests long after Usama Bin Ladin and his cohorts are killed or captured. Thus our strategy must match our means to two ends: dismantling the al Qaeda network and prevailing in the longer term over the ideology that gives rise to Islamist terrorism.

Islam is not the enemy. It is not synonymous with terror. Nor does Islam teach terror. America and its friends oppose a perversion of Islam, not the great world faith itself. Lives guided by religious faith, including literal beliefs in holy scriptures, are common to every religion, and represent no threat to us.

Other religions have experienced violent internal struggles. With so many diverse adherents, every major religion will spawn violent religious zealots. Yet understanding and tolerance among people of different faiths can and must prevail. The present transnational danger is Islamist terrorism. What is needed is a broad political-military strategy that rests on a firm tripod of policies to

- attack terrorists and their organizations;
- prevent the continued growth of Islamist terrorism; and
- protect against and prepare for terrorist attacks.

## More Than a War on Terrorism

Terrorism is a tactic used by individuals and organizations to kill and destroy. Our effort should be directed at those individuals and organizations.

Calling this struggle a war accurately describes the use of American and allied armed forces to find and destroy terrorist groups and their allies in the field, notably in Afghanistan. The language of war also evokes the mobilization for a national effort. Yet the strategy should be balanced.

The first phase of our post-9/11 efforts rightly included military action to topple the Taliban and pursue al Qaeda. This work continues. But long-term success demands the use of all elements of national power: diplomacy, intelligence, covert action, law enforcement, economic policy, foreign aid, public diplomacy, and homeland defense. If we favor one tool while neglecting others, we leave ourselves vulnerable and weaken our national effort.

Certainly the strategy should include offensive operations to counter terrorism. Terrorists should no longer find safe haven where their organizations can grow and flourish. America's strategy should be a coalition strategy that includes Muslim nations as partners in its development and implementation.

Our effort should be accompanied by a preventive strategy that is as much, or more, political as it is military. The strategy must focus clearly on the Arab and Muslim world, in all its variety.

Our strategy should also include defenses. America can be attacked in many ways and has many vulnerabilities. No defenses are perfect. But risks must be calculated; hard choices must be made about allocating resources. Responsibilities for America's defense should be clearly defined. Planning does make a difference, identifying where a little money might have a large effect. Defenses also complicate the plans of attackers, increasing their risks of discovery and failure. Finally, the nation must prepare to deal with attacks that are not stopped.

# The Responsibility to Protect

9.1

INTERNATIONAL COMMISSION ON INTERVENTION AND STATE SOVEREIGNTY

## The Case for Humanitarian Intervention

### The Responsibility to Protect: Core Principles

(1) BASIC PRINCIPLES

A. State sovereignty implies responsibility, and the primary responsibility for the protection of its people lies with the state itself.

B. Where a population is suffering serious harm, as a result of internal war, insurgency, repression or state failure, and the state in question is unwilling or unable to halt or avert it, the principle of non-intervention yields to the international responsibility to protect.

(2) FOUNDATIONS

The foundations of the responsibility to protect, as a guiding principle for the international community of states, lie in:

A. obligations inherent in the concept of sovereignty;

B. the responsibility of the Security Council, under Article 24 of the UN Charter, for the maintenance of international peace and security;

C. specific legal obligations under human rights and human protection declarations, covenants and treaties, international humanitarian law and national law;

D. the developing practice of states, regional organizations and the Security Council itself.

(3) ELEMENTS

The responsibility to protect embraces three specific responsibilities:

A. The responsibility to prevent: to address both the root causes and direct causes of internal conflict and other man-made crises putting populations at risk;

B. The responsibility to react: to respond to situations of compelling human need with appropriate measures, which may include coercive measures like sanctions and international prosecution, and in extreme cases military intervention.

C. The responsibility to rebuild: to provide, particularly after a military intervention, full assistance with recovery, reconstruction and reconciliation, ad-

---

From *The Responsibility to Protect* (Ottawa, Canada: International Development Research Centre, 2001).

dressing the causes of the harm the intervention was designed to halt or avert.

(4) PRIORITIES

A. Prevention is the single most important dimension of the responsibility to protect: prevention options should always be exhausted before intervention is contemplated, and more commitment and resources must be devoted to it.

B. The exercise of the responsibility to both prevent and react should always involve less intrusive and coercive measures being considered before more coercive and intrusive ones are applied.

## The Responsibility to Protect: Principles for Military Intervention

(1) THE JUST CAUSE THRESHOLD

Military intervention for human protection purposes is an exceptional and extraordinary measure. To be warranted, there must be serious and irreparable harm occurring to human beings, or imminently likely to occur, of the following kind:

A. large scale loss of life, actual or apprehended, with genocidal intent or not, which is the product either of deliberate state action, or state neglect or inability to act, or a failed state situation; or

B. large scale 'ethnic cleansing', actual or apprehended, whether carried out by killing, forced expulsion, acts of terror or rape.

(2) THE PRECAUTIONARY PRINCIPLES

A. Right intention: The primary purpose of the intervention, whatever other motives intervening states may have, must be to halt or avert human suffering. Right intention is better assured with multilateral operations, clearly supported by regional opinion and the victims concerned.

B. Last resort: Military intervention can only be justified when every non-military option for the prevention or peaceful resolution of the crisis has been explored, with reasonable grounds for believing lesser measures would not have succeeded.

C. Proportional means: The scale, duration and intensity of the planned military intervention should be the minimum necessary to secure the defined human protection objective.

D. Reasonable prospects: There must be a reasonable chance of success in halting or averting the suffering which has justified the intervention, with the consequences of action not likely to be worse than the consequences of inaction.

(3) RIGHT AUTHORITY

A. There is no better or more appropriate body than the United Nations Security Council to authorize military intervention for human protection purposes. The task is not to find alternatives to the Security Council as a source of authority, but to make the Security Council work better than it has.

B. Security Council authorization should in all cases be sought prior to any military intervention action being carried out. Those calling for an intervention should formally request such authorization, or have the Council raise the matter on its own initiative, or have the Secretary-General raise it under Article 99 of the UN Charter.

C. The Security Council should deal promptly with any request for authority to intervene where there are allegations of large scale loss of human life or ethnic cleansing. It should in this context seek adequate verification of facts or conditions on the ground that might support a military intervention.

D. The Permanent Five members of the Security Council should agree not to apply their veto power, in matters where their vital state interests are not involved, to obstruct the passage of resolutions authorizing military intervention for human protection purposes for which there is otherwise majority support.

E. If the Security Council rejects a proposal or fails to deal with it in a reasonable time, alternative options are:

   I. consideration of the matter by the General Assembly in Emergency Special Session under the "Uniting for Peace" procedure; and

   II. action within the area of jurisdiction by regional or sub-regional organizations under Chapter VIII of the Charter, subject to their seeking subsequent authorization from the Security Council.

F. The Security Council should take into account in all its deliberations that, if it fails to discharge its responsibility to protect in conscience-shocking situations crying out for action, concerned states may not rule out other means to meet the gravity and urgency of that situation – and that the stature and credibility of the United Nations may suffer thereby.

(4) OPERATIONAL PRINCIPLES

A. Clear objectives; clear and unambiguous mandate at all times; and resources to match.

B. Common military approach among involved partners; unity of command; clear and unequivocal communications and chain of command.

C. Acceptance of limitations, incrementalism and gradualism in the application of force, the objective being protection of a population, not defeat of a state.

D. Rules of engagement which fit the operational concept; are precise; reflect the principle of proportionality; and involve total adherence to international humanitarian law.

E. Acceptance that force protection cannot become the principal objective.

F. Maximum possible coordination with humanitarian organizations.

# *From "Yet Again" to "Never Again"*



GENOCIDE PREVENTION TASK FORCE

## Preventing Genocide: A Blueprint for U.S. Policymakers

*These are some of the policy recommendations made by the Genocide Prevention Task Force at the beginning of the Obama administration.*

## Leadership

### *To the President*

- Under presidential leadership, the administration should develop and promulgate a government-wide policy on preventing genocide and mass atrocities.
- The president should launch a major diplomatic initiative to strengthen global efforts to prevent genocide and mass atrocities.

### *To the Leaders of Congress*

- Congress should increase funding for crisis prevention and response initiatives, and should make a portion of these funds available for rapid allocation for urgent activities to prevent or halt emerging genocidal crises.

### *To the American People*

- The American people should build a permanent constituency for the prevention of genocide and mass atrocities.

## Early Warning: Assessing Risks and Triggering Action

- The national security advisor and the director of national intelligence should establish genocide early warning as a formal priority for the intelligence community as a means to improve reporting and assessments on the potential for genocide and mass atrocities.
- The State Department and the intelligence community should incorporate training on early warning of genocide and mass atrocities into programs for foreign service and intelligence officers and analysts.
- The State Department and USAID should expand ongoing cooperation with other governments, the United Na-

---

From *Preventing Genocide: A Blueprint for U.S. Policymakers* (Washington D.C.: U.S. Holocaust Memorial Museum, American Academy of Diplomacy, U.S. Institute of Peace, 2008), pp. 111–14.

tions, regional organizations, NGOs, and other civil society actors on early warning of genocide and mass atrocities.

## Early Prevention: Engaging before the Crisis

- Early prevention strategies should support development of institutions in high-risk states by supporting power sharing and democratic transition, enhancing the rule of law and addressing impunity, and reforming security forces.
- Early prevention strategies should aim to strengthen civil society in high-risk states by supporting economic and legal empowerment, citizen groups, and a free and responsible media.

## Preventive Diplomacy: Halting and Reversing Escalation

- The new high-level interagency committee—the Atrocities Prevention Committee—should meet every other month (and as needed at other times) to review the status of countries of concern and coordinate preventive action.
- Preventive diplomacy strategies should include the credible threat of coercive measures, should avoid an overly rigid "escalatory ladder," and should not dismiss potential benefits of rewarding "bad people" for "good behavior."

## Employing Military Options

- The secretary of defense and U.S. military leaders should develop military guidance on genocide prevention and response and incorporate it into Department of Defense (and interagency) policies, plans, doctrine, training, and lessons learned.
- The Departments of Defense and State should work to enhance the capacity of the United Nations, as well as the African Union, the Economic Community of West African States, and other regional and subregional bodies to employ military options to prevent and halt genocide and mass atrocities.
- The Departments of Defense and State should work with NATO, the European Union, and capable individual governments to increase preparedness to reinforce or replace United Nations, African Union, or other peace operations to forestall mass atrocities.

## International Action: Strengthening Norms and Institutions

- The secretary of state should launch a major diplomatic initiative to create among like-minded governments, international organizations, and NGOs a formal network dedicated to the prevention of genocide and mass atrocities.
- The secretary of state should undertake robust diplomatic efforts toward negotiating an agreement among the permanent members of the United Nations Security Council on non-use of the veto in cases concerning genocide or mass atrocities.

# *The Media and Foreign Policy*

9.3

WARREN P. STROBEL

## The Media and U.S. Policies Toward Intervention: A Closer Look at the "CNN Effect"

With the rise of "real-time" television in the 1980s, the growth of Ted Turner's 24-hour-a-day Cable News Network (CNN), and the deployment of news media technologies that can transmit video signals to and from virtually anywhere on the planet, government officials, legislators, media professionals, and scholars have voiced growing concern that journalists are exercising an irresistible control over western foreign policy.[1] It is said that dramatic images of starving masses, shelled populations, or dead American soldiers spark ill-considered public demands for action from elected officials. These temporary emotional responses may conflict with the more considered judgment of foreign policy officials, forcing them to take action that will soon have to be reversed or modified.

While the term "CNN effect" has numerous definitions and includes a range of phenomena, at heart it is understood to be a loss of policy control on the part of government policymakers.[2] CNN, it is said, makes, or at least exercises inordinate influence on, policy. * * *

This essay argues that these concerns, while understandable in the light of recent international changes, are misplaced. The CNN effect is grossly exaggerated, operating in few, if any, of the cases where it is most commonly cited. The media's effect on foreign policy is far more complex than the CNN-effect label would suggest, and far more dependent on the policy actions of government officials themselves than is seen to be the case. It is true that U.S. government policies and actions regarding international conflict are subject to more open public review than previously in history. But policymakers retain great power to frame events and solicit public support—indeed, CNN at times increases this power. Put another way, if officials do not have a firm and well-considered policy or have failed to communicate their views in such a way as to garner the support of the American people, the news media will fill this vacuum (often by giving greater time and attention to the criticism or policy preferences of its opponents). In this regard, little has changed since Daniel Hallin, studying the reporting of the Vietnam War, an

From *Managing Global Chaos: Sources of and Responses to International Conflict,* Chester A. Crocker and Fen Osler Hampson with Pamela Aall, eds. (Washington, D.C.: U.S. Institute of Peace Press, 1996).

era of much less sophisticated media technology, concluded that the news media's impact is intimately related to the consensus of society as a whole.[3] What *has* changed is the speed with which the news media can expose such gaps.

This analysis will examine the CNN effect as it applies to prospective or actual U.S. interventions in what are now called peace operations or operations other than war.[4] My conclusions are based on more than 100 interviews conducted during 1994–1995 with four main groups: senior policymakers from the Bush and Clinton administrations; military spokespersons and other U.S. officers (primarily from the Army and Marine Corps); print, radio, and television journalists, primarily from U.S. news organizations; and personnel from the United Nations, other international governmental organizations (IGOs), and nongovernmental organizations (NGOs). The findings can be summarized as follows:

- Graphic televised images hold no power to force U.S. policymakers to intervene in a civil conflict where there is no clear national interest.
- There seems to be an inverse relationship between the power of images on policymakers and the presumed costs of intervention. (At the time of the decision, the costs of U.S. action in Somalia appeared to be low.)
- Images do add to the pressures on policymakers to address humanitarian aspects of a crisis, but the news media are not the agenda-setters they are often portrayed to be. Government relief officials, other relief agencies, and U.S. lawmakers play key roles in drawing news media attention to such suffering.
- Because public and media pressures are not specific, policymakers often react with what might be called a minimalist response, attempting to signal more of a policy change than has actually taken place.
- There is evidence that the power of televised images to provoke emotional responses is diminishing as conflict and humanitarian need become ubiquitous features of the post–Cold War era, at least as portrayed on television.
- Media reports have a greater impact when executive branch policy is in flux or is poorly articulated.
- The prevalence of real-time media reports often contracts the policymaking process, giving officials less time before they must respond publicly. But this does not mean the media automatically determine policy outcomes.

In short, the CNN effect does not exist in many places where it is said to be found, and even where its traces can be detected, they are exaggerated, working only in combination with other factors.

* * *

## Stepping Back

* * *

The overarching U.S.-Soviet struggle provided a context within which administration officials could explain their policies to the news media and, in turn, helped the news media explain to readers and viewers the significance of complex and far-off events. The news media were more supportive than is usually remembered of U.S. foreign policy aims during the Cold War. Until the 1968 Tet offensive, the television networks and prestige newspapers such as the *New York Times* largely agreed with the White House's claim of the strategic importance of South Vietnam. Journalists such as the *Times*' David Halberstam criticized the means, not the ends.[5]

The end of the Cold War has deprived American administrations of a ready context in which to explain their policies and created a sort of meta-vacuum. This, the media have filled using their own professional ideology, which puts a high premium on crisis, drama, and unfilled humanitarian needs.[6]

* * *

## Somalia: Who Set the Agenda?

Because it is widely accepted that television images of starving civilians, especially children, forced President George H. W. Bush to dispatch U.S. military forces to Somalia in the fall of 1992, this is a good place to begin a more detailed examination of the news media's impact on U.S. intervention policy. This analysis challenges that widely held belief on three counts. First, the levels of television coverage were incompatible with the types of pressure usually associated with the CNN effect: Sharp increases in the levels of television reporting tended to *follow* administration actions, rather than precede them. Second, the television coverage (and other media attention) that did take place was almost always a result, not of media initiative and agenda-setting, but of deliberate and successful attempts by others to stir up media interest in Somalia in order to move policy. These "others" were a loose coalition of U.S. government relief officials, interested members of Congress, and representatives of NGOs and IGOs. Their efforts highlight the growing role in particular of nongovernmental or supragovernmental bodies in international relations.[7] Finally, interviews with numerous Bush administration officials made it clear that they intervened in Somalia largely because they expected it to be an exercise with low costs and high political benefit. Simultaneously, President Bush was wrestling with the question of a potential U.S. intervention in the former Yugoslavia, which senior officials agreed would require tens of thousands of U.S. ground troops. Somalia was chosen partly because it was easier and would relieve pressure for action in the Balkans.

Even a cursory look at patterns of coverage of Somalia by the three U.S. broadcast television networks and by CNN raises questions about the impact of these media on the decision to intervene in Somalia. President Bush's first major decision regarding Somalia, one that "created an activist consensus in the national security bureaucracy where none had existed earlier,"[8] was to begin an airlift of emergency food supplies to drought-affected areas in Somalia and northern Kenya. This decision was announced August 14, 1992, although it had been made two days earlier. Prior to August 14, there were only fifteen network evening news stories in 1992 that mentioned Somalia; six of them were merely fleeting glimpses of Somalia's plight as part of one-minute or forty-second "round-ups" of news from around the world. CNN coverage patterns were roughly similar, with the exception of a burst of coverage in May stemming from a single correspondent's ten-day visit to Somalia. Once the airlift decision was announced, television coverage jumped to unprecedented levels, remaining relatively high in September, and then almost vanishing in October, no doubt overshadowed by the upcoming 1992 presidential election. Rather than television bringing U.S. troops and airplanes to Somalia in the first place, it was Bush's policy action that attracted increased media attention, with dozens of journalists descending on the country to report on the airlift. Of course, once there, they sent back more reports about the horrible conditions in the countryside. This pattern was repeated in November, prior to Bush's November 25 decision to launch Operation Restore Hope, the dispatch of nearly 30,000 U.S. troops to guard relief supplies. Somalia returned to television's agenda in mid-November, but it was Bush's decision that sparked the most intense media coverage.

* * * Nonetheless, once the images of starvation appeared on American television screens, they did have some further effect. Secretary of State James A. Baker III asked the rhetorical question of whether Bush would have dispatched troops to Somalia in December 1992 absent those images: "We probably wouldn't have," he concluded.[9] The next question is why they had an impact. The answer seems to be that senior Bush administration officials all believed that the Somalia intervention would be low in costs, especially casualties, and high in benefit. One of those benefits was to ease the simultaneous pressure the administration was feeling in the fall of 1992 to engage in a potentially much more costly intervention: the former Yugoslavia. Baker; his successor, Lawrence Eagleburger; and Brent Scowcroft, National Security Adviser to George H. W. Bush, all used virtually the same words: There was an easy consensus within the administration on doing something about Somalia.[10] In other words, the images from Somalia operated only on a narrow portion of the spectrum of national security concerns: a humanitarianism crisis that seemed to be an "easy fix."

* * *

In summary, the case most often held up as an example of the CNN effect—Somalia—falls apart under close examination. It was not the media that set the agenda in the fall of 1992, but the Bush administration itself, the Congress, and relief officials in and out of government. The horrible images did have an effect, but a narrow one. Reflecting on the experience, [Assistant Secretary of State Robert] Gallucci said that pictures "don't come anywhere near" forcing an introduction of U.S. ground troops when it is known they will be in harm's way.

"When you're short of that, then the pictures are very useful in getting people to focus on it as a basis for humanitarian support." For anything more than that, "it's gotta answer the question, Why us?" It is to these limits of media power that we now turn our attention.

## Bosnia: The Limits of Images' Power

* * * [T]here were two points at which news media pressure for intervention [in Yugoslavia] were at their most intense. The first

was in August 1992, with the revelations, first by [Roy] Gutman in *Newsday* and then on Britain's Independent Television Network (ITN), of the murder and gross mistreatment of Bosnian Muslims in Serb-run concentration camps. The second, the televised bloody aftermath of the February 1994 "marketplace massacre" in Sarajevo, will be examined in a moment.

Gutman's Pulitzer Prize–winning reports in *Newsday* and the vivid ITN images of emaciated men behind barbed wire, recalling as they did the Holocaust, caused an emotional reaction around the world. In the United States, journalists, lawmakers, and other politicians—including presidential candidate Bill Clinton—demanded action to stop the abuses. Yet by this time, the Bush administration had looked at the question of intervention in the former Yugoslavia, and determined it was an abyss that would draw in thousands of U.S. ground troops for an indefinite period (Clinton would later come to this same conclusion). Two factors about this policy decision are important in determining why the media had so little effect: The decision was firmly held, and it was shared by all the senior members of Bush's national security team. As Warren Zimmermann, the last U.S. ambassador to Yugoslavia, put it: "It wouldn't have mattered if television was going 24 hours around the clock with Serb atrocities. Bush wasn't going to get in."[11] Eagleburger used virtually identical language, saying: "Through all the time we were there, you have to understand that we had largely made a decision we were not going to get militarily involved. And nothing, including those stories, pushed us into it. . . . I hated it. Because this was condoning—I won't say genocide—but condoning a hell of a lot of murder. . . . It made us damn uncomfortable. But this was a policy that wasn't going to get changed no matter what the press said."[12]

In other words, while it was difficult for policymakers not to respond to the news media reports and the outcry that they engendered, they decided it would be even more costly to respond. Politically, however, the Bush administration could not afford to be seen as doing nothing or as uncaring. On August 6, 1992, the day the ITN videotape aired, Bush demanded that the Serbs open the camps to international access. A week later, with U.S. support, the UN Security Council passed Resolution 770, demanding outside access to the camps and authorizing member states to use "all measures necessary" (that is, force) to ensure humanitarian relief supplies were delivered. The news media reports also played a role in the establishment of the first war crimes tribunals in Europe since World War II. While some things had changed on the surface, U.S. policy remained largely the same, defined by Bush's August 7 statement that the United States would not intervene with force. Bush recalled Vietnam, saying, "I do not want to see the United States bogged down in any way into some guerilla warfare. We lived through that once." Resolution 770 never was fully implemented.

This lack of real policy change was further confirmed in interviews with officials and reporters. Scowcroft said, "We did some marginal things, but there was a real consensus—and I think probably an unshakable consensus—to make a real difference . . . would require an American or NATO intervention that we did not see justified." Foreign Service officer George Kenney, who on August 25 publicly resigned to protest the lack of substantive U.S. action, said that government concern with the media "only extended to the appearance of maintaining we were behaving responsibly," while in reality refusing further entanglement in the Balkans. I asked journalist Roy Gutman, who actively tried to raise the alarm within the U.S. government once he had confirmed atrocities were taking place, for his assessment of his reports' impact. He curled two fingers in the symbol for a zero. "Really," he said. "What you had is a lot of reaction to reports, but never any policy change."[13] This is the minimalist response.

* * *

## Real-Time Intervention: The Sarajevo Market Massacres

Another facet of the loss of policy control associated with the idea of a CNN effect is the ability of modern news media to transmit graphic images almost instantaneously. This speed, it is said, overwhelms the traditional policymaking structures, forcing decisions that might not otherwise be made, perhaps before all the facts are in.

A good example of the impact of real-time media reports on intervention decisions is the gruesome footage of the February 5, 1994, "marketplace massacre," in which a mortar shell fired by an unknown party (but almost certainly Bosnian Serbs) landed in a crowded marketplace in Sarajevo, killing 68 people and horribly wounding nearly 200 others. In the aftermath of the attack and the public outcry, the United States abandoned its hands-off policy toward the Balkan conflict. It led NATO in issuing an ultimatum to the Bosnian Serbs to remove their heavy weapons from around Bosnia's capital (an extension of this threat would lead to NATO's first use of offensive force in Europe in its history) and established the five-nation "Contact Group," giving new momentum to the search for a diplomatic solution to the conflict. Sarajevens enjoyed a bit of normalcy after nearly two years of siege.

This clearly seems to be a case where videotaped images led the United States into, or at least toward, intervention. But while the images did have an impact, it was not the simple cause-effect one that this glance at events would indicate. At the time of the shelling, the United States already was moving toward a more active role in the Balkans, for reasons that included intense pressure from France and U.S. concern that the inability to affect the conflict was eroding the Atlantic alliance and American leadership. On February 4, the day *before* the shelling, Secretary of State Warren Christopher proposed that the United States lead a new diplomatic effort, combined with the threat of using force.[14] "I am acutely uncomfortable with the passive position we are now in, and believe that now is the time to undertake a new initiative," he wrote in a letter to Defense Secretary William Perry and National Security Adviser Anthony Lake.[15] "We had a real sense that we didn't have a Bosnia policy that was going anywhere," said a senior State Department official. Before the shelling, "We had already made the psychological determination [about] the direction we wanted to go." This official was in a series of meetings on fashioning a new policy toward Bosnia when the mortar attack occurred—and recalled worrying that the new policy would be seen, incorrectly, as an instant response to the massacre.[16]

This is not to say that the bloody images had no impact; media reports actually had three effects. First, according to White House spokesperson Michael McCurry, they galvanized and accelerated the decision-making process. "The impact of the marketplace bombing . . . was to force there to be a response much quicker than the U.S. government" routinely produces one, McCurry said.[17] Second, it provided ammunition for those, such as Christopher, who had been arguing in administration councils for action. Third, it provided a moment of increased public attention to Bosnia that made it easier for the administration to explain a more robust policy. "It was a short window. We took advantage of it. We moved the policy forward. And it was successful," said McCurry's predecessor, Dee Dee Myers.[18]

In summary, rather than forcing the Clinton administration into doing something (undertaking an intervention) that it did not want to do, the images from Sarajevo helped the administration take a step that some of its senior members were arguing for. The images had an impact because the structure they affected—Clinton Administration foreign policy—was itself in flux.

* * *

Perhaps the clearest lesson here is that, in an age of instant, 'round-the-clock television news, foreign policy leadership remains both possible and necessary—perhaps even more necessary than before. * * * There seems little doubt that CNN and its brethren have made leadership more difficult. Numerous officials spoke of the temptation to respond to dramatic video images and the intense public outcry that often can accompany them. These calls can be resisted, but at a political price. If policy is not well anchored, the temptation to respond to the calculation of the moment can be overwhelming. CNN, in particular, gives opponents of policy—whether in the U.S. Congress or in the streets of Mogadishu—a platform to make their views known instantly, thus complicating the life of today's policymaker. Television feeds on conflict, whether political or physical, emphasizing the challenge to policy.

* * *

Nonetheless, while it is neither possible nor advisable to suppress all challenges to policy, this paper has found a clear inverse relationship between leadership and news media impact. When policy is well grounded, it is less likely that the media will be able to shift officials' focus. When policy is clear, reasonably constant, and well communicated, the news media follow officials rather than lead them—by the rules of "objectivity," they can do nothing else.[19] * * *

In sum, the awesome powers of communication technology at the news media's disposal have not had as dramatic an impact on this critical aspect of foreign policy as it might seem at first glance. Each of the cases revealed how other, abiding factors played a central role in the decision about whether or not to intervene. These factors included the real potential costs in U.S. blood and treasure; the credibility of the United States on the international scene; the future of important alliances; and the goals and benefits of the proposed mission itself. Journalists have had an impact on the decision about whether or not the United States will send its men and women into combat for a long time, as the case of the Yellow Press,

McKinley, and the Spanish-American War shows. They still have an impact—and for the same reasons. What technology per se has changed is the pressures of time. If government officials allow others to dominate the debate, if they fail to communicate their policies and build support, if those policies fail, the news media will reflect all this, and officials will soon find that the impact of the media can be very real—and blindingly swift—indeed.

While the news media have made modern governance more difficult and more risky, Kennan's fears about the obsolescence of official prerogatives are exaggerated at best. Policymakers retain the power to set the agenda, to make policy choices and to lead. To do so, they need a sophisticated understanding, not simplistic descriptions, of the news media's complex role.

## Notes

[1]For our purposes, "real-time" means not only images that are broadcast as they are occurring (that is, live) but also those that reach policymakers and other audiences within twenty-four hours of the event. See Nik Gowing, *Real-Time Television Coverage of Armed Conflicts and Diplomatic Crises: Does it Pressure or Distort Foreign Policy Decisions?* Working paper 94-1, Joan Shorenstein Barone Center on the Press, Politics, and Public Policy, Harvard University, Cambridge, Mass., June 1994.

[2]Steven Livingston and Todd Eachus, "Humanitarian Crises and U.S. Foreign Policy: Somalia and the CNN Effect Reconsidered," *Political Communication* 12, no. 4 (October–December 1995): 415–416.

[3]Daniel Hallin, *The "Uncensored War": The Media and Vietnam* (Berkeley: University of California Press, 1986).

[4]"Peace operations" is the term employed by the Clinton administration in its May 1994 policy declaration, where it was defined as "the entire spectrum of activities from traditional peacekeeping to peace enforcement aimed at defusing and resolving international conflicts." "Operations other than war" (OOTWs), as used by the U.S. military, is somewhat broader, encompassing such activities as drug interdiction and relief missions such as those conducted in Bangladesh (Operation Sea Angel) or south Florida (Hurricane Andrew).

[5]Hallin, *The "Uncensored War."*

[6]*The Media and Foreign Policy in the Post–Cold War World* (New York: Freedom Forum Media Studies Center, 1993).

[7]Livingston and Eachus, "Humanitarian Crises"; and Eric V. Larson, *U.S. Casualties in Somalia: The Media Response and the Myth of the "CNN Effect"* (draft), RAND, Santa Monica, Calif., March 1995, p. 69.

[8]Herman J. Cohen, "Intervention in Somalia," *The Diplomatic Record 1992–1993* (Boulder, Colo.: Westview Press, 1994), pp. 62–63.

[9]Telephone interview with Baker, September 11, 1995.

[10]Interviews: Baker, September 11, 1995; Eagleburger, February 1, 1995; and Scowcroft, February 27, 1995.

[11]Interview with Zimmermann, June 8, 1995.

[12]Eagleburger interview.

[13]Scowcroft interview; interview with Kenney, January 26, 1995; and interview with Gutman, January 31, 1995.

[14]Elizabeth Drew, *On The Edge: The Clinton Presidency* (New York: Simon and Schuster, 1994).

[15]Elaine Sciolino and Douglas Jehl, "As U.S. Sought a Bosnia Policy, the French Offered a Good Idea," *New York Times*, February 14, 1994, p. A1.

[16]Background interview, February 3, 1995.

[17]Interview with McCurry, May 15, 1995 (at the time of the event, McCurry was State Department spokesperson).

[18]Interview with Myers, February 27, 1995.

[19]Hallin, *The "Uncensored War."*

# *The Global AIDS Crisis*

10.1

UNAIDS

## Report on the Global AIDS Epidemic

*The HIV response is critical to progress across the breadth of the global development agenda.* Success in addressing HIV will accelerate progress in achieving virtually all of the Millennium Development Goals. Satisfying the many political commitments made on HIV will require greater leadership, building on recent successes by taking account of lessons learnt, enhanced financial resources, improved coordination of effort, and effective action to address societal determinants of HIV risk and vulnerability.

### Status of the global HIV epidemic

*The global percentage of people living with HIV has stabilized since 2000.* However, the overall number of people living with HIV has increased as a result of the ongoing number of new infections each year and the beneficial effects of more widely available antiretroviral therapy. Sub-Saharan Africa remains most heavily affected by HIV, accounting for 67% of all people living with HIV and for 72% of AIDS deaths in 2007.

*The global epidemic is stabilizing but at an unacceptably high level.* Globally, there were an estimated 33 million [30 million – 36 million] people living with HIV in 2007. The annual number of new HIV infections declined from 3.0 million [2.6 million – 3.5 million] in 2001 to 2.7 million [2.2 million – 3.2 million] in 2007. . . .

*An estimated 370 000 [330 000 – 410 000] children under age 15 became infected with HIV in 2007.* The annual number of new HIV infections among children worldwide has declined since 2002, as services to prevent mother-to-child transmission have expanded. Globally, the number of children younger than 15 years living with HIV increased from 1.6 million [1.4 million – 2.1 million] in 2001 to 2.0 million [1.9 million – 2.3 million] in 2007. Almost 90% live in sub-Saharan Africa. Since 2003, the rate of annual AIDS deaths among children has also begun to fall. . . .

From *2008 Report on the Global AIDS Epidemic*, Executive Summary, http://data.unaids.org/pub/GlobalReport/2008/JC1511_GR08_ExecutiveSummary_en.pdf (accessed 9/24/09).

## Addressing societal causes of HIV risk and vulnerability

*Long-term success in responding to the epidemic will require sustained progress in reducing human rights violations associated with it, including gender inequality, stigma and discrimination.* Although these social factors differ in their manifestations, intensity and impact between and within regions, they are present to some degree worldwide and in all cases impede an effective, evidence-informed and rights-based response to the epidemic.

## Reducing gender inequality

*While many countries have begun to recognize gender issues in their HIV planning processes, substantial numbers continue to fall short in the areas of budget and policy support for such issues. . . .*

*Evidence-informed programmes to forge norms of gender equity should be brought to scale, with particular attention to interventions focused on men and boys.* A meta-analysis of programmes to promote gender equality found that those that expressly aimed to transform gender roles through critical reflection, role play and other interactions were most likely to be effective in producing changes in the targeted attitudes and behaviours. Norm-changing interventions should be supported by legal reform to prohibit gender violence, enhanced law enforcement to hold perpetrators of violence to account, and interventions to address the attitudes and conditions that may contribute to gender-based violence.

*Strategies to increase women's economic independence and legal reforms to recognize women's property and inheritance rights should be prioritized by national governments and international donors. . . .*

## Addressing stigma and discrimination

*In the epidemic's third decade, one third of countries lack laws protecting people living with HIV from discrimination. . . .*

*Most countries lack legal protections for the populations at highest risk. . . .*

*Much stronger financial and technical support is needed for capacity-building for organizations and networks of people living with HIV and groups most at risk of HIV. . . .*

## Preventing new HIV infections: the key to reversing the epidemic

*The global HIV epidemic cannot be reversed, and gains in expanding treatment access cannot be sustained, without greater progress in reducing the rate of new HIV infections.* Yet even as treatment access has steadily expanded in recent years, efforts to ensure robust HIV prevention activities have lagged. While 87% of countries with targets for universal access have established goals for HIV treatment, only slightly more than half have targets for key HIV prevention strategies.

*Existing prevention strategies can be effective in reducing the risk of HIV exposure.* Proven strategies exist to prevent every mode of HIV transmission – sexual, blood borne (including through injecting drug use and in health care settings), and mother-to-child. Recent years have seen the confirmation of medical male circumcision as a potentially valuable technology for HIV risk reduction in men. A cluster of HIV prevention strategies centred on antiretroviral medicines – including prevention of mother-to-child transmission, post-exposure prophylaxis, experimental regimens for pre-exposure prophylaxis, and probable secondary prevention benefits from therapeutic administration of antiretroviral medicines – has also emerged.

*Although young people, 15–24 years of age account for 45% of all new HIV infections in adults, many young people still lack accurate, complete information on how to avoid exposure to the virus. . . .*

*Major progress in the last two years in expanding access to services to prevent mother-to-child transmission suggests that this mode of transmission could be rendered extremely rare in the future with sufficient financing, commitment and strategic action. . . .*

*Prevention efforts should become more strategically focused on sexual partnerships, especially those that increase the risk of HIV exposure. . . .*

*Sustaining prevention gains represents one of the great challenges of HIV prevention. To maintain a robust prevention response, countries need to nurture a 'prevention movement,' build the human and technical capacity that will be needed to sustain prevention efforts, and work to stimulate greater demand for prevention services.* In every country where HIV infection rates have sharply fallen, community mobilization for HIV prevention has been a critical element of success.

## Treatment and care: unprecedented progress, remaining challenges

*In only six years, the number of people receiving antiretroviral medicines in low- and middle-income countries has increased ten-fold, reaching almost 3 million people by the end of 2007.* Many actors share credit in this achievement, most notably people living with HIV themselves, whose advocacy helped achieve what was once considered impossible. . . .

*Intensified action is needed to ensure timely delivery of HIV treatment to children, who are significantly less likely than adults to receive antiretroviral medicines.* Without treatment, approximately half of children with perinatal HIV infection will die by age 2. . . .

*Despite the existence of affordable medications, too few people living with both HIV and tuberculosis are receiving treatment for both conditions.* The failure to make optimal use of existing diagnostic and treatment regimens results in considerable illness and death. An estimated 22% of tuberculosis cases in Africa – and, in some countries in the region, as many as 70% – occur in people living with HIV.

*Weaknesses in health care systems are slowing the scale-up of HIV treatment programmes, underscoring the need for intensified action to strengthen these systems.* Evidence indicates that scale-up of antiretroviral medicine provision is helping drive significant improvements in health care infrastructure in resource-limited settings....

## Mitigating the epidemic's impact on households, communities and societies

*The epidemic continues to inflict significant damage on affected households, with particularly harmful effects on women and children.* The financial burden associated with HIV for the poorest of households in India represents 82% of annual income, while the comparable burden for the wealthiest families is slightly more than 20%. About 12 million children (under age 18) have lost one or both parents to AIDS in sub-Saharan Africa, and the number of children orphaned by the epidemic continues to rise.

*Although most high-prevalence countries have strategies in place to support children orphaned or made vulnerable by HIV, few national programmes reach more than a small minority of such children....*

*Ensuring educational opportunities for children is critical to mitigation of HIV-related vulnerability.* In 56 countries from which recent household survey data are available, orphans who had lost both parents were on average 12% less likely to attend school than non-orphans....

*The epidemic is having particularly harsh effects on women, requiring implementation of scaled-up measures to increase women's independent income-generating potential.* Women account for two thirds of all caregivers for people living with HIV in Africa, and women who are widowed as a result of HIV risk social ostracism or destitution. Enhancing women's financial options helps mitigate some of the epidemic's most harmful effects; 90% of women participating in microfinance initiatives reported significant improvement in their lives, including improved sense of community solidarity in crises and reductions in partner violence....

## Where do we go from here? Sustaining an effective, robust HIV response for the long term

*Moving towards universal access to HIV prevention, treatment, care, and support is an important step in the direction of an effective, sustainable HIV response....*

*To extend these scattered successes to more countries in all regions – and to sustain these achievements in the coming decades – the following key actions are needed.*

- *Base national action on sound evidence of what works to address documented national needs, ensuring full implementation of evidence-informed policies and programmes.* By basing decisions on strong public health surveillance, resource mapping and evidence of what works, effective national efforts pair evidence-informed strategies with documented national needs.

  Too often, however, national HIV expenditures do not match national needs. This is especially the case in many countries with low-level or concentrated epidemics, where rational funding would focus primarily on HIV prevention services for populations most at risk. In Latin America, where HIV prevalence is well below 1%, HIV prevention accounts for just 15% of HIV spending in 2007. Within the category of HIV prevention spending in concentrated epidemics, countries often opt for broad prevention programmes for the general population rather than for the more cost-effective interventions focused on populations most at risk. For concentrated epidemics generally, risk-reduction programmes focused on populations most at risk represent only 10% of overall HIV prevention spending. . . .

True leaders are not satisfied with only the development of sound policies but ensure full and timely implementation of strategic action frameworks. In only 69% of countries – far fewer than the 97% that report having a national strategy – have national strategies been translated into costed operational plans with programme goals, detailed programme costing and identified funding sources. In sub-Saharan Africa, only about half of national HIV strategies meet UNAIDS quality criteria.

- *Plan for the future, by implementing strategic planning and evaluation mechanisms that extend beyond three- and five-year time cycles.* Strong leadership on HIV remains focused on long-term objectives, refusing to permit intervening challenges to undermine the national HIV response. . . .
- *Couple programmatic scale-up with measures to reduce the societal factors that increase HIV risk and vulnerability, including gender inequities, stigma and discrimination, and social marginalization. . . .* Until sufficient political will exists to address the sources of HIV risk and vulnerability, the epidemic will continue to expand, undermining the sustainability of the HIV response.

  Confronting HIV requires addressing issues such as human sexuality, and drug use, that make many people uncomfortable. It also requires compassion and effective action with respect to groups that society often prefers to ignore. . . .
- *Mobilize sufficient financial resources to reach the global target of universal access, putting in place innovative mechanisms to sustain financing for the long term.* Robust HIV funding will be needed for decades. In low-income countries, international donors will need to provide most of the financing for HIV in the coming years.

10.2

# *The Planetary Emergency of Global Warming*

AL GORE

## An Inconvenient Truth

The relationship between human civilization and the Earth has been utterly transformed by a combination of factors, including the population explosion, the technological revolution, and a willingness to ignore the future consequences of our present actions. The underlying reality is that we are colliding with the planet's ecological system, and its most vulnerable components are crumbling as a result.

I have learned much more about this issue over the years. I have read and listened to the world's leading scientists, who have offered increasingly dire warnings. I have watched with growing concern as the crisis gathers strength even more rapidly than anyone expected.

In every corner of the globe—on land and in water, in melting ice and disappearing snow, during heat waves and droughts, in the eyes of hurricanes and in the tears of refugees—the world is witnessing mounting and undeniable evidence that nature's cycles are profoundly changing.

I have learned that, beyond death and taxes, there is at least one absolutely indisputable fact: Not only does human-caused global warming exist, but it is also growing more and more dangerous, and at a pace that has now made it a planetary emergency. * * *

The climate crisis is, indeed, extremely dangerous. In fact it is a true planetary emergency. Two thousand scientists, in a hundred countries, working for more than 20 years in the most elaborate and well-organized scientific collaboration in the history of humankind, have forged an exceptionally strong consensus that all the nations on Earth must work together to solve the crisis of global warming.

The voluminous evidence now strongly suggests that unless we act boldly and quickly to deal with the underlying causes of global warming, our world will undergo a string of terrible catastrophes, including more and stronger storms like Hurricane Katrina, in both the Atlantic and the Pacific.

We are melting the North Polar ice cap and virtually all of the mountain glaciers in the world. We are destabilizing the massive mound of ice on Greenland and the equally enormous mass of ice propped up on top of islands in West Antarctica, threatening a

From *An Inconvenient Truth: The Planetary Emergency of Global Warming and What We Can Do About It* (New York: Rodale, 2006).

worldwide increase in sea levels of as much as 20 feet.

The list of what is now endangered due to global warming also includes the continued stable configuration of ocean and wind currents that has been in place since before the first cities were built almost 10,000 years ago.

We are dumping so much carbon dioxide into the Earth's environment that we have literally changed the relationship between the Earth and the Sun. So much of that $CO_2$ is being absorbed into the oceans that if we continue at the current rate we will increase the saturation of calcium carbonate to levels that will prevent formation of corals and interfere with the making of shells by any sea creature.

Global warming, along with the cutting and burning of forests and other critical habitats, is causing the loss of living species at a level comparable to the extinction event that wiped out the dinosaurs 65 million years ago. That event was believed to have been caused by a giant asteroid. This time it is not an asteroid colliding with the Earth and wreaking havoc; it is us.

Last year, the national academies of science in the 11 most influential nations came together to jointly call on every nation to "acknowledge that the threat of climate change is clear and increasing" and declare that the "scientific understanding of climate changes is now sufficiently clear to justify nations taking prompt action."

So the message is unmistakably clear. This crisis means "danger!" Why do our leaders seem not to hear such a clear warning? Is it simply that it is inconvenient for them to hear the truth?

If the truth is unwelcome, it may seem easier just to ignore it.

But we know from bitter experience that the consequences of doing so can be dire. * * *

Today, we are hearing and seeing dire warnings of the worst potential catastrophe in the history of human civilization; a global climate crisis that is deepening and rapidly becoming more dangerous than anything we have ever faced.

And yet these clear warnings are also being met with a "blinding lack of situational awareness"—in this case, by the Congress, as well as the president.

As Martin Luther King Jr. said in a speech not long before his assassination:

"We are now faced with the fact, my friends, that tomorrow is today. We are confronted with the fierce urgency of now in this unfolding conundrum of life and history, there is such a thing as being too late.

"Procrastination is still the thief of time. Life often leaves us standing bare, naked, and dejected with a lost opportunity. . . ." But along with the danger we face from global warming, this crisis also brings unprecedented opportunities.

What are the opportunities such a crisis also offers? They include not just new jobs and new profits, though there will be plenty of both, we can build clean engines, we can harness the Sun and the wind; we can stop wasting energy; we can use our planet's plentiful coal resources without heating the planet.

The procrastinators and deniers would have us believe this will be expensive. But in recent years, dozens of companies have cut emissions of heat-trapping gases while saving money. Some of the world's largest companies are moving aggressively to capture the enormous economic opportunities offered by a clean-energy future.

But there's something even more precious to be gained if we do the right thing.

The climate crisis also offers us the chance to experience what very few generations in history have had the privilege of knowing: *a generational mission*; the exhilaration of a compelling *moral purpose*; a shared and unifying *cause*; the thrill of being forced by circumstances to put aside the pettiness and conflict that so often stifle the restless human need for transcendence *the opportunity to rise.*

When we do rise, it will fill our spirits and bind us together. Those who are now suffocating in cynicism and despair will be able to breathe freely. Those who are now suffering from a loss of meaning in their lives will find hope.

When we rise, we will experience an epiphany as we discover that this *crisis* is not really about politics at all. It is a moral and spiritual challenge.

At stake is the survival of our civilization and the habitability of the Earth. Or, as one eminent scientist put it, the pending question is whether the combination of an opposable thumb and a neocortex is a viable combination on this planet.

The understanding we will gain—about who we really are—will give us the moral capacity to take on other related challenges that are also desperately in need of being redefined as moral imperatives with practical solutions. * * *

This is not ultimately about any scientific discussion or political dialogue. It is about who we are as human beings. It is about our capacity to transcend our own limitations; to rise to this new occasion. To see with our hearts, as well as our heads, the response that is now called for. This is a moral, ethical and spiritual challenge. * * *

Imagine with me now that once again, time has stopped—for all of us—and before it starts again, we have the chance to use our moral imaginations and to project ourselves across the expanse of time, seventeen years into the future, and share a brief conversation with our children and grandchildren as they are living their lives in the year 2023.

Will they feel bitterness toward us because we failed in our obligation to care for the Earth that is their home and ours? Will the Earth have been irreversibly scarred by us?

Imagine now that they are asking us: "What were you thinking? Didn't you care about our future? Were you really so self-absorbed that you couldn't—or wouldn't—stop the destruction of Earth's environment?"

What would our answer be?

We can answer their questions now by our actions, not merely with our promises. In the process, we can choose a future for which our children will thank us.

# *NGOs*

10.3

MARGARET E. KECK AND KATHRYN SIKKINK

## Transnational Networks in International Politics: An Introduction

World politics at the end of the twentieth century involves, alongside states, many nonstate actors that interact with each other, with states, and with international organizations. These interactions are structured in terms of networks, and transnational networks are increasingly visible in international politics. Some involve economic actors and firms. Some are networks of scientists and experts whose professional ties and shared causal ideas underpin their efforts to influence policy.[1] Others are networks of activists, distinguishable largely by the centrality of principled ideas or values in motivating their formation.[2] We will call these *transnational advocacy networks.*

Advocacy networks are significant transnationally and domestically. By building new links among actors in civil societies, states, and international organizations, they multiply the channels of access to the international system. In such issue areas as the environment and human rights, they also make international resources available to new actors in domestic political and social struggles. By thus blurring the boundaries between a state's relations with its own nationals and the recourse both citizens and states have to the international system, advocacy networks are helping to transform the practice of national sovereignty.

* * *

Major actors in advocacy networks may include the following: (1) international and domestic nongovernmental research and advocacy organizations; (2) local social movements; (3) foundations; (4) the media; (5) churches, trade unions, consumer organizations, and intellectuals; (6) parts of regional and international intergovernmental organizations; and (7) parts of the executive and/or parliamentary branches of governments. Not all these will be present in each advocacy network. Initial research suggests, however, that international and domestic NGOs play a central role in all advocacy networks, usually initiating actions and pressuring more powerful

From *Activists Beyond Borders: Advocacy Networks in International Politics* (Ithaca, NY: Cornell University Press, 1998), ch. 1.

actors to take positions. NGOs introduce new ideas, provide information, and lobby for policy changes.

Groups in a network share values and frequently exchange information and services. The flow of information among actors in the network reveals a dense web of connections among these groups, both formal and informal. The movement of funds and services is especially notable between foundations and NGOs, and some NGOs provide services such as training for other NGOs in the same and sometimes other advocacy networks. Personnel also circulate within and among networks, as relevant players move from one to another in a version of the "revolving door."

Relationships among networks, both within and between issue areas, are similar to what scholars of social movements have found for domestic activism.[3] Individuals and foundation funding have moved back and forth among them. Environmentalists and women's groups have looked at the history of human rights campaigns for models of effective international institution building. Refugee resettlement and indigenous people's rights are increasingly central components of international environmental activity, and vice versa; mainstream human rights organizations have joined the campaign for women's rights. Some activists consider themselves part of an "NGO community."

* * *

Advocacy networks are not new. We can find examples as far back as the nineteenth-century campaign for the abolition of slavery. But their number, size, and professionalism, and the speed, density, and complexity of international linkages among them have grown dramatically in the last three decades. As Hugh Heclo remarks about domestic issue networks, "If the current situation is a mere outgrowth of old tendencies, it is so in the same sense that a 16-lane spaghetti interchange is the mere elaboration of a country crossroads."[4]

We cannot accurately count transnational advocacy networks to measure their growth over time, but one proxy is the increase in the number of international NGOs committed to social change. Because international NGOs are key components of any advocacy network, this increase suggests broader trends in the number, size, and density of advocacy networks generally.

* * *

Transnational advocacy networks appear most likely to emerge around those issues where (1) channels between domestic groups and their governments are blocked or hampered or where such channels are ineffective for resolving a conflict, setting into motion the "boomerang" pattern of influence characteristic of these networks; (2) activists or "political entrepreneurs" believe that networking will further their missions and campaigns, and actively promote networks; and (3) conferences and other forms of international contact create arenas for forming and strengthening networks. Where channels of participation are blocked, the international arena may be the only means that domestic activists have to gain attention to their issues. Boomerang strategies are most common in campaigns where the target is a state's domestic policies or behavior; where a campaign seeks broad procedural change involving dispersed actors, strategies are more diffuse.

## Political Entrepreneurs

Just as oppression and injustice do not themselves produce movements or revolutions, claims around issues amenable to international action do not produce transnational networks. Activists—"people who care enough about some issue that they are prepared to incur significant costs and act to achieve their goals"[5]—do. They create them when they believe that transnational networking will further their organizational missions—by sharing information, attaining greater visibility, gaining access to wider publics, multiplying channels of institutional access, and so forth. For example, in the campaign to stop the promotion of infant formula to poor women in developing countries, organizers settled on a boycott of Nestlé, the largest producer, as its main tactic. Because Nestlé was a transnational actor, activists believed a transnational network was necessary to bring pressure on corporations and governments.[6] Over time, in such issue areas, participation in transnational networks has become an essential component of the collective identities of the activists involved, and networking a part of their common repertoire. The political entrepreneurs who become the core networkers for a new campaign have often gained experience in earlier ones.

## The Growth of International Contact

Opportunities for network activities have increased over the last two decades. In addition to the efforts of pioneers, a proliferation of international organizations and conferences has provided foci for connections. Cheaper air travel and new electronic communication technologies speed information flows and simplify personal contact among activists.[7]

Underlying these trends is a broader cultural shift. The new networks have depended on the creation of a new kind of global public (or civil society), which grew as a cultural legacy of the 1960s.[8] Both the activism that swept Western Europe, the United States, and many parts of the third world during that decade, and the vastly increased opportunities for international contact, contributed to this shift. With a significant decline in air fares, foreign travel ceased to be the exclusive privilege of the wealthy. Students participated in exchange programs. The Peace Corps and lay missionary programs sent thousands of young people to live and work in the developing world. Political exiles from Latin America taught in U.S. and European universities. Churches opened their doors to refugees, and to new ideas and commitments.

Obviously, internationalism was not invented in the sixties. Religious and political traditions including missionary outreach, the solidarity traditions of labor and the left, and liberal internationalism have long stirred action by individuals or groups beyond the borders of their own state. While many activists working in advocacy networks come out of these traditions, they tend no longer to define themselves in terms of these traditions or the organizations that carried them. This is most true for activists on the left who suffered disillusionment from their groups' refusal to address seriously the concerns of women, the environment, or human rights violations in eastern bloc countries. Absent a range of options that in earlier decades would have competed for their commitments, advocacy and activism through either NGOs or grassroots movements became the most likely alternative for those seeking to "make a difference."

* * *

## How Do Transnational Advocacy Networks Work?

Transnational advocacy networks seek influence in many of the same ways that other political groups or social movements do. Since they are not powerful in a traditional sense of the word, they must use the power of their information, ideas, and strategies to alter the information and value contexts within which states make policies. The bulk of what networks do might be termed persuasion or socialization, but neither process is devoid of conflict. Persuasion and socialization often involve not just reasoning with opponents, but also bringing pressure, arm-twisting, encouraging sanctions, and shaming. * * *

* * *

Our typology of tactics that networks use in their efforts at persuasion, socialization, and pressure includes (1) *information politics,* or the ability to quickly and credibly generate politically usable information and move it to where it will have the most impact; (2) *symbolic politics,* or the ability to call upon symbols, actions, or stories that make sense of a situation for an audience that is frequently far away;[9] (3) *leverage politics,* or the ability to call upon powerful actors to affect a situation where weaker members of a network are unlikely to have influence; and (4) *accountability politics,* or the effort to hold powerful actors to their previously stated policies or principles.

* * *

## Information Politics

Information binds network members together and is essential for network effectiveness. Many information exchanges are informal—telephone calls, E-mail and fax communications, and the circulation of newsletters, pamphlets and bulletins. They provide information that would not otherwise be available, from sources that might not otherwise be heard, and they must make this information comprehensible and useful to activists and publics who may be geographically and/or socially distant.[10]

* * *

Nonstate actors gain influence by serving as alternate sources of information. Information flows in advocacy networks provide not only facts but testimony—stories told by people whose lives have been affected. Moreover, activists interpret facts and testimony, usually framing issues simply, in terms of right and wrong because their purpose is to persuade people and stimulate them to act. How does this process of persuasion occur? An effective frame must show that a given state of affairs is neither natural nor accidental, identify the responsible party or parties, and propose credible solutions. These aims require clear, powerful messages that appeal to shared principles, which often have more impact on state policy than advice of technical experts. An important part of the political struggle over information is precisely whether an issue is defined primarily as technical—and thus subject to consideration by "qualified" experts—or as something that concerns a broader global constituency.

* * *

Networks strive to uncover and investigate problems, and alert the press and policymakers. One activist described this as the "human rights methodology"—"promoting change by reporting facts."[11] To be credible, the information produced by networks must be reliable and well documented. To gain attention, the information must be timely and dramatic. Sometimes these multiple goals of information politics conflict, but both credibility and drama seem to be essential components of a strategy aimed at persuading publics and policymakers to change their minds.

* * *

## Symbolic Politics

Activists frame issues by identifying and providing convincing explanations for powerful symbolic events, which in turn become catalysts for the growth of networks. Symbolic interpretation is part of the process of persuasion by which networks create awareness and expand their constituencies. Awarding the 1992 Nobel Peace Prize to Maya activist Rigoberta Menchú and the UN's designation of 1993 as the Year of Indigenous Peoples heightened public awareness of the situation of indigenous peoples in the Americas. Indigenous people's use of 1992, the 500th anniversary of the voyage of Columbus to the Americas, to raise a host of issues well illustrates the use of symbolic events to reshape understandings.[12]

* * *

## Leverage Politics

Activists in advocacy networks are concerned with political effectiveness. Their definition of effectiveness often includes some policy change by "target actors" such as governments, international financial institutions like the World Bank, or private actors like transnational corporations. In order to bring about policy change, networks need to pressure and persuade more powerful actors. To gain influence the networks seek leverage (the word appears often in the discourse of advocacy organizations) over more powerful actors. By leveraging more powerful institutions, weak groups gain influence far beyond their ability to influence state practices directly. The identification of material or moral leverage is a crucial strategic step in network campaigns.

Material leverage usually links the issue to money or goods (but potentially also to votes in international organizations, prestigious offices, or other benefits).

* * *

Although NGO influence often depends on securing powerful allies, their credibility still depends in part on their ability to mobilize their own members and affect public opinion via the media. In democracies the potential to influence votes gives large membership organizations an advantage over nonmembership organizations in lobbying for policy change; environmental organizations, several of whose memberships number in the millions, are more likely to have this added clout than are human rights organizations.

Moral leverage involves what some commentators have called the "mobilization of shame," where the behavior of target actors is held up to the light of international scrutiny. Network activists exert moral leverage on the assumption that governments value the good opinion of others; insofar as networks can demonstrate that a state is violating international obligations or is not living up to its own claims, they hope to jeopardize its credit enough to motivate a change in policy or behavior. The degree to which states are vulnerable to this kind of pressure varies, and will be discussed further below.

## Accountability Politics

Networks devote considerable energy to convincing governments and other actors to publicly change their positions on issues. This is often dismissed as inconsequential change, since talk is cheap and governments sometimes change discursive positions hoping to divert network and public attention. Network activists, however, try to make such statements into opportunities for accountability politics. Once a government has publicly committed itself to a principle—for example, in favor of human rights or democracy—networks can use those positions, and their command of information, to expose the distance between discourse and practice. This is embarrassing to many governments, which may try to save face by closing that distance.

* * *

Domestic structures through which states and private actors can be held accountable to their pronouncements, to the law, or to contracts vary considerably from one nation to another, even among democracies. The centrality of the courts in U.S. politics creates a venue for the representation of diffuse interests that is not available in most European democracies.[13] It also explains the large number of U.S. advocacy organizations that specialize in litigation. * * *

## Under What Conditions Do Advocacy Networks Have Influence?

To assess the influence of advocacy networks we must look at goal achievement at several different levels. We identify the following types or stages of network influence: (1) issue creation and agenda setting; (2) influence on discursive positions of states and international organizations; (3) influence on institutional procedures; (4) influence on policy change in "target actors" which may be states, international organizations like the World Bank, or private actors like the Nestlé Corporation; and (5) influence on state behavior.

Networks generate attention to new issues and help set agendas when they provoke media attention, debates, hearings, and meetings on issues that previously had not been a matter of public debate. Because values are the essence of advocacy networks, this stage of influence may require a modification of the "value context" in which policy debates takes place. The UN's theme years and decades, such as International Women's Decade and the Year of Indigenous Peoples, were international events promoted by networks that heightened awareness of issues.

Networks influence discursive positions when they help persuade states and international organizations to support international declarations or to change stated domestic policy positions. The role environmental networks played in shaping state positions and conference declarations at the 1992 "Earth Summit" in Rio de Janeiro is an example of this kind of impact. They may also pressure states to make more binding commitments by signing conventions and codes of conduct.

The targets of network campaigns frequently respond to demands for policy change with changes in procedures (which may affect policies in the future). The multilateral bank campaign is largely responsible for a number of changes in internal bank directives mandating greater NGO and local participation in discussions of projects. It also opened access to formerly restricted information, and led to the establishment of an independent inspection panel for World Bank projects. Procedural changes can greatly increase the opportunity for advocacy organizations to develop regular contact with other key players on an issue, and they sometimes offer the opportunity to move from outside to inside pressure strategies.

A network's activities may produce changes in policies, not only of the target states, but also of other states and/or international institutions. Explicit policy shifts seem to denote success, but even here both their causes and meanings may be elusive. We can point with some confidence to network impact where human rights network pressures have achieved cut-offs of military aid to repressive regimes, or a curtailment of repressive practices. Sometimes human rights activity even affects regime stability. But we must take care to distinguish between policy change and change in behavior; official policies regarding timber extraction in Sarawak, Malaysia, for example, may say little about how timber companies behave on the ground in the absence of enforcement.

We speak of stages of impact, and not merely types of impact, because we believe that increased attention, followed by changes in discursive positions, make governments more vulnerable to the claims that networks raise. (Discursive changes can also have a powerfully divisive effect on networks themselves, splitting insiders from outsiders, reformers from radicals.) A government that claims to be protecting indigenous areas or ecological reserves is potentially more vulnerable to charges that such areas are endangered than one that makes no such claim. At that point the effort is not to make governments change their position but to hold them to their word. Meaningful policy change is thus more likely when the first three types or stages of impact have occurred.

* * *

## Issue Characteristics

Issues that involve ideas about right and wrong are amenable to advocacy networking because they arouse strong feelings, allow networks to recruit volunteers and activists, and infuse meaning into these volunteer activities. However, not all principled ideas lead to network formation, and some issues can be framed more easily than others so as to resonate with policymakers and publics. * * *

* * *

As we look at the issues around which transnational advocacy networks have organized most effectively, we find two issue characteristics that appear most frequently: (1) issues involving bodily harm to vulnerable individuals, especially when there is a short and clear causal chain (or story) assigning responsibility; and (2) issues involving legal equality of opportunity. The first respond to a normative logic, and the second to a juridical and institutional one.

* * *

## Actor Characteristics

However amenable particular issues may be to strong transnational and transcultural messages, there must be actors capable of transmitting those messages and targets who are vulnerable to persuasion or leverage. * * *

Target actors must be vulnerable either to material incentives or to sanctions from outside actors, or they must be sensitive to pressure because of gaps between stated commitments and practice. Vulnerability arises both from the availability of leverage and the target's sensitivity to leverage; if either is missing, a campaign may fail.

* * *

## Notes

[1]Peter Haas has called these "knowledge-based" or "epistemic communities." See Peter Haas, "Introduction: Epistemic Communities and International Policy Coordination," *Knowledge, Power and International Policy Coordination,* special issue, *International Organization* 46 (Winter 1992), pp. 1–36.

[2]Ideas that specify criteria for determining whether actions are right or wrong and whether outcomes are just or unjust are shared principled beliefs or values, Beliefs about cause-effect relationships are shared causal beliefs, Judith Goldstein and Robert Keohane, eds., *Ideas and Foreign Policy: Beliefs, Institutions, and Political Change* (Ithaca: Cornell University Press, 1993), pp. 8–10.

[3]See John D. McCarthy and Mayer N. Zald, "Resource Mobilization and Social Movements: A Partial Theory," *American Journal of Sociology* 82:6 (1977): 1212–41. Myra Marx Feree and Frederick D. Miller, "Mobilization and Meaning: Toward an Integration of Social Psychological and Resource Perspectives on Social Movements," *Sociological Inquiry* 55 (1985): 49–50; and David S. Meyer and Nancy Whittier, "Social Movement Spillover," *Social Problems* 41:2 (May 1994): 277–98.

[4]Hugh Heclo, "Issue Networks and the Executive Establishment," in *The New American Political System,* ed. Anthony King (Washington, D.C.: American Enterprise Institute, 1978), p. 97.

[5]Pamela E. Oliver and Gerald Marwell, "Mobilizing Technologies for Collective Action," in *Frontiers in Social Movement Theory,* ed. Aldon D. Morris and Carol McClurg Mueller (New Haven: Yale University Press, 1992), p. 252.

[6]See Kathryn Sikkink, "Codes of Conduct for Transnational Corporations: The Case of the WHO/UNICEF Code," *International Organization* 40 (Autumn 1986): 815–40.

[7]The constant dollar yield of airline tickets in 1995 was one half of what it was in 1966, while the number of international passengers enplaned increased more than four times during the same period. Air Transport Association home page, June 1997, http://www.airtransport.org/data/traffic.htm. See James Rosenau, *Turbulence in World Politics* (Princeton: Princeton University Press, 1990), pp. 12, 25.

[8]See Sidney Tarrow, "Mentalities, Political Cultures, and Collective Action Frames: Constructing Meanings through Action," in *Frontiers in Social Movement Theory,* p. 184.

[9]Alison Brysk uses the categories "information politics" and "symbolic politics" to discuss strategies of transnational actors, especially networks around Indian rights. See "Acting Globally: Indian Rights and International Politics in Latin America," in *Indigenous Peoples and Democracy in Latin America,* ed. Donna Lee Van Cott (New York: St. Martin's Press/Inter-American Dialogue, 1994), pp. 29–51; and "Hearts and Minds: Bringing Symbolic Politics Back In," *Polity* 27 (Summer 1995): 559–85.

[10]Rosenau, *Turbulence,* p. 199, argues that "as the adequacy of information and the very nature of knowledge have emerged as central issues, what were once regarded as the petty quarrels of scholars over the adequacy of evidence and the metaphysics of proof have become prominent activities in international relations."

[11]Dorothy Q. Thomas, "Holding Governments Accountable by Public Pressure," In *Ours by Right: Women's Rights as Human Rights,* ed. Joanna Kerr (London: Zed Books, 1993), p. 83. This methodology is not new. See, for example, David H. Lumsdaine, *Moral Vision,* in *International Politics: The Foreign Aid Regime* (Princeton: Princeton University Press, 1993), pp. 187–88, 211–13.

[12]Brysk, "Acting Globally."

# *The Triumph of Democracy*

11.1

FRANCIS FUKUYAMA

## The End of History?

In watching the flow of events over the past decade or so, it is hard to avoid the feeling that something very fundamental has happened in world history. The past year has seen a flood of articles commemorating the end of the Cold War, and the fact that "peace" seems to be breaking out in many regions of the world. Most of these analyses lack any larger conceptual framework for distinguishing between what is essential and what is contingent or accidental in world history, and are predictably superficial. If Mr. Gorbachev were ousted from the Kremlin or a new Ayatollah proclaimed the millennium from a desolate Middle Eastern capital, these same commentators would scramble to announce the rebirth of a new era of conflict.

And yet, all of these people sense dimly that there is some larger process at work, a process that gives coherence and order to the daily headlines. The twentieth century saw the developed world descend into a paroxysm of ideological violence, as liberalism contended first with the remnants of absolutism, then bolshevism and fascism and finally an updated Marxism that threatened to lead to the ultimate apocalypse of nuclear war. But the century that began full of self-confidence in the ultimate triumph of Western liberal democracy seems at its close to be returning full circle to where it started: not to an "end of ideology" or a convergence between capitalism and socialism, as earlier predicted, but to an unabashed victory of economic and political liberalism.

The triumph of the West, of the Western *idea,* is evident first of all in the total exhaustion of viable systematic alternatives to Western liberalism. In the past decade, there have been unmistakable changes in the intellectual climate of the world's two largest communist countries, and the beginnings of significant reform movements in both. But this phenomenon extends beyond high politics and it can be seen also in the ineluctable spread of consumerist Western culture in such diverse contexts as the peasants' markets and color television sets now omnipresent throughout China, the cooperative restaurants and clothing stores opened in the past year in Moscow, the Beethoven piped into Japanese department stores, and the rock music enjoyed alike in Prague, Rangoon, and Tehran.

From *National Interest* 16 (Summer 1989).

What we may be witnessing is not just the end of the Cold War, or the passing of a particular period of postwar history, but the end of history as such: that is, the end point of mankind's ideological evolution and the universalization of Western liberal democracy as the final form of human government. This is not to say that there will no longer be events to fill the pages of *Foreign Affairs*'s yearly summaries of international relations, for the victory of liberalism has occurred primarily in the realm of ideas or consciousness and is as yet incomplete in the real or material world. But there are powerful reasons for believing that it is the ideal that will govern the material world *in the long run.* To understand how this is so, we must first consider some theoretical issues concerning the nature of historical change.

* * *

Have we in fact reached the end of history? Are there, in other words, any fundamental "contradictions" in human life that cannot be resolved in the context of modern liberalism, that would be resolvable by an alternative political-economic structure? If we accept the idealist premises laid out above, we must seek an answer to this question in the realm of ideology and consciousness. Our task is not to answer exhaustively the challenges to liberalism promoted by every crackpot messiah around the world, but only those that are embodied in important social or political forces and movements, and which are therefore part of world history. For our purposes, it matters very little what strange thoughts occur to people in Albania or Burkina Faso, for we are interested in what one could in some sense call the common ideological heritage of mankind.

In the past century, there have been two major challenges to liberalism, those of fascism and of communism. The former[1] saw the political weakness, materialism, anomie, and lack of community of the West as fundamental contradictions in liberal societies that could only be resolved by a strong state that forged a new "people" on the basis of national exclusiveness. Fascism was destroyed as a living ideology by World War II. This was a defeat, of course, on a very material level, but it amounted to a defeat of the idea as well. What destroyed fascism as an idea was not universal moral revulsion against it, since plenty of people were willing to endorse the idea so long as it seemed the wave of the future, but its lack of success. After the war, it seemed to most people that German fascism as well as its other European and Asian variants were bound to self-destruct. There was no material reason why new fascist movements could not have sprung up again after the war in other locales, but for the fact that expansionist ultranationalism, with its promise of unending conflict leading to disastrous military defeat, had completely lost its appeal. The ruins of the Reich chancellory as well as the atomic bombs dropped on Hiroshima and Nagasaki killed this ideology on the level of consciousness as well as materially, and all of the proto-fascist movements spawned by the German and Japanese examples like the Peronist movement in Argentina or Subhas Chandra Bose's Indian National Army withered after the war.

The ideological challenge mounted by the other great alternative to liberalism, communism, was far more serious. Marx, speaking Hegel's language, asserted that liberal society contained a fundamental contradiction that could not be resolved within its context, that between capital and labor, and this contradiction has constituted the chief accusation against liberalism ever since. But surely, the class issue has actually been successfully resolved in the West. As Kojève (among others) noted, the egalitarianism of modern America represents the essential achievement of the classless society envisioned by Marx. This is not to say that there are not rich people and poor people in the United States, or that the gap between them has not grown in recent years. But the root causes of economic inequality do not have to do with the underlying legal and social structure of our society, which remains fundamentally egalitarian and moderately redistributionist, so much as with the cultural and social characteristics of the groups that make it up, which are in turn the historical legacy of premodern conditions. Thus black poverty in the United States is not the inherent product of liberalism, but is rather the "legacy of slavery and racism" which persisted long after the formal abolition of slavery.

* * *

If we admit for the moment that the fascist and communist challenges to liberalism are dead, are there any other ideological competitors left? Or put another way, are there contradictions in liberal society beyond that of class that are not resolvable? Two possibilities suggest themselves, those of religion and nationalism.

The rise of religious fundamentalism in recent years within the Christian, Jewish, and Muslim traditions has been widely noted. One is inclined to say that the revival of religion in some way attests to a broad unhappiness with the impersonality and spiritual vacuity of liberal consumerist societies. Yet while the emptiness at the core of liberalism is most certainly a defect in the ideology—indeed, a flaw that one does not need the perspective of religion to recognize[2]—it is not at all clear that it is remediable through politics. Modern liberalism itself was historically a consequence of the weakness of religiously-based societies which, failing to agree on the nature of the world's nationalist movements do not have a political program beyond the negative desire of independence *from* some other group or people, and do not offer anything like a comprehensive agenda for socio-economic organization. As such, they are compatible with doctrines and ideologies that do offer such agendas. While they may constitute a source of conflict for liberal societies, this conflict does not arise from liberalism itself so much as from the fact that the liberalism in question is incomplete. Certainly a great deal of the world's ethnic and nationalist tension can be explained in terms of peoples who are forced to live in unrepresentative political systems that they have not chosen.

While it is impossible to rule out the sudden appearance of new ideologies or previously unrecognized contradictions in liberal societies, then, the present world seems to confirm that the fundamental principles of sociopolitical organization have not advanced terribly far since 1806. Many of the wars and revolutions fought since that time have been undertaken in the name of ideologies which claimed to be more advanced than liberalism, but whose pretensions were ultimately unmasked by history. In the meantime, they have helped to spread the universal homogenous state to the point where it could have a significant effect on the overall character of international relations.

* * *

The passing of Marxism-Leninism first from China and then from the Soviet Union will mean its death as a living ideology of world historical significance. For while there may be some isolated true believers left in places like Managua, Pyongyang, or Cambridge, Massachusetts, the fact that there is not a single large state in which it is a going concern undermines completely its pretensions to being in the vanguard of human history. And the death of this ideology means the growing "Common Marketization" of international relations, and the diminution of the likelihood of large-scale conflict between states.

This does not by any means imply the end of international conflict *per se*. For the world at that point would be divided between a part that was historical and a part that was post-historical. Conflict between states still in history, and between those states and those at the end of history, would still be possible. There would still be a high and perhaps rising level of ethnic and nationalist violence, since those are impulses incompletely played out, even in parts of the post-historical world. Palestinians and Kurds, Sikhs and Tamils, Irish Catholics and Walloons, Armenians and Azeris, will continue to have their unresolved grievances. This implies that terrorism and wars of national liberation will continue to be an important item on the international agenda. But large-scale conflict must involve large states still caught in the grip of history, and they are what appear to be passing from the scene.

The end of history will be a very sad time. The struggle for recognition, the willingness to risk one's life for a purely abstract goal, the worldwide ideological struggle that called forth daring, courage, imagination, and idealism, will be replaced by economic calculation, the endless solving of technical problems, environmental concerns, and the satisfaction of sophisticated consumer demands. In the post-historical period there will be neither art nor philosophy, just the perpetual caretaking of the museum of human history. I can feel in myself, and see in others around me, a powerful nostalgia for the time when history existed. Such nostalgia, in fact, will continue to fuel competition and conflict even in the post-historical world for some time to come. Even though I recognize its inevitability, I have the most ambivalent feelings for the civilization that has been created in Europe since 1945, with its north Atlantic and Asian offshoots. Perhaps this very prospect of centuries of boredom at the end of history will serve to get history started once again.

## Notes

[1] I am not using the term "fascism" here in its most precise sense, fully aware of the frequent misuse of this term to denounce anyone to the right of the user. "Fascism" here denotes any organized ultranationalist movement with universalistic pretensions—not universalistic with regard to its nationalism, of course, since the latter is exclusive by definition, but with regard to the movement's belief in its right to rule other people. Hence Imperial Japan would qualify as fascist while former strongman Stoessner's Paraguay or Pinochet's Chile would not. Obviously fascist ideologies cannot be universalistic in the sense of Marxism or liberalism, but the structure of the doctrine can be transferred from country to country.

[2] I am thinking particularly of Rousseau and the Western philosophical tradition that flows from him that was highly critical of Lockean or Hobbesian liberalism, though one could criticize liberalism from the standpoint of classical political philosophy as well.

# *Ongoing Threats to Democracy*

11.2

SAMUEL P. HUNTINGTON

## The Clash of Civilizations?

### The Next Pattern of Conflict

World politics is entering a new phase, and intellectuals have not hesitated to proliferate visions of what it will be—the end of history, the return of traditional rivalries between nation states, and the decline of the nation state from the conflicting pulls of tribalism and globalism, among others. Each of these visions catches aspects of the emerging reality. Yet they all miss a crucial, indeed, a central, aspect of what global politics is likely to be in the coming years.

It is my hypothesis that the fundamental source of conflict in this new world will not be primarily ideological or primarily economic. The great divisions among humankind and the dominating source of conflict will be cultural. Nation states will remain the most powerful actors in world affairs, but the principal conflicts of global politics will occur between nations and groups of different civilizations. The clash of civilizations will dominate global politics. The fault lines between civilizations will be the battle lines of the future. * * *

### The Nature of Civilizations

During the cold war the world was divided into the First, Second and Third Worlds. Those divisions are no longer relevant. It is far more meaningful now to group countries not in terms of their political or economic systems or in terms of their level of economic development but rather in terms of their culture and civilization.

What do we mean when we talk of a civilization? A civilization is a cultural entity. Villages, regions, ethnic groups, nationalities, religious groups, all have distinct cultures at different levels of cultural heterogeneity. The culture of a village in southern Italy may be different from that of a village in northern Italy, but both will share in common Italian culture that distinguishes them from German villages. European communities, in turn, will share cultural features that distinguish them from Arab or Chinese communities. Arabs, Chinese and Westerners, however, are not part of any broader cultural entity. They constitute civilizations. A civilization is thus the highest

From *Foreign Affairs* 72.3 (Summer 1993).

cultural grouping of people and the broadest level of cultural identity people have short of that which distinguishes humans from other species. It is defined both by common objective elements, such as language, history, religion, customs, institutions, and by the subjective self-identification of people. People have levels of identity: a resident of Rome may define himself with varying degrees of intensity as a Roman, an Italian, a Catholic, a Christian, a European, a Westerner. The civilization to which he belongs is the broadest level of identification with which he intensely identifies. People can and do redefine their identities and, as a result, the composition and boundaries of civilizations change.

* * *

## Why Civilizations Will Clash

Civilization identity will be increasingly important in the future, and the world will be shaped in large measure by the interactions among seven or eight major civilizations. These include Western, Confucian, Japanese, Islamic, Hindu, Slavic-Orthodox, Latin American and possibly African civilization. The most important conflicts of the future will occur along the cultural fault lines separating these civilizations from one another.

Why will this be the case?

First, differences among civilizations are not only real; they are basic. Civilizations are differentiated from each other by history, language, culture, tradition and, most important, religion. The people of different civilizations have different views on the relations between God and man, the individual and the group, the citizen and the state, parents and children, husband and wife, as well as differing views of the relative importance of rights and responsibilities, liberty and authority, equality and hierarchy. These differences are the product of centuries. They will not soon disappear. They are far more fundamental than differences among political ideologies and political regimes. Differences do not necessarily mean conflict, and conflict does not necessarily mean violence. Over the centuries, however, differences among civilizations have generated the most prolonged and the most violent conflicts.

Second, the world is becoming a smaller place. The interactions between peoples of different civilizations are increasing; these increasing interactions intensify civilization consciousness and awareness of differences between civilizations and commonalities within civilizations. North African immigration to France generates hostility among Frenchmen and at the same time increased receptivity to immigration by "good" European Catholic Poles. * * *

The interactions among peoples of different civilizations enhance the civilization-consciousness of people that, in turn, invigorates differences and animosities stretching or thought to stretch back deep into history.

Third, the processes of economic modernization and social change throughout the world are separating people from longstanding local identities. They also weaken the nation state as a source of identity. In much of the world religion has moved in to fill this gap, often in the form of movements that are labeled "fundamentalist." Such movements are found in Western Christianity, Judaism, Buddhism and Hinduism, as well as in Islam. In most countries and most religions the people active in fundamentalist movements are young, college-educated, middle-class technicians, professionals and business persons. The "unsecularization of the world," George Weigel has remarked, "is one of the dominant social facts of life in the late twentieth century." The revival of religion, "la revanche de Dieu," as Gilles Kepel labeled it, provides a basis for identity and commitment that transcends national boundaries and unites civilizations.

Fourth, the growth of civilization-consciousness is enhanced by the dual role of the West. On the one hand, the West is at a peak of power. At the same time, however, and perhaps as a result, a return to the roots phenomenon is occurring among non-Western civilizations. Increasingly one hears references to trends toward a turning inward and "Asianization" in Japan, the end of the Nehru legacy and the "Hinduization" of India, the failure of Western ideas of socialism and nationalism and hence "re-Islamization" of the Middle East, and now a debate over Westernization versus Russianization in Boris Yeltsin's country. A West at the peak of its power confronts non-Wests that increasingly have the desire, the will and the resources to shape the world in non-Western ways.

* * *

Fifth, cultural characteristics and differences are less mutable and hence less easily compromised and resolved than political and economic ones. In the former Soviet Union, communists can become democrats, the rich can become poor and the poor rich, but Russians cannot become Estonians and Azeris cannot become Armenians. In class and ideological conflicts, the key question was "Which side are you on?" and people could and did choose sides and change sides. In conflicts between civilizations, the question is "What are you?" That is a given that cannot be changed. And as we know, from Bosnia to the Caucasus to the Sudan, the wrong answer to that question can mean a bullet in the head. * * *

Finally, economic regionalism is increasing. The proportions of total trade that were intraregional rose between 1980 and 1989 from 51 percent to 59 percent in Europe, 33 percent to 37 percent in East Asia, and 32 percent to 36 percent in North America. The importance of regional economic blocs is likely to continue to increase in the future. On the one hand, successful economic regionalism will reinforce civilization-consciousness. On the other hand, economic regionalism may succeed only when it is rooted in a common civilization.

* * *

As people define their identity in ethnic and religious terms, they are likely to see an "us" versus "them" relation existing between themselves and people of different ethnicity or religion. The end of ideologically defined states in Eastern Europe and the former Soviet Union permits traditional ethnic identities and animosities to come to the fore. Differences in culture and religion create differences over policy issues, ranging from human rights to immigration to trade and commerce to the environment. Geographical propinquity gives rise to conflicting territorial claims from Bosnia to Mindanao. Most important, the efforts of the West to promote its values of democracy and liberalism as universal values, to maintain its military predominance and to advance its economic interests engender countering responses from other civilizations. Decreasingly able to mobilize support and form coalitions on the basis of ideology, governments and groups will increasingly attempt to mobilize support by appealing to common religion and civilization identity.

The clash of civilizations thus occurs at two levels. At the micro-level, adjacent groups along the fault lines between civilizations struggle, often violently, over the control of territory and each other. At the macro-level, states from different civilizations compete for relative military and economic power, struggle over the control of international institutions and third parties, and competitively promote their particular political and religious values.

* * *

## The West Versus the Rest

The West is now at an extraordinary peak of power in relation to other civilizations. Its superpower opponent has disappeared from the map. Military conflict among Western states is unthinkable, and Western military power is unrivaled. Apart from Japan, the West faces no economic challenge. It dominates international political and security institutions and with Japan international economic institutions. Global political and security issues are effectively settled by a directorate of the United States, Britain and France, world economic issues by a directorate of the United States, Germany and Japan, all of which maintain extraordinarily close relations with each other to the exclusion of lesser and largely non-Western countries. Decisions made at the U.N. Security Council or in the International Monetary Fund that reflect the interests of the West are presented to the world as reflecting the desires of the world community. The very phrase "the world community" has become the euphemistic collective noun (replacing "the Free World") to give global legitimacy to actions reflecting the interests of the United States and other Western powers.[1] * * *

Differences in power and struggles for military, economic and institutional power are thus one source of conflict between the West and other civilizations. Differences in culture, that is basic values and beliefs, are a second source of conflict. V. S. Naipaul has argued that Western civilization is the "universal civilization" that "fits all men." At a superficial level much of Western culture has indeed permeated the rest of the world. At a more basic level, however, Western concepts differ fundamentally from those prevalent in other civilizations. Western ideas of individualism, liberalism, constitutionalism, human rights, equality, liberty, the rule of law, democracy, free markets, the separation of church and state, often have little resonance in Islamic, Confucian, Japanese, Hindu, Buddhist or Orthodox cultures. Western efforts to propagate such ideas produce instead a reaction against "human rights imperialism" and a reaffirmation of indigenous values, as can be seen in the support for religious fundamentalism by the younger generation in non-Western cultures. The very notion that there could be a "universal civilization" is a Western idea, directly at odds with the particularism of most Asian societies and their emphasis on what distinguishes one people from another. Indeed, the author of a review of 100 comparative studies of values in different societies concluded that "the values that are most important in the West are least important worldwide."[2] In the political realm, of course, these differences are most manifest in the efforts of the United States and other

Western powers to induce other peoples to adopt Western ideas concerning democracy and human rights. Modern democratic government originated in the West. When it has developed in non-Western societies it has usually been the product of Western colonialism or imposition.

The central axis of world politics in the future is likely to be, in Kishore Mahbubani's phrase, the conflict between "the West and the Rest" and the responses of non-Western civilizations to Western power and values.[3] Those responses generally take one or a combination of three forms. At one extreme, non-Western states can, like Burma and North Korea, attempt to pursue a course of isolation, to insulate their societies from penetration or "corruption" by the West, and, in effect, to opt out of participation in the Western-dominated global community. The costs of this course, however, are high, and few states have pursued it exclusively. A second alternative, the equivalent of "band-wagoning" in international relations theory, is to attempt to join the West and accept its values and institutions. The third alternative is to attempt to "balance" the West by developing economic and military power and cooperating with other non-Western societies against the West, while preserving indigenous values and institutions; in short, to modernize but not to Westernize.

* * *

## The Confucian-Islamic Connection

The obstacles to non-Western countries joining the West vary considerably. They are least for Latin American and East European countries. They are greater for the Orthodox countries of the former Soviet Union. They are still greater for Muslim, Confucian, Hindu and Buddhist societies. Japan has established a unique position for itself as an associate member of the West: it is in the West in some respects but clearly not of the West in important dimensions. Those countries that for reason of culture and power do not wish to, or cannot, join the West compete with the West by developing their own economic, military and political power. They do this by promoting their internal development and by cooperating with other non-Western countries. The most prominent form of this cooperation is the Confucian-Islamic connection that has emerged to challenge Western interests, values and power.

* * *

## Implications for the West

This article does not argue that civilization identities will replace all other identities, that nation states will disappear, that each civilization will become a single coherent political entity, that groups within a civilization will not conflict with and even fight each other. This paper does set forth the hypotheses that differences between civilizations are real and important; civilization-consciousness is increasing; conflict between civilizations will supplant ideological and other forms of conflict as the dominant global form of conflict; international relations, historically a game played out within Western civilization, will increasingly be de-Westernized and become a game in which non-Western civilizations are actors and not simply objects; successful political, security and economic international institutions are more likely to develop within civilizations than across civilizations; conflicts between groups in different civilizations will be more frequent, more sustained and more violent than conflicts between groups in the same civilization; violent conflicts between groups in different civilizations are the most likely and most dangerous source of escalation that could lead to global wars; the paramount axis of world politics will be the relations between "the West and the Rest"; the elites in some torn non-Western countries will try to make their countries part of the West, but in most cases face major obstacles to accomplishing this; a central focus of conflict for the immediate future will be between the West and several Islamic-Confucian states.

This is not to advocate the desirability of conflicts between civilizations. It is to set forth descriptive hypotheses as to what the future may be like. If these are plausible hypotheses, however, it is necessary to consider their implications for Western policy. These implications should be divided between short-term advantage and long-term accommodation. In the short term it is clearly in the interest of the West to promote greater cooperation and unity within its own civilization, particularly between its European and North American components; to incorporate into the West societies in Eastern Europe and Latin America whose cultures are close to those of the West; to promote and maintain cooperative relations with Russia and Japan; to prevent escalation of local inter-civilization conflicts into major inter-civilization wars; to limit the expansion of the military strength of Confucian and Islamic states; to moderate the reduction of Western military capabilities and maintain military superiority in East and Southwest Asia; to exploit differences and conflicts among Confucian and Islamic states; to support in other civilizations groups sympathetic to Western values and interest; to strengthen international institutions that reflect and legitimate Western interests and values and to promote the involvement of non-Western states in those institutions.

In the longer term other measures would be called for. Western civilization is both Western and modern. Non-Western civilizations have attempted to become modern without becoming Western. To date only Japan has fully succeeded in this quest. Non-Western civilizations will continue to attempt to acquire the wealth, technology, skills, machines and weapons that are part of being modern. They will also attempt to reconcile this modernity with their traditional culture and values. Their economic and military strength relative to the West will increase. Hence the West will increasingly have to accommodate these non-Western modern civilizations whose power approaches that of the West but whose values and interests differ significantly from those of the West. This will require the West to maintain the economic and military power necessary to protect its interests in relation to these civilizations. It will also, however, require the West to develop a more profound understanding of the basic religious and philosophical assumptions underlying other civilizations and the ways in which people in those civilizations see their interests. It will require an effort to identify elements of commonality between Western and other civilizations. For the relevant future, there will be no universal civilization, but instead a world of different civilizations, each of which will have to learn to coexist with the others.

## *Notes*

[1]Almost invariably Western leaders claim they are acting on behalf of "the world community." One minor lapse occurred during the runup to the Gulf War. In an interview on "Good Morning America," Dec. 21, 1990, British Prime Minister John Major referred to the actions "the West" was taking against Saddam Hussein. He quickly corrected himself and subsequently referred to "the world community." He was, however, right when he erred.

[2]Harry C. Triandis, *The New York Times,* Dec. 25, 1990, p. 41, and "Cross-Cultural Studies of Individualism and Collectivism," Nebraska Symposium on Motivation, vol. 37, 1989, pp. 41–133.

[3]Kishore Mahbubani, "The West and the Rest," *The National Interest,* Summer 1992, pp. 3–13.

# *Democratic Peace?*



EDWARD D. MANSFIELD AND JACK SNYDER

## Democratization and the Danger of War

One of the best-known findings of contemporary social science is that no democracies have ever fought a war against each other, given reasonably restrictive definitions of democracy and of war.[1] This insight is now part of everyday public discourse and serves as a basis for American foreign policymaking. President Bill Clinton's 1994 State of the Union address invoked the absence of war between democracies as a justification for promoting democratization around the globe. In the week following the U.S. military landing in Haiti, National Security Adviser Anthony Lake reiterated that "spreading democracy . . . serves our interests" because democracies "tend not to abuse their citizens' rights or wage war on one another."[2]

It is probably true that a world where more countries were mature, stable democracies would be safer and preferable for the United States. However, countries do not become mature democracies overnight. More typically, they go through a rocky transitional period, where democratic control over foreign policy is partial, where mass politics mixes in a volatile way with authoritarian elite politics, and where democratization suffers reversals. In this transitional phase of democratization, countries become more aggressive and war-prone, not less, and they do fight wars with democratic states.

The contemporary era shows that incipient or partial democratization can be an occasion for the rise of belligerent nationalism and war.[3] Two pairs of states—Serbia and Croatia, and Armenia and Azerbaijan—have found themselves at war while experimenting with varying degrees of partial electoral democracy. Russia's poorly institutionalized, partial democracy has tense relationships with many of its neighbors and has used military force brutally to reassert control in Chechnya; its electorate cast nearly a quarter of its votes for the party of radical nationalist Vladimir Zhirinovsky.

This contemporary connection between democratization and conflict is no coincidence. Using the same databases that are typically used to study the democratic peace, we find considerable statistical evidence that democratizing states are more likely to fight wars than are mature democracies or stable autocracies. States like contemporary Russia that make the biggest leap in democratization—from total autocracy to extensive mass demo-

From *International Security* 20.1 (Summer 1995).

cracy—are about twice as likely to fight wars in the decade after democratization as are states that remain autocracies. However, reversing the process of democratization, once it has begun, will not reduce this risk. Regimes that are changing toward autocracy, including states that revert to autocracy after failed experiments with democracy, are also more likely to fight wars than are states whose regime is unchanging.

Moreover, virtually every great power has gone on the warpath during the initial phase of its entry into the era of mass politics. Mid-Victorian Britain, poised between the partial democracy of the First Reform Bill of 1832 and the full-fledged democracy of the later Gladstone era, was carried into the Crimean War by a groundswell of belligerent public opinion. Napoleon III's France, drifting from plebiscitary toward parliamentary rule, fought a series of wars designed to establish its credentials as a liberal, popular, nationalist type of empire. The ruling elite of Wilhelmine Germany, facing universal suffrage but limited governmental accountability, was pushed toward World War I by its escalating competition with middle-class mass groups for the mantle of German nationalism. Japan's "Taisho democracy" of the 1920s brought an era of mass politics that led the Japanese army to devise and sell an imperial ideology with broad-based appeal.[4] In each case, the combination of incipient democratization and the material resources of a great power produced nationalism, truculence abroad, and major war.

Why should democratizing states be so belligerent? The pattern of the democratizing great powers suggests that the problem lies in the nature of domestic political competition after the breakup of the autocratic regime. Elite groups left over from the ruling circles of the old regime, many of whom have a particular interest in war and empire, vie for power and survival with each other and with new elites representing rising democratic forces. Both old and new elites use all the resources they can muster to mobilize mass allies, often through nationalist appeals, to defend their threatened positions and to stake out new ones. However, like the sorcerer's apprentice, these elites typically *find* that their mass allies, once mobilized, are difficult to control. When this happens, war can result from nationalist prestige strategies that hard-pressed leaders use to stay astride their unmanageable political coalitions.[5]

The problem is not that mass public opinion in democratizing states demonstrates an unvarnished, persistent preference for military adventure. On the contrary, public opinion often starts off highly averse to war. Rather, elites exploit their power in the imperfect institutions of partial democracies to create *faits accomplis*, control political agendas, and shape the content of information media in ways that promote belligerent pressure-group lobbies or upwellings of militancy in the populace as a whole.

Once this ideological connection between militant elites and their mass constituents is forged, the state may jettison electoral democracy while retaining nationalistic, populist rhetoric. As in the failure of Weimar and Taisho democracy, the adverse effects of democratization on war-proneness may even heighten after democracy collapses. Thus, the aftershock of failed democratization is at least one of the factors explaining the link between autocratization and war. * * *

## How Democratization Causes War

Why are democratization and autocratization associated with an increased chance of war? What causal mechanism is at work?* Based on case studies of four great powers during their initial phases of democratization, we argue that threatened elites from the collapsing autocratic regime, many of whom have parochial interests in war and empire, use nationalist appeals to compete for mass allies with each other and with new elites. In these circumstances, the likelihood of war increases due to the interests of some of the elite groups, the effectiveness of their propaganda, and the incentive for weak leaders to resort to prestige strategies in foreign affairs in an attempt to enhance their authority over diverse constituencies. Further, we speculate that transitional regimes, including both democratizing and autocratizing states, share some common institutional weaknesses that make war more likely. At least in some cases, the link between autocratization and war reflects the success of a ruling elite in using nationalist formulas developed during the period of democratization to cloak itself in populist legitimacy, while dismantling the substance of democracy. In explaining the logic behind these arguments, we draw on some standard theories about the consequences of different institutional arrangements for political outcomes.

We illustrate these arguments with some contemporary examples and with cases drawn from four great powers at early stages in the expansion of mass political participation: mid-Victorian Britain, the France of Napoleon III, Bismarckian and Wilhelmine Germany, and Taisho Japan. * * *

## Democratic versus Democratizing Institutions

Well-institutionalized democracies that reliably place ultimate authority in the hands of the average voter virtually never fight wars against each other. Moreover, although mature democracies do fight wars about as frequently as other types of states, they seem to be more prudent: they usually win their wars; they are quicker to abandon strategic overcommitments; and they do not fight gratuitous "preventive" wars.[6] Explanations for these tendencies focus variously on the self-interest of the average voter who bears the costs of war, the norms of bargaining and conflict resolution inherent in democracy, the moderating impact of constitutional checks and balances, and the free marketplace of ideas.[7]

However, these happy solutions typically emerge only in the very long run. In the initial stages of expanding political participation, strong barriers prevent the emergence of full-fledged democratic processes and the foreign policy outcomes associated with them. The two main barriers are the weakness of democratic institutions and the resistance of social groups who would be the losers in a process of full-fledged democratization.

Popular inputs into the policymaking process can have wildly different effects, de-

*Editor's Note: Autocratization is shifting away from democracy toward autocracy or other nondemocratic rule.

pending on the way that political institutions structure and aggregate those inputs.[8] It is a staple of political science that different institutional rules—for example, proportional representation versus single-member districts, or congressional versus executive authority over tariffs—can produce different political outcomes, even holding constant the preferences of individual voters. In newly democratizing states, the institutions that structure political outcomes may allow for popular participation in the policy process, but the way they channel that input is often a parody of full-fledged democracy. As Samuel Huntington has put it, the typical problem of political development is the gap between high levels of political participation and weak integrative institutions to reconcile the multiplicity of contending claims.[9] In newly democratizing states without strong parties, independent courts, a free press, and untainted electoral procedures, there is no reason to expect that mass politics will produce the same impact on foreign policy as it does in mature democracies.

* * *

## *Competitive mass mobilization*

In a period of democratization, threatened elite groups have an overwhelming incentive to mobilize allies among the mass of people, but only on their own terms, using whatever special resources they still retain. These have included monopolies of information (e.g., the German Navy's unique "expertise" in making strategic assessments); propaganda assets (the Japanese Army's public relations blitz justifying the invasion of Manchuria); patronage (British Foreign Secretary Palmerston's gifts of foreign service postings to the sons of cooperative journalists); wealth (Krupp steel's bankrolling of mass nationalist and militarist leagues); organizational skills and networks (the Japanese army's exploitation of rural reservist organizations to build a social base); and the ability to use the control of traditional political institutions to shape the political agenda and structure the terms of political bargains (the Wilhelmine ruling elite's deal with the Center Party, eliminating anti-Catholic legislation in exchange for support in the Reichstag on the naval budget).[10]

* * *

Ideology takes on particular significance in the competition for mass support. New participants in the political process may be uncertain of where their political interests lie, because they lack established habits and good information, and are thus fertile ground for ideological appeals. Ideology can yield particularly big payoffs, moreover, when there is no efficient free marketplace of ideas to counter false claims with reliable facts. Elites try out all sorts of ideological appeals, depending on the social position that they need to defend, the nature of the mass group that they want to recruit, and the type of appeals that seem plausible in the given political setting. A nearly universal element in these ideological appeals is nationalism, which has the advantage of positing a community of interest that unites elites and masses, thus distracting attention from class cleavages.

Nationalist appeals have often succeeded even though the average voter was not consistently pro-war or pro-empire.

* * *

## Implications for Policy

In light of these findings, it would be hard to maintain a naive enthusiasm for spreading peace by promoting democratization. Pushing nuclear-armed great powers like Russia or China toward democratization is like spinning a roulette wheel, where many of the potential outcomes are likely to be undesirable. However, in most cases the initial steps on the road to democratization will not be produced by the conscious policy of the United States, no matter what that policy may be. The roulette wheel is already spinning for Russia, and perhaps China, regardless of what the West does. Moreover, reversals of democratization are nearly as risky as democratization itself. Consequently, the international community needs a strategy not so much for promoting or reversing democratization as for managing the process in ways that minimize its risks and facilitate smooth transitions.

What might be some of these mitigating conditions, and how might they be promoted? The association of democratization with war is probabilistic. Democratization can lead either to war or to peace, depending on a variety of factors, such as the incentives facing the old elites during the transition process, the structure of the marketplace of foreign policy ideas, the speed and thoroughness of the democratic transition, and the character of the international environment in which democratization occurs. Some of these features may be subject to manipulation by astute democratic reformers and their allies in the international community.

One of the major findings of scholarship on democratization in Latin America is that the process goes most smoothly when elites that are threatened by the transition, especially the military, are given a "golden parachute."[11] Above all, they need a guarantee that if they relinquish power they will not wind up in jail. The history of the democratizing great powers broadens this insight. Democratization was least likely to lead to imprudent aggression in cases where the old elites saw a reasonably bright future for themselves in the new social order. British aristocrats, for example, had more of their wealth invested in commerce and industry than they did in agriculture, so they had many interests in common with the rising middle classes. They could face democratization with relative equanimity. In contrast, Prussia's capital-starved, small-scale Junker landholders had no choice but to rely on agricultural protection and military careers.

In today's context, finding benign, productive employment for the erstwhile Communist *nomenklatura*, military officer corps, nuclear scientists, and smoke stack industrialists ought to rank high on the list of priorities. Policies aimed at giving them a stake in the privatization process and subsidizing the conversion of their skills to new, peaceful tasks in a market economy seem like a step in the right direction. According to some interpretations, Russian Defense Minister Pavel Grachev was eager to use force to solve the Chechen confrontation in order to show that Russian military power was still useful and that increased investment in the Russian army would pay big dividends. Instead of pursuing this reckless path, the Russian military elite needs to be convinced that its prestige, housing, pensions, and technical competence will rise if and only if it transforms itself into a western-style military, subordinate to civilian authority and resorting to force only in accordance with prevailing international norms. Moreover, though old elites need to be kept happy, they also need to be kept weak. Pacts should not prop up the remnants of the authoritarian system, but rather create a niche for them in the new system.

A top priority must also be placed on creating a free, competitive, yet responsible marketplace of ideas in the newly democratizing states. Most of the war-prone democratizing great powers had pluralistic public debates, but the terms of these debates were skewed to favor groups with money, privileged access to the media of communication, and proprietary control over information, ranging from historical archives to intelligence about the military balance. Pluralism is not enough. Without an even playing field, pluralism simply creates the incentive and opportunity for privileged groups to propound self-serving myths, which historically have often taken a nationalist turn. One of the rays of hope in the Chechen affair was the alacrity with which Russian journalists exposed the true costs of the fighting and the lies of the government and the military about it. Though elites should get a golden parachute in terms of their pecuniary interests, they should be given no quarter on the battlefield of ideas. Mythmaking should be held up to the utmost scrutiny by aggressive journalists who maintain their credibility by scrupulously distinguishing fact from opinion and tirelessly verifying their sources. Promoting this kind of journalistic infrastructure is probably the most highly leveraged investment that the West can make in a peaceful democratic transition.

Our research offers inconclusive results about the wisdom of speed and thoroughness in transitions to democracy. On the one hand, we found that states making the big jump from autocracy to democracy were much more war-prone than those moving from autocracy to anocracy. This would seem to favor a strategy of limited goals. On the other hand, the experience of the former Communist states suggests that those that have gone farthest and fastest toward full democracy are less nationalistic and less involved in militarized quarrels. This is a question that needs more research.

Finally, what kind of ruling coalition emerges in the course of democratization depends a great deal on the incentives that are created by the international environment. Both Germany and Japan started on the path toward liberal, stable democratization in the mid-1920s, encouraged in part by abundant opportunities for trade and investment from the advanced democracies and by credible security treaties that defused nationalist scare-mongering in domestic politics. But when the international supports for free trade and democracy were yanked out in the late 1920s, their liberal coalitions collapsed. Especially for the case of contemporary China, whose democratization may occur in the context of sharply expanding economic ties to the West, the steadiness of the Western commercial partnership and security presence is likely to play a major role in shaping the incentives of proto-democratic coalition politics.

In the long run, the enlargement of the zone of stable democracy will probably enhance the prospects for peace. But in the short run, there is a lot of work to be done to minimize the dangers of the turbulent transition.

## Notes

[1]Michael Doyle, "Liberalism and World Politics," *American Political Science Review,* Vol. 80, No. 4 (December 1986), pp. 1151–1169; Bruce Russett, *Grasping the Democratic Peace* (Princeton: Princeton University Press, 1993). For skeptical views, see David E. Spiro, "The Insignificance of the Liberal Peace," *International Security,* Vol. 19, No. 2 (Fall 1994), pp. 50–86; and Christopher Layne, "Kant or Cant: The Myth of the Democratic Peace," *International Security,* Vol. 19, No. 2 (Fall 1994), pp. 5–49. They are rebutted by Bruce Russett, "The Democratic Peace: 'And Yet It Moves'," *International Security,* Vol. 19, No. 4 (Spring 1995), pp. 164–175.

[2]"Transcript of Clinton's Address," *New York Times,* January 26, 1994, p. A17; Anthony Lake, "The Reach of Democracy: Tying Power to Diplomacy," *New York Times,* September 23, 1994, p. A35.

[3]Zeev Maoz and Bruce Russett, "Normative and Structural Causes of the Democratic Peace, 1956–1986," *American Political Science Review,* Vol. 87, No. 3 (September 1993), pp. 630, 636; they note that newly created democracies, such as those in Eastern Europe today, may experience conflicts, insofar as their democratic rules and norms are not adequately established. See also Russett, *Grasping the Democratic Peace,* p. 134, on post-Soviet Georgia.

[4]Asa Briggs, *Victorian People,* rev. ed. (Chicago: University of Chicago, 1970), chaps. 2–3; Geoff Eley, *Reshaping the German Right* (New Haven: Yale University Press, 1980); Alain Plessis, *De la fête impériale au mur des fédérés, 1852–1871* (Paris: Editions du seuil, 1973), translated as *The Rise and Fall of the Second Empire, 1852–1871* (Cambridge: Cambridge University Press, 1985); Jack Snyder, *Myths of Empire: Domestic Politics and International Ambition* (Ithaca: Cornell University Press, 1991), chaps. 3–5.

[5]Hans Ulrich Wehler, *The German Empire, 1871–1918* (Dover, N.H.: Berg, 1985); Jack S. Levy, "The Diversionary Theory of War: A Critique," In Manus Midlarsky, ed., *Handbook of War Studies* (Boston: Unwin-Hyman, 1989), pp. 259–288.

[6]David Lake, "Powerful Pacifists," *American Political Science Review,* Vol. 86, No. 1 (March 1992), pp. 24–37; Snyder, *Myths of Empire,* pp. 49–52; Randall Schweller, "Domestic Structure and Preventive War: Are Democracies More Pacific?" *World Politics,* Vol. 44, No. 2 (January 1992), pp. 235–269.

[7]Russett, *Grasping the Democratic Peace;* Miles Kahler, "Introduction," in Miles Kahler, ed., *Liberalization and Foreign Policy* (forthcoming); Jack Snyder, "Democratization, War, and Nationalism in the Post-Communist States," in Celeste Wallander, ed., *The Sources of Russian Conduct after the Cold War* (Boulder: Westview, forthcoming).

[8]Kenneth Shepsle, "Studying Institutions: Some Lessons from the Rational Choice Approach," *Journal of Theoretical Politics,* Vol. 1, No. 2 (April 1989), pp. 131–147.

[9]Samuel Huntington, *Political Order in Changing Societies* (New Haven: Yale University Press, 1968).

[10]Snyder, *Myths of Empire,* pp. 103, 140–141, 205; Louise Young, "Mobilizing for Empire: Japan and Manchukuo, 1930–1945," Ph.D. dissertation, Columbia University, 1992.

[11]On the importance of bargaining with and co-opting old elites (giving them incentives, a "golden parachute," to depart from power), see the literature summarized in Doh Chull Shin, "On the Third Wave of Democratization: A Synthesis and Evaluation of Recent Theory and Research," *World Politics,* Vol. 47, No. 1 (October 1994), pp. 135–170, esp. 161–163.

# Credits

**p. 300:** From "Global Opinion in the Bush Years (2001–2008)," Dec. 18, 2008, p. 3, Pew Global Attitudes Project, a project of the Pew Research Center. Reprinted by permission of the Pew Research Center.

**p. 330:** Figure 1 – U.S. Foreign Policy Goals from "Troubled By Loss of Standing in the World, Americans Support Major Foreign Policy Changes," Global Views, 2008, The Chicago Council on Global Affairs. Copyright © 2008 by The Chicago Council on Global Affairs. Reprinted by permission.

**Graham T. Allison:** "Conceptual Models and the Cuban Missile Crisis" by Graham T. Allison from *American Political Science Review* 62.3 (September 1969).

**Bernard Brodie:** *Strategy in the Missile Age.* © 1959 The Rand Corporation. Published by Princeton University Press. Reprinted by permission of Princeton University Press.

**Lt. Gen. Roméo Dallaire:** From *Shake Hands With the Devil: The Future of Humanity in Rwanda.* Copyright © 2003 by Roméo Dallaire, LGen (Ret) Inc. Reprinted by permission of Da Capo/Carroll & Graf, a member of Perseus Books Group.

**Francis Fukuyama:** From "The End of History" by Francis Fukuyama, *National Interest* 16 (Summer 1989). Copyright © 1989 by Francis Fukuyama. Reprinted by permission of the author.

**John Lewis Gaddis:** From *The United States and the End of the Cold War: Implications, Reconsiderations, Provocations* by John Lewis Gaddis. Copyright © 1992 by John Lewis Gaddis.

**Leslie H. Gelb:** From "Vietnam: The System Worked" by Leslie H. Gelb, *Foreign Policy* 3 (Summer 1971). Reprinted by permission of the author.

**Genocide Prevention Task Force:** "Preventing Genocide: A Blueprint for U.S. Policymakers" (Washington D.C.: U.S. Holocaust Memorial Museum, American Academy of Diplomacy, U.S. Institute of Peace, 2008), pp. 111–114.

**Alexander George:** "Détente: The Search for a Constructive Relationship" from Managing *U.S.-Soviet Rivalry: Problems of Crisis Prevention* (Westview Press, 1983), pp. 19–28. Reprinted by permission of Copyright Clearance Center.

**Mikhail Gorbachev:** From Mikhail Gorbachev, et al., *Essays on Leadership* (Washington, D.C.: Carnegie Commission on Preventing Deadly Conflict, 1998). Reprinted by permission of the Woodrow Wilson Center.

**Al Gore:** Material taken from *An Inconvenient Truth* by Al Gore. Published by Bloomsbury Publishing Plc. Reprinted by permission of the publisher.

**Ole R. Holsti:** Excerpts from "Public Opinion and Foreign Policy," *International Studies Quarterly* 41.1.

**Samuel Huntington:** "The Clash of Civilizations?" Reprinted by permission of *Foreign Affairs*, 72:3 (Summer 1993). Copyright 1993 by the Council on Foreign Relations, Inc. www.ForeignAffairs.com.

**John G. Ikenberry:** "America's Imperial Ambition." Reprinted by permission of *Foreign Affairs* 81:5 (Sept./Oct. 2002). Copyright 2002 by the Council on Foreign Relations, Inc. www.ForeignAffairs.com.

**International Commission on Intervention and State Sovereignty:** "The Responsibility to Protect." Reprinted by permission of the International Commission on Intervention.

**Margaret Keck and Kathryn Sikkink:** "Transnational Networks in International Politics" by Margaret Keck and Kathryn Sikkink. Reprinted from *Activists Beyond Borders: Advocacy Networks in International Politics*, by Margaret E. Keck and Kathryn Sikkink. Copyright © 1998 by Cornell University Press. Used by permission of the publisher, Cornell University Press.

**George Kennan:** "The Sources of Soviet Conduct." Reprinted by permission of *Foreign Affairs* 25:4 (July 1947). Copyright 1947 by the Council on Foreign Relations, Inc. www.ForeignAffairs.com.

**Robert O. Keohane:** "Governance in a Partially Globalized World: Presidential Address, American Political Science Association, 2000," *The American Political Science Review*, 95(1) March 2001, pp. 1–13. Copyright © 2001 by the American Political Science Association. Reprinted with permission of Cambridge University Press.

**Henry Kissinger:** From "America Re-enters the Arena: Franklin Delano Roosevelt" by Henry Kissinger. Abridged with the permission of Simon & Schuster Inc., from *Diplomacy* by Henry Kissinger. Copyright © 1994 by Henry Kissinger. All rights reserved.

**Gabriel Kolko:** "The United States and World Economic Power" from *The Roots of American Foreign* Policy. Copyright © 1969 by Gabriel Kolko. Reprinted by permission of Copyright Clearance Center.

**Charles Krauthammer:** Excerpts from "The Unipolar Moment Revisited" by Charles Krauthammer from *The National Interest*, Winter 2002/2003. Reprinted by permission of the author.

**Walter LaFeber:** "The American New Empire" reprinted from *The New Empire: An Interpretation of American Expansion, 1860–1898, Thirty-Fifth Anniversary Edition, With a New Preface*, by Walter LaFeber. Copyright © 1963 by the American Historical Association; Preface to the 1998 edition © 1998 by Cornell University Press. Used by permission of the publisher, Cornell University Press.

**Melvyn P. Leffler:** "The American Conception of National Security and the Beginnings of the Cold War," *The American Historical Review* 89:2, pp. 346–381. Reprinted by permission of the University of Chicago Press.

**Michael Mandelbaum:** From *The Case for Goliath: How America Acts as the World's Government in the 21st Century*. Copyright © 2005 by Michael Mandelbaum. Reprinted by permission of PublicAffairs, a member of Perseus Books Group.

**Edward D. Mansfield and Jack Snyder:** "Democratization and the Danger of War," *International Security* 20:1 (Summer, 1995), pp. 5–38. © 1995 by the President and Fellows of Harvard College and the Massachusetts Institute of Technology. Reprinted by permission of MIT Press.

**Hans J. Morgenthau:** From *In Defense of the National Interest* by Hans Morgenthau (New York: Alfred A. Knopf, 1951). Copyright © 1951 by Susanna and Matthew Morgenthau. Reprinted by kind permission of Susanna and Matthew Morgenthau.

**Joseph S. Nye Jr.:** From *The Paradox of American Power: Why the World's Only Superpower Can't Go it Alone*. Copyright © 2002 by Joseph S. Nye Jr.

**Shen Pei-Jun:** Excerpt from "As China Sits, America Stands Off to the Side," *United Daily News*, April 8, 2009. Translated by John Wu, edited by Katy Burtner. From *Watching America*, www.WatchingAmerica.com.

**Arthur M. Schlesinger, Jr.:** Excerpted from *The Imperial Presidency* by Arthur M. Schlesinger, Jr. Copyright © 1973 by Arthur M. Schlesinger, Jr. Reprinted by permission of Houghton Mifflin Harcourt Publishing Company. All rights reserved.

**Tony Smith:** "The United States and the Global Struggle for Democracy," *America's Mission*. © 1994 The 20th Century Fund, Inc. Published by Princeton University Press. Reprinted by permission of Princeton University Press.

**Warren P. Strobel:** Excerpts from "The Media and U.S. Policies Toward Intervention: A Closer Look at the CNN Effect" by Warren P. Strobel from *Managing Global Chaos* edited by Chester A. Crocker and Fen Osler Hampson with Pamela Aall (Washington, DC: United States Institute of Peace Press, © 1996).

**Tribune India:** Excerpts from "PM Fully Booked" and "Don't Repeat Mistakes: PM," *Tribune India*, April 3, 2009 online edition.

**UNAIDS:** Excerpt from "2008 Report on the Global AIDS Epidemic, UNAIDS." Reprinted by permission of UNAIDS.

**Window of China News:** Excerpts from "Brazilian President Happy to Lend Money to IMF," online edition dated April 2, 2009.

# Glossary

***Afghanistan war*** Ongoing U.S. military action against the Taliban and the Al Qaeda terrorist network in Afghanistan that began in October 2001.

***African Union (AU)*** The major African regional organization, with fifty-three member states, founded in 2002 to replace the Organization for African Unity.

***Alien and Sedition Acts (1798)*** Legislation that silenced opponents of the war with France by limiting their freedom of speech and of the press.

***Alliance for Progress*** Foreign aid program established by the Kennedy administration in 1961, ostensibly to promote democracy and enhance economic cooperation with Latin America, but these policies gave way to support for military coups.

***alliances*** Associations of states for collective security or other mutual interest. Alliances against a common enemy are key components of both defense and deterrence strategies.

***Al Qaeda*** Osama bin Laden's terrorist network, which emerged during the 1990s and was responsible for 9/11 and a number of other attacks on the United States and other nations.

***American exceptionalism*** The belief that the United States has a uniqueness and special virtue that ground our foreign policy in Principles much more than the foreign policies of other countries.

***Amnesty International (AI)*** One of the leading human rights NGOs in the world.

***anti-apartheid*** An international movement, including economic sanctions, against South Africa's system of apartheid, which gave the white minority power over the black minority; strongly supported on American college campuses during the 1980s and by other activists in the United States, other countries, and within South Africa.

***anti-ballistic missile (ABM) defense systems*** Defense systems that use missiles to counter ballistic missiles. Concerns that such systems were destabilizing because they meant mutual destruction was no longer assured led to the 1972 ABM treaty as part of SALT I, committing both the United States and the Soviet Union to a limited number of systems.

***Asian financial crisis*** The crisis that struck in mid–1997, starting in Thailand and spreading to Indonesia, South Korea, and then throughout East Asia; also had a significant impact on American banks, companies, and exporters.

***Association of Southeast Asian Nations (ASEAN)*** Established in 1967 to promote economic cooperation among its members, which at that time were Indonesia, Malaysia, the Philippines, Singapore, and Thailand. ASEAN has since grown in membership and roles in regional cooperation.

***Atlantic Charter*** A joint statement by FDR and Churchill in August 1941 in which they described the principles and values that should define the post–World War II world.

***"axis of evil"*** The name given to Iraq, Iran, and North Korea by President George W. Bush in his 2002 State of the Union speech.

***balance of power*** A distribution of power among states in which no state can safely calculate that it can achieve dominance. Therefore, peace is preserved.

***Baruch Plan*** A U.S. proposal to the UN Atomic Energy Commission for establishing international control of nuclear weapons; rejected by the Soviet Union.

***Bay of Pigs invasion*** A U.S.-engineered invasion of Cuba in 1961 by exiled forces seeking to overthrow Fidel Castro. The invasion failed miserably and is one of the most often cited cases of flawed executive-branch decision making.

***belief system*** Worldview, made up of the analytic component of the conception of the international system, the normative component of the national-interest hierarchy, and the instrumental component of a basic strategy.

***biodiversity*** The number and variety of plant and animal species.

***bipolar system*** An international system in which there are two major powers.

***Bretton Woods system*** The international economic system set up after World War II based on the International Monetary Fund; the General Agreement on Trade and Tariffs (GATT) and its successor, the World Trade Organization; and the World Bank.

***BRIC*** An informal coalition of Brazil, Russia, India, and China, which began holding summit meetings in June 2009.

***bureaucratic politics*** The way in which the positions of executive-branch departments and agencies on an issue depend on the interests of that particular department or agency; "where you stand depends on where you sit."

***Camp David Accord*** A major breakthrough in Middle East peace brokering in 1979 between Egypt and Israel, negotiated by the Egyptian president Anwar Sadat, the Israeli prime minister Menachem Begin, and the U.S. president Jimmy Carter.

***cap and trade*** A policy for combating global climate change whereby companies and others agree to emission-cuts targets and can sell emissions permits to those who have trouble meeting their targets.

***Carter Doctrine*** A doctrine proclaimed by President Carter in January 1980 following the Soviet invasion of Afghanistan. The doctrine stated that the United States would use any means, including military force, to defend the Persian Gulf region.

***catastrophic terrorism*** The use of nuclear, chemical, or other weapons of mass destruction by terrorists.

***Centers for Disease Control and Prevention (CDC)*** A U.S. agency responsible for preventing, detecting, and controlling disease and promoting health and safety.

***Central American Free Trade Agreement (CAFTA)*** Negotiated in 2003–2004 among the United States, Guatemala, Honduras, Nicaragua, El Salvador, and the Dominican Republic as an intermediate step between NAFTA and a hemisphere-wide Free Trade Area of the Americas.

***China lobby*** During the Cold War, the anticommunist lobby supporting Taiwan and opposing "Red China." The term is still used, although now in reference to lobbies in current issues of U.S.-China relations.

***City on the hill*** The image related to American exceptionalism that the United States was to play a highly principled role in the world that would be both good for us and good for others; can be traced back to John Winthrop, governor of the Massachusetts Bay Colony, in 1630.

***civil-military relations*** Relations between political authorities and the military within political systems.

***civil society*** The voluntary civic and social organizations that are essential for a functioning society.

***clash of civilizations*** A theory developed by Samuel Huntington; states that the differences between peoples of different civilizations, such as religion and culture, are more fundamental than differences of political ideologies or economic systems and are a major source of war and other conflict.

***CNN curve*** The effect of the media on humanitarian crises: on the front end, the intensity focused on a crisis raises public awareness and puts pressure on officials to intervene quickly; on the back end, negative coverage of casualties decreases public support for the intervention and puts pressure on officials to withdraw quickly.

***coercive statecraft*** Measures used to exert power and influence without military force. These range from low-level actions, such as the filing of an official protest or issuing a public condemnation; to withdrawing an ambassador and suspending diplomatic relations; to imposing economic sanctions; and other, tougher measures.

***Cold War*** A period of political and military tension, including risks of nuclear war, between the Soviet Union and the United States with their respective allies. The Cold War lasted more than four decades after World War II, from 1945 to 1989 in some analyses, 1991 in others.

***colonialism*** Governing another country or territory without its people's consent and with the interests of the colonial power paramount over those of the colony.

***common but differentiated responsibility*** Part of the Montréal Protocol, principle whereby all nations of the world agreed to make environmental policy changes, but those that were the largest sources of the problem accepted proportional responsibility.

***compellence*** The act of getting another state to take a particular action that it otherwise would not.

***Comprehensive Test Ban Treaty (CTBT)*** Treaty building on prior limited bans that now seeks to ban all tests of nuclear weapons.

***containment*** A Cold War doctrine whereby the United States would counter any attempt by the Soviet Union to expand its sphere of influence or to spread communism beyond its own borders.

***counterfactual argument*** Argument based on a situation that did not happen but with strong logic and credible evidence demonstrating the plausibility of alternative outcomes; for example, used to argue that conflicts such as those in Bosnia or Somalia could have been prevented if other policies had been implemented.

***counterproliferation*** Efforts to combat the spread of weapons, particularly weapons of mass destruction, that go beyond the diplomacy of nonproliferation, often including military force.

***covert action*** The secret operations of intelligence agencies to overthrow another nation's government or achieve other foreign policy objectives.

***credibility gap*** The sense of skepticism that caused the public to lose faith in the truthfulness of its leaders about Vietnam.

***Cuban missile crisis*** A major confrontation in 1962 between the United States and the Soviet Union over Soviet missiles in Cuba in which the world came close to nuclear war. It is one of the most often cited cases of effective executive-branch decision making.

***cyber warfare*** The use of computers and the Internet as "weapons of mass disruption" to attack military systems, other sensitive systems, and day-to-day societal operations.

***declaratory commitments*** Foreign policy commitments derived from speeches and statements by presidents, such as the Monroe Doctrine.

***deforestation*** The removal of trees in forested areas, primarily by logging and/or burning.

***democracy promotion*** A strategy of spreading democracy to other countries; usually includes facilitating free and fair elections, helping build strong and accountable political institutions, strengthening the rule of law, protecting human rights, and helping cultivate a robust civil society.

***Democratic Idealism*** An international relations theory that emphasizes Principles and is rooted in two central tenets: in a tradeoff, "right" is to be chosen over "might," and in the long run, "right" makes for "might."

***democratic peace*** An international relations theory that asserts that promoting democracy also promotes peace because democracies do not go to war against each other. In other words, this theory claims that the world could be made safe *by* democracy.

***Department of Defense (DOD)*** The federal department created in 1947, combining previous separate Departments of War (including the Army) and the Navy, now also including the Air Force and Marines, headed by a civilian Secretary of Defense, with headquarters at the Pentagon.

***desertification*** Defined by the UN Convention to Combat Desertification as "the degradation of land in arid, semi-arid and dry sub-humid areas . . . caused primarily by human activities and climate variations."

***détente*** Literally, a "relaxation of tensions," the principal term used to characterize efforts during the 1970s to break out of the Cold War and improve relations between the United States and the Soviet Union.

***deterrence*** The prevention of war by credibly communicating sufficient will and capacity to retaliate as a second strike if attacked.

***diplomacy*** The process by which states conduct official relations, most often through ambassadors or other diplomatic representatives.

***diseases of mass destruction (DMD)*** Diseases with the potential to become pandemics and cause massive numbers of deaths worldwide.

***dispute-settlement authority*** The authority given to the World Trade Organization to impose binding settlements in trade disputes.

***divided government*** A government wherein one political party controls the White House and the other party holds the majority in one or both houses of Congress.

***Doha Round*** Multilateral trade negotiations launched in late 2001, which placed a greater emphasis than did past rounds on the issues most affecting developing countries.

***economic sanctions*** Restrictions on trade, finance, and/or other economic relations, imposed by one country to exert power or influence over another country.

***the end of history*** A thesis developed by Francis Fukuyama stating that democracy would be the last form of human government; therefore, the end of the Cold War meant that the big issues of world affairs had been settled once and for all.

***"the enemy of my enemy is my friend"*** An old adage suggesting that because two parties share a common enemy, they can use one another to promote their interests.

***energy security*** Concerns about U.S. economic and overall security due to threats from the supply side (price hikes by the OPEC cartel, wars, or other political instability) and the demand side (the insatiable global demand for energy).

***Espionage and Sedition Acts*** Legislation passed during 1917–18 that imposed broad prohibitions on speech and made it a crime to express dissent against World War I.

***ethnic "cleansing"*** A general term describing ethnically motivated mass killings, such as the murder of thousands of Bosnian Muslims from 1992–95

***euro*** The common currency of participating European Union countries, which are collectively known as the Eurozone.

***executive agreements*** International commitments made by the president that do not require a two-thirds Senate majority and usually do not require congressional approval.

***fast track*** A U.S. legislative mechanism that guaranteed that trade agreements negotiated by the president would receive expedited consideration in Congress. The fast track was developed during the 1970s to ensure passage of the Tokyo Round.

***foreign aid*** Economic or other type of assistance given from one country to another.

***Four Freedoms*** Proclaimed by FDR as the values underlying the war against Hitler and Nazism: freedom of religion, freedom of speech, freedom from fear, and freedom from want.

***free trade*** Trade between countries without tariffs or other barriers from government intervention.

***G7*** The "Group of Seven," an informal but influential institution created in the mid–1970s by the United States, Canada, Britain, France, Germany, Italy, and Japan for consultation and coordination on international economic issues.

***G8*** The Group of Seven plus Russia, which joined after the Cold War.

***G20*** An institution created in 1999 that included China, India, and a number of developing countries, but that did not play a prominent role until the 2008 global economic crisis.

***Gates Foundation*** A philanthropic organization founded by Bill and Melinda Gates with a principal focus on global health and poverty reduction.

***General Agreement on Tariffs and Trade (GATT)*** Established in 1944 as a mechanism for managing trade disputes so as to prevent their escalation to trade wars. GATT moved the world gradually toward freer trade through periodic "rounds" of negotiations. In 1995 GATT was folded into the newly created World Trade Organization (WTO).

***genocide*** The deliberate and intentional effort to eliminate a people, as in Nazi Germany during World War II or Rwanda in 1994.

**glasnost:** Literally, "openness," it meant greater political freedoms in the Soviet Union, including a degree of freedom of the press, the release of prominent dissidents, and an end to the Communist party's "leading role" in society.

***global climate change*** The gradual warming of the earth; the most pressing environmental issue today.

***global governance*** A broader and more flexible concept than the actions of government, it encompasses the rules, institutions, and cooperative problem-solving arrangements of state and nonstate actors.

***global governance gap*** The gap created when the interconnectedness of globalization outpaces policy capacities. Closing this gap is one of the major challenges that American foreign policy and, more broadly, the international community face.

***globalization*** The increasing interconnectedness of the world across nation-state boundaries; affects governments, businesses, communities, and people in a wide range of policy areas.

***global public health*** Health problems and issues that have international implications, not only for humanitarian concerns but also for national security concerns and considerations of Peace and Power.

***Great Depression*** The worldwide economic depression that began with the crash of the U.S. stock market on October 29, 1929 (Black Tuesday) and soon affected nearly every country in the world.

***greenhouse gases*** Gases in the atmosphere, the most prominent of which is carbon dioxide, that have contributed to global warming; some of these gases exist naturally but most are produced by human activities.

***groupthink*** A concept from social psychology that refers to the pressures within small groups for unanimity that work against individual critical thinking.

***Gulf of Tonkin Resolution*** Passed by Congress in 1964 in response to alleged North Vietnamese attacks on U.S. naval ships; gave the president an open-ended authorization to use military force, without any formal declaration of war by Congress.

***guns and butter strategy*** President Lyndon B. Johnson's attempt to pursue major domestic social programs while also escalating the Vietnam War, which caused the federal budget deficit to grow and led to stagflation.

***hegemon*** A leading power that can exert its influence and values throughout the world.

***Helsinki Accords*** Adopted in 1975 by the Conference on Security and Cooperation in Europe; gave the Soviets the recognition they wanted of territorial borders in central and Eastern Europe, but also established human rights and other democratic values as the basic tenets that the members agreed to respect.

***HIV/AIDS*** A global epidemic that affects the human immune system and has contributed to millions of deaths worldwide, particularly in sub-Saharan Africa.

***homeland security*** Term commonly used since 9/11 to refer to efforts to ensure the protection of the United States from both internal and external threats, through transportation security (air travel, ports), emergency preparedness, domestic intelligence, infrastructure protection, and related measures.

***humanitarian intervention*** Entry of armed forces into another country to protect citizens from human rights violations, mass killings, or other atrocities.

***hydrogen bomb (H-bomb)*** A nuclear weapon that is vastly more destructive than the atomic bomb (A-bomb). Its development was seen as necessary to maintain nuclear deterrence because the Soviets developed the A-bomb more quickly than expected.

***imperialism*** The subordination of a weaker state by a stronger political entity, frequently through conquest or territorial occupation.

***interbranch politics*** The relationship between the executive and legislative branches.

***interest groups*** Formal organizations or groups of people who share a common belief or interest and who work together to try to influence government policy.

***Intergovernmental Panel on Climate Change (IPCC)*** Established by the UN Environment Program and the World Meteorological Association to assess global climate change; shared the 2007 Nobel Peace Prize with former vice president Al Gore.

***International Atomic Energy Agency (IAEA)*** An agency created in 1957 to ensure that as nations develop nuclear energy, it would be used only for peaceful purposes such as nuclear power plants.

***International Criminal Court (ICC)*** A permanent criminal tribunal, founded in 2002 to prosecute individuals who commit the most serious crimes against the international community, including crimes against humanity, war crimes, and genocide.

***International Institutionalism*** A school of international relations theory that emphasizes both the possibility and the value of international institutions and other forms of cooperation for reducing the chances of war and other conflict.

***internationalism*** A foreign policy whereby a country takes an active role in world affairs.

***International Monetary Fund (IMF)*** The global organization that oversees the international monetary system, promotes international monetary cooperation and exchange-rate stability, and provides resources to help members in balance of payments difficulties or to assist with poverty reduction.

***International Trade Commission (ITC)*** An independent federal agency with broad investigative and quasi-judicial responsibilities on matters of trade.

**Intifada** Palestinian uprisings, the first of which was against Israeli occupation of the West Bank in Gaza from 1987 to 1993 and the second of which was from 2000 to 2004.

***Iran-contra scandal*** A secret deal worked out by Reagan administration officials whereby the United States would provide arms to Iran in exchange for Iran's help in getting the American hostages in Lebanon released. The profits from the arms sales were then used to fund the Nicaraguan contras, thereby circumventing congressional prohibitions.

***Iraq War*** The invasion of Iraq in March 2003, led by the United States along with Great Britain and a coalition of about forty countries. The invasion was based on the claim that Iraq possessed weapons of mass destruction.

***isolationism*** A foreign policy whereby a country minimizes its involvement in world affairs.

***Jackson-Vanik amendment*** Passed by Congress in 1974, linking most-favored-nation status for the Soviet Union to a prescribed increase in emigration visas for Soviet Jews.

***Janjaweed*** "Devils on horseback," the name given to the Arab tribesmen who, along with the Sudanese government, have burned villages and farms and killed and terrorized the people of Darfur.

***Japanese-American internment*** The imprisonment of 120,000 Japanese Americans during World War II, often cited as an example of civil liberties violations in the name of national security.

***jihad*** Translated from Arabic as "struggle," often interpreted as "holy war" and linked to Al Qaeda.

***Joint Chiefs of Staff*** Established during World War II to coordinate the military services; made up of the chairman, the vice chairman, the Chief of Staff of the army, the Chief of Naval Operations, the Chief of Staff of the air force, and the commandant of the Marine Corps.

***just war*** An ethical doctrine with bases in all major religions that claims war must meet certain criteria, including a just cause, proportionality of the military means, a strong possibility of success, and the use of force as a last resource.

***Kyoto Treaty*** The 1997 United Nations Framework on Climate Change; went into effect in February 2005 despite American opposition and has had a mixed record.

***League of Nations*** An international institution created after World War I as a result of the Treaty of Versailles. Its failure was due to two crucial errors: U.S. nonmembership and the weakness of its institutional design.

***liberal international economic order (LIEO)*** The relatively open, market-based, free-trade system created after World War II with a minimum of tariffs and other government-initiated trade barriers, and with international economic relations worked out through negotiations.

***loose nukes*** Nuclear weapons and materials, particularly from Russia, that could fall into the hands of rogue states or terrorists.

***Louisiana Purchase*** The acquisition of the western territory of the United States from France for $15 million in 1803.

***Ludlow Amendment*** A constitutional amendment proposed in 1938 that would have required a national referendum before any decision to go to war.

***manifest destiny*** A term coined in 1845 that refers to the "right" claimed by the United States to continental expansion.

***Marshall Plan*** The first major U.S. Cold War foreign-aid program, for the reconstruction of Western Europe after World War II and during the Cold War.

***massive retaliation*** A nuclear strategy doctrine pursued during the Eisenhower administration whereby the United States threatened to resort to nuclear weapons to counter any Soviet challenge anywhere of any kind.

***Mayaguez incident*** A 1975 incident involving the limited use of force against Cambodia to rescue an American merchant ship and its crew.

***McCarthyism*** Widespread public accusations of procommunist activity that gripped the country in the early 1950s, based on little evidence and often in violation of civil liberties.

***Mexican Revolution*** Civil war in Mexico that began in 1910, caused by corruption and social unrest, and in which the United States intervened militarily.

***Mexican War*** War between the United States and Mexico, 1846–48, that focused on the annexation of Texas, which had declared its independence from Mexico in 1836.

***military assistance*** The provision of weapons, advisers, financing, and/or other forms of aid to a government or rebel group.

***military-industrial complex*** A social and political subsystem that integrates the armament industry, the military-oriented science community, the defense-related parts of the political system, and the military bureaucracies.

***Military intervention*** The "small wars," or the use of military force in a relatively limited fashion, as in the overthrow of governments considered hostile to U.S. interests and the protection or bringing to power of pro-U.S. leaders.

***Millennium Development Goals (MDGs)*** Eight goals established by the UN at its Millennium Summit in 2000 to be achieved by 2015 or sooner; the goals are most fundamentally about poverty but also focus on the environment, women's rights, education, and health.

***Montréal Protocol*** A 1987 multilateral agreement whereby all the nations of the world acted collectively to address the problem of ozone depletion; generally considered a success for global environmental policy.

***multilateralism*** An approach to foreign policy that emphasizes acting with other nations (three or more is what distinguishes multilateral from bilateral) through processes that are more consultative and consenual as structured by international institutions, alliances, and coalitions.

***multipolar system*** An international system in which there are three or more major powers.

***Munich analogy*** A reference to the negotiations in Munich leading up to World War II; invokes the need to confront dictators and aggressors, using force if necessary, rather than making concessions and pursuing "appeasement."

***mutually assured destruction (MAD)*** A Cold War nuclear doctrine based on the fact that the United States and the Soviet Union had enough nuclear weapons to destroy one another. MAD was considered potentially stabilizing because neither country could launch a "first strike" without risking devastation by a "second strike."

***National Intelligence Estimate (NIE)*** Officially defined as "the coordinated judgments of the Intelligence Community regarding the likely course of future events," written with the goal of providing "policymakers with the best, unvarnished and unbiased information—regardless of whether analytic judgments conform to U.S. policy."

***national missile defense (NMD)*** A system intended to defend the United States from incoming intercontinental ballistic missiles.

***National Security Agency (NSA)*** The nation's cryptologic intelligence organization, dating back to the Cold War. The NSA gained attention for its role in a secret Bush program of warrantless wiretapping and electronic surveillance of hundreds or thousands of people within the United States.

***National Security Council (NSC)*** The president's principal forum for considering national security and foreign policy matters with senior national security advisors and Cabinet officials.

***NATO expansion*** Post–Cold War opening of NATO to former Soviet-bloc states.

***neocolonialism*** Extensive power exercised by one country over another through less direct control than colonialism.

***neoconservatism*** A belief system prevalent in the George W. Bush administration that strongly links Power and Principles and holds that America's role is to advance freedom through the exercise of its superior power, including military force.

***nongovernmental organization (NGO)*** An unofficial, nonprofit organization; NGOs have grown in numbers and roles as actors in foreign policy and international affairs.

***9/11 Commission*** An independent, bipartisan commission set up in late 2002 to investigate the September 11, 2001 terrorist attacks, including their causes and lessons.

***Nixon shock*** President Nixon's announcement on August 15, 1971 that the United States was unilaterally devaluing the dollar, suspending its convertibility to gold, and imposing a 10 percent special tariff on imports.

***nonstate actors*** Actors on the international stage that are not states yet have a major impact, whether as threats (terrorist groups such as Al Qaeda), or as problem solvers (Gates Foundation).

***North American Free Trade Agreement (NAFTA)*** Approved in 1993, created a free-trade area among the three North American countries: Canada, Mexico, and the United States.

***North Atlantic Treaty Organization (NATO)*** The first peacetime military alliance in American history. Created in 1949, NATO ensured a military commitment to keeping U.S. troops in Europe and the collective defense pledge that the United States would defend its European allies if they were attacked.

***NSC-68*** An influential security-planning paper developed in early 1950 by President Truman's National Security Council. NSC-68 called for three important shifts in U.S. strategy: globalization of containment, militarization of containment, and the development of the hydrogen bomb.

***nuclear deterrence*** Prevention of nuclear war by credibly communicating sufficient will and capacity to retaliate as a second strike if attacked.

***nuclear freeze movement*** A movement during the early 1980s based on widespread fear that the nuclear buildup had gone too far.

***Nuclear Nonproliferation Treaty (NPT)*** Approved by the UN General Assembly in 1968, allowing the five states that already had nuclear weapons—the United States, the Soviet Union, Britain, France, and China—to keep them, and prohibiting all other states from acquiring or developing them.

***Nuclear utilization targeting strategy (NUTS)*** In contrast with the doctrine of mutually assured destruction (MAD), this theory argued that only if the United States alone had the capacity to fight a "limited" nuclear war would deterrence be strengthened—and only then would the United States be in a position to "win" should it come to that.

***"One China" policy*** Established by Nixon and Kissinger as part of détente; signified that American policy shifted from its traditional support for Taiwan and supported the peaceful reunification of China.

***Open Door policy*** A demand made on the major European powers in the 1890s that the United States not be closed out of spheres of trade and influence in China; the United States claimed to be helping China against the encroachments of European colonialism, but was also self-interested.

***Operation Desert Shield*** Response to the 1990 invasion of Kuwait by Iraq, the most rapid buildup of U.S. military forces since World War II to protect Saudi Arabia from an invasion by the Iraqi armies of Saddam Hussein.

***Operation Desert Storm*** Followed Desert Shield, the U.S.-led coalition operation launched in January 1991 to drive the Iraqi armies of Saddam Hussein out of Kuwait; it was a formidable military victory, with Iraqi forces withdrawing from Kuwait in little more than a month and with few American and coalition casualties.

***Operation Restore Hope*** A largely humanitarian mission in which the United States sent twenty-seven thousand troops to Somalia in December 1992 to help restore order and bring food to the Somali people.

***Orange Revolution*** A series of protests in Ukraine in late 2004 that overturned Soviet-style rigged elections.

***Organization for Security and Cooperation in Europe (OSCE)*** The new name given to the CSCE in 1994, which expanded its membership to fifty-six states, enhanced its role in diplomacy and conflict management and resolution, and implied greater institutionalization.

***Organization of American States (OAS)*** The major regional organization of the Western Hemisphere, which currently has thirty-five member states; dominated by the United States during the Cold War, but less so since then.

***Organization of Petroleum Exporting Countries (OPEC)*** An organization that led an oil embargo in 1973, targeted at the United States and the Netherlands for their support of Israel in the Yom Kippur War, and a global price hike, actions that forever changed the economics of oil. OPEC led a second oil shock in 1979 during the Iranian Revolution.

***Oslo agreement*** Officially the Israeli-Palestinian Declaration of Principles, it was signed by Israel's prime minister Yitzhak Rabin and the Palestine Liberation Organization leader Yasir Arafat alongside President Bill Clinton in 1993 and marked a major breakthrough toward resolution of the Israeli-Palestinian conflict.

***peace enforcement*** Operation in a situation where there is no peace to be kept, but rather it must be imposed and enforced, as in Bosnia during the 1990s.

***peacekeeping*** Operation in which UN forces are brought in after the parties involved in a conflict have agreed to the terms of peace; with the consent of those parties, the UN forces ensure and facilitate the keeping of that peace.

***peace operation*** Operation conducted by soldiers assembled on a temporary basis from the national armies of UN member countries to establish or preserve peace.

***Pearl Harbor*** A U.S. naval base in Hawaii, the site of a surprise attack by the Japanese on on December 7, 1941 that precipitated U.S. entry into World War II.

**perestroika** Literally, "restructuring," it meant changes in the Soviet economy, allowing for more open markets with some private enterprise and foreign investments.

***Platt Amendment (1901)*** An amendment attached to the Cuban constitution to protect U.S. special interests in Cuba.

***policy enhancement*** Argues that the freedom of action the United States gives up by acting multilaterally tends to be outweighed by the capacity gained to achieve shared objectives.

***political institutions*** The ongoing governing structure essential for maintaining political stability, accountability, and good governance.

***political Islam*** Refers to Islam as not only a religious and cultural system, but also a political system. Political Islam has controversial implications for human rights and democratization.

***Powell Doctrine*** A term named after General Colin Powell that refers to the decisive use of force to end conflict quickly and minimize U.S. casualties, as in the 1990–91 Persian Gulf War.

***power transition*** A situation in which a dominant global power is at least somewhat declining and a new global power is rising. During a power transition, risks of conflict and even war can run high.

***preemption*** The use of military force anticipatorily against imminent threats.

***preponderance*** Similar to primacy; refers to the dominant position of a superpower.

***prerogative encroachment*** The concern that actions by the UN and other multilateral institutions infringe on American power and freedom of action.

***prevention*** In general, action to reduce chances of a future conflict; in military terms, the anticipatory use of force against a prospective but not an imminent threat.

***preventive diplomacy*** Early action to prevent a dispute from escalating or a problem from worsening; involves getting at problems at the root of violent conflict.

***primacy*** The dominant position of a major power.

***primordialist*** Refers to an explanation of the sources of ethnic conflict that sees ethnicity as a fixed and inherently conflictual historical identity.

***procedural legislation*** Process-specific legislation that spells out the procedures and structures through which foreign policy will be made.

***proliferation*** The spread of nuclear weapons to states that are banned from having them by the Nuclear Nonproliferation Treaty.

***protectionism*** An economic policy of restricting trade to protect businesses in one country from foreign competition, often through the use of tariffs.

***public diplomacy*** Efforts to influence perceptions and attitudes of foreign publics to foster favorable views of the United States and its foreign policy.

***purposive*** Refers to an explanation of the sources of ethnic conflict that acknowledges how history shapes ethnic tensions but stresses the ways in which demagogic leaders and others intentionally exploit, exacerbate, and escalate such tensions.

***Reagan Doctrine*** A U.S. foreign policy strategy developed by the Reagan administration as the basis for going beyond containment to seek to oust communist regimes that had come to power.

***Realism*** A school of international relations theory that emphasizes power as the objective of the state and conceives the international system as a competition for power.

***Reciprocal Trade Agreements Act*** First passed by Congress in 1934, delegating to the president authority to cut tariffs by as much as 50 percent if he could negotiate reciprocal cuts with other countries. This act laid the basis for a fundamental shift away from protectionism and toward free trade.

***Red Scare*** The period 1919–20 when the Wilson administration, led by Attorney General A. Mitchell Palmer, grossly overreacted to fears of internal subversion linked to "world communism'" with heavy-handed repression and blatant disregard for civil liberties.

***responsibility to protect (R2P)*** Emerging norm stressing that individuals must be protected from mass killings and other gross violations of their rights within states, the corresponding limits to claims of sovereignty by offending states, and the legitimacy of certain types of international intervention.

***revolution in military affairs*** A mastery of electronic and information technologies that gave the United States unprecedented conventional military capabilities during Operation Desert Storm.

***ripeness*** Refers to points(s) in the life cycle of a conflict at which that conflict is more conducive to possible resolution than at other times.

***rogue state*** Describes a state that is considered an extreme security threat and is not very susceptible to negotiations for ideological or other essential reasons.

***Roosevelt Corollary*** Set forth in 1904, claimed for the United States the "international police power" to intervene when instability within a Latin American country risked creating the pretext for an Old World power to act.

***rule of law*** A strong constitution and other legal guarantees that protect citizens against arbitrary acts by the state and lawless actions by other citizens.

***Russian Revolution*** The series of revolutions in 1917 against the Czarist government which led to the creation of the Soviet Union and the world's first communist state.

***Secretary of Commerce*** The head of the Department of Commerce, responsible for trade promotion and other areas of economic policy.

***Secretary of the Treasury*** The head of the Department of the Treasury and one of the president's principal economic advisers.

***security community*** An area in which strategic rivalries are attenuated and the use of force within the group is highly unlikely.

***self-defense*** Military action taken in response to already having been attacked.

***Shanghai Cooperation Organization (SCO)*** A quasi alliance initiated by China in 2001 with Russia and a number of Central Asian countries to balance against American power.

***shuttle diplomacy*** Secretary of State Henry Kissinger's method of intensive U.S. peace brokering during and following the 1973 Arab-Israeli war, working out cease-fires and other agreements among Israel, Egypt, Jordan, Syria and others in the region.

***Six-Party Talks*** A series of negotiations involving the United States, China, Russia, Japan, South Korea, and North Korea to peacefully resolve the nuclear proliferation threat posed by North Korea.

***Smoot-Hawley Tariff*** A protectionist tariff of 1930 that had disastrous effects, including contributing to the Great Depression.

***social capital*** A term used to describe a public spiritedness and community involvement that go beyond just voting; entails other forms of civic engagement, a sense of cooperation, and a shared ethic among citizens of helping and trusting each other.

***soft power*** The ways in which the values for which a nation stands—its cultural attractiveness and other aspects of its reputation—can be sources of influence in the world.

***sovereignty*** The authority of a state within its own borders, dating back to the seventeenth-century Treaty of Westphalia; debated today in terms of the rights of states to act autonomously and their responsibilities to their own people and the international community.

***Spanish-American War*** War in 1898 between Spain and the United States in which the United States gained dominance over Cuba and took the Philippines as a colony, and that also marked the beginning of the emergence of the United States as a world power.

***START (Strategic Arms Reduction Treaty)*** The first of the post–Cold War U.S.-Soviet nuclear arms control agreements, signed by President George H. W. Bush and the Russian president, Mikhail Gorbachev, in 1991. It cut strategic nuclear weapons from Cold War levels of 13,000 U.S. and 11,000 Soviet warheads to 6,000 on each side.

***State Department*** The federal department responsible for implementing the foreign policy of the United States.

***Strategic Arms Limitation Treaty (SALT I)*** Negotiations during the 1970s to limit U.S. and Soviet nuclear weapons. SALT I was signed and ratified during the Nixon administration.

***Strategic Arms Limitation Talks (SALT II)*** The follow-up agreement to limit U.S. and Soviet nuclear weapons. It was never finalized amid controversies over détente and then the Soviet invasion of Afghanistan.

***Strategic Defense Initiative (SDI)*** A Reagan-initiated program to build a nationwide defense umbrella against nuclear attack; also known as "Star Wars."

***substantive legislation*** Policy-specific legislation that spells out what the details of what foreign policy should or should not be.

***Summit of the Americas*** The series of regular summit meetings that bring together leaders from countries in North America, South America, and Central America, but which have not produced significant results.

***surge*** A major shift in strategy during the Iraq war, which involved a buildup of another thirty thousand troops combined with a revised counterinsurgency strategy; led by General David Petraeus.

***Sustainable development*** A policy approach that meets the needs of the present without compromising the ability of future generations to meet their own needs.

***Taiwan*** An island off the coast of mainland China to which the Jiang Jeishi (Chiang Kai-shek) government retreated after its defeat in the 1949 Chinese revolution; a strong U.S. ally during the Cold War, still backed by the United States but in the context of overall U.S. relations with Beijing and support for peaceful reunification.

***Tiananmen Square*** Site of massive prodemocracy protests in China in 1989 that culminated in violent repression, including the killing and injuring of hundreds of people gathered in this main square in Beijing.

***Tibet*** The home of the Tibetan people, who seek greater autonomy from China and possibly secession from China itself; a major human rights issue in U.S.-China relations.

***Tokyo Round*** A round of GATT global trade negotiations during the 1970s that not only lowered tariffs but also brought down some "nontariff barriers"—various governmental policies and practices that discriminated against imports and thus impeded free trade.

***trade deficit*** A negative trade value; increases when the growth in the value of exports does not keep up with the growth in the value of imports.

***trade promotion authority*** Approved by Congress in 2002, during the George W. Bush administration, to replace the more seemingly political term *fast-track authority*; delegated trade-negotiating authority to the president and committed Congress to expedited review and legislative procedures, but was not renewed in 2007.

***treaty*** A formal agreement between two or more states that is negotiated by the president and ratified by a two-thirds majority of the Senate.

***Truman Doctrine*** A U.S. commitment proclaimed in March 1947 to aid Greece and Turkey against Soviet and Soviet-assisted threats; key basis for containment.

***Uighurs*** A Turkic ethnic group living in China that has had tensions with the Han, China's ethnic majority. Those tensions exploded into violent riots in July 2009.

***unilateralism*** An approach to foreign policy that emphasizes actions that a nation takes largely on its own, or acting with others but mainly on its own terms.

***unipolar system*** An international system in which there is one major power.

***United Nations (UN)*** The principal global institution founded on June 26, 1945 by fifty-one countries to ensure peace. The UN now includes 192 countries and plays a key, often controversial, role in world affairs.

***U.S. Trade Representative (USTR)*** The president's principal trade advisor, negotiator and spokesperson on trade issues.

***veto*** The constitutional right of the president to refuse to approve legislation passed by the legislature.

***Vietnam War*** A hugely controversial war in Southeast Asia, fought mostly between 1965 and 1975, in which the United States allied with South Vietnam against communist North Vietnam and the Viet Cong. The war was a major defeat for the United States, the reasons for which are hotly debated.

***War of 1812*** The war between the United States and Britain along the Canadian border, the Atlantic coast, the Gulf of Mexico and on the oceans. British forces burned the White House.

***war on terrorism*** The war declared by President George W. Bush after the attacks on September 11, which he stated would not end "until every terrorist group of global reach has been found, stopped, and defeated," and of which the Afghanistan and Iraq wars have been part.

***war powers*** The constitutional power given to the president to serve as "commander in chief" and given to Congress to "declare war" and "provide for the common defense." Because these are not separate powers but rather shares of the same power, war powers have been a topic of recurring debate in foreign policy politics.

***War Powers Resolution (WPR) of 1973*** An act seeking to limit presidential war powers by tightening requirements for consulting with Congress; based on the lessons of Vietnam but has not had much actual impact.

***Washington consensus*** Policy view that prevailed in the 1990s at the World Bank and the International Monetary Fund whereby countries should give the highest priority to reducing barriers to international trade and investment, cutting their own government spending, reducing government regulations, promoting privatization, and taking other steps to gain the greater economic efficiency and competiveness that would promote economic growth.

***Watergate*** The political scandal which began with the arrest of five men for breaking into Democratic party offices at the Watergate complex in June 1972. The resulting investigation revealed that President Nixon and his cronies had lied and committed crimes, and led to Nixon's resignation.

***weapons of mass destruction*** Weapons, including nuclear, biological, and chemical weapons, that can kill very large numbers of people and cause other massive destruction.

***Weinberger criteria*** Six criteria laid out by Defense Secretary Caspar Weinberger in November 1984 that set the threshold for when and how to use military force; prompted by the failure of American troops in Lebanon.

***World Bank*** Formally named the International Bank for Reconstruction and Development, it initially focused on European reconstruction and later became a major source of development aid for Third World countries.

***World Health Organization (WHO)*** The principal UN agency dealing with HIV/AIDS and other global health issues.

***World Trade Organization (WTO)*** Established in 1995 as a significantly stronger multilateral institution to replace the General Agreement on Tariffs and Trade; responsible for multilateral trade policy.

***World War I*** A major world conflict, from 1914 to 1918, that the United States entered in 1917. The world powers organized into two opposing camps: the Triple Entente and the Triple Alliance. This war resulted in over 15 million casualties.

***World War II*** A major world conflict, from 1939 to 1945, in which the Allied powers fought against Hitler's Nazi Germany and imperial Japan, engaging in a war that resulted in 70 million deaths. The war was fought in both the European and Pacific theaters. The United States and the Soviet Union emerged as the world's superpowers.

# Index


Abbas, Mahmoud, 451, 453
ABC (anything but communism)
  ABT and, 418, 609–11
  Africa and, 192
  democracy and, 594–95
  human rights and, 165
  ideological bipolarity and, 130–33
  Kirkpatrick on, 181
  Vietnam and, 130–31, 154
Abdulaziz, Abdullah bin, 421
ABM (Anti-Ballistic Missile) Treaty, 34, 646
ABMs (anti-ballistic missiles), 164
abortion, 562
ABT (anybody but terrorists), 406, 418, 609–11
Abu Ghraib prison scandal, 427, 435, 615
Abu Sayyaf, 443
accountability, global governance and, 204, 205
accountability politics, 579, 696, 698
ACDA (Arms Control and Disarmament Agency), 35, 39, 139
Acheson, Dean, 114, 140, 144, 152, 157, 395
Adams, Brooks, 239
Adams, John, 34, 47, 73, 83, 88, 106
Adams, John Quincy, 41, 99
Adelman, Kenneth, 425
administrative trade remedies, 583–84
advocacy networks, 693–701
Afghanistan
  Al Qaeda and, 414, 416
  chemical weapons and, 314
  drug rings and, 318, 319, 436
  economic sanctions against, 303
  foreign policy and, 411
  Japan and, 377–78
  national interest and, 485
  nation building in, 482
  Obama administration and, 436, 439–41, 447
  Pakistan and, 381, 609
  Soviet Union and, 150, 167, 168, 170, 177, 188, 190, 192, 276, 381, 506
  swine flu and, 568
  United Nations and, 332
  war on terrorism and, 3, 406, 411–13, 415
Afghanistan War (2001)
  alliances in, 347, 357
  Bush and, 411–13, 436
  NATO and, 353
  public opinion and, 353–51
  UN Security Council and, 303
  war powers and, 31
Afghan Northern Alliance, 412
AFL-CIO, 171, 621
Africa
  AIDS in, 394, 564, 598, 688
  China and, 368, 369
  communism in, 115
  continental unity, 389–90
  Darfur and, 295, 354, 374, 392, 482, 510–15, 520
  decolonization of, 93
  democracy and, 390–91, 594, 595, 598, 621, 623
  geopolitics of, 389–94
  global economic crisis of 2008 and, 537
  human rights and, 602, 603
  hunger in, 562
  IMF and, 551
  national interest and, 485
  news media and, 59
  piracy and, 316
  population growth in, 577
  Soviet Union and, 169
  UN membership, 303
  war on terrorism and, 414
African Command, 457
African National Congress (ANC), 598, 634
African Union (AU), 394, 511, 513, 621
African Union Mission in Sudan (AMIS), 511, 513
Agency for International Development (AID), 139, 298, 620, 625
agenda setting, 59
*Agents of Influence*, 53
Agreed Framework, 310, 647
agriculture, 462, 544
Agriculture, U.S. Department of, 49, 583
Aguinaldo, Emilio, 93, 96
Ahmadinejad, Mahmoud, 446, 447, 600
Ahtisaari, Martti, 505–6, 506n
AID (Agency for International Development), 139, 298, 620, 625
AIDS
  Africa and, 394, 564, 598, 688
  China and, 375, 564
  Gates Foundation and, 566
  globalization and, 564–66
  India and, 382, 564

AIDS (*cont.*)
  public health and, 563, 564
  UNAIDS report on, 685–89
AIPAC (American-Israel Public Affairs Committee), 51, 54
air pollution, 576
Akil El-Kouedi, Mona, 614–15
Albania, 349, 593
Albright, Madeleine K., 47, 482
Alien and Sedition Acts, 73, 74, 106
Allende, Salvador, 169, 594
Alliance for Progress, 132, 556
alliances, foreign policy strategies and, 12, 83–84
Allison, Graham T., 48, 141, 221–22
Almond, Gabriel, 63
Almond-Lippmann thesis, challenges to, 223–30
Al Qaeda
  Chechnya and, 361
  Cold War and, 192
  Hussein and, 23, 423, 424, 468
  on information gathering, 463
  intelligence agencies and, 327
  Islamic fundamentalism and, 442, 611, 670–71
  languages used by, 418
  members of, 443
  national security and, 458
  Obama and, 444
  Pakistan and, 381, 436, 440–41, 609
  as true Enemy, 456, 670–71
  war on terrorism and, 3, 406, 410–13, 414, 416
  weapons of mass destruction and, 423
America First Committee, 52, 86
American Bar Association, 621, 626
"American Conception of National Security and the Beginnings of the Cold War, 1945-48, The" (Leffler), 246–52
American exceptionalism, 17, 90–95, 283, 285, 289
American-Israel Public Affairs Committee (AIPAC), 51, 54
American Legion, 52
"American 'New Empire,' The" (LaFeber), 239–45
*American People and Foreign Policy, The* (Almond), 63
"America's Imperial Ambition" (Ikenberry), 665–68
AMIS (African Union Mission in Sudan), 511, 513
Amnesty International, 52, 376, 602, 621, 629
anarchic view of international relations, 6–7
ANC (African National Congress), 598, 634
Andropov, Yuri, 189
Angell, Norman, 608
Angola, 53, 169, 391, 598
Annan, Kofi
  on Darfur, 511
  election of, 332
  on HIV/AIDS, 565
  human rights and, 629
  on interventions, 502
  on multilateralism, 286
  on national sovereignty, 490
  on poverty, 553
  "We the Peoples," 649–55
Annenberg Public Policy Center, 60
Antarctic Treaty (1959), 164n
anthrax-laden letters, 314, 415
Anti-Apartheid Act, 38, 635
anti-apartheid movement, 54
Anti-Ballistic Missile (ABM) Treaty, 34, 646
anti-ballistic missiles (ABMs), 164
anticommunism
  Helsinki Accords and, 162
  HUAC and, 144
  interest groups and, 143
  military assistance and, 12
  Taiwan and, 118
anti-globalization movement, 3, 54
Anti-Imperialist League, 52
antiwar groups, 52
anybody but terrorists (ABT), 406, 418, 609–11
anything but communism, *see* ABC (anything but communism)
apartheid in South Africa
  democracy and, 595
  economic sanctions against, 51, 634
  end of, 393, 633
  interest groups and, 52, 54
  overview of, 634–35
  Reagan and, 38
appointments, 30, 34–36
Aquino, Benigno, 28, 622
Aquino, Corazon, 28, 622
Arab-Israeli conflicts
  Arab-Israeli War, 19
  Clinton and, 405, 406, 450, 452, 453, 456
  foreign policy and, 411
  identity groups and, 51
  Obama and, 455
  overview of, 448–56
  peace and, 23, 405, 406
  Six-Day War, 172
Arab League, 512
Arafat, Yasir, 63, 405, 406, 449, 450, 452, 453, 633
Arbenz Guzman, Jacobo, 22–23

Argentina
democracy and, 593, 594, 600
export promotion and, 583
global economic crisis of 2008 and, 545
military coups in, 132
swine flu and, 568
transitional justice and, 627
Arias, Oscar, 191, 391
Aristide, Jean-Bertrand, 618
Arizona, 84
Armenia, 593
Armitage, Richard, 312
arms control
deterrence and, 257–58
Reagan and, 188–89
Soviet Union and, 190, 356
Arms Control and Disarmament Agency (ACDA), 35, 39, 139
Army, U.S., 218
Art, Robert, 490
Articles of Confederation, 74, 216
Asad, Bashar, 455
ASEAN (Association of Southeast Asian Nations), 383
Ashcroft, John, 462
Asia
Central Command and, 457
communism in, 115
decolonization of, 93
drug rings and, 318
financial crises in, 541, 546–48
geopolitics of, 368–83, 657
global economic crisis of 2008 and, 537
human rights and, 602–3
Pacific Command and, 457
population growth in, 577
power in, 101–3
*see also specific countries*
Asia Foundation, 621
Asian and Pacific Population Conference, 562
Aspin, Les, 47
Association of Southeast Asian Nations (ASEAN), 383
Atlantic Charter, 79, 80, 93, 236, 668
atomic bombs, *see* nuclear weapons
Atta, Mohammed, 443
AU (African Union), 394, 511, 513, 621
Aum Shinrikyo, 314
Australia, 420, 428, 568
Austria, 568
automobile industry, 175–76, 545
avian flu (H5N1), 4, 463, 567
"axis of evil," 445, 628, 646
Ayoob, Mohammed, 599
Azerbaijan, 623, 626

Bachelet, Michelle, 601
Baeza, Mario, 54
Baghdad Pact, 128
Bahrain, 599
Baker, James A., III, 45, 47, 466, 483, 503, 680
balance of power, 7, 236
Balkan wars, 360
Ball, George, 152, 230n12
Bao Dai, 131
Barak, Ehud, 453
Barbary pirates, 74–75
Barnett, Michael, 496
Baruch, Bernard, 118
Baruch Plan, 118
Bashir, Omar al-, 514–15
Basic Principles Agreement, 270
Bayard, Thomas F., 240
Bay of Pigs invasion, 45, 61–62, 128–29, 139–40
Beers, Charlotte, 415
Begin, Menachim, 450, 452
Beijing
Olympics (2008), 376
Tiananmen Square, 20–21, 374, 395, 591, 617
Belarus, 356, 593, 623
belief systems, 43–44
belligerent nationalism, 608
benevolent hegemony, 283, 288
Benton, Thomas Hart, 104
Berger, Samuel, 47
Berlin blockade, 115
Berlin Wall, 2, 160, 191, 280, 342, 590
Berlusconi, Silvio, 420
Beschloss, Michael, 61
Betts, Richard, 4, 141, 361–62, 410
Bhutto, Benazir, 440, 610, 611
Biden, Joseph, 325, 326, 360, 440–41
billiards metaphor, 8
Bill of Rights, 106–8, 457
bin Laden, Osama
background of, 411, 443
Cold War and, 192
crime syndicates and, 320
Lashkar-e-Taiba and, 381
on Obama, 444
Sudan and, 512
as true Enemy, 456
war on terrorism and, 3, 406, 410, 412, 413, 415

biodiversity, 5, 575
Biological and Toxin Weapons Convention (1972), 315–16
biological weapons, 314–16, 467, 485
Biological Weapons Convention, 309, 646
BioWeapons Prevention Project, 316
bipartisanship, 27, 135
bipolar systems, 7, 282, 290
Blaine, James G., 240
Blair, Dennis, 320, 326
Blair, Tony, 312, 347, 420, 443, 469
blogs, 328
Bolívar, Simon, 387
Bolivia, 317–18, 600, 601
Bolshevik revolution, 77, 78, 597
Bolton, John, 35–36, 284, 285, 311
B-1 bombers, 56–57
Bono, 563
Bosnia
  Bush and, 503–4
  Clinton and, 30, 301, 481, 503–4, 517, 683
  CNN curve and, 518–19, 680–82
  Dayton Accord and, 14, 301, 504
  democracy and, 593, 620
  ethnic conflicts in, 294–95, 297, 360, 480–81, 485, 486, 487, 488, 591, 682–84
  Herzegovina and, 360, 495
  interventions in, 480–81, 495, 501, 503–4, 680–82
  military force in, 408
  NATO and, 347, 352, 501, 504, 517
  peacekeeping costs in, 486–87
  United Nations and, 332, 506
  war powers and, 517
Botha, P. W., 634
Botswana, 566
Boutros-Ghali, Boutros, 508
Brandeis, Louis, 107, 108, 144
Brandenburg, Benjamin B., 614–15
Brazil
  China and, 368, 386
  democracy and, 593, 594, 601
  financial crises and, 547–48
  geopolitics of, 386–87
  global economic crisis of 2008 and, 537, 539, 545
  military coups in, 132
  overpopulation and, 562
  special drawing rights and, 550
  swine flu and, 568
  UN Security Council and, 305
Bremer, L. Paul, III, 425
Bretton Woods conference, 82, 211
Bretton Woods system, 320–21
Brezhnev, Leonid, 162, 166, 168, 189, 190, 267, 270, 273
BRICs, 540, 550, 551
Britain, *see* Great Britain
Brodie, Bernard, 120, 121, 253–58
Brooks, Stephen, 282, 290, 291
Brown, Archie, 190
Brownback, Sam, 520
Browne, Malcolm, 159
Broz, Josip, 131n
Brysk, Alison, 701n9
Brzezinski, Zbigniew, 36, 170
Buchanan, James, 41
Bulgaria, 349, 625
bully pulpit, 38
bureaucratic politics, 41, 44–49, 221–22, 469–70
Bureau of Decency, Labor and Human Rights, 396
Bureau of Democracy, Human Rights, and Labor, 620
Bureau of East Asian Affairs, 396
Bureau of Economics, Business, and Agricultural Affairs, 581
Burma, 318, 492–93
Burundi, 559, 595
Bush, George H. W.
  advisers to, 45–46
  appointments by, 35
  Arab-Israeli conflict and, 450
  assassination attempt on, 409
  Bosnia and, 503–4
  China and, 21, 374, 396, 617
  Cold War and, 2, 480
  economic sanctions and, 617, 618, 619
  foreign policy and, 42, 409
  Great Britain and, 347
  human rights and, 628
  interventions and, 480, 483, 679, 680
  NAFTA and, 582
Bush, George W.
  ABM Treaty and, 34
  abortion and, 562
  advisers to, 36, 46, 47–48
  Afghanistan War and, 411–13, 436
  agricultural subsidies and, 462, 544
  AIDS funding and, 565
  appointments by, 36, 286
  Arab-Israeli conflict and, 451, 454
  benevolent hegemony and, 283
  China and, 370, 371
  Darfur and, 511, 513
  democracy and, 600, 605–6, 608–9

Democratic Idealism and, 17
foreign aid and, 556–57
foreign policy and, 42–43, 330, 331, 436, 605
FTAA and, 545
global warming and, 574
Guantánamo Bay and, 461
homeland security and, 418
ICC and, 509, 510
India and, 382
interventions and, 481–82
Iran and, 445, 446
Iraq War and, 3, 23–24, 42, 48, 406, 419, 422–23, 426–28, 430, 434–35, 463–70, 472
Mexico and, 384
Moscow Treaty and, 356
national missile defense and, 307
national security and, 458, 459, 482, 485, 608–9, 663–64
NGOs and, 578
North Korea and, 310
oil and, 542
Pakistan and, 381, 440, 441, 609
Persian Gulf War and, 19, 407, 408
on preemption, 297, 416–17, 663–64
public opinion and, 297, 330, 331, 333, 348, 472, 648n1
Russia and, 355, 359, 360, 361, 362
September 11 attacks and, 3, 42, 333, 482
Somalia and, 391, 480, 515
START and, 356
Taiwan and, 398
on torture, 459
trade agreements and, 582–83
trade and, 544
trade deficit and, 541
unilateralism and, 282, 384, 646
Venezuela and, 387, 612
war on terrorism and, 406, 409, 411–18, 442, 472–73, 664
weapons of mass destruction and, 423, 424, 465, 467, 468
Wolfowitz and, 121
Bush Doctrine, 413–14, 416–17, 424–25, 500, 663–68
Byrd, Robert C., 465–66

Cable News Network (CNN), *see* CNN (Cable News Network)
CAFTA (Central American Free Trade Agreement), 545–46
California, 74, 620
Cambodia
communism in, 152
democracy and, 623
genocide in, 484–85
Khmer Rouge and, 154
Mayaguez incident, 185
transitional justice and, 627
United Nations and, 507
Campbell, Kurt M., 370
Camp David Accord (1978), 14, 301, 450, 452, 456
Camp David talks (2000), 453
Canada
democracy and, 621
NAFTA, FTAA, and, 545
peacekeeping operations and, 353
U.S. investments in, 209
CANF (Cuban-American National Foundation), 54
cap and trade policies, 574
capitalism, 189, 210, 540, 547
CARE, 554
Carothers, Thomas, 630, 631
Carter, Jimmy
advisers to, 36
appointments by, 35
B-1 bombers and, 57
belief system of, 43–44
Camp David Accord and, 14, 301, 452, 456
China and, 34, 395
dètente and, 167, 271, 272, 273
economic sanctions and, 634
Haiti and, 516–17
human rights and, 165, 170, 181, 213
Iran and, 445
Israel and, 450
Nicaragua and, 622–23
oil and, 542
public opinion and, 66
Reagan and, 66, 67
SALT II, 168
Taiwan and, 34
weapons of mass destruction and, 185
Carter Doctrine, 167
"Case for Goliath, The" (Mandelbaum), 343–44, 656–58
"Case for Humanitarian Intervention, The" (International Commission on Intervention and State Sovereignty), 672–74
Castillo Armas, Carlos, 22
Castro, Fidel, 22n, 54, 128–29, 139–40, 384, 387
CDC (Centers for Disease Control and Prevention), 568

CEELI (Central and East European Law Initiative), 626
Center for International Private Enterprise, 621
Center for Strategic and International Studies, 469
Centers for Disease Control and Prevention (CDC), 568
CENTO (Central Treaty Organization), 128
Central American Free Trade Agreement (CAFTA), 545–46
Central and East European Law Initiative (CEELI), 626
Central Command, 457
Central Intelligence Agency Act (1949), 137
Central Intelligence Agency (CIA)
  on Al Qaeda, 468
  Bay of Pigs and, 140
  Congress and, 137, 158
  covert actions and, 130, 132–33, 137, 192, 387
  creation of, 139
  debate over role of, 458
  Obama administration and, 327
  public health and, 564
  scandals in, 166, 327
  war on terrorism and, 412–13
Central Treaty Organization, 381
Central Treaty Organization (CENTO), 128
CFCs (chlorofluorocarbons), 571
CFR (Council on Foreign Relations), 366, 418, 469, 530
CFSP (common foreign and security policy), 348
Chad, 510, 511, 514, 559
Chamberlain, Neville, 155–56, 235
Chamorro, Violeta, 622, 623
Chan, Margaret, 568
Charles V, 667
Chávez, Hugo, 362, 387, 600, 612, 614
Chayes, Abram, 490
Chayes, Antonia Handler, 490
Chechnya, 357, 360–61, 414, 495, 502, 717, 718
chemical weapons, 314–16, 467, 485
Chemical Weapons Convention (CWC), 314–15, 316
Cheney, Dick
  bureaucratic politics and, 470
  Iran and, 446
  Iraq War and, 48, 419, 425, 468, 469–70
  Libya and, 312
  Pentagon planning document, 343
  on Russia, 362
  as senior adviser, 45, 47, 48
  on torture, 459
  on weapons of mass destruction, 423
Chernenko, Konstantin, 189
*Chesapeake* affair, 88
Chiang Kai-shek, *see* Jiang Jeishi
Chicago Council on Global Affairs, 329, 330
child mortality, 552, 555
Chile, 214, 546, 568, 593, 594, 601, 627–28
China
  Africa and, 368, 369
  AIDS in, 375, 564
  Brazil and, 368, 386
  Carter and, 34, 395
  chemical weapons and, 315
  Clinton and, 21, 370, 371, 374, 396, 617
  Cold War consensus and, 136–37, 143, 249
  communism and, 20–21, 115, 124–25, 157, 375
  crime syndicates in, 319
  Darfur and, 512, 515
  democracy and, 20–21, 374, 375–76, 620
  dètente and, 161, 166, 268
  economic sanctions against, 21, 374, 617–18
  environmental issues and, 322, 374, 570, 573, 574
  espionage and, 397
  financial crises in, 547
  foreign aid to, 562
  geopolitics of, 344, 368–76, 657
  global economic crisis of 2008 and, 537, 538, 545, 550
  human rights and, 20–21, 49, 375–76, 395–96, 398, 591, 628, 629
  IMF voting rights of, 550
  international commitments in, 138
  Internet service providers and, 617, 618
  Japan and, 372, 373, 379
  journalists and, 626
  Kosovo and, 502
  military and, 368–69, 371–72, 376, 378
  most-favored-nation status of, 20–21, 49
  North Korea and, 310–11, 373, 379
  nuclear weapons and, 310, 378
  oil and, 373–74, 396, 542
  poverty and, 553
  revolutions in, 103
  SARS and, 567, 568
  security threats and, 4
  Soviet Union and, 168–69
  special drawing rights and, 550
  Taiwan and, 369–71, 395, 398
  trade deficit and, 377, 396, 542
  treaties with, 101
  unipolarity and, 644, 645

UN Security Council and, 118, 304, 305, 395
U.S. economic relations with, 374
China lobbies, 143, 369, 394–99
Chinese Exclusion Act, 76
Chirac, Jacques, 420
chlorofluorocarbons (CFCs), 571
choice, 6, 9, 24, 27–68
Christopher, Warren, 15, 47, 355, 466, 487, 682, 683
Church, Frank, 166
Churchill, Winston, 79, 80, 81, 82, 93, 114, 235, 236–37, 246, 346–47
CIA, *see* Central Intelligence Agency (CIA)
CIA directors, 35, 42, 46, 138n
Cisco, 618
civil liberties
Lincoln and, 106
national security and, 107, 411
USA PATRIOT Act and, 456
civil-military relations, 625
Civil War, American
democratic peace theory and, 607
foreign policy significance of, 75, 76
France and, 99
military strength and, 88
reconstruction after, 76
slavery and, 109
Clancy, Tom, 364
"Clash of Civilizations, The" (Huntington), 591, 706–12
Claude, Inis, 13
Clausewitz, Karl von, 11
Cleveland, Grover, 109, 110
Clifford, Clark, 247
climate change, 571–74, 690–92
Clinton, Bill
advisers to, 46, 47
appointments by, 35
Arab-Israeli conflict and, 405, 406, 450, 452, 453, 456
Bosnia and, 30, 301, 481, 503–4, 517, 683
Chechnya and, 360–61
China and, 21, 370, 371, 374, 396, 617
CTBT and, 32, 33
Dayton Accord and, 14, 301
defense spending and, 295
democracy and, 215, 605–6, 608, 713
economic sanctions and, 445, 617, 618, 619
end of Cold War and, 480
foreign aid and, 556
foreign policy and, 42, 683, 713
FTAA and, 545
on globalization, 3
global warming and, 573
Great Britain and, 347
Haiti and, 516–17, 618, 619
India and, 382
international finance and, 547
interventions and, 480–81
Kosovo and, 505, 517
multilateralism and, 282, 284, 286, 287
NAFTA and, 582
national interest and, 284, 485
NATO and, 349
North Korea and, 311
nuclear arms deal and, 358, 359
Pakistan and, 609
Rabin and, 63
Rome Treaty and, 509
Russia and, 355, 359
Rwanda and, 497, 500
Somalia and, 30, 47, 391, 500, 515–16
Washington consensus and, 535n
Yeltsin and, 365
Clinton, Hillary Rodham
appointment as Secretary of State, 301, 325, 326
Democratic primaries and, 324
on drug trade, 386
human rights and, 628
Iraq War and, 465
NAFTA and, 385, 545
on "smart power," 302
Tibet and, 398
on war on terrorism, 442
women's empowerment policies and, 554
Clinton Doctrine, 505
Clooney, George, 520
CNN (Cable News Network)
CNN curve, 518–19, 677–84
impact of, 58
Iraq War and, 422–23
Persian Gulf War and, 408
coercive statecraft, 12, 494
Cohen, Bernard, 225
Cohen, William S., 47, 482
Colby, William, 35
Cold War
Africa and, 391, 598
alliances during, 12
American exceptionalism and, 92
bipartisanship and, 27
Bush on, 2, 480
covert actions and, 137

Cold War (*cont.*)
democracy and, 27, 616
détente and, 150, 160–70, 267–72, 273
deterrence during, 7, 119–29, 656–57
duck test and, 22
economic shocks of 1970s, 170–77
end of, 177–92, 273–75, 276–78, 342
foreign aid during, 557
foreign policy politics and, 135–46, 156–60, 193–94
foreign policy strategy and, 192
ideological bipolarity and, 130–33
liberal international economic order and, 133–35
military-industrial complex and, 56
national security and, 246–52
origins of, 114–15, 134, 246–52
orthodox view of, 115
political issue groups and, 51, 52
revisionist view of, 115, 246–52
system structure and, 8
transition from, 2
turbulence of, 150–51
United Nations and, 116–19
*see also* post–Cold War era
*Collapse* (Diamond), 322, 570, 571
collective action, 414, 569
collective defense, 124
Colombia, 95, 317, 318, 319, 546, 602
colonialism, 15–16, 102, 242
Commager, Henry Steele, 89
commerce, constitutional provisions for, 30, 36–37
Commerce, U.S. Department of, 49, 581, 584, 620
Commission on Sustainable Development, 570
Committee on the Present Danger, 52, 170
Committee to Defend America by Aiding Anti-Communist China, 395
Committee to Protect Journalists, 366
Committee to Warn of the Arrival of Communist Merchandise on the Local Business Scene, 143
common foreign and security policy (CFSP), 348
*Common Sense* (Paine), 216
communism
ABC and, 130–33
in Africa, 115
in Cambodia, 152
China and, 20–21, 115, 124–25, 157, 375
Cold War and, 115, 124–25, 247–48
containment policy and, 262
democracy and, 213, 594, 717–18
in France, 20, 122, 124
globalization and, 4, 127
in Guatemala, 22
Marshall Plan and, 20, 122, 124
revolutions and, 188
Roosevelt on, 114
Soviet Union and, 107
Vietnam War and, 152–53, 263, 265–66
compellence, 120
Comprehensive Anti-Apartheid Sanctions Act, 636
Comprehensive Test Ban Treaty (CTBT), 32–33, 284, 313–14
"Conceptual Models and the Cuban Missile Crisis" (Allison), 221–22
Conference of Defense Ministers of the Americas, 593
confrontation, 29
Congo, 391, 506, 595
Congress, U.S.
Afghanistan War and, 456
agricultural subsidies and, 544
and annexation of Texas, 104
Bosnia and, 517
CAFTA and, 546
Chinese espionage and, 397
Cold War consensus and, 135–38
CTBT and, 313
Darfur and, 520
on democratization, 620
economic sanctions and, 635–36
executive branch and, 184
genocide prevention and, 675
interest groups and, 53
Iraq War and, 428, 456, 462, 463–66
isolationism and, 86
Jay Treaty and, 27–28
Kosovo and, 517–18
Marshall Plan and, 20
military strength and, 87, 89
NAFTA and, 582
Obama and, 325
Pennsylvania Avenue diplomacy and, 29–37
pork-barreling by, 462
protectionism and, 109
public opinion influence and, 54
Somalia and, 679
trade agreements and, 581–83
United Nations and, 116–18
Vietnam War and, 153, 157–58
war powers and, 31–32, 186, 217–18
Congressional Black Caucus, 517
Congressional Research Service, 427
Congress of Vienna (1815), 345
Connally, John, 171
consensus

Cold War, 135–45, 158–60
foreign policy politics and, 28
senior advisers and, 44–45
conservatives, 170
Constitution, U.S.
on domestic surveillance, 458
drafting of, 216–20
First Amendment, 61, 460
foreign policy and, 29–37, 74
Fourth Amendment, 458
ICC and, 510
Second Amendment, 87
Third Amendment, 87
constitutionalism, 598
constructive compromise, 29
consumer product-safety problems, 5
containment
China and, 369
definition of, 120
détente and, 169, 275
in Europe, 191
power and, 119–29, 259–62
Reagan and, 192
in Third World, 192
contras, Nicaraguan, 183–84
Convention on the Prevention and Punishment of the Crime of Genocide (1948), 484
Converse, Philip, 224–25
Coolidge, Calvin, 232
cooperation, 29
*cordon sanitaire,* 115
Correa, Rafael, 601
corruption, 55, 625
Corwin, Edward S., 219
Costa Rica, 191
Council for a Livable World, 52
Council on Foreign Relations (CFR), 366, 418, 469, 530
counterfactual arguments, 488
covert actions
CIA and, 130, 132–33, 137, 192, 387
Cold War consensus and, 137
détente and, 166
France and, 12
power through, 12
Cox, Michael, 505
credibility, 254
credibility gap, 158
Creppy, Michael J., 460
crime syndicates, 5, 319–20
Croatia, 349, 352, 485, 487, 494, 503–4, 593
Crocker, Chester, 485
CSCE (Conference on Security and Cooperation in Europe), 162, 367, 500
CTBT (Comprehensive Test Ban Treaty), 32–33, 284, 313–14
Cuba
Bay of Pigs invasion, 45, 61–62, 128–29, 139–40
Castro and, 22n, 128–29, 139–40, 384, 387
democracy and, 593
geopolitics of, 384
Guantánamo Bay, 435, 442, 460–61
human rights and, 628, 629
journalists and, 626
military interventions in, 97, 99
U.S.S. Maine and, 105
Cuban-American National Foundation (CANF), 54
Cuban missile crisis
ExCom and, 140–41
Kennedy and, 2, 61, 129, 140, 143
nuclear war and, 2, 129
system structure and, 8
cultural influence of globalization, 533–34
CWC (Chemical Weapons Convention), 314–15, 316
cyber warfare, 296–98
Cyclone Nargis, 492–93
Cyprus, 506
Czechoslovakia
democracy and, 214, 594, 612
Guatemala and, 22
Havel and, 188, 191, 613
Munich analogy and, 155
"Prague Spring" in, 190
UN membership, 303
Czech Republic, 349, 353, 593, 631

Daalder, Ivo, 354
Daladier, Edouard, 155
Dalai Lama, 376, 396
Dallaire, Romeo, 489, 497, 498–99
Danforth, John, 36
Darfur, 295, 354, 374, 392, 482, 510–15, 520
Darfur Peace and Accountability Act, 513
Daschle, Tom, 462
da Silva, Luiz Inácio Lula, 304–5, 386, 537, 539, 601
*Day After, The,* 181
Dayton Accords (1995), 14, 301, 352, 360, 481, 495, 501, 504
D-Day, 82
debates over foreign policy, 72–73
on American exceptionalism, 90–95
on force and diplomacy, 294–302

debates over foreign policy (*cont.*)
on free trade vs. protectionism, 109–10, 580–81
on globalization, 529, 530–37, 539–40
on going to war, 103–6
historical context of, 73–83
IMF policies and, 548–50
on isolationism vs. internationalism, 83–87
on military strength, 87–90
on national security vs. Bill of Rights, 106–8
on prosperity and imperialism, 95–98
on relations with Latin America, 98–99, 101
on United States as Pacific power, 101–3
Debs, Eugene V., 107
decertification, 318
decision making, 140–41
decisive force theory, 178
"Declaration of a New International Economic Order," 173, 174–75
Declaration of Independence, 74
declaratory commitments, 34
Defense, U.S. Department of
bureaucratic politics and, 49
civil-military relations and, 625
creation of, 139
genocide prevention and, 676
interest groups and, 54
national security and, 459
news media and, 61
Defense Intelligence Agency, 139, 468
defense spending
great debates about, 87–90
post–Cold War era and, 295–97
deforestation, 576
de Gaulle, Charles, 82, 347
de Klerk, F. W., 633
Dell, 533
Dellums, Ron, 636
demilitarized zone (DMZ), 380
democracy
Africa and, 390–91, 594, 595, 598, 621, 623
Argentina and, 593, 594, 600
Bush and, 600, 605–6, 608–9
China and, 20–21, 374, 375–76, 620
Clinton and, 215, 605–6, 608, 713
Fukuyama on, 702–5
historical perspectives on, 594–95
human rights and, 593, 595–603, 620–33, 637
national interest and, 590–92, 706–12
Obama and, 438
in Pacific region, 102
Peace and, 604–9, 713–19
in Philippines, 28, 213, 214, 594
Power and, 609–16
Principles and, 211–15, 604–20, 713–19
Prosperity and, 617–20
Realism on, 11
Russia and, 215, 354, 364–67, 593, 594, 717–18
Soviet Union and, 593, 594, 608, 623
Wilson and, 94, 214
*Democracy in America* (Toqueville), 212
Democratic Idealism, 16–18
Democratic Party, 109, 110
democratic peace theory, 17, 604–9
Democratic Republic of Congo, 485, 495, 598
"Democratization and the Danger of War" (Mansfield and Snyder), 713–19
Deng Xiaoping, 375
Denmark, 557
desertification, 575–76
Destler, I. M., 36, 176, 580
détente
China and, 161, 166, 268
Cold War and, 150, 160–70, 267–72, 273
definition of, 160
Western Europe and, 191
"Détente" (George), 267–72
deterrence, 7, 253–54, 257–58, 297, 351, 656–57, 663
*see also* nuclear deterrence
developing countries, *see* Third World
Dialog, 630
Diamond, Jared, 322, 570, 571
Diamond, Larry, 624
Diem, Ngo Dinh, 131, 141, 154
diplomacy
Bush and, 297
China and, 368
coercive statecraft, 13, 494
definition of, 294
drug rings and, 318
enhancing, 298–99
foreign policy politics and, 322–34
of Metternich, 161
military force vs., 294–302
Obama and, 297, 299, 301–2, 447–48
"Pennsylvania Avenue," 29–37, 104, 135–38, 193
preventive, 493–96, 521
public opinion and, 66, 612
Realism on, 13
shuttle, 14, 301, 449, 452
*Diplomacy* (Kissinger), 86

direct action, 55
diseases of mass destruction (DMD), 567–68, 585
dispute settlement authority, 543
Djibouti, 595
DMD (diseases of mass destruction), 567–68, 585
DMZ (demilitarized zone), 380
DOD, *see* Defense, U.S. Department of
Doha Round, 544–45, 566
Dollar, David, 553
Dollar Diplomacy, 76, 77
domestic issues
  foreign policy politics and, 27–68
  multilateralism and, 289
  national security and, 462–63
  unilateralism and, 285
Dominican Republic, 78, 97, 99, 213, 214, 545–46
Donors Conferences, 453
Dorgan, Byron, 32
Downie, Leonard, 328
Doyle, Michael, 305–6, 606
*Dr. Strangelove*, 122
drug rings, 317–19, 436, 602
duck test, 22
Dulles, John Foster, 127, 177
dynamics of choice, 6, 24

Eagleburger, Lawrence, 680
Earth Day, 54
East Asia-Pacific Bureau, 49
East Asia-Pacific regional security, 372–73
Easterly, William, 558
Eastern Europe
  Cold War and, 115, 118, 276–78
  CSCE and, 162
  democracy and, 594
  global economic crisis of 2008 and, 537
  Gorbachev and, 190
  revolutions in, 186–89
  *see also individual countries*
East Timor, 591
Economic Cooperation Administration, 139
economic hegemony, 134–35
economic interest groups, 50–51
economic international institutions, 14
economic issues
  economic freedom and globalization, 3
  economic shocks of 1970s, 170–77
  global economic crisis of 2008, 537–40, 545
  gold standard, 171
  international economy and national security, 320–21
  internationalization of economy, 5
  liberal international economic order, 133–35, 146, 171, 173, 193
  New International Economic Order, 172–73, 174–75, 193
  OPEC shocks, 171–72
economic sanctions
  against Afghanistan, 303
  against apartheid, 51, 634
  bureaucratic politics and, 49
  Bush and, 617, 618, 619
  against China, 21, 374, 617–18
  decertification, 318
  democracy and, 617–20
  foreign policy politics and, 633–36
  against Haiti, 03, 618–19
  Iran and, 446
  against Iraq, 619–20
  power through, 12
  South Africa and, 51, 633–36
  UN Security Council and, 303, 310, 311, 446
Economism, 15
Ecuador, 132, 593, 600, 601
Edwards, John, 465
Egypt
  Arab-Israeli conflict and, 449, 450, 452
  Camp David Accord and, 14, 301
  chemical weapons and, 314, 315
  democracy and, 598–99, 615, 623
  foreign policy and, 411
  Iraq War and, 419, 421
  United Nations and, 305
  war on terrorism and, 416
Eisenhower, Dwight D.
  Arab-Israeli conflict and, 449
  Bay of Pigs invasion and, 128
  CIA covert actions and, 132
  Cold War consensus and, 135, 136–37
  foreign policy and, 41
  Guatemala and, 22
  massive retaliation doctrine, 129
  on military-industrial complex, 56
  national security state and, 139
  segregation and, 612, 616
  Stevenson and, 67
  on Vietnam War, 152
Eisenhower Doctrine, 128
El Baradei, Mohamed, 314
elections, 67, 622–24
Elliott, Kimberly Ann, 619
Ellsberg, Daniel, 62, 62n

El Salvador
  CAFTA and, 545–46
  death squads in, 181
  democracy and, 593, 620
  international commitments in, 138
  legislative aid and, 631
  peace accord in, 188, 191
  Sandinistas and, 178
  United Nations and, 507
  war powers and, 186
Elsey, George, 247
endangered species, 575
"End of History, The?" (Fukuyama), 591, 702–5
energy security, 321–22
engagement, 369–70
England, *see* Great Britain
Environmental Defense Fund, 575
environmental issues
  air pollution, 576
  biodiversity and, 5, 575
  deforestation, 576
  desertification, 575–76
  global climate change and, 571–74, 690–92
  globalization and, 568–77
  global warming, 5, 322, 571–74, 690–92
  oceans, 575
  political issue groups and, 52
  as threat to peace, 570
  United Nations and, 570, 571
  urbanization, 577
environmental mass destruction, 293
Environmental Performance Index, 574
EPA (Environmental Protection Agency), 581
equality, 598
Eritrea, 515, 626
Espionage and Sedition Acts, 28, 107, 108
essence of choice, 6, 9
*Essence of Decision*, The (Allison), 141
Estemirova, Natalia, 361
Estonia, 349, 367, 593
Ethiopia, 59, 169, 314, 392
ethnic cleansing and genocide, 520–21
  Bosnia and, 294–95, 297, 360, 480–81, 485, 486, 487, 488, 591, 682–84
  Cambodia and, 484–85
  Darfur and, 482, 511
  driving forces behind, 487–89
  humanitarian interventions and, 480–522, 675–76
  Kosovo and, 487, 505
  Rwanda and, 481, 488, 489, 496, 497–99, 591, 598
  during World War I, 484
  during World War II, 484
ethnicity, 5, 51
EU, *see* European Union (EU)
EU-3, 446
euro, 550
Europe, *see* Eastern Europe; Western Europe
European-Atlantic Partnership Council, 349
European Command, 457
European Union (EU)
  agricultural protectionism and, 544
  democracy and, 621
  environmental issues and, 322
  geopolitics of, 348, 657
  peacekeeping role of, 480–81
  tariffs and, 544
Evans, Gareth, 303, 493
Evans, William M., 96
exceptionalism, American, 17, 90–95, 283, 285, 289
ExCom team, 140–41
executive agreements, 34, 137–38
executive branch
  administrative trade remedies and, 583–84
  bureaucratic politics and, 41
  Cold War consensus and, 135–36
  constitutional power of, 37–38, 216–20
  détente and, 166
  foreign policy politics and, 41–49
  interest groups and, 54
  national security state and, 138–41
  Pennsylvania Avenue diplomacy and, 29–37
  presidential powers, 461
  Supreme Court and, 40
  Vietnam War and, 157–58
Executive Order 9981, 38
Export-Import Bank of the United States, 583
exports, *see* trade

factions, 55
Falun Gong, 376
fascism, 212, 594, 703, 705n1
fast-track authority, 176, 582
Fatah, 451, 453
Faulkner, William, 521
Fayyad, Salam, 455
FBI, *see* Federal Bureau of Investigations (FBI)
fear, freedom from, 93
Federal Bureau of Investigations (FBI)
  crime syndicates and, 320
  debate over role of, 458
  international criminals and, 5

Obama administration and, 327
war on terrorism and, 412–13, 418, 458–59
*Federalist Papers* (Hamilton), 31, 218, 219, 220
Federal Reserve Board, 532
Federal Trade Commission (FTC), 584
Fillmore, Millard, 102
"Final Report of the National Commission on Terrorist Attacks upon the United States," 669–71
Finnemore, Martha, 286
First Amendment, 61, 460
Food Board, 89
Ford, Gerald R.
containment and, 169
détente and, 177, 271
grain exports and, 165
Kissinger and, 44, 166
Solzhenitsyn and, 165
Vietnam War and, 153
weapons of mass destruction and, 185
*Foreign Affairs*, 99, 101, 120, 483, 703
foreign aid, 209, 356, 554, 556–58, 562
foreign investments, trade and, 209–10
foreign policy
Cold War consensus and, 135
Constitution and, 29–37, 74
debates over, *see* debates over foreign policy
Democratic Idealism on, 16–18
global environmental issues and, 568–77
globalization and, 528–29
historical chronology of key events in, 73–83
human rights and, 5
identity politics and, 5
imperialism and, 15–16
interest groups and, 49–58
Middle East and, 18, 405, 411
moralizing approach to, 198–201
neocolonialism and, 15–16
prosperity and, 15–16, 95–98
public health and, 463
public opinion and, 329–34
racism in, 94–95
security threats to, 4
setback from Vietnam War, 150, 151–60
"water's edge" myth, 27
*see also* "4 Ps" framework
foreign policy politics
aid to contras and, 183–84
China lobbies and, 394–99
Cold War and, 135–46, 156–60, 193–94
diplomacy and, 322–34
dynamics of choice and, 6
economic sanctions and, 633–36
executive branch and, 41–49
globalization and, 577–84
great debates over, 73, 103–10
interest groups and, 49–58
Iraq War and, 456, 463–72
news media and, 58–62, 518–19, 677–84
process of choice and, 6, 27–68
public opinion and, 62–67, 223–30
war powers and, 184–86, 515–18
"water's edge" myth, 27–29
foreign policy strategy
alliances and, 12, 83–84
Cold War and, 193
democracy and, 620–33
dilemmas of, 18
dynamics of choice and, 6, 24
essence of choice and, 6, 8, 24
great debates over, 72, 83–103
human rights and, 620–33
international system and, 6–8, 18
"4 Ps" framework and, 9–24
state structure and, 8
in time of transition, 2–7
on Vietnam War, 152–56
Foreign Service Institute, 61
Four Freedoms, 79, 87, 93, 667–68
Fourth Amendment, 458
Fox, Vincente, 384, 421
Fox News, 60
France
Alien and Sedition Acts and, 106
alliances with, 12, 73, 83
Arab-Israeli conflict and, 449
Berlin blockade and, 115
Bosnia and, 504
communism in, 20, 122, 124
covert actions and, 12
Darfur and, 512
global economic crisis of 2008 and, 545
Iran and, 446
Iraq War and, 346, 347, 419, 420
Jay Treaty and, 28
League of Nations and, 117
Limited Test Ban Treaty and, 164n
Louisiana Purchase and, 74
Mexico and, 76, 99
NATO and, 347, 353
nuclear weapons and, 310
power and, 88, 345

France (*cont.*)
treaties with, 34
unipolarity and, 644–45
UN Security Council and, 304
Vietnam and, 128, 131
Washington Naval Conference, 90
World War II and, 79, 80
Franco, Francisco, 80, 594
Franklin, Benjamin, 13
"Franklin D. Roosevelt and the Coming of World War II" (Kissinger), 231–38
Freedman, Lawrence, 417
freedom from fear, 93
freedom from want, 93
Freedom House, 593n
freedom of religion, 93
freedom of speech, 93
freedom of the press, 61–62, 461–62
free trade
anti-globalization movement and, 579
CAFTA and, 545–46
debates about, 109–10, 580–81
FTAA and, 545–46
LIEO and, 133
Pennsylvania Avenue diplomacy and, 37
poverty and, 553
protectionism vs., 109–10, 171, 580–81
Free Trade Area of the Americas (FTAA), 545–46, 582
Free Trade Union Institute, 621
Friedberg, Aaron, 373
Friedman, Edward, 375
Friedman, Thomas, 4, 528, 531–32
FTAA (Free Trade Area of the Americas), 545–46, 582
FTC (Federal Trade Commission), 584
Fuggers family, 530
Fukuyama, Francis, 4, 48, 432–33, 434, 590–91, 597, 702–5
Fulbright, J. William, 136, 152, 157
Fund for Peace, 503
Future of Iraq study, 469

Gaddis, John Lewis, 115, 167, 273–75, 431–32, 434
Gallatin, Albert, 88
Gallucci, Robert, 680
Gambia, 595
GAO (Government Accounting Office), 418
García, Alan, 601
Gardner, Lloyd, 433
Garrett, Laurie, 530
Garthoff, Raymond, 167–68
Gates, Bill, 563, 566, 577
Gates, Melinda, 563
Gates, Robert, 295, 325, 326, 378
Gates Foundation, 290, 564, 566–67
GATS (General Agreement on Trade in Services), 543
GATT, *see* General Agreement on Tariffs and Trade (GATT)
GDP, *see* gross domestic product (GDP)
G8, 537
Geithner, Timothy, 326
Gelb, Leslie, 152, 263–66, 466
gender inequality, 554, 555, 686
General Agreement on Tariffs and Trade (GATT)
administrative trade remedies and, 583
export promotion and, 583
foreign economic policy and, 15
interest groups and, 52
LIEO and, 133–34, 173
Pennsylvania Avenue diplomacy and, 37
Uruguay Round and, 542–43
voting rights and, 134
General Agreement on Trade in Services (GATS), 543
General Motors, 532, 540
general powers, 30, 37–39
Geneva Conventions, 435, 461
Geneva Protocol, 314
genocide, 484
*see also* ethnic cleansing and genocide
Genocide Convention (1948), 117–18, 484, 490, 513
Genocide Intervention Fund, 520
Genocide Prevention Task Force, 482, 487, 494, 675–76
geopolitics, 342–44, 399–400
of Africa, 389–94
Asian regional organizations and, 383
of China, 344, 368–76, 657
historical perspectives on, 345
of India, 380–83
of Japan, 376–79
of Korea, 379–80
of Latin America, 383–88, 391
Mandelbaum on, 343–44, 656–58
and NATO's future, 348–54
Nye on, 344, 659–62
OSCE and, 367
of Russia, 354–67
of Western Europe, the EU, and NATO, 346–48
George, Alexander L., 9, 160, 267–72, 494
Georgia, 349, 351, 362–63, 414, 593
Gephardt, Richard, 463, 465
Germany
alliance against, 103

arms race and, 344
Darfur and, 512
democracy and, 211, 213, 214, 594, 621
global economic crisis of 2008 and, 537
Iran and, 446
Iraq War and, 346, 348, 419
NATO and, 127, 347
power and, 345
reunification of, 276–78
revolutions and, 597
trade, peace, and, 608
UN Security Council and, 305
in World War I, 105
Zimmerman telegram and, 84
germ warfare, 315–16
Gerry, Elbridge, 217
Ghana, 389
Ghanem, Shukri, 312
Gheit, Ahmed Aboul, 305
Ginsberg, Benjamin, 58
glasnost, 190, 276
Global Alliance for Vaccination and Immunization, 567
global crime syndicates, 319–20
global governance, 204, 205, 293–94, 534–36, 569
global international institutions, 14
globalization
AIDS and, 564–66
anti-globalization movement, 3, 54
benefits of, 3
of communism, 4
debate over, 529, 530–37, 539–40
dimensions of, 532–34
dynamics of, 529, 531–32
environmental issues and, 568–77
financial markets and, 4
foreign policy and, 528–29
foreign policy politics and, 577–84
and global economic crisis of 2008, 537–40
global poverty and, 551–63
governance and, 202–5, 293–94, 534–35
historical perspectives on, 530–31
India and, 382
interest groups and, 51
international finance and, 546–51
NGOs and, 577–79, 693–701
policy dilemmas and, 534–36
public health and, 530, 563–68
terrorism and, 410
trade and, 3, 532, 540–46, 577–84
global population problem, 559–63, 577
global warming, 5, 322, 571–74, 690–92
*see also* Kyoto global warming treaty
Global Zero, 314
GNP (gross national product), 172, 173
Goldman Sachs, 530, 540, 554
gold standard, 171
Good Neighbor policy, 79, 383
Google, 375–76, 617, 618
Gorbachev, Mikhail, 66, 151, 187, 189–91, 274, 275, 276–78, 356
Gore, Al, 47, 572, 690–92
governance, 202–5, 293–94, 534–35, 569
"Governance in a Partially Globalized World" (Keohane), 202–5
Government Accounting Office (GAO), 418
Gowing, Nik, 328
Grachev, Pavel, 717
Graham, Billy, 520
Graham, Franklin, 520
Grant, Ulysses, 42, 457
Great Britain
as aggressor, 88
alliances with, 12
Arab-Israeli conflict and, 449
Baghdad Pact and, 128
Berlin blockade and, 115
Bosnia and, 504
Darfur and, 512
Germany and, 344
global economic crisis of 2008 and, 545
IMF voting rights of, 550
Iran and, 446
Iraq War and, 353, 420
Jay Treaty and, 27–28
League of Nations and, 117
Limited Test Ban Treaty and, 164n, 313
military assistance to, 12
NGOs and, 621
nuclear weapons and, 310
power and, 345
Revolutionary War and, 73, 83
swine flu and, 568
terrorist attacks in, 416, 443
trade, peace, and, 608
treaties with, 34
UN Security Council and, 304
War of 1812 and, 75
Washington Naval Conference, 90
World War II and, 79, 235
great debates, *see* debates over foreign policy
Great Depression, 78–79, 110

Greece, 122, 123, 594
greenhouse gas production, 572–73
Greenland, 571
Greer, 237
Grenada, 185
Gresham, Walter Quintin, 240
gross domestic product (GDP)
  crime syndicates and, 319
  economic sanctions and, 618
  financial crises and, 547
  Russia and, 365
  trade and, 532
gross national product (GNP), 172, 173
groupthink, 45, 469
G7, 537, 539
G20, 537, 539, 551
Guantánamo Bay, 435, 442, 460–61
Guatemala
  CAFTA and, 545–46
  CIA covert actions and, 132, 387
  Cold War and, 134
  human rights and, 627
  international commitments in, 138
  "4 Ps" trade-offs and, 21–23
  transitional justice and, 627
Gulf of Aden, 316, 317
Gulf of Tonkin Resolution, 157, 157n
Gutman, Roy, 681, 682

Haass, Richard, 286–87, 468
*habeas corpus*, 220, 461
Haditha killings, 427, 435
The Hague, 509, 621
Haig, Alexander, 634
Haiti
  democracy and, 623
  economic sanctions against, 303, 618–19
  interventions in, 76, 78, 97, 99, 495, 516–17, 618
  military force in, 408
  war powers and, 516–17
Halberstam, David, 679
Hallin, Daniel, 677–78
Hamas, 406, 447, 448, 451, 454, 456, 599
*Hamdi v. Rumsfeld*, 461
Hamilton, Alexander, 31, 37, 216, 217, 218, 219, 220
Hamilton, Lee, 28, 418
Han Chinese population, 376
Hannay, David, 486
Hariri, Rafiq, 297
Harrison, Benjamin, 42, 109
Harrison, William Henry, 42
Hart, Gary, 661
Hart, Jeffrey, 549, 553
Hart-Rudman Commission, 661
Havel, Vaclev, 188, 191, 304, 350, 612, 613
Hawaii, 102, 377
Health InterNetwork, 653
Hearst, William Randolph, 105
hedging, 372
hegemony, 98–99, 101, 134–35, 283, 288
Helms, Jesse, 32–33, 396, 636
Helsinki Accords (1975), 162, 269
Hemingway, Ernest, 572
Henkin, Louis, 38
Heritage Foundation, 428
Herzegovina, 360, 495, 593
Hezbollah, 443, 447, 448, 451, 454, 456
H5N1 flu, 4, 463, 567
Hickey, Donald, 104
Hill, Christopher, 311
Hinsley, F. H., 490
Hiroshima, 83, 120, 378, 703
*History of the United States Decision-Making Process on Vietnam Policy*, 62
Hitler, Adolf
  Atlantic Charter and, 93
  attacks on Britain, France, and Poland, 79, 80
  democracy and, 594
  election of, 597
  genocide and, 484
  Hussein and, 20, 463
  Munich analogy, 154, 155
HIV, *see* AIDS
Hobbes, Thomas, 6–7, 11, 199
Hobson, John, 15
Ho Chi Minh, 130–31, 154, 155
Hoffmann, Stanley, 483, 501
Holbrooke, Richard, 373, 504
Holder, Eric, 327
*Hollywood Goes to War*, 58
Holmes, Oliver Wendell, 107, 144
Holocaust, 446, 481, 484
Holst, Johan Jorgen, 452
Holsti, Ole R., 223–30
homeland security
  Bush and, 418
  terrorism and, 415–16
Homeland Security, U.S. Department of, 39, 445, 456
Honduras, 97, 132, 138, 388, 391, 545–46, 595, 600
H1N1 virus, 567–68
*Hotel Rwanda*, 520
House of Representatives, U.S., *see* Congress, U.S.

House Un-American Activities Committee (HUAC), 144
Howard, John, 420
HR 6646, 398
HUAC (House Un-American Activities Committee), 144
Hudson, Valerie M., 56n, 57
Huerta, Victoriano, 97
Hufbauer, Gary, 619
Hughes, Karen, 415
Hu Jintao, 537
Hull, Cordell, 116, 302
humanitarian interventions, *see* interventions, military and humanitarian
human rights
  Africa and, 602, 603
  Bush and, 628
  Carter and, 165, 170, 181, 213
  Chile and, 627–28
  China and, 20–21, 49, 375–76, 395–96, 398, 591, 628, 629
  democracy and, 593, 595–603, 620–33, 637
  genocide and, 484
  on Guantánamo Bay, 460–61
  Havel and, 188
  interest groups and, 54
  North Korea and, 380
  political issue groups and, 52
  Realism on, 11
  Third World and, 165
  United Nations and, 490, 628–29
  *see also* ethnic cleansing and genocide
Human Rights Council, 303–4, 629
Human Rights Watch, 52, 376, 384, 396, 621, 628, 629
*Human Security Report* (2005), 482
Humphrey, Hubcrt H., 66, 152
Humpreys, David, 91
Hungary
  democracy and, 593
  IMF and, 551
  invasion of, 127, 177
  Iraq War and, 428
  legislative aid and, 631
  NATO and, 349
  revolution in, 190
  transitional justice and, 627
Hunger Project, 554
Hunt, Michael, 94
Huntington, Samuel, 4, 10, 442, 591, 598, 706–12, 716
Hurricane Katrina, 427, 615, 616
Hussein, Saddam
  Al Qaeda and, 23, 423, 424, 468
  economic sanctions against, 619–20
  ending rule of, 312, 413, 415, 422, 425, 431, 434, 447, 472
  genocide and, 485
  Hitler and, 20, 463
  Iraq War and, 23–24, 424–25
  nuclear weapons and, 450
  peace and, 430
  Persian Gulf War and, 19–20, 407–9
  public opinion and, 65
  Russia and, 363
  weapons of mass destruction and, 23, 407, 409, 423, 424, 465, 467–68
Hutus, 481, 488, 495, 496, 497
hydrogen bomb, 127
Hyland, William, 271

IAEA (International Atomic Energy Agency), 14, 308, 309, 314, 316, 445–46
ICBMs (intercontinental ballistic missiles), 129, 357
ICC (International Criminal Court), 14, 284, 285, 289, 346, 508–10, 514–15
Iceland, 551
ICG (International Crisis Group), 512, 514
ICISS (International Commission on Intervention and State Sovereignty), 489, 492, 500, 502, 672–74
identities of mass destruction, 293
identity interest groups, 50, 51–52
identity politics, 5
Idris, King, 311
IFOR (Implementation Force), 352
Ignatieff, Michael, 431
Ikenberry, G. John, 288, 290, 291, 344, 416, 665–68
illegal drugs, 317–19, 385–86
*Illicit* (Naim), 536
IMF, *see* International Monetary Fund (IMF)
immigration, 460, 530–31, 534
IMO (International Maritime Organization), 317
imperialism, 15–16, 95–98
*Imperialism* (Lenin), 16
Implementation Force (IFOR), 352
imports, *see* trade
Imus, Don, 446
income distribution, 562
*Inconvenient Truth, An* (Gore), 572, 690–92
*In Defense of the National Interest* (Morgenthau), 10
India
  AIDS and, 382, 564
  Bush and, 382

India (*cont.*)
  China and, 368, 372
  environmental issues and, 573
  export promotion and, 583
  geopolitics of, 380–83
  global economic crisis of 2008 and, 537, 538, 545
  globalization and, 382
  nuclear weapons and, 307, 310, 382
  oil and, 542
  Pakistan and, 380–81
  peacekeeping and, 506
  poverty and, 553
  special drawing rights and, 550
  UN Security Council and, 305
individualism, 598
Indonesia
  democracy and, 599
  as emerging power, 383
  environmental issues and, 569
  financial crises in, 547
  global economic crisis of 2008 and, 545
  Jemaah Islamiyah and, 443
  overpopulation and, 562
  war on terrorism and, 414
  World Bank and, 559
Indyk, Martin, 312
infant mortality, 552, 555
influence, conversion of power to, 287–88
*Influence of Sea Power upon History, The* (Mahan), 89, 241
information politics, 696–97, 701n9
*In Retrospect* (McNamara), 151
INR (Intelligence and Research) Bureau, 467
institutional competition, 29
*INS v. Chadha,* 39, 40
integration, 344
intelligence agencies
  debate over roles of, 458
  domestic powers of, 457–59
  failures of, 467–68
  Obama administration and, 327
  *see also specific agencies*
Intelligence and Research (INR) Bureau, 467
InterAction, 52
Inter-American Democratic Charter (2001), 621
intercontinental ballistic missiles (ICBMs), 129, 357
interest groups, 49–58, 143
Intergovernmental Panel on Climate Change (IPCC), 571, 574
Intermediate Nuclear Forces treaty (1987), 188
International Atomic Energy Agency (IAEA), 14, 308, 309, 314, 316, 445–46
International Center for Human Rights and Democratic Development, 621
International Commission on Intervention and State Sovereignty (ICISS), 489, 492, 500, 502, 672–74
International Commission on Nuclear Nonproliferation, 313–14
international commitments, 137–38
International Court of Justice, 509, 621
International Criminal Court (ICC), 14, 284, 285, 289, 346, 508–10, 514–15
International Crisis Group (ICG), 512, 514
International Economic Emergency Powers Act, 633
international finance, 530, 533, 535, 546–51
international institutionalism
  multilateralism and, 285–87
  United Nations and, 116–19
international institutions
  foreign policy strategy and, 302
  LIEO components, 133–34
  overview, 13–15, 289
internationalism
  foreign policy and, 4–5, 228
  isolationism vs., 63, 64–65, 73, 83–87, 231–38, 329–31
  national interest and, 9
International Maritime Organization (IMO), 317
International Monetary Fund (IMF)
  environmental issues and, 569
  foreign economic policy and, 15
  global economic crisis of 2008 and, 538, 539
  international finance and, 533, 546, 547, 548–51
  as international institution, 14
  international system and, 7
  LIEO and, 133–34, 173
  policy debates over, 548–50
  special drawing rights and, 550
  voting rights and, 134, 550–51, 559n
  WTO and, 543
International Peace Cooperation Law, 377
International Press Institute (IPI), 626
international relations
  anarchic view of, 6–7
  Iraq War and, 431–33
  Realism and, 10–11
International Republican Institute, 621
International Security Assistance Force (ISAF), 353
international systems
  anarchic view of, 6–7
  belief systems and, 43

billiards metaphor, 8
foreign policy strategy and, 6–8, 18
system structure, 7–8
*see also* globalization
international trade, *see* trade
International Trade Commission (ITC), 37, 176, 584
International Union for Conservation of Nature (IUCN), 575
Internet
China and, 617–18
news media and, 327–29
internment camps, 28, 81, 108
interventions, military and humanitarian
attacks on aid workers in, 495
in Bosnia, 480–81, 495, 501, 503–4, 680–82
in Cuba, 97, 99
Darfur, 510–15
deciding on, 502–3
definition of, 11–12
effective, 503–10
genocide and, 480–522
in Haiti, 76, 78, 97, 99, 495, 516–17, 618
ICISS on the case for, 672–74
in Kosovo, 481, 487, 495, 502, 505–6
in Latin America, 76, 97–98, 99, 101
media and foreign policies toward, 677–84
in Mexico, 99
national interests and, 483–87, 521
national sovereignty and, 489–93
NATO and, 482
in Nicaragua, 76, 77, 97, 99
in Panama, 95
preemptive force and, 500–501
public opinion and, 334, 519–20
in Rwanda, 481, 495, 496–97, 500, 501
in Serbia, 392, 502
in Somalia, 480, 495, 515–16, 679–80
*intifadas*, 448, 450, 451, 453
intrafirm, 532
intraindustry trade, 532–33
IPCC (Intergovernmental Panel on Climate Change), 571, 574
IPI (International Press Institute), 626
Iran
alliances with, 12, 445
as "axis of evil," 445
Baghdad Pact and, 128
Bush and, 445, 446
chemical weapons and, 314, 315
CIA covert actions, 132–33, 446
Cold War and, 134
democracy and, 599–600
economic sanctions and, 446
Hezbollah and, 447
human rights and, 165, 628
international commitments in, 138
Iraq War and, 447
journalists and, 626
Khomeini and, 170
nuclear weapons and, 307, 310, 406, 445–47
Obama administration and, 447–48
Reagan and, 185, 445
Russia and, 363
weapons of mass destruction and, 424
Western Europe and, 346
Iran-Contra scandal, 184
Iranian hostage crisis, 60, 60n, 184, 185, 445
Iranian Revolution (1979), 19, 172, 321
Iran-Iraq War, 66, 185, 506
Iraq
Arab-Israeli conflict and, 449
Baghdad Pact and, 128
chemical weapons and, 314, 315
democracy and, 615
economic sanctions and, 619–20
foreign policy and, 456, 463–72
genocide in, 485
invasion of Kuwait, 19, 178
Israel and, 446, 450
nation building in, 482
nuclear weapons and, 310, 312
Persian Gulf War and, 407–9, 411
"4 Ps" and, 430, 434–35
Reagan and, 65–66, 185, 445
Russia and, 363
war on terrorism, 415
weapons of mass destruction and, 423–25
*see also* Hussein, Saddam
Iraq War (2003)
as "a cakewalk," 425
alliances in, 347, 419
Bush and, 3, 23–24, 42, 48, 406, 419, 422–23, 426–28, 430, 434–35, 463–70, 472
China and, 373
CIA prisoner abuses in, 327
Congress and, 428, 456, 462, 463–66
counterinsurgency doctrine and, 439
domestic politics of, 463–72
France and, 346, 347, 419, 420
Germany and, 346, 348, 419
international opposition to, 419, 420–21
international relations theory and, 431–33

Iraq War (2003) (*cont.*)
  international support of, 420, 428
  Japan and, 378, 428
  national sovereignty and, 492
  NATO and, 353
  news media and, 58, 422–23, 470–71
  Obama and, 3, 429, 465
  overview of, 419, 422–23
  "4 Ps" dissensus, 23–24
  public opinion on, 297, 332, 427, 428, 471–72
  ramifications of, 430, 434–35
  rationale for, 423–25
  results of, 425–30
  surge strategy and, 428–29, 439
  United Nations and, 23, 24, 303, 332, 419
  war powers and, 31, 463–66
  Western Europe and, 346
Irwin, Douglas, 580
ISAF (International Security Assistance Force), 353
Islamic fundamentalism
  Al Qaeda and, 442, 611, 670–71
  democracy and, 599, 609
  foreign policy and, 411
  Hamas and, 447, 448, 451, 454, 599
  Iran and, 599–600
  Khomeini and, 181
  Pakistan and, 411, 440, 609, 610
  Somalia and, 392
  threat of, 670
isolationism
  internationalism vs., 63, 64–65, 73, 83–87, 231–38, 329–31
  retreat into, in 1919 to 1941, 78–81
  World War II and, 81, 86
Israel
  Camp David Accord, 14, 301
  Hamas and, 406, 454
  historical overview of, 448–56
  Hussein and, 23
  interest groups and, 51–52, 54
  Iraq and, 446, 450
  Lebanon and, 406, 448, 451, 454
  nuclear weapons and, 310
  Obama and, 438
  OPEC and, 172
  war on terrorism and, 416
  *see also* Arab-Israeli conflicts
Israel-Gaza war (2008), 448
Israeli-Palestinian conflict, 346, 363, 443
Italy
  chemical weapons and, 314
  communism in, 20, 122, 124, 130
  crime syndicates in, 319
  democracy and, 594
  Iraq War and, 420, 428
  League of Nations and, 117
  Washington Naval Conference, 90
ITC (International Trade Commission), 37, 176, 584
IUCN (International Union for Conservation of Nature), 575
Iyengar, Shanto, 59
Izetbegovic, Alija, 504

Jackson, Andrew, 42, 212
Jackson, Henry M, 156
Jackson-Vanik Amendment, 165
Jamaica, 319
Janjaweed, 511, 512, 513, 514
Japan
  Afghanistan and, 377–78
  agricultural protectionism and, 544
  alliances with, 12, 103, 376–77
  chemical weapons and, 314
  China and, 372, 373, 379
  crime syndicates in, 319
  democracy and, 211, 213, 608, 620, 714
  environmental issues and, 573
  geopolitics of, 376–79
  global economic crisis of 2008 and, 537
  Hawaii and, 102
  IMF voting rights of, 550
  Iraq War and, 378, 428
  League of Nations and, 117
  military occupation of, 127–28
  North Korea and, 380
  nuclear weapons and, 83, 118, 120, 378–79
  Pearl Harbor attack and, 79, 81, 87, 103, 105, 108, 120, 231, 237, 406
  Persian Gulf War and, 19, 377, 407
  power and, 345
  prisoners of war and, 460
  Russia and, 376
  South Korea and, 379
  trade with, 102, 173–77, 377
  UN Security Council and, 305
  Washington Naval Conference, 90
Japanese-American internment camps, 28, 81, 108
Jay Treaty, 27–28, 73, 74
JDAMs (joint direct-action munitions), 411
Jefferson, Thomas
  on alliances, 84
  American exceptionalism and, 17

covert actions and, 12
foreign policy and, 41, 74–75
Havel on, 188, 612, 613
Madison's letters to, 31, 106, 218
War of 1812 and, 104
Jemaah Islamiyah, 443
Jervis, Robert, 43, 490
Jewish Americans, 51–52
Jews, 165, 481, 484
Jiang Jeishi, 118, 138, 143, 370, 394–95
jihadism, 392, 426, 442–43, 512
John Paul II, 191, 553
Johnson, Loch, 327
Johnson, Lyndon B.
McNamara and, 151
Pennsylvania Avenue diplomacy and, 37
Vietnam War and, 30, 152, 153, 154–55, 156–57, 158
Joint Chiefs of Staff, 46, 138n, 139
joint direct-action munitions (JDAMs), 411
Jones, Bruce, 497
Jones, James, 325, 326
Jordan, 416, 449, 450, 452, 599, 615
journalists, 626
judiciary branch, 460–61
*see also* Supreme Court, U.S.
Junichiro Koizumi, 379
justice, Rawls conception of, 206
Justice, U.S. Department of, 459, 620

Kagan, Fred, 428–29
Kagan, Robert, 282, 283, 346, 431
Kahn, Herman, 121–22
Kaiser, Robert, 328
Kant, Immanuel, 17, 604, 606, 607
Karzai, Hamid, 436
Kashmir, 307, 380–81
Kazakhstan, 356, 593, 623
Keck, Margaret, 578, 693–701
Kellogg-Briand Pact, 78, 79, 232–33, 647
Kennan, George F., 120, 122, 139, 248, 259–62, 369
Kennedy, Edward, 636
Kennedy, John F.
on Alliance for Progress, 132
Bay of Pigs invasion and, 61, 128, 139–40
Cold War consensus and, 135
Cuban missile crisis and, 2, 61, 129, 140, 143
Democratic Idealism and, 17
Diem and, 131
economic sanctions and, 634
foreign aid and, 556
McNamara and, 151
national security and, 139, 141–43
Vietnam and, 152, 154
Kennedy, Robert, 140
Kenney, George, 681–82
Kent State University, 158
Kenya, 410, 552, 570, 595
Keohane, Robert O., 9, 13, 14, 202–5, 289
Kepel, Gilles, 708
Kerry, John, 319, 465
Kessler, Gladys, 460
KGB, 189, 190n, 365–66
Khamenei, Ayatollah, 447, 600
Khartoum, 511, 512
Khatami, Mohammed, 599–600
Khmer Rouge, 154, 627
Khodorkovsky, Mikhail, 366
Khomeini, Ayatollah Ruhallah, 170, 181, 409, 445, 599
Khrushchev, Nikita, 61, 189, 190
Kim Dae Jung, 48
Kim Jong-il, 311
Kim Jong-un, 311
Ki-moon, Ban, 492, 554
King, Martin Luther, Jr., 691
Kirk, Ron, 326
Kirkpatrick, Jeane, 181
Kissinger, Henry
as adviser, 44, 45
appointments and, 36
on Berger, 47
China and, 369, 370, 395
on covert actions, 12
CTBT and, 313
détente and, 160–67, 168, 177, 267, 268–70, 271
on economic war, 171
"Franklin D. Roosevelt and the Coming of World War II," 231–38
Nixon and, 44, 45, 139
on planning during World War II for peace, 246
"quarantine of aggressor nations" speech and, 86
"shuttle diplomacy" of, 14, 301, 449, 452
Vietnam War and, 152, 153, 156
on witch hunts, 628
Kiva, 554
Klaus, Václav, 573
Kohl, Helmut, 191
Koizumi, Junichiro, 305
Kolko, Gabriel, 207–10
Koppel, Ted, 60n
Korb, Lawrence, 429
Koreagate, 55

Korean War, 379–80
China and, 115, 395
labor-union strike during, 40
lessons of, 127
public opinion and, 226
Truman and, 127, 136
UN Security Council and, 118, 303, 331, 464
Kosovo
Clinton and, 505, 517
ethnic conflicts in, 485, 486, 505
interventions and, 481, 487, 495, 502, 505–6
military force in, 408, 411, 412
NATO and, 347, 352, 360, 481, 487, 501, 502, 503, 505–6
Russia and, 360, 502
war powers and, 517–18
Kovalev, Sergei, 366
Kozyrev, Andrei, 355
Krasner, Stephen, 530
Krauthammer, Charles, 282, 283, 291, 644–48
Kravchuk, Leonid, 359
Krepinevich, Andrew F., Jr., 65, 441
Krishna, Anirudh, 563–64
Kristof, Nicholas, 511, 520, 554
Kristol, William, 282, 283, 431
Kubrick, Stanley, 122
Kumalo, D. S., 305
Kurds, 425, 426, 429, 485
Kurtz, Howard, 471
Kuwait
democracy and, 599
invasion of, 19, 178, 445
Persian Gulf War and, 407–9
Reagan and, 185
Kyoto global warming treaty, 284, 288, 289, 346, 573–74, 646
Kyrgyzstan, 414, 593, 611

labor unions, 171
LaFeber, Walter, 76, 95, 239–45
Laird, Melvin, 131
Lake, Anthony, 35, 47, 682, 713
Land, Richard, 520
land mines treaty, 346
Laos, 152, 318
Lapidus, Gail, 355
Laqueur, Walter, 246
Lashkar-e-Taiba, 381
Latin America
China and, 368, 369
Cold War and, 128, 132, 601
communism in, 115
democracy and, 213, 214, 593, 594–95, 600–602, 717
drugs and, 317–18
financial crises in, 547–48
foreign aid and, 556
of geopolitics, 383–88, 391
global economic crisis of 2008 and, 537
HIV and, 689
human rights and, 602
military interventions in, 76, 97–98, 99, 101
poverty in, 552
relations with, 78–79, 98–99, 101
revolutions in, 93
Southern Command and, 457
UN Security Council and, 305
U.S. investments in, 209
*see also individual countries*
Latvia, 349, 367, 593
Lavrov, Sergei, 362
Law of National Reconciliation (1996), 627
League of Nations
design of, 117
failure of, 116
founding of, 32
as international institution, 14
isolationism and, 232–33, 345
mandate system of, 91, 93
Wilson and, 32, 76, 85–86
Lebanon
Arab-Israeli conflict and, 449, 450, 454
containment policy and, 128
drug rings and, 318
Hezbollah in, 443, 447, 448, 451, 454
Iranian hostage crisis and, 184
Islamic fundamentalism and, 411
Israel and, 406, 448, 451, 454
Reagan and, 178
Lee, Euna, 311
Lee, Thea, 397
Lee, Wen Ho, 397
LeFever, Ernest, 54
Leffler, Melvyn P., 246–52
legislative branch, 38–39, 53–54
*see also* Congress, U.S.
Lemkin, Raphael, 484
Lend-Lease, 12, 80, 114, 554
Lenin, Vladimir Ilyich, 16, 354, 597
Lepgold, Joseph, 352
leverage politics, 579, 696, 697–98
Levgold, Robert, 363–64

*Leviathan* (Hobbes), 7
Levin, Sander, 578
Lewinsky, Monica, 33
*Lexus and the Olive Tree, The* (Friedman), 531–32
liberal international economic order (LIEO), 133–35, 146, 171, 173, 193
liberalism, 211, 212, 598
Liberia, 559, 591
Libya
 bombing of, 185
 covert actions and, 12
 democracy and, 598
 economic sanctions against, 303, 312
 human rights and, 629
 nuclear weapons and, 310, 311–13
 war on terrorism and, 414
LIEO (liberal international economic order), 133–35, 146, 171, 173, 193
*Life*, 141
life expectancy rates, 552
Limited Nuclear Test Ban Treaty (1963), 32, 164n, 313
Lincoln, Abraham, 75, 105, 106, 361
Lindsay, James, 38
Lindsey, Lawrence, 426
Ling, Laura, 311
Lippmann, Walter, 63, 141, 152, 223–24
Lithuania, 349, 593
*Lobby, The*, 51
lobbyists, 50, 53
Local Elected Officials for Social Responsibility, 52
local government, *see* state and local governments
Locke, Gary, 326
Locke, John, 219, 220
Lodge, Henry Cabot, 32
Lon Nol, 154
Lord, Kristin, 612
*Los Angeles Times*, 329
Lott, Trent, 33, 462–63
Louisiana Purchase, 74, 75
Louis XIV, 667
Louis XVI, 73
Lowell, James Russell, 95
Lowi, Theodore, 57–58
Luce, Henry, 141
Luck, Edward, 492
Ludlow amendment, 86
Lugar, Richard, 357, 441, 622, 635, 636
Luxembourg, 557

Maathai, Wangari, 570
MacArthur, Douglas, 214
Macedonia, 352, 367, 486, 500, 593, 661
Madison, James, 12
 Constitution and, 31, 217, 218, 219
 foreign policy and, 41
 on impulses of passion, 56
 on interest groups, 55, 57
 on liberty, 106
 War of 1812 and, 104
MAD (mutually assured destruction), 162, 180
*Maersk Alabama*, 316
Mahan, Alfred Thayer, 89, 102, 239, 241–42
Mahbubani, Kishore, 291, 616, 710
"Mainsprings of American Foreign Policy, The" (Morgenthau), 198–201
malaria, 563
Malaysia, 383, 414, 545
Mali, 414
Malthus, Thomas, 573
Manchuria, 103, 314
Mandela, Nelson, 390–91, 393, 590, 592, 595, 627, 632–33
Mandelbaum, Michael, 343–44, 483, 656–58
manganese, 207
Manhattan Project, 82, 90
manifest destiny, 75, 91, 94
Mansfield, Edward D., 608, 713–19
Mao Zedong, 103, 124, 166, 394–95
Marcos, Ferdinand, 28, 622
Marshall, George, 20n, 122, 144, 625
Marshall Plan (1947), 20n
 administration of, 139
 announcement of, 122
 approval of, 38
 Cold War consensus and, 134, 249, 556
 description of, 123–24, 134
 foreign policy strategy and, 20
 ideological bipolarity and, 130
 World Bank and, 134
Martin, Lisa, 289
Marx, Karl, 703–4
Masaryk, Tomas Garrigue, 613
massive retaliation doctrine, 129
Mauritania, 595
Maximilian, Ferdinand, 99
Mayaguez incident, 185
Mbeki, Thabo, 393, 566
McCain, John, 324, 444
McCarthy, Joseph, 144–45, 157, 395
McCarthyism, 28, 144–45, 193, 395
McGovern, George, 67
McKinley, William, 95, 109, 110, 242–44

McKinley Tariff Act, 76, 109
McMurry, Michael, 683
McNamara, Robert, 62, 65, 122, 151–52, 153, 162
McNeil, Dan, 413
MDGs (Millennium Development Goals), 554, 555–56, 562, 563
Mearsheimer, John, 10, 283, 284, 432
media, *see* news media
"Media and U.S. Policies Toward Intervention, The" (Strobel), 677–84
Medvedev, Dmitri, 356, 366
Mejia, Francisco, 96
Menchú, Rigoberta, 697
Menendez, Robert, 384
Menkhaus, Ken, 317
Metternich, Klemens von, 160–61
Mexican Revolution, 76, 77, 97
Mexican War, 31, 93, 95, 96, 104
Mexico
  democracy and, 602
  drug rings and, 317–18, 319
  drug wars and, 385
  financial crises in, 546–48
  France and, 76, 99
  geopolitics of, 384–86
  Iraq War and, 421
  military interventions in, 99
  NAFTA and, 385, 545
  peso crisis in, 548
  poverty in, 552
  Roosevelt and, 101
  swine flu and, 567–68
  Texas and, 84, 91, 104
MFN (most-favored-nation) status, 21, 21n, 49, 165, 617
Microsoft, 375–76, 577, 617, 618
Middle East
  Baghdad Pact and, 128
  Central Command and, 457
  China and, 368, 369, 373–74
  Cold War consensus and, 137
  decolonization of, 93
  democracy and, 598–600, 614–15
  foreign policy and, 18, 405, 411
  human rights and, 603
  Obama and, 435–48, 473
  oil and, 19, 373–74
  peace process in, 452
  Russia and, 363
  war on terrorism and, 414
  *see also individual countries*
Midway, Battle of, 81
military assistance, 12
military draft, 80
military force
  in Bosnia, 408
  China and, 368–69, 371–72, 376, 378
  diplomacy vs., 294–302
  drug rings and, 318–19
  great debates about, 87–90
  in Haiti, 408
  preemption and, 500–501
  public opinion on, 333–34
  war on terrorism and, 417
  Weinberger criteria for, 178–80
  when to use, 496–98, 500–503
military-industrial complex, 56–57, 56n, 154
military interventions, *see* interventions, military and humanitarian
*Military Times*, 427
Mill, John Stuart, 607
Millennium Development Goals (MDGs), 554, 555–56, 562, 563
Milosevic, Slobodan, 360, 486, 501, 504, 505, 509, 608
MIRVs, 164n, 166
Mitchell, George, 455
MNCs (multinational corporations), 50, 533
Mohammed, Khalid Sheikh, 459, 460
Moldova, 593
Mondale, Walter, 181
money laundering, 536
Monroe, James, 34, 41, 137
Monroe Doctrine, 34, 75, 99, 100, 101, 246
Montenegro, 593
Montesquieu, 607
Montréal Protocol (1987), 571
Morales, Evo, 601
moral hazards, 549
moralizing approach to foreign policy, 198–201
Moreno-Ocampo, Luis, 514–15
Morgan, Thomas, 136
Morgenthau, Hans J., 10, 154, 198–201, 616
Morgenthau, Henry, Sr., 484
Morison, Samuel Eliot, 89
Morocco, 414, 599
Moscow Treaty on Strategic Offensive Reduction, 356
Mossadegh, Mohammed, 128, 132–33, 134
most-favored-nation (MFN) status, 20–21, 21n, 49, 165, 617
Mother Teresa, 483
Mozambique, 507, 625
MTV, 471

Mubarak, Hosni, 421, 599, 623
Mueller, J. E., 226
Mugabe, Robert, 598, 630
Mullen, Michael, 295, 301, 325–26, 413, 439
multilateralism
 Clinton and, 282, 284, 286, 287
 definition of, 281
 freedom of action and, 284, 661
 unilateralism vs., 281–89
 United Nations and, 650
 war on terrorism and, 417–18
multinational corporations (MNCs), 50, 533
multipolar systems, 7, 290, 647
Munich Agreement, 80
Munich analogy, 154, 155
Munich Pact, 234
Muravcik, Joshua, 283
Murdoch, Rupert, 60
Murtha, John, 465
Musavi, Mir Hossein, 600
Museveni, Yoweri, 623
Musharraf, Pervez, 381, 440, 609–11
Muslim Brotherhood, 599
Mussolini, Benito, 82, 594
mutually assured destruction (MAD), 162, 180
MX missiles, 180
Myers, Dee Dee, 683
My Lai massacre, 154

NAFTA, *see* North American Free Trade Agreement (NAFTA)
Nagasaki, 83, 378, 703
Nagorno-Karabakh, 367
Naim, Moises, 536
Naipaul, V. S., 709
Namibia, 507, 566, 621, 623
Napoleon III, 75, 99, 667, 714
Napolitano, Janet, 325, 386
National Archives, 72
National Cattlemen's Beef Association, 462
National Commission on Terrorism, 410
National Commission on Terrorist Attacks Upon the United States, 327
National Conservative Political Action Committee, 183
National Defense University, 61
National Democratic Institute for International Affairs, 621
National Endowment for Democracy, 624, 630
National Guard, 427, 616
National Intelligence Director, 327, 459
National Intelligence Estimate (NIE), 467
national interests
 belief systems and, 43
 democracy and, 590–92, 706–12
 humanitarian interventions and, 483–87, 521
 Iraq War and, 23–24
 moral principles and, 198–99
 multilateralism and, 288–89
 "4 Ps" framework and, 9–18
 unilateralism and, 283–84
national missile defense (NMD), 307, 309
national security, 4
 Bill of Rights vs., 106–8
 civil liberties and, 107, 411
 Cold War and, 246–52
 cost of, 669
 crime syndicates and, 319–20
 energy security and, 321–22
 environmental issues and, 570, 574
 executive-branch politics and, 138–41
 freedom of the press vs., 61–62, 141–43
 international economy and, 320–21
 public health and, 564
 threats from nonstate actors, 316–20
 war on terrorism and, 457–63
 *see also* homeland security
National Security Act (1947), 137
national security advisers, 45, 46, 47, 138n
National Security Agency (NSA), 139, 458–59
National Security Council (NSC), 31, 138–39, 138n
National Security Strategy, 283, 482, 485, 608–9, 663–64
national solidarity, 28
national sovereignty, 489–93
National War Powers Commission, 466
nation building, 482
Native Americans, 74, 91
NATO, *see* North Atlantic Treaty Organization (NATO)
Navy, U.S., 87–90, 87n, 139, 185, 218
Nazism, 131n, 155, 594
NBC television network, 59
Negroponte, John, 36, 510
neocolonialism, 15–16
neoconservatism, 283, 431
Nestlé, 695
Netanyahu, Benjamin, 455
Netflix, 534
Netherlands, 172, 353, 557, 621
Neutrality Acts, 80, 233, 235, 236, 238n3
Newbold, Greg, 427

New Deal, 90, 213
"new empire," 76, 239–45
New International Economic Order (NIEO), 172–73, 174–75, 193
New Mexico, 84
*Newsday*, 681
news media
CNN curve and, 518–19, 677–84
Cold War consensus and, 141–43
foreign policy politics and, 58–62, 518–19, 677–84
Internet, blogs, and changes in, 327–29
Iraq War and, 58, 422–23, 470–71
national security and, 461–62
Persian Gulf War and, 58, 461, 470
Vietnam War and, 58–59, 159
*Newsweek*, 470, 583
*New York Times*
Bay of Pigs invasion and, 61–62
on Darfur, 511
on Diem, 141
on Europe, 84
Iraq War and, 471
NGOs, *see* nongovernmental organizations (NGOs)
Nguyen Van Thieu, 154
Nhu, Ngo Dinh, 131
Nicaragua
CAFTA and, 545–46
democracy and, 593, 601, 622–23
human rights and, 165, 170, 628
Iraq War and, 428
military interventions in, 76, 77, 97, 99
Ortega and, 184
peace in, 191
Reagan and, 177–78, 181, 188, 191
Nicolson, Harold, 294
NIE (National Intelligence Estimate), 467
NIEO (New International Economic Order), 172–73, 174–75, 193
Nigeria
crime syndicates and, 319
overpopulation and, 559, 562
piracy and, 316
United Nations and, 305
war on terrorism and, 414
*Nightline*, 60n
9/11 Commission, 424, 442, 669–71
9/11 terrorist attacks, *see* September 11, 2001, terrorist attacks
Nixon, Richard M.
advisers to, 36, 44
appointments by, 35
China and, 168, 370, 395
containment and, 169
détente and, 150, 160–70, 177, 267–70, 271, 325
foreign policy and, 42, 43
gold standard and, 171
Kissinger and, 44, 45, 139
McGovern and, 67
oil and, 542
Pentagon Papers and, 62, 62n
resignation of, 167
vetoes by, 38, 158, 185, 636
Vietnam War and, 43, 153, 154, 155, 156, 157–58
Watergate scandal and, 159, 167
Nkrumah, Kwame, 389
NMD (national missile defense), 307, 309
Nobel Peace Prize
Amnesty International and, 629
Arias and, 191
de Klerk and, 633
Gorbachev and, 191
Maathai and, 570
Mandela and, 633
Menchú and, 697
Roosevelt and, 14
Sakharov and, 190n
United Nations and, 191, 506
nongovernmental organizations (NGOs)
Agency for International Development and, 620
AIDS and, 565, 566, 567
China and, 376
corruption and, 625–26
Darfur and, 511, 514, 515
definition of, 52
democracy and, 621–22, 623
environmental issues and, 569
globalization and, 577–79, 693–701
human rights and, 602, 629
Poland and, 630
poverty and, 553, 554
Russia and, 630
women's empowerment policies and, 554
North, Oliver, 45, 184
North American Free Trade Agreement (NAFTA)
approval of, 39, 109
FTAA, CAFTA, and, 545–46
trade policy and, 582
North Atlantic Cooperation Council, *see* European-Atlantic Partnership Council
North Atlantic Treaty Organization (NATO)
Afghanistan War and, 353
Balkan wars and, 360

Bosnia and, 347, 352, 501, 504, 517
Cold War and, 12
creation of, 124, 211
CSCE and, 162
Darfur and, 520
description of, 125
European Command and, 457
expansion of, 349–51, 361–62
France and, 347, 353
future of, 348–54, 385
Germany and, 127, 347
Kosovo and, 347, 352, 360, 481, 487, 501, 502, 503, 505–6
Obama and, 301
Partnership for Peace, 349, 625
post-Cold War era mission of, 351–54
poverty and, 552
public ignorance on, 63
public opinion on, 144
Truman and, 136
Western Europe and, 346–48
Northern Alliance (Afghan), 412
Northern Command, 457
North Korea
chemical weapons and, 315
China and, 310–11, 373, 379
Japan and, 380
South Korea and, 310, 311, 379–80
UN Security Council and, 118, 310, 464
weapons of mass destruction and, 307, 310–11
North Vietnam, 131, 154, 157n, 168
Norway, 405, 557
NPT (Nuclear Nonproliferation Treaty), 308, 310, 311, 314, 315, 316, 358, 382, 445–46
NSA (National Security Agency), 139, 458–59
NSC-68, 125–27
NSC (National Security Council), 31, 138–39, 138n
nuclear deterrence
détente and, 162
foreign policy strategy and, 297
power and, 119–29, 162, 253–58
Reagan and, 180
revisionists on, 191
nuclear freeze movement, 181
Nuclear Nonproliferation Treaty (NPT), 308, 310, 311, 314, 315, 316, 358, 382, 445–46
nuclear utilization targeting strategy (NUTS), 180
nuclear war, 2, 129
nuclear weapons
arms race and, 358–59
China and, 310, 378
détente and, 164n
Hussein and, 450
hydrogen bomb, 127
India and, 307, 310, 382
Iran and, 307, 310, 406, 445–47
Japan and, 83, 118, 120, 378–79
Manhattan Project, 82, 90
Pakistan and, 307, 310
*see also* weapons of mass destruction (WMD)
Nunn, Sam, 313, 357, 516–17
Nunn-Lugar Cooperative Threat Reduction program, 357, 445
Nuremberg trials, 508
NUTS (nuclear utilization targeting strategy), 180
Nye, Joseph S., Jr., 17, 287, 344, 433, 611, 659–62
Nyerere, Julius, 389–90

OAS (Organization of American States), 387–88, 621, 632
OAU (Organization for African Unity), 394, 621
Obama, Barack
"Af-Pak" and, 436, 439–41
Africa and, 393
Arab-Israeli conflict and, 455
Brazil and, 386
Cairo speech (2009) of, 436, 437–39
China and, 370
climate change and, 574
conception of common security, 9
Congress and, 325
Cuba and, 384
Darfur and, 515, 520
defense spending and, 295
diplomatic strategy of, 297, 299, 301–2, 447–48
foreign aid and, 557, 562, 565
foreign policy and, 41, 324–26
Guantánamo Bay and, 461
Honduras and, 388
human rights and, 628
inaugural address of, 17, 435–36, 447
intelligence agencies and, 327
international support for election of, 299, 301
Iran and, 447–48
Iraq War and, 3, 429, 465
NAFTA and, 385, 545
nuclear nonproliferation agenda of, 313, 356
oil and, 542
public opinion and, 331
on the risk of a nuclear attack, 306
Russia and, 360
terrorism strategy of, 442–45

Obama, Barack (*cont.*)
on torture, 460
Venezuela and, 387
women's empowerment policies and, 554
Obasanjo, Olusegun, 514
oceans, acidity and, 575
O'Connor, Sandra Day, 461
Office of Price Administration, 90
Office of Strategic Services (OSS), 137
oil
China and, 373–74, 396, 542
détente and, 150
energy security and, 321
Iran and, 133, 134
Iraq and, 24, 426, 427
Middle East and, 19, 373–74
oil embargo, 150, 165, 172
Russian economy and, 354–55
Soviet Union and, 165
Sudan and, 512
trade deficit and, 542
*see also* Organization of Petroleum Exporting Countries (OPEC)
oil import bill (2008), 542
Olmert, Ehud, 451, 453–54
Olson, Mancur, 56
OPCW (Organization for the Prohibition of Chemical Weapons), 315, 316
OPEC, *see* Organization of Petroleum Exporting Countries (OPEC)
Open Door policy, 76, 77, 102
open society, 463
Operation Allied Force, 505
Operation Desert Shield, 407–9, 463, 464
Operation Desert Storm, 19, 407–9
Operation Provide Comfort, 515
Operation Restore Hope, 480, 680
Orange Revolution, 361, 612, 613–14, 623
Oregon Territory Treaty, 34
Organization for African Unity (OAU), 394, 621
Organization for Security and Cooperation in Europe (OSCE), 14, 362, 366, 367, 621, 623, 632
Organization for the Prohibition of Chemical Weapons (OPCW), 315, 316
Organization of American States (OAS), 387–88, 621, 632
Organization of Petroleum Exporting Countries (OPEC)
Arab-Israeli conflict and, 449
global economic crisis of 2008 and, 537
oil crisis and, 150, 165, 171–72, 321, 542
Organski, A.F.K., 344
organ trade, 536
Ortega, Dan, 184, 601, 622, 623
OSCE (Organization for Security and Cooperation in Europe), 14, 362, 366, 367, 621, 623, 632
Oslo agreement, 450, 452
OSS (Office of Strategic Services), 137
overpopulation, 559–63
overproduction, 16
Oxfam, 514, 553

Pacific Command, 457
Pacific region, U.S. power in, 101–3
Packer, George, 333, 468, 469
PACs (political action committees), 53
Page, Benjamin, 226
Paine, Thomas, 216
Pakistan
Afghanistan and, 381, 609
Al Qaeda and, 381, 436, 440–41, 609
Baghdad Pact and, 128
China and, 397
democracy and, 610–11, 615
drug rings and, 318
IMF and, 551
India and, 380–81
international commitments in, 138
Islamic fundamentalism and, 411, 440, 609, 610
nuclear weapons and, 307, 310
Obama and, 436, 439–41
peacekeeping and, 506
United Nations and, 305
war on terrorism and, 381, 414, 611
Palestine, 438, 443, 447, 448–56, 599
Palestine Liberation Organization (PLO), 63, 405, 449, 452
Palmer, A. Mitchell, 107–8
Panama
crime syndicates in, 319
democracy and, 593, 602
drug rings and, 317–18
military interventions in, 95
Panama Canal, 76, 77, 95, 98
Pan American Conference, 14, 101
pandemics, 567–68
Panetta, Leon, 326
"Paradox of American Power, The" (Nye), 659–62
Paraguay, 388, 593
Paris, Treaty of, 74, 153
Partnership for Peace (PFP), 349, 625
Paterson, Thomas, 102

Patolichev, Nikolai, 164n
patriotism, 333
Patterson, Robert P., 249
peace
  Arab-Israeli conflicts and, 23, 405, 406
  Cold War and, 116–19
  democracy and, 604–9, 713–19
  environmental issues and, 570
  globalization and, 4, 202–5, 528–29
  historical perspectives on, 345
  ICC and, 509
  Iraq War and, 23, 24, 430, 434–35, 469–70
  Marshall Plan and, 20
  military strength and, 87–90
  national interest and, 521
  Obama and, 301
  post-Cold War era and, 342
  poverty as threat to, 4
  power and, 10–11, 345
  principles and, 592, 604–9, 713–19
  "4 Ps" and, 9, 18, 23–24
  public health and, 564
  Reagan and, 177, 192
  trade and, 608
  Vietnam War and, 152–53
peace broker role
  in Bosnia, 481
  definition of, 14
  nuclear arms deal and, 358–59
peacekeeping operations
  costs of, 486–87
  Darfur and, 511
  NATO and, 347, 353
  troops provided for, 507
  United Nations and, 486, 489, 504, 506–8
Pearl Harbor attack, 79, 81, 87, 103, 105, 108, 120, 231, 237, 406
Pell, Clairborne, 463–64
Pelosi, Nancy, 396
Pennock, J. Roland, 203
Pennsylvania Avenue diplomacy, 29–37, 104, 135–38, 193
Pentagon, *see* Defense, U.S. Department of
Pentagon attack (2001), *see* September 11, 2001, terrorist attacks
Pentagon Papers case, 62
*People* magazine, 471
People's Liberation Army (PLA), 372
People's Republic of China (PRC), *see* China
PEPFAR (Presidentís Emergency Plan for AIDS Relief), 565
*perestroika*, 190, 276
Pérez, Andres, 387
Perle, Richard, 282
Perpetual Peace (Kant), 17, 604
Perry, Matthew C., 102
Perry, William, 313, 625, 682
Persian Gulf, 185
Persian Gulf War (1990-91)
  alliances in, 12, 347, 419
  Bush and, 19, 407, 408
  foreign policy strategy and, 19–20
  Japan and, 19, 377, 407
  military force and, 405, 411
  news media and, 58, 408, 470
  overview of, 407–9
  Powell and, 178, 408
  "4Ps" and, 407
  Russia and, 363
  UN Security Council and, 303, 332, 407, 408
  war powers and, 31
Peru, 317–18, 546, 593, 601
Peterson, Peter G., 164n
Petraeus, David, 428, 439
Pew Research Center, 60, 329
PFP (Partnership for Peace), 349, 625
Philippines
  Abu Sayyaf in, 443
  colonization of, 95, 102
  democracy in, 28, 213, 214, 594
  elections in, 622
  international commitments in, 138
  Iraq War and, 428
  legislative aid and, 631
  Spanish-American War and, 76, 84, 96
  swine flu and, 568
  war on terrorism and, 414
Phillips, Richard, 316, 317
Pinochet, Augusto, 627–28
piracy, 316–17
Pisar, Samuel, 628
PLA (People's Liberation Army), 372
Platt, Orville, 97n
Platt Amendment, 97, 97n, 99, 101
PLO (Palestine Liberation Organization), 63, 405, 449, 452
Point Four program, 556
Poland
  Cold War and, 115, 118
  crime syndicates in, 319
  democracy and, 593
  invasion of, 79, 80, 155, 235

Poland (*cont.*)
legislative aid in, 631
Lemkin and, 484
NATO and, 349, 353
NGOs and, 630
Solidarity movement, 188
Yalta summit on, 119–20
policy area international institutions, 14
policy enhancement, 286
policy makers, 60
Policy Planning Staff, 139
political action committees (PACs), 53
political calculations, 44
political institutions, 202–5, 624–26
political Islam, 599
political issue groups, 50, 52
political parties, 623–324
Polk, James K., Jr., 34, 104
pollution, 576
population growth, 559–63, 577
pork–barreling, 462
Portugal, 594
Posse Comitatus Act (1878), 457
post-Cold War era
defense spending and, 295–97
democracy and, 593–95
diplomacy and, 322–23
ethnic cleansing and, 482
geopolitics in, *see* geopolitics
international institutionalism and, 284
NATO and, 351–54
WMD proliferation, 306–16
postpolar systems, 290, 292
poverty
global economic crisis and, 320
globalization and, 3
public health and, 564, 653
sustainable development and, 551–63
terrorism and, 443, 485
as threat to peace, 4
Powell, Colin
bureaucratic politics and, 470
China and, 370
on Darfur, 511
decisive force theory of, 178
Haass and, 287
Haiti and, 516–17
Iraq War and, 48
North Korea and, 48
Persian Gulf War and, 178, 408
Russia and, 359
as senior adviser, 45, 47
on weapons of mass destruction, 423–24
Powell doctrine, 297, 408
power
in Asia, 101–3
balance of, 7, 236
democracy and, 609–16
globalization and, 528
historical perspectives, 345
identity groups and, 52
Iraq War and, 406, 430, 434, 470
Marshall Plan and, 20
military strength and, 87–90
morality and, 198–201
multilateralism and, 287–88
national interest and, 486, 521
nuclear deterrence and, 119–29, 162, 253–58
Obama and, 324
in Pacific for U.S., 102
peace and, 10–11, 345
Persian Gulf War and, 19
post–Cold War era and, 342
primacy of, 343–44
principles and, 283, 592, 609–16
"4 Ps" and, 9, 10–12, 18, 20–23
public health and, 564
Reagan and, 177–78, 180–81, 192
separation of, 30
soft, 17–18, 287, 611–12, 616, 631
unilateralism and, 282–83
United Nations and, 118
Vietnam War and, 153–54
war on terrorism and, 415
*see also* war powers
Power, Samantha, 481, 483, 485
power of the purse, 39
power transitions, 344
"Pre-Emption and National Security Strategy" (Bush), 663–64
preemption doctrine
Bush on, 416–17, 663–64
definition of, 11, 297
Ikenberry on, 665–66
Iraq and, 424–25
preponderance, 282
prerogative encroachment, 284, 286
"Present at the Creation" (Acheson), 114
presidency, *see* executive branch
President's Emergency Plan for AIDS Relief (PEPFAR), 565

"Preventing Genocide" (Genocide Prevention Task Force), 675–76
preventive diplomacy, 493–96, 521
preventive statecraft, 493
Price, David, 625
*prikhvatizatsiya*, 625
primacy, 7, 282, 343–44
primordialist view of ethnic conflict, 487–88
principles
  American exceptionalism and, 90–95
  democracy and, 211–15, 604–20, 713–19
  globalization and, 529
  identity groups and, 52
  ideological bipolarity and, 130–33
  Iraq War and, 23, 24, 434, 435
  Marshall Plan and, 20
  national interest and, 487, 521
  Obama and, 324
  Pacific region and, 102
  peace and, 592, 604–9, 713–19
  post–Cold War era and, 343
  power and, 283, 592, 609–16
  prosperity and, 592, 617–20
  "4 Ps" and, 9, 16–18, 20–23
  Reagan and, 181–83, 193
  Vietnam War and, 154
  war on terrorism and, 415, 418
*Problem from Hell, A* (Power), 481, 483
procedural legislation, 38, 39
process of choice, 6, 27–68
Proctor, Redfield, 243
prosperity
  democracy and, 617–20
  globalization and, 528, 585
  imperialism and, 95–98
  Iraq War and, 23, 24, 434, 435
  liberal international economic order and, 133–35
  Marshall Plan and, 20
  Obama and, 324–25
  Pacific region and, 102
  Persian Gulf War and, 19
  post–Cold War era and, 342
  principles and, 592, 617–20
  "4 Ps" and, 9, 15–16, 18, 20–23
  Reagan and, 183, 193
  Vietnam War and, 154–56
  world economic power and, 207–10
protectionism
  agricultural subsidies and, 544
  free trade vs., 109–10, 171, 580–81
  LIEO and, 134
  tariffs and, 36–37
"4 Ps" framework
  as complementary, 19–20
  dissensus and, 23–24
  Iraq and, 23–24, 430, 434–35
  national interest and, 9–18
  post–Cold War era and, 342–43
  Reagan and, 177–78, 180–83, 192–94
  trade-offs and, 20–23
  *see also* peace; power; principles; prosperity
public health, globalization and, 530, 563–68
public opinion
  Afghanistan War and, 353–51
  Cold War consensus and, 144–45
  foreign policy politics and, 62–67, 223–30, 329–34
  global, on U.S. foreign policy, 297, 300
  interest groups and, 54
  interventions and, 334, 519–20
  on Iraq War, 297, 332, 427, 428, 471–72
  news media and, 59–60
  post–Cold War era and, 329–34
  on United Nations, 117, 118, 289, 331–33, 471–72
  on Vietnam War, 54, 65, 158, 159–60, 226
"Public Opinion and Foreign Policy" (Holsti), 223–30
purposive view of ethnic conflict, 487, 488
Putin, Vladimir
  Bush and, 355
  Chechnya and, 361
  election of, 364, 365, 366
  Iraq and, 363, 421
  Moscow Treaty and, 356
  oil boom and, 355
  war on terrorism and, 357, 645
  Yeltsin and, 365–66
Putnam, Robert, 629

Qaddifi, Muammar, 185, 311–12, 313
Qaddifi, Seif el-Islam, 312
Qatar, 414, 599

Rabin, Yitzhak, 63, 405, 406, 450, 451, 452
racism in foreign policy, 94–95
Rally to Stop Genocide, 520
RAND Corporation, 122, 371, 469, 508
Rawls, John, 206
raw materials, 207–9
Rayburn, Sam, 137
Reagan, Ronald
  abortion and, 562
  arms control and, 188–89

Reagan, Ronald (*cont.*)
belief system of, 43–44
Carter and, 66, 67
Cold War and, 151, 177–92, 273–75
Democratic Idealism and, 17
détente and, 170
economic sanctions and, 634, 635, 636
on "evil empire," 191
foreign policy and, 28, 409
human rights and, 628
Iran and, 185, 445
Iraq and, 65–66, 445
national interest and, 485
nominees by, 54
Philippines and, 28, 622
South Africa and, 38
on totalitarianism, 182–83
vetoes by, 38
Reagan Doctrine, 177, 188, 192
Realism
definition of, 10–11
international institutionalism and, 286
new unilateralism and, 646–48
world view, 13
Realpolitik approach, 161, 246
Reciprocal Trade Agreements Act (1934), 36
Reciprocal Trade Agreements Act (RTAA), 110
reciprocity treaties, 109–10
Red Cross workers, murder of, 495
Refugees International, 52
regime change, 297
regional international institutions, 14
religion, freedom of, 93
"Report on the Global AIDS Epidemic" (UNAIDS), 685–89
Republican Party, 109, 110
*Responsibility to Protect, The,* 489
revisionist theories, 115, 189, 191
Revolutionary War, 11, 12, 73, 83
revolution in military affairs (RMA), 408
Ricardo, David, 580
Rice, Condoleezza
appointments and, 36
Darfur and, 513
democratic peace theory and, 605, 606
global warming and, 574
on Japan, 379
on national interest, 284
North Korea and, 311
on power, 282
on preemption, 425
on Russia, 362
as senior adviser, 47
Taiwan and, 398
on weapons of mass destruction, 423, 468
Rice, Susan E., 304, 306, 325, 513
Rio Treaty, 12
ripeness, theory of, 495
RMA (revolution in military affairs), 408
Roberts, Adam, 492
Rockefeller Brothers Fund, 4
Rockwell International, 57
Rogers, William, 45, 166
rogue states, 310, 311
Romania, 349, 593
Romero, Oscar, 181
Rome Treaty, 509
Rooney, Bethany, 418
Roosevelt, Franklin Delano
Big Three and, 81, 82, 114
Churchill and, 82, 236
on communism, 114
death of, 82
foreign policy politics and, 27, 77
Four Freedoms and, 79, 87, 93, 667–68
isolationism vs. internationalism and, 231–38
Latin America and, 78–79, 99, 101
peace and, 116
on Pearl Harbor attack, 105, 108
"quarantine of aggressor nations" speech of, 86
war powers and, 90
Yalta summit, 119–20
Roosevelt, Theodore
on bully pulpit, 38
letter to Turner, 239
Monroe Doctrine corollary and, 99, 100
Panama and, 95
peace broker role of, 14, 301
Russo-Japanese War and, 102, 102n
Spanish-American War and, 84
Roosevelt Corollary, 76, 77, 99, 100–101
Root, Elihu, 97n
Root-Takahira Agreement, 103
Roper, Elmo, 64
Rose, Gideon, 631
Rose, Richard, 630
Rossiter, Clinton, 220
Rothchild, Donald, 486
Royce, Ed, 398
RTAA (Reciprocal Trade Agreements Act), 110
Rubin, Robert, 549
Rudman, Warren, 661

rule of law, 598, 626–28, 631, 650–51
Rumsfeld, Donald
bureaucratic politics and, 470
Iraq War and, 48, 419, 425, 468, 469
Russia and, 359
as senior adviser, 47, 48, 326
Rusesabagina, Paul, 520
Rusk, Dean, 155
Russett, Bruce, 65
Russia
AIDS in, 564
alliance with, 355–57
Balkan Wars and, 360
chemical weapons and, 315
communism in, 107
corruption in, 365, 625
crime syndicates in, 319
Darfur and, 512
defense spending and, 295
democracy and, 215, 354, 364–67, 593, 594, 717–18
environmental issues and, 569, 570, 578
financial crises and, 354, 547–48
geopolitics of, 354–67
global economic crisis of 2008 and, 537, 545
Iraq War and, 363, 419, 421
Japan and, 376
Kosovo and, 360, 502
NATO and, 351, 361–62
NGOs and, 630
nuclear weapons and, 356–57, 358–59
revolutions in, 107, 115, 597
special drawing rights and, 550
START and, 356
unipolarity and, 644, 645
UN Security Council and, 304
U.S. foreign aid to, 356
*see also* Soviet Union
Russia-Georgia War, 349, 351, 356, 362–63
Russian Revolution, 76, 115, 597
Russo-Japanese War, 14, 77, 102, 102n
Rwanda
ethnic conflicts in, 297, 391–92, 485, 488, 489, 496, 497–99, 591, 598
interventions in, 481, 495, 496–97, 500, 501

Saakashvili, Mikhail, 362
Sachs, Jeffrey, 558, 661
Sadat, Anwar, 450, 452
Safire, William, 46
Sakharov, Andrei, 190, 190n
SALT I (Strategic Arms Limitation Treaty of 1972), 38–39, 164, 166, 269
SALT II (Strategic Arms Limitation Treaty of 1979), 168
Samoa, 102
Samuelson, Paul, 569
Sandinistas, 170, 177–78, 181, 188
*San Francisco Examiner,* 105
Sanger, David, 440
Santiago Resolution, 388, 394
Sarajevo Market Massacres, 682–84
SARS (severe acute respiratory syndrome), 375, 463, 567, 568
*Saturday Evening Post,* 107
Saudi Arabia
Arab-Israeli conflict and, 449
arms sales to, 38
democracy and, 598, 615
foreign policy and, 15, 411
global economic crisis of 2008 and, 538
Iraq and, 19, 407, 421
SAVAK, 133
Schelling, Thomas, 494
Schlesinger, Arthur M., Jr., 31, 140, 157, 166, 216–20, 285
Schlesinger, James, 45
Schroeder, Gerhard, 347
Schwarzkopf, Norman, 19, 407, 470
SCO (Shanghai Cooperation Organization), 369
Scott, David, 398
Scowcroft, Brent, 45, 166, 305, 680
SDI (Strategic Defense Initiative), 180, 188, 191
SDRs (special drawing rights), 550
SEATO (Southeast Asia Treaty Organization), 12, 128
Second Amendment, 87
secretary of commerce, 37
secretary of defense, 46
secretary of state, 41, 676
secretary of the treasury, 37, 46
security, *see* national security
security community, 350
segregation, racial, 612, 616
Selective Service Act (1917), 89
self-defense, military, 11
Sellers, Peter, 122
Sen, Amartya, 203
Senate, U.S., *see* Congress, U.S.
Senegal, 414
senior foreign policy advisers, 44–49
separation of powers, 30

September 11, 2001, terrorist attacks
  Bush and, 3, 42, 333, 482
  defense spending and, 295
  description of, 3
  foreign policy after, 456, 481–82
  hijackers' planning of, 463
  intelligence agencies and, 327
  lessons of, 482, 645–46, 670
  NATO and, 353
  news media and, 60
  9/11 Commission's report on, 669–71
  Obama on, 437
  patriotism after, 333
  shock of, 405, 645
  war on terrorism and, 406, 409–11, 671
Serbia
  Dayton Accord and, 504
  democracy and, 593
  economic sanctions against, 303
  ethnic cleansing and, 481, 487, 501, 504
  interventions and, 392, 502
  military aid to, 504
  Russia and, 360
severe acute respiratory syndrome (SARS), 375, 463, 567, 568
Seward, William, 245
SFOR (Stabilization Force), 352
Shanghai Cooperation Organization (SCO), 369
Shapiro, Robert, 226
Sharon, Ariel, 451, 453
Shelby, Richard, 35
Shelton, Hugh, 47
Shiite Muslims, 425, 426, 429, 431, 447
Shinseki, Eric, 425, 426
Shultz, George, 66, 178, 313
shuttle diplomacy, 14, 301, 449, 452
Sierra Club, 52
Sierra Leone, 591
Sikkink, Kathryn, 578, 693–701
Simon, Julian, 573
Singapore, 383, 616
Singh, Manmohan, 305, 538
Six-Day War, 172, 449
Six-Party Talks, 310–11, 373
Skidmore, David, 56n, 57
Slaughter, Anne-Marie, 466
slavery, 94, 109, 554
Slovakia, 214, 349, 593, 630
Slovenia, 349, 593
Smith, Adam, 580
Smith, Christopher, 617–18
Smith, Gerard C., 248
Smith, Tony, 211–15
Smoot-Hawley Tariff Act (1930), 36, 50, 79, 110, 329, 580
Snyder, Jack, 608, 713–19
Socialist Party, 107
soft power, 17–18, 287, 611–12, 616, 631
Soho.com, 375
Solidarity movement, 188
Solzhenitsyn, Aleksandr, 165
Somalia
  Clinton and, 30, 47, 391, 500, 515–16
  CNN curve and, 518–19
  ethnic conflict in, 391, 488, 598
  as a "failed state," 192
  geopolitics of, 392
  interventions in, 480, 495, 515–16, 679–80
  military force in, 408
  national interest and, 483
  piracy and, 316, 317
  United Nations and, 332, 506
  war powers and, 515–16
Somoza, Anastasio, 132, 165, 170, 181, 214, 628
"Sources of Soviet Conduct, The" (Mr. X [Kennan]), 120, 259–62
South Africa
  AIDS in, 564, 566
  apartheid in, *see* apartheid in South Africa
  democracy and, 213, 390–91, 595, 598
  economic sanctions and, 51, 633–36
  geopolitics of, 393
  global economic crisis of 2008 and, 539
  Mandela and, 390–91, 590, 592, 595, 627, 632–33
  transitional justice and, 627
  UN Security Council and, 305
Southeast Asia Treaty Organization (SEATO), 12, 128
Southern Baptist Convention, 520
Southern Command, 457
South Korea
  alliances with, 12, 379
  export promotion and, 583
  financial crises in, 547
  Iraq War and, 428
  Japan and, 379
  Koreagate, 55
  North Korea and, 310, 311, 379–80
  UN Security Council and, 118, 305
South Vietnam, 131, 168
sovereign immunity, 627
sovereignty, 489–93, 535, 568
Soviet Union

Afghanistan and, 150, 167, 168, 170, 177, 188, 190, 192, 276, 381, 506
Africa and, 169
alliances with, 12, 114, 380
arms control and, 190, 356
chemical weapons and, 314
China and, 168–69
Cold War and, 7, 115, 118, 248–49, 273, 275, 276–78
Cuban missile crisis and, 162
democracy and, 593, 594, 608, 623
détente and, 150, 160–70, 267–72
dissolution of, 186, 342, 354, 356, 590
end of Cold War, 186–92, 342
Guatemala and, 22
Helsinki Accords and, 162
human rights and, 628
Hungary and, 127, 177
Kennan on, 120
NATO and, 63, 124, 127, 351
nuclear arms race and, 127, 162
Persian Gulf War and, 407
post–Cold War era and, 322–23
public opinion influence on, 66
SALT treaty and, 39, 164
Truman Doctrine and, 122
UN General Assembly and, 119, 303
UN Security Council and, 117
Warsaw Pact and, 127
*see* also Russia
"Soviet Union's Crucial Role, The" (Gorbachev), 276–78
Spain
covert action against, 137
Cuba and, 99
democracy and, 594
power and, 345
swine flu and, 568
terrorism in, 416, 428, 443
U.S.S. *Maine* and, 105
Spanish-American War
Cuba and, 97
foreign policy significance of, 76, 77
great debates over, 105, 242–44
internationalism and, 84
manifest destiny and, 91
Philippines and, 76, 84, 96
political issue groups and, 52
war powers and, 31
Spanish flu, 530, 567
special drawing rights (SDRs), 550
species extinction, 573
speech, freedom of, 93
Spero, Joan, 549, 553
Speth, James "Gus," 576
*Sputnik* satellite, 129
Stabilization Force (SFOR), 352
stagflation, 156, 172
Stalin, Josef, 81, 82, 114, 115, 131n, 189
START (Strategic Arms Reduction Talks), 190, 274, 356, 358
Star Wars, 180
State, U.S. Department of, 37
bureaucratic politics and, 49
China and, 396
democracy and, 620
drug rings and, 318
expansion of, 139
genocide prevention and, 675–76
HUAC and, 144
interest groups and, 54
Iraq and, 66, 469–70
McCarthyism and, 144–45
news media and, 61
Rwanda and, 500
trade agreements and, 581
on Vietnam War, 153
war on terrorism, 416
state and local governments, 50, 52–53, 625
Statue of Liberty, 20
steel industry, 207, 544
Stevenson Adlai, 67
Stiglitz, Joseph, 535
stock markets, 547–48
Strategic Arms Limitation Treaty of 1972 (SALT I), 38–39, 164, 166, 269
Strategic Arms Limitation Treaty of 1979 (SALT II), 168
Strategic Arms Reduction Talks (START), 190, 274, 356, 358
Strategic Defense Initiative (SDI), 180, 188, 191
strategy, foreign policy, *see* foreign policy strategy
"Strategy in the Missile Age" (Brodie), 120, 253–58
Strobel, Warren, 518–19, 677–84
Strong, Josiah, 239
Students for a Free Tibet, 398
substantive legislation, 38–39
Sudan, 374, 482, 495, 510–15, 629
Suez War, 449
Suharto, President, 547
Suhrke, Astri, 497
Summers, Lawrence, 326

Summit of the Americas, 383
Sunni tribes, 425–26, 428, 429, 447
Sun Yat-sen, 103
Supreme Court, U.S.
  executive branch and, 40
  Guantánamo Bay and, 461
  on national security, 107, 108
  on presidential powers, 461
  as referee, 39–40
  *see also specific cases*
sustainable development, 551–63, 570
Sweden, 557
Sweig, Julia E., 384
swine flu, 567–68
Switzerland, 16
symbolic politics, 579, 696, 697, 701n9
Syria, 315, 318, 449, 452, 455–56, 598, 629

TAA (Trade Adjustment Assistance), 581, 584
Taiwan
  alliances with, 12
  anticommunism and, 118
  China and, 369–71, 395, 398
  Cold War consensus and, 136–37, 143
  détente and, 166
  treaty with, 34
  U.S. policy toward, 398
Taiwan Relations Act, 398
Tajikistan, 414, 593, 611
Talbott, Strobe, 93
Taliban regime
  Cold War and, 192
  Iran's opposition to, 447
  Pakistan and, 381, 440–41
  repression of women, 415
  war on terrorism and, 3, 406, 411–13
Tanzania, 389–90, 410
tariffs, 36–37, 50, 109, 110, 544
Taro Aso, 378–79
Taylor, Zachary, 42
telecommunications technology, globalization, and, 533
Tenet, George, 423, 433
territorial expansion, 74–76
terrorism
  ABT policy and, 406
  China and, 373
  Cold War and, 192
  Guantánamo Bay and, 435, 442, 460–61
  homeland security and, 415–16
  Iraq War and, 23–24, 456
  NATO and, 353
  Obama and, 442–45
  poverty and, 443, 485
  Qaddafi and, 185
  Sunnis and, 425–26
  tactical advantages of, 410–11
  as true Enemy, 456, 670–71
  *see also* September 11, 2001, terrorist attacks; war on terrorism
Texas, 73, 84, 91, 93, 96, 104
Thailand, 138, 318, 547, 568
Thatcher, Margaret, 190
Third Amendment, 87
Third World
  Cold War and, 151
  containment in, 192
  foreign aid and, 209–10
  foreign policy in, 168, 169
  human rights in, 165
  ideological bipolarity and, 130–33
  population growth in, 559
  poverty in, 552–54
  raw materials and, 207, 208–9
  redefining relations, 172–73
  Soviet Union and, 188
  UN Security Council and, 304–5
  World Bank and, 134, 558
  *see also specific countries*
Thomas, Norman, 86
"three Ds" threats, 292–93
Thucydides, 10, 282, 287
Tiananmen Square, Beijing, 20–21, 374, 395, 591, 617
Tibet, 376, 396, 398, 399
*Time*, 141
*Times of London*, 484
Tito, Josip Broz, 131n
Togo, 595
Tokyo Round, 176
Toqueville, Alexis de, 212
Tora Bora battle (2001), 412
torture, 459–60
totalitarianism, 182–83
Tower, John, 35
trade
  China and, 101, 396
  democratic peace theory and, 607
  developing nations and, 208
  foreign economic policies and, 15
  foreign investments and, 209
  GDP and, 532
  global economic crises and, 320, 537

globalization and, 3, 532, 540–46, 577–84
Japan and, 102, 173–77
peace and, 608
poverty and, 553
South Africa and, 635
Western Europe and, 346
*see also* free trade
Trade Adjustment Assistance (TAA), 581, 584
Trade and Development Agency, 583
trade deficit
Asia and, 542
China and, 377, 396, 542
Cold War and, 150
increases in, 540–41
Japan and, 377
stagflation and, 156
trade policy, 76, 579–84
trade promotion authority, 582–83
Trade Related Aspects of Intellectual Property Rights (TRIPS), 543
Trade Related Investment Measures (TRIMs), 543
TransAfrica, 634–35, 636
transitional justice, 626–27
"Transnational Networks in International Politics" (Keck and Sikkink), 693–701
Transparency International, 625
Treaty of Paris, 74, 153
Treaty of Versailles, 27, 32, 38, 43, 78, 79, 232
Treaty of Wangxia, 101
Treaty of Westphalia (1648), 490
Trident submarines, 180
TRIMs (Trade Related Investment Measures), 543
TRIPS (Trade Related Aspects of Intellectual Property Rights), 543
tropical deforestation, 576
Truman, Harry S.
on bombing Japan, 118
China and, 157, 395
Cold War and, 122, 135, 187, 249
executive power of, 38, 461
Korean War and, 127, 136
labor-union strike and, 40
Manhattan Project and, 90
NSC-68 paper and, 125, 127
Point Four program of, 556
United Nations and, 117
Truman Doctrine
Cold War and, 135, 167, 249
declaratory commitment and, 34
description of, 122, 123
ideological bipolarity and, 130
tuberculosis, 563
Tunisia, 414, 603
Turkey, 122, 123, 128, 138, 484, 551, 599
Turkmenistan, 593, 611
Turner, Frederick Jackson, 239–41
Tutsis, 481, 488, 496, 498
Twain, Mark, 95
Tyler, John, 104

UDHR (Universal Declaration of Human Rights), 111, 490, 602, 629
UFCO (United Fruit Company), 22, 97, 134
Uganda, 559, 623
Uighurs, 376
Ukraine
democracy and, 593, 613–14, 620, 623
IMF and, 551
Iraq War and, 428
NATO and, 349, 351, 362
nuclear weapons and, 356, 358–59
orange revolution, 361
swine flu and, 568
UNAIDS, 564, 565, 566, 685–89
UNAMID (United Nations Assistance Mission in Darfur), 515
UNAMIR (United Nations Mission in Rwanda), 496–97, 498–99
UNASUR (Union of South American Nations), 386
UNCCD (United Nations Convention to Combat Desertification), 575–76
UN Commission on Human Rights, 629
underconsumption, 16
unemployment, monetary policy and, 532
"Unexpected Ronald Reagan, The" (Gaddis), 273–75
UN Food and Agriculture Organization, 619
Unger, Roberto Mangabeira, 540
UNHCR (United Nations High Commissioner for Refugees), 303, 486, 621
UNICEF (United Nation's International Children's Emergency Fund), 303, 619
unilateralism
Bush and, 282, 384, 646
definition of, 281
Krauthammer on, 644–48
multilateralism vs., 281–89
war on terrorism and, 282
Union of South American Nations (UNASUR), 386
Union of Soviet Socialist Republics, *see* Soviet Union
"Unipolar Moment Revisited, The" (Krauthammer), 644–48
unipolar systems, 7, 282, 287, 343, 644–48

United Fruit Company (UFCO), 22, 97, 134
United Nations
  Annan on, 649–55
  Arab-Israeli conflict and, 449
  Bush and, 480
  creation of, 81, 83, 303
  Darfur and, 482, 511–12
  democracy and, 620–21
  on environmental issues, 570, 571
  foreign policy strategy and, 302–6
  on globalization, 532
  HIV/AIDS and, 564–66
  human rights and, 490, 628–29
  international institutionalism and, 116–19
  international regimes and, 14
  international system and, 7
  interventions and, 480–81, 482, 486, 521–22
  Iraq War and, 23, 24, 303, 332, 419
  national sovereignty and, 492
  Nobel Peace Prize and, 191, 506
  peacekeeping forces and, 486, 489, 504, 506–8
  Persian Gulf War and, 407, 408, 409
  prerogative encroachment and, 284, 286
  public opinion on, 117, 118, 289, 331–33, 471–72
  Russia and, 362
  weapons of mass destruction and, 424, 468
United Nations Assistance Mission in Darfur (UNAMID), 515
United Nations Atomic Energy Commission, 118
United Nations Charter, 116, 117, 118, 203, 303, 416–17, 490, 628–29, 649, 651
United Nations Convention to Combat Desertification (UNCCD), 575–76
United Nations Environmental Program, 14
United Nations Framework Convention on Climate Change, *see* Kyoto global warming treaty
United Nations General Assembly
  admission to, 118
  approval of NPT, 310
  authority of, 117
  Honduras and, 388
  initial membership of, 303
  John Paul II and, 553
  NIEO and, 173
  public opinion and, 331–32
  support for the United States, 119
  voting in, 559n
  WTO and, 543
United Nations High Commissioner for Refugees (UNHCR), 303, 486, 621
United Nations Information Technology Service (UNITeS), 653
United Nation's International Children's Emergency Fund (UNICEF), 303, 619
United Nations Mission in Rwanda (UNAMIR), 496–97, 498–99
United Nations Security Council (UNSC)
  Afghanistan War (2001) and, 303
  Arab-Israeli conflict and, 449
  China and, 118, 304, 305, 395
  Darfur and, 511–12, 514
  design of, 117
  economic sanctions and, 303, 310, 311, 446
  expansion of, 304–6, 386, 393
  Haiti and, 517
  interventions and, 502–3
  Iran and, 446
  Iraq War and, 303, 332, 346, 363, 419
  Korean War and, 118, 303, 331, 464
  national sovereignty and, 490
  Persian Gulf War and, 303, 332, 407, 408
  on piracy, 317
  vetoes and, 117–18, 304, 419
  war on terrorism and, 411, 417
"United States and the Global Struggle for Democracy, The" (Smith), 211–15
"United States and World Economic Power, The" (Kolko), 207–10
*United States v. Curtiss-Wright Export Corp.*, 39–40
UNITeS (United Nations Information Technology Service), 653
Universal Declaration of Human Rights (UDHR), 111, 490, 602, 629
universal jurisdiction, 627
UN Population Fund, 562
UNSC, *see* United Nations Security Council (UNSC)
UNSCOM (UN Special Commission), 407
urbanization, 577
Urquhart, Brian, 304
Uruguay Round trade agreement, 542–43, 542n
U.S. Chamber of Commerce, 621
U.S.-China Economic and Security Review Commission, 397
U.S. Institute of Peace, 469, 501
U.S. Post Office, 106
U.S. Trade Representative (USTR), 37, 139, 581
USA PATRIOT Act (2001), 456, 456n
USIA (U.S. Information Agency), 139
U.S.S. *Maine*, 105
USS *Abraham Lincoln*, 422

USS *Cole*, 410, 414
USSR, *see* Soviet Union
USTR (U.S. Tradc Representative), 37, 139, 581
Uzbekistan, 414, 593, 611

Van Buren, Martin, 41
Vance, Cyrus, 47, 170
Vandenberg, Arthur, 116, 135, 235
V-E day, 83
Vedrine, Hubert, 347
Vegas dilemma, 294, 568
Venezuela, 362, 387, 600, 612, 614
Versailles, Treaty of, 27, 32, 38, 43, 78, 79, 232
Veterans of Foreign Wars, 52
vetoes
  constitutional provisions for, 38
  legislative, 39
  presidential, 38
  of WPR, 158, 636
Vietnam, 128, 130–31, 154
"Vietnam" (Gelb), 263–66
Vietnam War
  foreign policy politics and, 27
  great debates over, 103–4, 263–66
  news media and, 58–59, 62, 159
  Nixon and, 43, 153, 154, 155, 156, 157–58
  political issue groups and, 52
  public opinion and, 54, 65, 158, 159–60, 226
  Reagan on, 181
  as a setback, 150, 151–60, 263
Villepin, Dominique de, 346
V-J day, 83
*Voices of America* (Lord), 612
voter education programs, 623

Walesa, Lech, 188, 191
Wali, Aminu Bashir, 305
Wallach, Lori, 578
*Wall Street Journal,* 164n
Walt, Stephen, 283, 344, 432
Waltz, Kenneth, 8
Wangxia, Treaty of, 101
want, freedom from, 93
war
  constitutional provisions for, 29–30
  democratization and, 713–19
  global governance and, 203
  great debates on going to, 103–6
  *see also specific wars*
war-crimes tribunals, 508
War Industries Board, 89
War Manpower Commission, 90
Warnke, Paul, 35
War of 1812, 31, 75, 88, 104, 405–6
war on terrorism
  Afghanistan and, 3, 406, 411–13, 415
  Africa and, 414
  Al Qaeda and, 3, 406, 410–13, 414, 416
  bin Laden and, 3, 406, 410, 412, 413, 415
  Bush and, 406, 409, 411–18, 442, 472–73, 664
  China and, 645
  CIA and, 412–13
  declaration of, 3
  Ikenberry on, 666, 667–68
  Japan and, 377
  national security and, 457–63
  Obama and, 442
  Pakistan and, 381, 414, 611
  Russia and, 357, 645
  September 11 terrorist attacks and, 406, 409–11, 671
  unilateral approach to, 282
war powers
  Bosnia and, 517
  Cold War consensus and, 136–37
  constitutional provisions for, 31–32, 217–18
  foreign policy politics and, 184–86, 515–18
  Haiti and, 516–17
  Iraq War and, 31, 463–66
  Kosovo and, 517–18
  Roosevelt and, 90
  Somalia and, 515–14
  Wilson and, 89
War Powers Resolution (WPR) of 1973
  Bush and, 463, 464
  failings of, 184–86
  Iraq and, 466
  Nixon and, 38, 636
  passage of, 157–58
  procedural legislation and, 39
  Somalia and, 516
War Production Board (WPB), 90
Warsaw Pact, 127, 131n, 162, 348, 349, 351, 352, 645
War Shipping Board, 89
Washington, George, 27–28, 42, 73, 74, 83–84, 85, 88, 91, 124, 216
Washington consensus, 535, 535n, 548, 558
Washington Naval Conference (1921-22), 89–90, 103
*Washington Post,* 61, 95, 328, 471, 472
Watergate scandal, 159, 167

"water's edge" myth, 27–29
weapons of mass destruction (WMD)
  Betts on, 4
  Bush and, 423, 424, 465, 467, 468
  Hussein and, 23, 407, 409, 423, 424, 465, 467–68
  Iraq and, 423–25
  Obama administration and, 445
  proliferation of, 4, 306–16
  Russia and, 357
  terrorists and, 410, 417
  *see also* nuclear weapons
Weber, Max, 49, 426, 490
Weber, Vin, 635
Weinberger, Caspar, 178
Weinberger criteria, 178–80
Weiss, Thomas, 306, 492
Western Europe
  CSCE and, 162
  democracy and, 594, 608
  détente and, 191
  geopolitics of, 346–48
  global economic crisis of 2008 and, 537
  isolationism and, 84–85
  Marshall Plan, 20, 124
  Persian Gulf War and, 19, 407
  *see also specific countries*
West Germany, *see* Germany
Westminister Foundation for Democracy, 621
Westphalia,Treaty of (1648), 490
"We the Peoples" (Annan), 649–55
"What the Founding Fathers Intended" (Schlesinger), 216–20
*White Man's Burden, The* (Easterly), 558
WHO (World Health Organization), 14, 303, 562, 565–66, 567–68, 576
Wiesel, Elie, 520
Wilhelm, Charles E., 318
Will, George, 572, 573
Willkie, Wendell, 236
Wilson, James, 217
Wilson, Woodrow
  American exceptionalism and, 17
  communism and, 107
  democracy and, 94, 214
  foreign policy politics and, 27, 43, 604
  Fourteen Points and, 91, 93
  Havel on, 613
  internationalism and, 84, 200, 211–12
  League of Nations and, 32, 76, 86
  Mexican Revolution and, 97
  on news media, 58
  peace and, 76
  war powers and, 89
  World War I and, 76, 84, 105, 116
Winthrop, John, 92
WMD, *see* weapons of mass destruction (WMD)
Wohlforth, William, 282, 290, 291
Wolfensohn, James D., 495–96
Wolfowitz, Paul, 121, 283, 359–60, 425, 426
women, 52, 415, 438, 554
Women's Action for New Directions, 52
Wood, Robert E., 86
World Bank
  foreign economic policy and, 15
  global poverty and, 558–59
  human development index of, 552
  as international institution, 14
  LIEO and, 133–34
  on Russia, 354
  voting rights and, 134, 559, 559n
  WTO and, 543
World Court, 14
World Economic Forum, 553
World Health Organization (WHO), 14, 303, 562, 565–66, 567–68, 576
world hunger, 559–63
world order, 13
World Trade Center attack (2001), *see* September 11, 2001, terrorist attacks
World Trade Organization (WTO)
  anti-globalization movement and, 3, 496
  China and, 396
  environmental issues and, 569
  export promotion and, 583
  globalization and, 542–45
  as international institution, 14
  multilateralism and, 288
  Oxfam and, 553
  protests at 1999 summit of, 577
World War I
  alliances in, 12, 77
  chemical weapons during, 314
  democracy and, 594
  Espionage and Sedition Acts, 28, 107
  genocide during, 484
  military strength during, 88, 89
  Pacific power and, 103
  U.S. entry into, 76, 105
  war powers and, 31
  Wilson and, 84
World War II
  alliances in, 12, 114

civil liberties and, 108
foreign policy significance of, 81–83
genocide during, 484
isolationism and, 81, 86
Lend-Lease program and, 114, 554
Marshall Plan and, 20
military strength during, 79, 88, 90
Munich analogy from, 154, 155
news media and, 58
political issue groups and, 52
war powers and, 31
World Wildlife Federation, 52
WPB (War Production Board), 90
WPR, *see* War Powers Resolution (WPR) of 1973
Wright, Jim, 184
WTO, *see* World Trade Organization (WTO)
WuDunn, Sheryl, 554

Xinjiang Province, 376
Yahoo, 617, 618
Yakasuni war memorial, 379
Yalta conference, 82, 119–20
Yanukovich, Viktor, 361
yellow journalism, 105
Yeltsin, Boris, 355, 359, 361, 364, 365–66, 633
Yemen, 314, 316, 410, 414
Yom Kippur War, 172, 449
*Youngstown Sheet and Tube Co. v. Sawyer,* 40, 461
Yugoslavia
ethnic conflicts in, 485, 488, 503–4
NATO and, 347, 349, 352
peacekeeping forces in, 382, 486
Tito and, 131n
UN membership, 303
Yukio Hatoyama, 379
Yushchenko, Viktor, 361, 612, 613–14, 623

Zaire, 192, 391, 485, 598
Zakaria, Fareed, 4, 291
Zardari, Ali, 440, 610, 611
Zartman, William, 495
Zelaya, Manuel, 388, 600
Zhirinovsky, Vladimir, 364, 713
Zhou Enlai, 124, 395
Zimbabwe, 595, 598, 629, 630
Zimmermann, Warren, 681
Zimmerman telegram, 84
Zoellick, Robert, 47
Zuma, Jacob, 393
Zyuganov, Gennadi, 364, 365

UNIVERSITY OF WINCHESTER
LIBRARY